# THEORY'S EMPIRE

# Breakfast Theory: A MORNING METHODOLOGY

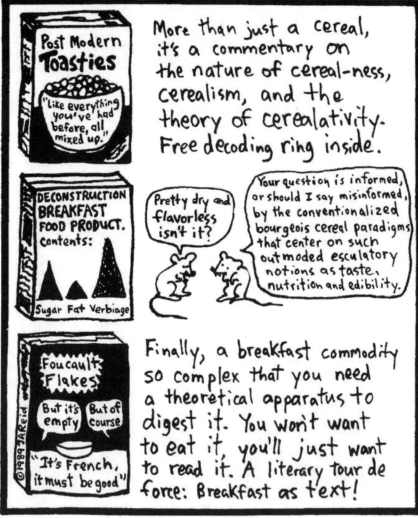

"Breakfast Theory: A Morning Methodology," by Jeff Reid. Originally appeared in *In These Times*, 29 March 1989.

# THEORY'S EMPIRE

## An Anthology of Dissent

EDITED BY

## DAPHNE PATAI AND WILL H. CORRAL

COLUMBIA UNIVERSITY PRESS

NEW YORK

Columbia University Press
*Publishers Since 1893*
New York   Chichester, West Sussex

The coeditors of this volume are deeply grateful for the financial assistance they received in
the preparation of this book from Lee R. Edwards, dean of the Faculty of Humanities and
Fine Arts at the University of Massachusetts Amherst, and from the Office of Research and
Sponsored Projects at California State University, Sacramento.

Library of Congress Cataloging-in-Publication Data
Theory's empire : an anthology of dissent / edited by Daphne Patai and Will Corral.
    p. cm.
  Includes bibliographical references and index.
  ISBN 0–231–13416–9 (alk. paper)—ISBN 0–231–13417–7 (pbk. : alk. paper)—ISBN
0–231–50869–7 (electronic)
    1. Criticism. 2. Literature—History and criticism—Theory, etc.  I. Patai, Daphne, 1943–

PN 81.T445 2004
801′.95—dc22

2004058252

∞

Columbia University Press books are printed on permanent and durable acid-free paper.
Printed in the United States of America

*Designed by Chang Jae Lee*

c 10 9 8 7 6 5 4 3 2 1
p 10 9 8 7 6 5 4 3 2 1

# CONTENTS

INTRODUCTION   1

PART I. THEORY RISING   19

INTRODUCTION   21

1.  Theory, What Theory?
    *Valentine Cunningham*   24

2.  Destroying Literary Studies
    *René Wellek*   41

3.  Traveling Through American Criticism
    *Tzvetan Todorov*   52

4.  The Rise and Fall of "Practical" Criticism:
    From I. A. Richards to Barthes and Derrida
    *Morris Dickstein*   60

5.  The Power and Limits of Literary Theory
    *Richard Freadman and Seumas Miller*   78

6.  Is Theory to Blame?
    *John M. Ellis*   92

7.  Theory, Theories, and Principles
    *Denis Donoghue*   109

PART II. LINGUISTIC TURNS   121

INTRODUCTION   123

8.  The Linguistic Unconscious:
    Saussure and the Post-Saussureans
    *Raymond Tallis*   125

9.  Literary Theory and Its Discontents
    *John R. Searle*   147

10. The Quandaries of the Referent
    *Vincent Descombes*   176

11. The Great Dichotomy
   *Wendell V. Harris* 190

12. The Deconstructive Angel
   *M. H. Abrams* 199

## PART III. EMPIRE BUILDING 213

### INTRODUCTION 215

13. The Grand Academy of Theory
   *Frederick Crews* 218

14. Theorrhea and Kulturkritik
   *J. G. Merquior* 234

15. Masters and Demons
   *Brian Vickers* 247

16. The Debate Over the Wartime Writings of Paul de Man:
   The Language of Setting the Record Straight
   *Alan B. Spitzer* 271

17. Presentism: Postmodernism, Poststructuralism,
   Postcolonialism
   *Graham Good* 287

18. Preface for a Post-Postcolonial Criticism
   *Erin O'Connor* 297

## PART IV. THEORY AS A PROFESSION 313

### INTRODUCTION 315

19. Author! Author! Reconstructing Roland Barthes
   *Clara Claiborne Park* 318

20. The French Intellectual Habitus and Literary Culture
   *Niilo Kauppi* 330

21. Social Constructionism: Philosophy for the
   Academic Workplace
   *Mark Bauerlein* 341

22. Bad Writing
   *D. G. Myers* 354

23. Everyman an Übermensch: The Culture of Cultural Studies
*Stephen Adam Schwartz* 360

24. The End of Theory, the Rise of the Profession: A Rant in Search of Responses
*Geoffrey Galt Harpham* 381

PART V. IDENTITIES 395

INTRODUCTION 397

25. The Cant of Identity
*Todd Gitlin* 400

26. The Gender Fallacy
*William C. Dowling* 411

27. Feminism's Perverse Effects
*Elaine Marks* 419

28. Queer Theory, Literature, and the Sexualization of Everything: The Gay Science
*Lee Siegel* 424

29. Battle of the Bien-Pensant
*Kwame Anthony Appiah* 441

PART VI. THEORY AS SURROGATE POLITICS 449

INTRODUCTION 451

30. Oppositional Opposition
*Harold Fromm* 454

31. Silence Is Consent, or Curse Ye Meroz!
*Richard Levin* 458

32. Criticism as Displacement
*Jeffrey Wallen* 476

33. Thick Aestheticism and Thin Nativism
*Russell Jacoby* 490

34. Casualties of the Culture Wars
*Eugene Goodheart* 508

PART VII. RESTORING REASON   523

INTRODUCTION   525

35.   Rationality/Science
      *Noam Chomsky*   528

36.   The Furor Over *Impostures Intellectuelles*: What Is All the
      Fuss About?
      *Jean Bricmont and Alan Sokal*   537

37.   The Sleep of Reason
      *Thomas Nagel*   541

38.   Staying for an Answer: The Untidy Process of Groping for
      Truth
      *Susan Haack*   552

39.   What Is Social Construction?
      *Paul A. Boghossian*   562

40.   Postcolonial Science Studies: Ending "Epistemic Violence"
      *Meera Nanda*   575

PART VIII. STILL READING AFTER ALL
THESE THEORIES . . .   585

INTRODUCTION   587

41.   Literature and Theory: Notes on the Research Programs
      of the 1980s
      *David Bromwich*   590

42.   Changing Epochs
      *Frank Kermode*   605

43.   Making Knowledge: Bioepistemology and the
      Foundations of Literary Theory
      *Nancy Easterlin*   621

44.   Literature and Fiction
      *Peter Lamarque and Stein Haugom Olsen*   636

45.   Literary Aesthetics and the Aims of Criticism
      *Paisley Livingston*   651

46.   Crisis in the Humanities? Reconfiguring Literary Study for
      the Twenty-first Century
      *Marjorie Perloff*   668

CODA    685

INTRODUCTION    687

47.    A Hippocratic Oath for the Pluralist
       *Wayne C. Booth*    688

LIST OF CONTRIBUTORS    691

INDEX    699

# THEORY'S EMPIRE

# INTRODUCTION

*Theory's empire [is] an empire zealously inquisitorial about every form of empire but its own.*          —CHRISTOPHER RICKS[1]

THIS ANTHOLOGY APPEARS at a moment when not only have theoretical discussions of literature become stagnant but articles and books are published in defense of the conceptual stalemates that have led to this very immobility. In the early years of the new millennium, theorists are busily writing about the impasse in which theory finds itself, discoursing on the alternatives as portentously as they once wrote about the death of the novel and the author. But there is one revealing difference between the predictably cyclical revisions of theoretical notions before structuralism and those present developments that can today be referred to simply as Theory, emblazoned with a capital T: the proponents of the latter tend to avoid acknowledging their own role in creating and dispersing the very theorizing that increasingly seems to lead to a dead end. To be sure, the 1990s witnessed the beginning of a few mea culpas. But this repentance has yet to distinguish between "a theory" as one approach among many, "theory" as a system of concepts employed in the humanities, and Theory as an overarching "practice" of our time. This failure has led to endless reassertions as critics vie for recognition that they are still "doing theory," understood as a superior and demanding labor.

From its inception, what is now called Theory aroused strong reactions. As early as the 1960s, caveats were heard regarding its foundations and practices. Yet such was the excitement generated by Theory as it promised, first, to revitalize literary study, and then, other humanistic fields that skeptical and dissenting voices went largely unheard or created no more than a brief stir destined soon to fade as the march of Theory continued. This was the milieu teachers of literature inherited, and that still surrounds them in this new century.

In the past few decades, however, vigorous critical challenges have been raised to Theory as it has come to be routinely practiced and taught. So numerous are these objections that it is impossible to represent in a single volume all the incisive and sensible adverse views that have surfaced since at least the time of the Picard-Barthes controversy of the 1960s. Yet so little impact has this dissidence had that compendia celebrating Theory continue to be published and to function as important vehicles for conveying to new generations of readers reigning ideas of what literature is and how it should be studied. These volumes are defined by the presumption that theory matters more than the literature it once interpreted, and that certain key figures, concepts, movements, and texts are beyond question. Meanwhile, the challenges that have been offered to this presumption are widely scattered in scholarly journals, books by individual authors, and a few small and little-known collections; hence they have been practically unavailable to students and teachers.[2] *Theory's Empire* proposes to fill this gap by showing how it came about that Theory and theorists ascended to their present eminence and by subjecting their claims to careful scrutiny.

Hazard Adams, one well-known critic and anthologist, wrote in the preface to the 1992 revised edition of his *Critical Theory Since Plato* of "the tendency among recent academic critics to spend far less time discussing what . . . used to be called 'literary' texts and more time debating each other's theories."[3] As if to bear out this observation, a conference on the present state of theory, held in April 2003 at the University of Chicago, saw some of the founders and promoters of Theory at pains to reinvigorate their propositions, including, in particular, their claims to be politically relevant. Their attempts to either absolve themselves of responsibility for their own excesses or to marshal forces to allow them to continue to claim centrality for the ideas they have long espoused simply confirmed our sense of the by-now entirely established nature of assertions about Theory. As Emily Eakin points out in her report on the Chicago meeting, "If theory's political utility is this dubious, why did the theorists spend so much time talking about current events?"[4] The recent *Norton Anthology of Theory and Criticism* (the first major compendium of this century) corroborates our perspective of Theory's still grandiose ambitions when it ends its introduction with the following assertion:

> There are very good reasons that, as Jonathan Culler observes, contemporary theory now frames the study of literature and culture in academic institutions. Theory raises and answers questions about a broad array of fundamental issues, some old and some new, pertaining to reading and interpretive strategies, literature and culture, tradition and nationalism, genre and gender, meaning and paraphrase, originality and intertextuality, authorial intention and the unconscious, literary education and social hegemony, standard language and heteroglossia, poetics and rhetoric, representation and truth, and so on.[5]

If even recent handbooks and reference works such as *The Edinburgh Encyclopedia of Modern Criticism and Theory* (2002) fail to acknowledge views opposing such inflated expressions of the purview of theory, it should come as no surprise that existing anthologies rarely include or even mention work that contests not only the applicability but also the very foundations of the theories presented and the claims made in their name. This failure is evident in most anthologies currently in use in theory classrooms. Examples are David H. Richter's *The Critical Condition* (second edition, 1998), Donald Keesey's *Con-*

*texts for Criticism* (third edition, 1998), K. M. Newton's *Twentieth-Century Literary Theory: A Reader* (second edition, 1997), and more widely known collections such as Julie Rivkin and Michael Ryan's *Literary Theory: An Anthology* (second edition, 2004), Philip Rice and Patricia Waugh's *Modern Literary Theory: A Reader* (fourth edition, 2001), and now the *Norton Anthology of Theory and Criticism,* whose aspirations are evident in the absence of the limiting term "literary" from its title.

In his review of the *Norton Anthology* Geoffrey Galt Harpham includes a list of omitted critics and theorists, and it is interesting to note who the major missing figures are. While his list in some particulars varies from our own, what can one say about the exclusion of Shklovsky, Empson, Trilling, and Steiner from a volume of over 2,500 pages in which ample space is given to a host of trendy but ephemeral contemporary figures?[6] Certainly a truly comprehensive survey of theory would include essays by Booth, Abrams, Ellis, Tallis, and Vickers (all absent from the *Norton Anthology*), critics whose work appears in the chapters that follow.

Readers of the standard anthologies would not know that since the late 1960s and in particular from the 1980s to the present, forceful efforts have been launched by scores of scholars to identify and analyze the gaps and wrong turns in the reigning approaches to criticism and theory. When noted at all, these critics have usually been dismissed with personal attacks and political tags intended to discredit them. Why they have been so treated seems to us no mystery. It is because the rhetoric of Theory has been successful in gaining the moral and political high ground, and those who question it do so at their peril. Vincent Descombes, whose work we include in our volume, alludes to this predicament in a recent essay:

> In the writings of American cultural critics, the word "theory" is used as an absolute noun. One does not need to specify what this theory is the theory of, nor how it relates to observation. This reflects a peculiarity of French usage in the 1960s (in particular in avant-garde journals of the time). Moreover, there are great resemblances between the older French usage and American usage today. The idea is that one can do one's work of critique (literary, film, etc.) in two ways: either without having a theory of one's object and one's practice, thereby succumbing to the illusion of "empiricism" and of "positivism," or by arming oneself with a theory that permits one to out-maneuver the ideological ruses by which the dominant "system" (with its arbitrary exclusions and preferences) tends toward the perfect reproduction of itself.[7]

Contrast these comments with what M. Keith Booker feels compelled to write in explaining the difficulties undergraduate students are likely to face in using *The Norton Anthology of Theory and Criticism*:

most of the students in courses that might be taught using *NATC* as a primary text will need to learn *some basics* about how to read literary theory and criticism before they can begin to appreciate the complexities and implications of the various selections assigned in the course. Instructors might, then, want to start the course with *some basic* comments on reading theory and criticism, alerting students that they will be confronting a new discourse that operates according to principles with which they might not be fully familiar.[8]

The proviso is well taken, but why suggest that students need only become "familiar" with (and not also critical of) the "new discourse" they are being taught? Why not expose these students to the work of Niilo Kauppi, for example, who explains the dynamics of postwar French intellectual culture and the pressure on ambitious intellectuals to come up with new ideas and to coin neologisms, which are taken by the French public to be "the main index of . . . originality and profundity"? Students struggling with the recondite formulations of Theory may learn much from Kauppi's comment that "clarity was not socially encouraged in this context of accrued competition," where "terms and schemas were borrowed in seeming disorder from other disciplines."[9]

Far from responding with reasoned argument to their critics, proponents of Theory, in the past few decades, have managed to adopt just about every defect in writing that George Orwell identified in his 1946 essay "Politics and the English Language." It is worth noting that Orwell was writing at a time when criticism seemed incapable of giving "an appearance of solidity to pure wind," as he said about political language.[10] By the early 1980s, self-appointed to the progressive side of the political spectrum, theorists projected a nihilistic tone for which "everything is language" became a central tenet.

The result is that we continue, today, in a state that M. H. Abrams described more than three decades ago:

> Each critical theorist, it can be said, pursuing his particular interests and purposes, selects and specializes his operative and categorical terms, and in consequence sets up a distinctive language-game whose playing field overlaps but doesn't coincide with that of other critical language-games and which is played according to grammatico-logical rules in some degree special to itself.[11]

The ensuing language games have usually been played by people lacking the necessary philosophical foundations but nonetheless eager to participate. One of the major lacunae we have encountered in the conventional theory anthologies of today is a direct discussion of the problem described by Abrams, specifically in terms of the contradictions between poststructuralist nihilism and the political agenda of much contemporary theory. If language creates reality, then we need only change our language to bring about political change. But, obviously, the proponents of postcolonialist, feminist, and queer theorizing do not endorse such a view in practice. The contradiction should be plain to all.

Because these and other paradoxical strands have not been untangled, many alert students of Theory have realized the arbitrariness of readings based on the theorists they study. When students notice that some theories work much better than others on particular texts, they will suspect that these theories aren't really *theory* but *approaches*, among which they—like the books that serve them as models—can pick and choose. True, dictionaries often list "idea" as the last definition of "theory," but clearly it is not this weak sense that proponents of Theory have in mind. Terms such as "approaches" or "perspectives" do not suggest the scope, explanatory power, or level of generalization one expects from a theory. Most theory anthologies and guides to the practical application of Theory do not address the incoherence in their use of the operative term. And, indeed, the incoherence exists *only* if one takes the work of theory seriously. If one replaces "theory" by "approach"—a word that lacks grandiose connotations—the problem vanishes, though the question of the legitimacy of a particular approach certainly remains. But if one uses the word "theory" in all its present high signification and believes its power to be on a par with (or superior to) that of theory in the sciences, then it's absurd to think one is free to pick and choose among theories, each of which purports to explain the same sort of object (a "text").

In point of fact, Theory as used in the literature classroom is often nothing more than an "idea"—which lets one try out this theory or that. Michael Ryan's *Literary Theory: A Practical Introduction* (1999) reveals the defects of this position.[12] In his preface, although Ryan uses the words "theory," "perspective," and "approach" interchangeably, he notes that a problem exists for Theory's claims when literary works are preselected as suitable for particular "theories."[13] Ryan faces this challenge and subjects the same three literary works to analysis by means of his chosen theories. As a result, competing readings of the same work frequently contradict one another. Equally telling, the effort to justify a given theory's applicability to any literary work is entirely abandoned in the tougher case of poetry. Here Ryan selects not the same poem but different poems by the same author, Elizabeth Bishop. It is the themes and images of particular poems that lead him to decide which theory to apply: formalism, structuralism, psychoanalytic theory, poststructuralism, Marxism, feminism, queer theory, historicism, or postcolonial studies. Thus Ryan begs the question he set out to explore.

In our experience, independent-minded students can sense that something is amiss with these shifting applications of theory to literary works. They detect the overdetermination in the selection of poems. In the case of novels and plays, students perceive how the critic strains to make the text compatible with each theory in the list of isms (occasionally skipping one if the task seems too difficult). They quickly catch on to the truth of an observation made by Frank Lentricchia a few years ago. Having decided to read literature as literature instead of as a vehicle for Theory, Lentricchia noticed that the Theory game was played by the formula "Tell me your theory and I'll tell you in advance what you'll say about any work of literature, especially those you haven't read."[14]

A quarter of a century ago Christopher Ricks, in his search for a thoughtful alternative to literary theory as practiced around 1980, wrote an illuminating review of several books by Geoffrey Hartman and Stanley Fish. Ricks noted an interesting contradiction. Theorists insist that we all do theory whether we recognize it or not (a point exemplified by Paul de Man's convenient statement that the resistance to theory *is* theory). At the same time, they are so eager to spread the Theory gospel that, as Ricks put it, they "practice baptism with a hose"—which suggests there aren't enough theorists to go around.[15] Ricks was proved right: the inevitability of Theory persists as an article of faith, and the proselytizing spirit nonetheless continues as well. The result has been the publication of ever more reiterative and derivative theories.

The sheer mass of this self-perpetuating glut has had the result that scholars skeptical of particular theorists (whether the latter are French *maîtres à penser* or their younger epigones such as Homi Bhabha and Judith Butler) or of entire schools of them (such as New Historicists) have been largely dismissed as politically conservative and out of touch, traditional, self-interested, exclusionary, and—ironically (given the generally unyielding tone of theorists)—intransigent. Labeling them thus has functioned, in turn, as a pretext for neglecting a whole range of complex, scrupulous, and often inspiring writings on theory, some examples of which appear in the chapters that follow.

We believe that in the thirty years between the publication of the first edition of Hazard Adams's *Critical Theory Since Plato* and the appearance of the *Norton Anthology of Theory and Criticism*, much has been lost with respect not only to theory and criticism that actually illuminate literary texts but also to the appreciation of criticism's actual contributions to academic discourse. That time span also saw the dissemination of theoretical principles in innumerable books aiming to ease readers' way into the arcane world of Theory, while in no way encouraging a love of literature. Elaine Showalter reminds us of the result of these developments.

> These days you need the chutzpah of a Terry Eagleton to have a stab at defining "literature" at all, and even he concedes that "anything can be literature, and . . . any belief that the study of literature is the study of a stable, well-definable entity, as entomology is the study of insects, can be abandoned as a chimera."[16]

Our book does not propose a return to an ideal past (nonexistent, in any case) of literary studies. Nor do we support a retrogressive or exclusivist view of a canon, classics, traditions, or conventions (the predictable charges hurled against critics of Theory). Rather, we have selected essayists who see the need—more urgent now than ever—to question today's theoretical orthodoxies and to replace them with open discussion and logical argumentation. Our authors also thoroughly examine the background and tenets of currently accepted Theory, and they do so in language most readers will understand. They do not represent a new version of what Harold Bloom has called a "School of Resentment,"[17] nor do they chime in with what Robert Hughes examined in 1992 as the "culture of complaint."[18] Indeed, what is particularly noticeable in our authors' writings is the general lack of ad hominem attacks, even when confronting some of the more preposterous and unreadably convoluted theories. They concentrate not on personality—as central an issue as Theory's stars have made this in cultivating their public personae—but instead on logic, reason, and evidence, concepts without which it is impossible to have any sort of fruitful intellectual exchange. They are mindful of the point made by Lamarque and Olsen (among our contributors) that the habit of many theorists to make claims without showing any awareness of the highly contentious nature of their premises and reasoning is a symptom of the poor standard of argumentation prevailing in modern literary theory.

When we began graduate work in literature in the late 1960s and 1970s a Marxist or, more generally speaking, sociological approach to literature was a new and promising area of study, excitingly different from the linguistic models of structuralism and formalism. North American scholars were (belatedly) discovering Gramsci, Brecht, Lukács, Adorno, Benjamin, and similar theorists, who quickly became icons of a critical establishment that pervaded literature departments and, to a lesser extent, related fields. In the years that followed, figures such as Althusser, Foucault, Derrida, Lacan, and Jameson (an intellectual "client of Europe," according to his fellow Marxist holdout, Terry Eagleton) became touchstones of the craft of literary analysis. "Power," "hegemony," "the Other," "the mirror stage," "deferred meaning," "the logic of late capitalism," and similar terms and phrases—by then inseparable from the authority of Theory—turned into the preeminent themes for exploration in and through literary texts.

At the same time, a feminist perspective became indispensable for literary scholars, starting with the work of such figures as Kate Millett and Shulamith Firestone and passing through French feminist critics, mainly Kristeva, Cixous, and Irigaray. Putting such figures on pedestals, however, also led to the elevation of lesser lights whose contributions were not so much to theoretical issues as to the promulgation of increasingly abstract (and often abstruse) forms of expression.

In the 1970s and well into the 1980s, reception aesthetics, narratology, critical theory (basically the Frankfurt School), postcolonialism, and an all-encompassing preference for political approaches (grounded in the theorists' own presumptively correct opinions) became the norm. Though not often cohering with an accelerating postmodernist rhetoric that saw the whole world as a "text," these approaches devolved into specializations and subfields such as subaltern studies, cultural studies, and, more recently, queer theory—all of which have spread beyond the area of literature—as is only to be expected once most everything has been reconceived as a "text."

What theorists of all these persuasions have in common, whatever their individual differences, is a decisive turning away from literature as literature and an eagerness to transmogrify it into a cultural artifact (or "signifying practice") to be used in waging an always antiestablishment ideological political struggle. This view of theory as practice, rooted in the political activism of the 1960s and acclaimed repeatedly in Theory texts from that time on, has by now found its way even into such standard anthologies as the *Norton*, as we shall see below.

At the same time an unmistakable grandiosity entered the discourse of literary theory. Professors trained primarily in literature began to claim for themselves a commanding position from which to comment importantly on any and all aspects of cultural and political life (and even on scientific research, which stood as the last bastion untouched by Theory) and thereby rise to stardom in the academic firmament. The eminence of these celebrities helps explain why so little scrutiny is given to propositions articulated by fashionable theorists whose terminology has been embraced and reiterated by their many followers. Claims to postmodernist relativism notwithstanding, the Theory world is intolerant of challenges and disagreement, which is perhaps why its rhetoric has been so widely parroted in the academy.[19]

The results of these developments have been unfortunate in many ways. As intellectual claims that at one time seemed new and exciting became ossified—reduced to the now-predictable categories of race, class, gender, and, later, sexuality—criticism and theory turned endlessly repetitive and hence otiose. A style of reading developed that, when not denying meaning altogether or seeing literary texts as inevitably about themselves, condensed complex works to an ideological bottom line drawn on their authors' perceived "subject position" and on the political leanings that could be teased out of—or imported into—their texts. Howard Felperin has referred to this process as "one of systematic misconstruction, a kind of textual harassment."[20] By now this approach has become a pervasive mindset, producing interpretations that invariably end at the same point: a denunciation of authors for their limitations vis-à-vis the orthodoxies of the historical moment and its preferred "voices," or, alternatively, a celebration of authors or texts for expressing the favored politics or for merely embodying the requisite identity. In view of all this, it is worth recalling a sane observation made by Frank Kermode (a contributor to this volume) in a recent essay:

> Despite the carping and the quarrels, despite the great variety of critical approaches that were becoming available—the American New Criticism, the Chicago Critics, the maverick Winters and the maverick Burke and the maverick Frye—there was still a fundamental consensus: literary criticism was extremely important; *it could be taught*; it was an influence for civilization and even for personal amendment.[21]

Most graduate students, we believe, and even many undergraduates in literature programs today would have little truck with such a viewpoint. For they have not failed to pick up some of what Theory is purveying. Even as newcomers in graduate programs, they have little difficulty producing the anticipated analyses in short order. Meanwhile, they acquire scant or no knowledge of formalist or stylistic criticism and have no acquaintance with aesthetics. Even if they suspect that not everything they are taught is beyond question, they are too often caught up in a mimicry of the contemporary theorists whose views they accept with more blindness than insight. Pondering such impoverishment in the study of literature, even theory enthusiasts such as Elaine Marks (who more than two decades ago was among the first to introduce French feminist theorists to an American audience) wrote with alarm and disappointment about what has happened to the academic study of literature (her essay, published in 2000, is among our selections).

Margaret Atwood recently wrote, "I think I am a writer, not a sort of *tabula rasa* for the Zeitgeist or a non-existent generator of 'texts.'"[22] Earlier still, in a 1986 interview, she explained how she had "tried for the longest time to find out what *deconstructionism* was. Nobody was able to explain it to me clearly. The best answer I got was from a writer, who said, 'Honey, it's bad news for you and me.'"[23] Her comments are emblematic of the reaction to Theory of most creative writers, whose status many theorists have been eager to usurp. Tension between critics and creative writers is hardly unusual, but it is resentful rivalry that seems to drive much academic theorizing of the past few decades.

The fantasies underlying much that goes on in the name of Theory are readily detectable in the declarations found in Theory anthologies. The preface to the *Norton Anthology of Theory and Criticism*, on its very first page, stakes its claim to relevance by equating theory with "engaging in resistance." And Rice and Waugh, coeditors of *Modern Literary Theory*, inform their student readers, in an introduction to one part of their book, that "scientific knowledge can be no more 'objective' than aesthetic knowledge."[24] These are typical assertions made in major Theory anthologies. Should readers passively assent to them?

Even books that set out to demystify theory make similarly tendentious claims. Lois Tyson's *Critical Theory Today: A User-Friendly Guide* (1999), far from promoting critical thinking, presents each of the theoretical positions she covers as a profound truth. Language, she says, "determines what we can see when we look around us and when we look at ourselves." She believes that "particular experiences [are] generated by language."[25] And yet, she affirms, all Theory is inherently political—the familiar non sequitur. If Tyson is unusual, it is only in that she wants also to teach her students something about the beauty of literature. Her "positive" aim, she claims, is to demonstrate that literature can be "ideologically appalling" and intensely beautiful as well.[26] And perhaps her sense of vulnerability in voicing such a concern in today's climate explains her eagerness to assure readers that she deplores power in all its guises.

This kind of teaching has been subjected to criticism for decades. Twenty years ago D. G. Myers, one of our contributors, concluded that "if we are serious in believing that the role of theory is to oppose cultural authority, if we are sincere in our objective of putting self-evident certainties under interrogation, what better way than by leading our students to struggle against the authorities that we ourselves have placed in their hands?"[27] Instead of this, as another contributor, Mark Bauerlein, puts it, today's political criticism is distinguished from earlier variants merely by the "broad methodological shift it brings about. Specifically, what political criticism does is center criticism on political content and render formal, disciplinary, methodological considerations secondary."[28] Frank Kermode makes a similar point in the essay cited earlier, comparing criticism half a century ago with what is written at the present time. Today's criticism, he notes, involves principles that "actually prevent it from attending closely to the language of major works (in so far as that description is regarded as acceptable)—to the work itself, rather than to something more congenial, and to some more interesting, that can be put in its place."[29]

Geoffrey Galt Harpham, in the review mentioned above, notes that even ostensible critics of Theory, such as Gloria Anzaldúa, Barbara Christian, and Jane Tompkins, who appear to have found the theory-obsessed academic scene to be repressive and alienating, do not actually suggest a turn to literature. To make their escape, Harpham points out, they chose "to focus on other things, such as themselves, the way it feels to be them, how people ought to be if they want to be like them."[30] Nonetheless, they typically attempt to remain within the glow of Theory by expanding its definition so as to include the writings of their favorites (mostly themselves and/or hitherto "marginalized voices"). Thus, poems, journals, commentaries, novels—when created by the right identity group—become "theory." In other words, Theory today is something everybody can claim to be "doing"; just expand its meaning to suit your predilections.[31]

More than eighty years ago, Boris Eichenbaum expressed the fear that formalism might degenerate and become the work of academic second-stringers who "devote themselves to the business of devising terminology and displaying their erudition." At least in the United States, this state of affairs (although unrelated to formalism, of course) is now commonplace. We think it telling that critics such as Frank Lentricchia, Edward Said, and Terry Eagleton in recent years started to question the practical implications of the theory they once preached and promoted.[32] For despite the surface diversity, the many schools of thought, and the variety of sexual and textual politics, what we really encounter today is the routine busy work of "dismantling," "unveiling," "demystifying," and so on, whether of the "unwitting" biases of an author, a group, or an entire culture, or of the spurious nature of disinterest and objectivity.

There is no need to reiterate at this juncture the institutionalization of Theory by the Modern Language Association or to examine press reports about the bizarre views that pass for literary interpretation in that organization's annual conference. We note, instead, that part of our sense of urgency about the need for *Theory's Empire* comes from our participation in academic searches to fill faculty positions, ostensibly in literature, over the past few decades. We see applicant after applicant present dossiers, dissertations, and job talks that are interchangeable and entirely predictable (in the last few years preferred themes have been the "construction of national identity," "globalization," "epistemic violence," and various versions of "border" crossings, while "transgressive sexuality," has remained in favor only by extending its boundaries to include ever new identity groups it purports to speak for and to). Largely untrained in historical methods, sociology, philosophy, and other human sciences, these young scholars often produce distressingly reductive readings—when they turn their attention to literature at all, that is. They may call their approach multi- or interdisciplinary or label it "cultural studies." But their writing is strong primarily on up-to-the-minute theory rhetoric, dutifully paying homage (if only in passing) to their chosen theory or theorist, while resolutely displaying political commitment and zeal. Such performances rarely suggest that these future teachers are inclined, or even equipped, to question their own conceptual templates, or that they have made themselves aware of the problematic aspects of the theory they have embraced.

We have composed *Theory's Empire* to provide students and faculty with materials that afford them a better understanding of theory from a fresh point of view. Ours is not a "back-to-basics" volume but rather one that intends to show how much broader a dialogue about theory has in fact unfolded over the past few decades than is usually encountered in literature and theory courses. The valuable tools supplied by dissenting theorists need to be incorporated into the curriculum. We think it crucial that if students are to continue to study developments in theory, they be exposed to reasoned critiques of it as well. As for the theoretical orthodoxies of the past few decades, they urgently require examination in a much more critical spirit, one that scrutinizes what is lost as well as what is gained by their adoption. Only when made aware of such critiques can students avoid feeling obliged to mirror the dominant discourse as a mark of their own sophistication or their membership in the club.[33] The alternative—which we have seen too often—is the student who asserts that any interpretation of a literary work is as valid as any other and blithely refers to "the bankruptcy of the Enlightenment project."

In various essays published in France and in his *Le Démon de la théorie: Littérature et sens commun* (1998) Antoine Compagnon has addressed students' fear of being out of fashion, noting the grave consequence of thereby producing generations of conformists. This is a point that many of our contributors also make as they observe how the inexact and rushed oscillation among disciplines creates a "drifting" (the term is Compagnon's) that jettisons expertise for opinions that sound far more substantial than they actually are.[34] A phenomenon seen by many humanists and social scientists as a major source of today's theoretical drifting is the spread of postmodernism's aggressive vocabulary of subversion, demystification, transgression, violence, fissures, decentered subjects, fragmentation, dismantling master narratives, and so on. This lexicon may promote an illusion of revolutionary upheaval (though in the name of what cause remains notoriously unclear). But it is hard to see how such militant rhetoric contributes to an understanding, much less to the solution, of the real political and social struggles going on in the world. Perhaps because it is so gratifying to display, this sort of political grandstanding seems to have no end. Thus, in the proceedings of the Chicago meeting referred to above, we read that one participant said, "What I'm suggesting is that the apparent collapse of theory and the distrust of cultural studies was already prefigured by endorsements that sought to place it within the system and make it a part of normal professionalization that had, and would have, no relationship to the world outside of the academy."[35] Apart from the clotted prose, this statement is a problem for innocent readers of Theory because its author seems to think he has invented the wheel while in fact he can offer nothing beyond the weary charges of scholars' "complicity" in the problems they seek to expose. Reading "outside the box" of incestuous journals, books, and conferences would reveal that similar "discoveries" have long been thoroughly scrutinized by other critics, among them our contributors J. G. Merquior, Brian Vickers, and John Ellis.

*Theory's Empire*, however, is not making an appeal to readers on political grounds—as has been done in recent years by Martha Nussbaum (in her criticisms of Judith Butler), Terry Eagleton (on Fish, Bloom, and Spivak), and others who have grown impatient with the kind of theorizing they find politically ineffective or plain frivolous. We believe that intellectual work in the humanities needs no strained justification—least of all the pretense that it can solve the problems of globalization or gender identity or racial divisions. But something larger is at stake here than the futility of such political pretenses. What the languages of present-day criticism and theory unmistakably do is undermine what should be a protected intellectual space—that of classroom teaching and learning—in which ideas can be explored and tried out with an extraordinary measure of freedom and safety. Such an environment, for the few short years that it is available to students, ought to be cultivated and cherished, rather than turned into an arena for waging ersatz politics. From frequent journalistic reports and our own and many of our colleagues' observation of the prevailing modes of instruction and critical writing in the humanities, it is evident that today's theoretical vocabulary has led to an intellectual void at the core of our educational endeavors, scarcely masked by all the posturing, political zealotry, pretentiousness general lack of seriousness, and the massive opportunism that is particularly glaring in the extraordinary indifference to or outright attacks on logic and consistency.[36]

Nothing we have written above should be taken to express an expectation, on our part, that Theory as currently conceived will meekly go out of fashion. Indeed, its status as accepted doctrine is pretty well secure. This in itself, however, creates a situation in which change is both inevitable and desirable. One sign of changes underway is that, as we and some of our contributors observe, more and more students these days approach theory as a tedious obligation, no longer as an exciting subject they wish to explore. In other words, theory in the classroom is, today, often little more than a routine practice, as predictable and dull as cafeteria food. Many professors, on the other hand, are still so wedded to the arcane rhetoric and turgid terminology that have characterized the Theory scene (and that, as some of our contributors suggest, account in no small measure for the mystique it exudes) that they are reluctant to let go of it. We strongly believe that the next decades will see the emergence of more and more open criticism of sanctioned theory in academic settings, and we hope *Theory's Empire* will contribute to it.

Having culled from a wide range of available sources materials that can help readers break out of the passive assent to established routines, we have brought together a challenging collection of essays, to be used as primary readings for those interested in theory debates and as a complement and corrective to anthologies such as the ones whose conceptual faults and gaps we have summarized above. Our chief aim is to provide students and interested readers with effective intellectual tools to help them redeem the study of literature as an activity worth pursuing in its own right. By subjecting Theory to sustained critical examination, they will—we believe—acquire a much more realistic sense of the place of theory in the world of intellectual and creative endeavors.

The essays we have gathered date from the 1970s to 2004 and cover the progression from structuralism to postmodernism and their by-products. Their authors include well-known critics and theoreticians as well as new or emerging authors from the United States, England, and other countries. All their work is fresh and—we are sure—innovative in the current context. In addition to the participation of dozens of literary scholars, we have also sought specialists in fields other than literature whose perspectives seem to us essential to understanding what has happened since the advent of Theory. The sociologist Niilo Kauppi, philosophers Paul Boghossian, Susan Haack, and John Searle, the mathematical physicists Alan Sokal and Jean Bricmont, the science studies specialist Meera Nanda, the historian Alan Spitzer, the cultural critics Russell Jacoby and Todd Gitlin, and the polymath physician Raymond Tallis—all included in our anthology—have in their large body of work contributed much to the growing skepticism regarding Theory. But their work also reveals how grave a situation we are now in. To make their case, these scholars have to spell out and reinforce some rudimentary arguments concerning facts and beliefs, evidence and truth, knowledge and opinion that should by right be considered commonplaces but are more often unfamiliar to most of our students. Like us, our contributors are trying to reach a generation of readers who have been made suspicious of these concepts and distinctions and who are confused as to what to put in their place.

Our contributors do not conceal the strong passions and deep commitment to reason and logic they bring to their critiques. Some take on the invocatory rhetoric of Theory; some provide historical and cultural explanations for its dominance; others analyze the problematic philosophical foundations on which much fashionable Theory rests. Many point out the contradictions, the paucity of evidence, the address to particular constituencies, the flagrant identity politics, and the ultimate incoherence of certain theorists. Some express their own second thoughts about theories that they had embraced at an earlier time; still others vigorously defend reason and science. And a few even reopen the subject of aesthetics, so neglected by Theory. All share an affection for literature, a delight in the pleasures it brings, a respect for its ability to give memorable expression to the vast variety of human experience, and a keen sense that we must not fail in our duty to convey it unimpaired to future generations.

## NOTES

1. Christopher Ricks, "The Pursuit of Metaphor," in *What's Happened to the Humanities?* ed. Alvin Kernan (Princeton, N.J.: Princeton University Press, 1997), 181.

2. Among the anthologies that have preceded ours, though much smaller in range, three stand out: Dwight Eddins, ed., *The Emperor Redressed: Critiquing Critical Theory* (Tuscaloosa: University of Alabama Press, 1995); Wendell V. Harris, ed., *Beyond Poststructuralism: The Speculations of Theory and the Experience of Reading* (University Park: Pennsylvania State University Press, 1996); and Kernan, ed., *What's Happened to the Humanities?* (see note 1). In general, these volumes identify the themes and figures common to the pessimistic cult of antihumanist thought during the last third of the twentieth century.

3. Hazard Adams, introduction to *Critical Theory Since Plato*, ed. Hazard Adams, rev. ed. (Fort Worth, Tex.: Harcourt Brace Jovanovich, 1992), 9. Adams also observes that the movements that argued for space in critical theory back then "are all locatable with respect to the matter of political and cultural critique, and they all grow out of the political and social ferment of the late sixties and the dominant interests of a generation now assuming power in the academic world" (6–7).

4. Emily Eakin, "The Latest Theory Is That Theory Doesn't Matter," *New York Times*, 19 April 2003. It is not unimportant that the questions of the legitimacy of theory or its demise have reached a nonspecialized public. See David Herman, "Silence of the Critics," *Prospect* 81 (December 2002): 38–41. The proceedings of the Chicago meeting are now in *Critical Inquiry* 30, no. 2 (Winter 2004).

5. *The Norton Anthology of Theory and Criticism*, ed. Vincent B. Leitch et al. (New York: W. W. Norton and Company, 2001), 28. Leitch defended his anthology in a forum published in *Symploke* 11, nos. 1–2 (2003): 242–53, and in various interviews, the most extensive of which are the sixth and seventh chapters of his *Theory Matters* (New York: Routledge, 2003), 49–67, 69–89.

6. Harpham's detailed review addresses the great gaps, arbitrariness, and presentism of the *Norton Anthology*, noting the tendentious introductions to the essays included and the tone celebrating the risky business of Theory. See his "From Revolution to Canon," *The Kenyon Review*, n.s. 25, no. 2 (Spring 2003): 169–87. Of course, the *Norton Anthology* is hardly unusual in its biases. For critiques of major reference works with similar agendas, see, for example, John Ellis's "In Theory It Works," a review of *The Penguin Dictionary of Critical Theory*, by David Macey, *Times Literary Supplement*, 29 September 2000, 6–7. Ellis demonstrates Macey's partisan view of his subject, especially deplorable in reference works, which, Ellis states, have a duty "to represent the real state of opinion in the field, and that means getting [the author's] own commitments under control so that he can present the full range of opinion in a reasonably balanced way." Ellis contrasts the state of "critical theory" with that of, say, linguistic theory or music theory, where the term "defines an area of knowledge, not an attitude or belief." By contrast, "critical theory" expresses a system of belief, one that these days "refers to ideas now dominant in university English departments." A similar criticism of a still earlier reference work appears in Brian Vickers's "Who's In, Who's Out," a review of the *Encyclopedia of Contemporary Literary Theory: Approaches, Scholars, Terms*, ed. Irena R. Makaryk, *Times Literary Supplement*, 15 July 1994, 8–9. Vickers notes the volume's failure to define what is meant by "contemporary literary theory." But worse still is its predictable ideological bias. In its pages, Vickers observes, "the words of the founding fathers and their hermeneuts are beyond criticism," an immunity that also "affects the fundamental issues of who or what is to be discussed." He concludes that "protective isolation prevents the growth of knowledge."

7. Vincent Descombes, "Rorty contre la gauche culturelle," *Critique* 622 (March 1999): 200n5 (our translation).

8. M. Keith Booker, *Teaching with* The Norton Anthology of Theory and Criticism: *A Guide for Instructors* (New York: W. W. Norton and Company, 2001), 3 (our emphases).

9. Niilo Kauppi, *French Intellectual Nobility: Institutional and Symbolic Transformations in the Post-Sartrian Era* (Albany: State University of New York Press, 1996), 78, 91. Kauppi points out that some French critics have written about the misuses of terms among the French intelligentsia, e.g., Georges Mounin analyzed the discourses of Lévi-Strauss, Lacan,

and Barthes; Marc Adriaens criticized Kristeva's use of formal models (91). For an opposing view, see Laurent Zimmerman, "Vive la théorie," *L'Infini* 84 (Autumn 2003): 75–84.

10.  George Orwell, "Politics and the English Language," in *I Belong to the Left, 1945*, vol. 17 of *The Complete Works of George Orwell*, ed. Peter Davison (London: Secker and War-burg, 1998), 430. For a feminist critique of Orwell, see Daphne Patai, *The Orwell Mystique: A Study in Male Ideology* (Amherst: University of Massachusetts Press, 1984). Now skeptical of the very notion embodied in the subtitle, Patai believes that what utility this book may still have today is owing primarily to the close reading and textual analysis undertaken. These is-sues are discussed in her recent essay, "Third Thoughts About Orwell?" in *George Orwell Into the Twenty-first Century*, ed. Thomas Cushman and John Rodden (Boulder, Colo.: Par-adigm Publishers, 2004), 200–211.

11.  M. H. Abrams, "What's the Use of Theorizing About the Arts?" (1972), in *Doing Things with Texts: Essays in Criticism and Critical Theory*, ed. Michael Fisher (New York: W. W. Norton and Company, 1989), 48–49.

12.  Michael Ryan, *Literary Theory: A Practical Introduction* (Oxford: Blackwell, 1999).

13.  We do not notice these or similar reservations in the generally enthusiastic exposi-tions collected in *Teaching Contemporary Theory to Undergraduates*, ed. Dianne F. Sadoff and William E. Cain (New York: The Modern Language Association of America, 1994). Ide-ally, in every theory course there should be a week or more of readings about the meanings of the word "theory"—all of which would help students understand the particular senses the term has and does not have in literary studies.

14.  Frank Lentricchia, "Last Will and Testament of an Ex-Literary Critic," *Quick Studies: The Best of* Lingua Franca, ed. Alexander Star (New York: Farrar, Straus and Giroux, 2002), 31.

15.  Christopher Ricks, "In Theory," *London Review of Books* 3, no. 7 (16 April–6 May 1981): 3.

16.  Elaine Showalter, *Teaching Literature* (Oxford: Blackwell, 2003), 21. In a review of Ea-gleton's *After Theory* (New York: Basic Books, 2003), which proposes replacing literary with "cultural theory," Showalter asserts that Eagleton's epitaph for his previous positions falls short of confronting questions emanating from within and without literary study. She won-ders, "why isn't literature, rather than theory, the best place to go for help about morality, love, evil, death, suffering, and truth, among other things?" See Elaine Showalter, "A Cham-pion of Cultural Theory?" *The Chronicle of Higher Education*, 23 January 2004, B9. Most re-views of Eagleton's recent treatise are negative and center on his making theory a lucrative trade. See, for example, Eric Griffiths, "The Pedlar's Wares," *Times Literary Supplement*, 17 October 2003, 6–8. More recently, James Wood, in "Textual Harassment," *The New Republic*, 7 and 14 June 2004, 28–35, has written that Eagleton's *After Theory* is "marked by the same intellectual cost-cutting, matey bombast, vulgar haste, and final incoherence that made [his] *Literary Theory* a less-than-finished work" (30). Wood goes on to say: "You would never guess, from [Eagleton's] either/ors, that Anglo-American criticism before 1960 had been both theoretical and cosmopolitan. . . . Eagleton regularly writes as if no one not prac-ticing his kind of theory can ever *really* be theoretical" (31; his emphasis). Compare Wood's conclusion to Jacques Barzun's overview of the reactions to the New Criticism: "In the en-thusiasm for the new its points of likeness to the old were scarcely seen. Because meaning was the goal, the same preoccupation with textual and verbal minutiae impugned in the former historical scholarship was now felt to be justified.  It was not seen that a new literal-

ism was developing as destructive of art as the old, and more congenial only because it was more anarchic. Everyone could preach and contemn, no one could argue or refute, for symbols were ambiguous and elusive and each vaunted method was at bottom arbitrary, indeed 'impressionistic.' Anyone brought up on explication de texte knows how much is 'found' by visceral fiat" (91). Barzun's conclusion is similar to arguments that some of our contributors make. His text is from 1958, but he could just as well be talking about today. See "The Scholar-Critic," in *A Jacques Barzun Reader: Selections from His Works*, ed. Michael Murray (New York: HarperCollins, 2002), 87–92.

17. Harold Bloom, "Literature as the Bible," *New York Review of Books*, 31 March 1988, 23–25.

18. Robert Hughes, *Culture of Complaint: The Fraying of America* (New York: Oxford University Press, 1993).

19. For a recent demonstration of such intolerance, see the irate protest against Jonathan Kandell's critical obituary of Derrida (*New York Times*, 10 October 2004). By late November, just as this book was going to press, more than four thousand individuals, ranging from graduate students to senior theorists, had signed on to the protesters' Web site, affirming their unqualified faith in the theorist's work and objecting to the tone of the article, which they found blasphemous. Evidently, proclamations of the death of theory are premature.

20. Howard Felperin, *Beyond Deconstruction: The Uses and Abuses of Literary Theory* (Oxford: Clarendon Press, 1985), 33.

21. Frank Kermode, "Literary Criticism: Old and New Styles," *Essays in Criticism* 51, no. 2 (April 2001): 194 (our emphasis). This essay is now included in Kermode's *Pieces of My Mind: Essays and Criticism, 1958–2002* (New York: Farrar, Straus and Giroux, 2003), 342–56.

22. Margaret Atwood, "If You Can't Say Something Nice, Don't Say Anything at All," *Saturday Night Magazine*, 6 January 2001.

23. Earl G. Ingersoll, ed. *Margaret Atwood: Conversations* (Princeton, N.J.: Ontario Review Press, 1990).

24. Leitch, ed., *Norton Anthology*, xxxiii; Philip Rice and Patricia Waugh, eds., *Modern Literary Theory: A Reader*, 4th ed. (London: Arnold, 2001), 449. After a brief account of the Sokal hoax, Rice and Waugh state with apparent approbation that now that sociologists of science have "joined forces" with more traditional philosophers of science, it is clear that "just as criticism constructs the 'literariness' of the text, so science constructs the shape of nature." Adding to the confusion of students of literature (who typically have little understanding of science), the editors state that "it is impossible to offer final proof that any scientific theory is actually in contact with what it purports to explain"—a phrase guaranteed to encourage students to dismiss science, rather than to explore the implications of "final proof" as applied to science. Thus the editors can conclude, "we cannot say that one theory is more true than another" (449). These issues will be taken up in detail in part 7, below.

25. Lois Tyson, *Critical Theory Today: A User-Friendly Guide* (New York: Garland Publishing, 1999), 203, 205. Immediately preceding this, Tyson writes, "our language *mediates* our experience of our world" (her emphasis), a very different claim. As an illustration of the increasing dogmatism that occurs as Theory trickles down, one could hardly do better than examine Tyson's work.

26. Tyson, *Critical Theory Today*, 429.

27. D. G. Myers, "On the Teaching of Literary Theory," *Philosophy and Literature* 18, no. 2 (October 1984): 334.

28. Mark Bauerlein, *Literary Criticism: An Autopsy* (Philadelphia: University of Pennsylvania Press, 1997), 104.

29. Frank Kermode, "Literary Criticism," 206.

30. Harpham, "From Revolution to Canon," 177.

31. As an example of the still-expanding ambitions of Theory, consider an announcement for a panel at the Modern Language Association meeting in December 2004. Called "Theorizing Retirement," the panel asks such questions as "How can a theorization of retirement inform our understanding of aging and ageism? . . . Is retirement anything other than an ageist construct? . . . In the body of literature that foregrounds the experiences of retirement, how is the experience theorized?" Sent to the Women's Studies E-mail List (wmstl@listserv.umd.edu) on 25 March 2004.

32. It is not surprising that these efforts have been along the lines of Paul de Man's posthumous *The Resistance to Theory* (Minneapolis: University of Minnesota Press, 1986), which generally prescribes defensive antidotes to aesthetic "manipulations." In "In Theory," quoted above, Ricks noted that "the case against literary theory begins with its overbearing insistence that there is no genuine case for anything else" (3). Edward Said's *Humanism and Democratic Criticism* (New York: Columbia University Press, 2004), especially its chapter "The Return to Philology," is a call for tolerance, albeit with a distinctly politicized charge.

33. This is why we cannot agree with Christopher Ricks, who, in his essay "The Pursuit of Metaphor," writes, "for to argue that current literary theory's claims are inordinate may be held to be—losingly therefore—engaging in current literary theory. And to argue that literary theory's claims deserve less attention than they have courted or extorted is, losingly again, to lavish yet more attention upon what (some of us believe) has been quite sufficiently garlanded with attentions already" (179). While sympathizing with Ricks's point, we believe it vital to make available to students, and other readers, the many grounds on which the reign of Theory can be, and has been, challenged. Ignoring a problem will not make it go away.

34. Antoine Compagnon, "La traversée de la critique," *Revue des Deux Mondes* 173, no. 9 (September 2002): 71–83. For Compagnon, *la French Theory* has delegitimized literature outside France and within it. François Cusset's *French Theory: Foucault, Derrida, Deleuze and Cie et les mutations de la vie intellectuelle aux États-Unis* (Paris: Éditions La Découverte, 2003) arrives at similar conclusions and expands on them by tracing the paradox of how what he calls "intellectuels français marginalisés dans l'Hexagone" (11) could become extremely successful in America, whereas in France their ideas were used to point out the dangers of "la pensée 68."

35. Harry Harootunian, "Theory's Empire: Reflections on a Vocation for *Critical Inquiry*," *Critical Inquiry* 30, no. 2 (Winter 2004): 399.

36. The necessity of a common, direct language in learning has been pointed out throughout the last half century. See, for example, Jacques Barzun, "The Language of Learning and of Pedantry," in his *The House of Intellect* (New York: Harper and Brothers, 1959), 216–49.

# PART I
## THEORY RISING

THE ESSAYS IN PART 1 prepare the ground for the contributions appearing later in this book. They all address the drastic change of focus forced upon the professional study of literature by the rise to unprecedented prominence of Theory and by the influence it commands in the academy. They argue for restoring a sense of balance, mindful of tradition and above all consistent with reason, to theorizing about literature. They also show—again and again—the cumulative drive that pushes theories to build upon one another as their authors' assumptions (ideological as well as conceptual) go unexamined.

The new theoretical trends that began in the 1960s and came to the fore in the 1970s and 1980s could not simply be ignored, for, as the star system in academe developed, major figures acquired a visibility, even in the mass media, that had to be acknowledged. The same decades also saw attempts by scholars of different backgrounds and preferences to address the many problems evident in the new theories and theorists. These scholars searched for a common basis on which to ground the discussion of literature under the onslaught of new ideas and articulated their objections to the growing irrationalism and abstruseness of contemporary Theory. Unfortunately, the potential impact of their work was stymied by the fear among academics (especially younger ones) of the charge of being "anti-theory." A further impediment was the reluctance of some dissenting critics (such as Christopher Ricks, cited in our general introduction) to engage in debates they came to consider futile and even unprincipled. This hesitancy still exists today—such is the force of the high status Theory has arrogated to itself.

Part 1 presents seven essays describing the transformation of theory into Theory. This mutation, while generating considerable excitement in the profession, was accompanied by the progressive relegation of literature and its study—not to mention the pleasure it afforded its devotees—to a lesser place by theorists whom most of our contributors perceive as dismissive of the humanistic values inherent in literature.

We begin with a recent essay by Valentine Cunningham, who questions the claim of Theory (the capital T is Cunningham's) to be an innovative, even revolutionary project. Not so, argues Cunningham. Theory always revisits, albeit in new guises, older critical concerns and practices, hence "theorizing about literature is always a palimpsest." Nonetheless, Theory is now ubiquitous in language and literature departments. But what, really, is Theory? Even its enthusiasts have difficulty defining it. And this, Cunningham states, is because theorists have gathered a host of subjects under the umbrella term "Theory." Conflating its many constituent parts into a set of "master tropes" held together by an "obsessive linguicity," Theory has easily penetrated kindred disci-

plines like history and architecture. This expansion beyond the realm of literature has made Theory "the greatest intellectual colonizer of all time."

René Wellek, whose essay was written more than two decades ago, cau-
tioned that literary studies were being destroyed from within. His warning has
been more than justified in the succeeding years and is therefore worth revisiting. Wellek delineates the varying motifs and aims of the attack: abolition of
the aesthetic, denial of literature's referentiality to reality, assaults on the authority of the text, blurring the distinction between poetry and critical prose,
rejection of the ideal of correct (as if this meant single) interpretations, the
displacement of artists by critics. Affirming the need for a clarification of principles and methods—the impulse that had led Wellek to write (with Austin
Warren) *Theory of Literature* (1949), the first book in English with this title—
Wellek notes that Theory has prevailed "with a vengeance," resulting in a loss
of interest in analysis, interpretation, and evaluation of literary works.

Next, Tzvetan Todorov offers a brief, highly critical survey of the state of
Theory in the United states in the mid-1980s. Both deconstruction (texts are
endlessly ambiguous, the world outside is inaccessible, only discourse exists)
and pragmatism (texts can mean anything, it is readers who give them meaning) fail, in Todorov's judgment, as viable critical stances, owing to their exag-
gerations, contradictions, confusions, ethical blind spots, and frivolity. It is
their very dogmatism, Todorov contends, that explains their success in the
academy: they offer formulas that can be applied to anything. What, then, remains for the critic who feels that literature bears some relation to the world
and insists that some values are better than others? Not Marxism, despite its
popularity in the academy, for it shares with deconstruction and pragmatism a
common antihumanist posture. It is antihumanism, then, that dominates
American criticism. To put this "regrettable episode" behind us, Todorov urges
critics to attend, once again, to this question: What does the text mean?

Morris Dickstein gauges the distance that has been traveled between I. A.
Richards's *Practical Criticism*, published in 1929, and the writings of today's
celebrated theorists. Like Cunningham, Dickstein perceives the arc that can be
traced from Richards to Barthes and Derrida as changes in the way we are
taught to read. The gap between readers and critics opened by New Criticism,
with its encouragement of a pedagogic style, was only widened by the advent
of poststructuralism, which for Dickstein was another turn of the wheel of a
modernist self-consciousness that arrived belatedly in France. Generous in his
appreciation of poststructuralists such as Barthes and Derrida, Dickstein sees
these figures as more perceptive than their method suggests. But the influence
of their writing on academic criticism, he concludes, has been numbing, leading, among other characteristics, to an "impenetrable elite jargon."

Richard Freadman and Seumas Miller present a revised and updated chapter of their 1992 book *Re-Thinking Theory*, which takes issue with the literary
theorizing of the 1980s. For Freadman and Miller, the more recent isms fa-

vored by Theory have exacerbated the problems of what they term "constructivist antihumanism," with its denial of referentiality, repudiation of the individual subject, and dissolution of substantive evaluative discourse. These are all features, they argue, inimical to constructing adequate literary theories. Instead, they propose connecting theory to the world by demonstrating how fictional discourse can furnish readers with significant truths.

In an essay targeting race, class, and gender criticism in particular, John Ellis insists that the deficiencies of some theoretical practices must not be held against theory in general. His charge is against Bad Theory, the kind that has replaced theory's true and original function—analysis—with mere assertion, blatant advocacy, and dismissive intolerance. In Bad Theory objectivity is held to be an illusion, all knowledge is socially constructed, diligent scrutiny is superseded by posturing and verbal tricks. Bad Theory soaks up ideas from other fields without having mastered them. Ellis concludes that this impoverished set of beliefs and practices has come to be wholly identified with theory itself—a mistake Ellis attempts to rectify.

Denis Donoghue's essay, with which part 1 closes, reminds us that the term "theory" has, in recent times, been appropriated by followers of what is, in essence, an institutionalized belief system claiming total explanatory force. To this pretense to holding the key to universal explanation he counterposes theory as an experimental or heuristic procedure, a theory always of *something* (not of everything), requiring argument and evidence. Donoghue's particular target in this essay is Derrida, whose deconstructionist dogma pronounced authoritatively on such fundamental matters as truth and falsehood, morality and immorality, law, politics—indeed on the entire realm of discourse. Accept this persuasion, Donoghue warns, and you will have abandoned the power of "adjudicating on true and false, right and wrong." Donoghue's essay thus seeks to elucidate what is at stake when theory rises to the level of an unyielding orthodoxy.

# 1.  THEORY, WHAT THEORY?

## VALENTINE CUNNINGHAM

*To read on a system . . . is very apt to kill what it suits us to con-*
*sider the more humane passion for pure and disinterested reading.*
     —VIRGINIA WOOLF, *"HOURS IN A LIBRARY"*

WE ALL—all of us readers—come after theory. Certainly. But what theory?
It's commonly said and assumed that we've lived through a theory revolution
in the last few decades. And this is correct. We live within an abundance of apparently novel theories, approaches, terminology, rhetorics. Theory is everywhere. It's rare to find anywhere now a published discussion or reading of literature, or to hear a lecture on a literary topic, certainly by a professional critic
from the academy, which doesn't deploy critical terms quite unknown before,
say, 1965, and which is not paying homage to named theorists of literature who
might well have been writing before then but were known only to a few close-
up chums and colleagues. A critical Rip Van Winkle waking up now after fifty
years of slumber wouldn't recognize the critical tower of Babel he'd returned
to. Cynics think that literary studies have always been too much in love with
neologisms, because we're all a bunch of pseudo-scientists desperate for a rationale for our work and so always on the *qui vive* for highfalutin important-
sounding terminologies to dazzle and confute our critics and opponents with.
If that is even nearly so, then the last few decades will have been peculiarly satisfying for insiders, for the literary-critical business simply bristles now with
critical neologisms, our readerly sky quite brilliantly alight with rhetorical
bravado. Our Theory lexicon certainly puts on a good show. Or a bad one, if
you're one of Theory's many enemies. (The terminological sword swings both
ways.)

You can easily spot "postmodernist" departments of literature, says the conservative U.S. National Association of Scholars, if their Course Catalogues use
any items from a list of 115 deplorable Theory items the Association (www
.nas.org) has helpfully drawn up. This long, shiny hit-list includes: agency,
AIDS, Baudrillard, bodies, canonicity, Chomsky, cinematic, classism, codes,
color, contextualism, decentered, Deleuze, de Man, Derrida, discourse, dominant, erotic, eurocentric, feminism, feminisms, feminist, Foucault, Freud,
Freudian, gay, gayness, gaze, gender, gendered, Guattari, gynocentric, hege-
mon, hegemonic, heteronormative, heterosexism, historicist, homoeroticism,

Valentine Cunningham. "Theory, What Theory?" Abridged from *Reading After Theory*, by Valentine Cunningham, 13–37. Oxford: Blackwell, 2002. Copyright © Valentine Cunningham 2002. Reprinted by permission of
the publisher.

identity, ideology, imperialism, incest, Lacan, lesbian, lesbianism, logocentric, Lyotard, maleness, marginalized, Marxism, modernism, oppression, otherness, patriarchal, patrimony, phallocentric, postcolonialism, postmodernism, poststructuralism, power, praxis, psychosexual, queer, queered, queering, race, sex, sexism, sexualities, slavery, structuralism, subaltern, subjectivism, theory, transgendered, transsexual, voice, whiteness, womanism, womyn.[1]

Merrily listing sixty of the NAS's terms, the London *Times Literary Supplement* (6 October 2000) chortled that you should apply to the colleges which evinced "the highest percentage" of such "postmodern" terminology "if this makes your brain cells shine with delight." But both the NAS and the *TLS* are missing the point; the historical point. For these terms and approaches to literature, the reading interests they suggest and promote, are simply everywhere in university departments of English and of other literatures, and in faculties and sub-faculties devoted to studies, such as Cultural Studies, which also use literature as evidence and certainly encourage the "reading" of social "texts" as an investigative method. They're normal and normative. Contemporary reading, certainly as that is attempted in universities, cannot, apparently, do without them—and many more of their ilk.

Theory of the kinds indicated by the NAS list—what I'm calling Theory with a capital T—is simply ubiquitous. Much of what comes under this title is not, of course, strictly speaking, theoretical—at least not in a scientific sense of a proposition, a model, a theorem, a description telling you in a testable, provable-disprovable fashion what literature and the literary are and how they or one or other of their branches function. But then poems, novels, genres of literature, are not like an enzyme, say, or an atomic sub-particle, or a chemical element, nor even like moons or that large rambling entity the human body (even though "body" is, of course, a favorite metaphor for literary things: "body of writings," we say; "body of work"; "in the body of the text"; and so on), so perhaps we would be simply wrong to expect theories of the literary to function as do scientific cognitive instruments, models, theorems, mathematical symbols, and equations. Which doesn't stop many Theorists wanting this scientificism. Some achieve something like it. The closer to linguistics the Theorist operates the more possible and convincing this is. The linguistic parts and structures and functions of writing—a dental fricative, it might be, or a phoneme, a dative, a signifier, a sentence—are not dissimilar in their knowability and boundedness to particles or moons, objects whose nature and behavior can be identified and predicted and truly theorized. It's quite a bit otherwise with Satire, or the Novel, or the Sixteenth Century.

Much of what is offered as literary theory, and Theory especially, poses as a set of genetic codes for literature, as what Gerard Genette has called a "constitutive" or "essentialist" poetics, as what E. D. Hirsch means by a "general hermeneutics." But in practice most "theory," and Theory not least, comes down to what Stanley Fish has called mere rules of thumb, or Genette's "conditionalist poetics," i.e., temporarily useful lines and avenues of reading approach, utilities of interpretation, simple practices of criticism (as Fish has suggested), principles of reading, mere matters of belief, of hunch even—the mess of useful assumptions I happen to have in my critical kitbag, postures and practices driven by contingency and pragmatism as much as by necessity, sometimes even downright blagues and try-ons, things the "theorist" has just thought of.[2]

Theorists don't like the charge of untheoretical messiness, and work hard to disprove it. Some have tried to lean on etymology for the strict meaning of their work, and invoke the originating Greek word *theoros,* spectator. So theory becomes spectator work, what onlookers and audiences do. And of course much Theory has invoked the defining authority and presence of "the interpretive community" and "reader responses" as well as various sorts of readerly "gaze" as fixable markers of the pursuit. But such invocations remain as slippery and elusive as so much else that interests Theorists, and they keep failing to harden up into the tough objects of the would-be scientific gaze their deployers crave. Indeed thinking of theory/Theory as a kind of spectator sport does rather give the game away. What precisely is an interpretive community? It's just one very loose cannon of a notion knocking about the Theoretical field. And loose cannons generate loose canons of Theory—more conditionalist than constitutive, to use Genette's distinction. Literary theorizing is generally at some remove from what the German vocabulary claims is *Literaturwissenschaft,* literary science. And this is so even when so-called scientists are attempting the theorizing. The psychiatrist Jacques Lacan, one of the modern masters of Theory, presented his literary theorizings as part and parcel of his scientific work, and his pages come littered with algebra, algorithms, seeking to express functions of language, and cognition, and so of reading. But that doesn't grant his speculations and his concepts theoretical status in a way an astrophysicist or a biochemist would recognize (which is, of course, as much a problem for psychiatry as for literary criticism).

But still we talk of theory, and I will talk of Theory. Notwithstanding the looseness of the term, vague, ultra-compendious, a huge flag of convenience, it has stuck, and in practice we know more or less what it covers. It does indeed comprise the loose assemblage of concerns and positions evinced by the NAS list, and the allied assumptions the list implies. We all know what it means. It has indeed come to mean what Jonathan Culler had more or less in mind when, back in 1982 in his book *On Deconstruction,* he suggested that "theory" *tout court* would be an apter label for contemporary literary business than "literary theory," and that "theory" was now a recognizable genre, and that "reading as a woman," say, would be a main way of "doing" theory, of entering into the essence of this "genre."

What's embraced by the label theory, what I mean by Theory, is what you expect to find and indeed do find in those proliferating university courses called "Theory" or "Introductions to Theory"; what you find in the exploding field of handy student handbooks and textbooks. The scope is, of course, Structuralism and Feminism and Marxism and Reader-Response and Psychoanalysis and Deconstruction and Poststructuralism and Postmodernism and New Historicism and Postcolonialism—the concerns of the various sections of Julian Wolfreys' volume, *Literary Theories: A Reader and Guide* (1999), in the order in which they appear. The modem gurus of Theory on these lines are, of course, the likes of Mikhail Bakhtin, Walter Benjamin, Roland Barthes, Louis Althusser, Jacques Derrida, Paul de Man, Jacques Lacan, Julia Kristeva, Luce Irigaray, Michel Foucault, non-anglophone thinkers all, but most notably French-speakers, the French men and women who poured the Word from Paris (as John Sturrock has aptly put it)[3] into eager anglophone ears from the 1960s onwards. (A key historical moment of delighted encounter and cultural insertion can even be dated exactly to the conference in 1966 at Johns Hopkins University intended to introduce French structuralism into the North American academy, when what turned up in practice was poststructuralism, including the momentously influential Jacques Derrida with his deconstructive vision of reading as a game forever poised between "two interpretations of interpretation"—on the one hand the weary old logocentric quest for meaning as truth, and on the other the zippier new expectation of meaning as imponderable, indeterminate, caught in the endless web, the maze, the labyrinthine tangle of meaning).[4]

Theory as we now know it, as the student guides have it, comprises, clearly, an awful lot of things. An awful lot; an aweful lot. Too many, you might readily think, for just one conceptual container; certainly too many for the minimalist pages of Jonathan Culler's *Literary Theory: A Very Short Introduction* (1997). Which is why Julian Wolfreys, for one, prefers Literary Theories. The great umbrella term "Theory" is not only too convenient to be altogether true, it simplifies too much by its unhelpful homogenizing.

> However implicitly, "literary theory" names a single focal point, rather than something composed, constructed or comprised of many aspects or multiple, often quite different identities. If we name several identities or objects as one, not only do we not respect the separateness or singularity of each of those subjects or identities, we also move in some measure towards erasing our comprehension of the difference between those objects and identities, making them in the process invisible.[5]

And that's well said (and like many other committed Theorists, Wolfreys is greatly distressed by any tendency to blunting the force of particular theoretical postures, deconstruction, feminism and so on, such as this homogenizing tendency represents). But still a kind of sense is served by this cramming-in label. For Theorists have indeed managed to pull off what is, by any standards, an astounding coup, or trick; have managed to wedge together a great many various subjects, concerns, directions, impulses, persuasions, and activities that are going on in and around literature, and squeeze them all under the one large sheltering canopy of "Theory." They have managed to compel so many divergent wings of what they call Theory under the one roof, persuaded so many sectional variants of interpretative work to sink their possible differences around a common conference table, in the one seminar with the sign Theory on its door. So while setting their faces, usually, against Grand Narratives and Keys to All Mythologies, as delusive and imperialist, and all that, Theorists have managed to erect the Grandest Narrative of all—Theory—the greatest intellectual colonizer of all time. How this wheeze was pulled off, how you can have the political and the personal subjects of literature—representations of selfhood and class and gender and race: the outside-concerns, the outward look of writing, the descriptive and documentary, the reformist intentions, and the ideological instrumentality of writing—envisioned and envisionable as part and parcel of the often quite opposite and contradictory functions of writing—the merely formal, or the technically linguistic, or (as often) a deeply inward, world-denying, aporetic writing activity—rather defies ordinary logic. Foundationalism and anti-foundationalism, shall we say roughly the Marxist reading on the one hand, and the deconstructionist on the other, make awkward bed-partners, you might think. But Theory deftly marries them off, or at least has them more or less cheerfully all registered as guests in the same hotel room.

The secret of these dangerous and strange liaisons, this hold-all capaciousness of Theory, is, of course, embedded in the truly versatile resources of Ferdinand de Saussure's *Cours de linguistique générale*, those potent lectures given in Geneva to tiny handfuls of escapees from nineteenth-century philology in the years up to and into the First World War, and cobbled together later for posthumous publication from students' notebooks. Saussure's wonderfully generous donation to literary theory, and quite foundational for Theory's wide field of interests, was a double-sided vision of linguisticity—on the one hand, a radical menu of definitions of language as such, which fired and fed concepts of signification as an activity on the inside only of language and so also of text; on the other, a pointing to a new science of signs in society, *semiotics*, a way of seeing and analyzing all human structures as like language, as in a deep way all textual. Here were the basics for literary theory's so-called linguistic turn and the basis of Theory's obsessive linguisticity. The Saussurean terminology and concepts were all set to be quite intellectually ravishing, and after the Second World War when they spread to Western Europe and the Americas (they'd mainly been taken up after the First World War in Eastern Europe) they became simply normative for literary study.

Saussure's brilliant suggestions caught on momentously. That language should be thought of as an affair of sign-systems rather than of words; that

these systems were organized as sets of binaries—linked pairings of opposites—so that signs were binaries of *signifiant*, signifier (the written or spoken
entity) and *signifié*, signified (the mental image or concept produced by the
sign); and the time and space of language, the language condition, were a binary of past and present, of the synchronic (language at any given moment)
and the diachronic (language in history, the history of language); and language
in existence was a binary of potential use and actual use (*langue* being the language *in potentia*, *parole* being language in action): all this became conventional wisdom, and a wisdom that quite ran away with Theory. Saussure said
(correctly) that his binaries could not be separated in practice, but he chose in
his lectures not to discuss signifieds or *parole* or diachrony. This was a mistake
so far as his eager Theorizing followers would be concerned, for soon Theorists were saying, and thinking, that those aspects of language had been quite
ruled out, didn't matter, and need not concern literary criticism. Reading literature did not need to take them into account, literature did not foreground
them, being about signifiers rather than about signifieds, and not-historical
(not of diachronic interest), and to do with *langue* rather than *parole*. These
formalist preoccupations of Saussure-inspired Theory certainly sound now a
bit crazy, a bit rich; but anyone who fails to credit them should glance at, say,
Terence Hawkes's influential *Structuralism and Semiotics* (1977), a founding
volume of the Methuen New Accents series of Theory paperbacks, and see
them being cemented firmly in place for the student audience. It was all a
cheeky traducing of Saussure, but a process furthered by more wrestings along
the same misreading lines. Signs are arbitrary, said Saussure, and have little
necessary link to what they denote—which has some truth in it: *cat* could easily be *dog*, to start with anyway—but quickly all of language, writing, meaning,
were being declared to be arbitrary, not grounded in any reality, a mere illusion
of language.

The "arbitrariness of the signifier"—a non-Saussurean phrase, for him it
was always the *arbitrariness of the sign*—set in as Theory's code for the linguistic life of literature, for literariness itself. Phonemes, the building blocks
of words, comprised, according to Saussure, and again with truth, a system
not of references but only of differences (*a* is not *b* is not *c*, and so on), but
soon all linguistic and textual stuff was being thought of as differential rather
than referential systems, cases of endless inward-looking deferrals of meaning, *mises en abyme* in the nice French coinage, writing plunging down for
ever and ever into black holes of retreating signification. And soon Jacques
Derrida was playing his astute game with the French word *différence*, to produce his coinage *différance*, so as to really bring home the deferral aspect of
differential meaning, and to confirm his idea of the mere *jeu*, or play, or game
of signifiers—a metaphor wrongly beefed up by his U.S. mistranslators as the
*freeplay* of signifiers, an idea not Derrida's, but one soon found on hundreds
of critical pages. And soon the old rhetorical term *aporia* was being brought

into play—into *this* play—to point to the same claimed effect of uncatchable meaning—though *aporia* actually means a dead end, an end-stop, a cul-de-sac of sense-making, not its total disappearance down some linguistic black hole. Jacques Lacan was quick to come up with talk of gaps and lacks, of *béances*, yawning holes of meaning—and soon every text possible was found to be full of those.

And, of course, this sequence of language-literature concepts was also getting itself applied to all the signifying practices out there in the world—the world of semiotics, of signs in society—as Saussure said they might. Soon everything was being seen as structured like a language, and language Saussureanly viewed. This was the high claim of Structuralism. The anthropologist Claude Lévi-Strauss became notable for reading, say, kinship structures as sets of Saussurean-type binaries. As revealed in tribal stories, these anthropological arrangements were of course linguistic and linguistified. Structural Anthropology was on its way. And Roland Barthes came to fame trying to read items of French culture (wrestling matches, and so on) as linguistic structures. His reading of French fashion magazines as a textualized system of the French fashion industry was more successful. But once started, this analytic furor need never stop its applications. The unconscious, for example, was also structured like a language, according to Jacques Lacan. Of course the structure was like a language on the Saussurean model as appropriated by literary Theorists—all signifiers and deferral. And Lacan, naturally, produced his own "algorithm" (he was fond of geometrical diagrams) for the current denigration of signifieds. The sign should be represented as $\frac{S}{s}$: big signifier over a very small signified, always sliding about deterringly and deferringly under the signifier that mattered more. Such was the rapid circulation of such notions across the Theoretical stage, literary critics were soon burbling happily about sliding signifiers (see Colin McCabe, for instance, on their presence in Joyce, in his *James Joyce and the Revolution of the Word*, 1978). The linguistic trades defined the others, and the others returned to boost the literary. A glorious, amenable circularity of concept. A slippery sliding contagion.

Analogy-drawing is, of course, perennially worrying in the history of interpretations. Analogies are slippery customers and too-easy friends, and the language model came with all of the useful casual attractions of analogy. But catch on this one certainly did. In structuralist readings of literature, construing writing as built on phonemic or morphological sentence models, on binary lines, and so on—stimulated no end by the Saussure-inspired Russian formalist Vladimir Propp and his *Morphology of the Folktale* (1928 in Russian, 1958 in English), a "morphological" examination of a collection of Russian folktales. Which was all logical enough, because literature is made of language and if it won't submit to linguistic models, what will? But here was a set of language analogies applied also to everything that was made by the human language user. Everything, it was soon being alleged and grasped, could be seen and read on language lines, as textual, as text. Or, as the concept held and fertilized, read as mere "rhetoric," as "discourse," as "story," or "narrative."

The analytic brilliance of Michel Foucault was to extend the notion of "discourse" across the whole globe of social constructs, but with particular fructifying force into his analysis of social areas where power operates to create social and individual subjugation, marginality, subalternity, in definitions of madness, illness, criminality, sexual deviance. The authoritarian arrangements of different periods, his arguments ran, were characterized by different "discourses" or epistemic arrangements, i.e., are interpretable and comprehensible as rather like, if not always very like, a language or language stuff.[6] Foucault's inherited French leftism—and all the major French Theorists have been more or less, as they say, *Marxisant*—thus found new force as older views of class and economic oppression were rigorously re-spun as the gaze of oppressive authority, organized to mark the oppressed Other (prisoner, madman, schoolchild, the sick, the gay): this gaze a politicized version of Lacan's psychologized gaze; these Others a politicization of Lacan's otherness, with links to the old Saussurean/new Derridean validation of difference. And how "power" became an absolutely universal critical concept. And how the panoptic gaze of oppression—after Foucault's historical allegorization of the panopticon prisons of the nineteenth century in his *Surveillir et Punir* (1975; in English: *Discipline and Punish*, 1977)—got everywhere. And, of course, this conceptual siding with the oppressed Other, with otherness, and with the socially different, readily linked hands with the analysis of *carnivalesque* by the exiled Russian Formalist Mikhail Bakhtin in his *Rabelais and His World* (1968)—which in turn fell off the tree, so to say, into the lap of the Derridean idea of textuality as game. And Foucault's work not only had this power of drawing in its own analogies, but fed vividly back into the politicized analyses out of which (like carnivalesque) it had come. So that feminism, not least, so powerfully defined for older literary criticism by writers from Mary Wollstonecraft to Virginia Woolf, took on new life rearmed as it were by Foucault's gripping rhetorics of the discourses of power. And the other strong analytical -isms which are still potently with us as mainstays of Theory were also force-fed by Foucault's influential concepts: studies such as postcolonialist ones, those angered investigations into imperialism fired originally by Marxism; and postcolonialism's twin, Black Studies, fired by equally angry analyses in the long aftermath of slavery, especially in the U.S.A; and New Historicism, instigated by groups of old Marxists who were looking around in the wake of deconstruction for a legitimation of their literary-cultural historicist yearnings; and (so-called) Cultural Materialism, invented by one-time pure British Marxists and products of the powerful Cambridge (England) Raymond Williams–F. R. Leavis axis which spawned Terry Eagleton as well, namely Alan Sinfield and Jonathan Dollimore; and, naturally, Queer Studies, utterly the godchild of Foucault's histories of sexuality. If Gender, Race, and Class have become a dominant trinity of literary-critical concerns (as well as of Cultural Studies), then it's Michel Foucault's work which brought them all brilliantly together (with the special emphasis, of course, on Gender and Race, especially in the U.S.A., where Marxism has never been allowed to take strong root and class-consciousness and class rhetoric are by British and European standards deeply confused, and even taboo).

This linguistic-textual turn has succeeded in being a set of popular master tropes or keys, of course, by its canny inclusivity, its seemingly unstoppable adaptability, and, obviously, its conceptual looseness. Henry Louis Gates Jr., the most interesting of black spokesmen for American Black Studies, referring to the theory of literature which we all as reading individuals inevitably bring to our reading (our unwitting hybrid of theories), called it "a critical gumbo as it were."[7] Clearly gumbo is a lovely, multivalent, tasty (and slavery-derived, postcolonial) mix that is most apt to Gates's postcolonial vision of the American cultural *olla podrida*. Gates has rightly likened gumbo to the ancient Roman *satura lanx*, the "full plate" of mixed edibles, sweet or sour, i.e., forced meat, farce-meat, stuffing, sausage-meat—what Americanistically Gates calls "hash"—which is one etymological root of *satire*, and which traditionally helps define the rich mix of that genre of writing.[8] Gumbo nicely captures the omnicomprehensiveness of Theory in our textualizing era. Here, and like *this*—mainly unfarcically, unsatirically, though with satirizable and farcical aspects—comes everything, potentially. And that's why Theory has spread so slickly, glibly even, into so many domains of the humanities—into geography (the surface of the earth is a text, and so are cities and weather systems and so on);[9] and history (historiography is writing, ergo it's to be theorized as narrative and story and rhetoric, all tropologically, and its practitioners slotted into the gender, race and class boxes);[10] and music (more textual product, subject to the squeeze, of course, of race and class and gender; gender especially; can a flattened third be gay? why yes indeed it can);[11] and theology (the Judaeo-Christian God and His Book, all easily deconstructable and narrativizable; and as for patriarchy and logocentrism, why here are their foundations; deconstruction begins, as it were, in the Book of Genesis);[12] and, of course, art history (all texts);[13] and architectural theory and practice (all texts again, and Daniel Libeskind deconstructs buildings!); and law (more text, and all deconstructable interpretative acts);[14] and medicine (the body is a text, after all).[15] Theory's gumbo-effect is why Cultural Studies, the study of anything and everything "cultural," can claim coherence. Anything at all, in short, which can be thought of as if made textually, imagined as imagined, as narrated, as constructed language-like, and thus "readable," is now being "read."

You do have to feel a bit sorry for the editors of the journal *Social Text*, so utterly taken in by Alan D. Sokal's spoof article "Transgressing the Boundaries: Toward a Transformative Hermeneutics of Quantum Gravity," a very large bowl of Theory gumbo indeed. But Sokal moved in on quantum mathematics making all the right-sounding Theoretical anti-foundationalist and anti-hegemonic noises: "Most recently, feminist and poststructuralist critiques have demystified the substantive content of mainstream Western scientific practice, revealing the ideology of dominance concealed behind the facade of 'objectivity.'" The assumptions of physics—"that there exists an external world, whose properties are independent of any individual human being and indeed of humanity as a whole; that these properties are encoded in 'eternal' physical laws; and that human beings can obtain reliable, albeit imperfect and tentative, knowledge of these laws by hewing to the 'objective' procedures and epistemological strictures prescribed by the (so-called) scientific method"— are just, Sokal burbled merrily, one more set of post-Enlightenment dogmas to be busted with the tools of up-to-scratch Theory brought over from the literary-linguistic domain.[16] And why not? After all, the editors of *Social Text* had long ago come to believe in the universality of Theory's vision. And if geography and music and theology and the rest had succumbed to Theory, why not mathematics and physics? Certainly, for Theorists, for Theory, all human pitches, and some non-human ones, have been as it were queered by the same analytical brush or brushes, and readily so. All of them "constructed like a language." And language, of course, skeptically regarded.

With Theory thus ecumenically conceived as being more or less all things to all women and men, offering something or other to more or less everyone of every gender and racial and class disposition and from every critical background, as some analytical touch or other for all textual occasions and seasons, the claim on the *necessity* of this or the other critical corner of Theory does indeed tend to dissolve into mere contingency, into questions of what's useful, or just handy, on any particular reading occasion. And of course handiness has been the key to Theory's success. Theory does open textual doors—with this key, if not quite that other one. The multiplying student guides mostly operate on this suck-it-and-see approach. You can have a go at "reading like a woman," as it were, whoever you are; but then again, you might try a Marxized reading, or this week you can write me an essay using a New Historicist approach, and of course there's a stimulating Lacanianized article you might look at for the week after that. Douglas Tallack epitomizes this Theoretical pragmatism, or opportunism, very nicely with his volume *Literary Theory at Work* (1987), in which the Nottingham University Theory Group run various Theoretical approaches, from narratological through political to deconstructive and psychoanalytic, across three texts, Conrad's *Heart of Darkness*, Henry James's *In the Cage*, and D. H. Lawrence's *St. Mawr*. And they all compel, more or less.[17]

"Which Theory?" asks Raman Selden in his *Practising Theory and Reading Literature: An Introduction*, and he means which Theory for me, for you, in this or any other reading situation. And the answer is a "*de facto* pluralism." "It may seem best to say 'Let many flowers bloom' and to treat the plenitude of Theories as a cornucopia to be enjoyed and tasted with relish."[18] Or dip into your gumbo, as you wish, in your own time. Selden disowns a "market economy" approach, he says, but that is what his view of Theory's multiplex of approaches suggests: shop around; roll your own; pick 'n' mix (excluding, it always goes without saying, a racist, male-chauvinist, fascistic, master-class approach). This liberalism is for many analysts the very essence of "postmodernity." It is, precisely, where Theory has arrived with its espousal of multivalence and multiculturalism and its suspicions of canons, and evaluation, and, in effect, truth-claims. It is, though, an eclecticism which naturally vexes many purists, who do survive among Theorists, for the various sections of Theory thus plundered often started out as very rigid kinds of analysis, steeped in the particulars of their ideological sources. Such and such are how language and the self really are, say Saussure and Freud and Marx and Lacan and Derrida and all the rest of the prophetic tribe, and so this and this is how writing and text actually are. And many Theorists, the really devout believers and ideologues, essentially claim that you should, you must, read like a deconstructionist, or a woman, or a lesbian, or a slave-emancipationist; for if you do not you are untrue to the nature of things, and of language, are obtuse and myopic about history and repression, and so on. Only thus and thus might criticism live up to the criticism implicit in its name.

The "domestication" of Theory evidenced by the handbooks and liberal university courses is just what worries Julian Wolfreys, for example—a good case of the Theorist who wants Theory to retain a radicalism of critique. The Theory Course acts, he complains, like a set of rabies shots; it's a quarantining effect; "an effective form of containment" working by a false flattening out and homogenizing. It's a sort of mere Theory tourism ("If this is week six it must be feminism").[19] But Wolfreys's own volume simply joins the long roster of guides ministering to this tourism effect. It props up the assumption of Theory as a mere self-service counter; sustains the cheerful pragmatism of Richard Rorty, for whom all hard-and-fast rules of reading are simply misguided (the "view that 'theory'—when defined as an 'attempt to govern interpretations of particular texts by appealing to an account of interpretation in general'—has got to go").[20]

The Old Bolsheviks, as we might call them, the true Theoretical believers, prize what they believe to be the absolute revolutionary force of the linguistic turn, especially in its high deconstructive mode. And many European Theorists, and not just the French, as well as some North Americans and lots of South Americans, did indeed start out as Old Leftists, committed to a basic notion of literary-critical hermeneutic truth as nothing if not revolutionary, as the ultimate turnaround. They found it easy, even necessary, to talk of absolute losses of old critical currencies, total disruptions of old positions by new ones, a "split in the psyche of traditional literary studies," a "true break" with, say, "the Romantic inheritance," and so on. (I take all of these firm *coupure/* cut/break terms almost randomly from Raman Selden's introduction to his *Practising Theory and Reading Literature*). Catherine Belsey—an Old Bolshevik of Theory if ever there was one—reminds us in her feistily dogmatic *Critical Practice* (1980) that Freud liked to think he'd made a Copernican revolution by unsettling old ideas of selfhood, and Lacan agreed with him. Belsey, though, devotes the last part of her book to arguing that it was Lacan's Saussureanized continuation of Freud's decentering of the self that was truly Copernican.[21] These revolutionary dreams are characteristic of our Theorists. But, in truth, there is nothing in Theory which has proved utterly revolutionary—all of it being, manifestly, new spins on old turns, a continuing affair of what T. S. Eliot in his 1930 conversion poem "Ash Wednesday" dubbed a turning and turning again.

In many ways there is only one history of literary theory—and wiser counsels increasingly realize it—as witnessed neatly in Chadwyck-Healey's 2001 *Literary Theory* database: "which traces literary theory and criticism from Plato to the present day,"[22] or from Aristotle to Derrida, as their publicity has it. Certainly everything that Theory comprises, operates in one zone or another, or in some combination, of what have proved the main continuing focuses of literary theory since poetics and discussion of aesthetics began with the Greeks and Romans. There's only ever been up for critical grabs, for theory, a simple trio of knowable, thinkable zones, corresponding to the three components of the basic model of linguistic communication. There is always, and only ever, a sender, a message, and a receiver—a writer, a text, a reader—the act of writing, the thing written, the reading of the written thing—the literary input, the literary object found to be "there," reader(s) attending to this thereness. Or, if you like: cause, consequence, effect. Only three; but a mighty three for all that. And the whole history of criticism, of theorizing, is merely a history of the varying, shifting preoccupation across the ages with these three zones, and with these three alone. These three, and only these three, define the range, the nature, of literary theorizing. It's what's done with them, the varying emphases and definitions which they have received over time, that defines the history, as it defines the politics, of theorizing.

Rarely has past critical fashion chosen to emphasize all three simultaneously. Critical fashion has always been notably picky and partial. The busy copresence of all three in Theory is one sign of the ways modern or postmodern theory is spun differently from the theorizing of the past: it's a marker of the greedy omnivalence of Theory's gumbo. But however partially or fully dwelt on in the theorizing of a given historical moment, these three—their avatars, their rejiggings and redefinings, their formulations and reformulations, their various turns and returns—are always the three, from the beginning to now, from theoretic Genesis to modern Theoretical Apocalypse, or (in those lovely words in *Finnegans Wake)* from guinesses to apolkaloops.

Only the temporary emphasis and focus shift—as a sketchy sketch map of the last two-and-a-half millennia of literary theory readily shows. But the theory position remains always one of emphasis and concentration on one or other of the Big Three rather than absolute neglect, and the "progress" of criticism and theory sticks at being a game with only three dimensions. So it went, and so it still goes. The great nineteenth-century critic Thomas Carlyle is, of course, immersed in textualities (his zany *Sartor Resartus* [1834] is as dotty on wild textuality as anything promoted by *Tristram Shandy* or *Shandy*'s postmodern admirers), but he's also a post-Romantic literary biographer and keen to promote poets as heroes of the age. Matthew Arnold, too, is interested in authors, and talks amply about text ("the best" that's been "thought and said"), but like most Victorians his main preoccupation is with poetry's moral and social effects. For Arnold, poetry is an acculturating mechanism. It educates and socializes. Above all, it consoles and instructs readers as a secular substitute for the instructions and consolations once provided by the texts and readings of the now challenged Christian religion. But the theoretical emphasis had switched away from the romantic stress on the poet as the main thing, and was now directed very much towards the reader, the context, the world, and bore strongly on personal, and so also on social construction, on up-building, or (to use the older and Christian term) edification. And that was as true of George Eliot as it was of Marx and those great Victorian survivors and inspirees, T. S. Eliot and F. R. Leavis.

Other emergers from the nineteenth-century went in for reaction and reemphasis rather than affirmation, of course. What made Ferdinand de Saussure open his *Cours* with a lengthy discussion of linguisticity as such was precisely a reaction against the nineteenth-century concentration on philology, on language in history, in the world outside of language (he was after all a Professor of Sanskrit). Saussure might even be thought of as catching the spirit of the late nineteenth-century reaction away from realism and towards symbolism, aestheticism, formalism, imagism, and the text burning with a hard gemlike flame purely and uncontaminated by the world. And the Russian Formalists Saussure inspired in his turn were steeped in that same reactionary spirit—which is why Formalism soon fell foul of the new Soviet regime that looked back with yearning on the nineteenth-century theorists' preoccupation with the work's dynamic relation to the context, out there where the readers were, as the source of all aesthetic good—which was a reaction against the modernist reaction: truly reactionary, as one might say. And, after all, the founders of Marxist aesthetics, Marx and Engels, were nothing if not High Victorians. And this quarrel between the formalizers and the politicizers became one of the twentieth century's recurrent causes of theoretical warfares. I. A. Richards, inventor of Practical Criticism, and his theoretical offspring the Chicago New Critics, vigorously resisted the politicizing and theologizing of reading that went on in the 1920s and 1930s hand in glove with Soviet doctrinism and/or its Fascist and Christian antagonists. The "verbal icon" was the only thing for the New Critics, the text as a self-subsistent "well-wrought urn," with all other critical preoccupations and emphases ruled sharply out as heresies.

Structuralism, and then deconstruction, descended more or less straight out of Saussure's formalism, with much theoretical support from the particular stress granted to the amazing narrative and rhetorical structures of the "dream text" by Saussure's great contemporary Sigmund Freud. Freud did, naturally, have real patients and their therapy in mind, real selves producing the dream texts whose interpretation would, *hoffentlich*, lead to actual cures. And so, arguably, did Jacques Lacan. But as Freud's work tended to get appropriated as a set of clues to mere textual penetration (Hamlet's problem "is" the Oedipus complex), so Lacan's most notable contribution to literary theory has been on the merely textual front (sliding signifiers; textual *béances*; and so forth); which has not stopped him also reinforcing the politicizers with their discourses of "the other." But then Saussurean difference has also been able to take on a political edge at the politicizers' behest; and Michel Foucault, the great inspirer of New Historicism and the rest, drew happily and profitably on such originally formalist notions to reinvigorate his own Marxism. Which brings us back, of course, to Theoretical gumbo, as well as potently illustrating the point about theoretical revision being more the norm than theoretical revolution.

Criticism always claims newness; it wants to be new. It's not just writers who want (as Ezra Pound put it) to "make it new." But criticism has never ever been quite new; and the history we're dealing with is all about swings and roundabouts, about the Big Three items going around and coming around, again and again, in a process of constant reaction, resurrection, rereading, repositioning, revision. Aristotle overturns Plato; Sidney takes on his Puritan contemporaries armed with polished-up Aristotelian tools; the formalists resist the realists who in turn object to formalism; Lacan rereads Freud; Althusser rereads Marx; Leavis wars with the New Critics, who fight the Marxists; Derrida moves away from Marxism and is repudiated by Foucault; Derrida reclaims the self and history and "presence" from his deconstructionist fans who reject those things in his name (and is welcomed back into the fold by Foucault). And so on, systole and diastole, fading and returning, on and on.

Revisionism is, of course, always striated with nostalgia. Soviet Socialist Realism, for example, wanted a simple nineteenth-century realism to return to displace rampant modernism and formalism. And our modern Theory has, more than any previous set of theoretical notions and practices, provoked in its adversaries the wish to reinstate some earlier period's theory and to return to a mythic period of greater theoretical or cultural purity before multiculturalism (or "multi-culti" with its deliberately pejorative ring of *cult* in it) arrived to derange what's thought of as an earlier homogeneity of language and disposition (a kind of aestheticized racism, this), before deconstruction (rhymes with destruction, of course, in its detractors' ears), before the "culture of complaint," as it's been dubbed, set in and whingeing feminists or black-studies students got loud. But no simple return to prelapsarian theoretical innocence is ever possible, for that never existed. There never was such a theory arcadia as Theory's opponents allege. The offensive concerns of Theory have always been present in some form or another, muted often, differently loaded frequently, but still there. Theory has always been fallen, as it were. What worries some, and excites others, about our recent Theory is by no means its innovativeness, but only what are in effect its strong renovations.

There certainly is strong renovation. Theoretical rereading is indeed rereading. Marx is Foucauldianized. Freud is indeed Lacanianized. The formalizings of old New Criticism get more forcefully reinstated as Structuralism. The "biographical fallacy" of the New Critics reappears more extremely as Barthes's Death of the Author. Russian Formalism feeds, in a real sense, into deconstruction, but more intensely. Old Historicism segues into New Historicism, but it's a historicism with grave doubts about history. And, of course, there is, and will be, inevitable revisionism of Theory's pushes. The intensity of the politicization of criticism was in many ways a reaction to the strength with which deconstruction's anti-foundationalism took hold. A once derided Humanism has rearrived as the Anthropological Turn.[23]

What deceives both those shocked, as well as those besotted by Theory, is that the returners, whether welcomed or despised, never wear exactly the same hat they wore to go away in. Raymond Williams once famously claimed, in an echo of Milton's vexed assertion in his *Areopagitica*, that "new presbyter" was "but old priest writ large," that new structuralism was but old New Criticism writ large. And he was right, but not quite right. The theoretical return is always contaminated by what went on meanwhile. Althusser is Marx put through the Saussurean wringer. Lacan sharply Saussureanizes Freud. New historicism is by no means a simple reprise of old historicism, but historicizing inevitably affected by the historically intervening supremacy of textuality, so that its founding guru Stephen Greenblatt, though recognizably still a Marxist of sorts, is one whose model of the historical input and output of writing is greatly complicated by an interest in the input rather of texts into texts, and in texts' output rather as textual (a "circulation of texts," as it's called, replacing other kinds of circulation—say of persons and things, materialities, into texts and out again into the world of persons and things). And twentieth-century Socialist Realism is far more narrow and exclusive than nineteenth-century social realism. And the Death of the Author concept is indeed several steps more murderous than the Biographical Fallacy—which never imagined a dead author, only one critics shouldn't talk about. And when the "new" biography sets in it is infected by the new gender issues, and foregrounds issues of hermeneutics, and expresses doubts about the authority of its stories in a metatextual way owing everything to Theory. And when the question of reader emotionality returns as a critical concern, though it will usually involve some discussion of Aristotelian catharsis, or pause over the Johnsonian repertoire of highly charged textual encounters, it is also differently inflected from all its earlier occasion—whether in, say, I. A. Richards's rejection of emotional response as a criterion of value in 1920s Cambridge, or in Wolfgang Iser's interest in readers' responses, or in the weight given to questions of emotion in the Canon Wars provoked by our Gender, Race, and Class debates. The returns of Theory are inevitably incremented.

For all that, theorizing about literature is always a palimpsest. Below the latest lines you can always still read the older inscribings. Theoretical memory is always stronger than Theory's would-be revolutionaries hope. The present trend of Theory is always a simultaneously present archeology or paleography. Theory's archive is perpetually open. As with the media of communication. We move from script to print to IT, but I still start writing this with a pen and pencil. Now I fly, now I drive my car, now I ride my bike, now I go on foot. While Concorde flies supersonically overhead, a canal barge goes by and a railway train, and, as Larkin has it in his poem "The Whitsun Weddings," there's always someone "running up to bowl."

In denying Theory's absolute innovativeness, I'm seeking to place it rather than simply denigrate it. And, to be sure, if Derrida and Foucault are, as it were, Theory's Concorde—if, for that matter, our Theory gumbo is like flying Jumbo—then it's easy to believe the excitement that Theory's turns and turnabouts have generated. And in truth, there has been, and there is the good, and the goods, of Theory.

## NOTES

1. National Association of Scholars, *Losing the Big Picture: The Fragmentation of the English Major Since 1964* (Princeton, N.J.: National Association of Scholars, 2000).

2. For Gerard Genette, see "Fiction and Diction," in his *Fiction and Diction*, trans. Catherine Porter (Ithaca, N.Y.: Cornell University Press, 1993), 1–29. For Hirsch and Fish, see Stanley Fish, "Consequences," in *Against Theory: Literary Studies and the New Pragmatism*, ed. W. J. T. Mitchell (Chicago: University of Chicago Press, 1985), 106–31.

3. John Sturrock, *The Word from Paris: Essays on Modern French Thinkers and Writers* (London: Verso, 1998).

4. Jacques Derrida, "Structure, Sign, and Play in the Discourse of the Human Sciences." One version of this lecture is in Derrida, *Writing and Difference*, trans. Alan Bass (London: Routledge & Kegan Paul, 1978), 278–93.

5. Julian Wolfreys, foreword to *Literary Theories: A Reader and Guide*, ed. J. Wolfreys (Edinburgh: Edinburgh University Press, 1999), x–xi.

6. The best bibliography of Foucault's writings is in David Macey, *The Lives of Michel Foucault* (London: Hutchinson, 1993).

7. Henry Louis Gates Jr., "Authority, (White) Power, and the (Black) Critic; or, It's All Greek to Me," in *The Future of Literary Theory*, ed. Ralph Cohen (London: Routledge, 1989), 334.

8. See Henry Louis Gates Jr., *The Signifying Monkey: A Theory of African-American Literary Criticism* (Oxford: Oxford University Press, 1988), 223.

9. See Derek Gregory, *Geographical Imaginations* (Oxford: Blackwell Publishers, 1994).

10. Hayden White led the way, of course, with his *Metahistory: The Historical Imagination in Nineteenth-Century Europe* (Baltimore, Md.: Johns Hopkins University Press, 1973), and *The Content of the Form: Narrative Discourse and Historical Representation* (Baltimore, Md.: Johns Hopkins University Press, 1987). Typical is the mass of work on representations of the Holocaust, e.g., Dominick LaCapra, *Representing the Holocaust: History, Theory, Trauma* (Ithaca, N.Y.: Cornell University Press, 1994).

11. See, for example, Philip Brett et al., eds., *Queering the Pitch: The New Gay and Lesbian Musicology* (London: Routledge, 1994); and Richard Dellamara and Daniel Fischlin, eds., *The Work of Opera: Genre, Nationhood, and Sexual Difference* (New York: Columbia University Press, 1997).

12. See, for example, George Aichele et al., eds., *The Postmodern Bible: The Bible and Culture Collective* (New Haven, Conn.: Yale University Press, 1995), which has a huge and most useful bibliography. For deconstruction and theology in particular, see Valentine Cunningham, "The Rabbins Take It Up One After Another," in *In The Reading Gaol: Postmodernity, Texts, and History* (Oxford: Blackwell, 1994), 363–410.

13. The large push of Theory into art history begins, I suppose, with Michel Foucault's inspection of Velásquez's *Las Meninas* in *Les Mots et les choses* (Paris: Gallimard, 1966), and Jacques Derrida's *La Vérité en peinture* (Paris: Flammarion, 1978), and Roland Barthes's *La Chambre claire* (Paris: Éditions du Seuil, 1980), all of which are available in English translation.

14. See, for example, Stanley Fish, *Doing What Comes Naturally: Change, Rhetoric, and the Practice of Theory in Literary and Legal Studies* (Oxford: Clarendon Press, 1989), and Maria Aristodemou, *Law and Literature: Journeys from Her [sic] to Eternity* (Oxford: Oxford University Press, 2000).

15. Any one of the numerous exhibitions on medical history, anatomy, the business of reading the body in history and in the present, which have become so commonplace through the 1990s, tells this story well. I was very impressed by *The Quick and the Dead* travelling exhibition and its catalogue under that title, ed. Deanna Petherbridge (Great Britain: Hayward Gallery/Arts Council, 1997).

16. Alan D. Sokal, "Transgressing the Boundaries: Toward a Transformative Hermeneutics of Quantum Gravity," *Social Text* 46/47 (Spring/Summer 1996): 217–52. See also Sokal's outrage at the ease of his deception: "A Physicist Experiments with Cultural Studies," *Lingua Franca* 6, no. 4 (May/June 1996): 62–64.

17. *Literary Theory at Work: Three Texts*, ed. Douglas Tallack (London: B. T. Batsford, 1987).

18. Raman Selden, *Practising Theory and Reading Literature: An Introduction* (Lexington: University Press of Kentucky, 1989).

19. Julian Wolfreys, "Introduction: Border Crossings, or Close Encounters of the Textual Kind," in *Literary Theories*, ed. Wolfreys, 1–11.

20. Richard Rorty, "Philosophy Without Principles," in *Against Theory: Literary Studies and the New Pragmatism*, ed. W. J. T. Mitchell, 132.

21. Catherine Belsey, *Critical Practice* (London: Methuen, 1980).

22.  Chadwyck-Healey, *Literary Theory* (database), www.umi.com/products/pd-product-LitTheory.shtml.

23.  See Wolfgang Iser, *The Fictive and the Imaginary: Charting Literary Anthropology* (Baltimore, Md.: Johns Hopkins University Press, 1993); and *The Anthropological Turn in Literary Studies*, ed. Jürgen Schlaeger, REAL: Yearbook of Research in English and American Literature, vol. 12 (Tübingen: Gunter Narr Verlag, 1996).

## 2.  DESTROYING LITERARY STUDIES

### RENÉ WELLEK

AT LEAST SINCE THE TIME of Aristarchus in Alexandria, who died one hundred forty-five years before Christ, a body of knowledge or, if you prefer, a "science of literature" has been built up over the centuries. The Renaissance revived and codified it and the Romantic movement gave impetus to its enormous expansion and institutionalization in the later nineteenth century. Though deep changes in methods and emphases came about in the first half of this century, one can say that literary scholarship has flourished uninterrupted—at least in all Western countries—for roughly two centuries.

One can distinguish among three main branches of literary study. First, there is theory, which is concerned with the principles, categories, functions, and criteria of literature in general. Theory is the term now preferred to the older "poetics," since "poetics" seems limited to writing in verse and has not shed the implication of prescriptive rules. Second, there is the study of concrete works of literature, which is sometimes identified with criticism or called "practical criticism" and which attempts to describe, analyze, characterize, interpret, and evaluate individual works of literature or groups of works, for example, of one author or in one genre. Interpretation is only one step in this process of criticism, though it has developed an enormous debate about its theory, for which the old theological term *hermeneutics* has been revived. And third, there is literary history, seen most frequently in the setting of political, social, and intellectual history. Literary biography is an established subgenre within literary history. These three branches of literary study implicate each other. There can be no literary theory without concrete criticism and without history; there is no criticism without some theory and history; and no literary history is possible without theoretical assumptions and without criticism.

René Wellek: "Destroying Literary Studies." Originally published in *The New Criterion* 2, no. 4 (December 1983): 1–8. Reprinted by permission of *The New Criterion*.

This growing body of knowledge, immense in its ramifications, anticipates and parallels the establishment of similar disciplines, such as the study of the fine arts (sometimes included in aesthetics or developed as history of art) and the study of music, musicology, the history of music, and so on. The study of the relationships among the arts and of their common traits has been a growing concern. It leads to aesthetics and to a philosophy of art.

Today this whole edifice of literary study has come under an attack that is not merely the normal criticism of certain aspects of a changing discipline but an attempt to destroy literary studies from the inside. The attempt seems to have succeeded in certain academic circles; it has enlisted the support of a number of journals and has affected many students, apparently all over the country. It has hardly dislodged or even modified up till now the practice of the vast majority of teachers and students of literature. But it has had considerable publicity and, if it should be generally effective and find many adherents among the younger generation, may spell the breakdown or even the abolition of all traditional literary scholarship and teaching.

I shall try to distinguish among the different motifs and aims of the attack, which is by no means uniform or directed from a single center, either institutional or ideological.

One rather old view that has gained new prominence is the simple denial of the aesthetic nature of literature. One can doubt the very existence of aesthetic experience and refuse to recognize the distinctions, clearly formulated in Immanuel Kant's *Critique of Judgment*, between the good, the true, the useful, and the beautiful. This attack on aesthetics goes back at least as far as the German theory of empathy, as Croce's intuition-expression doctrine, as Dewey's account of art as the experience of heightened vitality, and, in the Anglo-American critical tradition, as I. A. Richards's claim that there is no "aesthetic mode or aesthetic state" or "aesthetic emotion" and that there is no difference between reading a poem and "dressing in the morning." Richards held, in *Principles of Criticism*, that "the world of poetry has in no sense any different reality from the rest of the world and it has no special laws and no other-worldly peculiarities." Since this argument abolishes the distinction between plays, poems, and novels on the one hand and didactic, expository, informative prose on the other, we arrive at the conclusion that literary study includes everything in print.

Long before Richards, of course, the study of literature was often conceived as the study of the whole history of civilization. In *The Province of Literary History* (1931), for example, Edwin Greenlaw stated forcibly that "we [literary historians] are not limited to *belles lettres* or even to printed or manuscript records." This expansion of literary study has been justified, in part at least, by the fact that the branches of learning which should be studying the history of thought and sensibility and of social change have at least temporarily neglected to do so. English and American technical philosophy is notoriously antihistorical and has practically abandoned the study of the history of philosophy to English departments, to the "history of ideas" in Lovejoy's sense. And for a long time academic history departments have been preoccupied with diplomatic, military, and political events, though in recent decades one can speak of a strong revival of social and cultural history, partly under the influence of Marxism and the *Annales* group in France. Most of my own historical work is concerned with the history of ideas, with Immanuel Kant's influence in England, with the history of critical ideas, with the history of historiography and of specific key terms and concepts. There is nothing wrong with this except the danger that imaginative literature might be neglected.

But the old apprehension that literary study might be absorbed in general cultural and social history is now being replaced by a very different worry. The new theory asserts that man lives in a prison house of language that has no relation to reality. It seems to be suggested, or at least buttressed, by a few passages in Nietzsche where, for example, he speaks of truth as "a mobile marching army of metaphors, metonymies, and anthropomorphisms . . . , illusions of which one has forgotten that they are illusions," and by an interpretation of the *Cours de linguistique générale* of Ferdinand de Saussure, who considered the referential function of language irrelevant for a science of linguistics but who did not doubt language's relation to experience and reality. In its extreme formulation, which looks for the abolition of man, denies the self, and sees language as a free-floating system of signs, the theory leads to total skepticism and ultimately to nihilism. This accusation is not simply an invention of the detractors of "deconstructionism," as it is called. It has been expressly confirmed by its practitioners: by J. Hillis Miller writing in *Critical Inquiry* in 1977; by Paul de Man, who in *Blindness and Insight* elaborates in gloomy existentialist terms the view that poetry names the void, asserts itself as "pure nothingness"; and by Jacques Derrida, who describes the new theory as a "Nietzschean *affirmation*, that is, the joyous affirmation of the play of the world, . . . a world of signs without fault, without truth, and without origin . . . beyond man and humanism."

The view that there is "nothing outside of text," that every text refers or defers only to another text, ignores that texts—political, juridical, religious, philosophical, and even imaginative and poetic—have actually shaped the lives of men and thus the course of history. Denying the self and minimizing the perceptual life of man, the theory deliberately refuses to acknowledge that the relation of mind and world is more basic than language.

For literary studies, some consequences have been drawn that would spell their doom. If there is no distinction between imaginative literature and any other writing, if everything is a language game, the inclusive words *écriture* and "text" allow the claim that the critic is equal to the creative writer. A critic can feel himself to be on the level of Dante or Shakespeare. Actually, some of the new critics compare themselves and their friends constantly with the greatest names of the past, speaking in the same breath of themselves and of Car-lyle, Ruskin, or Pater. They revive the idea of "creative criticism" propagated by Oscar Wilde. No doubt there are aesthetic features in much critical writing: composition, style, evocative skill, and so on. And there were and are critics who feel strongly that they are artists expressing or displaying their personali-ties. Friedrich von Schlegel, William Hazlitt, and Sainte-Beuve are obvious ex-amples, and Oscar Wilde flaunted ostentatiously the view of the critic as artist. But the new view goes much further: it wants to make criticism indistinguish-able from fiction and it does not recognize that there is a definite work of liter-ature out there (whatever its mode of existence may be) which has to be un-derstood, which challenges and imposes on us. In the new theories there is no object but only an event in the mind—or, rather, in the language—of the critic. The critic engages in a free play with language.

Jacques Derrida is the philosopher who, for American students, has formu-lated this view most impressively. He rejects the whole tradition of Western thought, which he labels a "metaphysics of presence," by "presence" meaning its reliance on ultimate concepts such as Being, God, consciousness, self, truth, origin, and so on. He propounds the preposterous theory that writing pre-cedes speaking, a claim refuted by every child and by the thousand spoken lan-guages that have no written records. His view can be defended only by giving "writing" a deliberately deceptive new meaning. He argues that all philosophy is shot through by metaphors, ambiguities, "undecidables," as is all literature and criticism. This view was welcomed by some literary critics and students as a liberation, since it gives license to the arbitrary spinning of metaphors, to the stringing of puns, to mere language games. The model praised to the sky is Derrida's *Glas* (1981), which presents, in two columns, a string of quotations from Hegel's *Philosophy of Right* alongside Genet's *Thief's Journal*. As even an admirer admits, it is "a purely speculative chain of words and associations." In practice, it is a series of puns, beginning with the French pronunciation of Hegel as *aigle* (eagle) and wandering off to *seigle* (rye), the field the thief crosses, and to *sigle* (sign). The book falls between three stools: it does not give an aesthetic experience, it is not literary criticism, and it is not good philoso-phy. It is at most a display of ingenuity and wit, inspired (possibly) by Heideg-ger's etymologizing punning, by *Finnegans Wake,* Dada, and Surrealism. If this were an isolated instance of the whim of a learned man, it might be harmless. Unfortunately, it has been widely imitated, with less wit and learning, and has encouraged utter caprice, extreme subjectivity, and hence the destruction of the very concepts of knowledge and truth.

In practice, of course, these absurd consequences are often avoided by the-orists inventing new techniques or by their diverting attention to newly for-mulated problems. Thus, "deconstruction" is often an ingenious uncovering of ambiguities, contradictions, and inconsistencies in diverse texts, along with the monotonous conclusion that every work of literature is only "words about words," literature about literature. These writers have only just discovered an old and simple truth—that words are not things. Some time ago, Jonathan Swift satirized the project of carrying around "such things as were necessary to express the particular business they are to discuss on." These new critics refuse to understand that words designate things and not only other words, as they argue.

I am no defender of the Realist dogma. I have advocated the view that Realism is only one possible style of literature and I have always recognized the fantastic, the Utopian, the grotesque, the symbolic, and many other modes of representing reality. But literature does represent reality, however distorted and transformed. It both projects a world of its own creation and tells us something about our world. The deconstructionist theory is a flight from reality, and from history. Paradoxically, it leads to a new, anti-aesthetic ivory tower, to a new linguistic isolationism. Actually, the deconstructionists often ignore modern technical linguistics. In the writings of Paul de Man, for example, "deconstruction" amounts to a study of rhetoric, understood not as a technique of persuasion but as a study of figures and tropes, metaphors and metonymy. The entire question of meaning is bracketed. Thus, at least the rudiments of literary study are preserved, as the texts of a few suitable authors are attended to: Rousseau, Nietzsche, Proust, Mallarmé, and Rilke. There is no pretense here of creative criticism.

The second prominent motif of the new trends is abolition of the authority of the text, the rejection of the whole ancient enterprise of interpretation as a search for the true meaning of a text. We have learned since the New Criticism to look for ambiguities and paradoxes, and Ingarden and others (myself included) have defended the view that an accrual of meaning occurs in the course of history. The possibility exists of a conflict of interpretations that cannot be completely resolved in some cases, though there is always a limit to the freedom of interpretation. All this has been endlessly debated by E. D. Hirsch, who defends the criterion of the author's intention and the prescriptive role of genre, by J. P. Juhl, who believes that there is only one correct interpretation, and most learnedly by Hans Georg Gadamer in *Wahrheit und Methode* (1960; English: *Truth and Method*, 1975) and a whole new German school of hermeneutics. The so-called *Rezeptionsaesthetik* or reader-response criticism has shifted attention away from the work of literature to the process of reading, to the audience. In the theory propounded by the Konstanz group (mainly Hans-Robert Jauss, a learned student of medieval French literature, and Wolfgang Iser, a specialist in the English novel) we hear of a "fusion of horizons" between that of the reader or interpreter and that of the work of art. It is a compromise between the present-day assumptions and the historical definiteness of a work. *Rezeptionsaesthetik* recommends some good things: paying attention to the history of taste and criticism (which, needless to say, I fully approve) and to the implied reader addressed in the text. But the theory is unable to bridge the gulf between these two problems: the reader reactions and the signs of historicity—parody, imitation, allusion, conventions—embodied in the works themselves. In practice, *Rezeptionsaesthetik* lands in extreme relativism, though the emphasis on certain neglected aspects of readers' reactions seems to me welcome. But the theory of this school is not as new as it claims and is hardly a panacea for the presumed ills of literary history.

The most influential American reader-response theory, that of Stanley Fish, is another matter. It comes in several versions: in its most radical formulation it assumes that a work is completely contained in the sequential, linear reading process. It is a protest against what Fish regards as the reification and illegitimate spatialization of such concepts—or, rather metaphors—as the "verbal icon" or "the well-wrought urn." It has led him to make—in *Self-Consuming Artifacts* (1972)—farfetched, forced, and sometimes demonstrably mistaken readings of seventeenth-century texts. It is restated theoretically in his 1980 collection *Is There a Text in this Class?* There we are told that texts are so undetermined that we cannot decide their meaning at all, that "no interpretation can be said to be better or worse than any other." Thus, "interpretation is not the art of construing but the art of constructing. Interpreters do not decode poems: they make them." More recently Fish has seen that his theory leads to complete anarchy and extreme subjectivism, a consequence he tries to obviate or circumvent by an appeal to "interpretive communities." But he merely worsens the situation. By absolutizing the power of assumptions, he empties literature of all significance. Great critics have fortunately eluded "interpretive communities," resisted or contradicted them. Fish's theories encourage the view that there are no wrong interpretations, that there is no norm implied in a text, and hence that there is no knowledge of an object.

A few reflections should refute this view. There are patently absurd and wrong interpretations, for example, that Hamlet is a woman in disguise or that Hamlet is "mainly King James I," as Miss Winstanley argued. There are interpretations that can be shown to be wrong. For instance: D. H. Lawrence in his comment on Dostoevsky's "Legend of the Grand Inquisitor" in *The Brothers Karamazov* interprets Christ's kissing the Grand Inquisitor as meaning his acceptance of the Inquisitor's views, "Thank you, thank you, you are right, old man." But the kiss is rather the silent answer of religion that rejects and refutes the Inquisitor's diatribe. Alyosha immediately afterwards kisses Ivan, forgiving him for his atheism and Ivan reacts, "This is plagiarism from my poem." The rest of the book, the story of Zosima and his brother Markel, confirms this. Dostoevsky's journalistic writings confirm it and so do all the later novels. One can thus correct mistaken interpretations by appealing to the context of a book, of an author's work, and finally of a whole tradition. There are also, one should admit, puzzling cases. The end of *King Lear* has led to opposite conclusions. Blake's "Tiger" and Wordsworth's Lucy poem "A Slumber Did My Spirit Steal" have excited heated disagreements. But even here it is possible to adjudicate the differences: to explain them by the different approaches and implied assumptions of the interpreters. The Hegelian concept of tragedy assumed in A. C. Bradley will lead to different conclusions than will the Sartrean existentialist concept assumed in Jan Kott's *Shakespeare Our Contemporary* (Eng., 1964). Still, there are works or passages that are ambiguous, indeterminate, and even opaque and incomprehensible; but that should be a spur to discovering meaning rather than an argument for surrender. The otherness of a text, removed in time or place or both, or simply alien to our way of thinking, is a challenge to interpretation. To draw completely skeptical conclusions is simply to doubt the very possibility of knowledge, to deny the ideal of man ever understanding himself or other human beings and their creations. The world may be dark and ultimately mysterious, but the mind of man is not so narrowly limited that it cannot understand and illuminate its own creations. Vico, in the early eighteenth century, knew that, while nature may be impenetrable to man, we can have certain knowledge of our own works in history, in poetry, and in institutions. The recent attempts to increase our self-consciousness, to make us aware of our own situation in time and place, to see the "presenticentric predicament," to use the unlovely coinage of A. O. Lovejoy, is valuable if it diminishes rampant subjectivity and makes us more tolerant of other viewpoints. But it can also have a paralyzing effect, turning us into the famous centipede that did not know which foot to put first and thus encouraging the suppression of personality, which, whatever its excesses, is after all the source of insight and judgment.

This ideal of impersonal objectivity is only one of the motives for the current dismissal of evaluation in literary criticism. Evaluation used to be criticism's central task. It has been dismissed by a new group of students of literature with completely different assumptions: by would-be scientists, mainly linguists, by semioticians and some structuralists, and by Northrop Frye, who erected a complex system of archetypes that obliterates the distinction between the most trivial detective story and a play by Shakespeare. Evaluation seems especially irrelevant to these system builders, who are looking for examples of structures to incorporate in their schemes, scientific or imaginative. Recently evaluation has also been attacked as "elitism," as a defense of the tradition, and even as a method of oppression. But a little reflection should show that evaluation is a basic task of literary study. There is an insuperable gulf between great art and real trash.

The day-to-day task of criticism is the sifting of the enormous production of books, and even the ranking and grading of writers. That we teach Shakespeare, Dante, or Goethe rather than the newest best-seller or any of the romances, Westerns, crime, and detective novels, science fiction, and pornography on the racks of the nearest drugstore is an act of evaluation. We exercise choice the minute we take up even a classical text whose value is certified by generations of readers, in deciding what features we shall pay attention to, what we shall emphasize, appreciate, and admire, or ignore and deprecate. It is now unfashionable to speak of a love of literature, of enjoyment of and admiration for a poem, a play, or a novel. But such feelings surely must have been the original stimulus to anyone engaged in the study of literature. Otherwise he might as well have studied accounting or engineering. Love, admiration is, I agree, only the first step. Then we ask why we love and admire or detest. We reflect, analyze, and interpret; and out of understanding grows evaluation and judgment, which need not be articulated expressly. Evaluation leads to the definition of the canon, of the classics, of the tradition. In the realm of literature the question of quality is inescapable. If this is "elitism," so be it.

Recently, arguments have been advanced in favor of subliterature, of *Kitsch*, colportage, *Trivialliteratur*, or however we may call it. Nobody can deny that a study of subliterature throws light on the history of taste, or that detective stories, science fiction, and all the other genres can be studied for structural properties and even graded by aesthetic criteria. One may very well distinguish between good, mediocre, and bad science fiction, detective novels, and even pornography. Even the most vociferous enemies of evaluation judge and rank. In his *Anatomy of Criticism*, whose "Polemical Introduction" denounces value judgment and hopes for a "steady advance toward undiscriminating catholicity," Northrop Frye speaks of Aristophanes's *Birds* as "his greatest comedy" and of Burton's *Anatomy of Melancholy* as "the greatest Menippean satire in English before Swift." The mere fact that Frye and others have elected to study Milton rather than Blackmore, Shakespeare rather than Glapthorne, is sufficient to show that there is no criticism or even literary history without choice and judgment. Recently, we also find an influential critic, Leslie Fiedler, advocating in *What Was Literature?* a reversal of the canon, praising pulp science fiction, hard-core pornography, and fiction "not accepted in the canon of o.k. art": Conan Doyle, Bram Stoker, Rider Haggard, Margaret Mitchell. Fiedler is convinced that narrative skill and mythopoeic power are independent of formal excellence. Despising "upper-class" art and embracing "pop" art, Fiedler rejects his early admirations as so much hypocrisy. But even he has to make distinctions and evaluations. Though he tends always to side with the underdog, the proletarian, and the black man, he condemns Alex Haley's *Roots* as "prefabricated commodity *schlock*." But he has not told us why there should be, in what he considers upper-class art, no masterpieces to be pointed out and ranked, as he has ranked the examples of pop art he admires.

The need for evaluation is also obvious in literary history. In recent decades, literary history has often been dismissed as concerned only with the accumulation of external facts: bibliography, biography, influences, reputations, and so on. It has been ridiculed as a catchall of information on all subjects, as trivial antiquarianism. I count myself among the severest critics of literary histories (in reviews of Legouis-Cazamian's, A. C. Baugh's, and Grierson's histories of English literature and R. Spiller's *Literary History of the United States*). Many attempts have been made to remedy this situation. I must sketch the history of literary historiography to make the present situation comprehensible. There is a romantic tradition of nationalistic histories that sees literature as the expression of the national mind; there is a school of social explanation formulated memorably in Hippolyte Taine's triad—*race, milieu, moment*; finally, there are the schemes of internal evolution devised by Ferdinand Brunetière on the analogy of biology and by the Russian formalists and Czech structuralists who saw literary evolution as a dialectical process of shifts in structure. Little to my mind has been added to these schemes that is really new. T. S. Eliot's interpretation of the tradition has changed the evaluation of specific periods, styles, and groups of writers in the history of English poetry but has not changed the practice of literary history. The numerous writings of Harold Bloom have recently given a new twist to old problems. He is obsessed by the "burden of the past" (a phrase used in the title of W. J. Bate's book on the English romantics) and by what he calls "the anxiety of influence," the poet's revolt against his predecessors. Bloom restates the old convention-revolt problem in psychoanalytical terms: the poet has an Oedipus complex; he wants to slay his poetic father. "True poetic history is the story of how poets have suffered other poets," Bloom says in *The Anxiety of Influence* (1973). He makes elaborate distinctions among the ways a poet handles his relation to older poets, inventing fancy terms—*tessera, kenosis, daemonization, askesis,* and *apophrades*—and describing the whole history of poetry as "an endless civil war, indeed a family war." His criticism is "antithetical, revisionist," carried by prophetic pathos in defense of "visionary" poetry, the line he construes—in conscious antithesis to T. S. Eliot's—from Milton via Blake and Shelley to Whitman and Wallace Stevens. Unfortunately, this very individual scheme is marred by Bloom's adherence to the view that all interpretation is misreading ("misprision") and that "the true poem is the critic's mind." But Bloom cannot share the deconstructionists' rejection of poetry's relation to reality. "The theory of poetry is for him the theory of life," to borrow his quotation from Wallace Stevens.

The abolition of aesthetics, the blurring of the distinction between poetry and critical prose, the rejection of the very ideal of correct interpretation in favor of misreading, the denial to all literature of any reference to reality are all symptoms of a profound *malaise.* If literature has nothing to say about our minds and the cosmos, about love and death, about humanity in other times and other countries, literature loses its meaning. It is possible to account for the flight from literary studies in our universities. I am of course aware of other reasons, mainly economic, but the emptying of human significance, the implied nihilism, must be contributing to the decline of the appeal of subjects like English and foreign languages and encouraging the preference for more palpable and palatable subject matter not only in the sciences and their utilitarian applications but also in the social sciences, which are still concerned with a nonlinguistic reality. I would be misunderstood if I were seen simply as a *laudator temporis acti*, as recommending a return to the unreflective literary history that dominated the American universities when I first came to this country in 1927. After all, I wrote (with Austin Warren) *Theory of Literature* (1949), the first book in English with this title. In it I discuss the Russian formalists, Ingarden's phenomenological analysis of the work of art, Czech structuralism, German *Geistesgeschichte* and stylistics, and other Continental developments. Long before, in 1937, I got involved in a controversy with F. R. Leavis whom I had criticized for his boastful empiricism, for being suspicious of any theory. In the last chapter of *Theory* (later deleted), I criticized the American academic situation quite harshly. I cannot be suspected of enmity toward theory or Continental developments.

There is a recent book by an Englishman, Geoffrey Strickland, *Structuralism or Criticism?* (1981) which puts the choice bluntly, voting for criticism in Leavis's sense and rejecting structuralism mainly for its ambition to construe a closed system of literary signs. I agree with him on this point and can quote Hugo Friedrich, the eminent German *Romanist*, who wrote in 1967 that there cannot be a scheme or system, which would consider all phenomena of literature as limited by internal relations and combinations. But I don't see what can be said against the less universal structural analyses of Mukarovsky, Genette, Todorov, and Lotman. There is a new poetics in the making, particularly of the novel, called "narratology," which has profited from the structuralist approach. Strickland's *Structuralism or Criticism?* poses a false dilemma. The enterprise of structuralism, first clearly formulated by the Prague Linguistic Circle in about 1935, seems to me fully justified. It is inconceivable, however, without the criticism of concrete works, without analysis, interpretation, and ultimately evaluation. I cannot agree with Jonathan Culler, an enthusiast for structuralism, who says in *The Pursuit of Signs* that "the interpretation of individual works is only tangentially related to the understanding of literature." Only the collaboration, the exchange and necessary interaction of criticism and poetics, can guarantee a healthy development of literary studies. I reject the theories of some structuralists and poststructuralists who advocate "the abolition of man" (whatever that may mean), who are content with the presumed "prison house of language" and claim a complete systematization of all literature. Nor can I sympathize with the blurring of the difference between imaginative literature and criticism. I cannot advocate either a return to the anti-theoretical, almost instinctive kind of criticism practiced, say, by F. R. Leavis or Yvor Winters. I sometimes feel guilty of having helped to propagate the theory of literature. Since my book, theory has triumphed in this country and has, possibly, triumphed with a vengeance. Still, I approve the basic impulse behind theory of literature, the need for clarification of principles and methods, for an articulated rationale of literary study. But some of the recent developments in their extreme skepticism and even nihilism would destroy this ideal, "deconstruct," as they say, all literary study, interrupt tradition, dismantle an edifice built by the efforts of generations of scholars and students. Fortunately, one may hope that this new "absurdist" wave, as Hayden White has called it, has already crashed on the shore, even though its propounders still believe that they ride its crest.

## WORKS CITED

Bloom, Harold. *The Anxiety of Influence: A Theory of Poetry*. New York: Oxford University Press, 1973.

Culler, Jonathan. *The Pursuit of Signs: Semiotics, Literature, Deconstruction*. Ithaca, N.Y.: Cornell University Press, 1981.

De Man, Paul. *Blindness and Insight: Essays in the Rhetoric of Contemporary Criticism*. 1971. 2nd ed. Minneapolis: University of Minnesota Press, 1983.

Derrida, Jacques. *Glas*. Trans. John P. Leavey Jr. and Richard Rand. 1974. Lincoln: University of Nebraska Press, 1986.

——. "Structure, Sign, and Play in the Discourse of the Human Sciences"(1967). In *Writing and Difference*. Trans. Alan Bass. Chicago: University of Chicago Press, 1978, 278–93.

Fiedler, Leslie. *What Was Literature?* New York: Simon and Schuster, 1982.

Fish, Stanley. *Is There a Text in this Class?* Cambridge, Mass.: Harvard University Press, 1980.

——. *Self-Consuming Artifacts: The Experience of Seventeenth-Century Literature*. Berkeley: University of California Press, 1972.

Friedrich, Hugo. *Die Struktur der modernen Lyrik. Von der Mitte des 19. bis zur Mitte des 20. Jahrhunderts*. Reinbek bei Hamburg: Rowohlt, 1956.

Frye, Northrop. *Anatomy of Criticism: Four Essays*. Princeton, N.J.: Princeton University Press, 1957.

Greenlaw, Edwin. *The Province of Literary History*. Baltimore, Md.: The Johns Hopkins Press; London: Humphrey Milford, Oxford University Press, 1931.

Miller, J. Hillis. "The Critic as Host." *Critical Inquiry* 3, no. 3 (Spring 1977): 439–47.

Nietzsche, Friedrich. "Truth and Falsity in an Ultramoral Sense" (1873). In *Early Greek Philosophy and Other Essays*. Vol. 2 of *Complete Works of Friedrich Nietzsche*. Ed. Oscar Levy. London: T. N. Foulis, 1911.

Richards, I. A. *Principles of Literary Criticism*. London: Kegan Paul, Trench, Trubner, 1924.

Strickland, Geoffrey. *Structuralism or Criticism? Thoughts on How We Read*. Cambridge: Cambridge University Press, 1981.

Wellek, René, and Austin Warren. *Theory of Literature*. New York: Harcourt, 1949.

White, Hayden. "The Absurdist Moment in Contemporary Literary Theory." *Contemporary Literature* 17, no. 3 ( Summer 1976): 378–403.

Winstanley, Lilian. *Hamlet and the Scottish Succession; Being an Examination of the Relations of the Play of Hamlet to the Scottish Succession and the Essex Conspiracy*. Cambridge: The University Press, 1921.

## 3.  TRAVELING THROUGH AMERICAN CRITICISM

### TZVETAN TODOROV

WHEN A FOREIGNER VISITING FRANCE asks me "what's happening in French criticism these days?" I am at a loss: I either keep still or change the subject. I am in the dark about prevailing trends: the people I know are individuals who seem to be following their own separate paths. In the United States, on the other hand, where I spend only a few weeks a year, quite the reverse is true: there, I feel I am observing a coherent picture, and I would have no trouble at all answering the same question about American criticism. I had always attributed this contrast to my own personal vantage point: in France, I lack the distance a good observer needs, while in the United States, where I am a visitor, not a participant, I benefit from the privileged status Montesquieu attributed to Persians in Paris. But this privilege has its drawbacks, too (I lack in-depth knowledge and infallible intuitions), and these might have sufficed to keep me from ever venturing an opinion about American criticism had I not come across Robert Scholes's *Textual Power*.[1] The picture Scholes paints of the critical scene in the United States is so close to my own that it makes me wonder, in my readiness to pat myself on the back, whether the coincidence may not be based on the accuracy of the picture itself.

To formulate my impressions clearly, I need to begin by looking backward. Until roughly 1968, let us say, most American critics seemed preoccupied by one key question: "What does the text mean?" Confronted with a text calling for commentary, they shared the conviction that their most important task was to discover as exactly as possible what the text meant. (They began to disagree as soon as they had to choose one means or another, one approach or another, to finding the answer. Should they pay special attention to historical events contemporary with the book, or to stylistic features? to its author's motivations, or to the rules of its genre?) The only critics who did not share in this consensus were those that might be called didactic (and they were more often journalists than academics, though the two are not mutually exclusive): these critics were generally pursuing some personal goal through their own writing, and they used works from the past without caring much one way or the other about the accuracy of their interpretations.

Tzvetan Todorov. "Traveling Through American Criticism." Originally published in *Critique de la critique*. Paris: Éditions du Seuil, 1984. Reprinted from *Literature and Its Theorists: A Personal View of Twentieth-Century Criticism*, by Tzvetan Todorov, 182–91. Ithaca, N.Y.: Cornell University Press, 1987. Translated by Catherine Porter. Translation copyright © 1987 Catherine Porter. Used by permission of the publishers, Cornell University Press and Taylor and Francis.

Structuralism, the most recent arrival on the scene, had not brought about any basic changes in the underlying situation. Whether in Northrop Frye's version or the one inherited from the Russian Formalists, structural analysis, like its predecessors, sought to help find a better answer to the same question. Its approach was to call attention to the internal construction of literary works (which had the side effect of leaving their other aspects unexplored—but that was not unique to structuralism either).

Against such a background, then, the new trend in American criticism that I mentioned above was to emerge. The trend has been labeled *poststructuralism*, a term which strikes me as rather unfortunate: it implies both continuity (otherwise it would mean nothing) and progress (as if what comes after were always an improvement over what went before), whereas in fact we have extreme discontinuity. "Poststructuralism" has developed along two major lines (and in a large number of subsidiary variants and transitional forms) which have one thing in common: they make the earlier question, "What does this text mean?", completely irrelevant. The first—and the more dogmatic and elaborate—of the two main types is called "deconstruction." Oversimplifying somewhat, we might say that deconstruction renders the earlier question moot by invariably answering: "Nothing at all." The second type of poststructuralism, more cheerful but also more naive, is sometimes known by its advocates as "pragmatism." Pragmatism renders the question meaningless by replying: "Anything whatsoever." In the wake of either response, obviously, the question can hardly be raised again; it seems preferable to go on to something else.

Deconstruction appears to be characterized by three interrelated postulates.

(1) The world itself is inaccessible; discourse alone exists, and discourse refers only to other discourse. Statements of principle abound. "There is no such thing as an outside-of-the-text." "I don't believe that anything like perception exists" (Scholes, 92). The text "liberates us from the empirical object" (Scholes, 84). The text produces "a structure of infinite referral in which there are only traces" (Scholes, 95). Literature, Edward Said writes, is an "endless naming and renaming of the void."[2]

(2) Even so, we are not to believe that discourse is better endowed than the world: the latter may not exist, but the former is necessarily incoherent. Deconstructionist commentary always consists in showing that the text studied is internally contradictory, that its intentions are not carried out in actual practice. Thus there is an "insurmountable obstacle in the way of any reading or understanding" (Scholes, 78).

(3) As no discourse is exempt from these contradictions, there is no reason to prefer one sort over another, or to prefer one value over another. In fact, in

the deconstructionist perspective, any value-oriented behavior (criticism, the struggle against injustice, hope for a better world) becomes subject to ridicule.

A good deal might be said about this approach to criticism, and Scholes (like Abrams, Said, and others) does not hold back. The idea that texts are inconsistent is striking first of all for its dogmatism: all texts are implicated equally, with no distinction between literature, theoretical discourse (philosophy, law, ethics, politics), and empirical discourse (the sciences); here, everything becomes "literature." One may wonder, too, whether the deconstructionist idea may not be judged somewhat pretentious: to contradict oneself is human, to be sure, but is it plausible that the contradictions in question could have escaped the notice of thinkers like Plato, Rousseau, or Kant, while they leap to the eye of the first deconstructionist who comes along? When a scrupulous analyst sets out to "think with" Rousseau (as Goldschmidt and Philonenko have done in France, for example), many inconsistencies disappear and the place of the "unthought" is strikingly reduced.

The hypothesis of an inaccessible world is also somewhat overdrawn. It is a commonplace of epistemology, at least since Kant, to recognize the constructed character of knowledge and to challenge belief in a transparent perception of objects; thus both empiricists and positivists may legitimately be criticized. But to go on from there to deny any content whatsoever to perception is a step that ought to be carefully considered before it is taken. As Scholes says, there is something excessive in asserting "that sign-systems affect perception but that the world does not" (164). The discourse of knowledge does indeed have to do with the world, and not just with itself. In this connection Scholes has a delightful example of the independence of the "referent" with respect to the "signifier": the relation between the word "kangaroo" and the thing that jumped up and down around Captain Cook. He quotes eloquent examples of excessive skepticism, and concludes, quite rightly: "'From the perspective of deconstruction, there is nothing upon which we can ground an argument for evolutionary biology as opposed to fundamentalist creationism, since both are discourses, with their blindness and their insights" (99). Although literature for its part does not refer directly to particular objects, it is nevertheless not wholly lacking in truth value: if we continue to read Shakespeare today, it is because we have the feeling (even though we cannot explain it) that he offers us a better understanding of "human nature" or something of the sort.

The renunciation of judgment and of values leads to insurmountable aporias, as well. To make their own task easier, deconstructionists seem to have assimilated all values to religious values, thus rejecting the distinction between faith and reason, and they treat reason as an avatar—no more and no less—of God, thus wiping out several centuries of struggle with a single stroke of the pen. Or else they lump everything together under another umbrella-word, "power," which rules out any further distinctions between police-state repression and the exercise of reason, between violence and law. After all this, they can take refuge, without any pangs of conscience, in a "quietistic acceptance of injustice" (Scholes, 79).

Deconstruction is a "dogmatic skepticism,"[3] and it combines the worst of two worlds. It is skepticism, to the extent that it considers knowledge and judgment impossible, along with truth and justice. But it is also dogmatism, because it decides in advance what each text means—namely, nothing. Deconstructive readings are extremely monotonous, since the result is "always already" known, and since only the means used to reach that result are subject to variation. Deconstruction, according to one of its practitioners, more lucid or more naive than others (J. Hillis Miller), "is a demonstration that [the text] has already dismantled itself," and each reading "reaches, in the particular way the given text allows it, the 'same' moment of an aporia."[4] As Augustine, theoretician of another hermeneutic dogmatism, would say, the path the reader follows is not what matters; his interpretation is correct so long as it leads in the end to the reign of charity. Here the goal is different but the strategy remains the same: "Whatever track the reader follows through the poem he arrives at blank contradictions."[5] This dogmatic aspect is doubtless what accounts for deconstruction's extraordinary success in academic institutions: the formula has only to be applied to new subject matter to result in an "original" exegesis.

The other major variant of "poststructuralism," pragmatism (whose most prominent representative is Stanley Fish), does not suffer from the same monotony in its results. Its principal hypotheses are the following.

(1) A text means nothing in itself; it is the reader who gives it meaning. Here, clearly, we have two propositions. The first is negative ("there are no determinate meanings and . . . the stability of the text is an illusion")[6] and it links the pragmatists with the deconstructionists, except that their arguments differ. Deconstructionists maintain that discourse as a whole is inconsistent, while pragmatists argue that words have no meaning; the former cast their "suspicion" on the molecules of language, the latter on its atoms. The second proposition, on the other hand, is affirmative: the reader, and thus the critic, may indeed propose and impose a determinate and stable meaning. "Interpreters do not decode poems; they make them" (Fish, 327). The text, then, is no more than a sort of Rorschach test allowing readers, like Pirandello's characters, to choose their own meanings: "each in his own way." Of course, in this context, "the notion of a mistake, at least as something to be avoided, disappears."[7]

(2) What consequences does this choice have for the critical work itself? "It relieves me of the obligation to be right . . . and demands only that I be interesting," as Fish has said.[8] We are far removed from deconstructive monotony here: the field is wide open to creative imagination.

(3) More recently, Fish seems to have tempered his relativism into a historicism, claiming that it is not the individual reader who decides what the

meaning of the poem is, but rather the group to which the reader belongs: "It is interpretive communities, rather than either the text or the reader, that produce meanings and are responsible for the emergence of formal features" (Fish, 14).

The negative part of the first thesis is both empirically false and logically contradictory. It is false because it ignores the social nature of language: neither individuals nor special-interest lobbies are in a position to change the meaning of words. The most idiosyncratic usage, the most audacious metaphor, the most obscure of allusions all presuppose a common language, and this is precisely what dictionaries catalogue (if they did not, it is hard to imagine what they would contain). But the hypothesis is also internally contradictory, for it presupposes that we understand it, while explicitly denying the possibility of understanding. Hence the affirmative part of the statement seems hyperbolic: to be sure, readers necessarily read in a certain way; no reading is transparent. It does not follow, however, that readers produce the complete meaning (and here we return to the problem of perception).

The requirement to write interestingly rather than accurately is shocking only, if at all, because of the field to which it is applied. No one would be scandalized if such a requirement concerned literature itself, even though such a conception, which would raise the detective novel to the summit of the hierarchy, might not seem to do literature full justice. What is called into question by this view of criticism, and in fact of history in general, is its empirical ambition. But the formula is easier to put across when it is applied to criticism. Would anyone dare require historians to give up concern for truth, and only try to be interesting? Would anyone allow interest to be the single guiding principle for the discourse of a judge or a politician? And yet no one is upset about an irresponsible opinion so long as it merely applies to that amusement park known as literature.

Fish's initial conception transforms all reading into that sort of "picnic" Lichtenberg described with reference to Jakob Böhme's works: the author brings the words and the reader supplies the meaning. His later views bring us closer to the Humpty-Dumpty position: it is the master who decides what words mean. In this connection Scholes rightly alludes to the Orwellian world of *Nineteen Eighty-four*, in which the "interpretive community," i.e., the Party, decides on the meaning and nature of past events by constantly rewriting history. To say that there is no difference between facts and interpretations (that is, that "everything is interpretation") is in fact to see force ("the carrot and the stick" [Scholes, 156]) as the only way of imposing one's views. Raymond Aron warned against this confusion long ago: "It can no doubt be maintained, in the spirit of philosophical precision, that every historical fact is a construct and therefore implies selection and interpretation. When applied, these distinctions [facts vs. interpretations] preserve their full implications. It is either true or false that Trotsky played a considerable role in organizing the Red Army; it is either true or false that Zinoviev or Bukharin plotted the assassination of Stalin. . . . Every totalitarian state exaggerates, to the point of absurdity, the interdependence of fact and interpretation."[9]

Is it appropriate to bring these two critical tendencies together under a common label ("poststructuralism"), despite their theoretical and rhetorical divergencies? I think it is. They have common roots in Nietzschean philosophy. They have common enemies: on the one hand, universal values, justice, ethics; on the other, truth, knowledge, science. And they have shared affinities: the one revealed by the more or less explicit praise of force (hence the proximity with Harold Bloom, another militant Nietzschean), the other with subjective idealism (the world does not exist in itself, but only in my perception).

In the face of this critical school, what recourse is open to those who continue to believe that literary works have some relation to the world and that some values are better than others, that some are even worth fighting for? Curiously, the only intellectual movement in American criticism that maintains this other position seems to be Marxism, so that the choice boils down to a straightforward one between poststructuralism and Marxism. Scholes himself, who is not a Marxist, has some difficulty differentiating his own position from the Marxist one. Certain coincidences, however, may make us wonder whether the opposition is as radical as it first appears. The idea of an "interpretive community" that would control meaning and interpretation is not foreign to Marxist doctrine, for instance: that doctrine claims that everything depends upon class membership, after all. Communist totalitarianism does not arise from Marxism by accident.

Marxist-inspired criticism claims, of course, that literary works have a relationship with the world. But that is just the starting point; after all, common sense itself indicates that some sort of relationship must exist. Marxist criticism is based on a more specific thesis: what interests it is not the work as representation of the world or statement about it, but rather the world (or a portion of it) as the origin of the work. Marxist criticism is a genealogical criticism; if you say to a Marxist, "the salt is on the table," he never wonders "is it true?" but only "why is she saying that?" It is distinguished from other genealogical criticism (the Freudian version, for example) by its faith in the relevance of the notion of social class. In this game, consciousness always loses to "gut feeling," and every utterance, however universal its intention, is reduced to the particular circumstances of its enunciation; it is necessarily "historical," and that is what counts.

Marxist criticism recognizes the relevance of values, but only certain ones. Those presented as universal or "interclass" values arouse its particular animosity. The rhetorical device most often used to denigrate them consists in a combination of abstraction (liberty is liberalism; individual rights are individualism) and a tendentious particularization (liberalism is the right to fire workers whenever you feel like it; individualism is the right to send your children to the right schools). This is how "liberalism," "individualism," or "humanism" become dirty words. Any attempt to rise above a particular determination is reduced to its humble origins: humanism, for instance, is nothing more than a "suburban moral ideology," in the words of Terry Eagleton.[10] Marxism refuses to recognize the distinction of ethics from politics: in its view, politics is a responsible ethics, one that is taken seriously. And so it reduces all striving for values to the defense of group interests: what contributes to the "socialist transformation of the society" (Eagleton, 211) is deemed good, whatever the members of that society may think. And instead of celebrating right and justice, it gives its accolades to the forces of history.

To the universalist aspirations of science, Marxism opposes social and historical determinism; the politics of private interests takes the place of a common ethics. Marxist criticism thus recognizes the relation of literary works to the world and to values, but it rejects universality: truth and justice are grounded in history rather than reason. It is evident, then, that the Marxist opposition to poststructuralism is not as radical as it may have seemed: above and beyond their quarrels over specifics, both are fighting a common enemy called humanism—in other words, in this case, the attempt to ground science and ethics on reason and to practice them in a universal way. Now it is clear why there have been so many attempts to hybridize these two apparently opposed schools of thought: not only because of the superficial desire to be at the forefront of the avant-garde, but also because of deep affinities. Here is a test to try: who said that "the idea of justice in itself is an idea which in effect has been invented and put to work in different societies as an instrument of a certain political and economic power or as a weapon against that power"? No, it was not Terry Eagleton; it was Michel Foucault.[11]

American criticism is thus dominated by what we may as well call by its rightful name, antihumanism. The word may have unpleasant resonances, and it will be objected that its partisans do not usually resemble bloodthirsty ogres. I agree; even Marxists today take pains to dissociate themselves from socialism as it is practiced, and from Stalinist concentration camps. I can bear personal witness to the fact that Paul de Man was a delightful man, and Stanley Fish still is. I am not saying that they themselves are inhuman. I am simply saying that it is not possible, without inconsistency, to defend human rights with one hand and deconstruct the idea of humanity with the other.

What path remains open, then, to criticism today? The one indicated by Scholes might be called critical humanism. Scholes does a good job of highlighting the meaning of the word "critical" that counts here; I will add that that adjective has to serve as a precautionary device against fraudulent uses of the same program. This is not a trivial matter: we know that the humanist camouflage of European colonialism came close to undermining the humanist cause once and for all. Thus the relation of literature and the world has to be recognized: "the whole point of my argument," Scholes writes, "is that we must open the way between the literary or verbal text and the social text in which we live" (Scholes, 24). The relation of both to values has to be recognized as well: "we will have to restore the judgmental dimension to criticism, not in the trivial sense . . . of ranking literary texts, but in the most serious sense of questioning the values proffered by the texts we study" (Scholes, 14).

I should like to hope, though I cannot really believe it possible, that this regrettable episode of contemporary criticism might be quickly forgotten, so that we might begin to look critically at the earlier criticism—but in a different way. The question "what does the text mean?" is a relevant question, and we shall always have to try to answer it, without excluding any contexts, historical, structural, or other, that might help us in the task. But that is not a reason to fail to go beyond it. That question may be carried further by another twofold question, addressed to the response to the first: "Is it true?" and "Is it right?" In this way, we could transcend the sterile opposition between the specialist-critics who know, but do not think, and the moralist-critics who speak without knowing anything about the literary works they discuss. In this way, the critic could finally assume fully the role that is incumbent on him, that of participant in a double dialogue: as reader, with his author; as author, with his own readers—who in the process might even become somewhat more numerous.[12]

## NOTES

1. Robert Scholes, *Textual Power: Literary Theory and the Teaching of English* (New Haven, Conn.: Yale University Press, 1985).

2. Edward Said, *The World, the Text, and the Critic* (Cambridge, Mass.: Harvard University Press, 1983), 162 [editors' note: Said is here describing Paul de Man's view].

3. Eugene Goodheart, *The Skeptic Disposition: Deconstruction, Ideology, and Other Matters* (Princeton, N.J.: Princeton University Press , 1984; reprint, 1991), 14.

4. Quoted in M. H. Abrams, *Theories of Criticism: Essays in Literature and Art* (Washington, D.C.: Library of Congress, 1984), 25.

5. Abrams, *Theories of Criticism*, 28.

6. Stanley Fish, *Is There a Text in This Class?* (Cambridge, Mass.: Harvard University Press, 1980), 312.

7. Fish, quoted by M. H. Abrams, "How to Do Things with Texts," *Partisan Review* 46, no. 4 (1979): 577.

8. Quoted by Abrams, "How to Do Things with Texts," 580.

9. Raymond Aron, *History, Truth, Liberty: Selected Writings of Raymond Aron*, ed. Franciszek Draus (Chicago: University of Chicago Press, 1985), 345.

10. Terry Eagleton, *Literary Theory: An Introduction* (Minneapolis: University of Minnesota Press, 1983), 207.

11. Quoted in Said, *The World, the Text, and the Critic*, 246.

12. Feminist criticism is missing in the overview I have just presented, and I should like to account for its absence. Feminist criticism has undergone a significant development during the period in question: I have not included it not because of any negative judgment, but

because it is not defined on the same basis as the other trends considered here. A book of feminist criticism may be at the same time structuralist, or poststructuralist, or Marxist, or humanist; it is not characterized by what the critics call their method, but rather by the choice of certain themes and by the adherence to certain values. I trust that my intentions will not be misunderstood.

## 4.   THE RISE AND FALL OF "PRACTICAL" CRITICISM

### FROM I. A. RICHARDS TO BARTHES AND DERRIDA

### MORRIS DICKSTEIN

IN AN 1891 ESSAY on criticism, Henry James, who had long suffered from the obtuseness of reviewers, posed a dilemma which looms larger as the territory of criticism expands: "The bewildered spirit may ask itself, without speedy answer, What is the function in the life of man of such a periodicity of platitude and irrelevance? Such a spirit will wonder how the life of man survives it, and above all, what is much more important, how literature resists it."[1] For all his exasperation, James was no enemy of criticism, not the artist determined to keep the mysteries of his trade intuitive, unspoken. The prefaces he later wrote for the New York Edition of his novels aimed to provide a formal ground for the criticism of prose fiction. James could not anticipate the forest of signs and symbols that would grow from his formalist acorn, nor could he imagine that technical sophistication would one day pose as great a threat to literature as the philistine platitudes of reviewers. Once long ago, while I was looking for a thesis topic, a gust of inspiration picked me up and whispered in my ear the word "Conrad." I went to the Cambridge University library to scout the terrain, but soon gave way to an almost physical nausea at the sheer quantity of what had already been done, enough to weigh down and bury all inspiration forever.

Problems of quantity are quickly translated into problems of quality. Our understanding of both James and Conrad has benefited greatly from what Roger Gard describes as "the absolutely unprecedented increase in this century of 'professional' students of literature."[2] But as the amateur "gentleman of letters," who remained anonymous to protect his social status, gave way early in the century to the academic busywork of "practical criticism," the increase of knowledge threatened us with a bureaucratization of the imaginative, while

Morris Dickstein. "The Rise and Fall of 'Practical' Criticism: From I. A. Richards to Barthes and Derrida." From *Double Agent: The Critic and Society*, by Morris Dickstein. Copyright © 1992 Morris Dickstein. Used by permission of Oxford University Press, Inc.

artists, out of an instinct for self-preservation, stopped paying attention. It's easy to see why this quantitative explosion of criticism did not always contribute to the March of Mind. As literary criticism became academicized, scholastic work learned to stay within the parameters of the "field"; the existing literature, with its prevailing categories and methodologies, the whole discipline, with its hierarchical channels of certification and advancement, often became so much dead weight on the shoulders of the living. New views were encouraged to differ, but only minutely, from the academic consensus; when such views gained acceptance, they too became part of the conservatizing inertia of that body of received opinion.

In the secondary world of literary criticism, where everything is commentary, new views were not even required, only new "readings," only texts that could be "read" and re-"read" without going too obviously dead on you. Before exegesis was displaced by the changing fashions of literary theory, the specter that haunted practical criticism for decades was the plague of numbers, the proliferation of mediocrity, the multiplication of redundant readings to which theorists themselves now contribute so abundantly. Of what earthly use, outside the classroom and the certification rituals of the academy, was yet another reading of a poem or play that has been continuously understood and intuitively enjoyed for at least three centuries, or even three decades? Some forms of close reading had no relation to how anyone actually *read*. The New Criticism provided some excellent tools for pedagogy, but it also bound criticism over to the pedagogic spirit, while severing it from the free play of mind that gives the intellectual life its excitement and its value. This is what drew many of us to literature and criticism in college. Where history seemed in thrall to "the facts," the archives, the minutely circumstantial, criticism was the best possible arena of ideas. The philosophers might lose themselves in thickets of abstraction, remote from all immediate human concern, but literature could pose the largest issues of social and personal destiny in a vividly human context. The study of literature demanded a sheer love of language and storytelling for their own sake, yes, but the great writers also had something to say; the cognitive mysteries and affective intensities of the work of art lay before the young would-be critic like a land of dreams.

It didn't take many months of graduate school to disabuse the novice of these prospective ecstasies. The routines of professionalism and apprenticeship, combined with the pseudoscientific methods of positivist scholarship, quickly made an interest in ideas a hindrance, if not an irrelevance, and turned affective intensities into a distracting luxury. A personal stake in books had to give way to a personal stake in one's career, and to a casual facility masquerading as authority. During the seventies the graduate study of English closed down shop, a casualty of the job market, but the best that could be said about it even earlier, when it was thriving, was that a really deep love of literature could survive it, though it couldn't expect much encouragement. When the word "literature" was used in graduate school, it usually referred not to the work of art but—preceded by a definite article—the body of writing that has been secreted around it, like the biblical glosses which, sentence by sentence, made up the edifice of the true church.

Even by the early sixties, however, this traditional scholarship was on the defensive; the spirit of practical criticism, with its emphasis on the text itself, had made serious inroads even into such bastions as the scholarly journals and the major graduate departments. Yale, where I was a graduate student, had long been the redoubt of a softened, academicized version of the New Criticism, which combined a focus on literature itself with a proper respect for what everyone else had said about it. The New Criticism was already a tired movement, a toothless lion, well past old insurgencies. It had made its peace with the old scholarship, whose occasional value it acknowledged. Interpretation and critical thinking had by then acquired some status and respect even in graduate study. But the New Criticism itself was not interested in ideas, which it considered a little extrinsic to the literary work, and it showed relatively little interest in theory, except as an afterthought to justify its procedures of close reading.

There was a body of New Critical theory concerning such matters as organic form, the intentional fallacy, image and metaphor, and so on, but it followed on the heels of the movement's practical work. The New Criticism spread its influence more through textbooks like *Understanding Poetry* (1938) than through much later theoretical polemics like Wimsatt's *Verbal Icon* (1954). In Cleanth Brooks's *Well Wrought Urn* (1947) the theoretical chapters are a postscript to the exegesis of individual poems, and by the time of Wellek and Warren's *Theory of Literature* (1949) the battle was essentially over: the time for handbooks and codification had arrived. And as an academic procedure, churning out new "readings," the New Criticism could be as spiritually deadening as the old scholarship. By successfully turning the New Criticism into theory, Yale professors like Wellek, Wimsatt, and Brooks laid the ground for the insurgent theorists of the next generation, some of whom were their own students.

For all its formal sophistication, for all its attention to the stresses and internal contradictions of the literary work, the New Criticism, by objectifying and hypostatizing the text, never really broke with the positivism of the philologists and the source-and-analogue hunters. For the scholars the text was the sum of its traceable influences. René Wellek recalled taking a seminar on Goethe's *Faust* which began with sources so far back in time that it never reached Goethe. "All we ever established about *Faust*," he said, "was that it existed."[3] For the New Critics, those inheritors and exegetes of modernism, the text's existence was of more complex concern than its background or its relationship to other texts. Sources and analogues—*Quellenforschung*, philology, along with social and biographical contexts—belonged to the old historical scholarship. The New Critics heard the battle cry of modernism, MAKE IT NEW, and behaved as if this rupture had actually been achieved, or desired, by every significant work, past and present. Just as they tried to sever the practice of criticism from theory and ideas, they failed to see that in a way the scholars were right: the text was a living tissue of its manifold contexts. Everything that went into it—the mind that composed it, the language that articulated it, the literature that preceded it, the social moment that conditioned it, the generations that had put their mark on it, the minds that received it—were flickering, prismatic, and unstable. For all their lip service to a Coleridgean idea of organic form, the practice of the New Critics usually betrayed a surprisingly mechanical notion of form. Paradox and ambiguity were there *in the object*, existing not as fragments of internal drama, diversity, and self-contradiction but as elements of a higher unity, a conservative principle of order.

What finally signed the death warrant for the New Criticism was not its conceptual weaknesses but its practical triumphs. Like all successful movements, the New Criticism died when it was universally assimilated. Its techniques of close reading, its vision of formal coherence, its attention to patterns of metaphor and narrative personae, were integrated into the useful equipment of every teacher and critic of literature, and influenced many readers who had studied with them, some of whom became editors, journalists, book reviewers, and even authors. Few have ever suggested returning to the days of genteel impressionism or dry factual scholarship. But by the late fifties and sixties, many began to feel bored and constrained by the anatomical approach to literature. They were eager to see the work reconnected to the wider sphere of history and theory, politics and psychology, from which the New Critics had amputated it. They envied the broader horizons and grander ambitions of European criticism. Writers like Auerbach, Spitzer, Lukács, Poulet, and Bachelard were expected to become guides in the struggle of American critics to pass beyond formalism, but they were far too idiosyncratic to offer any easy new method, and their approach made fools of less learned and nimble men who tried to imitate them too directly. It was only the arrival of structuralism and deconstruction in the late sixties and seventies that seemed to provide a way out of the formalist impasse with new critical techniques. For all their formidable difficulty, the works of Lévi-Strauss, Foucault, Lacan, Barthes, and Derrida collectively breached the resistance to theory endemic among English and American critics. Sympathetic expositors sprang up at key American universities who themselves began to provide a body of theory rivaling the work of the Europeans in its daunting complexity and elusiveness of style.

Marxism, Freudianism, structural linguistics, deconstructionism—American critics threw themselves into difficult and often contradictory conceptual systems with a reckless zeal as strong as their previous resistance. Yet the critical utopia that these theoretical breakthroughs once seemed to promise failed to materialize. Americans learned to handle big European ideas, but they have not really translated them into convincing critical practices. Literary theorists have had a greater impact on legal interpretation than on the way readers read or writers write. They've had no effect on journalistic criticism, which mediates between writers and readers. The test of a critic comes not in his ideas about art, and certainly not in his ideas about criticism, but in the depth and intimacy of his encounter with the work itself—not the work in isolation, but the work in its abundance of reference, richness of texture, complexity of thought and feeling. If the New Critics inhibited themselves by objectifying the text and putting it under glass, the deconstructive critics display their ingenuity by evaporating the text into an infinite variety of readings and misreadings. We grant that no two readers read the same book. But by scanting the degree to which different readings may overlap, and even coincide, the deconstructive critics undermined the communal basis of practical criticism, which is grounded in the possibility of common perception and mutual assent. The provisional (rather than definitive) character of any reading does not therefore condemn us to an anarchy of arbitrary subjective difference. Cut off from a text that he can manipulate at will, isolated from an audience whose agreement he deliberately eschews, the deconstructive critic creates an almost impenetrable barrier—his style—which repels the uninitiated and becomes the self-fulfilling prophecy of separation from the language of the tribe.

There is much to be said against the Arnoldian public style which long dominated English and American criticism, especially for the air of objective authority it arrogates to itself. T. S. Eliot's essays, for example, don't bear examination as argument, despite his philosophical training; even his casual aphorisms read like dictatorial fiats. But the plain style is at least a communal style, not a specialist's jargon, and its transparency assumes that what matters about art is its relation to life. The public style not only aims to communicate but presumes what Jürgen Habermas calls a "public sphere," a liberal arena of citizenship, public opinion, policy debate, and civic responsibility. Deconstruction, on the other hand, especially among the imitators of Derrida, gave rise to an intensely literary style, an artifact style, that mimics the self-referential involutions of art's relation to itself. Sentences take a long, sinuous course before looping back upon themselves, donnish puns cascade over one another, hyphens separate syllables to highlight dubious etymologies. Having decided that art is not about life but only about itself, the deconstructionist then insists that criticism can't really be about art but only about itself, about the duplicities of language and representation. Life is a construct, a series of fictions; art is a discourse which helps create those fictions; and criticism is a competing discourse without genuine access to either art or "life"—an illusion created by language. The style of deconstruction reflects its rejection of the public sphere and the politics of liberal humanism.

Writing some of these sentences, I feel myself falling into the very jargon I have criticized. Words take on a life of their own, losing their referential grasp and their power to communicate something precise and concrete. In *Practical Criticism* I. A. Richards[4] quotes Blake's saying that "Virtue resides only in minute particulars," which could stand as a justification for the whole enterprise of practical criticism. To avoid dissolving into generalities, and to keep myself from foreclosing the possibility that poststructuralist theory, for all its disbelief in the idea of the individual author, will someday prove itself in the criticism of actual works, I'd like to take a closer look at Richards's book, which was a key influence on the New Criticism, and compare it to structuralism's most ambitious attempt at practical criticism, Roland Barthes's *S/Z*. Before doing that, however, I ought to explain at last what I mean by practical criticism, and sketch in some of the background of its development.

Students of criticism can't help but notice that they almost never encounter detailed analyses of individual works or passages in criticism written before the twentieth century. Before the beginning of the nineteenth century, even essays devoted to individual authors are a rarity. Unlike the history of art itself, the history of criticism is progressive and cumulative. Criticism builds on past work as art need not. But until the early nineteenth century the history of criticism is really a history of aesthetics, not of critical practice. Though there is no reason to think that men of taste and perception in past ages read more superficially than we do, the comments they left us often seem distant and external. With a few remarkable exceptions, they had no framework or rationale for detailed interpretation and evidential analysis. The exceptions are notable, and usually have a purpose apart from criticism itself: philosophical treatises on other texts, such as the Neoplatonic commentaries on Plato or medieval discussions of Aristotle; handbooks of rhetoric from the ancient world through the Renaissance; biographies of artists, such as Vasari's lives of Renaissance painters or Johnson's great *Lives of the Poets*, which forms the effective beginning of practical criticism in English; polemical or didactic forays, such as Rymer's comments on *Othello* or Addison's papers on *Paradise Lost*; early legal commentaries, such as Blackstone; and above all, religious hermeneutics and biblical commentary, which provided the model for both literary scholarship (texts, annotated editions) and critical interpretation. (Later, when the "higher criticism" of the Bible developed in the nineteenth century, it repaid this secular scholarship the compliment of imitation.)

Occasionally, a work of aesthetic theory such as Lessing's *Laokoön* would shade off into close textual commentary of a surprisingly modern kind. But by and large, practical criticism developed in response to the immediate needs of expanding middle-class cultural activity. During the Romantic period, reviewing became the mediating force between an increasingly difficult literature and an increasingly diverse audience; and a reviewer, then as now, was prompted to confront the individual work as the aesthetician had not. Serious reviewing begins in England with the founding of the liberal *Edinburgh Review* in 1802 and its Tory rival the *Quarterly Review* in 1809, but there was an upsurge of reviewing in monthly magazines and newspapers as well, embracing not only literature but theatrical performances and art exhibitions. As Kean walked the boards, Hazlitt, Leigh Hunt, and their friends were there to record their reactions to his acting, and even Keats, inspired by Kean to write a play, could at times contemplate earning his living as a literary journalist. In the midst of this journalistic hubbub, much of it trivial and mediocre, the "Advertisement" in the first number of the *Edinburgh Review* sounded exactly the note that would later be heard from the modern quarterlies and the founders of the *New York Review of Books*. Unlike other reviews, the *Edinburgh Review* would "be distinguished, rather for the selection, than for the number of its articles"; rather than try to review everything, it would confine itself "in a great degree, to works that either have attained, or deserve, a certain portion of celebrity"; the articles would be fewer, longer, more reflective, and hence would not have to appear at just the time of publication. Lord Brougham, one of the prime movers, stressed in his memoirs that these were meant to be essays occasioned by books rather than strictly critical reviews of the books themselves.

Today the early stalwarts of the great reviews remain only sour footnotes to the history of English Romanticism. Jeffrey, Lockhart, Croker, and Gifford are largely remembered for their savage attacks on Wordsworth, Shelley, Byron, Keats, and Hazlitt. Francis Jeffrey, who edited the *Edinburgh Review* from 1803 to 1829, who contributed literally hundreds of articles (including at least fifty on contemporary English literature), whose pieces were collected into library editions after his death, has come down to us as the man who opened his review of Wordsworth's *Excursion* with the ringing words "This will never do." A look at Jeffrey's articles on Wordsworth shows us immediately what makes them both impressive and insufferable, even when they're manifestly right, as on *The Excursion*. Jeffrey's crisp, authoritative tone verges on bullying. His cold fury at Wordsworth is redoubled because he acknowledges real talent in the poet, and because the poet has had the temerity to refuse his earlier advice. The level of vituperation exceeds anything in twentieth-century criticism. *The Excursion*, for example, is "a tissue of moral and devotional ravings . . . such a hubbub of strained raptures and fantastical sublimities, that it is often extremely difficult for the most skilful and attentive student to obtain a glimpse of the author's meaning."[5]

Just as the poetry of Wordsworth and Coleridge is one of the first examples of a conscious avant-garde, Jeffrey's reviews are perfect specimens of how critical theory, armed with precepts inherited from an earlier generation, interferes with practical criticism, especially during the time of a major revolution in taste. Jeffrey's obtuseness is partly rooted in snobbery, for the lower-class rural characters of Wordsworth reflected a social as well as poetic revolution. ("Why should Mr. Wordsworth have made his hero a superannuated Pedlar? What but the most wretched and provoking perversity of taste and judgment, could induce anyone to place his chosen advocate of wisdom and virtue in so absurd and fantastic a condition? Did Mr. Wordsworth really imagine, that his favorite doctrines were likely to gain anything in point of effect or authority by being put into the mouth of a person accustomed to [haggling] about tape, or brass sleeve-buttons?") But Jeffrey's snobbery is really an aspect of poetic theory; he brings to bear a classical standard of *literary* decorum which rules out low-born characters entirely, or at least requires that they be depicted in a way that is consistent dramatically and consonant with their social standing. Jeffrey charges Wordsworth with "revolting incongruity and utter disregard of probability or nature."[6] Wordsworth is "revolting" indeed, against the very notions of decorum and probability that blinker Jeffrey's criticism.

Before these passages make us complacent about our superior appreciation of Wordsworth and our more advanced critical subtlety, we ought to ask ourselves a small question. Are we really responding to the poet more deeply than Jeffrey did? Do our reverential commentaries really take in what is extreme and problematic about him? Can we even begin to understand his drastic affront to accepted taste? Aren't obtuseness and outrage the highest tribute conventional minds can pay to genius—particularly vanguard genius of the modern kind, which always *is* trying to "make it new"? This kind of sharp recoil wasn't limited to the bold, stylized products of Romanticism. The same obtuseness can be traced in reviews of Henry James later in the century, and in the initial responses to Beckett in our own time. I don't mean to elevate the angry rebuff of the offended philistine into the only true tribute to originality. As we follow the more positive reactions to Wordsworth from the comments of Ruskin and Mill, to the great statements of Arnold and Pater, along with the obligatory essays of the lesser Victorian critics like Leslie Stephen, Morley, Bagehot, and Lewes, we continue to feel the shock of recognition, the wrestling with the intractable that rarely intrudes into our modern academic assimilation of the poet. The plebeian sublimities that revolted Jeffrey became therapeutic and life-giving myths for Mill, Ruskin, and Arnold, but the personal stake of the critics never abates. The vitality of the poet radiates down through their work, as it rarely does in our academic discourses—despite the voluminous attention directed at Wordsworth by recent scholars.

Before we conclude that the discovery of close reading coincided with the loss of our ability to read, or at least to read deeply and feelingly, we ought to remind ourselves of James's response to his reviewers' tribute of incomprehension and disapproval: "a periodicity of platitude and irrelevance."[7] It would be hard to find a better phrase to describe the work of those heirs of Jeffrey who populate I. A. Richards's modern *Dunciad*, oddly misnamed *Practical Criticism* (1929). For several years in the late twenties Richards distributed a group of anonymous short poems to his undergraduate audiences at Cambridge, giving them a week to compose written comments, on which he subsequently lectured. Excerpts from these comments—or "protocols," as Richards calls them—make up the main part of *Practical Criticism*. Richards introduces this material modestly, as an experimental survey and "documentation," and his own comments on the protocols and the poems are spare and laconic. But others have followed his hints and asides to read recklessly large implications into his evidence. According to Stanley Edgar Hyman, who is no enemy of hyperbole, "what the protocols reveal, by and large, is probably the most shocking picture, exhaustively documented, of the general reading of poetry ever presented."[8]

Published more than sixty years ago, *Practical Criticism* has always been considered one of the landmarks of modern criticism, but like many assumed classics it's more respected than read. After all, what still shocked Hyman in 1948 could hardly surprise anyone who corrects undergraduate papers today. Instead, we are likely to be impressed by the technical sophistication and polemical eloquence with which the protocol writers, like their ancestor Francis Jeffrey, pursue lines of argument wholly irrelevant to any kind of fair-minded criticism. Well equipped with information about meter, rhyme, and verse forms, they unsparingly demolish poems whose rhythm departs even minutely from a regular standard. Often able to piece out difficult thematic configurations, they are quick to bully the poet with their own (irrelevant) point of view on the same subject. On one weak religious poem a writer comments: "I don't like to hear people boast about praying. Alfred de Vigny held that *to pray is cowardly, and while I don't go as far as this,* I do think that it is rude to cram religious ecstasies down the throat of a sceptical age" (90). Such a brave agnosticism makes clear that the writers are by no means hidebound and old-fashioned, despite their aversion to poetic rudeness. Their stern up-to-dateness is nowhere more evident than in their sharp attacks on "sentimentality," even in great poems like Lawrence's "Piano" where the sentiment is precisely qualified and vividly actualized.

Revealing much more than ignorance or the inability to read, the protocols, like the reviews of Romantic poetry of a hundred years earlier, demonstrate the drastic interference of critical theory with critical practice. Richards's readers are caught in a backwater of Romantic and Georgian taste just when the tide is running out. Quite able to take the measure of decorous minor nature poetry, they're utterly lost with Donne, Hopkins, and Lawrence, all figures who, whatever their dates, belong to the new modern sensibility of the 1920s, poets whose verse forms all fail the late-nineteenth-century test of musical regularity and artful literary diction. One reader describes a delightful Hopkins poem as "a nonsensical agglomeration of words. Expressed in jerky, disconnected phrases, *without rhythm.*" Another agrees that "*there doesn't seem to be the least vestige of a metrical scheme.*" Others have equal difficulty with what the poem is saying: "I read this ten times without finding any meaning in it and very little attraction" (82). Still others take a wild stab at what's happening in the poem, and then substitute their prose paraphrase for the poem itself, addressing all their subsequent comments to the paraphrase rather than the poem.

The main disability of Richards's readers is that they come to a poem with fixed ideas of what a poem ought to be, instead of attending to what is actually there. Richards is very amusing on this tendency of his readers to write substitute poems out of their own experience, which displace the poem on the page. This inattention to detail is matched in other readers by "dogmatic pronouncements upon detail irrespective of the final result"; both approaches tend to ignore plain evidence of the poet's intentions. Richards demonstrates in great detail how "critical preconceptions" and "technical presuppositions" can blind readers to the whole point of a work, especially if it is original in form or meaning. "The blunder in all cases," says Richards, "is the attempt to assign marks *independently* to details that can only be judged fairly with reference to the whole final result to which they contribute. It is the blunder of attempting to say how the poet shall work without regard for what he is doing" (277–78).

This emphasis on internal form and on the totality of the individual work was Richards's chief legacy to the New Critics. Richards had a great feeling for how poems are put together. His notion, developed in other books, of poetic statement as "pseudo-statement," emotive and provisional in character rather than cognitive and discursive, provided later critics with a rationale for objectifying individual works and isolating them from larger cultural contexts. Yet Richards himself, like the other great practical critic who emerged from the Cambridge English school in the twenties, F. R. Leavis, almost never confines himself to straight explication. Richards's work, for all the uses to which it has been put, offers a good deal that undercuts formalism and anticipates later developments, including structuralism. With his interest in psychology, linguistics, semantics, Basic English, literary theory, and Eastern thought, Richards is very much the nineteenth century Professor of Things-in-General. Every page in *Practical Criticism* that tells us that works have a unity of form also tells us that they have a diversity of meaning, that people will read them in different ways, in different moods, using different codes and assumptions.

This is especially true when readers encounter literary works without the provenance and cultural authority of a known, brand-name author. Richards's experiment in anonymous reading foreshadows the structuralist interest in a science of literature, as well as its dream of a literature without authors, cut loose from the mystifying bourgeois idealization of the individual artist, bathed instead in the semiological glow of a staggering variety of semantic codes and potential meanings. Though New Critical exegetes like William Empson and Cleanth Brooks took from Richards a sense of the inherent ambiguity of all texts, they saw these contradictions as inherent in the object itself rather than in our different ways of reading it. Richards, on the other hand, anticipates the recent interest in literature from the point of view of the reader, which the New Critics ruled out under the heading of the Affective Fallacy. For Richards, a science of literature is a subdivision of a science of life, a psychology of behavior and emotion. He sees emotion as the fundamental element in literary response and, unlike the New Critics, makes short shrift of the critical charge of "sentimentality" when it is simply a cover for disagreement or simple contempt. His reaction to the protocols, which is usually so oblique and understated—we never learn what Richards thinks of most of the poems he presents to his students—rises to a pitch almost of indignation when they use their critical sophistication to rend the emotional fabric of Lawrence's "Piano" (99–112). With his keen interest in emotion, and his sense that critical judgments are judgments about life as well as art, Richards is far from sharing the antiromantic, antisubjective bias Eliot and T. E. Hulme passed on to the New Critics.

I can't refrain from pointing out one other feature which gives *Practical Criticism* its contemporary feeling and keeps it a living work—its form. Cast as a report on a quasi-scientific experiment, "the record of a piece of field-work in comparative ideology" (6), Richards takes pains to avoid the belletristic pontifications of a conventional man of letters. In *The Rise and Fall of the Man of Letters* (1969), John Gross described the gradual professionalization of criticism and its attachment to the university. But it is hard to understand, apart from some personal animus, why he makes Leavis the chief character in his demonology while hardly mentioning Richards.[9] When Richards castigates "the attempt to assign marks *independently* to details that can only be judged fairly with reference to the whole final result to which they contribute" (277–78), he is describing not only the hapless efforts of his untutored students but the whole line of attack of periodical criticism and book reviewing from Francis Jeffrey to his own day, and well beyond. Just as Leavis never tired of assaulting the cultural authority of the British weeklies and Sunday papers, one key element of *Practical Criticism* is its origin in the university classroom and its dedication to his student "collaborators."

The fissure opened up by the new modernist sensibility, into which those same students stumble and fall, is closely related to the growing gap in England between the conservative taste of the periodical reviewers and the more advanced literary thinking that was developing in the universities. What a reversal from the time, not much earlier, when not only modern literature but *English* literature were barred from the university, when Arnold could become the first Professor of Poetry in Oxford to lecture in English rather than Latin. It's in the context of this split between the middlebrow metropolitan culture of book clubs and consumer guidance and the advanced literary culture of Cambridge that we must see Richards's rejection of the essayistic mode, his unwillingness even to make explicit his own judgments of the works he presents for study, as well as Leavis's astringent critical judgments and knotty Jamesian cadences. For both of them, reading is a more searching process than the glib Sunday reviewers imagine. Their styles suggest steady work, the resistance of literature to easy assimilation.

What Leavis achieves through surly exactitude—his writing is both exact and exacting—Richards accomplishes by withholding: by restraint, understatement, and irony. *Practical Criticism* is not an essay but a palimpsest—multilayered and unstable. Richards's spare voice becomes the continuous bass line beneath a polyphonic display of more assertive critical voices, whose very diversity dramatizes the manifold range of reading and meaning. Richards is most intrigued by how differences in human psychology and background are reflected in the different ways we read. Even after we pare away those readings based simply on ignorance—on what Richards calls failures in "construing"—the exchange between text and reader remains mercurial and dynamic.

There are serious weaknesses in the analytical part of the book, where Richards is sometimes tempted to assume the role of the village explainer. But in the documentation section the interplay of different poetic texts, the voices of the protocol writers, and Richards's own oddly personal tone of subdued irony, learned objectivity, and donnish whimsy makes the book a uniquely instructive and entertaining work, as bold in its form as it is unusual in content.

It would be tempting to round off our excursion into practical criticism by saying that Roland Barthes's staggering book *S/Z* bears the same relation to structuralism (and poststructuralist "narratology") that Richards's book does to the New Criticism. Both are idiosyncratic works, in surprising ways more like each other than like the work produced by critics who share their approach. I have already underlined Richards's differences from the New Critics, not least of which were his strong theoretical interests, which found little echo in the busywork of explication that became the New Criticism. Of course there's a long, dreary tradition of "explication de texte" in the French school system, from which Barthes takes pains to distinguish himself, but the advanced part of French intellectual life is highly theoretical, grounded in philosophical training, with no equivalent of the Anglo-American empirical tradition to provide ballast. Deconstructionists have been much less eager to apply themselves to literary texts than to spin out pure theory, or comb earlier thinkers like Rousseau, Marx, Nietzsche, Freud, or Bataille for anticipations of their own views. In *S/Z*, even more than in his books on Racine and Michelet, Barthes sets out not only to confront a literary work but chooses one as alien to his own modernism and structuralism as can be imagined.

The quasi-scientific, quasi-dramatic form of Richards's book finds its unexpected complement in Barthes's equally polyphonic performance. The New Critics rarely ventured beyond the manageable confines of the lyric and had meager luck with narrative fiction, but Barthes's line-by-line commentary on *Sarrasine*, a little-known novella by Balzac, makes that story one of the longest secular texts ever analyzed so exhaustively. And since the book quotes the entire text of the novella, dividing it into 561 separate units, or lexia, there's a constant interplay between the voice of the narration and the voices of the critic.

Like Richards, Barthes dedicates the book to his student collaborators, but their voices are never heard as they are in *Practical Criticism*: their views have been assimilated by Barthes, who intervenes with comments and miniature essays literally between the lines of Balzac's story. His goal is to dismantle the work, to demystify it, rather than to interpret it. As an experiment in reading as disintegration and deconstruction, *S/Z* is unique. Barthes follows the linear sequence of *Sarrasine* from first sentence to last, but rarely has a critic interceded in a literary work, *interrupted* it, so aggressively or so possessively. Barthes's stated aim is to avoid doing a conventional "reading" of Balzac's story, one that would reductively transpose it into the prose and the argument of the critic. He wants "no *construction* of the text: . . . [T]he *step-by-step* method, through its very slowness and dispersion, avoids penetrating, reversing the tutor text, giving an internal image of it."[10] Barthes's purpose is to preserve and extract the multiplicity of the text's meanings, the range of codes which make up a grid of interlocking significations. Like Richards he eschews belletristic continuity, preferring the appearance of a scientific analysis, and even constructs his title as a diagram, a symbolic paradigm, rather than a piece of writing.

But out of this very attempt to write an *open* book rather than a closed and seamless critical discourse, Barthes decomposes the Balzac story more thoroughly than any conventional exegete. A "reading" at least is a point of view, which we approach as argument, aware of its partiality; but the format of Barthes's interlinear commentary, like a page of the Interpreter's Bible, looks both exhaustive and official, for all its insistence on the text's inexhaustibility. Barthes even expresses annoyance that his readers are likely to want to read the Balzac story *first*, before turning to what he calls his "manhandling" of it. "Those who like a good story may certainly turn to the end of the book and read the tutor text first; it is given as an appendix in its purity and continuity, as it came from the printer, in short, as we habitually read it" (15). That is to say, Barthes's book, like some specially formed creatures in nature, must be entered from the rear. But when we turn to that aperture, the appendix—perhaps already ashamed of our perverse reading habits, our unseemly appetite for the original—far from finding the text "in its purity and continuity," we see it interrupted by 561 numerical superscriptions, denoting Barthes's lexical divisions. The critic's blows have landed even in the despised appendix; the "original" text has been typographically deconstructed.

We need to consider the origin of the deconstructive critic's rage at what Barthes calls the classical or "readerly" text—the realistic narrative accessible to naive consumption—which shows up in his critical procedure and the never-explained fury of his slashing tones. As a literary journalist Barthes had come to prominence as a modernist, an exponent of Brecht, Robbe-Grillet, and the *nouveau roman*. Barthes had ingeniously expounded the critique of illusionism and verisimilitude made by both of these writers. But in *S/Z* he sets himself the task of commenting on a traditional narrative, while still holding to the view that its "realism" is a mystification and a deception. The alien character of the text, its remoteness from what he officially likes—yet also his unacknowledged fascination with its themes of castration and sexual ambiguity—bring out the best and worst in Barthes as a practical critic.

Barthes's very distance from realistic storytelling, his profound suspicion of its unreflective enchantments, enables him to describe the sheer mechanics of fictional construction more intricately than anyone since Henry James. If James aimed to make readers more conscious and respectful of the *art* of fiction, Barthes is eager to alert them to its mesh of appealing deceptions, its false continuity and lifelikeness, "the 'glue' of the readerly" (172), which attaches "narrated events together with a kind of logical 'paste'" (156). If an observant, articulate, highly cerebral Martian had arrived on Earth and had immediately been handed a novel to read, this is the account of it he might have produced. Who else could describe the ordinary sequence of cause and effect, the elementary consistency of character and motivation, in which "everything holds together," in the following terms?

> The readerly is controlled by the principle of non-contradiction, but by multiplying solidarities, by stressing at every opportunity the *compatible* nature of circumstances, by attaching narrative events together with a kind of logical "paste," the discourse carries this principle to the point of obsession; it assumes the careful and suspicious mien of an individual afraid of being caught in some flagrant contradiction; it is always on the lookout and always, just in case, preparing its defense against the enemy that may force it to acknowledge the scandal of some illogicality, some disturbance of "common sense." (156)

Barthes transposes the concrete narrative into its abstract pattern and falls into overanalysis and wild hyperbole, yet somehow, quite wonderfully, he manages to create the frame of mind of a man reading a novel for the first time, amazed at the concatenation of "events" into the simulation of a story, of "life." In his very anger at this trompe l'oeil, Barthes has succeeded in pinpointing the almost indescribable feeling of wonder that lies at the root of our affinity for stories. But in doing this he also becomes the myopic viewer who stares too long and too closely at a painting, until it becomes just dots and patches of pigment. Finally, he projects on the narrative the very suspicion with which he himself greets and examines it.

The fear of "scandal," the conventionality that Barthes attributes to the classical narrative, may be news to those whose literary taste is guided by the Prix Goncourt, but most of us have long understood that realism is a set of literary conventions rather than a direct reflection of reality, that life rarely duplicates the pattern of a well-made plot, that dialogue is a stylized suggestion of the real, not naturalistic transcription, that realism, like all other conventions of discourse, has social and ideological presuppositions that should concern the critic.

It's disappointing that Barthes deals with realism only in its most naive sense—of art as a photographic duplication of "reality"—rather than with more subtle conceptions of social representation developed by Lukács, Auerbach, and others. Barthes's assault on realism, carried out within the textual terrain of one of its greatest practitioners, belongs with his demystification of the mythologies of popular culture, where he exposes images and texts that otherwise appear naive and natural as manipulative systems of signs. Performed virtually without reference to Balzac's other work, this reading is also an attack on the very idea of the Author, "that somewhat decrepit deity of the old criticism," who "can or could some day become a text like any other: he has only to avoid making his person the subject, the impulse, the origin, the authority, the Father" (211). But by denying the personal element in both narrative and authorship, by concentrating so much on the mechanics of verisimilitude, Barthes virtually jettisons the human element in literature, which everyone but the Martian can recognize and appreciate. Far from passing beyond formalism, he simply dilates its concern with technique into grander and more subjective terms.

This self-conscious emphasis on mechanics, on formal engineering at the expense of theme and emotion, is one of the weaknesses which practical criticism and poststructuralism share. Barthes might retort (with Foucault) that this notion of the human is itself ideological, but this would not diminish his own disability in the face of what really moves people in literature, an obtuseness he himself tried to correct in later books like *The Pleasure of the Text*. Practical criticism is both the shame and the glory of criticism, shameful because it is merely practical and obsessed with technique, glorious when it really gets close to the work of art in a life-giving interchange of both judgment *and* interpretation, will and understanding.

Here Barthes shows his superiority to most of poststructuralist criticism. We all know that literature is written in language, but many recent theorists were obsessed with language and tended to give literature a wholly self-referential character.[11] Everywhere this deconstructive critic turns, he or she finds writing about writing. In deconstructing the role of the author, the stance of the critic, and all naive assumptions about content and representation, poststructuralism represented another turn in the wheel of modernist self-consciousness, which arrived late in France but arrived with a paralyzing vengeance. And this critic's own involutions of style are a signal of his paralysis. Barthes, on the other hand, by grappling with the charms of the readerly, with the monster Balzac at his most lurid and exotic, with bizarre themes of sexual distortion and misplaced passion, undergoes the kind of unsettling confrontation that is the glory of practical criticism. (Before the end, in a chapter called "Character and Discourse," he even yields to the claims of the naive "realistic" reader.) In spite of himself he makes a neglected text vibrate with meaning, and develops a "reading" of it which can vivify and illuminate it even for someone who doesn't share his theoretical interests.

I myself take very little away from most deconstructive readings apart from the spectacle of a mind dancing on the head of a pin—if that kind of prose can be called dancing. The ingenious emphasis on minute details, framing devices, and conflicting subtexts, the rage to expose the mechanics and ideologies by which we are "taken in," can be numbing. It draws our attention to innumerable sideshows while we miss the main event. But because many brilliant critics have been attracted by poststructuralism, their work often tells us more about literature, peripherally, than their theory allows. Eliot once said that "there is no method except to be very intelligent,"[12] and deconstructive critics are frequently more intelligent than their method. An elegant example is Jacques Derrida's essay on Nietzsche, "Spurs," which pretends to be about style but also manages to build up a fascinating pattern, almost entirely by quotation, of Nietzsche's notions about women. Gradually, however, the seductive distance and alluring inaccessibility of Woman modulates into Derrida's assertion of the distance and inaccessibility of Truth, and Nietzsche's texts on women are appropriated to confirm Derrida's view that "there is no such thing either as the truth of Nietzsche, or of Nietzsche's text." To demonstrate this point that "truth is plural," Derrida settles on a few strange words written in quotation marks in one of Nietzsche's unpublished manuscripts: "I have forgotten my umbrella." Derrida observes that this text may be trivial or highly significant. It may be an utterly casual notation of someone else's words. It may mean everything or nothing. As a text it is merely a "trace," a detached remnant of something which may be irrecoverable.

> Because it is structurally liberated from any living meaning, it is always possible that it means nothing at all or that it has no decidable meaning. . . . It is quite possible that that unpublished piece, precisely because it is readable as a piece of writing, should remain forever secret. But not because it withholds some secret. Its secret is rather the possibility that indeed it might have no secret, that it might only be pretending to be simulating some hidden truth within its folds.[13]

From this exquisite miniaturization, however, Derrida leaps without warning to the largest generality: the possibility that "the totality of Nietzsche's text, in some monstrous way, might well be of the type 'I have forgotten my umbrella'" (133), since this illusory "totality," this whole body of work, is itself no more than a larger trace or remnant of what may also be irrecoverable. And the same may be true of Derrida's own "cryptic and parodic" text, which, he suggests, may be no more than a joke, a parody of his own ideas, and so on.

Derrida's aim, which he achieves beautifully, is to open up a vertigo of interpretation which forswears interpretation—by excess of interpretation to prove its very futility—so as to place a time bomb in the analytic baggage of all practical criticism. It's a brilliant performance, a feat of prestidigitation, but to agree with him we must abandon the plain evidence that a good deal more can be gleaned from Nietzsche's books, and even from Derrida's, than from the phrase "I have forgotten my umbrella" (though, as Derrida himself might say, the latter can be more important when it starts to rain).

With its emphasis on the subjectivity of interpretation, indeed, the impossibility of interpretation, poststructuralism was a deliberate affront to the empirical Anglo-Saxon tradition of the "common reader," what Leavis liked to call "the common pursuit of true judgment."[14] The skeptical theorist dismisses evidence of what two minds can share to underline all that separates and eludes them.

By making criticism more technical, the New Criticism had opened a wide gap between the academic study of literature and periodical criticism, which understandably emphasized the *feeling* of a work rather than its form. The emergence of a new generation of younger reviewers in the fifties and sixties, trained in close reading yet also alert to the ambiguities of consumption in the literary marketplace, began to close this gap and to make periodical criticism more sophisticated.

The arrival of poststructuralism, with its impenetrable elite jargon, made this gap wider than ever. As academic criticism became more technical and theoretical, it generated the very split it posited between reader and reader, between reading and meaning, between reviewer and text. If the effect of recent theory on practical criticism has been limited, its effect on reviewing and cultural journalism has been nil; to their credit, the best reviewers continue to look on literature as experience, whatever the formal mediations.

What really damages deconstructionist criticism is not the questions it raises about the status of texts and the possibilities of interpretation but rather its remoteness from texts, its use of them as interchangeable occasions for a theoretical trajectory which always returns to the same points of origin, the same indeterminacy and happy multiplicity. For Nietzsche and his umbrella we could substitute Rousseau and his ribbon, or any other text, and the point would be the same. What wouldn't change is the use of texts as opportunities for self-display, the abdication of responsibility that Steven Marcus once aptly described as a "cheerful nihilism." From the New Critical text as object we have simply shifted to the deconstructionist critic as subject, seeking out either naive texts whose duplicities can be easily exposed, or self-deconstructing texts which have already done half the critic's work for him. Skeptical of interpretation, the critic remains faithful to the sound of his voice, the invitation some texts offer to his resourceful cleverness.

NOTES

1. Henry James, "The Science of Criticism" (1891), in *Literary Criticism: Essays on Literature, American Writers, English Writers*, ed. Leon Edel, with Mark Wilson (New York: Library of America, 1984), 96.

2. Roger Gard, introduction to *Henry James: The Critical Heritage*, ed. Roger Gard (London: Routledge & Kegan Paul, 1968), 7–8.

3. Wellek said this in one of his Comparative Literature classes at Yale in the early 1960s, which I audited.

4. I. A. Richards, *Practical Criticism: A Study of Literary Judgment* (1929; reprint: New York: Harcourt, Brace & World, 1956), 284; italics in original.

5. Francis Jeffrey, in *The Romantics Reviewed*, ed. Donald Reiman, part A, vol. 2 (New York: Garland, 1972), 439, 440.

6. Jeffrey, in *The Romantics Reviewed*, 453.

7. Henry James, "The Science of Criticism."

8. Stanley Edgar Hyman, *The Armed Vision: A Study in the Methods of Modern Literary Criticism* (1948; rev. ed., New York: Vintage, 1955), 291.

9. John Gross, *The Rise and Fall of the Man of Letters: Aspects of English Literary Life Since 1800* (London: Weidenfeld and Nicolson, 1969), 269–84.

10. Roland Barthes, *S/Z*, trans. Richard Miller (New York: Hill and Wang, 1974), 12.

11. As Barthes himself says in his autobiographical *Roland Barthes by Roland Barthes*, trans. Richard Howard (New York: Hill and Wang, 1977), 79, he "wants to side with any writing whose principle is that *the subject is merely an effect of language*" (italics in original).

12. T. S. Eliot, "The Perfect Critic," in *The Sacred Wood: Essays on Poetry and Criticism* (New York: Alfred A. Knopf, 1930), 11.

13. Jacques Derrida, *Spurs: Nietzsche's Styles*, trans. Barbara Harlow (Chicago: University of Chicago Press, 1979), 131–33.

14. The phrase, from T. S. Eliot, became Leavis's credo. See F. R. Leavis, *The Common Pursuit* (1952; reprint: Harmondsworth: Penguin, 1962), v–vi.

## 5. THE POWER AND LIMITS OF LITERARY THEORY

### RICHARD FREADMAN AND SEUMAS MILLER

### INTRODUCTION

PUBLISHED IN 1992, our book *Re-Thinking Theory: A Critique of Contemporary Literary Theory and an Alternative Account* was an attempt to counter some of the key claims and attitudes of antihumanist literary theory, but without repudiating the theoretical enterprise altogether. Indeed we hoped that by offering a clear characterization of some of the modes and purposes of theory, and by conceptualizing the text as a substantive particular entity, we could "rethink" the relationship between theory and text, such that each would creatively inform the other. Above all, we argued that the text should not simply be reduced to the claims, preconceptions, and prescriptions of theory. Inevitably, the book has dated in the intervening years—a current discussion would need to take much more detailed account of postcolonial and cultural studies, queer theory, and other discourses—nevertheless, we believe that our critique of what we term "constructivist antihumanism" remains pertinent, and that the "alternative account" we offer still has merit.

Since in preceding chapters [of *Re-Thinking Theory*] we have taken issue with a series of positions currently associated with "literary theory" it is important at this point to remind the reader that this is not an "against theory" book. On the contrary, our argument has been with certain conceptions of literary theory, and certain forms that literary theory has taken, but not with the activity of literary theory as such. In fact, the aim of this chapter is to map out an alternative account, a third conception, of literary theory which we hope may help both to delineate the powers and also the limits of theory. A further hope is that it may help both to systematize and to extend (albeit modestly) existing forms of humanist critical practice. In this aspiration we may be distinguished, on the one hand, from the "Against Theory" theorists whose theory of meaning and intention leads them to propose that theory is a gratuitous exercise,[1] and, on the other, from the constructivist antihumanist theorists like the Althusserian Marxists and the (post-) Saussurean linguistic constructivists, who propose theories which are we believe inadequate.

In order to clear the way for an alternative account, we have attempted to isolate and target particular features of current theorizing which seem to us in-

Richard Freadman and Seumas Miller. "The Power and Limits of Literary Theory." Abridged by the authors from *Re-Thinking Theory: A Critique of Contemporary Literary Theory and an Alternative Account*, by Richard Freadman and Seumas Miller, 10–33. Cambridge: Cambridge University Press, 1992. Reprinted with the permission of Cambridge University Press.

imical to the construction of an adequate literary theory or theories. These features are: the denial of referentiality and therefore objective truth; the repudiation of the individual subject; and the dissolution of substantive evaluative discourse, both moral and aesthetic. We have termed this conjunction of claims, now so pervasive in literary studies, constructivist antihumanism. Before turning to our own counter-claims on referentiality, the subject and evaluation, we wish to reiterate two points relating to the now-notorious notion of humanism in literary studies.

The first is that we categorically reject the widespread assumption that literary theory and criticism can espouse emancipationist politics only if its exponents subscribe to the main tenets of constructivist antihumanism. This assumption is given characteristic expression in the concluding chapter of Terry Eagleton's *Literary Theory*.[2] Our point, by contrast, is that the incoherences of antihumanist theory—incoherences which in some instances Eagleton himself notes and criticizes—render it politically incoherent and, consequently, politically problematical. A key example here concerns the individual subject: how can "the strategic goal of human emancipation" be served or secured in the absence of a theoretical account of the emancipated individual subject? Needless to say, our further point is that "humanist" theory, as we have defined it, can be and in some instances is potently political; powerful in its commitment to emancipation. That it can be so is a consequence of the fact that it may seek to give adequately theorized accounts of the real (or desirable) world, of the emancipated subject, and of the moral claims entailed in the politics of emancipation. Now, not all "humanist" discourse is strong in these respects: too much of it is not. But there is no in principle reason why "humanist" criticism and theory cannot be strong in these areas, and it is our intention in what follows to give preliminary theoretical accounts of just these issues and thereby to offer a general account which is conceptually more plausible in emancipatory implication than those the constructivist antihumanists have produced.

Our second point concerns the whole issue of "humanism"—and the way it has been characterized by antihumanist theorists. As we have noted, it is now widely believed that the notion of theory entails antihumanism; or, to put it another way, that one cannot engage in theoretical discourse from a "humanist" standpoint. We have just said that this is wrong; we have also noted, and wish to repeat here, that the characterizations of "humanism" involved in these assertions are simplistic to the point of caricature. There is no necessary opposition between the political emancipationist and the humanistic; nor between theory and humanism. Humanism is a complex and varied phenomenon with an array of possible commitments, political and other. As we have said, our commitments in using the term are to the human individual, and to the securing of those values and conditions that are commensurate with humane and fulfilling lives. Such commitments are consistent both with theory and with social emancipation.

Having, as it were, deconstructed the oppositions between emancipationist politics and humanism, we turn now to the nature and role of theory, both in general and in literary studies.

## ELEMENTS OF A THIRD CONCEPTION OF LITERARY THEORY

### LITERARY THEORY

Let us begin with some elementary observations about the notion of theory in general and then see how this might relate to the issue of literature.

We need initially to make a distinction that is anathema to many avant-garde literary theorists: the distinction between a theory and its object. The theory itself will consist of a set of claims or principles in respect of some object or phenomenon; and the objects or phenomena may be widely varying in nature. In this instance, however, the object of theorizing is literature. It is in our view imperative to resist the temptation—and indeed the tendency—to collapse the distinction between object and theory. Theories or quasi-theories may strongly condition conceptions of their objects, but they cannot literally construct those objects or entirely determine our conceptions of them. Were they able so to construct and determine, we would be unable to apprehend, or even to posit the existence, of the object; and it would follow from this that theorizing would literally be inconceivable since there would be nothing to theorize about. Quite simply, a theory is a theory of something.

Now, in putting matters in this way, we do not wish to suggest that a theory of literature is going to take the same form as, say, a theory in the natural sciences. Indeed, it is essential to recognize that theories can take various forms and that they may differ in respect of rigidity of structure, descriptive precision, susceptibility to different kinds of testing and so on. Moreover, they can vary as to the degree of explanatory and predictive power which they purport to have in respect of their objects.

Having noted some of the important determinants of meaning such as convention and context, we need now to focus on the notion of meaning itself. Needless to say, the notion is as problematic as it is central, but any account of it would need to make certain fundamental distinctions. We shall offer a more detailed account of these in the next section. Here we propose a distinction between linguistic meaning and what we might call literary meaning. Linguistic meaning is that which can in principle be grasped by someone with elementary linguistic competence. Literary meaning, by contrast, presupposes linguistic meaning but also transcends it such that for the reader to grasp it would require more than simply linguistic competence; it would also at the very least require knowledge of literary conventions: for example, the ability to interpret symbolism, detect irony, recognize particular plot structures, and so on. At this point we need to make clear that while there is at the conceptual level a distinction to be drawn between the literary and the nonliterary, and to be drawn (at least in part) along the lines we have just indicated, the boundaries between the literary and the nonliterary are blurred. Most texts have both a literary and a nonliterary dimension; and in practice it is very difficult to characterize every given text as either (predominantly) literary or nonliterary or to isolate all the literary from the nonliterary elements within any individual text.

Now, in respect of linguistic meaning and/or literary meaning, we can distinguish (roughly) between structure and content. In fact, the distinction can be made in various ways. For example, at one level there must be some such distinction, since it is possible for the same plot structure to be associated with different plots, events, themes, and so on. At another commonplace linguistic level we can distinguish between the structure of the language the author is using and the particular meaning contents which he/she produces in conformity with that structure. A further level of content relates to the "views" which the author wishes to espouse in the work; still another, and one that needs to be distinguished from this, pertains to the ideological content of the work. As we have argued, there is in principle at least a distinction between these notions of content: the author's views are not necessarily reducible to ideology.

Needless to say, meaning (both linguistic and literary) is always meaning for someone, in this instance for reader and/or author. Now the triad of relationships—author, text, reader—is a complex one, and we shall be looking at it in more detail in the next section. Suffice it to say here that since we regard literature as a fundamentally communicative activity, we ascribe a central role to both author and reader. Moreover, in respect of both author and reader we shall be employing the kind of notion of the subject that we have proposed earlier: that is, a "thick" notion which refuses the reduction of the self to language, ideology, or discourse, which ascribes to the self agency, the capacity for rational deliberation and imaginative activity, and which, crucially, imputes moral and aesthetic dimensions to the self. As we have noted, the moral dimension involves an ability to distinguish between right and wrong, an ability to act on the basis of such a distinction, and so on.

We shall begin by provisionally characterizing theoretical accounts of literature in terms of a tripartite system of classification. We shall distinguish, therefore, between descriptive, explanatory, and normative theories. Let us take each in turn. A descriptive theory attempts to describe its object, but without purporting to prescribe or evaluate that object. Thus, so-called "generic theory" attempts to categorize literary texts according to genre, but without furnishing grounds for textual preferences. Now, in respect of descriptive theories we need to note a point that holds for other kinds of theories as well, namely, that there exists a wide range of theoretical tasks that can properly be termed descriptive. Thus, we can, like the reader-reception theorists, attempt to describe the cognitive and imaginative operations that take place within a reader as he/she reads. Again, one might have a descriptive theory of a range of interpretative practices—Leavisite, deconstructive, feminist—in which an account is given of the forms of critical practice in question: their underlying assumptions, the aspects of texts they concentrate attention on, and so on.

An explanatory theory, by contrast, is not concerned to describe how things are; rather, it wishes to account for their being as they are. Thus, the existence of the English novel in the eighteenth century may be accounted for with reference to (among other things) the rise of the middle classes. Again, in order to account for the customary content of Mills and Boon [i.e., Harlequin] novels, we might have recourse to sociological evidence about correlations between economic status and certain kinds of cultural fantasies and myths. Typically, explanatory theories are either causal or teleological in nature. That is, they seek to account for their objects in terms of antecedent causes, or in terms of some hypothetical end towards which things are alleged to be tending. An instance of causal explanation would be the Mills and Boon case where the proposition is that the sociological factors adduced cause the books to be written in the way they are. An example of a teleological kind might be drawn from Marxism; say, the proposition that dissonances in Brecht's plays foreshadow the self-destructive dissolution of capitalism prophesied by Marx. We could multiply examples of explanatory activity at great length since there are so many aspects of literature, and histories thereof, that might invite explanatory theorizing.

Let us now consider normative theories. A normative theory is one that does not stop at description or explanation but rather seeks to prescribe and evaluate its object. Thus a normative theory of interpretation, for example, does not simply seek to describe or explain the existence of some antecedent critical practice; it seeks to evaluate and recommend particular interpretative practices. In so doing, of course, it must have recourse to some descriptive and explanatory accounts of text, reader, and so on; moreover, its evaluations and prescriptions must be furnished with due justification and argumentation. Consider as an example a Marxist normative theory of interpretation. Such a theory will be normative if it enjoins one to interpret texts in a particular way, and to the exclusion of other interpretative modes. Thus, it will presuppose a certain theoretical description of the text, namely, that it is an ideological construct; it will then advocate a particular interpretative mode—its own—on the grounds that it, and it alone, can detect the presence of ideology in the text. An example here would be Catherine Belsey's discussion of Arnold's "The Scholar-Gipsy" in which, having presupposed that the text is ideological, she discerns a conflicted ideology of withdrawal and idealization therein.[3] As is the case with descriptive and explanatory theories, there can be a wide range of spheres in which normative theorizing may operate. Thus, a normative theory might tell us not only how we ought to interpret a text, but also, à la Leavis, how an author ought to construct a text, or, again à la Leavis, what constitutes a particularly valuable text.

It is apparent, then, that theorizing in relation to literature can take many forms and can address itself to various phenomena. If we ask what forms of activity have characterized so-called literary theory over the past three decades, we get an answer that is rather at variance with the rhetoric of some of its practitioners. Thus, such theory may, as in the case of Jonathan Culler's conception of "structuralist poetics,"[4] repudiate the notion and practice of interpretation; or, as in the case of Eagleton's Marxism or Derrida's deconstruction, repudiate substantive normative discourse. However, the fact of the matter is that most literary theorists, the above among them, have actually been offering normative theories of interpretation. Quite simply, they provide a theory of how to construe a text—deconstruct it, refuse its actuality, reduce it to economic or psychological determinants, and so on—and then recommend this interpretative practice over others. Indeed, the institutional politics of literary theory has provided a spectacular example of a commitment to specific normative theories which has been accompanied by an often savage disrecommendation of alternative theories.

## TEXT, AUTHOR, READER

We have already offered a preliminary definition of the text as a set of marks possessing meaning and significance, at least partly in virtue of literary and linguistic conventions. We have also noted that any given set of conventions permits an array of possible meanings. Further, we have argued that, in addition to convention, intra- and extratextual contexts are among the chief determinants of meaning. Finally, we offered a (very) preliminary distinction between linguistic meaning (that ascertainable through elementary linguistic competence) and literary meaning. We need now to give a more elaborate account of each of these things and of their relation to author and reader.

An initial distinction here is that between authorial intention and textual meaning. That there is some such distinction to be drawn is apparent from the fact that what an author intends to mean by the production of some sentence in a particular context can be different from the meaning of that sentence type according to standard linguistic conventions. Thus, if an author produces the sentence "he has gone down to the bank," he may mean that a character—say Huck Finn—has gone down to the river bank; however, this degree of specificity would not be forthcoming from a grasp of sentential meaning. So it is clear that there is a difference between the meaning of a sentence and what an author intends by it on some particular occasion.[5] Moreover, there is a further distinction to be made between what the author intends to mean by producing a particular sentence in a context, and what the sentence means in that context. An example here might occur in a novel where one character utters the sentence "he has departed." On the basis of convention and context the reader might legitimately infer that "he" in this sentence refers to Jim; but this may not be so: the author may not have given sufficiently clear indications as to the person in question and may actually have intended that the sentence refers to John. Needless to say, in drawing this distinction between intended meaning and sentence meaning we are not suggesting that intended and sentence meaning never coincide. Clearly, in the generality of instances they do coincide, since it is principally in virtue of the author's knowledge of convention and context that he/she is able to communicate his/her intentions to a reader. For his/her part, the reader determines meanings principally through knowledge of the same conventions and contexts.

We can now see precisely where Knapp and Michaels are in error.[6] They suppose that because in general the intended meaning is as a matter of contingent fact the meaning of the sentence in context, there is no distinction to be drawn between intended and sentence meaning. They reach this false conclusion on the basis of a fallacious argument. This argument is, roughly, that there is no such thing as sentential meaning (as distinct from intended meaning) because sentences which are not uttered on some occasion with a particular intention do not have any meaning. But unused sentences are grounded in intentions; namely, the intentions of the community which uses the language in question. Quite simply, a sentence means what the members of that linguistic community would intend it to mean were they to utter it. Knapp and Michaels offer an example of unauthored writing on a beach[7] to demonstrate their claim that meaning is only ever what someone intends by an utterance on some occasion. But, we submit, the example demonstrates nothing of the sort. The Wordsworth beach poem in question has sentential meaning. This is why we as speakers of English can make something of it. However, if the writing were some kind of freakish wholly unintended accident, then it follows that no one meant anything by it. Thus, there would be no authorial intention because there is no author.

We have now distinguished between the meaning of a sentence in context and what the author intends by it. We have also seen that in general intended and sentential meaning coincide. Moreover, we have noted that we construe a text as a structured set of speech acts or sentences in use, rather than as some freak of climate. In short, we construe the text as having an author and its meanings as having been intended.

Having considered linguistic meaning, let us now turn to the more problematic notion of what we have termed literary meaning. (It is problematic both in itself and in terms of its separability from linguistic meaning.) As we have so far defined it, literary meaning is dependent not just on narrow linguistic conventions and meaning but on literary conventions and devices, contexts of various sorts, and understandings, beliefs, and so on that are shared within a hermeneutic community. We do not need to elaborate on literary conventions and devices at length. They would clearly include such things as symbolism, irony, metaphor, narrative point of view and structure, particular poetic, dramatic and narrative forms, various rhetorical and stylistic techniques, modes of characterization, and so on.

Context, by contrast, would include an array of intertextual features such as stereotyped mythological and symbolic materials, standardized modes of narrative and rhetorical procedure, commonplace forms of patterning, and so on. These would combine with the specific intratextual context, together with extratextual context (including communal beliefs and assumptions), to produce a general contextual framework. It is the reciprocal interaction between linguistic meaning and this general contextual framework that allows literary meaning to be generated. Literary meaning is a very inclusive term. It can refer, for example, to symbolic, metaphoric, rhetorical, and other meaning. It can also involve various forms of implication, where there is a contrast between what is explicitly said or indicated and what has to be inferred. An example here would be Hemingway's story "The Snows of Kilimanjaro," where the conviction that love is essentially shallow is nowhere stated but everywhere heavily implied.

## TRUTH IN LITERATURE

Now we wish to claim that fictional literature can furnish significant truths about the world. But given that fictional discourse is by definition in some senses not true, the central task of our account will necessarily be to show how such discourse can be untrue at one level and true at another. It is to this problem that we now turn.

Before proceeding it needs to be noted that when we claim, as we wish to do, that fictional discourse can furnish significant truths about the world, we are not claiming that some sentences in the text may as a matter of fact be true, as we can see the sentence "London is south of Edinburgh" is true. (Though of course this latter claim about some sentences in texts is in fact true.)

Now, the speech acts which constitute the text are not themselves either true or false. Rather, in virtue of being pretended acts, they construct an imaginary world.[8] It follows from this that if there is truth in fiction it will have to exist in virtue of some relation between this imaginary world (of hypothetical objects) and the ordinary spatio-temporal world. It is obvious that some of the elements of this imagined world—characters, events, and so on—in varying degrees resemble elements of the ordinary world. But it does not follow from the fact that one thing resembles another thing that the first thing is true of the second. This color patch resembles that one, but the one is not true of the other. And even if someone draws a picture of a suburban street which fortuitously resembles very closely a particular suburban street, it does not follow that the drawing is a representation of that particular street, much less a true representation. If, on the other hand, the artist had done the drawing for a resident in the street and intended it to be taken as a representation, then it would be assessed in respect of truth/falsity, accuracy or inaccuracy. Translated into the case of literature, the question is whether certain conventions exist in virtue of which the author is taken as intending that these hypothetical objects (fictional entities) created by his pretend assertions are representations of aspects of the real world. (These conventions would of course be additional to those which (a) govern ordinary assertions, and (b) those which suspend the operation of these just-mentioned conventions, so as to enable pretend assertions to be performed.) The aspects in question could be particular individuals and events or general features; they could, that is, be particulars or universals. Quite clearly, the answer to this question is in general affirmative; and indeed this is one of the things that distinguishes fictional literature from other forms of pretense like (say) circus clowning, where it is not assumed that the activity performs any representational or instructive function. It is merely pretense for the sake of pleasure.

However, it is also clear that the degree and kind of representational intention would be taken by readers to vary from genre to genre. Thus, the conventions pertaining to extreme forms of free-verse associative poetry would cue the reader to expect only a very limited degree of representational intention, and probably intentions relating more to some mental state in the poet than to the external world. Conversely, the conventions of novelistic realism posit a high degree of representational intention; the writer is assumed to be intending to represent salient aspects of both the ordinary external world and the ordinary internal (psychological) world in his/her fiction.

We must beware, however, of using the notion of representation indiscriminately. In respect of representation in literature it is important to distinguish the question as to what degree of representational fidelity is characteristic of a certain genre from the question: which particular truths is the author concerned to impart? We can illustrate this point through a comparison of (say) Trollope and Beckett. It is obvious that the fidelity of Trollope's fictions to their social milieu is very (albeit selectively) high. Beckett's novels, by contrast, are relatively nonnaturalistic. However, it is equally obvious that Beckett is no less concerned to impart some form of truth about the world than is Trollope, even if the form of truth in question involves radical skepticism about the notion of truth itself.

Clearly, a further set of questions concerns the specific means by which representational content achieves representational power. At one relatively unproblematic level a narrative, in particular a realist narrative, can mirror certain events, character types, objects, and so on. Other and less direct means rely on techniques like symbolism, psychological notation, and so on. The degree of realism associated with a given genre type is determined by the extent to which constructions concretely mirror or resemble things in the world.

However, as we have noted, works in relatively "nonrealist" genres can equally be truth-bearing. Thus, Beckett's fictions penetrate various real but little-understood mental states. This is as we would expect, since in sophisticated literature authors generally impart truths by means of implication rather than direct representation. Thus, in a Shakespeare play the central insights are carried and ramify at all sorts of levels: through image patterns, recurrent syntactical forms, thematic vocabulary, configurations of events and response, elements of myth, psychological preoccupations of characters, and so on. There are also less-implicit means such as narrative commentary or dialogue in which themes are articulated; but a work cannot rely too heavily upon such explicitness without forfeiting aesthetic complexity and therefore the capacity to furnish compelling representations.

To conclude: if, as we have suggested, it is part of the conventionalized purpose and demonstrable capacity of fictional literature to communicate truth, then the value of such literature will in part depend upon whether it does in fact communicate truth rather than falsity; and, especially, whether the truth in question is of a significant kind.

## READING FOR THE ETHICAL

Before turning to a specific novel, let us recall in summary form relevant aspects of the general account of theory, criticism, and text offered to this point.

We have argued that theory informs but does not fully determine its object—some antecedent conception of the object is a prerequisite for theoretization—and that the object of literary theory, literature, must be conceived of as possessing specifically literary properties. Otherwise the theory in question will not be a theory of literature. We have suggested that there is a variety of interconnected theoretical tasks to be performed within the general area of literary theory, including that of constructing a theory of literary interpretation. Such a theory would presuppose and rely heavily on a theory of the literary text. It would also partially depend on a range of related theoretical considerations such as those pertaining to the nature and extent of authorial responsibility, the degree of importance ascribed to the ethical, and so on. While we do not offer a developed theory of literary interpretation here, it will by now be clear what our favored conception of literary interpretation is.

Such interpretation will address an array of textual and contextual features. It will include accounts of, for example, the sociohistorical causation of the text, the role of ideology in the production of the text, and more. It will also seek and discern in the text elements of literary meaning which are not the subjects of conscious authorial determination nor of individual and shared awareness on the part of author and reader: for instance, unconscious, implied, and inferred elements. It is, however, fundamental to our account that the text can simulate and embody salient aspects of the real; in particular, that it can offer authentic representations of the ethical realm. Indeed we believe that literature is centrally concerned with this realm, and that its powers in respect of this realm render it a central form of human enquiry. We have defined ethics as a concern with how one ought to live (a concern which involves interrelated questions about desirable modes of conduct of individual lives, on the one hand, and, on the other, desirable forms of interrelatedness between individuals), and we have argued both that the ethical is presupposed in the political and that the ethical entails particular political imperatives. On our account, the literary text represents the real in a manner that is particular to literature. This particularity resides, at least in part, in the concreteness and specificity of the representations literature can offer, and critical interpretation must attend sensitively to the nuanced specificity of the text: its representation of character, of the sociohistorical world (in this connection we have commended Greenblatt's "thick" sense of sociohistorical context), its deployment of literary conventions and techniques, and so on. We have stressed that critical interpretation is not an objective activity (in the sense that theory might ideally be), but that it is nevertheless constrained by objective fact. These objective facts include (among other things) the meanings of terms in the public language in which the text is written and certain shared understandings and beliefs of authors and readers. But it also needs to be emphasized that the meaning of a text is to some extent indeterminate and that the text's meaning is in need of completion by the reader. Accordingly, any interpreter will bring subjective elements to the incomplete and (to some extent) indeterminate thing that is the text. But the interpreter must not, in "completing" the text and determining its meaning, indulge in the kind of "textual harassment"[9] that distorts the text in the light of inappropriate prior ideological or personal preoccupations. A preoccupation which is, however, appropriate, and indeed essential, entails a substantive conception of individual agency; in particular, a conception of the moral agent. Let us elaborate on this conception here.

This agent is on our account characterized by the following minimal set of properties.[10] One, he/she possesses a capacity for rational and imaginative thought. This involves, among other things, a capacity to envisage hitherto unencountered situations and ways of behaving. It also involves the capacity for consistency in the making of ethical judgments. Two, the agent possesses freedom in the sense that he/she can make decisions on the basis of his/her rational thought processes and implement these decisions, even in the face of external resistance. Three, the agent experiences emotions such as sympathy for other people, compassion, love, and so on. Four, the agent possesses an awareness of him/herself, and this, together with his/her powers of rational thought and volition, enables the agent to conceive of his/her life as a totality, and to develop that life in particular ways. Five, the agent possesses a sense of ethical value. This includes the sense that certain things are worth doing and others not; and that certain actions are morally right and others morally wrong. Importantly, this sense exists and can be acted upon despite contrary personal inclinations and various forms of external social prohibition and pressure. Six, in virtue of the above properties, and especially the capacity for sympathy and a sense of justice, the agent is able to establish intrinsically valuable relations with other agents. Seven, the agent's values and standards must cohere with one another and persist over some significant period of time. Otherwise his/her ethical dimension will become conflict ridden and eventually disintegrate. Eight, the structure of ethical values internalized by the agent will be to some extent a response to and a result of the particular historical circumstances—including social circumstances—in which the agent finds him- or herself.

Though the description just offered ascribes a central place to the notion of a substantive individual agent, it should be clear—and indeed needs to be heavily emphasized—that our conception of the ethical ascribes equal importance to what might be termed the interpersonal domain; that is, the sphere of relations that includes both close personal relationships and those forms of relatedness that are characteristic of life in a community. In the picture we are giving, the individual agent will to some extent derive, but will not wholly derive, his/her characteristics and modes of behavior from the community. Moreover—and this point is consistent with the above—our picture ascribes to individuals the capacities of an agent: that is, the power of individual and collective rational judgment, decision making, and action. It is this capacity which makes possible the transformation of various forms of political and social organization in the manner prescribed by emancipatory politics. Indeed it should be noted here that if the doctrinaire Marxists were right in their denial of the self as agent, they must be wrong in recommending and prescribing revolutionary struggle. Only individual agents can be expected to accept and enact such recommendations in the face of the massive pressures of the society into which they have been inducted. That such pressures are at times massive, and that agents in repressive societies experience extreme restraints upon their freedoms, we would not, of course, wish to deny. Nor do we (needless to say) wish to imply that all agents in relatively "open" societies are equally free or privileged. Nevertheless, our view is that these minimal conditions will generally obtain in some measure and that, as an ideal, they ought always to obtain. A concluding point about our humanist conception is that it is a version neither of the atomistic bourgeois self nor of the socially constructed self of avant-garde theory.

Importantly, the fact that both readers and authors are moral agents so conceived means that, among other things, authors and their texts are not wholly determined by their sociohistorical context: though some textual meanings will be so conditioned, others will reflect the fact that authors can to some extent transcend their sociohistorical contexts. Similarly, readers can grasp these meanings in a manner not entirely so determined.

## MR. SAMMLER'S PLANET

Saul Bellow's writings in general, together with the kind of fictional contract operating in this work—an amalgam of moral-psychological realism and satire—is suggestive of a high degree of mimetic ambition, and a close, if not exclusive, accord between authorial and protagonist perceptions.

In *Mr. Sammler's Planet*[11] the "now," and with it the sense of apocalypse, is associated with three time frames. The first is the Holocaust, in which romanticism in its Nietzschean manifestation has achieved its nihilistic apotheosis. The second is contemporary America, specifically America in the late sixties (the novel was first published in 1969 and seems to be set in 1968). The third frame is the future. Moonshots have started and talk of leaving the tormented planet abounds. Sammler, the Wellsian time traveler, suspects that with such an end in view, with the final release from earthly constraint in prospect, the dark Romantic soul has embarked on an orgy of self-assertion:

> Of course at the moment of launching from this planet to another something was ended, finalities demanded, summaries. Everyone appeared to feel this need. Unanimously all tasted, and each in his own way, the flavor of the end of things-as-known. And by way of summary, perhaps, each accented more strongly his own subjective style and the practices by which he was known. (222–23)

Sammler, a Holocaust survivor, has perhaps more reason for favoring flight from his planet than most. Yet he finds that he is "mysteriously . . . powerfully, so persuasively drawn back to human conditions" (95). He cannot countenance escape. But in staying, in keeping faith with what may be a doomed civilization, he is compelled to try to comprehend the dark Romantic soul and the threat that its "accented . . . subjective style" poses to the ethical structures upon which the maintenance of social life on this planet depends.

To this extent *Mr. Sammler's Planet* is a philosophical novel in which the protagonist, an Anglicized Polish Jew living in postwar New York, is driven by his sense of tragedy, and by intimations of apocalypse, to ask again certain fundamental questions. Sammler, "the philosophical rambler out on Broadway" (118), wants to know what constitutes a human being ("Man is a killer. Man has a moral nature," 158), and how a human life ought to be lived. Intellectuals, he believes, should be "judges of the social order" (118). Such questions involve him repeatedly in contemplation of various kinds of ethical phenomena and issues. He wonders about the ethical inclinations, whether acculturated or intrinsic, of the self; about the nature of ethical codes and their proper or plausible authority over the individual; about the proper ends of a life and the virtues it should instantiate; he wonders about the nature, structure, and inter-relation of the virtues—of goodness, duty, loyalty, courage, integrity, sincerity, and so on; about the nature of evil, of friendship, familial relationships. And much else.

Such a list might sound more the stuff of moral philosophy than of fiction. But it is Bellow's contention that art in general, and novels in particular, can give us a special kind of access to ethical issues. In his 1976 Nobel Lecture he argues that the contemporary "intellectual public" has been "waiting to hear from art what it does not hear from theology, philosophy, social theory and what it cannot hear from pure science . . . a broader, more flexible, fuller, more coherent, more comprehensive account of what we human beings are, who we are, and what this life is for."[12] Recalling Proust's notion of art's "true impression," he continues:

> A novel moves back and forth between the world of objects, of actions, of appearances, and that other world from which these "true impressions" come and which moves us to believe that the good we hang on to so tenaciously—in the face of evil, so obstinately—is no illusion.[13]

If Bellow's notion of the "true impression"—the perception of a kind of underlying condition or moral order to which art can penetrate—is (understandably) somewhat vague, we believe his insistence upon the ethical powers of literature to be undeniable. Certainly, a novel like *Mr. Sammler's Planet* can embed and elaborate certain ethical notions—the moral agent, the virtues—in a manner unavailable to other discourses. It can give such notions embodiment; it can examine them in extended sociological contexts; and it can, through careful attention to particular personal contexts and contingencies, extend our sense of what such notions entail. Thus, in this particular novel, Bellow's narrative technique gives us a kind of complex dual perspective on the ethical. It gives us the world as seen by Sammler the ethical analyst; but it also gives us Sammler as ethical agent, immersed and acting in the ethical realm that so preoccupies his thoughts.

It is fundamental to the alternative account we offer in *Re-Thinking Theory* that our position cannot simply be given in the abstract. Our "theory" is in part an account of the dynamic process of interaction that occurs between heuristic theoretical presuppositions and the inner life of particular texts. The theory has therefore to be exemplified with respect to specific literary works. The concluding sections of *Re-Thinking Theory* comprise a detailed reading of *Mr. Sammler's Planet*—a reading informed by our "alternative account" of literary theory, and of its nonreductive relations to what we define as works of "literature."

NOTES

1.  W. J. T. Mitchell, ed., *Against Theory* (Chicago: University of Chicago Press, 1982).

2.  Terry Eagleton, *Literary Theory: An Introduction* (Oxford: Blackwell, 1983).

3.  Catherine Belsey, *Critical Practice* (London: Methuen, 1980), 118–24.

4.  Jonathan Culler, *Structuralist Poetics* (London: Routledge and Kegan Paul, 1975).

5.  A theory of intended meaning, sentential meaning, and of their relation is propounded by Paul Grice in "Utterer's Meaning, Sentence Meaning, and Word Meaning," *Foundations of Language* 4 (1968): 1–18.

6.  Stephen Knapp and Walter Benn Michaels, "Against Theory" in *Against Theory*, ed. Mitchell, 11–30.

7.  Knapp and Michaels, 15–17.

8.  John Searle, "The Logical Status of Fictional Discourse," *New Literary History* 6, no. 2 (Winter 1975): 319–32. An earlier version of this account of truth in literature appeared in Seumas Miller, "Truth in Fictional Discourse," *South African Journal of Philosophy* 10 (1991): 1–6.

9.  The term is Howard Felperin's, in his *Beyond Deconstruction: The Uses and Abuses of Literary Theory* (Oxford: Clarendon Press, 1985), 33.

10.  This set of conditions for moral agency first appeared in Seumas Miller, "Ethical Theory and Literature," *Redoubt* 14 (1991): 145.

11.  Page references below are to Saul Bellow, *Mr. Sammler's Planet* (Harmondsworth: Penguin, 1969).

12.  Saul Bellow, "The Nobel Lecture," *American Scholar* 46 (1977): 324–25.

13.  Bellow, "The Nobel Lecture," 325.

## 6.  IS THEORY TO BLAME?

### JOHN M. ELLIS

MANY PEOPLE BLAME THEORY for the present malaise in literary studies, and there is some empirical support for this view: the now predominant race-gender-class criticism is generally laden with theoretical jargon, and the critics seem less interested in considering what literary works have to say to us than in applying a particular theory to them. But it would be wrong to deduce from this that theory is the source of the problem. What is wrong here is not theory but *bad* theory.

Theory is unavoidable, and for reasons that are more compelling than the currently popular notion that some dark ideology lurks at the bottom of even

John M. Ellis. "Is Theory to Blame?" Abridged with permission of the author from *Literature Lost: Social Agendas and the Corruption of the Humanities*, by John M. Ellis, 181–203. New Haven: Yale University Press, 1997. Copyright © 1997 Yale University. Reprinted by permission of Yale University Press.

the most innocent pronouncements. Two aphorisms by Goethe put the point succinctly: "With every attentive look at the world we are theorizing" and "Everything that is factual is already theory."[1] To understand a particular case is already to have placed it among others. Kant makes the same point, but with movement going in both directions: "Thought without content is empty; perceptions without concepts are blind."[2] If the general is in the particular, the particular is in the general, too.

By contrast, current theory is largely a one-way street, going only from the general to the particular: the theory prescribes political and social attitudes as the basis of what criticism should do and literature should be, but it cannot allow for feedback from literature itself because that would show that there is more to literature than this particular theory can allow.

This idea of what theory is and what it does is too narrow in yet another way. Theory has two modes, one assertive, the other analytical. In the assertive mode, new general views of some aspect of criticism or literature are proposed: a particular theory is advocated. But in the analytical mode, ideas are examined and analyzed. The two modes are never entirely separate: new suggestions for the practice of criticism may originate from analysis, whereas a better analysis may also be a consequence of critical practice. At times when many have felt that criticism needed to change, work in theory has tended to become more assertive and prescriptive, but after the initial impetus for change has been spent, it generally returns to a more analytical mode. For example, around the time of World War II, theory was identified with the New Critics' proposals for criticism;[3] more recently, it has become identified with advocacy of social change. But this recurring tendency to identify theory with the agenda of a particular group is unfortunate, because analysis, not assertion, is the more fundamental of the two modes of theory. What makes theory valuable to us is the quality and depth of its analysis; the commitments to which that analysis may lead are a secondary concern. In the hands of race-gender-class theorists, however, the assertive mode predominates: for them, theory is knowing the right answers and applying them, not looking for a deeper analysis of the questions.

One result of this limitation is that when theorists from other fields look at the present state of literary theory, they are not impressed. The philosopher Guy Sircello suggests (to be sure, mainly on the basis of a single, indifferently argued, yet by no means completely atypical example) that literary theory contains more poetry than theory, because it generates ideas without the analysis and argument needed to support and explicate them.[4] He is right enough about the analytical incompetence of current literary theory, though his judgment of poetry sounds rather less reliable.[5] The point remains, however, that current deficiencies should not be taken to define the nature or scope of theory.

A focus on results that are politically desirable at present has also produced a discontinuity with the past and a neglect of much valuable work that is still relevant. Theory of literature is a body of knowledge and analysis that has accumulated over many years.[6] It is the result of a great deal of thought on all kinds of issues that arise in the study of literature: for example, the nature and function of literature and its relation to other aspects of a culture, the purposes and procedures of criticism, the relation of author and historical context to the meaning of a literary work, the validity of critical evaluation of literature, the nature of literary genres, and many others. There have been roughly three stages in its development. In the first, general reflections on the nature of literature and criticism were mainly sporadic by-products of the literary scene, often arising from manifesto-like writings of particular authors and literary groups or from contemporary commentary upon them. Herder's theory of cultural relativism, for example, originated in the launching of the German Sturm und Drang movement.

A new stage was reached when, in the early twentieth century, theory of criticism began to be more self-conscious and more independent of the creative writing of the time. The first organized groups of theorists for whom developing a conceptual framework for the understanding of literature became an issue in its own right were the Russian Formalists and the Prague Linguistic Circle. This more systematic attitude to theory spread to Germany, where a spate of theoretical works appeared in the 1920s as a result of the example of Oskar Walzel; to England, where I. A. Richards was a pioneer; and then to America, where former members of the pioneer groups of eastern Europe such as Roman Jakobson and René Wellek were influential. With the publication in 1949 of *Theory of Literature* by Wellek and Austin Warren, it was clear that the analysis of theoretical issues had become well developed and complex. Even so, theory of criticism remained a minority interest, and most critics were still indifferent or even mildly hostile to what they saw as abstract theorizing.

A third phase was reached in the 1970s, when a stagnant situation was energized by the influence of French thinkers such as Derrida and Foucault. There were gains and losses in this transition from the second to the third phase. For the first time, theory became accepted as an indispensable part of the knowledge and outlook of any critic—something the theorists of the previous phase had not been able to achieve—but this gain has to be weighed against the loss of analytical depth as theory became fashionable. And because France had been the most conservative of the major European nations in literary study, at first scarcely taking part in twentieth-century theoretical developments, French influence was not an unmixed blessing. The eventual catch-up was certainly energetic, but it did not build on analysis already done elsewhere. This fact, and the adoption of a new vocabulary, helped to sever links with the past. For example, the imported idea of the "death of the author" was crude compared to the results of the debate that had already taken place in America on the intentional fallacy.[7] As we shall see, when the recent treatment of most theoretical issues is compared with that of the earlier period, a consistent deterioration in analytical quality can be seen.

It has always been easy for theory of criticism to become involved in broad issues that arise in other disciplines. For example, questions about the objectivity of critical knowledge or the validity of evaluation take theory of criticism into areas explored more typically by philosophers; questions of style and meaning, into linguistic theory; questions of human behavior (both of authors and of fictional characters), into psychology; and questions of the social situations portrayed in literature, into political science and sociology. Theorists in some of these other fields (most notably Freud and Marx) have become the basis of particular schools of criticism. This presents both opportunities and dangers. Literary theorists find many useful ideas in adjacent fields, but to use them well they must master their meaning in the context of their origin. Because this mastery is rarely achieved, literary critics have always been prone to amateurish misuse of borrowed concepts.

Recent theory has relied increasingly on ideas imported from other fields, and that has led to a drastic increase in the incoherence that results when those ideas are not fully understood. For example, Ferdinand de Saussure's ideas about language achieved a considerable vogue among critics because of their use by Jacques Derrida, but (as I have shown elsewhere)[8] Derrida and his deconstructionist followers garbled those ideas disastrously, in no small part because they knew very little about their context in the history of linguistic thought.

Let us now measure the contributions of race-gender-class theorists to four major issues in theory of criticism against the full context of the debate and analysis already available from the second phase of literary theory. First, consider historical context and its relevance to the literary work, perhaps the most important issue that divides literary critics and theorists. Forty years ago a great theoretical debate had already taken place between those who argued that literary works are the product of a concrete historical situation, speak first and foremost to the concerns of that situation, and must be interpreted as such, and their opponents who argued that the transitory concerns of the place and time of composition would give too restrictive an account of a work's meaning, one that could not account for the vivid interest of readers who are no longer part of that context. According to this second view, the test of time resulted in the survival of only certain writings of a particular era, after the passions of that time had been forgotten. Writers who survive this test have produced work compelling enough to be of relevance not just to their own age but to a society conceived, more broadly, as continuing through time.

Historicist literary criticism originates in Herder's cultural relativism, according to which literature should be measured not by normative ideas such as those in Aristotle's *Poetics* but by the standards of its own time and culture.

This idea soon developed into the literary historical orthodoxy of the nineteenth and early twentieth centuries. Eventually a major problem emerged: How was one to determine what was relevant within the cultural and historical background? In the absence of a standard of relevance, historicist literary criticism easily slipped into triviality, because without it all facts of the writer's life and times were equally relevant. It was this lack of focus that helped to produce the reaction against historicist criticism known as the New Criticism.

What contribution have race-gender-class theorists made to this discussion? They have essentially adopted the first of these two positions—the historicist position—and then added to it three additional elements: first, a belief in a zeitgeist that closely determines what can be thought or imagined in a given epoch; second, an assumption that politics is the most important content of all literature; and third, an assumption that the most basic concern of politics is oppression through imperialism, economic inequality, and unequal power relations. This complex of positions and assumptions is called the New Historicism.

The one positive thing we can say here is that the New Historicism does not suffer a lack of focus. The second and third assumptions provide the clear standard of relevance conspicuously missing in the old historicism. Unfortunately, this solution raises more problems than it solves; as I have argued in previous chapters, these assumptions sharply reduce the content both of literature and of politics. This remedy for what had been a continuing problem is therefore worse than the original malady.

The contribution of race-gender-class scholars to the more general question of historicism as a theoretical position is no more encouraging. In the case of a much-analyzed issue such as this, a distinctive new contribution might consist either in new arguments for historicism or in new rebuttals to old objections. We get neither. The acknowledged leader among New Historicists, Stephen Greenblatt, brushes aside the problems of historicism by insisting that the only alternative is a belief in "a conception of art as addressed to a timeless, cultureless, universal human essence" or in "the self-referentiality of literature."[9] These are not only crude caricatures of the issues that historicism raises but unoriginal ones at that; they are a reprise of the lowest level the old debate reached. A valid contribution to the debate would have to deal with the strongest versions of the arguments against historicism, not the weakest.

The most difficult problem in historicism concerns the quality of a writer: if all writing simply reflects and responds to the problems of its age, on what basis can one say that only some writing is important and valuable? But instead of dealing with the essential logic of this tough issue, race-gender-class theorists usually avoid the question with the suggestion that it arises only from the psychological need of some critics to indulge in hero worship. For example, when Paul Cantor raised this issue in a critique of Stephen Greenblatt's work, Greenblatt replied that admiration for Shakespeare's art is "better served by historical understanding than a hierophantic *o altitudo*."[10] From the standpoint of theoretical analysis this response is no response at all. Greenblatt seems unable to grasp the problem and so cannot contribute to its analysis. Judgments about the quality of Shakespeare's writing and thought represent an altogether different mode of response to his work, not simply a failure to seek historical understanding. Historical understanding can extend equally to Shakespeare and political pamphlets, but only qualitative judgments can separate the two.

The assumption that a zeitgeist pervades all the phenomena of a particular age is important for the New Historicism, because it is the presumed vehicle through which the climate of race-gender-class assumptions exercises its all-powerful effects. And that, in turn, provides support for the notion that these themes must be central to all literature.[11] The trouble is that this pervasive zeitgeist is part of a theory discredited several decades ago; once more, New Historicists seem unaware of the devastating arguments that put an end to it.

The German philosopher Wilhelm Dilthey was the founder of the theory in question. It was well known in Germany during the first half of this century as *Geistesgeschichte*, a reasonable translation of which would be "history of the spirit of the age."[12] Dilthey's theory was at the height of its popularity in Germany between the two World Wars until even the resolutely historicist Germans realized that it reduced all the diverse phenomena that make up an era to an artificial and unrealistic uniformity. Moreover, the need to make one idea fit an entire period led to ideas so general that they could be made to apply to anything. Consequently, the Germans largely abandoned it. This chapter in the history of theory was not hard to find; the story is told, for example, in the classic *Theory of Literature*, by Wellek and Warren. Yet the New Historicists picked up this old and long-since discarded theory, evidently unaware that it was a blind alley we had been down before.[13]

On the question of historicism, then, the New Historicism contributes not new theoretical analysis but only dogmatic assumptions to support the unlikely proposition that, as Edward Pechter puts it, literary works are "generated from and directed toward the politics of a historically remote period."[14] And the anachronism of judging sixteenth-century Europe by modern post-Enlightenment standards means that even as history the New Historicism suffers from an elementary incompetence.

One of the best-explored theoretical topics is that of biography and the author's intention; what is the contribution of race-gender-class theorists here? "The Intentional Fallacy," the seminal article by W. K. Wimsatt and Monroe Beardsley, is among the most celebrated essays in the field.[15] Wimsatt and Beardsley argued that the intention of the author was neither available nor desirable as a standard by which to interpret and judge the literary text. Two major themes supported this conclusion. First, authors are not necessarily the best judge of what they have done; an author's closeness to the text may be outweighed by the wider perspective of a critic. Second, the text communicates its meaning through the conventions of language, and those conventions are public, not personal, in nature. A text means what it actually says, not what its author later thinks he meant to say but perhaps did not.

What had precipitated the debate was a habit that biographically oriented critics had increasingly adopted, that of using brief statements by authors as the key to a literary text, forgetting that the fullest, most explicit, and most relevant evidence of authorial intent was the language of the text itself. The discussion that followed the publication of this article constituted the most extensive theoretical exploration ever undertaken in the field.

The core of the theoretical issue here is the special status of literary texts. Ordinary uses of language have no fixed boundaries, so that it is possible to seek amplification or clarification of any sequence of words by looking more broadly at what came before and after it. But if literary texts have firm boundaries (say, the first and last pages of a novel), then the question arises, Can a critic in effect add more text taken from the author's other pronouncements? The logic of the intentionalist case requires one answer, the anti-intentionalist another.

Once again, race-gender-class theorists are a disappointing letdown after such a productive debate, and the reason for the disappointment is easy to see. Instead of immersing themselves in the logic of the question and trying to carry it further, they are content to find some snippet that can be made to support their agenda and carry it off. The superficiality of this approach to the problem of intention can be illustrated by two feminists who use different snippets from the debate to attack male hegemony, with the result that they end up on opposite sides of the theoretical question. One argues that to take a text in the context of its author's intent is to be committed to a patriarchal notion of authority and that feminists should resist this "arbitrariness of patriarchal hegemony" by putting in question "the authority of authors, that is to say the propriety of paternity." But the other argues that to ignore author is to ignore gender and that to oppose "male critics' trivialization, contempt or neglect of the author . . . is one of the first steps in an emerging feminist critic's rebellion against the critical establishment."[16] In both cases the use of theory is opportunistic and superficial, and neither makes any real contact with the issues that are present in the well-developed argument and analysis that already existed.

The most common theme of race-gender-class theory with respect to authorial intention is an attack on the idea that an author's intention is a means to an objective account of a text, the truth about it. Such is the import of the dramatic phrase "the death of the author." But looked at more closely, this has nothing to do with the classic debate on intention, because its thrust is not a shift from one kind of valid evidence about the meaning of a text to another. On the contrary, it is part of an argument against the validity of any evidence for an account of a text's meaning.[17] In effect, race-gender-class scholars are not making a contribution to the debate between intentionalists and anti-intentionalists at all but, rather, are taking a radical and uncompromising stance on a different theoretical question: that of truth or objectivity in knowledge. Let us therefore turn to their contribution to the exploration of that question.

Here the position of race-gender-class scholars can be stated simply: they argue that objectivity and truth are naive illusions of traditional scholars and, more generally, of the Western tradition and that they have demystified these ideas. There are no value-free facts, they argue, because all knowledge is socially constructed.[18]

The odd thing about this position is that it is diametrically opposed to the reality of what both newer and older groups have actually done: first, as I have argued before, the race-gender-class scholar's commitment to his and her truths about the reality of sexism, racism, and oppression is as rigid as anything could be; and second, traditional scholars—both philosophers and critics—have often been skeptical about truth and objectivity. In point of fact, one of the most persistent questions in theory of criticism has been whether criticism gives us knowledge of the kind we get from other fields of inquiry. Philosophers, too, have a long history of concern with the question What is truth? The results in both cases long ago reached a level of sophistication that goes well beyond the simple dogma of the race-gender-class rejection of objectivity.

The most persistent opinion about objectivity in criticism has been Harry Levin's assertion that literary criticism is not an exact science.[19] From time to time, however, groups of critics and theorists have tried to establish criticism as a more systematic endeavor. These two basic positions have generally alternated as action and reaction. Race-gender-class critics constitute the most recent phase of this cycle, but far from being pioneers in their denunciation of objectivity, they represent only a reprise of the majority view of the past.

The orthodoxy of the nineteenth century represented a synthesis of both positions: literary history and biography afford genuine knowledge, but criticism in the sense of a critic's writing about the meaning and impact of a literary text is an impressionistic, subjective matter. It was precisely this fundamental skepticism about objectivity in criticism that made the literary historian cling to the objectivity of biographical and historical fact. At the turn of the century this orthodox synthesis began to break up, though two different tendencies emerged in its place. In Germany, critics began to question one half of the synthesis, namely, the assumed quasi-scientific objectivity of literary history. Reacting against what had become a rigidly positivist climate, Wilhelm Dilthey argued that literary history was unlike science in that it demanded empathy and imagination if one was to grasp the spirit of an age. But elsewhere the challenge was mostly to the other half of the older synthesis—the notion that criticism was irredeemably subjective.

A major thrust of the New Criticism was a rejection of the older defeatism about knowledge of the text and a consequent intense attention to texts through "close reading." The New Critics' refusal to rely on biography was in large part due to their rejection of the concomitant view that text-oriented criticism could only be impressionistic. That is why Wimsatt and Beardsley, in another notable article, entitled "The Affective Fallacy," argued that the qualities of the text, not the response of the reader, were the central concern of criticism.[20] The culmination of the search by Anglo-American New Criticism for a more systematic study of literature is Northrop Frye's *Anatomy of Criticism*, an ambitious attempt to develop a taxonomy of literary forms, now more admired for its ambition than its accomplishment.[21]

Even before the New Critics, the Russian Formalists had also attempted to make literary study more systematic, and when, many decades later, a belated reaction against nineteenth-century literary historicism finally appeared in France, it took a similar form, beginning with Claude Lévi-Strauss's attempt to analyze the basic patterns of narratives.[22] In conscious imitation of the mode of empirical science, Lévi-Strauss looked for the basic building blocks of narrative. Doubts about his system soon appeared, however, as his choice of underlying patterns came to seem arbitrary; some details of the plot of a narrative were declared essential, whereas others were discarded to make those that remained fit a common pattern. It was hard to justify radically different treatment of plot elements that were not inherently different at all.

As before, the overambitious systematizing tendencies of Frye and of French structuralism provoked a reaction, and by the 1960s the newest version of antiobjectivism had appeared. It is this latest swing of the pendulum that race-gender-class scholars are part of. Another manifestation of the same reactive development is reader-response criticism, which stresses the creative role of the reader in supplying meaning to an inherently indeterminate text. Still another is the strain of deconstructionism that stresses the infinite deferral of meaning in language.[23]

It is perhaps fair to say that this area of literary theory has not been analyzed with the same penetration that has been evident in others, and that the mood swings of the field—from attraction to controlled scientific methods to distaste for them and back again—have been more noticeable than serious analysis of the issue. It has also been hampered both by unrealistic notions of the mechanical quality of scientific procedure that do not allow for imagination and creative ideas in the development of scientific hypotheses and by equally unrealistic notions of criticism as a uniquely imaginative activity that has no place for controlled thought.

Even so, the best work does give the sense of a struggle to solve real problems. Leo Spitzer gave due weight to both imagination and systematic thought when he suggested that the procedure of criticism was circular: it went from general impressions of the text to scrutiny of particular passages and back again.[24] Modification and refinement could take place in each part of the cycle: thought about particular passages could suggest modifications of general interpretive ideas, and those modifications would in turn suggest a closer look at other passages that now became crucial.

This is very interesting theory, and if we compare it to, say, reader-response theory, its superiority is clear. In reader-response criticism, the reader's response is single and final and does not develop, whereas Spitzer shows us how thought about a text progresses. Interestingly, although Spitzer thought he had demonstrated that criticism was unlike scientific work, he had really shown that they are closer than we often think. His critical circle was much like that of hypothesis and experiment. By making contact with broader principles of inquiry that go beyond literary criticism, Spitzer had in fact broken through the barrier that had kept the literary critic's ideas about critical knowledge at a fairly primitive level.

By contrast, the race-gender-class view of this issue gives no sense of a productive struggle with real problems. It is excessively simple, consisting only in a denunciation of objectivity; it is uninformed, because unaware of more complex prior analysis and of the commonplace nature of its own contribution; and it is inconsistent, in that social activism requires a suspension of skepticism if a social goal is to be pursued with the necessary conviction that that goal is desirable.

The race-gender-class denunciation of objectivity and truth goes beyond literary criticism to encompass philosophical and scientific truth, but in this broader sphere, too, a strong Western philosophical tradition of questioning the nature of truth is ignored. Indeed, this persistent strain in philosophy could well be called an obsession, and the scope of the resulting conceptual explorations make the race-gender-class contribution seem small indeed.

The legacy of Charles Sanders Peirce is especially relevant to recent claims by race-gender-class scholars. Peirce looked at Descartes's deductive view of scientific knowledge, with its assumption that we proceed from the known to the unknown, and saw that it contained a major error: new knowledge is not simply added to old knowledge but can profoundly change our understanding of what we thought we knew.[25] For this reason, Peirce saw the impossibility of producing a final test of the truth of any proposition and concluded that all knowledge is in the nature of a hypothesis and that the only test of the validity of a scientific proposition is the always provisional assent of the scientific community. This view of science was in fact older than Peirce; Goethe first set it out nearly two hundred years ago, and Peirce acknowledged that his first philosophical reading was from the German classical age.[26]

Attitudes such as these have been part of the basic framework of the philosophy of science for some time, but when Thomas Kuhn popularized them in his *The Structure of Scientific Revolutions* (1962), they finally reached scholars in the humanities, with bizarre results.[27] The trouble was that the humanists who now took up these ideas knew nothing of their context and development and therefore did not realize that they had long since become familiar to philosophers of science. Instead, they thought that something cataclysmic had happened: for humanists, the nature of scientific truth itself seemed to have been undermined. Stanley Fish, for example, includes Thomas Kuhn in his list of "anti-foundationalists," along with Derrida, Heidegger, Foucault, and, of course, himself, and suggests that making the criterion for good science the assent of the scientific community is "Kuhn's rhetoricization of scientific procedure."[28] Yet all that had really happened was that some scholars in humanistic fields had finally made contact with what modern philosophy of science had to say about scientific objectivity.

A parallel development in historiography is the vogue of Hayden White's *Metahistory*,[29] a work that race-gender-class scholars found appealing because it suggested that in history, too, "all interpretation is fundamentally rhetorical."[30] Once again, the objectivity of historical scholarship was undermined with the help of the false opposition of final truth, on one hand, and the imagination of the historian, on the other. White is candid about the anti-Western impulse in his position: "In short, it is possible to view historical consciousness as a specifically Western prejudice by which the presumed superiority of modern, industrial society can be retroactively substantiated."[31] The link to race-gender-class orthodoxy is clear.

In fact, earlier writers on historiography had often stressed the historian's shaping hand[32] and even claimed that the best history is an aesthetically satisfying whole, though one still answerable to the relevant facts. Literary historians, too, had often claimed to have synthesized knowledge to make it an aesthetically satisfying whole. The literary historian, said Robert Spiller, "uses many of the methods of the literary artist."[33] No one ever thought that this was inconsistent with a sense that getting the facts wrong, generalizing from the wrong facts, not knowing enough of them, or not understanding them would produce bad and inaccurate history. But White took this familiar partial truth and pressed it to its limit: historical interpretation was now fundamentally rhetorical, and its determinants were tropes, literary figures, and styles of narrative. Hans Kellner summarizes White's position: "White can find no reason to prefer one account over another *on historical grounds alone.* The version of the past we choose depends rather on *moral and aesthetic values*, which ground both the historian and the audience and are beyond the call of historical evidence."[34] (Kellner is a highly sympathetic interpreter of White.) Someone with moral or aesthetic values differing from our own (Charles Manson? Adolf Hitler?) might, therefore, also legitimately interpret the past differently. In White's theory, the distinction between history and a novel disappears: we are no longer able to learn from history as *history*. A necessary distinction vanishes.

The fourth and last of these illustrative topics is evaluation. Here again we see the contrast between a long history of struggling with difficult logical issues and the assertion by race-gender-class critics of a logically unsophisticated position that is immediately contradicted by their own actions. Although theoretically against judgments of literary value, they are, in practice, perfectly content with their own; having argued that hierarchies are elitist, they nonetheless create one by adding Alice Walker or Rigoberta Menchú to their course reading lists. They vacillate between the rejection of all value judgments and the rejection of one specific set of them—that which created the Western canon.

Race-gender-class orthodoxy on the matter of evaluation is so inconsistent and so driven by what a particular prejudice demands that it can hardly be called theory at all; and it does not begin to confront the body of thought on this topic that already existed. The three phases of theory I distinguished above have markedly different emphases with regard to evaluation. In the first, evaluation of works of art was simply assumed to be central to criticism. There was a strong interest in normative theories of poetry (for example, how should a tragedy be constructed?) and in concepts used to evaluate works of art (such as beauty). In the second stage, however, skepticism arose about the justification for both normative poetics and value judgments,[35] and criticism itself became correspondingly more descriptive in character. The normative writings of the previous period now tend to be regarded as descriptions of the practice of a particular school, each new manifesto showing the arbitrariness of its predecessor. In the third and most recent phase, value is seen largely as a question of the political interests of socially dominant groups, no other kind of value being recognized.

It was the second stage that began the serious business of examining the logic of evaluation and distinguishing it from the logic of descriptive statements: the latter, but, it was thought, not the former, could be verified by observation. For this reason, the logical positivists thought that evaluations were mere expressions of emotive response without cognitive content. Northrop Frye, a key figure of the second phase of critical theory, evidently followed this ranking when he said that descriptive criticism was a form of knowledge, unlike evaluative criticism, which was the province of journalists.[36] For Frye, as for the logical positivist A. J. Ayer, evaluative language was something of an indulgence.[37]

But this view seemed unable to account for some real facts of experience— for example, the fact (for so it must always seem to be) that Shakespeare is a writer of enormous stature. And so later analytic work tried to rescue evaluative statements from this low status. One attempt to do this distinguished different valid uses of language, one descriptive, the other appraisive.[38] This rehabilitation was not completely convincing, however, because it still allowed evaluative statements to fall short of full cognitive status.

My view is that evaluative statements are factual and do have cognitive content but that they are rather like brief summaries of a great deal of more specific information.[39] For this reason it must always seem unsatisfying to regard them as lacking in cognitive content. A brief summary can only hint at the full cognitive content of what is summarized, but it has a practical use: it allows one to make decisions such as whether to take one novel rather than another on a vacation and whether to include one book rather than another in a syllabus. The key to much of the theoretical problem posed by evaluations is this: they are not grandiose conclusions that everything leads up to but a quick orientation and starting point that must be left behind if we are to think more precisely. Only the general feeling that their greater weight should indicate a cognitive superiority misleads us.

Even in an area of theory that has been somewhat inconclusive, the contrast between the simplicity of race-gender-class thought and the relative complexity of what preceded it is striking. Instead of a genuine struggle with a difficult logical problem, we are offered only opportunistic uses of diametrically opposed attitudes to evaluation; instead of original analysis, we find only a reprise of the crass measure of literature according to its current political value that has always been used to censor and silence writers.

If we add to these four illustrative topics in theory others where the race-gender-class contribution has been seen—for example, the definition and function of literature—then the inescapable conclusion is that race-gender-class theory when seen against the context of the field as a whole is poor theory. Yet this impoverished theory has managed to become so identified with theory in general that even many of its detractors accept that identification. How did this illusion arise? How did this anti-theory become identified with theory? To answer these questions, we must look at the history of the field.

As we have seen, theory of criticism began to emerge as a distinct field only in this century, for prior to this time it had been largely a sporadic by-product of events in the contemporary literary scene. Theory then began to drift away from the practice of criticism, until, by the 1960s, most literary critics were mildly hostile to what they saw as abstract theorizing. The sudden popularity of French thought in the early 1970s was less a theoretical revolution than an anti-theoretical coup; critics who had not been involved in the more self-consciously analytical phase of theory now returned it to a much closer relationship with the ideological currents of the contemporary critical scene. The result of this shift was that the word *theory* became identified with one of those ideological currents rather than with the activity of analysis. This development really turned the word *theory* upside down, as could be seen when Paul de Man claimed that opposition to deconstructionism was a "resistance to theory."[40] Given that theory must imply analysis, it was de Man himself who was really resisting theory, by treating his own position as sacrosanct and refusing to accept the possibility that it might be further analyzed.

As theory became fashionable, there arose a theory cult in literary studies, and its leadership became a kind of theory jet set, a professional elite with a carefully cultivated aura of au courant sophistication. In this atmosphere, only recent theory counted; anything from earlier times was wooden and out-moded. The persistent ignorance of prior theory was therefore no accident but an essential feature of this new development.

The new elite shared a set of assumptions but not a penchant for analysis. One recognized members not by their analytical skill but by the standardized quality of their attitudes. All went through similar motions to come to similar conclusions. Theory was no longer about exploration but about conformity. Stanley Fish's *Doing What Comes Naturally* was typical both in its predictable positions and its ignoring the past: in this book, philosophy of science begins with Thomas Kuhn, serious questions about the idea of truth and the posi-tivist theory of language begin with Derrida, jurisprudence begins with the radical Critical Legal Studies movement, and cultural relativism is a bright new idea without any previous history.

The theory culture also has its own language, which all aspirants to member-ship must learn to speak and which functions to preserve an otherwise unstable situation in many ways. It cuts off new theory from older thought—which is useful, since if the same terms were used, the limitations of the new would be much easier to see. It identifies those who speak it as insiders and those who do not as old-fashioned outsiders who lack the required level of sophistication. Those who have learned the language demonstrate their mastery of theoryese in titles of conference papers that are full of verbal tricks and gyrations. (Unfor-tunately, this also draws the attention and the well-deserved derision of the gen-eral public.) In addition, the new language serves as a protective device in that its remoteness from ordinary speech camouflages triviality or absurdity.

The drawback is that standardized language means standardized thought. Oddly enough, race-gender-class critics insist on the limitations imposed on thought by the use of a particular system of terms in all other contexts. An im-portant part of their mental apparatus is Foucault's notion of a discourse, by which he means a standard set of terms that are both the expression of a par-ticular mind-set and the mechanism that perpetuates that mind-set. Fou-cault's own examples are rarely convincing, because the normal vocabularies of both English and French are too large and varied to channel thought so rigidly. A convincing illustration of Foucault's point would require a special-ized terminology that was able to shut out the rest of the vocabulary of a lan-guage. We need not look far to find such a case: the perfect example of Fou-cault's discourse and its stultification of thought is the highly restricted and arcane terminology of theoryese: re-presentations, marginalize, decenter, re-vision, difference, discursive practices, hegemony, phallocentrism, the "other," and so on. Genuine thought requires more than the rote learning and inge-nious manipulation of a special vocabulary.

A deeper problem is that theorists do not run in packs; they are individuals who set out to crack particular theoretical problems by thinking hard about them. Their work is solitary; it is never fashionable and must always be estranged from orthodoxies. It follows that a theory elite can arise only when theory has ceased to function effectively and when the individuals who are a part of it no longer act like theorists. Real theorists thrive on the concept of argument and counterargument that is central to theoretical analysis, but race-gender-class scholars show a marked tendency to avoid facing the substance of the arguments of their critics. Sometimes, they just seem to hide: as support for deconstruction has eroded under the pressure of recent analyses and disclosures, many of its leading figures have fallen silent.[41] Yet scholars like J. Hillis Miller, Geoffrey Hartman, and Jonathan Culler, who have enthusiastically urged deconstruction upon students and colleagues for some time, surely had an obligation to defend it publicly or to recant; edging quietly toward the door when things begin to look bad is not what theorists do.

Dissent from the current orthodoxy is routinely met with ad hominem attacks on allegedly ignoble motives that avoid the substance of arguments. Critics are said to be hostile to progress for women and minorities or simply conservative, as if no further analysis were necessary. Real theorists would want to meet and engage arguments put forth against their positions by academic colleagues and to take part in the internal debate that is now under way. The only conclusion to be drawn from this survey is that what now passes for theory is a degraded and corrupt shadow of what theory should be.

## NOTES

1. Goethe, *Goethes Werke*, ed. Erich Trunz, 12th ed., 14 vols. (Munich: Beck, 1981), 13:317: "Und so kann man sagen, dass wir schon bei jedem aufmerksamen Blick in die Welt theoretisieren"; and 12:432: "Das Höchste wäre zu begreifen, dass alles Faktische schon Theorie ist."

2. Ernst Cassirer, ed., *Immanuel Kants Werke*, 11 vols. (Berlin: Bruno Cassirer, 1912–23), vol. 3, *Kritik der reinen Vernunft*, 80: "Gedanken ohne Inhalt sind leer; Anschauungen ohne Begriffe sind blind."

3. See, e.g., René Wellek and Austin Warren, *Theory of Literature* (New Haven, Conn.: Yale University Press, 1949).

4. Guy Sircello, "The Poetry of Theory: Reflections on *After the New Criticism*," *Journal of Aesthetics and Art Criticism* 42, no. 4 (Summer 1984): 387–96. The example is Frank Lentricchia's *After the New Criticism* (Chicago: University of Chicago Press, 1980). Sircello confesses to inadequate knowledge of the field as a whole, and he does not grasp the fact that although Lentricchia's book is representative of the present state of the field, it is decidedly not "a good orientation to the whole field" (387) in the sense of being a guide to its most distinguished and enduring work.

5. Inadequacies of this kind have led occasionally to the blanket claim that theory of criticism is not a useful activity. See W. J. T. Mitchell, ed., *Against Theory* (Chicago: University of Chicago Press, 1985). Stanley Fish makes an argument for the irrelevance of theory a leading issue in his book *Doing What Comes Naturally* (see note 28, below), but it is logically

unimportant in that context. An older version of this rejection of theory can be found in the critical pluralism that advocated an eclectic acceptance of all critical approaches, a view that precluded any analysis of their relative strengths and weaknesses. For arguments against this position, see my *Theory of Literary Criticism* (Berkeley: University of California Press, 1974), chap. 1.

6. A survey of the field and outline of an analysis of major issues is contained in my contribution ("Theory") to *The Princeton Encyclopedia of Poetry and Poetics*, ed. Alex Preminger and T. V. F. Brogan, 3rd ed. (Princeton, N.J.: Princeton University Press, 1993), 1282–90. See also my *Theory of Literary Criticism* for further development of issues briefly raised here.

7. This debate began in earnest in 1946 with the essay "The Intentional Fallacy," by W. K. Wimsatt with Monroe C. Beardsley, republished in their collected theoretical essays, *The Verbal Icon: Studies in the Meaning of Poetry* (Lexington: University of Kentucky Press, 1954). Michel Foucault, "Qu'est-ce qu'un auteur?" *Bulletin de la Société Française de Philosophie* 63, no. 3 (1969): 73–104, appeared more than two decades later. An English version, "What Is an Author?" appeared in 1977 in *Language, Counter-Memory, and Practice: Selected Essays and Interviews,* trans. and ed. Donald Bouchard (Ithaca, N.Y.: Cornell University Press, 1977), 113–38.

8. John Ellis, *Against Deconstruction* (Princeton, N.J.: Princeton University Press, 1988), chap. 2.

9. Stephen J. Greenblatt, *Renaissance Self-Fashioning: From More to Shakespeare* (Chicago: University of Chicago Press, 1980), 4; and "Invisible Bullets: Renaissance Authority and Its Subversion," *Glyph* 8 (1981): 56.

10. "Is a New Historicist Free?" (exchange of letters between Stephen Greenblatt and Paul Cantor), *Academic Questions* 7, no. 2 (Spring 1994): 5–6.

11. See Paul Cantor's excellent discussion of this point in "Stephen Greenblatt's New Historicist Vision," *Academic Questions* 6, no. 4 (Fall 1993): 21–36.

12. For details, see John M. Ellis and Evelyn W. Asher, "German Theory and Criticism: Twentieth Century to 1968," in *The Johns Hopkins Guide to Literary Theory and Criticism,* ed. Michael Groden and Martin Kreiswirth (Baltimore, Md.: The Johns Hopkins University Press, 1994), 348–52.

13. It is worth noting that the original proposal for the graduate program in the "History of Consciousness" at the Santa Cruz campus of the University of California was simply an exposition of Dilthey's *Geistesgeschichte.*

14. Edward Pechter, "The New Historicism and Its Discontents: Politicizing Renaissance Drama," *PMLA* 102, no. 3 (May 1987): 299. Pechter continues: "When addressed to the left-liberal academic community, for whom the monarchy is an anachronism, feminism an article of faith, and colonialism a source of embarrassed guilt, these critical versions cannot help draining the plays of much of their potential to involve an audience."

15. Wimsatt, with Beardsley, *The Verbal Icon,* 3–18.

16. These two contradictory viewpoints, which are both obsessed with male wrongdoing but which find it in diametrically opposed places, occur in the same anthology of feminist writing: Gayle Greene and Coppélia Kahn, eds., *Making a Difference: Feminist Literary Criticism* (London: Methuen, 1985). The writers are Nelly Furman, "The Politics of Language: Beyond the Gender Principle," 71; and Sydney Janet Kaplan, "Varieties of Feminist Criticism," 41.

17. For an extended discussion of this strain in recent theory, see chap. 5 of my *Against Deconstruction*.

18. The number of race-gender-class scholars who have expressed this view is overwhelming. One example will suffice: Lorraine Code, *What Can She Know? Feminist Theory and the Construction of Knowledge* (Ithaca, N.Y.: Cornell University Press, 1991).

19. Harry Levin, *Why Literary Criticism Is Not an Exact Science* (Cambridge, Mass.: Harvard University Press, 1967).

20. Wimsatt, with Beardsley, *The Verbal Icon*, 21–39.

21. Northrop Frye, *Anatomy of Criticism: Four Essays* (Princeton, N.J.: Princeton University Press, 1957).

22. E.g., Claude Lévi-Strauss, *Anthropologie structurale* (Paris: Plon, 1958).

23. Another strand of deconstructionist criticism suggests a different goal for criticism, however; it asserts that all texts undermine their surface meaning and embrace the reverse of what they appear to say. Here, meaning has a much more determined shape, one knowable to readers if they will only read in a certain way. This strand is analyzed in my *Against Deconstruction*, chap. 3.

24. Leo Spitzer, *Linguistics and Literary History* (Princeton, N.J.: Princeton University Press, 1948).

25. See the excellent discussion of Peirce's "Assault on Cartesianism," in W. B. Gallie, *Peirce and Pragmatism* (Harmondsworth: Penguin, 1952), chap. 3.

26. Gallie, *Peirce and Pragmatism*, 35. See also the two aphorisms cited above, note 1.

27. Thomas S. Kuhn, *The Structure of Scientific Revolutions*, 2d ed. (Chicago: University of Chicago Press, 1970).

28. Fish, *Doing What Comes Naturally: Change, Rhetoric, and the Practice of Theory in Literary and Legal Studies* (Durham, N.C.: Duke University Press, 1989), 345 and 487. Part of the blame here must go to Kuhn, who does not mention Peirce in the course of his book and appears not to have known the source of his own ideas.

29. Hayden White, *Metahistory: The Historical Imagination in Nineteenth-Century Europe* (Baltimore, Md.: The Johns Hopkins University Press, 1973). White's position is developed in two further books: *Tropics of Discourse: Essays in Cultural Criticism* (Baltimore, Md.: The Johns Hopkins University Press, 1978); and *The Content of the Form: Narrative Discourse and Historical Representation* (Baltimore, Md.: The Johns Hopkins University Press, 1987).

30. This is the summary of Hans Kellner in his "Hayden White," in *The Johns Hopkins Guide to Literary Theory and Criticism*, 728–29.

31. White, *Metahistory*, 2.

32. E.g., E. H. Carr, *What Is History?* (New York: Macmillan, 1961).

33. Robert E. Spiller, "Literary History," in *The Aims and Methods of Scholarship in Modern Languages and Literatures*, ed. James Thorpe (New York: MLA, 1963), 53.

34. Kellner, "Hayden White," 728; emphasis in original.

35. A typical instance here is the collection of essays *Aesthetics and Language*, ed. William Elton (Oxford: Blackwell, 1954).

36. See Northrop Frye, "Literary Criticism," in *Aims and Methods of Scholarship in Modern Languages and Literatures*, ed. James Thorpe (New York: MLA, 1963) , 57–69.

37. A. J. Ayer, *Language, Truth, and Logic*, 2d ed. (London: V. Gollancz, 1946), chap. 6.

38. E.g., P. H. Nowell-Smith, *Ethics* (Harmondsworth: Penguin, 1954).

39. This view is discussed in my *Theory of Literary Criticism*, a somewhat belated contribution to the second phase of literary theory. Its underlying logic is set out much more explicitly in my *Language, Thought, and Logic* (Evanston, Ill.: Northwestern University Press, 1993).

40. Paul de Man, *The Resistance to Theory* (Minneapolis: University of Minnesota Press, 1986).

41. See my *Against Deconstruction* and David Lehman's *Signs of the Times: Deconstruction and the Fall of Paul de Man* (New York: Poseidon Press, 1991).

## 7. THEORY, THEORIES, AND PRINCIPLES

### DENIS DONOGHUE

IN 1912 THE PHILOSOPHER Ralph Barton Perry published a book called *Present Philosophical Tendencies*; it was subtitled *A Critical Survey of Naturalism, Idealism, Pragmatism, and Realism, Together with a Synopsis of the Philosophy of William James.* In the first chapter Perry distinguished between belief and theory, evidently because he thought his colleagues were confusing those terms in the zeal with which they pursued them. Perry deemed belief, or rather "established belief," to denote faith, in the sense of "conviction favorable to action." He regarded theory as an altogether smaller consideration, mainly because it should not—or at least not immediately—issue in action or otherwise change one's life. He deemed a theory to be experimental, a notion to be taken up or put down as it proved useful or not to a particular task. The theorist, he said, can enjoy the experiences of doubt, interrogation, conjecture, irresponsibility, "a certain oscillation of mind between hypothetical alternatives." But it is wise, Perry maintained, "to surrender belief reluctantly," and it is a grave matter "to substitute one's own theory, however well reasoned, for another man's belief." While theories "may be changed with little cost and with certain gain, that is not true of beliefs." Here "the cost is more certain than the gain."[1]

I have referred to Perry's book because it points to a certain distinction that we would do well to recall or to propose afresh. There is a good deal of evidence that Theory as an institution in our profession is being advanced as if it amounted to a belief, and with the insistence that normally accompanies the expression of a belief. There is no merit in being for or against Theory unless we know what it is we are for or against. It makes a difference if we are for or against

Denis Donoghue. "Theory, Theories, and Principles." Originally published in *The Practice of Reading*, by Denis Donoghue, 20–33. New Haven: Yale University Press, 1998. Copyright © Yale University, 1998. Reprinted by permission of Yale University Press an activity of mind for the most part speculative or conjectural; or, alternatively, if we are for or against an activity of mind as a result of which it is suggested that we should change our beliefs and thereby change our lives. If a theory is merely experimental or, as we say, heuristic, we do well to take it to mind if not to heart, and give it a run for whatever money we risk on it. But if it is offered to us as a creed or a vision or a doctrine, we should approach it much more skeptically and estimate the consequence of taking it to heart and soul.

It may be prudent to distinguish between Theory as an institution, which comes armed with the coercive force of a capital letter, and theories, which are more modest plays of mind, local notions. There are hundreds of theories, and they appear to do useful work. Svetlana Alpers has a theory of seventeenth- and eighteenth-century Dutch painting: or rather, she has an explanation for our relative failure to see such paintings properly; she thinks we are excessively impressed by the Italian notion that a painting should tell or imply a story. Many Dutch paintings don't. Alpers's theory helps to rid our minds of irrelevant expectations when we look at Dutch paintings. Northrop Frye had a theory of fiction: he thought that there were four forms of fiction—five if you included *Finnegans Wake*—and that we should not confuse them. While reading a romance or an anatomy, we shouldn't become tetchy because the book doesn't fulfill our expectations of reading a realistic novel. Schoenberg had a theory about twelve-tone music, the rules of its composition, and why it doesn't sound like a sonata by Beethoven. Kierkegaard had a theory of irony, the kind of stance an ironist would take up, and why he would hold that ground, if he could. J. L. Austin had a theory about felicitous and infelicitous uses of language. Conor Cruise O'Brien has a theory about nationalism, which he applies to every country except Israel. Gilles Deleuze and Félix Guattari developed a theory of "minor literature," works written from a marginal position in relation to a major language: Kafka writing in German, Prague's German; Mangan writing in English, Ireland's English. These are local theories that refer to particular forms of life, particular activities; they don't claim to be universally applicable. If you challenge such a theory you ask for immediate verification, you appeal to a specific body of evidence. It wouldn't be damaging to Alpers's theory of Dutch painting if you showed that it didn't work well for Japanese line drawing or Italian Renaissance sculpture. It wouldn't harm our lives if we discarded the theory.

We are moving toward Theory as an institution when the considerations we're offered are supposed to refer to large-scale entities and perhaps to life itself. But there are degrees of scale before we reach that extreme position. T. S. Eliot's theory of the "dissociation of sensibility" claims that something happened in the seventeenth century in England—it probably had to do with the Civil War—as a result of which the English language from the later seventeenth to the nineteenth century no longer facilitated thinking as a development of feeling. Thinking became one activity, and feeling another. If that were true, it would be a point of great interest to many people, but to more than those many it would make little or no difference. William Empson had a notion about poetic language, that it was all the better for being ambiguous, since in that respect it testified to the incorrigibly ambiguous character of life itself. There is no need to estimate the number of people who would find that notion worth losing sleep over. I. A. Richards had a theory about the neutralization of Nature in the middle of the nineteenth century: he claimed that writers who continued to think of Nature in neo-Wordsworthian terms were at best bizarre creatures, perhaps geniuses—like Lawrence and Yeats—but daft nonetheless. Jean-François Lyotard had a theory about postmodernism—whatever that might be—that it was chiefly characterized by a general incredulity toward metanarratives, large-scale stories that claimed total explanatory power. Ferdinand de Saussure had a theory that enabled him to distinguish in language between *langue* and *parole*. Bourdieu has a theory to explain the social provenance of taste, how one work is appreciated rather than another. Stanley Fish has held a theory that meaning can't be established intrinsically but only by agreement among the members of an interpretive community. I don't think he still holds to that view, but that's another issue: if he has abandoned it—as in *Professional Correctness*—no matter. These ideas are theoretical, but none of them constitutes Theory because none of them claims total explanatory force.

This is the main distinction between a theory of something—Dutch painting, twelve-tone music—and Theory as an institution. Theory as an institution is like Theology in one respect: it makes foundational claims, it starts from a posited ground and works up and out from that source. It differs from Theology mainly because it hasn't anything to say of first and last things. Theory is related to Philosophy, but the relation is juridical rather than discursive: it doesn't take part in a conversation. Instead, it aspires to the condition of a system, a metadiscourse, and longs to have the attributes of a science or a myth. If reality is widely thought to be political, Theory sets itself up as a critique of ideology. It seeks evidence wherever it chooses, often in texts of metaphysics, philosophy, literature, and politics. That is to say, Theory aspires to universal application.

The theories that claim to constitute Theory in the past two centuries include Kant's Third Critique, Hegel's *Aesthetic*, Nietzsche's *Beyond Good and Evil*, Marx's *Capital*, Freud's *Civilization and Its Discontents*, Heidegger's *Being and Time*, Sartre's *Being and Nothingness*, Derrida's *Of Grammatology*, and de Man's *Allegories of Reading*. The list is not exhaustive. Even if one of these works seems to refer only to local considerations, as *Capital* does, it claims endlessly allusive power of explanation and prophecy; it sets no limit on its rhetorical scale.

The main arguments we hear against Theory, as distinct from local theories, are these. It is maintained that Theory is arrogant in claiming that not to think theoretically is not to think at all. Theory is chiefly interested in spinning larger and larger webs of its own vocabulary. Christopher Ricks has argued that Theory is characterized "by its degree of elaboration, concatenation, completeness, abstraction, self-consciousness, explicitness, regression, recession and technicality."[2] In this respect, while not amounting to a philosophy, it mimes philosophy. It does not accommodate contradiction or allow for the different view a rival might take of the matter at hand. It feels no misgiving about the mode of autonomy it claims. A further argument might be mentioned, which I find in Geoffrey Hill's *Lords of Limit*. In an essay on T. H. Green, Hill quotes H. J. Laski remarking that "Green and his followers emphasized not the individual over against the process of government, but the individual in the significant totality of his relations with it." Laski's sentence prompted Hill to this development: "There is a case to be made for the suggestion that one of the major discoveries of modern criticism has been the method of transferring 'significant totality of relations' to a contextual plane and of conferring a consequent distinction upon those authors or individual works which fulfil most completely that kind of expectation: Keats, in the Odes, George Eliot in *Middlemarch*, or the poems of Green's sometime pupil Gerard Manley Hopkins."[3] It would be difficult to claim for Theory, as distinct from literary criticism, that it has worked to transfer significant totality of relations to a contextual plane. It has worked rather to limit such relations and to isolate, as far as possible, the constituents of attention that might form relations. The very fact that we can so easily think of Theory as a body rather than as a set of mutually invigorating relations speaks to this charge.

But there is a further consideration that seems to me at least as cogent as those I have mentioned: that is, the claim of Theory—at least in its most insistent forms—to act juridically in relation to knowledge. I find such a claim in Derrida's essay on Kant's *Conflict of the Faculties* (1799). Kant wrote the book under the following circumstances. In 1793 he committed the misdemeanor of publishing *Religion Within the Limits of Reason Alone*. He was free to hold whatever religious convictions he wished, provided he kept them to himself, but he was not free to spread uncertainty and dissension among the citizens by publishing those convictions. Several theologians protested that he had invaded their territory. In June 1794, Kant wrote, but did not publish, a partial reply in the form of an essay, "The Conflict of the Philosophy Faculty with the Theology Faculty." Not surprisingly, Minister of Justice Wöllner sent him a Cabinet Order, dated October 1, 1794, accusing him of having misused his philosophy in publishing *Religion Within the Limits of Reason Alone* and of having distorted and disparaged "many of the cardinal and basic teachings of the Holy Scriptures and of Christianity."[4] Kant didn't answer these charges till 1799, when he published as *The Conflict of the Faculties* three essays, the long one on the conflict of the philosophy faculty with the theology faculty, and two short ones on the conflict of the philosophy faculty with the faculties of law and medicine.

In his reply, Kant concealed the fact that his ultimate motive was to establish philosophy as superior to theology, law, and medicine. He pretended to concede that those three faculties deserved the power they exerted as instruments for the government of the citizens. They should stick to their practical, bureaucratic jobs; they should continue to be supervised by the government they served; and the criteria applied to their teachings should be civic, not philosophical. But the government should guarantee to the philosophy faculty the right to pronounce freely upon the true and the false. Philosophy would have no executive power—nor should it seek it—but it should have the right to pronounce on all matters of truth and falsehood: it would enjoy the right of free judgment on questions of theory and discourse. "The Philosophy Faculty . . . must be conceived as free and subject only to laws given by reason, not by the government"[5] Besides, Kant claimed that he had written *Religion Within the Limits of Reason Alone* as a treatise for his colleagues. The public would find it unintelligible, a closed book. His only interest was to arrange that proper or what he called legal conflicts among the faculties of the university should be adjudicated, so far as they pertained to true and false, right and wrong, moral and immoral, by the philosophy faculty. As Derrida notes, "The first examples that Kant gives—the ones that visibly preoccupy him the most—pertain to the sacred, to faith and revelation; it is the responsibility of the philosophy faculty, as Kant claims, 'to examine and judge publicly, with cool reason, the origin and content of a certain supposed basis of the doctrine, unintimidated by the sanctity of the object.'"[6]

Kant's aim was to propose a rational religious faith, as Ian Hunter has noted, "by developing a purely moral exegesis of the scriptures."[7] The only part of the scriptures that Kant valued was the part that could be turned to moral use; the rest was sensuous narrative, historical accretion, interesting, no doubt, but inessential. Besides: "The Biblical theologian says: 'Search the Scriptures, where you think you find eternal life.' But since our moral improvement is the sole condition of eternal life, the only way we can find eternal life in any Scripture whatsoever is by putting it there. For the concepts and principles required for eternal life cannot really be learned from anyone else: the teacher's exposition is only the occasion for him to develop them out of his own reason."[8] In effect, Kant wanted to use philosophy to remove from Christianity every trace of its doctrines. The Christian narrative must be expounded only in the interests of morality, "and yet"—as he wrote in *Religion Within the Limits of Reason Alone*—"(because the common man has an enduring propensity within him to sink into passive belief) it must be inculcated painstakingly and repeatedly that true religion is to consist not in the knowing or considering of what God does or has done for our salvation but in what we must do to become worthy of it."[9] The Bible deserves to be read, "put to moral use, and assigned to religion as its guide, *just as if it is a divine revelation*" (emphasis in original).[10]

Ian Hunter concludes his analysis of *The Conflict of the Faculties* by arguing that "the Kantian image of 'man' as a pure mind encumbered by an impure sensibility is . . . an anthropology for a caste defined by a practice of intellectual self-purification-clarification." Might we also suggest, he wonders, that "this practice can count among its offspring the intellectual exercises of critical theory and deconstructive criticism?": "Certainly, in framing the problem of the university in terms of an idea whose object has been delayed by history or occluded by representation, these discourses set the 'task' of an exemplary self-decipherment of this object."[11] And so it appears, on the evidence of Derrida's essay on *The Conflict of the Faculties*, except that he presents his commentary not in terms of self-purification-clarification but in terms of juridical privilege and moral responsibility.

My synopsis of Kant's essay, and of Derrida's commentary on it, must be brief and in other respects partial. Only an approximate account is possible here. My concern is not with the detail of Derrida's commentary but with the claim that it makes for Deconstruction. Derrida repeats, in favor of Deconstruction, the claim Kant made for the faculty of philosophy on all questions of true and false, right and wrong, moral and immoral. Derrida says:

> If, then, it lays claim to any consequence, what is hastily called deconstruction *as such* is never a technical set of discursive procedures, still less a new hermeneutic method operating on archives or utterances in the shelter of a given and stable institution; it is also, and at the least, the taking of a position, in work itself, toward the politico-institutional structures that constitute and regulate our practice, our competencies, and our performances. Precisely because deconstruction has never been concerned with the contents alone of meaning, it must not be separable from this politico-institutional problematic, and has to require a new questioning about responsibility, an inquiry that should no longer necessarily rely on codes inherited from politics or ethics.[12]

I construe this last claim, remarkable indeed, as corresponding to Kant's claim to rise above the specious prerogatives of theology and the merely mundane uses of law and medicine. Just as Kant hoped that one fine day the last would be first and the lowest faculty, philosophy, would be granted such privilege in the jurisdiction of truth and falsehood that it would exercise power by the sheer force and truth of its pronouncements, so Derrida claims for Deconstruction the unique privilege of pronouncing on questions of true and false, right and wrong, moral and immoral. Further, he insists on making these pronouncements by prescribing responsibility, in practice, and without relying on codes inherited from politics or ethics. Deconstruction, he maintains, "is limited neither to a methodological reform that would reassure the given organization, nor, inversely, to a parade of irresponsible or irresponsibilizing destruction, whose surest effect would be to leave everything as is, consolidating the most immobile forces of the university."[13] As if that program were not enough, Derrida asserts that the boundary between legal and illegal conflicts among the faculties that Kant spoke of is no longer tenable: there is no longer a feasible distinction between "war" and "conflict," as Kant still hoped there might be. So we must appeal—or rather, Derrida appeals—"to a *surplus* of responsibility" (emphasis in original): "This surplus of responsibility—for me, the very experience of deconstruction—leads to interrogating, suspecting and displacing those tranquil assurances in whose name so many moralisms, today more than ever, organize their courts, their trials and their censures. So long as those assurances are not interrogated or put to the test of a vigilant deconstruction, these moralisms will signify above all else a repressive violence, dogmatism and irresponsibility: the very irresponsibility that claims to speak in the name of responsibility, the well-known immorality of edifying moralism."[14] It seems strange to me that Derrida, speaking in the name of Deconstruction, should prejudge the values and motives of other people to the extent of writing off their consciences as "tranquil," their acts of mind as "assurances," their moral concerns as "moralisms," their professional activities as "the most immobile forces of the university." Who are these dreadful people? And while we're engaged in rooting them out, we are to give Deconstruction the right of becoming metapolitics, metaethics, metalaw, indeed metadiscourse. Is it impertinent to recall that Levinas insisted that ethics precedes ontology and becomes, in effect, a new and better metaphysics; and that he showed no sign of despising the codes of ethics he inherited?

I find it surprising, too, that Derrida quotes Friedrich Schelling's objection to Kant's high claim for the faculty of philosophy but doesn't take it as seriously as it deserves. Derrida admits that it is a serious problem—that the "essence of the university, namely philosophy, should also occupy a particular place and a faculty within the university topology, or that philosophy in and of itself should represent a special competence." He then quotes Schelling's objection:

> To the extent that the sciences obtain, through and in the state, an effectively objective existence, and to the extent that they become a power, the associations formed by each in particular are called faculties. As for their mutual relations—and a comment here is particularly necessary since Kant, in his work on *The Conflict of the Faculties*, strikes us as having treated the issue from an altogether unilateral point of view—it is clear that theology, as a science where the heart of philosophy is found to be objectified, should occupy the first and highest place; and to the extent that an ideal power is higher than a real one, it follows that the faculty of law precedes the faculty of medicine. As for a faculty of philosophy, however, it is our thesis that there is not, nor can there be, any such thing, the proof ly-

ing in the simple fact that something which is everything cannot, for that very reason, be anything in particular.[15]

This objection seems far more cogent to me than it evidently does to Derrida. Schelling is not objecting to the existence of a faculty of philosophy but to the hubris of such a faculty as Kant has called for, and to Kant's claims for it. If Derrida proposes to make the same claim for Deconstruction, as a faculty deserving to act in a superior relation to all forms of discourse, legal and illegal, one might transpose Schelling's objection and say that Deconstruction, as something which is everything, cannot, for that very reason, be anything in particular.

Of course it is something in particular; but what is it, if we don't concede its claim to be the modern form of the Kantian faculty of philosophy, with the moral privilege that such a claim would entail? This question may be answered in various tones, and I would prefer to be urbane, if that is possible. Instead of answering in my own perhaps truculent behalf, I prefer to quote from a recent essay by Ian Hunter that seems to me notably just and civil. His theme is the relation between Theory, in its institutional sense, and politics. He says:

> Similarly, in recognizing that literary theory relates to empirical politics not as a positive knowledge or intervention but as a counter-political defense of a particular spiritual deportment, we have effectively reframed the debate around literature and politics. Arguments over which variant of literary theory will best decipher and liberate the divided energies of an ideal political community therefore become idle, while the important question becomes why every variant assumes that politics entails deciphering man's occluded ethical being and dialectically reconciling the fragments of a once and future humanity. The answer, it seems to us, is that literary theory's "political" discourse is actually a means of converting political situations into hermeneutic occasions.[16]

The aim of these hermeneutic occasions, according to Hunter, is not to discover what is in the text but to form a "certain spiritual or intellectual comportment of the subject." If this is the case, and Hunter's evidence is impressive, there are two possible consequences. One is that literary discourse is bound to suffer from the weightlessness of which Edward Said complained, in *Culture and Imperialism*, when he said that "policy-oriented intellectuals who have internalized the norms of the state" find their mirror-image in academic "cults"—"post-modernism, discourse analysis, New Historicism, deconstruction, neo-pragmatism." The self-interested and self-enclosed jargon of these cults—as Hunter, too, puts the case—cuts them off from the political world and induces what Said calls "an astonishing sense of weightlessness with regard to the gravity of history and individual responsibility."[17] Another consequence is that Deconstruction, far from enforcing the claims that Derrida has made by appeal to Kant's faculty of philosophy, must take its chances along with other worldly forms of discourse. If, as Hunter maintains, Deconstruction converts political situations into hermeneutic occasions, it cannot claim any ex officio privilege in relation to true and false, right and wrong, moral and immoral: it must put up with the constraints of intervening just as any journalist does in the editorial or op-ed pages of the *New York Times*. There are no privileges, now that the conflict of faculties is incorrigible. Said may claim, in a desperate attempt to give weight to weightlessness, that "all these hybrid counter-energies, at work in many fields, individuals, and moments provide a community or culture made up of numerous anti-systemic hints and practices for collective human experiences . . . that is not based on coercion or domination."[18] But Hunter's reply to Said is decisive: "Were we to hold this appeal to a self-governing community accountable to any particular governmental problem, such as that faced by the United Nations in dealing with the 'anti-systemic hints and practices' of the warring communities in Bosnia, we would find it connected to the actual political situation by only the slenderest of threads: the theorist's moral prestige. For this appeal too is neither more nor less than a counter-political projection of the theorist's own spiritual comportment."[19] To Bosnia in that sentence one might add, with similar cogency, any political forces that ignore their translation into a hermeneutic occasion. I am not an Irishman for nothing.

But a question remains to be asked: What, or rather whom, does Derrida have in mind as the most immobile forces of the university? Does he really believe that Deconstruction is the only evidence of mobility, or that anyone who does not practice Deconstruction is by definition a tranquil, irresponsible adept of moralism? Let me quote, as an instance of one professor's activity within a university, Empson's brief commentary on a stanza from Thomas Gray's "Elegy Written in a Country Churchyard":

> Full many a gem of purest ray serene
> The dark, unfathomed caves of ocean bear;
> Full many a flower is born to blush unseen
> And waste its sweetness on the desert air.

What this means, Empson says, is that eighteenth-century England had no scholarship system or *carrière ouverte aux talents*:

> This is stated as pathetic, but the reader is put into a mood in which one would not try to alter it. (It is true that Gray's society, unlike a possible machine society, was necessarily based on manual labor, but it might have used a man of special ability wherever he was born.) By comparing the social arrangement to Nature he makes it seem inevitable, which it was not,

and gives it a dignity which was undeserved. Furthermore, a gem does not mind being in a cave and a flower prefers not to be picked; we feel that the man is like the flower, as short-lived, natural, and valuable, and this tricks us into feeling that he is better off without opportunities. The sexual suggestion of *blush* brings in the Christian idea that virginity is good in itself, and so that any renunciation is good; this may trick us into feeling it is lucky for the poor man that society keeps him unspotted from the World. The tone of melancholy claims that the poet understands the considerations opposed to aristocracy, though he judges against them; the truism of the reflections in the churchyard, the universality and impersonality this gives to the style, claim as if by comparison that we ought to accept the injustice of society as we do the inevitability of death. Many people, without being communists, have been irritated by the complacence in the massive calm of the poem, and this seems partly because there is a cheat in the implied politics; the "bourgeois" themselves do not like literature to have too much "bourgeois ideology."[20]

Christopher Ricks has quoted that passage from Empson to maintain that in criticism we want principles, not theories; or rather, in my terms, that we want principles rather than the institution of Theory. He has a point, though not one as decisive as he thinks. The principles he celebrates are moral principles, applied in a piece of literary reading and criticism. If they are moral principles, how has Empson come by them? It won't do to point to Samuel Johnson and say that he is the supreme English critic because he brought his moral sense to bear on every literary consideration. Aren't we back in the argumentative world in which John Rawls wrote *A Theory of Morals* and a thousand readers of that book questioned the theory? If by Empson's principles Ricks merely means his good old-fashioned English decency, I would remind him of the many occasions on which that virtue failed Empson or he failed it, when Christianity was the object of attention and Empson vented his hatred on it and his disgust for its adherents. I admire Empson's commentary on Gray's stanza just as much as Ricks does, and for similar reasons: it is morally impressive to have a critic being as just to a piece of writing as Empson is even as he disapproves of the political attitude on which the poem proceeds. Edifying, too, to find Empson taking such care to decide what he feels about the poem and its attitudes, and how much he feels, and why. In that chapter of *Some Versions of Pastoral* Empson starts from Pope's feeling that the *Aeneid* was a puff for Augustus: its "dreamy, impersonal, universal melancholy" made the puff a success. So with Gray's "Elegy." What makes Empson's commentary great criticism is that he recognizes Gray's trickery and knows that it is not mere trickery: it would be easy to show that Gray is sincere in holding the mixture of sentiments in a decent degree of order. Feelings about destiny, as in the flower's being "born" to a particular one, are mixed with the recognition that this destiny involves what any decent person is bound to see as "waste." The sweetness of the flower is also that of a woman who would in better circumstances have allowed a man to enjoy her sweetness and respond to it in kind. And so on. There is more to be said along Empson's lines.

I am aware that Empson, despite Paul de Man's essay on the alleged "dead end of formalist criticism," is sometimes thought of as a Deconstructionist before the letter of Grammatology. If that view has any merit—though it seems to me not to have much—it might suggest that Empson's commentary on Gray's "Elegy" is just the sort of post-Kantian faculty work that Derrida has in mind for Deconstruction; pronouncing on the truth and falsehood, right and wrong, moral and immoral quality of a piece of writing. But Empson's books show that, to pronounce in this spirit, there is no need to set up a special faculty and make an outlandish claim for it as a matter of principle. Empson did a lot of such work without making a fuss about it and certainly without claiming that he should have institutional privilege over his rivals. He was prepared to argue with anyone. He didn't ask for special consideration from Helen Gardner, F. A. C. Wilson, John Dover Wilson, or any of his opponents. That strikes me as a principle contiguous to the principles Ricks has in view, and good enough to be going on with.

The moral of the story is perhaps a simple one. There is no need to outlaw a theory or a principle or even to discourage the institution of Theory. But it seems important to decide, on each occasion, what is at stake. Is it a matter of belief, on which we may have to change our lives? The language of spiritual adherence allows for several degrees: we speak of belief, but we also speak of credence, which is not the same thing. We apprehend an idea or a belief or a notion, but we may also entertain each of these; again, this marks a different relation to the object in question. It seems desirable, and perhaps more than desirable, to know not just what the words we read and write mean and what their sense is—to use a crucial distinction of Vygotsky's—but to determine their status as forces that enter our minds. Is their entry a matter of life and death or an issue of little account or a notion that may be useful on a later occasion but not now? Or is Hunter right in his implication that the translation of brute facts into hermeneutic occasions is the only practice we're any good at?

But I may remark, to end with, that when I first read Derrida's early books and tried to take account of their complex relations to those of Husserl and Heidegger, I thought they belonged to the history of skepticism and might safely be allowed to find their place in that story. But Derrida's recent books and essays seem to me not to belong to the history of skepticism but to the history of politics. They retain their skepticism, but now as a quality that should justify an appeal not just to other skeptics but to the polity at large. The deconstructive scruple is now offered as if it were the basis of a political program. It appears that Deconstruction is offering itself not as a political party like any other, but as a political party unlike any other; unlike, because of its more radical stance in epistemology. If we vote for this party, we are to give it the power of adjudicating on true and false, right and wrong, precisely the authority that Kant claimed for philosophy against theology, medicine, and law.

## NOTES

1. Ralph Barton Perry, *Present Philosophical Tendencies: A Critical Survey of Naturalism, Idealism, Pragmatism, and Realism, Together with a Synopsis of the Philosophy of William James* (1912; reprint, New York: George Braziller, 1955), 7–8, 21–23.

2. Christopher Ricks, *Essays in Appreciation* (Oxford: Clarendon, 1996), 322.

3. Geoffrey Hill, *The Lords of Limit: Essays on Literature and Ideas* (New York: Oxford University Press, 1984), 107.

4. Immanuel Kant, *The Conflict of the Faculties/Der Streit der Fakultäten*, trans. Mary J. Gregor (New York: Abaris, 1979), 11.

5. Kant, *Conflict of the Faculties*, 43.

6. Kant, *Conflict of the Faculties*, 55. Quoted in Jacques Derrida, "Mochlos; or, The Conflict of the Faculties," in *Logomachia: The Conflict of the Faculties*, ed. Richard Rand (Lincoln: University of Nebraska Press, 1992), 27–28.

7. Ian Hunter, "The Regimen of Reason: Kant's Defence of the Philosophy Faculty," *Oxford Literary Review* 5, no. 17 (1995): 70.

8. Kant, *Conflict of the Faculties*, 63.

9. Immanuel Kant, *Religion Within the Limits of Reason Alone* (New York: Harper, 1960), 123. Quoted in Hunter, "Regimen of Reason," 73–74.

10. Kant, *Conflict of the Faculties*, 119.

11. Hunter, "Regimen of Reason," 80.

12. Derrida, "Mochlos," 22–23.

13. Derrida, 23.

14. Derrida, 202.

15. Friedrich Schelling, *Vorlesungen über die Methode des akademischen Studiums* (Jena: University of Jena, 1802). Quoted in Derrida, "Mochlos," 33–34.

16. Ian Hunter, "Literary Theory in Civil Life," *South Atlantic Quarterly* 95, no. 4 (Fall 1996): 1129.

17. Edward Said, *Culture and Imperialism* (New York: Knopf, 1993), 366–67. Quoted in Hunter, "Literary Theory in Civil Life," 1108.

18. Said, *Culture and Imperialism*, 406.

19. Hunter, "Literary Theory in Civil Life," 1124.

20. William Empson, *Some Versions of Pastoral* (1935; reprint, New York: New Directions, 1974), 4–5.

# PART II
## LINGUISTIC TURNS

IN THE FIELD OF PHILOSOPHY, "the linguistic turn" is the name generally given to the view that philosophical problems are primarily problems about language. Exemplified by Ludwig Wittgenstein's comment "The limits of my language are the limits of my world" (from his *Tractatus Logico-Philosophicus* [1921]) and by the tradition of analytic philosophy associated with his work, the phrase "the linguistic turn" was given currency starting in 1967 by a collection of essays of that title edited by Richard Rorty.[1] Further broadening the phrase, contemporary Theory has vastly inflated, and often misunderstood, the insights drawn not only from analytic philosophy's focus on language but also from Ferdinand de Saussure's foundational writings.

The notion that literature is made out of language would seem to need no elaborate defense. All students of literature today learn (or should learn) about Russian Formalism and the American New Critics, whose focus was precisely on the language of literature and the way literary texts work. But something quite other than this is meant by the appeal to the "linguistic turn" as it became prominent in the study of literature starting in the 1960s. Drawing principally on the work of Derrida, the "turn" has gone to extreme lengths to expand the notion of literature-as-language, to the point of treating literature as mere "marks" on paper. Even students who have never read Derrida at first hand confidently affirm nowadays that no word can have a determinate meaning. Far from needing to argue that literature is made of language, what needs bolstering today is the notion that something more than language exists in the world of literary studies. This is the issue taken up by the essays in this section. (The corollary extreme—that literature can be reduced to politics—is taken up in part 6.)

Raymond Tallis has for some years been investigating human consciousness, a subject marginalized by Theory today. In the essay selected for this volume, Tallis traces some of the claims about language popularized by Theory to their authors' fundamental misconceptions of Saussure's work, misconceptions Tallis shows to be typical of "post-Saussurean thought." After delineating Saussure's key contributions, Tallis analyzes the distortions—by now widely disseminated—of these ideas in the work of Barthes, Benveniste, and, above all, Derrida. Against the assault on consciousness and self-presence that these men have promoted in some of their most famous writings, Tallis affirms the subtlety of Saussure's understanding of the arbitrariness of the linguistic sign. Thus, contrary to the claims repeated by many theorists today, Tallis sees Saussure's work as crucial for illuminating how language is embedded in the physical world, a world that can never be reduced to "discourse."

John Searle approaches some of the same issues from a different perspective. He argues that key confusions in literary theory derive from theorists' ignorance of principles and distinctions commonly accepted in logic, linguistics, and the philosophy of language. Literary theorists thus have failed to note that their disagreements about textual meaning may result from the fact that they address different questions and that their questions themselves rest on some conceptual confusions. Searle lays out eight principles that literary critics and other theorists would need to understand about language if they were to engage in fruitful discussion, and applies these principles to the work of Knapp and Michaels and Derrida.

Whereas both Tallis and Searle posit a "background" and assert that only against it can language and its use make sense, Vincent Descombes focuses on arguments about the *referent*—a term that has replaced the older *object of representation*. He attributes the need to define the referent to the combined and inseparable rise of linguistic theory and semiotic analyses. Proceeding from the question, To what is the referential function of language attached in a sentence like "Caesar crossed the Rubicon"? he proposes avoiding a "dialectic of the Other" to understand the relation between language and reality. In tracing misconceptions regarding the referent, he parallels Tallis's view of the progression of the Saussurean legacy and implicitly demolishes the deconstructionist position that things are not truly present. Using as a metaphor the relationship between a chit and a coat in a cloakroom, which changes in different contexts, Descombes explains the inescapability of symbols and why their denial must lead to nihilism. The problem of the referent results from the particular model chosen by scholars and does not entail the conclusions they have drawn. Thus, he concludes, what needs to be criticized is not language or its symbolic function but rather the indifference of theorists to what grammarians clearly see as the division of the parts of speech.

The great dichotomy Wendell Harris undertakes to expose in his essay of the same name is the one between those writers (the "hermetic" or poststructuralist group) who view all meaning as indeterminate and who disconnect words from an extralinguistic reality, and those (the "hermeneutic" group) who attempt to elucidate how intended meanings do in fact adequately communicate and connect to a reality "out there." Contrasting the core doctrines of contemporary hermetic theorists with the central concepts associated with the word "hermeneutics," Harris notes that these two groups in fact address different questions. He argues that the absolute barriers that hermetic writing (intended for initiates only) see in language do not apply to language-in-use, as speech-act theory helps us to recognize.

One of the liveliest and clearest challenges to the linguistic turn's rapidly gaining ascendancy in Anglo-American criticism in the 1970s is M. H. Abrams's essay, "The Deconstructive Angel," with which this section closes. First presented as a paper at a session of the MLA convention in 1976, Abrams here responds to J. Hillis Miller's criticisms of Abrams's humanistic approach and reveals the underlying incoherence in some key precepts of deconstruction as promoted by Derrida and embraced by Hillis Miller and others. Abrams points to the confidence in language and its ability to communicate meaning that is exhibited on a daily basis by Hillis Miller and other deconstructionists as they engage in such practical activities as reading, commenting on, criticizing, and defending their own and one another's work.

## NOTE

1. Richard Rorty, *The Linguistic Turn: Essays in Philosophical Method* (Chicago: University of Chicago Press, 1967).

## 8. THE LINGUISTIC UNCONSCIOUS

### SAUSSURE AND THE POST-SAUSSUREANS

#### RAYMOND TALLIS

LANGUAGE IS HUGE, extraordinary, ungraspable; mysterious in its instances, stupendous in its range. It is easy to see why thinkers over the millennia have so often defined humanity in terms of it, describing Man as the Speaking Animal. As I have argued elsewhere,[1] this is mistaken: language is the most striking thing about us, yes, but it is in turn symptomatic of something else that is also expressed nonlinguistically; namely, the propensity to make things explicit. Although it is almost absurd to put it thus, we may see language, at the very lowest estimate, as a kind of tool, an infinitely pliable instrument for ensuring, among other things, maximum cooperation between members of a species engaged in common purposes. Language enables individuals to draw on a powerful communal consciousness to serve their needs better than their own unassisted minds. The extension of oral communication by means of writing and other systems of enduring signs enables information to be stored, not only outside the moment of its production, but also outside the human body.[2] This has permitted humankind to develop at an extraordinary rate, quite independently of changes in genetic structure, bodily composition, or the physiological parameters within which the body operates. As George Steiner put it: "Man has talked himself free of organic constraint."[3] Language has driven a widening wedge between human history and animal evolution, between culture and nature.

The fact that written language outlives its moments of utterance allows it to be used as a means of asserting group solidarity among those who share a common tongue against those who do not. Moreover, written language is the supreme means of raising self-awareness. It is as if consciousness, in depositing itself in objects and events—written signs and spoken sounds—that are outside of itself, is able to encounter itself more clearly and so become more self-conscious. Self-knowledge and self-awareness, the individual and collective sense of self at the highest level are mediated through language. This was why, in the previous paragraph, I hesitated to speak of language as a mere "tool": it is not merely used, and constituted by, subjects; it is also, in a sense, constitutive of them.[4]

The protean manifestations and influences of language tempt one to think of it as coterminous not only with human society but with human conscious-

Raymond Tallis. "The Linguistic Unconscious: Saussure and the Post-Saussureans." From *Enemies of Hope: A Critique of Contemporary Pessimism*, by Raymond Tallis, 272–89. New York: St. Martin's Press, 1997. Reproduced by permission of Palgrave Macmillan.

ness above the level of the most primitive, formless sensations. "My languages are my world," to modify Wittgenstein's dictum. The intimate relation between language and consciousness and self-consciousness works both ways. Not only does language seem to be the bearer of most of human consciousness, but linguistic acts, under the usual conditions, seem to be uniquely the product of consciousness, of deliberation and voluntary choice. Discourse is signally infused with consciousness and self-consciousness and is, apparently, deliberate and nonautomatic to a unique degree. It seems, therefore, to be a conspicuous sign of a self-present individual, a final redoubt against the assaults from thinkers such as Marx, Durkheim, and Freud on the centrality of the conscious, rational agent.

This view of the special status of linguistic acts has, however, been challenged by certain post-Saussurean thinkers, notably Derrida. Post-Saussurean thought—which encompasses not only such poststructuralists as Derrida but also structuralists such as Lévi-Strauss, Benveniste, and Todorov, and writers such as Foucault, Barthes, and Lacan who seem to fit into both categories— minimizes the role of intention and the status of the individual human being as a free, deliberate agent. More comprehensively than Marx, Durkheim, or even Freud, post-Saussurean thinkers question whether the individual can ever know what she is doing. Some, such as Lacan—who claimed to read Freud correctly by structuralizing the unconscious, making it into a language—even have a theory of how the individual acquires the illusion that she does know what she is doing, and the deeper illusion that she is a "she" at the center of her knowings and doings, to which the various knowings and doings of her life can be attached.[5]

The Saussurean revolution in linguistics, like the Durkheimian revolution in sociology, was marked by a shift from an item-centered to a system-centered approach. The post-Saussurean revolution in thought about man and society was characterized by a similar shift, based on the belief that language was the paradigm of society as a whole, the latter being simply a larger system of signs that included language. The analysis of society and of the individuals within it thus became, in Edmund Leach's words, a kind of "cultural linguistics."

Post-Saussurean thinkers drew their inspiration from Saussure's writings on theoretical linguistics. To what extent do Saussure's writings license these large assumptions about human nature? I have previously argued that there is nothing in Saussure to justify post-Saussurean thought.[6] I concluded that a handful of careful distinctions would have caused roomfuls of post-Saussurean steam to condense into a few drops of water. It is necessary to reiterate some of the main points of the argument against the post-Saussureans here.

At the heart of Saussure's vision of a system-based, as opposed to an item-based, analysis of language is a recognition of the arbitrariness of the linguistic sign. Individual linguistic signs have no natural connection with that which they signify; "dog" does not look or sound like a dog, and so on. Saussure was not the first to draw attention to this feature of language, nor did he say that he was; he claimed only to be the first to appreciate "the numberless conse-quences" that flow from it. Since linguistic signs do not derive their signifying power from being naturally associated with the things they are used to signify, they must derive it from somewhere else.

According to Saussure, the source of the signifying power of signs is the *system* to which they belong. A sign has two aspects—the signifier, correspon-ding roughly to the phonetic aspect, and the signified, corresponding roughly to the semantic aspect—and it consequently belongs to two systems, the system of sounds and the system of meanings. Neither the signifier nor the signified enjoys an independent existence outside of the system of language. The linguis-tic system is *a set of differences* and its component signifiers and signifieds, being purely differential, are essentially negative. They can be grasped only through the network of other units. This crucial point warrants further elaboration.

Consider first the signifier. According to Saussure, this is a set of contrasting features realized in sound opposed to other contrasting features realized in other sounds: it is a bundle of phonic *differences*. The recognition that actual words (spoken or written tokens) served as the physical realization of abstract, contrasting sound-features opened the way to numerous advances in our un-derstanding of phonological relationships between languages and of the way the brain extracts verbal tokens from the acoustic material served up to its ear.

The signified, too, is not a naturally occurring entity but a "concept" (a term Saussure uses in a special sense), and one whose boundaries are determined only within the linguistic system by its opposition to other concepts. It is not, however, intrapsychic—a mental entity such as a mental image: like the signi-fier, it is not a thing but a *value*; and it has value only within the system where it coexists with other opposing or different values. The denial of the pre-linguistic reality of the signified is the most revolutionary aspect of Saussure's theory. The signified is not a "thing" "out there"; nor is it a prelinguistic psy-chological entity. The signified is purely relational:

> The conceptual side of value is made up solely of relations and differences with respect to the other terms of language . . . differences carry significa-tion . . . a segment of language can never in the final analysis be based on anything except its non-coincidence with the rest. *Arbitrary* and *differential* are two correlative qualities.[7]

So verbal meaning is specified not in virtue of an external relation between a sound and an object, but of an internal relation between oppositions at the phonetic level and oppositions at the semantic level.

So far so good. Few people would dispute that language is more of a system than a word heap and that its component signs are arbitrary in Saussure's sense. And it is perfectly obvious that the semantic catchment area of individual terms rarely corresponds either to patches of space-time or to "natural kinds" (or "types of patches of space-time"). Most people would be prepared to accept that linguistic value, as Saussure meant it, is negative or differential and that it is the differences between linguistic units rather than their positive contents, that carries verbal meanings.

Most of the errors in, and much of the excitement of, post-Saussurean thought derive, paradoxically, from thinkers overlooking Saussure's fundamental doctrines: for example, the fact that the signifier does not strictly correspond to a sound and the signified does not strictly correspond to the meaning. The signifier-signified relationship should not be confused with that between a sign—an uttered sound or written mark—and an external, extralinguistic object. Therefore, the intralinguistic and arbitrary nature of the former cannot be taken to imply the intralinguistic and arbitrary nature of the latter. To think that the one implies the other is also to confuse the language system with the use of that system by an individual on a particular occasion in generating a particular speech act.

This seems obvious; nevertheless, as a result of this confusion, several un-Saussurean conclusions have been drawn from Saussure's work. They underpin a radical assault on the central role of consciousness (and consciously formed intentions) in everyday life and, more particularly, on those actions—speech acts—that seem supremely volitional and governed by intention. Saussure, it is correctly argued, has shown that behind every speech act—indeed, every discourse act—lies a language system of which speakers are largely unconscious. But then it is incorrectly argued that, since the signifier and the signified are internal to the linguistic system, discourse is closed off from the extralinguistic world. From this it follows that discourse is only a series of moves within a system of which speakers and writers are unaware and that such meaning and reference as discourse has is to this hidden system. The meaning of individual utterances (and other linguistic and nonlinguistic signs) is not merely achieved through the implicit or hidden system, but indeed is that system. Speakers don't know what they are talking about. Derrida, for example, has argued that behind every specific text—written or spoken, a novel or a chance remark in a conversation—is "the general text." This text is not a collection of words but a condition of the possibility of discourse; since this condition cannot be specified, all specific texts remain "undecidable."[8]

One of the best-known applications of what is taken to be post-Saussurean, but is actually non-Saussurean, thought is in the writings of Lévi-Strauss. Saussurean phonology licensed his structuralist analysis of myths. We have seen how, according to Lévi-Strauss, the meaning of myths lay not in their individual, manifest content, but in the group or system to which they belonged. This group had an enormous scope, stretching across millennia and straddling continents. Myths were recounted by individuals not, as those individuals may have thought, in order to convey their content, but in order to realize part of a form whose totality, hidden from everyone except the structuralist mythologizer, was the structure of the human mind itself.

Less spectacular, but of more direct importance for the present discussion, is the post-Saussurean dissolution of the speaking (or discoursing) subject. The scope of the claims advanced under this heading varies from writer to writer, but we may identify three types of claim:

1. The denial (associated in particular with Barthes) of the originality and unitary nature of the author.
2. The denial (associated with Derrida) of the presence of the speaker (or his/her intentions) in the speech act.
3. The assertion (associated with Benveniste) that the self, the self-present I, the centered ego, is the product of language and (according to Lacan and Derrida) is therefore illusory.

I should like to deal with each of these in turn.

## THE ABSENT AUTHOR

According to Barthes,[9] readers of texts, especially officially approved texts that belong to the literary canon, believe that behind the text there is a rather special person called an "Author." The Author has several characteristics: he/she is the true origin of the text (he/she is an original creator); he/she has a unity represented in his/her distinctive presence throughout his/her text (or, indeed, his/her *oeuvre);* and he/she is the authority on the definitive meaning of his/her text. In short, he/she shares most of the properties of a deity and is in truth an Author-God. Barthes denies the author these extraordinary properties and, on the basis of this, argues that there is no such thing as an author of a text. The text is merely "a multi-dimensional space in which a variety of writings, none of them original, blend and clash." And the author is merely a site through which language passes: he/she does not use language to write his/her text; rather, language uses him/her to write the text.

The dissolved Barthesian Author is a straw person, who may be alive and well in the French educational system but has little life elsewhere. His/her death would go unremarked in most parts of the world. The ordinary everyday author remains alive and well. Roland Barthes may not have created his texts *ab initio* (he cannot take exclusive credit for all the dubious ideas in them), but he is infinitely closer to being the author of them than I who quote from and comment on them. No one would wish to claim that he has the last word on their meaning or that his unique personality is uniformly present throughout them. Most literature (even a short, much revised poem) is put together out of scattered moments of inspiration that have no more claim to be uniquely expressive of their author than do the products of other, less literary moments.

## The Absent Speaker

Barthes's attack on the Author—once regarded as revolutionary bordering on scandalous because of his semideliberate confusion between the Author-God and the author-in-ordinary—and on the presence of the author in the text is not too upsetting to ordinary thought. What writer would wish to claim that she is fully present in passages she wrote a decade, or even a minute, ago? One of the benefits of writing is that it enables us to clarify and extend our ideas and distance ourselves from them. (This would not be possible for Barthes's all-pervasive Author-God.) The text is a product in which the craftsman is only metaphorically present. At best, past moments of consciousness are embodied in this product.

However, one of the arguments used by Barthes to bump off the Author—namely, that we do not use language to speak/write, rather that language speaks/writes through us—has become the basis of a more radical attack on the presence and self-presence of the speaker/writer:

> once the conscious subject is deprived of its role as a source of meaning—once meaning is explained in terms of conventional systems which may escape the grasp of the conscious subject—the self can no longer be identified with consciousness. It is "dissolved" as its functions are taken up by a variety of interpersonal systems that operate through it.[10]

This implication is at work in Derrida's critique of the idea of expression and self-expression in discourse. Derrida begins with a radicalization of Saussure. He draws out what he considers to be the logical consequences of Saussure's vision of language—consequences from which he believes Saussure shied away. Language, Derrida points out, is difference-riddled: the meaning of a signified is owed entirely to its difference from, its noncoincidence with, the other signifieds. Signification therefore depends on the domination of absence over presence—the absent system dominates over the present signifier or signified. Derrida then takes three steps which enable him to get to his position that speakers are not expressed in (are indeed absent from) their speech:

(1) He extends the domination of difference (absence, negativity) from the signifier and the signified taken singly (where they are indubitably the playthings of absence) to the sign-as-a-whole (a step specifically warned against by Saussure),[11] and thence to the completed speech act. This is nonsense, of course—the speech act does not belong to the systems of signifieds and signifiers. It uses the systems, but is not part of them. The confusion between the system and its use, between *langue* and *parole* (especially unforgivable in writers who claim to be familiar with Saussure, as it was one of the latter's great achievements to distinguish these things), has complex consequences that one can trace through the whole absence-presence argument.

In fact, presence in a speech act is due to the actual presence of the speaker. This is not merely a question of bodily presence (otherwise one would have to consider an individual vocalizing in a coma as being self-present) but also of being-consciously-here. The latter is also the necessary basis of the closure of general meaning to specific reference to particulars. The implicit *deixis* of the physical situation of the speaker, and of "the story so far," provides the coordinates of a closed universe of actual discourses, which is quite unlike the boundless universe of Derrida's disembodied text floating freely in a limitless sea of other texts. The *system*, of course, lacks deixis, knows no referents and has only the general possibilities of meaning at its disposal. It is quite without presence, achieved meaning and reference.[12]

In order to draw the conclusion that discourse and discoursers are empty in the way that Derrida argues that they are, it is necessary, as has already been said, to conflate the system with the actual discourse acts that utilize it. In order to do this, it is necessary to conflate the components of the system with the use of the system on particular occasions; to conflate the meaning and reference of signs with the means by which meaning and reference are achieved; to conflate the system (which is hidden from users) and the use of that system in particular speech acts; to conflate signifier and signified with the-sign-as-a-whole, the type with the token, the sign with its meaning and/or reference on a particular occasion of use, etc. All of this Derrida and his poststructuralist followers gladly and repeatedly do.

Consider, for example, this argument from a prominent British literary theorist, Terence Hawkes.[13] All systems, he says, including language, "act to maintain and underwrite the intrinsic laws which bring them about, and to 'seal off' the system from reference to other systems." Consequently, language

> does not construct its formations of words by reference to the patterns of "reality" but on the basis of its own internal and self-sufficient rules. The word "dog" exists, and functions within the structure of the English language, without reference to any four-legged barking creature's real existence.

If this were the case, we would expect the strings "The dog is barking," "The dog is quacking" and "The dog is reading *Of Grammatology* with pleasure and profit" to occur with approximately equal frequency.[14] As it is, their respective frequencies seem to reflect the frequencies with which the extralinguistic situations to which they refer occur in real life.

(2) Derrida introduces a new term—*différance*, which compounds both difference and deferral: the meaning of an utterance is never reached, so that deferral is indefinite. There is thus a double absence in discourse—the difference upon which it is based and the endlessly deferred meaning that it never reaches.

On closer examination, however, the meaning that is eternally deferred by Derrida is a special sort of meaning—an absolute closure that would bring the search for further meaning to an end. Ordinary meaning, by contrast, does seem to be available within the lifetime of the speaker—indeed, within the sentence-time of the speaker—and so is not a serious source of absence. And even if Derrida were referring to the ordinary delay that occurs in the fulfilment of the meaning of an utterance (having to wait to the end of a sentence or paragraph to arrive at some more or less definite meaning), this would not make speech acts any different from other acts such as walking. When I walk to the pub, I undertake numerous acts which, though they contribute to the goal, the overall meaning, of my behavior, are not themselves endowed with the full meaning. Crossing the road to avoid someone who will delay my arrival at the pub has a relationship to the overall meaning of my behavior no less remote than that of a participle to the final meaning of the sentence.[15]

(3) Derrida considers the fact that the meaning of an utterance is determined not solely by the words of which it is composed and the order in which they are placed, but also by their social context. The utterance "I do" has a very particular meaning in the course of a marriage ceremony, which it does not have outside of this. The felicity conditions that will ensure that the utterance "I do" is valid as a marriage vow are extraordinarily complex and largely hidden from the utterer. Generalizing from this, Derrida argues that the context that determines, or gives determinacy to, the meaning of an utterance is boundless and, consequently, is unavailable to the speaker. More specifically, since I cannot know the infinitude of conditions that would ensure that my utterance had one meaning rather than another, I am not in control of the meaning of my utterance. How, then, can I say that I am expressed in my utterance, when the determinants of its meaning lie beyond my ken?

One can answer this question by considering the fact that I don't know whether my legs are going to work or, even less, how my legs work. In the present state of ignorance of physiology, nobody, least of all myself, could state the conditions necessary for walking. Specifically to address Derrida's point, we need only to remember the distinction between the context that makes an utterance felicitous and the meaning meant by the person uttering it; between the conditions of meaning and the meaning that is meant. The fact that my utterance turns out to be invalid (the vicar had been unfrocked, the woman was already married, an edict has just been issued banning all marriages, etc.) does not in any way attenuate my intention to get married, sever my speech act from that intention, or diminish the extent to which I am expressed in, or present in, the act. Indeed, these things, precisely by being so obviously unknown to me, can be clearly separated from my intention. Just as the referential opacity of most terms (for example, water which is also $H_2O$), does not prevent me from referring to water.

## THE ABSENT SELF

We may conclude that Derrida's grounds for denying the presence of the speaker in the speech act—so that absence is the hallmark of discourse, and writing, in which the originator is explicitly absent, becomes the paradigm of discourse—and for denying that speech acts realize intentions are to say the least dubious. Nevertheless, his ideas have been extremely influential and represent the most important contemporary attack upon the centrality of the individual's consciousness in ordinary life. For if even speech acts are not importantly conscious and deliberate, what is? The displacement of the speaker's expressive intentions from the center of his/her speech acts becomes the basis for a wider displacement of the individual and his/her intentions from his/her acts. Intention is pushed to the margins of behavior. Because we cannot formulate the context that gives our actions their meanings, we cannot be said truly to intend what we do.

A further assault on consciousness and the centrality of the conscious self deriving from Saussurean linguistics is the assertion (associated with Derrida, Lacan, and the linguist Benveniste) that the self, the self-present I, the centered ego, is the product of language. According to Derrida, the illusion of self-presence, and so of unmediated presence, is based on the accident of hearing oneself speak. The closed circuit whereby speakers hear themselves without mediation creates a (false, illusory) sense of being present to oneself. For Lacan, the unconscious is structured like a language and the sense of self is inscribed in "an endless chain of signifiers" to which there corresponds no signified. The *symbolic* self is the successor to the *imaginary* self derived from catching sight of oneself in a mirror. The infant enters the realm of the imaginary by identifying (incorrectly, according to Lacan) with its mirror image. This imaginary self subsequently enters the symbolic realm, at least in part as a strategy to resolve the Oedipus complex. These views (which I have discussed extensively elsewhere)[16] entrain the errors common to all post-Saussurean notions about the relationship between the speaker and the linguistic system plus faults of their own. The most explicit attempt to found the self, the sense of I, in language is that of the influential French linguist Émile Benveniste.[17]

For Benveniste, the act that constitutes the "I" is a linguistic act. Catherine Belsey succinctly summarizes his position:

it is language which provides the possibility of subjectivity because it is language which enables the speaker to posit himself or herself as "I," as the subject of a sentence. It is through language that people constitute themselves as subjects.[18]

Since individuals do not invent the language that they use (and are anyway used by, rather than users of, it) they are constitut*ed* rather than constitut*ing*.

The "I" is consequently caught up in the play of difference that is the essence of language, a play of which nobody is master.

In the essay in which he most explicitly advances his views about the relation between the self and language,[19] Benveniste begins by pointing out that discourse consists essentially of an *exchange*. In contrast with Derrida et al., he recognizes that the exchange, which lies between individuals, cannot be due to the properties of language itself—of the system rather than of individual speech acts. But he draws a rather extraordinary, and distinctly post-Saussurean, conclusion from this:

> "subjectivity," whether it is placed in phenomenology or in psychology . . . is only the emergence in the being of the fundamental property of language. "Ego" is he who *says* "ego." That is where we see the foundation of "subjectivity," which is determined by the linguistic status of "person."
>
> (224)

Subjectivity, however,

> is not defined by the feeling which everyone experiences of being himself (this feeling, to the degree that it can be taken note of, is only a reflection).
>
> (227)

A reflection, that is, of a subjectivity primarily established in and through language. Linguistically constituted subjectivity, however, accounts for the self as "the psychic unity that transcends the totality of the actual experiences it assembles and that makes the permanence of consciousness" (Benveniste, 224). This is what holds together all the various experiences attributed to the self and makes them experiences had by that self. The "establishment of subjectivity in language creates the category of person both in language and also . . . outside of it as well" (224). Thus, according to Benveniste, being a subject, along with some aspects of feeling that one is a (unified) "self," result from one's entry into language as a speaker. The individual's engagement in dialogue constitutes him as a person. Conscious personhood is an inner reflection of the oppositional status the speaker has when he engages as an "I" in dialogue:

> Conciousness of self is only possible if it is experienced by contrast. I use *I* only when I am speaking to someone who will be a *you* in an address. It is this condition of dialogue that is constitutive of a *person*, for it implies that reciprocally *I* becomes *you* in the address of the one who in his turn designates himself as *I*.
>
> (224–25)

The physically or bodily differentiated individual becomes *I* by positing himself as "I" opposed to "you."

For Benveniste, then, the actual feeling of subjectivity, of being *this* self rather than another, of being *this enduring thing*, is a secondary aspect of subjectivity, a mere reflection of actual subjectivity, which has an origin (in language) unappreciated by the subject. The fact that the subject should be mistaken as to his/her true nature suggests another severe limitation placed on consciousness and self-consciousness—one yet more drastic than those suggested by Marx, Durkheim, and Freud.

Even if one allows the starting assumption—that the self is experienced not positively but only differentially, that it exists (like a linguistic unit) by contrast with the not-self—it does not follow that it is experienced, or exists, only in opposition to the *verbal* "you." For the not-self includes nonverbal objects (material things outside its body) as well as entities apprehended verbally. Benveniste's position would not hold up even if he were to retreat to the claim that his "I" were only the grammatical "I" understood as the subject of a sentence. For the purely oppositional and commutative relationship that Benveniste refers to is not confined to *you*: "I" may also be opposed to *it, he, we, that (over there)*, etc.

It seems that Benveniste does at times intend the "subject" to be construed in the narrower sense of the grammatical subject, in which case his achievement is even less impressive. For it is, of course, easy to decenter the self linguistically if one either begins with the assumption that the "I" is a linguistic entity, or if one takes it for granted that the self is to be identified with the grammatical subject. The assertion that it is through language that people constitute themselves as subjects becomes a mere tautology if the term "subject" is employed only to indicate the grammatical subject of a sentence. You couldn't make yourself the subject of a sentence if there were no sentences to be the subject of.

Benveniste draws some surprising conclusions from the status of the first-person singular personal pronoun:

> What does *I* refer to? To something very peculiar which is exclusively linguistic: *I* refers to the act of individual discourse in which it is pronounced. . . . The reality to which it refers is the reality of the discourse. It is in the instance of discourse in which *I* designates the speaker that the speaker proclaims himself as "subject." And so it is literally true that the basis of subjectivity is in the exercise of language.    (226)

It is, of course, untrue that "I" refers to a particular linguistic act; on the contrary, it mobilizes the deictic coordinates in order to arrive at its true referent, which is the individual generating the act—the speaker. The conclusion that language itself is the referent of the pronoun is based upon a mistake we have already noted as being widespread and crucial for establishing many of the startling ideas associated with post-Saussurean theory: that of confusing the *referent of discourse* with the *means by which reference* is achieved. If the means of access to the referent of "I" is confused with the actual referent, then it only requires the observation that the means of access is linguistic (the speech act itself) in order to arrive at the conclusion (quoted above) that the referent of "I" is linguistic and that "the basis of subjectivity is in the exercise of language."

That there is an elementary error at the root of Benveniste's claim that subjectivity has a linguistic origin will come as no surprise to those who feel that, whatever construction one puts on the "subject" or the self, it seems implausible that the totally fortuitous and unexplained existence of handy pronouns used to refer to oneself should play such a central part in the creation of the self. The unconvinced will be puzzled as to how language—and especially dialogue—could arise in the absence of preexisting subjects. Or how a speaker could appropriate to himself an entire language by designating himself as "I" if he were not already a self.

Benveniste himself seems undecided on this crucial point; for at one place in the essay he says: "Language is possible only because each speaker sets himself up as a *subject* by referring to himself as *I* in his discourse" (225). From this, it would appear that the subject, far from being "a tropological construct" (to use a favorite post-Saussurean term)—the mere product of language—is itself the source of language; for language seems to depend upon the subject "referring to himself." The speaker, it seems, is not only prior to the subject but also to language, and is, indeed, the very condition of its possibility. Language is predicated upon the prior existence of speakers: a most curious state of affairs that raises innumerable questions. Among them is the question of how the speaker could refer to himself or herself—or want to do so—unless he or she existed in the first place: self-reference must presuppose some kind of preexisting self to refer to.

The Benveniste circuit—language creates the self that creates language; self-reference generates the pronouns that in turn create the self that is referred to by pronouns—illustrates the problems that arise when one wishes to dissolve the self entirely into a social system or institution such as language. For those systems and institutions would seem to require the interaction of subjects to bring them about and keep them in play; and such an interaction between subjects must imply that they preexist the system, however much they are bound up with or shaped by it.

The primacy of self-presence and of consciousness—that I am this thing, that I am here—is not, therefore, impugned. For, as already noted in the discussion of post-Saussurean thinkers, successful linguistic acts depend, ultimately, upon determinations of meaning and reference that cannot be performed through the system alone. In the end, deictic coordinates have to be brought into play. These are implicit in the individual's bodily location and historical situation; but they are explicit only in his or her sense that "I am this thing"—and its consequences: "I am here and now," etc. The centered self tethers language to the actual; it is essential for reference to be secured. As we have already noted, the system itself has no referential powers.

It would be difficult to exaggerate the significance of the tendency of system-based discourse theorists—those who give the system priority over the speaking subject, so that the latter is subordinated to the former ("Language speaks us," "We are not the authors of our sentences, we are constituted through the General Text")—to overlook deixis. It is this symptomatic omission that confers a temporary plausibility upon even the most outrageous claims about the relationship of the self to language. When Dragan Milovanovic asserts that "Language speaks the subject, providing it with meaning at the cost of being,"[20] he is only following out the consequences of this fatal omission. A moment's thought would reveal that, in order to speak meaningfully, we have to mean (transitively) what we say. As Grice[21] has pointed out, meaning is active. The meaning of what I say is not merely the meaning my uttered signs happen to have, as clouds may mean rain or spots mean measles. It is the meaning *I intend*; and in trying to determine what I mean, you will be interpreting what I intended to mean. And this interpretation will be heavily dependent upon what you know of me as an individual and certain specifics, such as our shared immediate context, my tone of voice, etc. This presupposes my presence in what I say. The meaning of utterances emerging from an absence possessed by the discursive system would be literally undecidable. Meanings, in short, are produced as well as consumed; and without the notion of the individual producer and without reference to the deixis implicit in his/her situation, to the existential context of the production, the meaning of an utterance would be simply undecidable. Communication cannot take place without both meaning-producer and meaning-consumer mobilizing the deictic coordinates in the speaker's situation.

To say this is to envisage the spoken word as primary and the written word as secondary, and so to fly in the face of the entire post-Saussurean framework of assumptions. Notoriously (and counterintuitively), Derrida asserted that Writing, in which the apparent origin of the discursive chains was absent, had primacy over Speech, in which the apparent origin of the discursive chains was apparently present. For Derrida, Speech was merely an instance of the former or, rather, of "Writing-in-General" and the absence of an originating source of the discursive chain, evident in writing, was actually a characteristic of all discourse.

I have set out Derrida's arguments, and my own view of the fallacies upon which they are based, elsewhere[22] and will not repeat them here. Suffice it to say that even the most fervent post-Saussureans feel uneasy about them. For example, Milovanovic seems to wobble uneasily between the speaking subject as the patient and the agent of discourse:

Much contemporary semiotic analysis is divided between a self-referential and a referential view. The former arguing for a semiotic system in which the reference of the sign is exclusively the system of signs itself and the latter for some external referent to which the sign points. The constitutive elements of the sign—signifier and signified—are also implicated in the subject taking up a position as an *I* in an utterance. Benveniste and Lacan have argued that what appears as an *I* in a statement is but a presence of an absence, the absence being the producer of the discursive chain itself.

(8–9)

Milovanovic, who allies himself with the self-referential party (indeed, he entertains "visions of an empowered democracy in which a new concept of subjectivity reigns," based upon Lacan and Benveniste's ideas), is clearly uncertain as to whether or not the discursive chain—a particular utterance—is produced, or simply happens, or is generated by the system, understood as a general absence instantiated in, or alighting upon, a particular individual. The latter is a difficult and even self-contradictory notion, being that of a not-here (or even a not-anywhere, or a not-anywhere-in-particular) taking root in a here and still retaining its status as a not-here.

The whole question of presence and absence in speech cannot be answered in general, unless one believes that anyone who participates in any rule-governed activity is somehow absent from the acts that result—that they have no choice in what occurs and are not represented personally in their acts. The untenability of this position becomes evident when one compares, for example, my comparative presence in my words when I make a statement calculated to impress, convince or persuade someone else, with my comparative absence from: the words I shout out in a dream; the sounds I babbled associatively as a child and may babble meaninglessly if I am demented in my old age; the words I have taped on a dictaphone and someone plays many years after my death; Homer's words (which I have not yet read). Post-Saussurean thought does not allow for these distinctions: we are all ego-less babblers, soluble fish in the sea of language.

Contrary to the claims of the post-Saussureans, the systematic nature of language does not deny us freedom of expression through it or insist that we are first dissolved in it before we can have freedom of expression, so that our freedom is freedom only to express the selves that are constituted through language. As a speaker, I am always outside of language: my existential situation is that of someone whose being is not fully consumed by the meanings that are embodied in the utterance I am engaged in. At the very least, my bodily weight and position, its numerous unexpressed sensations, the physical world around me with its endless source of novelty, and its inexhaustible particularity, distance me from the meanings that I offer for consumption and make me, as producer, the source of meaning and distant from it. There is no question of vanishing from actuality into the world of possibility and the system of language, of giving myself up to general meaning at the cost of my particular being. The rules are enabling constraints, not straitjackets, that permit communication. They are necessary, just as the friction that makes walking into hard work is necessary in order that walking should be possible. We do things with words, but we can do them because we obey the rules that make communication possible.[23]

This is illustrated if we consider the most commonplace, off-the-shelf utterances, the kinds of things that would seem likely to show us as speakers at our most limited, constrained, system-bound, and "constituted in language." Saying "Hello" would seem to fit this description: it is almost a linguistic reflex and, as a phatic word, free of informational content and triggered by certain stereotyped situations; it would seem, if any utterance is, to be something that chooses the speaker rather than vice versa, an example, if there are any examples, of language speaking us rather than we speaking language. And yet we have the option of exerting an extremely complex and deliberate freedom through saying, or refraining from saying, "Hello." We have a choice of degrees of warmth. We may assume a variety of accents to impress or amuse. We may speak it quietly so as not to be heard saying it and betray a relationship we would rather conceal ("strangers when we meet") or so as not to wake the children or out of respect for the occasion in which the word is uttered. We have a choice, when we are approaching someone, of the distance at which we say the word and we exercise our judgment—based upon the respective relationships between us, actual or to be asserted or underlined—as to who we think should say it first. We may say it in a certain way to mock the pretensions of others; or to remind us of the occasion many years ago when we said it in a certain tone of voice and so to assert our solidarity through this signal of the duration of our relationship. In summary, this simple greeting may express, or be used to express, an infinitely elaborated and highly personal consciousness of another person.

From this we may draw two non-post-Saussurean conclusions. First, language is used by us to express selves that are not anticipated by, or nodes in, the language system. And, secondly, we are explicit animals whose ability to develop our explicit consciousness of things, including what we feel ourselves to be at a particular time, or over time, may be elaborated indefinitely. We are free agents when we use language: the rules of language do not specify what we shall say in a given situation—except within very broad constraints—and certainly not the way in which we say it. This is at least in part because language does not tell us what the situation is—what, for example, my relationship is with this woman coming towards me down the road that will, along with many other things (such as how I am feeling at present, my recent and remote history), determine if, when, and how I shall say "Hello" to her. Using language—even the most stereotyped elements of it—we can unravel more and more complex modes of explicitness.

Saussure himself emphasized that the act of speech (*parole*) is an individual act of intelligence and will[24] in which the speaker's freedom of choice is only loosely constrained by the possibilities available in the linguistic system (*langue*). The choice is still the individual's, and the choosing is still conscious or part of an act that is conscious. Far from decentering the self, *parole* requires a centered self in order that the speech act shall be spoken and enacted. The post-Saussurean claim that it is language which speaks (presumably *langue* that *paroles!*), which we have seen cannot be sustained even for stereotyped utterances such as "Hello," sounds even less plausible (and, indeed, downright odd) when one thinks of ordinary discourse: whether one says or wishes to say "Pass me the salt please" versus "Pass me the pepper please" versus "Get your elbows off the table" is obviously not determined by the system, which could neither provide a reference for "me" nor legislate over its use on a particular occasion. *Parole*—actual talk—is always rooted in particular occasions, and those occasions are not intralinguistic—as if everything that was said was a series of stereotyped responses between priest and congregation. The rules of language do not specify what we say, even less how we should say it, precisely because so much of what we say is prompted by events whose occurrence is not regulated by the rules of discourse.[25]

In placing the arbitrariness of the linguistic sign at the center of his understanding of language, Saussure's instincts were surely correct. And his intuition that the consequences of his "first principle" of language are "numberless" is absolutely right. It is therefore a shame that so many of his followers have misunderstood the arbitrariness of the linguistic sign and have focused on its nonconsequences. For there is even more to be understood about arbitrariness than is indicated in Saussure's writings. It is connected not only with the nature of human language, but also with the nature of human consciousness. The arbitrariness of the linguistic sign sets discourse off from the associative net that would embed language in the causal nexus of the physical world. Arbitrariness is a pervasive manifestation of the status of linguistic signs as *explicit signs* and of their role in making explicitness (consciousness) explicit. Arbitrariness creates the essential distance across which reference is possible and on the basis of which expression, rather than reaction, representation rather than duplication, can be enacted. If linguistic signs were not arbitrary, they could not carry an increasing burden of explicitness and many things, amongst them the formulation of theories of language, would not be possible. Thus, as I have argued in more detail elsewhere, a true understanding of Saussure's thought would see that it emphasizes, rather than dissolves, the relationship between discourse and individual consciousness, between speech acts and individual intentions.[26]

NOTES

1. Raymond Tallis, "Consciousness Restored," *The Explicit Animal* (London: Macmillan, 1993).

2. This claim has to be treated with a good deal of non-literal-minded care. See Raymond Tallis, *Psycho-Electronics* (London: Ferrington, 1994), especially the entry "Information."

3. George Steiner, *After Babel* (London: Faber, 1974).

4. I owe this way of putting the matter to an anonymous referee of an earlier draft of this section. Her/his criticisms have been invaluable. It is important to note the *two-way* relationship: the self constitutes language as well as being constituted in/by language. I would not wish it to be thought that I subscribe to the notion that "language speaks us"—the very viewpoint that I criticize later in this section.

5. This claim is subjected to critical examination in the chapter on Lacan in Raymond Tallis, *Not Saussure* (London: Macmillan, 1995).

6. See *Not Saussure.* Shorter versions of my critique are available in *Theorrhoea and After* (Houndmills: St. Martin's Press, 1999); and Raymond Tallis, "A Cure for Theorrhoea," *Critical Review*, 3, no. 1 (Winter 1989): 7–39.

7. Ferdinand de Saussure, *Course in General Linguistics*, trans. Wade Baskin (rev. ed., London: Fontana, 1974), 117–18.

8. See Stephen Cox, "Devices of Deconstruction," *Critical Review* 3, no. 1 (Winter 1989): 56–76, for a clear exposition and critique of the Derridean notion of the General Text. This notion, according to Derrideans, ruins any project of interpretation. We shall encounter in due course the argument that, because language is intrinsically undecidable, definite meanings can be derived from statements only through coercively imposing such meanings upon them. All (definite) meaning is therefore "Fascist."

9. This belief is most famously expounded in Roland Barthes, "The Death of the Author," in *Image–Music–Text*, ed. and trans. Stephen Heath (London: Fontana, 1977).

10. Jonathan Culler, *Structuralist Poetics* (London: Routledge and Kegan Paul, 1975), 28. Culler is, of course, a secondary source, but the formulations in his extremely (and deservedly) popular expositions have had enormous influence. The lucid (if deeply uncritical) texts of Terence Hawkes and Terry Eagleton have also been crucial mediators between the gurus and the congregation.

11. "The statement that everything in language is negative is true only if the signified and the signifier are considered separately; when we consider the sign in its totality, we have something that is positive in its own class. . . . Although both the signifier and the signified are purely differential and negative, when considered separately, their combination is a positive fact: it is even the sole type of facts that language has" (Saussure, *Course*, 120–21).

12. The crucial role of deixis in ensuring reference to particulars—or in ensuring that (general) meanings have particular referents—is significantly overlooked by post-Saussureans. Without the explicit deixis of the present speaker or the implicit deixis (anaphora), parasitic upon the notion of explicit deixis, of the absent narrator in a written story, reference—the cash value of language—would fail. Deixis is not just a matter of the body being available as the 0,0,0 of a set of coordinates, as the basis of "here" and "now" and so of the determination of specific, unique (i.e., actual) referents. Deixis has to be mobilized, exploited, *meant.* This shows how wide of the mark are characteristically post-Saussurean claims such as Dragan Milovanovic's assertion that "Language speaks the subject, providing it with meaning at the cost of being" (*Postmodern Law and Disorder: Psychoanalytic Semi-*

*otics and Juridic Exegeses*, [Liverpool: Deborah Charles Publications, 1992], 7). This is something to which we shall return. (See also note 15.)

13. Terence Hawkes, *Structuralism and Semiotics* (London: Methuen, 1977), 16–17.

14. I have discussed this passage in more detail in *Not Saussure*, 70–79.

15. It is worthwhile spelling this out a little bit further, with reference to Derrida's notion of the transcendental signified. The term is introduced in a seemingly crucial but very obscure passage in his *Of Grammatology*, trans. Gayatri Chakravorty Spivak (Baltimore: The Johns Hopkins University Press, 1976), 50:

> Since one sign leads to another *ad infinitum*, from the moment there is meaning, there are nothing but signs. *We think only in signs.* Which amounts to ruining the notion of the sign at the very moment when, as Nietzsche says, its exigency is recognized in the absoluteness of its right.

One is left only with "play"—the free play of the signifier:

> the absence of the transcendental signified as the limitlessness of play, that is to say as the destruction of onto-theology and the metaphysics of presence.

The chain of signs never terminates at anything that is simply present; it always points to the next sign, so that it is reduced to signs of itself—to traces. More generally, we never touch presence unmediated by signs—immediate presence, presence itself. Immediacy is an impossible, elusive dream. Thus Derrida.

It is, of course, untrue that the emergence of "meaning" in signs results in the evaporation of presence to traces of traces. The paw marks are a sign to me of a lion. But, over and above their character as signs of a *general* meaning, they have *particular* existence as depressions in the dust. They are that which means "lion," they carry the meaning "lion" on this occasion; but that is not all that they are. They continue to exist when they are not meaning and they have features that are quite independent of their meaning, or that are not involved in the specification of the meaning "lion." Their location two inches rather than two feet from a particular bush, their being dampened by rain, their being seven in number rather than six, etc., are not features relevant to the discrimination of their general meaning. So, existing and signifying, being present and signifying something that is absent, are not alternative states. On the contrary, being a sign is predicated upon being an existent that is present.

We are no more entitled to infer from the fact that one sign may lead to another *ad infinitum* that the signified is never reached than to conclude from the fact that since every effect is itself a cause and the causal chain is interminable that there are no effects—that the chain of causes never "arrives at" effects. Of course, there is no "transcendental effect" which would bring the causal chain to an end; but this does not mean that there are no effects at all. *Omne causa de causis*—all causes themselves arise from causes—does not imply that there are "no effects/things/events." The fact that the signifier does not reach a "transcendental signified" should be cause for concern only if the signifier were the sign itself and the "transcendental signified" were a referent. And manifestly they are not.

The "transcendental signified" is a useful smokescreen. It is used, variously, to mean: the signified; the meaning of a sign; the referent of a chain of signs in use; or the ultimate termination of the chain of signs in plenitude or closure of meaning, in absolute presence or in God. So those who believe in the reality of the signified and do not believe that language is an endless chain of signifiers apparently also believe in the transcendental signified; and to believe in the transcendental signified is to believe that the chain of signs comes to an end, that a final meaning can be reached and that the place where the latter is reached is identical to the place where signs give way to absolute presence—to believe, in other words, in God, Who is both absolute presence and final meaning. Since most contemporary readers are liable to be atheists and since, too, Husserlian "absolute presence" is so elusive, merging the notion of the signified with that of the *transcendental* signified is certain to discredit it and to give plausibility to the idea that discourse is an endless chain of signified-less signifiers. The concept of the "transcendental signified" enables Derrida to move almost imperceptibly from the position that no sign opens directly on to a plenitude of meaning/presence, i.e., is underwritten by God, to the claim that there is no signified at all, or none, anyway, that the linguistic signifier can reach out to.

Incidentally, Derrida, and his epigones, endlessly repeat the unfounded assertion that the notion of (unmediated) presence is a specifically Western illusion. This is factually incorrect, as this passage indicates:

> In the [Eastern] mystical consciousness, Reality is apprehended directly and immediately, meaning without any mediation, any symbolic elaboration, any conceptualization, or any abstractions; subject and object become one in a timeless and spaceless act that is beyond any and all forms of mediation. Mystics universally speak of contacting reality in its "suchness," its "isness," its "thatness," without any intermediaries; beyond words, symbols, names, thought images.
>
> (*Quantum Questions*, ed. Ken Wilber [Boulder and London:
> New Science Library, Shambhala, 1984], 7.)

16.  See "The Mirror Stage, A Critical Reflection," in *Not Saussure*.

17.  See Émile Benveniste, "Subjectivity in Language," in *Problems in General Linguistics*, trans. Mary Elizabeth Meek (Coral Gables, Fla.: University of Miami Press, 1971). See also, "Changes in Linguistics" and "Man and Language," in the same collection.

18.  Catherine Belsey, *Critical Practice* (London: Methuen, 1980), 59.

19.  Benveniste, "Subjectivity in Language," 224.

20.  Milovanovic, *Postmodern Law and Disorder*, 7. It was, of course, Heidegger, rather than the post-Saussureans, who first asserted that language speaks us—"Die Sprache spricht," as he said in his essay on Georg Trakl. He has been a major influence on postmodernist thought, as are the hermeneutic philosophers such as Gadamer and Ricoeur, who were themselves influenced by Heidegger. For the latter, language constitutes us and we are unable to break out of the hermeneutic circle within which understanding moves. This notion has been an all-pervasive one, linked with Derrida's infamous assertion that "there is nothing outside of the text" and Rorty's popular relativization of truth to "interpretive communities." Moreover, it has a venerable ancestry—being premodern, as well as postmodern. The most relevant ancestors are, of course, the Counter-Enlightenment thinkers Hamann and Herder. It was Hamann who asserted that "language was the organ and criterion of truth." And for Herder, thought was inseparable from language, and hence from the culture expressing and expressed in the language. Truth resided in the world picture, the spirit of the *volk*.

The political expressions of organicist, anti-universalist, *völkisch* thought should not need spelling out, but it is surprising how few post-Saussurean thinkers seem to be aware of the potential consequences of their liberation from the notions of transcendent truth and from, in Lyotard's words, "the grand narratives of emancipation and enlightenment." Paul de Man's intellectual affiliations are regarded as an anomaly and Heidegger's politics quite separate from the philosophical notions that have been so powerfully influential on post-Saussurean thinkers. The relationship between postmodernism and far-right-wing thought has been set out with exceptional clarity by Rainer Friedrich, in "The Deconstructed Self in Artaud and Brecht," *Forum for Modern Language Studies* 26, no. 3 (July 1990): 282–95. What is not often appreciated is that the excited postmodernist gigglers are too shallow even to be right-wing; or to notice that they are not on the side of the (progressive) angels.

21. Grice's theory of discourse—with its emphasis on the production as well as the reception of meaning and the role of the recipient's understanding of the producer's intentions, of what the producer intends to mean, in ensuring communication—is crucial to an understanding of the errors in post-Saussurean discourse theory. I have discussed Grice's theories and their metaphysical implications in *The Explicit Animal*, chapter 8, "Recovering Consciousness."

22. See the chapter on Derrida ("Walking and Difference") in *Not Saussure*.

23. This notion of an "enabling constraint" (a term I owe to a generous, and painstaking, anonymous referee of an earlier version of this section) is a cousin of the Chomskeian notion of "rule-governed creativity." Chomsky's achievement was to recognize a problem that no one else had fully appreciated—which is that of explaining how it is that we are all inducted, through language, into a common world organized in roughly the same way for each of us. It is, as Gellner points out, the same problem as Durkheim's, except that Chomsky considers not only major categories, such as "God," "Man," etc., but also "the rank and file of our conceptual army." There must be constraints upon the ways in which we organize experience, and those constraints come from language. This raises the further problem of how we acquire the syntactic and semantic rules of language. Associationist psychology is simply unable to account for the fantastic number of rules regulating the use of individual words and the generation of verbal-strings that a five-year-old child has acquired in its short life. Associationism is the road not to the shared world but to private delirium. "All our concepts," Gellner points out, "are compulsively disciplined" (*Reason and Culture* [Oxford: Blackwell, 1992], 126). According to Chomsky, we are endowed with a Language Acquisition Device built into the brain that is primed to extract from the sloppy phonetic and semantic material served up to us a set of general principles, so that we are able to combine a restricted set of phonetic elements in a phonetically, syntactically, and semantically disciplined, and yet creative, way. Within these constraints, we are able to generate an infinity of novel sentences that meet our individual communicative needs.

Gellner worries that this account of the constraints built into language means that "Language has its reasons of which the mind knows nothing" (124):

> We mainly, or exclusively, think through language; but if our speech is bound by deep rules of which we know nothing (and the unraveling of which is the object of linguists' inquiries which are arduous and highly contentious), then it would seem that we are not and cannot be in control of our own thought.                (127)

The examples we have already given indicate that, in practice, things are not as bad as Gellner fears. Theoretical considerations cannot abolish the distinction between ordinary, seemingly deliberate, chosen talk and a fever of words shouted out in a delirium. Nor can they undermine the fact (discussed in the next paragraph of the main text) that I can, and frequently do, use even off-the-shelf "empty" phrases such as "Hello" to express very complicated and calculated communicative intents. What Chomsky has done is not to produce evidence that we do not express ourselves through language but to show that our self-expression is even more mysterious than we thought it was. Likewise a physiologist's demonstration of the existence of reflexes does not prove that there is no such a thing as deliberately walking to one place rather than another, only that the interaction between mechanisms and free action (or the use of mechanisms to bring about free action) is yet more puzzling.

24. "Language [*langue*] is not a function of the speaker; it is a product that is passively assimilated by the individual. . . . Speech [*parole*], on the contrary is an individual act. It is wilful and intellectual" (*Course*, 14).

25. The displacement of the self by language—summarized in the assertion that language speaks us rather than vice versa—has recently lost some of its fashionability, since it has been recognized that making language a "concrete entity" and an agent is no more convincing than ascribing concreteness and agency to the self. As Geoffrey Galt Harpham has expressed it:

> It is now easier than it once was to see in the new discourse on language not a severely literal description but a dense mesh of metaphors of intentional agency that were necessarily drawn from the only possible model for such agency, the old-fashioned subject. Without anyone's remarking on the fact, the "concrete entity" of language had implicitly been described . . . as a "who" making choices, guiding decisions, encouraging values, giving and taking orders.
>
> ("Who's Who," *London Review of Books*, 20 April 1995, 12–14.)

In short, behaving like a "who" rather than a "what." This is an example of what I have elsewhere characterized as the Fallacy of Misplaced Explicitness, whereby consciousness, agency, deliberation, etc., which are denied in the place where they are intuitively to be found, are ascribed to material objects or automatic processes (see the relevant entry in Tallis, *Psycho-Electronics*).

What, of course, goes missing from the self or subject when it is replaced by discourse is the personal coherence that characterizes a self; for example, the link between my being a witness to an accident (because of being in a particular place) and feeling obliged to call for help; or between my undertaking to do something at time t and my actually doing it at time t'.

26. See *The Explicit Animal*, "Recovering Consciousness," where the relationship between the arbitrariness of linguistic signs and the limitless human capacity for developing self-consciousness, for making things explicit, is set out in greater detail.

## 9.  LITERARY THEORY AND ITS DISCONTENTS

### JOHN R. SEARLE

### I

I WANT TO DISCUSS literary theory, and it is important to say "literary *theory*" and not "literary *criticism*." I will discuss, not in great detail, three different approaches to questions concerning textual meaning—Stanley Fish's claim that the meaning of a text is entirely in the reader's response;[1] the claim made by Stephen Knapp and Walter Michaels that the meaning of a text is entirely a matter of the author's intention; and the view of Jacques Derrida that meaning is a matter of, well, what? Meanings are "undecidable" and have "relative indeterminacy," according to Derrida. Instead of fully determinate meanings, there is rather the free play of signifiers and the grafting of texts onto texts within the textuality and the intertextuality of the text.

It is an odd feature of the extensive discussions in contemporary literary theory that the authors sometimes make very general remarks about the nature of language without making use of principles and distinctions that are commonly accepted in logic, linguistics, and the philosophy of language. I had long suspected that at least some of the confusion of literary theory derived from an ignorance of well-known results, but the problem was presented to me in an acute form by the following incident. In a review of Jonathan Culler's book *On Deconstruction* (1982) that I wrote for the *New York Review of Books*,[2] I pointed out that it is not necessarily an objection to a conceptual analysis, or to a distinction, that there are no rigorous or precise boundaries to the concept analyzed or the distinction being drawn. It is not necessarily an objection even to theoretical concepts that they admit of application *more or less*. This is something of a cliché in analytic philosophy: most concepts and distinctions are rough at the edges and do not have sharp boundaries. The distinctions between fat and thin, rich and poor, democracy and authoritarianism, for example, do not have sharp boundaries. More important for our present discussion, the distinctions between literal and metaphorical, serious and nonserious, fiction and nonfiction, and, yes, even true and false, admit of degrees and all apply *more or less*. It is, in short, generally accepted that many, perhaps most, concepts do not have sharp boundaries, and since 1953 we have begun to develop theories to explain why they *cannot*. Indeed, in addition to examinations of the problem of vagueness, there have been quite extensive discussions of family resemblance, open texture, underdetermination, and indeterminacy. There has

John R. Searle. "Literary Theory and Its Discontents." Originally published in *New Literary History* 25, no. 3 (Summer 1994): 637–67. Reprinted by permission of the author.

even developed a booming industry of fuzzy logic whose aim is to give a precise logic of vagueness.

When I pointed out that Derrida seemed to be unaware of these well-known facts, and that he seemed to be making the mistaken assumption that unless a distinction can be made rigorous and precise, with no marginal cases, it is not a distinction at all, he responded as follows: "Among all the accusations that shocked me coming from his pen, and which I will not even try to enumerate, why is it that this one is without doubt the most stupefying, the most unbelievable? And, I must confess, also the most incomprehensible to me."[3] He goes on to expound his stupefaction further:

> What philosopher ever since there were philosophers, what logician ever since there were logicians, what theoretician ever renounced this axiom: in the order of concepts (for we are speaking of concepts and not of the colors of clouds or the taste of certain chewing gums), when a distinction cannot be rigorous or precise, it is not a distinction at all. If Searle declares explicitly, seriously, literally that this axiom must be renounced, that he renounces it (and I will wait for him to do it, a phrase in a newspaper is not enough), then, short of practicing deconstruction with some consistency and of submitting the very rules and regulations of his project to an explicit reworking, his entire philosophical discourse on speech acts will collapse even more rapidly.                                      (123–24)

I will gladly yield to his authority when it comes to "the taste of certain chewing gums"; but, alas, I have to disappoint him and not "renounce" his "axiom," for the reason that, logically, in order to renounce something you must first have believed it, and I have never believed it. Indeed he is perhaps the only living philosopher I know who still believes this "axiom," for he writes: "It is impossible or illegitimate to form a *philosophical concept* outside this logic of all or nothing" (117). Further, he writes: "I confirm it: for me, from the point of view of theory and of the concept, 'unless a distinction can be made rigorous and precise it isn't really a distinction.' Searle is entirely right, for once, in attributing this 'assumption' to me" (126). And then he continues (somewhat more plaintively), "I feel close to those who share it. I am sufficiently optimistic to believe that they are quite numerous and are not limited, as Searle declares, with rather uncommon condescension, to 'audiences of literary critics' before whom he has 'lectured'" (126).

It is clear from this discussion that Derrida has a conception of "concepts" according to which they have a crystalline purity that would exclude all marginal cases. It is also clear that on his view intentional states also have this feature, and they even have what he calls "ideal self-presence."

He is mistaken in supposing that these views are widely shared. In fact, I cannot think of any important philosophers of language who now hold such views, and it is not surprising that he gives no examples. The very opposite has been more or less universally accepted for the past half century, and I will shortly give some reasons why Derrida's conception of "concepts" could not be correct. For reasons I will explain at the end, when Derrida makes remarks like these he reveals not only his ignorance of the history of the philosophy of language, but his commitment to a certain traditional pre-Wittgensteinian conception of language.

I believe that Derrida's ignorance of the current philosophical commonplace that concepts are in general quite loose at their boundaries is typical of a more widespread ignorance of certain fundamental linguistic principles. In what follows, I will argue that if you get certain fundamental principles and distinctions about language right, then many of the issues in literary theory that look terribly deep, profound, and mysterious have rather simple and clear solutions. Once you get the foundations right, many (though of course not all) of the problems are solved. So what I am going to do, rather tediously I fear, is to state about half a dozen principles, all but one of which are taken for granted by people who work in linguistics and the philosophy of language, as well as in psychology, psycholinguistics, and cognitive science generally, but which are not always well appreciated in literary studies.

Now let me say in advance that, of course, there is nothing sacred about these principles. Perhaps we can refute all of them. But I also have to tell you in advance that there are certain rules of investigation. The first is this: If I say, for example, "There is a distinction between types and tokens," it is not enough to say, "I call that distinction into question." You actually have to have an argument.

## II

So much by way of introduction. I will now list half a dozen principles, and then I will conclude by applying these very general principles to literary theory and to questions concerning the nature of textual meaning.

### THE BACKGROUND OF INTERPRETATION

The first point that I want to mention is the most controversial, and though I have been arguing for this thesis for almost twenty years, many people whose opinions I respect still disagree with me about it. I call it the thesis of the Background:[4] The functioning of meaning in particular and intentionality in general is possible only given a set of background capacities, abilities, presuppositions, and general know-how. Furthermore, in addition to the pre-intentional background, the functioning of meaning and intentionality generally requires a rather complex network of knowledge, beliefs, desires, and so on. Speech acts in particular cannot be fully determined by the explicit semantic content of a sentence or even by the speaker's intentional content in the utterance of the sentence, because *all meaning and understanding goes on within a network of intentionality and against a background of capacities that are not themselves part of the content that is meant or understood, but which is essential for the functioning of the content.* I call this network of intentional phenomena "The Network" and the set of background capacities "The Background."

The utterance of any sentence at all, from the most humble sentences of ordinary life to the most complex sentences of theoretical physics, can be understood only given a set of Background abilities that are not themselves part of the semantic content of the sentence. One can appreciate this point if one thinks of what is necessary to understand utterances of simple English verbs. Consider, for example, the utterance "Cut the grass." Notice that we understand the utterance of the word "cut" quite differently from the way we understand the occurrence of "cut" in "Cut the cake" (or "Cut the cloth," "Cut the skin," and so on), even though the word "cut" appears univocally in both sentences. This point is illustrated if you consider that if I say to somebody, "Cut the cake," and he runs a lawnmower over it, or if I say, "Cut the grass," and he runs out and stabs it with a knife, we will, in each case, say that he did not do what he was literally told to do. How do we know, as we do know, which is the correct interpretation? We do not have different definitions of the word "cut," corresponding to these two occurrences. We understand these utterances correctly because each utterance presupposes a whole cultural and biological Background (in addition to a Network of beliefs, etc.). Furthermore, for some simple occurrences of "cut" we simply do not understand the sentence at all because we lack a Background that would fix the interpretation. Suppose I hear the sentence "Cut the mountain." I understand all the words, but I do not understand the sentence or the corresponding speech act. What am I supposed to do if I am told to "cut the mountain"? To put the point generally, both literal meaning and speaker meaning only determine a set of conditions of satisfaction—that is, they only determine what counts as, for example, obeying an order, what counts as a statement's being true, what counts as a promise being kept—given a set of Background capacities.

I believe, furthermore, that it is impossible, in principle, to put the Background presuppositions into the literal meaning of the sentence. You can see this point if you consider actual examples. Suppose I go into a restaurant for a hamburger. Suppose I say, "Give me a hamburger, medium rare, with ketchup and mustard, no relish." That utterance, we may suppose, is intended almost entirely literally. I have said more or less exactly what I meant. But now suppose they bring me the hamburger encased in a solid block of concrete. The block is a yard thick and requires a jackhammer to open it. Now, did they do what I literally asked them to do? My inclination is to say "No."

One might object: "Well, you didn't tell them everything, you didn't say 'no concrete.'" But this objection starts one down a road one does not wish to follow. Suppose I go in next time and I say "Give me a hamburger, medium rare (and so on), and this time NO CONCRETE." There are still an indefinite number of ways they can misunderstand me. Suppose they bring me a three-thousand-year-old petrified Egyptian hamburger. They might say, "Oh, well you didn't say it had to be a *new* hamburger. This is a genuine King Tut hamburger. What's wrong with that?"

It will not be adequate for me to say, "Well, I'll block that—next time I'll say 'No concrete and no petrified hamburgers.'" There will still be an indefinite number of possible ways to misunderstand my utterance. Next time they might bring me a hamburger that is a mile wide so that they have to knock down a wall of the restaurant and use a lot of trucks and cranes to get the edge of it near me. And so—more or less indefinitely—on.

I am not saying: perfect communication is impossible and we cannot fully say what we mean. On the contrary, our communications are often perfectly adequate; and we can, at least in principle, say exactly what we mean. What I am saying is: meanings, concepts, and intentionality *by themselves* are never sufficient to determine the full import of what is said or thought because they function only within a Network of other intentionality and against a Background of capacities that are not and could not be included in literal meaning, concepts, or intentional states. In my technical jargon: intentionality, intrinsic or derived, determines conditions of satisfaction only within a Network and against a Background.

I said earlier that many valid distinctions are not rigorous and precise, but it is a consequence of the thesis of the Background that in the traditional Fregean sense according to which a concept is a kind of pure crystalline entity that allows for no marginal cases, there simply cannot be any such concepts. Any use of any concept is always relative to a Background, and consequently a concept can determine its conditions of satisfaction only relative to a set of Background capacities. What goes for concepts and meanings also goes for intentional mental states. If I am right about the Background, there are no such things as intentional states having the kind of purity they were alleged to have by the traditional authors on intentionality in the phenomenological tradition, such as Husserl.[5]

I think several philosophers who have become dimly aware of the thesis of the Background find it very disconcerting, even threatening. They correctly see that it renders a certain type of context-free account of meaning and intentionality impossible, and so they mistakenly conclude that any theory of meaning is impossible. This is especially true of those who see the *contingency* of the Background.[6] Our ways of acting do not have to be the way they in fact are; there is nothing transcendentally necessary about them. But it is a mistake to conclude from this that theorizing is thereby rendered impossible. The Background does not make theory impossible; on the contrary, it is one of the conditions of possibility of any theorizing, and where language and mind are concerned it is one of the chief objects of the theory.

At the beginning of our discussion it is important to get clear about (a) the basic idea of the Background and (b) the distinction between meaning as representational content on the one hand and Background as nonrepresentational capacity on the other, because all of the other principles and distinctions I am going to make depend on these points.

## THE DISTINCTION BETWEEN TYPES AND TOKENS

I believe the distinction between linguistic types and linguistic tokens was first formulated by Charles Sanders Peirce. If, for example, I write the word "dog" on the blackboard three times, have I written one word or three? Well, I have written one *type* of word, but I have written three different *token* instances of that word. That is, the token is a concrete physical particular, but the type is a purely abstract notion. We need this distinction because the identity criteria for types and tokens are quite different. What makes something a case of "the same token" will be different from what makes it "the same type." You might think that this is such an obvious distinction as to be not worth making, but in fact a fair amount of the confusion in literary theory rests on a failure to get that distinction straight. Derrida introduces a notion that he calls *iterabilité*, the idea that linguistic forms are, in his sense, iterable. But the notion is very ill defined in his work. He is unable to say clearly what the domain of its application is, that is, what entities exactly are iterable. He speaks of "marks" and "signs," but actual marks and signs, that is, actual physical tokens, are precisely not iterable. It is, rather, the *type* of mark that can have different instantiations. This is one way of saying that it is types and not tokens that allow for repeated instances of the same. Derrida lacks a clear answer to the question, "What is it that gets iterated?" in part because he seems to be unaware of this distinction.

The distinction between types and tokens, by the way, is a consequence of the fact that language is rule-governed or conventional, because the notion of a rule or of a convention implies the possibility of repeated occurrences of the same phenomenon. The rules of syntax, for example, have the consequence that the same type can be instantiated in different tokens. There are further type-token distinctions within the type-token distinction. Thus, for example, when Hemingway wrote *The Sun Also Rises*, he produced a token, which inaugurated a new type, his novel, of which your copy and my copy are two further tokens.

## THE DISTINCTION BETWEEN SENTENCES AND UTTERANCES

A third crucial distinction is that between a *sentence*, or any other linguistic element, and an *utterance* of a sentence or other linguistic element. A sentence, type or token, is a purely formal structure. Sentences are defined formally or syntactically. But an utterance of a sentence is typically an intentional action. To utter a sentence is to engage in a piece of intentional behavior.

We need this distinction, in addition to the distinctions between types and tokens, because, though every utterance involves the production or use of a token, the same token can function in quite different utterances. To take an example from real life, there is a man who stands on a street corner at a school near my house, and every so often he holds up a sign on which it says "STOP." He is protecting small children from passing motorists. Each time he holds up the stop sign, he is making a separate utterance and thus is performing a separate speech act. But he uses one and the same sentence token for each different utterance. Thus, the identity criteria for the elements of the sentence/utterance distinction do not exactly match the identity criteria for the domain of the type/token distinction. Once again, we need this distinction between the sentence or other symbol, on the one hand, and the intentional utterance of that sentence or symbol, on the other, because the identity criteria are quite different.

## THE DISTINCTION BETWEEN USE AND MENTION

A fourth distinction, common in logic and philosophy, is that between the use of expressions and the mention of expressions. If, for example, I say, "Berkeley is in California," I use the word "Berkeley" to refer to a city. If I say, " 'Berkeley' has eight letters," I am mentioning the word "Berkeley" and talking about it. It should be obvious that the use-mention distinction allows for the fact that one can sometimes both use and mention an expression in one utterance. Consider, for example, the occurrence of "stupid" in the following utterance: "Sam is, as Sally says, 'stupid.' "[7]

Now, when Derrida speaks of what he calls *citationalité*, one would think that he is talking about the use-mention distinction, but as with *iterabilité*, he does not give a coherent account of the notion, and this leads him to say things that are obviously false. For example, he thinks that when a play is put on, the actors in the play do not actually use words but are only citing them. The production of a play is a case of *citationalité*. This mistake reminds me of the freshman student who liked Shakespeare well enough but was dismayed to find that Shakespeare used so many familiar quotations in his plays. In the standard case of producing a play, the actors produce the words written by the playwright, they actually *use* the words, they do not *mention* or *cite* them.

## COMPOSITIONALITY

A crucial principle in understanding language is the principle of compositionality. Syntactically, the principle says that sentences are composed of words and morphemes according to grammatical formation rules. Semantically, the principle says that the meanings of sentences are determined by the meanings of the elements and by their arrangement in the sentence. Thus, for example, we understand the sentence "John loves Mary" differently from the way we understand the sentence "Mary loves John," because, though each sentence has the same morphological elements, they are combined differently and thus each sentence has a different meaning.

Both the syntactical and the semantical aspect of compositionality are crucial to any account of language. If you have certain sorts of rules[8] for combining linguistic elements, then the syntactical aspect of compositionality has the consequence that with a finite stock of words and a finite list of rules for combining them into sentences, you can generate an infinite number of new sentences. The semantic consequence is that you can take familiar words with familiar meanings and get completely new semantic units, new meaningful sentences, whose meanings you have never encountered before, but will understand immediately, given that you understand the meanings of the words and the rules for combining them. Most of the sentences you hear, by the way, you have never heard before. One can easily produce a sentence that one has never heard before and that one is unlikely ever to hear again. For example, if I now utter the sentence, "I just found a Chevrolet station wagon at the top of Mount Everest," I have uttered a sentence that you are unlikely to have heard before and are unlikely ever to hear again; but it is easily recognizable as an English sentence, and you have no difficulty in understanding it. This is an important principle because, among other reasons, it has the consequence that any attempt to define the meaning of a sentence in terms of the *actual* intentions of actual speakers is bound to fail. There is an infinite number of meaningful sentences that no actual speaker ever has uttered or ever will utter with any intentions at all.

## THE DISTINCTION BETWEEN SENTENCE MEANING AND SPEAKER MEANING

It is crucial to distinguish between what a sentence means, that is, its literal sentence meaning, and what the speaker means in the utterance of the sentence. We know the meaning of a sentence as soon as we know the meanings of the elements and the rules for combining them. But of course, notoriously, speakers often mean more than or mean something different from what the actual sentences they utter mean. That is, what the speaker means in the utterance of a sentence can depart in various systematic ways from what the sentence means literally. In the limiting case, the speaker might utter a sentence and mean exactly and literally what he or she says. But there are all sorts of cases where speakers utter sentences and mean something different from or even something inconsistent with the literal meaning of the sentence.

If, for example, I now say "The window is open," I might say that, meaning literally that the window is open. In such a case, my speaker meaning coincides with the sentence meaning. But I might have all sorts of other speaker's meanings that do not coincide with the sentence meaning. I might say, "The window is open," meaning not merely that the window is open but that I want you to close the window. A typical way to ask people on a cold day to close the window is just to tell them that it is open. Such cases, where one says one thing and means what one says, but also means something else, are called "indirect speech acts." Another sort of case where there is a split between the sentence meaning and the speaker meaning is the case where the speaker utters a sentence, but does not mean what the sentence means literally at all, but means the utterance metaphorically. So, for example, somebody in a diplomatic context might say, "The window is open," meaning that there are opportunities for further negotiations. In yet another sort of case, a speaker might utter the sentence ironically, meaning, if all the windows were closed, the opposite of what the sentence means. In all of these sorts of cases there is a systematic set of relations between speaker meaning and sentence meaning. *It is absolutely crucial to understand that metaphorical meaning, ironical meaning, and indirect speech act meaning are never part of sentence meaning.* In a metaphorical utterance, for example, none of the words or sentences changes their meanings; rather, the speaker means something different from what the words and sentences mean.

Now, it is tempting to think—and especially tempting to think when one is analyzing literary texts—that there must be an answer to the question, "Which is prior, literal sentence meaning or speaker meaning?" But, as usual, one has to be very careful about these questions. The answer depends on what one means by "prior." If by the question one means, "What are the conditions of possibility of being able to communicate with sentences at all?" well then, of course, sentences have to have standing, conventional sentence meanings in order that we can use them to talk with. In that sense, communication in actual natural languages requires standing sentence meanings in order that there can be particular speaker meanings in particular utterances.

On the other hand, in any actual speech situation, what matters for the identity of the speech act is the speaker meaning, and that is what sentences are for. Sentences are to talk with. A sentence type is just the standing possibility of an intentional speech act. So in one fundamental sense, speaker meaning is prior, since the speech act is the basic unit of communication, and the identity criteria for the speech act are set by speaker meaning.

Having said that, however, one does not want to give the impression that a person can just say anything and mean anything. Furthermore, for any complex thought it will not in general be possible to have, much less communicate, that thought unless there is some conventional device, unless there is some conventional sentential realization of the possible speaker meaning. For example, suppose I want to say to somebody the equivalent of: "If only Roosevelt had not been so sick at the time of the Yalta conference in 1943, no doubt the situation in the Eastern European countries in the postwar decades would still have been unfortunate in the extreme, but it seems reasonable to suppose that the sequence of disasters and catastrophes that overcame those countries would at least have been less onerous than it in fact was." Now try to imagine what it would be like to think that thought, only without any words, or to try to communicate that thought to someone without any words but just by gestures. The point I am making here is that there is an extremely complex set of relations between the conventional sentence meaning and the realized or articulated speaker meaning. In one sense, speaker meaning is primary, since the main purpose of the whole system is to enable speakers to communicate to hearers in the performance of intentional speech acts. But it would be a mistake to conclude that communication can be separated altogether from conventional sentence meaning. It is possible to communicate, or even to think, complex thoughts only given a structure of sentence meanings.

I have already said in passing what I now want to make fully explicit. Sentence meaning is conventional. Only given a knowledge of the conventions of the language can speakers and hearers understand sentence meanings. The relationships between sentence meaning and speaker meaning depend on a set of principles and strategies by means of which speakers and hearers can communicate with each other in ways that enable speaker meaning to depart from sentence meaning. I gave several examples of that earlier: metaphor, indirect speech acts, and irony. In all these cases, there is a systematic set of relations between the conventional meaning of the sentence and the particular historical speaker's meaning, as determined by the speaker's intentions on particular historical occasions.[9]

What, then, is the role of the hearer? The speech act will not be successful unless the hearer understands it in the way that the speaker intended it. And sometimes, of course, the speaker fails to communicate, and hearers understand his or her utterance in ways that are quite different from the way that he or she intended. Anyone who has ever written or spoken on a controversial subject knows this to be the case. And it is, of course, impossible to correct or prevent all of the potential misunderstandings. There will always be some ingenious ways of misunderstanding that you could not have foreseen. Any teacher who has ever read students' examination answers will know that there are ways of misunderstanding your views that you would have thought inconceivable if you had not actually found them there on the final exam. The role of the hearer, then, is crucial for the successful performance of the speech act. In the ideal speech situation, the speaker says something, he or she has a certain speaker meaning that may or may not coincide with the sentence meaning, and the hearer understands that meaning, that is, he or she understands the illocutionary intentions of the speaker.

In the previous sentence I say "illocutionary intentions" because, although speaker meaning is entirely determined by speakers' intentions, not just any old intention with which a sentence is uttered is relevant to meaning. For example, the intention to speak loudly or to annoy the hearer is not an illocutionary intention and therefore is not a meaning intention. It is a very tricky task to try to identify meaning intentions precisely.[10]

## THE DISTINCTION BETWEEN ONTOLOGY AND EPISTEMOLOGY

I promised half a dozen claims, but there are two more. It is crucial to distinguish questions of what exists (ontology) from questions of how we know what exists (epistemology). The failure to make this distinction was the endemic vice of Logical Positivism, and such a failure is built into any form of verificationism. Where language is concerned, often we cannot know what someone meant or intended by an utterance, but this has no relevance to the question whether there was a definite meaning and intention in his utterance. Epistemic questions have to do with evidence, and though they are immensely important to biographers, historians, and critics, they are of very little interest to the theory of language. Roughly speaking, as theorists we are interested in the ontology of language, and the epistemological question—how do you know?—is irrelevant.

This purely theoretical distinction between ontology and epistemology is immensely important for the practice of textual criticism for the following reason. If we are having difficulty in interpreting a text because of lack of evidence, say about the author's intention, we are in an epistemic quandary and can reasonably look for more evidence. If we are having difficulty with a text because there is simply no fact of the matter about what the author meant, we are dealing with an ontological problem of indeterminacy, and it is fruitless to look for more evidence. The standard mistake is to suppose that lack of evidence, that is, our ignorance, shows indeterminacy or undecidability in principle. I have been amazed to see how often this mistake is made, and I will give examples later.

## SYNTAX IS NOT INTRINSIC TO PHYSICS

One last point: though every sentence token is indeed a physical entity, it does not follow that syntactical categories are physical categories. Every sentence token is physical, but "sentence token" does not identify a physical natural kind. There are, for example, no acoustic, chemical, gravitational, electromagnetic, etc., properties that all and only sentences of English have in common and that could therefore serve to delimit the class of sentences of English.

This has the consequence that the relations between textuality and intentionality can become complex, as we shall see.

## III

I now want to use the apparatus that we have developed in these eight principles and distinctions to demonstrate that many of the controversial issues in literary theory have clear and simple solutions, once these principles are kept in mind. I begin with a simple example. Knapp and Michaels's claim that a sequence of marks found, say, on a beach could not really be words or even examples of language unless produced intentionally. They make this claim as the first step in their attempt to show that all meaning is intended speaker meaning and that, in consequence, the meaning of any text is necessarily what the author or authors intended it to mean.

Suppose you found on the beach a set of marks that looked exactly like this:

> A slumber did my spirit seal
> I had no human fears:
> She seemed a thing that could not feel
> The touch of earthly years.[11]

Now these marks certainly look as if they constituted a sentence composed of English words, but according to Knapp and Michaels in their article "Against Theory," published in 1982, there are no words, sentences, or even language unless the marks were produced intentionally.[12] Naturally, they agree, one would seek an explanation of the marks, but there would be only two possibilities: "You will either be ascribing these marks to some agent capable of intentions (the living sea, the haunting Wordsworth, etc.), or you will count them as nonintentional effects of mechanical processes (erosion, percolation, etc.). But in the second case—where the marks now seem to be accidents—will they still seem to be words? Clearly not. They will merely seem to *resemble* words." And later: "*It isn't poetry because it isn't language.*"[13]

So, according to Knapp and Michaels, what look like words and sentences are not such and are not even language! They announce this remarkable claim as if it were a discovery of considerable theoretical significance. But if what I have said is correct, there cannot be any substance to the issue as to whether or not a given formal structure is a string of words or a sentence and thus an example of *language*. The answer must follow trivially from the definition of wordhood and sentencehood. In linguistics, philosophy, and logic, words and sentences are standardly defined purely formally or syntactically. That is, words and sentences are defined as formal types that can be instantiated in different physical tokens. It could not be the case that the formal sentence types require the intentional production of tokens in order to be sentences, because there is an infinite number of formal types and only a finite number of actual human intentions. But from the definition of formal types, it follows trivially that a formal type can be instantiated in a concrete physical token, independently of the question whether or not that token was produced as a result of human intentions. So, on the standard definition of wordhood and sentencehood, it is simply not true that in order for a physical token to be a word or sentence token it must have been produced by an intentional human action.

On the standard definition, in short, Knapp and Michaels's claim is simply false, because they are confusing sentences with utterances. They might, however, be proposing an alternative definition for these notions. In that case, the issue cannot be a substantive one; it can only be a question of whether or not one wants to make an intentional utterance part of the criterion for wordhood and sentencehood. So it follows from what I have just said that what they say is either just a confusion (that is, they are confusing intentionally uttered tokens with tokens) or, if it is not a confusion, then it amounts to a proposal for altering our standard definitions.

Thus, what they present as a *discovery* amounts to either an obvious *falsehood* or a proposal for a *redefinition*. Notice, in this case, that once the distinctions are made clear, the other points fall into place; it then becomes an easy question whether or not some object that has the structure of a word or sentence really is a word or sentence token.

This same criticism of Knapp and Michaels was made by George Wilson in an article in 1992.[14] In their reply to Wilson, Knapp and Michaels claim that they were not interested in such general issues in the philosophy of language but only in the interpretation of texts, and that they never intended to deny "that the physical features of a set of marks intrinsically determine whether that set of marks is a token of a sentence type in a given language."[15]

This answer to Wilson will not do, first because it is inconsistent with everything they say in their 1982 article and second because it cuts the ground from under their thesis that all textual meaning is necessarily speaker meaning.

To see these points, let us go back to the beach and examine the marks in the sand. In the passages quoted above they explicitly deny that the marks in question, unless produced intentionally, constitute words, and they even deny that they are an instance of language. The marks are not poetry because *a fortiori* they are not even language. Such claims are made throughout the article: "For a sentence like 'My car has run out of gas' even to be recognizable as a sentence, we must have already postulated a speaker and hence an intention" (727). And about the sentences on the beach: "what had seemed to be an example of intentionless language was either not intentionless or not language" (728). Again, "Our point is that marks produced by chance are not words at all but only resemble them" (732). So what are we to conclude? Are the intentionless marks on the beach really a sentence of English regardless of how they were produced (as they admit in 1992), or are the marks not even words at all, but only marks resembling words (as they claimed roundly in 1982)? Whatever the answer, the two accounts are inconsistent.

In their 1982 article, as part of their general attack on intentionless meaning, Knapp and Michaels attack me precisely because I make the distinction between the conventional meaning of a sentence and the intentional meaning of a speech act, between sentence meaning and speaker meaning. I argue in numerous works that the meaning of a speech act is determined by the author's illocutionary intentions, in contrast to the meaning of a sentence, which is determined by the rules of the language of which the sentence is a part. They are at some pains to reject this distinction and to argue that I did not go far enough. According to them I was correct in stating that something was a speech act only if produced with illocutionary intentions, but I failed to see that something was a word, language, and so on, only if it was also produced with speaker's intentions. Indeed, I debated Walter Michaels on precisely this point when he lectured to the Berkeley Cognitive Science Group. A relevant passage in Knapp and Michaels's 1982 article is worth quoting in full:

> Even a philosopher as committed to the intentional status of language as Searle succumbs to this temptation to think that intention is a theoretical issue. After insisting, in the passage cited earlier, on the inescapability of intention, he goes on to say that "in serious literal speech the sentences are precisely the realizations of the intentions" and that "there need be no *gulf* at all between the illocutionary intention and its expression." *The point, however, is not that there need be no gulf between intention and the meaning of its expression but that there can be no gulf* [Italics added]. Not only in serious literal speech but in *all* speech what is intended and what is meant are identical. In separating the two Searle imagines the possibility of expression without intention and so, like Hirsch, misses the point of his own claim that when it comes to language "there is no getting away from intentionality." Missing this point, and hence imagining the possibility of two different *kinds* of meaning, is more than a theoretical mistake; it is the sort of mistake that makes theory possible. It makes theory possible because it creates the illusion of a choice between alternative methods of interpreting.[16]

This passage makes it crystal clear that Knapp and Michaels are denying that there can be a gulf between the speaker's intended meaning and the meaning of the sentences that the speaker uses to express that meaning, and thus they are denying that there are "two different *kinds* of meaning," sentence meaning and speaker meaning, just as the earlier quoted passages make it crystal clear that in their 1982 article they denied that a string of marks found on the beach but produced without any intentionality is a string of "words" or even "language" at all.

They cannot consistently say that Searle is wrong to distinguish between the identity criteria of speech acts in terms of speakers' meaning and the identity criteria of sentences in terms of the conventions of a language and at the same time argue that they have accepted this distinction all along.

Nor will it do to retreat from "word" and "language" to "text," as Knapp and Michaels do in their 1992 article, because the same sort of problem arises for "text" and even "literary text" that arose for "sentence." That is, if "text" is defined in such a way that the author's illocutionary intentions are essential to the identity of the text and the "meaning of the text" is defined in such a way that it is identical with the author's intentions in the production of the text, then their thesis follows trivially. This is an acceptable definition, and one I used in *Expression and Meaning*,[17] but the point I am making now is: However defined, a text consists of words and sentences, and they continue to have a *linguistic* meaning, whatever the intentions of the author. Furthermore, it is also possible to define "text" syntactically, as a set of words and sentences, however produced. And in that case the meaning of a text can be examined quite apart from any authorial intentions, because the meaning of the text consists in the meanings of the words and sentences of which it consists.[18]

Knapp and Michaels announce, "At the center of our account of interpretation is the view that an interest in the meaning of any text—when it really is an interest in the text's meaning and not in something else—can never be anything other than an interest in what the text's author or authors intended it to mean."[19] Construed one way this is trivially false; construed another way it is trivially true. It is possible to regard any text as a collection of words and sentences and to examine its meaning as such. So construed, their view is trivially false. It is also possible—and, I have argued, it is really essential—to regard a text as the product of speech acts and to insist on understanding the author's intentions in understanding the text. So construed, their view is trivially true. *But once they concede, as they do in their 1992 article, that "the physical features of a set of marks intrinsically determine whether that set of marks is a token of a sentence type in a given language," then they have already conceded what they claim to be denying, namely that there are at least two types of meaning, the conventional sentence meaning and the intentional speaker's meaning.*

For this reason, Knapp and Michaels are mistaken in criticizing E. D. Hirsch for recommending the course they adopt. They criticize him for recommending that interpreters of literary texts should look for the author's intentions, because they claim "the object of inquiry is *necessarily* the author's intended meaning."[20] They criticize Hirsch for recommending what they regard as inevitable, but on their own account (1992), it is not inevitable. They recognize that a set of marks can be a *fully meaningful* token of a sentence type in a given language without any intentionality by way of which those marks were produced. But to say that implies that the meaning of such sentences can be examined independently of any intentionality of speakers. This allows for precisely the possibility that they have been claiming to deny, namely, that a text can be regarded as either a string of sentence tokens and its meaning examined independently of any authorial intent, or a text can be regarded as a product of an intentional speech act and its meaning examined in terms of the intentions of the author.

Many critics interested in textual meaning have been concentrating on the meanings of words and sentences for decades. This may produce bad criticism, but it is not a logical impossibility—or, rather, it is a logical impossibility only given a certain definition of "text."

Nor will it evade these inconsistencies to say that Knapp and Michaels are interested in the problems of literary theory only as an "attempt to govern interpretations of particular texts by appealing to an account of interpretation in general,"[21] and that they were not interested in these abstruse questions about language in general. This will not do for two reasons: First, they do in fact make claims about language in general and not just about literary texts. Indeed, they even criticize other authors—me, for example—who are not especially concerned with literary texts, and they use examples such as "My car ran out of gas" that have no special connection with literary texts. In short, their claims about literary interpretation in 1982 were a consequence of more general claims about language. And second, it is impossible to be interested in questions of texts, meaning, interpretation, and so on, without making certain theoretical assumptions, because all of these notions are defined in terms of certain theoretical principles and distinctions. Once you get the principles and distinctions straight, most of the conclusions fall out trivially and unproblematically. Unless these principles and distinctions are made explicit, confusion is almost bound to ensue, as I hope the example of Knapp and Michaels illustrates.

To summarize, in their 1982 article Knapp and Michaels make three claims relevant to our present inquiry: (1) Marks are only words, language, sentences, and so forth, if produced intentionally. (2) Linguistic meaning is entirely a matter of speakers' intentions. There are not two kinds of meaning—sentence meaning and speaker meaning. There is only intentional speaker meaning. (3) For this reason interest in the meaning of a text is necessarily an interest in the author's intention. There is no other possibility.

I have argued as follows: On the standard account of linguistic meaning as articulated in the first half of this article, all of these claims are obviously false. It is important to see, however, that once Knapp and Michaels concede, as they do in their 1992 response, that it is possible to construe something as a sentence token even though it has not been produced intentionally (contrary to claim 1), then claims 2 and 3 collapse, because once you concede that something is a sentence token, you concede that it has a linguistic meaning. But once you allow that sentence tokens have linguistic meaning independently of their intentional production, then you allow that any literary text can be construed as a set of sentences and these sentences have a linguistic meaning. Like Hirsch's claims, Knapp and Michaels's claim amounts to a recommendation that we should concentrate on intended author's meaning. But they have not shown that any such concentration is necessary or inevitable.

Though claim 1 of Knapp and Michaels is not acceptable as it stands, there is a much deeper truth underlying it. From the fact that every syntactical token is a physical entity, such as an acoustic blast or a physical mark, it does not follow nor is it the case that syntactical categories are categories of physics. Notions such as "sentence of English" cannot be defined in terms of, for example, acoustics or mechanics. There are no acoustic properties, for example, that all and only English sentences have in common. There is a deep reason for this, and that is that the entire system of syntax exists only relative to human intentionality, including the Network and the Background. It is only given a knowledge of the rules of the grammar and the Background ability to use that knowledge that there can be such a thing as a formal or syntactical definition of sentencehood in the first place. So, though Knapp and Michaels are mistaken in thinking that every sentence token requires an intentional production in order to be a sentence, they are right if they think that intentionality is crucial to the existence of syntax as a system.

IV

I now want to use the results of our discussion of Knapp and Michaels to draw some general conclusions regarding issues in literary theory. A recurring controversy in literary theory has been over the question "What is the role of the author's intention in determining the meaning of a text?" In the history of this subject, a series of competing answers has been proposed to this question, sometimes giving rise to polemical disputes about the relative merits of the different answers. What I want to suggest is: In many cases the different answers are not competing answers to the same question, but noncompeting answers to quite different questions. So, for example, if the question is, "Does the author's intention determine the meaning of the text?" the answer will depend on what criteria of identity we adopt for "the text." Do we count the sequence of sentence tokens that instantiate particular sentence types as constituting the text? If what constitutes a text is simply a sequence of sentences, then the answer to the question has to be "no." It does not matter what intentions the author had when he produced particular tokens of those types, because if we are just looking at the tokens as instantiations of sentence types, and if sentence meaning is conventional, it follows, again trivially, that the sentences of the text have a meaning that is quite independent of any authorial intention. Once the question is made precise in this way, it is easily answered.

But, of course, there is another question, and that is, "Does the author's illocutionary intention determine what speech acts he or she is performing, that is, what intentional speech acts he or she is performing in the production of the text?" Does authorial intention determine speaker's meaning? To this question, I hope it is obvious that the answer is "yes." The author's intention determines which intentional act the author is performing. So the answer to this question has to be trivially and obviously "yes" in the same way that the answer to the previous question has to be trivially and obviously "no." And, of course, there are still further questions that we could ask.

A third question could be: "Does the author's intention determine how the text is interpreted; does it determine the meaning that the hearer understands?" I hope it is obvious that the answer to this question is "no." Notoriously, authors are understood in ways that are quite different from what they actually intended.

Now, these three different claims—that meaning is a linguistic property of the text, that meaning is a matter of authorial intention, and that meaning is in the reader—certainly look like competing theories. The first view says that the meaning of the text is strictly a matter of what the words and sentences mean in the language. This, I take it, is the formalist view of the "New Critics." The second view says that the meaning of the text is entirely determined by authorial intention, and this is the view of Knapp and Michaels in their 1982 essay "Against Theory." The third view says that the meaning of the text is entirely a matter of the reader's response to it, and this is (or was) the view of Stanley Fish and the so-called "reader response" theories of criticism.

Now, these certainly look like competing answers to the question "What is the meaning of the text?" And, in particular, they look like competing answers to the question "What is the role of authorial intention in determining the meaning of the text?" But if what I have said is correct, the appearance of disagreement is at least partly an illusion. Once this question is made sufficiently precise, it will be seen that there are three different questions to which three different answers are being offered.

Well, one might say, "So much the better. We welcome this ecumenism and perhaps everybody can go home happy." The problem, however, is that in the literature on this subject, very strong claims are made on behalf of these different answers, and these claims tend to exceed what has in fact been proved. For example, Stanley Fish in his book *Is There a Text in This Class?* makes the following statement, "Whereas I had once agreed with my predecessors on the need to control interpretation lest it overwhelm and obscure texts, facts, authors, and intentions, I now believe that interpretation is the source of texts, facts, authors, and intentions."[22] I am afraid that this paragraph contains an exaggeration. From the correct observation that the effect of a text on a reader or hearer is not always determined either by the literal meaning of the sentences or by the intentions, conscious or unconscious, of the speaker or author, it does not follow that, for example, texts, facts, authors, and intentions have their source in interpretations. The claim is absurd. The fact that, for example, Mount Everest has snow and ice near its summit is in no way dependent on anybody's interpretations. And as far as texts and authors and intentions are concerned, I, for example, have on frequent occasions been an author, I have created texts and I have had intentions. Often communication broke down because, to a greater or lesser extent, I failed to communicate my intentions, or they were unclear even to me, or my intentions were poorly expressed. But the interpretations were the source of neither text nor author nor intention. My existence as an author and the existence of my texts and intentions were in no way dependent on the understandings and misunderstandings that my readers may have experienced in encountering my texts.

Similarly, it seems to me that Knapp and Michaels make claims that are much too strong. They claim to have shown that the meaning of a text is entirely determined by the intentions of the author. But, as we have seen, the meaning of the speech act performed in the production of the text should not be confused with the meaning of the actual sentences that are constitutive of the text. The sentences have a conventional meaning independent of whatever authorial intentions they may have been uttered with.

## V

I now turn to the most obscure of these cases, Derrida's attempt to "deconstruct" the notion of meaning that occurs, for example, in the theory of speech acts and in particular the idea that the intentions of the speaker suffice to determine the meaning of the utterance and hence the identity of the speech act. The argument is not easy to summarize. In part, at least, it is the mirror image of the claim made by Knapp and Michaels. They claim that something is not even a text unless it is produced with authorial intention. Derrida claims that since the very same text can function totally detached from any authorial intention, the author cannot control the meaning of his or her utterance. Because the sign is subject to "iterability" and "citationality," the horizon of the author's intention is insufficient to control the free play of the signifiers.

The "argument," if I may so describe it, occurs at various places in Derrida's writings, but since it is never stated clearly as an attempt to present a valid argument, the best way to convey it is to quote some representative passages and then summarize its drift:

[The sign] is constituted in its identity as mark by its iterability.[23]

The possibility of its [the mark] being repeated *another* time—breaches, divides, expropriates the "ideal" plenitude or self-presence of intention, of meaning (to say) and, a fortiori, of all adequation between meaning and saying. Iterability alters, contaminating parasitically what it identifies and enables to repeat "itself"; it leaves us no choice but to mean (to say) something that is (already, always, also) other than what we mean (to say), to say something other than what we say *and* would have wanted to say, to understand something other than . . . etc.[24]

My communication must be repeatable—iterable—in the absolute absence of the receiver or of any empirically determinable collectivity of receivers.[25]

Such passages raise two questions: First, why does Derrida suppose that intentions have what he calls " 'ideal' plenitude or self-presence"? On my view intentions could never have such mysterious properties, because intentions can never function in isolation. Intentions—along with other biological phenomena such as beliefs, desires, and so on—function only within a highly contingent Network of other intentional states and against a preintentional Background of capacities. So, for the purpose of this discussion, which has to do with Derrida's criticisms of my views, we just have to ignore the claim about ideal self-presence. He simply misunderstands my position. The second question is: What does he mean by "iterability"? Here is part of his answer: "Let us not forget that 'iterability' does not signify simply, as Searle seems to think, repeatability of the same, but rather alterability of this same idealized in the singularity of the event, for instance, in this or that speech act."[26] Furthermore, he writes:

> The iterability of the mark does not leave any of the philosophical oppositions which govern the idealizing abstraction intact (for instance, serious/non-serious, literal/metaphorical or sarcastic, ordinary/parasitical, strict/non-strict, etc.). Iterability blurs a priori the dividing-line that passes between these opposed terms, "corrupting" it if you like, contaminating it parasitically, qua limit. . . . Once it is iterable, to be sure, a mark marked with a supposedly "positive" value ("serious," "literal," etc.) can be mimed, cited, transformed into an "exercise" or into "literature," even into a "lie"—that is, it can be made to carry its other, its "negative" double. But iterability is also, by the same token, the condition of the values said to be "positive." The simple fact is that this condition of possibility is structurally divided or "differing-deferring [*différante*]."[27]

These passages occur in a polemic that Derrida wrote against me, as well as against J. L. Austin. The argument is so confused that for a long time I could not believe he was actually advancing it. But such passages as those quoted exhibit his confusions clearly. Here is the argument in summary:

> There are a series of distinctions made by analytic philosophers, the distinction between metaphorical and literal, between true and false, between meaningful and meaningless, between felicitous and infelicitous, between parasitical and non-parasitical, and so on. All of these distinctions are undermined ("corrupted," "contaminated,") by the phenomenon of iterability. Here is how it is done Any mark or sign must be iterable, but because of this iterability, the sign or mark can always be disrupted from its point of origin and used for some completely different purpose. What was true can be false. What was literal can be metaphorical. What was felicitous can be infelicitous. What was meaningful can be meaningless, and so on. There-

fore, all of the original distinctions are undermined. Furthermore, this undermining cannot be avoided since iterability is the condition of possibility of something being a mark in the first place.

What is wrong with this argument? Roughly speaking, everything. Most important, from the fact that different tokens of a sentence type can be uttered on different occasions with different intentions, that is, different speaker meanings, nothing of any significance follows about the original speaker meaning of the original utterance token. Nor does anything follow that contaminates the basic distinctions I mentioned earlier. None of these distinctions is "contaminated" or "corrupted" or anything of the sort by the possibility of producing different tokens of the same type with different speaker meanings. Since the issues are of some interest and since Derrida's argument reveals a neglect of the distinctions I cited earlier, I will go through it slowly by stating my views in contrast to his.

On my view, if I say, "It is hot in here" or "Give me a hamburger," it is up to me, *modulo* the Network and the Background, what I mean. If I say, "It is hot in here," and I mean, "It is hot in here," then that is a matter of my illocutionary intentions. If I say, "It is hot in here," and mean ironically that it is cold in here, that is up to me as well. Of course, on my view I can't say just anything and mean just anything. There is a complex set of relations between sentence meaning and speaker meaning, and all meaning and intentionality depend on relations to the Network and the Background. It is a consequence of my view that meaning and intentionality have a much more radical form of indeterminacy than is conceivable to Derrida, because they have no independent functioning at all: they function only relative to a nonrepresentational Background. However, given a fixed set of Background capacities and a Network of intentionality, including a shared mastery of a common linguistic apparatus between speaker and hearer, meaning and communication can be completely determinate. When I complain about the heat or order a hamburger, I am, in general, able to do so without ambiguity or vagueness, much less indeterminacy. Within the constraints set by the conditions of the possibility on the speech act, I can say what I want to say and mean what I want to mean.

This account preserves intact the basic distinctions between metaphorical/literal, true/false, and so on. Derrida thinks that iterability refutes this account. He thinks that because marks and signs are iterable, that is, repeatable and alterable on subsequent occasions, that somehow or other the original speaker has lost control of his utterance and that he therefore has no choice "but to mean (to say) something that is (already, always, also) other than what we mean," and so on, and so on.

I believe that his argument is a massive tissue of confusions and that if we apply the distinctions I have been trying to elucidate, his various points simply dissolve. Suppose I say, "It's hot in here," meaning: it's hot in here. Now, what follows about my speaker meaning from the fact that the sentence type, of which my utterance was a token, is, in his sense, iterable and citable? Nothing whatever follows.

I uttered a sentence token that exemplified a particular sentence type. My utterance had a sentence meaning that is determined by the operation of the principles of compositionality operating over the conventional elements that composed it, including such structural elements as intonation contour, word order, and sentence boundary. My utterance had a particular speaker's meaning, which in this case coincided with sentence meaning. All of this apparatus functions within the Network and against the Background. If communication is successful, I will have succeeded in performing a serious, literal, nondefective speech act. What follows from the fact that I or somebody else might take a completely *different* token of the same sentence *type* and do something completely different with it? To repeat, nothing whatever follows. The intentionality of the speech act covers exactly and only that particular speech act. The fact that someone might perform *another* speech act with a *different* token of the same type (or even another speech act, with the same token) has no bearing whatever on the role of speaker's utterance meaning in the determination of the speech act.

Derrida holds the bizarre view that speech act theory is somehow committed to the view that the intentionality of the particular token speech act must somehow control every subsequent occurrence of tokens of the same sentence types. Since the idea that speakers' intentionality might achieve such a thing is quite out of the question, he thinks he has uncovered a weakness in the theory of speech acts. But speech act theory—my version or anybody else's—is not committed to any such view, and his failure to grasp this point derives from his failure to grasp the type/token distinction, the sentence/utterance distinction, and the speaker meaning/sentence meaning distinction. It is just a simple confusion to suppose that from the fact that I say something and mean something by what I say, and somebody else might use other tokens of those very words and sentences to mean something completely different, it follows that somehow or other I have lost control of my speech act.

I will give one more example. Someone once wrote a poem that began, "A slumber did my spirit seal. . . ." Now, suppose I decide I want to use that line to call my dog. "A slumber did my spirit seal!" I shout around the neighborhood until my dog comes home. Is the fact of my doing so supposed to show that Wordsworth has lost control of *his* meaning, of *his* speaker meaning?

There are lots of places where Derrida makes this mistake, but one of the clearest is in his book *Spurs*. There he discusses the following example.

The German for "I have forgotten my umbrella," with quotation marks around it, was found in Nietzsche's *Nachlass*, that is, among his unpublished manuscripts. The discussion of this token occupies several pages of Derrida's book. I will not quote all of it, but enough, I hope, to give the flavor of the text. He begins with an epistemic claim.

> It might have been a sample picked up somewhere, or overheard here or there. Perhaps it was the note for some phrase to be written here or there. There is no infallible way of knowing the occasion of this sample or what it could have been later grafted onto. We never will know *for sure* what Nietzsche wanted to say or do when he noted these words, nor even that he actually *wanted* anything.[28]

So far, this seems correct. But so far, it is merely an epistemic point. There are facts of the matter for which we lack evidence, and, consequently, we cannot know them for sure. But Derrida tries to derive ontological conclusions from this epistemic point. He writes:

> The remainder (*restance*) that is this "I have forgotten my umbrella" is not caught up in any circular trajectory. It knows of no proper itinerary which would lead from its beginning to its end and back again, nor does its movement admit of any center. Because it is structurally liberated from any living meaning [*vouloir-dire vivant*], it is always possible that it means nothing at all or that it has no decidable meaning. There is no end to its parodying play with meaning, grafted here and there, beyond any contextual body or finite code. It is quite possible that that unpublished piece, precisely because it is readable as a piece of writing, should remain forever secret. But not because it withholds some secret. Its secret is rather the possibility that indeed it might have no secret, that it might only be pretending to be simulating some hidden truth within its folds. Its limit is not only stipulated by its structure but is in fact intimately con-fused with it. The hermeneut cannot but be provoked and disconcerted by its play.[29]

It is not surprising that the "hermeneut" is disconcerted, because the hermeneut in question does not know enough philosophy of language to give an intelligent account of the fragment. There is a rather large number of mistakes in this passage, and I will simply list the three most obvious:

(1) The German sentence type has a conventional meaning in German. Given the Network and the Background, the sentence meaning is quite determinate. In a different Background culture, where all umbrellas were made of chocolate and eaten for dessert after use in rainstorms, the literal sentence meaning could be understood differently (it might mean: I have forgotten the taste of my umbrella); but given the existing cultural, biological, and linguistic situation in the late nineteenth century, the literal interpretations are unprob-

lematic. (Do I have to go through them?) It is, by the way, only because we know the meaning of the German sentence that we are so confident of its translation into French and English.

(2) The sentence token actually found in Nietzsche's *Nachlass* exemplifies the type and consequently shares with it this conventional meaning. It is just a mistake for Derrida to say, "it is always possible that it means nothing at all." Or rather it is more than a mistake, because he has no idea what the "it" is of which he says that it might "mean nothing at all"—type? token? utterance? speech act? At the very least he is confusing sentence meaning with speaker meaning. That is, from the fact that Nietzsche might not have meant anything by the production of the token (speaker meaning) it does not follow that the token might "mean nothing at all" (sentence meaning).

(3) For accidental historical reasons, we do not know what, if anything, Nietzsche intended by this sentence token. In particular, we do not know if he intended it as a speech act or if he was simply considering the sentence itself. But from the epistemological limitations, from our lack of evidence, nothing whatever follows about the ontology. If Nietzsche had a determinate speaker's meaning, then he had it. Whether or not we can know it is of biographical rather than theoretical interest. To put this point quite simply, the lack of empirical evidence has no bearing whatever on the issue of indeterminacy or undecidability in principle. Indeterminacy and undecidability in principle are problems that arise *given perfect knowledge*, given that all of the epistemic questions have been solved. It is simply a confusion to apply these notions in an epistemic fashion.[30] Derrida is here confusing epistemology with ontology.

In short, Derrida fails to show that the occurrence of this fragment in Nietzsche's *Nachlass* is of any theoretical interest whatever. Once all the distinctions are brought to bear, the only remaining difficulties are epistemic, and, consequently, though they may be of practical importance to biographers, historians, and critics, they are of no theoretical interest in developing a theory of language. The idea that there is some mystery or some tremendously obscure and difficult point that will disconcert the hermeneut only shows that the hermeneut is confused to begin with.

My impression is that a fair amount—not all of course, but a fair amount—of what passes for passionate controversies and deeply held divisions within literary theory is in fact a matter of confusions having to do, as I said earlier, not with competing answers to the same question, but with noncompeting answers to different questions, different questions that happen to be expressed in the same vocabulary because the authors are not making the distinctions that I am urging. In the most extreme cases, it seems to me that a lot of what passes for profundity and enormous obscurity and insight into deep and mysterious matters is in fact dependent on a series of rather simple confusions. These confusions derive in turn from the lack of a theoretical apparatus within which to pose and answer the questions that preoccupy us. No doubt the apparatus I have proposed is in various ways inadequate, but without some such apparatus we cannot clearly pose or intelligibly answer the questions. Once those confusions are sorted out, then much of the pretension just dissolves like so much mist on a hot day.

## VI

I have suggested that a good deal of the confusion in literary theory derives from a lack of awareness of familiar principles and results. How is this possible? Well, partly it derives from the hyperspecialization of contemporary intellectual life. It is not easy for someone specializing in twentieth-century American literature, for example, to become knowledgeable about the invention of the predicate calculus by Gottlob Frege in Germany in the late nineteenth century. But the normal ignorance due to disciplinary boundaries is aggravated by the fact that among the people in literary studies who have written on issues in linguistics and the philosophy of language and have been taken as authorities on these issues, there are some who don't seem to know very much about these subjects. I earlier cited some mistakes that Derrida seems to be making, and I believe these are typical of deconstructionist authors. I believe the mistakes derive not only from neglect of the principles I have mentioned but also from a general lack of familiarity with the recent history of the philosophy of language, as well as recent linguistics.

"The philosophy of language," as we now use that expression, begins only in the late nineteenth century with Frege, and continues through the works of Russell, Moore, Wittgenstein, Carnap, Tarski, Quine, and others right up to the present day. Earlier philosophers often wrote about language, but their contribution to contemporary discussion in the philosophy of language is minimal, unlike their contribution to most other areas of philosophy. As far as I can tell, Derrida knows next to nothing of the works of Frege, Russell, Wittgenstein, and so on, and one main reason for his incomprehension of Austin's work, as well as of mine, is that he does not see how we are situated in, and responding to, that history from Frege to Wittgenstein. When Derrida writes about the philosophy of language he refers typically to Rousseau and Condillac, not to mention Plato. And his idea of a "modern linguist" is Benveniste or even Saussure. All of these are important and distinguished thinkers , and their work should certainly not be neglected, but you will not understand what is happening today if that is where your understanding stops. Derrida is himself a very *traditional* philosopher in a sense that one can state briefly but precisely by saying that his work proceeds from assumptions that are pre-Wittgensteinian. For example, only a pre-Wittgensteinian philosopher could have made those remarks I quoted at the beginning of this article about the purity of concepts.

The fact that he is a traditional philosopher in this sense has three consequences for the present discussion: First, when Derrida sees the failures of the traditional assumptions, he thinks something is lost or threatened. He thinks, for example, that the possibility of misunderstandings creates some special problem for the theory of speech acts beyond the commonsense problem of trying to figure out what people mean when they talk. Furthermore, in desperation, he invents new jargon to try to deal with the failures of the old. "Iterability" and "*différance*" are just two examples. But this jargon does not enable him to overcome the foundationalist assumptions of the philosophical tradition. At best it provides a temporary disguise for the failures of the assumptions.

Second, in all of his quite lengthy attacks on speech act theory, both mine and others', Derrida still cannot grasp that this work does not proceed from his traditional philosophical assumptions. He finds it literally incomprehensible ("stupefying" is his word) that I do not accept the traditional assumptions. For example, he thinks that if I use the notion of intentionality I must be engaged in some Husserlian foundationalist project; he supposes that where I make distinctions, the very enterprise must exclude the possibility of marginal cases; and he has nothing to say about my theory of the Background and its importance for the philosophy of language. Since he appears to know next to nothing of the history of the philosophy of language over the past hundred years, he has not grasped that in everything I write I take these works, and especially the works of the later Wittgenstein, *for granted*. One of my many problems is: given that certain traditional foundationalist approaches to problems in philosophy are now more or less out of the question, how does one now, in a post-Wittgensteinian era, construct a theory of mind and language? Derrida, working from assumptions that are pre-Wittgensteinian, seems unable to comprehend what it would be like to construct a post-Wittgensteinian theory of speech acts or intentionality. He thinks any such theory must be traditional in the way that, for example, Husserl was a traditional philosopher. For these reasons, perhaps the best way to answer Derrida is not to provide a list of his mistakes, misunderstandings, and omissions, but to expose the traditionalist assumptions that make them inevitable.

Third, because of their lack of familiarity with the advances made and the distinctions drawn during the past century or so, Derrida and other deconstructionist authors tend to lack credibility in contemporary philosophy and linguistics.

In deconstructionist writing in general and Derrida in particular, the intellectual limitations of the background knowledge do not prevent a certain straining of the prose, an urge to achieve a rhetorical effect that might be described as the move from the exciting to the banal and back again. The way it works is this: Derrida advances some astounding thesis, for example, writing came before speaking, nothing exists outside of texts, meanings are undecidable. When challenged, he says, "You have misunderstood me, I only meant such and such," where such and such is some well-known platitude. Then, when the platitude is acknowledged, he assumes that its acknowledgement constitutes an acceptance of the original exciting thesis. I will conclude by illustrating this rhetorical move with three examples.

The first and most obvious is his claim that writing ("archewriting," which "communicates with the vulgar concept of writing") comes before speech, that written language precedes spoken language. "I shall try to show that there is no linguistic sign before writing," he promises.[31] But the claim that writing precedes speaking is obviously false, as any historical linguist can attest. Of course, Derrida does not mean this. What he means in large part is that many of the features of written speech are also features of spoken language. When this point is acknowledged, he then supposes that he has demonstrated the original thesis. From the exciting to the banal and back again.

A second case concerns his discussion of meaning. Derrida is notorious for the view that meanings are unstable. He even uses words such as "undecidability" and "relative indeterminacy" in these discussions.[32] This view has the consequence, for example, that all readings are to some degree misreadings, that all understandings are misunderstandings, and so on. But when challenged he tells us that he did not mean any of that at all. Now he says that he meant to remark only that "the essential and irreducible *possibility* of *mis*understanding or of '*in*felicity' must be taken into account in the description of those values said to be positive."[33] So the original daring thesis now amounts to the platitude that misunderstandings and infelicities are always possible. But this does not seem to prevent him or his followers from continuing to use the original formulations.

A third example of the same rhetorical maneuver is his claim that nothing exists outside texts "[*il n'y a pas de hors-texte*]." Here is what he says about it: "[*il n'y a pas de hors-texte*] means nothing else: there is nothing outside context."[34] So the original preposterous thesis that there is nothing outside of texts is now converted into the platitude that everything exists in some context or other. As Austin once said, "There's the bit where you say it and the bit where you take it back"[35]

## NOTES

The first version of this paper was delivered as a Romanell-Phi Beta Kappa lecture in Berkeley in 1987. Several people made helpful comments on earlier drafts. I am especially indebted to Isabelle Delpla, Hubert Dreyfus, Jennifer Hudin, Stephen Knapp, Dagmar Searle, Charles Spinosa, and George Wilson.

1. I gather that Fish no longer believes this. But it doesn't matter for our present discussion, which is designed to use this and other examples to illustrate certain general themes.

2. John R. Searle, "The Word Turned Upside Down," *New York Review of Books*, 27 October 1983, 74–79.

3. Jacques Derrida, "Afterword: Toward an Ethic of Discussion," in *Limited Inc*, ed. Gerald Graff (Evanston, Ill.: Northwestern University Press, 1988), 123.

4. I have discussed these points in much greater detail in other writings. See especially Searle, "Literal Meaning," *Erkenntnis* 13 (1978): 207–24; "The Background of Meaning," in *Speech Act Theory and Pragmatics*, ed. John Searle et al. (Dordrecht: Reidel, 1980), 221–32; *Intentionality: An Essay in the Philosophy of Mind* (Cambridge: Cambridge University Press, 1983); and *The Rediscovery of the Mind* (Cambridge, Mass.: MIT Press, 1992).

5. For brevity I state this position baldly. I argue for it in more detail elsewhere, especially in *Intentionality*.

6. The first philosopher known to me who had something like the idea of the Background was Hume. He saw that rationality depended on custom, practice, habit, etc. The philosopher most impressed and most unhinged by the radical contingency of the Background was Nietzsche. An important text on the Background is Ludwig Wittgenstein's *On Certainty* (New York: Harper & Row, 1969).

7. There are different ways of characterizing this distinction. The standard characterization in the logic textbooks is to say that when a word is mentioned and not used, the word itself does not actually occur at all; rather its proper name occurs. So, for example, if I write "Berkeley" with quotation marks around it, I have produced the proper name of the word and not the word itself. I think this characterization is mistaken. I think that the quotation marks do not create a new word but rather indicate that in the quoted occurrence the word is being mentioned and not used. On my view, the word does not suddenly get swallowed up into a proper name of itself just by writing quotation marks around it. But many respectable philosophers, Quine, for example, think that the word "Berkeley" no more occurs in this sentence than the word "cat" occurs in the word "catastrophe." They would agree that the sequence of letters occurs but the word itself does not occur; only its proper name occurs. I do not accept this part of the standard textbook account of the use-mention distinction, but in any case, it is crucial to get clear that there is a distinction between the use and the mention of expressions. For details, see Searle, *Speech Acts* (Cambridge: Cambridge University Press, 1969), especially chap. 4.

8. The rules have to be recursive. By itself, compositionality does not imply infinite generative capacity.

9. Searle, *Expression and Meaning* (Cambridge: Cambridge University Press, 1979), is in large part devoted to explaining these relations.

10. For a recent attempt, see Searle, *Intentionality*, chap. 6.

11. William Wordsworth, "A Slumber Did My Spirit Seal," in *William Wordsworth: The Poems*, ed. John O. Hayden, 2 vols. (New Haven, Conn.: Yale University Press, 1981), 1:364.

12. See Stephen Knapp and Walter Benn Michaels, "Against Theory," *Critical Inquiry* 8, no. 4 (Summer 1982): 723–42.

13. Knapp and Michaels, 728; my emphasis.

14. George M. Wilson, "Again, Theory: On Speaker's Meaning, Linguistic Meaning, and the Meaning of a Text," *Critical Inquiry* 19, no. 1 (Autumn 1992): 164–85.

15. Stephen Knapp and Walter Benn Michaels, "Reply to George Wilson," *Critical Inquiry* 19, no. 1 (Autumn 1992): 188.

16. Knapp and Michaels, "Against Theory," 729–30.

17. In analyzing the status of *fictional* texts, I wrote, "There used to be a school of literary critics who thought one should not consider the intentions of the author when examin-

ing a work of fiction. Perhaps there is some level of intention at which this extraordinary view is plausible; perhaps one should not consider an author's ulterior motives when analyzing his work, but at the most basic level it is absurd to suppose a critic can completely ignore the intentions of the author, since even so much as to identify a text as a novel, a poem, or even as a text is already to make a claim about the author's intentions" (*Expression and Meaning,* 66).

18. In 1987 they consider the possibility of defining textual identity on syntactical grounds alone but reject it for the strange reason that "if this criterion of textual identity were applied consistently, then any text could mean anything; indeed, any text could mean anything any other text could mean" (Stephen Knapp and Walter Benn Michaels, "Against Theory 2: Hermeneutics and Deconstruction," *Critical Inquiry* 14, no. 1 [Autumn 1987]: 58). This statement is not true. If the syntax of a sentence is defined relative to a language construed synchronically, it is simply not true that, for example, the sentence "The cat is on the mat" could mean anything. In some other language it might mean something else, but in the English of 1994, it has a quite definite meaning.

19. Knapp and Michaels, "Reply to George Wilson," 187.

20. Knapp and Michaels, "Reply to George Wilson," 187.

21. Knapp and Michaels, "Against Theory," 723.

22. Stanley Fish, *Is There a Text in This Class?* (Cambridge, Mass.: Harvard University Press, 1980), 16.

23. Jacques Derrida, "Signature Event Context," In *Limited Inc,* ed. Gerald Graff (Evanston, Ill.: Northwestern University Press, 1988), 7.

24. Derrida, "Limited Inc a b c . . . ," in *Limited Inc,* ed. Gerald Graff (Evanston, Ill.: Northwestern University Press, 1988), 61–62 (emphasis in original).

25. Derrida, "Signature Event Context," 7.

26. Derrida, "Afterword: Toward an Ethic of Discussion," 119.

27. Derrida, "Limited Inc a b c . . . ," 70 (Derrida's brackets at end of quotation).

28. Jacques Derrida, *Spurs: Nietzsche's Styles,* trans. Barbara Harlow (Chicago: University of Chicago Press, 1978), 123 (emphasis in original).

29. Derrida, *Spurs,* 131–33.

30. It is no accident that Gödel's famous incompleteness proof is given in a paper about *undecidable sentences* (Kurt Gödel, "Über formal unentscheidbare Sätze der Principia Mathematica und verwandter Systeme, I," *Monatshefte für Mathematik und Physik* 38 [1931]: 173–98) because he shows that in *Principia*-type systems there are true assertions that are not theorems. The point has nothing to do with lack of evidence.

31. Jacques Derrida, *Of Grammatology,* trans. Gayatri Chakravorty Spivak (Baltimore, Md.: Johns Hopkins University Press, 1976), 14.

32. Derrida, "Afterword: Toward an Ethic of Discussion," 145.

33. Derrida, "Afterword: Toward an Ethic of Discussion," 147 (emphasis in original).

34. Derrida, "Afterword: Toward an Ethic of Discussion," 136

35. Quoted in Richard Rorty, *The Consequences of Pragmatism: Essays, 1972–1980* (Minneapolis: University of Minnesota Press, 1982), 97.

## 10.  THE QUANDARIES OF THE REFERENT

### VINCENT DESCOMBES

THE FOLLOWING SHOULD BE READ as an outline for a historical and logical note on the notion of the referent.

Critics and philosophers are often called upon to take a stance on what might be called the "referential function of language." They must, for instance, decide whether in reading a text we refer back to *referents* (or to *the referent*) outside the text, whether we refer to other texts, or whether we must instead remain within the text we are reading.

I intend to show that such discussions need not be taken seriously. Does language turn outward toward something else, or inward toward itself? Does a book refer to the world, or only to *a* world constructed in the book? To find any single answer to these questions would be quite surprising. It is far more interesting to try to understand why we feel a need to speak of the referent, and what help we can expect from this concept.

### THE LINGUISTIC TURN

At the end of the last century, the focus of discussion was not the referent, but the *object*: the object of representation. The question posed was that of the limits of our representational capacity, and the urgency of the question came from the priority then given by philosophers to the epistemological question: How can I know something? If our ability to represent things is limited, so also will be our ability to know them. Hence the question in relation to any given thing: How can this thing become the object of my representation?

The epistemological question thus mandated a return to the examination of the mental faculties of the subject engaged in representational activity. But this meant entrusting the foundation of all knowledge to a single discipline that was, moreover, naturalistic. This in turn gave rise to the objection of psychologism. Another way of approaching the problem had to be found. Philosophers, for their part, defined that other way of examining the limits of representation a *transcendental* examination. Such a philosophical path was, obviously, speculative and unsatisfactory to those "researchers" who sought a positive or quasi-scientific solution to the problem. It was at this point that

Vincent Descombes. "The Quandaries of the Referent." Originally published in French as "Les Embarras du référant," *MLN* 101, no. 4 (September 1986): 765–80. Copyright © The Johns Hopkins University Press. Reprinted by permission of The Johns Hopkins University Press. English translation by Gwen Wells, originally published in *The Limits of Theory*, edited and with an introduction by Thomas M. Kavanagh, 51–75. Stanford: Stanford University Press, 1989.

there occurred what has been called "the linguistic turn in philosophy"[1] and the rise of linguistic theory.

If we were to take this linguistic turn seriously, we would assign the following significance to the exchange of the new *referent* for the old *object*. So long as there was talk of the object, we would say, it was imagined that human beings had direct access to things. The mind looked out onto things, as does a window onto a garden. It was believed that man could envision things, and situate himself in their midst, independently of language. This belief was contingent upon the unquestioning acceptance of a particular model: that of a *perception* in which the perceiver and the perceived are understood to confront each other directly. All mental activity (memory, imagination, thought, and so on) was laboriously reduced to this paradigm of a direct encounter between subject and object.

Today, we say *referent* rather than *object*. "Referent" means: an object to which reference is made by means of an expression belonging to language and used in discourse. Implicit in this definition is the assumption that our access to things is mediated through language. It is this language that must be analyzed if we are to determine anything whatsoever about the relation between a person and the world.

Such is the argument we might make to convey the essence of the linguistic turn. Curiously, this argument bears a strong resemblance to that used by the old philosophy—the "philosophy of representation"—against an adversary that was, at the time, called "common sense" or "naïve realism." The "turn," then, was an "idealistic turn in philosophy." Prior to this idealistic turn, naïve realists believed that they apprehended things directly, oblivious to the fact that things are given to us only in the representation we have of them. But the representation we have is that which we *can* have, given the constitution of our capacity to represent.

*Language* has replaced *representation*, but the "philosophy of representation" is perhaps not faring so badly. In any event, we can use the term "semiological hypothesis" to describe the widespread conviction that we today possess an adequate theory of the sign, a sure means of analyzing the "functioning" of "systems of signs" or of "symbolic systems."

## THE SEMIOLOGICAL HYPOTHESIS

The hypothesis is that we know today how to analyze symbolic systems. Since when have we known this? Some semiologists attribute our mastery of the symbolic to progress in the area of logic, others to progress in linguistics. In any case, our semiological science enables us to define that which is necessary in order that a group of signs function within an act of communication. It is here that the concept of the referent is introduced. Oswald Ducrot and Tzvetan

Todorov provide a good definition of this concept as it is generally used in texts of a semiological orientation:

> Since extra-linguistic communication often has an extra-linguistic reality as its object, a speaker must be able to designate its constituent objects: this is *the referential function of language* (the object or objects designated by an expression make up its referent). However, this reality is not necessarily *the* reality, or *the* world. Natural languages have in effect this power to construct the universe to which they refer: they can thus provide themselves with an imaginary *universe of discourse.* Treasure Island is a possible object of reference, just as is Grand Central Station.[2]

This indeed seems to be the accepted meaning of the term within the semiological school. Two particularities of this usage should be noted.

1. *An uncertainty regarding the user of the referential function.* The definition just proposed is of a hypothetical-deductive order. If, hypothetically, language exists in the service of communication, it must have a referential function because we must be able to designate referents. The referent is clearly the object designated as the object of the communicative act. But upon whom is it incumbent to do the designating? Who refers to the referent? Sometimes it is speakers who designate objects, sometimes it is natural languages that refer to a universe. (In this context, we would have to understand that, for example, the French language refers to *a* universe—necessarily one among other possibilities—and, furthermore, to a universe that it has itself constructed.)

2. *The initiation of a dialectic between outside and inside.* "Extralinguistic reality" is not necessarily reality plain and simple. It is the outside reality *of* the sequence of language under consideration rather than the reality *outside* the sequence in question. The sequence might be, for instance, *Treasure Island.* In the novel, reference is made to a treasure island. If we consider reality plain and simple, all we find is the material text of the novel and, outside of the text, no treasure island. This treasure island has no reality outside the novel's text, except within the novel itself. The extralinguistic reality referred to must thus be sought not outside, where the text says it is, but inside, where the text speaks of it. That which is outside must be sought inside. That which is in fact found within is given inside as if it were outside, and so on. This dialectic is a familiar one.

## THE FRENCH SCHOOL OF SEMIOLOGY

The French semiological school draws its inspiration chiefly from Ferdinand de Saussure. The word *referent*, however, is not used in the *Cours de linguis-*

*tique générale.*[3] The word seems to owe its favor in France to the translation into French of various articles by Roman Jakobson, among them his 1960 article on linguistics and poetics.[4] It should be recalled that, in this text, Jakobson distinguishes five functions of language, including a referential function. Jakobson, however, indicates that his analytic model, with its five functions, is an extension of Karl Bühler's, who in fact proposed three: *Darstellung* (corresponding to the third person), *Ausdruck* (corresponding to the first person), and *Appell* (corresponding to the second person). Bühler thus followed what today we would call a *pragmatic* model, in the sense that it was derived from the system of personal pronouns *I, you, he. Presentation, expression,* and *invocation*—this model can be expressed in a formula that distinguishes three necessary positions in any communicative act:

*Someone / speaks / about something / to someone.*

These three positions have more recently been labeled: addressor, referent, addressee. This formula clearly shows the necessarily relative nature of the referent: the referent corresponds to the *about something.* It is not, for instance, a flower or an island, but rather a flower that is spoken about, or an island that is mentioned somewhere.

One might ask what would happen if linguistic theory were to take another tack—one suggested, for instance, by a model such as the following:

*Someone / says / something / to someone / about something.*

In this configuration, the three persons of the singular are no longer sufficient to identify all the positions that must be occupied for communication to take place. The addressor, referent, and addressee are no longer adequate; there must also be a *says something.* Something must be said. This suggests that pragmatism will not suffice in all cases. The semantic conditions of a discourse cannot be reduced to a set of pragmatic instances (identify who is speaking, to whom, and so forth). It is this realization that enables us to speak of an *autonomy of grammar.*

If we nonetheless follow Bühler's pragmatic model (as he proposed it, or as it was completed by Jakobson), we are deriving our notion of the referent from our notion of the third person; *he, it*—that which is neither the source of the message nor the person to whom it is addressed. If this is the case, the referent must be conceived of in terms of a person (even if it is Émile Benveniste's "non-person," the person who cannot take part in the conversation). If it is not a person, it is a thing that can be individuated and identified.

Semiologists, however, do not speak of "the referential function of certain linguistic expressions" but rather, following Jakobson's example, of the referential function of language. For Jakobson, the five linguistic functions are attached to the totality of the message; specifically, the referential function corresponds to "the message's orientation toward the context."

Here again we encounter the difficulty mentioned previously: of what is the referent the referent? A moment ago, the possibilities were: of the speaker or of the language. Now they are: of certain expressions of the language (specifically, those that can be substituted for the personal pronouns and that are sometimes called "designators"), or of the message in its entirety.

## The Analysis of Language

Let us consider the following message:

> Caesar crossed the Rubicon.

What is its referent? In other words, to what in this message is the referential function of language attached? To the subject of the sentence? The referent would then be Caesar. To the whole sentence? The referent would then be an event: the crossing of the Rubicon by Caesar. These answers are *logically* different, which means that they correspond to two logically distinct concepts of the "referent." The word *Caesar* is a name, a designation. If this proper name refers to anything whatsoever, it must do so in conformity with the logic of proper names. Yet the event of Caesar's crossing the Rubicon, if it is the referent of anything at all, is not the referent of a name or a designation. The event is not *designated*, but rather *signified* by means of a nominalization of the initial message. To speak of an event (and thereby make it an object of discourse), one must start with a narrative proposition (for example, *Caesar crossed the Rubicon*) and change it into a name-like phrase (by adding, for example, *the fact that* to the beginning of the original sentence).

The difference between these two notions of the referent is thus the same as that between the logic of the name and the logic of the proposition.

1. The "referent" of the message is Julius Caesar if the word "Caesar" in the message is used, in the language of the message, to designate someone, and if that someone is Julius Caesar.

2. The "referent" of the message is the event of Caesar's crossing the Rubicon, not if these words are used to designate an event and that event is the one indicated, but rather if the sentence is true.

These two analyses are not in competition with each other. The second presupposes the first. In general, determining the reference of a linguistic expression is part of its logical analysis. In fact, the beginning of wisdom, in matters of logical analysis, is the realization that a sentence does not have *one and only one* logical form. Nothing prevents us from analyzing it sometimes one way, sometimes another. All we can legitimately require is that the analyses be compatible (for want of which the proposition will have to be rejected as equivocal).

It can be said that the message given as an example has, among other functions, that of referring us to Caesar. Yes, the message refers to Caesar if it is part of a biography of Caesar. But this does not prevent it from also referring us to the Rubicon: the sentence might be included in a summary of facts about the river. The referents of the message might well be both Caesar and the Rubicon, as in a more general history taking into account the fates of both Caesar and the Rubicon.

It is normal that several analyses be possible. It is true *of Caesar* that he crossed the Rubicon; it is true *of the Rubicon* that Caesar crossed it; it is true *of Caesar* and *of the Rubicon* that the first crossed the second; it is true *of the crossing* that this is what Caesar did in regard to the Rubicon; and all of these things are true, finally, because it is true *that* Caesar crossed the Rubicon. If it were false, it might be because the proper name *Caesar* referred to no one, or because the proper name *Rubicon* referred to nothing, or because the narrative was untrue. (Note that it is utterly futile to talk in terms of an "imaginary referent" or of the "construction of reality.")

If this is true, it must be admitted that a message's referent is something relatively indeterminate. The referent is not fixed once and for all but depends on the context of the sentence (a history of Caesar, a history of the Rubicon, a history of Rome, a history of coups d'état, and so forth). This is true, but why is the referent so nebulous?

It would be a mistake at this point to indulge in any *dialectic of the Other*, since that would fatally color our understanding of the relation between language and reality. This dialectic establishes itself all too easily as soon as we begin to talk *about* language as such in its relation to reality as such, forgetting that we started out with a simple sentence. Language would not be language if there were not something else besides language; language is thus the language of the Other of language (objective genitive). The Other of language would not be the Other of language if it depended on language. But the Other of language would depend on language if it were only that—that is, if it were that which language requires outside of itself in order to be language. But this Other of language required by language is not the simple nonlanguage relative to language that does in effect depend on the position of language; it is, rather, an authentic and absolute Other. Conclusion: the Other supposed by language is that which supposes itself in a language of the Other (subjective genitive). We can easily recognize here a Fichtean exercise of the Self and the non-Self. But this sort of dialectic need not emerge at all. If the referent of a message is problematic, it is quite simply because the referent has been defined as being "what a message is about," and this very notion of "what a message is about" is imprecise.[5]

## The Original Misconception of the Notion
### of the Referent

The current common usage of the term "referent" may well have been introduced by C. K. Ogden and I. A. Richards in *The Meaning of Meaning*.[6] This work celebrated the advent of a science of symbolism. The authors proposed the now-famous triangle whose apexes were labeled: *symbol, reference,* and *referent*. These three technical terms replaced the three more commonplace words that made up the title of the first chapter: "Thoughts, Words, and Things." Ogden and Richards explained in a note why they chose the English word *referent*: "It has seemed desirable . . . to introduce a technical term to stand for whatever we may be thinking of or referring to" (9).

*Referent,* they state, will therefore replace terms such as *thing, object, entity, ens*. It should be emphasized that, at the time of their writing, the translation of Gottlob Frege's term *Bedeutung* by *reference* had not yet been proposed. When, in the same work, Ogden and Richards mention Frege's distinction between *Sinn* and *Bedeutung*, they follow Bertrand Russell's distinction between *meaning* for *Sinn* and *indication* for *Bedeutung* (274).[7]

The constitutive flaw in the theory of the referent proposed in *The Meaning of Meaning* is obvious. It becomes apparent even in the diagram given by the authors on page 11: where side a is labeled *Stands for (true)*, side b is labeled *Symbolizes (correct)*, and side c is labeled *Refers to (adequate)*. In other words, the symbol replaces or *stands for* a referent (and this symbol is true if it is, in fact, the one that corresponds to the referent for which it is being used). The symbol *symbolizes* a thought, correctly or incorrectly. Finally, the thought *refers* to the referent, adequately or inadequately.

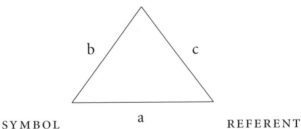

If we confine ourselves to this diagram, it seems natural to conclude that the symbol in question is propositional in nature. The referent in the diagram will thus be the fact corresponding to the particular clause. This is precisely what is suggested by an example given later in the book (62): I strike a match and I expect that match to light. My expectation consists of a certain "thought," which can be "symbolized" by a "symbol," specifically, the sentence *the match will light*. This symbol will be true if the match does in fact light, and false if the match does not light. In this example, the symbol is propositional and the referent is a fact.

However, the example given by Ogden and Richards immediately after their diagram is quite different. In this example, the symbol is the word *Napoleon*, the referent is the Emperor Napoleon, and the reference is the *idea* of Napoleon. Here, the symbol is a proper name and the referent is an individual. Hence we find again the common understanding of something like "the object of reference" meant in the sense of: that about which one is speaking in a singular proposition whose subject is a *proper name*. But if we try to apply the concepts established in the diagram to this example, we end up with absurd results. Granted, we can label the apexes of the triangle: Napoleon's name, Napoleon the person, and the idea of Napoleon. So far, so good. But the sides of the triangle become unintelligible. It would be necessary for the name *Napoleon* to be true or untrue of Napoleon. How can a proper name be true or false? There appears to be total confusion here between naming and predicating. If we could say that the word *Napoleon* were true of the individual Napoleon, we should be able to say, for the same reason, that the word *Talleyrand* is untrue of Napoleon. Now, we happen to know that Napoleon was not a liberal. The predicate *is liberal* is therefore untrue of Napoleon. If *is liberal* is untrue of Napoleon, it follows that the predicate *is not liberal* is true of Napoleon. But if we were able to say that the name *Talleyrand* was untrue of Napoleon, we ought to be able to say that the name *non-Talleyrand* is true of Napoleon. Inversely, if Napoleon cannot be designated by using the expression *non-Talleyrand*, it is because it is absurd to qualify the relation between the name and the named entity with the adjectives *true* or *false*.

## The Semiological Apologue of the Cloakroom

This fundamental misconception of the referent has its counterpart in an equally longstanding misconception of the sign itself. People speak about the sign, but we are never told whether the science of signs (or of sign systems) is dealing with signs in the sense of symbols that "stand for" something (and thus with the sign as name), or rather with signs in the sense of their being what one uses to signify, to say something. The quandaries of the referent are thus also very much the quandaries of the sign. The first tenet of the semiological hypothesis seems to be that the sign replaces the thing: *the symbol stands for a referent*. This assumption informs not only the work of Ogden and Richards, but also, if his remark cited below is indicative, Jakobson's theories of the sign: "Modern structuralist thought has clearly established the fact that language is a system of signs; linguistics is an integral part of the science of signs, *semiotics* (or, in Saussurean terms, *semiology*). Our era has resurrected the medieval definition of the sign—*aliquid stat pro aliquo*—and shown it to be valid and fruitful."[8]

Thus, wherever something stands for something else, there is a sign. This "definition" of the sign (which invites us to equate signification and substitution) favors the following observation: signs enable us to designate and describe things that are absent in the here and now. Proper names make it possible to refer to absent people and distant places. They enable us to apply the predicative system of language to what happens not here but elsewhere, not today but in another time, and so on.

It is in this context that a particular sophism came to play a decisive role: signs are indispensable when we wish to communicate about things that are absent, *therefore* signs are useless when it comes to dealing with things that are present—or at least signs would be useless if the things signified were really present.

The immediate consequence of this: *Since* in fact signs are useful and even indispensable in all communication, whether their subject is absent or present in the setting of the conversation, *therefore* things are never truly present.

> *A statement of the sophism*: The use of signs is necessary to represent that which is absent; *therefore* the absence of that which the sign signifies is necessary to any use of signs.

One more step and we end up with Hegel's famous dictum, on which Alexandre Koyré, Alexandre Kojève, Jean Hyppolite, Maurice Blanchot, Jacques Lacan,[9] and so many others have commented:

> The word is the murder of the thing.

Semiological theory has multiplied the paradoxes surrounding the referent. One might say of these paradoxes exactly what Freud said of delirium. For the people around the madman, the outbreak of delirium is the signal of madness; it is the best proof of an actual derangement. But, continues Freud, this symptom is also the hallmark of improvement, for the madman's delirium reveals his desire to be cured, a desire that expresses itself in his "corrected" reconstruction of reality. In much the same way, the paradoxes of the referent are semiology's delirium; they, too, are efforts to correct a model that was aberrant from the beginning. Each such paradox represents an additional contortion imposed on a model substituting the sign for the referent, in order that the model might somehow meet the demands made upon it—that is to say, so that it might furnish us with an adequate explanation of the workings of semiotic systems. There comes a time, however, when the model has been so thoroughly corrected and twisted that it cancels itself out.

The following apologue will allow us to observe the strange fate of the semiological model. Let us say that signs are like the chits given out in a cloakroom. The "cloakroom system" works in the following way: In exchange for your overcoat, you are given a chit identified by a number corresponding to the hanger on which your overcoat will be hung. By pure convention, this chit represents your overcoat. The main features of the system are as follows:

1. The association between the chit and the overcoat is *arbitrary*. One cannot wear a chit, nor can one put an overcoat in one's pocket.

2. The chit is, as we might expect, *the murder of the overcoat*. When the cloakroom system is functioning as it should, I cannot have both my chit and my overcoat—the sign and the thing itself—at the same time. If I have my coat, it means either that I haven't yet received my chit or that I have already returned it. If I have my chit, I am entitled to a coat.

3. A distinction must be made between the *diachronic* and *synchronic* points of view. Prior to the exchange of a particular overcoat for a particular chit, no relation existed between the two. All there was in the "treasury of the cloakroom" was a reserve of chits, *all different* and *all diacritical*, but none predestined to take the place of such and such an overcoat. When the exchange of overcoats for chits has taken place, a certain state of the system becomes fixed (and it will be revised each time an overcoat is reclaimed by its owner). After the exchange, a certain assimilation takes place between the chit and the overcoat. If this chit takes the place of my coat, I will be as attached to the chit as I was to my coat. As long as the coat remains in the cloakroom, the chit is a pledge of my coat, the promise that it will be returned to me.

Such is the cloakroom system when it is functioning normally. Within its normal functioning, this system is incapable of representing the workings of language as such. At most, this model represents a kind of language game that is one possible game among many others.

Suppose, however, that we wished to defend a definition of the linguistic sign as a substitute or as a *chit*. To do this, we would have to modify the cloakroom to reflect many obvious aspects of human language: the cloakroom would have to become paradoxical.

First, we would have to ask why the chit is assumed to be the symbol of the overcoat, and not the opposite. What is there to prevent us from seeing the overcoats as symbols and the chits as referents? Answer: There is, in principle, nothing to prevent this. The cloakroom chit is the symbol of the overcoat because, as it happens, we attach more value to overcoats than we do to chits in and of themselves. Now let us imagine a tyrannical cloakroom attendant who decides she is no longer going to return coats in exchange for chits. The chits would no longer be convertible but would be totally devalued, like Russian bonds. Or, in an inverse scenario, suppose that, following some fashion craze, the chits from a particularly chic cloakroom came to be admired and hoarded by collectors. In this case, one can imagine aficionados rushing to exchange their shabby overcoats for one of the precious chits.

The conclusion we are forced to draw is that, in a system of substitutions like that of the cloakroom, nothing predestines certain things to serve as symbols and others to serve as referents. There is, therefore, no *ultimate referent* in the sense of something that can be obtained through an exchange but that can, in itself, no longer be exchanged for something else. Only empirical considerations dictate that we stop with the exchange of the overcoat for the chit. Neither does there exist any *ultimate word*. There is no last word, no word of all words, with which we might obtain the ultimate referent. We must therefore begin to speak of a *nihilism of the cloakroom*. Nothing exists that cannot be exchanged; there is nothing such that one would not or could not exchange it "for anything in the world." All things can become chits. All things can be established as substitutable for something else. This brand of nihilism is not in fact a radical philosophical reversal, but merely one property of the model adopted here to describe symbolization.

Nothing escapes symbolization, nothing escapes a trip to the cloakroom—except, perhaps, such metaphysical words as *nothing* and *something, nothingness* and *being*. It is true that, in the cloakroom, there is no ultimate referent, unless it be by habit or convention. All things can become signs. There is no ultimate word, no sign of an ultimate referent or, if one does not distinguish between signified and referent, no sign of a "transcendental signified." Unless, that is, we take the words *nothing* and *something* as chits of a different order. They are signs, and therefore chits, but they are metaphysical chits. The *nothing* chit will be exchanged in the cloakroom for: nothing. The *something* chit will be exchanged in the cloakroom for: again, nothing. For if, in the cloakroom, I was given *just any* overcoat in exchange for the *something* chit, I would at the same time be receiving a specific overcoat that corresponded to a specific chit, and that chit would then be deprived of its referent.

The model must undergo a second correction if we are to represent language as a symbolic system—in other words, as a system of chits. The cloakroom could no longer function if people were to receive a chit without surrendering an overcoat or to recover an overcoat without returning a chit. The substitutions of chits and overcoats are perfectly defined. On this point, the assimilation between cloakroom chits and linguistic signs breaks down. Each speaker has symbols at his disposal, but how did he acquire them? What have I given up in exchange for the words given to me? Have I, for instance, somewhere deposited the "things" whose "names" I know? I do not remember any such exchange. According to the semiological conception of language, we are a bit like people waking up the morning after a rough night about which we remember nothing. We find mysterious cloakroom tickets in our pockets. We do not know where we received these tickets, nor what we exchanged for them. If I have a ticket, I have the right to a corresponding exchange that is corollary to the first exchange from which I saved the ticket. It is sufficient to know that the ticket is a ticket. I can thus use symbols without having the least idea of the referents corresponding to them.

How then, might we conceive of *the origin of language*—in other words, of the episode during which we received our first chits? Two versions of this episode might be suggested. The first claims to be positive; the second admits to being allegorical.

THE POSITIVE VERSION. Symbols were acquired during the language-learning process. Since I do not remember it, this prehistoric event must be reconstructed by reasoning out what must have taken place. That an exchange did take place is the very substance of the semiological hypothesis: the signs are chits. It is hard to see how this exchange could have taken place as we learned a specific word. To learn a specific word, one must first have acquired the language. We must therefore go back to the learning of a "first word" or, better still, to the origin of the symbolic faculty itself. The *first chit* is a word that can be exchanged for anything whatsoever; it is our very faculty of effecting an exchange in the form of a babylike babbling that is in the process of becoming articulated language. What has been given up in exchange for this ability to exchange? The alternative of *not* effecting an exchange, of *not* using the cloakroom. In the initial exchange, therefore, one gives up the ability to not exchange, to not make a trip to the cloakroom. The initial exchange is the one in which we give up the power to not exchange in order to receive the chits that will be the necessary currency of all future exchanges.

The way is now open to psychologize this structuralist schema: we might call the (imaginary) power not to exchange "phallic power," the fact of escaping the laws of the semiotic cloakroom "incest," and the ordeal of exchange "castration." In an unabashedly psychological version of the scenario, we would not hesitate to say that the ultimate referent of all exchanges is none other than the lost paradise of possessing all the women within the group. As concerns a psychology of the child, this woman is the mother. In the ethnologist's eyes, she would be, rather, the daughter or the sister. This is, moreover, unimportant: if the wife takes the place of the incestuous object, that object itself refers back to nothing. Everything signifies it, but it signifies nothing.

THE ALLEGORICAL VERSION. In fact, the story of the origin of language cannot be told, except in a fable. Even the so-called positive version cannot avoid making use of an image, of an "as if" in the conditional. A subtler strategy would be to give a figurative version of events—that is, to frankly concede that our story is only a tale or a manner of speaking about things that are in fact not like our representations of them.

The original exchange of the *thing itself* for the *word* never took place. Nothing has been left behind in the cloakroom. Chits were not given out in exchange for an object to be held. The chits are things, like others, that one uses to represent other things, which themselves replace still others, and so on ad infinitum. There is no thing itself, no ultimate thing. Everything is, in one way or another, *in the place* of another thing. The thing itself, if it existed, would be that which stood for nothing and existed in perfect self-sufficiency. Therefore we have left nothing behind, lost nothing. Nonetheless, signs are chits (a fact that the semiological hypothesis would not dream of questioning). Thus we cannot help but conceive of language as having symbolically replaced things themselves. The very nature of language inevitably gives rise to this illusion, this "transcendental appearance." Hence the sign is that which stands for something else; a thing that is not a sign is that which stands for nothing. The thing is *always already* lost. This loss has always already taken place, meaning that it has never happened in the present. The chits we hold in our hands bear the memory of this primordial exchange; they are the *traces* of an exchange that "will have taken place." They are the pledges of a restitution that has been due since the beginning. Meanwhile, in the interlude between the lost paradise and the awaited parousia, there is only the reign of an endless circulation of signs.

To say "transcendental appearance" is necessarily to call for a critique of this concept. If the hypothesis of originary substitution were a theoretical error committed by certain semiologists, it could be corrected. But if this hypothesis is inevitable, if it is integral to all "theories of the sign," then the critique of semiology must be a critique of language (just as the critique of rational metaphysics must be a critique of pure reason if the sophisms of that metaphysics are inevitable illusions). The critique of language directly concerns the illusion of the referent: the illusion of something that must bring together the two attributes by which the thing itself is defined, specifically:

1. That it serve as the referent of a sign.
2. That it not serve as sign for another referent.

As we can see, the *critique of pure language* remains very much justified so long as the illusion of a possible exchange between language as a whole and reality as a whole is a necessary error of the human mind.

I have tried in this essay to suggest that the illusion of an *ultimate referent* of *language per se*—of what dialecticians call the Other of language—is not a transcendental appearance. If the preceding remarks are justified, the illusion in question reflects, instead, the inadequacy of the chosen paradigm. At the origin of this illusion there is nothing that is necessary, only a cascade of *reductions*. All signs have been treated as words. All words have been treated as names. All names have been treated as symbols. What must be critiqued is not so much "language" or "the symbolic function" as it is the longstanding indifference of our contemporary theoreticians toward what grammarians call the division of the *parts of speech*.

NOTES

This essay and its notes were translated by Gwen Wells.

1. Richard Rorty, *The Linguistic Turn: Recent Essays in Philosophical Method* (Chicago: The University of Chicago Press, 1967).

2. Oswald Ducrot and Tzvetan Todorov, *Encyclopedic Dictionary of the Sciences of Language*, trans. Catherine Porter (Baltimore, Md.: The Johns Hopkins University Press, 1979), 242.

3. Ferdinand de Saussure, *Course in General Linguistics*, trans. Wade Baskin (New York: Philosophical Library, 1959).

4. Roman Jakobson, "Linguistics and Poetics"; first published in 1960, this article is reprinted in *Language in Literature*, ed. Krystyna Pomorska and Stephen Rudy (Cambridge, Mass.: Harvard University Press, 1987), 62–94. The model proposed by Bühler is described in his "Die Axiomatik der Sprachwissenschaften," *Kant-Studien* 38 (1933): 19–20.

5. Nelson Goodman, "About," *Mind* 70 (1961): 1–24; reprinted in Nelson Goodman, *Problems and Projects* (Indianapolis: Bobbs-Merrill, 1972).

6. C. K. Ogden and I. A. Richards, *The Meaning of Meaning: A Study of the Influence of Language Upon Thought and of the Science of Symbolism* (London: Kegan Paul, Trench, Trubner, 1923).

7. As a translation for *Bedeutung*, *indication* is peculiar, but *reference* is also problematic; on this point, consult Peter Geach and Max Black, "Glossary," in *Translations from the Philosophical Writings of Gottlob Frege*, 3rd ed. (Oxford: Blackwell, 1980); and Michael A. E. Dummett, *The Interpretation of Frege's Philosophy* (Cambridge, Mass.: Harvard University Press, 1981).

8. Roman Jakobson, "L'Aspect phonologique et l'aspect grammatical du langage dans leurs interrelations," in *Essais de linguistique générale* (Paris: Les Éditions de Minuit, 1963), 162.

9. See Alexandre Koyré, "Hegel à Iéna," in *Études d'histoire de la pensée philosophique* (Paris: Colin, 1961); Alexandre Kojève, *Introduction to the Reading of Hegel*, ed. Allan Bloom, trans. James H. Nichols Jr. (Ithaca, N.Y.: Cornell University Press, 1969); Jean Hyppolite, *Logique et existence: Essai sur la logique de Hegel* (Paris: PUF, 1953); Maurice Blanchot, *La Part du feu* (Paris: Gallimard, 1949); and Jacques Lacan, *Séminaire I: Sur les écrits techniques de Freud* (Paris: Seuil, 1975).

## 11. THE GREAT DICHOTOMY

### WENDELL V. HARRIS

*It is no doubt possible to justify the most extreme "liberty of inter-preting" when criticism is frankly concerned with the practical uses to which poems may be put by readers irrespective of their authors' intentions in composing them; they can then be made to say or mean whatever is most relevant to our interest or needs; and who can rightly object if this is what we want to do and is plainly advertised as such?* —RONALD S. CRANE[1]

*Shared communication proves the existence of a shared, and largely true, view of the world. But what led us to demand the common view was the recognition that sentences held true—the linguistic representatives of belief—determine the meaning of the words they contain.* —DONALD DAVIDSON[2]

NOTHING IN THE HISTORY of literary studies is stranger than the great dichotomy that has grown up in the last twenty-five years: that between writers who for the most part have sought either to show that all meaning is indeterminate or to somehow disconnect linguistic meaning from extralinguistic reality, and those who have labored to show *how* intended meanings are communicated with sufficient clarity and that such meanings are connected to a reality consisting of much more than language systems. The currents making up what is generally called poststructuralism have been the dominant ones, but during the same years that the greater part of the best-known theorists and a host of epigones have played variations on the principles of indeterminacy and infinite deferral of meaning, a significant number of theorists have devoted themselves to a variety of researches into what makes possible that communication the denial of which the poststructuralists seek constantly to communicate.

Part of the oddity of the situation is that, while some publishers and professional journals have chosen sides, many have been happily indiscriminate, publishing studies based on both of these incompatible positions with fine tolerance. The situation is rather like one portion of the medical profession devoting itself to studying how viruses induce diseases while a more influential portion is denying the existence of viruses; the parallel comes even closer if we assume that the second group in practice relies on modes of treatment that assume the existence of viruses.

Although the field of literary studies is too complicated fully to fit this central dichotomy—which seems, happily, to be breaking up—the basic opposition has been so striking and continues to exert so widespread a residual force that it requires explicit statement. The difference can be described in terms of philosophical allegiances, but the usual approach to the poststructuralist view of the world from Nietzsche, Freud, Husserl, and Heidegger to Derrida tends to lose certain basic differences amid the subtleties of metaphysical speculation. For the purpose of analyzing the oppositions, it is useful simply to recognize that two different questions are being asked. The poststructuralist (or hermetic) question is this: given the theory that the system of language is divorced from extralinguistic reality, what devices can be found to demonstrate that language is neither interpretable nor explanatory of reality? The very different question asked by what I will call the hermeneutic group is: what principle or principles make possible our understanding of individual instances of language use? My word choices in setting up these formulations have been deliberate. "Theory," "explanation," and "language-as-system" (Saussure's *langue*) as associated with hermetics are contrasted with the hermeneutic "principle," "understanding," and "language-in-use" (Saussure's *parole*).

## HERMETICS

Structuralism—though it served as a convenient rubric for a variety of intellectual perspectives—was in itself so short-lived that to follow the usual practice and call the large-scale phenomena that followed it "poststructuralist" is rather like calling contemporary literature post-Dadaist. That is why I prefer the term "hermetic." The appropriateness of the word was suggested to me by essays of Umberto Eco, who learnedly traces the magical tradition of hermeticism as associated with the writings of Hermes Trismegistus.[3] Eco parallels much in contemporary criticism and theory with hermeticism's suspiciousness, its search for secrets, the accompanying inclination to seize on any similarity as a clue, and, since the rooting out of more and more hidden meanings inevitably produces contradictory meanings, the belief that texts have indeterminate meanings. I find the term "hermetics" satisfying because it suggests the rather diverse phenomena behind which stands a highly esoteric, primarily occult tradition. Hermetics has always been associated with belief that the world (or reality) is very different from what it appears to be and that its nature is sealed from ordinary human understanding. Moreover, hermetics suggests the recondite, philosophically oriented theories that lie behind much of poststructuralist thought, restricting full access to a circle of initiates, the academic group within which members write primarily for each other.

The core doctrines of contemporary hermetics are well enough known to be summarized quite briefly (I give each in its strongest form):

1. The denial that language connects with anything beyond itself together with the assertion that it is meaningless to talk about a reality outside language since all we can know and speak of is linguistically formulated.

2. The denial of the possibility of determining meaning, which entails not only the denial of the possibility of saying true things about literature but of any adequate communication. The interpretation of texts and the interpretation of (attempted) interpretations both become impossible.

3. The denial of the author and the reader as thinking, willing subjects able to think about what they are thinking and willing and will what they are thinking. The notion of a discrete unitary human mind is regarded as a myth, since what appears to be a mind is an unstable collection of linguistically determined concepts. This doctrine manifests itself in two rather different ways. The first is in the denial of the efficacy of authorial intention. If there are such things as communicative intentions, so the argument runs, they can never be usefully known, necessarily embody self-contradictions engendered by the very structure of language, and in fact alter their substance in being embodied in writing since writing may function in the absence of either the author or the reader(s) for whom the text was intended. The second form of the doctrine is the assertion that what a reader finds is wholly the function of the reader's interpretive strategies.

4. The assumption of the equal validity of whatever relations or analogues any portion of the text suggests to the reader.

5. The belief that thought takes place within frameworks such that communication across frameworks is impossible. As a corollary, it is misleading if not meaningless to refer to historical fact since all such facts are the result both of linguistically determined perspectives and related culturally determined perspectives.

## HERMENEUTICS

Hermeneutics is an awe-inspiring word. It tends to scare undergraduates, light up the eyes of Ph.D. students seeking a talisman, and, often enough, annoy solid old scholars who have in fact given their days in its service. Of little help is the tendency to talk about hermeneutics in the sort of way exemplified by Paul Ricoeur's statement that the purpose of hermeneutics is "to reconstruct the internal dynamics of the text and to restore to the work its ability to project itself outside itself in the representation of a world that I could inhabit."[4]

Hermeneutics is in fact one of those words that has been pressed into such various services over time that one can hardly use it without attaching an immediate explanatory gloss. It now carries about it suggestions of the search for figurative meanings in Philo, Origen, and Augustine; of Schleiermacher's canons of interpretation; of Dilthey's more definite movement toward psychological interpretation through the recreation of "lived experience"; of Heideggerian views of hermeneutics as an interpretation of the existential world, not simply of individual texts; of Hans-Georg Gadamer's view of hermeneutics as an exercise in the fusion of the cultural horizons of author and interpreter; of Paul Ricoeur's interest in opening hidden levels of meaning; of Fredric Jameson's use of negative hermeneutics as the recognition of ideology and positive hermeneutics as "the symbolic representation of a specific historical and class form of collective unity";[5] and of Richard Rorty's view of hermeneutics as an endless process of discussion. The history of hermeneutic theorizing is thus an extremely complicated one (a history nowhere better summarized than in the introduction to Kurt Mueller-Vollmer's *Hermeneutic Reader*).[6] Nevertheless, although theorizing that invokes the term hermeneutics has become increasingly philosophical, it is not necessary to import the full library of hermeneutic thought of philosophers like Husserl, Heidegger, Gadamer, and Ricoeur into the question of understanding literary meaning. The questions addressed by what has come to be called philosophical hermeneutics have finally to do with what have traditionally been regarded as metaphysical questions about truth and reality—thus Heidegger extends hermeneutics to encompass the interpretation of Being. As Mueller-Vollmer has argued, the concepts of hermeneutics formulated by these philosophers, fashionable as they are, "have become most problematic when we consider their usefulness within the context of literary hermeneutics."[7]

Nevertheless, if we regard the core about which most of the uses of "hermeneutics" have entwined themselves—a notion that combines translation, interpretation, and clarification—we have a very useful word to which none of those three partial synonyms is quite equivalent: the human endeavor to understand the intended meaning of verbal utterances and, more especially, written texts. Additionally hermeneutics has the advantage of having always been associated not with the system of language but with language-in-use, the language we daily encounter. Much in the following exposition of the elements of hermeneutics as I employ the word will be well-known to many readers, but I wish to make my understanding of these elements as transparent as possible.

The *OED* defines "hermeneutics" as "The art or science of interpretation, esp. of Scripture. Commonly distinguished from exegesis or practical exposition." The phrase "especially of Scripture" of course refers to the difficulties of biblical interpretation that gave rise to the earliest explorations of the problem of understanding and explanation. The words "practical exposition" are of particular importance in distinguishing intended meaning from relationships to modes of thought external to the text. Such a distinction is set out by the nineteenth-century theorist of hermeneutics, Philip August Boeckh in the

*Encyclopedia and Methodology of the Philological Sciences* (1877). Hermeneutics' aim is to understand the text in itself while the purpose of criticism is "the establishment of a relation or reference to something else so that the recognition of this relation is itself the end in view."[8] But Boeckh saw clearly that nothing can be understood wholly in itself: "When we assign to hermeneutics the task of understanding the subjects themselves, we surely do not imply that anything can be understood without reference to much besides. For interpretation many auxiliaries must be used" (45).

Which brings us to E. D. Hirsch's twentieth-century adaptation of Boeckh's distinction, one which is essential to hermeneutics. Boeckh's "interpretation" is specifically defined as the construction of the author's intended meaning. Stipulating that he will use "meaning" only to designate "verbal meaning," that is, intended meaning, Hirsch states his central formulation precisely in *Validity in Interpretation*: "Verbal meaning is whatever someone has willed to convey by a particular sequence of linguistic signs and which can be conveyed (shared) by means of those linguistic signs."[9] The second portion of that sentence—"which can be conveyed (shared) by means of those linguistic signs"— is as important as the first. It is what Steven Mailloux calls the "operative intention": "the actions that the author, *as he writes the text*, understands himself to be performing in that text and the immediate effects he understands these actions will achieve in his projected reader."[10]

As for Boeckh's use of the term "criticism," Hirsch retains its designation of relationships between the text and external sources of judgment and explanation while expanding it far beyond the correction of texts that Boeckh had primarily in mind. Thus for Hirsch it includes all patterns and relationships found by the reader that cannot be attributed to authorial intention. These patterns and relationships, which in general speech are also called "meanings," Hirsch names "significances"; these, he explicitly recognizes, are of at least as much interest to readers as authorially intended meanings. Although Hirsch's constitutes the best-known statement of the difference between authorially intended and other meanings, pretty much the same distinction has been made by many others. The most sophisticated is probably that of H. P. Grice. In the statement "a temperature of 103 degrees means that the patient is seriously ill," the patient's temperature is interpreted without the thermometer or patient intending to mean anything. Grice calls this "natural" meaning (intentional meaning is "nonnatural"), although the term "symptomatic" which the above example suggests is probably the more useful.[11] Depending on specific use, Hirsch's "significance" sometimes seems the most appropriate term for nonintentional meaning, while at other times Grice's "symptomatic" seems clearer. I shall employ the two as synonymous (with the warning that this use of symptomatic is much broader than Louis Althusser's).[12] If we define hermeneutics as the reconstruction of authorial intention, the recognition of significances or symptomatic meanings can be called "symptomatics."

As for *the process of finding* intended meaning, Schleiermacher, the father of modern hermeneutics, started from the recognition that speech acts and acts of understanding are correlated in that "every act of understanding is the reverse side of an act of speaking, and one must grasp the thought that underlies a given statement."[13] This was to be accomplished through the mutually supporting operation of the two tasks of understanding. In "grammatical" interpretation, "more precise determination of any point in a given text must be decided on the basis of the use of language common to the author and his original public" (First Canon, 117) while "the meaning of each word of a passage must be determined by the context in which it occurs" (Second Canon, 127).

Schleiermacher's grammatical task evidently assumes that a use of words different from what the intended readers could interpret on the basis of their own competence would be somehow made clear by the author. His second task, the technical, he also called "psychological," describing it at one point as "a moment in the development of the person" (99). Many readers have thus been led into thinking that Schleiermacher was simply looking to the individual personality of the speaker. However, as Mueller-Vollmer notes, Schleiermacher's full discussion of the psychological side of interpretation evidently includes not only the author's individuality, but the particular genre and historical circumstances embodied by the text.[14] Hermeneutical theorizing since may be regarded as a lengthy series of attempts to determine the methods and limits of carrying out these practices.

It is perhaps an index of the degree to which our age is enchanted by the paradoxical, counterintuitive, inexplicable, and occultly motivated that the term hermeneutics has been driven farther from its sense as the recovery of intended meaning at the very time that speech-act theory, discourse analysis, and reader-response theory have been clarifying the operation of Schleiermacher's second canon. The basic problem such investigations address is simply this: granted that a knowledge of the semantic possibilities and accepted syntactic structures of the time a text was written (Schleiermacher's first canon) is not enough for full understanding, what more must the interpreter know? The question thus becomes more practical than philosophical. Unfortunately, lacking the attractions of the kind of sweeping, paradoxical speculation now in fashion, work on the answer to this question has caught the eye of relatively few literary critics. As useful as they are undramatic, hermeneutic analyses of this kind are represented by investigations as different as those in John Searle's *Speech Acts* (1969), M. A. K. Halliday and Ruquaiya Hasan's *Cohesion in English* (1976), George Dillon's *Language Processing and the Reading of Literature* (1978), Louise M. Rosenblatt's *The Reader, the Text, the Poem: The Transactional Theory of the Literary Work* (1978), Kent Bach and Robert M. Harnish's *Linguistic Communication and Speech Acts* (1979), and Gillian Brown and George Yule's *Discourse Analysis* (1983). In essence, all these begin by asking not about the abstract structure of language, but how it is that we get on with the processes of interpretation upon which we constantly rely. Once one asks the question in this way the characteristics of language that hermetic criticism asserts to be absolute barriers are seen not to apply to language in use. A composite answer to the question of what the interpreter of actual discourse requires besides grammatical knowledge emerges; interpretation depends on a *communicative contract* based on the total context (background knowledge, occasion, etc.) that author and reader could reasonably expect the other would take into consideration. J. L. Austin, the founder of speech-act theory, noted in 1955, "for some years we have been realizing more and more clearly that the occasion of an utterance matters seriously, and that the words used are to be 'explained' by the 'context' in which they are designed to be or have actually been spoken in a linguistic interchange."[15]

A good bit of confusion can be avoided by drawing on speech-act theory to sort out quite different aspects of what is generally packed together in our notion of an intended meaning. By "locution" is meant simply a string of spoken or written words (an utterance). By "proposition" is meant the combination of reference and predication that produces the bare content of the utterance. By "illocutionary force" is meant the relation of that proposition to the utterer and addressee (is the utterer promising, ordering, describing, asking?). Austin explains that the illocutionary force is that of the act performed *in* saying something as contrasted with the act *of* saying something (that is, uttering a locution expressing a proposition) (99). "Perlocutionary effects" are the effects produced by an utterance. Obviously there may be a difference between the effect intended and that produced: a proposition with the illocutionary force of an assertion intended to have the effect of convincing may in fact amuse or irritate. By "perlocutionary intent" is meant that effect which the proposition together with its illocutionary force is intended to produce. Thus, "Hermetic theories of literature are based on egregious fallacies" is a locution that expresses a proposition about hermetic theorizing; depending on circumstances it may carry any of a number of kinds of illocutionary force intended to produce any of a number of effects. For instance, it could be uttered with the force of an assertion and with the perlocutionary intent of opening an argument. Its actual effect could only be known if and when it was uttered in an actual situation. Austin explicitly confines his use of "meaning" to the sense and reference of individual words and the proposition thus expressed, preferring to distinguish illocutionary force from meaning (100); however, since the illocutionary force of an utterance is part of authorial intention, I will include it under the umbrella of authorial meaning.

Austin had noted that utterances with such conventionally understood consequences as promising or betting can be accomplished indirectly (32). "I'll be there" can be a promise; "Five pounds on Middlesex" can be a bet. In an article that has been highly influential among students of speech acts but hardly so among literary critics, H. P. Grice found indirect meaning to be dependent on what he has called the Cooperative Principle.[16] Both the speaker and hearer know, that is, that an utterance is expected to be as relevant to the topic at hand, as truthful from the point of view of those engaged in the discourse, as appropriate in length, as suitable in manner and tone as possible. What is reasonable in each characteristic is culturally defined—within each culture one learns what is reasonable under which circumstances (for instance, when it is appropriate to speak to a stranger, how detailed to be when giving directions to persons with different backgrounds, etc.). Violations of the Cooperative Principle that are obviously intentional signal that one's meaning is indirect. "I've never liked Bartok" is an indirect answer to the question "Are you going to the concert?" if both speakers know that Bartok is to be on the program.

I have omitted to mention that the terms hermeneutics and hermetics are both distantly derived from the god Hermes. As the messenger of the gods he both transmitted and translated messages; in addition he was the god of both thieves and merchants. He was in short both a conveyor of meanings and a transmuter of them, indispensable but not wholly trustworthy. To remember Hermes' problematic character and try to distinguish the cunning and mischievous from the undistorted and valuable was essential for any mortal having dealings with him. Hermeneutic understanding being always probabilistic, always fallible, the possibility of error is never absent, but that ought to put us even more on guard against any hermetic theorizing that denies the possibility of error on the grounds that there is no alternative to it—that we are indeed in endless error hurled.

## NOTES

1. Ronald S. Crane, *The Languages of Criticism and the Structure of Poetry* (Toronto: University of Toronto Press, 1953), 33.

2. Donald Davidson, "The Method of Truth in Metaphysics," in *After Philosophy: End or Transformation?* ed. Kenneth Baynes, James Bohman, and Thomas McCarthy (Cambridge, Mass.: MIT Press, 1987), 168.

3. See Umberto Eco et al., *Interpretation and Overinterpretation*, ed. Stefan Collini (Cambridge: Cambridge University Press, 1992). Roger Scruton, in "Public Text and Common Reader," in *Reconstructing Literature*, ed. Laurence Lerner (Oxford: Blackwell, 1983), uses "hermetic" to refer to criticism dependent on a professional argot (52–53).

4. Paul Ricoeur, "On Interpretation," in *After Philosophy*, ed. Kenneth Baynes, James Bohman, and Thomas McCarthy (Cambridge, Mass.: MIT Press, 1987), 377.

5. Fredric Jameson, *The Political Unconscious* (Ithaca, N.Y.: Cornell University Press, 1981), 291.

6. Kurt Mueller-Vollmer, ed., *The Hermeneutics Reader* (Oxford: Blackwell, 1986).

7. Kurt Mueller-Vollmer, "Understanding and Interpretation: Toward a Defense of Literary Hermeneutics," in *Literary Criticism and Philosophy*, ed. Joseph P. Strelka (University Park: Pennsylvania State University Press, 1983), 42. Mueller-Vollmer's position on the philosophical school of hermeneutics deserves serious consideration. "Its adherents claim to have uncovered the historical and ontological roots of hermeneutics and to have laid new

ground for the sciences of man. Indubitably, important new insights and a renewed interest in the philosophy of these sciences have sprung from hermeneutic philosophy, yet, from the point of view of literary studies, these claims have little value if they are held against the actual accomplishments of nineteenth-century hermeneutics" (44).

8. August Boeckh, *On Interpretation and Criticism*, trans. and ed. John Paul Pritchard (Norman: University of Oklahoma Press, 1968), 121.

9. E. D. Hirsch Jr., *Validity in Interpretation* (New Haven, Conn.: Yale University Press, 1967), 31.

10. Steven Mailloux, *Interpretive Conventions: The Reader in the Study of American Fiction* (Ithaca, N.Y.: Cornell University Press, 1982), 99; my italics.

11. See H. P. Grice's "Meaning," in his *Studies in the Way of Words* (Cambridge, Mass.: Harvard University Press, 1989). Although some of the subtlety of Grice's argument is lost by substituting "symptomatic meaning" for his "natural meaning" and "intentional meaning" for "nonnatural meaning," Grice's terms tend to be confusing when transported outside the context of his essay. Full-scale analysis of the different meanings of meaning would require consideration of at least two other of Grice's essays: "Utterer's Meaning and Intention," and "Utterer's Meaning, Sentence-Meaning, and Word-Meaning," both reprinted in *Studies in the Way of Words*.

12. Louis Althusser, *Reading Capital*, trans. Ben Brewster (London: NLB, 1970). Althusser's notion of "symptomatic reading" derives from the Freudian concept of repression: "I suggested," writes Althusser, "that we had to submit Marx's text not to an immediate reading, but to a *'symptomatic' reading*, in order to discern in the apparent continuity of the discourse the lacunae, blanks, and failures of rigour, the places where Marx's discourse is merely the unsaid of his silence, arising in his discourse itself" (143). Such a form of reading is of course perfectly legitimate, but it produces just one of many possible significances or symptomatic meanings as I am using those terms.

13. Friedrich Schleiermacher, *Hermeneutics: The Handwritten Manuscripts*, ed. Heinz Kimmerle, trans. James Duke and Jack Forstman (Missoula, Mont.: Scholars Press, 1977), 97.

14. Mueller-Vollmer, *The Hermeneutics Reader*, 11.

15. J. L. Austin, *How To Do Things with Words*, ed. J. O. Urmson and Marina Sabisá (Cambridge, Mass.: Harvard University Press, 1975), 100.

16. H. P. Grice, "Logic and Conversation," in *Studies in the Way of Words* (Cambridge, Mass.: Harvard University Press, 1989).

## 12. THE DECONSTRUCTIVE ANGEL

### M. H. ABRAMS

*DEMOGORGON.*—*If the Abysm*
*Could vomit forth its secrets:—but a voice*
*Is wanting . . .* —*SHELLEY*, PROMETHEUS UNBOUND

WE HAVE BEEN INSTRUCTED these days to be wary of words like *origin*, *center*, and *end*, but I will venture to say that this session [of the MLA, in 1976] had its origin in the dialogue between Wayne Booth and myself which centered on the rationale of the historical procedures in my book, *Natural Supernaturalism*. Hillis Miller had, in all innocence, written a review of that book; he was cited and answered by Booth, then re-cited and re-answered by me, and so was sucked into the vortex of our exchange to make it now a dialogue of three. And given the demonstrated skill of our chairman in fomenting debates, who can predict how many others will be drawn into the vortex before it comes to an end?

I shall take this occasion to explore the crucial issue that was raised by Hillis Miller in his challenging review. I agreed with Wayne Booth that pluralism— the bringing to bear on a subject of diverse points of view, with diverse results— is not only valid, but necessary to our understanding of literary and cultural history: in such pursuits the convergence of diverse points of view is the only way to achieve a vision in depth. I also said, however, that Miller's radical statement, in his review, of the principles of what he calls deconstructive interpretation goes beyond the limits of pluralism, by making impossible anything that we would account as literary and cultural history.[1] The issue would hardly be worth pursuing on this public platform if it were only a question of the soundness of the historical claims in a single book. But Miller considered *Natural Supernaturalism* as an example "in the grand tradition of modern humanistic scholarship, the tradition of Curtius, Auerbach, Lovejoy, C. S. Lewis,"[2] and he made it clear that what is at stake is the validity of the premises and procedures of the entire body of traditional inquiries in the human sciences. And that is patently a matter important enough to warrant our discussion.

Let me put as curtly as I can the essential, though usually implicit, premises that I share with traditional historians of Western culture, which Miller puts in question and undertakes to subvert:

M. H. Abrams. "The Deconstructive Angel." Originally published in *Critical Inquiry* 3, no. 3 (1977): 425–38. Reprinted by permission of the author, from *Doing Things with Texts: Essays in Criticism and Critical Theory*, by M. H. Abrams, edited and with a foreword by Michael Fischer, 237–52. New York: W. W. Norton and Company, 1989. This essay was first presented as a paper at the 1976 MLA meeting.

1. The basic materials of history are written texts; and the authors who wrote these texts (with some off-center exceptions) exploited the possibilities and norms of their inherited language to say something determinate, and assumed that competent readers, insofar as these shared their own linguistic skills, would be able to understand what they said.

2. The historian is indeed for the most part able to interpret not only what the passages that he cites might mean now, but also what their writers meant when they wrote them. Typically, the historian puts his interpretation in language which is partly his author's and partly his own; if it is sound, this interpretation approximates, closely enough for the purpose at hand, what the author meant.

3. The historian presents his interpretation to the public in the expectation that the expert reader's interpretation of a passage will approximate his own and so confirm the "objectivity" of his interpretation. The worldly-wise author expects that some of his interpretations will turn out to be mistaken, but such errors, if limited in scope, will not seriously affect the soundness of his overall history. If, however, the bulk of his interpretations are misreadings, his book is not to be accounted a history but an historical fiction.

Notice that I am speaking here of linguistic interpretation, not of what is confusingly called "historical interpretation"—that is, the categories, topics, and conceptual and explanatory patterns that the historian brings to his investigation of texts, which serve to shape the story within which passages of texts, with their linguistic meanings, serve as instances and evidence. The differences among these organizing categories, topics, and patterns effect the diversity in the stories that different historians tell, and which a pluralist theory finds acceptable. Undeniably, the linguistic meanings of the passages cited are in some degree responsive to differences in the perspective that a historian brings to bear on them; but the linguistic meanings are also in considerable degree recalcitrant to alterations in perspective, and the historian's fidelity to these meanings, without his manipulating and twisting them to fit his preconceptions, serves as a prime criterion of the soundness of the story that he undertakes to tell.

One other preliminary matter: I don't claim that my interpretation of the passages I cite exhausts everything that these passages mean. In his review, Hillis Miller says that "a literary or philosophical text, for Abrams, has a single unequivocal meaning 'corresponding' to the various entities it 'represents' in a more or less straightforward mirroring." I don't know how I gave Miller the impression that my "theory of language is implicitly mimetic," a "straightforward mirror" of the reality it reflects,[3] except on the assumption he seems to share with Derrida, and which seems to me obviously mistaken, that all views of language that are not in the deconstructive mode are mimetic views. My view of language, as it happens, is by and large functional and pragmatic: language, whether spoken or written, is the use of a great variety of speech acts to accomplish a great diversity of human purposes; only one of these many purposes is to assert something about a state of affairs; and such a linguistic assertion does not mirror, but serves to direct attention to selected aspects of that state of affairs.

At any rate, I think it is quite true that many of the passages I cite are equivocal and multiplex in meaning. All I claim—all that any traditional historian needs to claim—is that, whatever else the author also meant, he meant, at a sufficient approximation, at least *this*, and that the "this" that I specify is sufficient to the story I undertake to tell. Other historians, having chosen to tell a different story, may in their interpretation identify different aspects of the meanings conveyed by the same passage.

That brings me to the crux of my disagreement with Hillis Miller. His central contention is not simply that I am sometimes, or always, wrong in my interpretation, but instead that I—like other traditional historians—can never be right in my interpretation. For Miller assents to Nietzsche's challenge of "the concept of 'rightness' in interpretation," and to Nietzsche's assertion that "the same text authorizes innumerable interpretations (*Auslegungen*): there is no 'correct' interpretation."[4] Nietzsche's views of interpretation, as Miller says, are relevant to the recent deconstructive theorists, including Jacques Derrida and himself, who have "reinterpreted Nietzsche" or have written "directly or indirectly under his aegis." He goes on to quote a number of statements from Nietzsche's *The Will to Power* to the effect, as Miller puts it, "that reading is never the objective identifying of a sense but the importation of meaning into a text which has no meaning 'in itself.' " For example: "Ultimately, man finds in things nothing but what he himself has imported into them." "In fact interpretation is itself a means of becoming master of something."[5] On the face of it, such sweeping deconstructive claims might suggest those of Lewis Carroll's linguistic philosopher, who asserted that meaning is imported into a text by the interpreter's will to power:

> "The question is," said Alice, "whether you *can* make words mean so many different things."
>
> "The question is," said Humpty Dumpty, "which is to be master—that's all."

But of course I don't at all believe that such deconstructive claims are, in Humpty Dumpty fashion, simply dogmatic assertions. Instead, they are conclusions which are derived from particular linguistic premises. I want, in the time remaining, to present what I make out to be the elected linguistic premises, first of Jacques Derrida, then of Hillis Miller, in the confidence that if I misinterpret these theories, my errors will soon be challenged and corrected. Let me eliminate suspense by saying at the beginning that I don't think that their radically skeptical conclusions from these premises are wrong. On the contrary, I believe that their conclusions are right—in fact, they are *infallibly* right, and that's where the trouble lies.

1

It is often said that Derrida and those who follow his lead subordinate all inquiries to a prior inquiry into language. This is true enough, but not specific enough, for it does not distinguish Derrida's work from what Richard Rorty calls "the linguistic turn"[6] which characterizes modern Anglo-American philosophy and also a great part of Anglo-American literary criticism, including the "New Criticism," of the last half-century. What is distinctive about Derrida is first that, like other French structuralists, he shifts his inquiry from language to *écriture*, the written or printed text; and second that he conceives a text in an extraordinarily limited fashion.

Derrida's initial and decisive strategy is to disestablish the priority, in traditional views of language, of speech over writing. By priority I mean the use of oral discourse as the conceptual model from which to derive the semantic and other features of written language and of language in general. And Derrida's shift of elementary reference is to a written text which consists of what we find when we look at it—to *"un texte déjà écrit, noir sur blanc* [a text already written, black on white]."[7] In the dazzling play of Derrida's expositions, his ultimate recourse is to these black marks on white paper as the sole things that are actually present in reading, and so are not fictitious constructs, illusions, phantasms; the visual features of these black-on-blanks he expands in multiple dimensions of elaborately figurative significance, only to contract them again, at telling moments, to their elemental status. The only things that are patently there when we look at the text are "marks" that are demarcated, and separated into groups, by "blanks"; there are also "spaces," "margins," and the "repetitions" and "differences" that we find when we compare individual marks and groups of marks.

By his rhetorical mastery Derrida solicits us to follow him in his move to these new premises, and to allow ourselves to be locked into them. This move is from what he calls the closed "logocentric" model of all traditional or "classical" views of language (which, he maintains, is based on the illusion of a Platonic or Christian transcendent being or presence, serving as the origin and guarantor of meanings) to what I shall call his own graphocentric model, in which the sole presences are marks-on-blanks.

By this bold move Derrida puts out of play, before the game even begins, every source of norms, controls, or indicators which, in the ordinary use and experience of language, set a limit to what we can mean and what we can be understood to mean. Since the only givens are already existing marks, "*déjà écrit*," we are denied recourse to a speaking or writing subject, or ego, or cogito, or consciousness, and so to any possible agency for the intention of meaning something ("*vouloir dire*"); all such agencies are relegated to the status of fictions generated by language, readily dissolved by deconstructive analysis. By this move he leaves us no place for referring to how we learn to speak, understand, or read language, and how, by interaction with more competent users and by our own developing experience with language, we come to recognize and correct our mistakes in speaking or understanding. The author is translated by Derrida (when he's not speaking in the momentary shorthand of traditional fictions) to a status as one more mark among other marks, placed at the head or the end of a text or set of texts, which are denominated as "bodies of work identified according to the 'proper name' of a signature."[8] Even syntax, the organization of words into a significant sentence, is given no role in determining the meanings of component words, for according to the graphocentric model, when we look at a page we see no organization but only a "chain" of grouped marks, a sequence of individual signs.

It is the notion of "the sign" that allows Derrida a limited opening-out of his premises. For he brings to a text the knowledge that the marks on a page are not random markings, but signs, and that a sign has a dual aspect as signifier and signified, signal and concept, or mark-with-meaning. But these meanings, when we look at a page, are not there, either as physical or mental presences. To account for significance, Derrida turns to a highly specialized and elaborated use of Saussure's notion that the identity either of the sound or of the signification of a sign does not consist in a positive attribute, but in a negative (or relational) attribute—that is, its "difference," or differentiability, from other sounds and other significations within a particular linguistic system.[9] This notion of difference is readily available to Derrida, because inspection of the printed page shows that some marks and sets of marks repeat each other, but that others differ from each other. In Derrida's theory "difference"—not "the difference between a and b and c . . ." but simply "difference" in itself—supplements the static elements of a text with an essential operative term, and as such (somewhat in the fashion of the term "negativity" in the dialectic of Hegel) it performs prodigies. For "difference" puts into motion the incessant play (*jeu*) of signification that goes on within the seeming immobility of the marks on the printed page.

To account for what is distinctive in the signification of a sign, Derrida puts forward the term "trace," which he says is not a presence, though it functions as a kind of "simulacrum" of a signified presence. Any signification that difference has activated in a signifier in the past remains active as a "trace" in the present instance as it will in the future,[10] and the "sedimentation" of traces which a signifier has accumulated constitutes the diversity in the play of its present significations. This trace is an elusive aspect of a text which is not, yet functions as though it were; it plays a role without being "present"; it "appears/disappears"; "in presenting itself it effaces itself."[11] Any attempt to define or interpret the significance of a sign or chain of signs consists in nothing more than the interpreter's putting in its place another sign or chain of signs, "sign-substitutions," whose self-effacing traces merely defer laterally, from substitution to substitution, the fixed and present meaning (or the signified "presence") we vainly pursue. The promise that the trace seems to offer of a presence on which the play of signification can come to rest in a determinate reference is thus never realizable, but incessantly deferred, put off, delayed. Derrida coins what in French is the portmanteau term *différance* (spelled *-ance*, and fusing the notions of differing and deferring) to indicate the endless play of generated significances, in which the reference is interminably postponed.[12] The conclusion, as Derrida puts it, is that "the central signified, the originating or transcendental signified" is revealed to be "never absolutely present outside a system of differences," and this "absence of an ultimate signified extends the domain and play of signification to infinity."[13]

What Derrida's conclusion comes to is that no sign or chain of signs can have a determinate meaning. But it seems to me that Derrida reaches this conclusion by a process which, in its own way, is no less dependent on an origin, ground, and end, and which is no less remorselessly "teleological," than the most rigorous of the metaphysical systems that he uses his conclusions to deconstruct. His origin and ground are his graphocentric premises, the closed chamber of texts for which he invites us to abandon our ordinary realm of experience in speaking, hearing, reading, and understanding language. And from such a beginning we move to a foregone conclusion. For Derrida's chamber of texts is a sealed echo-chamber in which meanings are reduced to a ceaseless echolalia, a vertical and lateral reverberation from sign to sign of ghostly nonpresences emanating from no voice, intended by no one, referring to nothing, bombinating in a void.

For the mirage of traditional interpretation, which vainly undertakes to determine what an author meant, Derrida proposes the alternative that we deliver ourselves over to a free participation in the infinite free-play of signification opened out by the signs in a text. And on this cheerless prospect of language and the cultural enterprise in ruins Derrida bids us to try to gaze, not with a Rousseauistic nostalgia for a lost security as to meaning which we never in fact possessed, but instead with "a Nietzschean *affirmation*, the joyous affirmation of the play of the world and of the innocence of becoming, the affirmation of a world of signs without error [*faute*], without truth, without origin, which is offered to an active interpretation. . . . And it plays without security. . . . In absolute chance, affirmation also surrenders itself to *genetic* indeterminacy, to the *seminal* chanciness [*aventure*] of the trace."[14] The graphocentric premises eventuate in what is patently a metaphysics, a world view of the free and unceasing play of *différance* which (since we can only glimpse this world by striking free of language, which inescapably implicates the entire metaphysics of presence that this view replaces) we are not able even to name. Derrida's vision is thus, as he puts it, of an "as yet unnamable something which cannot announce itself except ... under the species of a non-species, under the formless form, mute, infant, and terrifying, of monstrosity."[15]

2

Hillis Miller sets up an apt distinction between two classes of current structuralist critics, the "canny critics" and the "uncanny critics." The canny critics cling still to the possibility of "a structuralist-inspired criticism as a rational and rationalizable activity, with agreed-upon rules of procedure, given facts, and measurable results." The uncanny critics have renounced such a nostalgia for impossible certainties.[16] And as himself an uncanny critic, Miller's persistent enterprise is to get us to share, in each of the diverse works that he criticizes, its self-deconstructive revelation that in default of any possible origin, ground, presence, or end, it is an interminable free-play of indeterminable meanings.

Like Derrida, Miller sets up as his given the written text, "innocent black marks on a page"[17] which are endowed with traces, or vestiges of meaning; he then employs a variety of strategies that maximize the number and diversity of the possible meanings while minimizing any factors that might limit their free-play. It is worthwhile to note briefly two of those strategies.

For one thing Miller applies the terms *interpretation* and *meaning* in an extremely capacious way, so as to conflate linguistic utterance or writing with any metaphysical representation of theory or of "fact" about the physical world. These diverse realms are treated equivalently as "texts" which are "read" or "interpreted." He thus leaves no room for taking into account that language, unlike the physical world, is a cultural institution that developed expressly in order to mean something and to convey what is meant to members of a community who have learned how to use and interpret language. And within the realm of explicitly verbal texts, Miller allows for no distinction with regard to the kinds of norms that may obtain or may not obtain for the "interpretation" of the entire corpus of an individual author's writings, or of a single work in its totality, or of a particular passage, sentence, or word within that work. As a critical pluralist, I would agree that there is a diversity of sound (though not equally adequate) interpretations of the play *King Lear*, yet I claim to know precisely what Lear meant when he said, "Pray you undo this button."

A second strategy is related to Derrida's treatment of the "trace." Like Derrida, Miller excludes by his elected premises any control or limitation of signification by reference to the uses of a word or phrase that are current at the time an author writes, or to an author's intention, or to the verbal or generic context in which a word occurs. Any word within a given text—or at least any "key word," as he calls it, that he picks out for special scrutiny—can thus be claimed to signify any and all of the diverse things it has signified in the varied forms that the signifier has assumed through its recorded history; and not only in a particular language, such as English or French, but back through its etymology in Latin and Greek all the way to its postulated Indo-European root. Whenever and by whomever and in whatever context a printed word is used, therefore, the limits of what it can be said to mean in that use are set only by what the interpreter can find in historical and etymological dictionaries, supplemented by any further information that the interpreter's own erudition can provide. Hence Miller's persistent recourse to etymology—and even to the significance of the shapes of the printed letters in the altering form of a word—in expounding the texts to which he turns his critical attention.[18]

Endowed thus with the sedimented meanings accumulated over its total history, but stripped of any norms for selecting some of these and rejecting others, a key word—like the larger passage or total text of which the word is an element—becomes (in the phrase Miller cites from Mallarmé) a *suspens vibratoire*,[19] a vibratory suspension of equally likely meanings, and these are bound to include "incompatible" or "irreconcilable" or "contradictory" meanings. The conclusion from these views Miller formulates in a variety of ways: a key word, or a passage, or a text, since it is a ceaseless play of anomalous meanings, is "indeterminable," "undecipherable," "unreadable," "undecidable."[20] Or more bluntly: "All reading is misreading." "Any reading can be shown to be a misreading on evidence drawn from the text itself." But in misreading a text, the interpreter is merely repeating what the text itself has done before him, for "any literary text, with more or less explicitness or clarity, already reads or misreads itself."[21] To say that this concept of interpretation cuts the ground out from under the kind of history I undertook to write is to take a very parochial view of what is involved; for what it comes to is that no text, in part or whole, can mean anything in particular, and that we can never say just what anyone means by anything he writes.

But if all interpretation is misinterpretation, and if all criticism (like all history) of texts can engage only with a critic's own misconstruction, why bother to carry on the activities of interpretation and criticism? Hillis Miller poses this question more than once. He presents his answers in terms of his favorite analogues for the interpretive activity, which he explores with an unflagging resourcefulness. These analogues figure the text we read as a Cretan labyrinth, and also as the texture of a spider's web; the two figures, he points out, have been fused in earlier conflations in the myth of Ariadne's thread, by which

Theseus retraces the windings of the labyrinth, and of Arachne's thread, with which she spins her web.[22] Here is one of Miller's answers to the question, Why pursue the critical enterprise?

> Pater's writings, like those of other major authors in the Occidental tradi-
> tion, are at once open to interpretation and ultimately indecipherable, un-
> readable. His texts lead the critic deeper and deeper into a labyrinth until
> he confronts a final aporia. This does not mean, however, that the reader
> must give up from the beginning the attempt to understand Pater. Only by
> going all the way into the labyrinth, following the thread of a given clue,
> can the critic reach the blind alley, vacant of any Minotaur, that impasse
> which is the end point of interpretation.[23]

Now, I make bold to claim that I understand Miller's passage, and that what it says, in part, is that the deconstructive critic's act of interpretation has a beginning and an end; that it begins as an intentional, goal-oriented quest; and that this quest is to end in an impasse.

The reaching of the interpretive aporia or impasse precipitates what Miller calls "the uncanny moment"—the moment in which the critic, thinking to deconstruct the text, finds that he has simply participated in the ceaseless play of the text as a self-deconstructive artifact. Here is another of Miller's statements, in which he describes both his own and Derrida's procedure:

> Deconstruction as a mode of interpretation works by a careful and cir-
> cumspect entering of each textual labyrinth. . . . The deconstructive critic
> seeks to find, by this process of retracing, the element in the system studied
> which is alogical, the thread in the text in question which will unravel it all,
> or the loose stone which will pull down the whole building. The decon-
> struction, rather, annihilates the ground on which the building stands by
> showing that the text has already annihilated that ground, knowingly or
> unknowingly. Deconstruction is not a dismantling of the structure of a
> text but a demonstration that it has already dismantled itself.[24]

The uncanny moment in interpretation, as Miller phrases it elsewhere, is a sudden "*mise en abyme*" in which the bottom drops away and, in the endless regress of the self-baffling free-play of meanings in the very signs which both reveal an abyss and, by naming it, cover it over, we catch a glimpse of the abyss itself in a "vertigo of the underlying nothingness."[25]

The "deconstructive critic," Miller has said, "*seeks* to find" the alogical element in a text, the thread which, when pulled, will unravel the whole texture. Given the game Miller has set up, with its graphocentric premises and freedom of interpretive maneuver, the infallible rule of the deconstructive quest is,

"Seek and ye shall find." The deconstructive method works, because it can't help working; it is a can't-fail enterprise; there is no complex passage of verse or prose which could possibly serve as a counterinstance to test its validity or limits. And the uncanny critic, whatever the variousness and distinctiveness of the texts to which he applies his strategies, is bound to find that they all reduce to one thing and one thing only. In Miller's own words: each deconstructive reading, "performed on any literary, philosophical, or critical text . . . reaches, in the particular way the given text allows it, the 'same' moment of an aporia. . . . The reading comes back again and again, with different texts, to the 'same' impasse."[26]

It is of no avail to point out that such criticism has nothing whatever to do with our common experience of the uniqueness, the rich variety, and the passionate human concerns in works of literature, philosophy, or criticism—these matters are among the linguistic illusions that the criticism dismantles. There are, I want to emphasize, rich rewards in reading Miller, as in reading Derrida, which include a delight in his resourceful play of mind and language and the many and striking insights yielded by his wide reading and by his sharp eye for unsuspected congruities and differences in our heritage of literary and philosophical writings. But these rewards are yielded by the way, and that way is always to the ultimate experience of vertigo, the uncanny *frisson* at teetering with him on the brink of the abyss; and even the shock of this discovery is soon dulled by its expected and invariable recurrence.

I shall cite a final passage to exemplify the deft and inventive play of Miller's rhetoric, punning, and figuration, which gives his formulations of the *mise en abyme* a charm that is hard to resist. In it he imposes his fused analogues of labyrinth and web and abyss on the black-on-blanks which constitute the elemental given of the deconstructive premises:

> Far from providing a benign escape from the maze, Ariadne's thread makes the labyrinth, is the labyrinth. The interpretation or solving of the puzzles of the textual web only adds more filaments to the web. One can never escape from the labyrinth because the activity of escaping makes more labyrinth, the thread of a linear narrative or story. Criticism is the production of more thread to embroider the texture or textile already there. This thread is like the filament of ink which flows from the pen of the writer, keeping him in the web but suspending him also over the chasm, the blank page that thin line hides.[27]

To interpret: Hillis Miller, suspended by the labyrinthine lines of a textual web over the abyss that those black lines demarcate on the blank page, busies himself to unravel the web that keeps him from plunging into the blank abyss, but finds he can do so only by an act of writing which spins a further web of lines, equally vulnerable to deconstruction, but only by another movement of the pen that will trace still another inky net over the ever-receding abyss. As Miller remarks, I suppose ruefully, at the end of the passage I quoted, "In one version of Ariadne's story she is said to have hanged herself with her thread in despair after being abandoned by Theseus."

3

What is one to say in response to this abysmal vision of the textual world of literature, philosophy, and all the other achievements of mankind in the medium of language? There is, I think, only one adequate response, and that is the one that William Blake made to the Angel in *The Marriage of Heaven and Hell*. After they had groped their way down a "winding cavern," the Angel revealed to Blake a ghastly vision of hell as an "infinite Abyss"; in it was "the sun, black but shining," around which were "fiery tracks on which revolv'd vast spiders." But no sooner, says Blake, had "my friend the Angel" departed, than "this appearance was no more, but I found myself sitting on a pleasant bank beside a river by moon light, hearing a harper who sung to a harp." The Angel, "surprised asked me how I escaped? I answered: 'All that we saw was owing to your metaphysics.'"

As a deconstructive Angel, Hillis Miller, I am happy to say, is not serious about deconstruction, in Hegel's sense of "serious"; that is, he does not entirely and consistently commit himself to the consequences of his premises. He is in fact, fortunately for us, a double agent who plays the game of language by two very different sets of rules. One of the games he plays is that of a deconstructive critic of literary texts. The other is the game he will play in a minute or two when he steps out of his graphocentric premises onto this platform and begins to talk to us.

I shall hazard a prediction as to what Miller will do then. He will have determinate things to say and will masterfully exploit the resources of language to express these things clearly and forcibly, addressing himself to us in the confidence that we, to the degree that we have mastered the constitutive norms of this kind of discourse, will approximate what he means. He will show no inordinate theoretical difficulties about beginning his discourse or conducting it through its middle to an end. What he says will manifest, by immediate inference, a thinking subject or ego and a distinctive and continuant ethos, so that those of you who, like myself, know and admire his recent writings will be surprised and delighted by particularities of what he says, but will correctly anticipate both its general tenor and its highly distinctive style and manner of proceeding. What he says, furthermore, will manifest a feeling as well as thinking subject; and unless it possesses a superhuman forbearance, this subject will express some natural irritation that I, an old friend, should so obtusely have misinterpreted what he has said in print about his critical intentions.

Before coming here, Miller worked his thoughts (which involved inner speech) into the form of writing. On this platform, he will proceed to convert this writing to speech; and it is safe to say—since our chairman is himself a double agent, editor of a critical journal as well as organizer of this symposium—that soon his speech will be reconverted to writing and presented to the public. This substitution of *écriture* for *parole* will certainly make a difference, but not an absolute difference; what Miller says here, that is, will not jump an ontological gap to the printed page, shedding on the way all the features that made it intelligible as discourse. For each of his readers will be able to reconvert the black-on-blanks back into speech, which he will hear in his mind's ear; he will perceive the words not simply as marks nor as sounds, but as already invested with meaning; also, by immediate inference, he will be aware in his reading of an intelligent subject, very similar to the one we will infer while listening to him here, who organizes the well-formed and significant sentences and marshals the argument conveyed by the text.

There is no linguistic or any other law we can appeal to that will prevent a deconstructive critic from bringing his graphocentric procedures to bear on the printed version of Hillis Miller's discourse—or of mine, or of Wayne Booth's—and if he does, he will infallibly be able to translate the text into a vertiginous *mise en abyme*. But those of us who stubbornly refuse to substitute the rules of the deconstructive enterprise for our ordinary skill and tact at language will find that we are able to understand this text very well. In many ways, in fact, we will understand it better than while hearing it in the mode of oral discourse, for the institution of print will render the fleeting words of his speech by a durable graphic correlate which will enable us to take our own and not the speaker's time in attending to it, as well as to reread it, to collocate, and to ponder until we are satisfied that we have approximated the author's meaning.

After Hillis Miller and I have pondered in this way over the text of the other's discourse, we will probably, as experience in such matters indicates, continue essentially to disagree. By this I mean that neither of us is apt to find the other's reasons so compelling as to get him to change his own interpretive premises and aims. But in the process, each will have come to see more clearly what the other's reasons are for doing what he does, and no doubt come to discover that some of these reasons are indeed good reasons in that, however short of being compelling, they have a bearing on the issue in question. In brief, insofar as we set ourselves, in the old-fashioned way, to make out what the other means by what he says, I am confident that we shall come to a better mutual understanding. After all, without that confidence that we can use language to say what we mean and can interpret language so as to determine what was meant, there is no rationale for the dialogue in which we are now engaged.

NOTES

1. M. H. Abrams, "Rationality and Imagination in Cultural History: A Reply to Wayne Booth," *Critical Inquiry* 2, no. 3 (Spring 1976): 456–60.

2. J. Hillis Miller, "Tradition and Difference," *Diacritics* 2, no. 4 (Winter 1972): 6.

3. Miller, "Tradition and Difference," 10–11.

4. Miller, "Tradition and Difference," 8, 12.

5. Miller, "Tradition and Difference," 12.

6. Richard Rorty, ed., *The Linguistic Turn* (Chicago: University of Chicago Press, 1967).

7. Jacques Derrida, "La Double séance," in *La Dissémination* (Paris: Éditions du Seuil, 1972), 203.

8. Derrida, "La Mythologie blanche: La métaphore dans le texte philosophique," in *Marges de la philosophie* (Paris: Minuit, 1972), 304. Translations throughout are my own.

9. Ferdinand de Saussure, *Course in General Linguistics*, trans. Wade Baskin (New York: Philosophical Library, 1959), 117–2l.

10. Derrida, "La Différance," in *Marges de la philosophie* (Paris: Minuit, 1972), 12–14, 25.

11. Derrida, "La Différance," 23–24.

12. In the traditional or "classic" theory of signs, as Derrida describes the view that he dismantles, the sign is taken to be "a deferred presence . . . the circulation of signs defers the moment in which we will be able to encounter the thing itself, to get hold of it, consume or expend it, touch it, see it, have a present intuition of it" (ibid., 9). See also "Hors livre" in *La Dissémination* (Paris: Éditions du Seuil, 1972), 10–11.

13. Derrida, "La Structure, le signe et le jeu dans le discours des sciences humaines," in *L'Écriture et la différance* (Paris: Seuil, 1967), 411.

14. Derrida, "La Structure, le signe," 427. Derrida adds that this "interpretation of interpretation," which "affirms free-play . . . tries to pass beyond man and humanism." On the coming "monstrosity," see also Derrida, *De la grammatologie* (Paris: Minuit, 1967), 14.

15. Derrida, "La Structure, le signe," 428. "We possess no language . . . which is alien to this history; we cannot express a single destructive proposition which will not already have slipped into the form, the logic, and the implicit postulates of that very thing that it seeks to oppose." "Each limited borrowing drags along with it all of metaphysics" (412–13).

16. J. Hillis Miller, "Stevens' Rock and Criticism as Cure, II," *Georgia Review* 30, no. 2 (Summer 1976): 335–36.

17. J. Hillis Miller, "Walter Pater: A Partial Portrait," *Daedalus* 105, no. 1 (Winter 1976): 107.

18. See, for example, his unfolding of the meanings of *cure* and *absurd* in J. Hillis Miller, "Stevens' Rock and Criticism as Cure, I," *Georgia Review* 30, no. 1 (Spring 1976): 6–11. For his analysis of significance in the altering shapes, through history, of the printed form of a word, see his exposition of *abyme*, ibid., 11; also his exposition of the letter *x* in Miller, "Ariadne's Thread: Repetition and the Narrative Line," *Critical Inquiry* 3, no. 1 (Autumn 1976): 75–76.

19. Miller, "Tradition and Difference," 12.

20. See, e.g., Miller, "Stevens' Rock, I," 9–11; "Walter Pater," 111.

21. Miller, "Walter Pater," 98; "Stevens' Rock, II," 333.

22. Miller, "Ariadne's Thread," 66.

23. Miller, "Walter Pater," 112.

24. Miller, "Stevens' Rock, II," 341. See also "Walter Pater," 101, and "Adriadne's Thread," 74.

25. Miller, "Stevens' Rock, I," 11–12. The unnamable abyss which Miller glimpses has its parallel in the unnamable and terrifying monstrosity which Derrida glimpses.

26. Miller, "Deconstructing the Deconstructors," *Diacritics* 5, no. 2 (Summer 1975): 30.

27. "Stevens' Rock, II," 337.

# PART III
## EMPIRE BUILDING

AS THE ESSAYS in this section demonstrate, it was primarily the celebrity status of a core group of French theorists that consolidated theory's sovereignty and invited imitation throughout the English-speaking world. Niilo Kauppi (whose work is included in part 4, below) has stressed how important it was to the development of Theory that postwar French intellectuals coined a set of neologisms that could be associated only with their particular names—a stratagem used not only by leading figures such as Althusser, Lacan, Foucault, Derrida, Kristeva, Deleuze, Baudrillard, and Bourdieu, but also by their non-French followers such as Spivak, Bhabha, and Butler. And perhaps it is fitting that those who see words as the preeminent elements of life should seek to put their imprint on language. As Thorstein Veblen might have said, "Vocabulary is the intellectual's form of conspicuous consumption."

Frederick Crews opens this section with an essay occasioned by Quentin Skinner's *Return of Grand Theory in the Human Sciences* (1986). Crews's analysis of this influential collection shows that critical thinking was dominated not by big ideas but by "a growing apriorism," that is, "a willingness to settle issues by theoretical decree." Drawing on loose readings of Kuhn's *Structure of Scientific Revolutions* (1962), this "theoreticism," that is, the "frank recourse to unsubstantiated theory"—as Crews calls it—expressed a mood of "antinomian rebellion and self-indulgence" inherited from the 1960s. More directly, it was inspired by French poststructuralists, whom Crews characterizes as "cognitive minimalists" who disdained empirical justification. The "dogmatism of intellectual style" evident in their Anglo-American epigones is plainly rooted in their French sources. Even as intellectual fashions shifted from one figure to another—Althusser, Lacan, Derrida, Foucault—the habit of unquestioning belief in these *maîtres* continued. Now, nearly twenty years after the original publication of Crews's essay, it is clear that the period in which he wrote witnessed the consolidation of Theory's empire, abetted by the patron-client syndrome endemic among intellectuals and driven by what Crews calls "our long romance with theory for theory's sake."

J. G. Merquior's essay, also dating from the mid-1980s, targets the "literalization of thought" launched by poststructuralism. Merquior's essay takes issue with Jonathan Culler's *On Deconstruction* (1982) for urging that literary theorists should play "the central role" in intellectual life. Such a posture (which Alan Megill at that time identified as "literary-critical imperialism"), Merquior comments, is typical of academic literati who function as purveyors of "theorrhea": that is, grandiose theoretical pronouncements resting on slipshod thinking and feeble analysis. Although some scholars have found their way out of this trap to a more humanistic stance (Todorov is an example), the field has continued to be dominated by cult figures such as Lacan, Foucault, and Derrida who reject the clarity of the social sciences in favor of hermetic pronouncements, even as they cover their words with a scientific gloss (a theme to which we will return in part 7 of this volume). While these theorists tilt at modern society and its values, their real victim, Merquior argues, is the rational intellect itself and the guiding role it should play in human affairs.

The concluding chapter of Brian Vickers's *Appropriating Shakespeare* (1993), presented here, explores a troubling phenomenon in literary theory: the readiness of critics nowadays to attach themselves wholeheartedly to a reigning master and his system of ideas. Deploring this tendency as a form of "slavehood in the history of thought," Vickers portrays autocratic leader figures (Derrida, Lacan, Foucault, Althusser, and so on) as intellectual dogmatists—absolutist in their opinions, prophetic in their pronouncements, dismissive of rivals, self-centered, and isolated from the world of observation. Their followers, in turn, he says, are trusting, simplistic, and yet aggressively partisan. Taking his examples from some recent readings of Shakespeare, Vickers shows how hanger-on scholars routinely misrepresent the texts they study by using an adopted system of thought as a template with which to assess the meaning and worth of a literary work. Exaggeration of the significance of their discoveries leads to intolerance toward competing interpretations. Vickers concludes with a reflection on the polarizing impetus imparted by this zealotry to professional conduct in literary studies.

An episode from the late 1980s sharply illuminating the Theory world and challenging its authority is explored by the historian Alan Spitzer in his essay about the late Paul de Man, the most influential proponent of deconstruction in the United States. Several years after his death in 1983, de Man became the center of controversy when it was discovered that in the early 1940s he had contributed to the pro-Nazi press in his native Belgium. While protesting the dismissal of a scholar's later work by revelations relating to his activities decades earlier, Spitzer is particularly struck by the contradictory behavior of de Man's defenders, leading deconstructionists all, who unhesitantly adopted the language of "setting the record straight." Faced with the job of defending de Man's reputation, they had no choice but to attempt to rest their case on conventional criteria of accuracy—an ironic reflection, this, on the gap between Theory's rhetoric and theoreticians' actual practice.

Listening to fashionable theorists, one cannot help perceiving how they strain always to be up-to-the-minute in their thinking. This drive has played a considerable role in their preeminence and in the eagerness of their followers to echo them. Graham Good's essay explores a common element in contemporary Theory: a dogmatic presentism that turns the realization that the past cannot be known fully into an insistence that it cannot be known at all. Complementary to the dismissal of the past is Theory's rejection of visions of the future, including the idea of human progress. In these ways presentism distorts the relationship of what came before to what is now, leading critics to their obsession with *post*ness while ignoring pastness. This distortion is especially evident in postcolonial studies, which concentrate on the negative aspects of European (but no other) imperialism. New Historicists, too, show their lack of a coherent view of history by juxtaposing incomplete fragments from the past in order to arrive at their key themes of power and suppression. History, to them, is merely a series of "past presents."

An important sense in which "empire" has played a key role in literary studies over the past few decades is as a thing to be relentlessly pilloried and deplored. This might seem an odd undertaking for literary scholars, but, as we will see in part 6, Theory has had an active life as surrogate politics. Here we offer Erin O'Connor's challenge to postcolonial criticism. O'Connor takes issue with the "globalizing" impulse in literary studies, which sets out to turn literary works into allegories for nonliterary endeavors such as imperialism and nation building. Nowhere is this reductive impulse more prevalent than in the treatment of the Victorian novel by postcolonial critics such as Gayatri Spivak and her followers. O'Connor shows how they misrepresent and distort, mostly in the form of "majestic generalities." Such "Victorientalism," as O'Connor calls it, cries out to be replaced by a genuinely post-postcolonial criticism that is neither censorious nor prescriptive and that recognizes Victorian literature's thematic subtleties, structural indeterminacies, and intellectual rigor.

## 13.  THE GRAND ACADEMY OF THEORY

### FREDERICK CREWS

IT HAS BEEN MORE than a quarter-century now since C. P. Snow first told us that we educated Anglo-Americans belong to two mutually uncomprehending and antagonistic cultures, one scientific and the other humanistic. In 1959, with the beeping of Sputnik still echoing in the public ear, no one expected Snow to accord the two camps equal sympathy, and he did not. The forbidding technical intricacy of the sciences, he declared in *The Two Cultures and the Scientific Revolution*, was hardly a sufficient reason for humanists to turn their backs on science, retreating into spiteful ignorance and misrepresentation.[1] Nonscientists grumbled under Snow's tongue-lashing, but many of them secretly agreed with the consensus that they had better mend their ways. Certainly it would have been an unpropitious moment for anyone to launch a major counteroffensive against scientific authority.

That episode came to mind as I was reading the Cambridge political scientist Quentin Skinner's introduction to a collection of essays by various hands on influential recent thinkers, portentously titled *The Return of Grand Theory in the Human Sciences* (hereafter *RGT*).[2] Snow's name is never invoked, but the idea of the two estranged cultures pervades Skinner's introduction, which spells out for us how radically the academic mood has altered. Moreover, Skinner begins his story just around the time that Snow's polemic appeared.

In those days, we are reminded, the most prestigious general model of explanation was logical positivism, the view that the meaningfulness of a statement is vouchsafed by its testability. Judged by that criterion, much of what had long passed for important discourse had to be dismissed as vacuous. Consequently, a generation of no-nonsense philosophers abandoned metaphysics for more modest pursuits, including, for example, clarification of the exact meaning of scientific terms. Social scientists, caught in the same wave, declared an "end of ideology" and steeled themselves to perceive only narrow empirical issues. And historians followed Sir Lewis Namier in rejecting all theoretical "flapdoodle," as he had called it, and in fixing their attention on "the detailed manoeuvres of individual political actors at the centres of political power" (*RGT*, 3). Thus, while most academics may have been as scientifically illiterate as Snow alleged, their own work implicitly honored what they took to be the heart of science, namely, deference to the almighty fact.

Frederick Crews. "The Grand Academy of Theory." Originally published in the *New York Review of Books*, 29 May 1986. Reprinted in *Skeptical Engagements*, by Frederick Crews, 159–78. New York: Oxford University Press, 1986. Used by permission of the author.

But by now, Skinner reports, a dramatic change has occurred. Among recent "general transformations" in the "human sciences,"[3] "perhaps the most significant has been the widespread reaction against the assumption that the natural sciences offer an adequate or even a relevant model for the practice of the social disciplines. The clearest reflection of this growing doubt has been the revival of the suggestion that the explanation of human behaviour and the explanation of natural events are logically distinct undertakings" (*RGT*, 6). Thus,

> During the past generation, Utopian social philosophies have once again been practised as well as preached; Marxism has revived and flourished in an almost bewildering variety of forms; psychoanalysis has gained a new theoretical orientation with the work of Lacan and his followers; Habermas and other members of the Frankfurt School have continued to reflect on the parallels between the theories of Marx and Freud; the Women's Movement has added a whole range of previously neglected insights and arguments; and amidst all this turmoil the empiricist and positivist citadels of English-speaking social philosophy have been threatened and undermined by successive waves of hermeneuticists, structuralists, post-empiricists, deconstructionists and other invading hordes.    (*RGT*, 5–6)

Anyone who has been close to the Anglo-American humanities and social sciences in recent decades will know what Skinner is talking about here. The paragraph, however, is arresting as an index both to the feelings stirred by its subject matter and to a resultant confusion in *RGT*. A quick reading could give the impression that Skinner is caught up in the irresistible energy of an ascendant movement, but his choice of language points elsewhere: to bewilderment, turmoil, threats, underminings, successive waves, invading hordes. Skinner sounds rather like a hostage on videotape, assuring the folks at home that he is being exposed to a lively new slant on things, meanwhile signaling with grimaces, *These people mean business!*

This mixed impression deepens when we realize that the "invading hordes," clearly of uppermost concern to Skinner, are only spottily represented by the nine figures treated in the volume he has edited: Hans-Georg Gadamer, Jacques Derrida, Michel Foucault, Thomas Kuhn, John Rawls, Jürgen Habermas, Louis Althusser, Claude Lévi-Strauss, and Fernand Braudel.[4] What, for example, do Marxists, Freudians, feminists, and deconstructionists have to do with Gadamer, the tradition-minded seeker of interpretive certainty, or with Rawls, the Kantian ethical philosopher who deduces rules of justice from an imagined social contract, or with Braudel, the student of geographic necessities that transcend and outlast all linguistic networks? Why, on the other hand, are such idolized system builders as Jacques Lacan and Gilles Deleuze not afforded chapters of their own? Lacan is mentioned only in passing, Deleuze not at all. One wonders if Skinner wants to allay his doubts about the "invading hordes" by putting them into the most respectable company he can find.

Not surprisingly, some of the contributors to *RGT* appear less than comfortable with Skinner's vague notion of Grand Theory. Thus Barry Barnes deems it "ironical" to include Thomas Kuhn, whose "mental universe could scarcely be more distant from that of Althusser, or even Habermas" (*RGT*, 98). And Mark Philp observes that Michel Foucault's presence in the book "might seem paradoxical," since "his work is above all iconoclastic in intent" (*RGT*, 67). Skinner himself perceives this latter problem, confessing that it "may well sound dangerously like missing the point" to characterize as grand theorists those extreme relativists who seek "to demolish the claims of theory and method to organize the materials of experience" (*RGT*, 12).

This anomaly remains in place after Skinner has lamely tried to banish it, first by claiming that iconoclasm is itself Grand Theory, then by calling its *influence* grand, and finally by hazarding that the iconoclasts at any rate "cleared the ground" (*RGT*, 13) for other thinkers who have reopened such classic topics as "the character of the good life and the boundaries of a free and just society" (*RGT*, 14). Here we are apparently being invited to imagine that a figure like Rawls must have been made possible by groundbreakers like Derrida and Foucault. But even a surface acquaintance with the latter pair would show the absurdity of such a suggestion. If Derrida and Foucault lead anywhere, it is not to social contracts and laws of human nature but to a ban on recourse to such flagrantly bourgeois concepts.

As a set of introductions to important figures, *RGT* is a sober and useful work, distinguished for the most part by clarity, fair-mindedness, and bibliographical helpfulness. In one contribution, James Boon's on Lévi-Strauss, it passes beyond utility to significant insight and eloquence. But as a case for a specific return of Grand Theory within determinate limits of time and place, the book is drastically fuzzy. It cannot even make up its collective mind about the meaning of its basic terms or the scope of their application.

In France and Germany, the homelands of all but two of the figures treated, modern philosophical and sociopolitical thought never surrendered to positivism and thus never reverted to sweeping speculation. Heidegger and Sartre, for instance, surely had more to say about "grand" issues of human fate than Foucault and Derrida do. If the new movement arrived with, say, Gadamer's *Truth and Method* in 1960, then we must exclude Lévi-Strauss, whose anthropological researches were already under way in the thirties. And if Braudel is to be counted, Grand Theory began at least as early as 1947, the year that *The Mediterranean* was submitted as a *thèse*, and possibly as far back as 1929, when the *Annales* school of historiography first became known. What kind of "return" would that be?

The editorial muddle behind *RGT* is worsened by a general reluctance to admit that some currents of theoretical enthusiasm are already weakening in their Continental homelands. In one instance, Susan James's chapter on the structuralist Marxist Louis Althusser, such discretion passes over into apparent disingenuousness. Not only does James fail to report that Althusser's intricately deterministic and top-heavy system of thought has come to be almost universally repudiated in France; she employs the present perfect tense (Althusser "has revised," "has held fast," etc.) to suggest that his position is still being articulated at this hour. But as every "Western Marxist" knows all too well, the curtain rang down on Althusser's career in 1980 when he strangled his wife and was judged mentally incompetent to stand trial. That culminating shock, in Martin Jay's words, "spelled the end [in France] of structuralist Marxism, whose obituary some observers in fact had written as early as 1969."[5]

Again, the diffuse idea of Grand Theory obscures a crucial shift of values within the career of Jürgen Habermas, the leading successor to the Frankfurt School, whom Skinner can appreciate only as the harbinger of our brisk Freudian and Marxist renaissance. Anthony Giddens's chapter on Habermas, though competent and informative so far as it goes, is less candid about Habermas's self-oppositions than is a still more recent essay of his.[6] In RGT Giddens appears to be restrained by the book's kidgloves decorum and by the group effort to accentuate "grandeur." His newer essay, by contrast, is more attuned to Habermas's dilemma of trying to reconcile traditional intellectual loyalties with a nascent impulse to ideologize knowledge.

For whatever reason, Skinner has confounded two reactions against positivism, one thematic and the other attitudinal, that are only casually and inconsistently related. The first is Grand Theory proper, the addressing of those general ethical and political questions that positivism had declared senseless. The other is a new peremptoriness of intellectual style, emboldening thinkers to make up their own rules of inquiry or simply to turn their whim into law. Such liberation from the empirical ethos can result in Grand Theory, but it can just as easily lead to a relativism that dismisses the whole idea of seeking truth. Skinner has chosen to minimize the fact that one thinker (Rawls, for example) can be "grand" in scope but flexible in intellectual style, whereas another (Derrida, for example) can be "anti-grand" in a way that brooks no dissent.

It seems obvious which of Skinner's themes is the more significant for an understanding of our present intellectual climate. The major shift we have witnessed over the past generation is not a growing taste for big ideas but a growing apriorism—a willingness to settle issues by theoretical decree, without even a pretense of evidential appeal. In 1960 nearly everyone, despite the widening fissure between Snow's two cultures, would have concurred with R. S. Crane's observation that one of the most important marks of the good scholar is "a habitual distrust of the a priori; that is to say, of all ways of arriving at particular conclusions which assume the relevance and authority, prior to the concrete evidence, of theoretical doctrines or other general propositions."[7] But today we are surrounded by *theoreticism*—frank recourse to unsubstantiated theory, not just as a tool of investigation but as antiempirical knowledge in its own right.

To appreciate the theoreticist climate, it is essential to recognize a distinction between two related conceptions of empiricism. Philosophers have used the term in several senses, one of which is a faith in "scientific method" or a "logic of verification"—that is, in the availability of neutral grounds for infallibly showing which of several hypotheses or theories is "closest to the truth." For excellent reasons, belief in that "foundationalist" empiricism has all but vanished in the past twenty years.[8] In a broader sense, however, science remains thoroughly empirical; even its most formalized reasoning is ultimately answerable to the testing of predicted consequences. Thus we both do and don't live in a "postempiricist" age, depending on which kind of empiricism is intended.

The empiricism that stands in some jeopardy today is simply a regard for evidence—a disposition to consult ascertainable facts when choosing between rival ideas. In practice, of course, the individual investigator never collects enough evidence to guarantee that a given idea is the best one going. Consequently, the heart of empiricism consists of active participation in a community of informed people who themselves care about evidence and who can be counted on for unsparing criticism.

Now, our theoreticists pride themselves on being resolutely "antipositivist"—that is, opposed to the restriction of meaningfulness to verifiability in the foundationalist or "scientific method" sense. They think of themselves as staving off a persistent threat of positivist incursion upon human studies. But there must be something else going on here, since by now one might have to repair to the graveyard to find an authentic positivist to kick around. What "antipositivism" really comes down to is a feeling of nonobligation toward empiricism in the broad sense—that is, toward the community that expects theory to stay at least somewhat responsive to demonstrable findings.

In the rhetoric of theoreticism, that community often gets conveniently merged with "science." To be a good contemporary antipositivist, then, is to resist the encroachment of science on human studies—to deny, as Skinner puts it, "that the natural sciences offer [us] an adequate or even a relevant model." This can be done in either of two ways. First, one can *declare the human studies off-limits to scientific rigor* by saying, in Skinner's phrase, that they are "logically distinct" from science. Or, more radically, one can *deny that science itself is really empirical*. Both methods make ample room for willful assertion, but the second, as we will see, leads to more spectacular theoretical claims.

We can observe the first of these strategies at work by looking at the early Habermas's so-called hermeneutic argument for making use of Marxism and psychoanalysis in social thought. According to hermeneutics, science seeks permanent cause-effect relations between physical objects, whereas hermeneutic insight consists of empathy with social-historical actors or with texts. Some hermeneuticists go on to assert that different standards of corroboration therefore apply to the two realms. Habermas's novelty in his first major treatise, *Knowledge and Human Interests* (1968), was to redescribe Marxism and psychoanalysis as nonscientific so that they could be absolved from empirical scrutiny and employed for utopian speculative ends.[9]

Freud and Marx thought of themselves as scientific lawgivers, codifying psychic etiology and cure in the one case and political economy and historical development in the other. Habermas, however, managed to convince himself and quite a few readers that Freud and Marx had made causal claims only through a kind of inadvertence or "scientistic self-misunderstanding." Properly understood, he explained, their visions must be regarded as context-dependent, self-certifying interpretive techniques, or "historical-hermeneutic disciplines." Their justification thus resides not in whatever empirical plausibility they may possess—an issue Habermas unceremoniously swept under the rug—but rather in their capacity to produce experiences of liberating "self-reflection."

In retrospect it seems clear that the acclaim bestowed on this argument owed much to the *Zeitgeist*—the emerging climate of theoreticism—and little to Habermas's reasoning, which was wishful in the extreme. As Adolf Grünbaum has shown, Habermas first misconstrued the bounds of science, wrongly decreeing that any historical phenomenon, such as a patient's therapeutic progress, automatically falls outside the scientific purview. Then he entangled himself in such absurdities as the claim that the *etiological causality* behind a neurotic symptom is rendered void once the symptom has been cured—as if determinism itself, fully efficacious at one early time, could then be retroactively unraveled.[10] In short, Habermas had sacrificed logical cogency to his overriding value in the sixties, "emancipation."[11]

Nonetheless, we can see that Habermas, whose political evolution soon caused him to begin rethinking the whole liberationist approach to knowledge, had scarcely gotten started down the theoreticist path. He was quite satisfied, for example, with the relatively mild epistemic relativism professed by Marx and Freud. That is, both of those observers faulted the majority for dwelling in occluded consciousness, but they did so—and Habermas approved—in the name of a truer, unrepressed consciousness that could be made accessible through private or mass re-education. Habermas was already placing his faith in human powers of cognitive adjustment to conditions that could be rationally brought to light.

Moreover, even in 1968 Habermas was concerned to employ only the most plausible-looking features of Marxism and psychoanalysis—which is to say, necessarily, the least deterministic ones.[12] His affinity was not for iron laws either of history or of psychobiological compulsion but for holistic humanism, ego psychology, and the mundane actualities of the therapeutic transaction. In all these respects he was showing resistance to theoreticism, whose purest impulse is toward positing ineluctable constraints on the perceptiveness and adaptability of everyone but the theorist himself.[13] Habermas's ethic of widening the individual's range of conscious choice armed him against that temptation.

It was fitting, however, that Habermas was trying to advance the particular doctrines of Marxism and psychoanalysis when he took his first tentative steps toward theoreticism. Of course the immediate explanation lies in his involvement with the Frankfurt School, which had already diluted Marx with Freud to explain the unfulfillment of Marx's prophecies. (If the Western proletariat was not arising on schedule, its unconscious must have been in thrall to the oppressor.) Yet it is surely no coincidence that when more committed theoreticists than Habermas have laid claim to antiempirical "sciences" of their own, their choice has almost always been for some permutation of Freudianism or Marxism. It is important to understand why.

While classic Marxism and psychoanalysis insist upon their observational basis, they also constitute inside critiques of received knowledge (it is distorted by "false consciousness" or "repression"), and they bestow epistemic privilege on a group of deep knowers (the revolutionary vanguard, the analyzed) who possess an antidote to chronic error. Try as they may to blend into the wider scientific community, Marxists and Freudians know that they have a head start toward truth; and they also know why the uninitiated may be compelled (by class interest, by fear of the repressed) to resist that truth. These two movements may have accumulated some well-founded tenets along their troubled roads, but in origin and spirit they are *countersciences*—creeds that use a dry mechanistic idiom and an empirical façade to legitimize "deep," morally engaged revelations, which can always be placed on some new footing if their original claims turn out to be baseless.

We have seen that Habermas's way of shielding his countersciences from empirical audit was to shift them to the nonscientific or hermeneutic side of the ledger. Such an evasion cannot satisfy an all-out theoreticist, since it leaves unchallenged the sovereignty of established science. The more thoroughgoing "antipositivist" strategy, then, is to defy empiricism in general by declaring it inoperative even within science. Practitioners of human studies need only catch distant rumors of philosophers' assaults on the foundationalist logic of verification to leap to a happy conclusion: we now live in a time "when science itself is recognizing that its own methods are ultimately no more objective than those of the arts."[14]

When this obituary for empiricism is accompanied by an argument, the latter usually rests on a loose reading of Thomas Kuhn's *The Structure of Scientific Revolutions* (1962), the most frequently cited academic book of modern times.[15] Kuhn, we are told, demonstrated that any two would-be paradigms, or regnant major theories, will be incommensurable; that is, they will represent different universes of perception and explanation. Hence no common ground can exist for testing their merits, and one theory will prevail for strictly sociological, never empirical, reasons. The winning theory will be the one that better suits the emergent temper or interests of the hour. It follows that intellectuals who once trembled before the disapproving gaze of positivism can now propose sweeping "Kuhnian revolutionary paradigms" of their own, defying whatever disciplinary consensus they find antipathetic and trusting that tomorrow's "sociology" will validate their choice.

One can gauge the emotional force of theoreticism by the remoteness of this interpretation from what Kuhn actually said, especially in the second edition of his book and in subsequent clarifying articles.[16] Kuhn happens to be a fervent believer in scientific rationality and progress, which, he argues, can occur only after a given specialty has gotten past the stage of "theory proliferation" and "incessant criticism and continual striving for a fresh start."[17] By incommensurability Kuhn never meant that competing theories are incomparable but only that the choice between them cannot be entirely consigned to the verdict of theory-neutral rules and data. (What looks like a "mistake" in one theory's terms may be a legitimate inference in the terms of its rival.) Transitions between paradigms—which in any case are mere problem solutions, not broad theories or methodologies—must indeed be made globally, through "gestalt switches," but the rationality of science is not thereby impaired. As Kuhn asked, and as he has continued to insist with mounting astonishment at his irrationalist fan club, "What better criterion than the decision of the scientific group could there be?"[18]

Nothing Kuhn can say, however, will make a dent in theoreticism, which is less a specific position than a mood of antinomian rebellion and self-indulgence. That mood comes down to us from the later sixties—from a sense of criminal inhumanity in science and technology, a revulsion against dry rationality, a cherishing of direct intuitive belief, and a willing surrender to intellectual, political, and spiritual counterauthorities. Such inwardness can include an unarticulated feeling that one at least deserves the haven of an all-explanatory theory, a way of making the crazy world cohere.

Of course the direct intellectual inspiration for most theoreticism has come from such French thinkers as Lévi-Strauss, Barthes, Lacan, Althusser, Foucault, and Derrida, representing various currents of structuralism and poststructuralism. Anglo-American academics, who seem only dimly aware that structuralism became *vieux jeu* in Paris shortly after they discovered it around 1966, continue to draw liberally on both structuralist and poststructuralist authorities. In doing so they have absorbed a dogmatism of intellectual style that is plainly apparent in their sources. For, while the gurus of theoreticism differ sharply among themselves, in another sense they are much alike: all of them neglect or openly dismiss the principle of intersubjective skepticism, the core of any empirical commitment.[19]

Consider, for example, the "structural-Marxist" Althusser and the "structural-psychoanalyst" Lacan. Unlike Habermas, both were absolutists who aimed at cleansing Freud's and Marx's founding texts of their bourgeois-accommodationist elements, establishing by fiat what was truly scientific in them, and cross-breeding the result with a rigid structural determinism. Observational considerations were totally extraneous to those projects. Indeed, Althusser's bookish "return to Marx" was explicitly modeled on the equally scholastic "return to Freud" effected by his sometime psychoanalyst, Lacan.

Althusser, reacting against Sartre's sentimental "Marxist humanism," arbitrarily excised Marx's own Hegelian humanism from the corpus of his work, claiming that Marx was being himself only when he was coldly systematic and structuralist—in other words, when he was Althusser. (Hence the title of the most damaging attack on Althusser by a former disciple: André Glucksmann's "A Ventriloquist Structuralism.") *Capital*, Althusser brazenly decreed, expounds a science as fundamental as physics and mathematics. Then, taking his methodized and depersonalized *Capital* as irrefutably true, Althusser found within it proof that the philosophy of dialectical materialism is itself scientifically validated. With some changes of terminology, the whole circular argument could have been devised in the thirteenth century.

Similarly, Lacan, repelled by the emphasis on middle-class normality in Freudian ego psychology, concocted a suitably "rigorous" counterpsychoanalysis. The concepts of Freud's that he endorsed (repression, the castration complex, the death instinct) were not ones that he had winnowed through his own clinical trial and error, but rather those he deemed most powerful—that is, most subversive of appearances. They represented the real, courageous Freud; ego psychology had come into being when a lesser, bourgeois Freud *repressed* those same unnerving notions. That act of diagnosis-at-a-distance epitomized Lacan's disdain for corroboration. Moreover, by then mapping the arbitrarily favored concepts, along with newly invented ones, onto a grid of Saussurean linguistic oppositions and paradoxes, Lacan largely abandoned the original reference of Freud's vision to actual neurotic suffering.

In Althusser's and Lacan's hands, then, both Marxism and psychoanalysis exchange an adaptive materialism for allegory. There is no point at which they unambiguously intersect experience and therefore no point where one of their contentions could be modified by behavioral data. They have become, not critiques of inhumane arrangements or guidelines for practical intervention, but master transcoding devices which will sort any text or problem into sets of formally opposed categories. And that is exactly how they have been used by phalanxes of humorless acolytes.

After the student uprising of 1968, neither Althusser nor Lacan could secure a compliant audience in France. To activists who felt betrayed by the conservative Communist party and by Althusser personally, every intellectual scheme, including the most radical-looking structuralist models, suddenly appeared complicit with a totalitarian principle uniting right, left, and center against the anarchic young. "Anything devoted to 'order,'" as James Boon remarks, "even covert marginalised orders of the social and linguistic unconscious, tended to be indicted as part of the establishment's will to oppress and repress" *(RGT,* 167).[20] The cry then arose for an end not just to oppression but to *theories about* oppression. The immediate beneficiaries on the intellectual *bourse* were poststructuralists, or cognitive minimalists, such as Derrida, Foucault, Jean-François Lyotard, and Gilles Deleuze.

At first glance, an advocate of empirical prudence might perceive such doubters as welcome allies. They have seen with pitiless clarity, for example, that Marxism is intellectually hobbled by its pseudo-objectivity, its moralized vision of history, its ineradicable utopianism, and its economic reductionism. Similarly, they have been largely immune to the scientific pretensions of psychoanalysis. To be sure, their complaint is an idiosyncratic one: that even Lacanian psychoanalysis wrongly presumes to posit real psychic energies and agencies beyond the play of signifiers, meanwhile referring all of its activity of finding structures to a falsely serene contemplative consciousness. But some wariness toward arbitrary claims is certainly better than none.

Unfortunately, however, poststructuralist cynicism is by no means the same thing as empirically based skepticism. We can see that divergence quite clearly in the writings of Derrida, whose "deconstructionist" viewpoint dominated vanguard opinion on both sides of the Atlantic throughout the seventies. Deconstruction, the technique of laying bare the metaphorical nature of all attempts to establish referential terms, holds that any use of language points only to further language and that the whole Western "metaphysics of presence" from Plato onward is erroneous. This is an arguable position, but in Derrida's hands it becomes an inverted metaphysics of its own, an unsupported contention that "*différance*," or the endless deferral of meaning, "constitutes the essence of life."[21]

Derrida's judgment that "there is nothing outside the text"[22] automatically precludes recourse to evidence. Hence he has no way of arriving at more fruitful ideas than the inherited ones he has doomed himself to deconstruct ad infinitum and thus to retain in a limbo of combined attention and nonassertion. His contentment with that annotative role marks him as an intellectual nihilist, though a learned and exuberant one. Both Derrida and his myriad followers think nothing of appropriating and denaturing propositions from systems of thought whose premises they have already rejected.[23] Why not, after all, when Western knowledge in general is an exercise in self-deception?

By now many theory-conscious academics are willing to admit the monotony and hermeticism of Derrida's "carrying off each concept into an interminable chain of differences."[24] All that is behind us now, they say, thanks to Foucault, who showed us a way out of the Derridean maze and back to concrete social reality. But Foucault's concreteness, such as it was, by no means entailed a belief in regulating his ideas according to the evidence he encountered. Indeed, though his historical works attach portentous significance to certain developments and details, his epistemological pronouncements appear to rule out the very concept of a fact.[25]

For Foucault the whole Enlightenment was a continuing nightmare of ever-harsher social control—a movement to draw "reasonable" distinctions (rational-irrational, sane-insane, innocent-criminal, normal-abnormal) so as to stigmatize and punish behavior that threatens bourgeois self-regard. Foucault's own delicate mission was to trace the origins of that mania without at the same time enlarging its dominion. Such a feat called for a determination not just to "escape the grasp of categories" but to "play the game of truth and error badly"[26]—in other words, to remain unbound by any norms of evidence and logic. Foucault could only hope that his books might serve as "Molotov cocktails, or minefields" that would "self-destruct after use."[27] The guerrilla imagery, evoking the Romantic antirationalism of May 1968, points not only to the wellsprings of the continuing Foucault cult but also to the common denominator of all theoreticism: a refusal to credit one's audience with the right to challenge one's ideas on dispassionate grounds.[28]

It is hard in any case to attach positive significance to the replacement of one revered master by another, when the very appetite for unquestioning belief lies at the heart of the problem. In the human sciences today, it is widely assumed that the positions declared by structuralism and poststructuralism are permanently valuable discoveries that require no further interrogation. Thus one frequently comes upon statements of the type: "Deconstruction has shown us that we can never exit from the play of signifiers"; "Lacan demonstrates that the unconscious is structured like a language"; "After Althusser, we all understand that the most ideological stance is the one that tries to fix limits beyond which ideology does not apply"; "There can be no turning back to naive pre-Foucauldian distinctions between truth and power." Such servility constitutes an ironic counterpart of positivism—a heaping up not of factual nuggets but of movement slogans that are treated as fact.

Our intellectual practices, rather than our choice of idols, will show whether we have begun to recover from our twenty-year romance with theory for theory's sake. Reasons for optimism are as yet hard to come by. I see no decline, for example, in the most curious practice of all, the Derridean habit of simultaneously using a theory and disclaiming responsibility for its implications. Many "human scientists" still assume that the only mistake you can make with a borrowed theory is to "privilege" it—that is, to take its ruling terms as a transcendent foundation or ultimate reality. If you aver that you wouldn't dream of privileging theory $x$ but are merely admitting it into the unsupervised playground of your mind, then any weakness in theory $x$ itself is not your problem. Typically, the writer announces that neither his theoretical methodology nor his subject matter will be privileged; each will keep the other from getting out of hand. Whereupon, of course, the methodology is put to work like a jackhammer.

The same license to subscribe to a theory without actually believing what it says also permits the ideologically committed to combine two or more doctrines which look to be seriously incompatible. Sectarian zeal, which now appears stronger than ever in the academy, provides all the guidance required to tell which tenets should be discarded or updated to match the latest political wisdom. Since no one is comparing a given theory to the state of research in its original domain, problems of empirical justification simply don't arise.

Take, for example, the use of imported theory in American academic film studies, which are now dominated by a pugnacious clique that regards itself as at once Lacanian, Marxist, and feminist. Its journals, which are as fawning toward radical system builders as they are implacable toward the patriarchal-capitalist order, allow little room amid the manifestoes for discussion of actual movies. To an outsider such fierce parochialism can be astonishing, and doubly so because it seems bizarre to commit the flamboyantly sexist Lacan into the care of feminists. But to an engaged theoreticist, that very discrepancy of consciousness offers opportunities for useful labor, namely, sex surgery on Lacan's "phallogocentrism" until it has been rendered suitably "gynocentric." No one suggests that a system needing such drastic repair might be unreliable in other respects as well; to do so would be to manifest a retrograde interest in connections between theory and observation.

Nor, unfortunately, is such insouciance restricted to ideologues. Many otherwise canny humanists and social scientists would now think it boorish and intolerant to care whether the ideas they invoke have received any corroboration, since only a soulless positivist would want to pass judgment on a theory before seeing what illuminating effects its application can provoke. A trial of sensibility is the only precaution needed: the theory will have demonstrated its cogency if it brings out meaning and coherence in a given text or problem. Of course such bogus experiments succeed every time. All they prove is that any thematic stencil will make its own pattern stand out.

With this self-centered approach to ideas—"everything comes together for me when I'm using this theory!"—we reach the mildest and most elusive refinement of theoreticist apriorism. But it is apriorism all the same: a refusal, this time on a pretext of open-mindedness, to adapt one's method to the intellectual problem at hand. And a subtle but ultimately impoverishing price is paid for it: a sense of artifice and triviality, of disconnection from the wider enterprise of rational inquiry.

Some readers, I know, will acknowledge this isolation but suspect that it is unavoidable in the realm of value-laden and fashion-sensitive human sciences. They should realize, however, that the global antithesis between scientific rigor and nonscientific diffuseness has been crumbling in recent years. We now know that individual subdisciplines, not the sciences en masse, become coherent and progressive when their practitioners have developed solutions to major problems and acquired a feeling for what Thomas Kuhn calls the "good reasons" that tacitly inhabit those solutions: "accuracy, scope, simplicity, fruitfulness, and the like."[29] Each of the human studies contains comparable specialties—research traditions that generate well-focused debate, high standards of reasoning, and even a degree of consensus. I suggest, not that we stop theorizing and expressing our sociopolitical views, but that we notice where our most substantial theories always originate: in concrete disciplinary engagement.

The age of positivism lies well behind us, and we are aware today that there is no algorithm for truth in any field. Science and nonscience are in the same epistemic fix: all we can ever rely on is a dedicated subcommunity that will address shared problems in rationally evolving ways. There can be no question, *pace* Quentin Skinner, of our deciding whether to humble ourselves before *the* scientific model of research. No such model exists. Across the intellectual spectrum, each subdiscipline hews to its uniquely appropriate way of addressing characteristic issues—except, of course, where the anti-investigative mood of theoreticism has taken hold.

In the Grand Academy of Lagado, where "projectors" are busy trying to soften marble for pillows and extract sunbeams from cucumbers, Lemuel Gulliver comes across "a most ingenious architect who had contrived a new method for building houses, by beginning at the roof and working downwards to the foundation." Presumably that project is as insensate as the others. But if Gulliver were to visit our own grand academy of theory, he could witness a like feat accomplished daily, with conceptual gables and turrets suspended on hot air and rakishly cantilevered across the void. And if C. P. Snow is perchance observing from a nearby cloud, it may occur to him that his two cultures stack up somewhat differently by now: not scientists versus nonscientists, but the builders of those floating mansions on one side and, on the other, empirical inquirers of every kind.

### NOTES

This chapter of my book *Skeptical Engagements* grew out of an opportunity to review a collection of essays intriguingly called *The Return of Grand Theory in the Human Sciences.* My essay became a general assessment of "theoreticism," the most notable—and, I believe, the most noxious—change in academic intellectual style over the past quarter-century.

1. C. P. Snow, *The Two Cultures and the Scientific Revolution* (Cambridge: Cambridge University Press, 1959).

2. Quentin Skinner, ed., *The Return of Grand Theory in the Human Sciences* (Cambridge: Cambridge University Press, 1985).

3. When John Stuart Mill's *System of Logic* (1843) was translated into German in 1863, his term "moral sciences" was rendered as *Geisteswissenschaften*, which in its turn got retranslated as "human sciences." As a thoroughgoing empiricist and determinist, Mill believed that "the phenomena of human thought, feeling, and action [and of society] cannot but conform to fixed laws" (John Stuart Mill, *A System of Logic, Ratiocinative and Deductive:*

*Being a Connected View of the Principles of Evidence and the Methods of Scientific Investiga-*
*tion,* 8th ed. [New York: Harper and Brothers, 1884], 607). Though such positivism on Mill's
part was ill-advised, we should note that the "human sciences" in their early development
sought the protection of scientific authority, not protection from it. I will use the more neutral term "human studies" below, meaning the social sciences and the humanities as usually
understood.

4. The contributors, in the same order, are William Outhwaite, David Hoy, Mark Philp,
Barry Barnes, Alan Ryan, Anthony Giddens, Susan James, James Boon, and Stuart Clark.
Most of the essays originated in a series of BBC radio talks organized by Skinner.

5. Martin Jay, *Marxism and Totality: The Adventures of a Concept from Lukács to Haber-*
*mas* (Berkeley: University of California Press, 1984), 397.

6. Anthony Giddens, "Reason without Revolution? Habermas's *Theorie des kommu-*
*nikativen Handelns,*" in *Habermas and Modernity*, ed. Richard J. Bernstein (Cambridge,
Mass.: MIT Press, 1985), 95–121.

7. Ronald S. Crane "Criticism As Inquiry; or, The Perils of the 'High Priori Road,'" in
*The Idea of the Humanities and Other Essays*, 2 vols. (Chicago: University of Chicago Press,
1967), 2:29.

8. "Today," as Hilary Putnam has remarked in *Reason, Truth, and History* (Cambridge:
Cambridge University Press, 1981), "virtually no one believes that there is a purely formal
scientific method" (125). The reasons are many, ranging from a consensus that theories are
invariably "underdetermined" by data; to W. V. O. Quine's demonstration that scientific
propositions are interlocked in networks and thus are never tested "sentence by sentence";
to a widespread realization that whole theories are not overturned by single failed predictions and that "counternormal" tenacity is essential for progress; to an awareness that, for
the most part, scientists simply don't submit very many of their beliefs to rigorous tests.

9. Jürgen Habermas, *Knowledge and Human Interests,* trans. Jeremy J. Shapiro (Boston:
Beacon Press, 1971).

10. Adolf Grünbaum, *The Foundations of Psychoanalysis: A Philosophical Critique*
(Berkeley: University of California Press, 1984), 7–44.

11. And this is to pass over the recklessness of granting any doctrine an intrinsic superiority to logical and empirical objections. As a fabric of mutually entailed reality claims, a
"historical-hermeneutic" system stands at the same risk of incoherence or disconfirmation
as any other.

12. I follow Donald Davidson, "Psychology as Philosophy," in *The Philosophy of Mind*,
ed. Jonathan Glover (Oxford: Oxford University Press, 1976), 101–10, and Jon Elster, *Ulysses*
*and the Sirens: Studies in Rationality and Irrationality.* (Cambridge: Cambridge University
Press, 1984), in believing that deterministic schemes of explaining human motives and
deeds are in principle unlikely to be well supported. What Davidson calls "psycho-physical
laws" overlook the fact that human beings, as "strategically rational actors" (Elster, 18), are
forever adjusting their plans to cope with a changing environment, including the changes
wrought by the popular diffusion of those very "laws." As Elster maintains, deterministic
schemes could at most account for the evolution of human capacities to behave strategically, not for specific strategic acts (Elster, 3).

13. Indeed, we could say with hindsight that in the very act of "hermeneutically" mis-
representing Freud and Marx as not having meant their causal claims very seriously,
Habermas was presaging his later withdrawal to still safer ground: from Freudian ego psy-

chology to Piaget's developmental theory, from Marx's sociology of oppression to Talcott Parsons's bland interactionism, from the privileged knowledge of the class-conscious and the analyzed to the commonsense universalist communication of speech act theory, and from "hermeneutic" special pleading to a virtual fetishizing of the empiricism advocated by that scourge of all radicals, Sir Karl Popper. It is hardly surprising that Habermas's admirers on the intellectual left have by now been reduced to a puzzled and edgy little band.

14. Howard Felperin, *Beyond Deconstruction: The Uses and Abuses of Theory* (Oxford: Clarendon Press, 1985), 88.

15. Thomas S. Kuhn, *The Structure of Scientific Revolutions*, 2nd ed. (1st ed., 1962), (Chicago: University of Chicago Press, 1970).

16. See Thomas S. Kuhn, "Logic of Discovery or Psychology of Research?" in *Criticism and the Growth of Knowledge*, ed. Imre Lakatos and Alan Musgrave, (Cambridge: Cambridge University Press, 1974), 1–23; "Reflections on My Critics," in *Criticism and the Growth of Knowledge*, ed. Imre Lakatos and Alan Musgrave, 231–77; and "Second Thoughts on Paradigms," in *The Structure of Scientific Theories*, ed. Frederick Suppe (Urbana: University of Illinois Press, 1974), 459–82.

17. Kuhn, "Reflections," 246, 244.

18. Kuhn, *The Structure of Scientific Revolution*, 2nd ed., 169.

19. That attitude is traceable in part to an antiexperiential school of reflection about science. In the Cartesian tradition, French scientific philosophers have tended to downplay recourse to experience, instead treating observations as mere applications of previously given theoretical postulates. Gaston Bachelard and Georges Canguilhem especially, who decisively influenced both Althusser and Foucault, presented the history of science as a sequence of ruptures between one self-exhausted "discourse" and its successor. They claimed, in fact, that every science begins precisely by breaking with experience by turning away from evidence of the senses and constructing a rival conceptual scenario that must follow out its internally plotted course. This helps to explain why an American Althusserian such as Fredric Jameson, for example, can declare in an axiomatic spirit that empiricism is only "the mirage of an utterly nontheoretical practice." See Jameson, *The Political Unconscious: Narrative As a Socially Symbolic Act* (Ithaca, N.Y.: Cornell University Press, 1981), 58; Gary G. Gutting, "Continental Philosophy of Science," in *Current Research in Philosophy of Science: Proceedings of the P.S.A. Critical Research Problems Conference*, ed. Peter D. Asquith and Henry E. Kyburg Jr. (East Lansing, Mich.: Philosophy of Science Association, 1979), 94–117; and Dominique Lecourt, *Marxism and Epistemology: Bachelard, Canguilhem, and Foucault*, trans. Ben Brewster (London: NLB, 1975).

20. When Gilles Deleuze and Felix Guattari devastated the already shrinking Lacanian camp in Paris with *The Anti-Oedipus* (1972), for example, they did not point out the complete absence of empirical controls in Lacan's work, but concentrated instead on his illicit wish to bring the irrational under intellectual domination. Deleuze and Guattari indicted Lacanian psychoanalysis as a capitalist disorder, and they pilloried analysts as the most sinister priest-manipulators of a psychotic society. The demonstration was widely regarded as unanswerable.

21. Jacques Derrida, *Writing and Difference*, trans. Alan Bass (Chicago: University of Chicago Press, 1978), 203.

22. Jacques Derrida, *Of Grammatology*, trans. Gayatri Chakravorty Spivak (Baltimore, Md.: Johns Hopkins University Press, 1976), 158.

23. Thus, in the same essay in *Writing and Difference* in which he calls psychoanalysis "an unbelievable mythology," one that must be cited "in quotation marks" (228, 197), Derrida credits Freud with the "discovery" of "the irreducibility of the 'effect of deferral'" (203)—in other words, with a realization that "the present is not primal but . . . reconstituted" (212). The "discovery" thus welcomed, drawn from such whimsical sources as Freud's abandoned "Project for a Scientific Psychology" and his "Note on the Mystic Writing-Pad," requires no more proof than the reflection that Freud was in this respect an early Derridean. And Derrida goes on to lay his blessing on Freud's creakiest psychophysical concepts, such as "repressed memory traces" and "cathectic innervations," simply because they evoke his own central notion of *différance*. In this manner he encourages the theoreticist habit of treating one's own system as received truth while dividing all other tenets into those that miss one's point (owing, perhaps, to "repression") and those that can be borrowed to adorn it.

As for Derrida's own "discoveries" of (a) an infinite regress of signifiers, rendering any intended meaning unstable, (b) the constitution of every "signified" by "traces" of its opposite, and (c) the "repression" of writing in all philosophy since Plato, see the decisive rebuttal by John R. Searle, "The Word Turned Upside Down," *New York Review of Books*, 27 October 1983, 74–78.

24. Jacques Derrida, *Positions*, trans. Alan Bass (Chicago: University of Chicago Press, 1981), 14.

25. Once having been rebuked by Derrida himself (in *Writing and Difference*, 31–63) for implying, in his *Madness and Civilization*, that insanity was a dimension of actual (prelinguistic) experience that the modern West had attempted to disown, Foucault thenceforth outdid his critic in proclaiming that all of existence is produced by discourse. "There is nothing absolutely primary to be interpreted," he wrote, "since fundamentally, everything is already interpretation" (quoted in Vincent Descombes, *Modern French Philosophy*, trans. L. Scott-Fox and J. M. Harding [Cambridge: Cambridge University Press, 1980], 117). As Allan Megill observes in *Prophets of Extremity: Nietzsche, Heidegger, Foucault, Derrida* (Berkeley: University of California Press, 1985), 202, in Foucault's works after 1963 "one is struck by the total disappearance of the concept 'experience.'"

26. Michel Foucault, *Language, Counter-Memory, Practice: Selected Essays and Interviews*, ed. Donald F. Bouchard (Ithaca, N.Y.: Cornell University Press, 1977), 190.

27. Quoted in Megill, *Prophets of Extremity*, 243.

28. Not coincidentally, it was immediately after 1968 that Foucault switched from his quasi-structuralist "archaeologies" of Western "epistemes" to more drastic Nietzschean "genealogies," reducing all truth claims to exercises of power. The attractive new ingredient in Foucault's thought was sixties paranoia toward the hidden, all-powerful oppressors whom he never attempted to identify.

29. Kuhn, "Reflections," 261.

## 14.   THEORRHEA AND KULTURKRITIK

### J. G. MERQUIOR

IT DOES NOT in the least follow that because our knowledge of the world pre-supposes interests and values the world itself is therefore but a product or a projection of those values and interests. As was only to be expected, literary theory hastened to build variants of such crass non sequiturs into the current dogmas of critical wisdom. Robert Scholes, always nimble in expounding or exposing the structuralist doxa, caught the gist of the matter. In olden times, claims Scholes, it was believed that fiction was about life and criticism about fiction. Now we know better: we have come to realize that all fiction is criticism (because it is about other fictions); and criticism proper is only about the impossibility of "aboutness": its real subject is "the impossibility of its own existence." As Scholes succinctly puts it: "there is no mimesis, only poesis."[1]

One could hardly say it more elegantly. But consider for a moment the kind of argument commonly used to justify the sacking of mimesis. The underlying assumption is that what we naively call correspondence to reality rests on no more than shared language which imposes on things a conformist adjustment to unconscious or manipulated social meanings rather than grasping their real nature (which is merely in any case a function of our "active interpretations"). The trouble is, it does not follow from this premise that "there is no mimesis." As Gerald Graff very sensibly remarks in that brave piece of critical dissent, *Literature Against Itself*:

> It is true that the idea of a "natural correspondence" between language and reality has often been used to justify the view of reality held by those wielding political power. But one can reject the ideological bias of such a justification without rejecting the principle of correspondence itself. Indeed, one can argue that the established ideology fails to correspond to reality, and go on to present an alternative view which corresponds more closely. In a similar way, the fact that our shared linguistic contracts often conceal ideological mystifications favorable to the interests of the ruling class is an argument for exposing these particular linguistic formulations, not for attacking the very concept of shared formulations.[2]

The real progress of modern criticism has been the increase in our sense of the meaningfulness of form. The advantage of its sundry methods of close

José Guilherme Merquior. "Theorrhea and Kulturkritik." Revised from the book *From Prague to Paris: A Critique of Structuralist and Post-Structuralist Thought*, by J. G. Merquior, 244–60. London: Verso, 1986. Copyright © J. G. Merquior 1986. Reprinted by permission of the publisher.

reading was that they enhanced our grasp of complex patterns of literary meaning and in so doing improved our ability to detect poetic or fictional value and gauge its degree. Yet nothing in the critical experience of meaningful form implied a denial of the relation between literature and life or its basic reference to the world. For this reason, the latest challenger of the formalist orthodoxy, A. D. Nuttall, is absolutely right in my view when he observes that the superiority of "transparent criticism," of criticism alive to the mimetic dimension of literature, over the formalist pieties of "opaque criticism" is partly a matter of inclusiveness, since "the Transparent critic can and will do all the things done by the Opaque critic but is willing to do other things as well."[3] In other words: transparent criticism will *both* pay attention to form *and* look through the text to the world of human experiences from which art takes its ultimate worth and most of its meaning.

The theoretical situation generated by "structuralist philosophy" is a comic reversal of the old positivist utopia of knowledge. Once upon a time, there was the positivist chimera of introducing into philosophy and social science the concept of truth and the scientific patterns found in hard science. Today, a growing number of "radical" thinkers dream of a dogmatic transposition into the realm of science of the indiscriminate skepticism about truth and objectivity that pervades the humanities. But Bouveresse, for one, thinks the game is not worth a candle. Indeed, he is sick and tired of this *Salonskeptizismus.* He prefers to say loudly "something that a relativist" (all poststructuralists being, obviously, fierce relativists)

> is well placed to understand, namely, that I have no sympathy at all with the kind of "progress" allegedly represented, in the view of certain (French) *maîtres à penser*, by the gradual liquidation of fundamental cognitive values such as coherence, truth, validity, objective confirmation or justification and I see no reason to accept as a historical fate what is, in reality, but the product of the historicizing and historicist conformism in which we live and moreover constitutes too local and parochial a cultural phenomenon.[4]

Nowhere more parochial than in the literary tribe of the humanities. For the literarization of thought created a climate of utter smugness in academic literary quarters. Listen, for instance, to the orotund self-satisfaction with which acolytes of the deconstructionist rite gravely aver that, in the ongoing surge of "theory," "it would not be inappropriate for *literary* theory to play the central role."[5] Not *a* role, not even a central role: nothing less than *the* central role. After all, if philosophy itself turned fictional, why should the literary clerisy stick to old boundaries and keep literature in its (admittedly very important) place? All one can do is denounce this and other pieces of guild paranoia as maneuvers within "a struggle for academic power" in which a "literary-critical imperialism" (in Alan Megill's phrase) increasingly raises its silly head.[6] Moreover, their small smattering of philosophy only increases the gullibility of teachers and students in modern literature departments when reacting to the fallacies and absurdities "theory" has come to indulge.

Those academic critics who have profited from structuralism without surrendering the rights of reason or sacrificing the intellect, as is so often required by poststructuralism, tend to be less enthusiastic about the present state of the art. Thus David Lodge has suggested that literary criticism has been damaged by the gulf between everyday language and technical discourse[7]—a gulf that the more jargon-laden brands of structuralese and poststructuralitis have widened into a chasm. Jargon has now made much of the humanities anything but humane—and the gain in knowledge is far from being, as a rule, substantial.

The poststructuralist literarization of thought has been accompanied by an overrating of the scope of literary theory. Departments of literature have become intellectual looms relentlessly weaving theoretical texts that are far from restricted to literary matters: their wild flux of standard theorizing—a veritable *theorrhea*—normally ploughs the open sea of loose but exceedingly ambitious philosophizing. Credulous inmates or naive bystanders of the literary academe may think that this theoretical boldness is a spillover from the power of literary theory at work on texts—but this is a pious illusion. Keener observers of contemporary literary criticism would agree with Arthur K. Moore: in our time, "if analytical criticism has surpassed rank impressionism, the gains have been owing more to improved reading than to improved theory: for theory has most evidently provided a pretext rather than a regulative principle."[8] The theorrhea of academic literati is not a projection of methodological success but an imperialist extension of humanist ideology.

In their boundless theoretical pontification, many literary theorists do not balk, as we have seen, at assigning a dominating role to their trade. Jonathan Culler, a successful apostle of deconstruction, tells us that this is only too natural, for three reasons: (a) Literary theorists are open-minded thinkers. Why? Because they are better placed—as outsiders—to welcome challenges to "the assumptions of orthodox contemporary psychology, anthropology, psychoanalysis, philosophy, sociology, or historiography." (b) Literary theory is self-conscious. Why? Because it "inexorably" explores "problems of reflexivity and metacommunication, trying to theorize the exemplary self-reflexiveness of literature." (c) Given that "literature takes as its subject all human experience" and its interpretive articulation, theory normally finds literature very instructive: "the comprehensiveness of literature makes it possible for any extraordinary or compelling theory to be drawn into literary theory."[9]

Even the most perfunctory examination shows this threefold claim to be a piece of appallingly poor thinking. Granted that literary theorists can look, as unprejudiced outsiders, at new ideas in a host of human sciences; but "psychologists, anthropologists, psychoanalysts, philosophers, sociologists, historians," as nonliterary researchers, can also look, without the bias of craft, at "contemporary literary theory." Seriously to suggest that the relationship is one-way, to the sole benefit of the literati, requires a touching leap of faith in the higher wisdom of the theory of literature—but that is grotesquely question-begging, for the entitlement of literary thinking to "the central role" was precisely what Culler was trying to justify in the first place. Either *all* the tribes in the humanities have their own craft-bound biases and (in principle) can look afresh at theoretical developments outside their purview, or they haven't and cannot—but if the first alternative is true, then the obvious upshot is a general tradeoff, not a privileged insight accruing to literary theorists.

Culler's second balloon can be popped even more easily, for claim (b) simply *takes for granted* the formalist-deconstructionist myth of literariness as self-reflexiveness. To equate theoretical acumen with a compulsive quest for aporia, alleged to be the quintessence of literature, is a very tall order but it is certainly not sufficient ground for giving modern literary thought the throne of Theory.

What about Culler's third (in his own list, emphatically the first) claim, namely, that literary theory must rule because literature deals with "all human experience?" Prima facie, the premise seems reasonable. Literature does indeed encompass all human experience. However, it does not follow that its comprehensiveness provides a clear-cut basis for a body of knowledge, let alone of *ruling* knowledge. For it is far from easy to transform the range of literature from a warrant of relevance and significance into a basis for theoretical cognition.

Nor does the matter end with the problem that literature's comprehensiveness, in terms of human relevance, is not readily translatable into theoretical cognition. The problem becomes still more complex or elusive because, while it is true that literature embodies comprehensive truth about the human condition, normally it is only (good) literature *as a whole* that does so. Consequently there is little point in suggesting that literary theory qualifies as higher knowledge simply because it deals with an art whose object is human experience: for literary truth (or, for that matter, literary beauty) cannot be predicated unconditionally of any single given work.[10] Therefore criticism cannot be invoked as a stable basis for literary theory as a knowledge of all matters human.

Humanist prophets such as Matthew Arnold used to think that, in his famous words "more and more mankind will discover that we have to turn to poetry to interpret life for us."[11] In their theoretical fervor deconstructionists seem eager to bestow this prerogative upon their overblown literary theory. They already see literary thought—a thought, incidentally, now only tangentially related to literature—as the dominating brand of Theory. Can one help seeing this, in turn, as an ill-founded attempt at domination? Lest this be reckoned an exaggeration, I hasten to recall that Paul de Man, the late godfather of the deconstructionist mafia in America, did not balk (in *Blindness and Insight*) at casting the net of the textual ideology wide enough to annex history itself to the rarefied realm of the suicidal meaning, the gist of self-reflexive literature. Coupling an axiomatic assertion that literature is endless aporia with a Nietzschean perspectivism ("no facts, just interpretations"), de Man hinted, to the apparent delight of avant-garde literary departments, that wars and revolutions are not empirical events (there is no such thing) but "texts" masquerading as facts.[12]

This book does not purport to discuss in any detail the fate of poststructuralism in America, although it is in America, from Yale deconstructionists to Californian Foucaldians, that Anglophone poststructuralism is strongest: my title is *From Prague to Paris*, not *From Paris to New Haven*. Suffice it then to say that de Man's preposterous reduction of history to a textual puzzle did not go unchallenged. The main challenger, Frank Lentricchia, earned prominence as a historian of criticism for whom—as he made clear in *After the New Criticism* (1980)—both structuralism and deconstruction originally contained radical promises belied and betrayed by their transatlantic acclimatization. Yet on close inspection the "radical" structuralism Lentricchia seems to have in mind is chiefly the work of Barthes in the *Mythologies* phase, still basically prestructuralist, as we saw; and his claim that Derrida's dismantling of meaning is far more rigorous than its American counterparts[13] cries out for substantiation. American deconstruction, says Lentricchia, "tends to be an activity of textual privatization,"[14] marking the critic's retreat from the social fray. But did we not see Foucault raise the same charge against Derrida himself? No wonder the tone of Lentricchia's objections got harsher in his next book, *Criticism and Social Change* (1983), where de Man plays villain to the hero, Kenneth Burke, who features as an American Gramsci. Then he stresses the "Prufrockian mood of current critical sophistication,"[15] an enterprise contrasted with the pugnacity of Foucault's new kind of social critique.

Much as I share Lentricchia's impatience with the ritualistic puzzle-mongering of deconstruction, I fail to see how poststructuralism qua genealogy (Foucault) can kill the virus of poststructuralism qua exegesis (Derrida). As Terence Hawkes notes, Foucault's idea of history is vulnerable to more than one of the strictures leveled against Derrida's way of wreaking anarchy upon texts[16]—scarcely surprising in view of their common Nietzschean stance in regard to knowledge and truth. Some Foucaldians, as is well known, set the avowed Nietzscheanism of their idol against Marxism, as an alternative form of critique. Others, however, tipsy on the Marxo-Nietzschean cocktail, deem Foucault's microphysics of power/knowledge to be the best way of rescuing Marxism from scientism or science tout court.[17] Lentricchia, who does not blush in equating "Marx without science" with "Marx without Stalin," and is happy to follow Richard Rorty in an attack on "a past of epistemological repression,"[18] obviously aligns himself with the Marxo-Nietzschean Foucaldians—to no visible analytical gain.

Fortunately, one can resist the spell of deconstruction—and the paranoid philosophizing of criticism as "theory"—without falling into rival irrationalisms; and I should like to end my remarks on the current predicament of literary theory by pointing to what looks like a case of mature self-criticism by an ex-structuralist: Tzvetan Todorov. We left him, many many pages ago, as a true believer in "linguisticism," a virulent form of formalist structuralism. Todorov has gone through much soul-searching since the days of his "structural analysis of narrative" and other similar ventures. In a recent book, *Critique de la Critique* (1984), he devotes the entire concluding essay to questioning the unexamined assumption of his erstwhile theorizing. In a nutshell, he confesses to having embraced structuralism, in early sixties Paris, because as a Bulgarian he was fed up with the ideological appropriation of literature usually prevalent in the socialist countries. "Discovering about me a literature enslaved to politics, I believed in the need for breaking all ties and keeping literature free from all contact with everything else." Hence his espousal of an "immanent" criticism coupled with the idea, of romantic ancestry, that literature is a language that finds an end in itself: immanent criticism—that is structuralism—was adopted in order to account for an autotelic verbal art.[19]

But Todorov now realizes that this might lead to as blind an alley as the narrowness of "dogmatic" criticism, be it Christian or Marxist.[20] After all, he says, literature deals with human life: it is a discourse geared towards truth and ethics. Sartre was right to call it an unveiling of humanity and the world. If literature does not just mirror ideologies, it is because it is itself an ideology, a statement about reality; and the critic's task is to analyze works without turning a deaf ear to such a statement, but without being afraid of contradicting it either. Above all criticism must recognize that, being caught up in the world, it, too, speaks about life and the conflict of values. Therefore, it should not be ashamed of a humanism conceived of as an "attempt to ground science and ethics in reason."[21] All that matters is that the attempt be conducted in a liberal, tolerant, judicious yet at the same time judicative way: for whereas dogmatic criticism ends in a critic's monologue, and immanent criticism in an author's monologue, humanist criticism proceeds through *dialogue* (the humanism Todorov opposes to the elision of world and subject in deconstruction has learned from Bakhtin's stress on dialogism, as well as from Paul Bénichou's concern for the ideological, as against the formal, element in literature).[22]

Todorov is aware that to a large extent he is rediscovering long-found Americas temporarily hidden by the conceptual fog of structuralist bigotry and by the hysterical denial of reference and reality promoted by poststructuralism. But this makes his self-criticism no less healthy, no less apposite. That such a leading figure in the formalist revival and the establishment of structuralism has decided to withstand the cacophony of poststructuralitis on grounds of reason and humanity, without in the least dropping the lucid, urbane style of his impressive previous output, is something to be welcomed wholeheartedly.

At most, one wishes that his plea for a new rational humanism in literary criticism were more sympathetic toward historical approaches, and less derogatory about Marxism. As a non-Marxist critic myself, I feel reasonably well placed to say that Todorov takes too unilateral a view in equating Marxism with relativism (in both knowledge and morals) on the grounds that it replaces reason with history, and is therefore no better than Foucault's Nietzschean dismissal of universal values.[23] Whatever its many shortcomings, Marxism—classical Marxism at least—has a core of strong universalist tenets, and an Enlightenment and Hegelian background, irreducible to the unabashed historicist relativism of the poststructuralist masters. Moreover, if we are to recover a sense of literature as a worldly discourse, and hence of the author's voice (conscious as well as unconscious), we shall also need to grasp the voice of the age, not as a lofty *Zeitgeist* but as a sum, often contradictory, of historical presuppositions and concrete conditions of literature. Historical materialism remains, as a powerful heuristics, the best available program for this necessary if not sufficient dimension of analytical criticism. To dare to judge without prejudice, a discipline of historical piety is mandatory; but it was the impact of historical materialism that taught us that the best historical piety is not an exercise in blind nostalgia, a romance of wistful empathy, but an intelligent grasp of the changing limits and constraints imposed on human experience.

But for all their deficiencies neither Todorov's anti-Marxism nor Lentricchia's pro-Marxism prevent them from contributing cogently to the supersession of the formalist environment revamped by the assault of deconstruction. Significantly, the model critics they propose—Burke, Bakhtin, Bénichou—represent seminal strands of analysis very distant from the cult of contentless forms and blank signifiers. Their joint revival would provide a natural antithesis to the influence of the main formalist axes: the lines of Shklovsky-Jakobson and Blanchot-Barthes. And it is no less instructive that none of the three mistook theoretical range (quite wide in all of them) for a license to treat texts as pretexts, for wanton philosophizing, in arcane jargons. In their different ways, Todorov and Lentricchia, together with critics like Jameson, Scholes, Graff, or Compagnon, are currently building a basis for effective dissent from a formalist orthodoxy disguised as rampant avant-gardism. For the moment, they lead the overdue rescue of literary theory from hubris and unreason.

## Toward a Sociology of Theorrhea

Poststructuralism has been the seat of theorrhea in the humanities—ambitious "theory" as a pretext for sloppy thinking and little analysis, fraught with anathemas against modern civilization. But how could the humanities be so hospitable to such an unpalatable scribbling? Here I can only sketch some suggested explanations. The trouble is that the humanities, outside of their natural fields of scholarship—history, philology, ethnography—have for too long felt insecure in the face of the growth of hard science. Humanist intellectuals, heirs of the ancient possessions of higher knowledge and literacy skills, nowadays face a society in which literacy is universal and world-shaping knowledge is beyond their ken. Little wonder if these displaced "artisans of cognition," as Ernest Gellner calls them,[24] fall for the kinds of lore and language that sound like their private property, and that may therefore enhance their status and self image in an increasingly narcissistic academic world.

If, in addition, the new skills revolve around *language*, so much the better. Language was the oldest flame of the humanist soul. Linguistics, after all, was virtually the only area in which humanists managed to produce decent science (as opposed to scholarship or erudition, best typified by history). Moreover, with the continuing "linguistic turn" of philosophy (Wittgenstein and Austin, Heidegger and hermeneutics), what could be more apposite than the advent of structuralisms, the brainchildren of Saussure? Logocracy held sway over the humanist guild. Humanity was no longer seen as lord of the logos, a sovereign *homo loquens*, but as the language-bound animal. However, something is amiss. As Roger Shattuck perceived, we don't really like surrendering everything to Mistress Language. We have therefore taken a subtle, hidden revenge on her spell. In order quietly to vindicate some sense of choice and individuality, we have embarked on an absurdist lusting after fantasy and rule-breaking. Our myths of transgression help us to bear the anonymous rule of language. Hence our latest cultural kit: the metaphysical picaresque.[25] The label seems tailor-made for grasping the essence of Lacan, Derrida, or Deleuze as well as the antirealist novelists Shattuck has chiefly in mind. But it goes without saying that theoretical clowning, for all its willful unruliness, turns into the rule. After all, it is just a mirror-image of logocracy. Dada theory, too, works as a language game.

Now in such a context, to say, as Paul de Man did as late as 1982, that the "terrorism" of "ruthless theory" would be an antiestablishment academic drive, could only be sheer rhetoric[26] or downright disingenuousness. For the spate of "theory" nurtured in literature departments may go on voicing its rhetoric of dissent and deviancy as loud as it pleases; the plain fact is that this noisy talk of transgression has become enormously ritualized—as ritualized as the stale avant-gardist breaks in the modernist-ridden art world that the new humanities chose to copy.

If I may stress the main point: as a cluster of intellectual mores, the structuralist/poststructuralist wave may pass for a theoretical avant-garde, but in reality it is rooted in strictly parochial traits of the humanities system. In a pithy recent essay[27] the sociologist Raymond Boudon has sketched an interesting explanation of the aestheticization of knowledge normally associated with what he dubs "the Freudian-Marxian-Structuralist movement" (FMS) in France. In a nutshell, Boudon accounts for the willful opacity of most masters of FMS by means of an institutional model of a specific kind of academic world that lacks some patterns of interaction usually present in centers of higher learning. In order for constant orientation toward sober knowledge-building to prevail, he claims, some institutional conditions have to be met, in social as well as natural science. These conditions imply a number of consequences for the role social scientists play: they impose a set of obligations to be clear and to comply with acceptable standards of objectivity. As they are supposed to address themselves primarily to their peers, authors in a cognitively oriented social science will normally try to abide by impersonal rules when justifying their theses or their findings: there is no question of suggesting that they are true just because the author is more clever or gifted than fellow experts. And, last but not least, academic advancement in each specialty depends on the observance of such codes of cognitive conduct.

Boudon submits that these institutional constraints have been very weak in the case of *French* social science, with the exception of history. The symbolic rewards and material resources available to the community of social scientists have been too restricted, the degree of differentiation between universities too low to foster social climbing through intellectual achievement. Hence theories that legitimize epistemological relativism (and not only methodological pluralism) thrive on the humanist side of French academe: for epistemological relativism (asserted with a vengeance by thinkers like Lacan, Barthes, Derrida, or Foucault) is just the ideological pendant to the lack of a true, self-conscious, and rule-bound cognitive community. And given the lack of a satisfactory social science system, the actual receivers of "social science" or literary theory are often not the equals of its senders. Rather they are a motley crowd of humanist intellectuals only loosely connected with the particular disciplines from which the new theoretical trends are coming: thus the *average* (and not just the occasional) reader of Lacan tends not to be a psychoanalyst, nor the reader of Foucault or Derrida a philosopher, and so on. As a result, the producer/consumer relationship becomes too asymmetrical, with the latter unable to assess the bibles of new thought with a modicum of competence. What is more, given such diffuse, unskilled audiences, the senders of theoretical messages are not likely to be penalized for indulging in opacity or intellectual permissiveness: on the contrary, their receivers are quite prepared to countenance their obscurity and arbitrariness, interpreting them as further evidence of their inferiority in relation to their chosen gurus.

In such circumstances, what tempts the gifted academic is not the career of an expert but the triumph of a prophet. But Boudon adds another perceptive remark. He notes that unlike, say, Marshall McLuhan or Wilhelm Reich (or Ivan Illich), the FMS gurus do not address themselves as authors directly to the public at large, over the heads of academic specialists. Hence a curious effect:

the FMS masters, Lacan, Althusser, Barthes, and so on churned out a highly aestheticized theory, one at a far remove from the stern rules of clarity and cogency demanded by institutionalized social science—and yet, they insisted on Science with a capital letter, flaunting their output as an arcane model of theoretical and methodological "rigor." The paradox of "aesthetic" knowledge wrapped up in scientistic guise is again explained by the social situation of the FMS masters—experts by origin but "prophets" by behavior (this paradox, in turn, accounts for the eventual shifts from scientism or near-scientism to open relativism in such authors as Barthes, Althusser, and Foucault). Only the nouveaux philosophes chose to behave like Reich or McLuhan, and therefore opted for a pop philosophy that retained the same degree of irresponsible intellectual bravado, but dropped opacity as the trademark of "creative" thinking. As for the FMS stardom, it is as esoteric as it is self-indulgent. "Theory" comes close to being no more than the diktats of abstruse gurus; theoretical revolutions strangely resemble logorrheic revelations. The main target is always the same: modern society and its values. The actual victim, however, is the quality of rational intellect.

## Poststructuralism and Kulturkritik

These sociological remarks help us to understand why theorrhea—sweepingly self-important theory—found fertile ground in a particular kind of academic culture, the burgeoning new humanities. But our own analysis is concerned less with the *why* than with the *what* of structuralist, and especially poststructuralist, theory. Accordingly, we should return at last to its ideological tenor. What wine is served in the opaque bottles of the new humanities?

As evident in my discussion of Allan Megill's gallery of the masters of *Kulturkritik*, most versions of poststructuralism stem from the radical aestheticism of Nietzsche. In a long and important recent work, *Der philosophische Diskurs der Moderne,* published in the same year (1985) as Megill's *Prophets of Extremity,* Jürgen Habermas, too, dwells on the Nietzschean heritage. He sees in Nietzsche the chief forerunner of "postmodern" reactions against the spirit of modern culture, the turning point in the history of our entry into a postmodern world.[28] Coming of age philosophically after the failure of the 1848 revolutions, Nietzsche renounced the historicist belief in the emancipatory power of philosophy (the gist of Hegel's "reason in history"). In addition, he rejected the compensatory role of high culture under capitalism—the idea of culture as, so to speak, the comforting sigh of society, what Bergson later called *un supplément d'âme,* allegedly desperately lacking in our technological society.

Given the failure of historicism, claims Habermas, Nietzsche found himself torn between the following theoretical alternatives: *either* he was to undertake an "immanent critique" of philosophical reason, in an attempt to rescue it from the shortcomings of historicist thought (a fair description of Habermas's own endeavor) *or* he could ditch philosophy's rational program altogether. Nietzsche chose the latter course. He adopted a paradoxical strategy of subverting reason. Boldly flaunting an uncompromising irrationalism, he denounced reason as a form of will-to-power and deprived value judgments of all cognitive force.

In so doing Nietzsche was not only the first to give a conceptual form to modernist aesthetics as a ludic, Dionysian mode of change and self-denial: he also built an alluring *aesthetocentric* redefinition of thought. Theory itself disparaged sustained logical analysis for the sake of "life" and wild insight. Whilst *logos* was played down, "myth" was given a free hand. Unlike Wagner, however, for whom myth became increasingly Christian and nostalgic, in Nietzsche the mythical element is given a futurist thrust, pledged against decadence and the repression of instinct. But this privileging of the aesthetic in turn contradicted the very spirit of the project of modernity. For the logic of western culture since the Enlightenment is predicated on the strict, Kantian autonomy of the three spheres of thought—knowledge, art, and morality. Science, artistic creation and ethics are supposed to operate within well-defined boundaries, however unstable the balance between them. By inflating aesthetic values into a resounding challenge to the very aims of knowledge (the sphere of truth) and morals (the sphere of duty), Nietzsche canonized *Kulturkritik*—the refusal of modernity—as a structure of thought in its own right.

Nietzsche himself often shifted between two courses in this supersession of rationalism. On the one hand, he contemplated the possibility of a new, skeptic history, a starkly critical genealogy of morals freed from every illusion about objective truth. On the other hand, he countenanced a critique of metaphysical assumptions that was still faithful to the idea of philosophy as a higher knowledge.

Nietzsche's posterity among the *Kulturkritiker* reproduces this bifurcation. Foucault (like Bataille before him) took the first path—of skeptical, openly irrational history; Heidegger, and nowadays Derrida, represent the second—the way of antimetaphysical philosophy.

In Heidegger this antilogos takes the form of a hermetic wisdom, an arcane renewal of ontology with a mystical accent. Derrida's version is far less assertive and soteriological: Being is no longer emphasized; meaning is forever shifting and ambiguous. Instead, all difference between logic and rhetoric is abolished: the aesthetic imposes its law on all concepts and categories. The distinction between concept and image, theory and art, still so dear to the negative dialectics of the first Frankfurt school, is swamped by the strange combination of "Nietzschean" perspectivism without the slightest hint of an antidecadent animus—the main motive of Nietzsche's thought.

Habermas's particular diagnosis of the centrality of the aesthetic is up to now the best discussion of postmodern and poststructuralist theory. Its advantage over those who correctly note the aestheticist nature of *Kulturkritik*, but leave it at that, is that unlike them Habermas sees that aestheticism, as far as cognitive standards go, is more of a problem than a solution. Moreover, as he is at pains to stress, aesthetocentric thought, whether in Nietzsche himself or in Heidegger, Foucault, or Derrida, overlooks the positive rational potential of modern culture—its humanizing, emancipatory horizon. In Habermas, the gallant attempt to reinstate reason as dialogue and "communicative action"[29] walks hand in hand with a qualified acceptance of the "modern project"— something very different from the wholesale repudiation of modernity to be found among the Nietzschean *Kulturkritiker*. (In the same way, he undertakes a stern critique of Horkheimer and Adorno's Nietzschean unmasking of the Enlightenment in their *Dialektik der Aufklärung*.)

Nevertheless, mere questioning of aesthetocentrism is far from enough. For it takes issue with a *response* to the crisis of modernity but scarcely examines the validity of the concept of crisis itself, as applied to modern culture. Habermas sensibly rejects the dismissal of cultural modernity root and branch; yet his own diagnosis gives pride of place to the idea of a "legitimation crisis" in-built in late capitalist culture. We can go further, and question the whole "humanist" claim that there is something basically wrong with modern *culture* as it actually is, in the developed, liberal capitalist societies of our time.

By stating that Foucault's anti-Enlightenment philosophical history, as well as Derrida's brand of irrationalism, are not only instances of a literarization of thought but also *a surrender of thought to modernist ideology*, that is, to the pious countercultural worldview of most modern art, I meant to stress how questionable are the assumptions that gave birth to the radical tradition within *Kulturkritik*. Do the many failures and shortcomings of modern culture actually warrant such a massive indictment of modernity's achievements? Can we really say that the historicist appraisal and approval of an industrial order, where knowledge, art and morals work as separate though obviously not wholly unrelated spheres, has been convincingly shown to be erroneous? Are there not sufficient grounds to present a case for what Hans Blumenberg has called "*die Legitimität der Neuzeit*?"[30] That a deep cultural crisis is endemic to historical modernity seems to have been much more eagerly assumed than properly demonstrated, no doubt because, more often than not, those who generally do the assuming—humanist intellectuals—have every interest in being perceived as soul doctors to a sick civilization. Yet is the medicine that necessary, or the sickness that real? Perhaps we should be entertaining second thoughts about it all.

NOTES

1. Robert Scholes, "The Fictional Criticism of the Future," *TriQuarterly* 34 (Fall 1975), quoted by Gerald Graff, *Literature Against Itself: Literary Ideas in Modern Society* (Chicago: University of Chicago Press, 1979), 172.

2. Graff, *Literature Against Itself*, 89.

3. A. D. Nuttall, *A New Mimesis: Shakespeare and the Representation of Reality* (London: Methuen, 1983), 80–98.

4. Jacques Bouveresse, *Le Philosophe chez les autophages* (Paris: Minuit, 1984), 117 (my translation).

5. Jonathan Culler, *On Deconstruction* (Ithaca, N.Y.: Cornell University Press, 1982), 10. Emphasis added.

6. Alan Megill, review of *On Deconstruction*, by Jonathan Culler, *Philosophy and Literature* 8, no. 2(October 1984): 285–89.

7. David Lodge, "Avoiding the Double Bind," review of *Reading Relations*, by Bernard Sharratt, *Times Literary Supplement*, 23 April 1982, 458.

8. Arthur K. Moore, *Contestable Concepts of Literary Theory* (Baton Rouge: Louisiana State University Press, 1973), 218.

9. Culler, *On Deconstruction*, 10–11.

10. The point is perspicuously discussed by Moore, *Contestable Concepts*, 212–14.

11. Matthew Arnold, "The Study of Poetry" (1880), reprinted as the opening essay in his *Essays in Criticism: Second Series* (London/New York: Macmillan, 1988).

12. Paul de Man, *Blindness and Insight* (Minneapolis: University of Minnesota Press, 1983), 165.

13. Frank Lentricchia, *After the New Criticism* (Chicago: University of Chicago Press, 1980), 209.

14. Lentricchia, *After the New Criticism*, 186.

15. Frank Lentricchia, *Criticism and Social Change* (Chicago: University of Chicago Press, 1983), 51.

16. Terence Hawkes, "The Anti-Historical Virus," review of *After the New Criticism*, by Frank Lentricchia, *Times Literary Supplement*, 17 April 1981, 444.

17. For brief comments on this issue among Foucault interpreters, see J. G. Merquior, *Foucault* (London: Fontana, 1985), 142–43.

18. Lentricchia, *Criticism and Social Change*, 13, 17.

19. Tzvetan Todorov, *Critique de la critique: Un Roman d'apprentissage* (Paris: Éditions du Seuil, 1984), 188 (my translation).

20. Todorov, *Critique de la critique*, 192.

21. See Todorov, "All Against Humanity," *Times Literary Supplement*, 4 October 1985, 1093. [Editors' note: A different translation of Todorov's essay is included in this book.]

22. Todorov refers to Bénichou's masterpieces of literary history from the point of view of ideology: *Morales du grand siècle* (Paris: Gallimard, 1948), *Le Sacre de l'écrivain* (Paris: Gallimard, 1973) and *Le Temps des prophètes* (Paris: Gallimard, 1977); *Critique de la critique* (143–77) contains a long interview with Bénichou [Editors' note: now in Tzvetan Todorov, "Literature as Fact and Value: Conversation with Paul Bénichou," in *Literature and Its Theorists: A Personal View of Twentieth-Century Criticism*, trans. Catherine Porter (Ithaca, N.Y.: Cornell University Press, 1987), 122–54].

23. See Todorov, "All Against Humanity," 1094.

24. See his essay on the crisis in the humanities in Ernest Gellner, *The Devil in Modern Philosophy* (London: Routledge and Kegan Paul, 1974) (quotation, 29).

25. Roger Shattuck, *The Innocent Eye: On Modern Literature and the Arts* (New York: Farrar, Straus, Giroux, 1984), 332–36.

26. As noted by Howard Felperin, *Beyond Deconstruction: The Uses and Abuses of Literary Theory* (Oxford: Clarendon Press, 1982), 141.

27. Raymond Boudon, "The Freudian-Marxian-Structuralist (FMS) Movement in France: Variations on a Theme by Sherry Turkle," *Revue Tocqueville* 2, no. 1 (Winter 1980): 5–23.

28. Jürgen Habermas, *Der philosophische Diskurs der Moderne* (Frankfurt: Suhrkamp, 1985), 104 ff.

29. For an overview of Habermas's oeuvre, see my *Western Marxism* (London: Paladin, 1986), 163–85.

30. Hans Blumenberg, *The Legitimacy of the Modern Age*, trans. Robert M. Wallace (Cambridge: MIT Press, 1983; first German ed., 1966).

## 15. MASTERS AND DEMONS

### BRIAN VICKERS

*I wish to emphasize from the very beginning that the attitude taken here is of a very personal character. I do not believe that there is any single approach to the history of science which could not be replaced by very different methods of attack; only trivialities permit but one interpretation.* —OTTO NEUGEBAUER[1]

LOOKING BACK THROUGH THIS BOOK [*Appropriating Shakespeare: Contemporary Critical Quarrels*], and reflecting on the very diverse range of material it has dealt with, one common element stands out, the degree to which critics pick up the ideas of a "Modern Master" and model their accounts of literature on the patterns he provides. Whether Freud, Derrida, Lacan, Foucault, Althusser, whether feminist or Christian, one thought-system is taken over as setting the standards by which Shakespeare should be read. Critics derive their assumptions about language and literature, their methodology (in some cases the renunciation of method), their attitudes to life even, from a law-giving individual or system. Adoption of the system usually seems to deprive them of the power to criticize it, or even to reflect on it critically. It is to be absorbed entire, demonstrated or validated through being imposed on this or that play. On the one side the master, on the other his pupils or slaves. The destructive effects of such allegiance were clearly shown by Francis Bacon in 1605:

And as for the overmuch credit that hath been given unto authors in sciences, in making them dictators, that their words should stand, and not counsels to give advice; the damage is infinite that sciences have received thereby, as the principal cause that hath kept them low, at a stay without growth or advancement.

In the mechanical arts, Bacon saw, a constant process of improvement and development takes place, but in philosophy all too often attention has been captured by the system of one thinker, which loyal exegetes "have rather depraved than illustrated. For as water will not ascend higher than the level of the first spring-head from whence it descendeth, so knowledge derived from Aristotle, and exempted from the liberty of examination, will not rise again higher than the knowledge of Aristotle." Bacon's conclusion is that "disciples do owe unto masters only a temporary belief and a suspension of their own judgment until they be fully instructed, and not an absolute resignation or perpetual captivity."[2] All too often today, it seems to me, the "absolute resignation" to a master system, "exempted from the liberty of examination" not only fails to advance thought but makes it shrink, as lesser wits "deprave" the original system by a mechanical and unimaginative reproduction of it.

The too loyal follower, passive and uncritical, seems to be imprisoned by the system he has adopted. To Bacon the bad effect of inquiry being restricted to a single system was shown by the medieval scholastics, whose

> wits being shut up in the cells of a few authors (chiefly Aristotle their dictator) as their persons were shut up in the cells of monasteries and colleges . . . did out of no great quantity of matter and infinite agitation of wit, spin out unto us those laborious webs of learning which are extant in their books.[3]

The same metaphor occurred to Edward Said in the 1980s to describe Foucault's concept of the ubiquity of power-structures making political engagement pointless: "Foucault's theory has drawn a circle around itself, constituting a unique territory in which Foucault has imprisoned himself and others with him."[4] At much the same time E. P. Thompson used a variant of the metaphor to convey his feeling of being "invited to enter the Althusserian theatre," where once inside "we find there are no exits." ("Men imprison themselves within systems of their own creation" also, Thompson writes, "because they are *self-mystified*").[5] Certainly their disciples are. I could wish for Shakespeare criticism in future more of the sturdy independence proclaimed by the American composer Virgil Thomson: "I follow no leaders, lead no followers."[6]

New perhaps in literary studies, the phenomenon of willing slavehood in the history of thought is ancient. Plato, Aristotle, Aquinas, Descartes, Hegel—many thinkers have attracted disciples, who have loyally expounded their works and reinterpreted contemporary issues in the same terms. In those cases a body of thought existed which was argued through, sometimes polemically and unfairly (Plato against the Sophists, say), but generally with due regard for evidence, accurate citation of instances, and the avoidance of self-contradiction. Not all of our current masters measure up to, or even accept these standards. Freud's work is notoriously speculative, a vast theoretical edifice elaborated with a mere pretense of corroboration, citing "clinical observations" which turn out to be false, with contrary evidence suppressed, data manipulated, building up over a forty-year period a self-obscuring, self-protective mythology. The system of Derrida, although disavowing systematicity, is based on several unproven theses about the nature of language which are supported by a vast expanding web of idiosyncratic terminology, setting up an auto-hermeneutical process which disguises the absence of proof or evidence adequate to meet external criteria. Lacan's system, even more vastly elaborated, is surrounded by another series of devices evading accountability, while Althusser's system has been judged "wholly self-confirming. It moves within the circle not only of its own problematic but of its own self-perpetuating and self-elaborating procedures."[7] As for Foucault, Thomas Pavel has acutely described his evasiveness on these issues as an " 'empirico-transcendental side-stepping,' which consists in conducting arguments on two levels at the same time without a system of transitions. If historical proof is missing in such a demonstration, the author will borrow from the language of metaphysics; when philosophical coherence is wanting, he will claim that the subject matter is only history." Foucault places himself beyond criticism with his nonempirical concepts of discursive formations and epistemes, but, as Pavel observes, this "transcendental discourse surreptitiously takes charge of an empirical domain. The excessive indetermination inherent in the quasi-transcendental leads to mistreatment of facts, which because they are innumerable and precise need completely different types of categories."[8]

One common element in these new masters is the confidence with which they proclaim their ideas, untouched by doubt, or else (Derrida, Foucault) absorbing skepticism into a system that remains, all the same, dogmatic. Perry Anderson observed that Althusser's "assertions of the scientific supremacy of Marxism had been more overweening and categorical" than anyone else's.[9] Such dogmatism, as Ernest Gellner observed of Freud, although intellectually speaking deplorable, can be effective with credulous and uncritical readers: "bare, brazen, unnegotiated assertion, if skilfully presented, can have a kind of stark authority."[10] It is a primitive rhetoric, of course, based on massive egotism, with a disdain for the petty details of argument and evidence, and to those aware of the great range of rational persuasion it is disappointing to see how successful mere assertion can be.

Frederick Crews, one of the shrewdest observers of contemporary culture, describes "the Grand Academy of Theory" that has arisen since the 1960s as marked by "a new peremptoriness of intellectual style, emboldening thinkers to make up their own rules of inquiry or simply to turn their whim into law. Such liberation from the empirical ethos," he observes, easily promotes "a relativism that dismisses the whole idea of seeking truth." Crews diagnoses in this period a growth of "apriorism—a willingness to settle issues by theoretical decree, without even a pretense of evidential appeal."[11] In 1960, he argues, most people would have agreed with R. S. Crane that an essential attribute of "the good scholar is 'a habitual distrust of the a priori; that is to say, of all ways of arriving at particular conclusions which assume the relevance and authority, prior to the concrete evidence, of theoretical doctrines or other general propositions.'"[12] (Many writers in many fields still share that distrust.) In the fashionable world of self-proclaimed new theory today, by contrast, participants practice "*theoreticism*—frank recourse to unsubstantiated theory, not just as a tool of investigation but as antiempirical knowledge in its own right." By empiricism Crews means (like E. P. Thompson) "simply a regard for evidence," choosing between rival ideas on the basis of observed phenomena, or an appeal to the text, a process in which the individual necessarily acknowledges the judgment of the scientific community. The basic justification for empiricism, he believes, "consists of active participation in a community of informed people who themselves care about evidence and who can be counted on for unsparing criticism."

In place of those principles—which to me constitute a genuine link between the humanities and the natural sciences, so different in other respects—Crews documents the presence of "wilful assertion" in modern theory, that "dogmatism of intellectual style" so evident in the work of Lévi-Strauss, Barthes, Lacan, Althusser, Foucault, and Derrida (164, 168). One quality these "gurus of theoreticism" share is their neglect or dismissal of what Crews calls "the principle of intersubjective skepticism." Althusser and Lacan were both "absolutists" who, under the guise of returning to their founding fathers, Marx and Freud, arbitrarily selected those elements that suited them and by "brazen decree" or *fiat*, with an explicit "disdain for corroboration," launched their own systems (169).

The dematerialization of a discipline, reducing it from reality to language, so to speak, is something that I have commented on several times in my discussion of these trends. The "poststructural cynicism" of Derrida and Foucault, as Crews describes it, deliberately distanced itself from the concepts of empiricism, evidence, and the notion of a community to whom interpretations are referred. Derrida's assertion that "there is nothing outside the text,"[13] Crews notes, "automatically precludes recourse to evidence," while in Foucault's historical works, although "portentous significance" is attached "to certain developments and details, his epistemological pronouncements appear to rule out the very concept of a fact" (171). This description echoes Thomas Pavel's analysis, just quoted, with remarkable accuracy. Rejecting any notion of positivism as privileging the natural sciences and their (once upon a time!) claim to objective certainties, I stand by the "empirical mode of intellectual practice," which appeals to the experience of reading in order to ground an argument by citing evidence from a (usually) printed text, available to all, subject to interpretation and open discussion. This principle maligned, the theoreticist is free to make whatever assertions he wishes.

The general effect of this absolutism among the Masters of the New Paradigm is to produce what Crews calls an "appetite for unquestioning belief" on the part of followers, matched by, or deriving from, the theorist's "refusal to credit one's audience with the right to challenge one's ideas on dispassionate grounds" (172). The result is the depressing state reached in the 1980s. As Edward Said independently observed, where once a critical consensus existed that at least disagreement could be confined within certain agreed limits, now there is "a babel of arguments for the limitlessness of all interpretation; . . . for all systems that in asserting their capacity to perform essentially self-confirming tasks allow for no counterfactual evidence" (230). If you have the system, what else do you need?

The 1960s iconoclasts quite consciously tried to guarantee a *carte blanche* for their own system-building by destroying the criteria of objectivity, empirical practice, evidence. Barthes was reporting on an established change of direction when he announced in 1963 the good news that

> the human sciences are losing some of their positivist obsession: structuralism, psychoanalysis, even Marxism prevail by the coherence of their system rather than by the "proof" of their details: we are endeavoring to construct a science which includes itself within its object, and it is this infinite "reflexiveness" which constitutes, facing us, art itself: science and art both acknowledge an original relativity of object and inquiry.[14]

Barthes was accurate in putting structuralism in first place. As the sociologist Simon Clarke showed in his penetrating study of that movement, Lévi-Strauss's first major work, *Les Structures élémentaires de la parenté* (1949; English translation 1969) offered a theory of kinship which was prophetic in having "no significant empirical content." To have an empirical content a theory "must tell us something about the world," both what it is like and what it is not like; that is, such a theory must be falsifiable. However, Clark argues, "Lévi-Strauss's theory of kinship is not falsifiable because it is consistent with any possible set of data." Rather than telling us "anything about the form or the operation of the kinship systems that we can find in actually existing societies," Lévi-Strauss's theories simply reduced "these systems to abstract models that are supposedly located in the unconscious," determining all observable structures.[15]

The task of science, according to structuralism, Clarke argues, is "not to create a view of the world that is true," but to find a theory which offers "a coherent and logical framework for discourse. . . . Thus positivism is preserved by turning into a form of rationalism" (103)—Barthes's pronouncement of the death of positivism was premature. The structuralist methodological separation of the ideal object from reality, although preferable to older and cruder positivism, Clarke judges, had "serious dangers." It allowed its users to preserve theories which could not be falsified by empirical evidence, however overwhelmingly opposed, such as Lévi-Strauss's kinship theories. Other followers protected their models by claiming that they existed "undetected and undetectable in the unconscious." This happened with Althusser's "symptomatic" reading of Marx, and his relegation of ideology to the unconscious, and it happened with Foucault's "epistemes," the construct of a "system of thought that is an ideal object, . . . only inadequately and incompletely expressed in the work of a particular thinker." (Foucault's theory can never be refuted by appeal to the evidence of a particular thinker's not corresponding to the episteme, for this merely shows that the thinker "had inadequately expressed it".) Throughout structuralism, Clarke concludes, "the rationalist development of positivism is the basis on which it is the theory that is made the judge of the evidence and not vice versa" (104).

This, I argue, is exactly the point at which Current Literary Theory has stuck. As—to use Barthes's words—"a science which includes itself within its object," it is self-contained and endlessly reflexive, not concerned with empirical enquiry into the makeup of the literary work, the complementary roles of writer and reader, the nature of genres, the possibilities of style, or the conventions of representing reality and human behavior. It pursues, as Clarke says, the "closed logical theory of an ideal object," ignoring any "correspondence between this object and a mythical reality." Attractive though this option may be to those who believe that Pure Theory is a superior object of study, it is very dubious that it could ever constitute a theory of literature. To begin with, any theory is already a selection from the phenomena to be discussed. No theory can explain everything, so some selection must be made in advance: every theory, as Clarke states, "is a theory about a part of the whole that is the world that we daily confront" (130). Current Literary Theory gets along, as I have pointed out several times, by simply ignoring large areas in linguistics, philosophy of language, and rival literary theories. The "part of the world" that it confronts is truly tiny. But what, in fact, is it a theory of? One basic principle of intellectual inquiry, Clarke notes, is that

> if a theory is to have any explanatory value it must be possible, in principle, to falsify the claims made by that theory empirically. Such falsification can only be achieved within the terms of the theory, and so can never be absolute. However if it is to be possible at all the theory must define its object independently of its explanations. (130)

As we have seen, that is precisely what the systems of Lacan, Althusser, Foucault and Derrida were designed not to do. As Clarke rightly observes, purely formal systems which refuse to define their object independently of their explanations can only be assessed "in relation to one another on formal grounds: the best theory is that which is simplest, most elegant," or whatever (137). On this basis the literary theory of Thomas Rymer might be judged superior to that of Coleridge, or Henry James. The corollary of a purely formal system, however, Clarke notes, is that "the isolation of the theory from the world of observation means that the theory has no purchase on reality" (130).

The unsatisfying nature of Current Literary Theory, I conclude, is that while being an *a priori* construct, largely made up of the negations of other theories, and while continuing to parrot the 1960s iconoclasts in scorning empiricism, it still claims to be telling us something about the world. What the theorists' pronouncements about decentered discourses, expelled subjects, absent presence, or nonreferential sign-systems are in fact proving is the accuracy of an observation made by W. G. Runciman, both a theoretical and practicing sociologist, namely that "there is in practice no escape for either the natural or the social scientist from a correspondence conception of truth," for to assert that any proposition is true (or not) "is to presuppose a relation of some kind between observation-statements and the state of the world," and therefore to employ a concept of truth.[16] This condition holds for all the assertions of Derrida, Foucault, and their followers, despite their attempts to evade accountability, about the nature of language, the incoherence of works of literature, and every other position either excoriated or recommended. Despite their attacks on objectivity, that concept remains inescapable in the human sciences, provided that it is properly understood. A. D. Nuttall recently wrote of the criterion of "objective truth," that if it is taken to mean " 'truth which . . . states itself, without regard to the nature and interests of the perceiver,' " then we could rightly reject it as superseded.

> If, on the other hand, "objective truth" means "truth which is founded on some characteristic of the material and is not invented by the perceiver," there is no reason whatever to say that [it] has been superseded. Indeed its supersession would mean the end of all human discourse, not just Newtonian physics but even *Tel Quel*. Objective atomism is dead but objectivity is unrefuted.[17]

Or, as Francis Bacon put it, "God forgive that we should give out a dream of our own imagination for a pattern of the world" (*Works*, 4:32–33).

Following through the history of the iconoclastic movement and its opponents since the 1960s it is heartening to see so much agreement between critics of very different training and background on its attempt to offload any notion of empiricism. To the Marxist classicist Sebastiano Timpanaro, the system-breakers, from Bachelard and Lévi-Strauss to Foucault and Derrida, merely managed "to blur together under the pejorative label of 'empirical' both 'lived experience' in the irrationalist sense and the 'experimental.'" They made an *a priori* definition of science "as anti-empiricism, as pure theory," ignoring its function as "knowledge related to action through a process of reciprocal verification,"[18] a fundamental mistake. Another Marxist critic, Perry Anderson, has commented on the way Derrida and Foucault took up "the philosophical legacy of the late Nietzsche, in its relentless denunciation of the illusion of truth and the fixity of meaning," trying to escape from "the tyranny of the veridical" towards "a free-wheeling nescience,"[19] glorying in a state beyond meaning or verification. Yet, he responds, "without untruth truth ceases to be such," indeed "the *distinction* between the true and the false is the unelim-inable premise of any rational knowledge. Its central site is evidence," a related concept disdained by structuralism and its successors, which claimed the li-cense to indulge in "a play of signification beyond truth and falsehood" (48). Evidence is particularly important in the historical sciences, however: as E. D. Hirsch points out, in their domain "decisive, falsifying data cannot be gener-ated at will," as in the natural sciences, so that the interpreter is often faced with the choice between two hypotheses, each having some evidence to sup-port it.[20]

For works of literature, to return to our main interest, the evidence cited de-rives from the text, which needs to have been accurately edited—a supposedly "factual" scholarly procedure, but which depends on all kind of interpretive hypotheses, including ideological ones (but that is another story). Secondly, citations from the text need to respect its overall meaning, and to reproduce the author's argument reliably. As I showed in chapter 4 of *Appropriating Shakespeare*, Stephen Greenblatt regularly misrepresents the texts he cites, in order (I surmised) to justify a New Historicist *ressentiment*. Although literary criticism has its own procedures, it shares with other subjects in the humani-ties a responsibility to describe the objects it studies accurately, as the first stage of interpretation. W. G. Runciman's outstanding study of social theory has identified some recurring instances of "misdescription" which can be used to sum up several of the failings I have documented in current Shakespeare criticism. Runciman divides misdescription into "misapprehension," involv-ing "incompleteness, oversimplification and ahistoricity"; and "mystification," involving "suppression, exaggeration, and ethnocentricity" (244–49). *Incom-pleteness* arises from an observer neglecting "an aspect of the institutions and practices of the society he is studying which is only peripheral to his own the-oretical interests but is of much closer significance to 'them.'" *Oversimplifica-tion* is seen when the researcher fails to realize that "the beliefs and practices connected with the behavior" he describes "are more complex than his account of it" would suggest. Social anthropology guards against this failing by developing "systematic participant-observation as the basic technique." *Ahistoricity* arises when the researcher forgets that a report on "the behavior of the members of an earlier society" may be accurate but "will be a misdescription if so presented as to imply that they were capable of conceptualizing their own experiences to themselves in the idiom of a later one."

These were instances of "misapprehension." The first mode of "mystification" is *suppression*, the researcher's deliberately failing to "include reports which would make the description which he presents less favorable to his chosen cause." *Exaggeration*, likewise, "typically arises when the researcher overstates a description to make a case for purposes of his own." *Ethnocentricity*, finally, "arises where the assumptions of the observer's own period or milieu are read into the experience of the members of another in which they do not in fact have any place." This is particularly likely when the description concerns that earlier society's values, when, for instance, the modern historian applies to them his "own taken-for-granted distinction between the natural and the supernatural"—or, we can add, a modern notion of witches as marginalized and therefore admirable people. Less specific, but rather similar criteria for interpretation, as we have seen, were suggested by E. D. Hirsch (legitimacy, correspondence, generic appropriateness, coherence), and S. M. Olsen (completeness, correctness, comprehensiveness, consistence, and discrimination).[21]

Although the literary critic is dealing not with societies, past or present, but with literary works, the same criteria apply, in particular the need to recognize the specificity or individuality of a play or novel, the fact that it has a unique dynamic structure, a growth, complication, and resolution of conflicting forces that is different from every other work (unless they belong to the type of *Trivialliteratur* written to a formula, when a description can be made of the genre as a whole). Given the potential uniqueness, at least, of every literary work, it follows that interpretation should begin at the beginning. Not in the sense that the critic's written account must always start with Act One, scene one, but that his reading should begin there, and the resulting interpretation should recognize the fact that every action has its consequences, and that to understand these it is necessary first to understand the action, the motives behind it, whether or not it was an initiating act or one in reply to, or in retaliation for, some preceding act. Drama, like life as Kierkegaard once defined it, is lived forwards but understood backwards, in retrospect. Plays certainly need to be experienced forwards, as evolving out of clearly defined human desires and their fulfilment or frustration. The first scene of *King Lear*, the first scene of *Othello*, are decisive for the subsequent events and their outcome. For a critic to *start* her account of the latter play with Iago's hypocritical words to Othello, "I am your own forever" (3.3.476), or for another to base a reading of *Coriolanus* on two brief passages taken out of context is to forfeit any chance of understanding it properly.

Equally, the evidence that a critic draws on concerning the play's individual structure involves him in reliably registering the various levels of plot, and how they interact. In *A Midsummer Night's Dream*, for instance, Shakespeare organizes four layers of plot in parallel. First, the impending marriage of Theseus and Hippolyta, "four happy days" off when the play begins (1.1.2). Secondly, the dispute between Egeus and his daughter Hermia, supposed to marry Demetrius but in love with Lysander. (Fortunately Helena loves Demetrius, and after various comic mistakes both couples achieve their desires.) Thirdly, the dispute between the King and Queen of the fairies, which Oberon resolves to his advantage with the help of a herb that makes Titania fall in love with Bottom. Fourthly, the company of artisans rehearsing their play of Pyramus and Thisbe, duly performed before the concluding nuptials (5.1). Any attentive reader can see how skilfully Shakespeare sustains these four plot-elements in parallel, bringing them all to a happy resolution in Acts 4 and 5.[22]

For some recent politically minded critics, however, the truly significant element in the play is that involving the artisans—not for its connection with the illusion basic to theatrical performance (which Theseus discusses in a famous speech), but for its relevance to immediate social unrest. In her book *Shakespeare and the Popular Voice*, Annabel Patterson has argued that the play should be interpreted in the light of the Oxfordshire Rising of 1596 and the midsummer disturbances in London of 1595, which some sources claim to have involved up to a thousand rioters, a mixture of artisans and apprentices.[23] Terence Hawkes reviewed Patterson's book favorably,[24] endorsing her notion that the artisans in the *Dream* offered to Shakespeare's audience "the worrying potential of the presence on the stage of a number of such persons," Bottom's "sexual triumph with Titania" constituting "an enactment in fantasy of upper-class fears regarding the potency of the lower elements both of society and the body." The artisans' play is now "thrust into new prominence," as Hawkes puts it, for their "mocking and sharply focused performance—capable of making its aristocratic audience as uncomfortable as the performance of 'The Mousetrap' does in *Hamlet*—takes up virtually the whole of the Fifth Act of the play, and the rehearsals for it resonate in the rest of the action to such a degree that they drown out much of the rather tedious framing plot."

This may be a demonstration of turning the margin into the center, but it certainly distorts the play. There is no evidence that the grievances of some working men in 1595–6 are echoed in this or any other play by Shakespeare. His presentations of social unrest (2 *Henry VI*, *Julius Caesar*, *Coriolanus*) derive from historical sources, and are never keyed to contemporary events. Far from airing their grievances, these craftsmen are entirely preoccupied with their play, and with the aesthetics of illusion. It is obvious that the artisans' play is comic, a parody of outdated verse style, absurd diction, and wooden dramaturgy. Hawkes's parallel with "The Mousetrap" in *Hamlet* could hardly be less appropriate, if we recall the subject-matter of that play, "the image of a murder done in Vienna . . . a knavish piece of work," and its intended (and successful) effect on Claudius. Far from being made "uncomfortable" by the playlet, Theseus and his courtiers keep up a rapid-fire series of deflating comments which are sometimes amusing. The crowning gesture in Hawkes's attempt to appropriate the play for a political reading, his claim that the artisans' rehearsals "resonate" so strongly that "they drown out much of the rather tedious framing plot," is another example of the ruthlessness involved in ideological interpretation these days, the seizing of that part of the play which fits your preoccupation and the contemptuous disposal of the rest. Patterson believes that the play's audience is faced with the dilemma of whether or not to join with the aristocrats in their mockery of the artisans. This partial reading of the play, trying to appropriate it for a politico-social ideology, exemplifies all the vices of misdescription that our sociologist identified: incompleteness, oversimplification, ahistoricity, suppression, exaggeration, and ethnocentricity. Ethnocentricity and ahistoricity are also, as we have abundantly seen, the defining marks of Freudian and (old-style) feminist criticism, from which the other faults soon follow.

Shakespeare criticism needs to take stock of the ideologies and systems to which it passively attaches itself: that much, I hope, has become clear. It has taken over elements from the general intellectual upheaval dating from the 1960s without reflecting on the methodological consequences of following Foucault, Althusser, or whomever. In absorbing their polemical attitudes to previous philosophies or systems, each group of literary critics today finds itself in opposition not just to all past Shakespeare critics but also to every other group working now. The result, as several experienced commentators have noticed, is an atmosphere of fragmentation and rivalry. The critic and historian of criticism, Denis Donoghue, adapting a phrase from Wallace Stevens ("the lunatic of one idea"), writes that "literary critics of our time are lunatics of one idea, and . . . are celebrated in the degree of the ferocity with which they enforce it." Donoghue chooses Kenneth Burke rather than Derrida, for instance, "because I prefer to live in conditions as far as possible free, unprescribed, undogmatic. Burke would let me practice a mind of my own; Derrida would not."[25] Derrida forces a choice on us, Donoghue writes,

> because he has a quarrel on his hands; he feels alien to the whole tradition of metaphysics. So he has driven himself into a corner, the fanatic of one idea. So far as he has encouraged other critics to join him there, turning an attitude into an institution, he has ignored the fact that, as Blackmur has said, "the hysteria of institutions is more dreadful than that of individuals." So is the fanaticism. What we make, thus driven, is an ideology, the more desperate because it can only suppress what it opposes; or try to suppress it.                                                    (207)

A younger commentator on recent developments in literary criticism sees them as a series of "competing orientations, each claiming to produce a more radical break with past conventions than the others." This struggle to get out in front of the field has established irritable disagreement as the norm: "the peevishness of critical debate in literary studies today can sometimes seem absurdly out of proportion to what is finally at stake."[26] What is at stake, though, is a whole range of cultural goods: egos, careers, identities, the supremacy of one's group.

The basic problem in current criticism, as I see it, is that many critics cannot experience—or at any rate, professionally discuss—a play or novel "direct," in itself. They have to impose between themselves and it a template, an interpretive model, some kind of "enchanted glass," in Bacon's striking phrase. But what that yields, once the reading has been performed, is not the play but the template, illustrated or validated by the play. All that such readings prove, as Crews puts it, "is that any thematic stencil will make its own pattern stand out."[27] This felt need for a guide or model can be found in much criticism over the last fifty years. What is new is the desire for collective templates, each group wanting its own magic glass to screen out material irrelevant to its own concerns and give back a reduced, but still clearly discernible mirror of itself, which other users can then reproduce in still smaller forms (the technique known as the "*mise en abyme*," a term from heraldry, as Hillis Miller points out).[28] As Wendell Harris observed, critical groups naturally select those works that can best exhibit "the power of their approach." Deconstructionists like texts that can be "pried open to suggest gaping contradictions," neo-Marxists and New Historicists like texts that "can be shown to reveal unsuspected workings of political power. Practiced New Critics, deconstructionists, and Marxists," he added, "can, of course, *read almost any text in a way that supports their own allegiances*."[29] To one critic that's just how things are; to others it could signify the denial of literary criticism. Edward Said asserts the contrary principle that

> criticism modified in advance by labels like "Marxism" or "liberalism" is, in my view, an oxymoron. The history of thought, to say nothing of political movements, is extravagantly illustrative of how the dictum "solidarity before criticism" means the end of criticism.[30]

Recent developments in the world of letters certainly bear out that verdict.

One result of the politicization of literary criticism is that readers now cannot afford to be unaware of the groupings and the polemical techniques that each uses to advance its own cause and frustrate its enemies'. (A knowledge of rhetoric is useful.) One popular ploy has been to pronounce a critical approach or methodology that you disapprove of "dead," or "finished." As Thomas Pavel has shrewdly observed, "the Rhetoric of the End" is a metaphor recently "much used and abused" to declare that its user "is in a position—or at least a posture—of Power." In claiming that an era is over, such narratives perform an aggressive act, for to "conceptualize the end" of a period—or "the entire metaphysical tradition—amounts to inflicting an ontological degradation on the sequence supposedly ended, relegating it, through rhetorical artifice, to the level of passive narrative material." If used "from within history and about history, the notion of an end points less to a *fact* than to a *desire*; far from achieving a real closure, it instead opens a polemic."[31] In simple vernacular terms it means "drop dead! Make room for me." This assertive technique can be seen very clearly in all the work of de Man.

Despite their claim to modernity, contemporaneity, or whatever, these polemical strategies hark back to a much older and cruder thought-world. As Pavel brings out, "for Lévi-Strauss to label his adversaries 'prescientific' was tantamount to pronouncing a symbolic death-sentence, to marking out their narrative end" and the advent of his new regime in anthropology. This was not so much a scientific gesture, however, as a magical or religious one,

> such is the force of excommunicative utterances. To proclaim the end of other groups and systems exorcizes the fear of having to confront them. . . . When the rhetoricians of scientific salvation announce the end of the infidels, they disguise the desire to annihilate the adversary and ensure complete mastery. (11, 13)

Thus Derrida's placing of Rousseau in "ethnocentric Western ontotheology," another commentator observes, "amounted to an impeachment, for Derrida's bracketing is the equivalent of a casting out or a death sentence."[32] The primitive nature of such expulsions is well described in Ernest Gellner's comment that in "pre-scientific societies"—this is now an ethnographic description, not a dismissal—

> Truth is manifested for the approved members of the society, and the question of its validation is not posed, or posed in a blatantly circular manner (the theory itself singles out the fount of authority, which then blesses the theory). Those who deviate, on the other hand, are *possessed* by evil forces, and they need to be exorcized rather than refuted.

It is only in modern "technological/industrial society," Gellner adds, "the only society ever to be based on sustained cognitive growth, that this kind of procedure has become unacceptable."[33]

Unacceptable indeed, but disturbingly prevalent in Current Literary Theory, which has developed a distinctly authoritarian streak. As S. M. Olsen has shown, such theory now "represents a form of theoretical imperialism," in that "conflicts between theories, or more often conflicts between skeptical critics with no supporters of some special theory" turn into an "ideological struggle" between incompatible value-systems.

> If one rejects conclusions yielded by a Marxist or psychoanalytic theory of literature one is blinded by a bourgeois ideology or by psychological defense mechanisms which will not permit one to recognize things as they really are. Protesting against the unreasonableness of deconstructionist readings, one is accused of being a liberal humanist who feels his individuality threatened.[34]

In this respect, then, Current Literary Theory, Olsen says, "is authoritarian in a way that theories of the natural sciences are not." E. P. Thompson described Stalinism as a doctrine which "blocks all exits from its system by defining in advance any possible exit as 'bourgeois,'"[35] and several Marxist critics produced many examples of Althusser using this ploy. Demonization (the first stage to exorcism) of the adversary is now a cliché of literary polemics. For A. D. Nuttall "the most typical vice" of twentieth-century ideological criticism is the abuse of "undercutting" explanations, setting down an opponent's weaknesses as being determined by psychological or social factors, hoping to neutralize the opposition "by ascribing to such explanations an absolute, exhaustive efficacy."[36] True enough, when Nuttall's book was mentioned by one Cultural Materialist he described it as "espous[ing] a positivistic conservative materialism which rejects the specificity of history."[37]

Abuse and defamation are, however, things that commentators on the cultural scene nowadays must learn to live with. The republic of letters, or the academy, is now leased out to a host of competing groups, engaged in the old practices of epideictic rhetoric, laus and vituperatio: praise for oneself, scorn for the others. One exponent of literary theory asserts that in the coming age it will "play the central role" in literary studies.[38] J. Hillis Miller, then president of the Modern Language Association of America, was more insistent. Celebrating "the triumph of theory" with a hypnotic repetition of that phrase, and engaging the rival Marxists in close-quarter combat, Miller asserted that "the future of literary studies depends on maintaining and developing . . . deconstruction."[39] For

> deconstruction and literary theory are the only way to respond to the actual conditions—cultural, economic, institutional, and technological—within which literary study is carried out today. . . . Theory is essential to going forward in humanistic study today.  (250)

And so on through many more "onlys." But of course the Marxists have a different version. For Fredric Jameson, "only Marxism" can offer what we need, since the Marxist perspective "is the absolute horizon of all reading and all interpretation," and constitutes "something like an ultimate *semantic* precondition for the intelligibility of literary and cultural texts."[40] None of these advocates is lacking in self-confidence.

Which of them shall we believe? Each makes a claim for our attention—no, for our total and absorbing involvement in their discipline before, or indeed to the exclusion of, all others. For Norman N. Holland, veteran Freudian campaigner, "the fantasy psychoanalysis discovers at the core of a literary work has a special status in our mental life that moral, medieval, or Marxist ideas do not. . . . The crucial point, then, . . . is: the psychoanalytic meaning underlies all the others."[41] In other words, fantasies are the first and best, moreover the source from which all other forms of thought develop. Close your Marx, open your Freud. In the struggle to gain, and keep our attention what matters is not logical argument but force of utterance, insistence, emphasis. On behalf of the feminists hear Ann Thompson:

> It is important for feminist critics to intervene in every way in the reading and interpretation of Shakespeare and to establish, even more securely than they have already done, that their approach is not just another choice among a plurality of modes of reading, not something that can be relegated to an all-woman ghetto, but a major new perspective that must eventually inform *all* readings.[42]

Given such intense jockeying for attention, each group trying to gain and retain that portion of the intellectual space that seems theirs by right, quarrels are inevitable. The feminists, for instance, have fallen out with the New Historicists. Whereas American feminists had hoped for an alliance with this new wave, their one-time allies in the fight against the establishment soon turned out to be making a new establishment, and furthermore a male enclave of their own. Peter Erickson, writing in 1987, reported—and it is a revealing comment on the febrile intensity with which cultural-political movements are discussed in American universities that he could write the chronicle of a three-year time-span—that "by the mid-nineteen-eighties both feminist criticism and new historicism had . . . entered a transitional stage marked by uncertainty, growing pains, internal disagreement, and reassessment." At a seminar on "Gender and Power" at the 1985 meeting of the World Shakespeare Conference (in West Berlin), apparently an "impasse" emerged over the relative importance of gender. Feminists attacked the New Historicists for being "more interested in power relations between men than between the sexes," and for not acknowledging the "absolutely central" position of gender. The dispute is a political one—in the current sense of "cultural politics" as the activity of self-constituted critical groups—and is rather parochial, if extremely bitter. Erickson accuses New Historicism of abusing its "capacity to confer legitimacy," sacrificing "intellectual integrity" to its "territorial imperative."[43] Another feminist, Lynda Boose, has complained that New Historicists are exclusively involved with "the absolutist court and its strategies of male power," choosing cultural texts "to privilege over the literary one[s]" that are all the same, "male-authored—hierarchical—patriarchal."[44] A feminist colleague, Carol Neely, accuses them of "re-producing patriarchy" and dooming women to silence (few readers will have noticed much silence in American feminism). The New Historicists' desire for mastery, Neely alleges, can be seen in their continuing "focus on the single and most visible center of power, the monarch," a choice that may attempt to conceal but in fact reveals "the widespread cultural anxiety about marriage, women, female sexuality and power engendered by the women's movement and feminist criticism."[45]

The New Historicists have defended themselves, of course, or proclaimed their innocence.[46] To some readers these group-disputes will seem tedious, and they may feel like exclaiming, with Mercutio, "a plague on both your houses!" But anyone concerned with the present, and more important, the future of Shakespeare criticism must take note of them. The danger is that collective animus can reach the point where a group "targets" anyone who evaluates their work by independent criteria as an enemy, a person of no worth or merit, whose motives can only be of the most dubious kind. That my diagnosis is actual, not hypothetical, nor hysterical, can be seen from the reaction to Richard Levin's essay on "Feminist Thematics and Shakespearean Tragedy." This is a challenging but fair and properly documented analysis of a dozen or so recent books and essays, in which Levin showed that some feminists tend to impose their own beliefs about gender on to the tragedies, indicting the main male characters as patriarchal misogynists whose (usually insecure) masculinity is the source of the tragic catastrophe. Levin's essay appeared in *PMLA* for March 1988. A correspondent in the October issue complained that the readings offered by Levin (and by the feminists) were "partial," that is, both "incomplete" and "partial in the sense of taking a position on one side of the gender divide."[47] The correspondent concluded that "masculinity is a malady. It is the gender, not the sex, that is the problem." In reply Levin objected to the feminists' claim to possess "a key to all human behavior," in which the "cause of the masculine malady" is located in men's "infantile experience with mothering," or even (in a recent feminist reading of *Coriolanus),* in "their fetal tissue"(!). The problem, then, "may be sex and not gender after all, and biology can once more become destiny, but this time only for the men"—a sad prospect, many would feel. Levin ended by congratulating *PMLA* (which has given much space to feminist criticism in recent years) for having published his article in the first place.

But that amicable conclusion was short-lived, for the issue of January 1989 included a truly virulent letter signed by no less than twenty-four feminists.[48] Rather than applauding *PMLA,* the writers indignantly queried why it had "chosen to print a tired, muddled, unsophisticated essay that is blind at once to the assumptions of feminist criticism of Shakespeare and to its own." From pure abuse the writers moved on to *ad hominem* arguments, professing to be "puzzled and disturbed that Richard Levin has made a successful academic career by using the reductive techniques of this essay to bring the same predictable charges indiscriminately against all varieties of contemporary criticism." Such smears debase themselves, of course, but for the record, Levin's work includes many studies of Renaissance drama besides his analyses of the distorting and deadening effects of some unexamined assumptions in contemporary literary criticism.

The letter writers' indignation shows that they are really concerned with the contemporary political issue, expressing "the serious concerns about inequality and justice that have engendered feminist analyses of literature." What they seem unable to realize is that other women, and other men, may share those concerns but still feel that their polemical expression in literary criticism can only produce a distorted reading of literature from the past, which is held up to blame for the ills of the present. There is no sign in this letter of that self-examination or rethinking of premises and assumptions which Levin's essay could have provoked. The signatories merely repeat the distortion to which Levin originally referred, the imposition of misogyny as a standard personality trait which is not only untrue to the characters concerned but erodes their individuality, giving them all "the same stereotypical male sickness." It is the men, the men who are to blame.

There is no need to summarize Levin's reply, which is in the public domain. The one point I pick out is his observation that the writers of the letter evidently want *PMLA* "to deny publication to any criticism of them that they disapprove of." Any right-minded reader will agree with Levin that a journal which thinks of itself as being open to debate cannot be "subject to the veto of any group." That would be to close off critical exchange, and human dialogue, from the outset. Not that Levin expects (any more than I do) to "convince the signers or others who share their feelings. For them, critiques of feminist criticism are permissible from within the fold . . . , but not from 'a cultural other.'"[49] This is surely the most depressing aspect of the current situation, the belief that no outsider has the right to criticize the group, that this right belongs exclusively to members of the group—who would risk, however, being expelled from it. . . . That way lies chauvinism, wars of religion, persecution.

Levin's reply did not, of course, settle the issue, which raged on in the press, on panel meetings at further conferences, and in print.[50] In the next installment, delivered at another MLA meeting in January 1990 and subsequently published, Levin and various critics exchanged further arguments. Addressing the dilemma of the politicization in literary studies that so many commentators have been deploring, Levin proposed a peace treaty based on the triple principles of objectivism, rationalism, and pluralism. By objectivism he means the ability to attain knowledge of a literary text without the resulting interpretation being "always determined by the interpreter's ideology." By rationalism he means the possibility that "rival ideologists in their attempt to persuade can invoke rational standards that are themselves not ideological"—otherwise, one would imagine, the automatic rejection of the other group's arguments on the ground of ideology would result in a true *dialogue des sourds.* And by pluralism Levin means the belief that various critical approaches can attain knowledge valid in their own terms, not positing "a necessary connection between these approaches and political ideologies," yet allowing us "to live together and talk to each other because we can understand and respect our different approaches."[51]

I personally welcome Levin's suggestions as moderate, lucidly argued, not attempting to appropriate a larger or better furnished space in the contemporary scene. But in the present climate all peace treaties seem doomed. As Levin shows, Marxists reject pluralism as a "formalist fallacy" since "they are not seeking peace but victory. They do not want Marxism to be regarded as one among several valid approaches; they want it to be the *only* valid approach, as can be seen in their frequent references to it as 'scientific' (which means all other approaches are unscientific" (18–19). Both Marxists and feminists display what Levin calls

> the genetic fallacy, which claims that our views of the world are caused by our race, gender, class, and similar factors, and that they therefore must be judged on the basis of those causes. But both of these claims are false. Our views may often be influenced by such factors, but are not necessarily determined by them. If they were, there would be no male feminists, or female anti-feminists, no bourgeois radicals or proletarian reactionaries.
>
> (54)

The diversity of human temperaments and persuasions is far greater than these deterministic models would allow. But "even if our views were caused by these factors," Levin adds, "it does not follow that they must be judged on that basis"; this would simply divide the world into the lowest common denominators of gender, class, age, and judge their products accordingly. The principle at issue here is that in all intellectual debates there must be reference points independent of the participants' biographical situation or ideological adherence. If there are no criteria for evaluating methodology, the use of evidence, procedures of argument, the truth or falsity of the conclusions, then intellectual pursuits become impossible, and unnecessary. Truth will simply be handed down from those in power, while the rest of us acquiesce in its dissemination. Who would want to live in such a world?

The politicization of discourse means that disagreements are regularly reduced, as A. D. Nuttall and Stein Olsen observed, to some putative underlying motive, psychological (the critic reveals his own "anxiety"), or political. In his original essay, as he recalls, Levin criticized those feminists' formalist readings of Shakespeare's tragedies because "some of them ignored parts of the text that did not fit their thesis" (55). The relevant response would have been for them, whether as a group or as individuals, to show either that they did not ignore the part in question or that it really did fit the thesis. Instead, as we have seen, a whole battery of bitter *ad hominem* arguments were ranged against Levin, and continue to be; one respondent argued that his article should have been denied publication because he "failed to understand the feminist cause."[52] Levin retorts that he does in fact support feminism but that "a just cause cannot justify interpretive faults" (55). The larger issue is this new tendency in ideology-dominated discourse, the "defensive move from criticism to politics." Whoever takes the new ideologues to task for some unsatisfactory critical interpretation is instantly accused of sexist bias, or any of the other demonized labels (essentialist-liberal-humanist-bourgeois . . . ). But this self-protective tactic has damaging effects; "Marxists and feminists seem to claim a special privilege for their approaches, on political grounds, that grants immunity from the kind of scrutiny to which other approaches are subjected and so would amount to a denial of pluralism," which would mean in turn that only members of a group could criticize other members (55–56). These are the depressing but predictable results of the slogan that Edward Said excoriated, "solidarity before criticism."[53] The survival of any intellectual discipline depends on there being some external terms of reference by which it can be judged, a language which is comprehensible to those outside the group, a community at large that can evaluate achievements. The alternative is already visible around us, the inbreeding of Derridians, Lacanians, Foucauldians, Althusserians, unable and unwilling to understand anyone else's language or concerns. It can be seen in so many places in current Shakespeare criticism, as groups align themselves and polarize the scene into an us/them division.

The last instance of polarization that I shall cite, which also expresses a satisfied feeling of group-consensus, having rejected alternative views as prescientific, imperialistic ("add demons here," as one of the ancient magical recipes would say), is Howard Felperin's recent description of the new, or "current" view of *The Tempest*. Felperin describes the change as having taken place since the mid-1970s, when "anti-authoritarian, anti-elitist, and anti-aesthetic doctrines were in the wind in a recently politicized academia." The resulting change to our perception of this play is phrased by Felperin in a series of rhetorical questions:

> What Shakespearean now would be oblivious or audacious enough to discuss *The Tempest* . . . from any critical standpoint other than a historicist or feminist, or more specifically, a post-colonial position? Would anyone be so foolhardy as to concentrate on the so-called "aesthetic dimension" of

the play? To dote thus on such luggage would be to risk being demonized as "idealist" or "aestheticist" or "essentialist" by a critical community increasingly determined to regard itself as "materialist" and "historicist."[54]

Whether Felperin is making fun of the new orthodoxy or endorsing it is not immediately clear from his text, but others certainly use those "scare quotes" to demonize their collective enemies. When I read such attempts at stigmatization, I must admit, a certain stubborn independence rises in me, and I feel tempted to retort: "Go ahead then! Demonize me! See if I care!" In more sober language, I would have to say that the "luggage" so contemptuously rejected[55] is essential accompaniment for a critic, or reader, the ability to receive a play or novel as an experience in itself, over and above our current, ephemeral, and limited concerns.

Felperin describes the views of "a critical community," but it is only one of many, although it may believe it possesses the exclusive source of knowledge. All schools, however, no matter how self-assured or polemical, would do well to accept that other approaches have a validity, and that no one has a monopoly over truth. "*Patet omnibus veritas,*" Ben Jonson wrote (adapting Vives), "Truth lyes open to all; it is no mans *severall.*"[56]

No one is about to grant New Historicists, materialists, me, or anyone else an immunity to criticism, an exclusive license to practice the one true mode of interpretation and outlaw all the others. Peace would be desirable, perhaps, but only if all parties grant each other the right to read Shakespeare as they wish, and be taken to task if they distort him.

This has been a book about the practice of Shakespeare criticism, and the effect on it of some current theories. I would like to end with some words from Edward Said's book *The World, the Text, and the Critic,* where he argues that "criticism is reducible neither to doctrine nor to a political position on a particular question," literary or otherwise.

> In its suspicion of totalizing concepts, in its discontent with reified objects, in its impatience with guilds, special interests, imperialized fiefdoms, and orthodox habits of mind, criticism is most itself, and . . . most unlike itself at the moment it starts turning into organized dogma.                                    (29)

Criticism, Said believes, should be "constitutively opposed to every form of tyranny, domination, and abuse; its social goals are noncoercive knowledge produced in the interests of human freedom," for "the moment anything acquires the status of a cultural idol or a commodity, it ceases to be interesting" (29–30). While recognizing that all readings derive from a theoretical standpoint, conscious or not, Said urges that we avoid using dehumanizing abstractions:

it is the critic's job to provide resistances to theory, to open it up toward historical reality, toward society, toward human needs and interests, to point up those concrete instances drawn from everyday reality that lie outside or just beyond the interpretive area necessarily designated in advance and thereafter circumscribed by every theory.                    (242)

The danger, as we see around us, is that literary theory can "easily become critical dogma," acquire "the status of authority within the cultural group" or guild, for "left to its own specialists and acolytes, so to speak, theory tends to have walls erected around itself" (247). A necessary counter to that tendency is for us "to move skeptically in the broader political world," to "record the encounter of theory with resistances to it," and, among other things, "to preserve some modest (perhaps shrinking) belief in noncoercive human community." These would not be imperatives, Said remarks, but "they do at least seem to be attractive alternatives. And what is critical consciousness at bottom if not an unstoppable predilection for alternatives?"

NOTES

1. Otto Neugebauer, "The History of Ancient Astronomy: Problems and Methods," *Journal of Near Eastern Studies* 4, no. 1 (January 1945): 2 (repr. in Otto Neugebauer, *Astronomy and History: Selected Essays* [New York: Springer-Verlag, 1983]).

2. Francis Bacon, *Works*, ed. James Spedding et al., 14 vols. (London: Longmans, 1857–1874), 3:289–90.

3. Bacon, *Works*, 3:285.

4. Edward W. Said, *The World, the Text, and the Critic* (Cambridge, Mass.: Harvard University Press, 1983), 245.

5. E. P. Thompson, *The Poverty of Theory and Other Essays* (London: Merlin Press, 1978), 32, 165.

6. Letter of 11 November 1977, in *Selected Letters of Virgil Thomson*, ed. T. and V. W. Page (New York: Summit Books, 1988), 363.

7. Thompson, *Poverty of Theory*, 12

8. Thomas Pavel, *The Feud of Language: A History of Struturalist Thought*, trans. L. Jordan and T. Pavel (Oxford: Basil Blackwell, 1989), 85, 93–94.

9. Perry Anderson, *In the Tracks of Historical Materialism* (London: Verso, 1983), 29–30.

10. Ernest Gellner, *The Psychoanalytic Movement, or, The Cunning of Unreason* (London: Paladin, 1985), 42–43.

11. Frederick C. Crews, "The Grand Academy of Theory," in *Skeptical Engagements* (New York: Oxford University Press, 1986), 163, 164. [Editors' note: This essay is included in this volume.]

12. R. S. Crane, "Criticism as Inquiry; or, The Perils of the 'High Priori Road,'" in *The Idea of the Humanities and Other Essays*, 2 vols. (Chicago: University of Chicago Press, 1967), 2:25–44.

13. Jacques Derrida, *Of Grammatology*, trans. G. C. Spivak (Baltimore, Md.: Johns Hopkins University Press, 1976), 158

14. Roland Barthes, *Critical Essays*, trans. R. Howard (Evanston, Ill.: Northwestern University Press, 1972), 277–78.

15. Simon Clarke, *The Foundations of Structuralism: A Critique of Lévi-Strauss and the Structuralist Movement* (Brighton, Sussex: Harvester Press, 1981), 54.

16. W. G. Runciman, *A Treatise on Social Theory*, vol. 1: *The Methodology of Social Science* (Cambridge: Cambridge University Press, 1983), 8.

17. A. D. Nuttall, *A New Mimesis: Shakespeare and the Representation of Reality* (London: Methuen, 1983), 12.

18. Sebastiano Timpanaro, *On Materialism*, trans. L. Gardner (London: NLB, 1975), 186

19. Anderson, *In the Tracks of Historical Materialism,* 46–47.

20. E. D. Hirsch Jr., *Validity in Interpretation* (New Haven, Conn.: Yale University Press, 1967), 181.

21. Hirsch, *Validity*; Stein Haugom Olsen, *The Structure of Literary Understanding* (Cambridge: Cambridge University Press, 1978).

22. See G. K. Hunter, *John Lyly: The Humanist As Courtier* (London: Routledge and Kegan Paul, 1962), chapter 6, "Lyly and Shakespeare" (298–349), for one of the best accounts of Shakespeare's comedies yet written (318–30, on *MND*), and David P. Young's full study of the play, *Something of Great Constancy: The Art of* A Midsummer Night's Dream (New Haven, Conn.: Yale University Press, 1966).

23. Annabel Patterson, *Shakespeare and the Popular Voice* (Oxford: Basil Blackwell, 1989).

24. Terence Hawkes, "Bardbiz," *London Review of Books*, 22 February 1990, 11–13. This review gave rise to a long-running correspondence, in which the virtues and faults of Cultural Materialist Shakespeare criticism were freely debated. Some of the most cogent observations came from James Wood: see, e.g., his letters of 22 March, 25 April, 24 May, and 16 August 1990.

25. Denis Donoghue, *Ferocious Alphabets* (Boston: Little, Brown, 1981), 205–6.

26. Don E. Wayne, "Power, Politics, and the Shakespearean Text: Recent Criticism in England and the United States," in *Shakespeare Reproduced: The Text in History and Ideology*, ed. Jean E. Howard and Marion F. O'Connor (London: Methuen, 1987), 57.

27. Crews, *Skeptical Engagements*, 173.

28. "*Mise en abyme* is a term in heraldry meaning a shield which has in its center *(abyme)* a smaller image of the same shield, and so, by implication, ad infinitum, with ever smaller and smaller shields receding toward the central point"; J. Hillis Miller, "Stevens' Rock and Criticism as Cure, I," *Georgia Review* 30, no. 1 (Spring 1976): 11.

29. Wendell V. Harris, "Canonicity," *PMLA* 106, no. 1 (January 1991): 116; my italics.

30. Edward Said, *The World, the Text, and the Critic*, 28.

31. Pavel, The *Feud of Language*, 9.

32. George McFadden, review of *Allegories of Reading*, by Paul de Man, *Journal of Aesthetics and Art Criticism* 39 (1981): 339.

33. Gellner, *The Psychoanalytic movement*, 120.

34. Stein Haugom Olsen, *The End of Literary Theory* (Cambridge: Cambridge University Press, 1987), 203.

35. Thompson, *Poverty of Theory*, 133.

36. Nuttall, *A New Mimesis*, 7.

37. John Drakakis, ed., *Alternative Shakespeares* (London: Methuen, 1985), 16.

38. J. G. Merquior, *From Prague to Paris: A Critique of Structuralist and Post-Structuralist Thought* (London: Verso, 1986), 246, citing Jonathan Culler, *On Deconstruction* (Ithaca, N.Y.: Cornell University Press, 1982), 10.

39. J. Hillis Miller, "The Triumph of Theory, the Resistance to Reading, and the Question of the Material Base," *PMLA* 102, no. 3 (May 1987): 289.

40. Fredric Jameson, *The Political Unconscious: Narrative as a Socially Symbolic Act* (Ithaca, N.Y.: Cornell University Press, 1981), 19, 75

41. Cited by Olsen, *The Structure of Literary Understanding*, 204.

42. Ann Thompson, " 'The Warrant of Womanhood': Shakespeare and Feminist Criticism," in *The Shakespeare Myth*, ed. Graham Holderness (Manchester: Manchester University Press, 1988), 84.

43. Peter B. Erickson, "Rewriting the Renaissance, Rewriting Ourselves," *Shakespeare Quarterly* 38 (1987): 330, 329.

44. Lynda E. Boose, "The Family in Shakespeare Studies; or—Studies in the Family of Shakespeareans; or—The Politics of Politics," *Renaissance Quarterly* 40, no. 4 (Winter 1987): 731, 732.

45. Carol Thomas Neely, "Women and Men in *Othello*: 'What should such a fool / Do with so good a woman?' " in *The Woman's Part: Feminist Criticism of Shakespeare*, ed. Carolyn Ruth Smith Lenz, Gayle Greene, and Carol Thomas Neely (Urbana: University of Illinois Press, 1980), 7, 15.

46. See, e.g., Jonathan Goldberg, "Perspectives: Dover Cliff and the Conditions of Representation," in *Shakespeare and Deconstruction*, ed. G. Douglas Atkins and David M. Bergeron (New York: Peter Lang, 1988), 245–66.

47. *PMLA* 103, no. 5 (October 1988): 817–18, from Alberto Cacicedo, with Levin's reply at 818–19. One feminist *topos* in Cacicedo's letter that I object to is his assertion that in *Othello* Emilia is "marginalized, objectified, literally utilized by her husband," made to keep quiet "despite her mistress's anguish." Cacicedo also complains when, in the comedies, women characters say little in the final scenes. But this is to apply yet again standards of modern egalitarianism to matters governed by theatrical exigencies. To demand that writers give women "an equal say" is to impose political demands on creative activity.

48. *PMLA* 104, no. 1 (January 1989): 77–78, with Levin's reply at 78–79. I must express regret that at least two of the signatories agreed to do so, their work being notable (so far, at least) for its historical depth and absence of vindictiveness.

49. *PMLA* 104, no. 1 (January 1989): 79.

50. See, e.g., "A Traditionalist Takes on Feminists Over Shakespeare," *New York Times*, 1 March 1990. [Additional note (2004): see now Richard Levin's collection, which traces the whole course of this controversy: *Looking for an Argument: Critical Encounters with the New Approaches to the Criticism of Shakespeare and His Contemporaries* (Madison, N.J.: Fairleigh Dickinson University Press, 2003).]

51. Ivo Kamps, ed., *Shakespeare Left and Right* (London: Routledge, 1992), 16, 20, 18.

52. This tactic is used by other defenders of exclusive systems. As Frederick Crews says of Derrida's selective borrowings from Freud, "he encourages the theoreticist habit of treating one's own system as received truth while dividing all other tenets into those that miss one's point (owing, perhaps, to 'repression') and those that can be borrowed to adorn it": Crews, *Skeptical Engagements*, 176n9. An example of this practice comes from Malcolm Bowie, a loyal exponent of Lacan, who dismisses all criticism of the master by declaring that

"most published [hostile] responses to which his thought gives rise . . . are trivial and written by self-righteous bystanders who have tried and failed, or simply failed to read what Lacan writes." Of the criticism by Sebastiano Timpanaro (a distinguished classical philologist) that " 'in Lacan's writings charlatanry and exhibitionism largely prevail over any ideas of comprehensible, even if debatable nature,' " revealing " 'an erroneous and confused knowledge' " of linguistics, Bowie merely retorts that "Timpanaro's remarks show signs of a limited knowledge of Lacan and premature judgement" (Malcolm Bowie, "Jacques Lacan," in *Structuralism and Since: From Lévi-Strauss to Derrida*, ed. John Sturrock [Oxford: Oxford University Press, 1979], 147). This is to make life too easy for yourself. For demonstration of Lacan's ignorance and misuse of linguistics see, e.g., Georges Mounin, *Clefs pour la linguistique* (Paris: Seghers, 1968), 13, and Vincent Descombes, *Objects of All Sorts: A Philosophical Grammar*, trans. L Scott-Fox and J. M. Harding (Oxford: Basil Blackwell, 1986), 177–87.

53. Said, *The World, the Text, and the Critic*, 28.

54. Howard Felperin, *The Uses of the Canon: Elizabethan Literature and Contemporary Theory* (Oxford: Oxford University Press, 1990), 171.

55. Frank Kermode's edition of *The Tempest* is similarly demonized, a by now ritual gesture in some quarters, for having such subheadings in its introduction as "pastoral tragicomedy," "art and nature," and "masque elements." Summarizing the course of "Shakespeare criticism" as "having recognized itself over the past decade . . . to be at one of those moments . . . when a 'return to history' is on the agenda," Felperin describes the current mood among New Historicists and cultural materialists as being one which "is not about to linger before such aesthetic luggage . . . without historicizing [it] anew" (172). I find it strange that just the dimension being mocked here is the history of literature, genres, and conventions. What crimes are perpetrated in the name of history!

56. *Timber*, in Ben Jonson, *Works*, ed. C. H. Herford, P. Simpson, and E. M. Simpson, 11 vols. (Oxford: The Clarendon Press, 1925–1952), 8:567.

## 16. THE DEBATE OVER THE WARTIME WRITINGS OF PAUL DE MAN

### THE LANGUAGE OF SETTING THE RECORD STRAIGHT

### ALAN B. SPITZER

*No reading is conceivable in which the question of its truth or falsehood is not primarily involved.*  —PAUL DE MAN

IN 1987, PAUL DE MAN, a literary scholar and critic of international distinction, was discovered to have written articles for the collaborationist press in Belgium in 1941 and 1942. Testimony at a ceremony in his honor, after his early death in 1983, expressed veneration for a teacher whose intellectual austerity was remembered as moral rectitude. The revelation that in his early twenties de Man had been a cultural critic for the Belgian paper *Le Soir*, after it was taken over by the Propaganda Abteilung of the Wehrmacht, came as a terrible shock, especially in the light of his contribution to an issue devoted to virulent anti-Semitism. The response to these revelations is an example of how traces of the past can emerge to reconstruct the present.

The young Belgian scholar Ortwin de Graef, who uncovered the articles while doing research for a work on de Man, brought it to the attention of people who had been closely associated with him, including Jacques Derrida and others in what I will loosely identify as deconstructionist or postmodernist literary circles. They decided to publish all of de Man's contributions during the occupation of Belgium—some 169 pieces for *Le Soir*, ten articles for the Flemish-language journal *Het Vlaamsche Land*, book notes for the publishing house *Bibliographie Dechenne*, as well as his preinvasion contributions to student publications. In addition, thirty-eight literary theorists and other scholars responded to a request for reflections on the issue, and these essays were published in a volume entitled *Responses: On Paul de Man's Wartime Journalism*.[1]

The revelations about de Man's wartime behavior aroused sufficient interest to be headlined in the *New York Times*, "Yale Scholar Wrote for pro-Nazi Newspaper,"[2] and then led to controversial exchanges in more or less popular journals and, with increasing emotions, in highbrow publications like *Critical Inquiry*, where academics engaged in acrimonious conflict. If the teapot was small, the tempest was certainly intense.

Alan B. Spitzer. "The Debate Over the Wartime Writings of Paul de Man: The Language of Setting the Record Straight." Abridged by the author from *Historical Truth and Lies About The Past: Reflections on Dewey, Dreyfus, de Man, and Reagan*, by Alan B. Spitzer. Copyright © 1996 The University of North Carolina Press. Used by permission of the publisher. www.uncpress.unc.edu.

All of this discussion inevitably produced a commentary on the controversy by the partisans themselves and by more or less dispassionate observers. Most commentaries identify several distinct, if overlapping issues. Here is my list: (1) a characterization and interpretation of what de Man actually wrote in the collaborationist press; (2) the implications for the evaluation of de Man as a human being—that is, for his posthumous reputation, with reference not only to his behavior during the war but also to why he concealed it; (3) the implications for reading de Man's immensely influential writings, for both evaluating and understanding them in the light of what preceded them; and (4) the implications of the writings of an author in his early twenties for an intellectual movement with which he was closely associated some thirty years later.

I am primarily concerned with the first issue—that is, with historical argument, but I do believe that anyone loyal to classic criteria of logical and temporal coherence would repudiate some prima facie condemnations of de Man's later writing because of what he wrote in his youth. The damning of deconstruction in the light of what de Man wrote thirty years prior to that movement seems an even more egregious non sequitur.

This tendentious and illogical projection of the past onto the present certainly fueled the indignation aroused by the journalistic exploitation of the scandal, but the defenders of de Man were also eager to refute misrepresentations of his wartime behavior and of his wartime writings. Their arguments to this effect were in turn harshly criticized as disingenuous special pleading.

The exchange has been accompanied by a powerful dose of what people used to call argument ad hominem. In his open letter to Jon Wiener, J. Hillis Miller characterized the "violence" of the denunciation of de Man and of deconstructionism as

> a reaction to the genuine threat posed by de Man's work and by that of the so-called deconstuctionists generally to a powerful tradition of ideological assumptions about literature, about history, and about the relation of literature to human life. Fear of this power in "deconstruction" and in contemporary theory generally, in all its diversity, accounts better than any other explanation for the unreasoning hostility, the abandoning of the canons of journalistic and academic responsibility, in articles like yours and the many other subsequent attacks on de Man, on "deconstruction," and on critical theory as such.[3]

Operating from the opposite side of the politico-cultural barricade, Roger Kimball characterized Geoffrey Hartman's troubled essay in the 7 March 1988 issue of the *New Republic* as an early contribution to a massive campaign of "damage control":

That this paragon [de Man] of chic academic achievement should stand revealed as the author of anti-Semitic articles for pro-Nazi publications at the height of Hitler's power has been a major embarrassment for his many epigones. The reason is obvious: the frequently heard charge that deconstruction is essentially nihilistic has now acquired existential support of the most damaging kind. . . . It is clear that whatever remorse or chagrin Professor de Man's admirers experienced has been completely overshadowed by a concerted effort at creative exculpation—that is to say, at damage control.[4]

This sort of rhetoric constitutes one version of what is currently called historicity. That is, the antagonists are, in the words of the historian Joan Scott, emphasizing "the relevance of the position or situatedness of subjects to the knowledge they produce and the effects of the difference on knowledge."[5] Or, to be exact, the situatedness of the other fellow. In this debate, people historicize each other with a vengeance. I cling to the old-fashioned notion that even if both parties have correctly described their antagonists' (conscious or unconscious) motives, I have yet to hear convincing arguments about the factual content or the moral implications of de Man's behavior from 1940 to 1942. Which is to say that there is something to the genetic fallacy.

Those who objected to the "irresponsible" exploitation of the scandal would not, and could not, confine their polemic to crude or subtle arguments ad hominem. This was not only because the audience they wished to convince would not have been convinced by such arguments but also because they shared an ethic that distinguished bad from good arguments, factual distortions from accurate reconstructions, misrepresentations from reasonable descriptions, and lies from truth.

To those who objected to what they saw as a biased, vindictive, unfair, and irresponsible treatment of what de Man actually did during the Occupation years, there was no choice but to engage in the language of "setting the record straight." These are the very words used in articles and pieces by outstanding figures in the movement labeled deconstruction or postmodernism, and the idea was implied in others. Three of the early contributions to the controversy—by Jonathan Culler, Christopher Norris, and J. Hillis Miller—strikingly illustrate the commitment to conventional standards of accurate reporting, legitimate inference, and respect for fact.[6]

Jonathan Culler published a statement in the *Chronicle of Higher Education* for 13 July 1988: "It's Time to Set the Record Straight About Paul de Man and His Wartime Activities for a Pro-Fascist Newspaper." Christopher Norris placed a piece in the *London Review of Books* entitled "Paul de Man's Past," in which we again find the statement, "It is important to set the record straight." Those precise words do not appear in J. Hillis Miller's deeply felt essay in the

*Times Literary Supplement,* but the essay is vibrant with indignation over the irresponsible handling of facts by those who so readily denigrated de Man: "One would have thought that in a case of such gravity a little checking of facts and rereading of the evidence would have been in order, especially of the past of those journalists who are also professors, professionally committed to a sober truth-telling."

The apparent discrepancy between the radical skepticism of the deconstructionist luminaries and their ad hoc insistence on rigorous evidentiary standards has provided considerable ammunition for their critics, who accuse them of a rhetorical double standard. This is an issue I will pursue, not so much to identify abstract philosophic contradictions, but to consider the choice of the grounds for convincing argument in the particular circumstances of the de Man case. Those concerned with setting the record straight had no choice but to appeal to conventional criteria of truth. To the extent that they affirmed such standards, they joined a certain community—one that is conceptually and ethically committed to "an adequate reading of the facts of the case," as J. Hillis Miller put it.

This deference to the authority of historical documentation was shared by the antagonists in the widening debate. The sharing is what made the debate possible. This is not to say that the conflict might have been settled by superior documentation. That conflicting conclusions were drawn from the same evidence might seem to support the currently influential view that historical narratives are essentially incommensurable, that they cannot simply be reduced to the sum of their "propositional assertions."[7] Variously plotted narratives do, however, often overlap, not only (as in this case) with regard to what constitutes relevant evidence but also with regard to what matters in constituting the narrative and what counts toward establishing the argument embedded in it. Indeed, some such overlapping is necessary for there to be an intelligible historical controversy.

Even though radically different histories of de Man—stories of his life— were fashioned out of the knowledge of his wartime behavior, they proceeded from the common assumption that such a narrative had been irreversibly transformed in the light of new evidence, and from a common identification of the moral and rational grounds for debating the implications of the evidence. The debate depended, for example, on the assumption (still not universally shared) that writing for a collaborationist journal was prima facie deplorable. As for rational grounds, the implicit consensus on what matters and what counts is what allows Culler and others to write in the language of setting the record straight.

The extent to which they succeeded in their campaign remains disputable, partly because there was considerably more to the record than Culler and the others had realized when they undertook to set it straight. It became apparent that the reference to innocuous passages could not simply cancel out the damaging passages.

From the beginning, the most vulnerable essay—not only an embarrassment but the source of personal pain to de Man's Jewish friends and students—was "Les Juifs dans la littérature actuelle," which was framed by articles far uglier than his in an issue of *Le Soir* introduced by the paper's proud affirmation of an anti-Semitism that was not merely social but racial—"Notre antisémitisme est d'ordre racial."[8]

De Man's essay deplores a "vulgar anti-Semitism" that condemns European literature as degenerate and decadent because Judaized. The Jews themselves have contributed to the myth of Jewish dominance, interpreted as one of the disastrous consequences of the First World War. But literature has been healthier than that, because it followed its own logic, especially in the psychological realism practiced by such exemplars as Gide, Kafka, Hemingway, and Lawrence (much will be made of this incongruous list). Jews have had relatively little influence on this development, despite their cerebral qualities, which might have been appropriate to the work of lucid analysis that novels require. In France, for example, Jewish writers have always been of the second rank. Here de Man presents a list from which the name of Marcel Proust is notable by its absence. This phenomenon should comfort Western intellectuals, whose civilization has demonstrated its health through preserving its original character, "despite Semitic interference in all aspects of European life."

This article concludes with the notorious passage luridly illuminated by the hindsight that de Man could not have possessed in 1941: "What's more, one can thus see that a solution to the Jewish problem that would lead to the creation of a Jewish colony isolated from Europe would not have regrettable consequences for the literary life of the West. It would lose, in all, some personalities of mediocre worth and would continue, as in the past, to develop according to its higher laws of evolution."

The assumption that only this piece referred to Jews turned out to be incorrect. In a survey of contemporary German fiction in *Het Vlaamsche Land*, 20 August 1942, de Man contrasts two forms of postwar literary composition that were materially separated by the events of 1933:

> The first of these groups celebrates an art with a strongly cerebral disposition, founded upon some abstract principles and very remote from all naturalness. The theses of expressionism, though remarkable in themselves, were used here as tricks, as skillful artifices aimed at easy effects. The very legitimate basic rule of artistic transformation, inspired by the personal vision of the creator, served here as a pretext for a forced, caricatured representation of reality. Thus [the artists of this group] came into an open conflict with the proper tradition of German art which had always and be-

fore everything else clung to a deep spiritual sincerity. Small wonder then, that it was mainly non-Germans, and specifically Jews, who went in this direction.[9]

Aside from these passages, there was a cumulatively damaging dossier of reviews and essays asserting the acceptance of German hegemony as a historical necessity, affirming a certain cultural nationalism with a racialist coloring, praising the accomplishments of Italian fascism, comparing French culture and politics unfavorably to German, and urging collaboration with the conqueror as simple realism. The reviews of French authors constitute a list of what Jeffrey Mehlman called the "Nazi hit parade"[10]—Robert Brasillach, Pierre Drieu La Rochelle, Jacques Chardonne, Marcel Jouhandeau, Alfred Fabre-Luce, Bertrand de Jouvenel, and Jacques Benoist-Méchin—most of whom were on the *Gesamtliste des fördernswerten Schrifttums*, the list of "publications worthy of support" compiled by the Wehrmacht's Propaganda Abteilung in France.

It became apparent to the defenders of de Man that this evidence required a sophisticated interpretation. As this conviction dawned, Jacques Derrida was summoned to the lists.

Derrida answered the summons in a sixty-two page essay in *Critical Inquiry*[11] that would provide a dialectically ingenious reading designed to draw the sting from the criticism of de Man's most vulnerable articles. Whatever its consistency with the expository principles of Derrida's other writings, his essay on de Man would appeal to conventional criteria of responsible argument, to those standards of "caution, rigor, honesty" violated by newspaper journalism and by "certain academics."

To the extent that Derrida was engaged in the refutation of those who had violated the standards of rigor and honesty, he fashioned a language appropriate to the task. He privileged (as postmodernists like to say) conventional criteria of veridicality—the publicly accessible text that constrains interpretation, if it does not impose legitimate readings; the drawing of plausible inference from relevant evidence and the rules of logical coherence.

To be sure, Derrida does not completely depend on the authority of dispassionate argument and scholarly paraphernalia. The pervasive use of the first-person singular carries the claim to a different sort of authority—the authority of moral indignation at the "newspaper war," and the authority of the pathos of personal implication, of the pain of reading a friend's text that first inflicted "a wound, a stupor, and the sadness that I would neither dissimulate or exhibit."[12]

One might accept the evident sincerity of the self-revelation and the pathos while noting their polemical function—that is, to contribute an emotional authenticity to Derrida's central argument, which grants the deplorable implications of de Man's most shocking texts in order to legitimate a mitigating reading of them. This strategy is embodied in a presentation of, "on the one hand"—evidence as to de Man's serving the German rulers by writing for a paper under their control—and "on the other hand"—the material conceivably containing ambiguity, irony, and double meaning, allowing an interpretation that suggests not merely considerable qualification of his Nazi or Fascist or even pro-German sympathies, but doubt about his having been a collaborationist at all.

The salient instance of Derrida's method is his rereading of the notorious piece "Les Juifs dans la littérature actuelle."[13] Having said "on the one hand" that "nothing . . . will heal over the wound I right away felt" when first reading the anti-Semitic passages, which seemed "in the *dominant* context in which they were read in 1941" to produce a dominant effect "in the direction of the worst," Derrida provides a close reading in support of his "on the other hand," suggesting that de Man subtly contrived to undermine his ostensible message.

The key to Derrida's countervailing interpretation is the hypothesis that de Man's dismissal of "vulgar anti-Semitism" might be read as implicitly condemning anti-Semitism *tout court*, inasmuch as anti-Semitism is "always and essentially vulgar":

> What does this article say? It is indeed a matter of criticizing vulgar antisemitism. That is the primary, declared, and underscored intention. But to scoff at vulgar antisemitism, is that also to scoff at or mock the vulgarity of antisemitism? This latter syntactic modulation leaves the door open to two interpretations. To condemn vulgar antisemitism may leave one to understand that there is a distinguished antisemitism in whose name the vulgar variety is put down. De Man never says such a thing, even though one may condemn his silence. But the phrase can also mean something else, and this reading can always contaminate the other in a clandestine fashion: to condemn "vulgar antisemitism," *especially if one makes no mention of the other kind*, is to condemn antisemitism itself *inasmuch as* it is vulgar, always and essentially vulgar. De Man does not say that either. If that is what he thought, a possibility I will never exclude, he could not say so clearly in this context. One will say at this point: his fault was to have accepted the context. Certainly, but what is that, to accept a context? and what would one say if he claimed not to have fully accepted it, and to have preferred to play the role there of the nonconforming smuggler, as so many others did in so many different ways, in France and in Belgium, at this or at that moment, inside or outside the Resistance? [emphasis in original]

Critics of Derrida's essay subsequently observed that his hypothesis immediately hardens to the flat description of the article as "non-conformist." Then, categorically, "it is a matter of condemning antisemitism *inasmuch as it is vulgar*." The other brutally anti-Semitic articles on the same page support the hypothesis, because even if de Man's article is "contaminated by the forms of vulgar antisemitism that frame it, *these coincide in a literal fashion, in their vocabulary and logic, with the very thing that de Man accuses,* as if his article were denouncing the neighboring articles."

Derrida's disposition of "Les Juifs dans la littérature actuelle" functions as an argument a fortiori. If the article on the Jews, perceived as the worst case, isn't as bad as it seems, the lesser offenses are diminished. Hereafter, Derrida applies the working principle—that all of de Man's "propositions carry within them a counter-proposition"—to other salient texts, to the same effect.

However one assays the balance of Derrida's judgment on de Man's wartime behavior, it is apparent that Derrida identifies some contemporary behavior as far worse than what de Man did under the pressures of historical circumstance. "To judge, to condemn the work or the man on the basis of what was a brief episode, to call for closing, that is to say, at least figuratively, for censoring or burning his books is to reproduce the exterminating gesture which accuses de Man of not having armed himself against sooner with the necessary vigilance. It is not even to draw a lesson that he, de Man, learned to draw from the war."[14] What Derrida first presented more or less tentatively, his successors in *Responses* and elsewhere argued categorically.[15]

Such an approach was applied to other potentially reprehensible articles in *Le Soir* and *Het Vlaamsche Land.* With the republication of all of de Man's contributions to these journals, as well as the reviews and book notes for the *Bibliographie Dechenne,* considerably more palliative "on the other hands" would be required to draw the sting from so many "on the one hands." This task was shouldered in a most thorough and literal-minded manner by Ortwin de Graef, almost as if to expiate his sin in opening the cover of the tomb. De Graef scrupulously uncovers various apparently collaborationist pieces, while finding a reason to suggest in each case that "matters are certainly not as simple as they might appear at first sight."[16] A second reading, de Graef argues, suggests that de Man "never uncritically praises any of the collaborationist books he reviews, but characteristically preserves a tellingly indeterminate margin of disagreement." De Graef thus considers some twelve examples that seem to express collaborationist and pro-German sentiment, including the two anti-Semitic passages, all accompanied by a mitigating gloss. The very length of the list suggests the problem of serial exculpation, and this is not an exhaustive list.

After sufficient communion with this style of argument, one begins to get the hang of it, as I hope I am about to demonstrate.

In a brief book note published in the *Bibliographie Dechenne* in September 1942, de Man reviewed Lucien Rebatet's *Les Décombres,* a French best-seller in 1942 and 1943. Rebatet was a French fascist, without apology or qualifications, whose condemnation to death at the end of the war was commuted because sufficient time had passed to render the death penalty unpopular. *Les Décom-*

bres—"the ruins," or "the rubbish"—was a diatribe against all of the mistakes and blunders that led to the catastrophic decline of France, and an affirmation of the virtues of fascism. It was the vehicle of a vicious anti-Semitism ornamented by such passages as this: "After one hundred and fifty years of Jewish emancipation, these evil impure beasts carrying within themselves the germs of every plague ought to be returned to the prisons where the secular wisdom had once incarcerated them."[17] Here is what de Man had to say about the book:

> Lucien Rebatet, like Robert Brasillach, is one of those young French intellectuals who, during the years between the two [world] wars, worked with all their might to combat a politics whose catastrophic and ill-fated orientation they had understood. The entire sum of bitterness and indignation accumulated over the course of those years of vain combat finally overflows [déborde] in this thick volume, an immense pamphlet of brilliant verve and vigor. One by one, all the guilty parties of the current French decay, whatever the milieu or party to which they belong, are looked over and shot down in a few lapidary and definitive sentences. But this great work of destruction also contains constructive elements: in walking among the ruins [les décombres] of a bankrupt era, Lucien Rebatet also dreams of reconstruction; and this is why without a doubt his ferocious book ends in words of hope.[18]

On the Derrida model, the approved way to handle this hot potato might go something like this:

> On first reading, this seems to be a recommendation to the Belgian reading public of an unequivocally profascist and viciously anti-Semitic work. Nothing can excuse that, above all in the light of consequences not foreseen by de Man, but it is not enough to stop with condemnation, which would be to speak the language of the totalitarian spirit voiced by Rebatet. One should allow at least the possibility of an, unverifiable but necessary, alternate reading. As obnoxious as it is, Rebatet's obscene text does not recommend the extermination of the Jews but only their incarceration in a worldwide network of ghettos. Furthermore, to recommend the work, or apparently to recommend the work, is not necessarily to commend it. De Man is simply describing it, and in language that is not unambiguously positive. Here the key word is overflow (déborde)—an overflow obviously refers to an excess. That is to say that there is something excessive about Rebatet's work against which, in his subtly defiant manner, de Man is warning the readers. We know that de Man believes that this is a ferocious book. He hasn't said that he shares its words of hope. Furthermore, what effect could the review have had? It's hard to believe that Belgians in this

period of dearth ran out to spend their francs on a book just because a young reviewer recommended it.

And so forth, with special emphasis on the incipient totalitarianism of those who would condemn, without qualification, de Man's blurb for a very nasty piece of work.

This rhetoric of partial admission, followed by a tentative mitigation that hardens into categorical exculpation, has the flavor of plea-bargaining by the hard-pressed attorney for the defense. Geoffrey Hartman, for example, appeals to the principle of "reasonable doubt" and the spirit of the First Amendment:

> To condemn the articles on the basis of their ideas would mean we clari-fied what was called *délit d'opinion* in the French purges after Liberation. In a democracy we do not prosecute ideas as such. Proof is required that they directly incited criminal or treasonous activities. . . . I do not think we have that proof. The essays stick to cultural issues and do not support par-ticular measures of the occupier or denounce individuals or groups.[19]

Since there is no proof that de Man denounced individuals or groups, he de-serves the benefit of the doubt. And so too, presumably, does every other writer who affirmed the realism of collaboration, identified the Hitlerian soul with the German soul and praised the works of fascist authors, but who brought no one in particular to the attention of the Gestapo.

There is an even more radical disjuncture between Jacques Derrida's dis-claimers and his line of argument.

> I have said why I am not speaking here as a judge, witness, prosecutor, or defender in some trial of *Paul de Man*. One will say: but you are constantly delivering judgment, you are evaluating, you did so just now. Indeed, and therefore I did not say that I would not do so at all. I said that in analyzing, judging, evaluating this or that discourse, this or that effect of these old fragments, I refuse to expand these gestures to a general judgment, with no possibility of appeal, of Paul de Man, of the totality of what he was, thought, wrote, taught, and so forth.

Apparently the repudiation of the general judgment with no possibility of ap-peal still licenses Derrida to appeal to the "unquestionable fact" that

> a statement can never be taken as a presumption of guilt or evidence in a trial, even less as proof, as long as one has not demonstrated that it has only an idiomatic value and that no one else, besides Paul de Man or of Paul de Man's signatory of the 1940–42 texts, could have either produced this statement or subscribed to it. Or inversely, that all statements—their

numbers are not finite and their contexts are highly diverse—could not be signed and approved by authors who shared nothing of Paul de Man's history or political experiences.

Having entered this ingenious demurrer, Derrida gives up "this petty and mediocre game," a technique he applies in various places to disavow inappropriate arguments he has just made. Thus he disclaims any appeal to his own background, which might authenticate his argument in favor of de Man, remarking that he was Jewish, persecuted during the war, known for his leftist opinions, and so forth, but then assuring the reader that "such declarations are insufficient."[20]

The technique of ritual disclaimer followed by arguments designed to undo it is a recurrent tactic for all of those who begin by saying that what de Man did was inexcusable and then go on to excuse what he did. This approach is fortified by the evidentiary double standard. As Marjorie Perloff observes, not all statements of witnesses who speak well of de Man are subject to the stringent scrutiny applied to the damaging evidence. When this technique is applied directly to the texts, "positive readings are cognitive, negative ones are merely judgmental and moralistic."[21]

The most convincing argument in de Man's defense depending on reference to historical fact speaks to the actual context for behavior that is all too easy to condemn from complacent hindsight. In the characteristically pugnacious words of Andrzej Warminski, "What do you know about the man, his circumstances, the place, the time? Who are you to draw a line between good man and bad man, resistance and collaboration?"[22] This question has considerable force that echoes beyond the circle of de Man's militant defenders, but it resonates differently if directed to his surviving coevals, such as his prewar condisciples at the *Cercle du libre examen* who chose a different path.

There are, however, Belgian contemporaries who do speak in defense of de Man, arguing that the choices under the German occupation were inescapable and extremely difficult. The absolutely clinching contextual factor, according to de Man's defenders, is the fact that he was not indicted by the Belgian postliberation courts, whose treatment of collaborationists was harsher than that of most of the other countries under German occupation—far harsher than in France. However, the historical context of de Man's wartime writings—the daily experience of the Occupation in Belgium, the body of writings published under the Nazi aegis, the course of the war and of world events—is precisely what has been emphasized in a critical reaction to the more or less sympathetic reassessments of de Man as a collaborationist.

Indeed, those apologists who perceive an Aesopian subtext in de Man's wartime writings exhibit a remarkable lack of interest in contemporary reader response. To postulate some subversive subtext as a mitigation of apparently offensive texts is to assume not only an audience that might have decoded it but also a censorship that misread it. The assumption that the Propaganda Abteilung censors were more obtuse than our contemporary critics may be valid but scarcely relevant; and the conjecture that they were bamboozled by de Man is dubious, although familiar enough among those intellectuals who believe that they are cleverer than the people they serve. Of course, it is possible that de Man was such an intellectual.

The situation in Belgium can be illuminated with reference to that in France, where such specialists as Otto Abetz preferred a low-key "realistic" acceptance of German hegemony to an embrace of French Nazism. This was the sort of regime under which de Man wrote essays that were not always "in conformity with the premises of Nazi politics." As long as de Man's writings, to use Derrida's words, "*most often and in a preponderant fashion*" conformed to official rhetoric, they served the purposes of the Propaganda Abteilung. Whatever his intention, he contributed to the soft sell—to the lowering of "the threshold of acceptability" of the intellectual collaboration.[23]

The context of the course of events outside of Belgium also speaks to the nature of de Man's "realism" in assimilating the fact of German hegemony. That is, until Stalingrad and the Allied landings in North Africa, after which de Man dropped out, meeting the deadline of the Belgian government-in-exile, which promised to exempt writers from prosecution if they severed relations with the collaborationist press by the end of 1942. His successor at *Le Soir* was assassinated. From 1943 until the end of the war, de Man and his family survived, apparently without a paying job.

The defense of Paul de Man has claimed the epistemological authority of evidence, logic, and context, fortified by an assumption of hermeneutical mastery, occasionally falling back on postmodern indeterminacy to the point of self-parody.

Here is Samuel Weber:

> What exactly are we talking about? What does it mean to talk, to ask "about" . . . ? For instance, about the "character" of an individual man? About a practice of language, of reading and rewriting, known as "deconstruction"? About a war fought some half a century ago? About Nazism? Fascism? Collaboration? About academic institutions and academic intellectuals? What about the word "about," that relates the question to its object? To talk "about" something is to position ourselves in its vicinity, to be sure, and yet nevertheless: outside it, alongside perhaps, but still at a certain remove from what we are talking about.[24]

According to Andrzej Warminski (who makes quite categorical judgments of critics of de Man, who have, he says, crawled out "from under the rocks of their pathologies"), "Reading suspends: it suspends knowledge and it suspends judgment, and it suspends, above all, the possibility of ever knowing whether we are doing one or the other."[25] Here the key term, the very touchstone is "reading"—that is, "attentive" reading, in contrast to inattentive reading or not reading at all. Once again, Derrida provides the paradigm. In his diatribe— and that is not too strong a term—against the critics of his first piece in *Critical Inquiry*, the clinching charge is that they *ne pveut pas lire*—fusing *pouvoir* and *vouloir* into a neologism for "they neither can nor wish to read," thus accruing the authority of Derridean wordplay.[26] Derrida's own gloss on de Man's "The Jews in Contemporary Literature" was, according to Rodolphe Gasché, "merely . . . an act of attentive reading of what this text unmistakingly tells us."[27]

In postmodernist discourse, especially in the most admired, mature works of Paul de Man, to read attentively is to emphasize the indeterminacy of texts; but in these condemnations of "self-righteousness at the expense of attentive, sustained reading"[28] or of ignoring "the first and most elementary rule," which is "to read,"[29] it is easy enough to read "attentive" as right and "inattentive" as wrong. Hans-Jost Frey nails this down. Resigned to "the readiness of non-readers to pass judgment and the refusal of those who would judge to read," he concludes: "Against these judgments one can simply say that, to the extent that they are based on the refusal to read precisely, they are invalid."[30]

The overriding responsibility to read did not especially detain those who cite in his favor de Man's 1955 letter to the Harvard Society of Fellows in response to an anonymous denunciation.[31] Even after the full text of the letter was available, Geoffrey Hartman was able to write, "The ethical situation of de Man differs from that of Heidegger in that there was no retrospective falsification, unless his silence is taken to be that."[32] Whether de Man should be condemned for not having called the equivalent of a press conference to present his mea culpa, or whether his silence about his past was the finest response to it, the fact is that when asked, he lied.

In the letter, de Man refers to his uncle Henri as his father. Whatever one makes of this, it is a falsehood. And his claim to have left *Le Soir* in 1941 rather than 1942 is not a trivial inaccuracy. All over Europe, there were people resigned to the German occupation through 1941 who were involved in active resistance by the following year. His statement that he wrote some literary articles in *Le Soir* and that "like most of the other contributors, I stopped doing so when Nazi thought control did no longer allow for freedom of statement" is not simply disingenuous but categorically false. The Nazis always exercised thought control over the paper, even when they did not apply preventative censorship. After this was applied on 20 August 1942, de Man contributed fourteen additional articles to *Le Soir*, one more to *Het Vlaamsche Land*, and assorted book notes to the *Bibliographie Dechenne*.

Those who cite in de Man's favor his assertion that he left the paper when the Nazis applied censorship and at the same time conjecture that he must have written the anti-Semitic essay under pressure contradict themselves.

The cumulative effect on this reader of the apologetic literature has been decidedly negative. While I cannot pretend to an initial neutrality (I once picketed Kirsten Flagstad),[33] I am not alone. Dubious defensive polemics have done more to reinforce a negative perception of what the deconstructionists (or so-called deconstructionists) are about than have all the attempts to establish some sinister linkage between de Man's collaborationism and the postmodernist project.

The criticism of the cohort that rallied to the standard planted by Miller, Culler, and Derrida is not confined to their antagonists but has also been expressed by those who deplore the weak logic and ignorance of the journalistic denunciations of de Man and deconstruction.[34] Dominick LaCapra, a historian open to postmodernist themes, and an admirer of writers he treats in an article on the affair, deplores "the self-serving hyperbole, tendentiousness and Schadenfreude" of the opponents of de Man and deconstruction but concludes: "Still, the strained attempt to show that the early journalistic articles were occasions for admirable silence, powerful scenes of self-deconstruction or even acts of resistance itself unconsciously tends to lend credence to the charge that deconstruction can be used to justify or rewrite anything—a charge that most applies, in my judgment, to abuses of deconstruction from which no one is altogether immune."[35] In his criticism of various apologists for de Man, LaCapra identifies their essential source, in psychoanalytic terms, as "transference," and he regrets their failure to "work through the trauma of distressing revelations by acknowledging and mourning the specific losses it involves." This approach patronizes, rather than refutes, their arguments, which in my view do not so much exemplify the presumption that deconstruction can be used "to justify or rewrite anything" as the assumption that any argument of a master rhetorician is self-validating.

But to conjecture that the dubious arguments of these distinguished scholars reflect a failure of self-analysis, or the arrogance of the hermeneutical elect, or some other conscious or unconscious motives, is not to speak to the substance of their historical discourse. As this discourse claims the authority of conventional empirical and rational standards, there can be no reputable evasion of their requirements. Once committed to the rules of a certain game, one is responsible to those rules. I don't use the word "game" to trivialize the epistemological or ethical content of the argument. The people who are indignant over what they take to be misrepresentations of de Man's past are not simply choosing one set of rhetorical conventions over another; they are saying what they think is true and doing what they think is right. To observe this is not to deny the potential complexities in identifying facts relevant to a particular case, drawing appropriate inferences from them, or deriving plausible interpretations from the inferences. The complexities are inherent in the argument.

## NOTES

1. Werner Hamacher, Neil Hertz, and Thomas Keenan, eds., *Wartime Journalism, 1939–1943, by Paul de Man* (Lincoln: University of Nebraska Press, 1988). Werner Hamacher, Neil Hertz, Thomas Keenan, eds., *Responses: On Paul de Man's Wartime Journalism* (Lincoln: University of Nebraska Press, 1989).

2. *New York Times*, 1 December 1988.

3. J. Hillis Miller, "An Open Letter to Professor Jon Wiener," in *Responses*, ed. Hamacher, Hertz, and Keenan, 342.

4. Roger Kimball, "Professor Hartman Reconstructs Paul de Man," *New Criterion* 6, no. 9 (May 1988): 37. Kimball is referring to Hartman's "Paul de Man, Fascism, and Deconstruction," *New Republic*, 7 March 1988.

5. Joan W. Scott, "The Evidence of Experience," *Critical Inquiry* 17 (Summer 1991): 783.

6. Jonathan Culler, "It's Time to Set the Record Straight about Paul de Man and His Wartime Articles for a Pro-Fascist Newspaper," *Chronicle of Higher Education*, 13 July 1989, section 2; Christopher Norris, "Paul de Man's Past," *London Review of Books*, 4 February 1988, 7; J. Hillis Miller, Guest Column, *Times Literary Supplement*, 17–23 June 1988, 676.

7. Louis O. Mink, "Philosophy and Theory of History," in *International Handbook of Historical Studies: Contemporary Research and Theory*, ed. Georg G. Iggers and Harold T. Parker (Westport, Conn.: Greenwood Press, 1979), 25.

8. The page of the 4 March 1941 issue of *Le Soir* on which de Man's article appeared is reproduced in *Wartime Journalism*, ed. Hamacher, Hertz, and Keenan, 286–92; de Man's review is also reproduced (45).

9. De Man, "People and Books: A View on Contemporary German Fiction," *Het Vlaamsche Land*, 20 August 1942, 325–26.

10. At least as quoted by Jon Wiener, "Deconstructing de Man," *Nation*, 9 January 1988. For a fair and balanced survey of de Man's favorable reviews of works by French and Belgian collaborationists, "realists," and fascists by a former student of de Man, see Alice Yaeger Kaplan, "Paul de Man, *Le Soir*, and the Francophone Collaboration (1940–1942)," in *Responses*, ed. Hamacher, Hertz, and Keenan, 266–84.

11. Jacques Derrida, "Like the Sound of the Sea Deep Within a Shell: Paul de Man's War," *Critical Inquiry* 14, no. 3 (Spring 1988): 590–652; this is reproduced with slight changes in *Responses*, ed. Hamacher, Hertz, and Keenan, 127–64. My citations are from the *Critical Inquiry* version. Derrida refers to the phone call from *Critical Inquiry* which proposed that he be the first to speak ("Like the Sound of the Sea," 596).

12. Derrida, "Like the Sound of the Sea," 600.

13. Derrida, "Like the Sound of the Sea," 621–32.

14. Derrida, "Like the Sound of the Sea," 651.

15. Ian Balfour, " 'Difficult Reading': De Man's Itineraries," Thomas Fries, "Paul de Man's 1940–1942 Articles in Context;" Peggy Kamuf, "Impositions: A Violent Dawn at *Le Soir*," in *Responses*, ed. Hamacher, Hertz and Keenan 8–9, 197–98, 264.

16. Ortwin de Graef, "Aspects of the Context of Paul de Man's Earliest Publications," followed by "Notes on Paul de Man's Flemish Writings," in *Responses*, ed. Hamacher, Hertz, and Keenan, 96–126. In a subsequent publication de Graef finds a motive for de Man's collaborationism in a sort of misplaced scientism, an insight that "allows us to address this collaboration along lines that are less overdetermined by the rhetoric of outright denunciation

or circuitous exculpation" (De Graef, *Serenity in Crisis: A Preface to Paul de Man, 1939–1960.* [Lincoln: University of Nebraska Press, 1993], 13). "Circuitous exculpation" perfectly characterizes de Graef's contribution to *Responses.*

17. Lucien Rebatet, *Les Décombres* (Paris: Éditions Denoel, 1942), 566. For a description of Rebatet and the bowdlerization of later issues of the 1942 work, see Alice Yeager Kaplan, *Reproductions of Banality: Fascism, Literature, and French Intellectual Life* (Minneapolis: University of Minnesota Press, 1986), 125–41. See also Robert Belot, *Lucien Rebatet: Un itinéraire fasciste* (Paris: Seuil, 1994), 282–301.

18. *Bibliographie Dechenne* (September 1942); *Wartime Journalism,* ed. Hamacher, Hertz, and Keenan, 366.

19. Geoffrey Hartman, "History and Judgment: The Case of Paul de Man," *History and Memory* 1, no. 1 (Spring–Summer 1989): 63. Hartman does not extend this argument to the anti-Semitic passages, which he cannot extenuate.

20. Derrida, "Like the Sound of the Sea," 631, 642, 648.

21. Marjorie Perloff, "Response to Jacques Derrida," *Critical Inquiry* 15, no. 4 (Summer 1989): 774.

22. Andrzej Warminski, "Terrible Reading (preceded by 'Epigraphs')," in *Responses,* ed. Hamacher, Hertz and Keenan, 388.

23. Zeev Sternhell, *Neither Right nor Left: Fascist Ideology in France,* trans. David Maisel (Berkeley: University of California Press, 1986), xiii; Gérard Loiseaux, *La Littérature de la défaite et de la collaboration* (Paris: Publications de la Sorbonne, 1984), 500.

24. Samuel Weber, "The Monument Disfigured," in *Responses,* ed. Hamacher, Hertz, and Keenan, 404. See Kenneth Asher, "The Moral Blindness of Paul de Man," *Telos* 82 (Winter 1989–1990): 197–205, who characterized the passage from Weber as "unintentional parody."

25. Warminski, "Terrible Reading," 392.

26. Derrida, "Biodegradables. Seven Diary Fragments," *Critical Inquiry* 15, no. 4 (Summer 1989): 823, 827.

27. Rodolphe Gasché, "Edges of Understanding," in *Responses,* ed. Hammacher, Hertz, and Keenan, 209.

28. De Graef, *Serenity in Crisis,* 119.

29. Aris Fioretos, "To Read Paul de Man," in *Responses,* ed. Hammacher, Hertz, and Keenan, 171.

30. Hans-Jost Frey, "Literature, Ideology," in *Responses,* ed. Hamacher, Hertz, and Keenan, 192.

31. The letter is reprinted in *Responses,* ed. Hamacher, Hertz, and Keenan, 475–77.

32. Hartman, "History and Judgment," 78.

33. The puzzled response to this reference reminded me that I stand on the aged edge of the generation gap. Kirsten Flagstad, the great Wagnerian soprano, had been accused (perhaps incorrectly) of sharing the politics of her husband, a Norwegian collaborationist.

34. James T. Kloppenberg, "Objectivity and Historicism: A Century of American Historical Writing," *American Historical Review* 94, no. 4 (October 1989): 1030; Paul Morrison, "Paul de Man: Resistance and Collaboration," *Representations* 32 (Fall 1990): 71–72; Russell A. Berman, "Troping to Pretoria: The Rise and Fall of Deconstruction," *Telos* 85 (Fall 1990): 15–16.

35. Dominick LaCapra, "The Personal, the Political, and the Textual: Paul de Man as Object of Transference," *History and Memory* 4 (Spring–Summer 1992): 30.

## 17.  PRESENTISM

### POSTMODERNISM, POSTSTRUCTURALISM, POSTCOLONIALISM

### GRAHAM GOOD

*From the totalitarian point of view history is something to be cre-*
*ated rather than learned. . . . Totalitarianism demands in fact the*
*continuous alteration of the past, and in the long run probably de-*
*mands a disbelief in the very existence of objective truth.*
—GEORGE ORWELL, "THE PREVENTION OF LITERATURE"[1]

PRESENTISM IS THE BELIEF in the primacy of the present, and the refusal to be guided by a vision either of the past or of the future. It repudiates historicism and holds that we cannot know the truth of the past "as it really was" (in the German historian von Ranke's phrase), and that the past never has been knowable, though nineteenth-century historians pretended or believed that it was. Now, says presentism, we know better. We know that the past is unknowable. So we give up the effort and accept what survives of the past as simply a repository of "heritage" motifs and styles, to be used in the present for amusement or "retro" novelty. Past modes of architecture, art, or dress can be pastiched or collaged or appropriated or reinterpreted at will. The past is reshaped by the present to suit present political purposes. Political correctness in the present has replaced the idea of historical correctness, which, although ultimately unreachable, is an ideal that humanistic study should constantly strive for.

Of course it is true that the past cannot be known fully or exactly. Presentism takes this truth and converts it into the dogma that the past cannot be known at all. All versions are equally valid, though in practice the politics of the present determines which version is acceptable. Much of the inspiration here comes from Nietzsche's idea, challenging the historicism of his century, that the past can and should be used to increase the present power of those actually in power. What does it matter if the image of the past created by the now-powerful is historically inaccurate, if it enables them to relish their vitality and strength and dominance? Nietzsche saw the quest for historical truth as not only impossible in itself, but often part of a slave-conspiracy against the strong. For him, the painstaking quest for historical accuracy is contemptible pedantry compared to the empowering vitality of myth.

However, presentism has reversed Nietzsche's political allegiances. When we hear that history is written by the winners, it's implied that theirs is a selective, biased account—though, Nietzsche, of course, would approve of this. But he also foresaw the eventual victory of the weak, and the consequent rewriting of history by the former losers, after the eventual success of their conspiracy against the strong and free. He would undoubtedly see contemporary Theory as part of the rewriting process, which makes it doubly ironic that he has canonical status with theorists. Logically, history as rewritten by the former losers must be as much a "construct" as the winner-history it replaces. Both sides ask, "Why bother to acknowledge facts that are inconvenient to your case? Why not ignore, deny, or distort them if it makes your myth more powerful?" Nietzsche and Theory share the excitements of forget-the-facts myth-making, despite being on opposite sides politically.

Presentism, rejecting the vision of historicism on one hand, rejects visions of the future on the other. The latter is formulated as a rejection of teleology (in philosophical terms), of human destiny (in religious terms), and of overall human progress (in political terms). The most influential version is Lyotard's repudiation of "*grands récits*" or Grand Narratives, which include the Biblical journey from Creation to Apocalypse, the "Whig" view that humanity is gradually progressing, despite setbacks, toward a higher and better state, and the Marxist vision of proletarian revolution, the withering away of the state and the end of history. A recent example of the "*grand récit*," Francis Fukuyama's brilliant Hegelian work called *The End of History*, was dismissed unread by most theorists despite (or because of) its offer of a coherent and persuasive vision of where we are in human history. If any further justification were needed for the dismissal, it was provided by the news that Fukuyama worked for the U.S. State Department. So why bother with study, argument, or disproof?

Any long-term view of human history or destiny is anathema to presentism, which is our generation's version of the *trahison des clercs*. Without some vision of the future, some sense of overall development, some ideal, end, or goal, the present becomes simply a jumble of short-term activities. In particular, the Marxist coloration of Theory becomes mere pastiche, and Marxism is reduced to a scatter of terms and concepts that are meaningless without the system they belong to. Theorists adopt the vivid abuse-vocabulary of Marxism ("bourgeois," "reactionary") as a set of labels to stick on anything they dislike. Theorists use "progressive" as a positive term, while attacking the notion of human progress that gives it its significance.

Theory jettisons most of the genuinely progressive ideas of the last five hundred years: liberalism, humanism, individualism, realism, and science are all explicitly attacked or regarded with suspicion and hostility. The culture of Theory is neomedieval, and the style of its discourse is neoscholastic. The citation of received authorities is more important than direct personal inquiry

and independent verification. For Theory, there is no individuality, no originality, no independence: the prefix *re-* dominates the vocabulary, along with
its companion *post-*. Everything is always already a repetition, a re-reading, a
re-writing. This climate of staleness and belatedness is a paradoxical result of
presentism; without a narrative linking the present to the future and the past,
there can be no development, only repetition.

But in practice, something has to determine the theoretically indeterminate. Even presentism has to give some orientation to the theoretically future-
less and pastless present. The solution is this: instead of pastness, *post*ness. The
three *post*s that situate Theory for itself are Post-modernism, Post-structuralism, and Post-colonialism. POMO, POSTO, and POCO, like three characters
in a Beckett play. In the absence of a concept of history, the present can only be
characterized by the immediately preceding phase or period, the still-in-view,
just-finished recent past which the present is *just after*.

The difficulty of periodization (in practice a necessity in academia) without
a concept of history is amply manifest in the many attempts to distinguish
postmodernism from modernism, to give some meaning to this supposedly
important distinction, beyond the banality that one is simply later than the
other. Perhaps because of their shakiness, the two concepts themselves are
rarely "called into question," though there is much dispute about how to characterize them. Postmodernism is a shaky construct because its basis, modernism, is equally so. Modernism is so widely accepted as a period concept for
the literature and art of 1910–1930 or 1900–1940, that many do not realize that
it only became fully established as a usage in the 1970s. Before that, we only had
"modern" literature. Movements like futurism, vorticism, and imagism existed
at the time, but not modern*ism*. In fact, modernism in art was known as post-
impressionism, perhaps the first time a new tendency was identified solely in
terms of what it followed, and perhaps a precedent for the term postmodernism.

Modernism, like other period concepts, requires an emphasis on discontinuities and a neglect of continuities. Writers like Joyce, Lawrence, and Forster
were initially seen as further extending *realism* to an unprecedented and disturbing degree. For example, Henry James in his 1914 essay "The New Novel,"
placed Conrad and Lawrence with Bennett and Wells in terms of their *continuation* of the realist tradition.[2] Only later was this emphasis reversed and, starting with Virginia Woolf's 1924 paper "Mr. Bennett and Mrs. Brown," a radical
break created between the Edwardians (Bennett, Wells, Galsworthy) and the
Georgians (Forster, Eliot, Joyce, Lawrence, Strachey, and Woolf herself), later
to be known as the modernists. Even here, it is worth noting that Woolf's
ground for preferring the Georgians was that they were better at creating vivid,
believable characters. Woolf accepted the basic goal of realism, claiming that
her means, or the Georgians' means, were superior to the "external" methods

of Bennett.[3] The dissolution of the "old stable ego," in Lawrence's words, was not made a defining feature of modernism until much later. This led to a neglect of the formal and intellectual sophistication of the Victorians and Edwardians in order to set them up as epistemologically naive and formally conventional, in contrast with the radical innovations of modernism.

But then, from the 1970s on, came the companion concept of postmodernism. Once the open-ended "modern" had become the safely periodized "modernism," the period following it needed naming. Modernism was gradually repositioned where it had previously positioned the Victorians and Edwardians: as a conservative foil to the even more radical, experimental, skeptical, self-reflexive, parodistic, allusive postmodernism. The trouble is that, in the novel at least, everything that has been identified as postmodernist can be found in the *first* European novel, *Don Quixote* (1605, 1615). Throughout its history and in most of its best examples, the novel as a genre has combined realism and experiment. Realism is not the naive, conventional, bourgeois form of the theorists' caricature; rather, realism is itself a never-ending experiment, though critics are always trying to separate realism and experiment into different periods. Presentism needs to see the present as a radically new period, and thus stereotypes the recent past as conservative. Postmodernism repeats the heroic "breakthrough" myth of modernism, but with modernism now in the conservative role. It is astonishing how theorists who claim to "call into question" virtually everything have exempted the concepts of modernism and postmodernism from challenge. These ideas are actually foundational for a perspective that claims to have no foundations, and constitute indispensable period concepts for an outlook that claims to have dispensed with history as coherent narrative.

Poststructuralism shares the same weakness as postmodernism: an excessive dependence on the concept it postdates. Structuralism had its heyday in the late 1960s and early 1970s, and for a while it seemed that literature would finally be subjected to a scientific method, akin to the "structural anthropology" of Claude Lévi-Strauss. But just as academia was examining this prospect, Derrida came up with something much more exciting: he discovered that even Lévi-Strauss's "rigorous" structuralism was self-contradictory—in fact, all texts were. Academia also recoiled from structuralism because there wasn't enough work in it: once all plots had been reduced to mathematical equations, what would remain to be done? Deconstruction offered a lot more material for literature professors seeking publication: show how *every* text is self-contradictory. Where before 1970 they had discovered more and more hidden unity (of image, symbol, theme, plot) in literary texts, now they went into reverse and found *dis*unity in all the same texts. Even better, this included *critical* texts. So the way was open to infinite chains of texts, each showing the contradictions of the previous ones. Every professor could add a commentary to Lacan on Derrida on Foucault on Poe. There was very little need for primary texts; in fact a small group of already much discussed texts by Proust, Rousseau, or Poe would be better, because these offered more layers of commentary. Critics began to feel more than equal to the authors at the bottom layer. Critics, too, were creators of texts, as important and interesting as the texts they started from. They, rather than authors, were the people that graduate students wanted to see, hear, and read. A Derrida, Fish, Jameson, or Culler could fill more lecture halls than any mere poet or novelist.

But while the base of primary texts was contracting in one area, it was expanding in another: the tremendous flowering of creative writing in countries once colonized by the European powers. Unfortunately these new literatures, within the Western academy, fell under the sway of the third *post*: postcolonialism. Like the other two, this *post* is an inadequate response to the literature it aims to "cover" or theorize. Anxious to move beyond thematic and descriptive criticism (now denigrated as unsophisticated), postcolonial critics have adopted, often uncritically, the terminology and concepts of poststructuralism. This framework is then *applied*, not to the small handful of canonical Western texts favored by deconstruction, but to work from a wide variety of cultural backgrounds. Thus while decrying Eurocentrism, postcolonialist critics are constantly citing European theorists like Foucault, Barthes, Lacan, and Derrida. The theoretical reorientation in the English-speaking world often amounts to no more than a shift from Anglocentrism to Francocentrism.

Postcolonialism, like postmodernism and poststructuralism, inherits the structures of what it is *post*. The former British colonies are extremely diverse in culture, and about all they have in common is having been governed by Britain. By maintaining this imposed grouping, postcolonialism reproduces colonial patterns. For example, it is rare to find courses that study African literature as a unity. Anglophone, Francophone, and Lusophone literatures are treated separately from each other and from work in African languages.

Postcolonialism's dependence on colonialism also leads to a lack of historical depth. Presentism conceals from view almost everything before the nineteenth century. Thus Roman imperialism is rarely discussed despite its obvious importance for later European imperialism. Negative Eurocentrism (seeing Europe as the only guilty party) conceals from view non-European examples of imperialism like the Islamic conquests in Africa and India, Japanese annexations of Korea and parts of China, the Chinese invasion of Tibet, or the Indonesian invasion of East Timor.

The case of Indian literature shows up the limitations of the postcolonial framework, which neglects the three-thousand-year traditions that predated and survived the British Raj. This long-term context is vital for most works of recent Indian literature, while the international postcolonial one is insufficient by itself. A related obstacle is Theory's hostility to religion (this hostility is perhaps the strongest common trait shared by Marx, Freud, and Nietzsche); this attitude is a serious barrier in approaching a culture imbued with religious belief and practice to an extent unimaginable to Eurocentrism.

The study of postcolonial literature in English is united as a field by a negative Anglocentrism which often goes beyond attacking British imperialism to a general attack on British culture as such. A favorite hypothesis is that Britain is in a terminal *cultural* decline as a necessary corollary of the rise of postcolonial cultures, a perception whose main support is simply to ignore contemporary British writing. Furthermore, wealthy white-settler countries like Canada and Australia are classed as postcolonial along with countries which suffered the real brunt of imperialism, thus giving POCO intellectuals from these countries the luxury of presenting themselves as members of the oppressed. Postcolonial theorists in these countries cannot seem to reach a balanced view of their British heritage or their present relation to Britain. There is little consciousness of ironies like the fact that Australia and Canada are more affluent than postimperial Britain, much of whose population would gladly emigrate to them if given the chance, or the fact that much of the British media is owned by Canadian or Australian tycoons like Conrad Black or Rupert Murdoch.

The myth of British cultural decline is also inconsistent with the charge of continuing cultural imperialism. There is more evidence for the reverse hypothesis, that Britain is culturally dominated by its former colonies. Besides the matter of media ownership, it is clear that the cultural establishment is extremely open to postcolonial talent. The list of writers, critics, publishers, and TV presenters from former colonies who occupy powerful roles in British culture would include Clive James, Peter Conrad, Germaine Greer, Michael Ignatieff, Ben Okri, Salman Rushdie, V. S. Naipaul, and the list could continue. This is more a case of the Empire Moves In than the Empire Writes Back. But rather than commend Britain on its openness to foreign talent, postcolonialists, ignoring the equal abundance and quality of contemporary "native" British writers, have seen it as a further sign of cultural eclipse, also neglecting the awkward question of why so many gifted postcolonial writers would be attracted to a supposedly moribund center.

The poverty of postcolonial theory (as opposed to the richness and diversity of the literature itself) is shown in one of its key texts, *The Empire Writes Back* (the phrase is Salman Rushdie's), coauthored by three academics based in Australia. After two hundred pages of unremitting hostility to British culture and even language-use, it ends with a vision in which "the English canon is radically reduced within a new paradigm of international english [*sic*] studies."[4] Among the authors remaining in this reduced canon, Haggard and Kipling, as instructive examples of overt proimperialism, would replace the standard Victorian classics like Hardy and George Eliot in courses on British literature. In fact, to add those authors to courses (though not at the expense of the others) would be worth doing; Kipling, in particular, deserves more study for aesthetic reasons. His support of imperialism has been treated as much less forgivable by literary academics than (for example) Pound's fascism and Eliot's anti-Semitism. The purpose of selecting Kipling, however, is not to increase aesthetic appreciation of his work but to inculpate nineteenth- and twentieth-century British culture.

A similar purpose motivates Edward Said's *Culture and Imperialism* (1993), which maintains that every work of nineteenth- and early-twentieth-century European literature, including Jane Austen's novels, is complicit with imperialism, whether it is mentioned or not. The book should actually be entitled "*European* Culture and Imperialism," since it has little to say, aside from a prefatory acknowledgment of their existence, about Russian, Islamic, Chinese, or Japanese imperialism. The guilt is focused on the West, and for Said this taints all of its "cultural production" in this period, however remote a work's themes might appear to be.

In the postcolonial perspective, glimpses of earlier literature are confined to those works that, like *Robinson Crusoe*, can be made to bear the burden of imperial guilt. *The Tempest* seems to be virtually Shakepeare's only play, to judge from the frequency of its appearance in reading lists influenced by postcolonialist thinking. Equally, the Calibanic interpretation—seeing Caliban as the innocent victim of the imperialist Prospero—seems to be the only current interpretation, disregarding Shakespeare's obvious intent to show Prospero as a wise, though flawed, ruler. In general, Shakepeare is seen as an object of judgment by the present, which has the right to condemn any divergences from current standards of rectitude. The Signet Classics have recently added to the collections of critical essays in their Shakespeare editions an article that in effect gives each play a rating according to its degree of racism, sexism, and homophobia.

For some, not just Shakespeare but the whole Western tradition is put on trial and found guilty. Postcolonialism combines with presentism to inculpate the past as a substitute for trying to understand it. The past is guilty—guilty of not being present. History becomes simply a repository of grievances, whose historical truth gets an exemption from the otherwise general view that historical truth cannot be established. Students get the idea that Western culture is uniquely guilty of racism, sexism, homophobia, ecocide, and imperialism. This kind of negative Eurocentrism would certainly be modified by a genuinely global outlook, which would show these abuses and prejudices as widespread in world history.

The one apparent exception to the prevailing presentism is the so-called New Historicism. The Old Historicism would set the past work in the context of its period, and the period in relation to the present through a coherent overall view of history, whether the "Whig" view of gradual progress, the conservative view of gradual or catastrophic decline, or the Marxist view of continual class struggle erupting into eventual revolution. The New Historicism, lacking any such overall perspective, uses a collage technique to juxtapose a literary with a nonliterary text from the same period and provide a feeling of moving outside the realm of fiction. This technique started in the field of Renaissance studies, where drama is the dominant literary genre, and this led to the habit of placing a scene from a play next to a "scene" from public life. The opening of Foucault's *Discipline and Punish* (in French, 1975; in English, 1977) was influential here, recording in detail how the French regicide Damiens was tortured, dismembered, and burned in 1757. The typical New Historicist article begins with a quoted description of an opulent pageant or a spectacularly brutal punishment, executes some transitional theoretical "moves" involving power/desire, and arrives at a play with a spurious air of "freshness" and "political relevance." "History" is simply a juxtaposed image, a gesture, a cross-reference.

The basic tenets of the New Historicism are conveniently and succinctly described in the introduction of H. Aram Veeser's *The New Historicism: A Reader*. The five key assumptions are "1) that every expressive act is embedded in a network of material practices; 2) that every act of unmasking, critique, and opposition uses the tools it condemns and risks falling prey to the practice it exposes; 3) that literary and non-literary 'texts' circulate inseparably; 4) that no discourse, imaginative or archival, gives access to unchanging truths nor expresses inalterable human nature; 5) that a critical method and a language adequate to describe culture under capitalism participate in the economy they describe."[5]

If we examine these tenets individually, we find that the third is identical with the idea that there is no essential difference among types of text; "literature" is simply an arbitrary construct from the romantic period onwards which serves bourgeois ideology. This leaves the New Historicist free to juxtapose any quotation from a poem or play with any quotation from a historiographical text, usually with the effect of guilt by association: in this way, any literary text can be implicated in the evils that were going on nearby. The "embeddedness" thesis is derived from the Marxist idea that culture reflects economic realities, but gives a localized version of it, without the overarching narrative of Marxist history, and without necessarily giving priority to the economic level as the ultimate *cause* of cultural expressions. This again enables the New Historicist practice of arbitrary juxtaposition. New Historicism creates an intertextual and contextual web around a text which ultimately consists of thematic parallels of the kind the New Critics of the earlier period used to discover *within* texts.

The fourth thesis, asserting that there is no continuous human nature underlying cultural change, reflects the antihumanist thinking prevalent in contemporary Theory. Of course, it is true that human behavior and creativity change over time, but it is also true that that there is a continuing human condition which enables us to understand and learn from works very remote from us in time and culture. In a fashion typical of Theory, the New Historicism takes one truth and rejects the other, producing an unbalanced view of creativity as *wholly* determined by culture.

The second and fifth theses we can consider together as the doctrine of *necessary complicity*. Resistance to the system is part of the system. To expose a practice is partially to reproduce that practice. Criticism is dependent on what it is criticizing. There is no independence and no innocence. All intellectual activity in a capitalist society is complicit with capitalism.

Taken together, the five tenets show the results of abandoning the idea of autonomy: the autonomy of the self and the autonomy of the work. Of course, this autonomy is limited by culture and many other factors, but the freedom of the artist and the critic are nevertheless realities. In a sense, the autonomy lost by the self and the work is displaced by New Historicism onto culture, the culture of a specific area and period, which becomes all-powerful, all-creative, and all-explaining. Culture becomes God, the individual nothing, in this strange antihumanist religion. Yet culture is also divided into self-contained compartments according to period, nationality, and so on: they do not connect with each other into a coherent narrative. History becomes a disconnected series of "past presents" waiting to be configured and reconfigured to suit the predilections of the actual present.

The central project of the New Historicism is, using textualist as well as presentist ideas, to cancel or reverse the Renaissance. Besides the rise of the "autonomous self," this period also saw enormous progress in "accurate representation" in both art and science. Unified perspective, realistic depiction of the human face and figure, navigation and map-making, classification in botany and zoology, all made dramatic advances toward consistency and reliability. These systems of accurate representation coincided with, and partially enabled the emergence of, humanism by enhancing humanity's ability to describe and represent its experience of the world in a referential way. The power to represent reality accurately and *verifiably* was a tremendous liberating force, not discredited by the use of some if its techniques in the furtherance of colonialism. These referential, verifiable representations gradually took over from ideological representations, that is, those which expressed and projected pre-existing beliefs about the cosmos or humanity. The new genre of the novel was created in *Don Quixote* by contrasting the chivalric "constructions" of the deluded hero with the harsh realities of Spain in 1600, rendered in the new referential prose. Similarly, in science, scholastic proofs validated by invoking the authority of Aristotle were gradually replaced by empirical proofs supported by repeatable experiments. Truth was no longer established intersubjectively by faith or ideology, but objectively and individually, with no authority other than the experiment itself.

The astonishing progress made on the basis of these systems of accurate representation is imperilled by current intellectual trends. Realism (artistic or scientific) and individualism are the twin mutually supporting creations of the

Renaissance, and are now equally in discredit. The period of the dominance of these two ideas, the seventeenth to twentieth centuries, is in disfavor. It is inculpated through its association with the rise of European colonialism, while the huge progress that was made toward social equality and prosperity is forgotten. New Agers and Deep Ecologists see the period as a spiritual disaster, emphasizing the desacralization of the world and the exploitation of natural resources, while forgetting the Reformation's pioneering of more individualistic forms of spirituality and romanticism's powerful revival of respect for nature, which led to preserving parks and areas of natural beauty. Presentism claims to have dispensed with Grand Narratives, but actually has one of its own about the last five centuries, whose achievements are reduced to the twin disgraces of imperialism and patriarchy, occluding all of the period's positive aspects.

In certain respects, the presentist rejection of the humanist centuries and their legacy coincides with the conservative perspective of someone like T. S. Eliot. Eliot saw the period as a disaster for poetry, due to the "dissociation of sensibility" which supposedly took place in the mid-seventeenth century and split thought from feeling. His ideal society was the medieval Christendom of Dante. Eliot was also hostile to liberal humanism. Where current Theory sees individual freedom as an illusion produced by bourgeois ideology, Eliot saw it as real but socially corrosive, destroying the hierarchical unity of medieval society. Eliot, like many theorists, sees culture as creating poetry, rather than the other way round. For both parties, culture is something already in place, not something to be achieved, as in liberal humanism. Both are hostile to literary individuality: where Eliot saw the poet's mind as simply a passive vehicle for combining ideas and images, Theory sees poetry as just another textual "effect" of the discourse system. Eliot's traditionalism resembles Theory in seeing the new artwork as simply a recombination or recycling of existing themes. Both are suspicious of, or hostile to, individualism and realism in art, as well as to any idea of originality.

Presentism denies historical agency to individuals and even to groups. It lacks the onward momentum supplied by class struggle in Marxism, and is thus at a loss to explain why one discourse system or regime changes into another. "Resistance" is about as active as it is possible to get in this view, and even this form of dissent is hard to explain within the assumptions of Theory. At times dissent is explained as a safety-valve in the system, a device for letting off pressure through an illusory subversiveness, and thus preserving the system all the more effectively. When radical academics apply this theory to their own "subversive" activities, the result may be a confession (we are all necessarily complicit) which amounts to a shrug. The radical claims of Theory seem to be based on the idea that exposing the injustices of a system will somehow lead to its being changed. But since Theory views all systems as total and all thought as an "effect" of the system, it cannot explain how or why injustice can *ever* be exposed. Theory is self-confessedly "ineffectual": as an effect of the system, it cannot affect the system to any significant extent. Thus claims of radical dissent are alternately advanced and withdrawn: they can neither be substantiated nor abandoned. The total nature of the condemnation of Western society coexists with cynical acceptance and professional careerism.

We have seen how presentism fails to accord an active role in history either to the individual or to groups and collectivities, as well as refusing to see any impersonal, inevitable direction to history, of the Christian, Hegelian, Marxist, or liberal kind, all of which are classified as outmoded Grand Narratives. This leaves only the lame and evasive solution of constituting periods by what they follow, simply adding the prefix *post*. The human situation, for presentism, seems to be helpless, powerless, and directionless, completely subjected to ideological control. The result is a kind of fatalism where culture plays the role of fate. Literary and cultural studies need a more balanced and progressive outlook than this.

### NOTES

1. George Orwell, "The Prevention of Literature," in *The Penguin Essays of George Orwell* (Harmondsworth: Penguin, 1984).

2. Henry James, "The New Novel," in *Henry James: Selected Literary Criticism*, ed. Morris Shapira (New York: McGraw-Hill, 1965).

3. Virginia Woolf, "Mr. Bennett and Mrs. Brown," in her *Collected Essays*, vol. 1 (London: Hogarth Press, 1967), 319–37.

4. Bill Ashcroft, Gareth Griffiths, and Helen Tiffin, *The Empire Writes Back: Theory and Practice in Post-Colonial Literatures* (London and New York: Routledge, 1989), 196.

5. H. Aram Veeser, ed., *The New Historicism: A Reader* (New York and London: Routledge, 1989), xi.

## 18.  PREFACE FOR A POST-POSTCOLONIAL CRITICISM
### ERIN O'CONNOR

THIS ESSAY TAKES as its point of departure the double valence of its subject, "globalizing literary studies." In common critical parlance, to speak of the "globalization" of literary study is to speak of doing criticism with an awareness of literature's contingent, historically specific relations to geography; in other words, it aims to account for the global relations embodied in the pro-

Erin O'Connor. "Preface for a Post-Postcolonial Criticism." Adapted by the author from *Victorian Studies* 45, no. 2 (Winter 2003): 217–46. Reprinted by permission of Indiana University Press.

duction, dissemination, and consumption of literature. Gayatri Spivak calls this type of critical approach "worlding"; Edward Said calls it "contrapuntal reading." Whatever the name, the project always involves articulating the roles of history, politics, and empire in the creation, publication, and study of literature. In what follows, I will explore a less obvious but equally significant aspect of this project: the tendency, in efforts to expand understanding of literature, to make that expansion contingent on a corresponding expansion of analytical focus. "Globalizing literature" frequently goes hand in hand with globalizing *about* literature; indeed, much of the project of postcolonial literary history depends on a set of globalizing statements about literature's theoretical relation to imperialism.

Some of the more famous of these statements have run like this: Edward Said has written that "texts are worldly,"[1] Abdul JanMohamed that "colonialist fiction is generated predominantly by the ideological machinery of the Manichean allegory,"[2] Fredric Jameson that "all third world texts are necessarily . . . to be read as . . . national allegories,"[3] and Homi Bhabha that "Nations, like narratives, lose their origins in the myths of time and only fully realize their horizons in the mind's eye."[4] Paraphrasing Bhabha, Said has written that "Nations themselves *are* narrations."[5] There are two things to notice about these formulations. The first is that they *are* formulas: globalizing is here synonymous with generalizing. The second is that the idea of narrative licenses these generalizations about narrative. Whether invoking "fiction," "allegory," "narration," or the "text," each formula explains literature's extraliterary dimensions as a literary process—a move that simultaneously reifies the literary as a mode of apprehension and makes literature as such peculiarly inaccessible: as narrative becomes a metaphor for ideological process, it ceases to be accessible as a particular form of writing with its own unique, irreducible ways and means. Such maneuvers are embedded in postcolonial literary theory, which routinely makes "narrative" into a figure for the textual dimension of nation-building, even as it takes individual narratives for exemplary allegories of narrative's role in nation-building.[6] The upshot is a globalization of literature—of the literariness of literature—accomplished by making literary texts into allegories for nonliterary processes (imperialism, nation-building, and so on), while metaphorizing those processes as literary forms in their own right (allegory, narration). Making literature into a small but paradigmatic aspect of a far larger system of narration has thus been one of the central tasks of postcolonial literary history.

Nowhere is the tautological quality of this logic more problematic than in postcolonial treatments of nineteenth-century British literature, which has been a primary subject for such globalizing ever since Gayatri Spivak's 1985 essay "Three Women's Texts and a Critique of Imperialism" established a model for treating the Victorian novel as a local instance of widespread imperialist sentiment. Announcing that "it should not be possible to read nineteenth-century British literature without remembering that imperialism, understood as England's social mission, was a crucial part of the cultural representation of England to the English," Spivak set the tone for subsequent postcolonial approaches to Victorian culture, which tend to read the novel as a cipher for imperialist ideology.[7] As Edward Said puts it in *Culture and Imperialism,* "the novel [is] *the* aesthetic object whose connection to the expanding societies of Britain and France is particularly interesting to study" (xii). The nineteenth-century British novel has been taken as both a prime example of what Spivak calls the "imperialist narrativization of history" (244) and as an originary moment in the production of that narration. Under the guise of realism, the argument goes, the nineteenth-century British novel, more than any other cultural form, generated an insularity so tightly sealed that it has refused ever since to reveal its foreign policy to even its finest critics. What is needed, the argument concludes, is a literary history that can illuminate the imperialist underpinnings of narratives that often neither know they have such underpinnings, nor care.

In recent years, it has become the self-imposed task of the postcolonial critic—by and large not a specialist in nineteenth-century literature or history—to describe the British novel's more worldly dimensions, i.e., to place it in a context that properly illuminates imperialism's determining influence on its ideology and its form. In so doing, postcolonial debate has assigned a very particular role to the Victorian novel, which, in providing a historical origin for a recognizably modern mode of imperialist thinking, has enabled postcolonial studies to ground itself in both a literary criticism and—it follows—a literature. That grounding has in turn revolved around a reading; what the Victorian novel is and does is as central to postcolonial theory as nineteenth-century colonialism itself.

It is the peculiar conjunction of a pressing contemporary politics with a comparatively arcane literary history that I wish to take up here. For if that conjunction has come to feel like familiar territory, well-traveled ground whose theoretical pathways have by now become deeply entrenched in thinking about both the history of imperialism and the geopolitics of the Victorian novel, that is exactly my point: it should not seem at all natural, or inevitable, that the Victorian novel would play such an extensive role in this theoretical project. My purpose in this essay will be to revisit the canonization of the Victorian novel as postcolonial theory's favorite stomping ground (the genre it loves to hate), tracking the terms of the novel's absorption into mainstream postcolonial literary theory in order to suggest that the success of the postcolonial project has come, at least in part, at the expense of Victorian studies.

I approach my subject not as a postcolonial critic, then, but as a student of Victorian literature and culture. My central concern is not to critique postcolonial criticism *per se,* though something of the kind is unavoidable here, but rather to ask what the postcolonial project has meant for thinking about the nineteenth-century British novel. My most basic contention is that the postcolonial narrative of literary history has largely overwritten the Victorian novel, that it has ignored—even at times denied—the genre's thematic subtleties, structural indeterminacies, and genuine intellectual rigor in order to make the novel into the means of establishing broadly applicable theoretical paradigms. The majestic generality of positions such as Spivak's and Said's is after all a generic one: the assumption that culture and imperialism can be adequately and responsibly thought through the novel is an assumption that takes the novel *to be*, in form and content, a categorical generalization *of* these otherwise bafflingly enormous categories. In order to uncover the terms of that generalizing impulse, I have chosen to center my analysis on one particularly telling moment in the Victorian novel's global literary history.

## VICTORIENTALISM: COLONIZING *JANE EYRE*

Gayatri Spivak's "Three Women's Texts and a Critique of Imperialism" may be understood as a primal scene of postcolonial reading, the place where many of the guiding assumptions and logical premises of postcolonial thinking about Victorian fiction were born. First published in a special issue of *Critical Inquiry* in 1985 and reprinted numerous times, the essay has had a distinctly worldly career, setting the agenda for much subsequent postcolonial work by offering what has become the definitive postcolonial reading of *Jane Eyre* (1847).[8] Since then, every piece on *Jane Eyre* and race has paid homage to it, alternately developing, refining, and deferring to Spivak's claims. Just about all postcolonial work on nineteenth-century literature and culture has had to contend with Spivak's ideas; her work has been instrumental in enabling critics of nineteenth-century literature and culture to speak casually of what Ann McClintock calls—with representative aplomb—"the planned epistemic violence of the imperialist project."[9] Studies that have overlooked Spivak's work have, by contrast, suffered at the hands of reviewers.[10] In short, this essay rules, and it is the reign of Spivak's essay that interests me here.

I'll begin at the beginning, with the first sentence of the first paragraph of the first attempt to trace the logic of a postcolonial literary history. For that is what Spivak claims to inaugurate when she opens with what she calls two "obvious 'facts'"—one, already cited: "it should not be possible to read nineteenth-century British literature without remembering that imperialism, understood as England's social mission, was a crucial part of the cultural representation of England to the English"; and two, "the role of literature in the production of cultural representation should not be ignored." From these " 'facts'" Spivak makes an observation and draws a conclusion: "These two obvious 'facts,'" she writes, "continue to be disregarded in the reading of nineteenth-century British literature. This itself attests to the continuing success of the imperialist project, displaced and dispersed into more modern forms"

(242). From this conclusion Spivak derives not a critical theory, but a critical theorem: "If these 'facts' were remembered, not only in the study of British literature but in the study of the literatures of the European colonizing cultures of the great age of imperialism, we would produce a narrative, in literary history, of the 'worlding' of what is now called 'the Third World'" (242). This reasoning—with its movement from "'facts'" (acknowledged, by scare quotes, to be premises rather than demonstrable truths) to conclusions (truths to which the aforesaid "'facts'" "attest") and back again to the hypothetical reality contained by the "if . . . then" formulation of her last point—has all the compact authority of a mathematical proof. At once unassailable in its logic and unverifiable, it is densely intriguing. Spivak's "rule" consists in the statement of a rule; the power of the essay is in no small part due to the certainty with which it lays out two bold assertions (the "'facts'") and an equally bold conjecture about how awareness of those "'facts'" would change literary history.

Spivak demonstrates just how an awareness of these "'facts'" would change literary history through a concise application of her thesis to that "cult text of feminism," *Jane Eyre*, supplemented by readings of Jean Rhys's *Wide Sargasso Sea* (1966) as "*Jane Eyre*'s reinscription," and Mary Shelley's *Frankenstein* (1818) as an "analysis—even a deconstruction—of a 'worlding' such as *Jane Eyre*'s" (244). The plot of the essay is simple. Spivak's reading of Brontë centers on brief examinations of a few select scenes: "the beautifully orchestrated opening of *Jane Eyre*" (which supplies a spatial map of "Jane's self-marginalized uniqueness" [246]); Bertha Mason Rochester's appearance to Jane (which supplies a physical anatomy of how "Brontë renders the human/animal frontier as acceptably indeterminate" [247]); and the conclusion, whose "*allegorical* language of Christian psychobiography . . . marks the inaccessibility of the imperialist project as such to the nascent 'feminist' scenario" (249). These readings are intended to punctuate Spivak's sketch of the novel's guiding sequential arrangement, Jane's progression from counter-family to family-in-law to community of families: "In terms of the narrative energy of the novel, how is Jane moved from the place of the counter-family to the family-in-law? It is the active ideology of imperialism that provides the discursive field" (247). The investment: around 1,800 words (in the Gates edition, this comes to approximately three and a half pages, nearly one third of which is taken up by block quotation). The yield: a reading of *Jane Eyre*, a theory of "the nineteenth-century British novel" that *Jane Eyre* synecdochically invokes, *and* a manifesto for postcolonial literary history itself.

Spivak was right about what would happen if her "'facts'" were remembered. They have become the guiding premises for much subsequent work on *Jane Eyre*, which has tirelessly dedicated itself to filling in the gaps in Spivak's sweeping history. There are Spivak-inspired studies of *Jane Eyre*'s relationship to Jamaica, to India, to Ireland, and to Africa; to colonialism, to Orientalism, and to racism; to slavery and to sati.[11] Together, they comprise a massive effort of retroactive documentation. Indeed, reading postcolonial studies of *Jane Eyre* since 1985 is virtually synonymous with watching Spivak's approach gradually get consolidated as scholars quietly provide the context and the close reading Spivak left out. Committing themselves to supplying the evidence for Spivak's broadest conjectures (to producing the narrative of literary history she desires), rather than to questioning the viability of an argument made without the benefit of evidence, scholars not surprisingly wind up producing readings that replicate Spivak's rather than generating substantially new ones. Indeed, what is most peculiar about postcolonial work on *Jane Eyre* is how uniformly it tends to bolster Spivak's argument, so much so that even critics who take issue with some of Spivak's premises do so in ways that enable her most basic claims to remain intact. Susan Meyer, for instance, argues that *Jane Eyre* questions the ideology of imperialism before finally upholding it, a thesis that differs from Spivak's only in order to fine-tune it. Instead of testing or challenging Spivak's claims, critics have set out to defend (by developing) a version of literary history that they have effectively accepted on faith.

The reasons for this tacit collective acceptance of Spivak's shaky reasoning lie in Spivak's condemnation of feminist Victorian studies as complicit with the Victorians' imperialist mentality. Feminist scholars' responses to Spivak get their urgency from their need to prove their political awareness and theoretical capability in the face of the worst accusation that can be leveled in today's academy: that of racism. When thinking about criticism, Spivak resorts to a logic as expansively mobile as when she is thinking about nineteenth-century British literature. As *Jane Eyre* is her point of origin for theorizing literature, so that novel's most influential critics to date, Sandra Gilbert and Susan Gubar, are the starting point for her thoughts about criticism. Noting that the "worlding" of Third World literature, its gradual recovery, interpretation, translation, and inclusion on English language syllabi, has thus far been conducted in such a way that it merely "expands the empire of the literary discipline" rather than challenging or changing it (243), Spivak directs her frustration straight at feminist Victorian studies:

> It seems particularly unfortunate when the emergent perspective of feminist criticism reproduces the axioms of imperialism. A basically isolationist admiration for the literature of the female subject in Europe and Anglo-America establishes the high feminist norm. It is supported and operated by an information-retrieval approach to "Third World" literature which often employs deliberately "nontheoretical" methodology with self-conscious rectitude.
>
> In this essay, I will attempt to examine the operation of the "worlding" of what is today "the Third World" by what has become a cult text of feminism: *Jane Eyre*.                    (243–44)

Spivak's stated wish is to talk about literary critics' treatment of Third World literature. But her stated plan is to talk about this by talking about something else: feminist criticism of *Jane Eyre*. She moves from lamenting the contemporary treatment of marginal literature—a treatment she describes as a form of disciplinary imperialism—to attacking a particular branch of contemporary criticism, the "isolationist" outlook of academic feminism. And she moves from this to *Jane Eyre* itself, which, by the end of these two short paragraphs, has mysteriously morphed into the origin—possibly even the cause—of late twentieth-century critical approaches to Third World literature, of "the 'worlding' of what is today 'the Third World.'" Aligning nineteenth-century British imperialism, "understood as England's social mission," and twentieth-century literary history, which pursues its own social mission with "self-conscious rectitude," Spivak argues that the "empire of the literary discipline" (243) participates in the imperialist project insofar as it fails to consider literature's historical relationship to empire. Because feminist theory has, to Spivak's mind, done a great deal to perpetuate, strengthen, and expand that disciplinary empire, it has a lot to answer for.

We should not be surprised, then, that the ready adoption of Spivak's ideas about Victorian literature has been led by feminist critics of Victorian literature: it was their political integrity Spivak specially maligned, and it has since been their aim to show that feminism is not after all incompatible with postcolonial critique, that feminist critics can indeed comment knowledgeably—and appropriately—on how Brontë and other women writers registered and responded to empire. As such, much of the criticism that has come out of Spivak's essay has an essentially conciliatory tone. No one argues with Spivak's claim about how the novel operates within the ideology of imperialism. What they do dispute is her suggestion that feminist criticism somehow replicates the patterns we see in the nineteenth-century novel. As Jenny Sharpe has noted, *Jane Eyre* has become "a contested site for establishing the relationship between feminism and imperialism" (29)—an observation that not only tells us that *Jane Eyre*'s privileged position as a "contested site" is not itself contested, but also tells us that there is no substantial debate about whether a single novel can sustain such a far-reaching project. Such "contestation" as there is centers not on whether the project is a viable one, but rather on how best to carry it out. Feminist critics have thus made reading and rereading *Jane Eyre* into a means of adapting Spivak's accusatory argument to their own ideological mission.

A paradox: this is an approach to literary history that operates inductively rather than deductively. Instead of generalizing from carefully amassed specifics, the postcolonial criticism that has grown out of Spivak's essay amasses specifics in order to support generalizations that are already in place. Contextualization is tactical, designed to support an existing thesis rather than to gather the evidence that would allow a thesis to be proposed. Another paradox: specifying the postcolonial reading of *Jane Eyre* has made Spivak's model more, rather than less, generalizable. Several scholars have built books around their *Jane Eyre* essays, extending their feminist-friendly version of Spivak's paradigm to other work by Brontë, other Victorian novels, other Victorian genres (particularly poetry and nonfiction prose), and even to literature from other periods.[12] It is the exemplary quality of this work that is most appealing to critics. What Elsie Michie finds most "admirable" about Susan Meyer's *Imperialism at Home* (1996) is not what Meyer has to say about the Victorian novel, but how she "keeps both [race and gender] in view at the same time."[13] What Paula Krebs admires about that same book is how it rises to the challenge Spivak posed for feminist literary scholarship.[14] Firdous Azim justifies devoting four out of seven chapters in *The Colonial Rise of the Novel* (1993) to Brontë by asserting that her reading "can be extended to the nineteenth century as a whole" (173). Just as Spivak equates *Jane Eyre* with the novel, so such books make the novel equivalent to *Jane Eyre*.

The exemplary utility of Spivak's argument holds for less explicitly feminist work as well. Spivak's use of a minor, undeveloped plot line as a sign of a major ideological subtext has become common currency in postcolonial literary criticism. In *Culture and Imperialism*, Said does unto *Mansfield Park* (1814) what Spivak did unto *Jane Eyre*. Reading Austen's marginal treatment of Antigua—the West Indian source of Sir Thomas Bertram's wealth—as evidence that Austen is "repress[ing] a rich and complex history" that she "would not, could not recognize" (93), Said opens his renowned study with a reading that owes its rationale and basic form to Spivak. Clearly taken by the aggressive elegance of her model, Said speaks of the potential for such readings to expand our understanding of domestic novels; he is particularly exercised about the interpretive possibilities of *Great Expectations* (1861), his comments about which inspired the Australian novelist Peter Carey to undertake a creative version of the by-then stock critique. In 1997, Carey published *Jack Maggs*, a novel about *Great Expectations'* "Bertha Mason figure," the transported convict who uses his ill-gotten colonial gains to fund Pip's conversion into a "gentleman."[15] Coming at *Jack Maggs* primarily through postcolonial theory and only secondarily through Dickens (whose novel Carey first read through Said's lens), Carey is decidedly—if unwittingly—Spivakian in the way he extends a thoroughly domestic novel's "exotic" subplot into an entire work of postcolonial fiction.

Most recently, critics have begun giving Spivak's model a materialist twist by focusing on the place of exotic goods in domestic fiction. Elizabeth Gaskell's *Cranford* (1853), with its India-rubber bands, silk turbans, and green tea; and Wilkie Collins's *The Moonstone* (1868), with its eponymous Indian diamond, have lent themselves readily to such readings.[16] Less obviously congenial novels have also yielded a surprising amount of analytical plunder.

Elaine Freedgood has read the "Negro-head tobacco" smoked in *Great Expectations* as the key to the novel's discourse of race. And, as if to bring Spivak's project back home, she has also turned her attention to *Jane Eyre*, treating the novel's fine mahogany furniture as the decadent spoils of deforestation and slavery abroad.[17]

As these examples suggest, Spivak's has become *the* basic model for doing postcolonial readings of nineteenth-century fiction. Whether developing Spivak's formulations or adapting them for new applications, whether close reading marginal ethnic characters or talking up passing mentions of imported things, critics have been busily carrying out a job whose parameters were set years ago by Spivak. That Spivak need no longer be formally cited (Said, for one, fails to acknowledge her obvious influence on his work) speaks to how thoroughly her approach has defined the postcolonial project—and it is indeed a *project*, a group effort, cooperatively and collectively pursued. That this should be the case becomes all the more troubling when one reflects that Spivak's argument is more polemical than it is historical, that it is finally more an argument about what literary history should say, than about how literary history ought to be done; or, to be more precise, it is an argument about how to do literary history in such a way that it conforms to a predetermined sense of what literary history should say.

The rote character of this branch of Victorian studies might be read as an analytical version of the leveling that has accompanied the colonialist spread of Western mass culture, the devastating loss of tradition, ritual, and belief that has become one of the principal preoccupations of postcolonial writing. Cultural imperialism may even be said to find its interpretive analogue in the critical imperialism of postcolonial literary studies, whose profitable investments in the Victorian novel may be read as a textual instance of reverse colonization. As such, the sheer uniformity of this work should alert us to the possibility that something akin to Said's Orientalism is at work here. Call it Victorientalism—the mining of a distant, exotic, threatening, but fascinating literature to produce and establish a singularly self-serving body of knowledge elsewhere, a body of knowledge that ultimately has more to tell us about the needs of its producers than about its ostensible subject matter.

Spivak initiates this Victorientalist endeavor by making *Jane Eyre* the object not of analysis, but of analytical expansion. As we have seen, the power of Spivak's reading comes less from compelling interpretation than from the compulsive momentum of synecdoche: *Jane Eyre* is the nineteenth-century novel is nineteenth-century culture is where imperialism is imagined; therefore, *Jane Eyre* is where imperialism is imagined. So, too, are Gilbert and Gubar equated with feminist literary criticism, which is in turn equated with the "empire of the literary discipline." The movement of the essay is one of pure growth. In this way, Spivak makes generalization the means—and end—of globalizing literary studies: "worlding" literature is a process that takes place by thinking globally—expansively, broadly, sweepingly—about texts. Spivak's is an argument predicated on the fantastic reach of marginal details, such that particular moments in one particular text yield—even seem to demand—broad conclusions about the place of the novel in literary history and—crucially—the place of literary history in the history of imperialism.

The message of Spivak's incremental synecdochal logic is clear: in their failure to connect Victorian stories to empire, critics have perpetrated an irresponsibly insular literary history.[18] And, by extension, what is needed to make literary criticism more worldly is a new Victorian studies (one populated at least in part by scholars from other fields). Spivak's relentlessly synecdochal reasoning thus amounts to a profoundly territorial mode of thought. If it raises legitimate questions about what constitutes a "field," about who qualifies to work within a field, and about who has the authority to decide what direction a field should take, it also behaves in a manner that is utterly, unrepentantly symptomatic of the problems it presumes to expose. Indeed, one could argue that Spivak's essay has done to Victorian studies something very like what she claims the Victorian novel has done to imperialism. Subjecting *Jane Eyre* to the very sort of "information-retrieval approach" (243) that she accuses politically naive critics of bringing to the study of Third World literature, Spivak may be said to have exchanged one set of oversimplifications for another: in order to produce her account of the nineteenth-century novel's "worlding," particularly as it relates to questions of feminism, individualism, and empire, she has chosen to simplify, and so objectify, the novel itself. There is a certain majesty to Spivak's tactics, one that can only be called imperial (calling Victorian literary studies imperialist could, after all, be seen as Spivak's own colonizing gesture). There is also a definite strategy: Spivak casts the field as a fundamentally backward area, incapable of governing, or thinking, for itself, and hence in need of enlightenment from beyond.

## INTERLUDE: MINUTE ON METHODOLOGICAL MISSION

In 1835, Macaulay delivered his infamous "Minute on Indian Education," a hortatory speech endorsing an English curriculum in Indian schools. "I have no knowledge of either Sanscrit or Arabic.—But I have done what I could to form a correct estimate of their value," he said; "I am quite ready to take the Oriental learning at the valuation of Orientalists themselves. I have never found one of them who could deny that a single shelf of a good European library was worth the whole native literature of India and Arabia."[19] Macaulay's idea was that a Westernized curriculum would teach Indian students to identify with European values, and so to identify with the project of imperialism: we must "do our best," he continued, "to form a class who may be interpreters between us and the millions whom we govern; a class of persons, Indian in blood and color, but English in taste, in opinions, in morals, and in intellect"

(729). Spivak's equally concise "Minute on *Jane Eyre*" partakes of a similar missionary brevity, a moralistic zeal whose urgent desire for reform takes shape as the leveling of nineteenth-century British culture into a single representative, and singularly provincial, class of writing: the domestic novel. Authorizing an English syllabus designed to train its students to recognize the invidious ways and means of empire, Spivak makes the nineteenth-century novel the object of a sort of intellectual imperialism, a native structure that, in embodying the distinctly unworldly qualities of its culture, needs to be rescued by the civilizing mission of the postcolonial critic, whose transformative exertions oddly resemble those of the missionary work they critique. (Where Macaulay envisions an Indian population eager to assimilate, so Spivak expects *Jane Eyre* to yield to the totalizing logic of her reading, itself a moral treatise that finds in the novel an exemplary ignorance to be tamed and, presumably, trained through an unrelenting course of [de]constructive criticism.) As with Macaulay's native, so with Spivak's novel: neither is politically viable, and both are infinitely in need of moral and intellectual enlightenment. In this manner, the Victorian habit of making natives responsible for their own domination finds its postcolonial echo in a theoretical invective that sees in the nineteenth-century novel the imaginative origins of our present world crisis and believes its own far-flung criticisms to contain the seeds of change.

There is something inhuman in the suggestion of an equivalency between postcolonial management of the nineteenth-century novel and nineteenth-century administration of empire. But without reducing people to popular fictions, or elevating fiction to unreasonably anthropomorphic heights, I do want to suggest that if there has been a casualty in postcolonial theory's revisionary effort, that casualty has been the nineteenth-century English novel, which has, in the missionary hands of political criticism, come perilously close to being delivered of its own existence (I call this special brand of extermination genrecide). As such, it is the very inhumanity of my own claim that matters here: novels are not people (neither are they ciphers for culture or imperialism) and hence the violence that can be done to them—and the truths that can be extracted from them—must be measured differently than we have yet done. The point of my analogy is not to compare novels to "natives," but rather to compare their historical construction as apposite Others: where the novel presumably helped cast the native as Other, so the postcolonial critique of othering frequently treats the Victorian novel as its epistemological Other, as a metonymic embodiment of all that the revisionary project officially and expressly resists. To paraphrase Spivak's own words: my reading does not seek to undermine the postcolonial project. But it will, if successful, incite a degree of rage that that project should have assigned both the Victorian novel and its critics so abject a script.[20]

To the extent that Spivak's essay has proved to be a formative one for postcolonial literary studies, especially for work on the Victorian novel, it has incited a condescension that manifests itself as an assumption that the Victorian novel is a simple thing indeed, a largely symptomatic repository of "culture" that is by definition always also an "allegory of empire."[21] One might go so far as to say that the complexity of this branch of postcolonial thought depends on what it perceives to be the profound simplicity of the Victorian novel, which, for all its wordy variety, always seems to wind up telling the same old story. Since Spivak first modeled this logic, the nineteenth-century novel has been put to work in the service of an interpretive mission whose enabling premises include an *a priori* assumption that the Victorian novel needs—like some recalcitrant—to be put definitively in its place.

## CODA

The censorious dimensions of this scholarship scream the need for a genuinely post-postcolonial criticism, an earnest effort to conceive of the Victorian novel's relationship to empire that would, above all, resist the twin temptations to berate the novel (for having bad politics) and to badger the critic (by prescribing a properly politicized reading practice). Such a criticism would refuse the by-now reflexive urge to seek paradigms for reading (as if works of art were interchangeable parts, and as if thinking responsibly about literature could be done by recipe). Such a criticism would thereby avoid the distressingly common practice of using individual works of literature to illustrate theoretical principles or to stage exemplary approaches. Finally, such a criticism would reassess, as honestly and dispassionately as possible, the project of postcolonial criticism as it has been practiced over the last two decades.

A. S. Byatt has written of the "fatal family likeness" that plagues so much contemporary criticism.[22] That likeness is in no small part due to the rise of paradigmatic thinking about literature's ideological investments. The distorted, distorting idea that literary criticism should be about modeling politicized styles of thought is not confined to postcolonial criticism; it prevails in Marxist, feminist, New Historicist, and queer criticism, too. It is, indeed, simply the way of our fraught, unhappy field. I would argue, too, that it is a major reason why our field is as fraught and unhappy as it is. A post-postcolonial criticism would—could—help launch a much-needed process of disciplinary reform, one that would begin by acknowledging the damage that agenda-driven scholarship has done to the fragile, increasingly embattled field of literary study.

The politicization of literary criticism is the means by which literature has been made to participate in a variety of progressive interpretive projects. This paradigm recruits literature to its cause by simplifying and distorting, by reducing literature to formula. Take it away, and literary criticism can begin to address the complexity that several decades of paradigmatic thinking have deliberately and devastatingly obscured. Citing the radical theoretical movements of the 1980s as a cause of profession-wide stagnation, Mark Taylor is eloquent about the need to abandon old formulas, to learn to think about systems and processes not as that which may—must—be simplified into models and paradigms, but as that which must be understood as complex: "A complexity that can be reduced to simplicity is no complexity at all."[23] This is a paradox we would do well to learn to live with and work within: sometimes the best way to manage complexity is to let it be simply and unapologetically complicated.

Such a realization has yet to penetrate Victorian studies, which has been the scene of some of the most rigidly formulaic thinking to come out of the humanities in recent years. Some scholars have begun to question the governing paradigms of the field, most notably Amanda Anderson and Eve Kosofsky Sedgwick.[24] But as a rule, even critics of Victorian studies' interpretive paradigms have tended to avoid concluding that paradigms are themselves the problem; instead, they make their analysis of faulty paradigms into the basis for proposing new, ostensibly improved ones. Anderson, for example, devotes her most recent book to promoting "detachment" as an alternative to the popular theoretical rubric of "cosmopolitanism," while Sedgwick concludes her remarkable skewering of the "hermeneutics of suspicion" that dominated criticism in the 1980s and 1990s by recommending a new-age psychoanalytic approach derived from Silvan Tomkins's little-known cybernetic work on shame.[25] But as Sedgwick's peculiar solution shows, the quest for a perfect paradigm is a quest for a methodological grail.

For too long, too many critics have devoted their careers to seeking that which does not—and cannot—exist. It's time to recognize how the interpretive prescriptions that lie at the heart of contemporary criticism have forced intellectual stasis on a field in the very moment of attempting to open up new imaginative and analytical possibilities. My own sense is that the future of Victorian studies—and of literary study—depends on our willingness to abandon the stasist security of paradigmatic thought and to search earnestly for more dynamic, less scripted ways of reading, writing, and teaching about literature.

A truly post-postcolonial criticism would be part of a larger effort of reclamation. It would aim to restore literature to its rightful place at the heart of English, treating it not as an embarrassing adjunct to theory, not as a crutch for armchair activism, not as so much undifferentiated "text," but as a unique, irreducible art form with a rich and colorful history. In other words, such a criticism would understand the dedicated, unapologetic study of literature as a viable, worthwhile, eminently respectable end in itself. A post-postcolonial contribution to that effort of reclamation would begin by divorcing the project of globalizing literature from the tactic of globalizing about literature. It would instead adopt a more humble and searching exploration of particularities; it would be far more closely and open-mindedly engaged with the details of author's lives, beliefs, and writing patterns; with the specificities of events and the unpredictable paths of their impact; with the complex mechanics of individual works. The aim of this criticism would be not to conflate knowing with containing, classifying, and controlling; it would be to honor the sheer complexity of literature, of history, and of the uncertain, shifting relationship between the two by allowing the material we work on to guide the way we work on it. A post-postcolonial criticism of this sort would be more work. It would be work fewer people could do well. But it would also be genuine scholarship rather than clever partisanship, honest inquiry rather than advocacy masquerading as inquiry. It would have dignity, and it would have substance. It would allow us to see things we have not already seen. It could even produce new knowledge. Who knows where it could lead?

## NOTES

1. Edward Said, *The World, the Text, and the Critic* (Cambridge, Mass..: Harvard University Press, 1983), 4.

2. Abdul R. JanMohamed, "The Economy of Manichean Allegory," in *"Race," Writing, and Difference*, ed. Henry Louis Gates Jr. (Chicago: University of Chicago Press, 1985), 102.

3. Fredric Jameson, "Third World Literature in the Era of Multinational Capitalism," *Social Text* 15 (Fall 1986): 78.

4. Homi Bhabha, ed., *Nation and Narration* (London and New York: Routledge, 1990), 1.

5. Edward Said, *Culture and Imperialism* (New York: Knopf, 1993), xiii.

6. An example of the wholesale reproduction of these framings in subsequent postcolonial work: in *Culture and Imperialism*, Said simply quotes Bhabha's paradigm as justification for conflating "culture," "imperialism," and "the novel."

7. Gayatri Chakravorty Spivak, "Three Women's Texts and a Critique of Imperialism," in *Critical Inquiry* 12, no. 1 (Autumn 1985): 243.

8. Since its original publication, Spivak's essay has been endlessly reprinted in anthologies dedicated to both feminist and postcolonial studies.

9. Anne McClintock, *Imperial Leather: Race, Gender, and Sexuality in the Colonial Contest* (New York: Routledge, 1995), 16.

10. For a representative example, see Chris Bongie's review of *Imperial Archive: Knowledge and the Fantasy of Empire*, by Thomas Richards, *Victorian Studies* 38, no. 3 (Spring 1995): 463–69.

11. *Jane Eyre*'s ethnohistory includes the following: May Ellis Gibson, "The Seraglio or Suttee: Brontë's *Jane Eyre*," *Postscript* 4 (1987): 1–8; Penny Boumelha, " 'And What Do the Women Do?': Jane Eyre, Jamaica, and the Gentleman's House" *Southern Review* 21, no. 2 (1988): 111–122; Laura E. Donaldson, "The Miranda Complex: Colonialism and the Question of Feminist Reading," *Diacritics* 18, no. 3 (Fall 1988): 65–77; Susan L. Meyer, "Colonialism and the Figurative Strategy of *Jane Eyre*" *Victorian Studies* 33, no. 2 (Winter 1990): 247–68; Elsie B. Michie, " 'The Yahoo, Not the Demon': Heathcliff, Rochester, and the Simianization of the Irish," *Outside the Pale: Cultural Exclusion, Gender Difference, and the Victorian Woman Writer* (Ithaca, N.Y.: Cornell University Press, 1993), 46–78; Joyce Zonana, "The Sultan and the Slave: Feminist Orientalism and the Structure of *Jane Eyre*," *Signs* 18, no. 3 (Spring 1993): 592–617; Sophie Gilmartin, "The Sati, the Bride, and the

Widow: Sacrificial Woman in the Nineteenth Century," *Victorian Literature and Culture* 25, no. 1 (1997): 141–58.

12.  For a sampling of this work, see Jenny Sharpe, *Allegories of Empire: The Figure of Woman in the Colonial Text* (Minneapolis: University of Minnesota Press, 1993); Susan Meyer, *Imperialism at Home: Race and Victorian Women's Fiction* (Ithaca, N.Y.: Cornell University Press, 1996); Deirdre David, *Rule Britannia: Women, Empire, and Victorian Writing* (Ithaca, N.Y.: Cornell University Press, 1996); Firdous Azim, *The Colonial Rise of the Novel* (New York: Routledge, 1993); and Suvendrini Perera, *Reaches of Empire : The English Novel from Edgeworth to Dickens* (New York: Columbia University Press, 1991).

13.  Elsie B. Michie, review of *Imperialism at Home: Race and Victorian Women's Fiction*, by Susan Meyer, *Modern Philology* 97, no. 2 (1999): 304.

14.  Paula Krebs, review of *Imperialism at Home: Race and Victorian Women's Fiction*, by Susan Meyer, *Clio* 28, no. 1 (Fall 1998): 110.

15.  Michael Noonan's *Magwitch* (New York: St. Martin's, 1983) anticipates this project.

16.  See, for example, Jeffrey Cass's " 'The Scraps, Patches, and Rags of Daily Life': Gaskell's Oriental Other and the Conservation of *Cranford*," *Papers on Language and Literature* 35 (Fall 1999): 417–33; and Ashish Roy's "The Fabulous Imperialist Semiotic of Wilkie Collins' *The Moonstone*," *New Literary History* 24, no. 3 (Summer 1993): 657–82.

17.  Elaine Freedgood, "Mahogany Furniture as Sadistic Souvenir: Deforestation and Slavery in *Jane Eyre*," delivered at the University of Pennsylvania, 17 April 2001, and "What Goes Around: Negro-Head Tobacco and Aboriginal Genocide in *Great Expectations*," delivered at the Marxism 2000 conference, University of Massachusetts, Amherst, September 2000.

18.  Spivak's essay is thus in part a critique of Gilbert and Gubar's concept of the woman writer and her dark double. Others have taken this cue: Said positions *Culture and Imperialism* as a book Raymond Williams might have written, but did not. Simon Gikandi's *Maps of Englishness: Writing Identity in the Culture of Colonialism* (New York: Columbia University Press, 1996) also claims to be a correction of Williams's insular cultural history.

19.  Thomas Babington Macaulay, "Minute of 2 February 1835 on Indian Education," in *Macaulay: Prose and Poetry*, selected by G. M. Young (Cambridge Mass.: Harvard University Press, 1957), 721.

20.  Spivak's own phrasing: "my readings here do not seek to undermine the excellence of the individual artist. If even minimally successful, the readings will incite a degree of rage against the imperialist narrativization of history, that it should produce so abject a script for her" (244).

21.  This phrase—originally Kipling's—has become a central one in postcolonial criticism. Sara Suleri opens *The Rhetoric of English India* (Chicago: University of Chicago Press, 1983) with a discussion of it, it provides the title for Jenny Sharpe's book on the subject, and it is, as we have seen, a formative image for critics as diverse as Fredric Jameson and Abdul JanMohamed.

22.  A. S. Byatt, *The Biographer's Tale* (New York: Knopf, 2001), 2.

23.  Mark Taylor, *The Moment of Complexity: Emerging Network Culture* (Chicago: University of Chicago Press, 2001), 60.

24.  See, for example, Amanda Anderson's "Cryptonormativism and Double Gestures: The Politics of Post-Structuralism," *Cultural Critique* 21 (Spring 1992): 63–95, and the introduction to *The Powers of Distance: Cosmopolitanism and the Cultivation of Detachment*

(Princeton, N.J.: Princeton University Press, 2001). In "Paranoid Reading and Reparative Reading; or, You're so Paranoid, You Probably Think This Introduction Is About You," in *Novel Gazing: Queer Readings in Fiction*, ed. Eve Kosofsky Sedgwick (Durham, N.C.: Duke University Press, 1997), 1–37, Sedgwick thoroughly challenges the "hermeneutics of suspicion" that she helped to establish and that has dominated progressive criticism since the 1980s.

25. See Sedgwick's "Paranoid Reading and Reparative Reading," and Sedgwick and Adam Frank's essay "Shame in the Cybernetic Fold: Reading Silvan Tomkins," *Critical Inquiry* 21, no. 2 (Winter 1995): 496–522.

# PART IV

# THEORY AS A PROFESSION

No ACCOUNTING OF ACADEMIC LIFE in recent years can fail to mention the changes Theory has brought to humanities departments in the academy. The rise of a star system within the liberal arts faculties has delivered increased, ultimately unprecedented, prestige to programs of language and literature, which had been all too aware of their lowly position in the eyes of colleagues and administrators. But a sort of "laughingstock effect" also made its appearance, of which Carol Christ, then provost of the University of California at Berkeley, warned. On every campus, she quipped, "there is one department whose name need only be mentioned to make people laugh; you don't want that department to be yours." Narrowing Christ's focus, Andrew Delbanco in 1999 added: "everyone knows that if you want to locate the laughingstock on your local campus these days, your best bet is to stop by the English department."[1]

The essays in this part explore the professionalization of Theory in an effort to explain this double effect. Postwar French ideas and professional habits having gained enormous influence beyond their own borders, they were uncritically adopted in English-speaking universities, even though the Anglophone setting offered no institutional or collegial scene comparable to the French intellectual stage. At first misfits in their Anglo-American setting, Theory intellectuals soon became a vanguard in the undermining of traditional disciplines, the aim being to carve out all-inclusive niches for themselves. Combining arcane vocabularies with pretensions (however rhetorical) to radical political agency, these professors became academe's version of media stars. At about the same time, identity groups stepped forward to associate themselves with the Theory project, seeing their prospects brightened by the reflected glow. In this way the French allure blended with a Third Worldism, the global reaches of which proved especially attractive to the expanding goals of American academic politics. The resulting conflation can be observed today in the conversion of language and literature departments into catchall sites where teaching and research often have little or nothing to do with literature. Understandably, these developments have aroused strong feelings among observers, as will be evident to readers of the following essays.

Part 4 begins with Clara Claiborne Park's discussion of Roland Barthes's famous essay on the death of the author, which she examines in the context of the unusually restrictive intellectual environment of French high academic culture. It made sense, Park writes, for Barthes to set out to dethrone the author, for in France—unlike in the English-speaking countries—authors are indeed granted extensive authority, occupying an exalted status consecrated by the French Academy. Although Barthes's ideas, arising from this situation and directly relevant to it, have circulated widely in the English-language Theory world, Parks discloses how fundamentally different is the American intellectual scene, which never (until the advent of Theory itself, we would add) granted particular literary figures such imperial influence over language and its products.

The sociologist Niilo Kauppi notes that in France, sophisticated cultural analysis must move beyond the high degree of personalization that characterizes cultural production. He therefore begins his analysis with an explanation of the French "intellectual field," a shared symbolic and social background for cultural production and consumption. Eager to break with the Sartrian model that until the 1950s dominated the philosophical and literary scene, figures such as Lévi-Strauss and his followers (the early Barthes, Derrida, and Foucault) could wrest status away from Sartre, and gain it for themselves, only by adhering to the demands of the French cultural heritage while vying for the rising rewards of celebrity that placed ideas and their expounders "on the market" as never before. In this case study of the 1950s and 1960s, Kauppi explores some aspects of the French intellectual field. Only by understanding its intricacies, he argues, can one grasp the mechanisms that allowed the second postwar generation of French intellectuals to emerge as a new intellectual nobility, "professionals of the symbolic."

Mark Bauerlein provides a critique of social constructionism from an unusual point of view. Noting that it serves as a "tribal glue" for humanities professors—for whom "knowledge is a construct" has become an article of faith—and finding no philosophical basis for this belief, Bauerlein tests his hunch that the attraction to an idea that confuses the contents of knowledge—its truth—with the external circumstances of its production can best be explained by its institutional setting. As a theory, social constructionism bolsters the status of humanities departments by disparaging science and its truth claims. More important, Bauerlein thinks, as a practice it substantially simplifies and speeds both work and the evaluation of work within the humanities. With its ready-made conclusions and unexacting research agendas, in which speculation and the play of rhetoric are valued more highly than fact finding and erudition, social constructionism saves time. It is, Bauerlein concludes, "the epistemology of scholarship in haste."

The adoption of a distinctively turgid and rebarbative style of Theory writing leads D. G. Myers to reflect on the prevalence of "Bad Writing." Acknowledging that problems with academic writing existed in the past, Myers notes that something new has happened over the past few decades, as incomprehensibility became a value in itself and obscurantism led particularly bad writers to stardom. Indeed, among the worst offenders against clarity and taste were some of the most renowned Theorists of our time. Myers describes the harmful effect of Bad Writing on younger scholars who feel obliged to imitate it and connects this trend with the conformity prevailing in the departments in which these scholars hope to make their careers.

A currently important and ever-expanding area that is a publishing gold-mine for academics is "cultural studies." Stephen Adam Schwartz analyzes the rise and evolving claims of this new "anti-discipline," using its "bible," the 1992 volume *Cultural Studies*, as a baseline. Schwartz argues that the notion of culture uniting all the essays in that large collection is both idiosyncratic and flawed, but he finds that it has nonetheless been immensely useful in the profession in establishing academic reputations. Cultural studies' principal effect is that it effaces distinctions. Once the differences between literature and non-literature have been rendered untenable—indeed, once the very concept of culture is attacked as tyrannical and all differentiations are reduced to reflections of "power" (and hence to be rejected)—it follows that curricula and research agendas must be made to accommodate all subjects and interpretations—as long as the right discourse is adopted. Thus cultural studies makes everyone an expert. Ironically, as Schwartz points out, this current fad embraces core values of American society, rooted as it is in liberalism and promoting, to an unprecedented degree, individual self-expression.

Geoffrey Galt Harpham, whose essay closes this section, unleashes a "rant" against the star system in academe. How, he asks, did leading universities become the haunt of overpaid "sybarites," while much of the teaching is done by a "proletarianized" helotry of lower-level faculty and adjuncts? The answer, he argues, lies in the rise of Theory and the prestige it brought to its practitioners. Harpham analyzes the typical moves in the Theory game, in which, under the inspiration of masters such as Foucault and Derrida, all knowledge has been reconfigured so as to allow "discoveries" made in one field to be "shoehorned" into other academic areas. The resulting hybrid, unrestrained by disciplinary or any other kinds of boundaries, is now an alluring academic pursuit, called simply "Theory." Its further utility is that it acts "in ghostly forms" as a way of legitimating types of studies that could not gain legitimacy on their own. Harpham urges us to think in two directions at once: toward the particular and the general, the "gritty details" as well as the larger structures and, in this way, transform the profession.

NOTE

1. Andrew Delbanco, "The Decline and Fall of Literature," *The New York Review of Books*, 4 November 1999, 32, where he also quotes Christ's words.

# 19. AUTHOR! AUTHOR!

## RECONSTRUCTING ROLAND BARTHES

### CLARA CLAIBORNE PARK

WHEN THE AUTHOR DIED in France in 1968, it was Roland Barthes who with his essay "La mort de l'auteur" administered the *coup de grâce*. Jacques Derrida had already warned, in *Of Grammatology*, of the frivolity of thinking that " 'Descartes,' 'Leibniz,' 'Rousseau,' 'Hegel,' are names of authors," since they indicated "neither identities nor causes," but rather "the name of a problem." Michel Foucault would later record an "author-function" arising out of the "scission" between "the author" and "the actual writer." The subtext for all three shimmered in the Parisian spring, when the students took to the streets and even the sacred *baccalauréat* felt the tremor. Barthes's way of putting it was somewhat more inspiriting than the transmogrification of authors into functions or problems: "We know now that a text is not a line of words releasing a single 'theological' meaning (the 'message' of the Author-God) but a multidimensional space, in which a variety of writings, none of them original, blend and clash." What Barthes was celebrating, in language permeated with the rhetoric of liberation, was release from the very idea of an origin; it was nothing less than that staple of the sixties, the death of God.

Barthes made sure his language told the story. The Author is "believed in"; his image is to be "desacralized," and with it his theological meaning. He is the God, "the origin, the authority, the Father" (as Barthes would write two years later), and not a very nice one. Literature is centered on him "tyrannically"; his "sway" is "powerful"; the new literature, now to be renamed *writing*, "liberates"; the Author is a myth it is "necessary to overthrow." Criticism, as Barthes would tell *L'Express* in 1970, could participate in "a kind of collective action." (Asked what it did, he answered, "It destroys.") The text, and the reader, are prisoners in the Bastille. With the erasure of the Author-God, the text, escaped from its Great Original, is revealed as an infinite regress of prior traces, of language, of ideas, of societal memories and assumptions. For "to give a text an Author is to impose a limit on that text, to furnish it with a final signified, to close the writing," and the reading with it. To dissolve the Author is to inaugurate that exhilaratingly "anti-theological activity," the conversion of literature

Clara Claiborne Park. "Author! Author! Reconstructing Roland Barthes." Reprinted by permission from *The Hudson Review* 43, no. 3 (Autumn 1990): 377–98. Copyright © 1990 Clara Claiborne Park. Abridged by permission of the author. This essay also appears in *Rejoining the Common Reader: Essays, 1962–1990* by Clara Claiborne Park. Evanston, Ill.: Northwestern University Press, 1991.

to *écriture*, which "ceaselessly posits meaning ceaselessly to evaporate it." It is "an activity that is truly revolutionary since to refuse to fix meaning is, in the end, to refuse God and his hypostases—reason, science, law."

To the reader coming in late, and from over the water, the excitement may be somewhat hard to understand. Is this Author-God, this Freudian Father ("a somewhat decrepit deity," as Barthes would later call him) anybody we know?

Sixty years ago, like many American children, I had a game of Authors. It was geared to seven-year-olds—a pack of cards with four suits, headed by Henry Wadsworth Longfellow, John Greenleaf Whittier, Edgar Allan Poe, and Oliver Wendell Holmes. (Not Melville back then, not Whitman, not Dickinson or Thoreau—an early lesson in the temporality of canons.) From the cards we learned such truths as that Longfellow wrote *Evangeline* and Holmes *The Autocrat of the Breakfast Table*. Naturally, we did not learn to think of the Author as God, Father, or even (*Whittier?*) as an Authority. And had we been English children, with a deck displaying Shelley, Keats, Tennyson, and Browning, we wouldn't have learned it either. To be able to associate authors with God, let alone with his institutional hypostases, you have to be French.

In 1635, in a book significantly entitled *De l'esclaircissement des temps,* a portrait appeared of the powerful politician who the year before had founded the Académie Française, Armand Jean du Plessis, duc de Richelieu. From the cardinal's head, as if prefiguring the Sun-King whose effulgence his policies prepared, shone forty rays of light. Each of those rays bore the name of an Academician—an Author.

Shall we try to imagine an analogous representation in an English-speaking context? No English prime minister has ever exercised Richelieu's absolute power. Had he done so, it remains inconceivable that the most sycophantic artist could ever have rayed forth from his head the names, say, of Milton, Dryden, Shadwell, and thirty-seven more, to Enlighten the Times with their harmonious brightness. Nor can we conceive of an English prime minister—still less an American president—concerning himself to create, as Richelieu did, an institution to regularize the national language, guard its purity, and impose upon its primary public literature, the drama, binding rules of literary practice. Long before Barthes, before Derrida, before Foucault, Richelieu had made the connection between Authors and Authority, between language and power. The relation of the dramatic Unities to monarchical unity, of literary Decorum to political and social conformity, was neither coincidental nor the expression of a vague French Zeitgeist. As David Kramer has shown, the Academy and its projects were a deliberate response to the exigencies of an absolutism emerging from a century of fragmentation and religious war. The rules, literary and linguistic, imposed by Richelieu's Academy expressed the absolute vision of what was to be Le Grand Siècle while helping to bring it into being.

It was Richelieu's Academy indeed. Perceiving their potential usefulness—or danger—he had by fiat institutionalized the cheerfully intellectual discussions of a group of literary friends into an assembly of forty so-called Immortals. Some wished to decline the honor, but since Richelieu had forbidden unlicensed assemblies they thought better of it. The Immortals, when not raying directly from Richelieu's head, were in his pocket. He awarded pensions at will. "No one could be so much as proposed for election unless he was 'agréable au protecteur.'" The Academy's first and continuing project, the codification and purification of French, was initially undertaken so that the conquering tongue could be more readily learned by those whom the Cardinal's military campaigns were to subject to the crown. This was the original impetus for the great French Dictionary. Language was a means of control; French was to spread French *civilisation* abroad, as Latin had. It would equally set limits on what could be written—and thought—at home. We may, if we like, imagine a world in which Dr. Johnson composed his Dictionary not to make the money he told Boswell every sane man wrote for, but to enhance the glory of the Hanoverian monarchy. That done, we have to imagine him thinking of himself as one of forty immortals and not laughing.

It was, then, more than the afflatus of the sixties that impelled Barthes to kill the Author, and rebel against "a language political in its origin" . . . "born at the moment when the upper classes wished . . . to convert the particularity of their writing into a universal language." Though there were contemporary reasons to proclaim liberation from the heavy rod of the Father-God, Barthes's sense of urgency was rooted deep in the historic soil of France. Only in France would it be possible to claim, as Barthes already had in "Authors and Writers" (1960), that "for the entire classical capitalist period, i.e. from the sixteenth to the nineteenth century . . . the uncontested owners of the language, and they alone, were authors"; that "no one else spoke." *No one else spoke.* The outrageousness of the hyperbole bespeaks its urgency. For when Barthes describes a "literary discourse subjected to rules of use, genre, and composition more or less immutable from Marot to Verlaine, from Montaigne to Gide," it is not hyperbole, but a truism of French literary history. "The certitudes of language . . . the imperatives of the structure of the genre"—these are not Barthes's own dismissive sarcasms, but the words of Professor Raymond Picard, a critic sufficiently infuriated by the originality of Barthes's criticism to call his "Nouvelle Critique" a "Nouvelle Imposture." Outside France, Barthes's essay *On Racine* wouldn't have raised an eyebrow. But in France those certitudes and imperatives *exist*, for everything from drama to orthography; one challenges them at one's peril. The walls of the prison house of language are far thicker in France.

What rayed from Richelieu's head was exactly that clarity later to be called Cartesian, the absolute and simple brightness of the "clear and distinct ideas" that Descartes thought he could find in his own mind and from them validate a universe; *la clarté cartésienne* was the visual manifestation of what Foucault calls "the great utopia of a perfectly transparent language." Barthes had already written, in *Mythologies*, of that "blissful clarity," how it "abolishes the complexity of human acts," giving them "the simplicity of essences," organizing "a world without contradictions because it is without depth, a world . . . wallowing in the evident." The myth was so powerful, even in America, that an American graduate student could be told to read Kant in a French translation, because it was impossible to be obscure in French. Clarity was the glory of that class monopoly, "the great French language," whose "lexicon and euphony," Barthes notes, could be "respectfully preserved" even through that "greatest paroxysm of French history," the Revolution. Though nineteenth-century authors might broaden that language, they were still its "acknowledged owners." Let us reactivate our English-speaking incredulity: it is quite simply inconceivable to us that authors, of all people, could even in imagination own a language. We speak and write a language that is the product not of authority but of receptivity, of foreign influence and invasion, that from the time of its greatest poet, and in his person, has been defined by its rich intransigence, its resistance to purity or purification. For us as for Shakespeare, language has been the product not of Authors, but of people talking,

But Barthes, with Derrida and Foucault and fifty million other Frenchmen, grew up within the secure structures of the great French language. There were forty Immortals in their youth, and there are forty Immortals today, two hundred years after that revolutionary paroxysm which nevertheless scarcely interrupted the Academy's guardianship over the integrity of French. Americans from time to time are made aware of the Immortals, as during the flap over the admission of the late Marguerite Yourcenar, and we are reminded that this is something that seems to matter—to matter less, presumably, than when three brilliant French minds were being formed by an educational system whose director was said to have claimed that he knew what page in what book every French schoolchild was turning on a given day, but still far more than we can readily imagine. The Quarante Immortels are still at work on their Dictionary. A centralized educational system still guarantees that a whole nation invests its emotions in the idea of an authoritative language. Summering in a country village, the astonished foreigner is lectured on what is and is not permissible French by the man who retails fish from door to door. Someone encountered in a train, asked to explain a word he has probably known all his life, defines it, then quickly adds, "But that's not French." It is, of course, *argot*—rich and self-renewing like any popular speech. When Victor Hugo introduced a few phrases of thieves' argot into *Les Misérables*, he appended thousands of words of justification. Authority is defined by power, and power is defined by its ability to forbid. That the vocabulary of classic French drama is confined to some 2,500 words (2,000, says Barthes, for Racine) as against Shakespeare's 25,000 is not just a quirk of literary history, still less of national character. It is the product of conscious decision. Though the vocabulary of permissible French is of course very much larger today, it is still defined by exclusion.

Helen Vendler has described the "intellectual formation of a French child attracted to literature"—the *cahier* (the obligatory blot-free notebook), the *dictée*, the *manuel littéraire* enshrining every received idea of literary history— and has noted Barthes's own awareness of "how little he could escape from this training." Barthes, in *S/Z*, describes it considerably more abstractly: "a predetermination of messages, as in secondary school education." But the structures of French civilization are formed long before its elite attends the lycée. The certitudes and imperatives of French are encountered much earlier. Few of the children whose education Lawrence Wylie describes in his *Village in the Vaucluse* would ever reach secondary school. Yet in their elementary classroom the Cartesian light still shone, clear and sharp, mandating a dedication to abstract formulation, to analysis, to classification that readers of contemporary French theory will find eerily familiar.

"Children," Wylie observes, "are not encouraged to formulate principles independently on the basis of an examination of concrete cases. They are given the impression that principles exist autonomously . . . always there: immutable and constant. One can only learn to recognize . . . and accept them." French education is not Baconian; its motion is not inductive but deductive. English-speaking readers may recall a flicker of surprise upon discovering that "empirical" is not, for French theorists, a word of praise. "Logical," however, is. "No attempt is made to understand or to appreciate the text which is presented to the class until it has been thoroughly . . . analyzed, . . . broken down into its logical divisions, and the author's purpose in each division . . . explained. . . . To approach problems with these assumptions is to approach them sensibly, reasonably, logically, and therefore . . . correctly."

French, of course, "is recognized as the most important subject taught. . . . Any other subject may be slighted or sacrificed in order to increase the time for drill" in the proper use of *la langue maternelle*. Wylie notes how hard it is for an Anglo-Saxon "to comprehend how essential this language study is to the French." Yet this is what we must comprehend if we are to appreciate the sense of free air breathed at last that pervades Barthes's *écriture*. Though so difficult a writing must severely, if regretfully, limit Equality and Fraternity, Liberty's banner floats triumphant, celebrating freedom from the Author/Father/God, from his "predetermined messages," his tyrannical intentions; from the imposed interpretation that wallows in the evident; from consistency; from logic. To rebel against the Author is to challenge Authority in a way neither imaginable nor necessary in an educational culture which valorizes the wayward and the polyphonic, and where no author (just ask one) has authority over language or anything else.

Barthes opens *Le Plaisir du texte*, his celebration of the delight of reading, with imagining an individual . . . who would abolish within himself all barriers, all classes, all exclusions, . . . by simply getting rid of that old specter: *logical contradiction*; who would mix up all kinds of languages, even those thought incompatible; who would mutely endure all the accusations of illogicality, of infidelity; who would remain impassive in the face of Socratic irony (which works by leading the other to the supreme opprobrium: *to contradict oneself*) and of legal terrorism (how much penal evidence is founded on a psychology of consistency!). That man would be in our society the lowest of the low; the courts, the school, the asylum, ordinary conversation would make him a stranger: who endures contradiction without shame?

Any reader whose pleasure has been taken largely in texts written in English will detect an accent, even in translation. From Chaucer to Sterne to Salman Rushdie, the glory of English has been the mixing up of languages thought incompatible. And only in French could "illogicality" be associated with "infidelity." The translator of the American edition was forced to render *infidélité* as "incongruity" lest he stymie the English-speaking reader in mid-sentence. *Infidelity*? To whom? To whom but the Author-God, with his "hierarchical sentence," his tyrannical meanings; with his hypostases of law, science, reason; with his fixation on logical consistency. God is *French*. That great rebel against the Rules, Victor Hugo, could still write with perfect naturalness in *Les Misérables* that "artistic peoples are logical peoples," since "the ideal is nothing but the culmination of logic, just as beauty is the apex of truth." No wonder Barthes complained, defending *Sur Racine*, that the *classes supérieures*, universalizing their own ideal of language, put forward "la 'logique' française" as "une logique absolue." The disclaiming quotes are, of course, Barthes's own.

*Who endures contradiction without shame?* Barthes's language vacillates here, as he likes it to do, with its initial suggestion that it's the representatives of school, court, and asylum who can't bear to be contradicted by Barthes's "counter-hero," the reader-writer taking his free pleasure. But "shame" takes us back to that *abjection* which I have translated as "the lowest of the low," to the shame of a Frenchman who has been caught out in a logical contradiction. *Ce n'est pas logique!*

Who, then, can endure the shame of logical contradiction? English shouts its answer. Emerson can endure it ("A foolish consistency is the hobgoblin of little minds"); Whitman can endure it ("Do I contradict myself? Very well then I contradict myself"); Blake can endure it; the metaphysicals can endure it. Shakespeare can endure it. Sir Philip Sidney, cosmopolite and aristocrat, his own French almost accentless, rejected a "mungrell Tragy-comedie" that mingled kings and clowns. Shakespeare went right ahead, befouling the purity of tragedy with comic gravediggers who spoke the people's prose. Voltaire hated the gravediggers, though there were a lot of things he admired in Shakespeare; you don't come across such barbarities in Racine.

French intellectuals, of course, do not read Emerson or Whitman; they read Poe, who is *plus logique*. And they generally read in French. Barthes refers to "The Purloined Letter" in Mallarmé's translation. Though he does quote Blake (a single Proverb of Hell) he quotes in French, and his reference is not to *The Marriage of Heaven and Hell* but to a book (in translation) by Norman O. Brown. He seems unaware of the literature of modernism in English; there is an extraordinary passage in *Plaisir* in which he describes the experience of sitting in a bar, amusing himself by enumerating its "whole stereophony" of "music, conversations, noises of chairs, of glasses," the "little voices" which dissolve the hierarchical sentence into the "nonsentence." It is as if Joyce's "Sirens" had never been written—or translated. "Why," Barthes asks in his autobiography, "so little talent for foreign languages?" English at the lycée was "boring (*Queen Mab, David Copperfield, She Stoops to Conquer*)." The candor is characteristic and disarming; still, so comfortable an admission is unexpected from someone who feels so intensely the difference between one word and another, and emphasizes the distinction between denotation and connotation as if he had discovered it. Though he excoriated the "narcissisme linguistique" of the guardians of the "idiome sacré," French is for him "nothing more or less than the umbilical language." It is in French he writes, in French he reads (with occasional hints of German and Italian); it is to the readers and writers of *la langue maternelle* that he addresses his *écriture*.

So it is curious that it is not in France that his work has acquired its maximum power. There the liberation of the text from the structures of decorum, of consistency, of logic could be felt as an exhilarating duty. Let its false and deceptive coherence dissolve, its meanings float free, in "a paradise of words," a "happy Babel," in which "one may hear the grain of the gullet, the patina of consonants, the voluptuousness of vowels," and exult in the amorous perversity (his word) of an *écriture* that "granulates, . . . crackles, . . . caresses, . . . grates, . . . cuts," and at last, joyously, "*comes.*" But how perverse is that perversity for readers whose experience of literature has been formed by the happy Babel of Chaucer, of Shakespeare, of Carroll and Lear and Joyce? What needs exploring is why these quintessentially French linguistic preoccupations have found so warm a welcome in an educational culture so different from, even antithetic to, that of France.

After all, it's been fifty years and more that English and American criticism has been preoccupied with language; with metaphors and metaphorical systems (Caroline Spurgeon got us started in 1930); with the referentiality of poetic statement (I. A. Richards and T. S. Eliot in the twenties); with the layered suggestiveness which makes words rejoice as they fend off all attempts at paraphrase. French students learn that their greatest playwright wrote the speeches out in prose to cast into alexandrines; in classical French "no word," wrote Barthes (*Writing Degree Zero*) "has a density by itself." Here, few students who undergo Introduction to Literature escape an exercise expressly designed to raise their consciousness of verbal densities. The distinction between denotation and connotation has been a staple of freshman writing texts ever since this year's retirees can remember. The inseparability of content and form is a truism: as Cleanth Brooks wrote in 1939, "the experience that [the poet] 'communicates' is itself created by the organization of the symbols he uses," so that "the total poem is therefore the communication, and indistinguishable from it." The sentence, including its suspicion of communication, could be Barthes's own. As he would put it decades later, with characteristic abstraction, "signification [is] the union of what signifies and what is signified . . . neither form nor content, but the proceedings between them."

Barthes's Author-God emitted "messages" in 1968: Brooks and Robert Penn Warren had warned American students to stop hunting them thirty years before. Barthes put the Author's intentionality in question; "the intentional fallacy" hit American criticism in 1946. Did New Critics direct us away from the poet to The Poem Itself? In 1963, so did Barthes, rejecting traditional criticism's interest in "coordinating the details of a work with the details of a life" in favor of an "immanent analysis" functioning "in a realm purely internal to the work."

In French, ambiguity is not a positive value: my *Larousse de poche* defines it as "a defect of that which is equivocal." In 1963 Barthes converted defect to virtue: "each time we write ambiguously enough to suspend meaning . . . writing releases a question, . . . gives the world an energy, . . . permits us to breathe." Indeed, breathing wasn't all that easy; Barthes would soon have to defend against professorial attack his "right" (imagine it!) to read in Racine's "literal discourse" "other senses which [he was still stepping gingerly] do not contradict it." But though his valorization of ambiguity might be news to the French Academy, the American academy had started amusing itself with seven types of ambiguity in 1930. Thrilling as it is to read of language as "an immense halo of implications" making "knowledge festive" with words "flung out as projections, explosions, vibrations, devices, flavors," readers whose language long before Hopkins embraced "all things counter, original, spare, strange" must take it as confirmation rather than battle cry.

Even deconstruction has a familiar ring. Excise the word "personal" from the following; guess the writer; guess the date: "That radical mode of romantic polysemism in which the latent personal significance of a narrative poem is found not merely to underlie, but to contradict and cancel the surface intention." In 1966, confronting Picard, Barthes was still leery of contradiction. In 1953, M. H. Abrams was as much at home with it as Blake had been in 1790.

Nor can Barthes's amorous embrace of the concrete, of the physical object seem radical, though it may surprise us as we persevere through aridities of abstraction which, while less extensive than those in Foucault and Derrida, are equally uninviting to the Anglo-American explorer. Empiricism informs English-speaking style as well as English-speaking epistemology. Freshman composition texts are as one in discouraging abstraction and enjoining specificity; like McGuffey before them, they do their best to get American students, in Wylie's words, "to formulate principles independently on the basis of an examination of concrete cases." Helen Vendler's examples of "compositional subjects of the sort set for French students—'Arrogance,' 'Ease,' 'Coincidence'"—would appear, if at all, only to illustrate the kind of subject to avoid. Barthes too believes in concreteness. Outraged when Picard accuses him of "an inhuman abstraction," he insists that "the works of *la nouvelle critique* are very rarely abstract, because they treat of substances and objects." Reversing the deductive method taught the French pupil, he "starts," he says, "from a sensuous object, and then hopes to meet in his work with the possibility of finding an *abstraction* for it" (italics his). He complains of the classic taste that considers objects "trivial," incongruous when introduced "into a rational discourse"; he commits himself to the object in full physicality he likes to call erotic; his "body," he says, "cannot accommodate itself to *generality*, the generality that is in language." The language is a bit warm for a freshman text, but the message is wholly familiar.

American critics, intellectual historians, and pedagogues, however, are not among the prior traces which constitute the text called Roland Barthes, which is entirely truthful in saying in 1963 ("What is Criticism?") that French criticism "owes little or nothing to Anglo-American criticism." (The Anglo-American texts Barthes does refer to address very different preoccupations: Bruno Bettelheim, D. W. Winnicott, Alan Watts, Norman O. Brown.) The relation of La Nouvelle Critique to The New Criticism is *post,* not *propter.*

What, then, explains our fascination? There is, of course, a peculiar pleasure in reencountering one's own *idées reçues,* especially when expressed with an elegant difficulty that lends them the dark glow of revelation. From New to Nouvelle was an easy transition. The transatlantic breezes started blowing just as the New began to seem old hat. Barthes was affirming, with supremely French intelligence, the pieties of English 101.

But of course there's more to it. In retrospect, the New Critics seem surprisingly modest. They might distrust "messages," but they were comfortable enough with meanings. They left epistemology alone; they had no aspirations to philosophy or psychology. Though they discouraged biographical approaches, though they directed attention from poet to speaker and novelist to narrator, though they might (some of them) bracket authorial intentions, they didn't meddle with the idea of the self. But if authorial selves are (in the words of Vincent Leitch) "fabrications . . . interpretations . . . effects of language, not causes," why should our own selves be any different? A risky idea, the dissolution of the self, if personal responsibility dissolves along with it.

Because there *is* more to it than old wine in new bottles. There is true exhilaration about the breaking of tablets. The New Critics had scarcely been revolutionaries, literary or philosophical, least of all political. Yet the familiarity of their ideas could pave the way to the Paris of '68. Though the shadow of the Author-God did not reach across the sea, though these were French texts speaking to the French, still they had their message for American intellectuals living in a country whose imperial impositions were increasingly difficult to ignore or justify. They aimed at the Author, but their target was Power. We could imagine with them a grand international democracy of power-free language—or if that were an impossible dream, we could at least proclaim our awareness of the invisibly tyrannical habits of our discourse. There were new, progressive uses for our old New Critical techniques. They could be applied to any writing. "Literature" was only a category, as artificial as any of those frozen seventeenth-century genres. Guilt over nationality, class, and gender could revivify a tired scrutiny. For there is a politics of language. Orwell had told us that in 1946, in his blunt, concrete, English way; thirty years after, we could examine the matter with new French subtlety.

And somewhere in the last paragraph irony gives way to appreciation. Barthes would have recognized the movement: of reversal, of the statement no sooner made than put in question, of contradiction not merely acknowledged but embraced. One may—I do—question the cost-free radicalism of our American warriors of theory, called to no undertaking more heroic than the reading of these admittedly exigent texts and the acquisition of a *parole* which now, in universities all over the country, itself exerts the power to require, insist, and exclude. For academics who have joined the club, the return of grand theory has brought not risk but a bonanza of renewal, liberating them into a hermeneutic paradise of publication where the professional reader is Adam, forever encountering beasts that invite him to name them anew. Critical theory, I'm told, is a game; you don't have to play it unless you enjoy it. But power games are rarely optional. Barthes, like Foucault, like Derrida, had something more radical in mind than the substitution of one linguistic tyranny for another.

For they were French. A true radicalism goes to the root; theirs attacked the root assumptions of an unusually restrictive socio-politico-linguistic culture. There was a heroism in their assault on *clarté*, their determination to validate a darkness all the richer by contrast with that vaunted *esclaircissement*, to honor the category of what Foucault called "the unthought." It's even explicable that stylistic obscurity should join the other insignia of liberation, the *étandards sanglants* of their good fight.

Their status as revolutionaries was helped, of course, by the unique history of the French seventeenth century, which permitted such a ready association of oppressive structures of literature with oppressive structures of economics and of class. A phrase like Barthes's "the entire classical capitalist period" won't work in England or America, neither of which has a classical tradition you could put in your eye. In France it is at least intelligible. With "capitalist" functioning as negative shorthand in literature as well as economics, Barthes could claim a radicalism as genuine as Sartre's, and a lot more subtle. Though Susan Sontag admires Barthes, she calls him a dandy. That's not wholly fair. When he rejects political engagement for a different responsibility, the responsibility to his umbilical language, it is more than mere aestheticism. The radicalism was genuine, the status as outsider absolutely real. In his fragmentary autobiography, Barthes defines himself as his culture had defined him: religiously, sexually, and academically marginal. "Who does not feel how *natural* it is, in France, to be Catholic, married, and properly accredited with the right degrees?" He wasn't, he tells us, even right-handed. We should not forget that the game American insiders now play was originally an enterprise of risk.

Barthes meant it about power. His essays were *essais* in Montaigne's original sense, tentative, trials of ideas. In his last decade even these came to seem too domineering, too insistently coherent, too "classical"; better to relax, to group paragraphs under topic headings, in alphabetical order, open to the aleatory air. Thus *The Pleasure of the Text, Roland Barthes by Roland Barthes, A Lover's Discourse*. They slide from under the essay's assertive form—thesis, argument, conclusion—into something more wavering, more faithful to the moods of thought—*his* thought—how it's always escaping, from reader, from writer, yet can't escape its paradoxical consistency, its message, its loyalty to the values of a lifetime. The older you get, the more everything you write and do connects, yes, into a self. What Keats, who didn't get old, called soul-making.

"All this must be considered as if spoken by a character in a novel." In *Roland Barthes by Roland Barthes* these are the first words we encounter. Yet he arranged for the words to appear not in print but in his own fine rapid cursive, most personal of signatures. Nothing impersonal about these last books except the use of the third person; they are rich with his highly individual sensitivities, likes, dislikes. He liked the letter Z, for instance. He called it "The letter of deviance" and made it his own. First the straight line of assertion, then the zigzag of "reversal, contradiction, reactive energy"; *but, on the other hand, yet*. So too the Author zigzags back in *The Pleasure of the Text*; though "as an institution" he's dead, yet "lost in the midst of the text (not *behind* it, like a god from the machine) there's always the other, the author." For (emphasis again his) "*I desire* the *author*"—"*d'une certaine façon.*"

When the Author died in France in 1968 it seemed a local matter. But as the report spread and discipline after discipline faced the demands of grand theory, the game turns serious. The insouciant critic gives way to the sober philosopher; people get nervous. In 1989 the lead article in the journal of the American Historical Association called "authorial presence" a "dream"; invoked Barthes, and after him Foucault and Derrida; worried whether, the author absent, intellectual history could be written at all. The simplicity of the answer may perhaps startle; the writer confesses that "it is beginning to look as if *belief* in the author may be our best response" (italics his). "Writers from a variety of disciplines are now suggesting that, if we hope to make sense of any text, we must first attribute to it an author." He had to read an awful lot to get to that point; my grandmother called it going round your elbow to get to your thumb.

"Of all the intellectual notables who have emerged since World War II in France," writes Susan Sontag, "Roland Barthes is the one whose work I am most certain will endure." If so, it is because he is the one whose writing can be read, at least intermittently, for pleasure. Pleasure of the text and pleasure of the author, no god and no authority, but a human being to be enjoyed, for his commitment to freedom, to multiplicity, and to delight, for his intelligence, and for the generosity of his intentions. He desired the author. So do we.

## WORKS CITED

[Editors' note: For certain quotations from Barthes, Park has slightly modified the published translation.]

Barthes, Roland. "Authors and Writers." 1960. In *Critical Essays*, trans. Richard Howard, 143–50. Evanston, Ill.: Northwestern University Press, 1972.

——. *Critique et verité*. Paris: Tel Quel, Éditions du Seuil, 1966.

——. "The Death of the Author." 1968. In *Image, Music, Text*, ed. and trans. Stephen Heath, 142–49. New York: Farrar, Straus and Giroux, 1977.

——. *A Lover's Discourse: Fragments*. 1977. Trans. Richard Howard. New York: Farrar, Straus and Giroux, 1978.

——. *Mythologies*. 1957. Trans. Annette Lavers. New York: Farrar, Straus and Giroux, 1972.

——. *On Racine*. 1963. Trans. Richard Howard. New York: Farrar, Straus and Giroux, 1964.

——. *The Pleasure of the Text*. 1973. Trans. Richard Miller. New York: Farrar, Straus and Giroux, 1975.

——. *Roland Barthes by Roland Barthes*. 1975. Trans. Richard Howard. New York: Farrar, Straus and Giroux, 1977.

——. *S/Z*. 1970. Trans. Richard Miller. New York: Farrar, Straus and Giroux, 1974.

——. "What Is Criticism." 1963. In *Critical Essays*, trans. Richard Howard, 255–60. Evanston, Ill: Northwestern University Press, 1972.

——. *Writing Degree Zero*. 1953. Trans. Annette Lavers and Colin Smith. New York: Farrar, Straus and Giroux, 1972.

Brooks, Cleanth. *Modern Poetry and the Tradition*. Chapel Hill: University of North Carolina Press, 1939.

Derrida, Jacques. *Of Grammatology*. Trans. Gayatri Chakravorty Spivak. Baltimore, Md.: The Johns Hopkins University Press, 1977.

Foucault, Michel. "What Is an Author?" In *Language, Counter-Memory, Practice: Selected Essays and Interviews*, trans. Donald F. Bouchard and Sherry Simon, ed. Donald F. Bouchard, 113–38. Ithaca, N.Y.: Cornell University Press, 1977.

Kramer, David Bruce. "'Tis a Drama of Our Own Invention: Dryden's Theatrical Practice and the French." Ph.D. diss., Princeton University, 1987.

Leitch, Vincent. *Deconstructive Criticism: An Advanced Introduction*. New York: Columbia University Press, 1983.

Picard, Raymond. *New Criticism or New Fraud?* Trans. Frank Towne. Pullman: Washington State University Press, 1969.

Sontag, Susan. "Writing Itself: On Roland Barthes." In *A Barthes Reader*. New York: Hill and Wang, 1982.

Vendler, Helen. "The Medley Is the Message." *New York Review of Books*, 8 May 1986.

Wylie, Lawrence. *Village in the Vaucluse.* Cambridge: Harvard University Press, 1957.

## 20.   THE FRENCH INTELLECTUAL HABITUS AND LITERARY CULTURE

### NIILO KAUPPI

> One needs, in order to write well, habits as well as ideas; and though the ideas may be born in solitude, the forms taken by these ideas, the images one uses to render them understandable, almost always belong to the memories of one's upbringing and of the society in which one has lived.
>
> —MADAME DE STAËL-HOLSTEIN,
> DE LA LITTÉRATURE CONSIDÉRÉE DANS SES RAPPORTS
> AVEC LES INSTITUTIONS SOCIALES

> Lévi-Strauss hasn't written any novels, and no one knows the poems of Foucault. Each occupies his compartment, and it is devilishly difficult to get one of them to come out to take a bit of air. The specialist is in power!
>
> —GILLES LAPOUGE

ONLY IN A CONTEXT such as the French intellectual field[1] could Gilles Lapouge label Foucault's *oeuvre* that of a specialist. But foreign observers of French cultural life, although not constrained by local etiquette and conventions, only rarely analyze ideas in relation to the *modus operandi* of cultural production, that is, to practices and habits of thinking prevalent in the context of creation. The explanation for this lies partly in the fact that the production of high culture in France is personalized to a degree that makes more sophisticated cultural analysis of it difficult. Yet in order to understand the singularity of a work, even that of a Claude Lévi-Strauss[2] or a Michel Foucault,[3] and the

Niilo Kauppi. "The French Intellectual Habitus and Literary Culture." Revised by the author from *French Intellectual Nobility: Institutional and Symbolic Transformations in the Post-Sartrian Era*, by Niilo Kauppi, 25–33. Albany: The State University of New York Press. Copyright © 1996 State University of New York. All rights reserved. Reprinted by permission.

subtle complicities and oppositions between ideas, individuals, and institutions, it might not suffice to concentrate only on the individual who produced the work. What needs to be grasped is the state, at a precise moment in time, of the whole intellectual field as a shared symbolic and social background for cultural production and consumption. Only then can we distinguish the particular from the universal and the extraordinary from the ordinary. Whereas a strict sociology of science does not take into account wider cultural dynamics, a theoretical reading of "structuralism" or "poststructuralism" leads to nothing more than an intellectual parade—a purely formal presentation of well known, recycled facts. For the thousandth time, Saussure, Foucault, Derrida, and Lévi-Strauss (the antecedents) are made to march in the first row (occasionally one can "discover" somebody still relatively unknown), followed by the minor prophets; in the third row come the contemporary commentators, including the author of the work him- or herself. For a sophisticated analysis of cultural production, the human and social sciences should be analyzed in relation to the broader transformations of the intellectual field. In the pages that follow, I will examine, using as a case study the 1950s and 1960s, some aspects of this shared symbolic and social background: the French intellectual habitus and French literary culture as central elements in the reproduction of the French intellectual field.

Beginning in the 1950s and 1960s, a new generation of thinkers, composed of the social- and human-scientific intelligentsia[4] and of avant-garde writers representing the *nouveau roman*, rose into positions of power in the French intellectual field. This succession coincided with a redefinition of the relationship between state-created and market-created intellectuals. The former, mainly academics and writers, were reproduced through the French Republican education system in elite schools such as the Écoles Normales Supérieures, the breeding ground of the local intellectual elite since their establishment at the end of the eighteenth century.[5] Market-created intellectuals, on the other hand, came into being with the expansion of, and qualitative changes in, the cultural market, the audience, the press, and publishing starting from the 1950s. Thus, the human and social sciences as new academic disciplines and intellectual fame as a legitimate cultural resource emerged simultaneously. To label this period, as Régis Debray has,[6] the age of media, creates a misleading picture in its excessive emphasis on cultural mediators.

In terms of cultural production, as young scholars and writers turned from the traditional humanities and from psychological literature to the developing human and social sciences and avant-garde literature, a conversion of schemas and ideas also took place. This second generation of postwar intellectuals developed a scientific style, structuralism, which spread to a growing student audience for whom the new and dangerous also had to be antibourgeois.[7] Literary scholars, such as Gérard Genette, moved from traditional literary history to literary theory; linguists, such as A. J. Greimas, from lexicology to linguistic theory and semiology; and philosophers, such as Pierre Bourdieu and Michel Foucault, to sociology and history, respectively. Armed with concepts and theories provided by linguistics, authors like Foucault and Julia Kristeva challenged traditional literary and philosophical culture.

In order to challenge the dominant Sartrian model of the so-called total intellectual, a generalist who combined politics with literature, journalism, and philosophy,[8] members of the new intellectual generation had to fulfill certain intrinsic requirements. This was especially true in humanities disciplines that did not prepare for professions and whose social function involved mainly the transmission of a cultural heritage. Those working in these areas had to conform to the inherited conventions of French intellectual legitimacy, an imperative frequently overlooked by outside observers. As Vincent Descombes has put it: "The great undertaking of each generation is to settle the debts handed down by the preceding one. *The sins of the fathers are visited upon the sons.*"[9]

The emotional need of the new aristocracy of culture to be part of the legacy was reflected in its members' ambitions, often connected with venerated institutions that embodied this tradition. Although anthropologist Claude Lévi-Strauss regretted never having written a novel or composed an opera, his description of his subjective aspirations with respect to the Collège de France, the most esteemed academic institution in France, is revealing:

> I was seized with a sudden desire. Nowhere else, I thought, would I rather spend my days than in the spacious, silent, and secret rooms, which still retained the aura of the mid-nineteenth-century library or laboratory. That was how I saw the Collège de France I aspired to enter: the workplace of Claude Bernard, Ernest Renan.[10]

For this second postwar generation, it was precisely science and objectivity which enabled the question of one's relationship with the past to be settled. Lévi-Strauss, the founder of structural anthropology, challenged Sartre with the authority of science, which had made a business out of finding the inevitabilities in human life. The movie director Jean-Luc Godard criticized precisely this tendency in the thinking of the most visible intellectuals of the moment:

> It [a text by Pier Paolo Pasolini on film] is beautiful, like [Michel] Foucault's text on [a painting by Diego] Velázquez. But I fail to see its necessity. Other things could be equally true. If I do not like Foucault, it is because he says: "At this period of time people thought such and such, and starting from this date, people thought that" . . . why not, but can one be so sure? It is precisely for this reason that we make movies, in order to prevent a future Foucault from affirming things like that with such presumption. Sartre does not escape this reproach either.[11]

This imperative of finding certainties, "structures," at any price, was, according to Godard, coupled with another requirement, alienation from real life. Roland Barthes's work *Système de la mode* (1967) exemplified this faith, this habit of rationalizing: "All this makes me think about Barthes's book on fashion. It is unreadable for one simple reason. Because Barthes reads a phenomenon which has to be seen and felt because it is *worn*, thus *experienced*."[12] Science, and more precisely, linguistics, inspired the brightest stars of the 1960s: Barthes, Jacques Derrida, and Foucault. In this sense, they were Lévi-Strauss's followers. Science also permitted the esteemed role of the intellectual to be reproduced. The idealized myth of the human- and social-scientific intelligentsia as a scientific avant-garde was a self-perception that organized the behavioral strategies of individuals.[13] Popularized scientific discourse enabled the requirements of the dual model of cultural dynamics to be fulfilled via an aggressive and even arbitrary redefinition of intellectual activity and its value hierarchies.

Fulfilling the internal demands of the French cultural heritage gave the new generation the authority to oust Sartre, to reject resolution of the conflicts between intellectual and political commitment, and to reinvent the man or woman of letters. In the 1960s, Sartre's philosophy became too humanistic; that is, it did not permit the radicalization necessary for scientization. His philosophy was considered too loose, not rigid enough. Sartre's discourse was seen as lagging behind modernity in its vocabulary: identification followed a dual model of culture. Lévi-Strauss was idolized while Sartre was ridiculed.

Continually updating the collective habitus was both a subjective and an objective requirement for legitimate symbolic creation because the challenge of past achievements had to be met; bulimia[14] was a central feature of intellectual activity. Bulimia was a sign of a high level of dynamism. In practice, bulimia became eclecticism as individuals combined all intellectual goods to be found at a given moment that corresponded to the cultural practices and restrictions relative to the individuals' positions.[15] This symbolic characteristic stemmed from well-known structural features of the French intellectual field that permitted structured change to take place: first, a high level of interaction between the two poles of the field, the academic and the literary; second, centralization within a relatively restricted geographical area, Paris; third, relatively high and dense population; fourth, rapid circulation of models and ideas, which is related to highly differentiated reciprocal emulation and transcoding mechanisms; fifth, relatively homogeneous intellectual training of individuals and a fund of knowledge tied to literary culture and the Écoles Normales Supérieures; and sixth, a common ideal, the man or woman of letters, challenged constantly by numerous symbolic subcodes, such as the discourses of politics, journalism, and science.

However, in the 1960s, this dominant habitus also evolved as internal channels of ascension relative to both the literary and university fields began to be challenged by the expansion of an intermediary sector. The media and cultural journalism made possible accumulation of financial gains and cultural fame with less investment, and, in fact, dislocated the dynamics of the intellectual field, breaking the previous regularities.

The internal division of the field, which is both a symbolic and institutional space, reflected a more general structural tension between a declining literary culture—embodied by the man or woman of letters—representing a relatively uncodified field of activity, literature, and a more highly codified one, scientific discourse, along with ascending scientific culture. The symbiosis of these two partly contradictory dimensions—that is, the interplay of the *littérateur* and the *savant* as ideals of cultural production—combined with the expansion in volume of the whole intellectual field, made possible, in the 1950s, the radical detachment of young thinkers from the dominant models. It resulted in the creation of new models which fulfilled the internal requirements of legitimacy. Young intellectuals such as Bourdieu, Derrida, and Foucault combined the institutional signs of the legitimate intellectual[16] and those of the marginal academic. They were able to take advantage of the rising value of celebrity as a cultural resource. As a French journalist and writer observed, "ideas are now on the market."[17]

With the development of this market of ideas and the subsequent decline of philosophical and literary culture in school programs, a gradual modification in cultural dynamics in favor of audiovisual culture and media-culture took place. As one example of this transformation, partly in response to technological innovations in cultural production, a side industry of cultural video films sprang up, as the following advertisement for Scherzo publishers indicates. The photographs of some of the great thinkers, Pierre Bourdieu, Jacques Derrida, Edmond Jabès, and Claude Lévi-Strauss, accompanied the advertisement:[18]

You know their works . . . now discover the men! Presented by *La Sept*, "Contemporary Profiles" presents, on film, these enlightened minds of our time. They respond to the testimony and interpellations of those whose lives or work they have influenced. From their responses, rich, profound, and often surprising portraits emerge through which the man behind the author and thinker is revealed. A live presence, documentary evidence that cannot be found on television: A new means to create for yourself a living archive. At last, video cassettes that you have every reason to include in your library. "Intelligence and television are not necessarily incompatible." These films, rich in content, finally show your VCR its true vocation: that of intelligent tool, the source of live, current documentation, not to be found elsewhere. These video cassettes are very simply presented, suitable for the library of today's "gentleman." You may order these directly by mail at a special "publisher's price," very reasonable for material of this quality, currently available only at Scherzo Publishers.

This example demonstrates how cultural consumption shaped and was shaped by a gendered book culture that cultivated specific conceptions of distinction and value.

It is in the sociohistorical context sketched above, with the structural tensions created by the dynamic between the *littérateur* and the *savant*, that the emergence of new variations in the French intellectual habitus—that is, the simultaneous rise of movements such as "structuralism" and "poststructuralism" and of groups such as the human- and social-scientific intelligentsia—must be analyzed. The symbolic dominance of human and social scientific discourse has not been reproduced since because, among other factors, of the absence of teaching of the social sciences at the pre-university level, the strength of literary culture, and changes in the interests of the young public, notably the rise of an audiovisual culture.[19] More general mechanisms of cultural reproduction have to be examined in order to fully understand under what conditions the second postwar generation of intellectuals succeeded the first generation.

## INTERGENERATIONAL SYMBOLIC TRANSMISSION

*Mystery is not one of the possibilities of reality. Mystery is what is necessary for reality to exist.*

—*MAGRITTE*

Sartre and Lévi-Strauss were the main representatives of the two intellectual generations, the literary and the scientific, in the 1960s. These generations engaged in numerous symbolic struggles beginning in the 1950s.[20] Precisely because they had different gods, the representatives of "structuralism" and "poststructuralism" were considered legitimate successors to Sartrian philosophy. If they had shared Sartrian philosophy's precepts, the structuralists and poststructuralists would have been mere followers. Very important social and psychological incentives prompted the second postwar generation of intellectuals to perceive itself in terms of filiation and rebellion against the previous dominant worldview represented by Sartre. As such, joining this intellectual generation implied an act of faith. This conception of one's own role as an intellectual enabled one to comply with an order of succession and with certain rules relative to symbolic domination. These rules of symbolic domination were related to the fact that the dominant habitus had been defined by men who had a certain formal and informal education. Not surprisingly, questions of ethnicity, gender, and religion were absent. According to the rules, surpassing the previous generation could be done only in relatively specific ways. As "techniques" do not exist in the humanities and philosophy in the same way as they exist in science, and as the members of the new generation were trained in the classical humanities, the only way to succeed Sartre in the 1950s and 1960s was to propagate the fresh, new start provided by science, that is, by something universal and disinterested, with new concepts and theories and the role of the *savant* that went with them. More general restrictions on succession were imposed by the very nature of legitimate symbolic domination.

Symbolic domination means domination by and through symbols. Domination is the likelihood of being obeyed, following Max Weber's definition. Symbolic violence is mediated and made possible by symbolic credit: one's "due." Symbolic credit has as much to do with values, trust, respect, and reputation, which are often results of a lifetime of work, as with gender, organizational structures, or socioeconomic class. It is that which is self-evident, tacitly agreed upon—for instance, via the canons of a discipline or of a subculture. It may be the immediate value given to Saussure in the 1950s and 1960s, or the reputation of intellectuals like Lévi-Strauss. This credit also has to do with the social valuation of certain institutions like the Écoles Normales Supérieures, the alumni of which are objects of added value; of certain noble traditions like philosophy, in the classical humanities, or structural linguistics, in the social and human sciences; or of certain authors and their works, considered classics. In short, credit is attributed according to a gerontocratic order.

In contrast to practices that constitute strongly codified and structured social worlds, the French intellectual field is characterized by unregistered trademarks and numerous quali-signs (such as "philosopher"), backed by institutional charisma. This charisma is the highest mark of intellectual excellence, the specific social resource over which individuals and groups struggle. It is a personalized quality that is manifest in extraordinary and undefinable deeds. It is the opposite of everything that is codified and explicated directly in manuals or indirectly in the reconstruction of canons such as those of the history of philosophy or sociology. Codified criteria are transmitted from one generation to another explicitly and unequivocally through objectification. Because they are accessible to everybody, they are always considered inferior to the unique and personal qualities necessary for the creation of ideas. In this sense, there is a sharp contrast between these criteria of excellence and those relative to specialized disciplines, which emphasize mastery of specific techniques. From the point of view of tradition and innovation, of intergenerational transmission of cultural values, and of the future patterns of innovation, the problem is how to transmit and protect the value of this charisma, that is, to reproduce in time the essence of intellectual activity, creation, which is by definition unique and singular. Charisma, following Max Weber,[21] is transmitted through routinization, by the integration of acts and qualities considered as extraordinary into the everyday world.

But rarity exists only in relation to other acts, qualities, or miraculous works.

In the French intellectual world, rarity could have to do with having been the student or follower of a hero, and thus being endowed with a patronymic or associated with an eponymous hero like Claude Lévi-Strauss, who symbolized intellectual modernity; with having published in a prestigious review like *Critique* that presented reviews of French and foreign publications, or with having defended a thesis at a young age in a highly respected institution. All these acts give intellectuals symbolic credit and contribute to their individual pedigrees. Another general criterion is precocity, tied to temporal structures, that is, to the rhythms of cultural production and consecration. Precocity is often coupled with a pretentious style. Consider Derrida's over one-hundred-page introduction to Edmund Husserl's *Origin of Geometry*. Writing this kind of inflated introduction to a master's work is still, in this environment, an accepted way of showing one's talents. In other contexts, where philosophical culture does not have the same status, modesty is *de rigueur* for a beginner. To the individual who embodies these qualities, rarity thus means becoming the object of transfer of credit, trust, or respect; that is, the object of social and psychological investments on the part of others. In the 1950s and 1960s, Lévi-Strauss provided an excellent example of this. Rarity involves accumulating exterior signs of superiority: to be, for diverse reasons, destined to stand out.

Separating the individual from the social involves going back to individual methodologism or sociologism and psychologizing charisma, a frequent criticism addressed to Weber.[22] In contrast, conceptualizing charisma in terms of symbolic credit and intellectual value enables us to look at charisma as a cultural phenomenon. Creative power is transmitted through the collective construction of certain extraordinary acts and qualities which are only partially and negatively codified. Most often, qualities collectively invented have their sole *raison d'être* in the numerous individual and group interests connected to their existence. Reproduction occurs through the transmission of belief in the existence of certain qualities to individuals (the elect) whose interest in believing in this existence is structural. In the 1960s, these qualities could be "rigorous," "systematic," and "scientific." But these qualities have to be relatively vague, thus accessible to those designated. Only in this way can they can be effectively transmitted to the next generation.

The dominant academics and writers, who comprise a symbolic gerontocracy, represent traditions and the weight of history. They are one of the privileged specialized groups in intergenerational transmission not only of values but also of aspirations and ambitions. Indeed, Sartre's intellectual achievements could be reversed in the French intellectual field of the 1950s and 1960s only by an equally panoramic and fundamental endeavor, the structuralist project. It had its canons—language and structure instead of subject and freedom—and prophets—Lévi-Strauss, instead of Sartre, as its figurehead. The originality of these generations has to do with the evolving system of symbolic and material transmission within the French intellectual field. Dominant intellectuals transfer symbolic power by presenting youth, the privileged stratum of transfers of credit, under the aegis of the old. Nobody really knows *what* they transmit, but in fact what they transmit is, from the point of view of creation, altogether secondary. What is transmitted can be advice, invitations to publish, personal relations, or other services. But it is the fact that dominant intellectuals serve as guarantors that is crucial for access to dominant positions. In contrast to a shoemaker, whose power (can this term even be used?) derives from a practical function, the power of dominant intellectuals seems to derive mostly from the fact that nobody really knows what they do. Symbols of something important that surpasses the comprehension of laymen, they are the flesh and blood representatives of timelessness, the future marble busts of hallowed sites of memory.[23]

For professionals of the symbolic, what is common or ordinary can be reproduced by more or less general standards and criteria; what stays outside such transmission is worthy of being called charisma, that is, something abstract which stirs the imagination. The function of many academic and literary rituals is to impress through form and to maintain the illusion of an undefinable excellence, legitimate because it is universal. Symbolic artifacts such as gifts or charisma are culturally created. From the very beginning, they start to develop a life of their own and to affect the actions of individuals. Distance guarantees the aura of magic.

But the illusion is effective because of the multiple material and symbolic interests of the individuals implicated in its reproduction. Their interests, like those of the politicians and pollsters who define public opinion, is to reproduce and reinforce the constitutive illusion. The magical power of the cultural resource is sustained by multiple processes the purpose of which is to promote and keep up a subjective, intuitive, inexplicable—in a word, magical[24]—relationship to this valued cultural resource. Paradoxically, subjectification, as a specific cultural operator, offers the surest means—because it imposes itself in silence and imposes silence (tacit acceptance)—to reproduce this intellectual excellence over time. Through subjectification, the criteria of this excellence will stay in a definitive position of extraterritoriality as something undefinable.

While ambitions are transmitted through education, outcomes can only be individual, subjective works. The ways in which the signs of excellence are combined with the rules of accessibility to works fulfilling the criteria of excellence are context-bound. For intellectuals, the problem is always how to show and affirm the existence of these qualities without falling into vulgarity and thus violating the fragile rules of worthiness. The signs of intellectual excellence are most often created in the struggles for recognition between diverse groups, anxious to promote others in order to promote themselves. In the French intellectual field, this unspoken complicity united the heterogeneous group of intellectuals that formed the new generation in the 1960s. Their mutual recognition served to create the extraordinary, a cocktail of bluff, eclecticism, and obscurity. Theoretical sophistication sufficient to surpass the previous generation was an *illusio* to which all the challengers in the field were attached. Even the most virulent denouncers, whose strategy[25] was to appear to distinguish themselves from the crowd by revealing the opportunism or conformism of the others, bought into it. Recognition followed specific rules of etiquette, which were only exceptionally violated.[26]

A critique of French academic and literary rituals will not "bite" in today's cycle of transmission because it would be integrated in this cycle, and would in the last instance only reinforce the illusion in which symbolic work is grounded in this context. However, it is possible to produce, from a distance, cumulative and critical information about the processes that uphold the specific interests, that maintain the illusion, even if the observer intervenes, following Weber's image, *post festum*, after the bottles have been emptied and the lights put out.

I have analyzed some aspects of the reproduction of the French intellectual field in the 1950s and 1960s. The dominant French intellectual habitus was defined by intellectuals, mostly men who had a specific kind of informal and formal education. The new intellectual nobility combined seemingly contradictory aims: on the one hand, popularizing scientific work, which many conceived in structuralist binary form, and, on the other hand, radicalizing political discourse. But the new nobility also reproduced and updated French literary and philosophical culture and its habits of thinking. These had included a penchant for the beauty of literary and philosophical form (conceptual romanticism or theoreticism) and an aversion to anything too empirical or technical. By colonizing the media, publishing theoretical essays, and creating new career combinations, the second postwar generation of French intellectuals partly renewed the traditional means by which the local intellectual nobility had been formed.

## NOTES

The term *habitus*, developed by a variety of authors such as Émile Durkheim, Max Weber, Norbert Elias, and Pierre Bourdieu, refers to a mechanism that enables individuals to adapt themselves to social life and "do the right things" without necessarily having explicitly learned them. For an analysis, see for instance Niilo Kauppi, *The Politics of Embodiment: Habits, Power, and Pierre Bourdieu's Theory* (Frankfurt am Main and New York: Peter Lang, 2000). By *culture* I mean shared understanding, common ways of doing and looking at things. See for example Howard S. Becker, "Culture: A Sociological View," *The Yale Review* 72 (Summer 1982): 518. Culture is also the object of struggles between individuals and groups striving to define cultural canons and values so as to favor their own assets.

1. By *intellectual field* is meant the institutional positions and discourses occupied by individuals considered as being intellectuals. Definitions of the intellectual abound. What they have in common is that an intellectual is usually a learned individual who takes part in public debate. In France, the history of the intellectual is tied to that of another cultural role, the writer. See for instance Alain Viala, *Naissance de l'écrivain: Sociologie de la littérature à l'âge classique* (Paris: Éditions de Minuit, 1985).

2. David Pace. *Claude Lévi-Strauss: The Bearer of Ashes* (London: Routledge and Kegan Paul, 1983).

3. Alan Sheridan, *Michel Foucault: The Will to Truth* (London and New York: Tavistock Publications, 1980).

4. For this concept see Wolf Lepenies, *Between Literature and Science: The Rise of Sociology*, trans. R .J. Hollingdale (Cambridge: Cambridge University Press, 1988), 7.

5. See for instance Robert J. Smith, *The École Normale Supérieure and the Third Republic* (Albany: State University of New York Press, 1982).

6. See for instance Régis Debray, *Le Pouvoir intellectuel en France* (Paris: Gallimard, 1986).

7. Tony Judt, *Past Imperfect: French Intellectuals, 1944–1956* (Berkeley: University of California Press, 1992), 299. For an English language presentation of the ideas of some of the most important thinkers, cf. R. Macksey and E. Donato, eds., *The Language of Criticism and the Sciences of Man: The Structuralist Controversy* (Baltimore, Md.: Johns Hopkins University Press, 1970). For an alternative point of view to intellectual production, see Pierre Bourdieu, *The Field of Cultural Production: Essays on Art and Literature*, ed. Randal Johnson (New York: Columbia University Press, 1993) and Niilo Kauppi, *The Making of an Avant-Garde: "Tel Quel"* (Berlin/New York: Mouton de Gruyter, 1994).

8. Anna Boschetti, *The Intellectual Enterprise: Sartre and "Les Temps Modernes,"* trans. Richard C. McCleary (Evanston, Ill.: Northwestern University Press, 1988).

9. Vincent Descombes. *Modern French Philosophy*, trans. L. Scott-Fox and J. M. Harding (Cambridge: Cambridge University Press, 1980), 3, emphasis in original.

10. Claude Lévi-Strauss, *Conversations with Claude Lévi-Strauss*. With Didier Eribon. Trans. Paula Wissing (Chicago: University of Chicago Press, 1991).

11. Jean-Luc Godard, "Luttes sur deux fronts: Conversations avec Jean-Luc Godard." *Cahiers du cinéma* 194 (1967): 13–28, 66–70.

12. Godard, "Luttes sur deux fronts," p. 21.

13. For an analysis of these strategies in another context, see J. M. Lotman, L. I. Ginsburg, and B. A. Uspenskij, *The Semiotics of Russian Cultural History*, ed. Alexander D. Nakhimovsky and Alice Stone Nakhimovsky (Ithaca, N.Y.: Cornell University Press, 1985), 94.

14. To use Lévi-Strauss's coinage. Lévi-Strauss, *Conversations with Claude Lévi-Strauss*, 91.

15. These restrictions followed the criteria of reception of certain parts of the public and of inherited literary culture.

16. Alumni of the École Normale Supérieure and *agrégé/é* in philosophy forming elements of a heritage shared by individuals having these same properties.

17. Jean-Marie Domenach, *Enquête sur les idées contemporaines* (Paris: Seuil, 1981), 111.

18. Advertisement for Scherzo Publishers, *Libération*, 13 December 1990, 49.

19. The effects of literary culture include the difficulty in publishing social scientific works in the cultural press once their novelty has faded. Cf. also *Les Pratiques culturelles des français* (Paris: La Documentation française, 1989).

20. Cf. Pace, *Claude Lévi-Strauss*, 109–17.

21. Max Weber, *Economy and Society*, trans. Ephraim Fischoff et al. (Berkeley: University of California Press, 1978), 1144.

22. Cf. for instance Edward Shils, "Charisma, Order, and Status," *American Sociological Review* 30 (1965): 199–213.

23. See Pierre Nora, ed., *Les Lieux de mémoire.* 7 vols. (Paris: Gallimard, 1984–1992).

24. For a more nuanced analysis of this, see Marcel Mauss, *A General Theory of Magic,* trans. Robert Brain (London: Routledge and Kegan Paul, 1972).

25. By *strategy* I mean the implementation of actions which are not necessarily conscious or premeditated but rather adapted to certain structural conditions, combining habitus and social structure.

26. A notorious case of violation of the rules of behavior that resulted in effect in a social suicide was the autobiography of Louis Althusser (*L'Avenir dure longtemps; suivi de, Les Faits* [Paris: Stock/IMEC, 1992]), one of the canonical thinkers of the new generation and the creator of structural Marxism. Written in the mental hospital where Althusser had been incarcerated after he strangled his wife, it revealed that his knowledge of Marxism was in reality quite superficial, and that he had read carefully only a few passages from Marx's work. In the 1960s, given the demand for radical ideas and Althusser's institutional position as a teacher of philosophy at the École Normale Supérieure of the rue d'Ulm in Paris, this rudimentary knowledge was sufficient to transform Althusser into the authority in the matter.

## 21. SOCIAL CONSTRUCTIONISM

### PHILOSOPHY FOR THE ACADEMIC WORKPLACE

### MARK BAUERLEIN

NOTWITHSTANDING THE DIVERSITY trumpeted by humanities departments these days, when it comes to conceptions of knowledge, one standpoint reigns supreme: social constructionism. It is a simple belief system, founded upon the basic proposition that knowledge is never true per se, but true relative to a culture, a situation, a language, an ideology, or some other social condition. Its catchphrases circulate everywhere, from committee meetings to conference programs. Truisms like "knowledge is a construct" and "there is no escaping contingency" echo in book prefaces and submission requests as if they were prerequisites to publication. Professors still waging a culture war against the Right live and work by the credo "Always historicize!" Neopragmatists, poststructuralists, Marxists, and feminists insist upon the situational basis of knowledge, taking the constructionist premise as a cornerstone of progressive thought and social reform. Graduate students mouth watchwords about subject-positions and antiessentialism as if they were undergoing an

Mark Bauerlein. "Social Constructionism: Philosophy for the Academic Workplace." Originally published in *Partisan Review* 68, no. 2 (Spring 2001): 228–41. Reprinted by permission.

initiation ceremony, meeting admissions requirements, and learning the tools of a trade. The standpoint functions as a party line, a tribal glue distinguishing humanities professors from their colleagues in the business school, the laboratory, the chapel, and the computing center, most of whom believe that at least some knowledge is independent of social conditions.

This is why it is a mistake to treat social constructionism as preached in the academy as a philosophy. Though the position sounds like an epistemology, filled with glib denials of objectivity, truth, and facts backed up by in-the-know philosophical citations ("As Nietzsche says . . ."), its proponents hold those beliefs most *un*philosophically. When someone holds a belief philosophically, he or she exposes it to arguments and evidence against it, and tries to mount arguments and evidence for it in return. But in academic contexts, constructionist ideas are not open for debate. They stand as community wisdom, articles of faith. When a critic submitted an essay to *PMLA* that criticized constructionists for not making arguments in their favor, the reader's report by Richard Ohmann rejoined that since constructionism is universally accepted by academic inquirers, there is no need to argue for it anymore. A phrase from Eve Kosofsky Sedgwick's *Epistemology of the Closet* nicely encapsulates this credulousness. Referring to Foucault's argument that "Western culture has placed what it calls sexuality in a more and more privileged relation to our most prized constructs of individual identity, truth, and knowledge," she proclaims she will proceed "in accord with Foucault's demonstration, whose results I will take to be axiomatic." This is a strangely empirical language to apply to Foucault. Only those already adopting a Foucauldian outlook would judge the speculations in *The History of Sexuality* to mark a "demonstration" that yields "results." No matter how controversial are Foucault's contentions, or how frequently historians, anthropologists, and philosophers have disputed them, to Sedgwick they are axioms, starting points for inquiry. Though Sedgwick suggests that Foucault's ideas have only a provisional justification—"I will take," she says—she still places them first, and never stops to ask, *What if they are wrong?* Such constructionist notions are so ingrained in the humanities mindset that nobody bothers to substantiate them at all. Save for a few near-retirement humanists and realist philosopher holdouts, academics embrace constructionist premises as catechism learning, axioms to be assimilated before one is inducted into the professoriate. To believe that knowledge is a construct, that truth, evidence, fact, and inference all fall under the category of local interpretation, and that interpretations are more or less right by virtue of the interests they satisfy is a professional habit, not an intellectual thesis.

One can prove the institutional nature of social constructionism by noting how easy it is to question. The weakness of social constructionism as an epistemology lies in the fact that one can agree with the bare premise that knowledge is a construct, but disagree with the conclusion that objectivity is impossible and that the contents of knowledge are dependent upon the social conditions of the knower. Of course, knowledge is constructed. It must be expressed in language, composed methodically, conceived through mental views, all of which are historically derived. Constructionists extend the fact that knowledge materializes in cognitive and linguistic structures which have social determinants into the belief that knowledge has no claim to transcend them. That knowledge cannot transcend the conditions of its origination stems from the notion that cognition is never innocent, that cognition has designs and desires shaping its knowledge-building process, that knowing always has an instrumental purpose. This human dimension is local and situational, constructionists argue, a historical context for knowledge outside of which the knowledge has no general warrant. Even the most ahistorical kinds of knowledge, the principles of logic, mathematics, and science, have a social basis, one obscured by thinkers who have abstracted that knowledge from its rightful setting and used it for purposes of their own. Thus Martin Heidegger claims in a well-known illustration in *Being and Time*, "Before Newton's laws were discovered, they were not 'true'. . . . Through Newton the laws became true." We only think the laws preceded Newton's conception because, Heidegger explains, that is how entities "show themselves."

But even though Newton's laws arose at a particular historical moment, in one man's mind, why assume that the laws are inextricable from that moment? There is abundant evidence for believing that the truth of Newton's laws is independent of Newton's mind, language, class, education, etc. The simple fact that persons of different languages and cultures implement those laws effectively implies their transhistorical and cross-cultural capacity. Engineers and physicists confirm the laws daily without any knowledge of Newton's circumstances. Three hundred years of experimentation and theory have altered Newton's laws only by restricting their physical purview. In short, Newton's laws have been justified in vastly different times and places. Yes, scientists and engineers have dehistoricized Newtonian knowledge, pared it down to a few set principles (nobody actually reads the *Principia*). But though abstract and expedient, the laws of Newtonian physics still have a truth-value, and that value is related not to Newton's world, but to how well the laws predict outcomes, how reliably they stand up to testing, how useful they are in physical domains.

To think otherwise is to deny the distinction between the contents of knowledge and the context of their emergence. This is an old logical mistake, namely, the genetic fallacy: the confusion of a theory's discovery with its justification. Social constructionists overlook this distinction between discovery (the circumstances of a theory's origin) and justification (the establishment of its truth). To them, the idea of separating truth from origin depletes thought of its historical reality, and ultimately smacks of formalist methods and mandarin motives. Constructionists grant that the discovery/justification point may be logically correct, but in slighting historical context, it can lead to a kind of neglect, whereby the abstract consideration of theories like Newton's laws allows us to forget, say, the race, class, and gender privileges that freed Newton to excogitate upon falling bodies. Epistemologists counter by saying that historical inquiry is one thing, truth-determination is another, but for scholars raised on Foucault and Rorty, the division is never so neat and clear. The history of scholarship itself reveals too many instances of ideas once thought to be true later exposed as alibis for social inequities, as having more institutional-use value than abstract-truth value. Only a punctual inventory of a theory's historical entanglements has saved scholars from misusing the theory, from fomenting its implicit and perhaps malignant politics. That is the real animus behind social constructionist commitments—not a philosophical belief about knowledge, but a moral obligation to social justice.

Take another familiar example, the popular study of literary theory by Terry Eagleton, *Literary Theory: An Introduction*, first published in 1983. The preface to Eagleton's readable discussion declares, "This book sets out to provide a reasonably comprehensive account of modern literary theory," and the chapter headings—"Phenomenology, Hermeneutics, Reception Theory," "Post-Structuralism," "Psychoanalysis"—suggest that a survey of competing schools of thought will follow. But in fact, the conceptual analysis is thin, the methodological description hasty. Instead, the book reads like a textbook case of commentary by genetic fallacy and ethical consequence. To the patient exposition of terms and concepts Eagleton prefers the oblique adumbration, as when he writes, "Leavis and Husserl both turn to the consolations of the concrete, of what can be known on the pulses, in a period of major ideological crisis [the post-World War I revolutions]." Expounding the poetics of this or that theory, Eagleton minimizes intellectual heritage and reckons ideas by their political affiliations. He attributes New Criticism to a Southern agrarian reaction to Northern industrialism, calling it "a full-blooded irrationalism, one closely associated with religious dogma . . . and with the right-wing 'blood and soil' politics of the agrarian movement." The intellectual fathers of New Critical aesthetics—Kant, Hegel, and Coleridge—play no role in this genesis. In the chapter on poststructuralism, Eagleton spends little time detailing the arguments of founding texts and instead strings together deconstructive platitudes—"Meaning, we might say, is thus never identical to itself"—and then summarizes, "Post-structuralism was a product of that blend of euphoria and disillusionment, liberation and dissipation, carnival and catastrophe, which was 1968." Again, a political context stands as source and explanation.

In turn, when assessing these theories, Eagleton focuses on their ethical results. New Critical method he reduces to "a recipe for political inertia, and thus for submission to the political status quo," one that licenses practitioners not to "oppose McCarthyism or further civil rights." Poststructuralism comes down to "a convenient way of evading such political questions [as Vietnam, Guatemala, Stalinism] altogether." How the definition of a poem as a verbal icon or as a play of signs kept one from storming the Columbia University administration building Eagleton does not say. But the fact that one could draw parallels, however factitious, between a formalist analysis that asked no political questions and a general political quietism suffices for Eagleton to indict New Criticism and deconstruction as reactionary bad faith. How one reads a poem and how one engages in political life are all of a piece. Daniel Bell may claim to be "a socialist in economics, a liberal in politics, and a conservative in culture," and the art historian Anthony Blunt may have counseled students to downplay politics in their studies, all the while serving as a postwar Soviet operative in England, but ultimately, Eagleton presses, inquirers have no latitude to modulate their actions, for there is no real disjunction between scholarship and social conduct, between teaching and voting. One cannot be a progressive on issues of, say, gun control and abortion rights and a conservative in matters of scholarly method.

*Literary Theory: An Introduction* hardly counts as a serious discussion of literary theory, but its tactics have come to dominate humanities criticism. Commentaries on ideological origins and ethical results far exceed conceptual analyses and logical expositions. Evaluating concepts and arguments by their political backgrounds and implications has become a disciplinary wont, a pattern of inquiry. It is the natural method of constructionist epistemology, the outlook that will not distinguish between a truth and its origination, which is to say the outlook that is not really an epistemology at all. It speaks an epistemological language, but it has no epistemological principles. This is one of the curiosities of social constructionism, and why people err in attacking it on epistemological grounds, that is, on grounds of truth, evidence, and objectivity. Constructionists affirm that truth is a construct, dependent upon the conditions of its discovery. This is a flat contradiction, since truth by definition is independent of the means by which it is discovered. If constructionists mean by "truth" merely "what passes for truth," then the contradiction disappears, but now we are no longer talking about truth in epistemological terms, but in historical terms, that which is accepted as truth in this or that time and place. The acceptance of something as true is one thing, the truth of that belief is another. Establishing the latter is a routine epistemological task. Documenting the former is a traditional historical endeavor, carried out by Gibbon as well as by Sedgwick. In this distinction lies the novelty of social constructionism: in a word, constructionism disregards it, mingling history and epistemology, fusing what is true and what passes for true, identifying discovery with justification.

For this reason, inquirers sensitive to such distinctions accuse constructionism of philosophical confusion and methodological incorrectness. Philosopher-antagonists like John Searle and Susan Haack express contempt for the logical credentials of constructionist arguments, while conservative critics like Roger Kimball mock their sophomoric relativism. But the continued popularity of the school of thought in the academy indicates that those charges, however accurate, miss the point. They rest upon standards of coherence and clarity that constructionists delimit as themselves constructs not binding to their own way of thinking. Besides, advocates aim to convince not by their dubious logic or their relativist beliefs. They do not subscribe to any foundations except the one which rules "There are no foundations." The concepts and distinctions that opponents attack them for mishandling, social constructionists have already negated. They commit the genetic fallacy time and again, but so what? Since they define knowledge as bound to the context of its construction, the genetic fallacy is not a mistake—it is a policy.

The real questions to put to social constructionists are not those of truth, but of tactics. Acknowledging the irrelevance of philosophical disputes, we must ask: If canons of logic do not apply to constructionist thinking, on what does it base its assertions? If all knowledge is bound by time and place, how does constructionist persuasion work outside *its* time and place? If discovery and justification are one, how does constructionist inquiry justify itself?

One answer may be found in the rhetorical patterns of constructionist statements. Because constructionist maxims are decreed so ritualistically in academic discourse, they tend to assume a customary verbal form, one whose import is often borne by seemingly non-substantive words and locutions. For example, in the following two citations, notice the word "surely." First, in a roundtable discussion on evidence in *PMLA* (1996), Stephen Orgel comments, "Surely historical evidence depends on interpretation. Even scientific evidence does." Second, in a *Christian Science Monitor* review of a book on the acceleration of modern life, Tom Regan writes, "*Faster* [the book under review] will help us think about the way we 'construct' time—for it surely is a construct." Time and evidence are the main objects in these sentences, but "surely" does most of the work. That historical and scientific evidence are interpretive and that time is a construct are, to say the least, complicated propositions. But the "surely" rules out any clarification or debate, and does so not on logical or definitional grounds, but on the grounds of the unfaltering surety of the speakers. "Surely" signifies not a premise or a piece of evidence, but an attitude. Orgel and Regan believe in what they say, and believe in it with certainty. Added to each proposition is a state of mind, an assurance that disallows objection. Marking the statements as dubitable only by wrongheaded people, "surely" automatically dismisses those who believe otherwise. Anybody who disagrees with the propositions faces the task of refuting them *and* surmounting the certitude of Orgel and Regan.

This excess of confidence is a key to social constructionist argumentation. The "surely" here is an explicit instance of the tacit, blank temerity of expression typical of the idiom. Given the breadth of constructionist ideas, proponents might submit them tentatively as speculations, hypotheses, or opinions, but in fact, this spirited confidence phrases them as bare simplicities whose contradiction is intellectually indefensible, and perhaps politically motivated. The aplomb turns the issue from the truth or falsity of the premises to the mindset of the antagonists. Since no enlightened mind would doubt the premises, dissent from them can only stem from the wrongheadedness of the dissenters. As the intentions of the other side come under scrutiny, the premises themselves remain untouched. A philosophical quarrel becomes a psychological speculation. Consider, for example, how these two statements take constructionist ideas for granted, and cast doubt on the temper of those who do not:

> nothing in today's colleges seems to have enraged traditionalists more than the idea of the contingency of knowledge.

> For after all, the pragmatist believes in the sufficiency of human practices and is not dismayed when those practices are shown to be grounded in nothing more (or less) than their own traditions and histories; the impossibility of tying our everyday meanings and values to meanings and values less local does not lead the pragmatist to suspect their reality, but to suspect the form of thought that would deny it.

The first citation, by Paul Lauter, comes from an afterword to the instructor's guide to *The Heath Anthology of American Literature*, in which Lauter reflects upon the canon, undergraduate education, and the contingent status of knowledge. Nowhere in the piece does Lauter demonstrate the contingency premise, nor does he mention any arguments against it. He simply assumes the former and pigeonholes anticontingency responses as rage. Again, the opponent's attitude substitutes for his reasoning, and because rage implies helplessness, Lauter's characterization suggests that there is no valid reason to counter the contingency premise. That someone would deny contingency dispassionately on epistemological grounds is out of the question.

The second citation, by Stanley Fish, appears in the afterword to a collection of essays on neopragmatism, and recites the same shift from philosophical debate to psychological inspection. The remarkable thing about the passage is how breezily Fish affirms this bullying maneuver. First, he asserts the impossibility of meanings and values transcending their locale. This "no transcendence" thesis is a logical necessity and/or an empirical given, period. Next, anybody who fails to recognize this fact is not just mistaken or confused, his entire "form of thought" is "suspect." When challenged by those who think that local meanings and values are "unreal," Fish's pragmatist does not counterargue *for* the reality of local meanings and values, but instead wonders whether his antagonist is ideologically blinded or psychologically disabled.

What could lead otherwise responsible academics to implement such narrow-minded, accusatory, cocksure tactics when it comes to constructionist ideas? How has constructionism licensed inquirers to abandon protocols of debate, specifically, the civility that requires learned combatants to listen to each other? Constructionist notions have become so patent and revered that their articulation need no longer happen, except as reminders to professors who stray from the party line (many utterances begin with "We must remember that . . ."). Those who raise objections soon find themselves trapped in debates shaped by us versus them forensics, enunciated in an idiom of brazen philosophical avowals and insinuations about the character of adversaries. Nonconstructionists feel not so much refuted as ostracized. The humanities become a closed society, captive to a weak epistemology with a mighty elocution.

This polarizing, personalizing rhetoric indicates that social constructionism has an institutional basis, not a philosophical, moral, or political one. It tramples on philosophical distinctions and practices an immoral mode of debate. Though it declares a political goal for criticism, it is not a political stance, for no political movement has issued from constructionist thinking. It has won few converts outside literature and "studies" departments, much less outside the university walls. Instead, what has emerged from social constructionism is not a philosophical school or a political position, but an institutional product, specifically, an outpouring of research publications, conference talks, and classroom presentations by subscribers. For many who have entered the humanities as teachers and researchers, social constructionism has been a liberating and serviceable implement of work, a standpoint that has enhanced the productivity of professors. It has provided academics with axioms and assurances necessary to their labors. Herein lies the secret of constructionism's success: the critical method that follows from constructionist premises has proven eminently conducive to the exigencies of teaching, lecturing, and publishing. In a word, it is the school of thought most congenial to current professional workplace conditions of scholars in the humanities.

The most obvious advantage constructionism provides lies in its territorial nature, for by undermining truth and objectivity, constructionism bolsters the humanities as an academic whole, carving out a space in the university for practices of interpretation and subjectivity. One can witness this turf function in critiques by literary and cultural theorists of their institutional competitors—the scientists. This cultural critique of science often goes by the name of "science studies," a project directed at the political subtleties of scientific practices—for example, the presence of ideologically charged metaphors in scientific discourse. Its goal is to reveal science itself as a construct, one especially dangerous in that it casts scientificity as neutral and *non*constructed. The institutional goal of science studies is to delimit the sciences to one knowledge domain, to show that they speak not for reality, but for certain constructions of reality. If the university is to reflect the different knowledges of the universe, then containing the purview of scientific knowledge to empirical practice preserves the humanities as a distinct way of knowing.

But while the defensive position of the humanities in the university promotes the use of social constructionism as a stock in trade, in fact, the pressures favoring constructionism are often more quotidian and prosaic than that of arts versus science competition. They affect professors individually, not as representatives of a department or an outlook; I mean the circumstances of graduate student aid, grant-giving, job-hiring, tenure, leave time, teaching load, and salary increases. Professors and graduate students have papers to grade, lectures to prepare, applications to evaluate, books to read, undergraduates to meet, and most importantly, essays and chapters to write. Their success rests in how well they handle students, maintain collegiality, and meet research expectations, with wellness frequently being measured by the number of students they attract, the number of committees on which they serve, and the number and girth of publications they produce. A school of thought whose practice accords neatly with the times and the money, numbers, and paperwork of academic labor becomes a material resource, especially in a field trading in words and ideas. If the methods of research and argument that follow from a set of terms and principles fit the schedules and competitions of professional life, subscribing to them marks an intellectual belief *and* a career decision.

At first sight, this attribution of an intellectual standpoint to institutional demands may appear reductive and tenuous. The hypothesis denigrates the reasons academics believe in this or that system and forecloses questions such as that of the genetic fallacy. But the goal here is to explain the popularity of constructionism, not its truth. Social constructionism as academic common sense needs to be analyzed. One prefers an institutional explanation to an intellectual one because this school of thought has settled into a critical dogma and adopted ad hominem tactics. Indeed, it is the fact that questions like the genetic fallacy one are *not* deliberated openly, that the cards are all stacked in favor of a constructionist answer, that makes one wonder about the state of the institution in which they are posed. When a school of thought has become so popular that it succeeds without really trying, it is time to interrogate the polity supporting it. The thing to do is to find concrete institutional situations that uncover how social constructionism helps professors function within academe.

One of the more intense and complicated moments of academic life is the tenure meeting. There, behind closed doors, senior faculty decide the fate of a junior colleague. The candidate looks upon the decision as a do-or-die threshold, with success meaning security for life, failure meaning years of scrapping at adjunct posts, or expulsion from the teaching ranks forever. Senior faculty regard their vote as a vote on the livelihood of a colleague, in comparison to which any objections they have to the record shrink to pettiness. Outside reviewers asked to evaluate the research materials all too often treat their task with obvious distaste, sending to the department perfunctory letters filled with the standard clichés about brilliance and potential. Administrators oversee each step of the process with one question in mind: "How will this look in a courtroom, or in a *Lingua Franca* article?" Economic hardship, legal fears, professor burnout, and personal feelings all conspire to make the tenure meeting a dreadful affair, in which supporters overpraise and sentimentalize the candidate while critics descend into a surly skepticism. Meanwhile, the candidate huddles in a paranoid freeze, six years of graduate school and six years of junior teaching adjudicated by a two-hour colloquy down the hall.

Of course, people and institutions always find ways of coping. Of late, at many universities senior faculty and administrators have discovered a mechanism that frees the decision-makers of responsibility and isolates for the aspirant *the* hurdle for advancement: the book. As long as the candidate proves an inoffensive teacher and a reasonable department member, only one question sits on the meeting room table: Is the research project finished? If the junior colleague has a book in hand or an acceptance letter from the director of a university press, tenure is a fait accompli. If the work remains in manuscript, promising but incomplete, no promotion. That is the employment equation. Tenure has boiled down to a six-year composition scheme. Junior faculty now face a demystified production schedule, and senior faculty enter the tenure meeting with a one-checkbox form in their heads. No more messy discussions about quality. No more anxiety about whether the department has enough discernment, or too much. Administrators have an objective criterion to point to should any outsiders challenge the proceedings. Judgment has been externalized, handed over to university editorial boards. The assistant professor has inherited a job task that takes priority over teaching students, that is, marketing his revised dissertation to academic press editors.

While the book criterion has clarified the tenure process, it has fundamentally altered the nature of scholarship in the humanities. The system discourages research that is time-consuming, that involves tracking down information secreted in libraries and archives, that may yield numerous dead ends before a discovery occurs. Junior faculty must envision book-length projects that can be executed well in advance of the crucial tenure meeting, which takes place in the middle of the candidate's sixth year of employment. With university presses sometimes taking two years to decide upon a manuscript, pretenure scholars have three and a half years from the time of their hiring to complete their opus. Books that require lengthier inquiries do not get written. Recent hires acclimating themselves to a new campus, building up their teaching repertoire, and learning the ropes of department service do not have time to bury themselves in manuscript collections or to pursue dubious trails of evidence. Clear-sighted professors will avoid empirical methods, aware that it takes too much time to verify propositions about culture, to corroborate facts with multiple sources, to consult primary documents, and to compile evidence adequate to inductive conclusions. They will seek out research models whose premises are already in place, not in need of proof, and whose exercise proceeds without too much deliberation over inquiry guidelines. Speculation will prevail over fact-finding, theory and politics over erudition. Inquirers will limit their sources to a handful of primary texts and broach them with a popular academic theory or through a sociopolitical theme. In sum, facing a process that issues in either lifetime security or joblessness, junior faculty will relax their scruples and select a critical practice that fosters their own professional survival, a practice that offers timely shortcuts to publication and still enjoys institutional sanction.

Social constructionism is one such expedient method. It has widespread support in the humanities, and so practitioners need waste no paragraphs validating it. It scoffs at empirical notions, chastising them as "naive positivism" and freeing scholars from having to prove the truth of constructionist premises and generalizations. It lightens the evidentiary load, affirming that an incisive reading of a single text or event is sufficient to illustrate a theoretical or historical generality. Objectivity as an ideal collapses, for while objectivity requires that one acknowledge opposing arguments and refute them on logical or empirical grounds, constructionism merely asks that inquirers position themselves as a subject in relation to other subject-positions. True, constructionism proposes to study phenomena as historical constructs, a proposal entailing a method of enumerating historical particulars and their convergence in this or that object. But in fact, constructionist analysis typically breaks the object down into theoretical, political, and (a few) historical constituents, most of which are common currency in academic parlance. In analyzing the text or event as a construct, inquirers suspend the whole question of the reality of the thing and the truth of the construction. All that counts is the particular version of the thing, and with no objective standard by which to measure the version, the laborious process of justification dissolves.

Last month a scholarly journal asked me to assess a submission on Jacques Lacan's adoption of certain semiotic principles of Charles Sanders Peirce. After reading the essay, I recommended publication, but added that Lacan largely misconstrued Peirce's arguments and that the author needed to discuss the misrepresentations. He replied that whether Lacan was right or wrong was beside the point. He was only interested in how Lacan "appropriated" Peirce. To focus on whether Lacan understood Peirce correctly would sway the discussion from Lacan's creative uses of Peircean ideas, he said. Of course, the author's defense was epistemologically dubious, but it was institutionally beneficial. Although it put the author in the position of purveying Lacan's misconstruction of Peirce uncritically, it simplified his task enormously, saving him the trouble of checking Lacan's appropriations against Peirce's voluminous, difficult corpus. If only conservative evaluators would agree to the constructedness of Lacan's notions, not their truth, then the essay could proceed to publication.

Apologias like this one are rampant in the humanities, and the books and articles that they enable flood the scholarly marketplace. University press catalogues, booknotes and ads in periodicals, and "list of contributors" pages in journals announce these publications as breakthough efforts and necessary reading, but despite the praise, most of them soon disappear into the library stacks never to be heard from again. They are hastily conceived and predictably argued, and notwithstanding the singularity promised on their dust jackets, they are all of a type. They begin with approved constructionist premises, bolster them with arguments from authority ("According to Richard Rorty . . ."), and attach them to standard generalities about power, race, and gender. They vary only in their subject matter, the texts and events selected for commentary. They also suffer from the stylistic and design flaws characteristic of scholarship pushed into production too quickly. Last year, I read six book-length manuscripts for university presses, five of them by junior faculty. All five I returned to the press with detailed instructions for developmental editing. The authors possessed considerable intelligence and earnest motives, but they obviously tried to compose too fast. Sentences were unpolished and contained uniform expressions. Transitions were jumpy and casual, as if the chapters succeeded one another with "Now, let's look at . . ." The introductions were elliptical and rambling, as if the authors had not yet settled the question of what concerns the projects were aimed at resolving.

But however rough and incoherent, such manuscripts often make it into print and the authors win promotions. This is the research result of the productivity requirements of the profession. Junior faculty scramble to get dissertations published before their time, and the market is saturated with scholarly ephemera. Younger humanities professors no longer spend ten years investigating a subject, sharpening their theses, and refining their prose. Lengthy archival studies and careful erudite readings no longer appear. Career trajectories of figures like René Girard, M. H. Abrams, Paul de Man, and Meyer Shapiro are eschewed, for none of those talents produced enough work early in their professional lives to merit tenure under the present system. Penalized for selecting long-term projects, assistant professors have too little time to embark upon studies such as *The Mirror and the Lamp*.

This book-for-tenure requirement affects professors primarily at research institutions, but the general trend it represents—the acceleration of scholarship—reaches into all areas of academic life. Whenever faculty observe annual salary increases tied to their productivity for the year, and whenever graduate students face tuition support packages due to expire after four years, they will opt for a method of inquiry that ensures their professional livelihood. Whenever academic press editors favor topical culture studies over archival research, ambitious scholars will follow practices that help them keep pace with intellectual current events. Whenever hiring committees and funding agencies emphasize their interest in innovative, nontraditional forms of inquiry, applicants will fashion themselves accordingly, mindful of the ever more tenuous line between the avant-garde and the old hat. In each case, a commitment to painstaking induction and catholic learning proves disastrous.

This is the bare and banal advantage of social constructionism: it saves time. Truth, facts, objectivity—those require too much reading, too many library visits, too much time soliciting interlibrary loan materials, scrolling through microfilm records, double-checking sources, and looking beyond academic trends that come and go. A philosophy that discredits the foundations of such time-consuming research is a professional blessing. It is the belief-system of inquirers who need an alibi for not reading the extra book, traveling to the other archives, or listening to the other point of view. This is why constructionism is the prevailing creed in the humanities today. It is the epistemology of scholarship in haste, of professors under the gun. As soon as the humanities embraced a productivity model of merit, empiricism and erudition became institutional dead ends, and constructionism emerged as the method of the fittest. Scholars may have initially embraced constructionism as a philosophical position, but the evolution of constructionism into a brash institutional maneuvering indicates that it now functions as a response to a changing labor environment. How unfortunate that humanities faculty did not fight back against the productivity standard as soon as it arose and insist that scholars need time to read, time to reflect, time to test ideas in the classroom and at conferences if they are to come up with anything lasting. What a shame that they were able to concoct a mode of thought that cooperated with the quantification system, a plan of survival that now stands as the academic wisdom of the age.

## WORKS CITED

Eagleton, Terry. *Literary Theory: An Introduction.* Minneapolis: University of Minnesota Press, 1983.

Fish, Stanley. "Truth and Toilets: Pragmatism and the Practices of Everyday Life." In *The Revival of Pragmatism: New Essays on Social Thought, Law, and Culture,* ed. Morris Dickstein. Durham, N.C.: Duke University Press, 1998.

Heidegger, Martin. *Being and Time.* Trans. John Macquarrie and Edward Robinson. New York: Harper, 1962.

Lauter, Paul. Afterword to *Instructor's Guide to The Heath Anthology of American Literature.* Boston: Houghton Mifflin, 1994.

Orgel, Stephen. "The Status of Evidence: A Roundtable." *PMLA* 111, no. 1 (January 1996): 7–31.

Regan, Tom. Review of *Faster: The Acceleration of Just About Everything,* by James Gleick. *Christian Science Monitor,* 26 August 1999.

Sedgwick, Eve Kosofsky. *Epistemology of the Closet.* Berkeley: University of California Press, 1990.

## 22. BAD WRITING

### D. G. MYERS

BAD ACADEMIC WRITING is nothing new. Back in 1912, the critic Brander Matthews damned the scholarship of his day for its "endless quotations and endless citations and endless references," its "entangled" facts, its shameless taste for "interminable controversy over minor questions," its careless assumption that every reader had an "acquaintance with the preceding stages of the discussion."

But though it still commits these faults more often than not, bad academic writing nowadays has become something worse than an aesthetic offense. Matthews may have been right to complain about his contemporaries' neglect of style. Academic writing in our own time, however, exhibits a disregard, not merely for style, but for truth. Once upon a time, no matter how badly they wrote, scholars imagined that they were contributing to knowledge. But no longer. Much of the scholarship now published in the humanities—primarily in English and comparative literature, but increasingly in history, musicology, art history, and religious studies—has no other purpose than to confirm the scholar's own status and authority. It is not a contribution to knowledge, but to political power.

Consider, for example, Judith Butler. Every year since 1994 the journal *Philosophy and Literature* has held a Bad Writing Contest, asking its readers to submit "the ugliest, most stylistically awful" sentences they've found. And this year's winning entry comes from Judith Butler, a full professor at the University of California, Berkeley, and author of five books including her widely quoted *Gender Trouble* (1990).[1]

Best known for this book's idea that gender is a performance rather than the expression of a prior reality, Butler is on practically everybody's short list of the most influential "theorists" now writing. She is routinely placed in the company of Friedrich Nietzsche, Martin Heidegger, Michel Foucault, and Jacques Derrida. Here is her award-winning sentence:

> The move from a structuralist account in which capital is understood to structure social relations in relatively homologous ways to a view of hegemony in which power relations are subject to repetition, convergence, and rearticulation brought the question of temporality into the thinking of structure, and marked a shift from a form of Althusserian theory that takes

D. G. Myers. "Bad Writing." Originally published in the *Weekly Standard* 4 (10 May 1999): 36–39. Used by permission of the author.

structural totalities as theoretical objects to one in which the insights into the contingent possibility of structure inaugurate a renewed conception of hegemony as bound up with the contingent sites and strategies of the rearticulation of power.[2]

When *Philosophy and Literature* announced Butler's victory last December 22 [1998], the story was carried in over forty newspapers and magazines. The *New York Times, US News and World Report,* the *Chronicle of Higher Education,* the *Economist,* the *Chicago Tribune,* the *Times Literary Supplement,* the *Toronto Globe and Mail,* and the *Wall Street Journal* all reported the contest, and National Public Radio broadcast a segment on it.

And then, in the February issue of the *New Republic,* Martha Nussbaum demolished Butler's pretensions as a thinker, calling her work sophistry rather than philosophy, a parody of original thought. Although trained as a philosopher at Yale, Butler is read and respectfully cited "more by people in literature than by philosophers," leading to the question whether she "belongs to the philosophical tradition at all." In its chic and willful obscurity, Butler's writing is an example of "hip quietism," Nussbaum concluded, which "collaborates with evil."[3]

The combination of popular press mockery and Nussbaum's reproach was too much, and Butler took to the op-ed pages of the *New York Times* on March 20 to defend herself. Scorning *Philosophy and Literature* as "a small, culturally conservative academic journal," she aligned herself with "scholars on the left" who focus on "sexuality, race, nationalism and the workings of capitalism." Although she agreed that even leftist scholars "should be able to clarify how their work informs and illuminates everyday life," Butler insisted that academic writing needed to be "difficult and demanding" (her words) in order to "question common sense"—the truths which are so self-evident that no one thinks to question them—and so to "provoke new ways of looking at a familiar world."[4]

If the only choice is between academic obscurity and the pseudo-clarity of "common sense," who wouldn't choose the former? But who said that's the only choice? In the limited range of options she offers us, Butler reveals much about the real politics behind bad academic writing.

The notion that difficult and demanding styles of writing are politically revolutionary—and that "plain" writing is hidebound and reactionary—is not just dubious, but tiresomely familiar. A variation on Ezra Pound's modernist credo Make It New, it has been offered by every pretender to artistic and philosophical originality this century. The desire to "question common sense" is merely the self-congratulation of someone whose "sense" is different, but no less "common." Although Butler wishes to disrupt "the workings of capitalism," the effect of her writing is exactly the opposite. Its effect is to safeguard the power and privilege of academic capitalists—among whom she is one of the great robber barons.

The ninety-word sample that won *Philosophy and Literature*'s Bad Writing Contest suggests as much. It is something more than the "ugly" and "stylistically awful sentence" demanded by the contest's rules. What Butler's writing actually expresses is simultaneously a contempt for her readers and an absolute dependence on their good opinion. The problem is not so much her lack of concern for clarity; it's her lack of concern for *clarification*. If Butler took seriously her academic responsibility—her duty to teach—she would take pains to make herself clear. Her concern, though, is not to clarify a difficult subject but to justify her position in the front ranks. Hers is not writing to be read and understood; it is a display of verbal majesty, which is to inspire awe and respect. Its one purpose is to confirm Butler's authority as a leader of the academic left.

At first blush, it seems remarkable that such writing finds *any* admirers. Warren Hedges, an English professor at Southern Oregon University, once declared that Butler is "one of the ten smartest people on the planet."[5] But Hedges's admiration breaks down when forced to confront academic writing simply as writing. The second-prize winner in this year's Bad Writing Contest was from a recent book by the post-colonial scholar Homi K. Bhabha:

> If, for a while, the ruse of desire is calculable for the uses of discipline soon the repetition of guilt, justification, pseudo-scientific theories, superstition, spurious authorities, and classifications can be seen as the desperate effort to "normalize" formally the disturbance of a discourse of splitting that violates the rational, enlightened claims of its enunciatory modality.[6]

Asked by the *Chicago Tribune* to parse and explain this sentence, Hedges admitted, "[It] doesn't make a lot of sense to me."[7] Two years ago, *Newsweek* named Bhabha as one of its "One Hundred Creative Individuals Most Worth Watching." How is it possible that a writer bears watching, but his writing does not? The likely explanation is this: When such writing is separated from its purpose of confirming academic authority, it just doesn't make a lot of sense.

Academic writing wasn't supposed to be this way. Even at its most stylistically absurd, it was supposed to seek truth. Instead, what we have in academic writing nowadays is the circulation of authority—the replacement of the ideals of scholarship and academic community with the principle of a political party.

An instructive example of this assault on truth in the name of party occurred last year [1998] at a Yale symposium on psychoanalysis. Frederick Crews, Butler's colleague at Berkeley, read a paper in which he criticized the circularity of Freudian theory, which confirms itself by means of evidence manufactured by the very premises it seeks to confirm. Such reasoning, Crews said, is "a scandal for anyone who subscribes to community standards of rational and empirical inquiry."[8]

By "community standards," Crews was invoking not an organic, social community, but rather the very principle of the university: an association of persons who are related to one another by virtue of their common pursuit of truth. During the discussion following his paper, however, Crews was willfully misunderstood by Judith Butler. Pouncing on the phrase "community standards," Butler declared that it entails—as Crews summarized her position—"a tendency to fall in line with social 'normativity' in general, especially as it applies to the imposing of heterosexist values and rules on people who should be left in peace to pursue their own goals and pleasures."

There's a certain truth to the distinction Butler is making. It is the distinction between a *formal* community like a city, in which everyone obeys the same laws, and a *substantive* community like a baseball team, in which everyone pursues the same goals. And Crews's understanding of rational inquiry is in fact a substantive one, implying a mode of association—the university—that exists to promote a common undertaking.

But the lie in Butler's response is the notion that she is somehow advocating merely formal associations among university scholars. In summarizing her attack upon him, Crews put it neatly:

> What was very interesting . . . about my statement of ordinary rational principles—and the point was not lost on Butler's audible rooting section in our conference hall—was my self-alignment with social oppression. The hint was placed deftly and inconspicuously, but there it was: "community standards" meant homophobia.[9]

In Butler's university community, just as in Crews's, everyone pursues the same good. But in her community, the standard is not a common devotion to ordinary rational principles, but a devotion to party.

We could call this party the "liberationist party." What is required for membership is voluble solidarity with the party's claim to liberate us from "social oppression." To have any kind of career in the university today is to be compelled to sit in the "audible rooting section," booing the likes of Crews and cheering the likes of Butler.

Over a century ago Matthew Arnold mocked this sort of call to party unity:

> Let us organize and combine a party to pursue truth and new thought, let us call it the liberal party, and let us all stick to each other, and back each other up. Let us have no nonsense about independent criticism, and intellectual delicacy, and the few and the many; . . . if one of us speaks well, applaud him; if one of us speaks ill, applaud him too; we are all in the same movement, we are all liberals, we are all in pursuit of truth.[10]

You can catch some of the flavor of this party feeling in the attacks made on *Philosophy and Literature*'s Bad Writing Contest. In her *Times* op-ed, Butler observed that the contest winners, beginning with the Marxist critic Fredric Jameson in 1994 (he won again two years later), were "restricted to scholars on the left." Writing earlier in the on-line magazine *Salon*, Christopher Hitchens had made much the same point, suggesting that the contest betrayed a "certain easy populist hatred for the 'politically correct' Left, and a certain Anglo-Saxon and anti-intellectual contempt for the French."[11] A professor from Germany went even farther, associating the contest with *Völkisch* anti-intellectual populism.[12] The implication is obvious: To criticize the bad writing of "scholars on the left" is Fascist.

But you can sense the strength of Butler's party even more clearly among those who support the Bad Writing Contest. In the last two years, at least five young scholars have submitted entries, asking that their names not be released if they should win. In an unsigned June 1997 letter, one entrant confessed that he was "loathe to upset senior scholars in my field," since alienating them could do "significant damage" to his career.

> I share this information not merely "to expose" the folly of current writing—there's enough bad writing going around that adding one more sentence won't really change much—but to let you know the terror under which many graduate students and junior faculty live. In the current crisis of hiring freezes and intense pressure for tenure, the need to publish is perhaps greater than any time before. Yet to publish in most journals means flinging the jargon, toeing the party line (which is somewhere to the left of gibberish), and quoting the usual suspects (Benjamin, Foucault, Derrida, Said, Jameson, Butler, *etc.*). I'm often appalled at my own writing, but since jargon, rather than substance, gains a publication, I succumb to verbiage.[13]

The problem, finally, is not that academic writing is "ugly" and "stylistically awful." It's rather that bad academic writing conceals the political reality of contemporary universities. No longer defined by the common attachment to ordinary rational principles, they have become institutions of one-party rule. To canvass for this party is to promote your career; to dissent from it is to put your career at risk. Young scholars must conform in their writing—and pay a protection fee to the party bosses in the form of quoting them. And "to succumb to verbiage" is really to succumb to "the terror under which many graduate students and junior faculty live."

In such a climate, the party leaders are effectively insulated from criticism. *Philosophy and Literature*'s Bad Writing Contest does, in fact, what Butler and cohorts always claim (and fail) to do: criticize entrenched power in the name of community. It is one means—however minor and satirical—of discharging the old-fashioned academic obligation to correct error and reprove negligence; that is, to criticize bad writing.

## NOTES

1. See "Philosophy and Literature announces winners of the Fourth Bad Writing Contest (1998)," available at: http://aldaily.com/bwc.htm.

2. Judith Butler's prize-winning sentence appears in her essay "Further Reflections on Conversations of Our Time," *Diacritics* 27, no. 1 (Spring 1997): 13–15.

3. Martha C. Nussbaum, "The Professor of Parody—the Hip Defeatism of Judith Butler," *The New Republic*, 22 February 1999: 37–45.

4. Judith Butler, "A 'Bad Writer' Bites Back," *New York Times*, 20 March 1999.

5. Warren Hedges, available at http://www.sou.edu/English/IDTC/People/Intros/butlrint.htm.

6. Homi Bhabha's sentence is from his essay, "Of Mimicry and Man: The Ambivalence of Colonial Discourse," in his *The Location of Culture* (New York: Routledge, 1994), 85–92.

7. See Ron Grossman, "In This Writing Contest, It's Good to Be Bad." *Chicago Tribune*, 28 January 1999.

8. Frederick Crews, "Unconscious Deeps and Empirical Shallows," *Philosophy and Literature* 22 (1998): 274.

9. Frederick Crews, "Unconscious Deeps," 278.

10. Matthew Arnold, "The Function of Criticism at the Present Time," in his *Essays in Criticism* (London and Cambridge: Macmillan and Co., 1865), 1–41.

11. Christopher Hitchens, "Sentenced to Death," in the online journal *Salon*, 25 June 1997. Available at: http://archive.salon.com/june97/media/media970625.html.

12. Joerg Gruel, "Bad Writing Contest," PHIL-LIT, post #21063 (May 20, 1997).

13. Private communication to Denis Dutton, editor of *Philosophy and Literature* and founder of the Bad Writing Contest, June 15, 1997.

## 23.  EVERYMAN AN ÜBERMENSCH

### THE CULTURE OF CULTURAL STUDIES

### STEPHEN ADAM SCHWARTZ

*The utmost emphasis on distinctions of value, in all the things that*
*man makes and does, is not an emphasis on inequality of being.*
                                        —RAYMOND WILLIAMS[1]

THE RISE OF CULTURAL STUDIES within North American universities has
been greeted with some measure of disquiet and not only on the part of tradi-
tionalists unwilling to move with the times. Though a certain pressure to stay
up to date is without a doubt making itself felt, it is still unclear what this
movement means for the future of those departments traditionally devoted to
the study of modern languages and literature. Indeed, even as the announce-
ments of jobs for specialists in cultural studies proliferate on the MLA job list,
the question of exactly what such specialists *do* is as yet poorly defined. While
this question continues to work itself out within classrooms, hiring committees and editorial boards, it nevertheless behooves us to ask the question:
"What is cultural studies?"

Its practitioners have long been loath to offer much in the way of a definition for reasons that, they tell us, have everything to do with the intellectual
originality of the burgeoning field. As the editors of the influential collection
*cum* stocktaking *Cultural Studies* take pains to point out, cultural studies "is
not merely interdisciplinary" but "is often . . . actively and aggressively anti-
disciplinary." It is also antimethodological—its "method" being a kind of
*bricolage*—and this is so by design.[2] To ask what cultural studies is, they imply,
is to misunderstand this fundamental anti- or postdisciplinarity. Nevertheless,
some work fits easily under the rubric of cultural studies and some work does
not. A critical leftist rhetoric of "progressivism," "activism," and "intervention"—"'cultural reading' as an act of resistance,"[3] for example—is clearly a
necessary and perhaps even a sufficient condition for having one's work accepted as work in cultural studies. Moreover, the cultural studiers themselves,
for want of a better term, do have a relatively clear idea of what does and does
not count as work in cultural studies, despite the persistence of borderline
cases—work on traditional "high" culture from a progressive perspective, for
example—and a certain anxiety that cultural studies might turn out to be

"every damn thing."[4] Indeed, one is encouraged to find the editors of the aforementioned collection assert that although cultural studies "resists . . . definition" it "cannot be just anything,"[5] since, given the imposing size of the volume and the general explosion in publications in cultural studies, one might well have had doubts about the matter.

My discussion of cultural studies will focus on the 788-page *Cultural Studies* volume cited above. This volume comprises the proceedings of an important conference on the future of the antidiscipline held in 1990 and featuring many of the major stars of the field. The forty essays it contains provide a wide sampling of perspectives that have been characterized as belonging to cultural studies by those in the mainstream of the field. Yet, what is striking about the essays in this collection is that, despite the wide range of topics discussed, the various disciplinary backgrounds of the contributors, and the many issues that divide the cultural studiers, the underlying premises and particularly the conception of culture remain remarkably consistent. I believe that this conception and those premises have not evolved in the intervening years and that the questions that continue to exercise the cultural studiers do nothing more than play out the consequences of a logic already in place in 1990.

Given that cultural studies is neither nothing nor just anything at all, and given its widening influence in literature departments, it is not only possible but also desirable to examine the presuppositions and implications of the notion of culture that it utilizes. In the absence of any precise methodology or disciplinary rigor, it is likely the conception of their object of study—culture—that holds together the various cultural studies approaches. I intend to argue that this notion of culture is both idiosyncratic and flawed in ways that the rhetoric of cultural studies would never lead one to expect.

The most tangible effect of the rise of cultural studies is the opening of the curricula and research agendas of literature departments to vast areas beyond the study of literature itself: not only popular art but everything from gas stations to drag racing to drag queens. This is, of course, in addition to the rise of the variety of politically motivated approaches. If there is one idea that is meant to justify this move from *Literary Into Cultural Studies*, as the title of Antony Easthope's book would have it, it is the notion that the specificity of high cultural categories like "literature"—the distinction between literature and nonliterature—is untenable and that therefore a radical opening of the field covered by what used to be called literary study is not only salutary but necessary. Indeed, a failure to carry out such an opening is *unjustifiable*: "the binary which excludes popular culture as an outside while conserving as an inside a canon of specially literary texts simply cannot be sustained as a serious intellectual argument."[6] A somewhat less radical claim that one often finds in work in cultural studies and related fields is that if not the specificity, then at least the *value* attributed to the works called "literature," as opposed to subaltern works, is unjustifiable. At first glance, these two views would appear to be incompatible in their ultimate aims. Those who seek to attack the principles on which the value of "literature" is based (generally through assessments like: "those works are no better than others that have therefore been unfairly excluded"), would argue logically enough for an *expansion* of the literary canon to include valuable subaltern or otherwise marginalized works. Those, like Antony Easthope, who, on the other hand, argue against the specificity of "literature" (e.g., "there is nothing at root that separates these works from other cultural productions") seek instead the *explosion* of the canon, an utter and complete leveling in which anything and everything to which significance can be attributed—any "signifying practice"—is a worthy object of study for a new antidiscipline. The seeming incompatibility between these two positions evaporates upon further examination.

Most work in cultural studies proceeds from the notion that the specificity of categories like literature derives from positive evaluation, that the specificity is unthinkable outside of the hierarchy that grants, for example, the works in the "Literature" section of American bookstores a prestige that it denies to the more pedestrian offerings of the "Fiction," "Mystery," and "Science Fiction" sections. Easthope, for example, writes that "the high culture/popular culture opposition was founded in a conception of value: while literary value is present in the canonical work, it is absent from the texts of popular culture."[7] Concepts without clear boundaries like "literature" and "art" are notoriously difficult ones to get a handle on. Easthope and others working in cultural studies see terms like "literature" and "art" as exclusively honorific, so that at bottom the ontological category has no other basis than the favorable judgments of those "tastemakers" in positions of authority: critics, editors, gallery owners, et al. This view has a long pedigree. The emphasis on "literature" as an honorific category where the term is only correctly applied to works of "genius" and "masterpieces" is a hallmark of romantic aesthetics from Novalis through Heidegger and remains a respectable, if contested, position today.[8] The emphasis on the institutional procedures by which art works become "enfranchised" as art works, on the other hand, has been the defining feature of what is known as the "institutional theory" in the philosophy and sociology of art since the early 1960s.[9]

Cultural studies not only combines these two ways of thinking about art—the romantic aesthetics of value and institutional theories of arthood as enfranchisement—in an original way, it extends them to areas far beyond categories like "literature" that are relatively vague and difficult to discern. For its partisans, not just "literature," but all "identities," all putative "facts" have their basis in enfranchised value judgments. Following the perspectivism of Nietzsche and his contemporary heirs, they see all facts as merely solidified or crystallized values, which is what they mean when they say, as they often do, that "reality is culturally constructed."[10] Just as, in their view, the fact of literature's distinction from nonliterature is rooted in the superiority, as perceived by those in positions of authority, of what is called "literature" relative to what does not receive this title, all other distinctions have this same genealogy: facts are merely values in disguise. One contributor, for example, argues in *Cultural Studies* that "since the concerns and issues of women of color are so rarely included in prevailing definitions of 'reality,' any analysis which suggests that 'reality,' or 'knowledge,' is not simply given but rather produced, seems to me particularly welcome."[11] "Concerns and issues" here can only mean "values and interests," and reality itself—rather than the beliefs we have about it or the questions we ask of it—is held to be unsatisfactory for somehow reflecting the concerns and issues of some but not all.

The view that facts are crystallized values is clearly meant to pose a challenge to modern notions of knowledge as objective and disinterested. In this, cultural studies would seem to have a view not so far removed from that attributed to most of the world's belief systems by anthropologists like Louis Dumont. Dumont argues that within every society—with the limited exception of modern, Western societies—ideas and values, *être* and *devoir-être* are indissociable.[12] In Dumont's schema, a traditional society is one in which values are embedded in facts, so that the values of the culture are held to derive from the very nature of things. A modern society, by contrast, is one in which facts and values are rigidly separated to the extent that this is possible, so that questions of what *should be* are never to be justified by what *is* and, conversely, the assessment of what is the case is not to be affected by the desires or interests of the assessor. In this light, the cultural studies reduction of fact to value would appear to be resolutely *postmodern*: opposed to the modern separation of *être* and *devoir-être* yet without for all that representing a return to a traditional and *hierarchical* rooting of value in fact within a "Great Chain of Being." Indeed, cultural studies is in many ways a postmodern hybrid of the traditional and the modern, a recoupling of fact and value but in a way adapted to an individualistic and egalitarian society. In its view, facts are derived from and genealogically reducible to the values of the individuals who hold that they *are* facts.

In practice, this reduction of fact to value has as a consequence that the arguments put forward by the partisans of cultural studies consistently confuse fact and value. On the one hand, they attack the specificity—the relative yet porous self-identity—of categories like literature so as to undercut their value. On the other hand, they attack the value so as to undercut their specificity. Nevertheless, the form of these arguments is relatively consistent. They generally run as follows:

(1) The specificity/prestige of literature has no basis. It is not *grounded*, for it lacks the metaphysical foundation that would guarantee its stability. In other words, the category called literature is infinitely protean and malleable with no

essence or set of necessary and sufficient conditions that would hold it together. It is, in a word, not "natural" but "socially constructed." Therefore,

(2) The specificity/prestige of literature relative to nonliterature is an ideological mystification. From this it follows that we need to:

(3a) abandon the study of the arbitrarily limited and ungrounded category of literature in order to turn our attention to the broader field of signifying practices, and/or,

(3b) unmask the manifold ways in which this ideological category both serves and bolsters the interests of "dominant groups."

Both the argument for the *expansion* of literary studies and the more radical one for their *explosion* therefore share a point of view. Invariably they assume that the justification for the choice and demarcation of a disciplinary object of study must be a consequence of a prior positive evaluation. For cultural studies, this specificity is seen as having proven to be an ideological mystification rooted in positive evaluation (e.g., the books that have been judged to be "great" by those in positions of authority—that reflect their "concerns and issues"—are called "literature"; those judged less great do not qualify). As a result, not only should curricula and research agendas be opened to hitherto devalued forms of cultural production (mystery novels, grade B movies, pop songs, etc.), but the object of study within what used to be literature departments must become culture taken at the greatest level of generality, that of all signifying practices. In other words, categories like "literature" and "art" are rooted in value judgments: of the manifold potential or putative "works" produced by humankind, only those to which the highest value is attributed are bestowed with the honorific term "art." It follows that the very notion of "bad art" is a contradiction in terms. Cultural studies shares this premise with some unlikely bedfellows—Matthew Arnold, F. R. Leavis, and Immanuel Kant come to mind—while seeking to cut its legs out from under it by means of the mordant genealogical question: "Whose values?"

If it is the case that facts are only values in disguise, one might expect an endeavor calling itself "cultural studies" to see hierarchy as the uneliminable "really real," the underlying and irreducible substrate by which our seemingly immediate experience is always conditioned. For hierarchy is the systemic form that evaluation takes within a culture. Cultural studies might then be a kind of comparative anthropology: an exploration of the differences in the hierarchies by which all societies are structured. Yet far from embracing the notion of hierarchies of value as the defining trait of culture, the partisans of cultural studies speak of hierarchy in unremittingly hostile terms, seeing their task as one of "resisting the subordination of human beings in hierarchical relations of power."[13] In the cultural studies view, all hierarchies and the kinds of subordination they entail can be seen only as the result or the embodiment of "rela-

tions of power."[14] Much of the tension within work in cultural studies originates in the attempt to do two incompatible things at once: to reduce fact to
value and nature to culture while at the same time flattening all values and leveling all hierarchies, treating both fact and hierarchy as mystifications that
must be destabilized. This contradiction is constitutive of the notion of culture
employed by cultural studies. It is one that is resolved by a further reduction: a
reduction of culture and the hierarchies of value it entails to the results of *relations of force* and, thereby, to the results of *political struggle*. For it is inconceivable to cultural studiers that any hierarchy might not be something that
has been *imposed* and *enforced*, given that our shared cultural hierarchies are
not something that any of us have freely chosen. It is as if the natural or ideal
state of a culture were one in which there would be a perfect absence of hierarchy and a perfect equality and equivalence of all opinions and comportments.
If we have hierarchies and systems of evaluation which virtually none of us has
had a say in, if we are confronted with facts that we are powerless to change,
then it can only be because they have been forcibly imposed on us by those
they benefit.

In short, what cultural studies often refers to as the "social construction of
reality" amounts to the following: First, a reduction of reality to the social or
cultural. This is the upshot of the claim that there is no value-free perspective
and that all so-called "facts" are value-laden in ways that have been socially and
culturally determined. Second, a reduction of the social and the cultural to the
result of the agglomeration or shaking out of competing interests in a power
struggle. What we call "society" or "culture" amounts to the putting into place
of illegitimate and arbitrary hierarchies, hierarchies that are illegitimate because they are arbitrary. All of which can be summed up in three formulas that
describe the underlying premises of cultural studies:

(1) knowledge = belief + power
(2) social norms/hierarchies of value = interests/values + power
(3) belief = interest (where "=" in all cases means "reduces to")

According to (1), of the manifold beliefs that people hold or may hold, the
ones held by people with the power and authority to impose them are what
come to be called "knowledge."[15] According to (2), the interests and personal
values of those who have the power to impose them are what come to be taken
as "norms" and hierarchies by the rest of us. And the extreme utilitarianism of
point (3) follows from these two: once one has eliminated, as Henry Giroux
characterizes it, the ideological view that knowledge consists in "some kind of
correspondence with a self-enclosed objective reality,"[16] and one sees it as
mere belief enfranchised by power, one is hard put to provide any source for
belief itself other than self-interest. Each of us believes what it is in his or her

interests to believe, so that not only objectivity but even disinterestedness is impossible. Or, as John Fiske puts it: "The social norms, or that which is socially acceptable, are of course neither neutral nor objective; they have developed in the interests of those with social power, and they work to maintain their sites of power by naturalizing them into commonsense—the only—social positions for power."[17]

After Foucault, to view "the production of knowledge in the context of power"[18] amounts to reducing the former in large measure to the latter. Or, as Foucault put it, "truth is already power."[19] Just as "fact" is a mask for the values that underlie it, "knowledge" is merely power in disguise: the power to *impose* one's beliefs and, ultimately, one's values on others who do not share them and are thereby both *marginalized* and *dominated* by this "imposition of a particular view of the world."[20] The agglomeration of these dominant values amount to what cultural studies' partisans often and interchangeably call "the dominant culture" or "the dominant ideology." Power is then above all a catalyst, a kind of Philosophers' Stone that is able to turn the dross of individual beliefs and interests into the gold of collectively shared knowledge and norms. Absent power, those beliefs and interests are all equivalent: in itself, none is superior to another. And since facts are held to be mere values in disguise (formula 3), it follows that formula 1 reduces to formula 2: all "knowledge" is then simply normative, a constraining rule of conduct, and a form of control. The content of those rules is the simple manifestation of the interests of those who have the power to impose them. Interest and power or, more precisely, power in the service of interests—which together define politics in the cultural studies perspective—are the two key concepts for understanding culture.

All of this is at work in a theme that recurs constantly throughout *Cultural Studies*, usually as a prelude to an inspiring set of imperatives, namely, that because distinctions and categories are not *natural* they can only be *political*: "Identities are not found but *made* . . . they are not just there, waiting to be discovered in the vocabulary of Nature, but . . . have to be culturally and politically *constructed* through political antagonism and cultural struggle."[21] This amounts, as another contributor to *Cultural Studies* pertinently points out, to "redefining what counts as political": in the case the author is discussing, the cultural studier will attempt to displace " 'science education' from 'the exposition of natural facts' to revealing it as the imposition of a particular view of the world."[22] Science itself can then be exposed as merely "one purveyor of a view of the world from a particular vantage point," a "knowledge" that "is often able to masquerade as 'natural fact,' a powerful means by which its vision of hierarchical human relationships is learned and internalized."[23] "Political" here and for most of the cultural studiers means "power struggle among competing interests" (i.e., interests + power). Since power struggle is everywhere that one finds "facts" and the norms to which they are reduced, it follows that everything is "political."[24]

Here, as in many of the essays in this collection, science, like "positivism," is a caricatural bogeyman. In the cultural studies lexicon, it represents a "naive" belief in "nature," the "reality of the real," and the possibility of separating facts from values, understanding from both opinion and free-floating interpretation, the way things are from *someone's* interested view of the way they ought to be. One can easily cut to the heart of the worldview implied by the cultural studies position by asking the question: If what science education "exposes" amounts to the unwarranted "imposition of a particular view of the world," then why should we expect the "revelation" of this "fact" not to suffer the same defect, i.e., to be anything more than an "imposition" in the guise of revelation? If all revelation—including science, the modern paradigmatic instance of such revelation—is in fact imposition, and if all knowledge is a power play, then how can the unmasking and demystifying carried out by cultural studies itself escape this fate? Is it not itself just another imposition?

The originality of cultural studies lies in fully accepting the abyssal consequences of this position, rather than shying away from them. For cultural studies aims to be a "knowledge" demystified regarding the basis of knowledge in power. It thereby also aims to be a force to be reckoned with. If "all knowledge is a condensed node in an agonistic power field," the findings of researchers in cultural studies and the distinctions drawn by them are not themselves removed from power but are, rather, themselves a power play.[25]

Although many of the contributors to *Cultural Studies* stress the need for actual political work outside of the confines of the academy, given that cultural studies has its power base within English departments it is not surprising that the terrain on which these power struggles are supposed to be waged is that of language and representation, where "identities are made." Taking poststructuralist theories of language as articles of faith, the cultural studiers stretch Saussure's thesis of the arbitrariness of the sign to its furthest extreme, concluding from the fact that the relationship between linguistic signifiers and their signifieds is *arbitrary* that signifiers are therefore essentially indeterminate in their relation to meaning. Since all signifiers are thus "floating signifiers"[26] and since there is no "transcendental signified," all signifiers must have had their meanings somehow assigned to them. Why do our words mean what they mean and not something else? "Who decides? Who has the power to decide?"[27] The cultural studies hypothesis meant to answer this question is that the meanings can only have been imposed by power: "language . . . cannot be abstracted from the forces and conflicts of social history" and is "always implicated in power relationships,"[28] for "the meaning of texts, discourses, and political events is a continuing site of struggle."[29] If our words mean what they mean, this can only be because it serves the interests of someone and has been imposed on those whose interests it does not serve. Since cultural studies explicitly sees itself as "a mode of study which is engaged and which seeks not the truth, but knowledge and understanding as a practical and material means of communicating with and helping to empower subordinate social groups and movements," it makes sense that it would see its task as "attempting to recast . . . terms by inflecting new meanings and by prizing apart and disentangling old ones."[30] In other words, language and the meanings of words and symbols are themselves sites of contestation. From this the cultural studiers conclude that, through language, *everything*—all human meaning, all identities—is "political," in the sense in which they use this word. And yet, because it is almost exclusively through language and the inflection of its meanings that "everything is political," one often gets the impression that *only* language is political: "To be empowered is to be 'other,' to be read as different by making the sign your own. What it means to be disenfranchised shifts accordingly: to be disempowered is to be 'conventional,' that is, to lose possession of the sign."[31] No doubt this is a comforting thought for political activists whose praxis happens to take place within the relatively isolated confines of literature departments where "taking possession of the sign," at least for faculty, is a fairly simple matter and being empowered by being "other" and unconventional is tolerated and even rewarded. But the overwhelming emphasis on the "politics of meaning" to the exclusion of serious institutional and social analysis gives the heavy "political" emphasis of the essays in *Cultural Studies* a somewhat frivolous and ineffectual cast.

As we have seen, in the view of the cultural studiers, all knowledge and the very meanings of our words are nothing more than relations of force. The cultural studies viewpoint is no exception. Disabused of all illusions regarding "truth" and "objectivity" (whose truth? whose objectivity?) it sees itself not as an attempt to discover or uncover anything in particular about its objects of study, but as an *intervention* or *performative discourse*, an attempt to impose a view and a set of interests, "to reshape knowledge according to the strategy of transgression."[32] It aims "to do more than just study mass-produced culture, but change it."[33] The word "studies" in "cultural studies" would then seem to be something of a misnomer: "insurgency" might be more accurate. As the editors of *Cultural Studies* put it: "In virtually all traditions of cultural studies, its practitioners see cultural studies not simply as a chronicle of cultural change but as an intervention in it, and see themselves not simply as scholars providing an account but as politically engaged participants."[34] Against the "imposition of a particular point of view" that "masquerades as natural fact," cultural studies seeks to impose a different view, attempting to fill what one contributor calls

> the need for forms of cultural theory and politics that will concern themselves with the production and placing of forms of knowledge—of functioning truths—that can concretely influence the agendas, calculations, and procedures of those entities which can be thought of as agents operating within, or in relation to, the fields of culture concerned.[35]

In the end it turns out that it is not the imposition of particular points of view in the guise of natural fact *per se* that cultural studies criticizes as illegitimate or otherwise puts in question. Notions like "illegitimacy" would imply a kind of juridical, liberal, bourgeois view based in other notions like "right" that have been abstracted from power and particular interests and that cultural studies therefore rejects.[36] There can be no question of opposing the illegitimate power of the "dominant ideology" with a "legitimate" or more "just" power, for what counts as "legitimate" is itself also seen as a function of power and interest. Notions like legitimacy lack sense because they are merely masks for interests enforced by power, serving no ends beyond their own propagation. That particular points of view come to impose themselves—to *be imposed by others*—as natural facts, rather than being a lamentable state of affairs whose unmasking would be the first step in the formation of a more just society possessed of nonideological meanings (meanings not based in power) and nonoppressive norms, instead turns out to be the metaphysical condition of all "knowledge" production as an effect of power. Since there are no "natural facts" that are not, at root, impositions of particular points of view, what is objectionable to the cultural studiers cannot be the imposition of particular points of view by means of power. To object to that would amount to objecting to what they see as our human condition. What is objectionable, rather, is the imposition of the particular points of view of *others*: the "truth"—or what passes for it—shall only enslave ye. The difference between knowledge and ignorance is then only a difference in force: not the relative logical or persuasive force of the arguments produced by those we call "knowledgeable" and those we call "ignorant," but the authority of the people who voice them and the positions of power from which they do so. Not only does might make right (in both the juridical and epistemological senses of the word), but there are no possible grounds for objecting to or opposing this state of affairs: one can only seek to be mighty and authoritative oneself.[37]

Here the individualist presuppositions of cultural studies begin to peer out from behind the "social" and "cultural" curtain by which they are often obscured. Cultural studies, in keeping with what the name implies and its roots in the work of thinkers like Raymond Williams and E. P. Thompson, makes much of what it calls the social or historical construction of reality. Its insight, which it shares with well-established positions in traditional fields like philosophy and sociology, lies in its knack for depicting norms, values, and significations as collectively and locally determined and its eagerness to investigate what Foucault called "the contingency that has made us what we are."[38] Its rhetoric is almost always one of attentiveness to the social, historical, and, above all, *collective* constitution of meanings and forms: "cultural studies . . . takes a keen interest in the social conditions underpinning the production and consumption of popular literature, the social relations of taste and evaluation that are embedded in everyday culture."[39] It just as frequently maligns the "concept of the individual" which one contributor claims to "reject entirely" because it "brings with it all the baggage of ahistoricism, free will, enlightenment rationalism and so on."[40] In short, at the same time that it constantly promotes the social constitution of everything, cultural studies also "[rejects] the mainstream humanist assumption that the individual is both the source of all human action and the most important unit of social analysis."[41]

Yet this relatively benign rhetoric of anti-individualist social constructionism sits poorly with the radical interventionist aims of cultural studies. In fact, the cultural studies position differs from that of social constructionists in better-established disciplines in its attempt to maintain two things at once: that all reality is socially constructed *and* that these constructions are also *ipso facto* oppressive. In other words, the talk about the "social construction of reality" is really no more than a prelude, a kind of pep talk meant to prepare the atomized troops for the real call to arms: If all reality is a social construction, then who decided that it would be this way rather than another? Why not me? Yet "troops" is certainly not the best metaphor here, for the call is addressed each time to an army of one. Saying that reality is socially constructed, in the cultural studies milieu, is a way of denying its hold on us, of proclaiming its mutability as a necessary preliminary to willing that it be otherwise. The converse of this is that cultural studies focuses on one aspect of what are ordinarily called knowledge, truth, and norms: that they exercise a force on us. But it can only conceive this force in individualistic terms: as a power that must in fact be wielded by *someone else*, as something that can only have been "imposed" and "decided" by the members of "dominant groups" and that is, therefore, contestable if not "illegitimate" (for calling this imposition "illegitimate" would imply the possibility of a legitimacy not rooted in interest and power).

In fact, the political program of cultural studies is strikingly but not surprisingly content-poor, reducing in general to praise for transgression and well-meaning bromides about respect for "difference." Of course the cultural studiers oppose racism, sexism, homophobia, nationalism, and class discrimination, but beyond that they seem to have no politics more precise than that we "take up notions of political community in which particularity, voice, and difference provide the foundation for democracy."[42] "Voice" here is the crucial metaphor for the politics of cultural studies. It has little to do with democratic participation in public life, where particular voices are inevitably subsumed within a greater consensus or compromise. That model of democracy is viewed as oppressive. Its "rights" and "consensuses"—including the explicitly political results of democratic plebiscites—can be nothing more than incarnations of the dominant ideology, inevitably resulting in the abstraction from particularity, the silencing of dissenting voices, and the subsumption of difference. The cultural studiers emphasize the exclusions on which such rights and decisions are based, seeing them as a denial of difference and a kind of silence *imposed* on those who happen to have other views.[43] "Voice" is defined by one participant as the "authority or the power to define experience."[44] Here, contrary to the popular slogan, it is not that "the personal is the political" but rather that "the political is the personal." The possibility of expressing oneself, of "defining" (one's own?) experience, of freely choosing every aspect of one's existence is taken not simply as legitimate and desirable within limits, but as the rightful beginning and absolute end of all social and political life. Yet "voice" is also a particularly weak metaphor, let alone metaphorical basis, for a politics. Can it really be of no consequence what the voice is actually saying as long as it is one that has hitherto been silenced? Charles Taylor has argued that this sort of valorization of choice as an end in itself (without consideration for the things chosen), in which "all options are equally worthy, because they are freely chosen, and it is choice that confers worth," is self-defeating. Without the sort of hierarchy of ideals, values, and meanings "whereby some things are worthwhile and others less so, and still others not at all, quite anterior to choice," the "soft relativism" of cultural studies deprives the differences it upholds of the very significance it wants to claim for them.[45] The value of choice has meaning only within a context where what is chosen, at least potentially, is valuable independently of my will that it be so: that is, only in a culture.

In cultural studies, both "giving voice" and the transgression of cultural norms or the "dominant ideology" are seen as in themselves progressive or liberatory. It seems to me that there is only one condition under which this can be so, and that is if the very notion of a norm, a rule, an ideal, or a constraint on total self-expression is seen as reactionary or oppressive. This is clearly the case for cultural studies and it frequently leads to what would otherwise be surprising and far-fetched conclusions about what counts as "progressive," which one contributor bemoans as "sleuth-like searching for subversive practices where you'd least expect them."[46] For example, one contributor to the volume writes of the pornographic magazine *Hustler* that its "insistent and repetitive return to the iconography of the body out of control, rampantly transgressing bourgeois norms and sullying bourgeois property and proprieties, raises certain political questions," and that indeed such "bodily grossness operates as a critique of dominant ideology." She concludes that "it is *Hustler's* very political incoherence—in conventional political terms—that makes it so available to counter-hegemonic readings, to opening up new political alliances and strategies."[47] Another contributor claims that "television is an empowering artifact and discourse for people much younger than we" and on this basis advocates that it be moved "not only into the University but into high schools and grade schools as well."[48] But if norms are oppressive in themselves, then what is oppressive, in the cultural studies perspective, can be nothing less than culture itself: culture as a set of rules, beliefs, and hierarchies—i.e., what it is one learns when one adapts to another culture, what Raymond Williams called, in his famous formulation, the "entire way of life,"[49] or what Stuart Hall refers to as "the actual, grounded terrain of practices, representations, languages and customs of any specific historical society."[50]

This explains why the contributors to *Cultural Studies* can unselfconsciously claim such things as that "the social order oppresses the people"; that "cities are places built to organize and control the lives and movements of their 'city subjects' in the interests of the dominant";[51] and that "culture" is best thought of as "a historically specific set of institutionally embedded relations of government in which the forms of thought and conduct of extended populations are targeted for transformation."[52] At the very least, these views lack nuance, for they make no distinction whatever between traditionally hierarchical societies, on the one hand, where deviation from the norms of the social order is often all but inconceivable, and the protean arrangement of modern Western societies on the other, in which such deviation, particularly deviant *consumption*, is at least mildly encouraged in the form of "doing your own thing" and social mobility and personal freedom have taken on unprecedented dimensions. Indeed, one might argue, as Ernest Gellner has, that only in the West are the conditions propitious for the expression of the cultural studies critique itself.[53] In any case, the perspective of cultural studies is always a dyadic one, always confronting "the master narrative of a monolithic culture" with the "particular histories that will not fit into [it]."[54]

Because any view regarding the state of things or any rule determining what counts as an appropriate comportment is, for cultural studies, merely a particular view or interest, it follows that what we call "culture" is made up of only the most successful of such particular views and interests, those that have succeeded in imposing themselves by marginalizing all the alternatives. Liberation then—the "political community in which particularity, voice, and difference provide the foundation for democracy"—would consist in a perpetual transgression on the part of "particulars" of any "dominant ideology" that might happen to form. Cultural studies' political program can only be a kind of homeopathic cure, opposing the "imposition of particular points of view" with relentless promotion of different "particular points of view," which is why cultural studies can both criticize science as "the imposition of a particular view" and uphold "particularity" as a new basis for democracy. The ideal would be a kind of "heat death" or *degré zéro* of the imposition of views on others, a cacophony in which all voices speak at once and none takes precedence over any others.[55] In the end, Utopia comes to resemble a generalized incoherence where all "particular points of view" are equally valid and everyone is within his or her rights to "refuse to admit that their ways of knowing and experiencing the world are in any way subordinate or inferior."[56] Since knowledge itself and the distinctions it draws are in some sense a restriction on freedom, in the name of *radical* freedom all becomes absorbed—or, rather, *ought* to become absorbed—within a general indistinction.

One thing is clear: the possibility of adjudicating among the competing individual interests involved in power struggle is by no means given, since, in the cultural studies perspective, there is no such thing as a neutral position from or toward which to carry out such adjudication. Indeed, it is difficult to see how there is any room for a politics at all in this perspective, since there can be no question of ever collectively establishing a legitimate and just political order: a just apportionment of rights and resources or an equitable ordering of societal priorities, for example. Even a merely *acceptable* political order is out of the question, for politics invariably involves establishing a *hierarchy* among competing interests through compromise. Because in the cultural studies view there is only a struggle of wills and interests, any public compromise necessarily entails oppression in various degrees. In other words, a state of affairs that does not fully reflect my personal "concerns and issues" can only have been violently imposed against my will.

One is left with a war of all against all. Yet the cultural studiers themselves are vaguely dissatisfied with this consequence of their reduction of everything to interests and power, which is why they often stress the need for what they call a "politics of articulation,"[57] i.e., ways of bringing together my interests with your interests, my cause and yours, of putting back together what they initially tore asunder. The "dominant ideology," mysteriously enough, appears to have no need for such articulation or has at least discovered the secret of carrying it off.

By representing culture and reality itself as matters of choices and decisions imposed by the few on the many, cultural studies conceives of culture in strictly individualist terms, "defining culture as a contested terrain, a site of struggle and transformation,"[58] but always of struggle among individual interests and points of view. That the point of departure (as well as highest value) of the cultural studiers is always the *individual* and his or her preferences is evident not only in the constant emphasis on the transgressive or otherwise insubordinate "particular" but in the heavy emphasis placed on "difference." Culture is seen as the result of a struggle among competing interests, rather than as the context from which those interests, in very large measure, derive and in which they have their meaning. In other words, individuals—replete with a full set of interests, desires, and beliefs—come first and culture is something not only derived and secondary but pernicious and, therefore, ultimately unnecessary. Personal preferences—*someone's* choices—turn out to be lying behind all collectively shared categories. They are opposed only by the other personal preferences that they deny and the expression of which is then necessarily a liberatory transgression whenever the "dominant ideology" is not already in accord with them.[59]

In a sense, cultural studies represents less the sort of total politicization of the study of culture that it claims to be (and that its critics bemoan) than it does a generalized aestheticism: an extension of aesthetic—specifically Dada and surrealist—avant-gardism to intellectual work. The generalized call to transgression of all social norms; the sacralization of mundane and everyday cultural artifacts by a hyperarticulate and often arcane theoretical discourse; the formation of cadres on the basis of elective affinities; the radical posturing and apocalyptic, vanguardist rhetoric; above all the almost total absence of genuinely political aims and the almost complete political ineffectuality of the endeavor are all traits that cultural studies has in common with its surrealist precursors. This aesthetics is essentially a romantic one. The Jena romantics, for example, held that the work of art, qua work of genius, is necessarily a masterpiece that transcends all worldly categories and interests so as to reveal their underpinnings. It is thereby also profoundly liberatory. In this aesthetics, a version of which has arguably driven virtually all of the major aesthetic and avant-garde movements since the nineteenth century, the evaluative and descriptive uses of the word "art" are confused, so that only the great and transcendent work is worthy of the term. Arthood is then something that a work *merits*.[60] Although the romantic artist and his avant-garde successors usually see themselves as separated from the society they seek to change, the work itself has a prophetic and liberatory function and, at least in principle, can and ought to command a universal respect and assent. Cultural studies *individualizes* this aesthetics while removing its otherworldly and transcendent element. The work is no longer held to be an otherworldly form of ecstatic knowledge, but art retains its liberatory potential.

This functional definition (art as liberatory creation), as we have seen, comes to be combined with a procedural definition which holds that the enfranchisement of works as artworks is rooted in nothing more than the interested pleasure they provoke in those who judge them to be art. What counts as art depends on who is doing the judging and what their antecedent interests are. It follows that, in the cultural studies aesthetics, what counts as art (for me) is based in what I like and these preferences are in turn rooted in my self-interest. Those in positions of authority and power are then able to impose their self-serving preferences and choices on the rest of us: high art and its prestige are a function of the hegemony of the bourgeoisie. However, if arthood is in the end based on nothing more than personal preferences and certain procedures of enfranchisement and, at the same time, is functionally defined as liberatory, it follows, perversely enough, that whatever I like must by that very fact be liberatory. This would help to explain the incredible inventiveness of the cultural studiers in teasing out the "progressive" implications of *Rambo* and the like.[61]

Cultural studies has extended this particular, essentially romantic, aesthetics into both a metaphysics and a politics. The metaphysics holds that individual evaluation (bolstered by power) underlies all of our concepts and categories. The politics holds that one's own preferences and evaluations are no worse than anyone else's (and are, at least in the eyes of those whose prefer-ences they are, a good bit better than anyone else's) and therefore have an equal right to see themselves embodied as facts and norms. This "personalization" of social reality, to use Lipovetsky's term,[62] helps explain why so much of the scholarship in *Cultural Studies* is autobiographical and confessional in tone. If every norm or fact is oppressive insofar as it is a norm or fact that each of us has not invented on our own, the only thing a cultural studier can bring to the table are his or her personal interests and beliefs: "In order not to be authorita-tive, I've got to speak autobiographically."[63] The papers and discussions in the collection are rife with confessional, first-person narratives in which the au-thor or speaker makes a point or criticizes a position or state of affairs on the basis of nothing more than his or her feelings, likes, or dislikes. Bell Hooks's criticism of one paper is that she doesn't feel it applies to her: "I am frustrated by the binary opposition you make between the intellectual and the under-class, because I feel myself to be both working in the underclass in many ways and an intellectual. So that I feel all the more like an outsider here, at this con-ference that seems to me to be so much a mirroring of the very kinds of hier-archies that terrorize and violate."[64] Similarly, Jan Zita Grover's essay on AIDS begins with a two-page first-person narrative in place of an argument, the thrust of which is that the disciplinary constraints imposed by literary study and history are unacceptable because she found them unsatisfactory.[65]

Both the antidisciplinarity and the autobiographical method in cultural studies are merely logical consequences of the rejection of all normative con-straints as oppressive of particularity. The methodological norms and the de-limitation of a field of study that characterize academic disciplines are them-selves targets of critique insofar as they exclude other ways of proceeding and other objects of study: "At a minimum, cultural studies must pursue an anti-disciplinary practice defined by the repeated, indeed, endless rejection of the logic of the disciplines and of the universal subject of disciplinary inquiry. . . . This anti-disciplinary practice begins by rejecting the universal subject of dis-ciplinaryknowledge."[66] One can only conclude that "the universal subject of disciplinary knowledge" here rejected is the researcher who presumes that her findings will be accepted by others and, ideally, by everyone. This is an ideal that Donna Haraway also rejects: "I am arguing for politics and epistemologies of location, positioning, and situating, where partiality and not universality is the condition of being heard to make rational knowledge claims."[67] But is this ideal so easily done away with? Without it, all scholarship, including the work of the cultural studiers, not only can but *must* be dismissed with a "Sez you." Its effect, far from radicalizing and politicizing scholarship, is to atomize it, thereby rendering it utterly inconsequential.

Cultural studies, then, turns out to be an uneasy hybrid of two liberal ideals, both of which have been radicalized to the point where they contradict each other. On the one hand is an egalitarian ideal: taken to its extreme, all hierarchy and all discrimination (even in the benign sense of "distinction making") are seen as pernicious and unacceptable. On the other hand is an expressivist and libertarian ideal: taken to its extreme, any curtailment of individual self-expression (particularly the expression of one's preferences) and the exercise of individual will is also pernicious and oppressive. In their radical forms, these two ideals are incompatible: unless one is willing, as the cultural studiers are not, to accept a juridical equality that abstracts from particularity, any self-expression or exercise of will in some sense will either institute an inequality or be inconsequential. Short of that, the two can only be reconciled through the advocacy of perpetual, endless transgression for its own sake on the part of each individual. Add to the radicalization of these two ideals a dose of Nietzschean vitalist perspectivism according to which each of us, in principle, can and should "define our own experience" and you end up with an epistemological and political anarchism rooted in the purest individualist voluntarism. What is most peculiar is that this voluntarism is promulgated in the name of an egalitarianism and justice the watchword of which might be: Everyman an Übermensch.

The cultural studies conception of culture reflects these two ideals, conceiving of culture itself, insofar as it necessarily involves hierarchies, traditions, and normative constraints on conduct, as tyrannical. It is no surprise then that this antidiscipline has had its greatest success in cultures where *self-reliance* is arguably the core value, for this allows its practitioners to be simultaneously radically trangressive and comfortably middle-of-the-road. Despite its claims to seek the dismantling of all hierarchies of value and its avowed multiculturalism, cultural studies quite clearly places the two modern and Western ideals of egalitarianism and expressivism above all others. It differs from the mainstream consensus around these values only in its seeming radicalism. Yet it is much less radical than it at first appears, since the thrust of its critiques is always to call contemporary Western societies back to (the hyperbolic forms of) their own individualist core values: equality and individual freedom.[68] Although cultural studies is best viewed less as an attempt to study culture than as an attempt to overthrow through transgression all social and cultural constraints on particularity, this attempt is carried out in the name of ideals it shares with the society it would overthrow. As such, it offers little insight into contemporary Western culture except as an example, for it is merely the academic avatar of an "era of the individual"[69] in which the demand for individual autonomy and consequent atomization of social life have reached unprecedented dimensions. Strange as it may seem, this methodological individualism makes of cultural studies a form of ethnocentrism. Incapable of relativizing the values at its core which it treats as universal desiderata, unable to see them as the culturally determined preconditions for its own enterprise, cultural studies cannot tell us much about contemporary Western culture or any other, for it is a symptom of what it claims to analyze, a modern form of culture in which the individual is the highest value.

## NOTES

1. Raymond Williams, *Culture and Society, 1780–1950,* 2nd ed. (New York: Columbia University Press, 1983), 318.

2. Cary Nelson, Paula A. Treichler, and Lawrence Grossberg, "Cultural Studies: An Introduction," in *Cultural Studies,* ed. Lawrence Grossberg, Cary Nelson, and Paula A. Treichler (New York: Routledge, 1992), 1–2.

3. Michele Wallace, "Negative Images: Towards a Black Feminist Cultural Criticism," in *Cultural Studies,* ed. Grossberg, Nelson, and Treichler, 656.

4. Stuart Hall, "Cultural Studies and Its Theoretical Legacies," in *Cultural Studies,* ed. Grossberg, Nelson, and Treichler, 292.

5. Nelson, Treichler, and Grossberg, "Cultural Studies: An Introduction," 4, 3.

6. Antony Easthope, *Literary Into Cultural Studies* (London: Routledge, 1991), 5–6.

7. Easthope, *Literary Into Cultural Studies,* 42.

8. For a thorough history and critique of this notion, see Jean-Marie Schaeffer, *Art of the Modern Age: Philosophy of Art from Kant to Heidegger,* trans. Steven Rendall (Princeton, N.J.: Princeton University Press, 2000).

9. See Arthur Danto, "The Artworld," *Journal of Philosophy* 61 (October 1964): 571–84; George Dickie, *Art and the Aesthetic: An Institutional Analysis* (Ithaca, N.Y.: Cornell University Press, 1974); as well as Howard S. Becker, *Art Worlds* (Berkeley: University of California Press, 1982). This tradition is not one to which the cultural studiers refer.

10. Jan Zita Grover, "AIDS, Keywords, and Cultural Work," in *Cultural Studies,* ed. Grossberg, Nelson, and Treichler, 238.

11. Wallace, "Negative Images," 659.

12. Louis Dumont, "On Value, Modern and Nonmodern," in *Essays on Individualism: Modern Ideology in Anthropological Perspective* (Chicago: University of Chicago Press, 1986), 248–49.

13. Jennifer Daryl Slack and Laurie Anne Whitt, "Ethics and Cultural Studies," in *Cultural Studies,* ed. Grossberg, Nelson, and Treichler, 576.

14. The work of Louis Dumont, particularly the fundamental distinction between (hierarchical) status and (political) power, provides a crucial antidote to much of the flabby thinking in cultural studies today. See the introduction to his *Homo Hierarchicus: The Caste System and Its Implications,* rev. English ed., trans. Mark Sainsbury, Louis Dumont, and Basia Gulati (Chicago: University of Chicago Press, 1980), as well as his *Essays on Individualism.*

15. To take only one example, Ellen Rooney argues against the "ideology of free and objective inquiry, of knowledge beyond power, which structures the liberal university and conceals many of its social and political functions." She concludes that cultural studies must follow the lead of feminist studies in carrying out a "critique of the politics of knowledge production" which in her view will lead to a "recognition of the interested nature of all knowledge, of every construction of an object, and of every inquiring subject's position." Ellen Rooney, "Discipline and Vanish: Feminism, the Resistance to Theory, and the Politics of Cultural Studies," *Differences* 2, no. 3 (1990): 17, 21, 22.

16. Henry A. Giroux, "Resisting Difference: Cultural Studies and the Discourse of Critical Pedagogy," in *Cultural Studies*, ed. Grossberg, Nelson, and Treichler, 202.

17. John Fiske, "British Cultural Studies and Television," in *Channels of Discourse*, ed. Robert Allen (Chapel Hill: University of North Carolina Press, 1987), 257. It is unclear what Fiske thinks it would mean for a norm to be *objective*.

18. Giroux, "Resisting Difference," 202.

19. Michel Foucault, "Truth and Power," in *Power*, ed. James D. Faubion, trans. Robert Hurley et al., vol. 3 of *Essential Works of Foucault, 1954–1984* (New York: The New Press, 2000), 133.

20. Emily Martin, "Body Narratives, Body Boundaries," in *Cultural Studies*, ed. Grossberg, Nelson, and Treichler, 418.

21. Kobena Mercer, " '1968': Periodizing Postmodern Politics and Identity," in *Cultural Studies*, ed. Grossberg, Nelson, and Treichler, 427.

22. Martin, "Body Narratives," 418.

23. Martin, "Body Narratives," 411.

24. This definition of "political" as "the imposition of a particular, interested point of view by means of power" is idiosyncratic at best, and, at worst, useless. What is important for our purposes—and what gives the use of this word in cultural studies much of its rhetorical force—is that what is "political" in the cultural studies argot is above all "not immutable," is subject to change, and, therefore, is an appropriate object of "struggle" by intellectual means. For a cogent critique of the idea that "everything is political," see Vincent Descombes, "Philosophie du jugement politique," *La Pensée politique* 2 (1994): 152–57.

25. Donna Haraway, "Situated Knowledges: The Science Question in Feminism and the Privilege of Partial Perspective," *Feminist Studies* 14, no. 3 (Fall 1988): 577.

26. Angela McRobbie, "Post-Marxism and Cultural Studies: A Post-script," in *Cultural Studies*, ed. Grossberg, Nelson, and Treichler, 722.

27. Nelson, Treichler, and Grossberg, "Cultural Studies: An Introduction," 13.

28. Giroux, "Resisting Difference," 203.

29. Nelson, Treichler, and Grossberg, "Cultural Studies: An Introduction," 13.

30. McRobbie, "Post-Marxism and Cultural Studies," 721, 726.

31. Slack and Whitt, "Ethics and Cultural Studies," 578.

32. Giroux, "Resisting Difference," 202.

33. Constance Penley, "Feminism, Psychoanalysis, and the Study of Popular Culture," in *Cultural Studies*, ed. Grossberg, Nelson, and Treichler, 496.

34. Nelson, Treichler, and Grossberg, "Cultural Studies: An Introduction," 5.

35. Tony Bennett, "Putting Policy Into Cultural Studies," in *Cultural Studies*, ed. Grossberg, Nelson, and Treichler, 32.

36. "Under the rubric of equality and freedom, the liberal version of assimilation wages 'war' against particularity, lived differences, and imagined futures that challenge culture as unitary, sacred, and unchanging, and identity, as unified, static, and natural" (Giroux, "Resisting Difference," 207).

37. The consequential respect and approval for the manifestations of power on the part of one's friends are merely the flipside of the denunciation of such exercises on the part of others. This might explain why the cultural studiers, so adept at rooting out effects of power and authority everywhere, seem oblivious to naked albeit benign displays of the "power-knowledge" dyad in their very midst. Homi Bhabha, a contributor to the Urbana conference

(of which the papers are collected in *Cultural Studies*) and undeniably a major "star" of the field, presented what has to be one of the most opaque "communications" ever put forth, filled with declarations such as: "It is the ambivalence and liminality enacted in the enunciative present of human articulation . . . that results in the signs and symbols of cultural difference being conjugated (not conjoined or complemented) through the interactive temporality of signification" ("Postcolonial Authority and Postmodern Guilt," in *Cultural Studies*, ed. Grossberg, Nelson, and Treichler, 58). Although his talk spurred one questioner to avow finding Bhabha's paper to be "of forbidding difficulty," apparently no one saw fit to call into question publicly the sort of charismatic authority and power one must possess to put such bombast over on a live audience.

38. Michel Foucault, "What is Enlightenment?" trans. Catherine Porter, in *The Foucault Reader*, ed Paul Rabinow (New York: Pantheon Books, 1984), 46.

39. David Glover and Cora Kaplan, "Guns in the House of Culture? Crime Fiction and the Politics of the Popular," in *Cultural Studies*, ed. Grossberg, Nelson, and Treichler, 223.

40. John Fiske, "Cultural Studies and the Culture of Everyday Life," in *Cultural Studies*, ed. Grossberg, Nelson, and Treichler, 172.

41. Giroux, "Resisting Difference," 204–5.

42. Giroux, "Resisting Difference," 209.

43. Bell Hooks, statement during discussion after presentation of Hall, "Cultural Studies and Its Theoretical Legacies," in *Cultural Studies*, ed. Grossberg, Nelson, and Treichler, pp. 293–4.

44. Wallace, "Negative Images," 668.

45. Charles Taylor, *The Ethics of Authenticity* (Cambridge, Mass.: Harvard University Press, 1991), 37–38.

46. Bennett, "Putting Policy Into Cultural Studies," 32.

47. Laura Kipnis, "(Male) Desire and (Female) Disgust: Reading *Hustler*," in *Cultural Studies*, ed. Grossberg, Nelson, and Treichler, 376, 387.

48. Janice Radway, "Mail-Order Culture and Its Critics: The Book-of-the-Month Club, Commodification and Consumption, and the Problem of Cultural Authority," in *Cultural Studies*, ed. Grossberg, Nelson, and Treichler, 530.

49. Williams, *Culture and Society*, 18.

50. Stuart Hall, "Gramsci's Relevance for the Study of Race and Ethnicity," *Journal of Communication Inquiry* 10, no. 2 (Summer 1986): 26.

51. Fiske, "Cultural Studies and the Culture of Everyday Life," 157, 160.

52. Bennett, "Putting Policy Into Cultural Studies," 26.

53. Ernest Gellner, *Postmodernism, Reason, and Religion* (London: Routledge, 1992), 79.

54. Giroux, "Resisting Difference," 209.

55. Only in the light of this ideal can one make sense of the complaint of a graduate student participant in the Urbana conference (one that, significantly, went unanswered) during the discussion after Stuart Hall's presentation that "in its structure, the conference most definitely privileges certain people, empowering them to speak while disempowering others" (Hall, "Cultural Studies and Its Theoretical Legacies," 293).

56. Fiske, "Cultural Studies and the Culture of Everyday Life," 165.

57. Bennett, "Putting Policy Into Cultural Studies," 24.

58. Giroux, "Resisting Difference," 202.

59. It is true that cultural studiers often emphasize race, gender, class, nationality, and sexual preference as sources of interests and beliefs. Yet if these categories are to be sources of interests, then they are open to the same dissenting critique as is the "dominant ideology," since my views or interests may always differ from and be marginalized by those that I am "supposed to" have as a function of my race, class, gender, etc. The emphasis on these categories, it seems to me, serves rather a compensatory function, allowing, except in the case of class, for the forging of collective identities on the basis of individual traits while giving a veneer of fatality to what is essentially a voluntarist conception of culture. These "groups" are ways of collectivizing what is at root a profoundly individualistic notion of culture.

60. Schaeffer, *Art of the Modern Age*, 284–85.

61. William Warner, "Spectacular Action: Rambo and the Popular Pleasures of Pain," in *Cultural Studies*, ed. Grossberg, Nelson, and Treichler, 686.

62. Gilles Lipovetsky, *L'Ère du vide: Essais sur l'individualisme contemporain* (Paris: Gallimard, 1983).

63. Hall, "Cultural Studies and Its Theoretical Legacies," 277.

64. Hooks, statement during discussion after presentation of Fiske, "Cultural Studies and the Culture of Everyday Life," 171. bell hooks's very name could be the emblem for the philosophy underlying cultural studies. If norms are in themselves oppressive, it is a deeply political and emancipatory act—"a rebellious gesture" that is "part of a strategy of empowerment"—to flout the convention whereby proper names are capitalized in English (Hooks, "To Gloria, Who Is She: On Using a Pseudonym," in her *Talking Back: Thinking Feminist, Thinking Black* [Boston: South End Press, 1989], 163).

65. Grover, "AIDS, Keywords, and Cultural Work," 227.

66. Rooney, "Discipline and Vanish," 22.

67. Haraway, "Situated Knowledges," 589.

68. "Our two cardinal ideals are called equality and liberty." Dumont, *Homo Hierarchicus*, 4.

69. Alain Renaut, *The Era of the Individual: A Contribution to a History of Subjectivity*, trans. M. B. DeBevoise and Franklin Philip (Princeton, N.J.: Princeton University Press, 1997).

## 24.  THE END OF THEORY, THE RISE OF
## THE PROFESSION

### A RANT IN SEARCH OF RESPONSES

### GEOFFREY GALT HARPHAM

IF YOU WORK in a university, you may sometimes wonder what your administrators are reading at night. I can tell you. Eyes popping, covers drawn up, they are eagerly devouring by flashlight lurid accounts of the bad effects of "the star system," by which a few conspicuously useless queen bees absorb vast resources that might go to building the institution. "The professoriat is being proletarianized," as the late Bill Readings summarizes this sense of things in *The University in Ruins*, "and the number of short-term or part-time contracts at major institutions increased (with the concomitant precipitation of a handful of highly paid stars)."[1] Such comments are echoed everywhere, especially in publications such as the *Chronicle of Higher Education* and MLA's *Profession*. Tulane University, where I worked for sixteen years, produced in the late 1990s an "Environmental Scan" that noted a "continuing trend toward the development of a winner-take-all market in which institutions vie for the services of 'star' faculty through generous salary and benefit packages. Star faculty," this document continues, "are recruited for their prestige; competition for their presence allows them to craft unique employment contracts which often limit their teaching loads to allow for greater time for research pursuits." A mighty prestige-machine, the university is being gutted by its own product, becoming hostage to "research."

Jetting from Bellagio to Berkeley—touching down everywhere, it seems, but at the institution that pays them—stars confer a reflected glory on their universities by virtue of their manifest uselessness: what sort of glorious entity must it be, the world wonders, that places such a high value on cognition that it could devote such immense resources to supporting someone whose only human function is to think, or at least to talk? What sort of entity, indeed, the "proletarianized" assistant and associate professors ask themselves bitterly, as they rise before dawn to grade scores of papers, having tossed in their beds for hours, pursued in their dreams by vengeful promotion and tenure committees that are skeptical and even contemptuous of their efforts. Stars, they might well conclude, wreck institutional efficiency, cripple institutional flexibility,

Geoffrey Galt Harpham. "The End of Theory, the Rise of the Profession: A Rant in Search of Responses." Originally published in *Professions: Conversations on the Future of Literary and Cultural Studies*, edited by Donald E. Hall. Copyright © 2001 by the Board of Trustees of the University of Illinois Press. Used with permission of the University of Illinois Press.

and give a wildly distorted view of the academic life; if only universities could get rid of those wretched stars, the wealth could be spread more evenly, incentives and rewards could be offered to those who need and deserve them, the university could rationalize its operations, and everything would be great.

Alas, they're tenured, and the university has not found an alternative currency comparable to cultural and intellectual prestige. So we're stuck. The whole miserable situation is like Brueghel's *Parable of the Blind Men*, with the entire line of sightless men, led by sightless administrators, tumbling one by one into the ditch. Brueghel does not, in this work, depict the stars themselves, but perhaps the massive composition called *The Peasant Wedding*, with its memorable images of gustatory and amatory repletion, the merry guests served platters of food carried on long boards by straw-haired graduate students, suggests the ethos of life at the top.

How did this happen? How did the university, the spiritual home of unremunerated idealism, come to germinate a whole class of overcompensated sybarites? The answer, I believe, is counterintuitive but inescapable: theory. At least in the humanities, *theory gave birth to the star system*.

In the beginning—the late sixties—theory promised a new beginning for the humanities, a transdisciplinary enterprise with great implications for future growth. The university was delighted to welcome theory into the fold, in part because theory represented a challenge to the increasingly encrusted autonomy of departments, a principle of communication between disciplines, and, as feature stories in national publications on such figures as Derrida, Foucault, Barthes, de Man, Fish, and the "Yale School" began to testify, a way of making headlines beyond the campus and thus of commanding the kind of respect reserved for celebrity. During the seventies and eighties, theory became a synonym for the exciting, the new, the postmodern. The theoretical "project" was the very site of individual and institutional ambition, the point at which the activities of the academy began to impinge on those of the world, and where the values of the world were most visibly operative in the academy.

In its immediate institutional effects, theory represented, then, a point of coalescence between the university and the outside world. Exactly why this might have been so is a bit obscure to me, but one interesting possibility is that, in contrast to other university pursuits centered on "research," the arduous re-finding of the various lost objects that presumably represented the essence of the university's mission, theory was in essence a forward-looking and synthetic activity. Theory acted as a universal solvent on those repositories of lost objects, history, and nature, whose orderings and hierarchies could be demonstrated to be "in theory" contingent or constructed rather than natural or given. The theoretical perspective leveled things that, when encountered in the world, had seemed to be formed into relations of higher or lower, weaker or stronger, valuable or worthless, essential and derivative, and so promoted the kind of skepticism about distinctions that characterized its institutional and extra-institutional effects.

Moreover, theory was intrinsically skeptical about identity, about the right or capacity of anything to determine what it was or how it could be understood, or about any kind of value or function that a thing, a practice, or a text might acquire in the course of its worldly existence. Theory posed the question of identity by treating all actual things not as themselves but as instances of some emergent general principle. Thus a meditation on a given text might become theoretical by giving way to a meditation on textuality itself, or a discussion of rhetorical figures in Proust might theorize itself by widening the focus to include figurality as such. Theory requires examples, and the theoretical approach treats all particular things as though they harbor theories, general laws yearning to see the light of day.

Often, theoretical skepticism takes the form of inverting some claim that had been thought to be crucial to the identity of a given thing or practice. This tendency is especially pronounced when it comes to the issue of whether something is concrete and material or conceptual and ideal. The rule of theory is that whatever a thing has been thought to be, it is in fact the opposite. Nothing is so utterly immured in specific, material, historical materiality that it cannot be seen otherwise, as a mere image, a concept, a tissue or film floating in zero G. "In theory," material things become liberated from the contexts in which they emerged, emancipated from their own most salient attributes, and free to enter into all manner of new configurations and relations. Thus, for example, prisons, when treated by Foucault, are transformed from monuments to the loss and lack of privilege, stone dungeons of banishment, into privileged figures or symbols of a radically conceptual "modernity." Derrida's account of Marx also falls into this category. Derrida emphasizes not the endless statistics of *Capital*, nor the insistence on economic and historical determinism, nor the calls to political transformation, but rather a persistent "spectrality" that runs through Marx's texts, as in the famous first line to "The Communist Manifesto": "A spectre is haunting Europe."

But theory can also materialize objects out of thin air. Derrida's early career as a theorist, we may recall, had been based on the insistence that texts, long held to be transparent records of mental events, testaments to spirit and genius, were in fact relentlessly and obdurately material entities, resistant to idealization and antithetical in their essence to anything like "consciousness." Early or late, spectralist or materialist, Derrida is always a theorist.

On one subject, theory is unequivocal. From the theoretical point of view, history can be suspended and the issues approached as if for the first time, with no baggage, no sense of an overriding natural or inevitable rightness. In one sense, history is the prey of theory, which relentlessly exposes its operations to be contingent, determined by power or force that has no "theoretical" justification. All historically settled interpretations of literary texts, for ex-

ample, were vulnerable to exposure by theorists not as the farthest point of refinement yet reached by human intelligence but as nonnecessary and provisional formulations achieved by various institutional and social agencies.
Whatever research had turned up concerning the whiteness of the whale,
Hamlet's indecision, or Satan's dark allure could be shown by some theorist to
be a mere reflex. Society or some uncognized force had tapped your knee, theory told interpreters, and you began to reproduce accounts for which no theoretical justification could be claimed.

This premise of reconfigurability extended beyond literary interpretation,
of course, to all sorts of other matters. Sexual identity, for example, was commonly understood to reflect one's inner disposition, one's "identity"; but, of
course, there was no solid theoretical reason why this should be: theoretically,
women were fully equal in endowment and rights to men, no matter what
their actual condition today or in history; theoretically, men could desire men
as well as women. The terms "feminist theory" and "queer theory" condense
into suggestive phrases the particularly strong alliance between the theoretical
and the minoritarian. And while history and theory are, as I noted, natural
predators, it could be said that each requires the other for support at crucial
moments. In the case of same-sex desire, theory corrodes the credentials of the
historical process that, in our society, has produced heterosexuality as a norm;
but history supports the theoretical claim by disclosing other cultures, or other
moments of our "own" culture, in which, for example, what we call "homosexuality" was felt to be not inconsistent with "normal" masculinity, even procre-
ative matrimony. Theory is nothing if not systematic, and the consistent argument of theory is that history is either more systematic than it appears to be, or
less systematic than it claims to be. In both cases, theory promotes the view,
which history—other histories, of other times and places—confirms, that
things could be otherwise than they are. The climate of theory is one of free
agency, in which all sorts of normative configurations are understood to be
historically constructed, pliable, and therefore susceptible to a previously unsuspected individual or collective agency.

Perhaps the exemplary instance of theory in the sense I'm talking about is
Saussure's linguistics. Saussure posited a new account of language; or rather,
he sought to delineate a new thing, which he called "language alone," as opposed to the language studied by comparative philologists and philosophers.
Comparative philologists had examined the internal evolution and geographical dissemination of various languages; philosophers, the origin or purpose of
language—historical in the first case, and radically historical in the second. Together, these two approaches combined to foster a kind of Hegelian view of
language as a historical product that yet could be traced to a single origin, perhaps even a divine endowment, an ultimate purpose, a definitively human nature. Saussure, by contrast, concerned himself with language as a present-tense
system of signs. According to Saussure, the sign system is fundamentally "arbi-

trary"; the system could have been constructed otherwise, and could, if the linguistic community so determined, be changed, albeit slowly. From this premise, only parts of which were retained in the discipline of linguistics as it subsequently evolved, other thinkers in various disciplines concluded that pretty much everything that has seemed fixed, given, natural, was in fact arbitrary and could be constructed differently—the essential premise, I am contending, of theory as such.

Perhaps the most exciting aspect of theory was that it operated by a kind of lever principle. "Discoveries" in one field could be shoehorned into another. In this way, the linguistics of Saussure could be made the basis for "advances" in the fields of psychoanalysis, political theory, philosophy, and literary criticism. Thus Saussurean premises had a "theorizing" impact on the hitherto empirical-philosophical discourse of linguistics; and this enabled linguistics to have a theorizing impact on other disciplines, as major "theorists" in such disciplines as history and philosophy happily conceded. Literature, the most empirical of fields in some respects, the closest to the untheorized world, was, perhaps for this very reason, the most hungry for theory and the most responsive to Saussure. As Paul de Man commented, literary theory "comes into its own . . . as the application of Saussurean linguistics to literary texts."[2]

In institutional terms, theory was power. In everyday parlance, theory and power might be antonyms, but within the university they rapidly became synonyms. And, through its sponsorship of theory, literary study went, almost overnight, from being the feminized outcast of the institution to the power center of the humanities, which were rechristened "the human sciences" in order to group them with social science and bring them more nearly into equivalence with the prestige and concreteness of the "hard" sciences. The prestige of theory was remarkably concrete. Theorists, especially foreigners, whose knowledge seemed different in kind as well as greater in quantity than that of natives, possessed the power of decree. Certain texts were literally required reading; smeary photocopies of articles recently published or freshly translated were passed around as samizdat productions. If you knew French or knew someone who did, you could acquire the cachet that accrues to the "subject supposed to know." I remember getting a mimeo on blue paper of a partial translation of Derrida's "Structure, Sign, and Play in the Human Sciences," and the feeling of power that rumpled bundle of paper gave me, even—in fact, especially—before reading it. Barthes's *Mythologies*, de Man's "The Rhetoric of Temporality," Lacan's *Écrits*, Kristeva's *Desire in Language*, Althusser's *Lenin and Philosophy*, Foucault's *Madness and Civilization*—if you hadn't read these, you just weren't in the game. Thus a dark luminosity spread from literature departments—or at least a favored few in those departments who were in possession of the right "texts"—outward.

Now the point is that this atmosphere of danger and charisma gave rise to the star system in the humanities: yesterday's renegade theorists are today's institutional stars. The most representative American figure in this scene is surely Stanley Fish, whose career reached a point of rare transparency with a series of articles and interventions in the mid-to-late eighties on the subject of professionalism. The most interesting of these, called simply "Anti-Professionalism," argued that since academics were properly and necessarily involved in professional structures, it made no sense to pretend otherwise. Those who for whatever reason deplored the professional context of knowledge-production were simply incoherent and self-confounding on the face of it.[3] Other messages from Fish to the universe, encouraging humanist academics to picture themselves behind the wheels of Porsches rather than pug-ugly Volvos, to think of themselves as players in the go-go atmosphere of corporate turbulence, swelling fortunes, and blockbuster mergers, further encouraged humanists, previously the most unworldly denizens of the ivory tower, to adopt a more aggressive posture, a more sharply delineated profile.

In one respect, Fish made a career of being against theory; as he said in the introduction to *Doing What Comes Naturally*, he was, time and time again, making "an argument in which the troubles and benefits of interpretive theory are made to disappear in the solvent of an enriched notion of practice."[4] But this hardly does away with theory. The most aggressive and capacious claim one can make on behalf of theory is that it is not a separate activity at all, but just ordinary practice, for this claim makes theory unconscious, inescapable, and impervious to critique. No practice would be immune to such a claim, as Fish demonstrated by making identical arguments not just about literature and its interpretation but also about linguistics, psychoanalysis, political philosophy, and legal theory. A thoroughgoing pragmatist, Fish actually instantiates many of the basic principles driving the theory revolution, including its tendency to level or erase distinctions and its ability to generate a transdisciplinary institutional power.

The forward thrust of the theoretical era effectively ended with the deaths of Barthes, Althusser, Lacan, de Man, and Foucault, but by then—1984, with all our Big Brothers gone!—all the elements of today's star system were in place. One of the many signs of the dominance of theory was the emergence of an academic discipline called, simply, "theory," and of various programs designed to propagate that theory. I was hired by Tulane University in 1986 as a "theorist," which was fine by me, and a year later, was given the job of inventing and then running the Program in Literary Theory, which I did from 1987 to 1993. The history of this program suggests the point I'm trying to make, and the next one as well. We got sizable and impressively engaged audiences at our hitherto sleepy university by inviting scholars who were thought to have something to say that was not just empirical but theoretical, not confined to the texts they were discussing but carrying a general import such that if you missed it, you might be history before you knew it, working in an outmoded paradigm. During those years, I invited people I considered to be established and rising stars: J. Hillis Miller, W. J. T. Mitchell, Robert Weimann, Naomi Schor, Jane Gallop, Hayden White, Judith Butler, Mary Poovey, Eve Kosofsky Sedgwick, Christopher Norris, Myra Jehlen, Martin Jay, Stanley Fish, Fredric Jameson, Walter Benn Michaels, Rodolphe Gasché, Slavoj Žižek, Homi Bhabha, and others. We missed a few, but we hit, I think, a fair percentage of the acknowledged intellectual leaders in the field. And they *were* acknowledged; their stature transcended their fields because that's the way theory worked.

What strikes me most forcibly about this list is that if I were running such a program today, a decade after I gave it up, I would invite many of the same people. To be sure, most of the people in this group are still in their primes, but I can think of very few emergent stars who will, in ten years' time, replace them. There is certainly no new *generation* of stars; what we now call "the profession" is not generating stars, so that yesterday's heavyweights remain today's, just a little heavier.

Similar things are going on all over. In his last decade, Sir Isaiah Berlin was fond of saying that there were no more geniuses around. And indeed, if one were to go back, say, to 1968, that amazing year, one could point to Martin Luther King, James Baldwin, the Beatles, Richard Feynman, Chomsky, Nureyev, Nabokov, Sartre, Borges. Another thirty years or so back, and you had Thomas Mann, Hemingway, Beckett, Duke Ellington, Schoenberg, Bogart, Picasso, Dietrich, Franklin Roosevelt, T. S. Eliot, James Joyce, Frank Lloyd Wright, Virginia Woolf. Peel off another thirty and you are looking at the birth of modern art, modern music, modern dance, modern poetry, modern science: Cézanne, Matisse, Degas, Picasso once again, Stravinsky, Dubois, Twain, the Wright Brothers, Thomas Edison, Marie Curie, Niels Bohr, Einstein, Bertrand Russell, Freud, Nijinsky, Rockefeller—giants were walking the earth. The world today has both expanded and shrunk; people have "access" to more information, but there is, it seems, less that is truly worth thinking about, less to become fascinated by or deeply committed to. All fields of cultural or intellectual endeavor, once heroic, now consider themselves "professions." And perhaps this is the true meaning of "postmodernism."

The portion of the academy that I'm talking about is, then, not alone in witnessing a certain flattening, or what Fredric Jameson called (speaking of postmodern culture) a "waning of affect."[5] Indeed, the history of literary criticism can profitably be studied from the point of view of the fortunes of affect. Eliot, of course, scrupulously eschewed affect, thereby creating a powerful "St. Sebastian" effect of pathos and fortitude. The most powerful subsequent critics—including I. A. Richards, Erich Auerbach, Edmund Wilson, Newton Arvin, F. O. Matthiessen, Leslie Fiedler, Raymond Williams—were also those whose rich affective life could be read as the photographic negative of their immersion in the facts of textuality and history. The demiurges of the theory revolution virtually drown in affect, sometimes expressed bluntly as in Derrida or Barthes, sometimes perceptible through its repression as in Foucault or de Man. Theory actually represented the liberation of affect; but the rise of professionalism made literary study available not just to aesthetically responsive scholars but to ambitious people who understood the structure and ethos of a posttheoretical professionalism that represents the form of postmodernism prevalent in the academy today. That spirit is corporate rather than controversialist, bureaucratic rather than charismatic, consolidating rather than exploratory.

It would, however, be a mistake to blame the spirit of professionalism for the death of theory, for theory was in trouble from the very beginning. The most effective theoretical pedagogue, de Man, himself wrote in a late essay that theory was in fact nothing other than "the universal theory of the impossibility of theory"; "nothing can overcome the resistance to theory," he wrote, "since theory *is* itself this resistance."[6] Of course, de Man had a highly idiosyncratic view of theory as the universal solvent of all identities, all totalizations, all "premature" thematizations; but it is interesting that, even at the acme of its institutional prestige, theory was attacking itself, issuing challenges to its own integrity. These challenges were taken up and amplified in a far less friendly and ironic spirit by those who, like Fish, Walter Benn Michaels, Stephen Knapp, Gerald Graff, and Frank Lentricchia, had no particular investment in theory's survival and in fact saw theory in a pre-Columbian spirit as an alien virus, an old-world microbe threatening the health of the indigenous peoples, their pristine pragmatism, their naive but sturdy moralism. Thus, during the past twenty years or so, the antitheoretical reaction has flourished and ramified, and theory has been supplanted by other critical discourses that make no grand systemic claims but do often claim moral rectitude and political efficacy. Since the nineties, the scene has been dominated by sex, especially homosex; by race, especially minorities; by culture, especially material culture; by performance, especially the performance of identity. The emphasis today is on the local, the particular, the concrete, the minority. Size does matter: the smaller, the better.

The discursive mark of the professionalized academy is the disappearance of controversy over fundamental principles and a general concentration on the cultivation of small plots of ground, little fields of specialization. There are no must-reads for a general audience. Instead, we have in-groups cultivating their social and institutional identities and reward systems. Everybody is preaching, but only to the choir, to smaller and precommitted audiences, because nothing applies generally. I was told by an editor at one of the major university presses that the largest-selling book at a recent MLA convention was a book on science and Victorian culture, a fact that confirmed, he said, his suspicion that literary scholars don't buy books in literary studies, but rather books in other fields. The reason for this, I think, is that literary scholars today don't feel the need to read anything else in literary studies—they just need to write.

The book on science may help them do that; the others are just competition, clogging the track.

The immersion in the specific and material forecloses any effort at speculative system building and fosters an intense effort at *description*, on the presumption that criticism properly consists of an accurate rendering, an account that "gives voice," "reconstitutes," or "celebrates." Cultural studies today is militantly empirical, with a settled preference for the material, the embodied, the visible, the localizable. The strong cultural critic today is typically, if not always, indifferent, even hostile, to theory. In a 1993 article entitled "Queer Performativity: Henry James's *The Art of the Novel*," Eve Kosofsky Sedgwick asserted that "the thing I *least* want to be heard offering here is a 'theory of homosexuality.' I have none and I want none."[7] An even more telling sign of the antitheoretical turn in this particular field is the conclusion to Judith Butler's influential book *Gender Trouble*, a book that became influential not through its dense and rigorous readings of Freud, Foucault, Lacan, and others but largely through its *envoi*, which made a sudden pivot toward "performance" as the key to gender identity and the dubious (as many feel) resolution of the "trouble" that had constituted the book's subject up to that point.[8] With this gesture, "queer theory" abruptly morphed into cultural studies.

By comparison with such classic theoretical terms as *text, form, determination, ideology, desire, value,* or *interpretation,* the very term *culture* is almost defiantly undertheorized. As Geoffrey Hartman notes in *The Fateful Question of Culture*, the term resonates with both *cult* and *agriculture*, and suggests, even in contemporary academic usages, a fascination with barbarism or archaism, a keen interest in the retrograde, as if authenticity were only to be found below radar or reconnaissance, down among the phenomena.[9] Recently, as chair of my department, I received a job application that referred to a dissertation entitled "Cannibalizing the Victorians: Racial and Cultural Hybridity in the Brontës and Their Caribbean Rewritings." A full and eager participant in the current academic scene, I could not suppress an involuntary moan of satisfaction, and regretted all the more that the position had not, after all, been funded.

Sometimes I can suppress the moan, as when, for example, theory is retained in ghostly forms as a way of legitimating studies that cannot legitimate themselves. I recently participated in a panel on the impact of cultural studies on literary study, and heard a speaker who, after making numerous judicious prefatory remarks about the importance and complexity of the interlocking questions of race, gender, class, et cetera, finally got down to the nub of the issue, her particular field of research. "White identity," she said, is an understudied component of racial self-articulation; and what is particularly understudied by the academy is the fact that whiteness is "performed" differentially. Within this general category of racial performance can be situated the further fact that some people seem not just white but super- or hyperwhite. And so, the professor settled in to speak of her work, which consisted of trolling the hallways of Los Angeles high schools in search of "nerds" to observe and interview. "The issue of nerd identity," she claimed, "involves many crucial theoretical questions." A trained and credentialed sociolinguist, this professor was in a position to assert that "different identity claims are being made by saying, 'tyotally cyool' as opposed to 'totally cool.' " On hearing this, my first thought, of course, was to call *Sports Illustrated* to offer the incident as a candidate for their feature, "This Week's Sign of the Apocalypse"; but then I reflected that the numerous theoretical issues buzzing around nerd identity, no matter how fascinating and urgent to me, would probably not interest most readers of *SI*.

I am not opposed to description. When criticism abandons descriptions it stands in danger of becoming like political philosophy, which neither analyzes nor describes anything concrete at all and is thus the most corrupt of all scholarly discourses. We must, however, continue to mark and to maintain the distinctions between description and inference, description and analysis, description and norm, description and speculation. Good criticism—that is, criticism that is judged to be good—will make the connections appear to be so tight that there seems to be almost no space between description and its others. But there must be, in the mind of the approving reader, some sense that an object is nested in the judgments or inferences that swarm around it, and that sense is produced only by description that seems to stand clear of those judgments and inferences. This is true even if the "object" in question is description, representation, or language itself, as it is in the case of a literary or philosophical text. Judgments, generalizations, theories have integrity only as generalizations from accurately described details.

But, I would insist, those details themselves acquired dignity and stature only in the firm embrace of some reasonable judgment, some tightly articulated general system, some powerful and suggestive theory. When the relations between description and its others are managed properly, the effect can be one of great power. When they are done poorly, when the distance between object and assessment, or description and inference, is collapsed, then the object of description has no autonomy from the mind of the critic; the reader of criticism is coerced, and the effect is one of absolute power, which, as is well known, corrupts absolutely.

Parenthetically, I would like to add that a collapse of distance in criticism is being accompanied and reaffirmed by a comparable collapse in the domain of teaching. If, today, one cannot theorize with the freedom of years past, neither can one deploy, in the classroom, old-style authority. It goes without saying today that one cannot claim superior wisdom or insight; one cannot intimidate; one cannot fail to befriend—in, of course, a strictly platonic sense. The only qualities valued are informality, accessibility, approachability, charm. Teaching must be easy listening. How different from my own experience! Most of my teachers, I confess, I merely tolerated; but a few earned my respect, even my fear and reverence. By these I was humbled and inspired and, eventually, guided. All these men—I had no women teachers after ninth grade!—retired long ago, but if they were teaching today, they would be considered woefully defective: after years of low or at best erratic evaluations with a high standard deviation, they would be advised by their chairs or deans to shape up, to get with the program, to conform themselves to their students' expectations. And whatever those students expected, it would not be a scholar. Students today do not, in general, seek out and read works their professors have written; at the undergraduate level, most students have a very uncertain sense of reputation or lack thereof. Professors are just there for them—not intellectuals but just graders. One inevitable consequence of the disappearance of distance in teaching is the disappearance of distance in the relation between teaching and research, which, as we are constantly hearing, are virtually identical activities, with the undergraduate classroom represented as the proper audience for scholarship.

We need, I believe, to restore the missing space. We need, that is, to create, to mark, and to maintain the kinds of contestable and nonabsolute distance— between object and description, description and inference, and even between teacher and student—that define criticism and pedagogy at their most powerful and indeed at their most dangerous. Without these distances, it is impossible to make the earth, or even the student, tremble, difficult to create the conditions for critical power or pedagogical inspiration.

Critical movements cannot arrange for their own succession, but they are capable of provoking reactions. And so we may hope that current practices might give way to a renewed attention to literature, especially to canonical literature. The big works earn their status not by their serene classicism but by their endless malleability, their generous sponsorship of an infinite number of arguments and interests. The deepest mystery of the aesthetic text is the way in which it combines a profound indifference to its own criticism and to any utilities that may be claimed for it with the keenest responsiveness to that criticism, those utilities. Stuck in the past, literature remains open to the future; it is progressive, even radical, because it includes among its energies a deep neutrality. It can provide a critique, a negative knowledge, because it has a certain monumentality, a profoundly material presence. We need to know more about all this.

The kind of inquiry I'm encouraging would be, first, an *inquiry*, undertaken in a spirit of passionate curiosity, a powerful desire to know and to create knowledge. Theory, or the theoretical impulse, would be essential to the latter, more active desire. I am not simply urging a return to the heyday of theory. To mark the difference, we could recall one of the more widely publicized arguments of those years concerning the "literary" component of philosophy and theory. Many construed this argument as meaning that literature had a kind of natural authority over these other discourses, but what it really means, or at least ought to mean according to me, is that no discourse is absolutely distinct from any other, and consequently that none has any predetermined priority or privilege over the others. Can we now begin to imagine a kind of dotted line between theory and literature; can we try to regard a theoretical formulation as an "example" of a literary one, or to see a conceptual statement as a clarifying instance of a statement whose native discursive home was literature?

I would like to cite the words of a particular hero of mine, my old teacher Robert Martin Adams, who was among the very greatest of American literary intellectuals. At the conclusion of his spacious and imposing work *The Land and Literature of England*, Adams comments on the reluctance of modern historians to generalize, and the consequent preference for studying family groupings or short-term behavior of actual people. "Putting a single faction, or single Parliament . . . under the microscope," he says, "we can almost persuade ourselves that there are no large-scale patterns in history, and that long-term developments, if they exist, don't count for anything." But, he argues, they do, and they count for plenty.

The chief trouble with atomizing history so completely is that it becomes, under these circumstances, an incomprehensible jumble of particulars of which the mind cannot form or retain a model. Schematizing it completely, on the other hand, flattens out all those living and complex particulars which really mark the behavior of men and raise the study of history above the interest of a diagram or a formula. Two simple rules of thumb (unfortunately antithetical if not contradictory) are that one must learn as much as possible of history's gritty details and incorporate them as largely as possible in a coherent vision of the past. Reconciling these two imperatives—one of which looks toward the past chiefly for its own sake, the other chiefly for the sake of our modern understanding—is the art of creative or compositional reading. Without this resilient, constructive activity, the perusal of reading lists, however long and elaborate, is mere accumulation of inert materials, a toilsome vanity.[10]

Adams stresses history, and I have emphasized theory, but the general project is the same: to attempt to think in two directions at once, to reach down and in toward a clear grasp of "gritty details" and to extend out and beyond to an understanding of the larger structures. To set the particular and the general, figures and concepts, narrative and nationality, on a flat surface, not in order to degrade or decompose them but in order to explore what sorts of relations they might enter into absent any presumptions of a natural discursive hierarchy—this would be not just to come up with new interpretations but to subject the very ideas of literature, history, and theory to new pressures and to expose each to new opportunities. Such a project would, I submit, constitute a viable and interesting agenda for the next generation, a project whose successful prosecution would make a star of anyone.

If there are, among those who read this, any respondents in search of a rant, or counter-ranters in search of an occasion, they might wish to pursue several lines of attack.

1. You seem opposed to professionalism. But isn't it true that professionalism is nothing other than a necessary attempt to claim respect for academic work in a cultural climate that is indifferent if not hostile to it?

2. Why are you so attached to theory? Theory was a corruption of literary study, not, as you say, a natural or inevitable form of it. How can you advocate both theory and the aesthetic? Your employment as a "theorist," whatever that may be, suggests an ulterior motive.

3. The lines between discourses secure the integrity of all discourses. To attempt, as you suggest, to imagine a "dotted line" between discourses or to attempt to think "in two directions at once" is simply to stop thinking productively at all. Are you contending that one can think omnidirectionally, without frameworks?

4. Postmodern culture is rapidly erasing the high modernism for which you seem so curiously nostalgic, and replacing it with more democratized forms of knowing to which you seem peculiarly hostile. Where do you get off?

5. Your insistent talk of heroes and geniuses and giants suggests a politically questionable and historically retrograde vision of higher education—a vision, in fact, of education as the virtual institutionalization of *height*, with a corresponding place reserved for the lowly. Doesn't this just confirm inequality as such, and work against the true goal of education, which is to eliminate such invidious differences?

6. Your obvious distaste for new areas of scholarly inquiry implies a mind embedded, like that of most boomers, in its own glorious past. You had your day, now why don't you just give it up and clear out?

7. Your touching defense of the aesthetic echoes some of the most mystified criticism of the past century, and coordinates nicely with the "aesthetic ideology" which is now known to have caused such confusion and damage. How can you distinguish your position from the right-wing ideologies that allied themselves with the aesthetic?

8. Isn't your argument about the dependence of theory on "gritty particulars" actually motivated by a desire to provide a brake on the kind of utopian theorizing that constitutes the proudest tradition of left intellectualism?

9. The way in which you insistently raise challenges from the left suggests that you feel particularly fortified on this front. In fact, however, aren't you more vulnerable to attacks from the right? Isn't, for example, your complaint about the "overcompensated sybarites" of the star system just a screen for a well-disguised if ill-advised populism that would, if installed in the university, destroy the very idea of merit and achievement and the respect that rightly goes with them?

10. The tone of this essay is difficult to assess, wavering as it does between massive self-assurance and a humble spirit of deference to one's betters. And you seem undecided about your attitude toward the star system. Do you really know what you're saying, or why you're saying it?

### NOTES

The above was published in a volume entitled *Professions: Conversations on the Future of Literary and Cultural Studies*, edited by Donald E. Hall (Urbana: University of Illinois Press, 2001). This volume was supposed to consist of a collection of conversations between scholars whose views would be divergent enough to produce an entertaining and perhaps illuminating exchange. The conversation in which I had been scheduled to participate never began, however, because just as arrangements were being finalized, my partner simply stopped responding to email or phone messages. With the deadline looming, the editor and I agreed that I would write a piece that would represent what I could project as my half of the conversation, without the resistance that would have been provided by a respondent. The result is this unopposed and unmoderated "rant."

1. Bill Readings, *The University in Ruins* (Cambridge, Mass.: Harvard University Press, 1996).

2. Paul de Man, *The Resistance to Theory* (Minneapolis: University of Minnesota Press, 1986), 8.

3. Stanley Fish, "Anti-Professionalism," *New Literary History* 17, no. 1 (Autumn 1985): 89–108.

4. Stanley Fish, *Doing What Comes Naturally: Change, Rhetoric, and the Practice of Theory in Literary and Legal Studies* (Durham, N.C.: Duke University Press, 1989), ix.

5. Fredric Jameson, *Postmodernism, or, The Cultural Logic of Late Capitalism* (Durham, N.C.: Duke University Press, 1991) 10.

6. Paul de Man, *The Resistance to Theory*, 19.

7. Eve Kosofsky Sedgwick, "Queer Performativity: Henry James's *The Art of the Novel*," *GLQ: A Journal of Lesbian and Gay Studies* 1, no. 1 (1993): 1–16.

8. Judith Butler, *Gender Trouble: Feminism and the Subversion of Identity* (New York: Routledge, 1990).

9. Geoffrey H. Hartman, *The Fateful Question of Culture* (New York: Columbia University Press, 1997).

10. Robert Martin Adams, *The Land and Literature of England: A Historical Account* (New York: Norton, 1983), 523.

# PART V
## IDENTITIES

ONE OF THE MOST STRIKING features of the ascendancy of Theory during the past few decades is its contradictory treatment of identity. Although the reigning ideas issuing from academic luminaries have attacked the very notions of stable identities (as well as stable meanings), this has in no way lessened these theorists' personal prestige. Despite this glaring contradiction, it is "subject positions"—not actual, coherent personhood—that have proliferated in academic debate. Thus, identity has come to be used as either a shield or a bludgeon, always, in the process, short-circuiting thought and replacing it with proclamations. This is where identity politics meets the assault on reason (to which we shall turn later). In the absence of a primary commitment to logic, rationality, and the force of evidence, how should competing claims be adjudicated? Identity leaps in to give the answer: it is not the content of ideas that counts but who has the right to speak about what.

Scholars have suggested that fairy tales help children discover their identity and calling. The essays in this part address another type of fairy tale: a story in which every character is situated in a place in the hierarchy of identities, while the value of individual contributions is judged on the basis of identity claims. As John Ellis noted in part 1, perhaps no other theoretical development has been more pernicious to the study of literature than the empowerment of identity flowing from privileging the ever-present threesome of race, class, and gender. Equally unproductive is the facile abandon with which "Third World" theorists have come to believe in that trinity and to use it to mimic "First World" theory. In the contemporary academic scene, identity politics has become a substitute for a careful examination of the validity of ideas, an indispensable tool that allows theorists to economize time and effort while claiming to occupy the moral high ground.

As the essays in this section show, identity politics for decades has been on a collision course with the serious study of literature. Perhaps the most expressive, and most familiar, emblem of this clash is the label "Dead White Males" with which the entire Western tradition (always excluding, of course, the still fashionable French *maîtres à penser*) is now routinely dismissed. The obverse of this blanket rejection is the "standpoint epistemology" that privileges, say, the writings of "women of color." The greater the claim for past oppression and marginalization, the greater the presumed validity of a group's contributions today.

The essays in this part describe the mechanisms of identity politics and its appropriation by Theory. We start with Todd Gitlin's account of the rise of this phenomenon and its roots in American life. All forms of identity politics, Gitlin asserts, attempt to distinguish insiders from outsiders and draw political advantage from this distinction. As identity issues narrow one's world, concern with language and imagery expands, and groups press the special merits of their separate "culture." Then, having reclaimed positive meanings for their beleaguered identities, identity groups move on to revel in separatism, engaging in defensive aggression, cultivating "a rapture of marginality." All this leads to an aggrandizement of "difference," which treats culture as politics and the university as a microcosm of the global struggle.

How such preoccupations play out in the study of literature is explored in the other essays in this section. Expecting benefits from identity—it is important to note—is a symptom that transcends literature classrooms and infects most areas in the humanities and social sciences, and even beyond. From Gitlin's account of the rise of identity politics we move to William C. Dowling's more detailed exploration of the incoherencies to which reading for (or from) identity leads. Drawing on Wimsatt and Beardsley's work, more than fifty years ago, on the "intentional fallacy," Dowling argues that these two scholars raised objections that contemporary gender criticism has not, to this day, adequately confronted. He demonstrates the problem with an examination of recent feminist readings of Alexander Pope's poem *Eloisa to Abelard* and of Diderot's *La Religieuse*. Gender criticism, driven by its ideological agenda, has failed to face what Dowling takes to be a crucial issue: the gender fallacy, which he identifies as a special version of the genetic fallacy (confusing a thing and its origins) that governs much criticism today.

Elaine Marks describes the practical consequences for literary studies of the frivolous embrace of identity (whether that of the writer, the reader, or the teacher) as a guiding principle. Her essay, published the year before her death in 2001, is of particular interest because Marks was one of the first scholars to introduce contemporary French feminist theorists to American readers (through her coedited book *New French Feminists* [1981]). But here Marks records her growing dissatisfaction with the exaggerated emphasis on "difference," which leads to simplistic trolling of literature for signs of the ubiquitous isms: sexism, racism, and so on. Lamenting the loss of the ability to respond imaginatively to literature, Marks also notes, ironically, that expressing such concerns today stigmatizes a scholar—even one with excellent feminist credentials—as "reactionary."

Next, Lee Siegel extends the discussion to another identity area: Queer theory. "Nowhere," he writes, "has the sexualization of reality proceeded so intensely and so relentlessly as in the seminar room." Volume 1 of Foucault's *History of Sexuality* has served as the bible of queer theory (contrary to Foucault's own intentions), resulting in an explosion of bad scholarship. Siegel's case in point is the work of Eve Kosofsky Sedgwick, the "mother of queer theory," and of her followers. He tracks in detail the forced readings that impose "queer" as a new kind of "normalcy" and deaden any appreciation of what

Siegel dares to refer to as "beauty and fineness of perception and fragile inner life."

This section concludes with K. Anthony Appiah's bemused contemplation of how moral judgments have entered into literary theory with a personal vengeance, so that the conduct of scholars and the presumed political implications of their work come under minute examination. Allied to identity politics, such scrutiny continually breaks out in print, at conferences, and in the classroom, as individuals are praised or blamed for their presumed commitment to or deviance from the normative attitudes on race and other identity issues. Appiah takes as an example the recent work of Susan Gubar, once heroine and now defendant in the endless game of identity politics. He concludes on an optimistic note, however: identity politics seems now to be falling into disrepute.

## 25. THE CANT OF IDENTITY

### TODD GITLIN

THE MORE VOCIFEROUSLY a term is trumpeted in public, the more con-testable it is under scrutiny. The automatic recourse to a slogan, as if it were tantamount to a value or an argument, is frequently a measure of the need to suppress a difficulty or a vagueness underneath. Cant is the hardening of the aura around a concept. Cant automates thought, substitutes for deeper assess-ments, creates the illusion of firmness where there are only intricacies, freezes a fluid reality. Cant is sincere, usually, and its sincerity also protects against scrutiny. Cant comforts. And cant tends to corrupt its opposition into coun-tercant. There is the cant of identity and the cant that rises with righteous and selective indignation against the "political correctness" of the Left, though not against that of the Right.

The cant of identity underlies identity politics, which proposes to deduce a position, a tradition, a deep truth, or a way of life from a fact of birth, physiog-nomy, national origin, sex, or physical disability. The hardening of one of these categories into cant begins with binary thinking—things are either raw or cooked, male or female, this or that—a propensity that may indeed be, as Lévi-Strauss maintained, universal. Anxiety generated by difference may well be embedded in the human condition; so may be the animosity that accompanies anxiety. Perhaps the capacity quickly to classify "the other" as same or differ-ent, friend or enemy, once conferred a benefit for survival. But whether or not it was originally a means of natural selection, this sort of binary thinking cer-tainly helps clans, elites, and nations maintain themselves. From binary think-ing follows a propensity for identity thinking, which categorizes strangers—this is a person of Type X, not Type Y. The identity thinking of the powerful reassures them that they deserve to rule; the identity thinking of the oppressed affirms that they are not who the rulers think they are. If the identity affirma-tion of the oppressed begins as a defense against claims of superiority, it can swerve into its own sense of superiority. All forms of identity politics are overly clear about who the insiders are—"*normal* Americans," "*the* people," "*la* Raza,"—and overly dismissive of outsiders. In either case, cant makes for effi-cient simplifications, but only at the price of rigidity. Cant is what we have when we think we know more than we do. Its opposite is curiosity.

Today, it is the cant of identity that many Americans espouse, and the ques-tion is why. The beginning of an answer is that identity does more than exclude. It transcends the self, affirms a connection with others. Erik H. Erikson, whose writings in the 1960s did a lot to popularize the notion of identity, put the matter this way: "The functioning ego, while guarding individuality, is far from isolated, for a kind of communality links egos in a mutual activation."[1] Identity extends through space, binding a person to fellow travelers in the human project. But identity also extends through time, linking the individual with past and future, extending beyond the mortal body. As Erikson wrote, "Psychosocial identity is necessary as the anchoring of man's transient existence in the here and now." Erikson warned against fossilizing identity, which, he said, "is never 'established' as an 'achievement' in the form of a personality armor, or of anything static and unchangeable."[2] But the cant retailed from his thinking spread rapidly throughout vertiginous America, a society founded on rootlessness, devoted to self-creation, worshipping evanescence, stuffing its spiritual voids with the latest gadgets.

Americans are obsessed today with their racial, ethnic, religious, and sexual identities. What is supposed to be universal is, above all, difference. And yet there is a peculiar blindness. Beneath the rhetoric, the functional assumption shared by virtually all Americans is that the market is the place to look for values, that what matters is "the bottom line." While Americans busily dig for roots, their economy is built on the steady replacement of old things with new things. The hypertrophy of difference, at least at the level of rhetoric, masks disrespect for the real thing.

## The Separatist Impulse

Identity politics based on race spawned identity politics based on ethnicity. The same model was adopted by the women's and gay liberation movements in 1968–69. The spirit of the New Left released long dammed-up forces of revolt. Subordination on the basis of sex and sexuality became the basis for a liberationist sequence: first, the discovery of common experience and interests; next, an uprising against a society that had imposed inferior status; finally the inversion of that status, so that distinct qualities once pointed out as proof of inferiority were transvalued into the basis for positive distinction. It is only this third stage—where the group searches for and cultivates distinctive customs, qualities, lineages, ways of seeing, or, as they came to be known, "cultures"—that deserves to be called identity politics.

Cut off from ecumenical political hopes, the partisans of identity politics became preoccupied with what they might control in their immediate surroundings—language and imagery. Thus the singular influence of literary and cultural studies and the virtually self-satirizing obsession with rectifying the language of opponents. Like the rest of American society, the practitioners of identity politics resorted to legalistic regulation to address social problems. They had, by now, many laws and administrative rulings on their side, and a tradition of fighting for more. Campaigning against pornography, they took up Puritan crusades against unholy expression. They promulgated on-campus speech codes and sought to regulate dating. Fights over appropriate language, over symbolic representation in curriculum and cuisine, were to them the core of "politics." Affirmative action substituted for economic reconstruction. The new academic Left tended to mistake strong language for steady, consequential political engagement. They spoke confidently, belligerently, of "disruptions," "subversions," "ruptures," "contestations." The more their political life was confined to the library, the more their language bristled with aggression.

The distinct identity groupings on campus, once institutionalized, found reasons to remain distinct. They radiated savoir faire and solidarity. They seemed to offer the satisfactions of intellectual companionship and political passion at the same time—a heady mixture. Having struggled to overcome silences, they developed their own methods of silencing. They were uncomfortable with self-contradiction and individual difference. They closed ranks and protected turf, for their struggle was never-ending. Identities, however strenuously declared, remained embattled, ever in need of shoring up. Separatism was no longer a stage on the way to some sort of intellectual and political reconciliation; it was an institution and an intellectual given. Difference was vital, commonality moribund. Demands for race and gender blindness and inclusion tipped toward demands for all-consuming race and gender consciousness. Difference was practiced, commonality barely even thought.

For the participants, the benefits of the pursuit of identity were manifold: a sense of community, an experience of solidarity, a prefabricated reservoir of recruits. Identity groups offered ready-made acquaintanceship. From the outside, they seemed bonded. From inside the identity groups, the world looked whole. Try telling someone who feels the hunger for wholeness that this is a totalitarian principle, that he or she had better get used to the overlap and complexity of attachments.

The result on campus was identity politics—the recognition of a collective hurt, followed by the mistaking of a group position for a "culture," followed by the mistaking of a "culture" for a politics. In a world where other people seemed to have chosen sides, and where, worse, they approached you—even menaced you—on the assumption that you were what your identity card proclaimed you to be, it seemed a necessity to find one's strength among one's people. From popular culture to government policy, the world had evidently assigned its memberships. Identity politics aimed to turn necessity to virtue. The demand for the respect for difference—for what came to be called multiculturalism—often swerved into the creation of parallel monocultures. Since the demands of identity politics were far more winnable in the university than elsewhere, the struggles of identity groups flourished there. The damage was both intellectual and political. For the recruits, the fierce pleasures of identity politics outweighed the rigors of cosmopolitanism. A political imperative to cut across academic boundaries and address poverty and inequality in the larger world? Not of interest, not sexy. Identity politics amounted to demobilization into a cloister.

While the Right was occupying the heights of the political system, the assemblage of groups identified with the Left were marching on the English department. They were seizing power in women's studies, African American studies, ethnic studies. Insurgencies that began in claims to dignity, recoveries from exclusion and denigration, developed a hardening of the boundaries. Isolated, frequently tenuous, scorned by and hostile to the prevailing university culture, these programs sustained a good deal of separatist rancor.[3] The best of these programs were committed to cosmopolitanism and produced excellent scholarship, though most of the best scholars found places among reformed departments in the old-line disciplines. Frequently, however, the separate programs nurtured a "culture" of exultation and victimization (exultation *through* victimization), a victimization the program felt itself, having to fight for funds against the hostility of established departments. They were consumed with factional disputes so bitter that the more cosmopolitan faculty frequently withdrew in sadness or disgust to their home departments.

The appeal of identity politics to an incoming student is easy to understand. Identity politics is already a tradition in its second generation, transmitted, modified, and transmitted again, institutionalized in departments and courses, supported by a critical mass of faculty and a surrounding, permissive ambivalence, embedded in living units, jargons, mentors, gurus, conferences, associations, journals, publishing subfields, bookstore sections, and jokes. By the time they arrive on campus, especially an elite, cosmopolitan, private campus, many students—particularly the political activists—have already absorbed the spirit of hard-edged identity politics from the media, secondary school, or home. Awaiting the perplexed is an identity package—academic studies, perspectivist theory, identity politics, social networks, "diversity" workshops—a whole world organized around identity culture. The newcomer arrives at the university disposed, in a common formulation, "to learn about herself," rather than to learn about the world and herself in it. She finds encouragement. She finds exclusive identity groups for partying, dancing , listening to music in a familiar style. She finds the Black Sociology Association and the Asian Business Association.

Protected by the academic superstructure as a relatively cheap alternative to disruptive protest, the separate programs cultivate a rapture of marginality. For identity-based movements, the margin is the place to be. Within each margin, there are always more margins to carve out. Postmodernist thought confirms that there is no center; or, rather, that those who claim the center—who claim a common truth or even the possibility that any common truth is attainable—are false universalizers, colonizers, hegemonists. The center, if there is one, is the malevolent Other. But this false center—so the argument goes—is only a margin in disguise. The margins are bastions from which to launch intellectual raids on a center that has no right to be central and has, moreover, lost confidence in itself. Summoning philosophical allies from Paris, the partisans of difference as a supreme principle tack together a ramshackle unity based not so much on a universalist premise or ideal as on a common enemy—the Straight White Male who, trying to obscure his power and interests, disguises himself as the human in "humanism." With the identity groupings, humanism is dead, a dirty word, a ghost that deserves to be put out of its misery.

The whole edifice of postmodern theorizing is topped by a spire flashing a single slogan: "Objectivity," in the words of a Berkeley activist, "is only another word for white male subjectivity." The reverence for difference ossifies into uniformity.

## Culture as Surrogate Politics, Campus as Surrogate World

Accused of politicizing everything, identity politics responds that politics is already everywhere; that interests dress up as truth but are only interests; that power is already everywhere and the only question is who is going to have it.

It was this new understanding—not the French thinker Michel Foucault's brilliance or his Gallic and gay aura—that accounts for the post-Sixties academic fascination with the "poststructuralist" theory of which Foucault remains the most influential representative. Americans not normally tempted by the arcana of social or philosophical theory, least of all the thick and erudite French variety, flocked to Foucault's lectures in the 1970s and early 1980s in New York, the San Francisco Bay Area, and elsewhere. Why was he all the rage and why has he remained so? Only partly because he was the Nietzschean lyricist of self-definition, self-revolt, and self-transcendence, with particular reference to sex; not solely because he was the all-knowledgeable master perspectivist on a grand scale.

The other reason why Foucault became a compulsory reference point, if not compulsory reading, was his insistence with great panache that every sphere of life—every profession, indeed, every field of knowledge—was saturated with power. Knowledge was "power/knowledge." So-called private relations were, in effect, ministates. All relations were power relations. Culture was governed— or "constituted"—by discourses that established who and what would be central or marginal, major or minor. The personal was, in short, political—perhaps so much so as to be nothing *but* political. Language was political. Clothing was political. "Lifestyles"—and sexual styles—were political. Whom one slept with, and how, was who one was, which in turn was what one believed. Indeed, for Foucault, "resistance" was merely another aspect of power, the means by which all-embracing power knew itself. In this fundamentally sadomasochistic world, resistance was swallowed up, doomed. In a time of political blockage on the broad scale, this was what the enclaves of the academic Left wanted to hear.

Then university life could come to feel like a consolation prize. If the Right held political power, what did it matter? This bad deal felt even better than compensation. It felt like an opportunity to change life—immediate, lived life—through direct action. And so the blurring of the line between culture and politics perfectly suited the movements that succeeded the New Left. They had vernaculars, turfs, sectoral music, and literature to protect and develop. There were now enough women and minorities at the university to feel like communities unto themselves. There were conferences to attend, journals to scrutinize, theoretical tendencies to compete with. From "the personal is political" it was an easy glide to "only the personal is really political"—that is, only what I and people like me experience ought to be the object of my interest. There was a swerve, in short, toward conventional interest-group politics, paralleling the philosophical swerve from universalism to the denial that any but group-bounded perspectives were possible. The universalism of the early women's movement, which sought for women the rights and powers guaranteed for all by the Enlightenment, yielded to a preoccupation with the inner life of feminism and the distinct needs of feminists. So, too, with people of color, especially blacks—the swerve from civil rights, emphasizing a universal condition and universalizable rights, to cultural separatism, emphasizing difference and distinct needs.

The dynamic of identity politics is self-confirming. A people against whom boundaries were drawn respond by fortifying those very boundaries. The newcomers gain dignity: they are a "culture." Cultures are not to be tampered with. Cultures are entitled to respect, recognition. By insisting on culture, one fights the power.

## THE PROFUSION OF IDENTITIES

Identity politics is not an alien excrescence. It is as American as the panoply of pies in the supermarket freezer. The multiplication of ethnicities stems from more than three centuries of human imports, starting with slaves. The campus centrifuge is the result of a long-deferred opening up of the professional classes. So is identity politics on the national scene, the demand that women and minorities be represented as such in government positions. This much excoriated emphasis is, in one sense, an extension of the normal pluralism of American politics—the practice of balancing tickets, for example, between North and South, urban and rural, Protestants and Catholics. On top of such rituals, the 1960s movements popularized identity labels; sociology played a part,[4] too, popularizing the concepts of "identity," "roles," "ethnicity"—describing a sense of social life that many people already intuited, helping make it legitimate and turn it to cant in rapid sequence. Who knows how many people would have told interviewers about their ethnic feelings if the interviewers hadn't asked in the first place?

But the contemporary passion for difference is also the consequence of unsettled psychological states. The American pace of change constantly eats away at identity—and just as reliably kicks up materials for the stitching together of new possibilities. The search for hard-edged social identities is surely an overcompensation. Americans have gravitated toward racial, ethnic, religious, sexual, and subcultural distinctions partly to build ramparts against confusion. They long to locate what T. S. Eliot called "a fixed point in the turning world." In fact, firmness of identity is hard to come by—so much so that the psychologist Robert Jay Lifton has rightly identified one of today's dominant psychological types as "protean."[5] Shape-shifting is normal. All this diffuseness and flux is unnerving. An intolerance for one's own confusion generates a frantic search for hard-and-fast identity labels. Beneath the flux, America has developed the countertendency toward a fundamentalist identity culture.

None of this is new, but in recent decades the pressures on traditional identities have mounted. The stabilities that cultivate firm (what David Riesman called "inner-directed") character have grown feeble. Old-line churches have lost their hold on religious life, to be replaced by the more up-to-date. Partly to find solid ground to rest on, legions of believers find solace in returning to fundamentals. They are—and what is this if not an identity that refuses identity?—"born-again." At the same time, family ties and gender roles have loosened. Correspondingly, the churn of identity has grown more rapid. Increases in divorce and remarriage, cohabitation and illegitimacy, multiple parentage, and a growing diversity of ethnic and religious attachments make for recombinant families. The forms of personality that develop within the crucible of the family develop in more complicated ways. Children find many—or no—models of adulthood in their vicinity. They belong to several families at a time, each of which makes its demands, requires its negotiations, incites its rebellions, and none of which makes unrivaled claims. The unsettling of American families, in turn, contributes to the disarray of other traditional fixities. One fruit of the feminist revolution is that there are today a larger number of legitimate ways of being female and male. The old strict polarities persist—homemaker versus breadwinner, frail versus muscular, emotional versus rational—but alternatives are visible. Many women and men mix and match the dizzying variants of gender identity.

What is "Americanization" into this churning nation, so multiplicitous, baggy, and overall purposeless? The choices multiply, the vertigo grows, and the market offers an apparently endless array of choices—Identities Lite. The "other-directed" personality, predisposed to rely on peers and the mass media for identity cues, was identified by David Riesman almost half a century ago,[6] but today this radar-driven modem, always in search of cues as to the right thing to feel or think, finds a bewildering variety of others to be directed by. The media rain down a storm of styles. Taste revision is routine.[7] Thanks to remote control devices, niche television, Internet chat groups, and specialized magazines, not only do style choices multiply, so does the ease of knowing what other styles are available and coasting from one to another. Media saturation and the marketing of youth culture institutionalize the cues for self-transformation into a veritable rebellion industry. Today's media, organized by targeted markets and consumption subcultures, capitalize on identity boundaries. Cable television drops black, Spanish-language, and other ethnically distinct programming schedules into more than 60 percent of American homes. Although ethnic marketing campaigns are nothing new, a considerable distance has been traveled from the "You don't have to be Jewish to love Levy's" rye bread ads of the fifties to Gatorade's "¡Lleno de gusto!" in the nineties. Half of the Fortune 1000 companies have ethnic marketing campaigns.[8] Procter & Gamble puts 5 percent of its massive advertising budget into ethnic-specific ads. AT&T advertises in twenty different languages. Today it remains true that immigrants want to assimilate, but the America into which they hope to do so is not the America of white bread. It is an America where the supermarket shelves groan beneath the varieties of bagels, sourdough, rye, seven grain, and other mass-produced loaves. One belongs by being slightly different, though in a predictable way.

Now, too, there are material incentives for preserving, or claiming, a version (however lite) of ethnic, racial, or religious identity, many of which, today, are paradoxical. Partly because the state legitimizes labels and allocates resources accordingly, people affirm them. "Ethnic pride" develops even where ethnicities have just been invented. "Asian American" is a newly devised category, and can therefore hardly be said to be a "culture" transmitted from generation to generation. What does it describe? Race—a substitute for the widely disliked term "Oriental"? If it describes the continent of national origin, should immigrants from the South Asian subcontinent be classified "Asian American"? If the category is cultural, does it make sense to group third-generation Japanese Americans with Hmong tribesmen, educated Koreans, and the newly arrived Hong Kong poor? People sort and resort themselves, even with respect to claims that, if they are to have any meaning, must logically be matters of fixed inheritance. The number of Americans reporting themselves as "American Indian" or "Native American" in the census grew by 255 percent between 1960 and 1990—from 552,000 to 1,959,000. Most of the growth must be among "new Indians," people choosing—or admitting to—the label. Between 1980 and 1990, the number of Cajuns leaped from 30,000 to 600,000, and the number of French Canadians from 780,000 to 2,200,000, while the number claiming French ancestry fell from 13 million to 10 million.[9]

If "culture" means anything, it is something that persists. But how long must it persist before it qualifies, and who is to say? Only in a fast-food setting, in a society that manufactures novelty, can one speak so casually of "hip-hop culture," "rock culture," "Asian-American" or "European-American culture." The invention of identity is easily mocked for its vagaries and inconsistencies. Yet an insurgent "culture" may succeed in winning the loyalty of large numbers of people, and at the start, who knows just how deeply it will reach, and for how long? The Deaf movement, barely one generation old, is representative of the strengths of post-1960s "ethnicization."

The practice of capitalizing Deaf signifies more than a new respect for those who cannot hear: it has become a sign of activism, with a popular base, with heroes and histories.[10] It includes a commitment to American Sign Language, an active bilingualism, a call for representation (marked in 1988 by the successful demand that the incoming president of Gallaudet University in Washington be a deaf person). It extends as far as the rejection of cochlear implants that are intended to restore a certain degree of hearing. The claim to a Deaf culture is, today, no laughing matter.

## THE AGGRANDIZEMENT OF DIFFERENCE

Are multiculturalism and identity politics nothing more than the impassioned reinvention of the ethnic- and religion-based local politics of a bygone era? Are universities, art museums, textbooks, and publishers' segmented lists today's equivalents of the working-class cities, with their foreign-language newspapers and specialized cuisines, where political tickets had to be balanced among the Irish, the Italians, and the Jews, and Nelson Rockefeller conspicuously wolfed down his knishes in Brooklyn on his way to the governor's mansion in Albany?

In certain ways, contemporary identity politics does resemble traditional pluralism, but there are crucial differences between today's obsessive elevation of difference and the long-standing ethnic diversity of the northern and Midwestern cities. The old mixed-ethnic urban slate was meant to create a working majority in politics; today's cultivation of cultural difference tends to detract from majoritarian thinking. Nothing is more responsible for the current impasse than the black-white divide, which is unlike any other. White Americans may not be frozen in their attachment to white supremacy, but the difference that does not melt is the yawning gulf, in opportunities and neighborhoods, in ways of life and worldviews, between black and white.[11]

In fact, one result of the ethnic revival was to eclipse the uniqueness of the African American experience. Once ethnicity was everywhere, it was, in a sense, nowhere, and the black experience was rhetorically neutralized. This blur was frequently well-meaning but it was also misleading, even euphemistic. It obscured the special antagonisms and discriminations that whites had imposed on blacks for more than three centuries. Black-white disparities in social condition remained sui generis, and they were likely to prove more intractable than any other racial or ethnic conflicts, past or present. For many blacks, the idea of multiculturalism, then, at first looked like something of a shield. If white racism had victimized many besides blacks, it was more convincingly criticized. The proliferation of "difference" and the rhetoric of multiculturalism permitted blacks to deflect the charge that they sought "special treatment." They could present themselves as one color in the rainbow.

But considering how important "difference" is supposed to be, this notion of "people of color" erased too many differences. In contrast to that of American-born blacks, in many respects the experience of today's Asian and Latin American immigrants—even black immigrants from the Caribbean—is closer to that of European immigrants a century ago. They confront discrimination fueled by economic distress. They cope with deprecation. They fight over scarce resources. But the black-white racial script, throughout its variations, carries a charge that was lacking from nineteenth-century tensions between, say, the native-born and the Irish or the Jews. What degree of racial and ethnic integration will take place in America from now on is, of course, unknowable. Because many taboos have broken down since the 1960s, it is even conceivable that the new Asian and Latin American—and Caribbean—immigrants and their descendants, over two or three generations, will succeed in assimilating, promoted socially to the status of "honorary whites," gaining acceptance within a remelted majority. Then the decisive gulf would be black/non-black—not to the advantage of the majority of the native-born black population. At a remove from the desperately poor blacks, a cosmopolitan professional class may be emerging, racially intermarried, ethnically complex, respectful of difference but not obsessed by it, half in the white world, half out, somehow at ease with its self-contradictions—yet a world away from the ghettos and racial furies that preoccupy the American black majority.

On campus, today's obsession with difference is distinguished, too, by the haughtiness of the tribes and the scope of their intellectual claims. Many exponents of identity politics are fundamentalists—in the language of the academy, "essentialists"—and the belief in essential group differences easily swerves toward a belief in superiority. In the hardest version of identity thinking, women are naturally cooperative,[12] Africans naturally inventive,[13] and so on. These pure capacities were once muscled into submission by Western masculine force—so the argument goes—then suppressed by rigged institutions, and now need liberating. Sometimes what is sought is a license to pursue a monoculture. Only the members can (or should) learn the language of the club. Only African Americans should get jobs teaching African American studies; conversely, African Americans should get jobs teaching *only* African American studies. Men, likewise, have no place in women's studies. As the T-shirt slogan had it: "It's a Black Thing, You Wouldn't Understand." As Sister Souljah rapped: "If my world's black and yours is white / How the hell could we think alike."[14] Essentialists, when they secede from the commons, dismantle it.

The cultivation of difference is nothing new, but the sheer profusion of identities that claim separate political standing today is unprecedented. And here is perhaps the strangest novelty in the current situation: that the ensemble of group recognitions should take up so much of the energy of what passes for the Left. It is often for good reason that differences have multiplied, making their claims, exposing the fraudulence of the universalist claims of the past. Not everyone is male, white, hearing, heterosexual. Very well. But what is a Left if it is not, plausibly at least, the voice of a whole people? For the Left as for the rest of America, the question is not whether to recognize the multiplicity of American groups, the variety of American communities, the disparity of American experiences. Those exist as long as people think they exist. The question is one of proportion. What is a Left without a commons, even a hypothetical one? If there is no people, but only peoples, there is no Left.

## NOTES

1. Erik H. Erikson, *Identity, Youth, and Crisis* (New York: Norton, 1968), 224.

2. Erikson, *Identity, Youth, and Crisis*, 42, 24.

3. A compelling treatment of women's studies programs is Daphne Patai and Noretta Koertge, *Professing Feminism: Cautionary Tales from the Strange World of Women's Studies* (New York: New Republic/BasicBooks, 1994).

4. Dennis H. Wrong, "The Influence of Sociological Ideas on American Culture," in Herbert J. Gans, ed., *Sociology in America* (Newbury Park, Calif.: Sage Publications, 1990), 19–30.

5. Robert Jay Lifton, *The Protean Self: Human Resilience in an Age of Fragmentation* (New York: BasicBooks, 1993). Even the ethnic identities affirmed with such sureness by college students shift, melt, and reform as one ages. Clarence Thomas is far from the only conservative middle-aged African American who went through a collegiate phase in which he admired Malcolm X.

6. David Riesman: *The Lonely Crowd* (New Haven, Conn.: Yale University Press, 1950).

7. Orrin E. Klapp, *Collective Search for Identity* (New York: Holt, Rinehart and Winston, 1969), 15–19, 74.

8. *Time*, "New Face of America," Fall 1993, "It's a Mass Market No More," 80–81.

9. Karl Eschbach, "Changing Identification Among American Indians and Alaska Natives," *Demography* 30, no. 4 (November 1993); Nampeo R. McKenney and Arthur R. Crewce, "Measurement of Ethnicity in the United States: Experiences of the U.S. Census Bureau," paper presented at the Joint Canada–United States Conference on the Measurement of Ethnicity, 1–3 April 1992, Ottawa, Canada, 189. Both are cited in Mary C. Waters, "The Social Construction of Race and Ethnicity: Some Examples from Demography," unpublished paper presented at American Diversity: A Demographic Challenge for the Twenty-First Century, Center for Social and Demographic Analysis Conference, Albany, New York, April 1994, 7–8.

10. Andrew Solomon, "Defiantly Deaf," *New York Times Magazine*, 28 August 1994, 38–45, 62, 65–68.

11. Herbert J. Gans, "Second Generation Decline: Scenarios for the Economic and Ethnic Futures of the Post-1965 American Immigrants," *Ethnic and Racial Studies* 15, no. 2 (April 1990): 173–92.

12. See Patai and Koertge, *Professing Feminism*, chapter 7.

13. Professor Molefi Kete Asante of Temple University, a leading "Afrocentrist" and editor of the *Journal of Black Studies*, writes that he wishes to "present the African as subject rather than object" ("Multiculturalism: An Exchange," *The American Scholar* 60, no. 2 [Spring 1991]: 270). But he also believes that the Arabs who invaded northern Africa more than a millennium ago are not "real" Africans (lecture, University of Iowa, 29 March 1994). That is, only blacks of "Negroid" features qualify as the founders of geometry, philosophy, and so on. If the Greeks produced anything of value, it is because they were "really" Africans. This poses for Dr. Asante a problem he does not seem to have faced: If Plato *was* black, why not read him? But what is most astounding about Asante's jerry-built cosmology and race-based idea of "knowledge" is that serious university professors fear to ask embarrassing questions of him. The fear of being considered "racist" cows them.

14. Quoted in Gregory Stephens, "Sister Souljah and the Issue of Black Racism," *In These Times*, 5 August–18 August 1992, 18.

## 26. THE GENDER FALLACY

### WILLIAM C. DOWLING

1

MY ARGUMENT WILL BE that the problem of "men writing the feminine," to borrow the title of a recently published collection of essays, involves a version of the genetic fallacy, what older logic texts explained as a confusion between a thing (an object of explanation) and its origins. As it happens, I think it is ultimately more useful to see the error as a kind of category mistake, an illegitimate jump between two separate universes of discourse. But there is a great deal to be gained, I think, by starting out with a sense that what is involved is in purely logical terms a fallacy, the sort of thing Wimsatt and Beardsley had in mind in speaking of the "intentional fallacy" some fifty years ago. Indeed, part of my point will be that the arguments Wimsatt and Beardsley raised then, in what we tend now to think of as an ancient episode in literary theory, pose objections to contemporary gender criticism that have yet to be answered in any convincing way.

The genetic fallacy as I want to consider it is usefully exemplified in an analysis of *Eloisa to Abelard* undertaken a few years ago by Ellen Pollak in a feminist study of the poetry of Pope and Swift. *Eloisa to Abelard* poses a genuine problem for feminist criticism precisely because Eloisa has to so many generations of readers seemed so real "as a woman." Crying out from the lonely walls of the convent to which she has been exiled by their tragic love affair, speaking to an absent and imagined Abelard with all the passion that she must have felt when she was younger and they were together, Eloisa has always been a poetic voice behind whom it has seemed difficult—or, what is perhaps the same thing, irrelevant—to hear the voice of an "actual" Alexander Pope.

Pollak, to her credit, does take into account the long tradition of response that has heard Eloisa's voice as wrenchingly "real," even noting the older tradition of biographical criticism that saw its emotional intensity as owing to Pope's own personal circumstances (specifically, his longing for the absent Lady Mary Wortley Montagu, with whom he was for a time wholly infatuated). But, Pollak concludes, given Pope's authorship of the poem, any appearance of emotional authenticity must be misleading. What is involved is necessarily ideological mystification, the male domination of women being carried out under the sign of a spurious empathy: "if anything is indulged here, it seems to me to be not the specificity of a woman's torment, or her display of erotic and emotional intensity, but rather a voyeuristic male appropriation of female eroticism in the service of a phallocentric ordering of desire in which both excess and lack are figured as female" (186).

There are several logical problems here. The first is that it is hard to see how, insofar as it begins from a notion of male writers as in some necessary sense misogynist, a properly feminist interpretation of *Eloisa to Abelard* could come to any other conclusion. Pollak herself explicitly raises this issue as part of the question whether Pope or Swift might not, in this or that isolated instance, have registered a genuine empathy with female experience. But it is not a suggestion she wishes to entertain. Even "to argue whether or not the texts of the two poets are misogynist is," she points out, "already to entertain the possibility that they (or some of them) may not be." And, "since these texts are the products of a phallocentric culture and of its authorizing sign-systems and codes" (183), it is something like an a priori certainty that they will mirror their misogynist origins.

Yet this raises a very great difficulty. Such a reading of Pope's poem will then have to depend in some strict and exclusive sense on its being, precisely, *Pope's* poem—that is, a text produced by a male author in at least the minimal sense that the hand holding the authorial pen was anatomically connected to a male body. The easiest way to see why this reading rests on the genetic fallacy is simply to explore what would happen in an imaginary scenario in which it had turned out, through some recently discovered documentation, that *Eloisa to Abelard* had been written not by Pope but by Lady Mary Wortley Montagu.

The scenario: having composed the poem—no great stretch of imagination called for here, Lady Mary having been a gifted poet in her own right, and one whose poetry includes Ovidian verse epistles like *Eloisa to Abelard*—and being on the point of leaving for a long absence in Constantinople, she is moved by aristocratic modesty to conceal her authorship and deliver the poem over to her friend Alexander Pope for publication in his 1717 *Poems*.

The problem for Pollak is obvious. Through an alteration of circumstances wholly external to the text, *Eloisa to Abelard* has suddenly gone from being a voyeuristic male appropriation of female emotional experience to (presumably) an authentic and moving expression of such experience. Yet not a word of the text has changed. To open an anthology and turn to *Eloisa to Abelard* is to find just the same poem as before.

## 2

"The Intentional Fallacy," wrote Wimsatt and Beardsley in 1951, "is a confusion between the poem and its origins, a special case of what is known to philosophers as the Genetic Fallacy" (21). In those more innocent days, their argument was against a historical or biographical criticism that wanted to move from information about an author, usually drawn from letters or journals or recollections of friends, to a claim about what some text bearing that author's name must mean, by virtue of embodying the traces of a unique personal or psychological history.

On the most general or abstract level, their counter to this notion would be the theory of literary autonomy: novels and plays and poems understood as worlds in themselves, obeying their own laws and their own logic and subject to violence and distortion when made to answer to doctrines or ideologies external to themselves.

The theory of literary autonomy as Wimsatt developed it in *The Verbal Icon* had a negative and a positive thrust. The positive idea was that of a speaker or narrator wholly internal to the work. Even the older biographical-historical critics against whom Wimsatt was writing had in certain obvious cases been compelled to make a distinction between author and speaker or narrator—the distinction, say, between Mark Twain and Huckleberry Finn, or Nabokov and Humbert Humbert, or Browning and Fra Lippo Lippi. To do so, as Wimsatt saw, was already in some sense to understand the work as a sphere of reality existing independent of the writer who had composed it.

Wimsatt's radical move in *The Verbal Icon* was to extend this distinction to anything understood as a literary work, to insist that the "Keats" who speaks in "When I Have Fears" is no less a voice within the text, created and sustained by its discourse and belonging to its world, than Huckleberry Finn or Fra Lippo Lippi. The "personal," on this account, even at its most intimate or self-revelatory, must always nonetheless be seen as an effect of language in its public aspect as literary discourse.

This distinction between author and speaker is not central to my present argument about the genetic fallacy, but I do want to note in passing that it suggests an immediate solution to the problem raised by Pollak's reading of *Eloisa to Abelard*. For at the time *The Verbal Icon* was written the usual way of insisting that the distinction was radical and constitutive was to say that a valid interpretation could survive any change in an attribution of authorship.

For instance, a reading of "To His Coy Mistress" that attributed to its speaker attitudes and opinions of the historical Andrew Marvell could not on this account survive the revelation, come to light in a newly discovered diary, that the poem had actually been composed by one Jonathan Smedwick, an obscure clergyman and contemporary of Marvell's living in Cornwall.

An interpretation taking the "I" of the poem as a mind or consciousness dwelling wholly within the text, on the other hand, would need no adjustment or alteration. The way this argument applies to Pollak's reading of Pope—that is, to evidence unexpectedly transferring *Eloisa to Abelard* from Pope to Lady Mary Wortley Montagu—does not, perhaps, need to be spelled out.

Still, it was the negative thrust of Wimsatt and Beardsley's argument, deriving from a purely logical or analytic insight, that gave it so enormous an influence in its day. This was the point that the problem of intention is illusory. The way Wimsatt and Beardsley put it is worth recalling. Imagine, they say, that a poet intends something and we want to know whether or not that intention was fulfilled in the text. How are we to find this out?

The answer: "If the poet succeeded in doing it, then the poem itself shows what he was trying to do. And if the poet did not succeed, then the poem is not adequate evidence, and the critic must go outside the poem—for evidence of an intention that did not become effective in the poem" (4). This point comes to bear with some cogency on a certain kind of argument—Pollak's "voyeuristic male appropriation," for instance, taken not as an argument about Pope but as a *form* of argument about literary meaning—common in contemporary gender criticism.

To bring the point to bear on the problem of gender in *Eloisa to Abelard*, we need only substitute "maleness" where Wimsatt and Beardsley speak of intention. If there is evident in Eloisa's voice some alien or dissonant element of maleness—"evident" in this case meaning "discernible by a competent reader who had not been told whether a man or woman wrote the poem"—a reading of *Eloisa to Abelard* as a voyeuristic male appropriation of female experience makes perfect sense.

If, on the other hand, nothing of Pope's maleness has made it through into the text—if, whether he or Lady Mary or somebody else altogether should happen to have written the poem, the "I" who speaks as Eloisa has been imagined in purely female or feminine terms—then such a reading will be a construction imposed upon the text, a signal instance of the genetic fallacy.

No better example of this point could be imagined, perhaps, than Diderot's *La Religieuse* as discussed by Beatrice Durand in the collection *Men Writing the Feminine*. For the circumstances in which Diderot's "novel" originated are so bizarre as to constitute a virtual parable of mystified or obscured authorship.

In very brief terms, here they are. The Marquis de Croismare, a member of Diderot's Parisian circle, in 1759 decided, to the regret of his friends, to retire to his estate in Normandy. Before leaving, the Marquis had taken up the cause of a young woman who had earlier been made to enter a convent against her will. He had intervened at court when she applied to renounce her vows. The appeal was lost.

The Marquis departed for his estate, and Diderot and his friends, in an effort to entice him back to the capital, sent him a series of heart-rending letters purporting to be from the young nun. The Marquis, wholly taken in, answered these letters. The correspondence continued at such length that it would later provide materials for the "memoirs" Diderot would compose as *La Religieuse.*

Here, one might reasonably suppose, we have hit upon a kind of Turing test of gendered textuality: a French nobleman, a literate and sophisticated man of the world wholly conversant with the codes and sign-systems of his society, has absolutely no intimation that he is reading texts composed by his own male friends. So sex or gender really do, in at least one signal instance to which we can point, leave no textual trace.

Yet this is not the conclusion drawn by Durand, for whom "Suzanne" as either the female voice speaking in the original letters to the Marquis or the narrator of the subsequent "memoirs" is not, "even if her character is credible," a "woman who speaks and writes." Suzanne is, on the contrary, "a man assuming a mask, the false identity of a woman. She is the image of the feminine that a male author must project in order to disguise himself as a woman" (90).

The great interest of *La Religieuse* thus lies, from this perspective, not in its relation to eighteenth-century French culture or other eighteenth-century texts but to the preoccupation of contemporary gender criticism with such matters as transvestitism and cross-dressing: "According to male transvestites who have been interviewed, one of the biggest satisfactions in cross-dressing is to 'pass,' to make oneself credible as a member of the opposite sex. . . . In conforming to the code of feminine voice and gestures, Diderot and his friends successfully 'passed': they were rewarded for their efforts by the response they received from the Marquis" (92).

The fallacy on which such arguments rest has no agreed-upon name in standard logic texts. I shall refer to it as *Omphalos* reasoning, borrowing the name from the episode in *Father and Son* in which Edmund Gosse's father, at once a brilliant natural scientist and a Christian fundamentalist, finds himself caught between his own deep religious belief and the unsettling new hypothesis of Darwinian evolution.

This is the situation in which, famously, Philip Gosse, suddenly glimpsing what he thought was a way out, would write the treatise *Omphalos*, arguing that God had indeed created the world during the six days described in Genesis, but had at the same time, to test the faith of a scientific age, strewn the geological record with fossil evidence to suggest a process of development requiring millions of years.

The argument, in short, is either that (1) God exists and the world shows that he exists—the standard physicotheological idea, summarized in works like Butler's *Analogy*, that nature reveals God's design—or (2) he must exist because he was there to construct the world in such a way as to imply that he does not exist.

The slide from genetic fallacy to *Omphalos* reasoning evident in Durand's analysis needs no extended comment. The idea is that the more successful Diderot was at effacing from the text every trace of his maleness, the more male it in some ineffable sense turns out to be, until a complete absence of textual evidence becomes, through a sudden twist or reverse of logic, an overwhelming weight of evidence.

3

Gender criticism has not been unaware that there is a problem here, or even that the problem may be associated with the attempt to impose modern ideological categories on poems and plays and novels existing quite independent of those categories. Yet it is not clear that anyone working in gender criticism has yet grasped that the problem arises from a version of the genetic fallacy that is evident in literally hundreds, perhaps thousands, of recent books and articles and reviews in scholarly journals, or in empty or *Omphalos* argumentation that derives from the genetic fallacy.

This is why, one suspects, there has been a tendency to misunderstand Nina Baym's point, in "Why I Don't Do Feminist Literary Theory," in objecting to such theory precisely because it "requires sexual difference as its ground" (quoted in Siegel, 61). The response of feminist critics to Baym typically betrays, as does that of Carol Siegel in *Men Writing the Feminine*, a note of honest puzzlement. Since the very idea of feminist criticism is based on the need to expose the illegitimate domination of women by men, how could it *not* require sexual difference as its ground?

There is, Siegel points out, a further consideration. Feminist criticism is not merely an area of intellectual inquiry—a discipline or "field" as such—but part of an ongoing political struggle: "As Toril Moi puts it, 'the feminist struggle must both try to undo the patriarchal strategy that makes "femininity" intrinsic to biological femaleness, and at the same time insist on defending women precisely as women'" (Siegel, 82).

The point that such a response misses is that Baym can be taken to be objecting not to any concern with gender in literary texts but to "sexual difference" as *Omphalos* reasoning. In the Diderot case, for instance, if one has grounds to suppose that the young woman in *La Religieuse* was originally a creation of Diderot and his male friends, then the argument from "sexual difference" will be that the text is an example of literary transvestitism or cross-dressing.

If evidence comes to light tomorrow in the Bibliothèque Nationale that "Suzanne" was an actual woman whom Diderot was protecting from retribution by her religious superiors—the originals of the letters to the Marquis turn up, let us say, in the handwriting of an eighteenth-century Frenchwoman whom scholars know to have been put in a convent against her will—then the argument from "sexual difference" will be that *La Religieuse* has suddenly been transformed into an authentic expression of female suffering.

If *these* letters turn out to be a literary hoax—a clever forgery by a modern collector who has seen a chance to make a financial killing, for example—then the argument from "sexual difference" will be that we have gone back to dealing with literary transvestitism. Yet through all these alterations, as in the case of the *Eloisa to Abelard* scenario, not a word of the text will have changed.

4

The occasional attempts to deal with this problem have come from outside gender criticism. In a noteworthy *Diacritics* essay published in 1988, for instance, Jefferson Humphries argued that much discussion of the body in feminist criticism has been a way of smuggling in an essentialist idea of gender that is, strictly speaking, forbidden to such criticism by its own postulates—a more generalized version, in short, of the genetic fallacy as discussed here.

To the extent that feminist criticism takes seriously the notion of the "female" as a cultural construction, Humphries argues, and to the extent that it is able to grasp textuality as a primary site of such construction, feminist criticism must by its own lights be guided by "a recognition that gender difference functions as a trope, subject to reversal and substitution" (26). This is the sense in which the literary work, even for the most politically engaged feminist critic, "already contains the antidote to phallocentrism" (27): its very textuality subverts the logic of essentialist or "natural" categories on which an ideology of domination must, on the account of gender criticism itself, be ultimately based.

The answer to this sort of argument by feminist theorists has been that it, too, is a mode of male domination. Thus, for instance, Teresa de Lauretis: "This kind of deconstruction of the subject is effectively a way to recontain women in femininity and to reposition female subjectivity *in* the male subject, however that will be defined" (24). Even to talk about a logic of textuality in relation to feminist criticism is, in short, to lapse into precisely the sort of abstract "male" rationality against which feminist criticism is engaged in perpetual struggle.

The point to which theory is brought by such a response resembles the controversy that in an earlier day raged around the Freudian concept of denial. The problem looks like this. Freudian psychoanalytic theory offers me an elaborate model of the workings of my own psychic economy, including the lawless sphere of instinctuality that is my unconscious. There is, as it follows from this, "denial," the absolute refusal of my conscious mind to register or acknowledge intolerable truths about myself.

I survey the Freudian model and remark that it seems to me not a theory at all, or even a very interesting body of speculation about human psychology. It seems, rather, a compound of medical quackery and Greek myth and fin de siècle irrationalism attempting to pass itself off as a science. And the psychoanalyst, or the one who has been appointed to speak for psychoanalytic theory, says, of course, now *that* is denial, and you will find it fully analyzed by Freud in his case study on . . .

There is, it may be, no way out of the impasse created by this move. To argue that contemporary gender criticism rests on the genetic fallacy is simply to make a theoretical point made long ago, as we have seen, by Wimsatt and Beardsley. But to be told that this sort of point is itself one of the ruses of masculinist or patriarchal domination—that theory as such, as de Lauretis says in an influential formulation, is a "technology of gender"—is abruptly to reach what at least feels like a dead end. As with the Freudian psychoanalyst, one does not see exactly how one could enter a meaningful objection to a system defended in this way.

Wimsatt and Beardsley were theorists of literary autonomy. That theory, though it has been politically denounced by Terry Eagleton and others, has not yet been shown on any persuasive theoretical grounds to be mistaken. In recognition of that fact, perhaps, even though they passed from the scene long before the arrival of gender criticism, Wimsatt and Beardsley may be permitted the last word: "The poem is not the critic's own and not the author's. It is detached from the author at birth and goes about the world beyond his or her power to intend about it or control it. The poem belongs to the public. It is embodied in language, the peculiar possession of the public, and it is about the human being, the object of public knowledge" (5).

WORKS CITED

de Lauretis, Teresa. *Technologies of Gender: Essays on Theory, Film, and Fiction.* Bloomington: Indiana University Press, 1987.

Durand, Beatrice. "Diderot and the Nun: Portrait of the Artist as Transvestite." In *Men Writing the Feminine: Literature, Theory, and the Question of Genders*, ed. Thaïs E. Morgan, 89–106. Albany: State University of New York Press, 1994.

Humphries, Jefferson. "Troping the Body: Literature and Feminism. *Diacritics* 18, no. 1 (Spring 1988): 18–28.

Morgan, Thaïs E., ed. *Men Writing the Feminine: Literature, Theory, and the Question of Genders*. Albany: State University of New York Press, 1994.

Pollak, Ellen. *The Poetics of Sexual Myth: Gender and Ideology in the Verse of Swift and Pope*. Chicago: University of Chicago Press, 1985.

Siegel, Carol. "Border Disturbances: D. H. Lawrence's Fiction and the Feminism of *Wuthering Heights*." In *Men Writing the Feminine: Literature, Theory, and the Question of Genders*, ed. Thaïs E. Morgan, 59–76. Albany: State University of New York Press, 1994.

Wimsatt, William K. *The Verbal Icon: Studies in the Meaning of Poetry*. Lexington: University of Kentucky Press, 1954.

Wimsatt, William K., and Monroe C. Beardsley. "The Intentional Fallacy." In *The Verbal Icon*, 3–20.

## 27.  FEMINISM'S PERVERSE EFFECTS

### ELAINE MARKS

THE TITLE BOTH REGISTERS my anxiety about the directions in which the fields of literary, cultural, ethnic, and women's studies have moved in the past ten years and suggests what I think we may have lost by following certain discursive directions proposed by "feminism" and rejecting others. I am myself a member of the executive committee in one department, French and Italian, and in two multidisciplinary programs, women's studies and Jewish studies, at the University of Wisconsin—Madison, and I have had a variety of experiences both in shaping the curriculum and in teaching undergraduate and graduate students during a period of sometimes intense debate about what it is we should be doing when we teach literature, culture, and language. I do not pretend to be objective in my evaluations, and, as in all writing, there will undoubtedly be "blind spots" in my arguments and even in my examples.

During the past four years I have begun each of my courses, whether graduate seminars in French, undergraduate and graduate classes in women's studies, or courses in literature in translation, with introductory comments to the students about my own unresolved questions. I warn them of my growing dissatisfaction with identity politics and studies, with the exaggerated emphasis

Elaine Marks. "Feminism's Perverse Effects." *Signs: Journal of Women in Culture and Society* 25, no. 4 (Summer 2000): 1162–66. Copyright © University of Chicago Press. Reprinted by permission.

on difference and inattention to commonalities, and with the separation into two opposing camps of cultural studies and literary studies, which mirrors a more troubling separation of the political and the poetic. If I were teaching language courses, I would add to this list the equally troubling separation of language and literature in our curriculum and in the pedagogical training of our students.

I was beginning to feel isolated in women's studies and fearful of being perceived in both women's studies and French and Italian as a closet conservative and traitor to my own pronouncements of the 1980s. And then, within the past year and a half, I discovered that I am not alone. Among those colleagues whose progressive positions I had always felt to be close to my own (e.g., Biddy Martin, Richard Rorty), as well as among those whom I had regarded at a distance as politically incorrect (Robert Alter and Harold Bloom), similar unresolved questions were being raised. Each one, in his or her own way, has deplored the reading of literature uniquely for signs of racism, sexism, anti-Semitism, uniquely as a document that reveals underlying discursive and cultural assumptions and presuppositions. As a student and teacher primarily of French language, literature, and culture, I have become increasingly hostile to readings of French literary texts whose unique goal seems to be to portray the French nation and French culture as villains whose main products for domestic and global consumption are sexism, racism, and anti-Semitism.

The January 1997 issue of *PMLA*, the journal of the Modern Language Association (MLA), is devoted to the teaching of literature. In her introductory essay, "Teaching Literature, Changing Cultures," Biddy Martin, the issue's editor, writes,

> Why devote a special issue to the teaching of literature? Why literature? Why now? The topic may strike readers as timely or outmoded, neutral or polemical, depending on their positions in the contentious debates over the status of literature and its relation to culture. I take a broad view of what literature entails, but the current shifting of literature departments in North American institutions to cultural studies makes me worry about the fate of reading practices that the term *literature* invites, permits or requires, the fate of reading that suspends the demand for immediate intelligibility, works at the boundary of meaning and yields to the effects of language and imagination. (8)

Similarly, in a "Point of View" column in the February 9, 1996, issue of the *Chronicle of Higher Education*, Richard Rorty writes,

> Academic disciplines are subject to being overtaken by attacks of "knowingness"—a state of mind and soul that prevents shudders of awe and makes one immune to enthusiasm. This may have happened to the teach-

ers of literature in American colleges and universities who make up what
the literary critic Harold Bloom has called "the School of Resentment."
These teachers are proceeding along the same path that led philosophers, a
few decades ago, to abandon inspiration for professionalism.

Harold Bloom, in his 1994 *The Western Canon*, sees his colleagues who
pursue "cultural studies" converting the study of literature into "one more
dismal social science"—thereby turning departments of literature into
dried-up academic backwaters. As he sees it, these teachers substitute resentment over societal failures for utopian vision.                    (A48)

It is no simple matter, in this millennial fin-de-siècle, to criticize certain tendencies in cultural studies or women's studies or ethnic studies without being
accused of participating in a conservative political agenda.

In 1994, when Bloom's controversial book appeared, I was shocked to discover how closely I had moved to positions from which I could have been expected (because of my long-standing affiliation with women's studies and the
feminist inquiry) to be very far removed. Although Bloom's lists of canonical
books were not the same as mine, in his opening chapter, "An Elegy for the
Canon," he makes a case for the role of imaginative literature's place within the
humanities curriculum that I can only applaud:

> Whatever the Western Canon is, it is not a program for social salvation. . . .
> The West's greatest writers are subversive of all values, both ours and their
> own. Scholars who urge us to find the source of our morality and our pol-
> itics in Plato, or in Isaiah, are out of touch with the social reality in which
> we live. If we read the Western Canon in order to form our social, political,
> or personal moral values, I firmly believe we will become monsters of self-
> ishness and exploitation. To read in the service of any ideology is not, in
> my judgment, to read at all. The reception of aesthetic power enables us to
> learn how to talk to ourselves and how to endure ourselves. The true use of
> Shakespeare or of Cervantes, of Homer or of Dante, of Chaucer or of Ra-
> belais, is to augment one's own growing inner self. Reading deeply in the
> Canon will not make one a better or a worse person, a more useful or more
> harmful citizen. The mind's dialogue with itself is not primarily a social
> reality. All that the Western Canon can bring one is the proper use of one's
> own solitude, that solitude whose final form is one's confrontation with
> one's own mortality.                                              (29–30)

The Association of Literary Scholars and Critics was formed four years ago
in response to what many of its adherents felt was the politicization of literary
studies in North America and particularly in the major organization for scholars and critics in North America, the MLA. Like many other active members of
the MLA, I initially considered the Association of Literary Scholars and Critics

to be composed mainly of reactionary scholars and teachers opposed to the opening of the canon and to many of the new approaches to literary texts that came to the United States from the European continent and Great Britain. The Association of Literary Scholars and Critics, as I understood its mission four years ago, wanted to take literary studies back to a precritical, pretheoretical moment in which the masterpieces of the Western literary tradition were transparent, and men and women, particularly men of good breeding and common sense, could discuss them among themselves in mutually satisfying ways without the noise provided by theory and noncanonical texts.

Imagine my surprise, then, upon reading the presidential address delivered by Robert Alter in November of 1997 to the Association of Literary Scholars and Critics and published in its entirety in the *Times Literary Supplement* on January 23, 1998. The title of the address, "The Recovery of Open-Mindedness and the Revival of the Literary Imagination," does suggest a nostalgic return to some golden age, a typical gesture of the ideological right. However, the essay's focus on "the literary imagination" also echoes the emphases of Biddy Martin, Richard Rorty, and Harold Bloom, and has the distinction of providing excellent examples from three very different texts: the David story in Samuel 1 and 2 of the Jewish Bible; *The Red and the Black* by Stendhal; and *Ulysses* by James Joyce.

The examples are preceded by Alter's attempt to define the literary imagination which,

> to borrow a formulation from the Frankfurt School critic Leo Lowenthal, is essentially "dialectic," dedicated to articulating critical challenges to, or subtle subversions of, regnant ideologies, received ideas and antecedent literary conventions and values. Great literary works thus will repeatedly surprise us—that is precisely the source of pleasure and instruction in reading them—as long as we do not insist on contorting them to fit the Procrustean bed of our own preconceptions. When we as an association proclaim that we honor the power of the literary imagination, that does not involve any mystification but, on the contrary, an empirical openness to the unanticipated ways in which an original writer, warts and all, can offer an odd and illuminating perspective on familiar topics, overturn bland assumptions, or startlingly recast the very instruments of literary expression.
>
> (15)

In each of the three examples, Alter points out how "the unpredictability of the literary imagination" surprises and subverts readers' expectations.

I would like now to give an example of my own. It comes from a classroom experience in which both my choice of certain texts and the manner of reading them were vigorously contested by a group of students. The text was *Dust Tracks on a Road* ([1942] 1991) by Zora Neale Hurston, assigned in a women's studies course called "Writing Women's Li(v)es." What seemed to disturb the hostile students was that Hurston's narrative did not focus sufficiently on what the students expected to read: the unrelieved story of Hurston's oppression as a black woman growing up in the South in the late nineteenth and early twentieth centuries. The class was composed entirely of women, and all of those who were angry with Hurston (and me) were white.

These angry students did not react with "surprise" at the discrepancy between their expectations and the words of the text but rather with hostility, in part because, through no fault of their own, they have had little or no training in the reading of a literary text. Like most readers, they tend to read uniquely for information, for historical or psychological "realism." Although the first text we had read together in that course was Nelly Furman's superb 1980 essay "Textual Feminism," which insists on the importance of words, language, and the signifier and attempts to show that literature has functions other than the referential, their habits of reading were not easily challenged. Indeed, these habits are often supported by ideological positions that students, in some of their classes, are taught to look for in all the texts they read. If the students do not find evidence of racism, sexism, or anti-Semitism, they tend to assume that either the writer or the teacher is guilty of a cover-up.

The other major reason many students have difficulty reading literary texts is that, because they are not omnivorous readers, they do not hear echoes of earlier texts in the texts they read; they do not know the pleasures of intertextuality. Those of us who teach literature have for some time noted the decline in our students' ability to recognize mythological or biblical references. This now extends to references, explicit or implicit, to much of the canon of Western literature. For several years, when this topic was raised by colleagues, I responded that although our students did not have literary culture, they have other kinds of culture, ones that we did not necessarily have. I no longer feel comfortable with this response.

In the case of *Dust Tracks on a Road*, it was impossible for some of the students to imagine that an African American woman writer might equate telling folktales and lying, might play frequently with signifiers, as in the story "Git back/Git black" (50), told by a female character called Gold, about how the races were given color, or might use pejorative words ironically, in a particular context, when naming African Americans. In a sense, the students were denying Hurston the right to write in a certain style, the right to write against the doxa and the discourse of her time and place. They could read *Dust Tracks on a Road* only in terms of racism and sexism. And because they could not find in it what they were looking for, they denied themselves the pleasures of discovering a new and different text, another mode of writing and reading.

These are some of what I consider to be the perverse effects of and caveats for feminism at the millennium.

WORKS CITED

Alter, Robert. "The Recovery of Open-Mindedness and the Revival of the Literary Imagination." *Times Literary Supplement*, 23 January 1998, 15–16.

Bloom, Harold. *The Western Canon*. New York: Harcourt Brace and Company, 1994.

Furman, Nelly. "Textual Feminism." In *Women and Language in Literature and Society*, ed. Sally McConnell-Ginet, Ruth Borker, and Nelly Furman, 45–54. New York: Praeger, 1980.

Hurston, Zora Neale. *Dust Tracks on a Road*. 1942. Reprint: New York: Harper Perennial, 1991.

Martin, Biddy. "Teaching Literature, Changing Cultures." *PMLA* 112, no. 1 (January 1997): 7–25.

Rorty, Richard. "The Necessity of Inspired Reading." *Chronicle of Higher Education*, 9 February 1995, A48.

## 28. QUEER THEORY, LITERATURE, AND THE SEXUALIZATION OF EVERYTHING

### THE GAY SCIENCE

### LEE SIEGEL

### I

I USED TO KNOW A woman who was in thrall to a particular anecdote. She told the tale again and again. Many years before, when her son was just a few years old, she had taken him and a couple of his playmates to a friend's house, where there were some little girls about the same age as her charges. After spending the afternoon there, my friend put her crew in the car and started to drive off. As they moved away, the girls ran to the edge of the front yard, waving to the boys. "Good-bye, penises!" they cried. And the boys waved back and cried, "Good-bye, vaginas!" Whenever my friend related her anecdote, she seemed surprised by her own wonder at it, and mysteriously consoled. In one fell swoop, the delightful story proclaims the elemental nature of sex and then demotes sex to a triviality. We all know that the pleasures of penises and vaginas are essential and significant and mysterious, but we also know that we amount to more than penises and vaginas. We also know that those pleasures are themselves more than the sum of our genitals, and also that our lives are more than the sum of our pleasures. We do know this. Don't we?

Lee Siegel. "Queer Theory, Literature, and the Sexualization of Everything: The Gay Science." Originally published in *The New Republic*, 9 November 1998, 30–42. Abridged by the author and reprinted by permission of the author.

Maybe we don't. To judge by American culture, there is only sex. My friend's tale might easily have been told of two groups of adults—Hollywood adults maybe, since Hollywood's idea of intellectual seriousness is often to discover sexual desire beneath all forms of political power and social convention; or maybe two groups of poets and novelists, since it seems that every other novel or book of poetry now has the sizzling word "desire" in the title; or legislators applying themselves to conduct in the workplace, or newspaper editors, or independent prosecutors. Just about every figure in the arena of our public life, it sometimes seems, wants a kinder, more genitally obsessed nation. But nowhere has the sexualization of reality proceeded so intensely and so relentlessly as in the seminar room. The contemporary academic obsession with sexuality and "the body" has nothing to do with the Freudian-inspired criticism of the 1940s and 1950s. On the contrary. For about the past fifteen years, some prominent and influential American academics, mostly literature professors, have applied ideas about language and literature to sexuality rather than the other way around. Queer theory, though nearly a decade old, is the thriving culmination of that development. Its scripture, its watershed source, is the first volume of Michel Foucault's *History of Sexuality*, which appeared in Paris in 1976, and in English translation in this country two years later. Foucault is to queer theory, and to the larger culture, what Freud has been to psychoanalysis, and to the larger culture.

## II

Of course, there was also the influence of the American scene. The legislation closing gay bathhouses and sex clubs, implemented at the height of the AIDS epidemic during the late 1980s and early 1990s, had a lot to do with the birth of queer politics and queer theory. Though many gays welcomed the regulations as life-saving and tragically overdue, "queers" saw them as attempts to suppress gay sexuality. Out of this controversy there arose anew the old 1960s conflict between gay reformers and gay liberationists, with the queers building on the ambitions of the latter. Driven by the engines of multiculturalism, the queer enterprise took off from there: queers use radical doubts about identity to revolutionize the idea of the "personal," just as, two or three decades ago, many present-day gay liberals used the radical certitudes of the personal to revolutionize the idea of the "political." Thus the ascendancy of queer theory over queer politics.

As the threat of AIDS has diminished, queer politics has subsided into what amounts to colorfully ineffective performance groups, such as the one calling itself Sex Panic. But queer theory has gained in its sense of mission. Queer theoretical ideas have their roots in long-repressed aspirations for a universal sexual transformation; for a recognition of the ubiquity of homosexual desire; for an end to marriage and "sex roles"; for a unifying theory exposing connections between sexual oppression, economic inequality, and colonialist domination. Like the liberationists of the 1960s, queer theorists have a totalizing framework; but they have no truck with 1960s notions of gay identity and gay pride. They wish to dissolve the categories of sexual identity and, with them, the way in which society has invested sexual identity with moral value, endorsing some sexual identities and stigmatizing others. Queers are engaged in a vast theoretical project of breaking up fixed sexual identities into the fluidity of sexual acts or practices. Instead of whom you have sex with, queer theory is interested in how you obtain sexual pleasure. Queer denotes "genitality," masturbation, and "fisting"; cross-dressing, transvestitism, and sadomasochism; and especially the meaning-neutral and value-neutral "body." Queers regard this shift in emphasis as a shift in historical paradigm. As Donald Morton observes in "Birth of the Cyberqueer":

> Rather than as a local effect, the return of the queer has to be understood as the result, in the domain of sexuality, of the (post)modern encounter with—and rejection of—Enlightenment views concerning the role of the conceptual, rational, systematic, structural, normative, progressive, liberatory, revolutionary, and so forth, in social change.

Morton's casual identification of "normative" with "revolutionary," of "progressive" with "liberatory," is representative of some of the confusions and contradictions (and so forth) in queer theory.

For Eve Kosofsky Sedgwick, similarly,

> the now chronic modern crisis of homo/heterosexual definition has affected our culture through its ineffaceable marking particularly of the categories secrecy/disclosure, knowledge/ignorance, private/public, masculine/feminine, majority/minority, innocence/initiation, natural/artificial, new/old, discipline/terrorism, canonic/noncanonic, wholeness/decadence, urban/provincial, domestic/foreign, health/illness, same/different, active/passive, in/out, cognition/paranoia, art/kitsch, utopia/apocalypse, sincerity/sentimentality, and voluntarity/addiction.

And Michael Warner, in his introduction to a volume of essays called *Fear of a Queer Planet*, writes that

> every person who comes to a queer self-understanding knows in one way or another that her stigmatization is connected with gender, the family, notions of individual freedom, the state, public speech, consumption and desire, nature and culture, maturation, reproductive politics, racial and national fantasy, class identity, truth and trust, censorship, intimate life and social display, terror and violence, health care, and deep cultural

norms about the bearing of the body. . . . Queers do a kind of practical social reflection just in finding ways of being queer.

With such gargantuan ambitions, it is no wonder that the ideal of queerness sometimes seems indistinguishable from the hormonal and glandular processes that make up sex itself. Indeed, for Sedgwick, "what it takes—all it takes—to make the description 'queer' a true one is the impulsion [*sic*] to use it in the first person." Identity and "impulsion"—that is, desire—fuse into a single entity. And if Eve Sedgwick has escaped the prison of contradiction, then David Halperin has escaped the prison of definition. In *Saint Foucault: Towards a Gay Hagiography*, Halperin goes Sedgwick one better and announces that queer is "an identity without an essence." Queerness is fluid, even as it dreams of fluids. Halperin, too, has a vision of global change: "Queer . . . envisions a variety of possibilities for reordering the relations among sexual behaviors, erotic identities, constructions of gender, forms of knowledge, regimes of enunciation, logics of representation, modes of self-constitution, and practices of community—for restructuring, that is, the relations among power, truth, and desire." Thus queerness, obsessed with transgression as the route to power, is finally a scatology in search of an eschatology. Michel Foucault, meet Norman O. Brown.

Naturally, the queer utopians reject the compromising liberal finitude of equal rights and equal protection under the law. They wish to "queer" society, to expose the essential "queerness" of everyone and everything. Queers do not want a place at the table. They want universal acknowledgment that the table has three legs. And yet, in queer writing, "queerness" always comes down to being gay. Worse, it often seems that calling oneself queer is a tactic for not acknowledging that one is merely gay, for not shouldering the burdens of coming out or the responsibilities that come with accepting the inevitable reality of a sexual identity and getting on with the rest of life. Queers defiantly want to bring the closet out into public view while adamantly refusing to leave it. That is why queers take the premises of gay identity politics to an extreme and proclaim an unending "politics of difference." They adopt the ugly slur "queer" so as to keep the gap between gay people and straight people wide and yawning, especially when it is in danger of being bridged. Yet their project of "queering" society, politics, history, and literature is the expression of a terrible fear of difference.

## III

In *The History of Sexuality*, volume 1—again, the bible of queer theory—Foucault offered a chastening and disheartening diagnosis of the situation of sexuality in society. His American followers have turned his pessimism into a prescription for a better world. For Foucault, modern society controls erotic life by broadcasting through various channels ever-evolving definitions of sexuality. Foucault called this complex network of domination the "deployment of sexuality." Such a process is part of the modern "discursive regime" that, like earlier discursive regimes throughout history, imposes what we take to be our identity through a web of social customs, moral and linguistic conventions, and official bodies of knowledge. Yet the domination is not all on one side. It is everywhere. In constructing types of sexuality—one man's simple desire for another man, say, becomes stigmatized as "homosexuality"—modern society also gives people an outlet for expressing their erotic desires through these regulated constructions. And so the Freudian model of repression is a false one. There is no "natural" sex urge that requires only to be sprung from confinement. Modern society will go on constructing desire from all points. It will go on simultaneously legitimizing, stigmatizing, regulating, and making available an assortment of sexualities, which themselves will demand a greater freedom of expression, but always through constructed and regulated channels of desire. With such a vision of life, Foucault obviously had no hope for a redeemed and perfected erotic world. He had a virtually pagan view of history as cyclical and nonprogressive. Of the discursive regimes cycling discontinuously through history there is no end. And there is no relief from the modern deployment of sexuality. That is why, toward the end of his life, Foucault found philosophical solace in the Stoic philosophers' ethic of self-cultivation through self-discipline. (Practically, he found it in sadomasochism's highly aestheticized rituals.) Not surprisingly, Foucault held sexual liberationists in contempt. He ends *The History of Sexuality*, volume 1, by declaring that "the irony of this deployment [of sexuality] is in having us believe that our 'liberation' is in the balance." Elsewhere in the same volume, he writes that "we must not think that by saying yes to sex, one says no to power." He disdains the modern tendency to think: "sex, the explanation for everything." He laments the "austere monarchy of sex," the way in which we have "become dedicated to the endless task of forcing [sex's] secret, of exacting the truest of confessions from a shadow." He regards it as pathetic that "we demand [of sex] that it tell us our truth." He believed (as did Christopher Lasch) that the most potent modern construction of sexuality was the endless Freudian-derived therapeutic obsession with sexuality.

Just as Heidegger wanted to return to a pre-Socratic purity of being, Foucault wanted to return to ancient pleasures, to a moment before the deafening modern invention and regulation of sexuality. He thought (bless him) that the time had come to stop thinking about sex. "The rallying point for the counterattack against the deployment of sexuality," this great pessimist wrote at the conclusion of *The History of Sexuality*, volume 1, with typical hyperbole, "ought not to be sex-desire, but bodies and pleasures." And the site for his "counterattack" was precisely the Stoic philosophers' faith in the private conditioning of private appetites.

Yet Foucault's followers, consecrated to absolute fluidity, prefer to ignore all this. "Foucault's 'self' . . . is not a personal substance," Halperin inanely insists in *Saint Foucault*, "or essence, but . . . a strategic possibility." And here is how Gayle Rubin uses Foucault in "Thinking Sex," one of the seminal essays behind queer theory, published in 1984: "The time has come to think about sex. . . . Contemporary conflicts over sexual values and erotic conduct . . . acquire immense symbolic weight. Consequently, sexuality should be treated with special respect in times of great social stress." You can hear the ghostly laughter wafting all the way down the Boulevard Saint-Germain.

This is where Eve Kosofsky Sedgwick, the mother of queer theory, and her chief disciple Michael Moon come in. Sedgwick's *Between Men: English Literature and Male Homosocial Desire* (1985) and *Epistemology of the Closet* (1990) are the keystones of queer thinking. In her books and her essays, she does not, like Gayle Rubin, make the semantic mistake of "thinking sex." Instead of saying yes to sex as a way of saying no to power, Sedgwick says yes to "bodies and pleasures" as a way of saying no to power. She makes "bodies and pleasures" the explanation for everything, dedicates herself to the endless task of forcing the secret of "bodies and pleasures" from a shadow, and demands that "bodies and pleasures" tell us our truth. In other words, she ends up like Rubin anyway, deploying the very deployment of sexuality that Foucault decried as a noisy plague on the erotic life. It is a dead end spawned by Foucault himself, though he turned to Greece and Rome and left his contradictions behind. Yet Sedgwick is in total intellectual and unironic servitude to what she has made of Foucault. From three different works by Sedgwick, written over the course of seven years: "Foucault's demonstration, whose results I will take to be axiomatic."; "A span of thought that arches at least from Plato to Foucault."; "the gorgeous narrative work done by the Foucauldian paranoid, transforming the simultaneous chaoses of institutions into a consecutive, drop-dead-elegant diagram of spiralling escapes and recaptures."

A lot has been written about the influence of Nietzsche and Heidegger on Foucault, but I don't believe anyone has pointed out the significant influences of French film and the *nouveau roman*. (Foucault's name probably first appeared in an American publication in 1963, in an essay that Susan Sontag originally published in *Partisan Review* on Nathalie Sarraute and the *nouveau roman*, where he pops up last in Sontag's list of French commentators on that new literary style.) Like Robbe-Grillet, Sarraute strove for a zero-degree objectivity that would reveal a zero-degree subjectivity. Robbe-Grillet wished for "the possibility of presenting with all the appearance of incontestable objectivity what is . . . only imagination." He invited the reader to supply gaps in meaning with the reader's own meaning; he juxtaposed isolated objects or "shots"; he plausibly imposed a crazy illogic. And he found in film the most felicitous vehicle for such expression.

Shortly after Robbe-Grillet publicized his ideas, Foucault began to offer his own. He insisted on filling in history's silences with the meanings that he chose for them; and he explained an entire society and culture by isolating from its context a cultural practice or institution; and he rested his rationally presented judgments on his presumption of a universal irrationality. That is to say, Foucault became the first cinematic philosopher. He jump-cut around history. This is exactly the intellectual style that Sedgwick has adopted in her weirdly mechanistic language. (You will find her matter-of-factly mentioning "adult/child object choice," for example, as just another option on the erotic menu.) She "presents with all the appearance of incontestable objectivity what is . . . only imagination." And this is fine, because—remember—"all it takes to make the description 'queer' a true one is the impulsion to use it in the first person." So all it takes to find a particular meaning in a literary work is the impulsion to wrench it from "silence"; to isolate it from anything else in the work; and then simply to say, in defiance of all common sense, that it is there. Once you isolate this particular meaning from its organic connections to the rest of the work, moreover, you may connect it to everything in the universe outside the work. This is because all identity and meaning are socially constructed, and because the way in which these constructions are fashioned and imposed is the key to all private and public "realities" in modern life. After all, Foucault says so. And what results from this sort of criticism is the "queering" of literature.

## IV

Consider Sedgwick's reading of this passage from Henry James's *Notebooks*, written during a visit to California when he was sixty-two:

> I sit here, after long weeks, at any rate, in front of my arrears, with an inward accumulation of material of which I feel the wealth, and as to which I can only invoke my familiar demon of patience, who always comes, doesn't he?, when I call. He is here with me in front of this cool green Pacific—he sits close and I feel his soft breath, which cools and steadies and inspires, on my cheek. Everything sinks in: nothing is lost; everything abides and fertilizes and renews its golden promise, making me think with closed eyes of deep and grateful longing when, in the full summer days of L[amb] H[ouse], my long dusty adventure over, I shall be able to [plunge] my hand, my arm, *in*, deep and far, and up to the shoulder—into the heavy bag of remembrance—of suggestion—of imagination—of art—and fish out every little figure and felicity, every little fact and fancy that can be to my purpose. These things are all packed away, now, thicker than I can penetrate, deeper than I can fathom, and there let them rest for the present, in their sacred cool darkness, till I shall let in upon them the mild still light of

dear old L[amb] H[ouse]—in which they will begin to gleam and glitter and take form like the gold and jewels of a mine.

For Sedgwick, this passage about the importance of reaching down into memory for literary creation is not about the importance of reaching down into memory for literary creation. No, the passage "shows how in James a greater self-knowledge and a greater acceptance and specificity of homosexual desire transform this half-conscious enforcing rhetoric of anality, numbness, and silence into a much richer, pregnant address to James's male muse, an invocation to fisting-as-*écriture*." Why, in heaven's name, did James hang fire on this topic for so long? Similarly, in *Wings of the Dove*, we find an older and wiser James "placing the reader less in identification with the crammed rectum and more in identification with the probing digit." Don't ask.

Sedgwick sees in history's silences an extraordinary amount of shit. (*Wings of the Pigeon.*) And it is all there because Sedgwick sees it there. And because she is "queer," marginal, "perverse," stigmatized, what she has seen has not been hitherto overlooked, it has been hitherto silenced, just as the queer Henry James had to silence himself. So now the real James (never mind that identity is constructed) will be heard; and now you will listen to Sedgwick because she has truth and virtue (never mind that all meaning is constructed) on her side. Sedgwick might go fancily on about how "queer" means so many different things, about how "genitality" is the antidote to the constrictions of "sexual identity," but her project always comes down to outing authors through their writing—to liberating them from their repressive historical moment. Needless to say, Henry James is the obsessive favorite for Sedgwick. His enigmatic sexuality makes him such a rich occasion for an analysis of the way in which "heterosexist" society buries same-sex desire under "compulsory" sexualities. And if no one knows for sure what James's sexuality was—alas, all we have are the novels, stories, essays, notebooks, and so forth—all the better. A hoarding, secretive anal eroticism can become James's calling card.

The legion of Sedgwick's disciples has adopted the anal strategy as their own, too. In *Novel Gazing: Queer Readings in Fiction* (1997), a collection of essays edited by Sedgwick, the Duke University graduate student John Vincent alerts us to the "face/butt metonymy" in Swinburne's poetry. Yet it is the rectum of the Master, brutally robbed of speech by history, in which one finds a veritable buried treasure of "recuperative" meanings. Here is the Duke University graduate student Renu Bora writing about James, also in *Novel Gazing*:

I picture James's head hovering over a consummated toilet, a glossy, smooth turd lolling in the waters, pride summoning lost pleasures. Perhaps it "passed" (a favorite James term) too perfectly. Perhaps it was less than slippery, and he gripped it within his bowels like a mischievous boy, playing peekaboo with the exit, hiding it upstairs, clinging to it as to a departing lover. Perhaps this dream only teased him.

The turd of independent minds.

Thus queer theory is partly about the more militant gay-liberationist goals of the 1960s "passing" into the tortured textual readings of the 1980s and the 1990s. Consider Sedgwick's theory of "homosocial desire." Propounded in 1985 in *Between Men*—it is more a feminist work than a queer one, with a faint but definite homophobic undercurrent—Sedgwick's theory rocked the groves of academe. It is not complicated. It holds that homosocialness derives from a sentence in Lévi-Strauss's *The Elementary Structures of Kinship*, quoted by Sedgwick in *Between Men*: "The total relationship of exchange which constitutes marriage is not established between a man and a woman, but between two groups of men, and the woman figures only as one of the objects in the exchange, not as one of the partners." Of course, Foucault is not far behind in Sedgwick's use of Lévi-Strauss. This, again, is because Foucault stressed the importance of making history's silences speak: "There is not one but many silences, and they are an integral part of the strategies that underlie and permeate discourses." That, for queer theory, is the carte blanche that launched a thousand bêtes noires. What meaning is being suppressed in Lévi-Strauss's formulation? Well, what meaning would you like him to be suppressing?

For Sedgwick, the analytical prize is this: men really desire each other, but society's prohibitions against homosexuality force them to repress that desire. Instead they marry women and channel their homosexual impulses into keeping women subordinate through marriage, while using marriage as a means to bond with other men for social advantage. The homosocial element lies in this bonding, which also causes homosexual panic whenever the forbidden homosexual impulse rises to the surface. In such a way, the entire structure of Western capitalism (Sedgwick looks to English literature to prove her theory, but she makes it obvious that she thinks it applies to Western civilization in general) is supported by a frustration of homosexual desire. Thus *Between Men* extracts its peculiar argument from one sentence in the work of a French structural anthropologist, who in fact never could prove the general truth of the proposition expressed in that sentence and never returned to it. And even riskier is Sedgwick's combination of Lévi-Strauss and Foucault. For Foucault saw the absurdity of applying the former's notion of primitive kinship structures to modern society long before Sedgwick went ahead and applied it. As Gayle Rubin puts it in "Thinking Sex," in a passage paraphrasing Foucault, "kin-based systems of social organization . . . [are] surely not an adequate formulation for sexuality in Western industrial societies."

But—and this is where things really get confusing—Rubin herself had used Lévi-Strauss's theory in just such a way a decade before, in an essay called "The Traffic in Women." In *Between Men*, Sedgwick acknowledges Rubin's earlier use of Lévi-Strauss's idea, even though Rubin had already disowned that idea and exposed its illogic. Don't these people have e-mail? This is the kind of thing that Michael Warner has in mind when he celebrates queer theory's "focus on messy representation."

Sedgwick cites also another important source for her theory of homosocial desire. It is Freud's essay on Dr. Schreber and "the mechanism of paranoia." Along with countless references to masturbation ("the Aesthetic in Kant is both substantively indistinguishable from, and at the same time definitionally opposed against, autoerotic pleasure") and to our friend the rectum, the subject of Freud's treatment of Schreber's paranoia appears throughout Sedgwick's work.

Freud notoriously claimed that all paranoia derived from an individual's repression of homosexual desire. Schreber's feeling that he was being persecuted by another man arose, for Freud, from Schreber's hidden desire for that man. Here is Freud's formulation of the paranoiac process: "The proposition 'I (a man) love him' is contradicted [repressed] by . . . 'I do not *love* him—I *hate* him.' . . . [T]he proposition 'I hate him' becomes transformed by *projection* into another one: '*He hates* (persecutes) *me*,' which will justify me in hating him.'" Such psychic slipperiness enables Sedgwick, in *Between Men*, to cite Freud on Schreber as justification for the way in which "this study discusses a continuum, a potential structural congruence, and a (shifting) relation of meaning between male homosexual relationships and the male patriarchal relations by which women are oppressed." In other words, Sedgwick can find homosocialness anywhere she wants to find it. Of course, by adopting Freud's theory, Sedgwick gets herself tangled up again. For if men marry women—or simply have sex with women—both to suppress their desire for each other and to bond with each other for social advantage, they can hardly be expressing, at the same time, their hatred for each other. Not to mention the fact that if Schreber's case exemplified homosocialness, society would fall to pieces in a New York minute. And what about mere friendship between men who do not desire each other sexually? Or genuine love and passion between men and women? But no matter. So Sedgwick contradicts herself. Queer theory contains multitudes.

Interestingly, Sedgwick's use of Schreber reverses Whitman: "And what I assume you shall assume, / For every atom belonging to me as good belongs to you." Queer theorists adore Whitman, but they are democracy's dark side. For their flaunting of their "difference" is driven by their belief that everyone is, or must be, the same as them—a belief that they find continually frustrated. The queer theorist's conviction that everyone desires everyone else is the obverse of the queer theorist's mission to accuse everyone of desiring everyone else. Perhaps that is why queer theory is flourishing at a moment when, in our culture, sexual recrimination has become a more instantly gratifying form of sexual indulgence.

V

Eve Kosofsky Sedgwick has complained about being "misspelled, misquoted, mis-paraphrased" by journalists who "wouldn't have been caught dead reading my work: the essay of mine that got the most free publicity, 'Jane Austen and the Masturbating Girl,' did so without having been read by a single one of the people who invoked it . . . the attacks on me personally were based on such scummy evidential procedures." I'm sure she's right. Sedgwick is one of the most influential academics at work today, and no one seems to read her closely, if at all. Still, if you do stay patiently and carefully with her writing, you find yourself in a twisting labyrinth of mad interpretations. Or is it that she does not read well, and took up theory and concocted those deliberately outrageous essay titles to disguise her deficiency? The first literary reading in *Between Men*, of Shakespeare's sonnets, is typical of the way that Sedgwick does literary criticism. Of the 154 sonnets, remember, the first 126 are addressed to a "fair youth," and all the rest but the last two spoken to the legendary "dark lady." The first part famously has a homoerotic undercurrent; but the poet also urges the fair youth to find a woman, marry, and have children.

As always, Sedgwick begins by laying down the theoretical framework. She adduces René Girard's notions of triangular desire. Marx appears. Lévi-Straussian binaries are posited and then deconstructed. There is an enveloping aroma of Foucault ("while genital sexuality is a good place to look for a concentration of language about power relationships"). Connect, connect, connect. She freezes the camera on "Marilyn Monroe": "the speaker treats the youth, rhetorically, as a dumb blonde." Isolate, isolate, isolate. The line "Thou single wilt prove none" does not mean, as it usually is taken to mean, that without marriage the young man will be alone, or will have no heirs. Rather, it means "essentially the same thing as the brutal highschool-boy axiom, 'Use it or lose it.'" Masturbation, as usual, appears; even though it actually is absent. Sedgwick claims that the dark lady is masturbating, and then she compliments herself for saying so by giving Shakespeare a pat on the back: "to attribute masturbatory pleasure to the woman is unusual in these poems—unusually benign and empathetic, I would say."

And then we get the essay's premise, which is also the essay's foregone conclusion: with the dark lady sonnets, "we are in the presence of male heterosexual desire, in the form of a desire [i.e., homosexual desire] to consolidate partnership with authoritative males in and through the bodies of females." This, Sedgwick tells us, is the significance of the phrase "the bay where all men ride," which the poet employs in trying to seduce the dark lady. The poet does indeed mean that the thought of other men having been in the dark lady's "bay" arouses him. But not for Sedgwick. She explains that if the poet's certainty that the dark lady has been with other men excites him, it must be because he has homosexual impulses. Never mind that men might like promiscuous women for another reason. Sedgwick's vaulting reductions do not only narrow the range of interpretive possibilities. They also narrow the range of erotic possibilities. And then there remains the biggest question that Sedgwick's elaborate cookie-cutter method of reading raises: Why would the poet want to use a common wench like the dark lady—she has, he tells us, a cumbersome gait, a bad complexion, and horrible breath—to bond with "authoritative males" when he has already "bonded" with the obviously powerful and highborn fair youth (who was also Shakespeare's patron)? And why would anyone want to write 154 sonnets about a business transaction, anyway? All Sedgwick tells us is that "male homosexual bonds may have a subsumed and marginalized relation to male heterosexuality similar to the relation of femaleness to maleness, but different because carried out within an already dominated male-homosocial sphere." Foucault disseminated his generalizations with a lot more flair; and he never dreamed of applying them to literature.

How does Sedgwick get away with this awful stuff? Her success is owed in part to her intermittent use of a reveal-all-hurts-and-wounds style of writing. After all, winning a reader's sympathy (as opposed to earning a reader's respect) is now a certified rhetorical stratagem; and the literary critic, too, has her uses for the confessionalism of the day. It enables her to write unsympathetically about subjects that have an elusive complexity. And anyone who cavils is vicious; an anti- or a -phobe.

> I can say generally that the vicarious investments most visible to me have had to do with my experiences as a woman; as a fat woman; as a nonprocreative adult; as someone who is, under several different discursive regimes, a sexual pervert; and, under some, a Jew.

> As a child, I hated and envied the frequent and apparently dégagé use my parents liked to make of the word *humiliating*, a word that seemed so pivotal to my life that I could not believe it could *not* be to theirs.

Sedgwick's preternatural sense of alienness is perhaps why she is so convinced that the "scummy evidential" reaction to "Jane Austen and the Masturbating Girl" reflected a dangerous opposition to onanism. True, she gravely concedes that "today there is no corpus of law or of medicine about masturbation; it sways no electoral politics; institutional violence and street violence do not surround it, nor does an epistemology of accusation." No, thank God, there is no street violence surrounding masturbation today. Still, trouble is brewing:

> Yet when so many confident jeremiads are spontaneously launched at her explicit invocation, it seems that the power of the masturbator to guarantee a Truth from which she herself is excluded has not lessened in two centuries. To have so powerful a form of *sexuality* run so fully athwart the pre-

cious and embattled sexual *identities* whose meaning and outlines we always insist on thinking we know, is only part of the revelatory power of the Muse of masturbation.

And yet, despite all the forces of darkness gathering out there, I have to report that "Jane Austen and the Masturbating Girl" does not live up to its promising title. And it is promising. For why shouldn't a literary critic write about masturbation? Or, for that matter, about rectums and excrement? Norman O. Brown's chapter called "The Excremental Vision" in *Life Against Death* analyzes with brilliance, wit, and style the role of the anus and human feces in Swift's writing. For the analysis of masturbation, I envision an essay starting with Rousseau and the connection between his idea of a totalizing "general will" and his bouts of masturbation; and moving on to Rilke's aimless, unemployed hands in the *Notebooks of Malte Laurids Brigge*; and then to Kafka's *The Trial*, where the words "hand" or "hands" are repeated dozens of times in a sophisticated, ironic burlesque of sexual and romantic frustration; and finally to Gide's *The Counterfeiters*, in which a young boy named Little Boris, a compulsive masturbator, kills himself.

It may be Sedgwick and her crowd are not comfortable with how great writers have consciously set out to portray one of the queers' favorite topics. Anyway, Sedgwick on Austen does not illuminate. I spent an entire, evidentially motivated day immersed in her fantasy about *Sense and Sensibility*. The essay's "point," if you can call it that, is that Marianne Dashwood's emotional and psychological distress is the result not of her rebuff by Willoughby, but of, yep, masturbation.

Sedgwick's argument consists of quoting a series of excerpts from a French medical text written about one hundred years after Austen wrote *Sense and Sensibility*. The author is one Demetrius Zambaco—a figure whom Sedgwick never discusses or even identifies—who describes what he believes are the effects of masturbation on two young girls. Some of these effects strikingly resemble Austen's dramatization of Marianne's malady. And therefore, Sedgwick reasons, Marianne must be masturbating.

Such an arcane analogy alone would be a shaky enough basis for an argument about literature and life. Worse, it appears that Sedgwick stumbled. Three years before Sedgwick delivered her paper on Austen to the MLA in 1989, Zambaco was exposed as a fraud by none other than Jeffrey Mousaieff Masson in *A Dark Science: Women, Sexuality, and Psychiatry in the Nineteenth Century*. The volume is a collection of nineteenth-century clinical writings that includes Zambaco's full text and a preface by Catharine MacKinnon. Yet Sedgwick went right ahead and published her paper in 1991 without making the slightest reference in her arguments to Masson's book, even to rebut him. She didn't even revise her paper to identify Zambaco. She merely mentioned Masson's volume in passing, in a brief footnote. Sedgwick's evasiveness is understandable. For, according to MacKinnon, Zambaco and the other writers in Masson's book "trade in half-truths." Their "diagnoses are not true because their etiology . . . is not true." Zambaco is a "sadomasochist." Masson writes that "Zambaco's view about the sexuality of the two girls is a fantasy"; and he considers Zambaco's text to be "shockingly brutal, offensive, and pornographic." It's impossible to disagree: Zambaco's treatment consisted of repeatedly applying a red-hot iron to the clitoris of one of the girls, until the patients were removed from his care. But Sedgwick uses Zambaco's diagnosis of the two girls' condition as a justification for her view that Austen is describing a similar condition for Marianne. In other words, Sedgwick believes that the sadistic, misogynistic doctor and the exquisitely profound novelist share the same understanding of women. This is the fumbled connection at the core of Sedgwick's notorious essay.

Oh, she does try to connect Marianne's masturbation with a lesbian relationship between Marianne and her sister Elinor, though "connect" is, in this context, far too merry a word:

> Is this, then, a hetero- or a homoerotic novel (or moment in a novel)? No doubt it must be said to be both, if love is vectored toward an object and Elinor's here flies toward Marianne, Marianne's in turn toward Willoughby. . . . Even before this, of course, the homo/hetero question is problematical for its anachronism . . . if we are to trust Foucault, the conceptual amalgam represented in the very term "sexual identity," the cementing of every issue of individuality, filiation, truth, and utterance *to* some representational metonymy of the genital.

And if Sedgwick could demonstrate that Marianne Dashwood has been masturbating—say, by the miraculous discovery of a letter from Jane to her sister Cassandra ("Mr. Plumptre walked home with us yesterday & ate soup and talked of Chawton—this morning after breakfast destroyed entire *chapter* with wedding of Marianne and Digit—Henry dines tonight with Mr. Digwood")? It would be like demonstrating that at a certain point in the novel Marianne is sitting on a chair rather than on the sofa upon which generations of scholars have believed her to be sitting. The novel would still be waiting to be read. And Marianne would still be in love with Willoughby, not with her finger.

Curiously, since Sedgwick published her essay on Jane Austen in 1991, she has more and more come to sound like the anti-Sedgwick. Consider her interest in Silvan Tomkins. (In 1995, she cowrote the long introductory essay for *Shame and Its Sisters: A Silvan Tomkins Reader*, a volume that she also coedited.) Tomkins was, essentially, an eccentric behavioral psychologist who, among other things, drew up personality evaluation tests for the Educational Testing Service. That is to say, he was just the sort of psychological expert that Foucault spent his life trying, fairly or unfairly, to expose. Yet Tomkins is also another kind of perfect guru for Sedgwick. For one thing, he describes sex in Sedgwick's mechanistic ("if love is vectored toward an object") and abstract terms. An excerpt from Tomkins:

> Many normal adults . . . utilize genital interpenetration as a way of heightening the oral incorporative wish or the earliest claustral wish. Sexual intercourse, as we shall see, lends itself as a vehicle to every variety of investment of social affect.

In other words, sex is an effect of affects. And the most primary "affect," for Tomkins, is shame. By using Tomkins, then, Sedgwick makes her publicly proclaimed feelings of "humiliation" theoretically more fundamental than the impossibly complicated matter of sex. And this is what Sedgwick and the queer theorists seem to have wanted all along: to turn the "body" ("the two writing bodies of Marx and Engels," says Michael Warner) into an impersonal, quantifiable spaceship in which they can flee from the emotional and psychological tumult of sex. That is, from themselves. Perhaps such a self-disowning is why, in the introduction to her book on Tomkins, published in 1995, Sedgwick sardonically turns against even Foucault.

> Some consequences of such readings of Foucault: The most important question to ask about any cultural manifestation is, *subversive* or *hegemonic*? Intense moralism often characterizes such readings.

But this is precisely the earth-shaking question that Sedgwick had been asking for her entire career! From Shakespeare to Jane Austen to Henry James: Sedgwick has subjected one literary work after another to an intensely moralizing interpretation.

Sedgwick may or may not be "straight," but she sure is full circle. For just as the homophobe strips the homosexual person of his human amplitude—the queer particularity of selfhood—and reduces him to his sexual practices, Sedgwick and her colleagues strip the homosexual person of his human amplitude and reduce him to his sexual practices. That is why the more you read the queers, the more their idea of "queer" sounds like a new kind of oppressive "normalcy."

## VI

Why am I being so hard, so mean? Because the result of Sedgwick's inestimable influence has been, among her followers—all of whom either are college teachers or will someday be college teachers—a deadness, not just to beauty and fineness of perception and fragile inner life, but also to human suffering. Michael Moon's new book, *A Small Boy and Others*, is interesting only as an illustration of this. Of the seven chapters of Moon's book, three are concerned with Henry James. (*A Small Boy and Others*, in fact, is the title of one of James's autobiographies.) In James's wonderful story "The Pupil," the touching and fairly uncomplicated relationship between a tutor and a young boy named Morgan in his care reveals, in Moon's expert hands, each one's sexual desire for the other. The story is not about what James seems to have meant it to be about: two injured souls supporting each other amidst the shabbily genteel Moreens' cruel manipulations of both the tutor and their son. And it is the boy's mother, Moon has discovered, who has extended to the tutor the "invitation to desire Morgan." This, Moon tells us, is because the mother herself has probably been engaging in incest with her eleven-year-old boy. Moon works up this last point by patiently and calmly explaining that the "*gants de Suède*" that Mrs. Moreen draws through her hands are made of a material that is described as "undressed kid" in "English-language guides to proper dress from midcentury forward." And "kid," Moon discloses, also means "child." (Impressive references to William Morris and the Earl of Shaftesbury drive home this point.) "Undressed kid," therefore, means "undressed child." Get it?

It follows from this that, in having Mrs. Moreen draw her gloves through her hands, James wants us to understand that she is unconsciously reenacting sex with her son. What role incest plays in this story, though, Moon never tells us. He merely "recuperates" it in this one isolated moment. And he never returns to it, which is not surprising, since a work of art can no more be split up into atomized particles than pleasure can be isolated from emotion, meaning, and value. As if to acknowledge this technical obstacle, Moon goes on to draw a helpful extraliterary conclusion from the story. With a kind of eerie remoteness, he writes:

> Like little Morgan and his tutor and the other "small boys" and young men that figure in these texts, we all often find ourselves possessing what seems to be both more knowledge than we can use and less than we need when we try to think about such difficult issues as our own relations to children and young people, including our students.

Comparing James's "The Pupil" to the film *Blue Velvet*, Moon describes Dennis Hopper's brutal beating of Kyle Maclachlan as representing "the two men's desire for each other that the newly discovered sadomasochistic bond that unites them induces them to feel." How the Master would have loved that scene! *Midnight Cowboy*, moreover, is not about the shelter of intimacy that the physically crippled Dustin Hoffman and the psychically wounded Jon Voight find with each other away from economic and sexual confusions; it is, says Moon, "a film about how two men can have a meaningful S-M relationship without admitting to being homosexuals." Moon has sadomasochism on the brain; I bet he faints at the slightest whiff of leather.

In *A Small Boy and Others*, the seventy-year-old James writes about how, as a young boy visiting the Louvre, he "felt myself most happily cross that bridge over to Style constituted by the wondrous Galerie d'Apollon . . . a prodigious tube or tunnel through which I inhaled little by little, that is again and again, a general sense of glory." Professor Moon has an orals question about this passage: "What's large enough for one to walk through and small enough to take into one's mouth?" And so the young James and his tutor are perhaps having sex. And the older James goes to a Yiddish play on the Lower East Side perhaps because he wants to have sex with the famous Yiddish actor Boris Thomashefsky. And on, and on, and on, and on, and on.

Queer America, I am putting my straight shoulder to the wheel, but I don't like what this is all about. For this cannot be literary criticism, and this cannot be life, and this cannot be sex. When we reduce our lives to "bodies and pleasures," we reduce bodies and pleasures to an ongoing debate about the meaning of our lives. And then we reduce love to work, and work, without the promise and reward of love, to a senseless finality. And the worst of it is that, as the effect of making a physical presence into a cold abstraction, we will start to become indifferent to—or perhaps connoisseurs of—physical pain in other people. Then we will have broken the sympathetic bond between the heart and the flesh. And then the taste of our own lips will be all that we can rely on to summon our erotic past out of distant memory. And then we will all be traveling away from ourselves and each other along a very dark road indeed. Sexualizing all of life takes all of life out of sex. Poor life, poor sex. Good-bye, penises. Good-bye, vaginas.

## WORKS CITED

Brown, Norman O. *Life Against Death: The Psychoanalytical Meaning of History*. Middletown, Conn.: Wesleyan University Press, 1959.

Halperin, David M. *Saint Foucault: Towards a Gay Hagiography*. Oxford: Oxford University Press, 1995.

Masson, Jeffrey Mousaieff, ed. *A Dark Science: Women, Sexuality, and Psychiatry in the Nineteenth Century*. Trans. Jeffrey Mousaieff Masson and Marianne Loring. New York: Farrar, Straus and Giroux, 1986.

Moon, Michael. *A Small Boy and Others: Imitation and Initiation in American Culture from Henry James to Andy Warhol*. Durham, N.C.: Duke University Press, 1998.

Morton, Donald. "The Birth of the Cyberqueer." *PMLA* 110, no. 3 (May 1995): 369–81.

Rubin, Gayle. "Thinking Sex: Notes for a Radical Theory of the Politics of Sexuality." In *Pleasure and Danger: Exploring Female Sexuality*, ed. Carole S. Vance, 267–318. Boston: Routledge and Kegan Paul, 1984.

——. "The Traffic in Women: Notes on the 'Political Economy' of Sex." In *Toward an Anthropology of Women*, ed. Rayna R. Reiter, 157–210. New York: Monthly Review Press, 1975.

Sedgwick, Eve Kosofsky. *Between Men: English Literature and Male Homosocial Desire*. New York: Columbia University Press, 1985.

———. *Epistemology of the Closet*. Berkeley: University of California Press, 1990.

———, ed. *Novel Gazing: Queer Readings in Fiction*. Durham, N.C.: Duke University Press, 1997.

Sontag, Susan. "Nathalie Sarraute and the Novel." *Against Interpretation and Other Essays*, 100–111. New York: Farrar, Straus and Giroux, 1966.

Warner, Michael, ed. *Fear of a Queer Planet: Queer Politics and Social Theory*. Minneapolis: University of Minnesota Press, 1993.

## 29. BATTLE OF THE BIEN-PENSANT

### KWAME ANTHONY APPIAH

1

ACADEMIC MORALISM IS ONE of the oldest traditions of the university, which began, after all, as an ecclesiastical institution whose students were mostly destined to be members of the clergy. In the early part of the twentieth century, the ethical voice in the American university was to be heard from the philosophy department as well as the divinity school, both of which were dominated by varieties of Protestantism. When William James or John Dewey spoke to the educated public on the conduct or meaning of life, they were only doing their job. They were not-so-terribly secular clerics, whose voices were heard alongside—occasionally even above—those of the official priesthood.

Sometime before the midcentury, however, professional philosophy in America became more centrally preoccupied with questions in epistemology and metaphysics, which were of less obvious relevance for their lay fellow citizens: the most influential figures in American philosophy in the decades after the Second World War were philosophers—some native, like W. V. O. Quine, some immigrant, like Rudolf Carnap—whose work was dauntingly technical and, by and large, not addressed to the moral life.[1] In becoming national and then international, the university had had also to become less sectarian and more secular; and so, as a result, the withdrawal of the philosophers from ethical questions left a gap that could no longer be filled by the divinity school. Questions of public ethical concern were increasingly the subject of the social sciences. But psychologists, sociologists, and economists often proclaimed their "value neutrality." (That was, to a degree, what made their pronouncements credible: they offered guides to living in the guise of technical, objective,

Kwame Anthony Appiah. "Battle of the Bien-Pensant." Originally published in *The New York Review of Books*, 27 April 2000, 42–44. Reprinted by permission of *The New York Review of Books*.

scientific information.) And so when someone had to speak up for values the literature faculty increasingly took up the slack.

It did not always do so comfortably. As the literary scholar John Guillory has observed, modern English departments represent the confluence of two nineteenth-century traditions: belles-lettres and philology. The scientific aspirations of the latter discipline gave rise to an emphasis on interpretative method and theoretical speculation. That focus on literature's mechanics—the medium rather than the message—now goes by the name of "literary theory." But these theorists never had the field to themselves; the spirit of moralism in academic literary criticism has a long pedigree in twentieth-century America, ranging across the continent, and alphabet, from Irving Babbit to Yvor Winters. And in the postwar period, as the United States assumed more confidently its global leadership, a professor of English like Lionel Trilling could speak for American values, for liberalism and democracy, and find them embedded, already waiting for us, in the high literary canon. The tone was that of a (progressive) gentleman's club; the signature color was tweed.

Today's academic moralism in the humanities sounds rather different. In the 1960s and 1970s of the last century, the liberation movements of blacks, women, and homosexuals often found their voice in literary work; this social fervor crossed the threshold of the English department just as the numbers of blacks, women, and open homosexuals increased at universities that had once been citadels of white and male privilege. The genteel cadences of old did not survive the resulting culture wars, for the liberationists aimed to dismantle the ethical consensus that earlier critics had assumed: Trilling's magisterial "we," once meant to conjure a moral community, came to be deplored as a blithe "exclusion of difference." "Essentialism" began as a word for criticizing anyone who assumed that all X's shared the same characteristics. And so, at the turn of the 1980s, the word was first used against nationalists of various sorts and women. There were black and Jewish essentialists, feminist essentialists, lesbian essentialists.

At the same time, in an ironic twist, "essentialist humanism" became a key term of opprobrium, an accusation flung at anyone who did not insist that society had created important differences between men and women, black and white, gay and straight, rich and poor, or who did not accept that those differences undermined the assumption of a shared humanity in the humanities. Now you could be an essentialist both for saying that people were different and for saying that they were the same. The result was to change not just the subject matter but the rhetorical tenor of academic criticism. Trilling, though he might have rejected William K. Wimsatt's approach to literature—which was text-centered and showed no interest in the author's psychological processes—would not for this reason have thought Wimsatt wicked. But if

African American literary criticism was an adjunct of Black Liberation—which, as a matter of dignity and justice, was obviously a business of the highest moral importance—then academic disagreements could easily spill over into conflicts more vulgarly political; and the dissemination of intellectual error might not only undermine the movement, it might also reflect bad character.

Of course, it wasn't the liberation movements that made literary study contentious. When Harold Bloom urged us to trace literary influences not as the transmission of tradition, the cultivation of a precious heritage, but as an Oedipal struggle of the sons against the fathers, his Freudian allegory was offered as an account of relations among poets. But one might be forgiven for suspecting that the idea came not from communing with the souls of Wordsworth and Blake but from Bloom's own experience of the struggle for existence in the groves of academe. Shelley may not have been battling Milton, but Harold Bloom, the author of *Shelley's Mythmaking*, was certainly battling Earl Wasserman, the author of *Shelley: A Critical Reading*. Individuality in scholarship, as in life, begins with defining yourself both within and against a tradition. What the new context added was the increasing moralization of the process of definition. Since academic generations always define themselves by resisting the interpretations of their predecessors, the moralization of intellectual differences (this is not just a point about the English department) was bound to lead to trouble.[2]

As you will have noticed, the alliance of liberation movements and literary study hasn't made criticism politically potent or politics critically informed: the revival of Zora Neale Hurston hasn't altered wage inequities; nor is her name one to conjure with in the primaries even of her native Florida. But this alliance did bring the conduct of literary scholars under minute "political" scrutiny, at least in the classroom, the conference, and the critical essay. It has raised the heat of literary debate, without always shedding more light. And the feminist shibboleth that the personal is the political—or perhaps one ought to say a particular construal of that shibboleth—has made the personal conduct of critics fair game for interpretation and "critique."

I once attended a conference on postcolonial criticism at which one of the speakers mistakenly addressed a young African professor as a graduate student and then left the conference early to catch a plane home. Both of these things were surely, at worst, lapses of manners: and yet the incident led to the publication of densely theoretical, fiercely denunciatory essays among the speaker's fellow Third World, poststructural, and Marxian theorists. It isn't easy, in such a setting, to distinguish the *ad feminam* from the substantive objection. Literature may not be, as Matthew Arnold thought, the "criticism of life," but literary scholarship is, often enough, the criticism of critics.

2

In 1979, Professors Sandra Gilbert and Susan Gubar published *The Madwoman in the Attic: The Woman Writer and the Nineteenth-Century Literary Imagination*, a work that shaped profoundly the then burgeoning field of feminist literary scholarship.[3] Ever since, this book has appeared regularly on reading lists in courses in departments of English around the country. It was not a work of high theory, but one of literary interpretation and textual recovery: it discussed a wide selection of nineteenth-century novelists and their critical reception. Beginning in 1988, Gilbert and Gubar published three further volumes, entitled *No Man's Land: The Place of the Woman Writer in the Twentieth Century*, which continued their earlier work and included such writers as Kate Chopin, Edith Wharton, Willa Cather, and Gertrude Stein. Some of them, such as Edith Wharton, were criticized for their criticism of the work of other women writers. In 1985, Gilbert and Gubar published the first edition of *The Norton Anthology of Literature by Women: The Tradition in English*, a work that helped shape, willy-nilly, a canon of women's writing for the next generation of students of English.

These books were feminist in aim, intention, and self-description. And part of their literary energy came from the fact that they were envisaged as part of the project of combating patriarchy and building a new feminist consciousness, especially for the young women in the classes where they were (and are) so widely used. In their 1979 opus, Susan Gubar and Sandra Gilbert castigated Harold Bloom for the ostensibly masculine bias of his account of literary relations—a man might attack his literary paterfamilias, but the literary relations among women, we were assured, were far more supportive. Far from seeking to overthrow their literary forebears, women writers were seeking a literary community; and the enemy was patriarchy, not their foremothers.

Despite their own experience of successful feminist collaboration, the response to their scholarly undertaking hardly confirmed this happy conviction. In later years, Susan Gubar writes, she has found herself (as part of "that curious entity called 'Gilbert and Gubar'") lambasted by various "insurgent" critics for various purported sins: she was "essentialist," didn't sufficiently acknowledge black women or lesbians, failed to keep pace with high theory—the list was no doubt long. (For example, it was pointed out that "Gilbert and Gubar" had made nothing of the fact that the madwoman in the attic of their title—Bertha Mason in Charlotte Brontë's *Jane Eyre*—was a Jamaican Creole.) To judge from her later book, *Critical Condition: Feminism at the Turn of the Century*, the experience has been demoralizing. The field of feminist criticism—a field she did much to establish—is now, she tells us, cluttered with alienating jargon and riven by divisive identity politics.[4]

*Critical Condition* has its origins in an episode that is sketched—I use this word advisedly—in the book's introduction. At some time (she does not say when) Professor Gubar was "a candidate for a senior position at a school to remain nameless." Informed by the chairman of the department that there was a risk that her appointment would be opposed by some of his more conservative senior colleagues—and assuming, as one gathers, that she could count on the support of the younger feminists—she gave a talk entitled "Who Killed Feminist Criticism?" in which she referred to some of the ideas of the critics who had attacked her. The talk, she tells us, cost her the job. And the opposition came not from the right but from the left. The visiting feminist progressive found herself condemned, astonishingly, as a troglodyte, perhaps even a racist. When she arrived she was Kate Millett; when she departed, John Rocker.

A final version of this talk is printed toward the end of the book as "What Ails Feminist Criticism?" (Dr. Gubar has, on sober reflection, taken the unusual step of moving the patient from the morgue back to the ICU.) She admits that the original paper was "probably written in too bellicose a manner." But if it was anything like the essay in this volume, it was its subject, not its tone, that was bound to cause trouble, and for at least two reasons. First, in considering feminist criticism, she objected (as she puts it here in the introduction) to "what Toni Morrison calls 'the calcified language of the academy.'" This confirmed the opinion of those who thought her insufficiently theoretical; since, if you object to academic language, it is often assumed that this is because you—unlike your more savvy colleagues—have a hard time understanding it.

But worse was to come; for Gubar also criticized "certain sponsors of African-American, postcolonial, and poststructuralist studies" for "subverting the term 'woman' that feminism needs to assure its political agency."[5] That is, she argued (to uncalcify the language a bit) that often, in the struggle for justice, what you need to insist on is not what divides women but what they have in common. Since what divides women, as she argued, was insistence on their differences, she could be pigeonholed by her critics with those essentialists who are allegedly hostile to women of color and lesbians. The effect of her remarks was thus only to confirm the worst suspicions of her detractors. A quondam insurgent critic fell victim to a new insurgency.

What Gubar had done was to respond to the major criticisms of her earlier work in the natural way: by attacking the works of her critics. The effect was only to inflame them. Given the new moralism, this led not just to vigorous disagreement but also to assaults upon her character. She did not give up: she read versions of the paper on several other occasions around the country and finally published it (in 1998) in *Critical Inquiry*, which is about the most visible journal in literary studies. After the response she reports, this was either courageous persistence or evidence of masochism.

Clearly Susan Gubar believes that her dogged criticism of the new insurgency has left her with a reputation (if only in some *soi-disant bien-pensant*— or at least *soi-pensant bien-disant*—quarters) as an essentialist and a reactionary. So her new book is both apology and apologia—or, to put it another way, it is an act of what's known, on Madison Avenue, as "positioning." The opening chapters feature sympathetic discussions of African American art (the quilts of Faith Ringgold, the conceptual art of Adrian Piper, the performances of Anna Deavere Smith); lesbian literature (the poetry of Marilyn Hacker and the "astonishingly diverse productions" of Jeannette Winterson); and her discovery of her own "inner ethnic" as she explores the relations of Judaism and feminism.

Each of these essays is a concession to "difference": to the recognition that women are, after all, not all the same. If, as the critics alleged, when "Gilbert and Gubar" wrote "woman" what they had unconsciously assumed was a female heterosexual of the white middle classes, then displaying the range of her interest in women who were neither straight nor white would seem to be a suitable act of clarification, if not atonement. At the very least, as Professor Gubar writes in the book's introduction, she hopes that her "positive engagement with the insights of African-American, postcolonial, and poststructuralist thinkers in what are now the opening chapters" will "free me from the allegation that I had dismissed or calumniated their labors." This book is driven by something other than the ordinary academic worry that one might be in error; it is, so to speak, Susan Gubar's soul, not her mind, that seems, to be up for judgment.

Well, I, for one, am happy to acknowledge the essential goodness of Professor Gubar's soul.[6] The question is why she has ended up having to defend herself before a tribunal that is largely unseen and unnamed. Discriminating between what is and isn't worthwhile is the purpose of intellectual judgment. Why, then, could she not criticize her critics without having her character impugned? The answer is, in part, that the intertwining of academic and social agendas has given rise to an outlandish rhetorical inflation, a storming-of-the-Bastille bombast brought to bear on theoretical niceties. Individuals get taken for kinds: a particular Third World literary feminist theorist comes to represent all women of color. Not teaching Jeannette Winterson is taken to mean excluding her from the canon, which is easily inflated into excluding lesbians from it; and soon we have unqualified talk of the "exclusion" of lesbians—or gays or blacks—which sounds as though you're keeping them out of the class, or the university, or running them out of the neighborhood. This is indeed moralism; but it is moralism run amok.

There is, to be sure, an argument lurking in the background here: it is that literal exclusion somehow stems from literary exclusion. Or, to speak more precisely, that much of the oppression in the world is the result of speaking and writing and thinking about people in the wrong way. If all men thought about women in the right way, fewer men would beat up their wives. I believe this is a truth, even a truism. But there remains a difference between thinking ill of a black woman's critical writings and thinking ill of her or of all black women. And there is yet a further distinction between thinking or speaking ill of people and beating them up. The point is that not every intellectual error about women—or blacks or lesbians—is as harmful as every other. Once you conflate errors of these different orders, you end up dissipating energy in pointless skirmishes while the vital battles are being lost all around you.

In her introduction, Susan Gubar worries that many women undergraduates today "do not define feminism as equity for women or an awareness of the social construction of gender or reproductive control or political agitation for the ending of sexual violence." Presumably these young women would be happy to identify with feminism if they did define it as "equity for women" and the like; and one is therefore inclined to ask why they do not. Professor Gubar suggests that at least part of the explanation has to do with the nature of recent feminist debates: what she describes as "mind-numbing battles in which so-called social constructionists faulted so-called essentialists for their naive totalizing, feminists of color blamed white scholars for their racism, lesbian critics accused straight thinkers of homophobia." Perhaps, if academic disputation looks to her students as it does to Professor Gubar, being a feminist doesn't seem like much fun.[7]

Neither, I suspect, does being a literary critic. In the last few decades, as countless cultural theories have jostled and collided, as the concept of literature itself has been relentlessly "interrogated," academic criticism—which is to say, literary scholarship and interpretation for its own sake and its own satisfactions—has lost a sense of cultural purpose. Accordingly, critics have increasingly turned to writing about each other. ("Garbage is garbage," a well-known philosopher used to say, "but the history of garbage is scholarship.") This soon becomes something of a tar pit: Susan Gubar's new book is, in no small part, criticism about criticism of criticism. Which, I suppose, means that what you're now reading is criticism of criticism about criticism of criticism. I'm sorry: it's just the spirit of the times.

Susan Gubar, it must be said, is clearly interested in literature as well as committed to political feminism. The book she's produced, however, tells us less about literature than about the social tensions in her profession at the end of the twentieth century. There is even a chapter, entitled "The Graying of Professor Erma Bombeck," devoted in part to discussing the personal and professional relations of older and younger women scholars. Such matters, I have come to feel, are probably better handled by practitioners than by critics of narrative: one finishes her book convinced that the most interesting version of *l'affaire Gubar* would be a novel by David Lodge or Molly Hite.[8] (Or Philip Roth, whose novel *The Human Stain* has much to say about the literary academy today.)

And, despite the generality of the reference to feminism in the book's subtitle, it is actually largely about literary feminism within the academy; which is, as Susan Gubar says in her introduction, "less an activist, more a scholarly enterprise." A review of her book is not, therefore, the place to discuss whether feminism outside the literary academy is dead, let alone ailing. But so far as the literary academy goes, my sense is that the heyday of the sort of Mau-Mauing to which Professor Gubar was subjected has passed, not just in feminist debates but also in those about race and sexuality as well. "Identity politics" has fallen into bad odor, at least among many members of university faculties (which does not guarantee, of course, that you recognize it when you do it yourself). Theory for its own sake, too, has lost some of its luster, another small victory for the spirit of belles-lettres in its apparently endless struggle with philology. Indeed, *mirabile dictu*, there are more and more literary critics— feminist and otherwise—who actually devote themselves to . . . literature. Susan Gubar's field may well be in a "critical condition," but there are signs that it is on the mend.

## NOTES

1. This process is described and lamented in Cornel West's *American Evasion of Philosophy: A Genealogy of Pragmatism* (Madison: University of Wisconsin Press, 1989). It's perhaps worth observing that, with John Rawls's *A Theory of Justice* (Cambridge, Mass.: Belknap Press of Harvard University Press, 1971), ethics once more assumed a place of honor in professional American philosophy and that philosophers of distinction have increasingly addressed not only moral theory—which can be as dense and difficult as the most abstruse metaphysics—but also practical ethics.

2. The struggle to overthrow the theories of one's predecessors is central, if in very different ways, to the natural sciences as well—at least, if either Karl Popper or Thomas Kuhn (who agree in this, if in little else) is to be believed. But what is at stake is not usually moralized in the natural sciences.

3. Reviewed by Helen Vendler, *The New York Review of Books*, 31 May 1990, 19–25.

4. Susan Gubar, *Critical Condition: Feminism at the Turn of the Century* (New York: Columbia University Press, 2000).

5. It is, in this context, a none-too-subtle reframing of the original talk—which did not mention Morrison—to put the first complaint into the mouth of the best-known living black woman writer.

6. This is probably the place to admit that her first chapter has an epigraph from an essay of mine; though, alas, the suggestions she quotes were glossed by me—in a phrase she does not cite—as "the proposals of a banal postmodernism."

7. It occurs to me that if these young women accept what Susan Gubar sees as feminism's goals, while rejecting the label, this might be accounted not a defeat but a victory.

8. This is something Gilbert and Gubar plainly know: their main joint work of the 1990s was *Masterpiece Theatre: An Academic Melodrama* (New Brunswick, N.J.: Rutgers University Press, 1995).

# PART VI
## THEORY AS SURROGATE POLITICS

SEVERAL ESSAYISTS in the preceding section deplored Theory's tendency to encourage its adherents to see their work as "political" and to use it as a substitute for the more laborious work of doing politics in the world outside the academy. We think it is a strange turn in modern intellectual life that "teaching" or "writing" have in many quarters become "my form of activism." But unlike some contributors to this book who lament this posture as a distraction from the practical activism that politics demands, what strikes us is the unquestioned authority that the arrogation of "politics" has gained for academic intellectuals. Celebrating their "oppositional" and "transgressive" aspirations—rhetorically and from the safety of the ivory tower—many followers of Theory now insist that by "doing theory" they are also "doing politics."

Twentieth-century history has clearly shown the problems that result from politicizing intellectual life and educators' role in it. The profession's failure to recognize these problems as they have appeared within the academy is, we think, a very serious dereliction. The essays in this section reveal just how extensive, and how damaging, the drive toward politicization has been for the humanities. Criticizing the conceit of scholarship-as-politics and recording the significant costs incurred, they expose the various ideological and cultural currents that have fed into what has become a broad stream of literary criticism with a political (or, many argue, pseudo-political) bent.

Not that protesting voices have been absent. One of these is that of Harold Fromm, whose polemical *Academic Capitalism and Literary Value* (1991), with which this section opens, confronts the dubious practices of academic intellectuals during the two preceding decades. "Oppositional Opposition," the chapter from that book included here, derides the use of literature to serve political ends by ironically portraying the activities of "vanguard intellectuals" as a form of manipulation of the academic marketplace where theories are their stock in trade. Claims to revolutionary action notwithstanding, their assaults on capitalism and patriarchy are—Fromm argues—little more than hypocritical posturing.

In "Silence Is Consent," Richard Levin analyzes the efforts of "oppositional" critics to depict traditional literary scholarship as complicit with the most deplorable aspects of the dominant ideology. Where texts do not offer any evidence of such an association, these critics discover "silences"—things that go unmentioned—which they deem to exhibit tacit acceptance of an evil status quo. Levin's cases in point are taken from recent Shakespeare criticism, where the "oppositional" stance places emphasis on political and social issues important to us today but ignored in the plays. Salient among the suspect "silences" are patriarchy, class exploitation, inequality, domination, colonialism—all seen as part of a monolithic and unchanging system of oppression. Regarding themselves as embattled in a "Manichean" struggle, oppositional critics exhibit much of the self-righteousness and truculence (including name-calling) of true believers, making genuine dialogue about competing theories impossible.

In "Criticism as Displacement" Jeffrey Wallen asks: Has the recent vogue for socially and politically engaged criticism broadened the appeal of literary studies? Can a criticism with such an emphasis move beyond the inner circle of experts to involve the wider reading public? Will it be politically effective? Or is it, rather, akin to a rite of purification for the critic? Focusing his analysis on Edward Said's reading of *Mansfield Park*, Wallen explains the failure of socially conscious criticism to open a productive debate: critics provide no intellectually respectable foundation for their belief in the necessity of social change; they don't engage their opponents in a fruitful dialogue; and they don't spell out the concrete changes they desire. Such answers as they can supply to the great social and political questions are predetermined by their assumptions. In these ways, Wallen argues, "literary criticism actually displaces debate away from the issues that most require it."

Russell Jacoby investigates the sources and manifestations of the widespread cynicism about truth and objectivity found in much intellectual work going on today. The anthropologist Clifford Geertz's technique of "thick description" serves Jacoby as a paradigm of the obliteration of differences between actual representation and fiction. Given Geertz's enormous influence in the humanities, the tendency to elide such distinctions and, in effect, aestheticize experience made quick headway among intellectuals. In turn, this has led to professional habits Jacoby holds responsible for breeding today's cynicism: cultural relativism, multiple truths and an inability to discriminate among them (all truths being constructed), a denial of universals, a blending of disciplinary categories, a tolerance for subjective, even narcissistic practices, and an exaggerated emphasis on power relations. For Jacoby, truths and facts are anything but relative, and he questions the tendency to see everything as a "text," open to self-indulgent "thick" interpretation.

In his essay "Casualties of the Culture Wars," with which this section closes, Eugene Goodheart makes a strong case for the merits of an aesthetic response to literature, a reading that "foregrounds the work and doesn't allow it to be devalued by one or another discourse." "Discourse," which in Goodheart's view is the forcing of a text into an ideologically freighted frame—feminist, postcolonial, and so on—has led to reductive readings (Goodheart labels them "the hermeneutics of suspicion"), to the degrading of disinterested knowledge, to a preoccupation with the circumstances of the production of a work, and to an obscure and often repellent style of writing. While recognizing the importance of political, social, and moral considerations in our responses to literature, Goodheart mourns the devaluing of aesthetic criticism, the devotees of which have now been put on the defensive—a position Goodheart's essay tries to reverse.

## 30.  OPPOSITIONAL OPPOSITION

### HAROLD FROMM

A MAJOR INFERENCE crying out for recognition in the course of the preceding chapters of my book *Academic Capitalism and Literary Value* is that the Academic Revolutionary is a fraud. Guaranteed a job for life through the tenure system regardless of subsequent performance, supported by dependable paychecks from the bureaucracy he pretends to scorn, relieved of some of the multiple anxieties of mortality by means of health insurance and a pension, and addicted as much as everyone else—if not more—to the perquisites of capitalism's shameless cornucopia, the revolutionary academic is no revolutionary at all. He is, rather, an exemplary specimen of capitalism in action. The marketplace of ideas, once only a metaphor, has literally become just that, a system of commodities. The Information Society, as Lyotard has so aptly insisted, is an exchange of ideas that is largely an Exchange of Ideas (as in "Chicago Mercantile Exchange"), where information commands a price and is traded like pork-belly futures.

The academic professional performs his function in the thick of the marketplace, enjoying it like crazy—flying around to conferences, aspiring to upper-middle-class tastes, benefiting from the cunning of technology (whether as computers, compact-disc players, xerography); indeed, today's academic is completely dependent on printouts, on-line retrieval systems, electronic bibliographies, so much so that one can hardly imagine an academic functioning without them, any more than one can imagine a contemporary supermarket without a scanner at the check-out. Today's academic is an artifact of capitalist technocracy.

By fancying himself to be a revolutionary, the "radical" academic superadds real vice to his relatively venial enchantment with technology and high living. It is surely a painful irony that his culture hero should be someone like Gramsci, who really was a revolutionary and paid a heavy price for it, his major work having been written from a place that few academics will ever experience firsthand, except perhaps as a penalty for drug pushing or murdering a spouse. Kierkegaard, had he lived in contemporary America, could have had wonderful new/old material for attacks against moral inauthenticity. Instead of exposing religious hypocrisy (e.g., the agent of Christ blesses the guns rather than protesting the war), he could have turned to its modern academic counterpart: phony radicalism. The radical academic exhibits the verbal trappings and forms of Marxist renunciation while acting as paradigmatic acquisitive capitalist: he needs the latest computer to write his jeremiads against technology and the marketplace, as well as grants (from government or private enterprise) for trips to European watering places where he can give and hear papers about hegemony and patriarchal oppression—all the while pretending to bite the hand that is paying his per diem. Or as Irving Howe has succinctly put it, "Marxism has gone to the universities to die in comfort."[1]

The Academic Revolutionary is not just an oxymoron but an ultimate betrayal of authentic ideals. In acting out with such precision the roles assigned to him by capitalist ideology while attacking the false consciousness of everyone else, he is pretty much in the same class as the television evangelist who pretends to be amassing millions for Jesus, even as he lives a life of luxurious debauchery.

Being a false revolutionary seems much worse than being a passive tool of oppression, for it is hard to be vigilant about vice while seeing oneself as always already virtuous. As for capitalism, though it has played a major role in producing the darker side of the American academy, its achievements are not *entirely* bad when seen against the range of past history, with its poverty, disease, and lives short and brutish. Like everything else, capitalism needs to be constantly subjected to criticism—its horrors are manifold, like the horrors of life itself—but total repudiation in the midst of wallowing enjoyment is worse than uncritical acceptance.

Finally, as if failure to acknowledge the hands that feed us were not bad enough, the use of literature as a weapon to fight this war against capitalism and patriarchy is too often a violation of the creative skills and larger consciousness behind the novels and poems that give us so much psychological nourishment. This is not to say that poets and novelists are transcendent, ahistorical souls uncontaminated by the clay of human deficiency and therefore beyond criticism or reproach. Works of literary genius emerge from the same human soil as everything else, and nothing is finally sacred, but reductive readings produce crabbed and crippled forms of aesthetic response, constricting rather than expanding consciousness. To read *Wuthering Heights* according to current political paradigms is to abort its multivalent and disturbing resonances by turning them into mere confirmations of today's vanguard political positions, positions that will rarely issue in worthwhile action, since a cheap sense of virtue (and marketability) is the "radically" operative motivation. If the reduction of art to politics is an evil in the totalitarian state, it is not so much less an evil when performed by ineffectual bourgeois intellectuals fueled by priestly resentments. If you believe in noblesse oblige, it comes off as rather worse.

Who could have guessed that academics would come to be as guilty of the commodification of culture as TV moguls and monolithic bookstore chains? But *this* betrayal of the clerks is more blameworthy than the ordinary vulgar doublecross, because the pretensions are so much greater. In the long run, atypical professors like Allan Bloom and E. D. Hirsch (whether we like their views or not)—as well as less categorizable thinkers like Russell Jacoby—may turn out to have contributed more to forcing intellectual issues into the forum of the real world than self-professed revolutionaries, who ultimately seem so domesticated and unthreatening, so easily defanged with dollar bills. Now, with the disappearance of the traditional person of letters, academia must also make an effort to supply the "independent intellectual" in addition to the partisan specialist (since we are all academics now), though it is difficult for most professors to be significantly "independent" because they are as corporately "bespoke" in their way as office personnel in theirs. It is just the *illusion* of independence that is stronger in their case, for how independent can you be when the demands of specialization lead you deeper and deeper into narrow professionalism's profound unfreedom.

For the present, at any rate, genuinely radical academics can be neither wholly Marxist nor feminist, neither wholly black nor Third World. The only radical position plausible right now is skeptical nonalignment, using a bit of this and a bit of that. Today's vanguard intellectual must learn to live without grandiose cosmic beliefs, entertaining local, temporary, and flexible viewpoints that can accommodate themselves to quotidian realities while resisting transcendental afflatus and bombast. This would be the only genuine heroism available to him, short of operating in the real world like Gramsci (who in today's comfortable America might well find himself incarnated as a fat-cat professor suited to a David Lodge novel). The vanguard intellectual claims, after all, to have accepted Nietzsche's message that God is dead and to have welcomed Derrida's modification of that message in the form of an assault on logocentrism. If it is no longer possible to believe in a center, whether as God, Essentialism, or Foundationalism, then fanatic insistence upon favored ideologies as ultimately true or right is no longer tenable and is today's most reprehensible form of intellectual hypocrisy. While one can and ought to "believe" in the truth or rightness of things in relation to the present needs of society, global theoretical assurances are simply preposterous, however plausible they may seem at any given moment to transient political interests. The categorical imperatives of radical feminism, for example, are no more in touch with What Is than patriarchy (though feminism has a great deal to offer and the best feminists know how to offer it), and when antirepresentationalists nevertheless go on to tell us how things really *are*, beating us over the head with their own essences, foundations, and representations, their mendacity is too serious to be brushed off with laughs.

Although one would have accepted the fruits of Nietzsche and Derrida to involve the embrace of radical skepticism, an abandonment once and for all of eternal verities, the big surprise is the trendy revival of polytheism, with biodegradable gods popping up all over the place. These gods rise and fall in the twinkling of an eye, as the needs of the academic job market produce sacred new truths to propel nascent careers. If today's consumers must throw out last year's cordless telephones because the newer models enjoy better transmission (and unlike theoretical artifacts, consumer appliances really do get better), so today's academic consumers must throw out Stephen Greenblatt (though he can still be peddled to undergraduates) because the New Historicism is entering its inevitable down-market phase. If the claims had been kept moderate, if the tenets of antirepresentationalism, antilogocentrism, and deconstruction had been synthesized as functional components of a generally skeptical understanding, the passionate conversions of true believers followed by rapid losses of faith would not have been necessary. Each theoretical movement has left us with worthwhile alterations of consciousness—but must we accept any of them as comprehensive accounts of the way things are, as their hard-sell proponents would have us believe? It is not really a question of accepting or rejecting theorizing altogether, as frequent debates on the subject propose, but a matter of recognizing the *constructedness* of theory, its pragmatic and instrumental nature. Theories can help us to deal with experience by providing models for behavior, in the way that thinking of the letter "H" can help us to shift the gears in a manual transmission, but theories cannot provide us with ultimate truths.

Today's radical intellectual, then, is in the final instance not radical enough, falling as he does into recidivist patterns of doctrinaire credulity. Though the doctrines themselves may be new, the mentality that generates them is old, tiresome, and effete. What is still to be learned is the art of playing it cool—as neither leftists nor rightists, neither specialists nor nonspecialists, neither feminists nor antifeminists, but an amalgam of all these: a critical intellectual. If "independence" is remotely possible for a creature who emerges from the primal mud, from his own genes, and from social and domestic history, then nonalignment looks to be the only Promethean way, and today's Prometheus can expect to have his entrails gnawed by all sides, since he or she would be opposed to them all and thus fair prey.

Nevertheless, for *now* the radically radical stance could hardly be clearer: alignments must be resisted so that *real* opposition may thrive.

### NOTE

1. Irving Howe, "The Treason of the Critics," *The New Republic*, 12 June 1989, 31.

## 31.   SILENCE IS CONSENT, OR CURSE YE MEROZ!

### RICHARD LEVIN

*These books do not pretend to political neutrality. This . . . involves
a claim that criticism which pretends to neutrality is in fact effacing its political orientation and that such a manoeuvre is normally
complicit with the dominant ideology.*

—ALAN SINFIELD, "LITERARY THEORY"[1]

*Neutrality in this case, is all one with opposition,* Curse ye Meroz,
curse the Inhabitants thereof, because they come not forth to
helpe, *silence is not always consent, but when we ought to speake
it is.*

—SAMUEL FAWCET[2]

BY NOW WE ARE ALL familiar with the argument invoked in my first epigraph, since we have been hearing many versions of it (usually without any
qualification like "normally") over the past fifteen years from many British
and American proponents of the new "oppositional" approaches to literary
criticism. Later in the same essay Sinfield also quotes with approval Terry Eagleton's assertion that conventional literary criticism "reveals its often unconscious complicity with [ideology], betraying its elitism, sexism or individualism in the very 'aesthetic' or 'unpolitical' language it finds natural to use of the
literary text," and that "it has helped, wittingly or not, to sustain and reinforce
[the] assumptions" of our "political system."[3] Criticism that is "assuming and
proclaiming its 'descriptiveness,' its 'disinterestedness,' its ideological innocence," says Peter Widdowson, serves "to reproduce 'and naturalize bourgeois
ideology as 'literary value.'"[4] Jean Howard's view of "the inevitably political
nature" of criticism is presented in a rhetorical question: "Self-effacement,
neutrality, disinterestedness—these are the characteristics privileged in the
Academy, but are claims to possess them more than a disingenuous way of obscuring how one's own criticism is non-objective, interested and political?"[5]
Malcolm Evans insists that in literary criticism "'disinterestedness' is always, at
best, an ideological flag of convenience," and that the supposedly disinterested
New Criticism has a "concealed political agenda" that "sustains . . . characteristic bourgeois concern[s]";[6] and Lynda Boose refers to "the overtly apolitical,
though inherently (if blandly) conservative, practice of 'New Criticism.'"[7] For

Richard Levin. "Silence Is Consent, or Curse Ye Meroz!" *College English* 59, no. 2 (February 1997): 171–90.
Copyright © 1997 The National Council of Teachers of English. Reprinted with permission.

Terence Hawkes, "traditional criticism pretend[s] to be politically neutral";[8] for Jonathan Dollimore, "traditional literary criticism" is "a politically conservative way of doing criticism" that is "spuriously impartial";[9] for David Margolies, "traditional character-imagery-plot [analysis] is reactionary" and "helps preserve the status quo";[10] and for Frank Lentricchia, "interpretation according to traditional humanism," with its " 'disinterested' ways of reading," really "is not . . . apolitical; in the strict sense it is politically conservative" and "shores up things as they are."[11]

There are many more versions. We are told by Catherine Belsey that "traditional Anglo-American critical practice . . . becomes the accomplice" of "the dominant ideology,"[12] and by Donald Morton that it "has an ideological investment in the status quo,"[13] and by Antony Easthope that it is "complicit" with "bourgeois ideology,"[14] and by Francis Barker and Peter Hulme that this ostensibly nonpolitical kind of criticism, when applied to *The Tempest*, has "often been complicit, whether consciously or not, with a colonialist ideology."[15] An older critic's praise of Shakespeare's plays as "profoundly moving, or spiritually restoring, or simply strangely enjoyable," according to John Drakakis, "subscribes tacitly to a teleological conception of Art not too far removed from the advice proffered by the Arts Minister . . . [that] 'You should accept the political and economic climate in which we now live,' "[16] and the older criticism of these plays, according to Kiernan Ryan, is "reinforcing the beliefs upon which our patriarchal, class-divided culture depends" and "the illusions underpinning the status quo."[17] Gayle Greene says that "it seems rather late in the day to have to point out that all critical positions are ideological" and that interpretations "are determined by political ideology," including those from "approaches which are more traditional" and "pass as 'neutral' and objective."[18] And Daniel Boyarin does not believe critics who "pretend that they are serving no interests" because it "should be by now commonplace . . . [that] they serve only the continued dominance of a particular gender, class, and culture" and are engaged in "a cynical attempt to enlist [others] as unwitting (and perhaps unwilling) allies in the reactionary protection of the privilege of that very gender, class, and culture."[19]

This argument, moreover, has become the standard reply to any protests against the focus on politics in the new oppositional approaches. And since these protests almost always come from proponents of the older historical or formalist approaches, the reply typically takes the form of *tu quoque*, asserting that this older criticism, even though—or rather, precisely because—it does not discuss politics or take a political position, is really just as political but is on the other (conservative/reactionary) side, since it supports what Sinfield in the epigraph calls "the dominant ideology" or, as he later puts it, "the maintenance of the status quo" that this ideology legitimates. This is a very powerful argument, and I believe it has played an important part in the current political polarization of our discipline since it seems to eliminate the possibility of any

discursive space outside the two warring poles, a point I will return to later. Indeed it has been repeated so often that many people assume it is now an established truth, as can be seen in the exasperated complaints, published in 1991, by
Boyarin that it "should be by now commonplace" and by Greene that "it seems
rather late in the day to have to point [it] out" (after pointing it out she adds, "I
find it astonishing that this needs repeating"). But since many of the critics
who keep repeating this argument also keep telling the rest of us that the doctrines we regard as established, commonplace, and obvious are the very ones
that should be "put in question," it seems only fair to subject their own argument to such an interrogation to see if it holds up. In this test I will draw most
of my examples from interpretations of Shakespeare, but I think it should apply to the interpretation of any literature of the past. I want to emphasize,
however, that it does not apply to all critics practicing the oppositional approaches, who are a very diverse lot; I am concerned here only with those who
use this argument, which is not integral to any approach—in fact we will see
that some oppositional critics reject aspects of it.

This argument really makes two distinct claims that are often conflated (as they
seem to be in several of the statements just quoted) but should be examined
separately. One claim is that supporting the dominant ideology and the status
quo is just as political as opposing them, which is certainly true, although we
may not realize it because in relatively stable societies such as ours this support
requires no special effort or even thought. Moreover, those who are satisfied
with the status quo tend to regard it as normal, just, or even natural, and therefore view its opponents as professional troublemakers with a sinister political
agenda, which accounts for the "outside agitator" trope. I can still remember
when the strikes accompanying the CIO organizing drive in the 1930s were
blamed on these agitators, as were the activities of the civil rights movement in
the 1960s. In both cases the people in power assumed that "their" workers or
blacks were just as happy with existing social arrangements as they themselves
were, and so must have been subverted by external political agents. (The same
rationalization is now employed to support their own Marxist status quo by the
people in power in China, who blamed the 1989 student demonstrations in
Tienanmen Square on the influence of "foreign reactionary forces";[20] and
Patrick Tyler reports that when tens of thousands of peasants rioted in Guizhou
Province in 1994 to protest against their living conditions, "Communist Party
officials blamed a handful of agitators who went from village to village to whip
up anti-Government sentiment.")[21] We have to recognize that the support of
the status quo and its ideology is itself political, even when we are not conscious
of it, and so we should be grateful to these new oppositional approaches for
helping to raise our consciousness about such a fundamental fact of life.

Problems arise, however, when we turn to the second claim of this argument,
that critics who do not discuss politics or take a political position in their treat-

ment of literary texts are supporting the dominant ideology and the status quo. This too may seem persuasive since it draws upon a very ancient and widely held belief embodied in the proverb "silence is (or gives or means) consent," and in such phrases as "unspoken agreement," "tacit consent," or "it goes without saying," and we can think of many instances in life and in literature where someone's silence is correctly interpreted in that way. In the closing scene of *As You Like It*, to take a simple example, when Duke Senior proposes that all his fellow exiles in Arden return to court with him, Jaques says he will remain in the forest but the others are silent, which we take to mean that they agree to return. In fact we are even surer of their consent here than in a similar situation in real life (those of us, that is, who have not wholly abandoned the useful concept of authorial intention), since we can assume that Shakespeare counted on the audience interpreting their silence as consent, and so would have had anyone else who did not consent speak out like Jaques, whereas in the real-life situation some nonconsenters might have other reasons for keeping quiet.

It is also true, however, that in most situations, real or fictional, we never think of interpreting a person's silence as consent to anything because there is nothing at issue that could be consented to. (Locke claimed that anyone living in a country "give[s] his *tacit Consent*" to obey its government,[22] but I do not think many of the oppositional critics who use the argument we are testing would consent to this application of it—Belsey clearly opposes it.)[23] There are even situations where silence has a negative meaning. During the chanting of slogans at a rally, a person's silence would probably mean dissent, and if the slogans were conservative, that silence would then be a tacit rejection of the chanters' acceptance of the status quo. This kind of tacit rejection of the surrounding community is also found in literature—in Hamlet's silence at the beginning of his first scene, for instance, or Iago's silence at the end of his last scene. And critics who were silent about the politics of literary works would be rejecting the dominant ideology if they practiced in the USSR during the reign of Zhdanov, who mandated the judgment of literature on political grounds. The significance of silence can also vary with the constituency: when opposition to the Vietnam War was widespread in colleges but not among the general public, the silence of some students on this subject might mean that they agreed with the prevailing view on campus, where this opposition "went without saying," and disagreed with the prevailing national view (although it could also mean that they did not subscribe to the campus orthodoxy but were unwilling to speak out); and when students are silent in class, no experienced teacher assumes that they all agree with the views she is propounding, since she knows that some may be opposed to them but afraid to challenge the person in power, or may be indifferent, or may not understand them. It seems evident, therefore, that the idea of silence meaning consent is not a general truth but only applies in certain specific contexts, which is how it is treated in our common law.[24]

We must then see if this idea applies in the context defined by the argument we are interrogating, where someone discusses a literary work without mentioning its politics or taking a political stand. It could hardly apply to an essay like Alice Walker's analysis of the printing of the quarto and folio texts of *Othello*;[25] she never refers to the politics of the play and does not even note that the compositors of both texts were white working-class males, yet I do not think even the most oppositional of the new oppositional critics would claim that this silence reveals her attitude toward the status quo because they would assume— and assume that she assumed—that such matters were not relevant to her bibliographical project. This is an extreme case, of course, but let us turn to an essay at the other extreme, Carol Sicherman's study of *Coriolanus*, where the project is clearly interpretive and the play clearly involves politics. One might have thought it was impossible to interpret this play without addressing its treatment of the conflict between patricians and plebeians or of the conceptions of masculinity and femininity, but that would be to underestimate the ingenuity developed by New Critical thematists in their final days when they were desperately searching for ever newer central themes to lick the older ones.[26] Sicherman finds that the play is "conduct[ing] an extended exploration of the often precarious correspondence of words and meanings,"[27] and then constructs a new close reading in terms of this "central problem" or "theme" that ignores the class and gender issues that seem so central to us today. Here, surely, we have a prime example of the kind of silence about politics that is supposed to indicate literary critics' support of the status quo or, in the terminology of several of the passages quoted at the beginning, their "complicity" with it.

There is a problem, however, because we must now determine *which status quo* these nonpolitical readings are supposed to be supporting or to be complicit with. Most of the people who employ this argument do not seem troubled about that question, even though in this case and others like it we have three different worlds, each with its own status quo: the world portrayed in the play (here republican Rome), the author's world (early modern England), and the world of postmodern America where the reading was produced. Presumably their argument refers to the third alternative, for they could scarcely claim that a critic today supports the social arrangements of Coriolanus's world or Shakespeare's, which are no longer available options. But how can they infer a critic's attitude toward the status quo of our own society from this silence about the politics of two earlier societies? Their most common strategy, so far as I can tell, is to treat the aspect of Shakespeare's society (and of the society presented in his play) that concerns them as if it has remained basically the same down to the present, often by translating it into an abstract social or political issue that seems to float free of history. This is curious because these oppositional critics regularly condemn the formalists for viewing human problems (like Sicherman's "precarious correspondence of words and meanings") as transcultural, transhistorical, essential, eternal, God-given, inevitable, natural, universal, unchanging, and so on, and regularly swear allegiance to the principles of historical or cultural specificity—indeed they are capable of producing, in other situations, detailed accounts of the differences between Renaissance and modern society, and even between Elizabethan and Jacobean society. But the nature of this argument about silence may lead us to suspect that a number of them are prepared to rise above their historical principles for the sake of their oppositional politics.[28]

That suspicion is confirmed by some of the critics themselves, for while their assimilation of the world of Shakespeare (and of his plays) to our own is often tacitly assumed without comment, they can sometimes be quite explicit about it. Margot Heinemann finds that the "causes of disaster" in *King Lear* lie in "the horror of a society divided between extremes of rich and poor" that Lear indicts in his speech on "houseless poverty" (3.4.26–36) and that "the indictment is still, for us, very direct and near the bone," which she proves by citing statistics on the number of homeless people in England in 1990,[29] as if the social etiology and significance (and, she implies, the remedy) of homelessness were the same in Lear's society and Shakespeare's and ours. Kiernan Ryan says that the "causes" of Lear's tragedy "are housed" in "the injustices of a stratified society" that was "class-divided . . . then as now," which has an "urgent bearing . . . on our own predicament,"[30] without noting that the class divisions are now very different and thus create a very different predicament. John Turner locates the cause of this tragedy in "the injustices of the system" of feudalism depicted in the play and then asserts that these same "injustices" operate in the societies of Jacobean and modern England,[31] which certainly are not feudal. In her study of *Troilus and Cressida* Gayle Greene takes the opposite tack to reach the same political goal—instead of extending feudalism forward she extends capitalism backward by explaining that the play has "relevance to the present" because "Cressida's fate is that of woman in capitalism," which "reduce[s] people to objects of appetite and trade,"[32] but she fails to explain how the play could have shown this before the advent of capitalism, or what capitalism could have reduced women from (the good old days of serfdom and *jus primae noctis*?). "That we are dealing with live issues" in *Macbeth*, Alan Sinfield maintains, "is shown by the almost uncanny resemblances between the Gunpowder Plot [of 1605] and the bombing in 1984 by the Irish Republican Army of the Brighton hotel where leading members of the British government were staying, and in the comparable questions about state and other violence that they raise,"[33] though one of the states we are dealing with is an aristocratic oligarchy and the other a bourgeois democracy. For Catherine Belsey, the problem of "the legitimate limit of state violence" raised in *Henry V* "is an issue which modern societies in the free West have still not satisfactorily resolved,"[34] which is not surprising since she defines it at such an abstract level that it is unresolvable. And Graham Holderness claims that *The Taming of the Shrew*, in its treatment of "Katherina's plight," is "capable of delivering . . . an urgent address to immediate and inescapable political realities,"[35] which are not identified, but the implication is that women today are in the same plight as Katherina, so that we confront the same political realities.

Some other oppositional critics assimilate Shakespeare's world to ours in terms of ideologies rather than social issues. Jonathan Dollimore tells us that *King Lear* presents and questions the values of "essentialist humanism" that we still suffer from today.[36] According to Linda Charnes's reading of *Antony and Cleopatra*, the "liberal humanist" mystification of "transcendent love," which is largely responsible for the difficulties of the titular characters, is still with us (in our Harlequin novels, among other things) and is responsible for many of the difficulties in contemporary gender relations.[37] We learn from Lisa Jardine that the "cultural construction of female guilt" in *Hamlet* "is still current" now,[38] and from Lynda Boose that "the ideology of the . . . family" and "family roles" that we find in Shakespeare "was still firmly in place some four hundred years later."[39] Marion Wynne-Davies begins her essay on the rape of Lavinia in *Titus Andronicus* by asserting that "the issue of rape appears to be founded upon certain [male] premises about women's sexuality which have remained unchanged for five centuries," quoting the judge's summing up of a 1986 rape trial as evidence, and she concludes that the play makes us "question the values of a society which allows such a violation to occur"[40] (I cannot tell if this refers to Lavinia's society or Shakespeare's or ours, but that does not matter since it is supposed to be true of all three). Even when we are not given such explicit statements merging the social problems or attitudes of the Renaissance with those of today, however, it seems clear that the argument being tested here claims that an interpreter's silence about the politics of Shakespeare's plays really supports the status quo or dominant ideology of our own society—in Lentricchia's words, it "shores up things as they are."

Some oppositional critics, including several quoted earlier, assert that formalist readings like Sicherman's support our status quo not only by their silence about politics, but also by their use of various prepoststructuralist concepts that belong to the "bourgeois ideology" (a.k.a. "liberal humanism") that underwrites this status quo: the concepts of literature as a special category, of essential or inherent qualities in literature and life, of autonomous subjects and literary characters, of authorial intention, objective meaning, and so on. They even try to divide critical approaches into two political camps, with the old formalism, which employs these concepts, on the Right and their own poststructuralism, which rejects them, on the Left; thus Toril Moi calls formalism an "inherently reactionary literary theory"[41] (compare Boose's statement, quoted at the outset, that the New Criticism is "inherently" conservative). But this simplistic scheme simply will not work. Marx and Engels themselves, no friends of the status quo, assumed many of these concepts in their comments on literature,[42] as did most of the Marxist critics until recently, as well as most of the early feminist critics. Some people on the Left have in fact protested that the politics of these concepts is not inherent in them (which a card-carrying poststructuralist like Moi should know) but depends on how they are used.[43] And many oppositional critics who attack these concepts are happy to invoke them in dealing with texts on their side: Malcolm Evans, for example, deploys the full poststructuralist arsenal against Shakespeare's plays and the older criticism of them throughout most of his book, but at the end when he takes up the radical authors Gerrard Winstanley and Abiezer Coppe, he becomes an old-fashioned intentionalist,[44] as do virtually all the new Marxists when they discuss Bertolt Brecht (Dollimore says that "it wouldn't make sense" to treat him otherwise).[45] Nor does the history of modern criticism bear out their scheme. There was a thriving group of Marxist formalists in the USSR before they were eliminated by Marxist socialist realists under Zhdanov, who are now scorned by Marxist cultural materialists because realism is bourgeois. The formalist New Critics in their heyday covered most of the political spectrum, and Frederick Crews demonstrates that there is no necessary theoretical or practical connection between poststructuralism and radical politics.[46] It seems, then, that this unsuccessful attempt to equate critical approaches with political positions does not really add anything to the basic argument that a critic's silence about politics means support of our status quo and its ideology.

We can now press on in our interrogation of this argument by asking *which aspects* of our status quo or its ideology are supported by the silence of these nonpolitical readings of Shakespeare. For the oppositional critics who use the argument never tire of reminding us that the dominant ideology of our society, or any other, is not a seamless web but an uneasy mixture of diverse and even contradictory components; and it should be just as evident that the status quo in our society, or any other, is not a monolithic, homogeneous entity but an evolving collocation of various institutions, relationships, and practices that are often in conflict. The argument, however, does not have to cope with such complexities because it seems to focus on only one aspect of our status quo and ideology. Sinfield does not explain what it is in the statement quoted as my epigraph, although we can infer that it must be a very bad aspect since support of or even neutrality toward it appears to be culpable (this is also implied by his term "complicit," which connotes guilt), but it is revealed in the foreword to *Political Shakespeare*, written by him and Dollimore, in a passage that begins with the same language:

> Cultural materialism does not pretend to political neutrality. . . . On the contrary, it registers its commitment to the transformation of a social order which exploits people on grounds of race, gender and class.[47]

Apparently, then, criticism that pretends to political neutrality (they say this applies to "much established literary criticism") does not oppose this exploitation and so is, in the words of the epigraph, "normally complicit" with it.

This accusation is confirmed by the people quoted earlier who specify (without Sinfield's "normally") what it is that nonpolitical criticism is supporting: for Boyarin it is the same "dominance of a particular gender, class, and culture"; for Ryan, patriarchy and class division; for Barker and Hulme, colonialism; and for Eagleton, "elitism, sexism or individualism" and the "assumptions" of our "political system"—a system that he defines earlier as one "in which considerable private wealth remains concentrated in the hands of a tiny minority, while the human services of education, health, culture and recreation for the great majority are torn to shreds."[48] These statements assume that critics who are silent about politics are always and only supporting the most deplorable aspects of our society, and this also seems to be what the other people I quoted have in mind, even though they do not specify it. They never accuse nonpolitical critics of complicity with freedom of speech or the writ of habeas corpus, which are parts of our status quo, or with the egalitarian strain in our dominant ideology, nor are such critics permitted to split their votes by supporting the better aspects of our status quo and ideology and opposing the worse ones (the typical liberal position), since the argument apparently does not recognize the existence of any better aspects. This selective blindness is conspicuous in Eagleton's wholly negative definition, just quoted, of the "political system" these nonpolitical critics are sustaining, which is not allowed any redeeming features. (It must have had some recently, however, for those "human services" could not be "torn to shreds" by the Thatcher administration unless they had been put in place by previous administrations. Would he then argue that a critic writing during the pre-Thatcher era who was silent about politics was complicit with the establishment of these services? A question not to be asked.) The same selectivity can be seen in the passages cited earlier that assimilate elements of Shakespeare's society to our own, since these are always bad: extremes of poverty and wealth, homelessness, class division, the reduction of women to objects of appetite and trade, state violence, the subjugation of "shrews," the construction of female guilt, the toleration of rape, and the ideology of essentialist or liberal humanism that supposedly legitimates such things. Apparently no good aspects of Renaissance society (if there were any) persisted down to the present for critics who are silent about the politics of Shakespeare's plays to support or to be complicit with.

We should also note that all these bad aspects of the Renaissance world and ours turn out to be injustices that are regarded by the people employing this argument as modes of "oppression" or "exploitation," usually based on class or gender. Moreover, many of their statements seem to treat these various modes of oppression as components or consequences of a single, transhistorical, all-powerful, all-pervasive, and utterly evil system, which is what their oppositional criticism opposes. For the Marxists, this is the system of class oppression—or, more simply, "capitalism"—which they tend to essentialize and demonize as the ultimate cause of all the injustices in early, middle, late, and postmodern society. Of course they recognize that it takes different shapes in different periods, which they can distinguish quite effectively when they are being historically specific, but behind these many shapes they usually see one Devil, and the Devil has no history. He is, according to Hamlet, a malevolent trickster who "hath power / T' assume a pleasing shape" to "abuse" us (2.2.599–603), and capitalism is, according to Peter Widdowson, a "huge confidence trick being played upon us," with an "infinitely protean dynamic" enabling it to "adapt and change" to "exploit" us;[49] but it is still the same old Devil.

Some feminist critics are also Marxists and therefore believe that class oppression is responsible for gender oppression and all other injustices.[50] But some other feminists find the ultimate cause of human problems, past and present, in a single, omnipotent, omnipresent, and wholly evil "sex/gender system"—or, more simply, "patriarchy"—that is, again, often essentialized and demonized. Like the Marxists, they recognize that it "takes a different form" in different periods, as Marianne Novy puts it,[51] and they too have given us effective accounts of these historical distinctions, yet behind the different forms they tend to see the same basic "patriarchy," the oppression of women by men, that is not defined historically because it is supposed to govern all history. (Jeanne Addison Roberts, for example, says that "the patriarchal system has shaped Western Culture for millennia" and "dominates all of Western written history" and is "still dominant in our culture.")[52] For both these groups, then, the question raised in this section about which aspects of our status quo are supported by nonpolitical criticism would be pointless, since they assume that there is only one significant aspect, the oppressive system based on class or gender (these two modes of oppression can be combined under the ideology of "humanism," which conveniently legitimates both capitalism and patriarchy and is invoked for this purpose in some of the passages quoted earlier). That is what concerns them in the status quo of our society and also what concerns them in the society and literature of the Renaissance. Although not all practitioners of the new approaches believe that this oppressive system is basically the same in both societies (see, for instance, the forceful objections of Stephen Greenblatt to the ahistorical treatment of capitalism and of Valerie Traub to the ahistorical treatment of patriarchy),[53] many of them do believe it, and this will explain how their argument can connect a modern critic's silence about the politics of Shakespearean drama to support of the present status quo, for the critic's failure to oppose this oppression in Shakespeare's world (or in the world of his plays) is equivalent to complicity with the same oppression today.

We must now address the next question raised by our interrogation of that argument: in determining the meaning of a critic's silence about the role of this oppression in the work being interpreted, what significance is attached to his or her *intentions or motives* for that silence? The passage taken from Sinfield for my epigraph begs this question, or rather stacks the deck, in its use of the terms "pretends," "effacing," and "manoeuvre," which indicate conscious intention and even deception, and this also applies to the terms "disingenuous," "obscuring," "flag of convenience," "concealed," "pretends," "spuriously," "accomplice," "pass as," and "cynical" in the initial quotations from Howard, Evans, Hawkes, Dollimore, Belsey, Greene, and Boyarin. If critics deliberately choose to be silent about this oppression in order to conceal their support of our status quo, then of course their silence must mean support of our status quo—that is a tautology. A number of these passages seem to be saying, or at least implying, that this is always the case, but surely that cannot be true. Many nonpolitical critics, especially those practicing before the theoretical revolution of the 1980s raised our consciousness, probably did not make a conscious decision to avoid politics in their readings of literature or to use those readings to support the status quo, which some of them may have opposed (or, as I suggested earlier, they may have opposed certain aspects of it and supported others). Moreover, when we read their readings we usually are not in a position to know or even infer what their motive was, and yet this argument requires us to judge them. That is the problem.

We can get some help in dealing with this problem of intention by returning to the two essays discussed earlier, Walker's analysis of the printing of the texts of *Othello* and Sicherman's New Critical reading of *Coriolanus*. I said that I did not think even the most oppositional of the new oppositional critics would maintain that Walker's silence about politics reveals her attitude toward the status quo, because she must have assumed that such matters were irrelevant to her bibliographical project. Why then could not formalist critics like Sicherman enter the same plea by deposing that they did not believe gender or class oppression was relevant to their thematic project, which focused on a quite different topic, and that they did not wish to support our status quo or at least its oppressive parts? Of course I cannot tell how everyone using this argument would respond to such a plea, but the answer of the argument, as it is usually deployed, seems to be that innocence is no excuse, that the silence of critics about this oppression makes them guilty of abetting it, regardless of their motives for being silent or their feelings about the oppression. (Perhaps this is the "theory of negative culpability" referred to in the student paper that Sandra Gilbert and Susan Gubar cite.)[54] Their motives and feelings apparently do not matter, since the argument assumes the old Marxist distinction between "subjective" intention and "objective" effect. We do not hear much about it today, probably because the new poststructuralist Marxists are not supposed to believe in objectivism, and perhaps also because they are embarrassed by the way this distinction was wielded by Marxist regimes to prove that people who "subjectively" defined themselves as liberals or social democrats or even communists of the wrong sect were "objectively" reactionary-counterrevolutionary-fascists who had to be liquidated. (This kind of thinking still survives: Adam Katz says that Gerald Graff is "a confirmed centrist" who is "actually reactionary";[55] Donald Morton and Mas'ud Zavarzadeh argue that Graff and Gregory Jay, since they "criticize us," are "reactionary" and so belong— along with Stanley Fish, Michel Foucault, Richard Rorty, and Andrew Ross— to the same camp as Rush Limbaugh;[56] and Morton, on his own, finds that Jonathan Arac and Jean Howard are "archconservative."[57] I too am called a "reactionary" by John Drakakis, while in another essay published in the same year he calls me a "self-confessed liberal,"[58] which is correct but sounds criminal.) It is implicit in this argument that critics' silence about oppression has the effect of complicity with it, even though they may not realize this and may not want to be complicit. The more generous of those quoted earlier (the ones who do not insist that these silent critics are just pretending to be neutral) refer to this as "unwitting" or "unconscious" complicity, but it is still complicity.

There is, however, a striking inconsistency in the way this argument is typically deployed, because most of the people who deploy it ask us to judge formalist criticism that is silent about politics in terms of its alleged conservative effect, regardless of the critic's intentions, but ask us to judge their own oppositional criticism in terms of their declared intention—namely, to produce an oppositional effect. Moreover, we have some reason to wonder how concerned they really are about the conservative effect of this nonpolitical criticism, since they merely assert it without producing any evidence. Undoubtedly a critical essay, like all other forms of human activity, has *some* political effect, but it is usually very small in the world outside the academy,[59] and it cannot be ascertained by looking at the essay itself because, like the politics of those supposedly "bourgeois" concepts discussed earlier, it is not inherent but always depends on the specific situation. One can imagine situations in which even Sicherman's essay on the "precarious correspondence of words and meanings" in *Coriolanus* might have an oppositional political effect—for instance, if it were invoked in the emancipatory struggle against the horrors of humanist logocentrism. The argument we are testing does not allow for such nuances, however, nor does it allow these nonpolitical critics to plead benefit of constituency by pointing out that their readings are written not for the general public but for a small group of colleagues, most of whom, one can assume, regard opposition to oppression as something that "goes without saying" and do not need more lessons on the subject. This plea, like the plea of innocence we just considered, would presumably be dismissed as irrelevant since the argument still requires all critics to perform their own oppositionality to oppression in every essay they write in order to avoid the charge of complicity with it, which could explain the continual repetition of the same unmaskings of the same oppression for the same audiences of the already converted that inflects so much of the new political criticism.

The new political critics, furthermore, do not seem to be very concerned about the political effects of their own criticism outside the academy, for while they regularly announce that it is intended to promote opposition to the status quo, they do not tell us why they believe—or expect us to believe—that it really does this. Some of them also try to assert this effect by calling their criticism "activist" and "transformative," as well as "oppositional," but again they fail to show that it produces any extramural activating or transforming (they even fail to reveal what specific action or transformation it is supposed to be producing). As John McGowan remarks, they "blithely claim political and material consequences for [their] theorizing that they never try to justify,"[60] because they seem to assume that their intention not only determines the meaning of their criticism (despite the poststructuralist anti-intentionalist creed that most of them profess), but also determines its effect, independent of the circumstances. Therefore they do not have to confront the question of what the effect of this "activist" criticism actually is in any particular situation, or to consider the possibility that in some situations it could have an effect very different from the one they claim for it—it might, for example, serve those who write it and those who read it as a displacement of or surrogate for real political activity. Wendell Harris observes that this kind of criticism "allows the critic to avoid wrestling with the difficulties of existing social, political, or economic problems" and "shifts energy from combatting the actual ills of the existing economic/political system."[61] But that is not relevant to the argument we are examining here.

Since this argument, in condemning critics who are silent about the politics of the works they interpret, does not and cannot ascertain the meaning of this silence from the critics' *intentions* or from the actual *effect* of their criticism, we must therefore return to the *context*, which we saw earlier will necessarily determine the meaning of any silence. This then raises the final question of our interrogation: how does the argument deal with the crucial problem of context? The issue can be clarified by a comparison with another argument against silence, which finally brings me to my second epigraph, taken from a Puritan sermon delivered during the crisis that led to the English Civil War (the text is Judges 5:23; where Deborah and Barak celebrate their victory over the Canaanites and curse those who did not join the battle). It may look like the argument we are testing but there is a very significant difference. Samuel Fawcet bases his case on the intense conflict that was dividing the nation into two warring sides and so provides the specific context for his assertion that "we ought to speake" now, since anyone who is silent about it, like the Merozites who sat out an analogous conflict, is giving "consent" to the other (Royalist) side, although he acknowledges that in other situations this proverb would not apply, as I too maintain. But the oppositional critics who use this argument cannot claim they are operating in a comparable specific and extraordinary context that is bringing us to the brink of civil war and could therefore justify their contention that those who do not take a political stand are giving aid and comfort to the enemy.

I have never seen any of these critics deal explicitly with this contextual problem, but the assumption that seems to underlie their argument—or would have to for it to be valid—is that there is always only one universal context, the aforementioned class/gender oppression, which, we have seen, is supposed to be an all-encompassing evil system dominating societies of the past and the present. From that assumption it logically follows that critics who do not oppose this oppression in interpreting the literature of an earlier society are supporting it in the status quo of our own society, and that it is the only aspect of our status quo they can support, and that they cannot split their votes by supporting some aspects of our status quo but not others. In the argument we are testing this universal context of oppression is what takes the place of Fawcet's specific context of crisis and thus obliges us to speak against it in our criticism, so that critics who produce interpretations that, for whatever reason, do not oppose this oppression are complicit with it and should themselves be opposed. Only if we buy this totalized view of the world can we claim that a critic's silence about politics must mean support of the present status quo and therefore must be political.

It should come as no surprise to learn that I do not buy this view. I do not believe, for reasons I already indicated, that the status quo of our society is a single, monolithic system that we must be either wholly for or wholly against, and while it certainly contains unjust and oppressive elements, I do not believe it is entirely evil. I suspect that the people who use this argument do not really believe it either, because their demand that critics must voice an opposition to our oppressive status quo acknowledges that the right to oppose our status quo is itself an element of our status quo—a nonoppressive element, clearly, and one they do not oppose. And in their everyday lives, when not writing "activist" criticism, they are not always acting against the status quo, certainly not against all aspects of it. Indeed I doubt if it is possible to be wholly against our status quo or wholly for it.[62] But if we reject this totalizing view, it does not logically follow that a critic's silence about politics *cannot* mean support of our status quo. Of course it can mean this, and sometimes it does, but it can also mean other things, depending on the specific context and the critic's intention. Therefore the argument we are interrogating, like the proverb it draws upon, is true in some instances but is not a general truth.

I do not want to close without mentioning another common argument that seems similar to this one and is sometimes combined with it. It also concerns the silence of the older critics, but a silence about theory rather than politics, and also frequently takes the form of a *tu quoque* rejoinder, in which the older critics' objections to the explicit—and often extensive—theorizing in the newer approaches are answered by the assertion that their own criticism is also based on a theory, even though they may not be conscious of it. I agree with this argument because, unlike the political one, it does not depend on any particular context or on anyone's intentions; it is a general truth that every critical approach assumes a theory of literature. I also believe that a wider acceptance of this argument would have a beneficial effect on our discipline, since it would lead those who are now "against theory" to examine and explain the theoretical foundations of their own approaches and therefore empower them to enter into a productive dialogue with adherents of the newer approaches, instead of grumbling in the corridors or joining the NAS. As Jean Howard points out, critics who are not "self-conscious about [their] theoretical position" and do not "examine it in the light of competing theories" will "fall back on the defense of common sense: i.e., the position that [their] critical practice depends on assumptions so self-evident that their truth is not in question."[63] This argument should also, incidentally, end the present monopolization of the term "theory" by these newer approaches.

Moreover, since critical theories, as we found earlier, do not neatly line up on two opposing sides, this argument should work against the polarization of our discipline that I noted at the outset, whereas the argument that we tested, and flunked, contributes to the polarizing (and is also in part a result of this polarizing, which operates as a self-confirming vicious circle that feeds on itself). It forces critics, not to articulate their own positions in a dialogue with colleagues, but to choose between two hostile camps, even if they do not want to, in a Manichean war of good against evil, and closes down dialogue by constructing a world where there is no other alternative, no neutral or intermediate ground, since "the only real question," as Michael Sprinker insists, is "Which side are you on?"[64] It also closes down any inquiry, because the basic principle of polarization is that all those who are not with us are against us, and so even the attempt to test the argument is relegated to the evil enemy camp (which I suppose will be the fate of this article). Still worse, it has a tendency to infect those using it with self-righteousness by giving them the illusion that the criticism they write is helping to bring about a "transformation" that will eliminate the very real injustices of our society, and it is designed to make the rest of us feel guilty for writing other kinds of criticism, which may be the postmodern secular equivalent of the biblical curse upon Meroz.

NOTES

1. Alan Sinfield, "Literary Theory and the 'Crisis' in English Studies," *Critical Quarterly* 25, no. 3 (Autumn 1983): 40.

2. Samuel Fawcet. *A Seasonable Sermon for These Troublesome Times Preached to the Right Worshipful Company of the Haberdashers Novem[ber] 23, 1641 in the Parish-Church of St. Mary Stainings in London* (London, 1641), 9–10.

3. Terry Eagleton. *Literary Theory: An Introduction* (Minneapolis: University of Minnesota Press, 1983), 196, quoted by Sinfield, "Literary Theory," 45.

4. Peter Widdowson, "Introduction: The Crisis in English Studies," in *Re-Reading English,* ed. Peter Widdowson (London: Methuen, 1982), 3.

5. Jean E. Howard, "The New Historicism in Renaissance Studies," *English Literary Renaissance* 16, no. 1 (Winter 1986): 43.

6. Malcolm Evans, *Signifying Nothing: Truth's True Contents in Shakespeare's Text* (Brighton: Harvester, 1986), 100, 262–63.

7. Lynda E. Boose, "The Family in Shakespeare Studies; or—Studies in the Family of Shakespeareans; or—The Politics of Politics," *Renaissance Quarterly* 40, no. 4 (Winter 1987): 709.

8. Terence Hawkes, *William Shakespeare: "King Lear"* (Plymouth: Northcote, 1995), 16.

9. Jonathan Dollimore, *Radical Tragedy: Religion, Ideology, and Power in the Drama of Shakespeare and His Contemporaries,* 2d ed. (Durham, N.C.: Duke University Press, 1993), xii–xiii.

10. David Margolies. "Teaching the Handsaw to Fly: Shakespeare as a Hegemonic Instrument," in *The Shakespeare Myth,* ed. Graham Holderness (Manchester: Manchester University Press, 1988), 52.

11. Frank Lentricchia, *Criticism and Social Change* (Chicago: University of Chicago Press, 1983), 10–11.

12. Catherine Belsey, *Critical Practice* (London: Methuen, 1980), 109.

13. Donald Morton, reply, "Forum" letters on "Birth of the Cyberqueer," *PMLA* 111, no. 3 (May 1996): 472.

14. Antony Easthope, "Poetry and the Politics of Reading," in *Re-Reading English,* ed. Peter Widdowson (London: Methuen, 1982), 147–48.

15. Francis Barker and Peter Hulme, "Nymphs and Reapers Heavily Vanish: The Discursive Con-texts [sic] of *The Tempest*," in *Alternative Shakespeares,* ed. John Drakakis (London: Methuen, 1985), 204.

16. John Drakakis, " 'Fashion It Thus': *Julius Caesar* and the Politics of Theatrical Representation," in *Materialist Shakespeare: A History,* ed. Ivo Kamps (London: Verso, 1995), 289.

17. Kiernan Ryan, *Shakespeare,* 2d ed. (London: Prentice Hall, 1995), 2.

18. Gayle Greene, "The Myth of Neutrality, Again?" in *Shakespeare Left and Right,* ed. Ivo Kamps (New York: Routledge, 1991), 24, 23.

19. Daniel Boyarin, "Critical Approaches, Political Positions," *PMLA* 106, no. 2 (March 1991): 315.

20. Xiao Cai, "China: Outward Conformity, Inner Despair," *Academe* 76, no. 3 (May–June 1990): 8, 11.

21. Patrick E. Tyler, "Deng's Economic Drive Leaves Vast Regions of China Behind," *New York Times,* 27 December 1995.

22. John Locke, *Two Treatises of Government,* ed. Peter Laslett, 2d ed. (Cambridge: Cambridge University Press, 1967), 2.8.119.

23. Catherine Belsey, *The Subject of Tragedy: Identity and Difference in Renaissance Drama* (London: Methuen, 1985), 120.

24. American Law Institute. *Restatement of the Law: Contracts.* 2d ed. St. Paul, 1981, sec. 69.

25. Alice Walker, *Textual Problems of the First Folio* (Cambridge: Cambridge University Press, 1953), 138–61.

26. See my "My Theme Can Lick Your Theme," *College English* 37, no. 3 (November 1975): 307–12.

27. Carol M. Sicherman, "*Coriolanus*: The Failure of Words," *English Literary History* 39, no. 2 (June 1972): 190.

28. An earlier version of this section appears in "The New and the Old Historicizing of Shakespeare," *Yearbook of Research in English and American Literature (REAL)* 11 (1995): 425–448 [440–43]. I must repeat that not all oppositional critics engage in this strategy and that some have objected to its abuses (see Dollimore, *Radical Tragedy*, xix–xx).

29. Margot Heinemann, "'Demystifying the Mystery of State': *King Lear* and the World Upside Down," *Shakespeare Survey* 44 (1992): 78.

30. Ryan, *Shakespeare*, 98, 102–4.

31. John Turner, "The Tragic Romances of Feudalism," in *Shakespeare: The Play of History*, ed. Graham Holderness, Nick Potter, and John Turner (Basingstoke: Macmillan, 1988), 109, 111, 117–18.

32. Gayle Greene, "Feminist and Marxist Criticism: An Argument for Alliances," *Women's Studies* 9, no. 1 (1981): 39–40.

33. Alan Sinfield, *Faultlines: Cultural Materialism and the Politics of Dissident Reading* (Berkeley: University of California Press, 1992), 106.

34. Catherine Belsey, "Richard Levin and In-different Reading," *New Literary History* 21, no. 3 (Spring 1990): 455.

35. Graham Holderness, "Production, Reproduction, Performance: Marxism, History, Theatre," in *Uses of History: Marxism, Postmodernism and the Renaissance*, ed. Francis Barker et al. (Manchester: Manchester University Press, 1991), 177.

36. Dollimore, *Radical Tragedy*, 191–95.

37. Linda Charnes, "What's Love Got to Do with It? Reading the Liberal Humanist Romance in Shakespeare's *Antony and Cleopatra*," *Textual Practice* 6, no. 1 (Spring 1992): 6, 11–12.

38. Lisa Jardine, " 'No Offence i' th' World': *Hamlet* and Unlawful Marriage," in *Uses of History: Marxism, Postmodernism and the Renaissance*, ed. Francis Barker et al. (Manchester: Manchester University Press, 1991), 139.

39. Boose, "The Family in Shakespeare Studies," 711.

40. Marion Wynne-Davies, " 'The Swallowing Womb': Consumed and Consuming Women in *Titus Andronicus*," in *The Matter of Difference: Materialist Feminist Criticism of Shakespeare*, ed. ValerieWayne (Ithaca, N.Y.: Cornell University Press, 1991), 129, 148.

41. Toril Moi, "Sexual/Textual Politics," in *The Politics of Theory*, ed. Francis Barker et al. (Colchester: University of Essex Press, 1983), 10.

42. See Lee Baxandall and Stefan Morawski, eds. *Marx and Engels on Literature and Art: A Selection of Writings* (St. Louis: Telos, 1973); Maynard Solomon, ed. *Marxism and Art: Essays Classic and Contemporary* (New York: Knopf, 1973); and R. S. White, "Marx and Shakespeare," *Shakespeare Survey* 45 (1993): 89–100.

43. See Lisa Jardine, " 'Girl Talk' (for Boys on the Left), or Marginalising Feminist Critical Praxis," *Oxford Literary Review* 8, nos. 1–2 (1986): 208–17; and Stephen Foley, "Nostalgia and the 'Rise of English': Rhetorical Questions," in *The Matter of Difference*, ed. Valerie Wayne (Ithaca, N.Y.: Cornell University Press, 1991), 242; on the role of women and working-class men in the institutionalization of literary studies, see Gerald Graff, "Co-optation," in *The New Historicism*, ed. H. Aram Veeser (New York: Routledge, 1989), 174; and Diana Fuss, *Essentially Speaking: Feminism, Nature and Difference* (New York: Routledge, 1989), xi–xii, on "anti-essentialist essentialism"; and Terry Eagleton, "The "Right and the Good": Postmodernism and the Liberal State," *Textual Practice* 8, no. 1 (Spring 1994): 6, on "the bugbear of the 'autonomous subject,' " which he associates with vulgar Marxism.

44. Evans, *Signifying Nothing*, 259–63.

45. Dollimore, *Radical Tragedy*, 277.

46. Fredrick Crews, "The End of the Poststructuralist Era," in *The Emperor Redressed: Critiquing Critical Theory*, ed. Dwight Eddins (Tuscaloosa: University of Alabama Press, 1995), 53–56.

47. Jonathan Dollimore and Alan Sinfield, "*Foreword*: Cultural Materialism," in *Political Shakespeare: Essays in Cultural Materialism*, ed. Jonathan Dollimore and Alan Sinfield, 2d ed. (Ithaca, N.Y.: Cornell University Press, 1994), viii.

48. Eagleton, *Literary Theory*, 196.

49. Peter Widdowson, "Terrorism and Literary Studies," *Textual Practice* 2, no. 1 (Spring 1988): 4.

50. Jennifer M. Cotter, "On Feminist Pedagogy," *Minnesota Review* 41–42 (1995): 119–21; Toril Moi, "Sexual/Textual Politics," in *The Politics of Theory*, ed. Francis Barker et al. (Colchester: University of Essex Press, 1983), 10; and Gayle Greene, "Feminist and Marxist Criticism," 41–42.

51. Marianne Novy, *Love's Argument: Gender Relations in Shakespeare* (Chapel Hill: University of North Carolina Press, 1984), 4.

52. Jeanne Addison Roberts, *The Shakespearean Wild: Geography, Genus, and Gender* (Lincoln: University of Nebraska Press, 1991), 16–17.

53. Stephen Greenblatt, *Learning to Curse: Essays in Early Modern Culture* (New York: Routledge, 1990), 151; Valerie Traub, "Jewels, Statues, and Corpses: Containment of Female Erotic Power in Shakespeare's Plays," in *Shakespeare and Gender: A History*, ed. Deborah E. Barker and Ivo Kamps (London: Verso, 1995), 136.

54. Sandra M. Gilbert and Susan Gubar, *Masterpiece Theatre: An Academic Melodrama* (New Brunswick, N.J.: Rutgers University Press, 1995), 83.

55. Adam Katz, "In Reply to Gerald Graff," in *Left Margins: Cultural Studies and Composition Pedagogy*, ed. Karen Fitts and Alan W. France (Albany: SUNY Press, 1995), 303.

56. Donald Morton and Mas'ud Zavarzadeh, "Yes, Exactly! If You 'Criticize' Us, You Are a 'Reactionary': An Open Letter to Gregory Jay and Gerald Graff," *Democratic Culture* 3 (1994): 32–33.

57. Morton, reply, 472.

58. See John Drakakis, "Terminator 2 1/2: or Messing with Canons," *Textual Practice* 7, no. 1 (Spring 1993): 64; and John Drakakis, untitled review, *Renaissance Quarterly* 46, no. 2 (Summer 1993), 406.

59. Stanley Fish, *Professional Correctness: Literary Studies and Political Change* (Oxford: Clarendon Press, 1995), 51–55, 96–101.

60. John McGowan, "Thinking about Violence: Feminism, Cultural Politics, and Norms," *Centennial Review* 37, no. 3 (Fall 1993): 453.

61. Wendell V. Harris, "Marxist Literary Theory and the Advantages of Irrelevance," *Sewanee Review* 104, no. 2 (Spring 1996): 224.

62. See Sacvan Bercovitch, *The Rites of Assent: Transformations in the Symbolic Construction of America* (New York: Routledge, 1993), 21; and David Rieff, "Multiculturalism's Silent Partner," *Harper's*, August 1993, 63.

63. Jean E. Howard, "Scholarship, Theory, and More New Readings: Shakespeare for the 1990s," in *Shakespeare Studies Today: The Horace Howard Furness Memorial Lectures*, ed. Georgianna Ziegler (New York: AMS, 1986), 135.

64. Michael Sprinker, "Commentary: 'You've Got a Lot of Nerve,'" in *Shakespeare Left and Right*, ed. Ivo Kamps (New York: Routledge, 1991), 116.

## 32.  CRITICISM AS DISPLACEMENT

### JEFFREY WALLEN

THE LITERARY CRITIC typically proceeds by applying a framework of interpretation to a literary text. Such a statement, which emphasizes our structures of thought rather than the "primary" work to which we respond, is not terribly controversial in the aftermath of literary theory. For the rise of literary theory has heightened our awareness of the interpretative frameworks that we employ and of the implications of our methodological choices. It is no longer respectable to presume that we could somehow dispense with the entire panoply of frameworks and schools of interpretation and achieve either an unmediated relation to "the text itself" or arrive at the "true" (and thus final) understanding of the work. The ability to generate critical readings by consciously employing such frameworks as deconstruction, New Historicism, postmodernism, and queer theory certifies one's professional competence.

The knowledge that we cannot transcend all interpretative frameworks (the set of concerns, the strategies of reading, the assumptions about texts, and the hopes for analysis that structure our criticism) has not led to a greater contentment with the prevailing models. Quite the contrary. Many critics want to break free from their constraint, particularly insofar as they have come to see the forms of interpretation as institutional, professional, and academic—as driven by the logic of the discipline and the university, rather than by the con-

Jeffrey Wallen: "Criticism as Displacement." Abridged by the author from *Closed Encounters: Literary Politics and Public Culture*, by Jeffrey Wallen, 115–42. Minneapolis: University of Minnesota Press. Copyright © 1998 The Regents of the University of Minnesota. Reprinted with permission of the University of Minnesota Press.

cerns of the larger society. This desire is no longer directed toward gaining an individual experience of the literary work, free from social or institutional mediation, but instead toward situating the "institution" within a societal context, in order to overcome all that insulates the literature professor from the world beyond the university. The aim is to re-orient, not deny, our interpretative frameworks, and to move beyond a preoccupation with issues that are "internal" to literary study in order to address matters of public concern.

Edward Said has been instrumental in this shift from literary theory to socially oriented criticism. Although his book *Beginnings* and his essays that helped introduce Foucault to an American audience established Said early on as a central figure in literary theory, he has long attacked theory, and he has advocated in contrast the role of the public intellectual. One instance of this appeal for a less insular criticism is Said's attack, in *Culture and Imperialism*, on the transformation of theory into an academic subspeciality:

> Cults like post-modernism, discourse analysis, New Historicism, deconstruction, new-pragmatism transport them [intellectuals in the American university] into the country of the blue; an astonishing sense of weightlessness with regard to the gravity of history and individual responsibility fritters away attention to public matters, and to public discourse.[1]

It is striking that Said published these remarks in 1993; they seem more apposite for 1983. He speaks as if the substantial changes in literary criticism of recent years had not taken place; as if race, class, and gender were not the most discussed topics of the day. The new critical orientation is almost entirely in the direction of "social justice," and embraces the leftish political concerns sketched by Said. He suggests that a more socially oriented and coherent literary criticism can fulfill an important public function: that of an educator and a conscience for the public. It is no longer sufficient, however, to discuss a criticism directed toward "public matters" in purely prospective terms.

For Said, the major barrier to a more socially significant literary criticism is the professional and theoretical self-absorption of the academic critic. He asserts that we now have:

> a steadily more powerful cult of expertise, whose main ideological burden stipulates that social, political, and class-based commitments should be subsumed under the professional disciplines, so that if you are a professional scholar of literature or a critic of culture, all your affiliations with the real world are subordinate to your professing in those fields. Similarly, you are responsible not so much to an audience in your community or society, as to and for your corporate guild of fellow experts, your department of specialization, your discipline. (321)

The issue here is that of the critic's *connections*: to the community, society, and the "real world"; or to the cult, the guild, and the profession. Said condemns interpretative frameworks based primarily on a theoretical and technical mastery insofar as they lead to a "cult of expertise," and to placing one's allegiance to the profession above all else.

Such arguments about the need for a more socially and politically engaged criticism have been well heeded; but what has been the result? Does the acknowledgement of social commitments by academic critics in any way "deprofessionalize" criticism or yield work that is not "subsumed under the professional disciplines"? What would it mean for such a subsumption "under the professional disciplines" not to take place? What would such a criticism look like?

I ask these questions because we now have in the universities a literary criticism that claims a strong responsibility to "community or society," even though it is still highly professional, academic, and addressed largely to "a corporate guild of fellow experts." I want to consider whether shifting the concerns of literary criticism—away from the "technical," professional interests of the discipline toward much broader cultural and social issues—will provide us with a more significant criticism, and one that is of interest also to those who are not professional critics. If literary critics are to do more than engage in "a powerful cult of expertise," not only must social concerns be brought into the critical arena, but the discussion must extend outward as well; otherwise we will have a politics just for literary criticism. Can literary criticism help begin a critical dialogue that confronts the concerns of those outside academia and encourage people other than professors (and their students) to participate in this much needed discussion?

Said argues that literary critics need to reestablish connections, and not just between the university and the "community or society," but also between the dominant cultural tradition and all that it has excluded, repressed, or ignored. One of Said's major aims is to get us to read texts such as Austen's *Mansfield Park* and Dickens's *Great Expectations*—texts that do not directly thematize imperialism as does Conrad's *Heart of Darkness*—with an awareness of all that connects culture to "the imperial process of which they were manifestly and unconcealedly a part" (xiv). He now often gets his wish. In his wake, readers now rarely look for a catachresis, an aporia, or a moment of undecidability with which to deconstruct a text, but instead resolutely seek out all the traces of imperialism in a novel in order to make their arguments.

I do not see how postcolonial studies (at least in American universities), or other new specialties such as queer theory or Chicano studies are less cultish or guildlike than ones that do not overtly stress a social connection. Postcolonial or gay studies is not simply an "area"—a group of texts that have something to do with imperialism or homosexuality—but an academically trained way of reading. Both a new-pragmatist and a postcolonial reading ask a set of questions and employ a set of techniques that have been defined and validated largely by previous scholars. A shift in interpretative frameworks does not bring about a criticism that is less oriented toward or less shaped by one's academic colleagues. Said, by downplaying the extent to which literary criticism has moved in the directions he advocates, avoids the heavy burden of either demonstrating that the new criticisms are in fact leading toward "the improvement and non-coercive enhancement of life in a community"—Said's goal for criticism—or explaining why they are not.

Is the attempt to address public matters through literary studies succeeding? Such new approaches as ethnic, feminist, gay, post-Marxist, cultural, and postcolonial criticism largely share a common paradigm. They focus above all on analyzing forms of inequality and domination, and they aim to envision and help bring about a more equal world, or in Said's words, "a community or culture . . . that is not based on coercion or domination" (335). Can the adoption of this paradigm generate a criticism that is socially engaged, politically effective, democratic, and liberatory?

My contention is that so far it has not and that literary analysis now offers a poor vehicle for debating political issues. The usual response by writers who seek a more socially significant criticism is that academics need to address a "public" audience, and forego their jargon, their merely technical interests, and their professional habits. I will argue instead that although the new interpretative frameworks are directly motivated by concerns that are at the center of social debate, the readings that flow from these frameworks do not stimulate a productive discussion of the ideas, suppositions, and desires behind the frameworks—the areas precisely where there is the most significant disagreement. Literary criticism actually displaces debate away from the issues that most require it.

The new criticisms hope to bring about social change by exposing the many forms in which our culture has condoned, sanctioned, and legitimated inequality. More specifically, they attack forms of inequality in precisely those areas where there now is no social consensus. When there is not already widespread agreement about the nature and basis of equality, it is essential to try to convince others about what constitutes domination, why it is wrong, and how it might be avoided or overcome; simply pointing out one's own favorite instances of domination or oppression will achieve little. This attempt at persuasion presupposes a dialogue with those who do not (yet) share one's viewpoint, since a commitment to equality (much less to academia) entails that others may, in fact, have compelling, even better ideas. A new political criticism, if it seeks to remedy inequality, needs to create a political and philosophical dialogue that can begin to do the work of formulating a viable foundation in a post–Cold War world for a "community or culture . . . that is not based on coercion or domination," and that can actively engage diverse perspectives and participants, so as to move beyond the historical polarizations of dominant and dominated. Above all, this requires an open dialogue about the possibilities of equality, a subject that is debatable at its core; there is no philosophical or political definition that can adequately respond to all the questions and decisions about equality that we face. The dialogues we have now, despite all the attention to conflict, hardly fulfill this need.

Literary criticism, instead of promoting such a discussion of equality, often employs the new frameworks to sniff out previously overlooked signs of domination and inequality in whatever the critic examines. The presuppositions of the critic are thereby confirmed more than interrogated. The work of the typical essay is to demonstrate, for instance, that the lens of postcolonialism can produce a new and vibrant interpretation of a much discussed novel. But a rich reading of a literary text does little to validate the theoretical underpinnings of the framework that shapes the reading. The new socially oriented interpretive frameworks are not simply critical strategies, but always also contain, whether implicitly or explicitly, a historical understanding, a social theory, a set of moral judgments, and an agenda for political change. It is these positions—not the actual interpretations of literary texts—that are most controversial, and it is around these topics that dialogue would be most beneficial.

Literary criticism rarely lays forth or persuasively argues for its social theory, its moral judgments, its political agendas. The literary analysis only demonstrates how important certain forms of inequality are for understanding culture; it does not confirm the social critique, the desirability and viability of whatever changes are envisioned. The new forms of literary criticism displace discussion away from the key areas of social, philosophical, and political disagreement and confine productive discussion to a few questions about the interpretation of literary texts. Competing readings of a literary text offer a meager terrain for fighting out the highly debatable nonliterary issues that are at stake in these interpretations.

I want to explore quickly why reading literature with an eye for unequal power relations has energized so many critics, even if, as I will be arguing, it does not generate the dialogues that would help to bring about the desired political changes. These new ways of reading appeal to the skills and training of critics, and also to the hope of making the "literary," in Terry Eagleton's words, again "the medium of vital concerns deeply rooted in the general intellectual, cultural and political life of [our] epoch."[2] Adopting the stance that inequities of power are to be remarked and criticized is in itself a means of opening a new political horizon of more egalitarian relations; the critique depends on imagining that things might be different. Gender, race, class, imperialism, and sexual orientation today provide the best axes with which to offer alternative and opposing perspectives, since they help us to see, instead of a seemingly "universal" point of view, female and/against male, black and/against white, non-Western and/against Western. The *asymmetry* of these paired terms generates their critical force, as they put into relief relations of domination and subordination whose logic is no longer accepted. The critic, to help raise the status of the historically subordinate group, now attempts to give voice to what previously had been ignored or suppressed.

The intellectual appeal of mapping a new, vital terrain is always joined with an expectation for social change. The point I wish to make is that whatever social changes are envisioned, the discussion around the literary work neither addresses the current sources of disagreement that stand in the way of such changes nor lays out a theory that would explain why new policies would help bring about a better society. The shift in the concerns of the critic is not enough to make literary criticism again a vital medium of social dialogue. The new frameworks of interpretation meet many of the demands and expectations of academic criticism, but they accomplish few of the social goals for regenerating a critical public sphere.

Literary critics hardly ever state what possible changes are presumed, desired, or envisioned in their criticism; it is implied that we already know what should change (and we must therefore raise people's consciousness to the existence of the problem), so that there really is no subject here for political debate (thus the critic can stick to demonstrating social problems through construing "cultural texts," rather than setting forth their theory of equality). I am not suggesting that literary critics ought to make explicitly "political" arguments. But when the analyses are motivated by a desire to be more socially significant and politically effective, they will add little to any debate if the sources of disagreement with others—the political premises—are hidden and not subject to scrutiny.

In contrast to earlier forms of literary criticism, where the "reading" worked to illustrate or "prove," or in the case of deconstruction to complicate, the theoretical framework, the readings that focus on forms of inequality, and the debates that ensue, do little to prove or disprove the suppositions of the interpretative framework. Despite the claim of a shift from aesthetics to politics in recent criticism, we have an almost aesthetic justification of political positions.

The discussions that ensue from the literary critique of inequality mainly distract us from addressing these issues, despite critics' claims to make the "literary" "the medium of vital concerns deeply rooted in the ... life of [our] epoch." The discussion remains insular, to the extent that the views of one's political and ideological opponents are rarely treated as principled arguments worthy of deliberation. The lack of a more productive dialogue, one that engages others in thinking through commonalities and differences, possible alternatives and next steps, is covered over by the necessarily conflictual nature of literary interpretation. The continual disagreements over textual interpretations, and now over even what texts to teach, supply only an appearance of meaningful political debate.

Amid the overwhelming thicket of academic publications, which multiply by performing only minor mutations to what has just preceded, it would be easy, now that political concerns are so prominent in literary criticism, to find example after example of political critiques of cultural texts in which there is hardly an acknowledgment of, much less an argument for, the political positions that are implicitly embraced. The institutionalization of socially or politically "aware" forms of reading necessarily dulls such "awareness," as disciplinary and formal concerns regulate the spread and the appropriation of new ideas. And it would be easy to insert such an argument within Said's attack on professionalism, in which even the attempt to engage social concerns still yields a criticism that is not sufficiently alert and open to the interests and ideas of those outside academia.

I want to make a much stronger argument, however: that contemporary literary criticism, even as the companion to an explicit political agenda, does not provide the vehicle for a dialogue on the "vital concerns" of the "intellectual, cultural and political life" of our epoch. For this reason, I will turn to Said's own criticism. He would seem to be the last person one might accuse of "displacing" political debate. Said's criticism is hardly epigonal; he cannot be accused of writing "political" literary criticism because it is fashionable, or of not considering or articulating his political vision. His literary criticism is central to the new "interpretative frameworks" I have been describing, and it lays the groundwork not only for postcolonial criticism, but for much of the engagement with the (foreign) other. Said would appear to set the example for literary discussion that might revitalize a critical public sphere.

In *Culture and Imperialism*, Said argues that imperialism is the major, in fact the "determining, political horizon of modern Western culture" (60). His project is to restore this political horizon to cultural analysis and to attack what he feels are the unwarranted claims for the autonomy of the aesthetic sphere. Said states:

> Instead we have on the one hand an isolated cultural sphere, believed to be freely and unconditionally available to weightless theoretical speculation and investigation, and, on the other, a debased political sphere, where the real struggle between interests is supposed to occur. To the professional student of culture—the humanist, the critic, the scholar—only one sphere is relevant, and, more to the point, it is accepted that the two spheres are separated, whereas the two are not only connected but ultimately the same.
>
> A radical falsification has become established in this separation. (57)

Said focuses particularly on the novel, since he believes that "[w]ithout empire, I would go so far as saying, there is no European novel as we know it" (69), and even more poignantly, "that the novel, as a cultural artefact of bourgeois society, and imperialism are unthinkable without each other" (70–71). If the European novel is so important for imperialism, a critical analysis of the novel can itself be a major step toward understanding and combatting imperialism.

Said has four major aims here: to support his claims for the strong inter-relation between modern Western culture and imperialism; to provide model interpretations that demonstrate what is revealed by analyzing key texts with regard to imperialism; to question what is at stake in our being able to see only now how important imperialism is for understanding culture; and, finally, to argue for an end to the "imperial ideology" that still permeates our society. The assertion that the cultural and political spheres "are not only connected but ultimately the same" gives great importance to the work of the cultural critic, since the culture that fostered and still continues to foster im-perialism must be radically critiqued if the desired social and political changes are to occur.

A similar description, with substitutions of only a few key words, could be supplied for many other influential works of contemporary criticism. In con-sidering an example of Said's criticism, I want to keep these similarities in mind, in order to raise the broader question of the political impact of aca-demic literary criticism. Said relies heavily on his exceptionalism, on his great difference from "the professional student of culture." What might it mean if the critical stance that grounds its insights on a resistance to the dominant ide-ology, and on giving critical weight to voices that have been largely ignored or suppressed, is no longer "marginal" in academia, but is in fact sanctioned, pro-moted, and rewarded? Have we thereby succeeded in regrounding and reener-gizing the spheres of culture and politics, or in disrupting imperial ideology? I want to examine Said's reading of Jane Austen's *Mansfield Park* in order to question—with regard to a project that openly avows its political aims and employs "the perspective provided by anti-imperialist resistance" (66)—whether such literary criticism still displaces debate away from the issues that most require it.[3] Or to use Said's terms, whether he achieves the following: "opposing and alleviating coercive domination, transforming the present by trying rationally and analytically to lift some of its burdens, situating the works of various literatures with reference to one another and to their histori-cal modes of being" (319).

Said argues that Austen's novel is "more implicated in the rationale for imperi-alist expansion" (84) than has previously been thought. The contention of his essay is that the estate in Antigua (owned by Sir Thomas Bertram, the propri-etor of Mansfield Park), which receives only glancing attention by the novelist (or as Said puts it, Austen "sublimates the agonies of Caribbean existence to a mere half dozen passing references to Antigua" [59]), is not merely a plot de-vice by which to get the head of the household off the scene for the first half of the novel, or simply a source of wealth for this particular baronet; rather, it is intimately and inextricably connected to the world of Mansfield Park. He writes:

> More clearly than elsewhere in her fiction, Austen here synchronizes domestic with international authority, making it plain that the values associated with such higher things as ordination, law, and propriety must be grounded firmly in actual rule over and possession of territory. She sees clearly that to hold and rule Mansfield Park is to hold and rule an imperial estate in close, not to say inevitable association with it. What assures the domestic tranquility and attractive harmony of one is the productivity and regulated discipline of the other. (87)

Domestic tranquility and attractive harmony are thus not only dependent on the profits from an oppressive colonial enterprise, but in fact require the same authority as that used to ensure "productivity and regulated discipline" overseas, that is, an authority that does not balk at sordid cruelty and slavery.

Said, with great care and sophistication, goes on to connect the major drama of the plot, the importation of the lowly cousin Fanny Price and her elevation into the guiding moral conscience of Mansfield Park, with the importation of the wealth derived from the Caribbean colony. Here, as elsewhere in *Culture and Imperialism*, his emphasis is *geographical*: Said highlights the "'out there' that frames the . . . action *here*" (93). He argues that the geographical process, "approved" by the novelist for its wholesome results of bringing Fanny from a distant though still English world into the domain of Mansfield Park, is not only analogous to, but interdependent with, the other, imperial process. Said states: "What was wanting within was in fact supplied by the wealth derived from a West Indian plantation and a poor provincial relative, both brought in to Mansfield Park and set to work. Yet on their own, neither the one nor the other could have sufficed; they require each other" (92). Said can therefore conclude that "Austen affirms and repeats the geographical process of invoking trade, production, and consumption that predates, underlies, and guarantees the morality" (93). Austen's complicity in imperialism is being established. Even if colonialism receives little direct attention in the novel and its morality is barely touched on, this very absence is significant. When Fanny asks about the slave trade, she is met by "such a dead silence!" which, for Said, is "to suggest that one world could not be connected with the other since there simply is no common language for both" (96). The task of criticism is now to reveal these connections and break the silence.[4]

The restoration of a political dimension to culture, of a foreign dimension to the domestic picture, and even of the "sublimated" cruelty that enables (and provides the money for) the gentility, opens up a range of issues neglected by most earlier critics. In the world described by Austen, where the matter of income is of such importance to so many characters, not only the quantity but the sources of Sir Thomas Bertram's income are certainly important. Scrutinizing Sir Thomas's role as father and proprietor, in light of his role as imperialist, poses significant questions: How does his management in one area relate to and help account for the success or failure of his management in the other? Or one might consider how, or if, his ownership of an Antiguan estate differentiates Sir Thomas from the other landholders in Austen's novels, and explore the role of colonial wealth among the landed gentry, who faced great changes in the early nineteenth century. More broadly, one might juxtapose the moral vision in Austen's writing to the debates about slavery already going on in England at the time, in order to probe further both the significance of Fanny's question, and the silence with which it was met. A focus on Sir Thomas's Antiguan estates also can help us to question what moral equivocations, and what views of non-European and nonwhite peoples, were required in order to sustain early British imperialism.

The critical act of "situating" the literary work, and of connecting it to a "complex history" that not only the characters in the novel but "Austen herself would not, could not recognize" (93), raises a wide array of questions. Yet the "connections" that Said establishes by situating the literary work in its imperial context do not provide the basis for an open discussion of the political, philosophical, economic, and cultural questions broached by the analysis of the literary text. I will address four of the ways in which the analysis of the literary text here works against the realization of such a dialogue: the answers to any new questions are for the most part already determined by the interpretative framework and its assumptions about imperialism and culture; any responses are further governed by the need to maintain an oppositional stance and not be complicit in imperialism; the literary text, as an example of a broader "imperial culture," only serves to explain the failures of culture and does not give us any ground for debating new alternatives; and the possibility of dialogue is itself undermined by the requirement to "go elsewhere," outside the domain of Western culture, for any genuine critical response.

In contrast to Said's interpretation, one might argue that colonial proprietorship does not underwrite the "attractive harmony" and "domestic tranquility" of Mansfield Park but is in fact responsible for the discord, rebellion, and poor transmission of values that results in a crippled heir, a disgraced, adulterous daughter who must seek refuge with her aunt, and another daughter who has eloped and is estranged from her father. The qualities that stand him in good stead as a colonial proprietor—imperial distance and otherness from those beneath him, firm authority and a strong sense of decorum—only teach most of his children to rebel against his example, and to flee (or transform, by making their home a theater, with the father's *sanctum sanctorum* now the theater's green room) the paternal hearth. One could suggest that the ways in which the colonial management of landed estates differs from the traditional domestic version (slavery and the employment of subjects, not citizens; absentee management and supervision through foreign overseers; and all the other aspects of colonial alienation) are embodied in the failings of the younger generation of the Bertram family; only the son who chooses his career in the church is unaffected. From here, one might even argue that *Mansfield Park* offers an implicit critique, rather than an affirmation, of imperialism.

Once one begins to interpret *Mansfield Park* through the framework of imperialism, there is a whole range of possible readings. But the differences between these interpretations finally do not much matter, since the guiding assumption of cultural criticism is that there is an alternative and an antidote to imperialist ideology that is so historically and morally obvious that one need not even articulate or defend it. The significance of any discussion is greatly curtailed when the answers to the most important questions are largely foreordained.

Said is less interested in supplying predictable answers, however, than in using cultural analysis as a tool for opposition and transformation. If the connection "Jane Austen and Empire" is to bear any fruit for the ongoing struggles against imperialism, the critique must demystify the powers of domination and resist the allures of culture. The reading of *Mansfield Park* is therefore only successful to the extent that it provides leverage for denouncing and distancing ourselves from imperial culture. At issue here is not simply a process of connection, but of linking something distasteful to something of the highest taste; that is, imperialism and a cultural masterpiece.

To increase this leverage, the linking of "culture" and "imperialism" must yield a picture of Western culture as *complicit* in imperialism and offer a possibility of positioning ourselves differently and of breaking from this cultural tradition—this is most easily accomplished by invoking an "elsewhere," a Third World, an " 'out there' that frames the genuinely important action *here*" (93). The aim is to make sure that one can no longer look at *Mansfield Park* without also seeing the sufferings of others; and more importantly, without also realizing that the *failure* to see connections between imperialism and culture is itself an *act* of complicity and even an authorization of "domestic imperial culture." The cultural critique performs the function of certifying that one is not complicit in processes of domination; criticism is now often akin to a rite of purification. No matter how the individual text is interpreted, we get a *reading for evil*, in which the critic always finds and condemns inequality.

Said first establishes the "connection" of *Mansfield Park* to imperialism by arguing that the proprietorship of an estate in Antigua cannot be *disconnected* from the novel. He then goes on to sketch an ever-widening series of "connections" in an effort to portray *Mansfield Park* as complicit in imperialism and all its consequences. Said writes: "[W]e must see 'Antigua' held in a precise place in Austen's moral geography, and in her prose, by historical changes that her novel rides like a vessel on a mighty sea. The Bertrams could not have been possible without the slave trade, sugar, and the colonial planter class" (94).

Said hopes to make explicit "what is hidden or allusive in Austen." What he finds "hidden," though, is not merely the cruelty of the slave trade, alluded to only by the "dead silence" that meets Fanny's question, but the entire aftermath of colonial slavery as well. Said remarks that in recent scholarship "slavery and empire are shown to have fostered the rise and consolidation of capitalism well beyond the old plantation monopolies, as well as to have been a powerful ideological system whose original connections to specific economic interests may have gone, but whose effects continued for decades" (94). The implication is that capitalism continues the exploitative practices of slavery and imperialism and that Austen's prose has contributed to a "consolidation of capitalism" whose ill effects still linger today.

Almost any fictional work could be condemned for contributing to "a powerful ideological system . . . whose [ill] effects continued for decades." Such readings will inform us of the failings of our culture, which countenances imperialism; they do not offer any arena for imagining equality. Envisioning new political structures and social ideals, anchoring this vision within the horizon of what may now be possible, and persuading others of the validity and justice of this outlook are much greater tasks. There is a disjunction between the effects of the critical act and the wider aims of the interpretative framework that guide it. Arguing against "imperial culture" by demonstrating "connections" between cultural texts and the systemic ills of our society is not equivalent to presenting arguments for any alternatives.

Said concludes his analysis of *Mansfield Park* by pointing out "a paradox here in reading Jane Austen which I have been impressed by but can in no way resolve": the paradox between "holding slaves on a West Indian sugar plantation" and the fact that "everything we know about Austen and her values is at odds with the cruelty of slavery" (96). This paradox does not, however, cause confusion or raise genuine questions for further discussion. Paradox is what the critic *must* find. If Austen's values were not "at odds with the cruelty of slavery," if we could not see *Mansfield Park* "in the main as resisting or avoiding that other setting" (96), but instead as either wholeheartedly endorsing or condemning brutality in Antigua, there would be no need for a sophisticated critique that brings to light what has been avoided and resisted by generations of readers. Nor would there be any opening for the critic's revaluation.

Reading for evil always uncovers a paradox, for the function of criticism is to disrupt ongoing complicity in systems of domination. The critic must argue that "great literary masterpieces" sanction attitudes and practices that are incompatible with the ideals of our culture (and with the ideals that these works help articulate); hence the utility of paradox. But the critic must also establish the obstacles and the resistances to achieving this insight in order to explain why the perspective of "that other setting" is required. If the apparent paradox were due to hypocrisy, and if the new insights could be supplied fully from within the discourse of the dominant ideology, there would be no need to turn elsewhere and no ground for a radical critique of the dominant culture. Some variant of liberalism and of the notion that "Western" culture can reform, critique, and improve itself would be sufficient. Contemporary cultural critics, like earlier deconstructive and even earlier "new" critics, thrive on paradox.

Said describes his method as reading *contrapuntally*, reading "with a simultaneous awareness both of the metropolitan history that is narrated and of those other histories against which (and together with which) the dominating discourse acts" (51). Said explicitly rejects a "rhetoric of blame" that attacks Austen "and others like her, retrospectively, for being white, privileged, insensitive, complicit," and states that we need to "see complementarity and interdependence instead of isolated, venerated, or formalized experience that excludes and forbids the hybridizing intrusions of human history" (96). Said's counterpoint itself alternates, however, between calling for us to listen to all voices and suggesting that for a genuine critique we now must turn only to those "unstinted in [their] hatred of implanted colonialism or the imperialism that kept it going" (18).

In his analysis of *Mansfield Park*, the "hybridizing intrusions of human history" are brought to bear only insofar as they cast a gruesome shadow on Western culture. The work of making connections, and of seeing complementarity and interdependence, always achieves the result of linking Austen, however weakly, to all that we now consider exploitative, if not evil. If "resistance" is the only legitimate critical position, the conclusions of the reading are, in a large sense, predetermined. Any discussion of the essential questions posed by the topic of imperialism—what can, and what ought to be, the relations between nations of unequal power and between different cultures—is constrained by the need to prove that one is not taken in by "imperial culture." And for those who disagree entirely with this view of imperialism, the most likely response is to strike the opposing attitude, demand proper reverence for the great works of culture, and insist that Austen's works not be sullied by the sins of others. No discussion of the widely divergent ideas concerning the proper uses of power—of the differences that underlie the opposing readings and approaches to Austen—will take place when the literary work is primarily a vehicle for upholding or resisting the dominant culture.

To what extent does Said's analysis oppose and alleviate coercive domination and transform "the present by trying rationally and analytically to lift some of its burdens"? The real accomplishment is one of de-legitimation. The political task of Said's work is to argue that we must now attend to other voices, must now listen to the voices neglected and suppressed by imperial culture, and must turn elsewhere for our intellectual wisdom and political vision. The only political force of this literary criticism is to critique, and finally to discredit, Western culture as complicit in domination. Despite the frequent calls for debate, critical exchange, and conversation, and despite the exhortations to listen to other voices, literary criticism now undermines more than it fosters the possible grounds on which such interchanges might take place.

Efforts to make literary criticism responsive to the needs of our communities and our society have not yet produced debates that have much significance beyond the domain of the participants. Literary critics may have learned to incorporate social concerns into their critical practices, but they have not achieved an effective social criticism. Locating "evil" is *not* the same as actually resisting it. Reading for evil is, however, eminently teachable, and students who miss all the subtleties and problematics of literary analysis easily come away with a powerful critical syllogism: colonialism is a horrendous evil; imperialism is the acceptance of other people's inequality and still permeates our culture; I am therefore fighting against imperialism (or any other "ism") by showing that it operates in literary texts. In this approach, literature is reduced to a frozen portrait of the thoughts of another era. Any ethical complexity is transformed into a Manichean division between abetting and resisting inequality, and the contemporary reader assumes a thoroughly unwarranted moral superiority. Said, in his masterly and often brilliant book, does not indulge in such trite forms of reading. Yet he helps to construct its fundamental logic. I do not look forward to the effects that *Culture and Imperialism* will have on literary studies.

I am certainly not advocating that readers of literature should ignore or condone manifestations of inequality. What I am really objecting to is less the "political" reading of literature than the political model that underlies it. For this model is one that is tailored for academic analysis: it postulates complicity, bad consciousness, and subjection as the norm and then declares a mode of *reading* as the path to political and intellectual authenticity. Said expresses "surprise" that "the quotidian processes of hegemony . . . yield surprisingly well to analysis and elucidation" (109). Of course they do! The conceit is always that hegemony triumphs over poorly trained readers, and that teaching students to analyze "the quotidian processes of hegemony" will radically challenge the prevailing consciousness. A cultural critique that requires the blindness of others for its own insights only perpetuates a system that discounts most people's ideas and brings us no closer to the discussions needed for making inequality any less intractable.

### NOTES

1. Edward Said, *Culture and Imperialism* (New York: Knopf, 1993), 303.

2. Terry Eagleton, *The Function of Criticism: From "The Spectator" to Post-Structuralism* (London: Verso, 1984), 107.

3. Said's *Culture and Imperialism* has been attacked for besmirching the honor and purity of Jane Austen. As Said puts it, he committed the "unforgivable sin" of arguing that *Mansfield Park* "also had something to do with slavery and British-owned sugar plantations

in Antigua" (*Representations of the Intellectual* [New York: Pantheon, 1994], xi). Susan Fraiman, in her essay "Jane Austen and Edward Said: Gender, Culture, and Imperialism," *Critical Inquiry* 21, no. 4 (Summer 1995): 805–21, provides a list of the many responses to Said's reading of *Mansfield Park*. I have no interest in protecting the aesthetic pleasures of reading Austen's work. I have chosen this section of Said's book since it offers a good opportunity for examining the possibilities and the results of the new awareness of colonialism for literary criticism.

4. Said slightly misquotes this passage, leaving out the exclamation mark after "silence" and presenting "there was such a dead silence" as a complete sentence. Said writes: "Fanny Price reminds her cousin that after asking Sir Thomas about the slave trade, 'There was such a dead silence.'" The Penguin edition from which he is quoting reads:

> "Did not you hear me ask him about the slave-trade last night?" [Fanny]
>
> "I did—and was in hopes the question would be followed up by others. It would have pleased your uncle to be inquired of farther." [Edward]
>
> "And I longed to do it—but there was such a dead silence! And while my cousins . . ." [Fanny]

See Jane Austen, *Mansfield Park* (Harmondsworth: Penguin, 1966), 213. Fanny, to enter into the world of Mansfield Park, must constantly regulate and suppress her desires and interests. The "dead silence" is that of the other characters who are everywhere being critiqued in the novel.

## 33. THICK AESTHETICISM AND THIN NATIVISM
### RUSSELL JACOBY

TODAY CYNICISM DRIVES INTELLECTUAL WORK, the belief that ideas only serve power and repression. Truth is obsolete; appeals to it sound almost embarrassing. "Around 1900," writes Peter Sloterdijk in his suggestive *Critique of Cynical Reason*, "the radical left wing caught up with the right-wing cynicism. . . . Out of the competition . . . arose that twilight characteristic of the present: the mutual spying out of ideologies." For Sloterdijk, this is the real source of the contemporary intellectual "exhaustion." The old ideas of truth stand "at a loss before this cynicism."[1]

The flight from naiveté into what Sloterdijk calls "ironic, pragmatic, and strategic realisms" can be charted in much liberal and left contemporary thought, for instance, in that of the philosopher Richard Rorty, a self-described ironist. He might be called a post–"end of ideology" thinker—

Russell Jacoby. "Thick Aestheticism and Thin Nativism." Abridged by the author from *The End of Utopia: Politics and Culture in an Age of Apathy*, by Russell Jacoby, 125–54. New York: Basic Books. Copyright © 1999 Russell Jacoby. Reprinted by permission of Basic Books, a member of Perseus Books, L.L.C.

"post" because he surrenders the liberal ideas that the 1950 thinkers championed; even the ghost of utopia dissipates. Rorty may believe in liberal ideas and their future, but his belief lacks conviction. He cites the socialist Raymond Williams, who praised George Orwell as a man who fought for "human dignity, freedom and peace." "I do not think," writes Rorty,

> that we liberals *can* now imagine a future of "human dignity, freedom, and peace." . . . We have no clear sense of how to get from the actual world to these theoretically possible worlds and thus no clear idea of what to work for.

For Rorty, this state of affairs must be accepted. "It is not something we can remedy by a firmer resolve, or more transparent prose, or better philosophical accounts of man, truth or history. It is just the way things happen to have fallen out."[2]

What remains of the philosophical project for an ironist? Not much. Terms like "just" or "rational" mean little "beyond the language games of one's time." For Rorty, "nothing can serve as a criticism of a final vocabulary save another such vocabulary. . . . Since there is nothing beyond vocabularies which serve as a criterion of choice between them, criticism is a matter of looking on this picture and on that."[3]

The charge of cynicism implies that liberals like Rorty and Michael Walzer or Charles Taylor or Clifford Geertz are splenetic debunkers. Yet they appear as open, bemused, tolerant, and thoughtful—and they are. Insofar as they have severed all links to utopian vision, however, aesthetic criteria come to the fore. Truth recedes before pose. What sounds interesting or feels sensible or looks provocative becomes the criterion. The break from universal and utopian categories leads to "aesthetization," an elevation of paradox, irony, and trivia, writes the German critic Hauke Brunkhorst. Interpretations compete on the basis of originality and cleverness.[4]

With half-hearted protests, Rorty and the others say as much. They exchange truth for art appreciation. In *Thick and Thin*, Michael Walzer writes of the eclipse of the "heroic" mode in philosophy, the search for big truths. Rather, Walzer calls for the "minimalist" approach where critics respond "in detail, thickly and idiomatically" to ordinary and local events. He suggests that "we ought to understand this effort less by analogy with what philosophers do than by analogy with what poets, novelists, artists and architects do."[5] Rorty agrees and tells us that the liberal ironist turns away from "social hope" and "social task" toward "private perfection." For this approach, what counts are novels and ethnologies, areas that "specialize in thick descriptions of the private and idiosyncratic."[6]

The references to "thick descriptions" in Walzer and Rorty allude to the anthropologist Clifford Geertz, who has championed the term. Geertz has had vast influence, not simply in anthropology but in fields like history and literary theory. "Thick description" sanctions layered portraits of singular events. It depreciates ambitious theories addressing broad issues, valuing instead modest observations describing small happenings; it encourages immersion in the stuff of everyday life, giving rise to history and anthropology that has more the feel of literature than of cold science. Yet Geertz adopts the term "thick description" from one of the virtuosos of arid theorizing, the Oxford philosopher Gilbert Ryle; and perhaps the concept has the last laugh. "Thick description" nourishes a literary approach; it also suggests the insular ruminations of self-satisfied professors.

In introducing the concept, Geertz cites Ryle's example of three boys, one winking; another, with a twitch; and a third, parodying the winker. For superficial thinkers, these three boys all appear to be winking. For deep thinkers, however, a host of "complexities" emerges. Winker, twitcher, and parodist may be embedded in a dense relationship of communications and miscommunications. For instance, the original winker might actually have been fake-winking to mislead others into imagining a conspiracy. As Ryle put it, "The thinnest description of what the rehearsing parodist is doing is, roughly, the same as for the involuntary eyelid twitch; but its thick description is a many-layered sandwich, of which only the bottom slice is catered for by that thinnest description."

Ryle offered other less-than-compelling examples of thick and thin descriptions like playing tennis, waiting for a train, humming, and clearing one's throat. What is a thick description of throat clearing? "I might clear my throat to give the false impression that I was about to sing." A thin description would miss the reference. "This throat-clearing is not a pretence throat-clearing; it is a pretence throat-clearing-in-preparation-for-singing."[7] Ryle spent his life meditating on such matters, an effort that Ernest Gellner long ago denounced as "Conspicuous Triviality." The Oxford approach, Gellner stated, was perfect for "gentlemen" philosophers. To those unsettled by ideas or real problems, it gave "something else to do."[8]

For Geertz, Ryle's approach opens up many avenues, but the term may not escape its roots in the Oxford clubs. To illustrate its richness Geertz provides "a not untypical excerpt" from his field journals. His days in the field must have been quite eventful for this typical selection reports a robbery and two murders with a vast cast of Moroccan Jews, Berbers, French troops, and several thousand sheep. The events offer much to chew on. For Geertz they demonstrate that anthropology is an "interpretative activity" akin to literary criticism requiring classifying of texts. "Here, in our text, such sorting would begin with distinguishing the three unlike frames of interpretation ingredient in the situation, Jewish, Berber and French."

Anthropology, then, is like literature, an act of interpretation, even imagination. "To construct actor-orientated descriptions of the involvements of a

Berber chieftain, a Jewish merchant, and a French soldier with one another in 1912 Morocco is clearly an imaginative act, not all that different from constructing similar descriptions of, say, the involvements with one another of a provincial French doctor, his silly, adulterous wife, and her feckless lover in nineteenth-century France." Geertz admits some differences. In *Madame Bovary* the acts may never have happened; in Morroco they are "represented as actual." Nevertheless, that is not crucial. "The conditions of their creation, and the point of it . . . differ. But the one is as much a *fictio*—'a making'—as the other."[9]

The difference between fictional representation and actual representation is not crucial for another reason: the Moroccan events may not have happened. At least Geertz evinces no interest in them as facts. His 1968 field report records a story told by a Jewish merchant, who must have been in his eighties, about some events six decades earlier, prior to World War I. Can this account be believed in all respects? Even the greenest investigator would raise questions about a sixty-year-old story of murder, robbery, and revenge, but Geertz never inquires whether any other accounts or records confirm these events. Facts are passé. Geertz offers no opinion about the trustworthiness of his informant. For Geertz these questions are immaterial; he has a text, ripe for a thick interpretation.

Is this anthropology? Is this history? For Geertz none of this matters. Yet his own thought hardly suggests cynicism. Like Rorty's, his style exudes a reflective bemusement as he moves from thought as insight to thought as art; he is a modernist content to juggle perspectives and savor texts. "There is no general story to be told, no synoptic picture to be had," Geertz writes in his recent intellectual autobigraphy. "It is necessary, then, to be satisfied with swirls, confluxions, and inconstant connections; clouds collecting, clouds dispersing." What "recommends" or "disrecommends" his own contributions is "their capacity to lead on to extended accounts which, intersecting other accounts of other matters, widen their implications and deepen their hold."[10]

Geertz writes engaging essays that tell us that the world is complex and the best we can do is talk to our neighbors to figure out what they are up to. His forte is describing unique and specific events; yet, pulled out from the larger context, the particular becomes not art but spectacle, something to gaze upon. His often cited essay, "Deep Play," on cockfighting in Bali, is a small tour de force, but it is as much a dazzling display of self as a penetrating discussion of its subject matter. "Early in April of 1958," begins this essay, "my wife and I arrived, malarial and diffident, in a Balinese village we intended, as anthropologists, to study." For Geertz, cockfighting is a text, "it is a Balinese reading of Balinese experience, a story they tell themselves about themselves," and Geertz, the anthropologist, is straining "to read over the shoulders" of the Balinese.

But what does he find? For this diffident observer everything evokes Shakespeare, poetry, and music.

To call the wind a cripple, as Stevens does, to fix tone and manipulate tim-
bre, as Schoenberg does, or closer to our case, to picture an art critic as a
dissolute bear, as Hogarth does, is to cross conceptual wires; the established conjunctions between objects and their qualities are altered, and
phenomena—fall weather, melodic shape, or cultural journalism—are
clothed in signifiers which normally point to other referents. Similarly, to
connect—and connect, and connect—the collision of roosters with the di-
visiveness of status is to invite a transfer of perception.[11]

An aestheticism drenches everything, a danger Geertz's critics have noted.
"Thick description as Geertz actually practices it," writes the anthropologist
Aletta Biersack, courts the danger of "aestheticizing all domains."[12]

To be sure, there is no direct route out of the maze of interpretations; the
problem is that Geertz seems happy to wander about. He puts it this way: "The
stance of 'well, I, a middle-class, mid-twentieth-century American more or less
standard, male, went out to this place, talked to some people I could get to talk
to me, and think things are sort of rather this way with them there' is not a retreat, it's an advance."[13]

The advance should not be depreciated. Against a tradition of dreary theorizing, Geertz wandered the byways of Indonesia and Morocco, asking, looking, and reflecting. Yet the advance harbored the danger of retreat, the anthropologist content to view and amuse, not fathom. Benedict Anderson, a
respectful critic of Geertz, cites a typical passage that begins this way. "I talked
to Djojo on the corner the other night about his marvellous grandfather. . . .
He said he was able to disappear magically." Anderson comments:

> This was a wholly new voice [in anthropology], and one that was to be
> widely imitated. The sympathetic, democratic American casually chats up
> a named individual, Djojo, on a street corner, "the other night," as if he
> were a neighbor, rather than a scientist or a colonial investigator. He is
> happy to let Djojo speak about magic, without contradicting him.

Yet in recent years, continues Anderson, the description seems pleased with
itself; culture gets reified. Little is explained. Rather, culture turns into art appreciation. He quotes a "marvellous" portrayal of a Javanese celebration,
which concludes, " 'The Meaning' of all this, just what was being said, and unsaid, by whom, to whom, with what purposes, in this parade of transgressions
bracketed with ritualisms, from Marceau's Bip, through Ionesco's 'Language
Lessons,' to Lucky's speech in *Godot*, is fairly well obscure. (It is very doubtful
that any of the participants had even heard of . . . any of these)."[14]

Some years after Geertz finished his field work in Bali, an unsuccessful
communist coup led to bloody riots in Indonesia with numerous killings. In
his piece on Balinese cockfighting only the last footnote alludes to these

events; and Geertz's language turns clumsy, as if the grim political facts mangle his aestheticism. His contorted footnote in the penultimate page of his book referring to the coup, riots, and deaths begins this way:

> That what the cockfight has to say about Bali is not altogether without perceptions and the disquiet it expresses about the general pattern of Balinese life is not wholly without reason is attested by the fact that in two weeks of December 1965, during the upheavals following the unsuccessful coup in Djakarta, between forty and eighty thousand Balinese ... were killed, largely by one another.[15]

Yet the point is not to wield the hammer of political reality against efforts to look at small chunks of the world. The tiniest fragment can yield the sharpest insights; conversely, the most expansive overview can yield the most banal platitudes. Indeed, the categories of small and large deceive, as if important thoughts derive from important subjects, and little ideas come from little subjects. It is not the size of the canvas that is at issue with Geertz or Rorty, but what they do with it. They are satisfied to sketch and paint, proposing minimal ideas about interpretation, diversity, and communication; their pose is increasingly aesthetic.

With and without the appeal to "thick descriptions," literary and aesthetic modes enjoy vast popularity in the social sciences and humanities. In anthropology, history, and English the talk is of tapestries of interpretations, imaginations of texts, the author as subject and poet, dialogic approaches. James Clifford, an anthropologist, writes that a literary and "dialogical" ethnology removes stability and objectivity. Subjectivity is the name of the game. The anthropologist's voice "pervades and situates the analysis, and objective, distancing rhetoric is renounced."[16] The anthropologist does not simply enunciate but, as a writer, participates in the discourse about representation.

Ernest Gellner, the late Cambridge University anthropologist, looked upon this with undisguised horror. Clifford, according to Gellner, has renounced studying other societies and cultures. "Clifford is not interested in the Navajo or Nuer or the Trobrianders, he is interested in what anthropologists say about them." From there it is a small step to study "what Clifford says about what others say," to analyze the representation of the representation of the represented; and, as Gellner notes, the step has been taken. For Gellner, this all makes for narcissistic, cloudy, and deficient anthropology. "What it means in literature does not concern me."[17]

What it means in literature is pertinent, however. The claim to be literary or poetic entails a renunciation of scientist truths. In return, the piece of work turns literary. Yet how do "thick" descriptions, instability, or multiple perspectives turn something into art or literature? Can art be reduced to the strategies and formulas these postmodernists claim? Do thick descriptions characterize

Kafka's writings? Is Joyce dialogic? Even if some of the terms fit, they do not apprehend the essence of art.

To put this differently, literary anthropology or history is not literature—and does not read like literature. In fact, the postmodern scholars are usually less readable than the more scientific predecessors they disdain. Nor should "readability" be understood simplistically. Works of literature are not always easy to read. Yet no one can confuse Faulkner or Joyce with literary postmodernism, which is unreadable in a precise sense: jargon-filled and half-written. These writings signal not the affirmation but the demise of literature.

The issue, however, is not simply one of style; it concerns the categories of truth. Art too has its truth, but this is ignored. The new literary scholars extol an artistic approach, which yields neither literature nor rigorous thinking about literature. The practitioners of a literary mode aestheticize reality. Art devolves into theories about art. Anthropologists become literary; historians imaginative. However, this is not art, but its debased form, a pretense to be artistic, as if multiple perspectives and self-referential writing constitute art.

The new literary professors abandon truth for art, and art for art appreciation. In their rebellion against scientism they alter the values but accept the terms. Objective is bad; subjective is good. In the name of subversion, they consign art to the reservation called subjectivity, in which it has long been imprisoned. Yet art is not simply subjectivity, multiple perspectives, and thick descriptions; it also partakes of truth, and hints of freedom and happiness. For this reason, poets like Wordsworth protested the casual talk of art as a taste, as if poetry did not also partake of truth and insight. The object of poetry, he stated "is truth, not individual and local, but general, and operative."[18]

Many scholars and academics have not only prospered in the marginality business, they have unloaded old, slow-selling stock. In the close-out sale, they drastically mark down concepts that hint of old world Enlightenment or out-of-the world utopia. The new lines dispense with balky universals and one-size-fits all engineering. Designed for local markets, the new items are smaller, easier to handle, neater.

A preference for the local and the specific is benign, even salutary. What is wrong with favoring the unique and distrusting universals? In the short run, nothing. Yet over time the suspicion of universals takes its revenge. Despite a rhetoric of subversion, it leads intellectuals down the path of acquiescence. Without an emphatic idea of freedom and happiness, a better society can scarcely be envisioned; utopia withers. Those who celebrate difference and discredit universals cannot think beyond the limited possibilities tossed up by history; at best they appreciate anything unique or non-Western; at worst they mythologize questionable practices.

They also relinquish the willingness to judge. Divested of a resolute idea of truth, political thinking turns murky. The new professors brag of their theoretical daring, but revel in unclarity; they confuse profundity and complexity. Proponents of cutting-edge theories do not acknowledge complexity as a stage in the process of thinking or recognize ambiguities as constituent of life and society. These become the goal or conclusion, proof of theoretical acumen.

To be sure, the issues preclude a brief discussion. All philosophy attends to the relationship of universals and particulars, which no formula can govern. In the domain of morality and politics the problems are no less dense. Do universal codes of justice and rights exist? And if they do, should they be used to criticize specific practices and acts? A case like that of Salman Rushdie, the English-Indian author, focuses the theoretical issues inasmuch as it seems to set a universal idea of human rights against the particular beliefs of several Islamic nations. His 1988 novel, *Satanic Verses*, provoked riots in India and censorship in several countries.

Iran's leader, Ayatollah Khomeini, issued a death sentence to Rushdie and "and all those involved in" the publication of the book. "I call on all zealous Muslims to execute them quickly, wherever they may be found, so that no one else will dare to insult the Muslim sanctities." To encourage the deed, heavenly defenders of the faith offered a secular million dollars to the successful assassin or assassins.[19] If the Rushdie affair were a test, however, many Western intellectuals would flunk.[20] As Robert Hughes has stated, "American academics failed to collectively protest," and he supposed this neglect was due to a politically correct relativism, the argument that "what they do in the Middle East is 'their culture.'"[21] This may be unfair, yet the writings on Rushdie by leftist academics are cautious to a fault. Confronted with sharply etched conflict, militant intellectuals with supercharged concepts reach for jargon and platitudes. The point is not that intellectuals come out on the wrong side in the Rushdie affair; they come out on no side.[22]

This is even true for some of the best and most lucid thinkers, like Charles Taylor, who frets that a Western standard of liberty may be inappropriate in the Rushdie dispute. "It goes without saying that there should be full freedom of publication," Taylor forthrightly states and then forthrightly retracts. "That applies to us," meaning North Americans and Europeans. In India, Iran, and elsewhere, other imperatives intrude. Perhaps no "abstract principle" of freedom applies. Diverse societies judge diversely what defines blasphemy and heinous insults. To stand above and outside "local conditions" with a single criterion implicitly endorses "the superiority of the West."

"I believe it is misguided to claim to identify culture-independent criteria of harm," he states. Where do these judicious thoughts lead Taylor? Nowhere. Since there is no "universal definition of freedom of expression," he argues, "we are going to have to live with this pluralism. . . . That means accepting solutions for one country which don't apply in others." Faced with a state-sponsored plan to assassinate a novelist, this stalwart liberal philosopher calls for acceptance and "some degree of understanding." He closes his reflections on Rushdie with mind-numbing clichés: "To live in this difficult world, the western liberal mind will have to learn to reach out more."[23]

Gayatri Spivak devotes an essay to the Rushdie affair that nimbly avoids any lucidity. In her inimitable style she cites her inimitable style. "Faced with the case of Salman Rushdie, how are we to read . . . ? I have often said, and said again in Chapter Two, that the (tragic) theater of the (sometimes farcically self-indulgent) script of poststructuralism is 'the other side.'" To nail down these statements she throws into the Rushdie controversy an account of Shahbano, a divorced Indian Muslim woman who sued for financial support from her ex-husband. To Hindu applause, the Indian Supreme Court found in her favor, but Shahbano in a change of heart protested the verdict in the name of Islam. As if this were not sufficiently illuminating, Spivak incisively concludes: "It is only if we recognize that we cannot not want freedom of expression as well as those other normative and privative rational abstractions that we on the other side can see how they work as alibis. It is only then that we can recode the conflict as Racism versus Fundamentalism, demonizing versus disavowal."[24]

A flight from universals, driven by simplistic notions of power and history, cripples political thinking. At the end of the twentieth century, vanguard thinkers hawk the most elementary ideas as revolutionary breakthroughs. The notion that history is complex is presented as late news; the idea that many perspectives constitute the world is discovered afresh. All this is written up in the clotted language of the new academics, who often deride coherency as inescapably repressive. "The demand for coherence," writes a feminist theorist, "requires the exclusion of any elements—such as ambiguity, conflict, and contradiction—which threatens coherence," as if Marx or Hegel did not discuss conflict coherently. Janet R. Jakobsen, who teaches women's studies, continues in the famous style of postcoherent thinkers, illustrating her point:

> I am not simply inciting a discourse which somehow focuses on all differences simultaneously, a move with universalizing tendencies that can reinstate a singular discourse by subsuming multiple sites of struggle; rather, I am suggesting that by reading for multiplicity and ambivalence it might be possible to articulate the "intersectionality" of differences—the points at which multiple processes of social differentiation come together to form nexuses of oppressions, as well as spaces in between the chasms of differentiation.[25]

Leftist thinkers monomaniacally extend the truism that power is powerful to the proposition that power is everything, as if this were a subversive notion. "In this book," goes a typical sentence by two cultural-studies practitioners, "we make the scandalous claim: *everything* in social and cultural life is fundamentally to do with *power*. Power is at the centre of cultural politics. . . . We are either active subjects . . . or we are subjected to . . . others."[26]

Scandalous claim? This is the wisdom of executive suites and abandoned streets. "Money talks." "The bottom line is . . ." "You're either with us or against us." "It's who you know . . ." The belief engenders a vision of the world of insiders and outsiders, those on top and those on bottom, all beyond good and evil. If history were only the story of contending power cliques, then every chapter would begin with a power struggle and end in blood, which is almost the case. Those out of power offer the same program as those in power, listing different individuals to be shot or imprisoned. That this is a recurring tale does not transform a truth into a critique.

Foucault redoubled the cynicism with his idea of total, not partial, power. Truth itself is a function of power. "Truth is what counts as true with the system of rules for a particular discourse," write several exponents of "postcolonial" literature. "Power is that which annexes, determines, and verifies truth. Truth is never outside power."[27] "To say that 'everything is political,'" stated Foucault, "is to affirm this ubiquity of relations of force. . . . To the vast new techniques of power correlated with multinational economies and bureaucratic States, one must oppose a politicization which will take new forms."[28]

The search for omnipresent power inspires some original research; it also opens the floodgates to demi-scholarship that endlessly rediscovers power. Traditionally political thinking began, not ended, with the recognition of power. Now the fact of power appears as a dazzling insight. The third chapter of Rousseau's *Social Contract* questioned the "right of the strongest." As Rousseau put it, the phrase is nonsense. "To yield to force is an act of necessity." No arguments need be adduced to hand over your purse to pistol-packing robbers, but where is the right? "If force creates right, the effect changes with the cause: every force that is greater than the first succeeds to its right. . . . But what kind of right is that which perishes when force fails?"[29]

The ability to distinguish what is from what should be, the *sine qua non* of political thinking, dwindles; the reality of a multifarious domination stuns liberal and leftist thinkers into reiterating the platitude that all categories deceive. A political theorist derides impartiality as a cloak for power. "The idea of impartiality," writes Iris M. Young, "legitimates hierarchal decisionmaking and allows the standpoint of the privileged to appear as universal."[30] Inasmuch as impartiality is rarely impartial, it never is and should be shelved. All universal categories serve as tools of power in history; since they are not uniformly realized, they are false.

Banal ideas of history supplement banal ideas of power. Critics incessantly observe that global intellectual diversity proves no idea is truer than any other, as if the fact of slavery justified its practice. The late bourgeois mind, Adorno proclaimed, is unable to comprehend validity and genesis in their simultaneous unity and difference.[31] To put this more crudely, the reality that all thought originates somewhere (genesis) does not constitute an argument for its false-ness (validity). Nor is something invalid because it is not generally recog-nized—or because it is misused. This may seem obvious, but left-leaning scholars regularly argue that global power and complexity disprove universals.

"The concept of universalism," state the editors of an anthology of a mar-ginalized literature, excludes the colonialized peoples.[32] In regard to music or poetry or fiction these sentiments could be easily multiplied; artists or writers of South America or Africa or Asia rightly object to being considered less than universal. The extension of this criticism from art to politics, philosophy, and science is questionable, however. While music or poetry may be culturally spe-cific, this is less true for scientific axioms and philosophic principles. Are hu-man rights invalid because they are violated or ignored—or unknown? If they are not recognized, does this makes them false? "The truth is also valid for those who contradict it, ignore it, or declare it unimportant," stated Max Horkheimer on behalf of a notion almost obsolete.[33]

To the modern academic, empirical diversity signifies multiple truths; im-perialism spawns "universal" truths. Human rights, states an anthropologist, Ann-Belinda S. Preis, are "culturally constructed." Observer and observed par-ticipate in a complex reality. What does this mean? "There is no objective posi-tion from which human rights can be truly measured." And the conclusion? "This ought to fundamentally challenge the current practice of establishing 'human rights records' of particular states (by organizations such as Human Rights Watch, Amnesty International, and the International Commission of Jurists) because such evaluations are always inherently partial, committed and incomplete."[34]

One vigilant anti-imperialistic scholar attacks "Western mathematics" as "the secret weapon of cultural imperialism." The reasoning is familiar. While it claims universalism, Western mathematics is a tool of domination and con-trol. "With the assumptions of universality and cultural neutrality," Western mathematics have been "imposed on the indigenous cultures." However, the world has produced other, equally valid systems of computation. "All cultures have generated mathematical ideas, just as all cultures have generated lan-guage, religion, morals, customs and kinship systems." According to Alan Bishop, a professor of education, "alternative mathematical systems" exist; for instance, in Papua New Guinea some six hundred systems of counting have been reported, including finger counting, body pointing, knotted strings, beads, and so on. This suggests we should recognize "ethnomathematics" as a "more localised and specific set of mathematical ideas" outside or against mainstream mathematics.[35]

Empirical observations of diverse mathematical and scientific practices across the globe can hardly be challenged. The conclusion that each society can and should have its own unique mathematics can be; and the notion that local obstacles inexorably yield effective solutions is delusional. Meera Nanda,

a science writer, protests the intellectual and political consequences of this position. It undermines cosmopolitanism and encourages dubious politics. She
cites Abdus Salam, the Pakistani Nobel Laureate in physics, affirming the universality of science. "There is no such thing as Islamic science, just as there is
no Hindu science, no Jewish science, no Confucian science . . . nor indeed,
'Western' science."[36]

Nanda, who is from India, finds that the criticism of scientific universalism
reinforces the most retrograde tendencies and groups. Hindu nationalism "in
my native India has definitely benefited from the cultural climate in which
even supposedly Left-inclined intellectuals and activists tend to treat all liberal
and modern ideas as 'Western,' inauthentic, and thus inappropriate for India."
She notes "the sad irony" of "the most 'radical,' cutting-edge thinkers in the
West giving intellectual ammunition to our nativists."[37]

From here it is a small jump to the Sokal brouhaha, an intellectual event
that fed or fed off of the idea of science as less than universal. As a leftist and a
physicist, Sokal wanted to expose the nonsense that much of the literary left
believed about science, in particular its lax notions about how scientific
knowledge was historical. To this end he contrived a patently inane essay that
hailed the cultural studies muck-a-mucks.[38] "I structured the article," Sokal
explained to the *New York Times*, "around the silliest quotes about mathematics and physics from the most prominent [cultural studies] academics, and I
invented an argument praising them and linking them together." He added
that this was easy to do for he ignored "standards of evidence and logic."[39]
*Social Text* loved it.

Afterwards, editors and other supporters scrambled to make the best of the
situation. They denounced Sokal, claimed he was "half-educated," or simply
blustered. The editors of *Social Text*, Bruce Robbins and Andrew Ross, who in
publishing the piece demonstrated they knew nothing about science, charged
that Sokal was "threatened" by cultural studies, as if the threat were the denunciation of shabby scholarship, not the shabby scholarship itself.[40] "Sokal's hoax
is a form of acting out," opined Homi K. Bhabha. "I detect in Sokal's essay—in
his rhetorical strategies, in his linguistic constructions—a displaced anxiety
about the contested 'autonomy' of science."[41]

Stanley Fish, executive director of Duke University Press, which publishes
*Social Text*, defended his editors; they all believe in the real world and its historical context in the same way they view baseball as both real and historical.[42]
Who could doubt that baseball is a historical construct, but are the laws of
physics that sustain it also historical, even imperialist?

"It is almost as if Fish were to astound everyone," grumbled Martin Gardner, a science writer, "by declaring that fish are not part of nature but only cultural constructs. Pressed for clarification of such a bizarre view he would then
clear the air by explaining that he wasn't referring to 'real' fish out there in real
water, but only to the word 'fish.'"[43]

With deep misgivings about universals, an unwillingness to judge on the basis of them, and a trite notion of history, leftist intellectuals drift into a major current of conservatism that includes Burkean traditionalism, German romanticism, and American regionalism. All repudiate abstract and uniform systems of thought, usually associated with the French Enlightenment, and champion the particular and the different.

The flat rejection of the universal leads to the rote affirmation of the unique and specific. History becomes the great excuse. This train of thought inexorably becomes conservative inasmuch as it sabotages the general propositions required to judge. Once writers and scholars isolate local conditions from universal categories, they lose the ability to evaluate them. They become cheerleaders, nationalists, and chauvinists. With equal enthusiasm Rajani K. Kanth, in *Breaking with the Enlightenment*, denounces the fraud of Western universalism and touts non-Western localism. In "Eurocapitalist societies" people demonize each other with broad categories. In the non-Western world, "people tied to each other by kinship, affinity, and affection (as, for instance, in tribal forms) are incapable, and unwilling, to abstractly demonize their fellows."[44] Does this prevent them from murdering each other? That war, violence, slavery, and caste are not Western monopolies, and that they do not improve when rooted in local situations does not seem to occur to Kanth.

The same distrust of universals pervaded American conservatives. It is not by chance that slavery became known by its defenders as "the peculiar institution"—peculiar inasmuch as it diverged from the universal rights established elsewhere.[45] American regionalists return to the same principles, upholding local and perhaps unjust realities against the abstract universals. "Unlike the America of the New World Order," runs a statement by the Southern League, a conservative group headquartered in Alabama, the League is "wedded, not to a universal proposition: democracy, or the rights of man, but to a real past of place and kin." The League "supports a return to a political and social system based on allegiance to kith and kin rather than to an impersonal state wedded to the idea of the universal rights of man."[46] A particularism that scorns universals inevitably ends by celebrating blood and race.

The Dreyfus case offers the classic example. Maurice Barrès, an anti-Dreyfusard, denounced intellectuals as "logicians of the absolute." He considered them "deracinated" internationalists who trade in abstractions like "Justice" and "Truth" and "who no longer spontaneously feel any rapport" with the nation. The next step seemed obvious: Dreyfus was Jewish; many of his supporters were Jewish. Deracinated Jews and intellectuals trade in abstractions. "For us," stated Barrès, "the nation is our soil and our ancestors; it is the land of our dead." For the Jewish intellectuals, on the other hand, nationalism is an "idea" or a "prejudice to destroy."[47]

Vanguard thinkers return to primal ideas, doubting any ideas that go beyond blood and place. Truth becomes "truth"; reason becomes "reason"; hu-

man rights "human rights." The quotation marks signify the subjective quality—as said by. Context is everything; truth is nothing. Today few could speak
the language of the Enlightenment: "We hold these Truths to be self-evident
. . ." For today's scholars these words hide as much as they state. No truths are
self-evident; they are constructed and invented. They emerge at specific times
and places; these are "truths" of eighteenth-century Europe and America. And
who is the "We?" A bunch of white patricians?

All "the constituting notions of Enlightenment metanarratives have been
exposed," writes a feminist political thinker, Jane Flax, referring to concepts
like reason and history. "True and false" are themselves obsolete, since "truth is
always contextual."[48] These platitudes enjoy great success. Yet it must be insisted upon: the universal also has its claims. Even, or exactly, the protest of the
individual against a political system taps into universal rights and equalities.
Without these universals, which weaken in the face of appeals to localism and
authenticity, the opposition crumbles. In the name of universals, the protest
not only protests but affirms a world beyond degradation and unhappiness; it
hints of utopia.

Herbert Marcuse's most visionary work, his 1955 *Eros and Civilization*,
brought out the links between utopia, protest, and universal categories. During the 1960s Marcuse championed what he dubbed "the absolute refusal," a
call to individuals to refuse cooperation with a deadly economic and social
system.[49] Despite its political and activist accents, the term "absolute refusal"
originated in his philosophical work *Eros and Civilization*, where Marcuse explored the utopian dimensions of art and imagination.

Drawing upon the surrealists, Marcuse argued that in repudiating a narrow
realism imagination and fantasy nurtured their own truths. "In its refusal to
accept . . . final limitations" to freedom and happiness and its "refusal to forget
what *can be*, lies the critical function of fantasy." Imagination transcends the
limited reality to glimpse its latent possibilities; it "comprehends reality more
fully" than realism. Conversely, on behalf of a narrow existing reality imagination is damned as untrue.

Marcuse compressed his analysis into what he called the "great refusal."

This Great Refusal is the protest against unnecessary repression, the struggle for the ultimate form of freedom—"to live without anxiety." But this
idea could be formulated without punishment only in the language of art.

In "realistic" philosophy and politics, the idea of life without anxiety would be
"defamed as utopia"[50]

Marcuse derived the phrase "the great refusal," which simultaneously invoked protest and utopia, from a discussion of universals by Alfred North
Whitehead. The English-American philosopher held that universals in art and
criticism transcend their particular cases. His language is a bit sticky, but the

argument is clear. "Every actual occurrence" must be set within an abstract realm that transcends it. "To be abstract is to transcend particular concrete occasions of actual happening." To transcend does not mean to be disconnected; indeed, the exact relationship of the universal and concrete is crucial. Any particular "red" flower falls short of the universal "red" by which we judge it. Yet the universal is not false.

> *The truth that some proposition respecting an actual occasion is untrue may express the vital truth as to the aesthetic achievement. It expresses the "great refusal," which is its primary characteristic* [my italics]. An event is decisive in proportion to the importance (for it) of its untrue propositions. . . . These transcendent entities have been termed "universals."[51]

The logic sticks in the craw of empiricists, postmodernists, and most leftists. Metaphysical universals inhere in the world, but transcend it. An individual event may be "untrue" in that it is contradicted by reality, but this untruth expresses its achievement or different truth, its basis in metaphysical principles.

Eugene Genovese, the historian, reminds us how "Fourth of July" celebrations caused problems in the slave South. During these events the glaring disjuncture between the idiom of universal freedom found in the Declaration of Independence and the fact of slavery gave rise to uneasiness.[52] In the North, abolitionists and ex-slaves appealed to its principles and daily violation. "Once, every year, in this land of the free, on Freedom's Natal day," stated a black petitioner to the Boston Legislature in 1853, "the people assemble in public convocation, and in intonations loud and long, proclaim to the despotism of the world, 'We hold these truths to be self-evident . . .'" But, continued William J. Watkins, "Your laws are founded in caste, conceived in caste, born in caste. Caste is the God whom this great Nation delights to honor." He thundered, "*Give us our rights. . . .* Treat us like men; carry out the principles of your immortal declaration."[53]

It was and is tempting to dismiss the festivities and its principles as bogus. "What, to the American slave, is your Fourth of July?" thundered Frederick Douglass in his 1852 speech, "The Meaning of July Fourth for the Negro." "I answer: a day that reveals to him, more than all other days in the year, the gross injustice and cruelty to which he is the constant victim. To him, your celebration is a sham, your boasted liberty, an unholy license . . . your shouts of liberty and equality hollow mockery."

This might sound very modern, a ringing attack on "Western" universals as frauds. On closer inspection, however, it is almost the opposite, a denunciation of the reality in the name of the ideas. Douglass damns slavery for betraying the ideas of liberty, not the ideas for betraying African Americans. The denunciation of the Fourth of July as hypocrisy appeals to the idea of equality; it bemoans the gap between the claim and reality.[54]

Like other abolitionists, Douglass drew "encouragement" from "the great principles" of the Declaration of Independence, and he saw them spreading throughout the world. No longer can "established customs of hurtful character . . . do their evil with social impunity. . . . No abuse, no outrage whether in taste, sport or avarice, can now hide itself from the all-pervading light."[55] Fifty years later Zola stated, "I have but one desire . . . seeing the light, in the name of humanity." All this sounds naive. What light? What principles? What humanity? Today the new generation of critics see through this stuff; they also see less.

## NOTES

1. Peter Sloterdijk, *Critique of Cynical Reason* (Minneapolis: University of Minnesota Press, 1987), xxvii, 3.

2. Richard Rorty, *Contingency, Irony, and Solidarity* (Cambridge: Cambridge University Press, 1989), 181–82.

3. Rorty, *Contingency*, 74, 80.

4. Hauke Brunkhorst, *Der entzauberte Intellektuelle* (Hamburg: Junius Verlag, 1990), 67–87.

5. Michael Walzer, *Thick and Thin: Moral Arguments at Home and Abroad* (Notre Dame, Ind.: University of Notre Dame Press, 1994), 51–52.

6. Rorty, *Contingency*, 94

7. Gilbert Ryle, "Thinking and Reflecting" and "The Thinking of Thoughts," in *Collected Papers*, vol. 2, *Collected Essays* (London: Hutchinson, 1971), 465–96.

8. Ernest Gellner, *Words and Things: An Examination of, and an Attack on, Linguistic Philosophy* (1959; London: Routledge & Kegan Paul, 1979), 267–73.

9. Clifford Geertz, "Thick Description," in his *The Interpretation of Cultures* (New York: Basic Books, 1973), 9, 16.

10. Clifford Geertz, *After the Fact: Two Countries, Four Decades, One Anthropologist* (Cambridge, Mass.: Harvard University Press, 1995), 2–3, 19.

11. Clifford Geertz, "Deep Play: Notes on the Balinese Cockfight," in *The Interpretation of Cultures*, 412–53.

12. Aletta Biersack, "Local Knowledge, Local History: Geertz and Beyond," in *The New Cultural History*, ed. Lynn Hunt (Berkeley: University of California Press, 1989), 81.

13. Clifford Geertz, " 'Local Knowledge' and Its Limits," *Yale Journal of Criticism*, 5, no. 2 (1992): 132.

14. Benedict Anderson, review of *After the Fact*, by Geertz, *London Review of Books*, 24 August 1995, 20. The passages appear in *After the Fact*, 145–51.

15. Geertz, "Deep Play," 452. For a criticism of Geertz's approach to Balinese violence see John Sidel, "Dark Play: Notes on a Balinese Massacre," *SEAP: Indonesia*, no. 63 (April 1977): 187–94; and the book it is discussing, Geoffrey Robinson, *The Dark Side of Paradise: Political Violence in Bali* (Ithaca, N.Y.: Cornell University Press, 1995).

16. James Clifford, "Introduction," *Writing Culture: The Poetics and Politics of Ethnology*, ed. James Clifford and George E. Marcus (Berkeley: University of California Press, 1986), 12.

17. Ernest Gellner, *Postmodernism, Reason, and Religion* (London: Routledge, 1992), 28–29.

18. William Wordsworth, Preface to *Lyrical Ballads* (1802) in *William Wordsworth*, ed. Stephen Gill (Oxford: Oxford University Press, 1986), 604–5.

19. For an account, see Daniel Pipes, *The Rushdie Affair: The Novel, the Ayatollah, and the West* (New York: Birch Lane Press, 1990).

20. Muslim intellectuals show themselves to be tougher and more lucid. See *For Rushdie: Essays by Arab and Muslim Writers in Defense of Free Speech* (New York: George Braziller, 1994). Bhikhu Parekh notes that in the Rushdie controversy British "political philosophers were largely silent." See Bhikhu Parekh, "The Rushdie Affair," *Political Studies* 38 (1990): 709.

21. Robert Hughes, *The Culture of Complaint: The Fraying of America* (Oxford: Oxford University Press, 1993), 115.

22. Of course, the situation is not so simple. Some intellectuals rallied to Rushdie; others rallied to his censors. For instance, Feroza Jussawalla, a professor of English, finds Rushdie guilty as charged, although it is unclear whether she wants him murdered. "Through stylistic wordplay . . . Rushdie attempts to escape the responsibilities of the monstrosities he perpetrates. . . . The Muslims of Bradford and Brick Lane . . . now find themselves further victimized by someone, who, to compound matters, is one of their own." Feroza Jussawalla, "Resurrecting the Prophet: The Case of Salman, the Otherwise," *Public Culture* 2, no. 1 (Fall 1989): 106–17.

23. Charles Taylor, "The Rushdie Controversy," *Public Culture* 2, no. 1 (Fall 1989): 118–22.

24. Gayatri Chakravorty Spivak, *Outside in the Teaching Machine* (New York: Routledge, 1993), 217–41.

25. Janet R. Jakobsen, "Agency and Alliance in Public Discourses about Sexualities," in *Feminist Ethics and Social Policy*, ed. Patrice DiQuinzio and Iris M. Young (Bloomington: Indiana University Press, 1997), 186–87.

26. Glenn Jordan and Chris Weedon, *Cultural Politics: Class, Gender, Race, and the Postmodern World* (Oxford: Blackwell Publishers, 1995), 11.

27. Bill Ashcroft, Gareth Griffiths, and Helen Tiffin, *The Empire Writes Back: Theory and Practice in Post-Colonial Literatures* (London: Routledge, 1989), 167.

28. Michel Foucault, *Power/Knowledge: Selected Interviews and Other Writings, 1972–1977*, ed. Colin Gordon, trans. Colin Gordon et al. (New York: Pantheon Books, 1980), 189–90.

29. Jean-Jacques Rousseau, *The Social Contract and Discourses*, trans. and intro. G. D. H. Cole (1950; rev. ed. New York: Dutton, 1973), chapter 3, 168.

30. Iris M. Young, *Justice and the Politics of Difference* (Princeton, N.J.: Princeton University Press, 1990), 116.

31. Theodor W. Adorno, "Zum Verhältnis von Soziologie und Psychologie," in T. W. Adorno, *Gesammelte Schriften*, vol. 8 (Frankfurt: Suhrkamp, 1972), 80.

32. Bill Ashcroft, Gareth Griffiths, Helen Tiffin, "Introduction," in *The Post-Colonial Studies Reader*, ed. B. Ashcroft et al. (London: Routledge, 1995), 55.

33. Max Horkheimer, "On the Problem of Truth," in *The Essential Frankfurt School Reader*, ed. Andrew Arato and Eike Gebhardt (New York: Urizen Books, 1978), 423. Translation slightly altered. Max Horkheimer, "Zum Problem der Wahrheit," in *Kritische Theorie der Gesellschaft*, vol. 1 (Frankfurt: Marxismus-Kollektiv, 1968), 248.

34. Ann-Belinda S. Preis, "Human Rights as Cultural Practice: An Anthropological Critique," *Human Rights Quarterly* 18, no. 2 (May 1996): 308

35. Alan J. Bishop, "Western Mathematics: The Secret Weapon of Cultural Imperialism," *Race and Class* 32 (October–December 1990): 51–65. A slightly abridged version appears in *The Post-Colonial Studies Reader*. Even a more judicious inquirer concludes we must move "beyond our Western mathematics." See Marcia Ascher, *Ethnomathematics: A Multicultural View of Mathematical Ideas* (Pacific Grove, Calif.: Brooks/Cole Publishing, 1991), 196.

36. The citation is from Abdus Salam's preface (iv) to Pervez Amirali Hoodbhoy's *Muslims and Science: Religious Orthodoxy and the Struggle for Rationality* (Lahore, Pakistan: Vanguard Books, 1991), which includes an eye-opening account of efforts to establish an "Islamic" science (169–87).

37. Meera Nanda, "Against Social De(con)struction of Science: Cautionary Tales from the Third World," in *In Defense of History*, ed. Ellen Meiksins Wood and John Bellamy Foster (New York: Monthly Review Press, 1997), 74–96.

38. Alan D. Sokal, "Transgressing the Boundaries: Toward a Transformative Hermeneutics of Quantum Gravity," *Social Text* 46–47 (Spring/Summer 1996): 217–52.

39. "Postmodern Gravity, Deconstructed, Slyly," *New York Times*, 18 May 1996.

40. For their statement, Sokal's reply and other comments, see "Mystery Science Theater: Sokal vs. *Social Text*, Part Two," *Lingua Franca* (July–August 1996): 54–64.

41. Homi K. Bhabha, "Laughingstock," *Artforum* 35, no. 2 (October 1996): 15–18.

42. Stanley Fish, "Professor Sokal's Bad Joke," *New York Times*, 21 May 1996.

43. Martin Gardner, "Physicist Alan Sokal's Hilarious Hoax," *Skeptical Inquirer* 20, no. 6 (November–December 1996): 14–17.

44. Rajani K. Kanth, *Breaking with the Enlightenment* (Atlantic Highlands, N.J.: Humanities Press International, 1997), 117–18.

45. Kenneth M. Stampp, *The Peculiar Institution: Slavery in the Ante-Bellum South* (New York: Random House, 1956).

46. Michael Hill, "President's Message: Kith and Kin," *Southern Patriot* 3, no. 5 (September–October 1996): 1–2.

47. Maurice Barrès, *Scènes et doctrines du nationalisme*, vol. 1 (Paris: Librairie Plon, 1925), 59, 49, 68.

48. Jane Flax, "The End of Innocence," in *Feminists Theorize the Political*, ed. Judith Butler and Joan W. Scott (New York: Routledge, 1992), 450–52.

49. Herbert Marcuse, *One Dimensional Man* (Boston: Beacon Press, 1964), 255–56.

50. Herbert Marcuse, *Eros and Civilization* (New York: Vintage Books, 1962), 136. The phrase in quotes is from T. W. Adorno, "Versuch über Wagner," in T. W. Adorno, *Gesammelte Schriften*, vol. 13 (Frankfurt: Suhrkamp, 1971), 145.

51. Alfred North Whitehead, *Science and the Modern World* (1925; New York: New American Library, 1948), 142–43.

52. See Eugene D. Genovese, *From Rebellion to Revolution: Afro-American Slave Revolts in the Making of the Modern World* (Baton Rouge: Louisiana State University Press, 1979), 126–37.

53. William J. Watkins, "Our Rights as Men. An Address Delivered in Boston Before the Legislative Committee on the Militia, February 24, 1853," reprinted in *Negro Protest Pamphlets: A Compendium*, ed. William Loren Katz (New York: Arno and New York Times, 1969), 7–10.

54. See generally Paul Goetsch and Gerd Hurm, eds. *The Fourth of July: Political Oratory and Literary Reactions 1776–1876* (Tübingen: Gunter Narr Verlag, 1992).

55. "The Meaning of July Fourth for the Negro" (July 4, 1852), in *The Life and Writings of Frederick Douglass*, ed. Philip S. Foner, vol. 2 (New York: International Publishers, 1950), 181–204.

## 34.  CASUALTIES OF THE CULTURE WARS

### EUGENE GOODHEART

THERE WAS A TIME in the recent past when a literary education required the cultivation of the critical faculty. Criticism, the interpretation and evaluation of works of literature, occupied a prominent place next to literary history and textual criticism. The practice of criticism continues in literary journalism, but it has lost its prestige in the academy. What has replaced criticism in prestige is discourse, that is, the transformation of works into texts and their placement in a rhetorical system based on ideology: Marxist, feminist, postcolonialist. Discourse doesn't interpret the work as a whole, but rather appropriates elements of it. Whether a work is good or bad, distinguished or mediocre, is usually irrelevant. Judgments are dictated by political or ideological interests. How does the text, formerly the work, illuminate or fail to illuminate the class struggle in nineteenth-century France or the plight of women in eighteenth-century England or the situation of Indians under the Raj? Interesting questions for scholarship and advocacy, but not to be confused with criticism.

The reasons for this transformation lie not only in the internal history of the discipline, but also in the political and cultural history of the past four decades. I have no desire to repeat a story that has already been told and retold. I want for the moment rather to focus on one reason, or perhaps more accurately rationalization, given for the change: the erosion of belief in the possibility of objective and disinterested knowledge. Given the vagaries of interpretation and judgment, how is it possible to establish the truth of an interpretation or the validity of an aesthetic judgment? Why waste time, so the argument goes, on an activity riddled with the caprices of subjective judgment? Discourse at least has the advantage of declaring its ideological interests; in its appropriation of texts to those interests it does not pretend to a nonexistent objectivity. Or so it rationalizes its practice. Actually, in making anti-objectivist arguments, it adopts the objectivist manner and tone.

Eugene Goodheart. "Casualties of the Culture Wars." Revised by the author from *Does Literary Studies Have a Future?* by Eugene Goodheart, 21–34. Copyright © 1999. Reprinted by permission of The University of Wisconsin Press. And from "Criticism in the Age of Discourse," by Eugene Goodheart, originally published in *Clio: A Journal of Literature, History, and the Philosophy of History* 32, no. 2 (2003): 205–8. Reprinted by permission of the publisher.

The history of criticism provides some support for this skeptical, indeed radically skeptical, view. Quarrels among critics have rarely, if ever, been adjudicated. Interpretations and evaluations abound and are often different from or in conflict with one another. The reputations of writers, determined by criticism, fluctuate, sometimes as wildly as the stock market in crisis. Matthew Arnold said that Shakespeare does not "abide our question," while other writers don't remain exempt from the vicissitudes of reputation. But even Shakespeare was subject to those vagaries before the nineteenth century. T. S. Eliot preferred the metaphysicals to Milton and had serious doubts about his greatness, only to change his mind. Eliot's views were determined by his own creative interests. F. R. Leavis disparaged Dickens as an entertainer, only to alter his view and acknowledge his greatness as a novelist without, I might add, ever accounting for the change of view. Melville's great reputation is of comparatively recent vintage. Instances of the vagaries of critical judgment abound. And one might argue that the vitality of literature depends upon the capacity of writers and critics to change their minds about the tradition in the light of changing interests and life experiences.

The radically skeptical view, however, tends to ignore the common ground that exists among critics in the matter of interpretation and in the endurance of reputations. For all the volatility that exists, Homer, Dante, Shakespeare, and Milton (a very partial list) have endured and helped form the culture in which we live. And even if one accepts the main force of the radically skeptical view of objectivity (which I do not), one need not accept its consequences for literary study. Criticism is not about the quest for a singular truth or a consensus view of its object. It presupposes a literary sensibility and its patient cultivation. It assumes a variety of critical temperaments and of personal, social, and historical experiences in critics. The disagreements as well as agreements that occur among critics presuppose a common ground of intelligence, training, open-mindedness, flexibility, sophistication, and taste, ideals not often realized. The critic is trained not to arrive at Truth, but to engage a work (not simply fragments of it) in as lively, perceptive, and discerning a way as possible. Objectivity is an element in critical discussion; it is not the whole story. It may be difficult to achieve, but not impossible. The more interesting achievement of criticism is the diversity of its engagement with the difficult passages (cruxes) that fascinate and confound the intelligence. I am suggesting that the reputation of criticism has suffered from misleading epistemological debates.

Most misleading is a false polarization between the work as an aesthetic whole devoid of political interest, on the one hand, and the work as a political or ideological expression, on the other. At issue are differing views about the relationship between art and politics or ideology in a work of art. Literary criticism does not necessarily exclude an interest in the political content or context of a work. (I say "not necessarily," because there is a formalist version that does.) What literary criticism necessarily resists is the idea that a work can be *reduced* to its political context. Literary criticism takes political and historical context into consideration, may even view it as a constraint upon the imagination, but rejects the idea that it determines its unfolding. Thus a knowledge of the social, political, and economic circumstances of Elizabethan England may contribute to an understanding of Shakespeare's achievement without, however, defining it.

But if politics occupies the entire space of discourse, you are no longer required to persuade others of the rightness of your views by appealing to reason (i.e., logic and evidence). Indeed, you cannot hope to persuade the other side, because of the assumption that what determines the opposing view are interests, hidden or open, that are not amenable to reason. Intellectual exchange becomes disdainful rhetorical encounters in which each side affirms itself without the prospect of common agreement. Differences between the like-minded can be adjudicated (i.e., among cultural conservatives or among cultural radicals), but between opposing sides, reasonable exchange is very difficult, if not impossible, precisely because "sociopolitical" rather than "epistemological justification" (Rorty's phrases) is the order of the day. Academic intellectuals are no longer required to justify knowledge; they need only tell us what they believe.

In my own discipline of literary studies, ideology critique rules the roost. It is a species of the hermeneutics of suspicion and one of the sources of the culture wars. There is nothing more aggressive than the effort to demystify the supposed illusions of others. As I have written previously, "real debate or dialogue becomes impossible, because the ground between demystifier and antagonist is not the problematic nature of truth [or an uncertainty about where the truth lies], but the difference between truth and illusion. The person who claims to know the truth and is *certain* that others with an opposing view are the captives of illusion is a potential despot."[1] Here is a paradox: Those who possess this certainty about the illusions of others usually call themselves antifoundationalists, antiessentialists, and antiuniversalists. And they are suspicious of all claims to objectivity. So where does their certainty about the mystifications of others come from? Apparently from a conviction about the moral superiority of their side in the cultural and political struggles. If mystification conceals motives of domination, then the moral task of criticism is to unmask these motives.

Unlike perspectivists who tend toward skepticism about all claims to objectivity, ideology critics equivocate on the question of objectivity. They would claim it for their demystifications, but at the same time share with perspectivists a sensitivity to the partiality and self-interestedness of all points of view. Ideology critique can be a valuable activity if it knows its limits, discriminating between what requires and what does not require demystification. In contemporary practice in the academy, it has become an imperial obsession with disastrous consequences.

One casualty of this obsession in literary study is the virtual disappearance of the practice of aesthetic criticism. A number of years ago at a Modern Language Association convention I was on a search committee interviewing candidates for a position in Victorian literature in our department. One of the candidates had done a dissertation on Christina Rossetti in which "Goblin Market" played a prominent role. As I recall, the candidate was putting forth a New Historicist or feminist argument about the poem, when one of my colleagues on the committee interrupted her with the question: "But is it a good poem?" The question took me by surprise, for I didn't remember such a question having been asked of students in years. It dumbfounded the candidate. She had apparently never considered the question. The poem was there as an occasion for . . . I was about to write interpretation or analysis, but it would be more accurate to say: a placement in a particular discourse—historicist, feminist, deconstructionist, ideological. The candidate's fluency about the poem came to a halt. She spluttered a few phrases about the power of the poem. She was unprepared to answer the question, having never been asked or taught to ask it by her teachers of any poem or novel or play that she had read.

We may not have been fair in our judgment of her. If we had been consistent and asked the same question of all the candidates, I do not think we would have met with greater success. Our candidate's disability was, indeed still is, built into the profession of literary studies at the present time. The distinction Jane Gallop makes between the New Criticism and poststructuralism is symptomatic of the current state of affairs: "When New Criticism held sway in the literary academy, the reigning values were aesthetic. By the mid-1980s the dominant discourse in the literary academy is poststructuralist and the reigning values are theoretical. Where once the academic feminist looked to Emily Dickinson, now she pins her hopes on Julia Kristeva."[2] The aesthetic can no longer achieve the dignity of theory; it has become its antonym. That aesthetic judgment is not one of the current professional practices is clear not only from its absence in the content of literary study but from the styles of the discoursers. No longer written in a vernacular style, criticism has become a species of sociological prose once held in contempt by literary scholars—ponderous, abstract, obscure, ungainly, jargonish. There are practitioners of New Historicism, ideology critique, and deconstruction who write well, but who seem to regard their own gifts of expression as incidental, and are not in the least discomfited by the bad writing of others.

Style is not an incidental matter. Orwell made a compelling case for its political and moral significance. In his classic essay "Politics and the English Language," he preached the virtues of plain speech, the transparent and elegant style as a mark of self-honesty. (Transparency makes it difficult to conceal your ideas from yourself.) In *Writing Degree Zero* and subsequent writings, Roland Barthes deconstructed, so to speak, the Enlightenment myth of transparency as a guarantor of honesty and truth. Reality was not as perspicuous to "natural" plain writing as the Enlightenment believed. Barthes's own style (rich, inventive, personal, alternately perspicuous and obscure) is that of an imaginative writer. I don't want to adjudicate the differences between Orwell and Barthes, but I should note what may not be obvious: they have a shared aesthetic concern with style, a concern that has virtually disappeared from academic discourse.

It should be noted that the hostility or indifference to aesthetic theory and criticism is nothing new. Gerald Graff quotes a scholar in 1901 who scorns attempts to make the study of literature a study of "the work as a work of art":

> Why then waste time and brains in thrashing over again something which is after all only subjective opinion? Mere aesthetic theorizing should be left to the magazine writer or to the really gifted critic who feels himself competent to tread in the footsteps of Lessing. My view has always been that the college (university) is a place for research, for scholarship, for finding out something hitherto unsuspected. Such is the object of our libraries and our seminary methods. The outside world hasn't the time to investigate; we must do the investigation.[3]

In trying to put literary study on a scientific basis, Northrop Frye in *Anatomy of Criticism* (1957) dismissively consigned aesthetic criticism to the capricious history of taste. One must, however, distinguish the grounds for hostility in its various expressions. For the ideology critics, the issue is not the lack of scientific rigor in aesthetic criticism, but rather the mystifying power of aesthetic illusion, its displacement or concealment of political motives. Aesthetic illusion is seen as a kind of cultural pathology.

It has become almost an embarrassment to speak in behalf of aesthetic value in the academy. One of the few unembarrassed exceptions is the voice of Harold Bloom, whose jeremiad *The Western Canon* begins defiantly with an affirmation of the aesthetic against its demystifiers: " 'Aesthetic value' is sometimes regarded as a suggestion of Immanuel Kant's rather than an actuality, but that has not been my experience during a lifetime of reading."[4] I take it that Bloom is saying that aesthetic value is an experience and not a theory. Indeed, if we insist on a theoretical justification of the aesthetic, we will end up speaking as does Barbara Herrnstein Smith of its contingent and subjective status (it is in the eye of the beholder and every beholder sees things differently) or we may find that the aesthetic is inescapably contaminated by political, moral, and philosophical interests. Bloom seems to me overconfident, even facile, in his insistence on the purity of aesthetic experience, but he is right to resist theoretical efforts to deny his experience of the sublime, which is for him the aesthetic emotion. The theoretical project of aesthetics may prove vulnerable, but its vulnerability is not proof against the actuality of aesthetic experience. There have been persuasive ways of talking and writing about it when confronting a work of art or, for that matter, a work of nature. Louis Armstrong had an instinctive knowledge of the limits of theory and of the actuality of experience when he responded to a request for a definition of jazz by saying that if you have to define it, you'll never know it.

It is true that the teaching of an aesthetic response to literature presents special difficulties. You do not in fact teach an aesthetic response, you practice it. What does it mean to practice it? Certainly not by the application of a method or a set of procedures, but rather by comments, indications, and gestures that accompany interpretation, the staple of literary criticism. Interpretation looks for patterns, significant coherences or incoherences that constitute the meanings of a text, but by itself is not a route to an apprehension of its beauty or power. In the course of an interpretation, the reader should be alert to surprises that reveal the wit, the ingenuity, the imagination of the work, the rightness and splendor of the language. The critic need not, indeed cannot, avoid talking about ethical, political, religious, or historical issues. What is decisive is the way he speaks or writes about the work, the kind of attention he gives to what count as aesthetic qualities. An aesthetic response foregrounds the work and doesn't allow it to be devalued by one or another discourse.

Literary criticism in the aesthetic sense is neither liberal nor conservative, progressive nor reactionary. Aesthetics may attach itself to politics as when fascists aestheticize power, or it may be experienced as a temptation to be avoided, as when Lenin refused to listen to Beethoven's music because he felt it distracted him from the task of making a revolution. But the aesthetic response has no necessary political applications. What may be the case is that there is a temperamental disaffinity between literary and political sensibilities, which could account in part at least for the sense of frustration and exasperation in current debates. Arguments cannot resolve differences between sensibilities.

Literary sensibility is not enough to constitute a discipline, which requires methods that can be exercised by its practitioners and into which its students can be initiated. The method of New Criticism, for all its inadequacies, proved to be an effective vehicle for its practitioners, particularly its most distinguished practitioners. But even in the New Criticism with its disposition toward formulas about paradox and ambiguity, a kind of mechanism of application developed which can easily betray the sensibility. We see this in the routinization of the criticism. In a way, literary criticism thrives to the extent that it resists academic professionalization. Methods and scholarship can produce certain kinds of knowledge about texts, but they are not guarantors of the experience of literary works. What is distressing about the current situation is that a literary sensibility is not requisite for professional entry into the discipline.

It is true that a discipline depends on method, and it may be a reason why the culture of the discipline has always had trouble accommodating the practice of aesthetic criticism. However, as I have already remarked, the current disrepute of, or uninterest in, aesthetic value may have less to do with theoretical disagreement about its constitution and how one might practice aesthetic criticism than with suspicion about its supposed ideological character. The demise of the aesthetic in the academy begins with the shift in focus from the New Critical concern with the individual work of art to the structuralist and poststructuralist attention to the conditions of its production. The structuralist and the poststructuralist (opposed as they are in other respects) care less for what the text says or does (the task of interpretation) than for the putative external factors that determine its existence and effects. From the perspective of the ideology critics, the aesthetic becomes little more than a mystification that conceals political, class, gender, or racial interests. How can we concentrate on the beauty and power of a work of art, if we are always supposed to look around it to discover its ideological biases and hidden motives? God forbid that we should be taken in by the surfaces of the work. Our failure to focus on "the ideology of the aesthetic" (the title of a book by Terry Eagleton) marks us out as naive or mystified.

Even some scholars who ally themselves with the ideology critics share a sense of loss or discomfort. Here is the testimony of George Levine in his introduction to a book entitled *Aesthetics and Ideology*:

> This book and this introduction have required that I face directly my own anxieties about what my passion for literature will seem like to the critical culture with which I want to claim alliance. . . . Beginning this book with the language of the affective, the sublime, the aesthetic, I hoped to rescue from the wreckage of the mystified ideal of the beautiful the qualities that allowed for such rich ambivalences. Eliot is anti-Semitic and worse. Arnold is both statist and snob. I wouldn't be without the writings of either of them. That, I recognize, puts me and this book under suspicion.[5]

The passage, I think, reveals more than Levine intends. What are we to make of allies who suspect the motives of a literary critic who employs the language of the affective, the sublime, the aesthetic? Levine's "anxieties" about taking an aesthetic stance in the presence of his ideologically motivated colleagues are so strong that he cannot avoid compromising his formulations about a "very small breathing space [why very small?] of free play and disinterest"[6] to the point of virtually conceding the futility of the effort.

> There must be a distinction between aspiration to some impossible ideal disinterested stance, and the effort to resist, in certain situations, the political thrust of one's own interests in order—in those situations—to keep

open to new knowledge of alternative possibilities and to avoid the consequences of simple partisanship. . . . Even if the Arnoldian and Bloomian ideal of intellectual free space is merely utopian and ultimately a mystifying and disguise of actual power, the notion that the university is not or should not try to be fundamentally different from partisan political institutions is merely absurd.[7]

One might wonder to the contrary: Is it not absurd to try to rise above the fray (i.e., "partisan political institutions") if the ideal of intellectual free space is mystification? If you wish to make a case for an aspiration to disinterestedness, it is self-defeating to characterize the object of the effort as "impossible," "ultimately mystifying," and a "disguise of actual power."

This is the place to say something about the contentious phrase "political correctness." Quarrels abound about whether it exists, the extent to which it exists, its content if indeed it does exist, and to whom it applies. My understanding of PC is that it does not or should not apply to the content of a position or theory, but rather to the way it is expressed. Evelyn Fox Keller is right to resist the "easy invocation of PC as shorthand for postmodernism, social constructionism, feminism and multiculturalism,"[8] for it is possible for those who adhere to these doctrines to be open to criticism and to refrain from imposing their views on others. It is also true that those who attack postmodernism may have their own brand of political correctness which they seek to impose on others. Neoconservative critics often display a closeminded vehemence that belies their claim to disinterestedness. Extreme versions of a doctrine on whatever side of the cultural or political spectrum tend to breed an ethos of political correctness and their effect may be disproportionate to their actual constituency. These versions have a way of haunting moderate and reasonable expressions of, for instance, postmodernism, as Levine's anxieties suggest.

Political correctness implies intimidation, for it places the offender outside the pale. Of course, it is always possible that the experience of PC is illusory and paranoiac, that it does not correspond to the facts of the case. But the evidence seems compelling when those in sympathy with a particular view find problems with it and experience fear or anxiety that they may offend those who hold the view unambivalently.

What is remarkable about a number of the essays in the Levine anthology is the defensiveness with which the claim of the aesthetic is articulated. Ideological suspicion informs even the best of the essays. Thus Peter Brooks in a fine essay, "Aesthetics and Ideology—What Happened to Poetics?," cites a passage from a prominent New Historicist in which he asks literary scholars to make a choice between two models of study: "Critical research and teaching in the Humanities may be either a merely academic displacement or a genuine academic instantiation of oppositional social and political praxis." Brooks's response is admirable, but not unexceptionable:

The terms in which the choice is posed create a kind of academic melo-drama, of the disempowered professorial wimp versus the macho resis-tance hero. Even if we want to align ourselves with the latter, and want to refuse definitively the notion of the critic as a genteel belated Victorian preaching sweetness and light, we may find that this version of the choice both plays into the hands of our enemies, and seriously undermines our ability to speak of literature with any particular qualifications for doing so.[9]

The contrast of styles between Brooks and the New Historicist alone should make it clear whom we are to trust. There is little to add to Brooks's incisive characterization of the false choices posed. But it is dismaying that the inci-siveness is marred by a wholly unnecessary concessiveness, "even if we want to align ourselves with the latter [the macho resistance hero]." Why, after what Brooks shows us to be false in the New Historicist's formulation, should we want to align ourselves with the latter? And why the concern about "playing into the hands of our enemies"? In citing a different passage from the same hapless critic, Brooks remarks that "one senses that this is material to hide from the eyes of such as Lynne Cheney or Hilton Kramer or Dinesh D'Souza, or other recent critics of the academic humanities, since it so readily confirms their intemperate view that the academy has become a conspiracy of aging Six-ties radicals made only slightly less dangerous by the fact that their prose can't shoot straight." If it confirms their view, how intemperate is it? This is culture war anxiety.

It may seem captious and ungrateful of me to fault Brooks for what is gen-erally an excellent essay. But it is precisely Brooks's excellence as a critic that makes the reader wonder about the allies he has chosen. There are reasons for him not to associate himself with Cheney, Kramer, and D'Souza, but what are his reasons for allying himself with the crude demystifiers of the aesthetic? With such friends, who needs enemies? (Levine, as I have shown, seems caught in a similar bind.) The only explanation can be that in a state of war one feels that one must choose sides, and there are apparently only two sides to choose from.

The quarrel or tension between ideology and aesthetics bears directly on the possibility of objectivity, for aesthetics in its classic formulation (e.g., Shaftesbury, Kant, Schiller) makes a claim for disinterestedness. As Jerome Stolnitz remarks, summarizing the main aesthetic tradition, we perceive beauty when it is the object of a "disinterested and sympathetic attention . . . and contemplation for its own sake alone [as in] 'the look of the rock,' the sound of the ocean, the colors in the painting."[10] Ideology critics have chal-lenged the claim of disinterestedness on grounds that have to be taken seri-ously. If all our activities are interest-driven, the plausible view of Nietzsche and William James among others, we cannot at the very least be complacent about assuming the existence of disinterestedness. But again we have the problem of how the issue is formulated. What do we mean by interest and disinterest? Ideology critics tend to see interest in its class or group-bound sense as serving the self or the constituency of which the self is a part. But interest can also be directed toward the cause of justice and the interests of humanity and in that sense can be conceived as aspiring to a value-laden disinterestedness. Disinterestedness, understood in this way, is uncommon, but possible.

In construing interest in the narrow self-interested sense, the ideology critics focus on the social, political, and economic conditions in which certain views arise. The question then becomes what to make of a knowledge of those conditions. Does it demystify the aesthetic theory of Shaftesbury to know that it arose out of a sense of personal "displacement" and "self-division" following the English Revolution?

> Henceforth it would be impossible for nobles to inhabit an aristocratic Lebensform regarded in the old, pre-seventeenth-century way as altogether natural, normative and problematic.
>
> Such nobles as Shaftesbury, whose family had risen to power and eminence on the dangerously volatile currents of the Restoration, would thereafter occupy a sphere of contingency and human construction where their status, titles, and house of assembly would conceivably be abolished anew, where the nobles recognize themselves at a deep level as now suffering the sufferance of the people.[11]

This passage describes the circumstances in which Shaftesbury conceived a utopia of aesthetic contemplation, freed of the contingencies of [his] social existence; it does not discredit his ideas. It may be true, as the writer of the passage argues, that "Shaftesbury's double displacement first of the political onto the ethical and then of the ethical onto the aesthetic would effectively obscure in later years the ideological role of his writing in assisting to legitimate the Whig consensual polity."[12] But Shaftesbury's work influenced the work of Kant, Schiller, and the Victorian social critics (it informs Arnold's conception of culture) and cannot be *reduced* to "Whig consensual polity."

I have cited Linda Dowling, whose short and excellent book *The Vulgarization of Art: The Victorians and Aesthetic Democracy* (an essay of only 100 pages) exemplifies what is admirable, but rare, in ideological interpretation. Her account of the conditions under which aesthetic ideas arise illuminates their motives, but does not cause her to prejudge the value of those ideas. Her view of the ideas themselves is complex. She appreciates their character as a moral critique of the constitution of society, particularly in her discussion of Schiller's *On an Aesthetic Education of Man*. Her engagement with the ideas is philosophical rather than ideological, when, for instance, she follows Alasdair MacIntyre in his view of how Shaftesbury's "rejection . . . of the traditional Aristotelian ideas concerning the essential nature and telos of human beings [and his reliance on 'the natural passions of the individual'] makes it henceforth impossible to supply anything like a traditional account of the virtues."[13] Dowling's work, influenced by current ideological concerns in the academy, displays the possibility of disinterestedness that is the occasion for her discussion.

There are lessons to be drawn from her account of the aesthetic tradition. From its very beginnings, there has been a tension between its emphasis on distinction (hence its elitism) and its ambition to become the spiritual basis of democracy, an expression of the *sensus communis* in Shaftesbury's phrase. This tension is evident in Arnold's aristocratic conception of cultural distinction, on the one hand, and his view of culture as a force that wishes "to do away with classes," on the other. Arnold wanted to democratize society on his high cultural terms. But democracy cannot exist without the consent of the people, who are formed by a mass culture and who may not be "in communication with the realm of transcendental value"[14] where beauty can be found or who may find beauty in sources other than the transcendental realm (popular culture, for instance). If the aesthetic sense is to have the power not only to express beauty, but to transform social reality (Schiller's view), it can do so only with the consent of the people, otherwise it would become another form of tyranny. We in the academy are the heirs to this unresolvable tension, which may not be an undesirable condition, so long as we understand that it cannot be resolved. The canon will always be under pressure, at once resistant and accommodating to change. The danger arises when the tension becomes a war in which adversaries try to resolve it one way or the other.

So long as this tension remains unresolved, debate will persist. I do not foresee (nor do I think desirable) a return to a time (largely imaginary) when the professional imperative was the contemplation of the aesthetic qualities of a work of art, exclusive of political, historical, and moral considerations—of the sort recently advocated by Harold Bloom in *The Western Canon*. Bloom, it should be remarked, does not deny the political and social dimensions of literary production:

> Canons always do indirectly serve the social and political, and indeed the spiritual, concerns and aims of the wealthier classes of each generation of Western society. It seems clear that capital is necessary for the cultivation of aesthetic values. Pindar, the superb last champion of archaic lyric, invested his art in the celebratory exercise of exchanging odes for grand prices, thus praising the wealthy for their generous support of his generous exaltation of their divine lineage. This alliance of sublimity and financial and political power has never ceased, and presumably never can or will.[15]

There are exceptions to the alliance of sublimity and financial and political power (Bloom mentions Blake and Whitman), but he has caught hold of a main truth that G. Wilson Knight anticipated in his discussion of Shakespeare. There is an imperial dimension in the greatest imaginations. Shakespeare's imagination fed on the expansive powers of Elizabethan political and social life, Dante's on the insurgent energies of the Italian cities in the Renaissance. The political and social are inescapable in experiencing and understanding the energies of art. Do we demystify the sublimity in order to show it to be a reflex or function of crude power, or do we appreciate the *sublimation* of power? Sublimity is the sublimation of power and to the extent that it resists demystification it is an object of aesthetic criticism.

In characterizing the aesthetic tradition, I focused on its major strain, that of Shaftesbury, Kant, Schiller, and Arnold: the strain of disinterested contemplation of the beautiful. There are other aesthetic discourses, for instance, those of Addison and Hogarth, as Ronald Paulson has demonstrated, that challenge the aesthetics of disinterestedness. In Paulson's account the aesthetics of Hogarth finds its way not only in Hogarth's practice as a visual artist, but also in the work of novelists and poets, among them Henry Fielding, John Cleland, Laurence Sterne, and Oliver Goldsmith. Even Dr. Johnson opposes the Shaftesburian aesthetic in "its distancing of art from life." Johnson valued art's involvement with human life.[16] It would be unfortunate if I was understood as proposing the aesthetic as a monolith and itself not a field of contention. My own disposition is more Shaftesburian than Hogarthean. What I am proposing, however, is a revival of interest in aesthetics. Ideology critique has taken as its object of attack aesthetics itself, not simply its tradition of disinterested contemplation of the beautiful.

Politics in and of art need not be the object of the demystifier's eye, searching for motives of domination. In our democratic age we should be able to appreciate what is valuable in the imagination of an aristocratic conception of life in the works of the ancient Greek poets or the spiritual aspirations in the religious imaginations of Dante and Milton. It is not history or politics that is inimical to the artistic imagination, but tendentious and impoverished conceptions of history and politics.

We should also be able to recover an idea of culture which provides a vantage point to criticize what is corrupt and degraded in contemporary political and social life. The new discipline of cultural studies promotes ideological criticism of what is seen as the pretensions of high culture. The cause of high culture has been largely taken up by neoconservatives outside the academy whose stridency often gives it a sectarian coloration that compromises its spirit. Left and right provoke stridency in each other. Robert Hughes neatly sums up the current situation: "Radical academic and cultural conservatives are now locked in a full-blown, mutually sustaining *folie à deux*, and the only person each dislikes more than the other is the one who tells them both to lighten up."[17] What we need to do is to disengage cultural criticism from the distortions in the current practices of left and right politics.

The vitality of a culture (its literature, music, and art) depends on the capacity of readers, spectators, and listeners to discriminate among their experiences. An intelligent criticism responsive to aesthetic value can instruct and inspire the confidence of artists in their own work. Newspapers, nonacademic and a few academic journals in their cultural columns continue to do the work of appreciation and discrimination with and without distinction.[18] (There is a division between nonacademic journalism and the academy that periodically flares up into outright hostility between them.) Journalism, however, is not a sufficient medium for aesthetic criticism, no matter how gifted some of its practitioners may be. For the most part, journalists lack the scholarship, the training, and the time for the kind of reflection necessary for serious criticism. The corrosive skepticism about aesthetic value in the academy (where the work of serious criticism is supposed to take place) necessarily has a harmful effect on the cultural life. If aesthetic appreciation and discrimination are not thought about and taught in the schools, they are bound to atrophy in the educated population.

Since nothing lasts forever, we might ask what will or should happen when the hermeneutics of suspicion will have exhausted itself and the desire for the pleasures of reading returns to the academy. Will we be able to revive the capacity for aesthetic response, and what form would the revival take? A return to the status quo ante (that is, to the time before the advent of critical theory) is neither possible nor desirable. To the ideology critics, the social theorists, the moral philosophers, the metaphysicians, Harold Bloom urges "a stubborn resistance whose single aim is to preserve poetry as fully and purely as possible."[19] But should we resist the political genius of Shakespeare's history plays, or the theological interest of *The Divine Comedy* or *Paradise Lost*, and simply regard it as trope or metaphor? Should we ignore the remarkable sociological and moral imagination of *Middlemarch*? Retrieving the literary from the ideology critics does not require us to return to a time when readers of Eliot, if not of Pound, turned a blind eye to his anti-Semitism or simply discounted it. It does require us to resist our premature impulse to pass moral and political judgment. Literary experience is not a pure thing; it is an amalgam of interests that includes the political, the historical, the ethical, and so on, but not necessarily at the expense of the aesthetic.

My argument represents an ongoing effort on my part to reenfranchise certain ideas that have become disreputable in the humanities: objectivity, disinterestedness, tradition, aesthetic appreciation. I think their loss of credit is a misfortune for the academy. They are or should be the common possession of scholars of whatever political or cultural persuasion: left, right, or center. Which is not to say that it is a bad thing for these ideas to have been put under the kind of pressure that forces a reformulation and strengthening of them. To agree on their necessity in intellectual exchange is not to agree about everything, but it may create the possibility of overcoming the current academic

Balkanization in which one always seeks the comfort zone of the like-minded or prepares to do battle with the enemy.

## NOTES

1. Eugene Goodheart, *The Reign of Ideology* (New York: Columbia University Press, 1996), 19.

2. Jane Gallop, "The Institutionalization of Feminist Criticism," in *English Inside and Out: The Places of Literary Criticism*, ed. Susan Gubar and Jonathon Kamholtz (New York: Routledge, 1993), 65.

3. Gerald Graff, *Professing Literature: An Institutional History* (Chicago: University of Chicago Press, 1987), 123–24.

4. Harold Bloom, *The Western Canon: The Books and School of the Ages* (New York: Harcourt, Brace, 1994), 1.

5. George Levine, "Introduction: Reclaiming the Aesthetic," in *Aesthetics and Ideology*, ed. George Levine (New Brunswick, N.J.: Rutgers University Press, 1994), 11.

6. Levine, in *Aesthetics and Ideology*, 21.

7. Levine, in *Aesthetics and Ideology*, 14.

8. Evelyn Fox Keller, "Science and Its Critics," in *The Future of Academic Freedom*, ed. Louis Menand (Chicago: University of Chicago Press, 1996), 204.

9. Peter Brooks, "Aesthetics and Ideology—What Happened to Poetics?" in *Aesthetics and Ideology*, ed. George Levine (New Brunswick, N.J.: Rutgers University Press, 1994), 158.

10. Jerome Stolnitz, *Aesthetics and the Philosophy of Art Criticism* (Boston: Houghton Mifflin, 1960), 34–35.

11. Linda Dowling, *The Vulgarization of Art: The Victorians and Aesthetic Democracy* (Charlottesville: University Press of Virginia, 1996), 4.

12. Dowling, *The Vulgarization of Art*, 13.

13. Dowling, *The Vulgarization of Art*, 10.

14. Dowling, *The Vulgarization of Art*, 61.

15. Bloom, *The Western Canon*, 33.

16. See Ronald Paulson, *The Beautiful, Novel, and Strange: Aesthetics and Heterodoxy* (Baltimore, Md.: Johns Hopkins University Press, 1996).

17. Robert Hughes, *The Culture of Complaint: The Fraying of America* (New York: Oxford University Press, 1993), 79.

18. See Morris Dickstein, "Journalism as Criticism," in *Double Agent: The Critic and Society* (New York: Oxford University Press, 1992), 55–67.

19. Bloom, *The Western Canon*, 18.

# PART VII
## RESTORING REASON

IT SHOULD COME as no surprise that in order to separate language from reality, and to treat words as the preeminent building blocks of life, a major assault on rationality and science had to be launched. Absent such an assault, the writings of Theorists would be too readily exposed for what they are: strategies to gain center stage. But if these Theorists could successfully convince other intellectuals that they, and they alone, had access to some fundamental understanding—that their expertise gave them exclusive tools with which to demystify the prestige of science and philosophy—they would have gained a great victory. And for a time it seemed as though such a prize had been won, as academics with limited or no training in science, philosophy, and related fields denounced these disciplines in a tone of easy superiority that has been characterized (as noted in Susan Haack's essay in this section) as the "Higher Dismissiveness."

In the past decade, however, the reaction against Theory's dismissive rhetoric has gained ever stronger allies. Even some of those who had themselves contributed to the attack on science (an assault institutionalized in academe under the name "science and technology studies") have had second thoughts. Thus we find Bruno Latour sounding a mea culpa in a recent issue of *Critical Inquiry*.[1] But Latour is hardly the first. Other voices have long been protesting against the irrationalism that today's "post-isms" seem not only to generate but to authorize. They are voices seldom heard in humanities seminars, however, where the claims of Theory still predominate.

In this part we offer more than ten years' worth of key statements aimed at the restoration of rational inquiry to the discussion of Theory. We start with Noam Chomsky's strong arguments against decades of intellectual posturing and "knowingness." Chomsky directly engages the issues and challenges the rhetoric predominant in attacks on science and reason—which he finds objectionable even when the attacks come from political allies and friends. He emphasizes the self-destructive potential of assaults on rational inquiry, to which, he argues, there are no viable alternatives. His warning is reiterated and extended by Meera Nanda at the end of this section.

Jean Bricmont and Alan Sokal, mathematical physicists both, attempt to explain once again why they wrote *Impostures Intellectuelles* (published in English in 1998 as *Fashionable Nonsense: Postmodern Intellectuals' Abuse of Science*). Their book grew out of Sokal's now-famous hoax that demonstrated how readily some leading American theorists of cultural studies accepted a deliberately senseless and pretentious piece of writing, as long as it attacked science and, buttressed by quotations from well-known theorists, claimed to prove that there is no "reality." Their essay explores reactions to their book, which documents in detail the misuse of scientific terminology by famous French theorists such as Baudrillard, Kristeva, Lacan, Latour, and Lyotard, among others.

Sokal and Bricmont's book is also the subject of Thomas Nagel's essay, which summarizes the downright charlatanism and abysmal ignorance of science replete in the work of prominent French intellectuals still much admired and taught today. Nagel examines why science is both envied and disparaged and how the work of philosophers of science such as Kuhn and Feyerabend, so influential in postmodernist writing, has been used to justify an extreme relativism, the fallacies of which he sets out.

Susan Haack takes on an idea that is virtually an orthodoxy in many humanities departments: there are no such things as truth and facts. Exploring our "epistemic situation," she argues against both the dismissal of all knowledge merely because it is fallible and the rejection of all evidence because it is tarred by subjectivity. Only by understanding the nature of rational inquiry, she contends, can we get beyond the "Higher Dismissiveness" so prevalent today in attacks not only on science but also on the very possibility of truth, fact, and evidence.

One of the consequences of skepticism about knowledge and evidence has been a compensatory effort to explain the world by other means. Currently, the most popular strategy for doing so is an extreme form of "social constructionism," and it is this concept that Paul Boghossian analyzes. He begins by distinguishing between constructionist propositions about things and facts, on the one hand, and, on the other, claims aimed at our beliefs, going on to take apart the arguments of a number of leading proponents of these points. While acknowledging the value of social constructionism when it is allied to sound scientific reasoning, Boghossian objects to it as a general theory of knowledge and offers several explanations to account for the appeal of what ought, by now, to be considered a discredited approach.

Concluding this section, Meera Nanda's essay provides a current example of the practical harm done in the developing world by attacks on science and reason and their demonization as "Western" impositions. Turning her attention to her native India, Nanda explores the influence of postcolonial theorists (such as Gayatri Spivak and her followers), whose work has contributed to the growing power of right-wing Hindu politicians. When postcolonial theory is allied to antirational science studies, Nanda argues, the result is an endorsement of dominant cultural-religious institutions that use the vocabulary of "local knowledges" to resist modernization and thereby consolidate their own power. The ironic, and potentially tragic, outcome is that progressive postcolonial and postmodern scholars become defenders of the conservative positions of traditional elites in postcolonial societies.

## NOTE

1.  Bruno Latour, "Why Has Critique Run out of Steam? From Matters of Fact to Matters of Concern," *Critical Inquiry* 30, no. 2 (Winter 2004): 225–48. Latour, a founder of the field of "science studies," these days worries that all political sides have learned to play the game of challenging facts, to the point that, as he puts it, "good matters of fact [are now] disguised as bad ideological biases!"

## 35.  RATIONALITY/SCIENCE

### NOAM CHOMSKY

THIS DISCUSSION [about science and reason] involves people with a large range of shared aspirations and commitments; in some cases at least, friends who have worked and struggled together for many years. I hope, then, that I can be quite frank. And personal, since, to be honest, I don't see much of independent substance to discuss.

I think I understand some of what is said in the six papers to which I am responding, and I agree with much of it.[1] What I don't understand is the topic: the legitimacy of "rationality," "science," and "logic" (perhaps modified by "Western")—call the amalgam "rational inquiry," for brevity. Frankly, I do not really grasp what the issue is supposed to be.

Many interesting questions have been raised about rational inquiry. There are problems about justification of belief, the status of mathematical truth and of theoretical entities, the use to which rational inquiry is put under particular social and cultural conditions and the way such conditions influence its course, and so on. These, however, are not the kinds of topics we are to address; rather, something about the legitimacy of the entire enterprise. That I find perplexing, for several reasons.

First, to take part in a discussion, one must understand the ground rules. In this case, I don't. In particular, I don't know the answers to such elementary questions as these: Are conclusions to be consistent with premises (maybe even follow from them)? Do facts matter? Or can we string together thoughts as we like, calling it an "argument," and make facts up as we please, taking one story to be as good as another? There are certain familiar ground rules: those of rational inquiry. They are by no means entirely clear, and there have been interesting efforts to criticize and clarify them; but we have enough of a grasp to proceed over a broad range. What seems to be under discussion here is whether we should abide by these ground rules at all (trying to improve them as we proceed). If the answer is that we are to abide by them, then the discussion is over: we've implicitly accepted the legitimacy of rational inquiry. If they are to be abandoned, then we cannot proceed until we learn what replaces the commitment to consistency, responsibility to fact, and other outdated notions. Short of some instruction on this matter, we are reduced to primal screams. I see no hint in the papers here of any new procedures or ideas to replace the old, and therefore remain perplexed.

Noam Chomsky. "Rationality/Science." Abridged from *Z Papers* 1, no. 4 (October–December 1992): 52–57.

A second problem has to do with the allusions to "science," "rationality," etc., throughout these papers. These targets are sharply criticized, but they are not clearly identified. True, they are assigned certain properties. But these are either irrelevant to the issue raised or unrecognizable to me; in many cases, the properties attributed to rational inquiry are antithetic to it, at least as I have always understood this endeavor.

Perhaps my failure to recognize what is called here "science," etc., reflects personal limitations. That could well be, but I wonder. For some forty years, I've been actively engaged in what I, and others, regard as rational inquiry (science, mathematics); for almost all of those years, I've been at the very heart of the beast, at MIT. When I attend seminars, read technical papers in my own or other fields, and work with students and colleagues, I have no problem in recognizing what is before me as rational inquiry. In contrast, the descriptions presented here scarcely resemble anything in my experience in these areas, or understanding of them. So, there is a second problem.

With regard to the first problem, I'm afraid I see only one way to proceed: by assuming the legitimacy of rational inquiry. Suppose that such properties as consistency and responsibility to fact are old-fashioned misconceptions, to be replaced by something different—something to be grasped, perhaps, by intuition that I seem to lack. Then I can only confess my inadequacies, and inform the reader in advance of the irrelevance of what follows. I recognize that by accepting the legitimacy of rational inquiry and its canons, I am begging the question; the discussion is over before it starts. That is unfair, no doubt, but the alternative escapes me.

With regard to the second problem, since what is called "science," etc., is largely unfamiliar to me, let me replace it by "X," and see if I understand the argument against X. Let's consider several kinds of properties attributed to X, then turning to the proposals for a new direction; quotes below are from the papers criticizing X.

First category. X is dominated by "the white male gender." It is "limited by cultural, racial and gender biases," and "establishes and perpetuates social organization [with] hidden political, social and economic purposes." "The majority in the South has waited for the last four hundred years for compassionate humane uses of X," which is "outside and above the democratic process." X is "thoroughly embedded in capitalist colonialism," and doesn't "end racism or disrupt the patriarchy." X has been invoked by Soviet commissars to bring people to "embrace regimentation, murderous collectivization, and worse"; though no one mentions it, X has been used by Nazi ideologists for the same ends. X's dominance "has gone unchallenged." It has been "used to create new forms of control mediated through political and economic power." Ludicrous claims about X have been made by "state systems" which "used X for astoundingly destructive purposes . . . to create new forms of control mediated through political and economic power as it emerged in each system."

Conclusion: there is "something inherently wrong" with X. We must reject or transcend it, replacing it by something else; and we must instruct poor and suffering people to do likewise. It follows that we must abandon literacy and the arts, which surely have the properties attributed to X as much as science does. More generally, we must take a vow of silence and induce the world's victims to do so likewise since language and its use typically have all these properties, facts too well-known to discuss.

Even more obviously, the crafts and technology should be utterly abolished. It is surprising that several of these critiques appear to be lauding the "practical logical thinking" of "technologists" who concentrate on "the mechanics of things," the technical knowledge ("T-knowledge") that is "embedded in practice" and rooted in "experience"; that is, the kind of thinking and practice which, notoriously, have been used for millennia to construct tools of destruction and oppression, under the control of the white males who dominate them (I say "appear to be," because the intent is not entirely clear). The inconsistency is startling, though admittedly, if consistency is to be abandoned or transcended, there is no problem.

Plainly, what I've reviewed can't be the argument; these cannot be the properties of rational inquiry that lead us to abandon (or transcend) it. So let us turn to a second category of properties attributed to X.

X is "E-knowledge"—expert knowledge or "episteme"—"obtained by logical deduction from firmly established first principles." The statements in X must be "provable"; X demands "absolute proofs." The "most distinctive component of Western E-knowledge" may be its "elaborate procedures for arriving at acceptable first principles." These are among the few attempts here to define or identify the villain.

Furthermore, X "claims to a monopoly of knowledge." It thus denies, say, that I know how to tie my shoes, or know that the sky is dark at night or that walking in the woods is enjoyable, or know the names of my children and something about their concerns, etc.; all such aspects of my (intuitive) knowledge are far beyond what can be "obtained by logical deduction from firmly established first principles," indeed well beyond the reach of rational inquiry now and perhaps ever, and is therefore mere "superstition, belief, prejudice," according to advocates of X. Or if not denying such knowledge outright, X "marginalizes and denigrates" it. X postulates dogmatically that "a predictable end point can be known in advance as an expression of X-achieved truth," and insists upon "grounding values in [this] objective truth." It denies the "provisional and subjective foundations" of agreement in human life and action, and considers itself "the ultimate organizing principle and source of legitimacy in modern society," a doctrine to which X assigns "axiomatic status." X is "arrogant" and "absolutist." What doesn't fall "within the terms of its hegemony . . . —anger, desire, pleasure, and pain, for example—becomes a site for disciplinary action." The varieties of X are presented as "charms to get us through the dark of a complex world," providing a "resting place" that offers a "sure way of 'knowing' the world or one's position in it." The practitioner of X "screens out feeling, recreating the Other as object to be manipulated," a procedure "made easier because the subjective is described as irrelevant or un-X." "To feel was to be anti-X." "By mid twentieth century the phrase 'it works' came to be enough for X-ists," who no longer care "why it worked," and lost interest in "what its implications" are. And so on.

I quite agree that X should be consigned to the flames. But what that has to do with our topic escapes me, given that these attributions scarcely rise to the level of a caricature of rational inquiry (science, etc.), at least as I'm familiar with it.

Take the notion of "E-knowledge," the sole definition of science presented here. Not even set theory (hence conventional mathematics) satisfies the definition offered. Nothing in the sciences even resembles it. As for "provability," or "absolute proofs," the notions are foreign to the natural sciences. They appear in the study of abstract models, which are part of pure mathematics until they are applied in the empirical sciences, at which point we no longer have "proof." If "elaborate procedures," or any general procedures, exist "for arriving at acceptable first principles," they have been kept a dark mystery.

Science is tentative, exploratory, questioning, largely learned by doing. One of the world's leading physicists was famous for opening his introductory classes by saying that it doesn't matter what we cover, but what we *dis*cover, maybe something that will challenge prevailing beliefs if we are fortunate. More advanced work is to a large extent a common enterprise in which students are expected to come up with new ideas, to question and often undermine what they read and are taught, and to somehow pick up, by experience and cooperative inquiry, the trick (which no one begins to comprehend) of discerning important problems and possible solutions to them. Furthermore, even in the simplest cases, proposed solutions (theories, large or small) "outrun empiricism," if by "empiricism" we mean what can be derived from experience by some procedure; one hardly has to move to Einstein to exhibit that universal trait of rational inquiry.

As for the cited properties of X, they do hold of some aspects of human thought and action: elements of organized religion, areas of the humanities and "social sciences" where understanding and insight are thin and it is therefore easier to get away with dogmatism and falsification, perhaps others. But the sciences, at least as I am familiar with them, are as remote from these descriptions as anything in human life. It is not that scientists are inherently more honest, open, or questioning. It is simply that nature and logic impose a harsh discipline: in many domains, one can spin fanciful tales with impunity or keep to the most boring clerical work (sometimes called "scholarship"); in the sciences, your tales will be refuted and you will be left behind by students who want to understand something about the world, not satisfied to let such matters be "someone else's concern." Furthermore, all of this seems to be the merest truism.

Other properties are attributed to X, including some that are presumably intended as caricature: e.g., that practitioners of X claim "that seventeenth-century Europe answered all the basic questions of humankind for all times to come." I've tried to select a fair sample, and apologize if I've failed. As far as I can see, the properties assigned to rational inquiry by the critics fall into two categories. Some hold of human endeavor rather generally and are thus irrelevant to the issue (unless we mean to abandon language, the arts, etc., as well); they clearly reflect the social and cultural conditions that lead to the outcome that is properly deplored. Others do not hold of rational inquiry, indeed are flatly rejected by it; where detected, they would elicit internal critique.

Several writers appear to regard Leninist-Stalinist tyranny as an embodiment of science and rationality. Thus, they argue, "the belief in a universal narrative grounded in truth has been undermined by the collapse of political systems that were supposed to [have] produced the New Socialist Man and the New Postcolonial Man." And the "state systems" that "used positive rationality for astoundingly destructive purposes" were guided by "socialist and capitalist ideologies"—a reference, it appears, to radically antisocialist (Leninist) and anticapitalist (state-capitalist) ideologies. Since "scientific and technological progress were the watchword of socialist and capitalist ideologies," we see that their error and perversity is deep, and we must abandon them, along with any concern for freedom, justice, human rights, democracy, and other "watchwords" of the secular priesthood who have perverted Enlightenment ideals in the interests of the masters.

Some of the commentary is more familiar to me. One contributor calls for "plural involvement and clear integration in which everyone sits at the table sharing a common consciousness," inspired by "a moral concept which is linked to social trust and affection in which people tell what they think they see and do and allow the basic data and conclusions to be cross examined by peers and non-peers alike"—not a bad description of many seminars and working groups that I've been fortunate enough to be part of over the years. In these, furthermore, it is taken for granted that "knowledge is produced, not found, fought for—not given," a sentiment that will be applauded by anyone who has been engaged in the struggle to understand hard questions, as much as to the activists to whom it is addressed.

There is also at least an element of truth in the statement that the natural sciences are "disembedded from the body, from metaphorical thought, from ethical thought and from the world"—to their credit. Though rational inquiry is rife with metaphor and (uncontroversially) embedded in the world, its intent is to understand, not to construct doctrine that accords with some ethical or other preferences, or that is confused by metaphor. Though scientists are human, and cannot get out of their skins, they certainly, if honest, try to overcome the distortions imposed by "body" (in particular, human cognitive structures, with their specific properties) as much as possible. Surface appearances and "natural categories," however central to human life, can mislead, again uncontroversially; we "see" the sun set and the moon illusion, but we have learned that there is more to it than that.

It is also true that "reason separates the 'real' or knowable . . . and the 'not real,'" or at least tries to (without identifying "real" with "knowable")—again, to its credit. At least, I know that I try to make this distinction, whether studying questions that are hard, like the origins of human knowledge, or relatively easy, like the sources and character of U.S. foreign policy. In the latter case, for example, I would try, and urge others to try, to separate the real operative factors from the various tales that are spun in the interests of power and privilege. If that is a fault, I plead guilty, and will compound my guilt by urging others to err in the same way.

Keeping to the personal level, I have spent a lot of my life working on questions such as these, using the only methods I know of—those condemned here as "science," "rationality," "logic," and so on. I therefore read the papers with some hope that they would help me "transcend" these limitations, or perhaps suggest an entirely different course. I'm afraid I was disappointed. Admittedly, that may be my own limitation. Quite regularly, "my eyes glaze over" when I read polysyllabic discourse on the themes of poststructuralism and postmodernism; what I understand is largely truism or error, but that is only a fraction of the total word count. True, there are lots of other things I don't understand: the articles in the current issues of math and physics journals, for example. But there is a difference. In the latter case, I know how to get to understand them, and have done so, in cases of particular interest to me; and I also know that people in these fields can explain the contents to me at my level, so that I can gain what (partial) understanding I may want. In contrast, no one seems to be able to explain to me why the latest post-this-and-that is (for the most part) other than truism, error, or gibberish, and I do not know how to proceed. Perhaps the explanation lies in some personal inadequacy, like tone deafness. Or there may be other reasons. The question is not strictly relevant here, and I won't pursue it.

Continuing with my personal quest for help in dealing with problems to which I have devoted a large part of my life, I read here that I should recognize that "there are limits to what we know" (something I've been arguing, in accord with an ancient rationalist tradition, for many years). I should advance beyond "panopticized rationality" (which I might happily do, if I knew what it was), and should not be "transferring God into knowable nature" (thanks). Since "it is now obvious" that its "very narrow and surface idea of rationality and rationalism" has undermined "the canon of Western thought," I should adopt "a new notation system which laid out moral and historical propositions" in a "rationality [that is] deepened" (thanks again). I should keep to "rebuttable axioms," which means, I take it, hypotheses that are taken to be open to question—the practice adopted without a second thought in all scientific work, unless the intent is that I should drop Modus Ponens and the axioms of arithmetic; apparently so, since I am also to abandon "absolutism or absolute proofs," which are unknown in science but, admittedly, sometimes assumed with regard to the most elementary parts of logic and arithmetic (a matter also subject to much internal controversy in foundational inquiries).

I should also follow the lead of those who "assert that there is a common consciousness of all thought and matter," from human to "vegetable or mineral," a proposal that should impinge directly on my own attempts for many years to understand what Hume called "the secret springs and origins, by which the human mind is actuated in its operations"—or might, if I had the slightest idea what it means. I am also enjoined to reject the idea that "numbers are outside of human history" and to regard Gödel's incompleteness theorem as "a situation of inability" of the twentieth century, which to my old-fashioned ear, sounds like saying that the irrationality of the square root of two—a disturbing discovery at the time—was "a situation of inability" of classical Greece. How human history or the way rationality "is presently defined" impinge on these truths (or so I thought them to be), I again fail to see.

I should regard "Truth" not "as an essence" but "as a social heuristic," one "predicated on intersubjective trust and story telling whether through narrative or numbers and signs." I should recognize that "scientific endeavor is also in the world of story and myth creation," no better or worse than other "stories and myths"; modern physics may "have more funding and better PR" than astrology, but is otherwise on a par. That suggestion does in fact help solve my problems. If I can just tell stories about the questions that I've been struggling with for many years, life will indeed be easier; the proposal "has all the advantages of theft over honest toil," as Bertrand Russell once said in a similar connection.

I should also "favor particular directions in scientific and social inquiry because of their likely positive social outcomes," thus joining the overwhelming mass of scientists and engineers—though we commonly differ on what are "positive social outcomes," and no hints are given here as to how that issue is to be resolved. The implication also seems to be that we should abandon "theories or experiments" favored "because of their supposed beauty and elegance," which amounts to saying that we should abandon the effort to understand the mysteries of the world; and by the same logic, presumably, should no longer be deluded by literature, music, and the visual arts.

I'm afraid I didn't learn much from these injunctions. And it is hard for me to see how friends and colleagues in the "nonwhite world" will learn more from the advice given by "a handful of scientists" who inform them that they should not "move on the tracks of Western science and technology," but should prefer other "stories" and "myths"—which ones, we are not told, though astrology is mentioned. They'll find that advice a great help with their problems, and those of the "nonwhite world" generally. I confess that my personal sympathies lie with the volunteers of Tecnica.

In fact, the entire idea of "white male science" reminds me, I'm afraid, of "Jewish physics." Perhaps it is another inadequacy of mine, but when I read a scientific paper, I can't tell whether the author is white or is male. The same is true of discussion of work in class, the office, or somewhere else. I rather doubt that the nonwhite, nonmale students, friends, and colleagues with whom I work would be much impressed with the doctrine that their thinking and understanding differ from "white male science" because of their "culture or gender and race." I suspect that "surprise" would not be quite the proper word for their reaction.

I find it depressing, frankly, to read learned left discourse on science and technology as a white male preserve, and then to walk through the corridors at MIT and see the significant results of the efforts to change that traditional pattern on the part of scientists and engineers, many of them very remote from the understanding of "positive social outcomes" that we largely share. They have dedicated serious and often successful efforts to overcome traditional exclusiveness and privilege because they tend to agree with Descartes (as I do) that the capacity for understanding in the "profoundest sciences" and "high feeling" is a common human attribute, and that those who lack the opportunity to exercise the capacity to inquire, create, and understand are missing out on some of life's most wonderful experiences. One contributor condemns this humane belief for labeling others as "defective." By the same logic, we should condemn the idea that the capacity to walk is a common human possession over a very broad range.

Acting on the same belief, many scientists, not too long ago, took an active part in the lively working-class culture of the day, seeking to compensate for the class character of the cultural institutions through programs of workers' education, or by writing books on mathematics, science, and other topics for the general public. Nor have left intellectuals been alone in such work, by any means. It strikes me as remarkable that their left counterparts today should seek to deprive oppressed people not only of the joys of understanding and insight, but also of tools of emancipation, informing us that the "project of the Enlightenment" is dead, that we must abandon the "illusions" of science and rationality—a message that will gladden the hearts of the powerful, delighted to monopolize these instruments for their own use. They will be no less delighted to hear that science (E-knowledge) is intrinsically a "knowledge system that legitimates the authority of the boss," so that any challenge to such authority is a violation of rationality itself—a radical change from the days when workers' education was considered a means of emancipation and liberation. One recalls the days when the evangelical church taught not-dissimilar lessons to the unruly masses as part of what E. P. Thompson called "the psychic processes of counter-revolution," as their heirs do today in peasant societies of Central America.

I'm sorry if the conclusion sounds harsh; the question we should consider is whether it is correct. I think it is.

It is particularly striking that these self-destructive tendencies should appear at a time when the overwhelming majority of the population regard the economic system as "inherently unfair" and want to change it. Through the Reagan years, the public continued its drift towards social democratic ideas, while the shreds of what existed were torn away. Furthermore, belief in the basic moral principles of traditional socialism is surprisingly high: to mention merely one example, almost half the population consider the phrase "from each according to his ability, to each according to his need" to be such an obvious truth that they attribute it to the U.S. Constitution, a text taken to be akin to Holy Writ. What is more, with Soviet tyranny finally overthrown, one long-standing impediment to the realization of these ideals is now removed.

With limited contribution by left intellectuals, large segments of the population have involved themselves in urgent and pressing problems: repression, environmental concerns, and much else. In these and numerous other cases, including domestic affairs and problems, the thoughts are individual and private; people have rarely if ever heard them publicly expressed. In part, that reflects the effectiveness of the system of cultural management; in part, the choices of left intellectuals. Quite generally, there is a popular basis for addressing the human concerns that have long been part of "the Enlightenment project." One element that is lacking is the participation of left intellectuals.

As left intellectuals abandon the field, truths that were once understood fade into individual memories, history is reshaped into an instrument of power, and the ground is laid for the enterprises to come.

The critique of "science" and "rationality" has many merits, which I haven't discussed. But as far as I can see, where valid and useful the critique is largely devoted to the perversion of the values of rational inquiry as they are "wrongly used" in a particular institutional setting. What is presented here as a deeper critique of their nature seems to me based on beliefs about the enterprise and its guiding values that have little basis. No coherent alternative is suggested, as far as I can discern; the reason, perhaps, is that there is none. What is suggested is a path that leads directly to disaster for people who need help—which means everyone, before too long.

NOTE

1. Editors' note: The original essays, by Marcus Raskin, Stephen Marglin, Ashis Nandy, Frédérique Marglin, Kate Ellis, and Wahneema Lubiano, with responses by Chomsky, Barbara Ehrenreich, and Michael Albert, were published in *Z Papers* 1, no. 4 (October–Decem-

ber 1992). They are available at http://www.zmag.org/ScienceWars/sciencetoc.htm. *Z Papers* was a quarterly periodical published by *Z Magazine* between 1992 and 1994. Although *Z Papers* is now defunct, *Z Magazine* continues.

## 36. THE FUROR OVER *IMPOSTURES INTELLECTUELLES*

### WHAT IS ALL THE FUSS ABOUT?

#### JEAN BRICMONT AND ALAN SOKAL

THE PUBLICATION IN FRANCE of our book *Impostures intellectuelles*[1] appears to have created a small storm in certain intellectual circles. According to Jon Henley in *The Guardian*, we have shown that "modern French philosophy is a load of old tosh."[2] According to Robert Maggiori in *Libération*, we are humorless scientistic pedants who correct grammatical errors in love letters.[3] We shall try to explain here why neither is the case.

Some commentators go farther, attacking not our arguments but our alleged motivations for writing the book. Julia Kristeva, writing in *Le Nouvel Observateur*, accuses us of spreading "disinformation" as part of an anti-French politico-economic campaign;[4] she was even quoted (we hope misquoted) by the Italian daily *Corriere della Sera* as saying that we should undergo psychiatric treatment.[5] Vincent Fleury and Yun Sun Limet, again in *Libération*, accuse us of seeking to divert research funds from the social to the natural sciences.[6] These defenses are curious: for even if our motivations were indeed as ascribed (and they most certainly aren't), how would that affect the validity or invalidity of our arguments? We have the modest hope that calmer heads will soon prevail among both our supporters and our critics, so that the debate can focus on the substantive content of our book.

Which is what? The book grew out of the now-famous hoax in which one of us published, in the American cultural-studies journal *Social Text*, a parody article chock-full of nonsensical, but unfortunately authentic, quotes about physics and mathematics by prominent French and American intellectuals.[7] However, only a small fraction of the "dossier" discovered during Sokal's library research could be included in the parody. After showing this larger dossier to scientist and nonscientist friends, we became (slowly) convinced that it might be worth making it available to a wider audience. We wanted to explain, in nontechnical terms, why the quotes are absurd or, in many cases,

Jean Bricmont and Alan Sokal. "The Furor Over *Impostures Intellectuelles*: What Is All the Fuss About?" Originally published in the *Times Literary Supplement*, 17 October 1997, 17. Reprinted by permission of the authors.

simply meaningless; and we wanted also to discuss the cultural circumstances that enabled these discourses to achieve such prominence and to remain, thus far, unexposed. Hence our book, the noise, and the furor.

But what exactly do we claim in our book? Neither too much nor too little. We show that famous intellectuals such as Jacques Lacan, Julia Kristeva, Luce Irigaray, Jean Baudrillard, and Gilles Deleuze have repeatedly abused scientific concepts and terminology: either using scientific ideas totally out of context, without giving the slightest empirical or conceptual justification—note that we are not against extrapolating concepts from one field to another, but only against extrapolations made without argument—or throwing around scientific jargon to their nonscientist readers without any regard for its relevance or even its meaning. We make no claim that this invalidates the rest of their work, on which we are explicitly agnostic.

Note that we do not criticize the mere use of words like "chaos" (which, after all, goes back to the Bible) outside of their scientific context. Rather, we concentrate on the arbitrary invocation of technical notions such as Gödel's theorem or compact sets or noncommuting operators. Also, we have nothing against metaphors; we merely remark that the role of a metaphor is usually to clarify an unfamiliar concept by relating it to a more familiar one, not the reverse. Suppose, for example, that in a theoretical physics seminar we were to explain a very technical concept in quantum field theory by comparing it to the concept of aporia in Derridean literary theory. Our audience of physicists would wonder, quite reasonably, what purpose such a metaphor served (whether or not it was apposite), if not merely to display our own erudition. In the same way, we fail to see the advantage of invoking, even metaphorically, scientific concepts that one oneself understands only shakily when addressing a nonspecialist audience. Might the goal be to pass off as profound a rather banal philosophical or sociological observation, by dressing it up in fancy scientific jargon?

A secondary target of our book is epistemic relativism, namely the idea—which is much more widespread in the Anglo-Saxon world than in France—that modern science is nothing more than a "myth," a "narration," or a "social construction," among many others.[8] (Let us emphasize that our discussion is limited to epistemic/cognitive relativism; we do not address the more difficult issues of moral or aesthetic relativism.) Besides some gross abuses (e.g., Irigaray), we dissect a number of confusions that are rather frequent in postmodernist and cultural-studies circles: for example, abusing ideas from the philosophy of science such as the underdetermination of theory by evidence or the theory-dependence of observation in order to support radical relativism.

We are accused of being arrogant scientists, but our view of the hard sciences' role is in fact rather modest. Wouldn't it be nice (for us mathematicians and physicists, that is) if Gödel's theorem or relativity theory did have immediate and deep implications for the study of society? Or if the axiom of choice could be used to study poetry? Or if topology had something to do with the human psyche?

The reaction in France thus far has been mixed. Kristeva and others have accused us of being Francophobes. But for us, ideas have no nationality. There is no such thing as French thought or any country's thought, though there may of course be fashions and fads in certain places and certain times. It is understandable that the individuals criticized in our book would like to paint it as a global attack against French culture, but there is no reason for their compatriots to fall for such a maneuver. No one should ever feel obliged to follow the "national line" of the place where he or she happens to have been born, and no one has the right to define such a "line" for others. And as for the notion of "French thought," what do philosophers such as Diderot and Deleuze have in common, anyway (apart from the language)?

Nor do we attack all of contemporary French philosophy. We limit ourselves to abuses of physics and mathematics. Such well-known thinkers as Althusser, Barthes, and Foucault—who, as readers of the *TLS* will be well aware, have always had their supporters and detractors on both sides of the Channel—appear in our book only in a minor role, as cheerleaders for the texts we criticize.

Pascal Bruckner, writing in *Le Nouvel Observateur* in defense of Baudrillard, contrasted "an Anglo-Saxon culture based on facts and information" with "a French culture that plays rather on interpretation and style."[9] Coming from a British or American commentator, that assertion would be an expression of national prejudice, an insulting confusion of *haute culture* with *haute couture*. Is it any better coming from a Frenchman?

But these "nationalist" reactions are not typical. Many French scientists of course agree with us, but many French social scientists and literary intellectuals do as well. That makes sense: far from being an attack on the human sciences or philosophy in general, the purpose of our book is to support serious workers in these fields by publicly calling attention to cases of charlatanism. Should criticism of Lysenko be viewed as an attack on biology? And if we had refrained from pointing out these abuses—even though we regularly criticize much less blatant errors in our own research fields[10]—wouldn't that constitute an insulting double standard, as if to say "Why bother, the social sciences are all nonsense anyway?"

The revelations contained in our book should serve merely as an eye-opener. Bertrand Russell once explained that, having been educated at Cambridge within a Hegelian philosophical tradition, he changed his mind when he read what the master (Hegel) had written about mathematics, which he regarded (rightly) as "muddle-headed nonsense."[11] This doesn't prove that what Hegel says about other subjects is rubbish, but it does make one think. Especially when beliefs are accepted on the basis of fashion or dogma, they are sensitive to the exposure of even a marginal part of them. Consider, by contrast, Newton's work: it is estimated that 90 percent of his writings deal with alchemy or mysticism. But, so what? The rest survives because it is based on solid empirical and rational arguments. If the same can be said for the work of our authors, then our findings are of marginal relevance. But if these writers have become international stars for sociological rather than intellectual reasons, and in part because they are masters of language and can impress their audience with a clever abuse of sophisticated terminology—nonscientific as well as scientific—then what we say may indeed be useful.

## NOTES

The following bibliographical notes did not appear in the *TLS* when this essay was originally published.

1. Alan Sokal and Jean Bricmont, *Impostures intellectuelles* (Paris: Éditions Odile Jacob, 1997). Subsequently published in the United States and Canada under the title *Fashionable Nonsense: Postmodern Intellectuals' Abuse of Science* (New York: Picador, 1998); and in the U.K. under the title *Intellectual Impostures: Postmodern Philosophers' Abuse of Science* (London: Profile Books, 1998).

2. Jon Henley, "Euclidean, Spinozist, or Existentialist? Er, no. It's simply a load of old tosh," *The Guardian*, 1 October 1997, 3.

3. Robert Maggiori, "Fumée sans feu," *Libération*, 30 September 1997, 29.

4. Julia Kristeva, "Une Désinformation," *Le Nouvel Observateur*, 25 September 1997, 122.

5. Ulderico Munzi, " 'Francesi, intellettuali impostori': Americani all'attacco di Parigi," *Corriere della Sera*, 26 September 1997. Julia Kristeva's views are quoted as follows:

> La prima a reagire con vigore, anche perché è viva e vegeta e intravede un inutile "crimine di lesa maestà", è Julia Kristeva, filosofa e critica letteraria. Dice: "Il sandinista Sokal e Bricmont fanno disinformazione. Oltre tutto sono dei francofobi". A suo parere, dovrebbero sottoporsi entrambi a cure psichiatriche.

6. Vincent Fleury and Yun Sun Limet, "L'Escroquerie Sokal-Bricmont," *Libération*, 6 October 1997, 5. For a reply to the dishonest claims in this article, see Jean Bricmont and Alan Sokal, "Réponse à Vincent Fleury et Yun Sun Limet," *Libération*, 18–19 October 1997, 5.

7. Alan D. Sokal, "Transgressing the Boundaries: Toward a Transformative Hermeneutics of Quantum Gravity," *Social Text* 46/47 (Spring/Summer 1996):   217–52.

8. Concerning misuses of the notion of "social construction," see Ian Hacking, "Taking Bad Arguments Seriously," *London Review of Books*, 21 August 1997, 14–16.

9. Pascal Bruckner, "Le Risque de penser," *Le Nouvel Observateur*, 25 September 1997, 121.

10. See, for example, the critique by one of us of the work of Prigogine and Stengers: Jean Bricmont, "Science of Chaos or Chaos in Science?" *Physicalia Magazine* 17, nos. 3–4 (1995). Available online in gzip'ed (compressed) Postscript.

11. Bertrand Russell, "My Mental Development," in *The Philosophy of Bertrand Russell*, ed. Paul Arthur Schilpp (New York: Tudor, 1951), 11.

## 37. THE SLEEP OF REASON

### THOMAS NAGEL

I

You will remember that in 1996 a physicist at New York University named Alan Sokal brought off a delicious hoax that displayed the fraudulence of certain leading figures in cultural studies. He submitted to the journal *Social Text* an article entitled "Transgressing the Boundaries: Toward a Transformative Hermeneutics of Quantum Gravity," espousing the fashionable doctrine that scientific objectivity is a myth, and combining heavy technical references to contemporary physics and mathematics with patently ridiculous claims about their broader philosophical, cultural, and political significance, supported by quotations in similar vein from prominent figures like Lacan and Lyotard, and references to many more. The nonsense made of the science was so extreme that only a scientific ignoramus could have missed the joke.

Sokal's article expressed deep admiration for the views of two editors of *Social Text*, Stanley Aronowitz and Andrew Ross, quoting at length from Aronowitz's crack-brained social interpretations of quantum theory. The article was published in a special issue of *Social Text* devoted to science studies, Sokal revealed the hoax, and nothing has been quite the same since. We can hope that incompetents who pontificate about science as a social phenomenon without understanding the first thing about its content are on the way out, and that they may some day be as rare as deaf music critics.

The book *Fashionable Nonsense*, published originally in French under the title *Impostures intellectuelles* is a follow-up to the article. Sokal and his coauthor, Jean Bricmont, a physicist at the University of Louvain, decided to produce a fuller discussion of the witless invocations of science and math by intellectuals in other fields. Since the most prominent culprits were French, they first published their book in France, but since the influence of these figures on American literary theory, feminism, and cultural studies is substantial, it is good that it has been translated into English.

Nearly half the book consists of extensive quotations of scientific gibberish from name-brand French intellectuals, together with eerily patient explanations of why it is gibberish. This is amusing at first, but becomes gradually sickening. There is also a long and sensible chapter on skepticism, relativism, and the history and philosophy of science. An introduction and an epilogue discuss the political and cultural significance of the affair. Sokal's hilarious

Thomas Nagel. "The Sleep of Reason." Originally published in *The New Republic*, 12 October 1998, 32–38. Reprinted by permission of *The New Republic*.

parody, with its 109 footnotes and 219 references, is reprinted as an appendix, together with comments explaining many of the travesties of science that appear in it.

There are a few differences from the French version. Apart from minor changes, the authors have left out a chapter on Henri Bergson and his misunderstanding of the theory of relativity, thought not to be of sufficient interest to English-speaking readers, and have added an article Sokal published in *Dissent* about his reasons for producing the parody. (This second article was submitted to *Social Text* but rejected "on the grounds that it did not meet their intellectual standards"—an unintended compliment.)

The book is somewhat repetitive: the basic idea is contained in the parody and Sokal's comments on it. But the parody alone is worth the price of the volume:

> Postmodern science provides a powerful refutation of the authoritarianism and elitism inherent in traditional science, as well as an empirical basis for a democratic approach to scientific work. For, as Bohr noted, "a complete elucidation of one and the same object may require diverse points of view which defy a unique description"—this is quite simply a fact about the world, much as the self-proclaimed empiricists of modernist science might prefer to deny it. In such a situation, how can a self-perpetuating secular priesthood of credentialed "scientists" purport to maintain a monopoly on the production of scientific knowledge? . . .
>
> A liberatory science cannot be complete without a profound revision of the canon of mathematics. As yet no such emancipatory mathematics exists, and we can only speculate upon its eventual content. We can see hints of it in the multidimensional and nonlinear logic of fuzzy systems theory; but this approach is still heavily marked by its origins in the crisis of late-capitalist production relations. Catastrophe theory, with its dialectical emphases on smoothness/discontinuity and metamorphosis/unfolding, will indubitably play a major role in the future mathematics; but much theoretical work remains to be done before this approach can become a concrete tool of progressive political praxis.

The chapters dealing in more detail with individual thinkers reveal that they are beyond parody. Sokal could not create anything as ridiculous as this, from Luce Irigaray:

> Is $E = Mc^2$ a sexed equation? Perhaps it is. Let us make the hypothesis that it is insofar as it privileges the speed of light over other speeds that are vitally necessary to us. What seems to me to indicate the possibly sexed nature of the equation is not directly its uses by nuclear weapons, rather it is having privileged what goes the fastest.

We are offered reams of this stuff, from Jacques Lacan, Julia Kristeva, Bruno Latour, Jean-François Lyotard, Jean Baudrillard, Gilles Deleuze, Régis Debray, and others, together with comments so patient as to be involuntarily comic. In response to Irigaray, for example, Sokal and Bricmont observe:

> Whatever one may think about the "other speeds that are vitally necessary to us," the fact remains that the relationship $E = Mc^2$ between energy $(E)$ and mass $(M)$ is experimentally verified to a high degree of precision, and it would obviously not be valid if the speed of light $(c)$ were replaced by another speed.

The writers arraigned by Sokal and Bricmont use technical terms without knowing what they mean, refer to theories and formulas that they do not understand in the slightest, and invoke modern physics and mathematics in support of psychological, sociological, political, and philosophical claims to which they have no relevance. It is not always easy to tell how much is due to invincible stupidity and how much to the desire to cow the audience with fraudulent displays of theoretical sophistication. Lacan and Baudrillard come across as complete charlatans, Irigaray as an idiot, Kristeva and Deleuze as a mixture of the two. But these are delicate judgments.

Of course anyone can be guilty of this kind of thing, but there does seem to be something about the Parisian scene that is particularly hospitable to reckless verbosity. Humanists in France do not have to learn anything about science, yet those who become public intellectuals typically appear on stage in some kind of theoretical armor. It even affects politics. I remember that at a certain point after Iraq's invasion of Kuwait, when the United Nations was working up its response, President Mitterand declared on French television, "*Nous sommes dans une logique de guerre.*"

Mitterand regarded himself as an intellectual, but at least it was fairly clear what he meant by this pretentious formulation. Yet listen to Baudrillard:

> In the Euclidean space of history, the shortest path between two points is the straight line, the line of Progress and Democracy. But this is only true of the linear space of the Enlightenment. In our non-Euclidean *fin de siècle* space, a baleful curvature unfailingly deflects all trajectories. This is doubtless linked to the sphericity of time (visible on the horizon of the end of the century, just as the earth's sphericity is visible on the horizon at the end of the day) or the subtle distortion of the gravitational field.

Sokal and Bricmont emphasize that their criticism is limited to the abuse of science and mathematics and that they are not qualified to evaluate the contributions of these writers to psychology, philosophy, sociology, political theory, and literary criticism. They merely suggest, cautiously, that the dishonesty and incompetence shown in the passages they examine might lead one to approach the writers' other work with a critical eye. Clearly all this name-dropping is intended to bolster their reputations as deep thinkers, and its exposure should arouse skepticism.

Sokal and Bricmont are playing it close to the vest here. They could no doubt find passages in these same works having nothing to do with science that are nonsensical, irresponsible, and indifferent to the meanings of words. Yet there is no direct way to refute a fogbank, and so they have adopted the safer strategy of focusing on the occasions when these writers rashly try to invoke the authority of science and mathematics by using a vocabulary that does have a clear meaning, and which could not serve their purposes, literal or metaphorical, unless it were being used more or less correctly. That also allows them to explain why the scientific material introduced, even if it were not completely garbled, would be irrelevant to the literary, psychological, or social topics being discussed.

I am not sure how many admirers of these writers, or of postmodernist thought generally, will read this book. It is important to follow up on the positive effects of the original hoax, but will teachers of cultural studies and feminist theory go through these patient explanations of total confusion about topology, set theory, complex numbers, relativity, chaos theory, and Gödel's theorem? The scientifically literate will find them amusing up to a point, but for those whose minds have been formed by this material, it may be too late. Or they may claim that these particular writers are not as important as the sales of their books suggest, and that other postmodern theorists don't misappropriate science. Derrida, for example, is absent from the book except for one quote in the original parody, because that was an isolated instance, produced in response to a question at a conference.

Yet the effect of a hatchet job like this, if it succeeds, is not just to undermine the reputations of some minor celebrities; it is also to produce a shift in the climate of opinion, so that insiders with doubts about the intelligibility of all this "theory" are no longer reluctant to voice them, and outsiders who have grumbled privately to one another for years have something concrete to which they can point. Anyone who teaches in an American university has heard similar inanities from students and colleagues in comparative literature or cultural studies. Sokal and Bricmont's book should have an impact at least on the next generation of students.

II

Although Sokal and Bricmont's book focuses on the abuse and misrepresentation of science by a dozen French intellectuals, and the cognitive relativism of postmodern theory, it broaches a much larger topic—the uneasy place of science and the understanding of scientific rationality in contemporary culture.

The technological consequences of mathematics, physics, chemistry, and biology permeate our lives, and everyone who has been around for a few decades has witnessed the most spectacular developments. That alone would give science enormous prestige; but it also reinforces the purely intellectual aura of science as a domain of understanding that takes us far beyond common sense, by methods that are often far more reliable than common sense. The problem is that it is not easy for those without scientific training to acquire a decent grasp of this kind of understanding, as opposed to an awareness of its consequences and an ability to parrot some of its terminology. One can be infatuated with the idea of theory without understanding what a theory is.

To have a theory, it is not enough to throw around a set of abstract terms or to classify things under different labels. A theory, whether it is true or false, has to include some general principles by which fresh consequences can be inferred from particular facts—consequences not already implied by the initial description of those facts. The most familiar theories embody causal principles that enable us to infer from present observation what will happen or what has happened, but there are other kinds of theories—mathematical, linguistic, or ethical theories, for example—that describe noncausal systematic relations. A successful theory increases one's cognitive power over its domain, one's power to understand why the particular facts are as they are, and to discover new facts by inference from others that one can observe directly. Most important of all, it provides an understanding of the unifying reality that underlies observed diversity.

You don't have to understand quantum mechanics to appreciate the nature of science. Anyone who has taken introductory chemistry and is familiar with the periodic table of the elements has some idea of how powerful a theory can be—what an extraordinary wealth of specific consequences can be derived from a limited number of precise but general principles. And understanding classical chemistry requires only a basic spatial imagination and simple mathematics, nothing counterintuitive. But it should be clear that not everything in the world is governed by general principles sufficiently precise and substantive to be embodied in a theory. Theories in the social sciences are possible which depend on principles, even if they are only probabilistic, that apply to large numbers of people; but to employ theoretical-sounding jargon in talking about literature or art has about as much effect as putting on a lab coat, and in most cases the same is true for history.

Unfortunately, the lack of familiarity with real scientific theories sometimes results in imitation of their outward forms together with denigration of their claim to provide a specially powerful source of objective knowledge about the world. This defensive iconoclasm has received crucial support from a radical position in the history and philosophy of science, whose authority is regularly invoked by writers outside those fields: the epistemological relativism or even anarchism found in the writings of Thomas Kuhn and Paul Feyerabend.

As Sokal and Bricmont explain, Kuhn and Feyerabend were writing in the context of an ongoing dispute over the relation of scientific theories to empirical evidence. The logical positivists tried to interpret scientific propositions so that they would be entailed by the evidence of experience. Karl Popper denied that this was possible, but held that scientific propositions, if they were to have empirical content, had to be such that at least their falsehood could be entailed by the evidence of experience. Yet neither of these direct logical relations appears to hold, because the evidentiary relation pro or con between any experience and any theoretical claim always involves auxiliary hypotheses—things apart from the proposition and the evidence themselves that are being assumed true or false. There is nothing wrong with relying on many assumptions in the ordinary case, but it is always logically possible that some of them may be false, and sometimes that conclusion is forced on us with regard to an assumption that had seemed obvious. When that happens with a truly fundamental aspect of our world view, we speak of a scientific revolution.

So far, none of this implies that scientific reasoning is not objective, or that it cannot yield knowledge of reality. All it means is that a scientific inference from evidence to the truth or falsity of any proposition involves in some degree our whole system of beliefs and experience; and that the method is not logical deduction alone, but a weighing of which elements of the system it is most reasonable to retain and which to abandon when an inconsistency among them appears. In normal inquiry, this is usually easy to determine; but at the cutting edge it is often difficult, and a clear answer may have to await the experimental production of further evidence, or the construction of new theoretical hypotheses.

This means that most of our beliefs at any time must in some degree be regarded as provisional, since they may be replaced when a different balance of reasons is generated by new experience or theoretical ingenuity. It also means that an eternal set of rules of scientific method cannot be laid down in advance. But it does *not* mean that it cannot be true that a certain theory is the most reasonable to accept given the evidence available at a particular time, and it does *not* mean that the theory cannot be objectively true, however provisionally we may hold it. Truth is not the same as certainty, or universal acceptance.

Another point sometimes made against the claim of scientific objectivity is that experience is always "theory-laden," as if that meant that any experience which seemed to contradict a theory could be reinterpreted in terms of it, so that nothing could ever rationally require us to accept or reject a theory. But as Sokal and Bricmont point out, nothing of the kind follows.

Suppose I have the theory that a diet of hot fudge sundaes will enable me to lose a pound a day. If I eat only hot fudge sundaes and weigh myself every morning, my interpretation of the numbers on the scale is certainly dependent on a theory of mechanics that explains how the scale will respond when objects of different weights are placed on it. But it is not dependent on my dietary theories. If I concluded from the fact that the numbers keep getting higher that my intake of ice cream must be altering the laws of mechanics in my bathroom, it would be philosophical idiocy to defend the inference by appealing to Quine's dictum that all our statements about the external world face the tribunal of experience as a corporate body, rather than one by one. Certain revisions in response to the evidence are reasonable; others are pathological.

Much of what Kuhn says about great theoretical shifts, and the inertial role of long-established scientific paradigms and their cultural entrenchment in resisting recalcitrant evidence until it becomes overwhelming, is entirely reasonable, but it is also entirely compatible with the conception of science as seeking, and sometimes finding, objective truth about the world. What has made him a relativist hero is the addition of provocative remarks to the effect that Newton and Einstein, or Ptolemy and Galileo, live in "different worlds," that the paradigms of different scientific periods are "incommensurable," and that it is a mistake to think of the progress of science over time as bringing us closer to the truth about how the world really is.

Feyerabend is more consistently outrageous than Kuhn, deriding the privileged position of modern science as a way of understanding the world. "All methodologies have their limitations," he says in *Against Method*, "and the only 'rule' that survives is 'anything goes.'" As Sokal and Bricmont point out, the first clause of this sentence may be true, but it does not in any way support the second. I was a colleague of Feyerabend's at Berkeley in the 1960s, and once it fell to the two of us to grade the German exam for the graduate students in philosophy. About twenty of them took it, and their papers were numbered to preserve anonymity. We discovered that the department secretary who assigned the numbers had considerately left out the number thirteen, and Feyerabend was appalled and outraged by this display of rank superstition. But his views developed, and both he and Kuhn have a lot to answer for.

Both of them are repeatedly cited in support of the claim that everything, including the physical world, is a social construct existing only from the perspective of this or that cognitive practice, that there is no truth but only conformity or nonconformity to the discourse of this or that community, and that the adoption of scientific theories is to be explained sociologically rather than by the probative weight of reasoning from the experimental evidence. Scientists don't believe this, but many nonscientists now do. For example, Sokal and Bricmont tell us that the sociologist of science Bruno Latour recently challenged as anachronistic the report of French scientists who examined the mummy of Ramses II that the pharaoh had died of tuberculosis, because the tuberculosis bacillus came into existence only when Robert Koch discovered it in 1882.

I do not think this is just a case of malign influence from bad philosophy. The radical relativism found in Kuhn and Feyerabend fell on fertile ground.

The postmodernist doctrine that there is nothing outside the text, no world to which it is tied down, seems plausible to the consumers of postmodernist writings because it is so often true of those writings, where language is simply allowed to take off on its own. Those who have no objective standards themselves find it easy to deny them to others.

## III

As Sokal and Bricmont point out, the denial of objective truth on the ground that all systems of belief are determined by social forces is self-refuting if we take it seriously, since it appeals to a sociological or historical claim which would not establish the conclusion unless it were objectively correct. Moreover, it promotes one discipline, such as sociology or history, over the others whose objectivity it purports to debunk, such as physics and mathematics. Given that many propositions in the latter fields are much better established than the theories of social determination by which their objectivity is being challenged, this is like using a ouija board to decide whether your car needs new brake linings.

Relativism is kept alive by a simple fallacy, repeated again and again: the idea that if something is a form of discourse, the only standard it can answer to is conformity to the practices of a linguistic community, and that any evaluation of its content or its justification must somehow be reduced to that. This is to ignore the differences between types of discourse, which can be understood only by studying them from inside. There are certainly domains, such as etiquette or spelling, where what is correct is completely determined by the practices of a particular community. Yet empirical knowledge, including science, is not like this. Where agreement exists, it is produced by evidence and reasoning, and not vice versa. The constantly evolving practices of those engaged in scientific research aim beyond themselves at a correct account of the world, and are not logically guaranteed to achieve it. Their recognition of their own fallibility shows that the resulting claims have objective content.

Sokal and Bricmont argue that the methods of reasoning in the natural sciences are essentially the same as those used in ordinary inquiries like a criminal investigation. In that instance, we are presented with various pieces of evidence, we use lots of assumptions about physical causation, spatial and temporal order, basic human psychology, and the functioning of social institutions, and we try to see how well these fit together with alternative hypotheses about who committed the murder. The data and the background assumptions do not entail an answer, but they often make one answer more reasonable than others. Indeed, they may establish it, as we say, "beyond a reasonable doubt."

That is what scientists strive for, and while reasonable indubitability is not the position of theories at the cutting edge of knowledge, many scientific results achieve it with time through massive and repeated confirmation, together with the disconfirmation of alternatives. Even when the principles of classical chemistry are explained at a deeper level by quantum theory, they remain indispensably in place as part of our understanding of the world.

And yet there is something else about the science produced over the past century that makes it more than a vast extension of the employment of commonsense rationality. The fact is that contemporary scientific theories describing the invisible physical reality underlying the appearances no longer represent a world that can be intuitively grasped, even in rough outline, by the normal human imagination. Newtonian mechanics, the atomic theory of matter, and even the basic principles of electricity and magnetism can be roughly visualized by ordinary people. Quantum theory and the theory of relativity cannot be so visualized, because they introduce concepts of space, time, and the relation between observed and unobserved states of affairs that diverge radically from the intuitive concepts that we all use in thinking about our surroundings.

Scientific progress has accustomed us to the idea that the world has properties very different from those presented to our unaided senses, but classical theories can still be understood through models that are based on what we can see and touch. Everyone understands what it is for something to be composed of parts, and there is no difficulty in extending this idea to parts that are too minute to be seen but are inferrable from other evidence, such as that of the chemical reactions between different types of substances. We can perceive the action of gravity and magnetic attraction, and electric currents can be roughly imagined by analogy with the flow of liquids. Yet the world of Einstein's special theory of relativity, in which the interval between two widely separated events cannot be uniquely specified in terms of a spatial distance and a temporal distance, is not one that can be intuitively grasped, even roughly, by a layman.

Our natural idea, an idea entirely suitable for the scale of ordinary experience, that things happen in a unique three-dimensional space and along a unique one-dimensional time order, is so deep a feature of our intuitive conception of the world that it is very hard to make the transition, required by relativity theory, to seeing this as just the way things appear from the point of view of a particular frame of reference. To account for the different spatiotemporal relations that the same events appear to have from different frames of reference in uniform motion relative to one another, it is necessary to postulate a reality of a different kind, relativistic space-time, which can be precisely mathematically described but not really imagined.

Special relativity is not a theory whose interpretation is contested. It reveals an objective reality very different from the way the world appears, but one with clear and definite properties. Quantum theory, by contrast, though it is extremely successful in predicting the observable facts—deriving from physics the phenomena described by classical chemistry, for example—seems to present conceptual problems even to the physicists who work with it, problems about how to conceive the underlying reality that the theory describes, which is so different from the observed reality that it explains. If one tries to use ordinary physical imagination to grasp the reality underlying the observations, the result always contradicts the observations. It is impossible to convey the problem without discussing the theory, but one gets a flavor of the difficulty from the usual gloss that in quantum mechanics, we seem forced to think of the basic facts as indeterminate among mutually incompatible observable states—as if a 50 percent chance of rain, for example, could be the most accurate description of yesterday's weather.

Physics continues to develop, of course, but these two theories have taken us to a conception of the real character of the world that can be grasped only through mathematical formulations and not even roughly by the ordinary imagination. As a result, scientific journalism often reads like mumbo jumbo. Not only does this prevent the assimilation of modern physics into the general educated understanding of the world, it also leads to grotesque misuse of reference to these theories by those who think of them as a kind of magic.

Thus quantum theory, via the Heisenberg indeterminacy principle, and to a lesser extent relativity, are often invoked to show that today even science has had to abandon the idea of an objective, mind-independent reality. But neither theory has this significance, however strange may be the reality that they describe and its interaction with observers. And this alienation will only increase if, as seems likely, science penetrates to less and less intuitively imaginable accounts of the reality that lies behind the familiar manifest world, accounts which rely more and more on mathematics that only specialists can learn.

## IV

Sokal and Bricmont are as much concerned with the general rise of irrationalism and relativism as with the abuse of science, and one of their motives is political. Sokal says that what motivated him to produce the parody was a belief that the infestation of the academic left in America with postmodernist relativism badly weakened their position as critics of the established order. To challenge widely accepted practices, it is not enough to say there is no objective truth, and then present an alternative point of view.

Sokal in particular emphasizes that he is an Old Leftist, and that he taught math in Nicaragua during the Sandinista government. Clearly he does not want to be confused with Allan Bloom. As Sokal and Bricmont rightly observe, there is no logical connection between any abstract theory of metaphysics or epistemology and any particular political position. Objectivity with regard to the facts ought to be regarded as essential for any view, left, right, or center, that presents itself as an account of how societies should be organized. Objectivity is implied by every claim that the justification for one system is better than that for another, because justification always involves, in addition to values that may be contested, appeals to the facts that reveal how well a particular system will serve those values. Objectivity should be valued by anyone whose policies are not supported by lies.

The embrace of relativism by many leftist intellectuals in the United States, while it may not be politically very important, is a terrible admission of failure, and an excuse for not answering the claims of their political opponents. The subordination of the intellect to partisan loyalty is found across the political spectrum, but usually it takes the form of a blind insistence on the objective truth of certain supporting facts and refusal to consider evidence to the contrary. So what explains the shift, at least by a certain slice of the intellectual left, to this new form of obfuscation?

Sokal and Bricmont attribute it partly to despair brought on by the course of history:

> The communist regimes have collapsed; the social-democratic parties, where they remain in power, apply watered-down neo-liberal policies; and the Third World movements that led their countries to independence have, in most cases, abandoned any attempt at autonomous development. In short, the harshest form of "free market" capitalism seems to have become the implacable reality for the foreseeable future. Never before have the ideals of justice and equality seemed so utopian.

This is a disturbing bit of rhetoric. Anyone whose hopes were dashed by the collapse of communism had either a very feeble grip on reality or a very distasteful set of values, and it is simply playing to the galleries to say that we are now all doomed to the harshest form of free-market capitalism. A return to old-fashioned standards of objectivity of the kind that this book favors would require the abandonment of a lot of left-wing cant, and that is not the same as abandoning the ideals of justice and equality.

Perhaps Sokal and Bricmont are right, and the appeal of relativism comes when one gives up the will to win, and settles for the license to keep saying what one has always said, without fear of contradiction. But I think there is a more direct link between postmodernism and the traditional ideas of the left. The explanation of all ostensibly rational forms of thought in terms of social influences is a generalization of the old Marxist idea of ideology, by which moral principles were all debunked as rationalizations of class interest. The new relativists, with Nietzschean extravagance, have merely extended their exposure of the hollowness of pretensions to objectivity to science and everything else. Like its narrower predecessor, this form of analysis sees "objectivity" as a mask for the exercise of power, and so provides a natural vehicle for the expression of class hatred.

Postmodernism's specifically academic appeal comes from its being another in the sequence of all-purpose "unmasking" strategies that offer a way to criticize the intellectual efforts of others not by engaging with them on the ground, but by diagnosing them from a superior vantage point and charging them with inadequate self-awareness. Logical positivism and Marxism were used by academics in this way, and postmodernist relativism is a natural successor in the role. It may now be on the way out, but I suspect there will continue to be a market in the huge American academy for a quick fix of some kind. If it is not social constructionism, it will be something else—Darwinian explanations of practically everything, perhaps.

WORKS CITED

Baudrillard, Jean. *The Illusion of the End*. Trans. Chris Turner. Cambridge: Polity Press, 1994.

Feyerabend, Paul. *Against Method*. London: New Left Books, 1975.

Irigaray, Luce. "Le Sujet de la science est-il sexué/Is the Subject of Science Sexed?" Trans. Carol Mastrangelo. *Hypatia* 2, no. 3 (1987): 65–87.

Sokal, Alan, and Jean Bricmont. *Fashionable Nonsense: Postmodern Intellectuals' Abuse of Science*. New York: Picador, 1998.

## 38.  STAYING FOR AN ANSWER

### THE UNTIDY PROCESS OF GROPING FOR TRUTH

### SUSAN HAACK

A FEW YEARS BACK I heard my (then) dean, a physicist by training, express his unease at the suggestion that the mission statement for the College of Arts and Sciences include the phrase, "concern for truth." The word makes people nervous, he warned, and they're bound to ask, "whose 'truth'?" A sociologist colleague, seconding the dean's reservations, remarked that, while of course his research advanced knowledge, he wasn't concerned with "truth." A couple of us pointed out that, unless your conclusions are true, they aren't really knowledge, only purported knowledge; and I did my best to explain that it doesn't follow from the fact that people disagree about what is true, that truth is relative to perspective. But the upshot was—a new Strategic Plan for the college specifying the curricular innovations required by the "fundamental questions" that have been raised "about the presumed universality and objectivity of 'truth.'"

Susan Haack. "Staying for an Answer: The Untidy Process of Groping for Truth." Originally published in the *Times Literary Supplement*, 9 July 1999, 12–14. Copyright © 1999 Susan Haack. Reprinted by permission of the author.

Probably most of you have heard, not exactly this story, but other stories essentially similar, only set in other places and with different characters; for the ideas this dean picked up are by now almost an orthodoxy in academia, taken in some quarters—admittedly, more often in the humanities and the social sciences than in the physics department!—as indications of intellectual sophistication and moral rectitude.

Naturally, proponents of this new almost-orthodoxy—the Higher Dismissiveness, in Anthony Gottlieb's nice phrase—differ among themselves on the finer points. But they agree that the supposed ideal of honest inquiry, respect for evidence, concern for truth, is a kind of illusion, a smokescreen disguising the operations of power, politics, and rhetoric; and that those of us who think it matters whether you care about the truth, who feel no need for precautionary scare quotes when we write of fact, knowledge, evidence, etc., are hopelessly naive. As if this weren't bad enough, the feminists and multiculturalists among them suggest that in our naiveté we are complicit in sexism and racism, and the sociologists and rhetoricians of science among them suspect us of reactionary conformism with the military-industrial complex.

Faced with such an intimidating double accusation of naiveté and moral backwardness, many take the ostrich attitude, apparently hoping that if they ignore the Higher Dismissiveness hard enough, it will go away. But an old-fashioned prig like myself begins to feel—well, rather like the proverbial cannibal among the missionaries.

A thoughtful cannibal will notice, at the heart of the Higher Dismissiveness, a profound intolerance of uncertainty and a deep unwillingness to accept that the less than perfect is a lot better than nothing at all. And so again and again true, fallibilist premises are transmuted into false, cynical conclusions: what is accepted as known fact is often enough no such thing, *therefore* the concept of known fact is ideological humbug; one's judgment of the worth of evidence depends on one's background beliefs, *therefore* there are no objective standards of evidential quality; science isn't sacred, *therefore* it must be a kind of confidence trick; etc., etc.

What is most urgently needed is a realistic understanding of our epistemic situation, of how complicated evidence can get and how difficult serious inquiry can be. For there's really no need to give up on the objectivity of truth, evidence, etc., provided you're fallibilist enough. Of course, this will be only the beginning of the work, for then there will be the questions of the place of the sciences within inquiry generally, of the differences between science and literature, of the roots of relativism, and of the claim of the Higher Dismissiveness to represent the interests of the oppressed and marginalized.

Evidence is complex and ramifying, often confusing, ambiguous, misleading. Think of the controversy over that four-billion-year-old meteorite discovered in Antarctica, thought to have come from Mars about 11,000 years ago, and containing what might possibly be fossilized bacteria droppings. Some space scientists think this is evidence of bacterial life on Mars; others think the bacterial traces might have been picked up while the meteorite was in Antarctica; and others again believe that what look like fossilized bacteria droppings might be merely artifacts of the instrumentation. How do they know that giving off these gases when heated indicates that the meteorite comes from Mars? that the meteorite is about four billion years old? that this is what fossilized bacteria droppings look like?—like crossword entries, reasons ramify in all directions.

How reasonable a crossword entry is depends on how well it is supported by its clue and any already-completed intersecting entries; how reasonable those other entries are, independent of the entry in question; and how much of the crossword has been completed. How justified a belief is, similarly, depends on how well it is supported by experiential evidence and by reasons, i.e., background beliefs; how justified those background beliefs are, independent of the belief in question; and how much of the relevant evidence the evidence includes.

The quality of the evidence for a claim is objective, depending on how supportive it is of the claim in question, how comprehensive, and how independently secure. A person's judgments of the quality of evidence, however, are perspectival, depending on his background beliefs. Suppose you and I are working on the same crossword puzzle, but have filled in some long, much-intersected entry differently; you think a correct intersecting entry must have an "F" in the middle, while I think it must have a "D" there. Suppose you and I are on the same appointments committee, but you believe in graphology, while I think it's bunk; you think how the candidate writes his "g"s is relevant to whether he can be trusted, while I scoff at your "evidence." Or, to take a real example: in 1944, when Oswald Avery published his results, even he hedged over the conclusion to which they pointed, that DNA is the genetic material; for the then-accepted wisdom was that DNA is composed of the four nucleotides in regular order, and so is too stupid, too monotonous, a molecule to carry the necessary information. But by 1952, when Alfred Hershey and Martha Chase published their results, the tetranucleotide hypothesis had been discredited; and then it could be seen that Avery already had good evidence in 1944 that DNA, not protein, is the genetic material.

Inquiry can be difficult and demanding, and we very often go wrong. Sometimes the obstacle is a failure of will; we don't really want to know the answer badly enough to go to all the trouble of finding out, or we really *don't* want to know, and go to a lot of trouble *not* to find out. I think of the detective who doesn't really want to know who committed the crime, just to collect enough evidence to get a conviction, of the academic who cares less about discovering the causes of racial disharmony than about getting a large grant to investigate the matter—and of my own disinclination to rush to the library to check out the article that might oblige me to redo months of work.

Other things being equal, inquiry goes better when the will and the intellect, instead of pulling in different directions, work together; that's why intellectual integrity is valuable. But even with the best will in the world, even when we really want to find out, we often fail. Our senses, imaginations, intellects are limited; we can't always see, or guess, or reason, well enough. With ingenuity, we can devise ways of overcoming our natural limitations, from cupping our ears to hear better, through tying knots in rope or cutting notches in sticks to keep count, to highly sophisticated electron microscopes and techniques of computer modeling. Of course, our ingenuity is limited too.

Everyone who looks into how some part or aspect of the world is—the physicist and the detective, the historian and the entomologist, the quantum chemist and the investigative journalist, the literary scholar and the X-ray crystallographer—works on part of a part of the same vast crossword. Since they all investigate the same world, sometimes their entries intersect: a medical researcher relies on an amateur historian's family tree in his search for the defective gene responsible for a rare hereditary form of pancreatitis; ancient historians use a technique devised for the detection of breast cancer to decipher traces on the lead "postcards" on which Roman soldiers wrote home.

So successful have the natural sciences been that the words "science" and "scientific" are often used honorifically, as all-purpose terms of epistemic praise. (To make sure we get the point, the actors in the television advertisements who promise that new, scientific Wizzo will get our clothes cleaner wear white coats.) Unfortunately, this honorific usage disguises the otherwise obvious fact that not all, or only, scientists are good, honest, thorough, imaginative inquirers. Some scientists are lazy, some incompetent, some unlucky, a few crooked; and plenty of historians, journalists, detectives, etc., are good inquirers.

Science is neither sacred nor a confidence trick. Standards of stronger and weaker evidence, better and worse conducted inquiry, are not internal to the sciences; and there is no mode of inference, no "scientific method," exclusive to the sciences and guaranteed to produce true, or probably true, or more nearly true, or more empirically adequate, etc., results. Nevertheless, as human cognitive enterprises go, the natural sciences have been remarkably successful; not because they use a uniquely rational method of inquiry, unavailable to other inquirers, but in part because of the many and various "helps" they have devised to overcome natural human limitations. Instruments of observation extend sensory reach; models and metaphors stretch imaginative powers; techniques of mathematical and statistical modeling enable complex reasoning; and the cooperative and competitive engagement of many people in a great mesh of subcommunities within and across generations not only permits division of labor and pooling of evidence but also—though very fallibly and imperfectly, to be sure—has helped keep most scientists, most of the time, reasonably honest.

Science, like literature, requires imagination. Scientists, like writers of literature, stretch and amplify the language they inherit: a nonproteinous substance in the nucleus of cells is dubbed "nuclein," and later comes to be known as "nucleic acid"; then we have "deoxyribose nucleic acid" then "ribonucleic acid," subsequently acknowledged to be "ribonucleic acids," in the plural; and then—almost a century after "nuclein" was coined—"transfer RNA," "messenger RNA," and so on. Scientists, like writers of literature, rely on metaphors: the chaperone molecule, the Spaghetti Hypothesis, the uncles-and-aunts experiments, parental investment, and so forth. But it doesn't follow, and it isn't true, that science is indistinguishable from fiction. The distinction between the imaginative and the imaginary is key.

Scientists engage in writing, and writers of literature engage in inquiry; but the word "literature" picks out a bunch of kinds of writing, while the word "science" picks out a bunch of kinds of inquiry. A scientist dreams of structures, classifications, and laws which, if he is successful, are real, and explanations which, if he is successful, are true. Imagination, and imaginative exploration of imagined explanations, comes first; but to go beyond mere speculation, appraisal of the likely truth of the imagined conjecture, itself often requiring imagination in the design of experiments, instruments, etc., must come after. And this requires that serious scientific metaphors, those that are not just picturesque speech but working intellectual tools, eventually be spelled out in literal detail: what, literally, is invested in reproduction? what constitutes maximizing return? is reproductive behavior as predicted?

Progress in the sciences is ragged and uneven, and each step, like each crossword entry, is fallible and revisable. But each genuine advance potentially enables others, as a robust crossword entry does; "nothing succeeds like success" is the phrase that comes to mind. Think of Crick and Watson checking their model of DNA using only a ruler and a plumb line, and then of Max Perutz, years later, checking his structure for the far more complicated hemoglobin molecule using a complex computer program; or of how, starting with the (relatively) simple X-ray, eventually we had the PET-scan, the CAT-scan, MRI.

Just about every inquirer, in the most mundane of everyday inquiries, depends on others; otherwise, each would have to start on his part of the crossword alone and from scratch. Natural-scientific inquiry is no exception; in fact, it is more so—the work, cooperative and competitive, of a vast intergenerational community of inquirers, a deeply and unavoidably social enterprise. But it doesn't follow, and it isn't true, that scientific inquiry is nothing more than a process of social negotiation in which scientists trade their theoretical loyalties for prestige, or that the entities postulated in scientific theories are nothing more than social constructions.

It is true, however, that both the internal organization of science and its external environment can affect how well or how poorly scientific work gets done. As ever more elaborate equipment is needed to make ever more recherché observations, scientific work tends to get more expensive. When only governments and large industrial concerns can afford to support science, when some scientists are tempted to go prematurely to the press, some find it possible to make fortunes from their work, and the expert-witness business booms, there is no guarantee that mechanisms which have thus far proven more or less adequate to sustain intellectual integrity will continue to do so. There are no grounds for complacency.

Some of the knowledge the natural sciences have achieved has the potential to cause grave harm—knowledge brings power, and power can be abused. Of course it doesn't follow, as some proponents of the Higher Dismissiveness are tempted to conclude, that the natural sciences haven't achieved genuine knowledge after all. But difficult moral and political questions about the distribution of resources, the applications of scientific knowledge, etc., cannot responsibly be left to scientists alone to settle. Again, there are no grounds for complacency.

In scientific inquiry, and in inquiry of every kind, what we take to be legitimate questions sometimes turn out to be flawed. Questions about the properties of phlogiston, for example, turn out to rest on a false presupposition, and so have no true answer; some texts turn out to be ambiguous in ways of which the author is unaware, and so have no uniquely correct interpretation; and so on. None of this has any tendency to undermine the objectivity of truth. Sometimes, speaking carelessly, we say that something is true for you, but not for me. But this has no tendency to undermine the objectivity of truth either; what we mean is only that the something—liking chocolate-chip cookie ice-cream, say, or being over six feet tall—is true of you but not of me; or else that you believe whatever-it-is, but I don't.

A statement or belief is true if and only if things are as it represents them to be; so everyone who believes anything, or who asks any question, implicitly acknowledges—even if he explicitly denies—that there is such a thing as truth. Truth is not relative to perspective; and there can't be incompatible truths (this is a tautology, since "incompatible" means "can't be jointly true"). But there are many different truths—different but compatible truths—which must somehow fit together. It doesn't follow that all the truths about the world must be unified in the logical positivists' strong sense of that term, that they must be reducible to a privileged class expressed in a privileged vocabulary; nor, in particular, that all the truths about the world must be expressible in the language of physics. Rather, physics supplies a contour map on which the social sciences, history, etc., superimpose a road map—the superimposed maps each representing, in its own "vocabulary," the same one, real world.

Though what is true is not relative to perspective, what is accepted as true is; though incompatible statements can't be jointly true, incompatible claims are frequently made. But a dreadful argument ubiquitous in the Higher Dismissiveness confuses what is accepted as true, what passes for truth, with what is true. From the true, fallibilist premise that what passes for truth, known fact, strong evidence, well-conducted inquiry, etc., is sometimes no such thing, but only what the powerful have managed to get accepted as such, the Passes-for Fallacy moves to the false, cynical conclusion that the concepts of truth, fact, evidence, etc., are ideological humbug.

Ruth Bleier, for example, complains that the claim by some neurophysiologists that there are differences in brain structure corresponding to the sex-related differences in cognitive ability (Bleier adds, the supposed differences), rests on "sloppy methods, inconclusive findings and unwarranted interpretations," not to mention "unacknowledged ideological commitments." Perhaps she's right. But if so, the reasonable conclusion would be: supposing that, after carefully reexamining its presuppositions, we determine that the question is a legitimate one, we need better investigation using rigorous methods, seeking more conclusive findings based on warranted interpretations and free of ideological commitments. Bleier, however, commits the Passes-for Fallacy, and draws the cynical conclusion: bias is everywhere, objectivity is impossible, and the "social production of knowledge" is inextricably conditioned by "gender, class, race, and ethnicity."

When it is stated plainly, the Passes-for Fallacy is not only obviously invalid, but also in obvious danger of undermining itself; for if, as the conclusion says, the concepts of truth, evidence, honest inquiry, etc., are ideological humbug, then the premise couldn't be really-and-truly true, nor could we have objectively good evidence, obtained by honest inquiry, that it is so. Usually, however, as shorthand for what is accepted as knowledge, what passes for truth, etc., the cynics write of "truth," i.e., so-called "truth," of "knowledge," i.e., so-called "knowledge," etc. The effect of the scare quotes is to neutralize the implication of success normally carried by these words; truth must be so, but "truth" needn't be; knowledge must be true, but "knowledge" needn't be. As the scare quotes become ubiquitous, the difference between truth and "truth," knowledge and "knowledge," facts and "facts," begins to blur; and what used to be success-words pick up that characteristic sneering tone: "known fact"—yeah, right!

As the distinction is blurred between truth and "truth," known facts and "known facts," etc., the Passes-for Fallacy begins to look like a valid argument; the idea that there can be incompatible truths begins to sound plausible; and certain forms of relativism begin to look inevitable. It makes sense to talk of what is taken for true, what is accepted as good evidence, what passes for known fact, only relative to some person or group of people. So, if you don't distinguish what is true from what is taken for true, etc., it will seem that truth, etc., must be subjective or relative.

Proponents of the Higher Dismissiveness aren't always or unambiguously relativist, however; often they shift up and back between relativism and tribalism: between denying that it makes sense to think of epistemic standards as objectively better or worse, and claiming that *their* (nonwhite, non-Western, nonmasculinist, nonscientific, etc.) standards are superior. Shielded by this strategic ambiguity, they can duck accusations that their relativism is self-undermining, and at the same time evade the necessity of explaining what makes their, tribalist epistemic standards better.

Among the most accomplished practitioners of this ducking and weaving is Richard Rorty, who evades accusations of epistemic relativism by shifting to a kind of tribalism according to which a belief is justified if and only if it is defensible by *our*, Western, epistemic standards. And it is thanks to Rorty that the Higher Dismissiveness has come to be associated with pragmatism. This, however, is very peculiar; for classical pragmatism was fallibilist, not cynical. Here is C. S. Peirce, the founder of pragmatism: "Out of a contrite fallibilism, combined with a high faith in the reality of knowledge, all my philosophy has always seemed to grow"; and William James, who made pragmatism well known: "Those of us who give up the quest for certitude do not thereby give up the quest or hope of truth itself."

But Rorty, who writes that "the pragmatist view is of . . . 'true' as a word which applies to those beliefs on which we are able to agree," and that "truth is entirely a matter of solidarity," offers an essentially opposite message. I won't even *mention* such self-styled neo-pragmatists as Stephen Stich, who writes that "once we have a clear view of the matter, most of us . . . will not see any value in having true beliefs"; or Louis Menand, who writes that pragmatism is the view that "the whole force of a philosophical account of anything . . . lies in the advertised consequences of believing it." Thanks to such other influential proponents as Sandra Harding, the Higher Dismissiveness has also come to be associated with feminism. This is no less peculiar than the kidnapping of "pragmatism"; and even more disturbing. The old feminism, emphasizing the common humanity of women and men, focused on equality, justice, opportunity. "The fundamental thing is that women are more like men than anything else in the world," wrote Dorothy Sayers, "they are human beings"; and went on to warn against the "error of insisting that there is an aggressively 'feminist point of view' about everything." Winifred Holtby declared her allegiance to a style of feminism committed, not to pressing the claims of a supposed "woman's point of view," but to "the primary importance of the human being." But contemporary academic feminism, turning the sexist stereotypes that old-fashioned feminists used to deplore into new-fangled "women's ways of knowing," or demanding "politically adequate research and scholarship" instead of honest inquiry, offers an essentially opposite message. And in a closely parallel *dérapage*, multiculturalism has transmuted from commitment to the admirable goal of mutual learning from cultural diversity into a flabby relativism or an arbitrary tribalism.

As radical feminists and multiculturalists have jumped on the bandwagon of the Higher Dismissiveness, it has come to be thought that to suppose that there is such a thing as truth, that it is possible to discover the truth by investigation, or that the natural sciences have made many true discoveries, must be to harbor regressive political tendencies. This is an idea as tragic as it is bizarre.

Yes, excessive confidence that what you take to be true, *is* true—the "blight of cocksureness," in Peirce's phrase—can be a tool of oppression, has sometimes served the purposes of sexism and racism. This reminds us that respect for evidence requires not only a disposition to give up a belief in the face of contrary evidence and to proportion the degree of your belief to the strength of the evidence, but also a willingness to envisage the possibility that you have been going about a question in the wrong way altogether, or that it isn't a legitimate question after all—and to acknowledge when you just plain don't know.

And yes, as we inquire, people's feelings will sometimes be hurt. As we fumble our way to the truth, incomplete evidence will sometimes mislead us into accepting hurtful falsehoods; and some of the truths we discover will be painful, unpalatable, not what we would have wished to be the case. But unless it is possible to find out how things really are, it is not possible to discover that racist and sexist stereotypes *are* stereotypes, not truths; nor to trace the roots of racist or sexist prejudices or figure out how to overcome them; nor to know what changes really would make society better.

Not all the reasons for the fashionable disenchantment with truth, evidence, etc., are intellectual; part of the explanation is sociological. Putting the last first and the first last, Jacques Barzun observes, "valuing knowledge, we preposterize the idea, and say: 'everyone must produce written research in order to live, and it shall be deemed a knowledge explosion.'" As preposterism has become the way of academic life, conceptions of "productivity" and "efficiency" more appropriate to a manufacturing plant than to the pursuit of knowledge have become firmly entrenched. The effect, inevitably, is a gradual erosion of intellectual integrity.

We are overwhelmed by bloated publishers' catalogues filled with glowingly incredible endorsements, by a bombardment of books and journals and a clamor of conferences and meetings in which it is close to impossible, except by sheer luck, to find the good stuff. No wonder, then, that many take the easy way out, conforming to whatever party line will best advance their career, or that many lose their grip on the demands of real inquiry, forgetting that you may work for years on what turns out to be a dead end, and that it is part of the meaning of the word "research" that you don't know how things will turn out.

Pseudo-inquiry is ubiquitous: both sham reasoning, making a case for a conclusion to which you are already unbudgeably committed at the outset, and, especially, fake reasoning, making a case for a conclusion to the truth-value of which you are indifferent. Long ago, Peirce predicted that when this happens, we will "come to look upon reasoning as mainly decorative. The result of this state of things is of course a rapid deterioration of intellectual vigor. . . . Man loses his conceptions of truth and of reasoning" (woman too, I am sorry to say). When pseudo-inquiry is ubiquitous, people are uncomfortably aware, or half-aware, that reputations are made as often by a clever defense of the indefensible or the incomprehensible as by real work, and become increasingly skeptical of what they hear and read. Soon those wretched sneer quotes, and the Passes-for Fallacy, are everywhere. And many, afraid of being duped or of being thought naive, manage to persuade themselves that honest inquiry isn't really possible or desirable anyway.

How has this factitious despair come to be thought to represent the interests of the oppressed and marginalized? In part because, as universities have tried to welcome women and blacks as full participants in the life of the intellect, we have allowed ourselves to be distracted from the entirely admirable goal of making a person's race or sex matter less to our judgment of the quality of his or her mind, and begun looking for ways in which a person's sex or race might itself be a qualification for intellectual work. As the stress on the interests of this or that class or category of person has waxed, our sense of our common humanity and our appreciation of individual differences has waned, until we are in danger of forgetting that fallible inquiry—the ragged, untidy process of groping for, and sometimes grasping, something of how the world is—is a *human* thing, not a white male thing. This is very sad.

For "howsoever these things are . . . in men's depraved judgements and affections, yet . . . the inquiry of truth, which is the love-making or wooing of it, the knowledge of truth, which is the presence of it, and the belief of truth, which is the enjoying of it, is the sovereign good of human nature." Thus Francis Bacon, who noticed how "factitious despair" of the possibility of finding things out "cuts the sinews and spurs of industry"; and, as he continued, "all for the miserable vainglory of having it believed that whatever has not yet been invented or discovered will never be invented or discovered hereafter."

## WORKS CITED

Bacon, Francis. "Of Truth" (1625) ("Howsoever these things are . . .").

———. *The New Organon* (1620), book 1, aphorism 88 ("factitious despair . . .").

Barzun, Jacques. *The American University*. New York: Harper and Row, 1968.

Bleier, Ruth. "Science and the Construction of Meanings in the Neurosciences." In *Feminism within the Science and Health Care Professions: Overcoming Resistance*, ed. Sue V. Rosser. Oxford: Pergamon Press, 1988. 91–104.

Gottlieb, Anthony. "The Most Talked-About Philosopher." Review of *Objectivity, Relativism, and Truth* and *Essays on Heidegger and Others*, by Richard Rorty. *New York Times Book Review*, 2 June 1991, 30.

Haack, Susan. *Manifesto of a Passionate Moderate: Unfashionable Essays.* Chicago: University of Chicago Press, 1998.

Harding, Sandra. *Whose Science? Whose Knowledge?* Ithaca, N.Y.: Cornell University Press, 1992.

Holtby, Winifred. Cited by Rosalind Delmar in the afterword to Vera Brittain's *Testament of Friendship.* 1945. Reprint: London: Virago, 1980.

James, William. *The Will to Believe and Other Essays in Popular Philosophy.* Dover: New York, 1956. 17.

Menand, Louis, ed. Introduction to *Pragmatism: A Reader.* New York: Vintage Books, 1997.

Peirce, C. S. *Collected Papers*, ed. Charles Hartshorne and Paul Weiss. 8 vols. Cambridge, Mass.: Harvard University Press, 1931–58. Vol. 1, para. 14. The passage is dated c. 1897.

Rorty, Richard. "Science as Solidarity." In *The Rhetoric of the Human Sciences: Language and Argument in Scholarship and Public Affairs*, ed. John S. Nelson, Allan Megill, and Donald N. McCloskey. Madison: University of Wisconsin Press, 1987. 38–52 ("the pragmatist view is . . ." ).

——. *Objectivity, Relativism, and Truth.* Cambridge: Cambridge University Press, 1991. 32 ("truth is entirely a matter . . .").

Sayers, Dorothy. "The Human-Not-Quite-Human." In *Unpopular Opinions: Twenty-One Essays.* New York: Harcourt Brace and Company, 1947. 142–49.

Stich, Stephen P. *The Fragmentation of Reason: Preface to a Pragmatic Theory of Cognitive Evaluation.* Cambridge, Mass.: Bradford Books, MIT Press, 1990. 101.

# 39.  WHAT IS SOCIAL CONSTRUCTION?

## PAUL A. BOGHOSSIAN

## SOCIAL CONSTRUCTION

SOCIAL CONSTRUCTION TALK is all the rage. But what does it mean and what is its point? The core idea seems clear enough. To say of something that it is socially constructed is to emphasize its dependence on contingent aspects of our social selves. It is to say: This thing could not have existed had we not built it; and we need not have built it at all, at least not in its present form. Had we been a different kind of society, had we had different needs, values, or interests, we might well have built a different kind of thing, or built this one differently. The inevitable contrast is with a naturally existing object, something that exists independently of us and which we did not have a hand in shaping.

There are certainly many things, and facts about them, that are socially constructed in the sense specified by this core idea: money, citizenship, and news-

Paul Boghossian. "What Is Social Construction?" Originally published in the *Times Literary Supplement*, 23 February 2001, 6–8. Revised by the author and reprinted by permission of the author.

papers, for example. None of these things could have existed without society; and each of them could have been constructed differently had we so chosen.

As Ian Hacking rightly observes, however, in his recent monograph, *The Social Construction of What?* (1999), social construction talk is often applied not only to worldly items—things, kinds, and facts—but to our beliefs about them. Consider Helene Moussa's "The Social Construction of Women Refugees" (1992). Clearly, the intent is not to insist on the obvious fact that certain women come to be refugees as a consequence of social events. Rather, the idea is to expose the way in which a particular belief has been shaped by social forces: the belief that there is a particular kind of person—the woman refugee—deserving of being singled out for special attention.

Talk of the social construction of belief, however, requires some elaboration of the core idea. For it is simply trivially true of any belief that we have that it is not necessary that we should have had it and that we might not have had it had we been different from the way we actually are. Consider our belief that dinosaurs once roamed the earth. It is obviously not inevitable that we should have come to this belief. We might never have considered the question. Having considered it, we might have arrived at a different conclusion, for a variety of causes: we might not have been interested in the truth; we might not have been as intelligent at figuring it out; we might never have stumbled across the relevant evidence (the fossil record).

These observations supply various boring senses in which any belief might be considered dependent on contingent facts about us. The important question concerns the role of the social once all of these factors have been taken into account: that is, keeping our skills and intelligence fixed, and given our interest in the question and our desire to learn the truth about it, and given our exposure to the relevant evidence, do we still need to invoke contingent social values to explain why we believe that there were dinosaurs? If the answer is "Yes"—if it's true that another society, differing from us only in their social values, would have arrived at a different and incompatible belief—then we could say that our belief in dinosaurs is socially constructed.

It is crucial, therefore, to distinguish between a constructionist claim that is directed at things and facts, on the one hand, and one that is directed at beliefs on the other, for they are distinct sorts of claim and require distinct forms of vindication. The first amounts to the metaphysical claim that something is real but of our own creation; the second to the epistemic claim that the correct explanation for why we have some particular belief has to do with the role that that belief plays in our social lives, and not exclusively with the evidence adduced in its favor. Each type of claim is interesting in its own way.

If a thing were shown to be socially constructed in the first sense, it would follow that it would contravene no law of nature to try to get rid of it (which is not the same as saying that it would be easy to do so—consider Manhattan). If a belief of ours were shown to be socially constructed in the second sense, it would follow that we could abandon it without fear of irrationality: if we have the belief not because there is adequate evidence in its favor but because having it subserves some contingent social purpose, then if we happen not to share the social purpose it subserves we ought to be free to reject it.

Much important work has been done under each of these headings, most significantly, it seems to me, for the topics of gender and race. Simone de Beauvoir (in *The Second Sex*), and other feminist scholars since, have illuminated the extent to which gender roles are not inevitable but are rather the product of social forces. Anthony Appiah has been particularly forceful in demonstrating that nothing physical or biological corresponds to the racial categories that play a pervasive role in our social lives, that these categories owe their existence more to their social function than they do to the scientific evidence.

Other claims are more controversial. Mary Boyle has argued that our belief in schizophrenia is socially constructed. Her claim is that there is no adequate reason to believe that the symptoms commonly lumped under this label are manifestations of a single underlying disease and, hence, that the search for its etiology by neurochemistry is doomed. Perhaps she is right: our understanding of mental illness is certainly in its infancy. On the other hand, there appears to be increasing evidence that the symptoms associated with schizophrenia are predictable significantly before their onset and that the condition is highly heritable. These facts point in the opposite direction.

In a flourishing research program, we find the expected mix of important and debatable work. What bears emphasis, however, is that while some particular social construction claims may be empirically controversial, the templates of which they are instances are in no way philosophically controversial. Both the abstract thought that some things are created by societies and the thought that some beliefs owe more to social values than they do to the evidence in their favor, are as old as reason itself. Whence, then, the widespread impression that social constructionists are antirationalist, antirealist, and antiobjectivist?

The answer is that it stems not from the forms of the claims themselves, and not from their application to this or that empirically debatable subject matter. It stems, rather, from the desire of some prominent theorists in this tradition to extend social construction talk to absolutely everything and, in particular, to the facts studied by, and the knowledge claims emanating from, the natural sciences. If we are to find our way through the muddy battleground on which these now famous science wars are being waged it will help to observe certain distinctions. I will begin with the claim about facts and things.

## SOCIALLY CONSTRUCTED THINGS

Money, citizenship, and newspapers are transparent social constructions because they obviously could not have existed without societies. Just as obviously, it would seem, anything that could have—or that did—exist independently of societies could *not* have been socially constructed: dinosaurs, for example, or giraffes, or the elementary particles that are supposed to be the building blocks of all matter and that physicists call "quarks." How could they have been socially constructed if they existed *before* societies did?

Yet when we turn to some of the most prominent texts in the social construction literature, we find an avalanche of claims to the effect that it is precisely such seemingly mind- and society-independent items that are socially constructed.

Take Andrew Pickering's book, *Constructing Quarks* (1984). As his title suggests, Pickering's view seems to be that quarks were socially constructed by scientists in the 1970s when the so-called "Standard Model" was first developed. And the language of the text itself does not disappoint: "the reality of quarks was the upshot of particle physicists' practice."

But how can this be? If quarks exist—and we are assuming for present purposes that they do—they would have had to have existed before there were any societies. So how could they have been constructed by societies?

Perhaps Pickering does not mean what he says; perhaps he intends only to be making a claim about our belief in quarks rather than about the quarks themselves, a thesis we shall also want to examine in due course. Whether or not Pickering intended the worldly claim, however, claims like that seem to be all around us. Here, just for another example, are Bruno Latour and Steve Woolgar on the subject of the facts studied by natural science: "We do not wish to say that facts do not exist nor that there is no such thing as reality. . . . Our point is that 'out there ness' is a consequence of scientific work rather than its cause" (180–182).

But it is not easy to make sense of the thought that facts about elementary particles or dinosaurs are a *consequence* of scientific theorizing. How could scientific theorizing have caused it to be true that there were dinosaurs or that there are quarks? Of course, science made it true that we came to believe that dinosaurs and quarks exist. Since we believe it, we *act as though* dinosaurs and quarks exist. If we allow ourselves some slightly florid language, we could say that *in our world* dinosaurs and quarks exist, in much the way as we could say that in the world of Shakespeare's *Hamlet*, Ophelia drowns. So, still speaking in this vein, we could say that science made it true that in our world there are dinosaurs and quarks. But all we could coherently mean by this is that science made it true that we *came to believe that* dinosaurs and quarks exist. And this no one disputes. Despite all the evidence in their favor, these beliefs may still be false and the only thing that will make them true is whether, out there, there really were dinosaurs and there really are quarks. Surely, science cannot construct those things; at best, it can discover them.

The views apparently on offer here hark back to the discredited "transcendental idealism" of Immanuel Kant. On Kant's picture (or at least on one influential way of reading it), there is a world that exists independently of human minds, so we do not have to go so far as to say that we created the world. But in and of itself this world is structureless: it is not broken up into things, kinds of things, or facts. We impose structure on the world by thinking of it in a certain way, by having one set of beliefs about it rather than another.

There are two different ways to understand the Kantian claim that we impose structure on the world. On the first, we literally make it the case that there are certain kinds of things in the world—mountains—by thinking of the world in terms of the concept "mountain," by believing there to be mountains. On the second, the structure remains entirely on our side of the divide: the claim that there are mountains is just a way of talking about what is true according to our conceptual scheme or language game. It is not even to try to make a claim about how things are in some mind-independent reality.

The first alternative, the one that Pickering's and Latour's language most closely suggests, is hopelessly bizarre. How could the mind carve the world out there into kinds? How could it create things and give them properties? And what happens when the world is carved up in two incompatible ways by two different societies? Some of us believe in immaterial souls and others of us do not. Does the world out there then both contain and not contain immaterial souls?

In writings that are much cited by social constructionists, however, Richard Rorty (1998) has suggested that talk of the social construction of facts and kinds is perfectly cogent provided it is understood along the lines of the second alternative:

> One reason the question of mind-independent reality is so vexed and confusing is an ambiguity in the notion of "independence." [My critics] sometimes [write] as if philosophers who, like myself, do not believe in "mind-independent reality" must deny that there were mountains before people had the idea of "mountain" in their minds or the word "mountain" in their language. But nobody denies that. Nobody thinks there is a chain of causes that makes mountains an effect of thoughts or words. . . . Given that it pays to talk about mountains, as it certainly does, one of the obvious truths about mountains is that they were here before we talked about them. If you do not believe that, you probably do not know how to play the language games that employ the word "mountain." But the utility of those language games has nothing to do with the question of whether Reality as It Is In Itself, apart from the way in which it is handy for human beings to describe it, has mountains in it.

Rorty is recommending that the social constructionist distance himself from the claim that we cause there to be mountains by talking about them. According to Rorty, the way to put the point is, rather, this: It pays for us to adopt some ways of talking over others. Among the ways of talking that it pays for us to adopt is one according to which there are mountains and they exist independently of humans. However, no way of talking could be said to be more faithful to the way things are in and of themselves than any other, because there is no way things are in and of themselves. There is just how we talk about how things are and the fact that some of those ways are better for our purposes than others. It is, therefore, correct to say that we do not make the mountains; that is a claim that is licensed by a way of talking that it pays for us to adopt. However, that does not mean that it is just plain true that there are mountains independently of humans; it never makes sense to say that anything is just plain true. All we can intelligibly talk about is what is true according to this or that way of talking, some of which it pays for us to adopt.

This, however, is an impossible view, as many critics have pointed out (see especially Thomas Nagel's *The Last Word*, 1997, and Bernard Williams's review of Nagel's book in *The New York Review of Books*, 1998). First, even Rorty doesn't succeed in distancing himself from any commitment to the idea that some claims are just plain true, and not just true relative to this or that way of talking; he simply commits himself to the implausible view that the only kinds of claim that are just plain true are claims about which ways of talking it pays for us to adopt, rather than claims directly about mountains. Otherwise, he could not simply assert, as he does, that it pays for us to talk about mountains, but only that it pays for us to talk about its paying for us to talk about mountains, and so on without end.

Second, if we accept his view that there is no higher authority concerning what's true than how it pays for us to talk, and if, as Rorty admits, it pays for us to say that science discovers a ready-made world, replete with mountains and giraffes, then there is simply no perspective from which he can also say, as he must if he is to express his distinctive view, that there isn't a ready-made world for science to discover, replete with mountains and giraffes. He can't have it both ways; but having it both ways is what his view requires.

## Socially Constructed Belief

If the preceding considerations are correct, social construction talk does not cogently apply to the *facts* studied by the natural sciences; does it fare any better when applied to the *beliefs* about those facts produced by those sciences?

The issue is not whether science is a social enterprise. Of course, it is. Science is conducted collectively by human beings who come equipped with values, needs, interests, and prejudices. And these may influence their behavior in a variety of potentially profound ways: they may determine what questions they show an interest in, what research strategy they place their bets on, what they are willing to fund, and so forth.

The usual view, however, is that none of this matters to the believability of a particular claim produced by science, *if that claim is adequately supported by the factual evidence*. Kepler may have become interested in planetary motion as a result of his religious and occult preoccupations, and, for all I know, he may have been strongly invested in getting a certain outcome. But so long as his eventual claim that the planets move in elliptical orbits could be justified by the evidence he presented for it, it does not matter how he came to be interested in the question, nor what prior investment he may have had. The view is now there, with a claim on our attention, and the only way to reject it is to refute the evidence adduced in its favor. It is irrelevant that Kepler would not have engaged in his research had it not been for preoccupations that we do not share or that he may have had extra-evidential motives for hoping for a certain outcome.

To put this point another way, we commonly distinguish between what philosophers of science call the "context of discovery" and what they call the "context of justification." And while it's plausible that social values play a role in the context of discovery, it's not plausible that they play a role in the context of justification. Social constructionists about knowledge deny this; for them it is naive to suppose that while social values may enter into the one context, they need not enter into the other.

Well, how could social values enter into the context of justification? There are four distinct ways of articulating the thought a constructionist may have in mind here; while all four may be found in the literature, they are not always sufficiently distinguished from one other.

To begin with, a constructionist may hold that it is not the factual evidence that does the justifying, but precisely the background social values. And while it may seem incredible that anyone could have seriously thought anything like this, there are certainly assertions out there that seem to demand just such a reading. Here is one, made by Kenneth Gergen: "The validity of theoretical propositions in the sciences is in no way affected by factual evidence."

However, anyone who really thought that, say, Maxwell's Equations could be *justified* by appeal to Maxwell's, or anyone else's, social or political beliefs would betray a complete incomprehension of the notion of justification. An item of information justifies a given belief by raising the likelihood that it is true. Admittedly, this is not an unproblematic notion. But unless we are to throw it out altogether, it is perfectly clear that one cannot hope to justify the fundamental laws of electromagnetism by appeal to one's political convictions or career interests or anything else of a similar ilk.

If one were absolutely determined to pursue something along these lines, a slightly better avenue, and the second of our four options, would be to argue that, although social values do not justify our beliefs, we are not actually moved to belief by things that justify; we are only moved by our social interests.

This view, which is practically orthodoxy among practitioners of what has come to be known as "science studies," has the advantage of not saying something absurd about justification; but it is scarcely any more plausible. On the most charitable reading, it stems from an innocent confusion about what is required by the enterprise of treating scientific knowledge sociologically.

The view in question derives from one of the founding texts of science studies, David Bloor's *Knowledge and Social Imagery* (1976). Bloor's reasoning went something like this: If we wish to explain why certain beliefs come to be accepted as knowledge at a given time, we must not bring to bear *our* views about which of those beliefs are true and which false. If we are trying to explain why *they* came to hold that some belief is true, it cannot be relevant that we know it not to be true. This is one of the so-called "Symmetry Principles" of the sociology of knowledge: treat true and false propositions symmetrically in explaining why they came to be believed.

It's possible to debate the merits of this principle, but on the whole it seems to me sound. As Ian Hacking rightly emphasizes, however, it is one thing to say that true and false beliefs should be treated symmetrically and quite another to say that justified and unjustified ones should be so treated. While it may be plausible to ignore the truth or falsity of what I believe in explaining why I came to believe it, it is not plausible to ignore whether I had any evidence for believing it. For some reason that is never explained, however, Bloor and his colleagues seem to think that the two principles are on a par and are both equally required by the enterprise of treating scientific belief sociologically. Bloor builds both into the very foundation of the subject: "[The sociology of knowledge] would be impartial with respect to truth and falsity, rationality or irrationality, success or failure."

However, absent an argument for being skeptical about the very idea of a good reason for a belief—and how could there be such an argument that did not immediately undermine itself?—one of the possible causes for my believing what I do is that I have good evidence for it. Any explanatory framework that insisted on treating not only true and false beliefs symmetrically, but justified and unjustified ones as well, would owe us an explanation for why evidence for belief is being excluded as one of its potential causes. And it would have to do so without undermining its own standing as a view that is being put forward because justified.

This is not, of course, to say that scientific belief must always be explained in terms of the compelling evidence assembled for it; the history of science is replete with examples of views—phrenology, for example—for which there never was any good evidence. It is simply to insist that scientific belief is sometimes to be explained in terms of compelling evidence and that the history and sociology of science, properly conceived, need have no stake in denying that.

This brings us to a third, milder conception of how social values might be indispensable for the justification of scientific belief. On this view, although evidence can enter into the explanation for why a particular view is believed, it can never be enough to explain it. Any evidence we might possess always *underdetermines* the specific belief that we arrive at on its basis. Something else must close the gap between what we have evidence for and what we actually believe, and that something else is provided by the thinker's background values and interests.

This idea, that the evidence in science always underdetermines the theories that we believe on its basis, has exerted considerable influence in the philosophy of science, even in nonconstructionist circles. In its modern form, it originated in the thought of the turn of the century French physicist and philosopher, Pierre Duhem. Suppose that an experimental observation is inconsistent with a theory that you believe: the theory predicts that the needle will read "10" and the needle does not budge from zero, say. What Duhem pointed out is that this does not necessarily refute the theory. For the observational prediction is generated not merely on the basis of the theory, but, in addition, through the use of auxiliary hypotheses about the functioning of the experimental apparatus. In light of the recalcitrant observational result, something has to be revised, but so far we do not yet know exactly what: perhaps it's the theory, perhaps it's the auxiliary hypotheses. Perhaps, indeed, it is the very claim that we recorded a genuinely recalcitrant result, as opposed to merely suffering some visual illusion.

Duhem argued that reason alone could never decide which revisions are called for and, hence, that belief revision in science could not be a purely rational matter: something else had to be at work as well. What the social constructionist adds is that this extra element is something social.

This is a clever argument that does not long conceal its difficulties. Is it really true that we could never have more reason to revise one of our theories rather than another in response to recalcitrant experience? Consider Duhem's example of an astronomer peering through his telescope at the heavens and being surprised at what he finds there, perhaps a hitherto undetected star in a galaxy he has been charting. Upon this discovery, according to Duhem, the astronomer may revise his theory of the heavens or he may revise his theory of how the telescope works. And rational principles of belief fixation do not tell him which to do.

The idea, however, that in peering at the heavens through a telescope we are testing our theory of the telescope *just as much* as we are testing our astronomical views is absurd. The theory of the telescope has been established by numerous terrestrial experiments and fits in with an enormous number of other things that we know about lenses, light, and mirrors. It is simply not plausible that, in coming across an unexpected observation of the heavens, a rational response might be to revise what we know about telescopes! The point is not that we might *never* have occasion to revise our theory of telescopes; one can certainly imagine circumstances under which that is precisely what would be called for . The point is that not *every* circumstance in which something about telescopes is presupposed is a circumstance in which our theory of telescopes is being tested, and so the conclusion that rational considerations alone cannot decide how to respond to recalcitrant experience is blocked.

Perhaps, however—to come to the fourth and final way in which belief and social values might be intertwined—the correct thought is not that the social must be brought in to fill a gap left by the rational, but simply that the rational itself is constitutively social. A good reason for believing something, according to this line of thought, only has that status relative to variable social factors—a sharp separation between the rational and the social is illusory.

This is currently perhaps the single most influential construal of the relation between the rational and the social in constructionist circles. What it amounts to is a relativization of good reasons to variable social circumstance, so that the same item of information may correctly be said to justify a given belief under some social circumstances, in some cultures, but not in others. It is nicely expressed in the following passage by Barry Barnes and David Bloor: "there is no sense to the idea that some standards or beliefs are really rational as distinct from merely locally accepted as such."

But this is an impossible construal of reasons for belief, as Plato understood some time ago (see his *Theaetetus*). We cannot coherently think of ourselves as believing and asserting *anything*, if all reasons for belief and assertion are held to be inexorably tied to variable background perspective in the manner being proposed. There are many ways to show this, but perhaps the most telling is this: not even the relativist would be able to adopt such an attitude towards his own view. For, surely, the relativist does not think that a relativism about reasons is justified only relative to his own perspective? If he did, why is he recommending it to us who do not share his perspective?

When we believe something, we believe it because we think there are reasons to think it is true, reasons that we think are general enough to get a grip even on people who do not share our perspective. That is why we feel entitled to recommend it to them. It's hard to imagine a way of thinking about belief and assertion that precluded the possibility of that sort of generality.

## THE CULTURAL AUTHORITY OF SCIENCE

Neither a generalized constructionism about the objects and facts investigated by the natural sciences, nor one about the reasons for belief provided by those sciences carries much plausibility. To what does this matter? Here are two contrasting views. Richard Rorty writes, in 1999:

> The science wars are in part a product of deep and long-lasting clashes of intuition, but mostly they are just media hype—journalists inciting intellectuals to diabolize one another. Diabolization may be helpful in keeping intellectuals aroused and active, but it need not be taken very seriously.

By way of contrast we have Dorothy Nelkin:

> Current theories about science do seem to call into question the image
> of selfless scientific objectivity and to undermine scientific authority,
> at a time when scientists want to claim their lost innocence, to be per-
> ceived as pure unsullied seekers after truth. That is what the science wars
> are about.

I think that Nelkin is closer to being right. As social constructionists realize
only too well, we would not attach the same importance to science if we came
to be convinced by constructionist conceptions of it.

In what does the cultural importance of science consist? This is, of course, a
vast subject, but there are, it seems to me, two central elements. First, and most
importantly, in matters of belief we defer to science. It would be hard to over-
estimate the significance of this practice, reflected as it is in what we are prepared to teach our children at school, to accept as evidence in courts of law and
to base our social policies upon. Second, we spend vast sums of money on basic scientific research, research that does not look as though it will have any
immediate practical payoff.

Rorty's laid-back attitude depends on the thought that neither of these
practices has any interesting philosophical presuppositions, and so cannot
be vulnerable to constructionist critique. But this seems wrong. For deference to make sense, it has to be plausible that science delivers the sort of
knowledge that everyone has reason to believe, regardless of their political or
more broadly ideological commitments. But this would be directly challenged by a constructionist thesis about reasons for belief, on any of its available versions.

If we look at the practice of spending vast sums on basic science, science
with no foreseeable practical payoff, it is arguable that an even greater amount
of philosophy is presupposed, that we have to hold not only that science delivers knowledge that everyone has reason to believe, but that it delivers true or
approximately true knowledge of the structure of an independently existing
reality. For if we ask why, given the many pressing social problems we face, we
should spend tens of billions of dollars to build a supercollider that will smash
ever smaller particles into each other in the hope of releasing ones that we have
never seen but which our theories predict, what could possibly be a compelling answer if not that doing so will help us to understand the fundamental,
hidden constitution of the universe, and that that is worth doing? If it doesn't
make sense to think that there is such a hidden constitution to probe, or even
if there is, if it doesn't make sense to think that science is capable of probing it,
what rationale could there be for spending such vast sums, when that money
could equally be spent on AIDS or on poverty? (To be clear: I am not saying
that a search for the fundamental truths automatically trumps all other con-

siderations, only that its coherence as a goal is required to make sense of the importance we attach to basic science.)

## CONCLUSION

At its best—as in the work of de Beauvoir and Appiah—social constructionist thought exposes the contingency of those of our social practices that we had wrongly come to regard as inevitable. It does so by relying on the standard canons of good scientific reasoning. It goes astray when it aspires to become either a general metaphysics or a general theory of knowledge. As the former, it quickly degenerates into an impossible form of idealism. As the latter, it assumes its place in a long history of problematic attempts to relativize the notion of rationality. It has nothing new to add to these historically discredited views; if anything, social constructionist versions tend to be murkier and more confused than their traditional counterparts. The difficulty lies in understanding why such generalized applications of social construction have come to tempt so many.

One source of their appeal is no doubt their efficiency. If we can be said to know up front that any item of knowledge only has that status because it gets a nod from contingent social values, then any claim to knowledge can be dispatched if we happen not to share the values on which it allegedly depends. There is no need to get into the often complex details.

But that only postpones the real question. Why this fear of knowledge? Whence the need to protect against its deliverances? Hacking writes of certain feminists, for example, who

> see objectivity and abstract truth as tools that have been used against them. They remind us of the old refrain: women are subjective, men are objective. They argue that those very values, and the word objectivity, are a gigantic confidence trick. If any kind of objectivity is to be preserved, some argue, it must be one that strives for a multitude of standpoints.        (96)

Hacking professes not to know whether to side with this thought. But he should know. Whatever legitimate worry may be at work here, it cannot be expressed by saying that objectivity and abstract truth are tools of oppression. At most what these observations entitle us to say is that there have been occasions when those concepts have been used as tools of oppression; and no one will want to dispute that. But the fact that a concept can be, and has been, abused can hardly be a basis for indicting the concept itself. Are we to be suspicious of the value of freedom because the Nazis inscribed "Arbeit Macht Frei" on the gate at Auschwitz?

The intuitive view is that there is a way things are that is independent of human opinion, and that we are capable of arriving at belief about how things are that is objectively reasonable, binding on anyone capable of appreciating the relevant evidence regardless of their ideological perspective. Difficult as these notions may be, it is a mistake to think that recent philosophy has disclosed any good reasons for rejecting them.

## WORKS CITED

Appiah, K. Anthony, and Amy Gutmann. *Color Conscious: The Political Morality of Race.* Princeton, N.J.: Princeton University Press, 1996.

Barnes, Barry, and David Bloor. "Relativism, Rationalism, and the Sociology of Knowledge." In *Rationality and Relativism*, ed. Martin Hollis and Steven Lukes. Cambridge, Mass.: MIT Press, 1982.

Beauvoir, Simone de. *The Second Sex.* Trans. and ed. H. M. Parshley. New York: Knopf, 1953. In French, 1949.

Bloor, David. *Knowledge and Social Imagery.* London and Boston: Routledge & Kegan Paul, 1976.

Boyle, Mary. *Schizophrenia—a Scientific Delusion?* New York: Routledge, 1990.

Gergen, Kenneth. "Feminist Critiques of Science and the Challenge of Social Epistemology." In *Feminist Thought and the Structure of Knowledge*, ed. Mary M. Gergen. New York: New York University Press, 1988.

Hacking, Ian. *The Social Construction of What?* Cambridge, Mass.: Harvard University Press, 1999.

Latour, Bruno, and Steve Woolgar. *Laboratory Life: The Social Construction of Scientific Facts.* Beverly Hills: Sage Publications, 1979.

Moussa, Helene. "The Social Construction of Women Refugees: A Journey of Discontinuities and Continuities." Ed.D. diss., University of Toronto, 1992.

Nagel, Thomas. *The Last Word.* New York: Oxford University Press, 1997.

Nelkin, Dorothy. "The Science Wars: What is at Stake?" *Chronicle of Higher Education*, 26 July 1996, A52.

Pickering, Andrew. *Constructing Quarks: A Sociological History of Particle Physics.* Chicago: University of Chicago Press, 1984.

Rorty, Richard. "Phony Science Wars." *Atlantic Monthly*, November 1999, 120–22.

——. "John Searle on Realism and Relativism." In *Truth and Progress.* Cambridge: Cambridge University Press, 1998.

Williams, Bernard. "The End of Everything?" Review of *The Last Word*, by Thomas Nagel. *New York Review of Books*, 19 November 1998.

## 40. POSTCOLONIAL SCIENCE STUDIES

### ENDING "EPISTEMIC VIOLENCE"

### MEERA NANDA

IN HER ESSAY "Can the Subaltern Speak?" which became an instant classic when it appeared in 1988, Gayatri Chakravorty Spivak identified a new species of violence that works without guns and without armies, but is, presumably, every bit as deadly. Invoking Foucault and Derrida, she called this genre of violence "epistemic violence"—that is, the violence of knowledge, or more properly, the violence of "discourse," which includes the complete apparatus of knowledge-production. She used the example of the British colonial administration's attempt to ban *sati* (widow immolation) in nineteenth-century India to illustrate how epistemic violence works. Spivak claims that in outlawing the practice of *sati*—that is, by classifying *sati* as a crime—the British committed an act of epistemic violence against the natives who tolerated and even "adulated" the practice as a sacred and heroic ritual. The self-immolation of widows, Spivak argues, "should have been" read in accord with local interpretations of Hindu sacred books and Hindu warrior traditions which allow it be understood as "[an] act of martyrdom, with the defunct husband standing in for the transcendental One; or [an act of] war, with the husband standing in for sovereign or state, for whose sake an intoxicating ideology of self-sacrifice can be mobilized. In actual fact, it was categorized [by the British] with murder, infanticide and the lethal exposure of the very old."[1] Put into simpler words, Spivak accuses the British of violence against traditions, because they reclassified what tradition condoned as a noble act, as an act of violence. The British, on this account, stand indicted of epistemic violence, because they tried to prevent actual violence against flesh-and-blood women.

This redefinition of a ritual into a crime amounts to violence against the "brown women whom the white men claimed to save from brown men" (to paraphrase Spivak), for it denied them even that thin veneer of courage and self-determination that the sacred traditions of Hindus conferred upon them, in however self-serving a manner. Women, however, were not the only or even the main targets. Rather, epistemic violence, which works "not by military might or industrial strength, but *by thought itself*,"[2] as Partha Chatterjee, another key figure in postcolonial studies, put it, is supposed to lie at the very heart of *all* colonialism, past, present, or future.

Meera Nanda. "Postcolonial Science Studies: Ending 'Epistemic Violence.'" Revised from Meera Nanda, *Prophets Facing Backward: Postmodern Critiques of Science and Hindu Nationalism in India*, 151–59. New Brunswick, N.J.: Rutgers University Press, 2003. Copyright © 2003 Meera Nanda. Reprinted by permission of Rutgers University Press.

Although Spivak's is one of the most influential voices connecting concerns about the "colonies" with fashionable poststructuralist theory, her idea of epistemic violence was not new. Starting around the early 1980s, a new crop of "amodern" or "nonmodern" intellectuals, upholding Mohandas Gandhi as an icon of alternative modernity, had already begun to emerge in India. In his well-known 1983 book, *The Intimate Enemy*, Ashis Nandy, the most prominent of these intellectuals, ascribed the political and economic power of the British imperialists to their "destruction of the unique gestalt of India," which he explicitly identified with a nonmodern, part-classical, part-folk Hinduism. Colonialism, according to Nandy, "won its victories [by] creating secular hierarchies incompatible with traditional order."[3] Thus colonialism was an act of violence against the nonsecular, nondifferentiated, nondualist view that had given meaning to ordinary people in India for centuries.

Following Nandy, another well-known book, again by an Indian intellectual, created a stir among postmodernist intellectuals around the world. This was Partha Chatterjee's 1986 *Nationalist Thought and the Colonial World: A Derivative Discourse?* In this book, Chatterjee argued that nationalist intellectuals, whether left-wing socialists like Nehru or right-wing religious nationalists like Bankim Chandra, were prisoners ("derivative") of a colonial mind-set, because both sides accepted the intellectual premises of the superiority of modernity and the necessity of modernization. The Fabian Socialist Nehru is as much a colonized mind as the Hindu nationalist Bankim because both accept the Western Enlightenment belief in progress through application of reason, the difference being that the former looked to the future for the evolution of reason in Indian society, while the latter looked to the heritage of the Hindu nation. On Chatterjee's account, both positions are equally problematic because both impose a Western teleology of progress and a Western conception of scientific reason on Indian culture. *The problem with the Hindu right, in other words, is not its backward looking, reactionary modernism, but its aspiration to modernity itself.* The only way to break out of the colonial mind-set is, according to Chatterjee, to break out of the Western "thematic"—that is, "Western justificatory structures, epistemological and ethical rules"—itself.[4] True anticolonialism lies in refusing the Western problematic (goals, possibilities) and the Western thematic (ways of thinking). On this account, India's nonmodern conceptual categories and epistemological and ethical rules should be used to study India and to allow India to chart its own future.

In yet another influential formulation, by Gyan Prakash, a subaltern-studies historian, to truly overcome the Orientalist biases, post-Orientalist historiography of India must take a postmodern turn and "repudiate the post-Enlightenment ideology of Reason and Progress."[5] Echoing Ashis Nandy and Partha Chatterjee, Gyan Prakash's view essentially comes down to the idea that India can be understood through its own indigenous conceptual categories. In a classic example of self-Orientalization, Prakash believes that a genuinely Indian history can be written only as "mythographies" which understand India from the Indian point of view. Again, colonialism is seen as acting through colonial knowledge.

Spivak, Nandy, Chatterjee, Gyan Prakash, and other postcolonial theorists were following in the footsteps of Edward Said's pathbreaking 1978 book, *Orientalism*. Drawing on the ideas of Michel Foucault, Said had argued that colonialism should not be seen merely as a project of territorial conquest and economic exploitation. Instead, colonialism should be seen as a project that constructs a new subjectivity—a new sense of what is real, normal, and good—among the colonized people that makes them available for control by the colonial powers. In the guise of producing "objective knowledge" of the people and places the West colonized, Western scholars created the Orient as something one "judges (as in a court of law), something one studies and depicts (as in a curriculum), something one disciplines (as in a school or prison), something one illustrates (as in a zoological manual)." The Oriental that the West constructed was "irrational, depraved (fallen), childlike, 'different'; [making the European appear in contrast as] rational, virtuous, mature, 'normal.'"[6] The West was able to control the Orient by "worlding" the subject peoples, that is, by substituting their version of reality with its own mode of understanding and structuring the world. It is through its claim to superior, objective, and universal knowledge that the West exerted its power.

This, then, is the pedigree of postcolonial studies, the latest entry into the jungle of post-marked areas of scholarship. The "postcolonialists" see themselves as creating a clearing where the power-knowledge of the West can be deconstructed and the colonized allowed—again—to see reality through "their own" conceptual frameworks. "Postcolonialism," in the words of Dipesh Chakrabarty, is a project of "provincializing Europe," showing that what the West claims as universally valid categories are actually provincial ideas of Europe which have acquired the status of universal truths because of Europe's economic and military power. Universal truths, like language, Dipesh Chakrabarty argues, are only "[provincial] dialects backed by an army."[7] If truth does not represent a reality outside of discourse, alternative, non-Western truths, if backed by the required trappings of power, can become alternative universals.

How is this task of provincializing and decolonization accomplished? The short answer is by deconstructing the universality of modern science. In this deconstruction, postcolonial theory joins hands (wittingly) with the social constructivist and feminist critiques of science, on the one hand, and (unwittingly) with the right-wing defenders of Hindu science, on the other.

At its most fundamental level, the postcolonial is an epistemological project. The postcolonial critique of the West is premised upon a repudiation of the objectivity, progressivity, and universalism of modern science. In general, postcolonial theorists take for granted what the assorted social constructivists, cultural studies and feminist critics labor so hard to argue, namely that scientific truths are social constructs and norms of justification depend upon the conceptual categories of a culture. Postcolonial theorists take it for granted that (to paraphrase Edward Said) there cannot be true representations of *anything*, because *all* representations are embedded alike in the language, culture, institutions, and the political ambience of the representer.[8] Truth, postcolonial theorists agree, is a dialect backed by an army; a "fact" becomes a fact because it is co-constructed with social power.

Lately, the alliance between postcolonialism and science studies, especially cultural studies and feminism, has become even more explicit. In her book *Is Science Multicultural?* Sandra Harding has argued that because modern science is both Eurocentric *and* androcentric, it is in the common interest of non-Western peoples and feminists everywhere to join forces to confront it. Because the colonized peoples and women alike have been driven to the margins of the modern world, they together offer a "standpoint epistemology" of the oppressed which can expose the blind-spots of modern science not visible to the beneficiaries of modernity.[9]

Harding is only belatedly echoing the postcolonial position of Ashis Nandy, who has long held Gandhi as an exemplar of how to build an alliance between the "other" West and nonmodern India. Like the generations of anti-Enlightenment romantics before him who found in India an escape from the instrumental, rational tendencies of the Western world, Nandy has argued that nonmodern India holds in "trusteeship" the softer, feminine, but repressed side of the West, namely, a relational view of the world, a noninstrumental search for knowledge that advances spiritual ends.[10] This provides grounds for a civilizational alliance between the marginalized selves of the West and the non-Western worlds. Like Harding and other feminists, Nandy believes that this alliance of the oppressed will rediscover the less dualistic, more interconnecting readings of nature which can then serve as alternative "technototems" of a more interdependent society.

The question still remains, in practical terms: how will postcolonial science differ from science-as-we-know-it? What difference will starting thought from the standpoint of postcolonial cultures, as Harding likes to put it, make on the ground?

Exhortations apart, real examples of ethnosciences in postcolonial science studies tend to be disappointing and limited mostly to defending the rationality of the local knowledge of peasants, shamans, midwives, herbalists, astrologers, and other ritualists within their own conceptual universes. The literature is vast and growing.[11] The objective of these new comparative studies in the postcolonial mode is to argue that "Western 'rationality' and 'scientificity' [cannot any longer] be used as the bench-mark by which other sciences can be evaluated. The ways of understanding the natural world that have been produced by different cultures and at different times should be compared as knowledge systems on an equal footing."[12] The theorists of alternative sciences quietly sidestep the issue of whether local knowledges can stand up to rigorous empirical testing with adequate controls. The standards of what constitutes evidence and what is a robust enough test are themselves treated as a part of the local context in all cases. How this position can escape a serious epistemological relativism is left largely unanswered, or answered with an attack on the political motives of those who raise the relativism question.

Reading this literature, it becomes clear that the underlying motivation is to give subaltern or marginalized social groups everywhere the right to challenge what the experts, bureaucrats, and those in power tell them. Scientific experts are seen not as serving truth but as glossing dominant interests in Western capitalist societies as facts of nature. Thus, postcolonial theorists, in the name of genuine openness and radical democracy, insist upon the right of prescientific traditions to question scientifically established knowledge. Dipesh Chakrabarty condemns as "hyper-rational" and colonized those Indian intellectuals who expect that only the peasant who understands the world in terms of ghosts and spirits has anything to learn from modern science and never the other way around. Nandy speaks for many in postcolonial science studies when he argues that non-Western cultures hold in trusteeship an alternative conception of knowledge which does not tear apart cognition from affect, facts from values, and does not reduce all knowledge for the sake of control and manipulation.[13] Clearly, the exhortation to cultural resistance against what modern science describes as normal and sane is motivated by the commendable political motives of enabling the weak to become the creators of their own symbolic worlds.

The problem, however, is that *what appears as marginal from the point of view of the modern West is not marginal at all in non-Western societies* which haven't yet experienced a significant secularization of their cultures. Local knowledges that Western critics assume to be standpoints of the "oppressed" are, in fact, deeply embedded in the dominant religious/cultural idiom of non-Western societies. Using local knowledges to challenge Western science may, however dubiously, illuminate the blind-spots of modern science in the West. But in non-Western societies themselves, such an affirmation of the scientificity of local knowledges ends up endorsing the power of the dominant cultural-religious institutions. Even worse, while the left-wing critics of science invoke local knowledges "strategically" in order to fight what they see as the bigger evil, that is, the West, the right wing can use the same logic and invoke the same local knowledges much more "authentically" and "organically," for it can mobilize all the traditional religious piety and cultural symbolism that go with local knowledges.

This is precisely what is going on in India today. It is not a mere coincidence that the Hindu right-wing supporters of Vedic science declare themselves to be a part of postcolonial studies. It is not a coincidence that the Hindu nationalists claim important postcolonial scholars, especially Ashis Nandy, Vandana

Shiva, Claude Alvarez, and Ronald Inden as their own.[14] Right-wing Hindu intellectuals have good reason to join the ranks of postcolonial scholars, for they, too, see themselves as fighting for the "decolonization of the Hindu mind." It is the de-Westernization of the national imaginary that they profess to fight for when they decry secularism and individual rights–based feminism and liberalism as signs of colonized minds. It is the cause of a "deeper" decolonization of the mind that they profess to defend when they rewrite science books to include astrology and *vastu* (building structures in alignment with the cosmic "life-force") as sciences, and when they find the Vedas to be the real source of all sciences.

There are, of course, clear differences between right-wing and left-wing postcolonialism, with two, in particular, worth noticing. First, the whole point of social constructivism, feminism, and postcolonialism has been to deny that there is any such thing as "the Hindu mind" or "the scientific method" that can escape the contingency of history and politics. While there are many examples of cruder varieties of gender and Third Worldist essentialism in the writings of some postcolonial theorists (especially Vandana Shiva and some other difference feminists), most postcolonial and feminist studies scholars have made strenuous efforts to distance themselves from essentialism. Scholars like Haraway, and more recently Spivak, have taken care to define subalternity or marginality not in terms of racial, gender, or national identities, but as "oppositional consciousness,"[15] or in terms of the ability to speak. According to Spivak, "everything that has limited or no access to cultural imperialism is subaltern— a space of difference," as are all those "cut off from upward—and in a sense 'outward' mobility."[16] Other postcolonialists share this nonessentialist view of subalternity. Gyan Prakash, for instance, wants to define subalternity as a "variety of shifting positions" that develop as an "effect of power relations expressed through a variety of means—linguistic, economic and cultural," rather than in static, essentialist terms like the "proletariat," "caste system," "Third World," or "Eastern," etc.[17] Thus defined, subalternity can cut across class and national lines, leading to a new "subaltern international" of sorts which defines itself in opposition to modernization and its constituent theme of reason and progress.

Yet, for all these disavowals of essentialism, even the best of postcolonial scholarship ends up taking shelter in what Spivak has called a "strategic essentialism." Strategic essentialism is essentially strategic. It amounts to saying that while we *know* that there are no real essences, no pure subjectivities, we can nevertheless "strategically use a positive essentialism in a scrupulously visible political interest."[18] The "visible political interest" is to give voice to the subaltern groups who have not been allowed to represent themselves. In this larger political interest, nearly all postcolonial studies fall back, strategically or otherwise, on a view of subaltern knowledge practices as essentially cyborgian, undifferentiated, nondualistic, and monistic. In postcolonial studies proper, subaltern rationality is accepted as a domain of "innocence" (Ashis Nandy), "community" (Partha Chatterjee), and an unproblematic unity of effect and analysis, values and facts (Ashis Nandy, Frédérique Marglin,[19] and Dipesh Chakrabarty)—all the traits that are supposedly lacking in Western, Enlightenment rationality. Take the last example: Dipesh Chakrabarty berates Indian critics of Hinduism as "hyper-rational" creatures of the Western Enlightenment who cannot empathize with the religious imagination of their countrymen. He complains that the secular critics simply fail to understand Hindu rationality, which does not split analysis from emotions, or nature from the supernatural. In this reading of difference, to separate these domains, to value the separation of facts from values, to aim for objectivity in knowledge is itself a mark of the colonial mind-set. However, if we grant the very foundations of objectivity to the West, are we not back to the old stereotypes of irrational, emotional natives?

The Hindu right wing is, of course, unabashedly essentialist. What is only "strategically" essentialist for the left-wing postcolonial theorists becomes part and parcel of the eternal "Hindu mind" in right-wing postcolonialism. The additional windfall for right-wing postcolonialists is that all the traits of nondifferentiated, interactionist knowledge that left-wing science critics defend fit very well with the holistic, undifferentiated antidualism of the Vedic worldview. The left-wing postcolonial scholars, in other words, have been doing the spadework for the right-wing postcolonial scholars. Highly visible scholars of international repute in progressive academic circles have been defending ideas that turn out to be the staple of a conservative, neo-Hindu understanding of Hinduism and Hindu sciences.

There is a second issue on which left-wing postcolonials can legitimately deny any overlap with right-wing Hindu nationalists. The left-wing postcolonials have no sympathy at all with the right-wing attempt to justify Hindu beliefs and practices as "scientific," as the right-wing defenders of Vedic science do. In fact, Ashis Nandy and Partha Chatterjee have been explicit in their denunciation of Hindu nationalists as mentally colonized by the West for justifying Hinduism against a Western episteme. Nandy and other left-wing postcolonialists want to reverse the direction of justification: they want the modern West to examine its conceptual categories in response to the subaltern categories. They see Hindu nationalists as distorting India's nonmodern gestalt by defending those elements of the Vedic tradition which can outdo the West in their "scientificity." For the left-wing postcolonialists, the right-wing discourse of Hindu science is modernist, and therefore a "derivative discourse" taken from the colonial masters.

But as I have been arguing, the Hindu right wing is modernist in a reactionary, anti-Enlightenment way. The right-wing movement for Hindutva (or Hindu-ness) is gobbling up modern science by declaring the Vedic knowledge systems to be at par with modern science in rationality and credibility. Proponents of Vedic science claim the Vedas to have presaged all the advances in modern science without admitting that, in fact, modern sciences challenge the metaphysical foundation of the Vedic view of the world.

The varieties of social constructivist critiques of science discussed in this chapter give aid and comfort to the Hindu right wing by providing philosophical arguments for the equality of modern science with other ways of knowing. By denying the reality and the possibility of progress in our knowledge of the natural world through the methodological and institutional innovations in modern science, these theories defend the worldview that *all* systematic attempts to learn about nature are equally scientific. By denying the fact that the scientific view of the world has put all metaphysics in question, these theories disarm the struggle for Enlightenment and secularization.

In this chapter I have shown that, despite strenuous denials, all varieties of social constructivism end up opening the door to a serious epistemological relativism. In each case, I have also shown that, despite their honorable political intentions, all varieties of social constructivism end up giving aid and comfort to Hindu chauvinists who display many symptoms of fascism.

I will close with two final clarifications. Some have argued that by laboring to establish this link with the Hindu right wing, I am censoring any attempt to reveal the role of social context/interest in science and therefore, indirectly, encouraging a return to a discredited "positivism." I believe that disclosing the social structuring of knowledge is a worthy enterprise, but it need not take a relativist turn. I believe that the undeniable fact of scientific progress in providing more adequate and transculturally true accounts of natural phenomena can serve—and should have served—as a pragmatist-realist check on social constructivist enthusiasm for empowering culture over nature. I also believe that the total and universal denunciations of the Enlightenment are just bad social theory, lacking any sense of the real history of non-Western societies. Those critics of science who uncritically embrace the ideals of nondifferentiated, "amodern" ways of knowing could have easily asked: How have the lives of real men and women been in societies under holist epistemologies and worldviews? Are individuation and objectivity really opposed to the interests of the oppressed? The social history of the subalterns in India could have shown that the subalterns have in fact struggled *against* the undifferentiated holism of Hindu cosmology and epistemology.

This brings me to the second clarification. It is true that the postmodernist and social constructivist critiques started out with the goal of deconstructing the hegemonic position of science in the West. The fate of science in the rest of the world was not their *primary* focus, even though there was always some concern with issues of science's contribution to imperialism. One cannot, therefore, some argue, hold these critics responsible for how their theories are used in the world outside the West.

This defense will not wash. As I have shown at length above, the evidence of the alternative rationalities of non-Western peoples has been an *integral* part of social constructivist arguments for denuding modern science of its special and universal stature. It is ironic that with all the emphasis on the social context of modern science, social constructivist theories, for the most part, have completely ignored the social context of alternative sciences in other parts of the world. Even a cursory familiarity with the social history of local knowledges in postcolonial societies could have shown the limits (both social and institutional) of these alternatives. Even a modicum of critical engagement with the "other" could have shown that the aspects of ethno-knowledges they admire have quite often been a part of the dominating, hegemonic cultures in non-Western societies. This knowledge is easily available. That it was not sought, or played down, is a result of the political biases of the postmodernist critics. It is simply bad scholarship.

My motivation for this engagement is to remind us of a simple truth: ideas have consequences. Those of us who trade in ideas have a responsibility to ensure that our ideas should do no harm. In the face of the rising threat of reactionary populism in India and many other parts of the developing world, it is high time critics of reason and Enlightenment ask themselves if they are fulfilling their responsibility.

## NOTES

1. Gayatri Chakravorty Spivak, "Can the Subaltern Speak?" in *Marxism and the Interpretation of Culture*, ed. Cary Nelson and Lawrence Grosssberg (Urbana: University of Illinois Press, 1988), 302.

2. Partha Chatterjee, *Nationalist Thought and the Colonial World: A Derivative Discourse?* (London: Zed books, 1986), 11.

3. Ashis Nandy, *The Intimate Enemy: Loss and Recovery of Self Under Colonialism* (New Delhi: Oxford University Press, 1983), 73.

4. Chatterjee, *Nationalist Thought*, 38.

5. Gyan Prakash, "Writing Post-Orientalist Histories of the Third World: Perspective from Indian Historiography," *Comparative Studies in Society and History* 32, no. 2 (April 1990): 404.

6. Edward Said, *Orientalism* (New York: Vintage Books, 1978), 40.

7. Dipesh Chakrabarty, *Provincializing Europe: Postcolonial Thought and Historical Difference* (Princeton, N.J.: Princeton University Press, 2000), 43.

8. Said, *Orientalism*, 272 and passim.

9. Sandra Harding, *Is Science Multicultural? Postcolonialisms, Feminisms, and Epistemologies* (Bloomington: Indiana University Press, 1998).

10. Nandy, *Intimate Enemy*, chapter 2 and passim.

11. For relatively recent overviews, see David J. Hess, *Science and Technology in a Multicultural World: The Cultural Politics of Facts and Artifacts* (New York: Columbia University Press, 1995); Laura Nader, ed., *Naked Science: Anthropological Inquiry into Boundaries,*

*Power, and Knowledge* (New York: Routlege, 1996); and Susantha Goonatilake, *Toward a Global Science: Mining Civilizational Knowledge* (Bloomington: Indiana University Press, 1998).

12. Helen Watson-Verran and David Turnbull, "Science and Other Indigenous Knowledge Systems," in *Handbook of Science and Technology Studies*, ed. Sheila Jasanoff et al. (Thousand Oaks, Calif.: Sage Publications, 1995), 115.

13. See especially Nandy, *Intimate Enemy*, chapter 2.

14. See Koenraad Elst, *Decolonizing the Hindu Mind: Ideological Development of Hindu Revivalism* (New Delhi: Rupa & Co., 2001); and Girilal Jain, *The Hindu Phenomenon* (Delhi: UBSPD, 1994).

15. Donna J. Haraway, *Simians, Cyborgs, and Women: The Reinvention of Nature* (New York: Routledge, 1991); and Harding, *Is Science Multicultural?*

16. Gayatri Chakravorty Spivak, "The New Subaltern: A Silent Interview," in *Mapping Subaltern Studies and the Postcolonial*, ed. Vinayak Chaturvedi (London: Verso, 2000), 325.

17. Prakash, "Post-Orientalist Histories," 400.

18. Gayatri Chakravorty Spivak, "Subaltern Studies: Deconstructing Historiography," in *Selected Subaltern Studies*, ed. Ranajit Guha and Gayatri Chakravorty Spivak (New York: Oxford University Press, 1988), 13.

19. Frédérique Marglin, "Rationality, the Body, and the World: From Production to Regeneration," in *Decolonizing Knowledge: From Development to Dialogue*, ed. Frédérique Apffel-Marglin and Stephen A. Marglin (Oxford: Clarendon Press, 1996), 146–82.

THE ESSAYS IN THIS SECTION consider the future of reading and the role of criticism once they are freed from the deforming constraints of Theory. Although they clearly function as skirmishes in a kind of rescue campaign launched against the subjugation of reading by theorizing, they are just as manifestly driven by a deep concern for the integrity of literature. Like other contributors to this book, the essayists in this section argue that literature is indeed a thing of the highest merit and that it must engage the critic in the service of its intrinsic value. In turn, critics are called upon to transmit the abiding worth of literature to the coming generations. If this does not happen, our essayists fear, the humane and life-enhancing properties of literary works will be lost to us as literary studies, and literature itself, are disfigured in the distorting mirrors of the fun house of theoretical posturing.

What standards remain for literary criticism, asks David Bromwich in the essay that opens this section, in the aftermath of Theory's assault on time-honored interpretive tools such as appreciation of complexity, tact, competence, and—yes—good instincts? Having deflated all these as "constructed" entities, postmodern theory turns literary criticism into a very different kind of pursuit. Meanings, genre divisions, historicity, even the human presence all dissolve. The "all or nothing propensities" of many Theory aficionados lead them, as observers of human life, to read culture as a "seamless general text," while these same theorists misleadingly give their own practices political labels. Bad theory, Bromwich points out, makes bad history. Once intelligibility is surrendered as an ideal, once equal weight is given to any aspect of a work, it makes little difference whether our analysis is of a work of art or of a mass-cultural product. Instead of capitulating to these debilitating trends, Bromwich argues, criticism should aim to comment—competently, sensibly, and richly—on literary texts in order to reveal in them, over and over, "the hidden power of living men and women."

Frank Kermode, in "Changing Epochs," addresses the consequences of the drastic cultural and institutional mutations occurring in our time. While noting that breaks of continuity (for example in the Renaissance) are not usually as abrupt and uncompromising as the disjunction postmodernist critics, in their arrogance, claim for their own rupture, he observes troubling breaks following upon the rise of the postmodern: the enfeeblement of literary studies, the loss of confidence in the civilizing agencies of the humanities, and the commodification of theory by its star practitioners and their trendy publishers. What to do? Kermode argues for the cultivation of a "literary sensibility"—a task whose difficulty he does not underestimate at a time when the past and its literature are often devalued, if not disdained.

Nancy Easterlin in her essay suggests that "bioepistemology"—the view that knowledge is related to the capabilities of human knowers—offers a solution to the stalemate between theory and practice now afflicting literary studies. Easterlin finds it nothing short of miraculous, in light of the denial of human agency that is now commonplace in much literary theory, that a field devoted to studying the artifacts of human culture has survived at all. To be meaningful, she affirms, discussion of these artifacts must be framed by our knowledge of human beings, not by artificial or incomplete notions of our world and our social experience. It is Easterlin's contention that a new humanism based in a bioepistemological perspective can reconnect literature with human life through scientific insight and allow us to speculate on the function and meaning of literature within the entirety of human knowledge.

Peter Lamarque and Stein Haugom Olsen argue for the recovery of literature's role as a repository of human values, without which it is meaningless. Literature, they note, appeals to readers because it promotes a special kind of interest in human life; this is what distinguishes it from fiction understood as invented stories and made-up descriptions. But poststructuralist theory has—through simple assertion, not analysis—undermined this vital distinction between literature and fiction (as Easterlin has also noted) in favor of the sweeping proposition that all literature is fiction in the sense that, as a product of language, it can make no claim to any kind of truth. Indeed, to Theory, the very possibility of "saying something about" does not exist. This denial, in turn, has led to the transformation of literary works into "texts," a shift that cancels out all distinctive properties of literature vis-à-vis every other kind of writing. Throughout their essay, the authors urge us to hold on to the concept of literature as an evaluative pursuit which, in representing life, speaks to us of things of lasting human interest.

Paisley Livingston makes an equally strong argument for a renewed vision of the aesthetics of literature, construed as "the appreciation of literary art *qua* art." Contemporary literary criticism is, he finds, poorly situated to serve that aim. Among its shortcomings is the conflict between epistemic responsibility and innovative claims, which scholars attempt to reconcile by occupying "the niche of 'theory,'" even if this means dissolving criticism into sociology, cultural history, and similar nonliterary fields. This leads to the "Very Big Claims characteristic of theory-driven literary readings," which, Livingston notes, escape the norms of humanistic or scientific inquiry by claiming for themselves the status of a kind of art. Ironically, then, these readings return us to the question of "the aesthetic." Livingston also warns against "instrumental" readings that focus on such sanctioned themes as gender, race, class, and Western metaphysics. While noting that there is no one right way to read literature, Livingston makes the case for attending to the intrinsic value—that is, the aesthetic and artistic qualities—of literary works.

In the searching essay with which this section concludes, Marjorie Perloff considers the "crisis in the humanities" by inquiring into the state of literature in our society. Why, she asks, the derogation of poetry in the academy? Perloff considers the abandonment of formalist criticism in the 1960s as an early cause. Later, cultural studies further stripped literature of its autonomy, disregarding its formal and rhetorical values, and ignoring its power and access to truth while emphasizing its merely instrumental function as a handy clue to the Zeitgeist. The uniqueness of literature as art, Perloff asserts, is beyond the grasp of contemporary criticism. In fact, the practice of cultural studies favored by theorists can dispense with literature altogether, as can race and gender studies, globalization, and other fashionable pursuits that now dominate English departments, where teaching "anything but literature" has been fostered in recent decades. Nonetheless, Perloff ends on an optimistic note, confident that the pleasures of poetry are such that they are bound to prevail.

## 41.  LITERATURE AND THEORY

### NOTES ON THE RESEARCH PROGRAMS OF THE 1980S

### DAVID BROMWICH

THEORY EXISTS NOW in a protected condition, in comparison with which the situation of literature as well as criticism in the past may look admirably unprotected. Still, it would be pointless to ignore the drift of things. The objects of study are gradually being redefined, both for advanced students of literature and for the students whom they instruct in turn. To isolate a single effect: someone informed by theory, and aiming to write on a certain author or a group of texts, will read more widely than he would have done a decade ago, but also more thinly. If, for example, the result is an article on *Frankenstein*, then Rousseau and Nietzsche may be brought in, together with several current theorists. In the economy of the argument, they displace other works by Mary Shelley and her contemporaries, as, in the thinking and reading that helped to construct the argument, a similar displacement is likely to have occurred. The visible result is a change in the look of interpretations—or interrogations, to use the up-to-date word. A larger and less obvious change has to do with the traits that are looked on as useful in a critic.

Tact was an available name to sum up these traits, but what did it mean? A competence, supported by an instinct. A critic who expected to persuade readers of the sense of an interpretation would show some feeling for the language in which the work was written, for the period in which its author wrote, and for the particular inflections that its style gave to the idiom it inherited and revised. A false hope on which this idea of criticism was premised, but a hope inextricable from the acceptance of literature as an academic subject, was that something as elusive as tact could somehow be taught. It could not be, any more than insight into personal lives can be taught to a psychologist. It ought to be taken to imply, therefore, nothing but a form of practical wisdom, which most critics wished to encourage. By contrast, few critics since the Enlightenment have believed that their efforts converged on a single right interpretation of a text. Their consensus was modeled, rather, on other sorts of common sense: in the reading of a literary work, there was such a thing as *getting things right*. This was linked with the conventions of making sense that governed more ordinary social practices as well. In literature, however, it related specifi-

David Bromwich. "Literature and Theory." Originally published as "Recent Work in Literary Criticism," *Social Research* 53, no. 3 (Autumn 1986). Copyright © *Social Research*. Abridged by the author and reprinted by permission of the author.

cally to the practice of honoring the complex over the simple, the worth-rereading over the not-worth-rereading. A clue to what has happened in criticism over the past several years is that every key word in this paragraph would now be challenged by many theorists: "sense," "competence," "instinct," "complexity," "practical wisdom." All these are constructed, the theorist can say, for purposes that theory exists to expose. It might be replied that one such purpose is the creation of works of art.

People in other academic disciplines often assume that making sense of a literary work and valuing it are activities on approximately the same level. In criticism, they think, it is all a matter of opinion anyway. To forestall this reaction and limit the truth I want to assert, it will help to give an example of what "a competence, supported by an instinct" may mean. In *Day of the Leopards: Essays in Defense of Poems*, W. K. Wimsatt relates the following anecdote.

> There was a student once who wrote a paper saying that a couplet by Alexander Pope, " . . . no Prelate's Lawn with Hair-shirt lined, / Is half so incoherent as my mind" (Epistle I.i. 165–66) ought to be read in the light of a couplet in another poem by Pope: "Whose ample Lawns are not asham'd to feed / the milky heifer and deserving steed" (*Moral Essays* IV. 185–86). Since I believe in the force of puns and all sorts of other verbal resemblances in poetry, I do not know quite how to formulate the rule of context by which I confidently reject that connection. But I seek first ineluctable confrontations, only later, if at all, rules.[1]

To Wimsatt, lawn (the fabric) simply was not answerable to lawn (the plot of land), notwithstanding their identity as sounds and their possible relationship as signifiers.

A sense of where such confrontations did occur was on this view the only guide one needed to point out the improbability of their occurrence somewhere else. But the sense in question did not apply to verbal resemblances alone. The social judgments which a text presumed, and to which it might allude subtly or openly, also ruled in certain critical statements as interesting, while it ruled out others as spurious. To keep for a moment with Pope: in the line "Or stain her honor, or her new brocade," the rhetorical scheme is zeugma, with abstract and concrete nouns sharing a verb. Now, a remark that Pope's uses of this scheme were concentrated disproportionately in his satires on women would be interesting if true; while a remark that, just when he wrote the line, brocade-sellers were flourishing in England as never before would be spurious even if true. Whatever the latter might add to the reader's view of the economic arrangements of the time, it would say nothing about what made Pope worth studying as a writer. In the two decades since Wimsatt wrote, however, the criteria he evoked for the pertinence of a statement have partly dropped away from criticism. The questions How could that matter? (said of an unjustified turn in an argument) and But where is it? (said of a piece of evidence conspicuously overlooked) are asked less often.

Thus a recent article in a respected critical journal proposed that *Jane Eyre* was an imperialist text.[2] The novel, that is, aimed to gain sympathy for a heroine whose passions were in complicity with the dominant prejudices of the age. It is not a startling general argument, and *Jane Eyre* is not the last place one would look for it to be tried. To make the case, Gayatri Spivak recalls the colonial origins of Mr. Rochester's mad wife, Bertha. Jane first sees Bertha Rochester's face reflected in a mirror, and the scene involves a repressed self-recognition. So far, the details and emphasis are familiar. The new element in this reading is the discovery that such a recognition could never be genuine since Jane Eyre herself is among the colonial oppressors. Her attitudes are established in part by an inquiry into her attachment to St. John Rivers, who is taken to represent the worst both of a male-dominated society and of an imperial ethic abroad. But here the *But where is it?* ought to stop one short. For the novel identifies Rivers as belonging to an evangelical sect that fought hard for the abolition of slavery: his parentage, though at a distance, includes men like Zachary Macaulay. If described as imperialist, it ought to be described carefully. Of all this the article says nothing. It is not treated as an irony or as a complicating fact.

At what point in arguing against procedures like these does one have to appeal to some version of reality or of objectivity in interpretation? There has been a long line of critics—at least beginning with Hume's essay "Of the Standard of Taste" and Johnson's *Lives* of Swift and Milton—who say that without ever arriving at such a point at all, one may coherently judge interpretations as well as literary works themselves. Emphatically included in their idea of judgment was a belief in the worth of correcting errors. The roots of academic criticism, however, were always in a different tradition, with its beginnings in Coleridge and German idealism. The modern concern with the single right interpretation and the unified text to be right about may be traced largely to Coleridge's belief in the perfect work as a mediatory object between man and God. It was a misfortunate, it seems to me, of the theoretical debates of the 1970s that critics who made similar emotional demands of truth were supposed to represent the common wisdom about interpretation; so that if one rejected them, one took oneself to be rejecting something like Hume's conception of taste or Johnson's of original invention, neither of which is committed to an epistemological way of truth. These writers, and many others after them, are so far from supposing their judgments will lack validity without a diffuse but substantial something called reality to anchor them that they suppose their judgments to be founded on merely the common habits of reading and the long duration of certain opinions that acquire the force of custom. Such critics were not "essentialists" about meaning, and they would not have seen essentialism versus relativism as a choice that confronted anyone. Yet in the debates I mentioned above, one side, particularly in the writings of E. D. Hirsch and Gerald Graff, chose to make the stability of critical judgments depend on the stability of their objects.[3]

The theorist wants, and Hirsch tells him he is right to want, all or nothing: if interpretations do not tend toward truth, then there is no such thing as getting things right. The developments I sketched at the start of this review are symptoms of a very quick passage from all to nothing. The dilemma was taken seriously, I think, because both sides agreed that criticism gave the method for tracing the discoveries of literature itself. The idea of method was the first mistake; the picture of someone following up clues was the second. It would have made better sense to think of criticism as a language for discussing representations of the way people live and think and feel. The language is secondary in that it comes later. But it aims to give fresh interest to a narrative that owes everything to life, as life owes everything to the narratives that put it within our grasp. The idea of criticism as a language, rather than a map to a special province of truth, might well have gained acceptance while the New Critics were still active, had they chosen Wittgenstein rather than Coleridge as their guide. His questions in the *Philosophical Investigations*, on the difficulties of a private language, fall in with arguments more familiar to critics, and written about the same time, on the difficulties of reckoning intention as part of meaning: "And how do you know what you are to give yourself an exhibition of before you do it? This *private* exhibition is an illusion." Again, the best aphorisms there are on interpretation itself as a perspective come from the *Investigations*: "What I can see something *as*, is what it can be a picture of." Criticism resembles the making of a picture by seeing something as something else; and the work is the sum of the things that the picture can be of. Wittgenstein defines the interpreted character of a figure, which one may take to stand for a work, by talking of its possible aspects: "The aspects in a change of aspects are those ones which the figure might sometimes have *permanently* in a picture."[4] A critic can say, in short, certain things the picture will *not* be, so long as sight, cognition, the passions and interests of the lookers-on, stay even roughly as they appear to be at present. But this does not limit the ways in which one can see a thing *as*.

Wittgenstein, as much as Hume, urges his readers to think of meaning as intelligible only in the light of habits or a more-than-private history of practices. He remarks in *Zettel* that it is a mistake "to say that there is anything that meaning something consists in." Saying a thing is a way of seeing what you mean; but meaning a thing is not seeing something that you do not say. "Only in the stream of thought and life do words have meaning."[5] In sentences like this and in the promptings, second guesses, and illustrations that enlarge them, Wittgenstein is the theorist who feels closest to the great, nonreligious, and nonepistemological critics from the eighteenth century to the present. Academic critics tend in practice to share their bias, and yet with rare exceptions for a critic like Empson or Wimsatt they are not close arguers, or conscious of the beliefs that their arguments presuppose. Faced by a question like "Do you believe in determinacy of meaning?" they sometimes fall back on memories of epistemological arguments, themselves modeled on religious beliefs, which have nothing at all to do with their practices. This may entail at first a ready assent to the sentence "If we know, we must be knowing something"—from which it may falsely be shown to follow that we know things as they are in themselves.

The influential attacks on the text-in-itself came not, where they might have been looked for, from social or intellectual historians, but from a tendency within theory, for which the best name anyone has offered is "textualism."[6] When Derrida said there was nothing outside the text, he meant there was nothing apparently discrete from the text that its words would assist in keeping so. It took only implication, the play of the rhetoric, the return of repressed opposites, to bring it inside. The chapters on Rousseau in *Of Grammatology* and on Plato in *Dissemination* proceed by translating such distinctions as that between voice and writing, or cure and poison, into the undistinguishable doubles they become when the concepts of philosophy are read with the ambivalences language can never exclude.[7] The opponent in these inquiries is every hierarchy of knowledge, whether it is figured as a progress from writing to speech, or from a rhetoric that conceals the forms of justice to a dialectic that reveals it. Because modern philosophy habitually abstracts arguments from the words that make them, and words themselves from the history they were conditioned by, Derrida's writing had a plainer moral for philosophers than for literary critics. His deconstructions came to this: a showing that epistemology only asserts what the language of its asserting must call into question. A recognition of the way that happens might be expected to provoke a close historical study of the languages by which the problems of philosophy are generated from age to age. It has had that effect, in a small degree. But the ambition of Derrida's writing was not confined to a discipline in any case. It suggested that what is called philosophy and what is called literature are not different in kind. When philosophy begins to be read as writing, literature may be read as thinking. The signs of such a response have begun to appear in a few studies of novels as moral philosophy—studies that take their motive from a belief that literature gives a density to examples that arguments alone cannot supply.[8] Yet the use of literary texts as a sort of primary material for philosophy was not what Derrida had in mind at all: as if novelists wrote to pose a problem ("the acknowledgment of others," for example) that had already been framed by philosophers. Within literature, Derrida's work has encouraged a reading of fictional and nonfictional, literary and philosophical, narrative and argumentative writings under their common aspects as texts.

In a review of Jonathan Culler's *On Deconstruction*, in the course of some extremely sensible comments on the all-or-nothing propensities of literary theorists, John Searle summarized an aim of deconstruction as the removal of metaphor from a marginal to a central position in language.[9] This was a good example of the all-or-nothing propensities of philosophers; and it brought out the persistence of the habits of mind that Derrida opposes. The point of his dealings with metaphor is that *any* rule separating the metaphorical from the literal will dissolve under scrutiny. Neither is central because neither can be prior, as the following illustration may attest: "The eminence was really an eminence when I saw him on the podium." Nobody ought to try to find the metaphor in the last sentence. And yet Shelley's "Defense of Poetry" is rich in suggestions like this concerning metaphor, as are many essays of romantic and modern criticism. What appears strange in the reception of Derrida's work is that it has been taken generally as saying something shocking about how criticism is done. One strong definition of literary power has always held that it impresses the reader with a specific gravity at every point while leaving its final emphasis unsettled.

About the status of Derrida's procedures there was always a puzzle. Was deconstruction a technique proper to the commentator, and necessary as a tactic against the naive constructionism of the author? Or was it something the author's writing practiced for itself, in which case the commentator's only role would be to tease out the language it had been speaking all its life? Derrida's interests did not require him to choose between these descriptions. But his mode of analysis became current in America, and later in Britain, largely through a long essay devoted to his reading of Rousseau, in Paul de Man's *Blindness and Insight*. There de Man appeared to choose the second description. Recounting Derrida's own argument against the metaphysics of presence, which had tracked the privilege of speech (as presence) against writing (as deception) from its prominent use in Lévi-Strauss back to its invention in the anthropology of Rousseau, "Jacques Derrida's Reading of Rousseau" pointed out that this and kindred oppositions were called into doubt in Rousseau's texts themselves. Rather than expose a self-deception, therefore, which literature shared with metaphysics, de Man vindicated literature as a place of self-suspicion that was exemplary for language in general. The same work was carried into de Man's later essays in *Allegories of Reading* and *The Rhetoric of Romanticism*; in the introductory chapter of the former book, on "Semiology and Rhetoric," de Man propounded his thesis unambiguously:

> A literary text simultaneously asserts and denies the authority of its own rhetorical mode, and by reading the text as we did we were only trying to come closer to being as rigorous a reader as the author had to be in order to write the sentence in the first place. Poetic writing is the most advanced and refined mode of deconstruction; it may differ from critical or discursive writing in the economy of its articulation, but not in kind.[10]

It is worth noting that the main points of this assertion—its leveling of text with commentary and its ranking of poetry, in degree, above criticism by virtue of its "rigor" and economy"—were made with a slightly different emphasis in the opening chapter of Empson's *Seven Types of Ambiguity*. Of ambiguity Empson wrote: "Meanings of this kind, indeed, are conveyed, but they are conveyed much more by poets than by analysts; that is what poets are for, and why they are important"; of the implicit statements of speech and writing he also remarked: "printed commonly differ from spoken ones in being intended for a greater variety of people, and poetic from prose ones in imposing the system of habits they imply more firmly or more quickly."[11] In the same way, Derrida's comments on the assimilability of all language to rhetoric may seem to recall Kenneth Burke's inquiries in the *Grammar* and *Rhetoric* he published in 1945 and 1950.

De Man's most impressive essay for me is "The Rhetoric of Temporality."[12] It argues that two dogmas have shaped critical thought about the literary object since the early decades of the nineteenth century: the conception of irony as a fixed perspective, and of the symbol as a fusion of image and idea that cannot be found in allegory. Hazlitt, Shelley, Lionel Johnson, Edward Thomas, and a good many others might be cited as critics outside the consensus that de Man writes against, but the people he really has in view are recent and synoptic literary historians: M. H. Abrams, for example, in his discussions of the symbol, and Wayne Booth in his treatment of narrative irony. After one has read this essay, one's sense of the uses of irony can never be quite the same, and there seems to be very little point in ever talking of the symbol again, except for the historical purpose of exhibiting the preoccupations of a school. The essays on romantic authors which de Man wrote soon after, particularly those on Rousseau, Shelley, and "Autobiography as De-Facement," add up to a denial of the consolations of writing. It is always pertinent, Iris Murdoch observed in *The Sovereignty of Good*, to ask of a philosopher, What is he afraid of? De Man in these essays asks the same question of writers, as the makers of inscriptions that are meant at once to outlast and to represent them. "Autobiography as De-Facement" starts from the Proustian datum that a life cannot speak to us as a life until it is inscribed on a monument; and yet the speaking monument is the author who, in order to address us, must imagine himself as already dead. Nor is this stance merely figurative. In writing his life, the author changes it from pure face to defacement, as all monuments are defaced or scarred by their inscriptions. Any testimony from a writer, then, which we receive concerning the writer's life, is a testimony from the point of view of death. Accordingly, the very words that mean to reflect a life must deform it in order to make its story come into existence at all. Once, however, we concede that "autobiography is a defacement of the mind of which it is itself the cause," it follows that "death is a displaced name for a linguistic predicament," for the discovery that autobiography hoped to gain through writing "deprives and disfigures to the precise extent that it restores."[13] Here again, though de Man's text is Wordsworth's *Essays on Epitaphs*, his recognition is familiar above all to readers of Proust. Phrased as a truism, it may be supposed to mean: every book leaves something out. Beneath this nevertheless one may discern the starker claim that there are no true stories.

An implication of most deconstructionist criticism is that an end of self-deception requires an end of the self. Writing and the self are said to confirm each other in the illusion that they can transcend the death that is another name for a linguistic predicament—the existence of what is called literature being the chief source of their positive reinforcement. It was understandable that the metaphysical-minded theorists of the 1970s should hope that a politics would materialize in the general direction their criticism seemed to indicate. A feature of the transition to the moralistic criticism of the 1980s—dominated as the latter has been by the writings of Michel Foucault—is that politically impressive conclusions are now trusted to emerge from a therapy of *nothing but* skeptical reading.

The effect is as follows. A promise of social analysis is made, tacitly by the tone itself of the criticism, more overtly by the choice of objects for analysis, yet the argument is foreshortened just at the point where what was promised might be performed. I have only a hunch about why this occurs, and since others have even less I will give it briefly. Deconstruction was a way to upset, from within, a system controlled by certain hierarchies of knowledge, which related in turn to hierarchies of power. Critics aware of what it could do to conventional linguistic arrangements saw how easily it might do something similar to conventional social arrangements. And yet here Foucault, whose *Discipline and Punish* has had a wide vogue in literary studies, proves to be as unrewarding a guide as Derrida. Talking about social arrangements, after all, means talking about the sorts of persons who live in them, and who suffer or profit by them. Talking about persons, however, is prohibited in advance by the exclusion that Foucault and Derrida alike enforce against comparable entities.

It is almost like talking about character, almost like talking about the self. And at this juncture, the theorist is apt to be inhibited by two leading conditions of the research program of theory itself: not only the antihumanism of some recent criticism but also a new tone, at once authoritative and clinical, that oddly resembles the tone of the very social-scientific texts that Foucault wrote with the hope of discrediting. Read either as social history or as history of ideas, his writings have tremendous power as an estrangement device; they were not meant to license a project of intellectual surveillance directed, this time, upon the guilty self of the author. But the tendency I am describing, though its vocabulary is largely Foucault's, has another and earlier source in the writings of Althusser. For it is from Althusser that contemporary theory has borrowed a vocabulary that incorporates persons only as the bearers of structures: a highly respected, plausible, Western constituent of an apology for the historical necessity of Stalinism.

This is a history that has been recounted in detail by E. P. Thompson in "The Poverty of Theory." Yet it may still be asked why such a theory should find its appeal just now, among advanced students of the humanities in America, who are seldom political enough to be either Stalinist or anti-Stalinist. The result owes much to the isolation of radical impulses in the teaching of advocacy subjects like "cultural studies," and much to the connection of individualist rhetoric now with the public-relations genius of the big corporations. But there is a less conspicuous cause for the appeal of antihumanism in theory: it seems to afford an understanding that is prior and, in consequence, superior to any historical agency. Further, it does so at a time when the distance between intellectuals (who can help to understand the world) and the working classes (for whom, in pre-Althusserian Marxism, the tasks of understanding it and changing it coincided) has widened to such a point that if it were not a cause of pride it would be a cause of shame. Thompson observes:

> What is so obvious is that this *elitism* stands as direct successor in the old lineage: Benthamism, Coleridgean "clerisy," Fabianism, Leavisism of the more arrogant variety. Once again, the intellectuals—a chosen band of these—have been given the task of enlightening the people. Whether Frankfurt School or Althusser, they are marked by their very heavy emphasis upon the ineluctable weight of ideological modes of domination— domination which destroys every space for the initiative or creativity of the mass of people—a domination from which only the enlightened minority of intellectuals can struggle free.[14]

In this respect the shift from Althusser to Foucault involves only a change of degree: a still further dimension of pessimism, with a still more attenuated emphasis on class. Together, these combine to make accounts of the domination by a mesh of power and knowledge over authors, readers, books, and the things a book can or cannot represent.

The emergent style has led to some remarkable examples of the interdisciplinary cross-sterilization of ideas. If I set out tomorrow to connect the Victorian decline of satire with the rise of sentimental comedy, the repression of women's sexuality, and the dietary practices that, with many other practices, controlled the arbitrary differences of a social order, I would need perhaps the following bits of evidence: an essay of eighteenth-century criticism that identified the satirical genres with the "acid" style; a textbook of etiquette for young ladies, published between 1830 and 1880, asserting that acidulous foods were particularly improper for persons of the female gender; and a letter from a standard Victorian author (Thackeray, say), with a comment in passing that satires tended to exacerbate rather than comfort people's resentments about their condition, and besides his wife had never enjoyed reading them. Whether these wire-drawn and empirical-looking hints carried conviction or failed to, the article in which I published them would not be attacked on the ground that connections like these could not possibly add up to anything cogent. They are the stuff the practice of theory is made of. Indeed, one's interest or lack of interest in the results is a master clue to the recent adoption, in discussions of the politics of interpretation, of the wholly misleading political terms of art "left" and "right." To want to make, as Benjamin did in his *Arcades* study, a direct inference from the duty on wine to Baudelaire's "L'Ame du vin," without adducing any intermediate chain of evidence, is a *left* position. To say of such a procedure what Adorno said of an early draft of the study, that it is "located at the crossroads of magic and positivism," is a *right* position.

An influential and much-discussed example of the left position is Fredric Jameson's 1984 *New Left Review* essay, "Postmodernism, or the Cultural Logic of Late Capitalism." In an earlier work, *The Political Unconscious*, Jameson had proposed an analysis of the utopian moment in the capitalist work of art—a category that itself was indebted to Benjamin's use of the "dialectical image," the figure that yields a coalescence of the archaic into the modern. When, in objecting to such terms, Adorno wrote of the dialectical image as regression, he meant that the only form of classlessness it uncovered was "a phantasmagoria of Hell." But the phantasmagoria of late capitalism that Jameson wants to explore for its utopian possibilities is not a moment but the imaginary space of a whole culture. Its lineaments, says Jameson, may be traced in "a new depthlessness, which finds its prolongation both in contemporary 'theory' and in a whole new culture of the image or the simulacrum; a consequent weakening of historicity, both in our relationship to public History and in the new forms of our private temporality."[15] Thus, scanning the contributions of video, television, the urban sprawl of shopping centers and the megalithic hotels that have squatted among the remnants of uprooted neighborhoods, Jameson composes an appreciative montage of what he calls "a new kind of superficiality in the most literal sense [sic]." As a defining trait of postmodernism, this has its avatar in Warhol's Campbell's Soup cans, which, Jameson says with emphasis, "*ought* to be powerful and critical statements." If they are not yet, it is the fault of the critics who have not made them so. Packages, simulacra, or works of commerce like Warhol's adequately represent the feelings of people now—feelings that, Jameson reflects, "it may be better and more accurate to call 'intensities'" since they "are now free-floating and impersonal, and tend to be dominated by a peculiar kind of euphoria."[16] Other features of the postmodernist look are a flat and affectless style of pastiche and "an omnipresent, omnivorous and well-nigh libidinal historicism." To give force to these impressions, Jameson then typifies postmodernism by an amalgam of objects and persons. "Cage, Ashbery, Sollers, Robert Wilson, Ishmael Reed, Michael Snow, Warhol or even Beckett himself" are all on this account postmodernist; so too are De Palma's *Blowout*, Polanski's *Chinatown*, Michael Herr's *Dispatches*, and all of the novels of E. L. Doctorow.

The list betrays a general tastelessness that is in harmony with the essay's ambition to read a culture as a seamless general text. Jameson draws his main exhibit not from literature or the arts but from the economic rescoring of a large city through the building of a gigantic architectural complex, John Portman's Bonaventure Hotel in Los Angeles. There, as in any postmodernist text, the structure induces in the reader a "feeling that emptiness is here absolutely packed, that it is an element within which you yourself are immersed, without any of that distance that formerly enabled the perception of perspective or volume. You are in this hyperspace up to your eyes and your body." Also, for the postmodern *flâneur*, there are escalators: "Here the narrative stroll has been underscored, symbolized, reified, and replaced by a transportation machine which becomes the allegorical signifier of that older promenade we are no longer to conduct on our own." But is not all of this irrelevant to the habits of the crowd in an older narrative, since their successors are excluded in advance by the very placement of the hotel? Instead of allowing such objections to halt the inquiry, Jameson deduces from this "new collective space" as such "a new collective practice, a new mode in which individuals move and congregate, something like the practice of a new and historically original kind of hyper-crowd." His is the sort of analysis that follows from a resolution to "think this development positively *and* negatively all at once; to achieve, in other words, a type of thinking that would be capable of grasping the demonstrably baleful features of capitalism along with its extraordinary and liberating dynamism simultaneously, within a single thought."[17] Jameson associates his strategy here with that of Marx. What Marx did not do, however, was advise his readers to think the negative features of a system positively. At this crossroads of magic and positivism, Marxism has grown indistinguishable from what it contemplates. To judge by the above description of being "immersed . . . up to your eyes and your body" in a space that is "absolutely packed," its aesthetic has likewise come to share certain traits with an aesthetic of fascism.

A moral of the foregoing pages may be that bad theory makes bad history. But there is more to it than that; and, as one takes stock of the books and articles that alter literary history to meet the new demands of social history or the history of *epistemes*, one may come to a less happy conclusion. Earlier, I alluded to Wittgenstein as a counterweight to the philosophers most influential in recent theory, and I have to quote here a final passage from *Zettel*:

What does it mean to say: "But that's no longer the same game!" How do I use this sentence? As information? Well, perhaps to introduce some information in which differences are enumerated and their consequences explained. But also to express that just for that reason I don't join in here, or at any rate take up a different attitude to the game.[18]

I have tried to point out how by gradual adjustments theory has been turning criticism into a game that is no longer recognizably the same. And I have tried to enumerate some of the differences, and to explain some of the consequences. If the description was adequate, my reasons will be plain for concluding, "Here is where I don't join in." A survey like this, however, would seem to me incomplete without some account of a proposition I believe is worth refuting, which many theorists either assert or do not want to be seen to challenge. It is, that once we give up the unity or complete intelligibility of the text as an attainable ideal, it makes less difference what texts we choose for analysis; so that the mass-cultural object has an equal claim with the work of art, all other considerations being favorable; and perhaps a better claim, if what interests us is the habits or projectable responses of the largest sheer mass of readers. I want to end by saying how this attitude came about and what may be wrong with it; and, finally, by defending the interpretation of great writing on nonaesthetic grounds.

The theoretical geniality toward mass culture is part of a larger history: it is the last chapter in the convergence of the avant-garde with the academy. The time lag between the advent of the new and its assimilation has grown shorter with every movement since the first appearance of an avant-garde around 1800. For Wordsworth, the period was forty years or so: almost the length of a career. For the younger American painters honored by museum retrospectives in the 1970s, it had shrunk to a little over a decade. What has been known about high art throughout this period is its equivocal indebtedness to popular culture and mass culture. It draws on these without being subservient to them. Now, by joining, in the name of "intertextuality," the work of art with the product of mass culture, critics level themselves with artists as exponents of the new. The practice has occasionally been employed against the valuations of any possible canon; the canon, it is said, acts in the service of mere ideology. Such arguments carry a persistent appeal even though they risk confusing mass consumption with democratic expression. But I believe that Adorno was right to maintain that a radical practice of criticism could not retreat from the defense of the work of art. He gave his own justification of "immanent criticism" in an essay entitled "Cultural Criticism and Society":

> Where [such criticism] finds inadequacies it does not ascribe them hastily to the individual and his psychology, which are merely the façade of the failure, but instead seeks to derive them from the irreconcilability of the object's moments. It pursues the logic of its aporias, the insolubility of the task itself. In such antinomies criticism perceives those of society. A successful work, according to immanent criticism, is not one which re-solves objective contradictions in a spurious harmony, but one which ex-

presses the idea of harmony negatively by embodying the contradictions, pure and uncompromised, in its innermost structure. Confronted with this kind of work, the verdict "mere ideology" loses its meaning.[19]

Adorno wrote from the perspective of modernism. And a few recent defenses of the modernist work of art have followed a similar pattern and rejected the interpretation of the mass-cultural object as a text like any other.[20]

The verdict of theory on itself may be summed up: "Literature dreams; theory knows." That what it knows may be dangerous to the order of things is a surmise, undertaken and destined to stay in the register of as-if. States have no objection to theorists until they propose the undoing of existing structures by more than textual means. But to do so means also to step outside theory once and for all. At the same time, literature itself remains manifestly dangerous. Ignored by theory, the works of a Kundera, a Konrad, a Milosz evoke keen interest from the customs agents at any number of borders, and are interdicted as the works of a Derrida or a Jameson are not. This still happens because there was always a volatile element in the very texture of romantic and modernist works that their appropriation by the academy has caused to pass from view but that is still recognized outside it. By asserting an unstable but strangely renewable connection with the past, they called into question the self-images of the present. And they did so at a time when the latter, either through censorship or the opinion-making efficacy of the media, were beginning to be rationalized under a new political authority.

"Who controls the past controls the future," goes the party slogan of Orwell's 1984, but it has a corollary: "Who controls the present controls the past." The modern state wants to control the understanding of the present. Literature and, when it chose to be active, criticism have been among the forces that stood in the way. Like the other slogans of the party, this one was drawn, as Orwell made clear, not only from the standard procedures of totalitarian states but also from emerging tendencies in America and Europe. What Orwell observed both in his novels and in many of his critical essays was that commercial democracies were starting to share certain aims with revolutionary dictatorships. They might see the aims as temporary, while the dictatorships saw them as final, but year by year anyway the damage was being done. The modern state wanted not merely to govern but to control; to control the present it was necessary to control the past; and if that meant obliterating the past, it would not shrink from doing so. Orwell's predecessor as a critic was Edmund Burke, who wrote: "People will not look forward to posterity, who never look backward to their ancestors." But the state has a gaze more flatly purposeful than the writer's. When an Eastern leader cites Tolstoy approvingly, or a Western leader cites Lincoln approvingly, the same thing is happening, and to capture it one needs another phrase of Burke's: "They unplumb the dead for bullets to assassinate the living."

The first mistake of theory has been to suppose that criticism can have a direct relationship with the political control of the present. A second mistake has been to suppose that its main rival is literature. Orwell and Burke together suggest a different idea of what criticism ought to do. It cannot itself attain, or even supply others with tools for attaining, control of the present. But it can insert itself between those who control the present and their wish to control the past. It can, that is, weaken the state's inertia and qualify its authority, by affording a few of its citizens a backward glance that is not the same as the look sanctioned by the state. To the degree that it teaches the differentness of the past, criticism acts on behalf of a future.

I am proposing that for criticism today a consciousness of the past as such performs a critical function. To believe this does not require a faith in the objectivity of interpretation or a prior belief that history is the sum total of positive facts. It presumes only that other times hold other persons in other situations which we may think of as alternative to ours: in some respects better, in some respects worse, in all respects different. And that these materials are not altogether tractable: they will not do everything we want them to. This last is what the modern state most needs to forget. And so it seems to me that literary criticism, when it matters, is not easily separated from cultural or social criticism. In the past few years, academic critics have seen all at once that they too are engaged in unclassifiable activities, and the recognition has led them to talk vaguely but ominously about power. Much of the talk conceives of power as a synonym for habits, customs, usages, practices of any kind, as if commentaries on texts could help people to live eventually without these things. The idea that they could is nonsense, with a short future in practice. Nevertheless, critics still do make a usable record of the ways people have thought and felt, or might think and feel, outside the mastery of the present. By translating, from a distant or otherwise hidden time, the testamentary parable or the unforeseen inheritance, they interpret for readers the hidden powers of living men and women.

## NOTES

This is a shortened version of an essay first published in 1986. I have cut some timely allusions and polemics that seem unnecessary today, without altering the general argument or the details that remain.—DB

1. W. K. Wimsatt, *Day of the Leopards: Essays in Defense of Poems* (New Haven, Conn.: Yale University Press, 1976), 196–97.

2. Gayatri Chakravorti Spivak, "Three Women's Texts and a Critique of Imperialism," *Critical Inquiry* 12, no. 1 (Autumn 1985): 243–61.

3. Se E. D. Hirsch Jr., *Validity in Interpretation* (New Haven, Conn.: Yale University Press, 1967); and Gerald Graff, *Literature Against Itself: Literary Ideas in Modern Society* (Chicago: University of Chicago Press, 1979).

4. Ludwig Wittgenstein, *Philosophical Investigations*, trans. G. E M. Anscombe, 3d ed. (New York: Doubleday, 1968), 103, 201.

5. Ludwig Wittgenstein, *Zettel*, trans. G. E. M. Anscombe (Berkeley and Los Angeles: University of California Press, 1970), 31.

6. See Richard Rorty, *Consequences of Pragmatism: Essays, 1972–1980* (Minneapolis: University of Minnesota Press, 1982), chap. 8.

7. The afterword to William James's essay "On Some Hegelisms," in *The Will to Believe* (New York: Longmans, Green, 1897) includes some notations on the circumstances of his temporary conversion to the Hegelian philosophy, under the effects of nitrous oxide gas: "Strife presupposes something to be striven about; and in this common topic, the same for both parties, the differences emerge. . . . *Yes* and *no* agree at least in being assertions," and so on. The leading vehicle for his conversion, as James describes it, was puns, and he gives as a specimen "What's mistake but a kind of take?" (295).

8. See, for example, Martha Nussbaum, "Flawed Crystals: James's *The Golden Bowl* and Literature as Moral Philosophy," *New Literary History* 15, no. 1 (Autumn 1983): 25–50.

9. John Searle, "The Word Turned Upside Down," *New York Review of Books*, 27 October 1983, 74–79.

10. Paul de Man, *Allegories of Reading: Figural Language in Rousseau, Nietzsche, Rilke, and Proust* (New Haven, Conn.: Yale University Press, 1979), 17.

11. William Empson, *Seven Types of Ambiguity*, 2d ed. (London: Chatto and Windus, 1974), 4.

12. Paul de Man, *Blindness and Insight: Essays in the Rhetoric of Contemporary Criticism*, 2d ed. (Minneapolis: University of Minnesota Press, 1983).

13. De Man, *The Rhetoric of Romanticism* (New York: Columbia University Press, 1984), 81.

14. E. P. Thompson, *The Poverty of Theory and Other Essays* (New York: Monthly Review Press, 1978), 185–86.

15. Fredric Jameson, "Postmodernism," *New Left Review* 146 (July–August 1984), 58.

16. Jameson, "Postmodernism," 64.

17. Jameson, "Postmodernism," 86.

18. Wittgenstein, *Zettel*, 60.

19. Theodor W. Adorno, *Prisms,* trans. Samuel and Shierry Weber (Cambridge, Mass.: MIT Press, 1981), 32.

20. Harold Rosenberg, "Art and Its Double," in *Artworks and Packages* (New York: Horizon, 1971), describes the mutual influences of the arts and the media as continuous throughout the modern period, but with the arts now on the brink of vanishing into the media. Thomas Crow, "Modernism and Mass Culture in the Visual Arts," in *Modernism and Modernity*, ed. Benjamin H. D. Buchloh, Serge Guilbaut, and David Solkin (Nova Scotia: Press of the Nova Scotia College of Art and Design, 1983), 215–64, sees the exchange as repeating a single pattern: "the appropriation of oppositional practices upward, the return of evacuated cultural goods downward."

## 42.  CHANGING EPOCHS

### FRANK KERMODE

SINCE THE TOPIC of changing cultural epochs, ends and beginnings, is in the fin-de-siècle air, it might be worth asking whether the one we may conceivably be experiencing is of a kind that will permit the survival of literary studies, a term I use in a sense that the sequel should make clear, or indeed of literature, a term I use in a sense that will still seem innocent to some, though condemned by many others as tainted by nostalgia for the aesthetic, redolent of a hateful elitism, an instrument of ideological oppression.

In Alain Robbe-Grillet's novel *Les Gommes*, published in 1953, there is a celebrated moment when the detective Wallas contemplates a tomato. Cut into quarters by a machine, it is, thinks the detective, "truly without flaw [*en vérité sans défaut*]," but then he notices that it does have a flaw: "*un accident à peine visible*," a barely perceptible unevenness, has occurred. An irregular piece of skin raised above the surface of the tomato now becomes its most interesting feature. Some suggest that it has been added in the act of description, that it is in the writing and not in the tomato; but the tomato is equally in the writing.

It may be relevant that *Les Gommes* genuinely was, in its way, an epoch-making novel; also that the criticism of the time, including Robbe-Grillet's own, found new ways of talking about fiction, about literature, attending very closely to the text—a practice much less usual now, as we shall see. Robbe-Grillet hated metaphor and would have objected to the use of this passage for purposes smacking of allegory.[1] Nevertheless I shall treat it as a motto for an essay which asks certain questions about mechanical *coupures*, which will to some extent dwell lovingly on the still perceptible irregularity, the accident of recalcitrant skin. The question is, shall we—I mean students and lovers of literature—survive a change of epoch, if only as an accident of that sort?

Does epistemic change come in different sizes or is it always catastrophic and total?

For a long time Hercules was represented in Arab star maps as wearing a short jacket and breeches rather than a lion's skin, and carrying a scimitar rather than a club. But in 1515 Albrecht Dürer published the first modern star map. It still depended to some extent on its Arab precursors, but Dürer's Hercules carried a club in his right hand and wore a lion's skin on his left shoulder. In much the same way he transformed an Arab Perseus, restoring his winged feet and making sure that the head the hero was carrying had been detached

Frank Kermode. "Changing Epochs." From *What's Happened to the Humanities?* edited by Alvin Kernan, 162–178. Copyright © 1997 Princeton University Press. Reprinted by permission of Princeton University Press.

not from some medieval demon but from the classical Medusa; indeed Dürer went out of his way to avoid misinterpretation by adding, in the appropriate position, the words "caput Medusae." He had restored to Hercules and Perseus their original iconographic attributes, and in doing so revived "the life and breath of paganism."

The gods had somehow survived through the long interval between antiquity and the fifteenth century, but they had lost their classical forms (Hercules became a monk with a tonsure). Now they were again as they had been originally, though incorporated in a modern—"state-of-the-art"—star map. "To recover the forms used by the ancients as well as their learning, their poetic imagination, and their knowledge of the universe—to reconcile, as they did, mythology and geometry—such was to be the dream of the greatest spirits of the Renaissance."[2]

Jean Seznec, from whose book I borrow these examples, boldly concludes that "we can speak of a Renaissance from the day Hercules resumed his athletic breadth of shoulder, his club and his lion's skin." Indeed, we can speak of "*the* Renaissance."[3] Then began a new epoch, consciously modern, aware that the achievements of the immediately preceding age were henceforth to be scorned and discounted, while the relics of antiquity, ever more anxiously sought out, were to stand as models, as examples, as guides though not as commanders, to the exponents of a self-proclaimed modernity. These were the materials chosen for a new age to fashion itself, once it had cut itself off from the in-between age, the *medium aevum*. The slicing was, we may say, mechanical, with seemingly little recalcitrant skin left over to call into question the efficacy of the machine that made the great *coupure*.

But we know well enough that the cut was not as clean as it looked to those who assumed and exulted in its cleanness. The Renaissance was in some perspectives an extension of the medieval it believed it was rejecting, although its self-conscious modernity derived, paradoxically, from *sacrosancta vetustas*, from a revival of the classic beginning with Petrarch. On further examination the cut left quite a lot of skin visible. Then was the Renaissance, after all, *sui generis* and a new age? There was a nineteenth-century tendency to continue its celebration as exactly that, but since then, and to this day, doubts persist about its extent, neatness, and uniqueness. A truly cardinal moment in history, a phenomenon so distinctive that we can confidently use it to take our historical bearings on Western culture—or simply one of a number of untidy, somewhat random cultural changes that could not be soberly be thought of as catastrophic upheavals?

After all, there are other rather similar cultural manifestations on record. Considering this possible objection, Erwin Panofsky distinguished between *Renaissances* and *Renascences*, using the latter term for less notable or less universal revivals of the antique, such as those of the Carolingian period and the twelfth century. He decided that *the* Renaissance *can* be quite sharply distinguished from the Renascences. It was different in that it manifested itself so generally, in so many areas of culture. It was different in that it was more fully conscious of historical perspective. It took some account of the gulf of time that separated it from the admired ancients. And although proudly inspired by the ancient world it was self-consciously "modern." Vasari, who celebrated a rebirth in painting (calling it *la rinascità*) praised Leonardo da Vinci for having "laid the foundations of that third style which I will call the modern"—so distinguishing it from the first style (Botticelli, Ghirlandaio) and the second (Perugino, Francia). *Modern* was not, as it happens, an exclusively modern word; like *new*, it could refer to something already rather old, as in *devotio moderna*, which was thriving around 1400. And it always seemed to carry the implication "with regard to an understood past." Perhaps what is genuinely modern always has a novel but powerful relationship with a past; preferably (my preference, at any rate) a relationship dialectical rather than abolitionist.[4]

Although it is mostly in respect of classical scholarship, literature, painting, sculpture, and architecture that these developments occupy the attention of cultural historians, we take it for granted when we talk about a new epoch or a new age that they were related to great changes in other departments of life—radical innovation and conflict in political thought; new technologies including printing; explorations, so damaging to received notions, of new worlds on earth and in the heavens (though these modernities also had their remembrances of appropriate pasts). Life in cities—directly involving the arts—was being transformed by changes in the social order, by new international trade and new money; this was the onset of the first age of capitalism. There were catastrophic religious conflicts, also affecting society and the arts, in which modern ideas of history and philology, individuality and rationality played their part. We can be sure not only that there was, cumulatively and generally, a great change in the times, but also that some people were aware that it was happening, without necessarily understanding what it was and meant.

It is of some importance that an epochal alteration can be announced, whether with pleasure or (as sometimes happened) with anxiety. However wrong they might have been about the details, some people knew that for good or ill they were living in a new age and said so. In this sense the Renaissance was not only a period but also a movement. E. H. Gombrich distinguishes between periods, or ages, and movements. "A movement," he remarks, "is something that is proclaimed."[5] The Renaissance was therefore a movement. A period can be imposed retrospectively. Nobody ever announced that he or she was living in the Middle Ages, and nobody ever proclaimed "the Mannerist Movement." It may well be that the proclamation is, at least in some respects, exaggerated or distorted. But so long as its contents are not seen to be false or absurd, the proclamation lends force to the view that it is permissible to speak of *the* Renaissance, though the phenomena will always be difficult to define precisely, and the cut will never again be thought clean.

By the same token it is acceptable to speak of modernism and, perhaps with more reluctance, of postmodernism also, unless it is to be thought of as an epiphenomenon of modernism.[6] Postmodernism has certainly been proclaimed, and to some extent its proclamation itself begets ideas and slogans that testify to the existence of what is proclaimed. There is a sort of program, put together ad hoc; the word presented itself, and it was provided piecemeal with a supporting lexicon and an ideology. It is antimodernist, opposed to notions of totality; it exhibits an "extreme epistemological skepticism which reduces everything—philosophy, politics, criticism and 'theory'—to a dead level of suasive or rhetorical effect where consensus-values are the last (indeed the only) court of appeal"; and it is scornful of such metanarrative survivals as reason and truth.[7] Even the distortions and falsities advanced by propagandists and enthusiasts are of historical interest; their proclamations are part of the validating record of the period. They may announce a clean break, they may omit judicious consideration of easily perceptible elements of continuity, but their insistence on a *coupure* is still, when cautiously handled, part of the evidence that there has been one. And it is easy enough to give it that larger context—technological, sociological, and philosophical—that is essential to concepts of epistemic break.

The epistemic, epochal break is now a very familiar conceptual instrument. Michel Foucault, who put into circulation a modern (and decidedly apocalyptic) form of an idea that has its origins in antiquity, and which has rarely been quite absent from historical thinking, applied a sharp knife: his tomato was permitted no roughnesses. It can be said (against some opposition, admittedly) that according to *Les Mots et les choses* there was no carry-over from one epoch to another; one episteme yielded absolutely to the next.

Of course Foucault was speaking of systematic formations at so deep a level that the Renaissance itself could probably be regarded as a superficial manifestation, much like Marx's thought, described by the same author as a mere storm in a children's paddling pool. It might be argued that the present discontents in the humanities, profoundly disturbing though they seem to all who have to deal with them, are fairly trivial according to this Olympian view. And it is true that we need to keep some such deeper perspective, for in the context of enormous change our local malaise can hardly be thought of as more than symptomatic. It may be that by making habitual resort to notions of continuity, and by demonstrating a professional inability to be rid of brainwashed notions of aesthetic value and truth, one is disqualified from profound epochal speculation. All the same there is, even among the rejectors, that habitual backward glance, stare, or glare. The haunting cultural memory, has, for good or ill, wanted or not, been part of the discourse of every episteme—obviously of the Renaissance, also of the Enlightenment; it is quite hard to imagine a break so clean that it will not recur. Of course it may take the form of a willed *anti-passéisme*, descended from the variety that in the early years of the century, especially in the form of Dada, was the twin of the revisionist historiographies of modernism.

Anyway, we may suppose that there is something to be learned from the Renaissance. It did happen, it transformed the arts and literature and scholarship. We are right to think it distinctive. But one must also remember the indisputably rough edge of its cut. Johan Huizinga remarked that what we call the Renaissance was only one aspect of sixteenth-century culture; a lot was going on that does not fit into the concept—a lot of rough skin, as it were, ignored by devotees of the clean cut. Much scholarship has been devoted to showing that Renaissance notions of antiquity, *sacrosancta vetustas*, were pretty chaotic, and the "break" from the late Middle Ages was, on inspection, much less complete than some contemporaries, and some nineteenth-century historians, may have thought. The same may turn out to be true of our own *coupure*. We are repeatedly and excitedly assured that our culture has also suffered a pretty clean historical break. This is, with important qualifications, admitted. But a lot else is going on. And we should here as elsewhere make allowances for the rhetoric of proclamation—it is rather thrilling, and it excites audiences, to assert that all continuity has gone, that the *grands récits* no longer have ethical or aesthetic or any other kind of paradigmatic force, that we can do as we please with the past. In a culture so saturated by advertising it is important not to take mere labels and slogans too seriously. They have their importance, but we should treat such proclamations critically.

It may be that the rejection of the past—which happens to some extent, though as I have suggested, nearly always imperfectly, in most ages, and is also a proclaimed feature of many of the art movements we admire—is now made more impatiently or arrogantly. It is less a reaction against something known, studied, and then declared obsolete than an attempt at total rejection of literature and certain ideas because they are past; an attack that is supported not by detailed dismissive study of documents but by grand theoretical efforts to occlude completely any consideration of them, for such consideration would be in danger of falling under the influence of paradigms already rejected in principle.

Here the prefix *post-* is of great value because it crudely situates whatever it adheres to in the admirable present, whereas whatever it cannot be applied to is obsolete and probably malign, like modernism to postmodernists. Respected works of modernism (Mallarmé, Joyce, Pound) can always be coopted as early or premonitory examples of postmodernism. As a way of justifying this historical kidnapping, it is sometimes argued that postmodernism logically precedes modernism, or at any rate that they can exist contemporaneously; so it may be that Dada was not so much a nihilistic form of modernism as an early postmodernism that simply assumed, without having much of a theory about it, the necessary demise of the *grands récits*. But this kind of talk is surely, in the end, unhelpful; it resembles the sort of thing that has been said about *Baroque*, first invented to name a historical period and then used more and more loosely to refer to anything perceived as having comparable stylistic characteristics. *Post-* is too malleable to tell us much.

Complaints about terminology are inevitable but barely scratch the surface of the problem. However one may wish to purge the new terminology and resist some theoretical claims (as I have tried in the past to do),[8] it can hardly be denied that the arts and the humanities generally, all of which depend on systems of communication, will be affected in unpredictable ways by technological changes so enormous that Gutenberg is useful only as a vague analogue. The power of individual communicators is now far greater (in extent and speed) than that afforded by moveable types, not in the measure that print surpassed the range of manuscript copies, but on a scale very much greater; and we are as yet only at the beginning of this revolution. The book is not yet dead and may not even be dying; but the Internet is not yet universal, digital television is still only a glorious promise, and we do not need much millennialist fervor to imagine, with joy or terror, what they may do to us and our children.

Though we cannot honestly make detailed predictions, post-McLuhanite reasoning suggests that the changes will not be simply quantitative. The modern condition of the arts requires them to live in change, to demonstrate that restlessness long ago deplored by Wyndham Lewis, who saw new fashions come and go like new models of washing machines. But postmodern change is no longer the simpler sort of thing he deplored, simply from one manifesto or one fashion to another. The claim is more drastic and of more universal scope, and it implies, among many other consequences, that attitudes toward the study of literature will be radically altered.

This is of course what we fancy we see happening all about us, a matter of common observation within the academy. Even before the times grew as intellectually turbulent as they now are, the academy, perhaps in the premonitory phase of epistemic change, was forced into the position of being virtually the sole site of serious reading and commentary. It has been the blessing and the curse of literary academics that they have been deputed to do the culture's reading for it. At one time there was an expectation that they would report back to their employers. But what Lionel Trilling called keeping the road open—ensuring, by proper provision of high journalism, the continuance of contact between experts and the educated public at large—is no longer thought a plain necessity of intellectual and social health, as it was in the nineteenth and early twentieth centuries. Communication from professors to the otherwise-educated laity has almost, if not quite, broken down. Their relationship to their students is also more problematical. This is partly the fault of the professors, the professionals, who notoriously speak to and write only for one another, inventing arcane dialects to keep out the uninitiated. They lament the ignorance of freshmen, but when they get them into graduate school ensure that they protect their careers by learning to talk as the teachers do—so maintaining the fence between academic criticism and the intelligent world outside.

There is a reciprocal decline of interest on the part of that lay audience, which no longer looks to professors for wisdom, nor assumes that the humanities offer a defense against the increasing horrors of modern life, as it was believed they did in the time of the great nineteenth-century periodicals. And there are few inducements of a gentler sort, that simply make the reading of literature seem a task in which the pleasure might conceivably outweigh the labor.

Consequently academic humanists, once so proud, so confident, may feel isolated, or dependent on the professional comfort of a school of thought or of theory. Meanwhile it is generally acknowledged that the students for whom they must care arrive in college having read much less, even in their own language, than their parents had; and if we consider their ignorance of other modern languages (to say nothing of the classical languages that were until quite recently assumed to be valuable instruments of humanistic culture), we see what a fearful task it must be to commence their education, supposing what is meant by that word remains roughly what it did a couple of generations back. For now books are less familiar objects, and nobody has much desire to explain why they were also privileged objects. And there may now be a majority of teachers in the humanities who would regard such explanations as in manifest bad faith, not worth contesting.

Wishing to examine, however cursorily, the conditions of epoch-change, we are obliged to try to connect these troublesome but relatively domestic difficulties with immense and obvious alterations in the world at large. We need to ask whether the cut is a clean one. It may not yet be clear how clean it is. Is it absurdly optimistic to suppose that, as with the Renaissance, it may turn out on mature inspection that the older culture, however impaired or scorned, will find a form in which it can survive? If a major change has been forced on us by technologies inimical to the old print culture, is it not at least possible that there can remain, at any rate for some, modes of useful communication with that culture and indeed with the past and with at least some of the *grands récits* (among which we can include literature)?

We see from the graphs and tables provided in the appendix to *What's Happened to the Humanities?* edited by Alvin Kernan [in which this essay originally appeared], that the numbers of students taking humanities courses are falling. In this reduced enrollment there may not be many who strike us, vanity apart, as being likely to fill our places in what we might think an adequate manner. Nevertheless one comes across wonderfully well-read young men and women, dedicated in their bright archaic way to canonical works of which they already apprehend the value; so there is at least likely to be what in other contexts might be called a saving remnant, willing to be despised as aesthetes or ideological innocents—as, in a bizarrely anachronistic way, dedicated to *literature*. It may be objected that such freaks could come to our aid merely by chance; but so does a great deal of literature.

Compelled into prediction, into gambling on the future, on the prospect that mere statistical probability may produce a few archaizing poetry-lovers, one cannot avoid pondering the operations of chance. We might well give more thought to the question of survival in art, to the chances that have to be taken when they come along. We have seven plays of Sophocles, selected from the whole corpus of over a hundred by an Alexandrian schoolmaster as texts for a grammar class and sold—in a unique copy—out of Constantinople just before the sack of 1453. Only then could virtuously preservative scholarship do its work. Of the tragedies of Euphorion, who beat Sophocles and Aeschylus in fair Athenian competition, no trace remains. The survival of the venerated objects of a culture has quite often depended on a hair-raising combination of luck and cunning. Improving on luck is part of the game for people who do not despise the past. Devotees of those objects must be valued in much the same way as the objects themselves; arriving by chance, these aliens must be cunningly fostered. They are the students who already have that intuition of value without which the task is nearly hopeless. Dr. Johnson ruled that it "ought to be the first endeavour of a writer to distinguish . . . that which is established because it is right from that which is right only because it is established." Some believe they have seen through this sturdy appearance of common sense; what is said to be right is so only because it is established. In that analysis Johnson's remark ceases to make sense. Our remnant will contest on instinct the opinion that value is never inherent but a fiction imposed by an oppressive institution, and that no other view makes sense.

What is now thought to make sense in literary studies? It is unnecessary at this stage to resume the debate about canons, a debate always in the end without much sense, since the opponents of canons, apart from a few total abolitionists, really just want their own canons, and the defenders, apart from a few extremists, do not in any case hold the reactionary views with which propaganda credits them. There is nothing in the least sacred or magical or, as the fashionable jargon has it, "mystified" about canons. There can be no objection in principle to any attempt to enlarge or alter reading lists and to include, say, the works of neglected women, Afro-American, and other "minority" writers. Canons are reading lists, but of course they are also rather more than that: they are necessarily selective reading lists. Everybody uses them. And it is always to be remembered that canons consist not of static texts alone—texts frozen in time, monuments in a heritage park, objects of a kind of snobbish archaeology—but also of continuing commentary on the texts; that is what preserves canonicity and makes the members of a canon as modern as yesterday's poem. Good commentary may of course cease, and the once canonical work can cease to be so. To ensure the entry of new works or the exclusion of old ones all that is needed is persuasive, perpetuating commentary on the one hand and neglect or informed hostility on the other.

It is, of course, a worry that the proponents of a new posthumanism have no regard for commentary (at its best, convincing exploration of particular texts or works), and concern themselves instead with such questions as canonicity, or what it is to read, or what distinguishes a work from a text, or what is the just relation of texts to their historical and ideological circumstances, and so on. At this stage the intoxicating impetus of literary theory in the last quarter century needs no description. The appeal of "theory" to large numbers of younger teachers may be pessimistically explained as a consequence of the drop in writing and reading skills that should have been acquired much earlier; this is the plausible view of Alvin Kernan. The decay of what used to be called literature is symbolized for him by the physical decay of thousands of books rotting in libraries, but also by the enormous piling up of new books that hardly anybody reads.[9]

The catalogue of Messrs. Routledge & Kegan Paul, publishers once proud of their Literary Criticism list, is now dominated by works more properly categorized as cultural materialism, feminism, popular culture, and poststructuralism. Bill Germano of Routledge's American office claims, in a recent interview, to be "making things happen in the culture." His interviewer says it is certain that "by spotting intellectual trends ahead of the curve and responding with a flash flood of suitable titles Germano has changed the face of academic publishing in the humanities." He has supplied "the software" needed for university programs in film studies, gay studies, and so on, courses with reading lists understandably dominated by Routledge books.[10] Of course the job of publishers is to supply—and if they can, even create—an audience, but in this instance, if one may borrow terms of abuse that are frequently employed in some of the books that appear in such lists, it might be proper to speak of commodification and colonialism.

Unlike Germano, I do not know where this "curve" is heading; the market glut and the restlessness of young academics, whose tenure can now depend on finding something new to say by way of Theory, guarantee fairly rapid change. It can hardly be otherwise in a community where one is obliged to be skeptical about everybody else's theory save one's own.

One of the books recently published by Routledge is Thomas Docherty's *After Theory* (1990). Docherty, as his blurb expresses it, contends that the Enlightenment project of emancipation through knowledge has ended in failure by allowing the academy to "become a prison-house for the institutionalization of critique." The agent of this imprisonment is Theory, so he contends that Theory needs liberating in its turn. After theory there needs to be a postmodernism that "questions every manner of binding or framing," which valorizes transgression and "error," "error" being " 'criminal' in the eyes of the white fathers, the acknowledged legislators behind the law of the imperialist enlightenment of the dark tropics of discourse; but the 'criminality' remains fully justified if we wish to reject the parameters of an imperialist mode of politics and an imperialist mode of conversation or social understanding." Finally Docherty wants thought to be liberated from *all* theory. "It is only in the refusal to be answerable to a governing theory that thought, and above all theoretical thought, becomes possible once more."[11] The dismissal of theoretical thought by means of posttheoretical thought in order to make theoretical thought possible, with the consequence adumbrated in the argument (theory liberated by posttheory, in order to be liberated again, and so on for ever) is a characteristically "oppositional" proposal. The association of older modes of thinking with imperialism simply goes without saying, and what used to be thought of as "primary" text is at no stage involved in the argument. Why should it be, when there simply is no such thing? It is a sign of the times that Docherty is described as a professor of *English*.

And so these new professionals spiral away from anything resembling what one stubbornly continues to describe as the study of literature. Practitioners of that study did of course have theories of criticism; the New Criticism had theories, and it flourished along with several rivals. But now theory is an opponent, and a difficult one, as hard to get around as Peer Gynt found the Boyg. It is many-headed, zealous, deliberately dark, and by no means all foolish. Our remnant will need literary theories, though of another stripe, founded in the literary text; they may find it best to avoid the Boyg's territory altogether.

In 1992 the Modern Language Association of America published a collection of essays entitled *Redrawing the Boundaries*, thus endorsing the argument that the area of studies over which it presides had indeed changed. The resulting volume makes the redrawing of boundaries look almost Yugoslavian, but there are hints that, as in the concept of the Renaissance, the tomato has not cut quite cleanly, that the *coupure* may still have interestingly ragged edges. Richard Marius, discussing "Composition Studies," reflects that Theory has made little difference to them; they are mostly in a terrible state, taught by ill-paid, reluctant, overworked part-timers using ill-written textbooks to instruct dismally inadequate students, who, far from needing instruction in Theory, need help to understand elementary written English. It is not really their fault; they are trying to learn too late what they should have been taught years before. To some of them reading is a new experience, and they can hardly be expected to begin instantly to meditate on what it means to read, or to expose the duplicity of the texts they are studying by deconstructing them, when the obvious sense, however simple—that Derridean guardrail—is still hard for them to hold on to. Meanwhile their instructors would almost certainly prefer to be doing something else, something expounded in the more exciting chapters of the MLA book. The gap between their students' performances and the rapt theoretical discourse of senior members of the institution is as unbridgeably wide as that between the discourse of those scholars and the interest of the educated laity.

It remains something of a surprise that not every article in the MLA book is curtly dismissive of older criticism. Some are, of course, but William Kerrigan, writing on seventeenth-century studies, is skeptical of some current developments. For example, he agrees with the author of the chapter on Renaissance/early modern studies (Leah Marcus) that Milton has proved a stumbling-block to opponents of "anti-author-ity"; but they differ about the significance of this. She seems on the whole content to think that as a consequence of this difficulty Milton must drop out of consideration unless and until postmodernism finds its own way of dealing with him—and, with a certain effect of oddity, she cites as hopeful evidence that this is beginning to happen B. Rajan's book on *Paradise Lost*, seemingly unaware that it was unpostmodernly published in 1947, not a date you would expect to find on a book worth reading. For his part Kerrigan takes an intelligent look at some postmodernist struggles with Milton but concludes, with evident but unfashionable satisfaction, that "the tradition lives." It is just the kind of remnant to match our remnant of literary students.

In their introduction to the MLA volume the editors, Stephen Greenblatt and Giles Gunn, ponder the general question of boundaries, alleging that the nature of their volume "obliged them to place a disproportionate emphasis on significant departures rather than important continuities." They modestly support the departures—canon changes, the disappearance of the author, attention to signifiers rather than signifieds, "the interrogation of boundaries." (I have noticed before a tendency for theory enthusiasts to treat dissident persons and ideas as political prisoners.) But they reasonably doubt whether the present degree of theoretical consensus, such as it is, can be maintained indefinitely. In their capacity as moderators they refrain from advocating any change, but they confidently expect it. They speak of "conversations" conducted over the shifting frontiers between literary studies and adjacent interests. Since they allow for the existence of "important continuities," it may be supposed that in principle they do not rule out a dialogue between the present of theory (with its uncertain future, its risk of sterile institutionalization) and the past (with its perhaps not yet totally exploded mythologies of authorship and "works").[12] There may be an interesting, as yet unquantifiable, remnant of skin.

All this may sound as if I am conceding that all who retain a somewhat different attitude, both to the criticism of literature and to the instruction of students, should just hang on and wait for better times, hoping against hope they will come around again before we die. But what would we be hanging on to and why, if unstoppable cultural forces are at work to deprive us (our remnant apart) of suitable students to teach and a suitable audience to address? And why does the very thought of hanging on tend to make us feel guilty, make us duck when we hear the word *elitist*? It has been plain for a long time that the writings humanists value as "literature" (now a contested category) are difficult in themselves, and that they are therefore primarily the preserve of what, in a probably vain attempt to avoid the facile imputation of elitism, we can call a *clerisy*. The word was invented by Coleridge and adopted by Emerson, but the idea existed independently of the word, and was associated with a nineteenth-century intellectual and cultural effort to escape from the advances of materialism—to reverse the apparently growing social and cultural decadence, often by a contemplation of literature.[13]

The tradition of a clerisy persisted and in England found a belated but embattled champion in F. R. Leavis. He made a celebrated assault on C. P. Snow for his lecture on the separation of the two cultures, scientific and humanist. In 1959 Snow—by profession a science administrator, by avocation a novelist—had given a lecture in Cambridge called "The Two Cultures and the Scientific Revolution," in which he compared, unfavorably, the social and political attitudes of literary people with those of scientists. He found the scientists humanly useful and the literary people uselessly frivolous; he pointed to the social advances that had come or were coming about everywhere as a result of technological advance and castigated as snobbery the literary habit of deploring the loss of amenity such an advance entailed. He despised our ignorance, famously asserting that he could ask a literary person to tell him the second law of thermodynamics in complete confidence that the humanist would be baffled.

In my experience Snow was a civil, friendly, though opinionated man. I remember him telling me with great emphasis how deplorable he found Virginia Woolf, and there is little doubt that she in her turn would have thought even less of his novels than she did of Arnold Bennett's. But this looked like a straightforward quarrel between the realist and the poetic or avant-garde novelist rather than a deep cultural divide. In Snow's living room there hung a large painting by the modernist Australian artist Sydney Nolan of the outback outlaw Ned Kelly, and I thought of this as some sort of measure of Snow's rebellion against what he took to be the cultural establishment of the day. Although he is now completely out of fashion his *roman fleuve Strangers and Brothers* was welcomed by the educated public of its time; and one novel of the sequence, *The Masters* (1951), about Cambridge college politics, had much success not only in Britain but also in the Soviet Union. He was a public figure respected as serious, and could hardly have foreseen that Leavis, with whom he had a polite acquaintance, would react with such vehemence to his lecture.

In his response, a lecture called "The Two Cultures: The Significance of C. P. Snow," Leavis described Snow as "portentously ignorant" and insisted that although he had been right about the advance of science and technology, he was quite wrong about its cost, and had failed to see that it brought with it "tests and challenges so unprecedented . . . that mankind—this is surely clear—will need to be in full intelligent possession of its full humanity." He added that he was not talking about "traditional wisdom," which would suggest a conservatism he also regarded as an enemy. What he meant was "intelligence, a power

. . . of creative response to the new challenges of time; something that is alien to either of Snow's cultures."

The argument was that Snow entirely neglected something preciously human, that kind of discourse which occupies the human space between men and women who belong to a community of language, a language which is recognized as "opening . . . into the unknown and itself unknowable." Where would one go to study this language if not to great literature? At the time the controversy was recognized as important; it continued for a long time and has recently been revived.[14]

I have been dwelling on what might seem, in the very large context of the present inquiries, a rather parochial dispute—a matter for the English, even a matter for the unrepresentative selection of the English who like to quarrel in Cambridge. But I take it to have a more general importance. The Anglophone countries have never quite managed to grant humanistic studies the dignity conferred on them in German usage by the title of *Geisteswissenschaften*. There is a science of what can only be known from within, as Dilthey expressed it, as when one "lives through" a poem;[15] and on some such argument the humanities can defend themselves against the incomprehension of scientists—some scientists, I should say, for there are many who know very well that the human sciences are necessary and complementary, and may even, on occasion, enrich "hard" science.

So there is reason, in the present context, to mention Leavis's conviction that society needs a highly intelligent humanist elite or remnant, sensibilities trained by an intense participation in literature (considered as the site of the most significant uses of language). The emphasis here is on literary study, but the position can be held in various ways. Francis Mulhern has argued that *Scrutiny*'s call for an embattled elite, engaged in a perpetual struggle with a society and a culture degenerating into a mechanical and polluted barbarism, was echoed by certain contemporary European protesters. For some "the critique of historical decline" centered on sociology rather than literature. Though *Scrutiny* did not neglect sociology, it was literary criticism in its Leavisian forms and with its Leavisian intentions—its certainty that deep critical involvement in great texts was essential—that distinguished the Cambridge school from their European cousins; but all parties felt the same need—to save the humanities from historical decline.[16]

It may be objected that these instances lack relevance to our immediate situation. Agreed, they were certain that the humanities were under threat, they proposed remedies for what they saw as their decay; but what has that to do with the situation now? Informed that there were still a great many people at college studying literature, Leavis would ask, knowing in advance the answer, how many were studying it with the requisite, intense, kind of attention, the kind of which Snow, though a prolific writer and critic, had shown himself incapable.

We may feel we are overfamiliar with this kind of talk of decadence, but it is reasonable to believe that on a Leavisian or any comparable estimate the situation really has grown worse. Simply to advocate intense reading may, in our circumstances, seem very inadequate. Epochal breaks, epistemic *coupures*, are shadows of apocalyptic thought, and it is easy to feel that the decadence is terminal, that we are closer to what feels like a decisive break rather than a gradual decline. The former vision of disaster lacked the decisiveness of apocalypse. A further sign of the enormous times may be that in the old days the threat seemed to be coming mostly from outside the humanities. Now—more pointed, more clearly abolitionist—it comes from within.

The imminence of the millennium has at least something of the effect observed earlier at the approach of certain dates; it is not that people do not understand their arbitrariness but that they cannot refrain from projecting onto them aspirations and anxieties that strictly have nothing to do with them. The date can be a death-substitute, an end-substitute, a moment beautifully apt for sensational *coupures*, whether for individuals or institutions; and I believe this fact now tends to color our own thinking, as well as the more exultant thinking of the abolitionists, about the shape of our studies: they had a beginning, they are still surviving in a middle, and why should they not have an end?

Or, if not yet quite an end, an immediate future much changed and diminished? Bernard Bergonzi speaks of "exploding English."[17] Taking notice of Catherine Belsey's remark that "only by closing the doors of the English Department against theoretical challenges from outside can we continue to ignore the 'Copernican' revolution which is currently taking place,"[18] he deconstructs it: "revolution" is an ambiguous trope, meaning something decisive, like the Copernican revolution or the French Revolution; or it may mean "a mere turning, continual movement without progress."

The solution Bergonzi proposes in his valuable and patient book is to split off conventional literary study from the activity now known as "cultural studies." He means that people who want to consider literature only as a discipline ancillary to some other disciplines or doctrines, as for instance "cultural materialism," should be educated separately from those who, whether for Leavisian or other reasons, want to read *literature*, and possess, or hope to develop, "literary sensibility."[19] It is a shamefully vague expression, but it corresponds to something that certainly exists; those who have it know it exists and easily recognize its absence in those who do not. In what measure it could be transmitted under the conditions prescribed by Bergonzi—and far more threateningly under an achieved new epistemic dispensation, when all our relations to the world must be drastically altered—is more than I can guess. But, like Bergonzi, I believe in the remnant.

Opponents will contend that notions such as "literary sensibility" are precisely part of the battered luggage of the past—loaded with the broken fragments of the aesthetic ideology, tradition, *grands récits*, canonical works distinguished from all others by centuries of bourgeois propaganda—that must be discarded. The "aesthetic ideology," they are sure, belongs to a superseded *episteme*. The problem of dealing with these dismissive arguments is that there is no common ground. The canonical works are not read by those who despise or mistrust them, tradition is irrelevant ex hypothesi, all is text (which is true if you allow that certain critical operations turn some texts into works, a point not to be conceded).

There may be little use in pretending to see, from where we now stand, the final effect of the change now believed to be under way. If we wanted to be truly apocalyptic we should even have to consider the possibility that nothing of much present concern either to "humanists" or to their opponents will long survive. But it is impossible that we should not be interested in and worried about our more local problem. There will be much argument, ultimately about value, and especially about value as attributed to that which, merely by being past, can be held to be without relevance, or certainly not to have relevance merely by virtue of its being past. As we may see from the current debasement of the word *heritage*, there is much popular confusion about what is valuable in the past, and why, and if anybody can sort it out it will be the old guard or what is left of it, not the new.

Comfort may come from the reflection that the great Renaissance, which dumped a long past into an epochal oubliette labeled the Middle Ages, brought about changes that, great as they were, turned out to be rather less total than it proclaimed, so that it even became possible to think of it as continuous with what its propagandists claimed to have dumped. Hercules got back his club and lion's skin, but remained in the same place in the star map. The tomato was not, after all, "*en vérité sans défaut*," and our recalcitrant strand of skin, our remnant, may finally turn out to be more interesting than the sharp regularity demanded by the slicers.

I had already written this essay when I found in the indispensable *Times Literary Supplement* a quotation from Julien Benda's *La Trahison des clercs*, a book published long ago and still famous, though as John Casey, the reviewer, remarks, no longer much read. "Our age is indeed the age of the intellectual organization of hatred."[20] Benda was of course thinking more of politics than of art; but in our present situation his sentence surely loses nothing of its force. For we all have colleagues who hate or despise literature and the study of literature; and institutional change has given them power. Our remnant will not have an easy life.

### NOTES

1. See, e.g., Stephen Heath, *The Nouveau Roman: A Study in the Practice of Writing* (London: Elek, 1972), 113–14; and John Sturrock, *The French New Novel* (Oxford: Oxford University Press, 1969), 196–97.

2. Jean Seznec, *The Survival of the Pagan Gods: The Mythological Tradition and Its Place in Renaissance Humanism and Art*, trans. Barbara F. Sessions, Bollingen Series 38 (New York: Pantheon Books, 1953), 185–88.

3. Seznec, *The Survival of the Pagan Gods*, 211–13.

4. Erwin Panofsky, *Renaissance and Renascences in Western Art*, 2nd. ed. (New York, Harper Torchbooks, 1969), 1–35.

5. E. H. Gombrich, "The Renaissance: Period or Movement?" in *Background to the English Renaissance*, by A. G. Dickens et al. (London: Gray-Mills Publishing, 1974), 9–30.

6. The tortuous business of nomenclature is well examined by Hans Bertens, *The Idea of the Postmodern: A History* (London: Routledge, 1995).

7. Christopher Norris, *What's Wrong with Postmodernism: Critical Theory and the Ends of Philosophy* (Hemel Hempstead, U.K.: Harvester, 1990), introduction, esp. 4.

8. Frank Kermode, *History and Value* (Oxford: Clarendon Press, Oxford University Press, 1988), 128–46.

9. Alvin Kernan, *The Death of Literature* (New Haven, Conn.: Yale University Press, 1990), 83, 135–36, and 151.

10. Robert S. Boynton, "The Routledge Revolution," *Lingua Franca: The Review of Academic Life* 5, no. 3 (April 1995), 24–32.

11. Thomas Docherty, *After Theory: Postmodernism/Postmarxism* (London and New York: Routledge, 1990), 27, 58, and 219.

12. Stephen Greenblatt and Giles B. Gunn, eds., *Redrawing the Boundaries: The Transformation of English and American Literary Studies* (New York: Modern Language Association of America, 1992), 1–11.

13. See Ben Knights, *The Idea of the Clerisy in the Nineteenth Century* (Cambridge: Cambridge University Press, 1978).

14. For a fuller account, see Ian MacKillop, *F. R. Leavis: A Life in Criticism* (London: Penguin Press, 1995), 314–25; but MacKillop argues that the disagreement between the two lecturers was, at bottom, about history (notably the Industrial Revolution) and, though I acknowledge the importance of this point, I prefer to understand them otherwise, as the sequel shows.

15. I find, a little to my surprise, that I developed this point at some length in an essay of 1965, "The University and the Literary Public," in *The Humanities and the Understanding of Reality*, ed. Thomas B. Stroup (Lexington: University of Kentucky Press, 1966), 55–74.

16. See Francis Mulhern, *The Moment of "Scrutiny"* (London: New Left Books, 1978), 305ff.

17. Bernard Bergonzi, *Exploding English: Criticism, Theory, Culture* (Oxford: Clarendon Press, Oxford University Press, 1990).

18. Catherine Belsey, *Critical Practice* (London: Methuen, 1980), 130.

19. Bergonzi, *Exploding English*, 100–101.

20. John Casey, "Canon to the Right of Them," *Times Literary Supplement*, 10 November 1995, 19.

## 43. MAKING KNOWLEDGE

### BIOEPISTEMOLOGY AND THE FOUNDATIONS OF
### LITERARY THEORY

### NANCY EASTERLIN

DESPITE THE PLURALITY of literary theories today, nearly all are guided by an assumption that is the legacy of structuralism: all modes of human behavior and thought, including all knowledge, are *constructed*. Few current biologists and psychologists would be much surprised by the general proposition that knowledge is somehow *made*, i.e., that knowledge is relative to the capacities and conceptual predispositions of human knowers while simultaneously subject to social values and interests. Such a view is what Paul R. Gross and Norman Levitt call "weak constructivism," and in this sense we are all likely to agree that knowledge is constructed.[1] But literary theorists generally resort to "strong constructivism"; according to this view, knowledge is not *made*, but *made up*, purportedly the exclusive product of power relations and/or consensus within cultures rather than the result of correspondences between hypotheses and outside facts observed over time.

Thus, in spite of the much-touted interdisciplinarity of present-day literary studies, the prevalence of strong constructivism in the field's theorizing attests otherwise, for such an extreme view of the formation of knowledge and behavior is in many ways at odds with the contrary evidence emanating from the sciences. It is a shame that Levitt and Gross, scientists both, adopt such a scornful tone toward literary scholars in *Higher Superstition*, for literary scholars skeptical about the value of science for their field are unlikely to be persuaded by contempt.

Theories and findings about the nature of the human mind have direct bearing on all domains of intellectual inquiry, and it is my purpose in this essay to demonstrate that psychological theories convergent with biological evolutionary theory can help us resolve the contradictions between theory and practice now besetting literary studies. Focusing first on the logic of strong constructivism, I will discuss its alliance with radical skeptical epistemology, a philosophical tradition whose claims about the impossibility of truth and knowledge undermine many current theorists' espoused goal of social action. I will then suggest that what philosophers of science call bioepistemology— the view that knowledge is related to the capabilities of human knowers—

Nancy Easterlin. "Making Knowledge: Bioepistemology and the Foundations of Literary Theory." Originally published in *Mosaic: A Journal for the Interdisciplinary Study of Literature* 32, no. 1 (March 1999): 131–147. Revised by the author and reprinted by permission of the publisher.

offers a solution to the impasse afflicting literary studies. Finally, drawing on discussions of narrative thought and binary construction now prominent in cognitive science, I will explore how these reflect just two of many ways in which we are predisposed, apparently *by nature*, to construct and therefore to know our world.

Traditionally, philosophical debates about knowledge have been cast in binary terms, with contenders on one side upholding faith in the possibility that humans can attain absolute truth and knowledge, and those on the other side maintaining that, given our perceptual and cognitive biases and limitations, humans cannot know anything at all. As linguist George Lakoff and philosopher Mark Johnson comment, this demarcation bears witness to a long history of neo-Platonism, and has resulted in our "mistaken cultural assumption that the only alternative to objectivism is radical subjectivity—that is, either you believe in absolute truth *or* you can make the world in your own image. If you're not being *objective*, you're being *subjective*, and there is no third choice."[2] In light of the proliferation of institutions of learning and the degree of industrial, technological, and medical innovation in the past several centuries, it is rather remarkable that the either/or construction of epistemological debate has kept our understanding of human knowledge at an impasse for so long.

Poststructuralism, though purportedly a radical undoing of the Western philosophical tradition, wholeheartedly adopted the binary terms of conventional epistemological debate, siding with radical skeptics over naive objectivists. For example, in his 1966 "Structure, Sign, and Play in the Discourse of the Human Sciences," which generally marks poststructuralism's supplanting of structuralism in literary theory, Derrida describes two opposing positions: on the one hand, a view of knowledge as absolute, objective, transcendent, and directly expressed in transparent language, embodied in the metaphysical tradition and implicitly intertwined with totalitarian being and consciousness, and, on the other, a radical skepticism manifest in the infinite undecidability of meaning, somehow implicitly liberating and democratizing.[3] In championing the instability of language, Derrida announces his allegiance to the latter tradition, because a theory of language asserting the endless deferral of meaning is necessarily embedded in a radically skeptical epistemology. Quite simply, if our medium for negotiating and making knowledge is endlessly malleable and unstable, we cannot share meanings, and without shared meaning, no real knowledge can be produced.

It did not take long for socially conscious literary theorists and philosophers alike to feel uncomfortable with deconstructive epistemology, for ethical action needs some groundwork of shared assumptions and values, which themselves imply shared knowledge. But although neopragmatists like Richard Rorty and Stanley Fish, among others, seek a liberal solution to the epistemological and ethical problems that deconstruction raises, they also adopt the either/or terms of traditional epistemological debate which baffle all attempts at a moderate and logical solution. Anxious not to base their arguments on universalizing claims—since, as Alexander Argyros points out, totalities, from this point of view, are inherently correlated with totalitarianism—these scholars provide the philosophical argument for strong constructivism, otherwise referred to as social or cultural constructivism or constructionism.[4]

According to this view, truth is a function of consensus within a given framework—that is, a community, culture, or institution—and the truths of one community are claimed to be radically incommensurate with those of another. In *Literary Knowledge*, a critique of poststructuralist epistemology from the perspective of philosophy of science, Paisley Livingston calls such cultural constructivism "framework relativism," and reveals the logical problem it entails:

> [such thinking] is incoherent when it asserts that truth always or necessarily comes in limited and incommensurable frameworks (and hence is limited and contingent truth), for this very assertion is an unlimited thesis about what is necessarily the case about knowledge and reality. When framework relativism avoids this contradiction, it typically reverts to saying that if you happen to see the world from its perspective, then you see the world from that perspective—which is trivial.[5]

Despite its flagrant illogic, framework relativism, a core feature of strong constructivism, pervades the humanities and social sciences today and influences literary theory in its selective borrowings from other disciplines.

For instance, there is great tonal contrast but little substantive difference between Rorty's theory of liberal irony and Michel Foucault's notion that power, disseminated through the structures of language, constructs truth, because both thinkers embrace, like Derrida himself, Nietzschean nihilism and its concomitant rejection of a correspondence theory of truth. Rorty claims that, in pondering the nature of reality, cultures create metaphors and stories that have meaning for those cultures while simultaneously bearing no correspondence to outside facts.[6] Rorty's suggestion that narrative and metaphor should replace a (presumably outmoded) concept of knowledge puts the problem in comfortingly soft focus, but through the mists one discerns the epistemological quicksand; Rorty's stories and metaphors, like Foucault's paradigms and "truths"—opinions really—originate inexplicably and are equally untestable. But if culturally generated truths cannot be inter- and intraculturally as well as temporally mediated, there is no ground for intellectual and moral judgments—only a matter of agreeing or, should anyone inconveniently disagree, exerting force or influence.

In short, neopragmatism, like deconstruction and Foucauldian New Historicism, eschews the belief that correspondences between human ideas and

the world lead to truth or knowledge at any level; in thus rejecting a correspondence theory of truth, neopragmatism envisions knowledge as *made up*
rather than *made*. As Michael Morton succinctly summarizes the case, "denial
of the possibility of genuine *knowledge* of what are and are not the *facts*" provides the radical skeptical basis for a wide variety of strong constructivist theories and philosophies now prevailing in the humanities:

> whether the preferred term be, for example, poststructuralism, decon-
> struction, postmodernism, antifoundationalism, neopragmatism, per-
> spectivism, relativism ("cultural" or otherwise), nominalism ("higher" or
> otherwise), the "strong program," or something else entirely . . . all these
> isms . . . are united in a common adherence to [epistemological-ontologi-
> cal denial].[7]

Certainly the most profound and disturbing contradiction of the strong constructivist perspective is that, while motivated by a moral desire for liberal or
radical social change, its underlying epistemology tells us that we cannot know
anything, which would include the ability to discriminate between better or
worse social conditions and to take remedial action.

But we are not really bound to choose between a naive objectivism and the
various forms of skepticism and relativism that redefine words like "truth" and
"knowledge" beyond all recognition. In fact, we risk nothing by giving up the
binary terms of a debate which traditionally displaces questions of knowledge
into an abstract realm beyond human experience; to the contrary, we have
everything to gain by recasting these questions within the perspective of
bioepistemology. Whereas orthodox dualism has long condemned debates
about epistemology to endless repetition—since metaphysical claims cannot
be tested and therefore neither proven nor disproven—bioepistemology holds
claims about the kind and nature of human knowledge accountable to our
growing understanding of the brain-mind. Thus, the monism and materialism
of bioepistemology, which assumes the unity of brain and mind, provides the
ground for a *truly* constructive approach to the question of knowledge.

Actually, although evolutionary epistemology can be seen as a challenge to
poststructuralism, chronologically the former long predates the latter. Darwin's formulations of evolutionary theory entail this perspective on human
knowledge, and bioepistemology is also apparent or nascent in the work of
other major nineteenth-century thinkers. In "Pragmatism and Common
Sense," William James defines as "common sense" a set of eleven concepts—including, for example, thing, kinds, bodies, and causal influences—that constitute the most ancient and fundamental level of human thought. Though
James does not claim that these ways of thinking are biologically based, his
sense of their universality and durability throughout human history leaves
him just short of an evolutionary perspective. Likewise, Leslie Stephen, ac-

cording to Joseph Carroll, can be credited with formulating bioepistemology's basic principles; "[Karl] Popper and Stephen agree on the elementary rule of falsification through experience, and they both locate this principle in the vital concerns of living organisms."[8] The scientific principle that a theory must be falsifiable in order to be proven true, in other words, is for Popper and Stephen both drawn from and justified by its basic centrality in the lived experience of animal species. The negative test yields scientific knowledge exactly as it yields practical knowledge.

That the theory of evolution has many disagreeable implications has been recognized since Darwin's day, but it is only recently, as at least one critic of current literary theory has commented, that humanists and social scientists have felt free to select theories based merely on their comfort with them.[9] Today, literary theorists and many other academics are reluctant to embrace evolutionary epistemology because it requires recognition of natural constraints on human thought and behavior; still, the explanatory strength of the Darwinian paradigm and its apparent truth must, I think, compel intellectuals to accept it as an encompassing theoretical framework or, alternatively, to provide another model of equally comprehensive explanatory power. Philosophers of science such as Roger Masters and Michael Ruse, following the initiative of sociobiologist E. O. Wilson, claim that philosophers can no longer ignore the implications of Darwinian theory and the biological basis of behavior for an understanding of human knowledge.

I would also add that humanists and social scientists, including literary theorists, who ignore the implications of evolutionary theory and biology do so at the cost of the increasing irrelevance of their disciplines. To be meaningful, discussion of the artifacts of human culture must be framed by our knowledge of human beings, not by artificial or incomplete notions of our world and our social experience. In light of the denial of human agency which has become commonplace in literary theory—primarily through the influence of Althusserian Marxism on Foucault and others—it is nothing short of miraculous that a field devoted to studying the artifacts of *human* culture has survived at all.

Bioepistemology represents one of the two basic theoretical positions within the more general category of evolutionary epistemology. The core assumption of bioepistemology is that, given evolutionary theory as the most plausible account of human origins, the human mind as a result of natural selection is predisposed in ways that have proven adaptively advantageous; from this central premise it follows that questions regarding the nature of human knowledge can be answered through an understanding of certain predispositions (e.g., cognitive adaptations). Human beings operate according to what Eugene d'Aquili calls a "cognitive imperative," a need to organize sensory input in a meaningful fashion.[10] Accordingly, the conceptual tendencies which enabled primitive man to overcome complexity and act in the interests of survival have direct bearing on the construction of knowledge within human culture.

Here, however, a distinction should be made between the current view that cognitive patterns or forms are universally evident in humans and an older (and anachronistic) philosophical belief in innate ideas, i.e., wired-in information about reality. As Wilson's conception of epigenetic rules suggests, the contemporary view of evolutionists is that our learning processes are governed by instructions for organizing information from the environment—that it is general *forms* of thought, not specific *content*, that is biogenetically given. These instructions for organizing are ancient human adaptations that evolved during the Pleistocene era, because they enhanced survival in that ancient environment. As today's leading evolutionary psychologists point out, this also means that our panhuman psychic architecture, of which our instructions for organizing are a part, does not rigidly determine behavior; to the contrary, plasticity in individual response to the environment is enabled by domain-specific competences.[11] In other words, without the inborn tendency to organize information in specific ways, we would not be able to experience choice in our responses. Chaos would take the place of experience, and our species would not have survived.

The second approach within evolutionary epistemology, called the conceptual approach, embraces the core assumption of bioepistemology and places it within a larger theoretical perspective. Whereas bioepistemology "starts within the human mind as a product of evolution through natural selection, and then works from there to try to understand the nature and development of science," the conceptual approach "sees the whole of existence as in some sense a developing phenomenon, with organic evolution as but one manifestation."[12] The conceptual approach, while not inconsistent with the biological approach, takes the added theoretical leap of presupposing a high degree of similarity and functional unity between the biological structures of individual organisms and systems and those of the larger physical universe. The conceptual approach thus complements, though by no means necessarily implies, an idealist teleological vision of the universe evolving toward greater and greater order and beauty.[13] Such an idealist teleology premised on evolutionary principles harks back to the work of nineteenth-century intellectuals who, in replacing static universals with developmental dynamics, optimistically saw continual moral and spiritual improvement in the order of things.[14]

The conceptual approach is therefore problematic for several reasons: first, history contradicts the correlation of evolution with improvement, and second, its conflation of models from biology, physics, and other sciences is questionable; we simply do not know enough to assert, with any degree of specificity, correlations between functions in individual organisms and vast universal systems of inert matter. Moreover, the strong implication of the conceptual paradigm that evolution works by design or in a design-like way is flatly rejected by scientists in the numerous fields (such as evolutionary psychology and paleoanthropology) who study specific adaptations and who generally see such a view as a relic of nineteenth-century misinterpretations of Darwin.

In addition to its theoretical shortcomings, the conceptual approach poses practical problems for the literary theorist. Precisely because of its universalizing vision, the conceptual approach prioritizes the physical universe models over the cognitive and behavioral (the human) ones, and therefore works best at the most generalizing level of theory, while it falls short on more specific literary theoretical and interpretive questions. Bioepistemology, in contrast, is concerned specifically with the human organism, seeking to uncover the biological mechanisms of cognition and thus focusing epistemological questions on how the naturally selected brain operates flexibly within parameters that both *enable* and *constrain* knowledge; it thus provides a crucial starting point for those who study the artifacts of human culture. As a basis for both a general epistemology and a practical body of knowledge, then, bioepistemology has distinct advantages over the conceptual approach. Although more cautious in its own knowledge, it has, apparently, more to offer.

As I have already noted, a biological approach to cognition can hardly be characterized as an eccentric fad within the philosophy of science; in addition to the nineteenth-century precedents for bioepistemology, its formulators in this century include the ethologist Konrad Lorenz and the developmental psychologist Jean Piaget, both of whom conducted studies seminal to the growth of their disciplines. Hence, the validity of such an approach is now taken for granted by most researchers in the hard and social sciences concerned with cognitive functioning.

Moreover, although a significant number of cognitivists retreat from or deny claims that our cognitive tendencies are the product of innate biological structures, their own research is strikingly consistent with that of scholars who make the logical assertion that such cognitive universals must have a biological basis. Like other strong constructivists, the strategy of those who deny the biological basis of the universal cognitive tendencies they study is to leave the origins of these universals an open question. This is simply an intellectually unsatisfactory evasion—a tactic, indeed, that seems especially disingenuous among those whose research daily reveals the strength and universality of such tendencies. Only by assimilating congruent research from cognitive science and evolutionary psychology with our growing understanding of the anatomical structures and physiological processes of the brain can we begin to answer the complex question of how humans construct knowledge.

Clearly, bioepistemology is not consistent with naive objectivism, for, being constrained by cognitive predispositions which work (or once worked) to adaptive advantage, we are preeminently *interested* knowers of our world; our knowledge is irreducibly human—that is, gathered and made in accordance with a specifically human orientation to the environment. Because this requires us to give up the notion of knowing the world-in-itself—of objective, transparent, unmediated knowledge—the question that arises is the one posed and answered by Ruse:

> Does this not plunge us into a world of subjectivity where anything goes, where there are simply no constraints on knowledge? Other evolutionary epistemologists fear so—and, today, in this they would probably be backed by various radical pragmatists like Richard Rorty. . . . However, Hume did not think he was plunged into such a quicksand and neither do I. We still have the real world, but it is the world as we interpret it.     ("View," 220)

Or, as Lakoff and Johnson put it, truth is relative to understanding. Ultimately, three things save bioepistemology from collapsing into the subjectivist stance: first, interpretation is not unconstrained but takes place within the parameters of "understanding"; that is, we organize according to certain rules or predispositions that, like fundamental aspects of human anatomy and neurophysiological functions, are cross-culturally shared; second, there is a fit—partial but significantly functional—between mind and world, to which the survival of our species attests; third, the cognitive tendencies which constitute understanding and interpretation are diverse, variable, and complex, so that, within the mind itself, there is a dynamic relationship between the tendency to simplify and hierarchize input and the recognition of real-world complexity. As William James, a true pragmatist, recognized, knowledge arises in interrelated dynamic processes ongoing between organism and environment (constituted by the physical world and other humans) and within the mind itself.

What, then, are the instructions for organizing that constitute understanding, orienting us in our experience of the world and defining our capacity for knowledge? Recent research in psychology, philosophy, and linguistics provides some striking insights into the nature of human thought. Perhaps first among these is the widely studied hypothesis that narrative plays a primary and indispensible role in mental and social life; events and mental states are not only given meaning by plot, as Jerome Bruner notes, but the construal of action and thought in narrative facilitates the retention of these phenomena in memory.[15] Drawing on several recent studies in language acquisition, Bruner furthermore observes that narrativity—defined as the ability to organize actor, action, goal, scene, and instrument into a sequential story—is a primary form of mentation inherent in social interaction prior to language acquisition. It is the impulse to shape his/her own meanings within the family that motivates the child to acquire language, and so to establish his/her influence within familial interaction. Thus, studies in language acquisition basically contradict poststructuralist textualism, the notion that language *creates* reality.

The basis of narrativity is causal thinking, one of the common sense categories identified a century ago by William James, and a cognitive mode whose crucial significance is now recognized by scholars in diverse disciplines. Linearizing, the most basic feature of narrative which Bruner tells us is built into the structure of every known grammar, is the product of our tendency to think causally. Argyros similarly draws a connection between narrative and causality, asserting that narrative is a powerful intersubjective map whose basic structure is the causal frame of actor-action-object.[16] This identification by linguists, cognitive scientists, and literary theorists of narrativity and the causal frame as primary to human thought and communication coincides with sociobiologist Wilson's identification of causal thinking as a discernable epigenetic rule. As Ruse points out, Wilson's rule here is consistent with Hume's observation that the human mind has a propensity to "[read] necessity into nature, thinking nevertheless it has found it as an objective facet of nature."[17] If narrative principally serves to give coherent shape to the events of social life, the imputation of necessity to nature suggests a profound predisposition to discover causal order in nature. Both are adaptive tactics, because the intelligibility of events resulting from narrative construal is correlated with a feeling of control and mastery.

Once again, however, if such order is not always a feature of nature but instead of the mind's constructions, does not this confirmation of the hypothesis that we project order onto nature erode the bioepistemological perspective? Are we in fact thrown back into subjectivism and radical skepticism? That the answer is "no" may be found in the promising fact that we are compelled, for reasons of survival, to perceive the discrepancy between a given human construal of events and an outside reality that seems not to support this construal. However stubbornly we hold to a story or version of things—and we most assuredly do this—we are not, in fact, caught in a hermeneutic circle when our interpretive tools fail repeatedly to yield practical results. True knowledge is preeminently the result of process, of repeated attempts to match mental constructions or theories to outside facts, of the interaction between humans and the apparent reality beyond them.

For example, if I attribute my allergic symptoms to the blooming crape myrtle tree in my yard and subsequently cut the tree down but experience no alleviation of my symptoms, I look for another cause. I conjecture that perhaps I have developed an allergy to my cats, or perhaps my symptoms are the result of an immunological breakdown, and therefore not attributable to any outside cause. We naturally subject our explanations of phenomena or events to a pragmatic test, changing—albeit sometimes with difficulty—beliefs that are not supported by external evidence.

In the case of my example, the first hypothesis is both the most probable and the most appealing, so my construction of it is guided by so-called subjective interests and objective considerations simultaneously. Having a history of pollen but not animal allergies, I logically infer that the tree is the source of my symptoms, an objective conclusion nonetheless conveniently reinforced by my subjective interests: I would be more distressed by the loss of my cats (members of my family), than by the loss of the tree, its beauty notwithstanding; but, being only human, I would probably be most upset by the prospect of some serious physiological danger to myself signalled by the breakdown of my immune system.

Self-interest and habit of mind affect profoundly our quest for knowledge, but they do not make knowledge impossible. As William James notes, and as the field in contemporary social psychology known as "consistency theory" corroborates, knowledge does grow, but it is a spotty process in which "we keep unaltered as much of our old knowledge, as many of our old prejudices and beliefs, as we can."[18] Likewise, in the example I have sketched here, the persistent form of my hypothesis, my attempt to identify a cause, indicates not abysmal subjectivism but the *relative adequacy* of human thinking; were there *never* a match between our stories and the world—were causal explanations nothing more than fictions—the predictions derived from our narratives, on which we base our present and future behavior, would certainly prove fatal.

I say the "relative adequacy," for science has also led us to an awareness of the limited nature of strictly causal and linear thinking. Thus, in the famous Chaos Theory example of sensitive dependence on initial conditions, it is reductively simplistic to identify the butterfly in Hong Kong as *the cause* of distant weather patterns.[19] The butterfly flapping his wings can send the system into chaos only because it has reached a critical state, so that all the factors contributing to the system's critical state (i.e., the initial conditions) might justifiably be considered causes as well. Modern science has attuned us to the crucial nature of context and condition, and thus modified our innate tendency to look for simple causes and unalterable physical laws.

As Bruner notes, narrative exhibits a shadowy epistemology, because it is our means of organizing both the real and the imaginary. And furthermore, narrative is, so to speak, a both/and phenomenon: because linearity is a function of the way we think as well as observable in real world events, different narratives can vary greatly in their degree of truth, sometimes intentionally and sometimes unintentionally. Unfortunately, because many humanists and social scientists regard *narrative* as synonymous with *fiction*, some contemporary literary theorists and philosophers like Rorty have concluded that human knowledge is storylike in an entirely fictional sense, that the literary critic or philosopher who is apprised of the fictionality of narrative understands the status of human knowledge better than the scientist who believes that his stories refer to phenomena and events in the real world. But literary critics who assert the storylike character of scientific theories and claim the absolute cultural relativism of the truth-value of such theories totalize the picture of narrative while ignoring the cultural purposes and uses of different kinds of narrative, a curious fact in light of the avowals of antitotalization and the much-announced cultural awareness so prevalent today.

In short, the argument of strong constructivists who conflate narrative and fictionality is specious because there are procedures for testing the truth claims of nonimaginative discourse to which scientific narratives are subject. If the theory of evolution is a story of our origins, if it is knowledge we have *made*, it is not *made up*, as is Dickens's *Bleak House*; and thus we test the theory of the descent of man against the fossil record and the behavior of primate species while, by contrast, the unlikeliness of spontaneous combustion in human populations embellishes rather than discredits the integrity of Dickens's fictional world.

Moreover, our ability to distinguish between fictional and nonfictional narratives is not a recent cultural invention or construct. Aristotle assumes it when he distinguishes the probable from the possible in literature: it is more important that an event be consistent with the internal logic of the drama than that there is an actual likelihood of its occurence.[20] For Aristotle, then, truth-value or correspondence to reality is not the criterion by which imaginative works should be constructed or judged, whereas the *Poetics* itself, whose critical/theoretical claims are based on inductive observation of the drama, should be judged precisely according to that set of data on which it is based—the actual features of Greek drama. Aristotle hopes and believes, based on his observations, that what he says about the relative unimportance of truth to reality in dramatic plots is in fact a true observation about literature. An innate ability to distinguish make-believe from factuality has, moreover, been refined and modified over the course of human cultural evolution, so that we bring very different sorts of expectations to fictional and scientific narrative, just as we use the narratives in strikingly dissimilar ways. And as children, we quickly learn the cultural conventions that separate fictional and nonfictional narratives.

Narrative is not our only strategy for organizing input and aspiring to knowledge, although it is probably our most basic, as Robert Storey notes, and one reason this innate way of knowing continues to thrive is because of its practical usefulness in the social sphere.[21] At the same time, the drive to produce meaning through a linear construal of events is also modified by other fundamental conceptual tendencies that make it impossible that human thought and knowledge struggle helplessly in the grasp of any single cognitive predisposition such as narrative.

Indeed, one of our most basic and primitive conceptual tendencies is probably binary opposition itself. Some time ago, in their 1974 *Biogenetic Structuralism*, Laughlin and d'Aquili suggested that the universal tendency to "order reality into pairs that are subjectively experienced as opposites" is based in the self-other dichotomy, and more recent research has also supported this contention. In *The Body in the Mind*, for example, Mark Johnson claims that the image schemata like binary pairing which underlie human conceptual structures have their origins in our bodily experience.[22] That this binary way of conceptualizing is deeply ingrained in our psyches and institutions is suggested by Carl Jung's theory of dream structure and Claude Lévi-Strauss's analysis of social institutions. We are, as Storey points out, predisposed "to both approach and avoidance"; the human animal "may be said to be an organism of natural divisions."[23] That is, humans are genetically predisposed toward both self-interest and sociality or helping, to conflict and consensus, and binary conceptualization is a reflection, on the cognitive plane, of this division in human nature. Essentially ambivalent about where and when to draw the line between the self and the group, we perhaps draw the line with remarkable clarity. What originates in a division between self and other, then, becomes a basic tendency of all human thought.

For our primitive ancestors, binary constructions must have contributed to survival in reducing and clarifying environmental input, allowing them to act quickly in response to environmental threats. Clearly, with the rise of culture the initial reason for such a tendency seems no longer to have much bearing on survival—and may, in fact, militate against it in a world where either/or thinking can have disastrous consequences—but just as clearly binarism remains a powerful and pervasive conceptual tendency. Thus a way of organizing based on a primitive opposition between self and other still shapes some of our most arcane intellectual arguments, those in literary theory included.

Both structuralist and poststructuralist literary theory, for example, are founded on assumptions about language that serve as stellar examples of the predisposition to binary construction as well as of its limitations. Structuralism asserts that language is structured in paired opposites (e.g., *l'histoire* and *discours*); poststructuralism concludes that, since structuralism's binaries collapse under the realization that such terms are not true opposites, language has no stable structure. But poststructuralism frames this very argument in an either/or fashion, and thus, like the initial structuralist assumptions about language, reflects the tendency to think in binary terms. In fact, language may be stable, even though its stability does not rest on a structure of binaries, and so in the deconstructive undoing of structuralism only *one* theory of linguistic structure has been, in the favorite phrase of our day, put into question. Yet several decades of literary theory and criticism have come to rest on the unwarranted overgeneralization of Derrida's "or."

I think that the lesson here is a fairly obvious one. If the natural world and the cultural world coextensive with it is not necessarily (or is only sometimes) organized in pairs of oppositions, then deconstruction's undoing of structuralism's binaries could have been much more than a decadent language game. What poststructuralist literary theorists failed to heed were the challenges to linguistic and anthropological structuralism put forth in the early 1970s by structuralists *across* the disciplines—for example, Piaget in psychology and Laughlin and d'Aquili in biological anthropology, all of whom called for an integration of the functional considerations of biological and psychological structuralism with the cultural analyses of anthropological structuralism.[24] Similarly, had poststructuralists taken a comprehensively interdisciplinary perspective and considered the implications of bioepistemology, they would have seen binary structure as an exaggerated but correctible tendency of human thought. Thus, instead of a nihilistic undoing of our own constructions into meaninglessness, poststructuralism could have discovered the renewed possibilities for meaning attendant upon a consciousness of our shared instructions for organizing.

Far from giving us cause for more self-indulgent radical skepticism, the insights we have gained into the mental predispositions of humans offer the opportunity for us to become much *better* knowers, who will reflect critically on our innate ways of construing the information we receive. Knowing that we have innate tendencies to organize reality in various ways—for instance, by creating narratives or by seeing things in paired oppositions—we can subject our hypotheses and theories in all disciplines to self-conscious scrutiny, asking whether they oversimplify, or indeed grossly misrepresent, the actual case.

Such intellectual self-reflection and self-correction is possible for two reasons. First, human cognition is not designed or logically engineered, but is comprised of a broad array of adaptations, including binary structure and narrativity. Since each adaptation evolved to solve a particular problem in the organism's adjustment to the environment, our cognitive predispositions do not always operate harmoniously with one another, and do in fact frequently conflict. To recall Storey's point, we are creatures of naturally divided impulses. For instance, though we strongly favor binary thinking, we are also predisposed to its opposite, the recognition of complexity. This leads to my second point, which is that we do test our hypotheses against the outside world—that is to say, we are still pragmatic animals today because the process of testing ideas against observed reality works—it has meant the survival of the species. And furthermore, because the world we test against has become a complex place, its very complexity has imposed upon us much need for self-correction.

Literary scholars now find themselves in a position to correct the limitations and oversights of structuralist and poststructuralist literary theory. As Mark Turner suggests, we need to reconstitute the profession of literature within an understanding of "language and literature as acts of the everyday mind" so that "our grounding activity [is] the study of language and of literature as expressions of our conceptual apparatus."[25] Turner aims at nothing less than restoring literary studies to a central position in culture and education;

somewhat more modestly, I would argue that, if anything will restore signifi-cance to literary study, it is a revised and informed humanism.

Rather than seeing human beings as evolution's greatest achievement and the center of the universe, a new humanism would be guided consciously—and with some humility—by the awareness that our knowledge is not absolute because it is inevitably human, the product of species-typical instructions for organizing such as narrativity and binarization. In contrast to traditional lib-eral humanism as defined by its critics, this new humanism will not have as its aim, as Terry Eagleton phrases it, "the nurturing of spiritual wholeness in a hostile world."[26] This new humanism, based in a bioepistemological perspec-tive, reconnects literature with human life through scientific insight, and thus leads not to the spiritualization of things human but to a biocultural perspec-tive that allows us to speculate on the function and meaning of literature within the entirety of human knowledge.

## NOTES

1. Paul R. Gross and Norman Levitt, *Higher Superstition: The Academic Left and Its Quarrels with Science* (Baltimore, Md.: Johns Hopkins University Press, 1994).

2. George Lakoff and Mark Johnson, *Metaphors We Live By* (Chicago: University of Chicago Press, 1980), 185.

3. Jacques Derrida, "Structure, Sign, and Play in the Discourse of the Human Sciences," in *The Structuralist Controversy*, ed. Richard Macksey and Eugenio Donato (Baltimore, Md.: Johns Hopkins University Press, 1972), 247–72.

4. Alexander Argyros, *A Blessed Rage for Order: Deconstruction, Evolution, and Chaos* (Ann Arbor: University of Michigan Press, 1991).

5. Paisley Livingston, *Literary Knowledge: Humanistic Inquiry, and the Philosophy of Sci-ence* (Ithaca, N.Y.: Cornell University Press, 1988), 59.

6. Richard Rorty, *Contingency, Irony, Solidarity* (Cambridge: Cambridge University Press, 1989).

7. Michael Morton, "Strict Constructionism: Davidsonian Realism and the World of Belief," in *Literary Theory After Davidson*, ed. Reed Way Dasenbrock (University Park: Penn-sylvania State University Press, 1993).

8. William James, *Pragmatism and Other Essays* (1913; New York: Pocket Books, 1963), 76; Joseph Carroll, *Evolution and Literary Theory* (Columbia: University of Missouri Press, 1995), 78–79.

9. Richard E. Levin, "The New Interdisciplinarity in Literary Criticism," in *After Post-structuralism: Interdisciplinarity and Literary Theory*, ed. Nancy Easterlin and Barbara Riebling (Evanston, Ill.: Northwestern University Press, 1993), 13–43, 17; Roger Masters, "Evolutionary Biology, Human Nature, and Knowledge," in *Sociobiology and Epistemology*, ed. James H. Fetzer (Dordrecht, Netherlands: Reidel,1985), 97–113; Michael Ruse, "Evolu-tionary Epistemology: Can Sociobiology Help?" in Fetzer, 250–65, and "A View from Some-where: A Critical Defense of Evolutionary Epistemology," in *Issues in Evolutionary Episte-mology*, ed. Kai Hahlweg and C. A. Hooker (Albany: State University of New York Press,

1989), 185–225; E. O. Wilson, *On Human Nature* (Cambridge, Mass.: Harvard University Press, 1978).

10. Charles Laughlin and Eugene d'Aquili, *Biogenetic Structuralism* (New York: Columbia University Press, 1974), 114.

11. Leda Cosmides and John Tooby, "The Psychological Foundations of Culture," in *The Adapted Mind: Evolutionary Psychology and the Generation of Culture*, ed. Jerome H. Barkow, Leda Cosmides, and John Tooby (New York: Oxford University Press, 1992), 19–130, 50–62, 113.

12. Ruse, "View from Somewhere," 204.

13. Among literary scholars, the conceptual approach is endorsed by Frederick Turner. See, for instance, *Rebirth of Value: Meditations on Beauty, Ecology, Religion, and Education* (New York: State University of New York Press, 1991).

14. Carroll, *Evolution and Literary Theory*, 185–91.

15. Jerome Bruner, *Acts of Meaning* (Cambridge, Mass.: Harvard University Press, 1990), 56. On the primacy of narrativic thought in human beings, see also Dan Edward Lloyd, *Simple Minds* (Cambridge, Mass.: MIT Press, 1989); Jean Matter Mandler, *Stories, Scripts, and Scenes: Aspects of Schema Theory* (Hillsdale, N.J.: Erlbaum Press, 1984); Roger C. Schank, *Tell Me A Story: A New Look at Real and Artificial Memory* (New York: Scribners, 1990).

16. Argyros, *Rage for Order*, 310.

17. Ruse, "Evolutionary Epistemology," 262.

18. James, *Pragmatism*, 74.

19. James Gleick, *Chaos: Making a New Science* (New York: Penguin Books, 1987).

20. Aristotle, *Poetics*, trans. and ed. James Hutton (New York: Norton, 1982).

21. Robert Storey, *Mimesis and the Human Animal: On the Biogenetic Foundations of Literary Representation* (Evanston, Ill.: Northwestern University Press, 1996), 84.

22. Lauglin and d'Aquili, *Biogenetic Structuralism*, 115; Mark Johnson, *The Body in the Mind: On the Bodily Basis of Meaning, Imagination, and Reason* (Chicago: University of Chicago Press, 1987).

23. Storey, *Mimesis*, 79.

24. Jean Piaget, *Structuralism*, trans. and ed. Chaninah Maschler (New York: Basic Books, 1970).

25. Mark Turner, *The Study of English in the Age of Cognitive Science* (Princeton, N.J.: Princeton University Press, 1991), 6.

26. Terry Eagleton, *Literary Theory: An Introduction* (Minneapolis: University of Minnesota Press, 1983), 199.

## 44.  LITERATURE AND FICTION

### PETER LAMARQUE AND STEIN HAUGOM OLSEN

### The Concept of Fiction in Literary Criticism

TOWARD THE END of the nineteenth century a new use of the concept of fiction as partially synonymous with the genre concepts of "novel" and "short story" spread rapidly in practical criticism. Whatever the reason for this new use, it forced authors who wanted to claim that the value of their literary works was at least in part due to their truth-telling function to formulate this claim as a paradox. Modernist novelists accepted the term "fiction" as a genre description of their works, but they insisted that *their* fiction (serious fiction, the fiction of the artist) was as *true* as, and perhaps *truer* than, history. "The only reason for the existence of a novel," says Henry James in his essay "The Art of Fiction," "is that it does attempt to represent life."[1] And in her essay "Modern Fiction," Virginia Woolf argues that fiction should not be governed by a conception of form but by the standard of life itself. Her charge against realist fiction is that it is merely conventional rather than true.[2] When the modernists stake their claim as serious artists, as elites with a message that the audience may not heed, but that they ignore at their peril, they use "fiction" to refer to what they create, but they emphasize that their task is to tell the *truth*.

Even though this technical identification of fiction with the discursive genres of literature was theoretically innocent, it created a situation where the possibilities for conceptual confusion were greatly increased. "Fiction" is plausibly applied to the narrative genres of literature only because it is widely recognized that these consist, at least to a large extent, of invented stories and descriptions. When the modernist novelists claim that their fiction must represent life, they trade on the strong sense of "fiction" to create their striking paradox: *in spite of* being fictions their works are true. There is a clear danger in this strategy for the novelist or theorist who wants to establish the point that literature aims at some kind of truth. By introducing the term "fiction" as an alternative name for the discursive genres of literature there is the risk of promoting exactly the opposite conclusion. For once established in literary criticism as a near synonym for "novel" and "short story," the term "fiction" invites the assumption that it is of the essence of these genres that they make no claim to truth. And given a certain combination of theoretical assumptions, the use

Peter Lamarque and Stein Haugom Olsen. "Literature and Fiction." Revised by the authors from *Truth, Fiction, and Literature: A Philosophical Perspective*, by Peter Lamarque and Stein Haugom Olsen, 268–88. Oxford: Clarendon Press. Copyright © Peter Lamarque and Stein Haugom Olsen, 1994. Used by permission of Oxford University Press.

of "fiction" might be construed as expressing a "profound" intuition about the cognitive status of literature. Such a combination of theoretical assumptions has dominated influential parts of modem literary theory.

Theories of literature from Aristotle onwards have worked with an overt or hidden assumption about the paradigmatic status of some particular genre of literature. For Aristotle it was tragedy. In the New Criticism the object of attention is poetry. The Semantic Definition of Literature, "a literary work is a discourse in which an important part of the meaning is implicit,"[3] applies *par excellence* to poetry, and the emphasis in New Critical practice was on the analysis of poems. Adopting the poem as the paradigm for all literary works, there was no danger that New Critical theory should introduce "fiction" as an alternative name for "literature." There is no critical usage of the term "fiction" to denote poetry.[4] In New Critical theory the relationship between literature and fiction therefore remained not only controversial but a central theoretical issue. Writing about "The Problem of Belief," in 1954, Arnold Isenberg could say: "the question, though not excessively clear, has been much debated; and it is possible to speak of 'sides.'" And he goes on, "I take one side, holding as I do the extreme view that belief and aesthetic experience are mutually irrelevant."[5] And the central theoretical work in the New Critical tradition, Monroe Beardsley's *Aesthetics*, published four years later, has one chapter on "Artistic Truth" (chapter 8) and one on "Literature and Knowledge" (chapter 9). However, the literary theories which can be subsumed under the labels "structuralism" and "poststructuralism" concentrate attention on discursive writing, in particular narrative, and the focus has been on the structure and other properties of narrative.

In these theories it is tacitly assumed that the paradigmatic kinds of literature are the novel and the short story. These theories therefore facilitate the identification of fiction and literature in a way that previous theories have not done. In addition, these theories rely on two further assumptions which make it seem natural that literature is fiction in the strong sense of being a description or a story that makes no claim to be true. It is assumed in these types of theory that literary works somehow have "meaning" and that this is what makes the literary work important.[6] And this assumption is combined with the further, formalist, assumption that meaning can be explained in purely formalistic, nonsemantic, terms based on relationships between signs rather than on referential or truth-bearing relations. If meaning is defined in this way, then a literary work can have meaning without being about anything in the world. Consequently, there is no reason for assuming that a literary work is a kind of discourse which in any way makes true or false statements. And the identification of fiction with literature, which the first assumption encourages, then seems unproblematic.

The three assumptions formulated above do not together *entail* the conclusion that the concept of "literature" is identical with the concept of "fiction," nor is there any weaker but logically sound inferential link from these three assumptions to that conclusion. They merely make the identification *seem natural* as long as it is not examined closely. Note what happens in the following passage where the view of literature and language expressed by the two last assumptions is taken for granted:

> For the statement about language, that sign and meaning can never coincide, is what is precisely taken for granted in the kind of language we call literary. Literature, unlike everyday language, begins on the far side of this knowledge; it is the only form of language free from the fallacy of unmediated expression. All of us know this, although we know it in the misleading way of a wishful assertion of the opposite. Yet the truth emerges in the foreknowledge we possess of the true nature of literature when we refer to it as *fiction*. All literatures, including the literature of Greece, have always designated themselves as existing in the mode of fiction; in the *Iliad*, when we first encounter Helen, it is as the emblem of the narrator weaving the actual war into the tapestry of a fictional object. Her beauty prefigures the beauty of all future narratives as entities that point to their own fictional nature. The self-reflecting mirror-effect by means of which a work of fiction asserts, by its very existence, its separation from empirical reality, its divergence, as a sign, from a meaning that depends for its existence on the constitutive activity of this sign, characterizes the work of literature in its essence.[7]

This critic turns the theoretically innocent fact that "we" refer to novels and short stories as "fiction," into a basic assumption on which a view of literature can be built, by first equating novels and short stories with "literature." This is an illicit move. "We" do not, as this critic assumes, refer to "literature" as "fiction"; "we" refer only to the genres of novels and short stories in this way. Second, this critic assumes that this use of "fiction" is expressive of a profound, shared intuition about the cognitive status of literature, an intuition that literary language is fictional discourse. "We," Paul de Man assumes, have the foreknowledge that literature is in the mode of fiction. But this is simply wrong. As has just been argued, the use of "fiction" as an alternative name for the discursive genres of literature is, in this respect, theoretically innocent. That usage does not signal "foreknowledge" of any kind. In particular, this use of "fiction" is not an expression of a shared intuition which is prior to and can support a formalist account of literary meaning. Nevertheless, in structuralism and poststructuralism, the identification of literature and fiction is not only a central feature, but it is also beyond argument. Proponents of these views do not argue the point, but assert magisterially, as does de Man in the quoted passage, that literature *is* fiction.[8]

The presence of the concept of fiction in literary criticism and the frequency with which it is used is not, then, expressive of any shared intuition about the cognitive status of literature. Literary works make use of invented stories and descriptions but this does not entail that literary works are works of fiction. Indeed, though in previous chapters of our book *Truth, Fiction, and Literature: A Philosophical Perspective* we have often analyzed passages in literary works that are fictive in the sense defined, it would be wrong to take for granted, without further argument, that any literary work must possess a fictive dimension. It does not seem to be part of the *definition* of literature that it be in the fictive mode or even have a fictional content. A premature and theoretically unsubstantiated identification of literature and fiction will disguise a central problem which the concept of literature raises: the problem of the relationship between the literary work and its representational powers. The relationship between literature and fiction is thus problematic rather than straightforward. It may very well be that the most reasonable position on the issue is to accept as a general presumption that for something to be a literary work it will also be a species of fictive utterance. However, this is no more than a presumption and still leaves us with the problem of literary value. Literature, unlike fiction, is an evaluative concept and a work is recognized as a literary work partially through the recognition of the intention to present something to the reader that is humanly interesting. This is not a necessary implication of the fictive stance. The highly valued works of the literary canon are recognized as such because they have something to say about the "human condition." If literature is closely bound to make-believe, then we have to offer an interpretation of the mimetic aspect of literature which, in spite of its fictive quality, does justice to this central aspect of literary value.

## The Attack on the Concept of Literature

When modern literary theory of the structuralist and poststructuralist type so easily assimilates literature to fiction without any further analysis of the process through which the assimilation comes about or any argument about the validity of the moves involved, this is because these types of theory rest on certain further assumptions that undermine the value of rational argument itself. It is instructive to note how in the passage from de Man the substitution of magisterial pronouncement for rational argument affects not only the way in which literature is identified with fiction, but also the way in which the illustration from the *Iliad* is presented. Even if one accepts without further argument that Helen in her first appearance in the third song of the *Iliad* is emblematic of the narrator of the story (she is weaving a cloak on which she pictures the battles fought for her), it is difficult to accept that she creates a "fictional object." What she seems to be doing is to picture a reality she sees before her. If she is indeed representative of the narrator, then his claim would seem to be exactly the opposite of that which de Man finds: i.e., that she tells a true story. It may, of course, be possible to interpret the scene in the way de Man does, but there is no *interpretative argument* in de Man's book to support his suggestion. In the quoted passage methodical argument is replaced by authoritarian tone. This substitution of assumed authority for rational argument is typical of de Man's book and indeed of much poststructuralist criticism. It is a natural consequence of a view that construes reason and objectivity as humanist myths which have to be discarded if the critic is to engage with the "open multisignificance of texts."

Behind this position lies the more general skeptical and antirealist stance that we have already examined and criticized.[9] This is the view that

> it [is] impossible any longer to see reality simply as something "out there," a fixed order of things which language merely reflected. On that assumption, there was a natural bond between word and thing, a given set of correspondences between the two realms. Our language laid bare for us how the world was, and this could not be questioned. This rationalist or empiricist view of language suffered severely at the hands of structuralism: for if, as Saussure had argued, the relation between sign and referent was an arbitrary one, how could any "correspondence" theory of knowledge stand? Reality was not reflected by language but *produced* by it: it was a particular way of carving up the world which was deeply dependent on the sign-systems we had at our command, or more precisely which had us at theirs.[10]

It is symptomatic of the poor standard of argument in modern literary theory that a well-known literary theorist should present this argument approvingly without showing any awareness of the highly contentious nature of the premises and reasoning.

In this passage one finds the first of three equivalences which are falsely construed as constituting the "profound" intuition that literature is identical with fiction. The series of equivalences, if unfolded, would run as follows. The world (reality) is organized through human linguistic systems: there is therefore no independently existing reality to which language refers (*non sequitur*). Since there is no real independently existing world to which language can refer, all uses of language are identical with fictional language (*non sequitur*). Literature being a type of discourse or language use is therefore fiction (*false conclusion*). It does not take much reflection to see that the argument as presented is unsound through and through. First of all, language may organize our reality without thereby creating it. Secondly, the distinction between fictional discourse and fact-stating discourse is a distinction between language functions (modes of utterance) and the outcome of the debate between realists, anti-

realists, and pragmatists about whether or not there is an independently existing world would not influence that distinction. There is, therefore, no epistemological ground, based on premises about knowledge of the world, for identifying literary language with fictional language. As we have seen, not only are
the concepts of literature and fiction distinct, but there are no formal qualities
of language which serve to define either.

Perhaps in the more extreme poststructuralists' rhetoric of irrationalism
these objections will simply be shrugged off as based on "logocentric" prejudices. But what would be the consequences for the concept of literature and
the activity of criticism if their position were to be accepted? One would be the
abandonment of a central defining feature of the institution of literature: the
requirement that literature should have something interesting to say about human life. Indeed, the whole concept of "saying something about" would become otiose. This is not a marginal or unimportant decision for those who are
concerned with literature. It is in effect a decision to reject the very concept of
literature that has been in operation in Western culture since the fifth century
B.C. Theories of the structuralist/poststructuralist type aim to replace the concept of a literary work with that of a text, using a value-free notion of "text."
The concept of literature is rejected precisely because it embodies, in its
creative-imaginative aspect as well as in its mimetic aspect, what are taken to
be unsupportable and undesirable humanist values.

The substitution of the concept of fiction for the concepts of novel and
short story, the poststructuralists would argue, is beneficial exactly because it
*does not* discriminate between literary works and other types of invented stories. The emergence of this use of the concept of fiction at the time when a new
mass-culture was in the making, is indicative, these theorists would argue, of
the challenge to the bourgeois concept of literary art and indeed of the dramatically diminished importance of this concept. Structuralism and poststructuralism are thus revolutionary theories, not in the sense that they offer
revolutionary new insights but rather in the sense that they attempt to revolutionize literary practice. What they offer is a strong recommendation that literary research should refocus on different sets of problems along with revised
assumptions about texts (rather than literature) which define these problems.

### In Defense of the Concept of Literature

There are two lines of argument against this "radical revision," if it can be
called a revision, of the concept of literature. The first line is to point out that
it is difficult to conceive that even the staunchest deconstructionist would
want to accept the full consequences of the rejection of those humanist values
embodied in the concept of literature. Some of the die-hard proponents of
structuralism have belatedly woken up to this fact and are now flaunting their
humanist credentials by arguing publicly, as does Tzvetan Todorov, that "it is

impossible (without being inconsistent) to defend human rights out of one side of your mouth while deconstructing the idea of humanity out of the other."[11] The point behind Todorov's observation is that the concept of literature as it is defined by the requirement of the creative use of the imagination and humanly interesting content has a central place in a scheme of values which defines the very idea of humanity. A radical revision of the concept of literature cannot take place without a radical revision of the concept of humanity. In particular, if one gives up all standards of coherence and unity, including such standards as define rational argument and individual identity, one also gives up any possibility of arguing and taking a reasoned stand against repression in all its forms as well as any possibility of defining and defending the rights of the individual. The second line of argument is to point out that the concept of "text" cannot bear the theoretical weight put on it by structuralism and poststructuralism. The concept of "text" is logically secondary to the concept of "work" or related concepts which designate types of text. A text is always a text of something, of a literary work, a philosophical treatise, a historical chronicle, a historical monograph, a medical article, etc. A text cannot be understood just as a text. Indeed, considered as a text, a text does not have any determinate textual (rhetorical) features at all. It gets determinate textual (rhetorical) features only when it is construed as a *work*.

Consider an example. In the first act of Shakespeare's *Julius Caesar* the tribunes Marullus and Flavius reproach the festive crowd they meet in the streets for celebrating Caesar's victory over Pompey's sons. Central in the scene is a speech made by Marullus which turns the mood of the crowd from high-spirited rejoicing to guilty shame. It is a set rhetorical speech with a pattern of hyperboles and repetitions apparently designed to work on the emotions of the crowd. The character of this episode as a textual (rhetorical) feature cannot be determined until one knows what one is reading. If *Julius Caesar* were read as a piece of reportive or fact-stating discourse, then this episode would be included in the text to establish certain propositions as true in the mind of the reader, to instil the belief that this is how two tribunes by the name of Marullus and Flavius behaved on a day in October of 45 B.C. in Rome during Caesar's triumph. (Not to complicate this point further, leave out of account that Shakespeare transfers Caesar's victory and celebration to March 15 the following year.) However, if *Julius Caesar* is read as a literary work, this episode must be construed differently and thus becomes a different rhetorical feature altogether. For then the confrontation of the tribunes with the crowd, focused in the set speech by Marullus, can be seen as foreshadowing the forum scene in which first Brutus and then Antony, through their respective speeches, change the mood of the crowd. It is part of a pattern of repetition which establishes, through three parallel scenes, the fickleness of the crowd and its role as an instrument of power that can be controlled through rhetoric. In a more comprehensive analysis of *Julius Caesar* one could show the point of giving the crowd this prominent role in the play, but it is not necessary to do that here. The textual characteristic of the episode described as an element in a pattern of repetition is dependent on the reader construing the text as a literary work just as the textual characteristic of the episode as a true or false account of actual historical events is dependent upon construing the text as fact-stating discourse.

If there is no such thing as a text in general, but only texts of works, then the theoretical basis for rejecting the concept of literature vanishes and the failure to deal with its *mimetic* aspect (which defines literature as an evaluative concept) must be seen as just that: a theoretical failure. It is possible to supplement this line of argument with the simpler but equally weighty argument that a radical revision of the concept of literature is merely a way of ducking the problem or changing the subject without admitting that this is what one is doing. Such a move does not merely amount to theoretical failure but also constitutes a form of intellectual dishonesty.

There are, then, various types of reason for rejecting the poststructuralist attack on the concept of literature. There is the epistemological reason that the premise on which rests the rhetorical chain supporting the identification of fiction and literature is dubious, even in its best and most qualified philosophical formulation. The degree to which language organizes "our world" is a controversial issue and it is arguable that antirealists and constructivists cannot really be said to have provided any clear account of what it might mean that the human mind, through language or in any other way, "posits" the reality a human being meets. Then there is the logical reason that the argument itself offered in support of the identification of literature and fiction is invalid in each of its steps. Thirdly, there is the evaluative consideration: the values embodied in the concept of literature are so closely connected with broader cultural and human values that it would be inconceivable for even the most committed deconstructionists to reject them. And, finally, there is the conceptual reason: one cannot substitute for the concept of literature a more general concept of text which can be characterized theoretically in an illuminating way.

What literary aesthetics has to deal with is an existing practice of literature within which are embodied the concept of literature and literary values. This practice has been accorded a central place in the culture that traces its roots back to classical Greece. In a broad sense, the values embodied in this practice are humanist values closely linked to the concept of an autonomous human individual possessing interests, goals, and powers of reason. The task for literary aesthetics is to clarify what is involved in the practice and give an explanatory account of the main aspects of those conventions defining literary practice. It is not possible to change the subject and still claim that one is saying something of interest to those who care about literature. That is simply an abdication of critical responsibility.

## FICTION AND LEVELS OF LITERARY DESCRIPTION

The relations between literature and fiction and literature and reality must, then, be a central theme in literary theory since these relationships are fundamental in the definition of how literature presents a humanly interesting content. In the formulation and discussion of these relationships it is useful to make three distinctions, which we will present in the following sections.

### LITERAL AND THEMATIC LEVEL

The first distinction is between two levels in the literary work itself: the literal level, or subject level, or level of reports, and the thematic level, or symbolic level, or level of reflection. The distinction used to be made as a matter of course in discussions of the cognitive status of literature, but has disappeared almost completely in recent literary theory when the problem of the cognitive status of literature was pushed to the sidelines.[12]

Every literary work contains sentences describing particular events, situations, characters, and places:

> The first account that I can Recollect, or could ever learn of myself, was, that I had wandred among a Crew of those People they call *Gypsies*, or *Egyptians*; but I believe it was but a very little while that I had been among them, for I had not had my Skin discolour'd, or blacken'd, as they do very young to all the Children they carry about with them, nor can I tell how I came among them, or how I got from them.
>
>     It was at *Colchester* in *Essex*, that those People left me; and I have a Notion in my Head, that I left them there (that is, that I hid myself and wou'd not go any farther with them) but I am not able to be particular in that Account.                    (Daniel Defoe, *Moll Flanders* [London, 1722], chap. 1)

The debate about fiction and the logic of fictional discourse has on the whole been carried out with reference to this type of utterance since it offers the clearest and most perspicuous illustration of problems of reference and truth. It is on this level that it seems unproblematic to say that at least some literary works are fictions: invented stories and not history, inviting make-believe. In this case the lines are written by Daniel Defoe, but are presented as coming from the pen of a character who never existed, Moll Flanders, and the events described never took place. The events, like the character, are made up. It is clear that the intention is that the reader should make-believe, not literally believe, their content. However, it is not immediately clear at the literal or report level that literary works at that level are *necessarily* to be construed as fictions:

> Five years have passed; five summers, with the length
> Of five long winters! and again I hear

These waters, rolling from their mountain-springs
With a soft inland murmur. Once again
Do I behold these steep and lofty cliffs,
That on a wild secluded scene impress
Thoughts of more deep seclusion; and connect
The landscape with the quiet of the sky.
The day is come when I again repose
Here, under this dark sycamore, and view
These plots of cottage-ground, these orchard-tufts,
Which at this season, with their unripe fruits,
Are clad in one green hue, and lose themselves
'Mid groves and copses.
> (William Wordsworth, "Lines Composed a Few Miles above
> Tintern Abbey, on Revisiting the Banks of the Wye during a Tour.
> July 13, 1798")

It is not at all obvious that these lines and the rest of "Tintern Abbey" are presented as fiction:

> "No poem of mine," [Wordsworth] said, afterwards, "was composed under circumstances more pleasant for me to remember than this. I began it upon leaving Tintern, after crossing the Wye, and concluded it just as I was entering Bristol in the evening, after a ramble of four or five days, with my sister. Not a line of it was altered and not any part of it written down till I reached Bristol." When he did reach Bristol it was written down at once and taken to Cottle, to be included in *Lyrical Ballads*, at the end of the volume. Not a line of it ever was altered, and the *Tintern Abbey* that we know today is identical with that composed on the Wye banks—an unusual occurrence in Wordsworth's poetry.[13]

"Tintern Abbey" was an outpouring by Wordsworth of descriptions and reflections at a specific time and with reference to specific visits to a specific place. The time and place of the visits are given in the title and in the poem itself. If these lines are nevertheless to be considered as presented in the fictive mode, we must assume that that intention, for some reason, can be seen as overriding the intention to describe his personal experience on revisiting the banks of the Wye during a tour, July 13, 1798. What is theoretically interesting about "Tintern Abbey" is that it does not present any propositions with which the reader has to agree or disagree. What makes the poem valuable is the presentation of nature and the speaker's reflections on the development of his own view of nature and its restorative power. It does not matter to the literary appreciation of the poem whether it is presented fictively or not. What is important is the theme that grows out of the presentation of subject in the poem.

There is a hint here of a possible interpretation of the mimetic aspect of literature which does not conflict with seeing literature as a creative-imaginative effort, but we shall have to leave that aside for the moment.

The problem whether the invitation to take up a literary stance necessarily
involves an invitation to take up a fictive stance rears its head on the literal
level of literary works in other ways as well. Many literary works not only contain descriptions of historical persons and events but might be based wholly
on historical situations. This has led some philosophers (as we saw in chapter
3 of our book) to conclude that literary works are a mixture of the fictional
and the nonfictional. "In *War and Peace*," says John Searle, "the story of Pierre
and Natasha is a fictional story about fictional characters, but the Russia of
*War and Peace* is the real Russia, and the war against Napoleon is the real war
against the real Napoleon."[14] In discussing such cases, from the point of view
of fiction, we proposed that it is helpful to draw on the distinction between
content and mode of presentation. Though some propositional content might
be factual in nature, it might nonetheless serve a fictive purpose, for example
in helping to characterize fictive states of affairs. We suggested at the time that
from the literary point of view there was a standing presumption that such
passages should be treated in this way. Both conventionally, in terms of the literary institution, as well as psychologically, Searle's position that works oscil-
late between fiction and nonfiction is unsatisfactory, since it means that the
reader of a literary work has to be seen as involved in a constant change of perspective, implying a constant change in the premises of the literary appreciation of the work. Note, however, that while it is natural to extend the fictive
mode in this way in the *War and Peace* case, where there is at least some undis-
puted fictional content, it is not obvious that a parallel move is desirable in the
"Tintern Abbey" case, which perhaps has no fictional content. A more extreme
proposal, which will be discussed later,[15] takes a quite different line: instead of
extending the fictive mode in some cases, it in effect denies it in all. On this
view literary works consist of statements, some of which are true and some
false, with the majority being true because they must be construed as saying
something about types of things (events, persons) in the world.

Though the problems of the relationship between literature and fiction
have no obvious solutions even when we deal with the literal or report level of
literary works, the problem itself is at least clearly defined in relation to the description of particular characters, situations, events, actions, plots, etc., which
constitute this level of a literary work. The problem becomes much less easy to
define once one leaves the literal level and moves on to the thematic or symbolic level. We have argued that it is a defining convention of literary practice
that the author should produce and the reader search for a humanly interesting content. It is arguable that this content can be formulated in a series of "reflections" or "thematic statements," generalizations over the characters, situations, events, actions, plots, etc., which are presented at the literal level of the

work. These reflections state the theme of the work. "Shakespeare's *Julius Cae-sar* presents the futility of opposing the forces of history through individual human action," would be such a thematic statement. But the reader does not always have to interpret the work himself. Sometimes the author generalizes the significance of the situations he presents:

> To each his sufferings; all are men,
> Condemned alike to groan:
> The tender for another's pain,
> The unfeeling for his own.
> Yet, ah! why should they know their fate?
> Since sorrow never comes too late,
> And happiness too swiftly flies.
> Thought would destroy their paradise.
> No more: where ignorance is bliss,
> 'Tis folly to be wise.

This is the final stanza of Thomas Gray's "Ode on a Distant Prospect of Eton College" where he draws the conclusion from the presentation of the happy boys he sees/remembers there and the host of cares and sufferings which he presents as waiting for them when they grow up.

## THEME AND SUBJECT

The example suggests that it is useful to introduce a second distinction, be-tween *theme* and *subject*. Subject is what the particular descriptions at the lit-eral or report level are *of*: the "chunks of experience" that the work presents to the reader, the concrete individual fates of the characters, the environment in which they move, the things they say, think, feel, etc. The subject of "Ode on a Distant Prospect of Eton College" is the happy boys whom the speaker imag-ines at play and work as he sees the school at a distance, as well as the memory which the speaker has of his youth there (the two are inseparable in the poem). This may seem a slightly artificial notion of subject, for subject, in critical dis-cussion, is often not separated from theme. And subject and theme do overlap, since once one starts talking about the subject of a work at a certain level of generality, thematic concepts have to be employed. However, the distinction between subject and theme can naturally be construed as a distinction be-tween the facts, experiences, etc., described in a work and the interpretation of these phenomena through abstraction and generalization. And it is this con-trast that is theoretically interesting in the present discussion.

Now it makes little sense to say that such content, which can be stated as a theme, is fictional. Nor does it make good sense to construe it as being amenable to evaluation as true or false. A theme is not a type of discourse, fictional or fact-stating, but rather a conception (of its subject) which discourse expresses. And different types of discourse define and express theme in different ways. Literature has its own highly characteristic way of doing so. There is, however, one way in which the question of the cognitive status may raise its head at the thematic level. It is a symptom of the poverty of the debate about fiction in recent literary theory that the problem was formulated over thirty years ago, once again by Beardsley, and needs to be rediscovered. Beardsley distinguishes between *theme* and *thesis*:

> A theme, then, is something that can be thought about, or dwelt upon, but it is not something that can be called true or false. What I shall mean by the perhaps awkward term "thesis," however, is precisely something about, or in, the work that *can* be called true or false, if anything can. Critics say, for example, that Shakespeare's *Tempest* embodies a mystical view of life; that Upton Sinclair's *The Jungle* is a protest against the injustices suffered by the poor under a free-wheeling economic system; that there is implicit Platonism in Spenser's "Epithalamion" and Shelley's "Epipsychidion." We speak of the philosophical, religious, ethical, and social ideas in Milton, Shaw, and Sartre. We debate whether Thomas Mann's *Doctor Faustus* is optimistic or pessimistic, how much there is of Schopenhauer and Bergson in Proust. And I take these ideological ingredients to be statable in a form in which we could say, though perhaps only with some hesitation, that they are true or false: even pessimism may be a view of life, not merely a feeling.[16]

While accepting something akin to the distinction between theme and thesis and agreeing that there is a theoretical problem to be formulated by the help of this distinction, one need not accept Beardsley's rather narrow conception of theme. The question which arises in any case is whether it is a convention of literary practice that the reader should expect a literary work to express a thesis, in Beardsley's sense of a bearer of truth, over and above a theme. Again this is a question which will be addressed later.[17]

### SAYING AND SHOWING

The third distinction which is useful in the discussion of the relationship between literature and fiction and between literature and reality is that between saying and showing or stating and presenting. It is sometimes held that even if literary works are fictional at the literal level, nevertheless the particular situations, events, objects, actions, plots, etc., which a work presents, provide the reader with insight into real life, and provide examples of possible modes of experience which the reader can engage. These insights or modes of experience, so the account goes, are not in the form of stable themes or propositions about human life, for literature does not deal in propositional knowledge. An interpretation can indicate what the mode of experience or insight is, but it cannot be a substitute for it. In *Julius Caesar* the tragedy of Brutus is that he is crushed by history. He is presented by Shakespeare as a fine man, a loyal friend, a dedicated and considerate husband, a kind master, and a good general. Nevertheless, in the role he is called on to play in the great drama of the transition from the Roman Republic to the Roman Empire, all his excellent human qualities come to nought. His role in this drama is defined by Shakespeare's play, but once the role is adopted, Brutus becomes its prisoner and his admirable human qualities cannot redeem him, nor do they count for anything. Through his presentation of Brutus Shakespeare offers the insight or the experience of what it is to be crushed by history. No interpretation of the play can offer this insight or experience. Only a thoughtful reading of the play can do that. This is what makes literature humanly and culturally important, what makes it a repository of human values.

## Conclusion

Let us summarize our principal conclusions. First of all, the relation between fiction and literature is complex and failure to recognize that complexity has laid down some false trails in literary theory. There is neither a definitional relation nor an identity between the two concepts. Literature is not defined as a mode of fiction—not all literary works are fiction, nor fictional works literary—and the concepts themselves are distinct because the concept of literature embodies values in a way that the concept of fiction does not. The practices that give life to the concepts are different. Theoretical attempts to replace the concept of literature with some supposedly value-free notion of "text" simply fail to mark discriminations among texts which are the starting point for any meaningful discussion of modes of cognition. To grasp what is interesting and distinctive about those texts designated "literature" it is more instructive to start with practices of reading—exploring what it is to adopt a "literary point of view" on a text—than to give exclusive attention to textual or rhetorical properties. Even where works of literature have a fictive element, as with novels and short stories, it is wrong to infer immediate consequences for the cognitive nature of those works. Questions of whether or how such works relate to, or make claims *about*, the real world remain open even in the face of an overtly fictional subject matter. The challenge for the theorist of literature is to explain how literary works can attain seriousness and interest not just in spite of but through their fictional content. Some preliminaries to that challenge have been outlined above, notably the thought that different levels of literary narrative should be distinguished. At a literal or subject level—the level of character and incident, or narrative content—fictionality is at its most overt. A full analysis of fictional discourse will seek to make sense of this special linguistic phenomenon, explaining how, to use a Kantian idiom, fiction is *possible.*

But this is not yet an analysis of literature. Only at the thematic level do specifically literary concerns emerge and here a crucial question is how the subject and thematic levels interact. There is no implication that fictionality at subject level determines fictionality at the thematic level. Those who want to explain the cognitive or even "mimetic" potential of literary fiction must address the status of a work's themes. Our own view is that an adequate account of the thematic level, satisfying most of the traditional demands of "mimesis," can be developed without appeal to the concepts of "truth" or "knowledge," at least as these terms are recognized in philosophy and science. But this ultimate rejection of the discourse of truth to characterize literary value has nothing whatever to do with the simpleminded identification of literature with fiction.

## NOTES

1. Henry James, "The Art of Fiction," in *"The Art of Fiction" and Other Essays* (New York: Oxford University Press, 1948), 5–6.

2. Virginia Woolf, "Modern Fiction," in her *Collected Essays* (London: The Hogarth Press, 1966), 2:106.

3. Monroe C. Beardsley, *Aesthetics: Problems in the Philosophy of Criticism* (New York: Harcourt, Brace & World, 1958), 126.

4. The use of the term "fiction" to denote poetry has appeared in certain poststructuralist critics. See, e.g., the first chapter, "Understanding Criticism," of Geoffrey Hartman, *Criticism in the Wilderness: The Study of Literature Today* (New Haven, Conn.: Yale University Press, 1980), where Hartman uses "fiction" consistently to refer to poems and other genres alike. However, the use seems forced and confusing: one is never quite sure what point Hartman is trying to make about *poetry.*

5. Arnold Isenberg, "The Problem of Belief," *Journal of Aesthetics and Art Criticism* 13, no. 3 (March 1955): 395–407; reprinted in Cyril Barrett, ed., *Collected Papers on Aesthetics* (Oxford: Blackwell, 1965), 125.

6. Though this is an assumption made by almost *all* theories of literature produced in this century, it is an assumption which is as problematic as the assumption that the paradigmatic kinds of literature are the novel and the short story. For it is not obvious why the semantic concept of meaning should be suitable as an explanatory concept in literary theory. See Stein Haugom Olsen, "Text and Meaning" and "The 'Meaning' of a Literary Work," in *The End of Literary Theory* (Cambridge: Cambridge University Press, 1987).

7. Paul de Man, "Criticism and Crisis," in *Blindness and Insight: Essays in the Rhetoric of Contemporary Criticism,* 2nd ed. (London: Methuen, 1983), 17.

8. Gerald Graff in the first three chapters of his book *Literature Against Itself* (Chicago: University of Chicago Press, 1979) diagnoses this malady in these areas of modem literary theory in an excellent way.

9. See Peter Lamarque and Stein Haugom Olsen, *Truth, Fiction, and Literature: A Philosophical Perspective* (Oxford: Clarendon Press, 1994), chapters 7 and 8.

10. Terry Eagleton, *Literary Theory: An Introduction* (Oxford: Blackwell, 1983), 107–8; emphasis in original.

11. Tzvetan Todorov, "All Against Humanity," review of *Textual Power: Literary Theory and the Teaching of English*, by Robert Scholes, *Times Literary Supplement*, 4 October 1985, 1094. [Editors' note: A different translation of this essay is included as chapter 3 of this volume.]

12. For versions of this distinction see standard traditional treatments of the problem such as Beardsley's chapter 9 of *Aesthetics*, or Morris Weitz, "Truth in Literature," *Revue Internationale de Philosophie* 9 (1955): 116–29. The distinction was put to use again in Stein Haugom Olsen, *The Structure of Literary Understanding* (Cambridge: Cambridge University Press, 1978), chapter 3, and Gerald Graff has remarked on the fateful consequences of ignoring it in *Literature Against Itself*, chapter 6.

13. Mary Moorman, *William Wordsworth: A Biography. The Early Years, 1770–1803*, 2 vols. (Oxford: Clarendon Press, 1957), 1:401–2.

14. John R. Searle, "The Logical Status of Fictional Discourse," in *Expression and Meaning: Studies in the Theory of Speech Acts* (Cambridge: Cambridge University Press, 1979), 72.

15. See Lamarque and Olsen, *Truth, Fiction, and Literature*, chapter 12.

16. Beardsley, *Aesthetics*, 404.

17. See Lamarque and Olsen, *Truth, Fiction, and Literature*, chapter 16.

---

## 45.  LITERARY AESTHETICS AND THE AIMS OF CRITICISM

### PAISLEY LIVINGSTON

ALTHOUGH CONTEMPORARY LITERARY SCHOLARS sometimes debate the place of "the aesthetic" in their field, surprisingly little attention has been paid in these discussions to the prior question of what that deeply ambiguous epithet should be taken as referring to, and remarkably enough, seldom is any reference made to the extensive literature in philosophical aesthetics on the topic.[1] In this essay I offer some clarification of "aesthetics" and "the aesthetic" in the context of a more general discussion of the relevance of these notions to literary criticism and research. In §1 I briefly survey some of the several senses of "aesthetic" in an attempt to identify some of the issues and options. In §2 I identify some conceptions of the relation between aesthetics and criticism, which leads to a discussion in §3 of some of the conflicting desiderata of contemporary literary criticism and research. The latter claims set the stage for a proposal in §4 regarding the scope and value of literary aesthetics.

---

Paisley Livingston. "Literary Aesthetics and the Aims of Criticism." Copyright © Paisley Livingston, 2002. Previously unpublished and used by permission of the author.

## 1. On the Several Senses of "Aesthetic"

To what does the expression "aesthetic" (and related terms in other languages) refer? In its attributive use, the adjective is applied to a wide variety of items, such as properties, qualities, values, objects, attitudes, and experiences, and it is far from apparent that a single aesthetic/nonaesthetic contrast holds with regard to all these cases—an issue which is skirted when literary theorists make predicative use of the adjective and write elliptically of "the aesthetic."[2] Philosophers have had various proposals to make concerning the correct way to delineate such a contrast. Two main options—of which there are many significantly different variants in the literature—may be identified. According to one conception, both natural and artificial phenomena have aesthetic qualities which can be the object of an aesthetic experience—a necessary condition on the latter being that the experience be an experience of precisely such qualities. How such properties and experiences are to be contrasted to nonaesthetic ones remains controversial. There is, for example, no consensus around the idea that aesthetic experience is the purely disinterested contemplation of sensory appearances—as the word "*aisthesis*" might suggest. It is sometimes contended that a special stance or attitude is necessary or even sufficient to aesthetic experience, yet the foibles of such theories have generated further controversy.[3]

The second basic option is the idea that "aesthetic" is a good label for all of those qualities by virtue of which something is a work of art—a move which logically subordinates the concept of the aesthetic to a prior conception of art.[4] A salient objection to this proposal is that differences between a work of art's artistic and aesthetic properties are thereby obscured. Carolyn Korsmeyer, for example, writes of a dilemma in this regard:

> either "aesthetic" means something fairly precise but does not accommodate the range of artistic value we feel is appropriate; or "aesthetic" is defined in terms of art, is expanded to include all sorts of artistic qualities, and loses whatever precision its contrast with other types of perception and other qualities of objects affords it.[5]

Korsmeyer proposes that a way out of the dilemma is to distinguish between artistic and aesthetic qualities, where the former embraces a broad range of values and properties of works of art, and the latter is restricted to a narrower range of qualities. A work of art's artistic properties, broadly construed, are those directly relevant to its appreciation *qua* work of art, i.e., those qualities that are either its aesthetic ones, or its artistic ones, narrowly construed. This latter, "narrow" conception of the artistic could be understood as artistry (centered, for example, in the case of the art of literature, on verbal wit, eloquence, style, technical skill and inventiveness, qualities relative to art-making traditions, etc.), while the broad conception of the artistic would embrace an even wider range of qualities possessed by works of art, including their aesthetic features, such as gracefulness and elegance.

It should be noted, however, that there is also a well-entrenched usage according to which the word "aesthetic" serves equally well to label the overarching category Korsmeyer evokes, so that both the work's narrowly artistic and narrowly aesthetic qualities are aesthetic ones, broadly construed. For example, Berys Gaut writes:

> In the narrow sense of the term, aesthetic value properties are those that ground a certain kind of sensory or contemplative pleasure or displeasure. In this sense, beauty, elegance, gracefulness, and their contraries are aesthetic value properties. However, the sense adopted here is broader: I mean by "aesthetic value" the value of an object *qua* work of art, that is, its artistic value. This broader sense is required, since not all of the values of an object *qua* work of art are narrowly aesthetic.[6]

To recapitulate: even at this most schematic and preliminary level, three distinct concepts, associated with only two terms, can be singled out:

1. Artistry, or specifically artistic qualities and values.
2. Aesthetic qualities and values in some narrow sense (requiring specification).
3. The full range of the specifically artistic and nonspecifically artistic qualities and values a work of art has *qua* work of art—to be called either "the aesthetic" or "the artistic" in some broad sense.

Of these (1) is perhaps the least problematic, but hardly so, given the notorious problem of elucidating the art/nonart distinction; (2) continues to be the object of much controversy, and though it is often suggested that (3) is a useful notion, we would do well to recall that whichever label for it we adopt, the idea in question embraces at least two other highly problematic notions.

A tempting thought in such a context is that reference to the realities of critical discourse and practice can provide the needed remedy to the inconclusive array of conceptual analyses, stipulations and arbitrary theoretical constructions. I consider this option in the next section.

## 2. THE TANGLED HIERARCHIES OF AESTHETICS AND CRITICISM

According to one conception, the primary task of philosophical aesthetics is the elucidation of the principles underwriting the discourses and practices of art criticism. This idea has at times been developed in terms of a tidy scheme of logical types. At the base of the logical hierarchy are the fine arts themselves, including, then, artists and their works. One level up we find criticism—the various descriptive, evaluative, and interpretative discourses that focus on the artistic and aesthetic properties of the items located at the first level. The second-order discourse of criticism in turn provides the object of a third-order discourse, that of the philosophical aesthetician.

Such a scheme has its attractions. It promises to relieve the philosophical aesthetician of the burden of providing accurate generalizations about the huge and complex domain of the fine arts. Instead, the philosopher finds a basis in the results achieved by the critical experts who have shouldered that burden. Yet there is still something for the philosopher to do, something which calls upon the specifically philosophical skills of conceptual analysis. Critical practice, with its emphasis on particular cases and the articulation of pretheoretical intuitions about them, does not explicitly develop general positions on a range of important issues—including issues to do with the nature and tasks of criticism. Yet as these more general issues are held to be latent within the critic's activities and pronouncements, the philosopher's explicit theory about art and its appreciation can be presented as an elucidation and extension of critical practice. Monroe C. Beardsley, for example, assumed that the essential business of the critic was "practical criticism" or the articulation of expert appreciations of particular works of art; the philosopher's task was that of elucidating and justifying this very critical practice, elaborating, on that basis, responses to theoretical questions about the identify, meaning, and values of art. Although the philosopher was not entirely uncritical in his discussion of critical practice (fallacies could be identified, and correct principles elucidated), his task was understood as being primarily a descriptive one.

A similar approach finds expression in more recent work in philosophical aesthetics as well. In *An Ontology of Art* Gregory Currie tells us that in approaching certain fundamental problems connected to the ontology of works of art, he intends to follow the example provided by Gottlob Frege's approach to the analysis of natural numbers.[7] This means, Currie continues, that he will evaluate proposed analyses in terms of their ability to deliver the judgments that we pretheoretically make. An overall aesthetic theory, Currie adds, will include such things as an analysis of the ways in which works of art are to be judged and appreciated, an account of what works of art are, and an analysis of appreciation. Some of these components of an overall aesthetic theory have a kind of priority in relation to others in that they weigh certain constraints on how we should think about them, at least in part because of the pretheoretical judgments we are inclined to make with regard to them. Currie tells us, for example, that the analysis of what works of art are is constrained by (a) an analysis of ways in which works are to be judged and appreciated, and (b) an analysis of the relations that hold between works and critics. Another item on the list is an account of which features of works of art are relevant to appreciation, which is said in turn to have important implications for a more general theory of appreciation. In accordance with his Frege-inspired approach, Currie claims that we have certain reliable intuitions about the target of appreciation (conceived, no doubt, as a combination of interpretation and evaluation), and these intuitions constitute the "bed" upon which a general theory of art, including an account of the ontology of individual works, must rest.

Such an understanding of philosophy's relation to the arts is appealing when it is contrasted to the many cases in the history of philosophy where philosophers have boldly generalized about the meaning and value of art without exhibiting any genuine knowledge of, or appreciation for, the diversity of the works and traditions. Even so, this conception is inadequate, because the philosophical aesthetician must reflect not only about criticism but about the arts themselves, but, more importantly, because the discourses and practices of criticism simply do not provide anything like a coherent and reliable ground of judgments and practices upon which a philosophical theory might be rested. Criticism is as a matter of fact too conflicted an affair for the descriptive model of aesthetics to be appropriate. It is also far too theoretically oriented and self-reflexive, as much of what might be called practical criticism today is already explicitly informed by some theoretical paradigm or model. Following that conception, aesthetic theory—or more accurately, that aspect of it which theorizes about criticism—does not simply reflect critical practice; on the contrary, it guides, directs, or dictates it. And well-known trends in critical practice have challenged the traditional idea that the central objects of criticism are works of art; instead, literary critics and scholars boldly investigate any and every aspect of "culture," it sometimes being assumed that neither literature nor the arts more generally should have any privileged status in their critical work.

In sum, my contention here is that it is implausible to hold that philosophical aesthetics can take as its goal the elucidation of an order constituted by critical practice taken as a systematic whole. An alternative to that conception of aesthetic theory is sketched in my final section, but first I shall provide a slightly more detailed diagnosis of the "conflicted" nature of literary critical discourse.

## 3. CRITICAL CONFLICTS

In evoking the specter of critical conflicts, my point is not the trivial observation that critics often disagree about the meanings and values of a given literary work, nor that they use strikingly divergent approaches and background assumptions in their interpretations and evaluations, for both of these observations are compatible with the idea of an underlying order or unity to current literary critical practice, and, indeed, it is important to identify what a wide range of critical practices do effectively have in common. My contention, instead, is that viewed globally, the current institution of literary criticism targets conflicting goals, and that certain problems and shortcomings emerge in critics' attempts to find strategies for dealing coherently with this situation.

Literary works are complex phenomena, and many different attitudes may usefully be adopted with regard to them. Yet it would be misleading to say that the critic freely chooses from an open-ended array of critical goals. Academic criticism, in particular, is not a purely individual matter since it is conducted within institutional contexts where certain goals and norms are brought to bear. For example, the development of innovative descriptive and explanatory claims based on intersubjectively controllable evidence is a goal inherited from a much older and more general scientific and scholarly tradition—a tradition in which the right to work as a scholar or researcher is only earned and kept if one makes something called "original contributions to knowledge." We can, then, identify goals common to academic critical practice, namely, that of making claims that are (a) epistemically justifiable, e.g., based on good and sufficient evidence or reasons (and ideally, true or correct), and (b) sufficiently new or innovative in the context in which they are made. The latter goal is anything but simple, as significantly different norms of innovation, applied in context-sensitive ways, need to be distinguished. For example, one, especially valued form of innovation is that of providing a different methodological model or example which enables colleagues to do work which will in turn count as innovative. It is one thing to come up with new things to say about the style and themes of a particular literary work, but something else to develop a way of writing about literature which can be applied in readings of many other works as well.

At least as a matter of institutional principle, all sorts of academic writing about literature share the epistemic goals of evidentiary adequacy and newness, and so are subject to corresponding norms and evaluations. Yet here a first critical conflict surfaces, as the two goals can in practice be hard to realize jointly: new claims may be unsound, and sound ones too familiar, given the limitations of extant evidence and the existence of a range of plausible accounts based on it. Just think how very difficult it is at this point to come up with a significantly new interpretation of *Hamlet* which respects the historical and textual evidence. If epistemically responsible and significantly innovative claims are to be made, something has to give: either the object of inquiry must be shifted, or the epistemic desiderata must be vitiated. Some of the most salient trends of literary criticism over the past few decades can be plotted as explorations of these two options.

One move which is sometimes made in this context is to introduce a distinction between criticism and literary scholarship (or literary research or science, as in "*Literaturwissenschaft*"), the idea being that the evidentiary and argumentative norms evoked above pertain only to the latter.[8] Yet if criticism is said to be unlike science or other forms of enquiry in that it need not track truths or make assertions supported by evidence and reasons, what positive account can be given of its central aims? One response is to say that the utterances of criticism are not assertions, but exhortations and invitations, it being added that no logical principles govern the disparate field of interpretative fancies. A problem with such proposals is that they do not match prominent features of critical practice—including those dimensions of criticism which might be singled out as specifically interpretative and evaluative. For example, the critics who utter statements about the artistic value and ethical significance of a poem by Charles Baudelaire do not generally allow that the contrary claims are equally acceptable: either the targeted aspects of the Baudelaire poem are "pornographic" or they are not; the poem either does or does not express the poet's renunciation of his own earlier, revolutionary ideals, and so on.[9] Critical debate is a matter of genuinely rival contentions, which are not, on the whole, effectively prefaced by some relativistic operator to the effect that both the claim and its contrary are equally correct.

If the critic's problem cannot be resolved by denying the very applicability of epistemic norms, another strategy is to reinterpret those norms in such a manner that the conflict is alleviated. If the evidentiary constraints are loosened sufficiently, innovative work becomes easier to produce. An example is the proposal that the "truth" or "justification" of critical claims is not a matter of arguments and evidence, but of social cohesion: the crux of justification and truth is conformity to the dictates of some "interpretive community." Such proposals raise a host of increasingly well-known problems, beginning with the question of how the judgments of "the" interpretive community are to be known, and why they should carry any epistemic authority. One can also ask how much work genuinely sociological notions of community do in this kind of theory.

Another, more successful option is to make room for innovation by shifting critical attention to the *significance* literary texts acquire in diverse contexts of reception (where "significance" is contrasted to "meaning" in E. D. Hirsch's sense).[10] If we respect the limited evidence on which historical claims can be based, it is inordinately difficult to say something significantly new about the meanings Shakespeare's works may have had for the bard himself or for his original audiences; yet the question of how Shakespearean texts have been staged and understood in diverse cultures and contexts over the past century remains an open and fertile field of sociocultural research, as the innovative and sociologically astute work of Michael D. Bristol clearly shows.[11] And by freeing themselves from the prior focus on the heavily investigated, central figures of the literary canon, critics further enhance the options for innovation.

Yet here we encounter a second major conflict which has been experienced and remarked upon by any number of critics involved in the shift towards "cultural studies": once the research agenda constituted by the historical appreciation of the canonical literary works has been abandoned, literary criticism effectively dissolves into sociology and cultural history, fields of research characterized by their own methods, research traditions, and topics. The critics' work may be both sound and innovative, yet it is no longer a matter of literary criticism. Or it may retain a literary quality, yet not constitute a sound contribution to social science. It is one thing to write informatively, for example, about the art of cinema, and something else entirely to publish well-researched findings about the politics and economics of the world entertainment industry in the last half of the twentieth century, as neither the background knowledge nor the methods appropriate to the one task suit the other. Literary scholars can, then, either retool and find ways of integrating their efforts into the relevant sociohistorical fields, or, if they choose instead to remain faithful to the background and skills specific to a literary training, they must find some other tack.

One such option is to leave the tedious empirical and theoretical work to the sociologists, economists, and political scientists and to specialize in verdicts, exhortations, and predictions, *Zeitgeist* critique and futurology being high on the agenda of some cultural studies theorists. Another option is to occupy the niche of "theory," where the latter refers to certain forms of generalizations which empirically minded historians and sociologists are not in the habit of risking. Yet here as well there is little or nothing in a literary education which is specifically suited to the task, unless, that is, the goal is given an additional specification, namely, that of elucidating and elaborating upon the theoretical significance of literary works: cultural studies becomes, then, cultural "poetics," in the sense that literary works remain at the center of the critic's attention for reasons that are not always apparent.[12]

In such a context, the goal of producing theoretically significant "content analysis" of literary works emerges as a salient strategy for literary-critical innovation. Roughly put, this is a matter of writing critical commentary of literary works which articulate theoretical propositions about one or more general conceptual or social issues, such as gender and power relations, the nature of language, meaning, value, desire, Western metaphysics, the subject, etc., where such propositions can be found in any of the many theoretical "isms" which have furnished twentieth-century intellectual history. Critical strategies oriented around this very general goal are facilitated by a number of contingent factors. One of these is that this strategy is recognized as having the virtue of the sort of "methodological" innovation evoked above: many new contributions are made possible by the more general model of applying new theoretical idioms to works in the canon. A second enabling factor has to do with the operation's apparent epistemic success: applying some set of theoretical doctrines in the elucidation of a literary work, the critic can appear to satisfy all the relevant evidentiary norms, enjoying an apparent moment of confirmation or "validity" when selective aspects of the text "resonate" with the background generalities brought to bear on the work.

Yet this very feature of the strategy brings it into potential conflict with the basic epistemic goal of making genuine contributions to knowledge. How, in performing a Lacanian reading of *Hamlet*, or a deconstruction of a poem by Baudelaire, have I made a contribution to knowledge? Is it a contribution to the knowledge *of literature*, or something else entirely? The authors of critical studies written in this vein tend, on the whole, not to be content with the contention that the apparently successful application of theory $T$ to text $t$ contributes to our knowledge of literary texts by establishing the applicability of $T$ to $t$; nor even is it usually enough to make the claim that the entities or properties identified by the theory have new, previously unknown instances "in" the target text. Such discoveries would, after all, be rather predictable and uninformative: if, for example, semantic indeterminacy of a certain sort (e.g., the variety yielded by "structures of supplementarity") is one of the "always already" or transcendental conditions of language, it comes as no surprise to learn that more of the same can be spotted in "the text of Baudelaire" or anywhere else. If, then, the critic's contribution is to be somewhat more momentous, i.e., genuinely innovative and sound, then he or she must uncover, in the theoretical elucidation of a work's contents, something of greater theoretical significance and value, i.e., truths of some moral or epistemic significance. Whence the Very Big Claims characteristic of theory-driven literary readings: it is not enough merely to indicate that Baudelaire's texts can be deconstructed along with everything else; instead, the texts are shown already to be engaged in a valuable deconstructive exploration of some important notion, such as "position," "freedom," "identity," "history," or "gender," and even though this exploration may be partial, incomplete, or "always already" doomed to failure, the critic's gloss on this aspect of the text's meanings, nonmeanings, or quasi-transcendental conditions can still be presented as a valuable contribution to our understanding of something important outside the target text.[13]

Those who have accepted the framework assumptions of the theory in question may accept the claims that are made for an interpretative amplification of that theory, especially when the sounding board is the work of a prestigious or canonical author. Yet for those who do not think that the deconstructionists' various contentions about language, meaning, metaphysics, ethics, etc., have even a prayer of being right (and, at this point, even the least bit innovative or interesting), another literary echoing of such messages hardly seems promising, and by strict standards ought not to count as a contribution to knowledge, literary or other. At some point no later than 1980, the Derrida-Foucault-Lacan et al. readings of literary works ought to have been generally recognized as being both unsound and profoundly unoriginal. Yet here is where the editorial and tenure committees introduce another twist of the institutional dialectic. Such theoretical readings of literary works are not always evaluated in terms of the norms of research characteristic of other fields, such as philosophy, historical enquiry, political science, etc., because it is thought that they are in fact contributions to an essentially "aesthetic" enterprise. Criticism isn't just about the arts, it is itself a kind of art. And as such, strong epistemic clauses are inapplicable. And so, oddly enough, we come full circle to the question of "the aesthetic." What in some cases is taken as justifying the literary critic's discourses, including his or her strident denunciations of "the aesthetic ideology" and the "autonomy of literary art," is their status as part of an aesthetic project having values and norms thought to be distinct from those of both scientific and humanistic enquiry.

Is that assumption correct? Are such critical readings in fact instances of literary appreciation? Or are they more properly understood as theoretical interventions, the primary aims of which are genuinely epistemic or political? Are some of the literary readings in this vein hybrids which "fall between stools" by failing to realize either aesthetic or epistemic aims? If such questions are to be raised, what is needed is a better sense of the nature of artistic appreciation and aesthetic experience, for only then can we meaningfully ask whether certain forms of critical practice genuinely correspond to them.

## 4. AESTHETICS AND CRITICAL ENQUIRY

Imagine, for the sake of the argument, that the nature of artistic appreciation or aesthetic experience was the object of a widespread and well-founded consensus; imagine, then, that we could know, in some particular case, whether a critic's encounter with a literary work was a genuine instance of aesthetic appreciation. The critic in question writes a description of this experience and of the qualities of the work that were central to it. In so doing, the critic makes an assertion about the work's artistic or aesthetic capacity to occasion a certain kind of experience. The critic's assertions could be wildly idiosyncratic or misleading with regard to the work's features, so there is a genuine possibility of epistemic failure. And in studying a work in its capacity to occasion an aesthetic experience, the critic would be focusing on the work of literature *qua* work of art, and would ideally satisfy aesthetic and epistemic desiderata at once. In short, the critic would potentially contribute to our knowledge of the art of literature—where "literature" is understood along broad, belletristic lines.[14]

How might the requisite notions of aesthetic experience, aesthetic value, and aesthetic quality be delineated? Only a sketch of a response can be provided here. My basic contention along these lines is to say that aesthetic experience, which embraces thought and imagination as well as perception and sensation, must be a direct, active contemplative attention to the qualities of some item, where this contemplation is an intrinsically valued experience.[15] An important background assumption here, which is often overlooked in discussions of aesthetic disinterestedness, is that it is not only possible but quite common to value something both intrinsically and instrumentally at the same time.[16] Aesthetic appreciation may, then, be accompanied by the pursuit of various practical or instrumental goals, so it is not a question of defending the ideal of a *purely* detached or disinterested attitude. The word "item" here is meant to serve as a highly neutral way of referring to the many different sorts of things that can be the object of aesthetic experience. We do not, in any case, want to say that we have aesthetic experiences only of works of fine art, nor of the arts more generally, or of some restricted category of properties or qualities. It will not do, for example, to stipulate that aesthetic experience is entirely a sensuous or perceptual affair, though it is clear that perceptual qualities are an important part of the basis of aesthetic qualities in general. One way to put this claim would be to say that aesthetic properties, such as gracefulness and awkwardness, emerge from lower-level perceptual qualities, such as line, physical texture, sounds, and color, and we experience the former only if we attend to the latter. Such a claim harmonizes with the truism that someone who has not actually seen a picture can hardly have had an aesthetic experience of it, but that point does not entail stronger theses as to the necessity or sufficiency of perceptual uptake in any literal sense.[17] It is the reader's eye that tracks down the wanted information in the newspaper in the case of nonaesthetic reading, while in the case of the aesthetic experience of poetry, an interpretation of propositional content, and not just seeing the letters or hearing the phonemes, is what is required. A literary work's aesthetic qualities supervene in part on the perceptual features of its language, but it is uncontroversial to observe that the "base" from which aesthetic qualities emerge is much broader than the phenomenal qualities of the text alone.[18]

An aesthetic experience of literature, I suggest, is an intrinsically valued experience occasioned by the contemplation of the qualities of a literary work of art. Such contemplation is what is lacking in nonaesthetic modes of reading. In the latter, the work or its text is read in a purely and exclusively instrumental spirit, or the intrinsic value attached to the experience does not find its basis in an attentive and apt attention to the features of the work.[19]

Given such an account of aesthetic experience and the corresponding notion of literary appreciation, two of the most central and controversial issues that arise are: (1) the relation between moral factors and aesthetic/artistic ones; and (2) the relation between cognitive and other qualities of literature. These are book-length topics, but a few remarks may be made here as an indication of the basic framework I have in mind.

On the former issue, I want to say that the moral content of a literary work should be acknowledged as being directly relevant to an appreciation of that work *qua* literary work, my principal reason being that in some contexts moral features directly influence the work's aesthetic function and value. Attempts to define the specificity of the artistic and aesthetic responses to works of fiction along purely formalist lines have been notoriously problematic, and any rejection of my claim will depend upon the development of a successful doctrine of this ilk. Although it certainly would be hard to prove that no such theory could ever be devised, the prospects seem dim, for one wonders why an adequate contemplation of a fictional work's features should *never* include a careful thinking through of the moral implications of the events and attitudes the writer has proposed for our make-believe. If, on the contrary, moral and political ideas are an intrinsic part of many literary works of art, their assessment would seem directly relevant to an evaluation of the works' overall merits.[20] What is more, since it is reasonable to think that our emotional (or quasi-emotional) reactions to works of fiction are directly relevant to the aesthetic dimensions of these works, moral considerations should be recognised as of *aesthetic* relevance, just as in a more standard and noncontroversial case, it would be correct to say that features contributing to a work's capacity to elicit laughter would be relevant to the aesthetic assessment of a work meant to belong to some comic genre.[21]

This line of thought has been labelled the "merited-response" argument by Gaut, who similarly uses it to isolate a kind of aesthetic failure that hinges on the presence in a work of ethically reprehensible content with a corresponding, targeted affective response.[22] The claim here is not that certain sorts of moral content are either necessary or sufficient to a highly positive evaluation of a work's aesthetic merit, but that in some contexts moral merits and demerits directly contribute to the complex weighing of values that go into the formation of an all-things-considered judgment. Arriving at such a judgment is no simple matter, and we must recognize that high measures of artistic excellence may be combined with serious moral failings, just as what may be taken as moral probity can be expressed in mediocre works of art.

An objection to this line of thought is that if all we are focusing on is the intrinsic value of a stretch of imaginative or contemplative experience, the contents in question have lost all of their genuine moral import. For example, *qua* genuine moral issue, Baudelaire's actual or depicted misogyny is irrelevant to the poetry's aesthetic value. In response, one wonders about the soundness of the meta-ethical assumptions on which the objection must rest. The claim is not that a rape fantasy is simply discordant or ugly, but that a properly moral rejection of this part of the intended make-believe directly influences the quality of our experience of the poem.[23] Perhaps there is some moral scheme in which the contents of one's thoughts and feelings are always ethically neutral, but I leave it to others to defend such a system.

Even more controversial, perhaps, given the state of the art in the literary disciplines in most of the world's institutions of higher learning, is the contention that many of the theoretically informed content analyses evoked in §3 have nothing to do with the work's qualities *qua* work of literary art and are not directly relevant to either the artistic or the aesthetic quality of the work— an implication of this verdict being that only normal scientific or scholarly epistemic norms ought to be applied in their assessment. Yet such is my claim. Its basis is not the observation that such interpretative flights of fancy are incompatible with authorial intention and are hence false if presented as claims about the work's meanings. After all, statements in this genre are frequently couched as ludic, transgressive, instrumental, or make-believe construals of possible significance that in some context may be associated with a text. So what one must say is why that sort of "free interpretive play" does not contribute to aesthetic appreciation, particularly given the fact that certain theorists have proposed to define the aesthetic precisely in such terms, i.e., as the suspension of standard hermeneutic norms and their replacement with a regime of polyvalence, polysemic perversity, tolerance, and "free association."[24] Do not unfettered semantic musings contribute directly to the sort of "inherently pleasurable contemplation" constitutive of aesthetic experience? Or to put it even more bluntly, isn't an unchained brainstorming over patterns of meaning the primary business of the poetry appreciation class?

In response to such queries, I would like to point out that it is one thing to have an aesthetic experience that is in any way whatsoever occasioned by some text, and something else to have an aesthetic experience *of a work of art*, i.e., one grounded in an attentive contemplation and knowledge of that work's features. An aesthetic experience that is not so grounded may even in part be causally occasioned by acquaintance with aspects of the work (e.g., some linguistic features of the text and its significance), yet still not count as an aesthetic experience or appreciation *of the work*. What is crucial here is an epistemic success condition, as well as the distinction between the text (or verbal performance) and the literary work, where the latter involves the intentional creation of a verbal artefact or performance in a given historical context by someone (or a group of persons) with a particular background and various aims and intentions. One can do all sorts of useful things with texts, but successfully to read a text as the text of a work of literature, one's contemplation of the text's features must be informed and guided by some understanding of the history and context of its production as part of an artistic achievement. Such a claim can be supported by the array of arguments set forth by Richard Wollheim in his distinction between criticism viewed as retrieval and criticism as revision, as well as by cognate considerations advanced by Jerrold Levinson, Gary Iseminger, Nicholas Wolterstorff, and others with an aim to separating the work's content from the world of possible posterior mobilizations and appropriations.[25] In short, the work is not a text's "effective history"; radical reinterpretings, ludic, pseudo-scientific, and other, no matter how otherwise intrinsically rewarding they may turn out to be, are distinct from literary appreciations.

The latter points hold, I want to claim, no matter what "the institution" says—or better, no matter what persons purporting to represent a given institution may say or write. Here I am in agreement with Stein Haugom Olsen's distinction between sociological and philosophical accounts of institutions, where the latter focus on norms constitutive of an institution's identity as opposed to various contingent activities, social arrangements, or regularities.[26] The key assumption here is that it is specific functions (as opposed to names and other extrinsic, historical continuities) that should be used to identify and individuate institutions, which would mean that it is the fulfilment of an array of artistic and aesthetic values and aims that make some institution's practices and roles worthy of the name "literary." And if persons claiming to represent some institution in fact fail to fulfil the functional roles constitutive of institutions of that sort, we should be critical of their claim to represent that institution.[27]

If what I have said accurately characterizes at least some of the institutional constraints within which academic literary critics are struggling, one may still ask why scholars would continue to claim that the results of such interpretative work deserve to be recognized as contributing to the aesthetics of literature, construed broadly as the appreciation of literary art *qua* art. This is, I think, a confusion motivated by some sense of where the institutional safety nets are located: exciting but evidentially challenged prose about gender, race, class, and the Western metaphysic—grounded, for example, in the text of *Hamlet*—may in fact fail to provide the epistemic and practical rewards promised. An aesthetical fig leaf nonetheless usefully provides a disciplinary rationale: I do not really need to show that the contents of Baudelaire's poem, as identified, deconstruct some aspect of Western metaphysics if all I am really after is an aesthetic exploration of some of the possible contents of the work of art's semantic structure. *If themes are just deep meanings we read into a text,* and if thematic patterns figure within those part-whole relations that give a work its overall unity or disunity, then thematic ruminations count as potential contributions to our apprehension of the unity in diversity that is arguably at the very heart of aesthetic appreciation. What is wrong with that argument is, however, the unsoundness of the part in italics, which overlooks the distinction between text and work, thereby smuggling the interpreter's extrapolations about textual significance into the domain of aesthetic experiences of the work.

To sum up, my claim about anachronistic, theory-driven interpretative writings is that they tend to conflate aesthetic, heuristic, sociopolitical (and in some versions, erotic) projects. To interpret a text with an eye to appreciating a work of literary art *qua* work of art is to attend to the aesthetic and artistic qualities that text has in relation to the context of its creation, where it is part of an artistic accomplishment. Whether this is *always* the most rewarding, new, and exciting way to read a text is a separate issue, an issue with regard to which the current needs of professors of literature do not provide the most reliable guide.

What I have sketched in the last part of this essay is a broad (but not all-inclusive) conception of aesthetic experience and of one kind of value that may be associated with works of literature. Such an account does not purport to elucidate ordinary usage or to identify a unitary concept latent in expert critical practice; nor is it adequately characterized as a "broad" form of philosophical analysis which offers minor correctives to a somewhat messy, but essentially sound prior usage. Instead, such an account is a revisionary reconstruction of concepts motivated by the values the target notions are meant to promote. Understood in this sense, aesthetics is not a theory or doctrine covering the entire range of critical discourse, but it does refer to an important, and arguably crucial part of it, namely, the part about the specifically aesthetic and artistic dimensions of literature.

NOTES

1. See, for example, George Levine, ed., *Aesthetics and Ideology* (New Brunswick, N.J.: Rutgers University Press, 1994). "The aesthetic"—usually employed elliptically and in scare-quotes, is designated in this collection quite variously as "a realm," "a part of a discourse of value," "a site of state power," "a radiant globe of material objects and attitudes," etc. In spite of the volume's purported goal of reexamining the place of "the aesthetic" in literary studies, not a single contributor refers to any of the relevant publications listed in my next note.

2. Publications on the issue include Monroe C. Beardsley, "What is an Aesthetic Quality?" *Theoria* 39 (1973): 50–70; Noël Carroll, "Aesthetic Experience Revisited," *British Journal of Aesthetics* 42, no. 2 (April 2002): 145–58; Ted Cohen, "Aesthetic/Non-Aesthetic and the Concept of Taste," *Theoria* 39 (1973): 113–52; T. J. Diffey, "Note on Some Meanings of the Term 'Aesthetic,'" *British Journal of Aesthetics* 35, no. 1 (January 1995): 61–66; Bohdan Dziemidok, "On the Need to Distinguish Between Aesthetic and Artistic Evaluations of Art," in *Institutions of Art: Reconsiderations of George Dickie's Philosophy*, ed. Robert J. Yanal (University Park: Pennsylvania State University Press, 1994), 73–86; Alan Goldman, "Aesthetic Qualities and Aesthetic Value," *Journal of Philosophy* 87, no. 1 (January 1990): 23–37; Nelson Goodman, *Languages of Art: An Approach to a Theory of Symbols* (Indianapolis: Hackett, 1988); Göran Hermerén, *The Nature of Aesthetic Qualities* (Lund: Lund University Press, 1988); Peter Kivy, "What Makes 'Aesthetic' Terms Aesthetic?" *Philosophy and Phenomenological Research* 36, no. 2 (December 1975): 197–211; Ruby Meager, "Aesthetic Concepts," *British Journal of Aesthetics* 10, no. 4 (October 1970): 303–22; Michael H. Mitias, *What Makes An Experience Aesthetic?* (Amsterdam: Rodopi, 1988); Michael H. Mitias, ed., *Possibility of the Aesthetic Experience* (Dordrecht: Martinus Nijhoff, 1986); David Novitz, "The Integrity of Aesthetics," *Journal of Aesthetics and Art Criticism* 48, no. 1 (Winter 1990): 9–20; J. O. Urmson and David Pole, "What Makes a Situation Aesthetic?" *Aristotelean Society Supplementary Volume* 31 (1957): 75–106; Frank Sibley, "Aesthetic Concepts," *Philosophical Review* 68 (1959): 421–50, and "Aesthetic and Non-Aesthetic," *Philosophical Review* 74 (1965): 135–59; Francis Sparshott, *The Theory of the Arts* (Princeton, N.J.: Princeton University Press, 1982), 467–86; Nick Zangwill, "Skin Deep or In the Eye of the Beholder? The Metaphysics of Aesthetic and Sensory Properties," *Philosophy and Phenomenological Research* 61, no. 3 (November 2000): 595–618.

3. David E. W. Fenner, *The Aesthetic Attitude* (Atlantic Highlands, N.J.: Humanities Press, 1996).

4. Such a view is advocated, for example, by Richard Wollheim in *Art and Its Objects*, 2nd ed. (Cambridge: Cambridge University Press, 1980), 91–104. Wollheim concedes that the experience of art has neither historical nor developmental priority, and his argument for its logical priority over aesthetic concepts involves claims about the foibles of attitude theories and the unfounded supposition that his opponent must hold that "the institution of art contributes nothing to human experience" (101). For a more convincing treatment of the issue, see Frank Sibley, "Arts or the Aesthetic—Which Comes First?" in *Approach to Aesthetics: Collected Papers on Philosophical Aesthetics*, ed. John Benson, Betty Redfern, and Jeremy Roxbee Cox (Oxford: Clarendon, 2001), 207–55.

5. Carolyn Korsmeyer, "On Distinguishing 'Aesthetic' from 'Artistic,'" *Journal of Aesthetic Education* 11, no. 4 (October 1977): 45–57, at 53.

6. Berys Gaut, "The Ethical Criticism of Art," in *Aesthetics and Ethics: Essays at the Intersection*, ed. Jerrold Levinson (Cambridge: Cambridge University Press, 1998), 182–203, at 183.

7. Gregory Currie, *An Ontology of Art* (London: Macmillan, 1989), 11–12.

8. An influential example in this vein is Roland Barthes, *Critique et vérité* (Paris: Seuil, 1966).

9. Richard D. E. Burton, *Baudelaire in 1859: A Study in the Sources of Poetic Creativity* (Cambridge: Cambridge University Press, 1999), 60, 134.

10. E. D. Hirsch Jr., *Validity in Interpretation.*(New Haven, Conn.: Yale University Press, 1967).

11. Michael D. Bristol, *Shakespeare's America, America's Shakespeare* (London: Routledge, 1990), and *Big Time Shakespeare* (London: Routledge, 1996).

12. For background on such discussions, and an example of an attempt to justify the "privileging" of literature along normative lines, see Brook Thomas, *The New Historicism and Other Old-Fashioned Topics* (Princeton, N.J.: Princeton University Press, 1991), 162.

13. I am hoping that my readers will have suffered through enough "high-theoretic" readings at literary symposia to be familiar with the target of these remarks. If by some chance you think I am making this up or that this sort of thing is no longer done, please consult Ulrich Baer, *Remnants of Song: Trauma and the Experience of Modernity in Charles Baudelaire and Paul Celan* (Stanford: Stanford University Press, 2000).

14. For a survey of conceptions of literature, see my "Literature," in *Oxford Handbook of Aesthetics*, ed. Jerrold Levinson (Oxford: Oxford University Press, 2003), 536–54; and for a more detailed presentation of a belletristic approach, "Aesthetic Experience and a Belletrist Definition of Literature" (forthcoming).

15. This basic insight has been expressed and defended by a variety of authors. One source is C. I. Lewis, *An Analysis of Knowledge and Valuation* (La Salle, Ill.: Open Court, 1946).

16. That this point was already clearly made by Plato is reiterated by Robert Stecker in his "Only Jerome: A Reply to Noël Carroll," *British Journal of Aesthetics* 41, no. 1 (January 2001): 76–80. Another philosopher who usefully emphasizes the link between intrinsic value and aesthetic appreciation is Gary Iseminger, "Aesthetic Appreciation," *Journal of Aesthetics and Art Criticism* 39, no. 4 (Summer 1981): 389–97. See also his informative survey, "Aesthetic Experience," in *The Oxford Handbook of Aesthetics*, ed. Jerrold Levinson (Oxford: Oxford University Press, 2003), 99–116.

17. For a detailed discussion, see my "On an Apparent Truism in Aesthetics," *British Journal of Aesthetics* 43, no. 3 (July 2003): 260–78.

18. As Roger Scruton put it, "any attempt to define aesthetic appreciation in sensuous terms will fail to explain the arts of poetry and narrative," *Art and Imagination: A Study in the Philosophy of Mind* (London: Methuen, 1974), 154. For a more recent recognition of this point, see Nick Zangwill, *The Metaphysics of Beauty* (Ithaca, N.Y.: Cornell University Press, 2001), 44–45. Zangwill, by the way, does not allow that literary works actually have aesthetic properties, which I take to be a serious problem for his manner of attempting to define aesthetic qualities (which also involves some tricky epistemic conditions that need not be gone into here).

19. For the distinction between text and work, see my "Texts, Works, Versions: Pierre Menard and the Ontology of Literature," in *Art and Intention: A Philosophical Essay* (Oxford: Clarendon: 2005).

20. Compare Colin McGinn: "Ethical questions, I contend, are integral to the study of literature, and it can only impoverish literary study to try to bracket such questions," "The Meaning and Morality of *Lolita*," *Philosophical Forum* 30, no. 1 (March 1999): 31–42, at 41; see also his *Ethics, Evil, and Fiction* (Oxford: Oxford University Press, 1997).

21. For an earlier statement of this line of thought, see Paisley Livingston and Alfred R. Mele, "Evaluating Emotional Responses to Fiction," in *Emotion and the Arts*, ed. Anne Mette Hjort and Sue Laver (New York and Oxford: Oxford University Press, 1997), 157–76.

22. See Berys Gaut, "The Ethical Criticism of Art," 182–203.

23. A similar point is made with regard to Baudelaire's work by Henry James; see his *Literary Criticism* (New York: Library of America, 1984), 157–58.

24. See, for example, Siegfried J. Schmidt, *Die Selbstorganisation des Sozialsystems. Literatur im 18. Jahrhundert* (Frankfurt: Suhrkamp, 1989).

25. Richard Wollheim, "Criticism as Retrieval," in *Art and Its Objects* (Cambridge: Cambridge University Press, 1968, 2nd rev. ed., 1980), 185–204; Jerrold Levinson, "Artworks and the Future," in *Music, Art, and Metaphysics* (Ithaca, N.Y.: Cornell University Press, 1990), 179–215; Nicholas Wolterstorff, "Resurrecting the Author," in *Meaning in the Arts*, ed. Peter A. French and Howard K. Wettstein, Midwest Studies in Philosophy, vol. 27 (Boston: Blackwell, 2003), 4–24.

26. See his "Conventions and Rules in Literature," *Metaphilosophy* 31, nos. 1/2 (January 2000): 25–42; *The Structure of Literary Understanding* (Cambridge: Cambridge University Press, 1978); and *The End of Literary Theory* (Cambridge: Cambridge University Press, 1987).

27. For a sophisticated proposal along these lines, see Julius Moravcsik, "Art and 'Art,'" in *Philosophy and the Arts*, ed. Peter A. French, Theodore E. Uehling Jr., and Howard K. Wettstein, Midwest Studies in Philosophy, vol. 16 (Notre Dame, Ind.: Notre Dame University Press, 1991), 302–13.

## 46. CRISIS IN THE HUMANITIES?

### RECONFIGURING LITERARY STUDY FOR THE
### TWENTY-FIRST CENTURY

#### MARJORIE PERLOFF

ONE OF OUR MOST COMMON genres today is the epitaph for the humanities. A few years ago, for example, Robert Weisbuch, the president of the Woodrow Wilson National Fellowship Foundation, declared:

> Today's consensus about the state of the humanities—it's bad, it's getting worse, and no one is doing much about it—is supported by dismal facts. The percentage of undergraduates majoring in humanities fields has been halved over the past three decades. Financing for faculty research has decreased. The salary gap between full-time scholars in the humanities and in other fields has widened, and more and more humanists are employed part time and paid ridiculously low salaries. . . . As doctoral programs in the humanities proliferate irresponsibly, turning out more and more graduates who cannot find jobs, the waste of human talent becomes enormous, intolerable.
>
> More broadly, the humanities, like the liberal arts generally, appear far less surely at the center of higher education than they once did. We have lost the respect of our colleagues in other fields, as well as the attention of an intelligent public. The action is elsewhere. We're living through a time when outrage with the newfangled in the humanities—with deconstruction or Marxism or whatever—has become plain lack of interest. No one's even angry with us now, just bored.[1]

Weisbuch tries to solve the problem with a series of practical solutions such as job creation for humanities graduates, but the more we probe the "humanities" question, the more apparent it becomes that, whereas schools of engineering or departments of economics have a specific curriculum and mandate, the "humanities" umbrella—at my own university, Stanford, the disciplines included are history, philosophy, religion, the various language and literature departments, art history, drama, and musicology—remains amorphous.

Marjorie Perloff. "Crisis in the Humanities? Reconfiguring Literary Study for the Twenty-first Century." Adapted from *Differentials: Poetry, Poetics, Pedagogy*, by Marjorie Perloff. Tuscaloosa: The University of Alabama Press, 2004. Originally published as "In Defense of Poetry," *Boston Review* 24, no. 6 (December 1999/January 2000): 22–26. Reprinted by permission of the University of Alabama Press.

CRISIS IN THE HUMANITIES? 669

What *does* the term *humanities* mean today? The mission statement of the National Endowment for the Humanities (NEH), found on its Web site reads as follows:

> *What are the Humanities?*
> The humanities are not any one thing. They are all around us and evident in our daily lives. When you visit an exhibition on "The Many Realms of King Arthur" at your local library, that is the humanities. When you read the diary of a seventeenth-century New England midwife, that is the humanities. When you watch an episode of *The Civil War*, that is the humanities too.

But if the NEH's claims for the humanities are dubious, they are also quite typical. At Stanford University for example, the Stanford Bulletin contains this description:

> The School of Humanities and Sciences, with over 40 departments and interdepartmental degree programs, is the primary locus for the superior liberal arts education offered by Stanford University. Through exposure to the humanities, undergraduates study the ethical, aesthetic, and intellectual dimensions of the human experience, past and present, and so are prepared to make thoughtful and imaginative contributions to the culture of the future.

The language used here is revealing. Whereas the social sciences (according to the Bulletin) teach "theories and techniques for the analysis of specific societal issues," and the "hard" sciences prepare students to become the "leaders" in our increasingly technological society, the humanities "expose" students to the "ethical, aesthetic, and intellectual dimensions of human experience." Exposure is nice enough—but also perfectly dispensable when leadership and expertise are at stake. Indeed, the humanities, as now understood and taught in our universities, no longer possess what Pierre Bourdieu calls "symbolic capital": an "accumulated prestige, celebrity, consecration or honour" founded on the "dialectic of knowledge (*connaissance*) and recognition (*reconnaissance*)."[2] In the capitalist and multicultural democracy of late-twentieth-century America, based as it is on money rather than on social class, "exposure" to the "intellectual dimensions of the human experience" is no longer a sine qua non of success or even of the Good Life. Our recent presidents from Jimmy Carter and Ronald Reagan to the two George Bushes and even the Rhodes scholar Bill Clinton are a case in point.

Consider the controversy about the NEH's invitation to Bill Clinton to deliver the 2000 Jefferson Lecture in the Humanities, an invitation Clinton declined in response to strong protest from the scholarly community. The annual

Jefferson Lecture, inaugurated in 1972 by Lionel Trilling, has been given by the likes of Jaroslav Pelikan, C. Vann Woodward, Vincent Scully, Caroline Walker Bynum, and Emily T. Vermeule—all of them serious scholars and outstanding intellectuals in their respective disciplines, ranging from architecture (Scully) to history (Woodward), to classics (Vermeule). Accordingly, when William Ferris, the chairman of the NEH, explained that his hope was that, in making the Jefferson Lecture a presidential event, "the humanities" would be brought "into the lives of millions of Americans who don't know what the humanities are and have no sense of the great work we do [at the NEH],"[3] what he was really saying was that the term *humanities* no longer means anything. At best, it seems, the term has a negative function, specifically, in the case of the Jefferson Lecture, giving the president a chance to make a speech that would not be overtly political but would deal with what are vaguely conceived as "humanistic" values. And of course this "lecture" would be written by the president's speechwriters—a situation that, in the scholarly community, would be classified as simple plagiarism.

Given this climate, perhaps we can think more seriously about the state of the "humanities" if we begin by getting rid of the word "humanities"—a word, incidentally, of surprisingly recent vintage. The first edition of the *Oxford English Dictionary* (*OED*), whose supplement appears in 1933, does not include it at all. *Humane, humanism, humanist, humanity, humanitarian*: these are familiar cognates of the word *human*, but *humanities* was not the term of choice for an area of knowledge and set of fields of study until after World War II. The more usual (and broader) rubric was Liberal Arts, Arts and Sciences, or Arts, Letters, and Sciences. The shift in terminology, reflected in the now-ubiquitous Humanities Centers, humanities special programs, and humanities fellowships, testifies, paradoxically, to an increasing perplexity about what these designations might mean.

When we study the roster of fellows at the various humanities centers and institutes in the U.S., a clear trend emerges: anthropology and history have taken over the humanities field. In 2003, I served on the selection committee for internal fellows at the humanities center of a leading Midwestern university, and although the staff very much hoped to attract candidates in art history, literature, musicology, and philosophy, the competitive applications came from what we might call the proto–social sciences, like environmental studies or human biology. Indeed, the top candidate in the pool was a professor from the law school.

How did we get into this bind? As someone trained in the discipline of English and Comparative Literature, I want to take a look at what traditionally has been one of the central branches of the humanities: the study of literature or, as I prefer to call it, *poetics*. "Literature" is an imprecise designator that came into use only in the eighteenth century,[4] whereas discussions of the poetic have a much more ancient and cross-cultural lineage. The discipline of poetics (which, from Plato through the nineteenth century, comprised narrative and drama as well as lyric) has been classified in four basic ways:

(1) The poetic may be understood as a branch of rhetoric. From Aristotle's profound understanding of *rhetoric* as the art (*techne*) of finding the available means of persuasion, to Cicero and Quintilian's division of rhetoric into three tasks—*docere* (to teach), *delectare* (to delight), and *movere* (to move)—and three faculties—*inventio* (the finding of arguments), *dispositio* (the arrangement into parts), and *elocutio* (style)[5]—to the handbooks of the medieval rhetoricians like Geoffrey of Vinsauf, to the late-eighteenth-century manuals of Hugh Blair and George Campbell, to the rhetorical hermeneutics of the contemporary Groupe Mu,[6] *rhetoric* has flourished as the study of *how* a piece of writing is put together. It has gradually evolved from its early prescriptive character (the description of rhetorical devices and strategies necessary to teach, delight, or move a given audience) to the more empirical study of what figures and devices actually *are* used in literary and nonliterary composition. Rhetoric thus means primarily *practical criticism*—the examination of diction and syntax, rhythm and repetition, and the various figures of speech.

But effective rhetoric, as Aristotle first demonstrated in what is still the great treatment of the subject, is no mere "ornament," as the tropes and rhetorical figures used to be called, but a matter of *ethos* and *pathos*: the artful presentation of a self designed to be persuasive to its audience, and the construction of an audience that will empathize with that self. To take some Renaissance examples, if Philip Sidney provides us with an excellent example of the ethical argument (in his case, the *sprezzatura* that makes us sympathize with Astrophel in the sonnet sequence *Astrophel and Stella*, as with the charmingly modest speaker of *A Defense of Poetry*), John Donne is the master of the pathetic argument: the urgent and passionate appeal to the poet's (and preacher's) fellow sinners to be at one with his suffering.

As such, rhetoric is at the very center of our discipline as literary scholars. No other discipline, after all, has as its central focus the issue as to how language actually *works* and what it *does*, whether in newspaper editorials or poems or the weather report. Conversely, inattention to rhetoric, as in Harold Bloom's otherwise powerful poetry criticism, downgrades the materiality of the text at the expense of its dominant myths and ideas, thus occluding the significant differences between, say, a Wallace Stevens poem and an Emerson essay. At the same time, the focus on the rhetorical dimension of a given text inevitably downplays the cognitive import of the poetic construct. Rhetoric, Michel Meyer argues in an interesting study, flourishes where ideologies fail, or, in Nancy S. Struever's words, it "reveals a deep commitment to question/response formations as more fundamental than concepts of referentiality in discursive exchange."[7] This points the way to the second frame for literary study.

(2) From Plato to Heidegger and Levinas, the *poetic* has often been understood as a branch of philosophy, and hence as a potential expression of truth and knowledge. Because poetry couldn't pass Plato's truth test—even Homer told false and salacious stories about the gods—the poets were ostensibly banished from the Republic. I will have more to say of this below, but for the moment, I note only that this conception of poetry is antithetical to the first. If the main purpose of a literary text is to convey knowledge or formulate truths, questions of form and genre take a backseat. Arthur Rimbaud's abandonment of the alexandrine, for example, in favor of free verse and then prose poetry would matter much less than the visionary content of those dense and oblique Rimbaldian texts, verse or prose. Again, if theories of poetry-as-rhetoric regard James Joyce and Ezra Pound as key modernists, the theory of poetry-as-philosophy would (and has) put Samuel Beckett or Paul Celan at that center.

The treatment of poetry as truth or knowledge has produced some marvelous criticism, especially in the romantic period and again after the Second World War when Heidegger came to prominence, but it has its own problems, perhaps most notably that it favors a limited corpus of literature at the expense of all others—the lyric of Wordsworth and Shelley, for example, at the expense of, say, a Jane Austen novel, which doesn't lend itself to comparable philosophical reflection. Then, too—and I shall have more to say on this below—the equation of poetry and philosophy tends to shortchange the former: when a given artwork is seen to exemplify or illustrate, say, Theodor Adorno's aesthetic theory or Louis Althusser's theory of interpellation, its heterogeneity is ignored, the pedagogical aim being one of exemplification rather than respect for the poem's own ontology.

(3) From antiquity to the present, poetry has also been classified as one of the arts (this time Aristotle is more important than Plato). In this configuration, poetry is placed in the context of the visual arts, music, dance, architecture, and so on. In the *Ion*, Plato argued that the practice of poetry involves *techne kai episteme*. *Techne* was the standard Greek word both for a practical skill and for the systematic knowledge or experience that underlies it. "The resulting range of application," Stephen Halliwell points out, "is extensive, covering at one end of the spectrum the activity of a carpenter, builder, smith, sculptor, similar manual craftsman, and, at the other, at least from the fifth century onwards, the ability and practices of rhetoricians and sophists."[8] So *techne* meaning "craft," "skill," "technique," "method," "art," coupled with *episteme*, meaning "knowledge," is the domain of the arts. But the discourse about poetry, Plato concludes in the *Ion*, doesn't seem to have sufficient *techne kai episteme*: unlike the shipbuilder or carpenter, the rhapsode demonstrates no special skill in speaking about Homer, and hence his ability to do so must be purely a matter of inspiration—in other words, an instinctive ability to interpret Homer that cannot be taught or learned—it simply *is*.

Criticism, by this account, is no more than a second-order discourse, a repetition, in diluted form, of what a given poem or artwork "says." Scientists and social scientists often hold this view of poetics. But the theory that poetry is a branch of the arts need not lead to such impressionism. On the contrary, to conceive of poetry as an art also implies that it is a form of discourse inherently *other*, that poetic language is to be distinguished from ordinary speaking and writing. This is the Aristotelian view: a tragedy or epic will be read, less for its potential truth value or its specific rhetorical properties, than as a unique aesthetic construct, whose "plot" or structure (*ton pragmaton systasis*) is coherent and characterized by what Aristotle called *to prepon* (fitness). The "formalist" analysis that such structures prompt is often associated with the New Critics, although their interest was primarily in thematic, rather than in formal or structural, coherence.

For real formalist criticism in our time, we must look less to the New Critics than to the Russian Formalists, whose object was to define *poeticity*—not in the individual poem but as a recurrent feature in poems across a wide spectrum. Indeed, the Russian Formalists studied the poetic function in a variety of genres and media, from the folk epic to the personal letter. A showpiece would be Roman Jakobson's "Marginal Notes on the Prose of the Poet Pasternak," which analyzes the role of passive verb constructions in creating the particular tone of a Pasternak short story, Jakobson's point being that "prose" can be just as "artistic" as "poetry."[9] The Formalist division between "literary" and "ordinary" language has been challenged from many quarters: for example, in Stanley Fish's famous essay "How Ordinary is Ordinary Language?" (1973), which argues that so-called "poetic" devices can be found in newspaper editorials as easily as in lyric poems.[10] But although most critics in the Formalist tradition would today concede that the distinction between literary and ordinary language is not hard and fast, they would argue that it is useful to concentrate on difference rather than similarity. "Do not forget," as Ludwig Wittgenstein put it in his box of notes called *Zettel*, "that a poem, although it is composed in the language of information, is not used in the language-game of giving information."[11]

(4) Formalist theory has often been accused of excessive technicality and aridity: in the politicized post-Vietnam era, it came under sharp attack from those who take poetics to be essentially a historical or cultural formation. Indeed in this fourth paradigm, formalism becomes a dirty word, a smokescreen for ignoring the ideology and political ethos of a given work. For the cultural critic, the only real justification for literary study is the concession that poems and novels can do "cultural work." From this perspective, a poetic text is primarily to be understood as a symptom of the larger culture to which it belongs and as an index to particular historical or cultural markers. Literary practices, moreover, are taken to be no different in kind from other social

or cultural practices. A poem or novel or film is discussed, not for its intrinsic merits or as the expression of individual genius, nor for its expression of essential truths, nor for its powers of persuasion, but for its political role, its exposure of the state of a given society. In this scheme of things, questions of value inevitably take the backseat, there being, in fact, no reason why Henry James's novels are a better index to or symptom of the cultural aporias of turn-of-the-century America than are the best sellers of the period—or, for that matter, early-twentieth-century domestic architecture, popular periodicals, or medical treatises. Read the list of topics currently being studied in university courses or at humanities centers and you will find that "literature" functions almost exclusively in this way.

Poetry as rhetoric, poetry as philosophy, poetry as an art, poetry as cultural production—what is at stake in adopting one of these classifications to the exclusion of the others? Interestingly, the first three inevitably incorporate the fourth into the discipline, in that they examine the history and cultural position of the different poetic, rhetorical, philosophical, and generic forms as well as the history and culture of their philosophical reception. But *history of* is very different from the transposition that views literature itself *as history*—the position of contemporary cultural studies, which is committed to the demolition of such "obsolete" categories as poetic autonomy, poetic truth, and formal and rhetorical value. Since cultural studies currently dominate the arena of literary study, I want to focus here on this particular approach.

We might begin by noting that the treatment of poetry as a branch of history or culture is based on the assumption that the poetry of a period is a reliable index to that period's larger intellectual and ideological currents. Beckett's *Endgame*, for example, testifies to the meaninglessness and horror of a post-Auschwitz, nuclear world. But as critics from Aristotle to Adorno have understood, the theory that imaginative writing is an index to its time ignores what is specific to a work of art, along with its powers of invention, transformation, and resistance. This is Aristotle's point in the ninth chapter of the *Poetics*:

> The difference between a historian and poet is not that one writes in prose and the other in verse. . . . The real difference is this, that one tells what happened and the other what might happen. For this reason poetry is something more philosophical and serious [*kai philosophoteron kai spoudaioteron*] than history, because poetry tends to give general truths while history gives particular facts.
>
> By a "general truth" I mean the sort of thing that a certain type of man will do or say either probably or necessarily. . . . A "particular fact" is what Alcibiades did or what was done to him.

It is clear, then ... that the poet must be a "maker" [*poietes*] not of verses but of stories, since he is a poet in virtue of his "representation," and what he represents is action. (no. 1451b)[12]

The meaning of the possible ("what might happen") is made clearer by Aristotle's response to Plato's complaint that poets are dangerous to the state because they tell lies. "The standard of what is correct," writes Aristotle, "is not the same in the art of poetry as it is in the art of social conduct or any other art. . . . It is less of an error not to know that a female stag has no horns than to make a picture that is unrecognizable" (no. 1461).

But of course Plato understood this distinction perfectly. The danger of poetry to the ideal republic, after all, is in direct proportion to its power, its charm, its magic: "We will beg Homer and other poets not to be angry if we cancel those and all similar passages [e.g., "false" stories about the gods], not that they are not poetic and pleasing to most hearers, but because the more poetic they are the less are they suited to the ears of boys and men who are destined to be free."[13] One could hardly endow the poetic with more power. And indeed, when in book 10 of the *Republic*, Plato takes up the ancient "quarrel between philosophy and poetry," so as to dismiss the latter from the well-governed state, he admits that "we ourselves are very conscious of her spell," "her magic." That magic reappears at the conclusion of the *Republic* with the poetic myth of Er, as if to let us know that, despite all the good reasons to the contrary, for Plato, poetry is finally the highest calling.

In distinguishing mimesis (representation) from diegesis (straightforward exposition or narrative in the author's own person), Plato, and Aristotle after him, isolate the *fictive* as the essential characteristic of the poetic construct: not what *has happened* but what *might happen* either possibly or probably. In his celebrated *Metahistory*, Hayden White taught us that, contra Aristotle, historical writing, even the "simplest" chronicle, also has a fictive element.[14] White places nineteenth-century historiography from G. W. F. Hegel and Jules Michelet to Friedrich Nietzsche and Benedetto Croce within the larger tradition of narrative fiction. But *Metahistory* was published over a quarter of a century ago (1973), and since then a major reversal has set in. For even as the notion of text as representation continues to be operative (there being no "reality" outside textual representation that one can access), in practice, the emphasis on representation has created, ironically enough, a situation where the *what* of mimesis has become much more important than the *how*. Subject matter—whether divine-right kingship in Renaissance England or the culture of condoms in early-twentieth-century America—becomes all.

At its best, the alignment of poetic and cultural practices has given literary study a new life. *Ulysses*, for example, was originally read as a parodic modern-day Odyssey or as an elaborate experiment in which plot and character are subordinated to the investigation of the possibilities of language. The structure of the novel, with its astonishing network of leitmotifs, allusions, cross-references, and symbolic threads, was examined from every possible angle. From the perspective of the new cultural studies, however, *Ulysses* is more properly read as an examination of the dynamics of race, power, and empire, as these play themselves out in the colonial Ireland of the early twentieth century—an Ireland whose very consciousness has been created by its subaltern position vis-à-vis its English oppressors. As such, Joyce's novel provides us with rich material about nationalism, colonialism, and imperialism, as well as specific gender and racial inequities: for example, the Joycean dialectic that regards woman as either virgin or whore. In the same vein, Joseph Conrad's *Heart of Darkness* and *Nostromo* are now read primarily as depictions of the horrors of colonial oppression under capitalist expansion, this time with respect to race in Africa and Central America; and here too the representation of gender (e.g., Kurtz's African woman versus his "Intended") has become the subject of interesting and useful critique.

The past decade has witnessed dozens of books on these subjects, there being plenty of room, within cultural studies, for debate on such issues as the relative complicity of Joyce himself with his colonial oppressors or the identification between Conrad and the notorious Kurtz. But in its zeal to unmask the hidden ideologies of these and related novels, critics seem to have forgotten what brought them to *Ulysses* or *Heart of Darkness* in the first place—namely, the uniqueness of these novels as works of art. Plenty of novels, poems, and plays deal with Irish nationalism and British oppression, but they have little of Joyce's appeal. Indeed, *Ulysses*, read as it is around the world by a steadily growing audience, is admired, first and foremost, for the brilliance, inventiveness, and power of its language and rhetoric, beginning with those absurd advertising jingles that go through Bloom's mind as he wanders the Dublin streets—jingles like "What is home without Plumtree's potted meat? Incomplete." And these slogans are never merely fortuitous: Bloom's own home, after all, is "incomplete" without Molly's "plums" and "potted meat." And the rhyme echo relates to the musical motifs associated with Molly and her lover, Blazes Boylan.

Then, too, despite all the "newness" of postcolonial theory, it is a question whether most discussions of nationalism and imperialism in *Ulysses* are really all that different from such early Joyce studies as William T. Noon's, *Joyce and Aquinas* or Kevin Sullivan's *Joyce Among the Jesuits*. Of the former, a recent reviewer, Cary McKinson, for Amazon.com writes:

> This book has been a classic in Joyce studies for many years. Joyce had said famously that if you wanted to understand his writing, you first had to understand Aquinas. Jumping off from this typically Joycean hyperbole, Noon explicates Joyce's Catholicism from the angle of Thomistic Aesthet-

ics. A technical/theological subject made very readable. A must for any wannabe Joyce scholar.

*Joyce and Aquinas* was published in 1957—a time when it was still assumed that to understand a novel meant to understand its author's "ideas." In the wake of structuralist and then poststructuralist theory, such notions went out the window: after all, it is argued, we cannot trust the author to understand the ideological formations that have shaped his consciousness, and it is hence up to the critic to unmask these. Yet, in the long run, the Thomistic philosophy on which Joyce was raised probably figures just as largely in his verbal universe as do his representations of nationalism or imperialism. *Ulysses* is, in any case, *sui generis* in its fusion of particular motifs and ideological markers. Even *Finnegans Wake* has a different radius of discourse.

It is this uniqueness of the artwork that cultural studies downplays. Indeed, in its more extreme incarnation, cultural theory can dispense with poetics altogether. Studies of consumerism, for example, can be based on the analysis of shopping malls or Home Depot layouts; no literary texts are required. Racial stereotyping manifests itself as readily in the newspapers or cartoons of a given period as in novels or plays. Teen culture can be explored through music, film, and computer games. The ideologies of globalization and nationalism can be profitably studied by examining network television and Internet discourse. And popular film is much more telling, so far as cultural theory is concerned, than are the art films of Federico Fellini or Jean-Luc Godard.

By the early nineties, in any case, English (and foreign language) departments found themselves in the odd position of teaching anything but literature. Indeed, I have seen job candidates, who are vying for the precious few tenure-track positions available, actually apologize for discussing a novel or poem and hurrying through these same discussions so as to get on to some important theoretical point relating to postcolonialism or queer theory or globalization. In this context, humanities centers inevitably find that the applications coming in from the anthropology department or the law school are more interesting than those from English or such related fields as musicology and art history. Inadvertently but surely, humanities has become social science without the statistics. No wonder, then, that foundation directors like Robert Weisbuch see the humanities—and especially literary study—as an embattled area, a field in crisis. No wonder that provosts and deans, having to make difficult budget decisions, cut positions that seem to be expendable.

But the crisis is not quite what we think it is. Poetics, we might say, abhors a vacuum: if the university doesn't offer courses on William Blake or Dante Gabriel Rossetti, on Ezra Pound or Samuel Beckett, the action moves elsewhere.[15] And here the impact of the Internet comes in. There are currently at least three Samuel Beckett Web sites, beginning with the "Samuel Beckett Online Resources and Links Page," hosted, amazingly enough, by Earthlink, which contains the texts of almost all of Beckett's works and a comprehensive set of secondary sources, including articles, reviews, commentaries, videos of the major plays, interviews—in short, an astonishing set of documents by and about Beckett. The site even produces seven parodies of *Waiting for Godot*, written over the years. Then, too, the Web site is interactive, allowing for discussion about the varying and constantly growing set of entries. A second Web site is *The Samuel Beckett Endpage*, founded by Porter Abbott at the University of California–Santa Barbara in 1996; this scholarly site contains recent Beckett news, scholarly notes from around the world, biographical material, thorough bibliographies of Beckett scholarship, and a good selection of the texts themselves online. And a third Beckett site—this one devoted to the scholarship—may be found at Literaryhistory.com.

Who is accessing these sites? Students, surely, but not only students or their professors. It seems that there are actually thousands of people "out there" who want to learn more about Beckett's work and share their interpretations of and enthusiasm for that work. And the same is true of Web sites devoted to Rossetti and Blake, to John Cage and Gertrude Stein and to movements such as Futurism or Dada. Futurist texts (e.g., F. T. Marinetti's manifestos), often out of print and unavailable, can be viewed on a beautiful British site called Futurism and Futurists, owned by the independent scholar Bob Osborn This site features all the major manifestos, artworks, photographs, the key writings, as well as a glossary of Futurist terms. There are also related Dada sites (for example, the Marcel Duchamp site *tout-fait*) and, perhaps above all, Kenneth Goldsmith's UbuWeb.[16]

Goldsmith is not himself an academic, and he does not apply for funding from the NEA or NEH so he need not compromise his values. Yet, within a five-year period or so, he has made UbuWeb an indispensable site for artists, poets, art historians, and literary scholars. As such, poetics is attracting a new generation of students who are coming to aesthetic discourses by the circuitous channels of the digital media. I use the word "aesthetic" advisedly here, for the audience in question is primarily interested in how Beckett's radio plays or Apollinaire's *calligrammes* actually function and what younger artists and poets can learn from these examples. In the context of actual art making, the relationship between poetry and its audience (the rhetorical) and the examination of the poem as formal, material construct will once again predominate. At the same time, as anyone who has used the *Wittgenstein Archives* [http://www.hit.uib.no/wab] at the University of Bergen in Norway knows, the relation of poetry to its philosophic analogues has never received as much attention as it is getting today.

What, then, of the "crisis" in the humanities? Given the astonishing interest in artworks and poetries manifested on the Internet, is the crisis perhaps more apparent than real? Yes and no. Within the academy, and especially in literature departments, it is real enough, as the shrinking enrollments and depressed job market indicate. But these phenomena may well be symptoms of something else—a bad fit between an outmoded curriculum and the actual interests of potential students. The main thrust of curriculum changes in English courses over the past few decades has been the shift in attention from major writers to minority ones and hence to include many more poems and fictions by underrepresented racial and ethnic groups as well as by women. But without clear-cut notions of *why* it is worthwhile to read literary texts, whether by established or marginalized writers, in the first place, the study of "literature" becomes no more than a chore, a way of satisfying distribution requirements.

"Theory" courses, as currently taught, exacerbate this problem. Suppose, for example, a class is assigned Peter Bürger's now-classic *Theory of the Avant-Garde*, along with some Marxist theory that provides background for Bürger's argument. The book posits that the early-twentieth-century avant-garde was a brave attempt to transform art but that it failed because it did not succeed in overturning the bourgeois institution of art as autonomous. But Bürger seems to equate the avant-garde with a few Dada and Surrealist works, for instance Duchamp's *Fountain*, and makes no mention of the Russian avant-garde that is arguably the very core of avant-gardism in the early twentieth century, the one avant-garde that fused, at least briefly, the radical aesthetic and the political critique that Bürger takes as a requisite for genuine avant-garde activity.[17] The narrowness of Bürger's definition puts his theory into serious question. But the student, who has yet to be exposed to the works themselves, French *or* Russian or otherwise), cannot possibly make a reasoned critique of Bürger's thesis.

Or take the current cult of Theodor Adorno, as presented to students who have no way of contextualizing his dense theoretical and critical commentary. When, for example, we read in Adorno's "On Lyric Poetry and Society," that "my thesis is that the lyric work is always the subjective expression of a social antagonism," and that "the objective world that produces the lyric is an inherently antagonistic world,"[18] we should be aware that Adorno's is a wholly Eurocentric position and that he takes nineteenth-century German poetry and philosophy as normative. But was the classical Chinese poem "the subjective expression of a social antagonism"? Are the lyrics in George Herbert's *The Temple* such an expression? And is it necessarily true that Heinrich Heine was not Baudelaire's equal because the former "surrendered more willingly to the flow of things; he took a poetic technique of reproduction, as it were, that corresponded to the industrial age and applied it to the conventional romantic archetypes, but he did not find archetypes of modernity"?[19] How can the student, who has probably never read either Heine or Baudelaire, tell?

Thus, the dominant cultural studies paradigm, combining, as it does, heavy doses of undigested European theory with American "minority" exemplars, can do little but confuse the student who would like to understand specific artworks and their relationship to one another. What is urgently needed—and here again Internet possibilities may lead the way—is a more "differential" and inductive approach to literary study, indeed to the humanities in general. This does not mean "covering" all periods of English (or whatever) literature or making one's way through as many canonical works as possible. But the wider one's reading in a specified area, the greater the pleasure of a given text and the greater the ability to make connections between texts.

It is interesting, in this regard, to see how pragmatic the premises of classical theory were. Plato's notion of what poetry does to move its audience was based on all the examples available to him, especially the example of Homer, who, so Plato thought, represented quintessential poetry more fully than any of his rival poets. Similarly, Aristotle's famous definition of tragedy in the *Poetics* ("A tragedy is the imitation of an action that is heroic, complete, and of a certain magnitude") is based on the examination of virtually dozens of compositions calling themselves "tragedies" that exhibited particular features. For example, is it because Greek tragedy did invariably include music and dance that Aristotle listed *melos* and *opsis* among its six elements and believed he had to examine their function?

I am well aware that Plato and Aristotle, Longinus and Horace had a much smaller corpus to deal with than does the Adorno of "On Lyric Poetry and Society." And indeed, the literary field is now so vast, heterogenous, and eclectic that it is obviously impossible to make universal choices as to which artworks to examine and how to organize meaningful curricula. But students can be taught—and here the question of expertise comes in—what the issues of analyzing poetry are; they can be taught narrative modes and lyric genres, the tropes and rhetorical figures to be found in any written text, the possibilities for rhythm and meter, "poetry" and "prose." In musicology and art history, such study is taken for granted: no one who cannot read a score or know the parts of the orchestra is likely to make pronouncements about a particular symphony But in poetics, we tend to assume that there is no vocabulary to master, that anyone can—and does—*read*.

The first step, then, would be to teach the student that *reading*, whether of a legal brief or the newspaper or even of an Internet ad, takes training. And that the methods learned, applied to one's own literature for starters and then to the really exciting literature of the past—allowing that past to be flexible, not confined to a narrow canon—will make the student see how language works in a given poem or play or novel. For language, which is, after all, the *material* of literature, as well as the means to its *fictiveness*, will be the central object of study—a study that involves all four of the paradigms outlined above. Such study, I believe, will come back into favor for the simple reason that, try as one may, one cannot eliminate the sheer *jouissance* or pleasure of the text. Thus, just at the moment when the common wisdom was that Marcel Proust was passé, what with his *longueurs*, his irritating snobbery and elitism, two new monumental biographies (by Jean-Yves Tadié [1996] and William C. Carter [2000]) appeared. Proust study groups sprang up in various cities. Newspapers talked of a Proust "revival," but of course it is more properly a Proust "survival." Proust won't go away because *À la recherche du temps perdu* is an encyclopedia of narrative forms, of complex language constructions, of historical and cultural ironies, as well as a psychological analysis of love and jealousy incomparable in its richness and passion. There may be little blips on the Proust radar screen—now he is up, now down—but the oeuvre is *there*, continuing to challenge and fascinate readers.

In chapter 4 of the *Poetics*, Aristotle discusses aesthetic pleasure, specifically the two pleasures he takes to be associated with artworks in whatever medium—the "pleasure of representation" and the "pleasure of recognition":

> Speaking generally, poetry seems to owe its origin to two particular causes, both natural. From childhood men have an instinct for representation, and in this respect man differs from the other animals in that he is far more imitative and learns his first lessons by representing things. And then there is the enjoyment people always get from representations.
>
> (no. 1448b).

The pleasure of representation is the basic human instinct one can observe most directly in young children who "play" at being someone else, who make up a story and pass it off as "true." It is the pleasure of invention, of fictiveness. The twin pleasure, that of recognition, is its mirror image, the pleasure of taking in the impersonations, fictions, and language creations of others and recognizing their justice. When, for example, Prufrock concludes his "love song" with the line, "Till human voices wake us and we drown," the most un-Prufrockian of us will recognize the aptness of the metaphor.

Pleasure was paramount for Aristotle as it was for the Plato who banished the poets from the Republic because their work produced too much pleasure and passion in its audience. But of course the pleasure calculus is complex: "one should not seek," we read in *Poetics* XIV, "from tragedy all kinds of pleasure but that which is peculiar to tragedy, and since the poet must by 'representation' produce the pleasure which comes from feeling pity and fear, obviously this quality must be embodied in the incidents" (no. 1453b). *Catharsis*, the purgation of pity and fear, is not an end in itself; it is a particular kind of poetic pleasure. And so on.

It is, I would argue, the contemporary fear of the pleasures of representation and recognition—the pleasures of the *fictive*, the *what might happen*—and its subordination to the *what has happened*—the *historical/cultural*—that has trivialized the status of literary study in the contemporary academy and shrunk the corresponding departments. Indeed, the neo-Puritan notion that literature and the other arts must be somehow "useful," and only useful, that the Ciceronian triad—*docere, movere, delectare*—should renounce its third element ("delight") and even the original meaning of its second element, so that *to move* means only to move readers to some kind of specific action, has produced a climate in which it has become increasingly difficult to justify the study of English or comparative literature at all.

Given this climate, we are now witnessing a deep pessimism, expressed in various jeremiads as to the death of humanistic studies in our time. In a recent essay, "The Humanities—at Twilight?", George Steiner argues that in contemporary technocratic mass culture, there may, alas, be no room at all for the humanities:

> Democracy and economic-distributive justice on a democratic plane are no friend to the autistic, often arcane, always demanding enterprise of "high culture." . . . Add to this the failures, the collaborative treasons of the clerics, of the arts, of the humanities in the fullest sense, during the long night of this century in Europe and Russia. Add to this the fundamental doubt . . . as to whether the humanities humanize, and the thrust of the crisis is inescapable.[20]

Interestingly, Steiner's elegiac essay never refers to a single work of art written since World War II: Adorno's adage that there can be no poetry after Auschwitz seems to be taken as a given. Again, Steiner seems to be wholly unaware of the digital media and their particular kinds of cultural production and dissemination of literature. This *retro Kulturdrang* strikes me as just as problematic as Weisbuch's "how-to" practicalities. For one cannot kill the basic human instinct to make poetry—the German verb *Dichten* is apposite here—and to enjoy the poetry making of others: indeed, the study of poetry has been with us much longer than any of the academic orthodoxies or philistine practices Steiner deplores. Some things, it seems, never quite vanish.

### NOTES

1. Robert Weisbuch, "Six Proposals to Revive the Humanities," *Chronicle of Higher Education*, 26 March 1999, B4–5.

2. See Randal Johnson, introduction to *The Field of Cultural Production: Essays on Art and Literature*, by Pierre Bourdieu, ed. Randal Johnson (New York: Columbia University Press, 1993), 7.

3. Cited by Patrick Healy, "Today's News," *Chronicle of Higher Education*, 20 September 1999. Internet version at http://chronicle.com.

4. According to the *OED*, literature (from the Latin *littera* or letter of the alphabet) as "Literary work or production; the activity or profession of a man of letters; the realm of letters," was first used by Samuel Johnson in the *Life of Cowley* (1779): "An Author whose pregnancy of imagination and elegance of language have deservedly set him high in the ranks of literature." The more restricted sense of literature, as a "writing that has claim to consideration on the ground of beauty of form or emotional effect," does not appear until 1812. *Literature*, in the sense of "the body of books and writings that treat a particular subject," is first found in 1860.

5. Aristotle, *On Rhetoric: A Theory of Civic Discourse*, trans. George A. Kennedy (New York and Oxford: Oxford University Press, 1991); Cicero, *Brutus*, trans. G. L. Hendrickson (Cambridge, Mass.: Loeb Classical Library, 1952); Quintilian, *Institutio Oratoria*, 4 vols., trans. H. E. Butler (Cambridge: Loeb Classical Library, 1921–1922).

6. Groupe Mu, *Rhétorique générale* (Paris: Larousse, 1970).

7. Michel Meyer, *Questions de rhétorique: Langage, raison et séduction* (Paris, 1993); Nancy S. Struever, "Rhetoric: Historical and Conceptual Overview," *Encyclopedia of Aesthetics*, 4 vols., ed. Michael Kelly, vol. 4 (New York: Oxford University Press, 1998), 151–55, esp. 155.

8. Stephen Halliwell, *Aristotle's Poetics*, 2nd edition (Chicago: University of Chicago Press, 1998), 44.

9. Roman Jakobson, "Marginal Notes on the Prose of the Poet Pasternak" (1935), in *Language in Literature*, ed. Krystyna Pomorska and Stephen Rudy (Cambridge. Mass.: Harvard University, Belknap Press, 1987), 301–17.

10. Stanley Fish, "How Ordinary is Ordinary Language?" *New Literary History*, special issue: "What is Literature?" 5, no. 1 (1973): 41–54; reprint, in Fish, *Is There a Text in This Class? The Authority of Interpretive Communities* (Cambridge, Mass.: Harvard University Press, 1980), 97–111. I discuss the problems of this essay in *Wittgenstein's Ladder: Poetic Language and the Strangeness of the Ordinary* (Chicago: University of Chicago Press, 1996), 54–57, 88–89.

11. Ludwig Wittgenstein, *Zettel*, ed. G. E. M. Anscombe and G. H. von Wright, trans. G. E. M. Anscombe (Berkeley: University of California Press, 1967), 28, no. 160.

12. Aristotle, *Poetics*, trans. W. Hamilton Fyfe (Cambridge, Mass.: Harvard University Press, 1960), 36–37. I have translated the word *philosophoteron* as "philosophical" rather than "scientific," which is misleading. Otherwise, I stick to the Fyfe translation, designating the traditional numbers for paragraphs.

13. Plato, *Republic*, in *The Collected Dialogues of Plato*, ed. Edith Hamilton and Huntington Cairns, trans. Lane Cooper et al., corrected edition (Princeton, N.J.: Princeton University Press, 1963), no. 387b, my emphasis. I give the standard paragraph number rather than page since there are so many translations and editions of *Republic*.

14. Hayden White, *Metahistory: The Historical Imagination in Nineteenth-Century Europe* (Baltimore: Johns Hopkins University Press, 1973).

15. Rossetti's work, both verbal and visual, is the subject of Jerome J. McGann's astonishingly comprehensive, beautifully produced, and learned *Rossetti Archive* at http://www.iath.virginia.edu/rossetti/.

16. See http://www.futurism.org.uk; http://www.toutfait.com; http://www.ubu.com.

17. See Peter Bürger, *Theory of the Avant-Garde*, foreword by Jochen Schulte-Sasse, trans. Michael Shaw (Minneapolis: University of Minnesota Press, 1984), esp. chapter 3.

18. See Theodor W. Adorno, "On Lyric Poetry and Society," *Notes to Literature*, vol. 1, ed. Rolf Tiedemann, trans. Shierry Weber Nicholsen (New York: Columbia University Press, 1991), 37–54, esp. p. 45.

19. Adorno, "Heine the Wound," *Notes to Literature*, vol. 1, 80–85; esp. 82.

20. George Steiner, "The Humanities—At Twilight?" *PN Review* 25, no. 4 (March–April 1999): 23. The essay (18–24) was originally presented as a lecture at Boston University on 2 April 1998.

# CODA

# INTRODUCTION

THROUGHOUT A LONG AND PRODUCTIVE career Wayne C. Booth has been the main voice of "ethical criticism," and his more recent books have developed a thoughtful approach to criticism that does not disdain humane values in reading. In the "Oath" reproduced here, first published in 1979 as an appendix to his book *Critical Understanding*, Booth offered a summary of his reflections in the form of a clairvoyant call for plurality and integrity in literary scholarship and interpretation.[1]

As our anthology draws to an end, we have chosen to open our book to the future—mindful of our own difficulty in approaching the high standard set by Booth—by recovering his call for integrity and honesty in theoretical and critical undertakings. The spread of Theory has made this call more necessary now than when it was written. That is probably why, in April 2003, on the occasion of a University of Chicago symposium on the future of criticism, Booth was moved to reiterate some of his lifelong principles and to remind his fellow scholars how much we need to insist on clear language, coherence, critical revelation, attention to close reading, a spirit of genuine inquiry, and respect for creative achievement.[2]

### NOTES

1. Wayne C. Booth, *Critical Understanding: The Powers and Limits of Pluralism* (Chicago: University of Chicago Press, 1979).

2. See Wayne Booth, "To: All Who Care about the Future of Criticism," *Critical Inquiry* 30, no. 2 (Winter 2004): 350–54.

## 47. A HIPPOCRATIC OATH FOR THE PLURALIST
### WAYNE C. BOOTH

I. I WILL PUBLISH NOTHING, favorable or unfavorable, about books or articles I have not read through at least once. (By "publish" I mean any writing or speaking that "makes public," including term papers, theses, course lectures, and conferences papers.)

The world is not at the moment in need of more words from me simply because they are mine, regardless of the subject and regardless of how little I know about it. To publish my opinion on Foucault—a rather strong one, as it happens—will help no one, not even myself, since I have not yet read more than about two dozen pages by Foucault.

[With one stroke, this self-denying ordinance wipes out at least a fourth of all published criticism. Perhaps a half. In any case, the worst part, however large or small. I can think of a score of comments on my own work that are here flushed down and out; those of you who have been publicly discussed, whether in seminars or in print, can think of others.]

II. I will *try* to publish nothing about any book or article until I have *understood* it, which is to say, until I have reason to think that I can give an account of it that the author himself will recognize as just. Any attempt at overstanding[1] will follow this initial act of attempted respect.

Many of us have learned, from various earlier new criticisms, to treat each poem with something like the attention its author hoped for. The arts of interpreting critical works, good and bad, are as difficult, manifold, and rewarding as the arts of what we call literary interpretation. Just as I must earn my right to criticize a poem by dwelling with it until I can find my dwelling *in* it, I earn my right to criticize criticism in the same way. Paraphrasing Coleridge: Before I damn a critic's errors, I will try to reconstruct his enterprise as if it were my own.

[With this ordinance, we wipe out, at a low guess, another fourth of what is published.]

III. I will take no critic's word, when he discusses other critics, unless he can convince me that he has abided by the first two ordinances. I will assume, until a critic proves otherwise, that what he says *against* the playing style of other critics is useful, at best, as a clue to his own game. I will be almost as suspicious when he presents a "neutral" summary and even when he praises.

Wayne C. Booth. "A Hippocratic Oath for the Pluralist." Reprinted from *Critical Understanding: The Powers and Limits of Pluralism*, by Wayne C. Booth. Chicago: University of Chicago Press, 1979. Copyright © University of Chicago Press.

"If we take in our hand any discussion by one critic of another, let us ask, *does it reveal any concrete reconstruction of the rival's enterprise? No. Does it reveal any proof that the rival's defeat (whether with open attack or 'friendly' reduction) is necessary to establish the new enterprise?* No. Commit it then to the flames: for it can contain nothing but sophistry and illusion."[2]

IV. I will not undertake any project that by its very nature requires me to violate Ordinances I–III.

### Corrolaries

a) I will not write any history of criticism, or analysis of the types of criticism, unless driven to it by thirteen demons and unless I decide to spend the lifetime required to do the job decently.

b) I will not write any history or analysis of general terms, like romanticism, pastoral, comedy, irony, rhetoric, understanding, or pluralism, unless driven by the same demons and unless I am willing to spend the years required. I will remember that if it took M. H. Abrams twenty years to write *Natural Supernaturalism*, a history of one poem by Wordsworth, it ought to take me at least as long to perform tasks no less complex.

[With this stroke, we eliminate at least half of the works remaining. It is in fact only by the most marvelous stroke of Providence that we do not wipe out *Critical Understanding*.

V. I will not judge my own inevitable violations of the first four ordinances more leniently than those I find in other critics.

Using these five simple ordinances, we could quickly reconstruct our experience of criticism: we would write and read only about one-fourth as many critical words; we would experience a renewed sense that our critical sanity does not depend on "covering" as many works as possible; and we would find leisure to enter full-heartedly into those that met or expanded our interest and heightened pleasure and profit from what we did read.

We could achieve all this, as a profession. But I will not allow my own practice to depend on the remote hope that we will.

### NOTES

1. Editors' note: As discussed in earlier chapters of *Critical Understanding*, "overstanding" refers to critics' sense of their own superior "understanding," which each then attempts to impose on others' texts. Although both understanding and overstanding are necessary, the former must precede the latter.

2. David Hume, *An Enquiry Concerning Human Understanding*, concluding paragraph.

DAPHNE PATAI was born in Jerusalem and emigrated to the United States as a child. She is professor of Brazilian literature at the University of Massachusetts Amherst, where she also teaches literary theory and utopian fiction. A recipient of fellowships from the National Endowment for the Humanities, the Guggenheim Foundation, and the National Humanities Center, she has written, among other books, *Professing Feminism: Education and Indoctrination in Women's Studies* (coauthored with Noretta Koertge; new, enlarged edition, 2003) and *Heterophobia: Sexual Harassment and the Future of Feminism* (1998). Her book *"What Price Utopia?" and Other Essays by a Recovering Feminist* is forthcoming with Rowman and Littlefield.

WILL H. CORRAL is a Latin Americanist who currently teaches at California State Univerity, Sacramento. He is the author of two books, the most recent of which is *El Error del acierto* (2005) and editor or coeditor of six others in his field. Born and bred in Ecuador, he received his Ph.D. from Columbia and has taught at the University of Massachusetts Amherst and Stanford University. He is the recipient of senior and distinguished Fulbright fellowships and a NEH fellowship. He is a regular contributor to cultural and academic journals in Spain and the Americas.

M. H. ABRAMS, Class of 1916 Professor of English at Cornell, emeritus, is the author of, among other books, *The Mirror and the Lamp: Romantic Theory and the Critical Tradition*; *Natural Supernaturalism: Tradition and Revolution in Romantic Literature*; *Doing Things with Texts: Essays in Criticism and Critical Theory*; and *The Correspondent Breeze: Essays on English Romanticism*. He is also general editor and an editor of the romantic period in *The Norton Anthology of English Literature*.

KWAME ANTHONY APPIAH teaches at Princeton, where he is a member of the philosophy department and the University Center for Human Values. In 2003, he published an introduction to philosophy entitled *Thinking It Through*; in 2005, he published *The Ethics of Identity*. His current work focuses on normative questions raised by relations between people across national borders.

MARK BAUERLEIN is professor of English at Emory University and director of research at the National Endowment for the Arts. His books include *Literary Criticism: An Autopsy* (1997) and *Negrophobia: A Race Riot in Atlanta* (2001). His essays and reviews have appeared in *Wall Street Journal*, *Yale Review*, *Partisan Review*, *The Weekly Standard*, *TLS*, and *Chronicle of Higher Education*.

PAUL BOGHOSSIAN is professor of philosophy and chair of the department at New York University. His research interests are in the philosophy of mind, the philosophy of language, and epistemology. He has published articles on topics including color, rule following, eliminativism, naturalism, self-knowledge, a priori knowledge, analytic truth, realism, and the aesthetics of music. He is currently at work on a book on the notion of objectivity.

WAYNE C. BOOTH is Distinguished Service Professor of English Emeritus at the University of Chicago. He is the author of numerous books on literary criticism, *The Rhetoric of Fiction* (1961, rev. 1983), *Modern Dogma and the Rhetoric of Assent* (1974), and *The Company We Keep: An Ethics of Fiction* (1988) among them. His most recent book is *The Rhetoric of Rhetoric* (2004).

JEAN BRICMONT is professor of theoretical physics at the University of Louvain (Belgium) and coauthor, with Alan Sokal, of *Fashionable Nonsense: Postmodern Intellectuals' Abuse of Science* (Picador USA, 1998).

DAVID BROMWICH is Housum Professor of English at Yale University and the author of *Hazlitt: The Mind of a Critic* and *Skeptical Music: Essays on Modern Poetry*. He has edited *On Empire, Liberty, and Reform: Speeches and Letters of Edmund Burke*.

NOAM CHOMSKY is an Institute Professor at MIT and the author of many books and articles on linguistics, philosophy, intellectual history, international affairs, and social and political issues.

FREDERICK CREWS is emeritus professor of English at the University of California, Berkeley. In addition to his satires on literary criticism, *The Pooh Perplex* and *Postmodern Pooh*, his books include several works bearing directly on theory: *Skeptical Engagements*; *The Critics Bear It Away: American Fiction and the Academy*; *The Memory Wars*; and (as editor) *Unauthorized Freud: Doubters Confront a Legend*.

VALENTINE CUNNINGHAM is professor of English language and literature at Oxford University. His publications include *Reading After Theory* (2002); *In the Reading Gaol: Postmodernity, Texts, and History* (1993); *British Writers of the Thirties* (1988); and *Everywhere Spoken Against: Dissent in the Victorian Novel* (1975).

VINCENT DESCOMBES is directeur d'études at l'Ecole des Hautes Études en Sciences Sociales (Paris). He is the author of *Modern French Philosphy* (1980); *Proust : Philosophy of the Novel* (1992); *The Barometer of Modern Reason* (1992); *The Mind's Provisions* (2001); and most recently *Le Complément de sujet* (2004).

MORRIS DICKSTEIN is Distinguished Professor of English at the Graduate Center of the City University of New York. He is a senior fellow of the Center for the Humanities, which he founded in 1993. His books include a study of the 1960s, *Gates of Eden* (1977); *Double Agent: The Critic and Society* (1992); and *Leopards in the Temple* (Harvard, 2002), a widely reviewed social history of postwar American fiction. His latest book is *The Mirror in the Roadway: Literature and the Real World* (Princeton, 2005).

DENIS DONOGHUE is University Professor and Henry James Chair of English and American Letters at New York University. He is the author or editor of numerous books in Anglo-American literatures, theory, and aesthetics, the most recent of which is *Speaking of Beauty* (2003).

WILLIAM DOWLING is University Distinguished Professor of English and American Literature at Rutgers University. He is author, most recently, of *The Senses of the Text: Intensional Semantics and Literary Theory* (1999). He is currently writing *Ricoeur on Time and Narrative: An Introduction to* Temps et Récit.

NANCY EASTERLIN, a professor of English at the University of New Orleans specializing in British romanticism and literary theory, is the author of *Wordsworth and the Question of Romantic Religion* as well as numerous essays on evolutionary and cognitive approaches to literature. She is coeditor of *After Poststructuralism: Interdisciplinarity and Literary Theory* and a member of the editorial board of *Philosophy and Literature*.

JOHN ELLIS is professor emeritus of German literature at the University of California, Santa Cruz. His books include studies of Kleist, Schiller, the brothers Grimm, and the German *Novelle* as well as *The Theory of Literary Criticism* (1974), *Against Deconstruction* (1989), *Language, Thought, and Logic* (1993), and *Literature Lost* (1998). He cofounded the Association of Literary Scholars and Critics.

RICHARD FREADMAN is professor of English and director of the Unit for Studies in Biography and Autobiography at La Trobe University. His principal research areas have been the English and American novel, literary theory, ethics, and life-writing. His most recent books are *Threads of Life: Autobiography and the Will* (Chicago, 2001), and a memoir, *Shadow of Doubt: My Father and Myself* (Bystander, 2003).

HAROLD FROMM is a visiting scholar in English at the University of Arizona, coeditor of *The Ecocriticism Reader: Landmarks in Literary Ecology*, and a regular contributor to *The Hudson Review*. He is currently writing on subjects involving Darwin and evolutionary psychology.

TODD GITLIN is a professor of journalism and sociology at Columbia University and the author of ten books, including *The Sixties: Years of Hope, Days of Rage*; *Media Unlimited: How the Torrent of Images and Sounds Overwhelms*

*Our Lives; The Whole World is Watching: Mass Media in the Making and Unmaking of the New Left;* and the award-winning novel *Sacrifice.*

GRAHAM GOOD teaches English and comparative literature at the University of British Columbia in Vancouver. His most recent book is *Humanism Betrayed: Theory, Ideology, and Culture in the Contemporary University* (McGill Queens University Press, 2001).

EUGENE GOODHEART is Edytha Macy Gross Professor of Humanites Emeritus at Brandeis University. He is the author of eleven books, among them *The Skeptic Disposition: Deconstruction, Ideology and Oher Matters; The Reign of Ideology;* and a memoir, *Confessions of a Secular Jew.* He has also contributed to numerous periodicals, including *Partisan Review, Sewanee Review,* and *New Literary History.*

SUSAN HAACK is Cooper Senior Scholar in Arts and Sciences, professor of philosophy, and professor of law at the University of Miami. Her books include *Evidence and Inquiry* (1993); *Philosophy of Logics* (1978); *Deviant Logic, Fuzzy Logic* (1996); *Manifesto of a Passionate Moderate* (1998); and *Defending Science—Within Reason: Between Scientism and Cynicism* (2003).

GEOFFREY GALT HARPHAM is president and director of the National Humanities Center in Research Triangle Park, N.C. He is the author of, most recently, *Language Alone: The Critical Fetish of Modernity* and *Shadows of Ethics: Criticism and the Just Society.*

WENDELL V. HARRIS began teaching at the University of Colorado in 1961, moved to Northern Illinois University as professor of English and associate provost in 1971, moved in 1979 to Pennsylvania State University as department head for six years, and retired from PSU in 1997. His books include *Interpretive Acts: In Search of Meaning; Dictionary of Concepts in Literary Criticism and Theory;* and *Literary Meaning: Reclaiming the Study of Literature.*

RUSSELL JACOBY is the author of *Social Amnesia, The Last Intellectuals, The End of Utopia,* and other books. His new book, *Thou Shalt Make No Graven Image,* is forthcoming from Columbia University Press. He teaches at UCLA.

NIILO KAUPPI is senior research fellow at the Academy of Finland. His publications include *The Making of an Avant-Garde:* Tel Quel (1994); *French Intellectual Nobility: Institutional and Symbolic Transformations in the Post-Sartrian Era* (1996); *The Politics of Embodiment: Habits, Power, and Pierre Bourdieu's Theory* (2000); and *The Battle for Europe: Social Resources and Political Power in the Construction of a Polity* (forthcoming, 2004).

FRANK KERMODE was formerly King Edward VII Professor of English Literature at Cambridge University.

PETER LAMARQUE is professor of philosophy and head of the department at the University of York, U.K. He has published widely on fictionality, the philosophy of literature, and aesthetics, including *Truth, Fiction, and Literature* (with S. H. Olsen) and *Fictional Points of View*. He edits the *British Journal of Aesthetics* and has also edited *Philosophy and Fiction: Essays in Literary Aesthetics*; *A Concise Encyclopedia of Philosophy of Language*; and (with S. H. Olsen) *Aesthetics and the Philosophy of Art: The Analytic Tradition: An Anthology*.

RICHARD LEVIN is professor emeritus of English at the State University of New York at Stony Brook. He is the author of *The Multiple Plot in English Renaissance Drama*; *New Readings vs. Old Plays: Recent Trends in the Reinterpretation of English Renaissance Drama*; and a collection of his recent essays, *Looking for an Argument: Critical Encounters with the New Approaches to the Criticism of Shakespeare and His Contemporaries*.

PAISLEY LIVINGSTON is professor of philosophy at Lingnan University in Hong Kong and senior lecturer in philosophy at the University of Copenhagen. He has published on various topics in aesthetics, cinema, and literary studies. His most recent book is *Art and Intention* (Oxford University Press, 2005).

ELAINE MARKS (1930–2001) was Germaine Brée Professor of French at the University of Wisconsin, Madison, until her retirement in 2000. She was the first chair of Wisconsin's Women's Studies Research Center and also chair of the Women's Studies Program. The recipient of numerous academic honors and awards, including France's Palmes académiques, she was coeditor of the acclaimed *New French Feminisms* (with Isabelle de Courtivron) and *Homosexualities and French Literature* (with George Stambolian). She also wrote books on Colette, Simone de Beauvoir, and French poetry and fiction. Marks's last book, *Marrano as Metaphor: The Jewish Presence in French Writing* (1996), was published by Columbia University Press.

J. G. MERQUIOR (1941–1991) was a Brazilian sociologist, philosopher, literary and cultural critic, diplomat, and an early respondent to contemporary theory. His books include *Rousseau and Weber*, *L'Esthétique de Lévi-Strauss*, *Foucault*, *Western Marxism*, and many others published in Portuguese, English, French, and Spanish. A selection of his essays was published in Portuguese as *Crítica 1964–1989: Ensaios sobre arte e literatura* (1990).

SEUMAS MILLER is professor of philosophy at Charles Sturt University and Australian National University (a joint position) and director of the Centre for Applied Philosophy and Public Ethics. His publications include *Rethinking Theory* (Cambridge, 1992), with Richard Freadman; *Social Action* (Cambridge, 2001); and *Corruption and Anti-Corruption* (Prentice Hall, 2004), with Peter Roberts and Ed Spence.

D. G. MYERS is the author of *The Elephants Teach: Creative Writing Since 1880* (Prentice Hall, 1996) and coeditor of *Unrelenting Readers: The New Poet-Critics* (Story Line, 2004). His essays and criticism have appeared in the *Weekly Standard*, *Commentary*, *American Literary History*, *Comparative Literature*, *Holocaust Literature: An Encyclopedia of Writers and Their Work*, and elsewhere.

MEERA NANDA is the author of *Prophets Facing Backward: Postmodern Critiques of Science and Hindu Nationalism in India* (Rutgers University Press, 2003). She is the recipient of a research grant from the Templeton Foundation and is working on a new book provisionally titled *The Science Question in Hinduism: "Holistic Science" in the Service of Hindu Nationalism*.

THOMAS NAGEL is the author of numerous books on philosophy. His most recent book is the collection *Concealment and Exposure, and Other Essays* (2002), which followed from *Other Minds: Critical Essays, 1969–1994* (1995).

ERIN O'CONNOR teaches, lives, and writes at a boarding school in Massachusetts. She is the author of *Raw Material: Producing Pathology in Victorian Culture* (Duke, 2000) and Critical Mass (www.erinoconnor.org), a Web site dedicated to issues in higher education.

STEIN HAUGOM OLSEN is (since 1997) Chair Professor of Philosophy and head of the Department of Philosophy at Lingnan University, Hong Kong. He previously (1985–97) held the chair of British civilization studies at the University of Oslo. He is an elected fellow of the Norwegian Academy of Science and Letters.

CLARA CLAIBORNE PARK retired from teaching English at Williams College. She continues publishing critical essays, some of which appeared in her 1992 collection *Rejoining the Common Reader*. She is also the author of *The Siege* and *Exiting Nirvana*, in-depth studies combining memoir and case history as she examines the development of her autistic daughter from babyhood to middle age.

MARJORIE PERLOFF is the author of many books, including *The Poetics of Indeterminacy*, *Wittgenstein's Ladder*, and, most recently, a memoir, *The Vienna Paradox* (New Directions, 2004) and a collection of essays entitled *Differentials: Poetry, Poetics, Pedagogy* (University of Alabama Press, 2004). She is Sadie D. Patek Professor Emerita of Humanities at Stanford University and currently scholar-in-residence at the University of Southern California.

STEPHEN ADAM SCHWARTZ teaches in the Department of French at University College Dublin. He is currently working on a book entitled *Post-Radical Thought: Philosophy in France Since 1980*.

JOHN R. SEARLE is Mills Professor of Philosophy in Berkeley. He is the author of fifteen books, and his work has been translated into twenty-one languages. He works in the philosophy of language, mind, and society. Recent books include *Consciousness and Language* and *Rationality in Action*.

LEE SIEGEL is a journalist and frequent contributor to *The New Republic* and other cultural journals.

ALAN SOKAL is a professor of physics at New York University. His main research interests are in statistical mechanics and quantum field theory. He is coauthor, with Roberto Fernández and Jürg Fröhlich, of *Random Walks, Critical Phenomena, and Triviality in Quantum Field Theory* (Springer, 1992) and coauthor with Jean Bricmont of *Fashionable Nonsense: Postmodern Intellectuals' Abuse of Science* (Picador USA, 1998).

ALAN SPITZER is professor emeritus of history at the University of Iowa. His publications on French history include *The Revolutionary Theories of Louis-Auguste Blanqui* (1957); *Old Hatreds and Young Hopes: The French Carbonari Against the Bourbon Restoration* (1971); and *The French Generation of 1820* (1987).

RAYMOND TALLIS is professor of geriatric medicine at the University of Manchester and a consultant physician in health care of the elderly at Hope Hospital, Salford. He has published extensively on stroke and epilepsy and was elected fellow of the Academy of Medical Sciences in 2000. He has been awarded honorary degrees as a doctor of letters at the Universities of Hull and Manchester for his contributions to the philosophy of mind and critiques of literary and cultural theory.

TZVETAN TODOROV is directeur de recherches at the Centre National de la Recherche Scientifique in Paris. Recent translations of his books in English include *Imperfect Garden: The Legacy of Humanism* and *Hope and Memory: Lessons from the Twentieth Century*, both with Princeton University Press.

BRIAN VICKERS is distinguished senior fellow at the School of Advanced Study, London University. He has recently published *'Counterfeiting' Shakespeare: Evidence, Authorship, and John Ford's Funerall Elegye* (Cambridge University Press, 2002) and *Shakespeare, Co-Author: A Historical Study of Five Collaborative Plays* (Oxford University Press, 2002), and is general editor of *The Collected Works of John Ford*, in preparation.

JEFFREY WALLEN is professor of comparative literature at Hampshire College and author of *Closed Encounters: Literary Politics and Public Culture*. He has also published widely on nineteenth-century literature and is completing a book on modes of influence in nineteenth-century culture. He was recently a visiting professor at the Free University in Berlin and also at the University of Toulouse.

RENÉ WELLEK (1903–1995) was a member of the Prague Linguistic Circle in the 1930s before moving to London and then to the United States, where he taught for many years at Yale University. He was one of the founders of the study of literary theory and of the field of comparative literature. Coauthor, with Austin Warren, of the seminal *Theory of Literature* (1949), he is also the author of (among many other books) the eight-volume *History of Modern Criticism: 1750–1950* (1950–93); *Four Critics: Croce, Valéry, Lukács, and Ingarden* (1981); and *The Attack on Literature and Other Essays* (1982).

Abbott, Porter, 678

Abrams, M. H., 4, 124–25, 325, 596, 689

absence: of author, 130, 328–29; of self, 134–38; of speaker, 131–33

academe, 8, 11; convergence with avant-garde, 601; effect of science on, 218–19; identity politics in, 401–3; ideological commitment and, 228–29; interpretive frameworks and, 476–77; junior faculty, 349–50, 381–82; link with outside world, 610–11; love of literature as unnecessary, 61–62; revolutionary academic, 454–57; star system, 21, 315, 317, 381–82, 385–87, 393; as surrogate world, 404–5; theoretical boldness, 235–38. *See also* professionalization; tenure system

*Academic Capitalism and Literary Value* (Fromm), 451, 454

academic moralism, 441–43; excesses of, 446–47; feminist criticism and, 444–48

Académie Française, 319–20

actor-action-object frame, 629

Adams, Hazard, 2, 6

Adams, Robert Martin, 392

addressee, 179, 196

addressor, 179

*ad hominem* arguments, 263, 265, 272

Adorno, Theodor, 499, 599, 679, 682

aesthetic criticism, 453; cultural distinctions and, 518–19; sublime, 512–13, 514; transparency and, 511–12

aesthetic experience, 652, 660–61

aestheticism: of Nietzsche, 243–44; of thick description, 493, 495–96

aestheticization of knowledge, 241–43

aesthetic qualities, 652–53, 660, 661

aesthetics, 65, 374, 393, 516, 588; critical inquiry and, 660–65; critics and, 43–44; hierarchies of, 653–55; moral factors, 661–62; senses of, 651, 652–53

*Aesthetics and Ideology* (Levine), 514–15

"Aesthetics and Ideology—What Happened to Poetics?" (Brooks), 515–16

*Aesthetics* (Beardsley), 637

aesthetic value, 653, 660, 661–62

aesthetocentric thought, 244–45

affect, 387–88, 438

"Affective Fallacy, The" (Wimsatt and Beardsley), 100

African Americans: criticism and, 442–47; identity politics and, 408–9; women writers, 422–24

Africans, 409, 411n13

*After the New Criticism* (Lentricchia), 238

*After Theory* (Docherty), 613–14

*Against Method* (Feyerabend), 547

"Against Theory" (Knapp and Michaels), 158–59, 164

agency, properties of, 88–89

ahistoricity, 254, 255

allegories, 298, 308

all-or-nothing thinking, 593, 594–95

Alter, Robert, 422

Althusser, Louis, 37, 198n12, 219–21, 250, 252, 341n26, 597–98; dogmatism of, 225–26

ambiguity, 325–26, 596

American criticism, 52–53, 123, 238; antihumanism and, 57–58; ineffectiveness of, 63–64; Marxism and, 57. *See also* New Criticism

Americans, identity politics and, 400–401, 408–9

analogies, 30–31, 206–7

anal strategy, 431–32

analysis of language, 180–81

analytical mode, 93, 104

analytic philosophy, 123, 147, 166

*Anatomy of Criticism* (Frye), 48, 100, 512

Anderson, Amanda, 309

Anderson, Benedict, 494

Anderson, Perry, 249, 254

Anglocentrism, 292

*Annales* school, 43, 220

anthropological turn, 38

anthropology, 495; social, 254–55; structural, 30, 332; thick description, 491–94

antiempiricism, 221–25

antiexperiential school, 232n19

anti-foundationalism, 38, 102
antihumanism, 22, 597–98; American criticism dominated by, 57–58; constructivist, 23, 78–79
anti-objectivist arguments, 508–9
antipositivism, 222–24
antiquity, revivals of, 605–6
antitheoretical reaction, 388–89
anti-Westernism, 102, 103
*Anxiety of Influence, The* (Bloom), 49
aporia, 29–30, 207–8, 238
Appiah, K. Anthony, 399, 564
*Appropriating Shakespeare* (Vickers), 216, 247, 254
apriorism, 215, 221, 229, 250, 254
arbitrariness, 127–28, 141, 185, 367; of sign, 29, 384–85
argot, 321
Argyros, Alexander, 623
Aristotle, 671, 680; *Poetics*, 631, 674–75, 681
Arnold, Matthew, 36, 237, 357, 443, 509, 518
Aron, Raymond, 56
Aronowitz, Stanley, 541
art, left and right positions, 599
art criticism, 653–55
arthood, 374
articulation, politics of, 373
artistic qualities, 664. *See also* aesthetics
arts, relationship among, 42
Asian Americans, 407, 409
assertive mode, 93
associationism, 145n23
Association of Literary Scholars and Critics, 421–22
Atwood, Margaret, 9
audiovisual culture, 334
Augustine, 55
Austen, Jane: *Mansfield Park*, 304, 452, 483–89, 490n4; *Sense and Sensibility*, 436
Austin, J. L., 166, 173, 196
author, 74, 192; absence of, 130, 328–29; defacement and, 596–97; denial of originality of, 130–31; as moral agent, 89–90; as voice within text, 413–14. *See also* death of author
Author-God, 130–31, 318–19; as French, 319–20, 323

authorial intention, 83–84, 97–99, 147, 192, 461; fiction and, 174–75n17; hermeneutics and, 194; illocutionary, 160–61; meaning of text and, 163–65. *See also* intentionality
autonomous self, 295
autonomy, literary, 413–14, 418
autonomy of grammar, 179
avant-garde, 66–67, 333, 601, 679
Avery, Oswald, 554
Ayer, A. J., 103
Azim, Firdous, 304

Background, 149–52, 163, 166, 174n6; intentionality and, 149–50, 167–68
Bacon, Francis, 247–48, 253, 561
Bad Theory, 23, 92, 104
Bad Writing, 316–17, 354–59; political agenda, 355, 357–58
Bad Writing Contest, 354–56, 358–59
Bakhtin, Mikhail, 31
Bali, 493–95
Balzac, Honoré de, 71–74
Barker, Francis, 459, 466
Barnes, Barry, 220, 571
Barrès, Maurice, 502
Barthes, Roland, 22, 30, 38, 238; Anglo-American interest in, 324–27; death of author and, 318–19, 330; on death of positivism, 251, 252; denial of author, 130–31, 315–16; historical context and, 319–22; as radical, 327–28; *Works:* "Authors and Writers," 320; "Nouvelle Critique," 320, 326; *Le Plaisir du texte* (*The Pleasure of the Text*), 74, 322–24, 328; *On Racine*, 320, 323; *Roland Barthes by Roland Barthes*, 328; *Système de la mode*, 333; *S/Z*, 65, 71–74, 322, 328; *Writing Degree Zero*, 512
Barzun, Jacques, 16–17n16, 560
Bate, W. J., 49
Baudelaire, Charles, 659
Baudrillard, Jean, 543
Bauerlein, Mark, 10, 316
Baym, Nina, 416–17
*béances*, 30, 37
Beardsley, Monroe C., 97–98, 100, 398, 411, 637, 648, 654; *Aesthetics*, 637. *See also* "Intentional Fallacy, The"; *Verbal Icon, The*
Beauvoir, Simone de, 564

Beckett, Samuel, 86, 87, 677–78
*Bedeutung*, 182
*Being and Time* (Heidegger), 343
belief, 119, 251, 363, 365; Network of, 150–51; scientific method and, 546; social construction of, 526, 563–64, 567–71; Theory as, 15n6, 23, 109–10
Bell, Daniel, 345
Bellow, Saul, 90–91
Belsey, Catherine, 34–35, 82, 134, 459, 461, 463, 618
Benda, Julien, 619
Benjamin, Walter, 599
Benveniste, Émile, 134–37, 139, 179
Bergonzi, Bernard, 618
Berlin, Isaiah, 386
*Between Men: English Literature and Male Homosocial Desire* (Sedgwick), 429, 430–38
Bhabha, Homi K., 298, 356, 378–79n37, 501
Biersack, Aletta, 494
Big Three items, 35–36, 37
binary constructions. *See* dualisms
bioepistemology, 588, 621–22, 629; basic principles, 624–25. *See also* epistemology
*Biogenetic Structuralism* (Laughlin and d'Aquili), 631–32
biographical fallacy, 38
biographical-historical criticism, 412, 413
"Birth of the Cyberqueer" (Morton), 426
Bishop, Alan, 500
Black Studies, 31, 32
Blake, William, 209
Bleier, Ruth, 558
Bloom, Allan, 550
Bloom, Harold, 7, 49, 57, 420–21, 443–44, 512–13, 518, 671
Bloor, David, 569, 571
Blumenberg, Hans, 245
Blunt, Anthony, 345
body, queer theory and, 425–29, 438
Boeckh, Philip August, 193–94
Boghossian, Paul, 526
Böhme, Jacob, 56
Bolsheviks, Old, 34
Booker, M. Keith, 3–4
Boon, James, 220, 226–27
Boose, Lynda, 262, 458, 464

Booth, Wayne C., 199, 596, 687
Bora, Renu, 431–32
Boudon, Raymond, 241–42
boundaries, 615; vagueness of, 147–49, 166–67
Bourdieu, Pierre, 332, 669
bourgeoisie, rejection of, 225–26
Bouveresse, Jacques, 235
Bowie, Malcolm, 269–70n52
Boyarin, Daniel, 459, 460, 466
Boyle, Mary, 564
Bradley, A. C., 47
brain, cognitive imperative, 625–26
Braudel, Fernand, 219, 220
Bricmont, Jean, 525–26, 541–44, 548, 550–51
Bristol, Michael D., 657
British imperialism, 292–93
British novel. *See* Victorian novel
Bromwich, David, 587
Brooks, Cleanth, 62, 325
Brooks, Peter, 515–16
Brougham, Lord, 66
Brown, Norman O., 324, 436
Bruckner, Pascal, 539, 540
Bruner, Jerome, 628, 629, 630
Brunetière, Ferdinand, 49
Brunkhorst, Hauke, 491
Bühler, Karl, 179
burden of the past, 49. *See also* past
Bürger, Peter, 679
Burke, Edmund, 602, 603
Burke, Kenneth, 238, 257, 596
Butler, Judith, 354–56, 357, 358, 389
Byatt, A. S., 308

Cacicedo, Alberto, 269n47
"Caesar crossed the Rubicon" example, 180–81
Cambridge school, 31, 39, 69, 70, 616–17
Campbell, Roger, 345
canny and uncanny critics, 205, 207–8
canonical literature, 391, 421–22, 518, 601, 612–13; Dead White Males, 397
Canon Wars, 39
"Can the Subaltern Speak?" (Spivak), 575–76
cant of identity, 400–401
Cantor, Paul, 96
capitalism, 327, 454, 467, 599; mass culture, 600–601

*Capital* (Marx), 226

Carey, Peter, 304

Carlyle, Thomas, 36

Carnap, Rudolf, 441

*carnivalesque*, 31

Carroll, Lewis, 201

Cartesianism, 320–21

Casey, John, 619

causality, 82, 143n15, 223, 629

center, as margin, 403–4

Cervantes, Miguel de, 290, 295

Chadwyck-Healey Web site, 35

Chakrabarty, Dipesh, 577, 579, 581

Chandra, Bankim, 576

charisma, intellectual, 336–38

Charnes, Lynda, 464

Chase, Martha, 554

Chatterjee, Partha, 575, 576, 581

Chicago New Critics, 36

China, 460

choice, 371

Chomsky, Noam, 145–46n23, 525

Christ, Carol, 315

citationality (*citationalité*), 153, 165

Cixous, Hélène, 7

clarification, 355, 356

clarity, 320–21

Clarke, Simon, 251–53

class, 57

classic theory of signs, 211n12

classification, tripartite system of, 81–83

clerisy, 616

Clifford, James, 495

Clinton, Bill, 669–70

cloakroom system model, 184–89

close readings, 61–63, 67, 100, 234–35

cognitive adaptations, 625

cognitive community, 242

cognitive imperative, 625–26

cognitive science, 622

Coleridge, Samuel Taylor, 592, 593

collaborationists, 271, 278–79, 281–82

Collège de France, 332

Collins, Wilkie, 304

colonialism, 291, 576–77. *See also* postcolonialism

*Colonial Rise of the Novel, The* (Azim), 304

common sense, 177, 355, 612, 624, 629

communication: extralinguistic, 176, 178; linguistic model, 35–36, 37; oral, 126

"Communist Manifesto, The" (Marx), 383

community standards, 356–57

Compagnon, Antoine, 12, 18n34

competence, 591

complexity, 591

compositionality, 153–54

composition studies, 614

concepts, 128; Background and, 151; boundaries of, 148–49

conceptual approach, 626–27

*Conflict of the Faculties* (Kant), 112–17

confusion, 147, 168–71

connections, 484, 485, 486, 488

Conrad, Joseph, 60, 478, 676

consciousness, 123, 136, 141; absent speaker, 131–33, 134; attack on, 129–30; influence of language on, 126–27. *See also* self; subjectivity

*Constructing Quarks* (Pickering), 565

constructivist antihumanism, 23, 78–79

content, 81

content analysis, 658, 662–63

context, 85. *See also* historical context

contingency premise, 347

continuity, 289, 294–95, 587, 608, 615. *See also* epistemic break

contradiction, 322–23, 325

contrapuntal reading, 488

Cooperative Principle, 196–97

correspondence theory of truth, 623–24

countersciences, 224

*Cours de linguistique générale* (Saussure), 28–29, 36, 43, 178–79

Crane, R. S., 221, 250

*Cranford* (Gaskell), 304

creative criticism, 44

creativity, rule-governed, 145–46n23

Crews, Frederick, 215, 249–50, 258, 269n52, 356–57, 465

*Critical Condition: Feminism at the Turn of the Century* (Gubar), 444–45

critical humanism, 58–59

critical imperialism, 305

*Critical Inquiry*, 43, 445, 525

*Critical Practice* (Belsey), 34–35

*Critical Theory Since Plato* (Adams), 2, 6

*Critical Theory Today: A User-Friendly Guide* (Tyson), 9–10

critical thinking, 215

criticism: all-or-nothing thinking, 593, 594–95; anti-theoretical, 50; characteristics of, 509; grandiosity and, 43–44; hermeneutics and, 194; as a language, 593; requirement to write interestingly, 55, 56. *See also* literary criticism

*Criticism and Social Change* (Lentricchia), 238

critics of Theory, 21; accusations of conservatism, 6, 420–21, 469; dismissive rhetoric used against, 1, 3, 6, 459–60, 469, 525; oppositional stance, 451–52; social constructionism and, 346–48. *See also* revolutionary academic

*Critique de la Critique* (Todorov), 239

*Critique of Cynical Reason* (Sloterdijk), 490

*Critique of Judgment* (Kant), 42

critiques of theory, by former practitioners, 11, 16n10, 50, 239–40, 419–21, 445–46, 525, 641–42

Culler, Jonathan, 2, 83, 142n10, 148, 236–37, 273; *Works: On Deconstruction*, 26, 147, 215, 594–95; *Literary Theory: A Very Short Introduction*, 27; *The Pursuit of Signs*, 50

"Cultural Criticism and Society" (Adorno), 601–2

cultural imperialism, 305

cultural linguistics, 127

cultural materialism, 31, 618

cultural poetics, 658

cultural production, 337–38; historical context, 330–31; poetry as, 674–76

cultural relativism, 94, 95

cultural sphere, 482–84

cultural studies, 11, 25, 679; as antidisciplinary, 317, 375, 389, 589, 618, 657–58; arguments of, 363–66; egalitarian ideal, 375–76; hierarchy, view of, 364–65, 373; indefinability of, 360–61; individualism and, 369–70, 373–74, 376, 380n59; knowledge, view of, 365–66; language as site of contestation and, 367–68; libertarian

ideal of, 375–76; metaphysics of, 374–75; as against norms and values, 371, 375; particularity and, 372–73; political struggle and, 365, 366, 378n24; politics of, 365, 374–75; power and, 366, 378–79n37; as resistance, 368–69; science, view of, 366–67; specificity of literature and, 361–64; transgression and, 371–74, 376; voice metaphor, 370–71

*Cultural Studies* (ed. Grossberg, Nelson, and Treichler), 317, 360–61, 363, 366, 367–76

cultural theory, 16n16

culture, 389, 398; campus as surrogate world, 404–5; high culture/popular culture opposition, 361–62; New Historicist view, 294–95; as oppressive, 371–72, 376; of Theory, 104–6

*Culture and Imperialism* (Said), 116, 293, 299, 304, 310n6, 477, 482–89, 489–90n3

culture of complaint (Hughes), 7, 37–38

culture wars, 508, 510, 515–16. *See also* ideology critique

Cunningham, Valentine, 21

Currie, Gregory, 654–55

cynicism, 490–91, 553

Czech structuralists, 49, 50, 94

Dada, 609

d'Aquili, Eugene, 625–26, 631–32

*Dark Science, A: Women, Sexuality, and Psychiatry in the Nineteenth Century* (Mousaieff), 436

Davidson, Donald, 231n12

*Day of the Leopards: Essays in Defense of Poems* (Wimsatt), 591

Dead White Males, 397

Deaf movement, 408

death, as polemical technique, 258–59

death of author, 38, 94, 315–16, 318–19, 326, 328–30; historical context, 319–21; race-gender-class theorists and, 98–99

Debray, Régis, 331

*Décombres, Les* (Rebatet), 278–79

deconstruction, 9, 22–23, 27, 37, 45, 290; aim, 595; American, 238; in Barthes, 71–74; characterization of, 53–54; deferral of meaning, 100, 108n23; denunciation of,

deconstruction (*continued*)
    272–73; dualisms and, 632–33; interpreta-
    tion and, 199–201; linguistic predicament
    and, 596–97; meaning, view of, 114–15,
    142n8, 165–70; politics and, 116–17, 119–20;
    postulates, 53–54; power, view of, 54–55;
    procedures, 207–8, 595; realism and,
    72–74; responsibility, view of, 114–15; style
    of, 64
deductive method, 326
"Deep Play" (Geertz), 493–94
defacement, 596–97
"Defense of Poetry" (Shelley), 595
deferral of meaning, 29–30, 100, 108n23,
    132–33, 204, 211n12
Defoe, Daniel, 644
de Graef, Ortwin, 271, 278, 285–86n16
deixis, 132, 136, 137–38, 142n11
Delbanco, Andrew, 315
Deleuze, Gilles, 110, 219–20, 232n20, 543
de Man, Paul, 43, 58, 144–45n20; deconstruc-
    tion of, 45, 104, 216, 238; defenses of, 273–
    75; Derrida's defense of, 276–78, 280–81,
    283; on fiction, 638–40; historical context
    of writings, 281–82; on Jewish writers,
    275–76; pieces in *Bibliographie Dechenne*,
    271, 278; pieces in *Het Vlaamsche Land*,
    271, 275–76; pieces in *Le Soir*, 271, 275;
    reader response and, 281–82; reviews of
    collaborationist books, 216, 278–79; rhet-
    oric of the end, 259; on theory, 6, 241, 385,
    388; wartime writings of, 271–86; *Works:
    Allegories of Reading*, 595–96; "Autobiog-
    raphy as De-Facement," 596–97; *Blind-
    ness and Insight*, 43, 238, 595; "Juifs dans la
    littérature actuelle, Les," 275, 277–78;
    "The Rhetoric of Temporality," 596
democracy, 370, 518, 602
*Démon de la théorie, Le: Littérature et sens
    commun* (Compagnon), 12
demonization, 259, 260, 266, 270n55
demystification, 515
Derrida, Jacques, 29–30, 37, 43, 119, 219, 290,
    544, 596; absent speaker concept, 131–33,
    134; on author, 318; *citationalité* concept,
    153; death of, 17n19; defense of de Man,
    276–78, 280–81, 283; on deferral, 211n12;

discourse, view of, 129, 130; distinctions,
    view of, 148–49; dualisms and, 622;
    equivocation of, 172–73, 227–28, 233n23,
    249, 280–81; essay on Kant, 112–17; on free
    play, 211n14; general text concept, 129,
    142n8; graphocentrism of, 204–5; influ-
    ence of, 22–23, 27; introduction to
    Husserl's work, 337; *iterabilité* concept,
    152, 172; linguistic premises of, 201–5; on
    meaning as undecidable, 147; metaphys-
    ics and, 204–5, 211n15, 244; misunder-
    standing of philosophy of language, 95,
    171, 173; Nietzsche and, 75–76, 254; noth-
    ing exists outside text concept, 173, 227,
    250, 594; origins and, 204; as pre-
    Wittgensteinian, 149, 171–72; priority of
    writing over speech, 202–3; procedures,
    595; response to Searle, 148; as traditional
    philosopher, 171–72; transcendental sig-
    nified and, 143–44n15; *Works: Dissemina-
    tion*, 594; *Glas*, 44; *Of Grammatology*, 318,
    594; "Jacques Derrida's Reading of
    Rousseau," 595; *Spurs*, 75–76, 168–69;
    "Structure, Sign, and Play in the Dis-
    course of the Human Sciences," 622. *See
    also différance*
Descartes, René, 101, 320
Descombes, Vincent, 3, 124, 332
description, 389, 390, 392
descriptive theories, 81–82, 103
designators, 180
desire, construction of, 428
determinism, 58, 231n12
diachronic point of view, 185
dialectical image, 599
dialectic of the Other, 181
dialogue, 239
Dickens, Charles, 304, 305
Dickstein, Morris, 22
Diderot, Denis, 398, 415, 417
*différance*, 29, 31, 132, 166, 172, 204–5, 227
difference, 128, 131, 203, 427; identity politics
    and, 398, 402, 408–10
Dilthey, Wilhelm, 97, 99, 617
disciples, 247–48
discourse, 31, 105, 508; confused with con-
    sciousness, 127; epistemic violence,

575–76; as exchange, 135; fictional *vs.* fact-stating, 640–41; as ideological framework, 452; types of, 548. *See also* language; polarization of discourse

discoveries, 385, 568; justification and, 343–44, 346

discursive chain, 138–39, 139

discursive regimes, 428

disinterestedness, 458–59, 514–15, 660. *See also* objectivity

dismissive rhetoric, 3; Higher Dismissiveness, 525–26, 553, 557–60

distinctions: ontology and epistemology, 157; sentences and utterances, 152–53; types and tokens, 152, 153; use and mention, 153

DNA example, 554

Docherty, Thomas, 613–14

dogmatic criticism, 239

Dollimore, Jonathan, 31, 459, 465–66

dominant ideology, 366, 458, 459; supported by silence, 460–62, 466–69; voice and, 370–71. *See also* status quo

domination, symbolic, 335–36

Donne, John, 671

Donoghue, Denis, 23, 257

*Don Quixote* (Cervantes), 290, 295

Dostoevsky, Fyodor, 46

Douglass, Frederick, 504–5

Dowling, Linda, 517–18

Dowling, William C., 398

Drakakis, John, 459, 469

dream texts, 37

Dreyfus case, 502

drifting, theoretical, 12

dualisms, 29, 400, 622–24, 631; deconstruction of, 632–33

Ducrot, Oswald, 177–78

Duhem, Pierre, 570

Dumont, Louis, 363

Durand, Beatrice, 415

Dürer, Albrecht, 605–6

*Dust Tracks on a Road* (Hurston), 422–23

Eagleton, Terry, 6, 11–12, 16n16, 31, 58, 418, 458, 466, 480, 634; *Literary Theory: An Introduction*, 79, 344–45

Eakin, Emily, 2

Easterlin, Nancy, 588

Easthope, Antony, 361, 362, 459

Eco, Umberto, 191

Écoles Normales Supérieures, 331, 333, 336

*écriture*, 202, 431. *See also* text

*Edinburgh Review*, 65–66

Edwardians, 289–90

Eichenbaum, Boris, 10–11

E-knowledge example (science), 530, 531, 535

"Elegy Written in a Country Churchyard" (Gray), 117–19

*Elementary Structures of Kinship, The* (Lévi-Strauss), 432–33

Eliot, George, 36

Eliot, T. S., 35, 36, 49, 64, 75, 296, 387, 406

elitism, 518, 615–16; evaluation as, 47–48, 103

Ellis, John, 15n6, 23, 397

*Eloisa to Abelard* (Pope), 398, 412–13, 417

emancipation, of subject, 79–80

embeddedness thesis, 294

emotion, practical criticism and, 69–70

empiricism, 222, 232n19, 250, 389, 531; antiempiricism, 221–25; dismissal of, 253–54; French view, 322, 325

Empson, William, 117–19, 596

*Encyclopedia and Methodology of the Philological Sciences* (Boeckh), 193–94

end, rhetoric of, 258–59

*End of History, The* (Fukuyama), 288

Engels, Friedrich, 36, 464

English Civil War, 470

Enlightenment, 228, 502, 512, 536

epigenetic rules, 626, 629

epistemes, 252, 530, 600, 608

epistemic break, 608–11, 617–18. *See also* continuity

epistemic relativism, 242, 538

epistemic situation, 526

epistemic violence, 575–76

epistemology, 54, 157, 169, 170, 176, 342, 594, 643; bioepistemology, 588, 621–22, 624–25, 629; either/or construction, 622–23; evolutionary, 625–26; postcolonialism and, 577–78; radical skeptical, 509, 621–22, 629; standpoint, 397, 578. *See also* knowledge

*Epistemology of the Closet* (Sedgwick), 342, 429

equality, interpretive frameworks and, 479–80
Erickson, Peter, 261–62
Erikson, Erik H., 401
*Eros and Civilization* (Marcuse), 503
essentialism, 409; feminist theory and, 442, 445–46; strategic, 580–81
ethical criticism, 687
ethics, 90–91, 115, 239; politics and, 58, 88; reading for the ethical, 87–90
ethnicity, 401, 407–8
ethnocentricity, 255
*ethos*, 671
etymology, 206
Eurocentrism, 291–92
evaluation, 47–48, 79, 643; cognitive status of, 103–4; cultural studies and, 364; as elitist, 47–48, 103; in literary history, 48–49; normative theories of, 81, 82–83; race-gender-class theorists and, 102–4
Evans, Malcolm, 458, 465
evidence, 157, 222, 553–54, 569
evil: political system as, 466–67, 471; reading for, 486–89
evolution, theory of, 625
evolutionary epistemology, 625–26
exaggeration, 255
explanatory theories, 81, 82–83
explicitness, 126, 140–41, 146n25
*Expression and Meaning* (Searle), 161
extralinguistic communication, 176, 178

facts, 205, 300–301; as values, 88, 363–66
Fallacy of Misplaced Explicitness, 146n25
fallibilism, 559
false consciousness, 224
falsification, 625
family, unsettling of, 406
fascism, aesthetic of, 600
*Fateful Question of Culture, The* (Hartman), 389
*Father and Son* (Gosse), 415–16
Fawcet, Samuel, 458, 470–71
*Fear of a Queer Planet* (ed. Warner), 426
Felperin, Howard, 8, 265–66, 270n55
female, as cultural construction, 417–18
"Feminist Thematics and Shakespearean Tragedy" (Levin), 262–63, 265

feminist theory, 7, 31, 59–60n12, 229, 305, 384, 398, 419, 573; academic moralism and, 444–48; arguments from sexual difference, 416–17; effects of on students, 423; essentialism and, 442, 445–46; French feminist theorists, 7, 9; Higher Dismissiveness and, 559–60; infighting, 444–46; New Historicism and, 261–62; origins, 444; political agendas, 261–65; as political struggle, 416–17; science, view of, 577–78; Shakespeare criticism and, 261, 262–63, 265; textuality as site of cultural construction, 417–18; Victorian studies, 302–3, 305. *See also* gender studies; *individual theorists*
Ferris, William, 670
Feyerabend, Paul, 545–46, 547
fiction: authorial intention and, 174–75n17; genre and, 636–38; levels of literary description and, 644–47; literature identified with, 639–41; narrative equated with, 630–31; truth of, 636–37. *See also* work
Fiedler, Leslie, 48
film, 229, 429–30
Firestone, Shulamith, 7
first principles, 530
Fish, Stanley, 25, 26, 55–57, 58, 111, 164, 501; career, 386; ignorance of historical context, 105, 106–7n5; on pragmatism, 347; reader-response and, 147; *Works:* "Anti-Professionalism," 386; *Doing What Comes Naturally*, 105, 106–7n5, 386; "How Ordinary Is Ordinary Language?", 673; *Is There a Text in This Class?*, 46, 164; *Self-Consuming Artifacts*, 46
Flagstad, Kirsten, 284, 286n33
Flax, Jane, 503
Fleury, Vincent, 537
form, 63, 70, 234–35
formalism, 10–11, 63, 234–35, 240, 464, 589, 673–74. *See also* Russian Formalists
formalist fallacy, 264
Foucault, Michel, 219, 220, 330, 332, 597; on author, 318; brilliance of, 31–32; on clarity, 320–21; concreteness of, 227–28; on contingency, 369; discourse, view of, 31, 105, 233n25; epistemes, 252, 608; evasiveness of, 249; French film's influence on,

429–30; Nietzsche's influence on, 254, 429; pessimism of, 427–28; popularity of, 404, 429; power, view of, 248, 366, 623; resistance, view of, 404–5; on sexuality, 342; silences and, 430, 432; social analysis of, 31, 58, 238, 369; *Works: Discipline and Punish*, 31, 294, 597; *The History of Sexuality*, 342, 398, 425, 427–28; *Les Mots et les choses*, 608

foundationalism, 28, 222

framework relativism, 623

frameworks, interpretive. *See* interpretive frameworks

France, science as attack against, 537, 539

Frankfurt School, 221, 224

Freadman, Richard, 22–23, 78, 91

Freedgood, Elaine, 305

Frege, Gottlob, 171, 182, 654

French Dictionary, 320

French educational system, 322, 326, 331

French feminist theorists, 7, 9. *See also* feminist theory

French intellectual habitus, 330–32; cultural consumption and, 334–35; institutional charisma, 336–38; intergenerational symbolic transmission, 335–39; internal demands of, 332–34; rarity of, 336–37; role of *savant*, 334–36. *See also* French intellectuals

French intellectuals, 3, 4, 52, 225; FMS movement, 241–43; historical context, 71, 94, 104, 220, 330–31; market- and state-created, 331, 334; Marxism and, 31; neologisms, 215; personalization, 330, 336; postwar generations, 331–32; professional habits, 315, 316; social context, 242–43. *See also* French intellectual habitus; structuralism; *individual theorists*

French language, 320–22

French literary history, 319–22

French school of semiology, 178–80

Freud, Sigmund, 34–35, 38, 233n23, 249, 433

Freudian-Marxian-Structuralist (FMS) movement, 241–43

Frey, Hans-Jost, 283

Friedrich, Hugo, 50

Fromm, Harold, 451

Frye, Northrop, 47, 103; *Anatomy of Criticism*, 48, 100, 512

Fukuyama, Francis, 288

Furman, Nelly, 423

fusion of horizons, 45

future, rejection of, 288

Gadamer, Hans-Georg, 45, 219, 220

Gallop, Jane, 511

Gandhi, Mohandas, 576, 578

Gard, Roger, 60

Gardner, Martin, 501

Gasché, Rodolphe, 283

Gaskell, Elizabeth, 304

Gates, Henri Louis, Jr., 32

Gaut, Berys, 653, 662

gaze, 26, 31

Geertz, Clifford, 452, 491–93

*Geistesgeschichte*, 97

Gellner, Ernest, 145n23, 241, 249, 259, 372, 492, 495

gender: identity politics and, 401, 406; textual traces of, 413–15; as trope, 417

gender fallacy, 398, 411–19

gender studies: on men writing the feminine, 411, 412, 415. *See also* feminist theory; race-gender-class theorists

*Gender Trouble* (Butler), 354, 389

generalization, 93, 658; importance of, 390, 392; in postcolonial literary studies, 303–4; postcolonial literary studies and, 298, 300

general text, 129, 142n8

generic theory, 81

Genet, Jean, 44

genetic fallacy, 264, 273, 398, 411–15; social constructionism and, 343, 344, 346

Genette, Gérard, 25–26, 331

Genovese, Eugene, 504

genre: fiction identified with, 636–38; representation and, 86–87

genrecide, 307

geographical process, 484, 486

geological criticism, 57

Georgians, 289–90

Gergen, Kenneth, 568

German intellectuals, 94, 97, 220, 592

Germano, Bill, 613

Giddens, Anthony, 221

Gilbert, Sandra, 302, 306, 444, 468

Giroux, Henry, 365

Gitlin, Todd, 397–98

globalizing literary studies, 297–98, 309. *See also* postcolonialism

Glucksmann, André, 226

Godard, Jean-Luc, 332–33

Goethe, Johann Wolfgang von, 93, 101

Goldsmith, Kenneth, 678

Gombrich, E. H., 607

*Gommes, Les* (Robbe-Grillet), 605

Good, Graham, 216–17

Goodheart, Eugene, 452–53

Gosse, Edmund, 415–16

Gottlieb, Anthony, 553

Graff, Gerald, 234, 512, 593

grammar, autonomy of, 179

grammatical interpretation, 195

grammatical subject, 136

Gramsci, Antonio, 454, 456

*grands récits*, 288, 296, 609

Grand Theory, 220–21, 249–50, 327

graphocentrism, 202, 204–5

Gray, Thomas, 117–19, 647

great dichotomy, 190–91

*Great Expectations* (Dickens), 304, 305

great refusal, 503–4

Green, T. H., 112

Greenblatt, Stephen, 38, 88, 96–97, 254, 467

Greene, Gayle, 459, 460, 463

Greenlaw, Edwin, 42

Grice, H. P., 137, 138, 145n21, 194, 196–97, 198n11

Griemas, A. J., 331

Gross, John, 70

Gross, Paul R., 621

Grover, Jan Zita, 375

Grünbaum, Adolf, 223

Guattari, Félix, 110, 232n20

Gubar, Susan, 302, 306, 399, 444–48, 468

Guillory, John, 442

gumbo metaphor, 32

Gunn, Giles, 615

Haack, Susan, 345, 525, 526

Habermas, Jürgen, 64, 219, 220, 221; hermeneutic argument, 222–24,
231–32n13; Nietzschean heritage, 243–45; resistance to theoreticism, 223–24

habitus, defined, 339n.

Hacking, Ian, 563, 568–69, 573

Hall, Stuart, 371–72

Halliwell, Stephen, 672

Halperin, David, 427, 429

Hamann, Johann Georg, 144n20

Haraway, Donna, 375

Harding, Sandra, 559, 578

Harpham, Geoffrey Galt, 3, 10, 317

Harris, Wendell, 124, 258, 470

Hartman, Geoffrey, 272–73, 280, 283, 389

Hawkes, Terence, 29, 132, 238, 256–57, 458

*Heart of Darkness* (Conrad), 478, 676

Hedges, Warren, 356

Hegel, G. W. F., 44, 539

Heidegger, Martin, 144n20, 220, 244, 343

Heinemann, Margaret, 463

Henley, John, 537

Hercules image, 605–6

Herder, Johann Gottfried von, 94, 95, 144n20

heritage, as term, 619

*Hermeneutic Reader* (Mueller-Vollmer), 193, 195, 197–98n5

hermeneutics, 41, 124, 191, 192–97; of Habermas, 222–24, 231–32n13. *See also* interpretation

hermeneutics of suspicion, 452, 510, 520

hermetics, 124, 191–92, 197

Hershey, Alfred, 554

hierarchies of aesthetics and criticism, 653–55

hierarchy, 364–65, 373

Higher Dismissiveness, 525–26, 553, 557–60

*Higher Superstition* (Levitt and Gross), 621

Hill, Geoffrey, 112

Hindu right-wing leaders, 526, 576, 578, 581; alignment with postcolonial studies, 579–83

*Hippocratic Oath for the Pluralist* (Booth), 688–89

Hirsch, E. D., 25, 45, 161, 194, 254, 255, 593, 657

historians, 199–200, 218

historical context: Barthes and, 319–22; of cultural production, 330–31; of death of author, 319–21; of de Man's writings, 281–82; of French intellectuals, 330–31; ignorance of, 95–97, 101–2, 105, 106–7n5; for knowledge, 342–43; of novel, 484–85; of text, 89–90

historical-hermeneutic system, 223, 231n11

historical interpretation, 200

historicism, 55–56, 95–97, 273

historiography, 49, 102; post-Orientalist, 576–77

history: of literary theory, 35–37, 104–5; reconfigurability of, 383–84; study of, 42–43; as textual puzzle, 238

History of Sexuality, The (Foucault), 342, 398, 425, 427–28

Hitchens, Christopher, 358

Hogarth, William, 519

Holderness, Graham, 463–64

Holland, Norman N., 261

Holtby, Winifred, 559

homosexuality, 384. See also queer theory

homosocial desire, 432–33

Hooks, Bell, 375, 380n64

Hopkins, Gerard Manley, 68

Horkheimer, Max, 500

Howard, Jean, 458, 472

Hughes, Robert, 7, 497, 519

Hugo, Victor, 321, 323

Huizinga, John, 609

Hulme, Peter, 459, 466

humanism, 218, 404, 467; critical, 58–59; defense of, 641–42; emancipation and, 79–80; ignorance of historical context, 101–2; Marxist criticism of, 58; values of, 643

humanities, 235–36, 241, 611; crisis in, 678–80; as term, 669, 670

"Humanities—at Twilight?" (Steiner), 682

human rights, 500

human sciences, 219, 230–31n3, 385

Hume, David, 174n6, 534, 592, 593, 629

Humphreys, Jefferson, 417

Hunter, Ian, 113–14, 116–17

Hurston, Zora Neale, 422–23

Husserl, Edmund, 337

Hustler, 371

Hyman, Stanley Edgar, 68

hyperspecialization, 171

"I," 134–37

iconoclastic movement, 220, 251, 253

idealism, transcendental, 565–66

idealist teleology, 626

identity, 383–84, 397–99; American pace of change and, 406–8; cant of, 400–401; fundamentalist, 406, 409; inner- vs. other-directed, 406–7. See also self; subject

identity politics, 399; in academe, 401–3; Americans and, 400–401, 408–9; campus as surrogate world, 404–5; difference and, 398, 402, 408–10; insiders vs. outsiders, 397–98, 400; objectivity and, 404, 510–11, 516; political ineffectiveness of, 402–3; profusion of identities, 405–8; race and, 401, 408–9; separatist impulse, 401–4; students and, 403

identity thinking, 400

ideology critique, 508–11, 516, 520; objectivity and, 510–11

Iliad (Homer), 639

illocutionary intentions, 156–59, 161, 167, 196

imaginary self, 134

imaginary world, 85–86

imagination, 100, 503–4, 519, 556

immanent criticism, 239, 243, 325, 601–2

Immortals, 319–20, 321

imperialism, 217, 292–93, 478; cultural, 292, 305; Indian education, 305–6; novel and, 482–83; Theory and, 235–36, 259–60; Victorian novel as instance of, 298–300

Imperialism at Home (Meyer), 304

Impostures intellectuelles (Bricmont and Sokal), 525–26, 537–44, 548, 550–51

incompleteness, 254

India, 306–7. See also Hindu right-wing leaders

Indian literature, 291

individual, identity politics and, 397

individualism, 295–96; cultural studies and, 369–70, 373–74, 376, 380n59

inequality, literary critique of, 478–81

inquiry, 391–92

instinct, 591

institutional theory of art, 362

instrumentalism, 588, 589

intellectual, defined, 339n1

intellectuals: anxiety about colleagues, 514–15; common ground, 509–10; dogmatism of, 215, 216, 225; German, 94, 97, 220, 592; misuse of knowledge, 538–42; public intellectuals, 477. *See also* French intellectuals; left intellectuals

intellectual style, 221

intention: illocutionary, 156–59, 167; self-presence, 165–66; silence and, 468, 470

intentional fallacy, 94–95, 97–98, 398, 411, 413, 418

"Intentional Fallacy, The" (Wimsatt and Beardsley), 97–98, 413, 418

intentionality, 127, 138, 414, 645; Background of, 149–50, 167–68; meaning and, 83–84, 158–59, 163–68, 593; Network and, 150–51; sentences, 152–53; standard definition of sentence/word and, 158–59; of token speech act, 167–68. *See also* authorial intention

Internet, 610, 677–78

interpersonal domain, ethics and, 88, 89

interpretation, 8, 27, 41, 45–46, 87; aesthetic criticism and, 513; Background of, 149–52; criteria for, 254–55; debates, 46–47; facts *vs.*, 56–57; general text and, 142n8; grammatical, 195; linguistic, 200; as misinterpretation, 206; normative theory of, 82; psychological, 195; as rhetorical, 102; as source of text, 164–65; subjectivity of, 75–76; thick description, 452, 491–96; truth and, 592–93. *See also* hermeneutics; interpretive frameworks

interpretive communities, 26, 46, 56, 111, 144n20, 657

interpretive frameworks, 476–77; academically trained ways of reading, 478–79, 482; de-legitimation, 488–89; displacement of debate away from issues, 483, 485, 486, 488; paired terms, 480–81; professionalization and, 477–78, 482; reading for evil, 486–89; social issues and, 478–79, 489

intertextuality, 601

*Intimate Enemy, The* (Nandy), 576

intuition, science and, 549–50

*Ion* (Plato), 672

Irigaray, Luce, 7, 542

ironical meaning, 155, 156

irony, 596, 623

Isenberg, Arnold, 637

Iser, Wolfgang, 39, 45

*Is Science Multicultural?* (Harding), 578

iterability (*iterabilité*), 152, 165–67, 172

*Jack Maggs* (Carey), 304

Jacoby, Russell, 452

Jakobsen, Janet R., 498

Jakobson, Roman, 179, 183, 673

James, Henry, 60, 289, 430–32, 439–40, 636; "The Art of Fiction," 636; "The New Novel," 289; *Notebooks*, 430–31; "Pragmatism and Common Sense," 624; "The Pupil," 439

James, Susan, 221

James, William, 559, 604n7, 624, 628

*James Joyce and the Revolution of the Word* (McCabe), 30

Jameson, Fredric, 232n19, 298, 358, 599

"Jane Austen and the Masturbating Girl" (Sedgwick), 434, 435–36

*Jane Eyre* (Brönte), 300–306, 592

JanMohamed, Abdul, 298

Jardine, Lisa, 464

jargon, 22, 64–65, 76, 92, 105, 236

Jauss, Hans-Robert, 45

Jay, Martin, 221

Jefferson Lecture in the Humanities, 669–70

Jeffrey, Francis, 66–67

*jeu*, 29

Jewish writers, 275–76

Johns Hopkins University conference, 27

Johnson, Mark, 622, 628

Johnson, Samuel, 519, 592, 612

journalism, literary, 520, 610

Joyce, James, 675–77

*Joyce and Aquinas* (Noon), 677

judgments, 399, 592–93

Juhl, J. P., 45

"Juifs dans la littérature actuelle, Les" (de Man), 275, 277–78

juridical privilege, 112–14

Jussawalla, Feroza, 506n22

justification, context of, 568–71

Kant, Immanuel, 42, 93, 112–14, 565–66
Kanth, Rajani K., 502
Katz, Adam, 469
Kauppi, Niilo, 4, 215, 316
Keats, John, 66
Keller, Evelyn Fox, 515
Kellner, Hans, 102
Kepler, Johannes, 568
Kermode, Frank, 9, 10, 270n55, 557
Kernan, Alvin, 612, 613
Kerrigan, William, 615
keywords, 206
Khomeini, Ayatollah, 497
Kierkegaard, Soren, 255, 454
Kimball, Roger, 272
Kipling, Rudyard, 292–93
Knapp, Stephen, 84, 147
Knapp and Michaels, 158–65
Knight, G. Wilson, 519
knowingness, 525
knowledge, 41–42, 54, 573; aestheticization of, 241–43; as construct, 316, 341, 342–43, 621; contingency premise, 347; cultural studies view of, 365–66; historical context for, 342–43; as hypothesis, 101; local, 526, 578–79; as normative, 365, 366; original contributions to, 656–57, 659; as power, 404; truth, relationship to, 552–53. *See also* epistemology; science; social constructionism
*Knowledge and Human Interests* (Habermas), 223
*Knowledge and Social Imagery* (Bloor), 569
Konstanz group, 45
Korsmeyer, Carolyn, 652–53
Kott, Jan, 47
Kramer, David, 319
Krebs, Paula, 304
Kristeva, Julia, 7, 332, 511, 540n5; science writings, 537, 539, 543
Kuhn, Thomas, 101–2, 108n28, 215, 219–20, 224–25, 229–30, 545–47
*Kulturkritik*, 243–45

labyrinth metaphor, 206, 207, 208
Lacan, Jacques, 26, 30, 35, 37, 127, 219–20, 229, 232n20; appropriation of Peirce, 351; dis-
missal of skepticism, 250; dogmatism of, 225–26; evasiveness of, 249; science writings, 543
LaCapra, Dominick, 284
Lakoff, George, 622, 628
Lamarque, Peter, 588
*Land and Literature of England, The* (Adams), 392
language: claims about, 161–62; consciousness and, 126–27; explicitness and, 126, 140–41; five functions of, 179–80; as identical with fictional language, 640; instability of, 622, 632; as means of control, 320; Other of, 181, 188; philosophy of, 124, 171, 173; as political, 368; reality and, 4, 10, 17n25, 43, 124, 177, 191–92, 234; self as product of, 130, 134–38; social nature of, 56, 205; syntax as relative to, 161, 175n18. *See also* discourse
language acquisition, 145n23; allegorical version, 187–89; narrativity and, 628–29
Language Acquisition Device, 145n23
language-as-system. *See* linguistic system
language games, 4, 43–44, 207, 209, 241, 566
language-in-use, 193
language rules, as enabling constraint, 139–41, 145n23
language speaks us (concept), 138, 141, 144n20, 146n25
*langue*, 29, 131, 146n24
*Laokoön* (Lessing), 65
Lapouge, Gilles, 330
Laski, H. J., 112
*Last Word, The* (Nagel), 567
Latin Americans, 409
Latour, Bruno, 525, 527n1, 547, 565
Laughlin, Charles, 631–32
Lauretis, Teresa de, 417–18
Lauter, Paul, 347
Lawrence, D. H., 46, 68, 70, 290
Leach, Edmund, 127
Leavis, F. R., 31, 36, 37, 50, 76, 616–17; as practical critic, 69, 70, 71
left intellectuals, 355–56, 401–2; cynicism of, 490–91; flight from universals, 497–98, 500–502; opposition to rational inquiry,

left intellectuals (*continued*)
528–36; scientists, 550–51. *See also* identity politics
Left position, 599
"Legend of the Grand Inquisitor" (Dostoevsky), 46
legitimacy, 369, 528–29
legitimate intellectuals, 334
Leitch, Vincent, 326
Leninist-Stalinist tyranny, 532
Lentricchia, Frank, 6, 11, 106n4, 238–39, 240, 459
Leonardo da Vinci, 607
Lessing, Gotthold, 65
Levin, Harry, 99
Levin, Richard, 262–64, 451–52
Levinas, Emmanuel, 115
Levine, George, 514–15
Lévi-Strauss, Claude, 30, 100, 129–30, 219–20, 251, 259, 290; *The Elementary Structures of Kinship*, 432–33; marriage as exchange between men, 432–33; model of, 330, 333, 337
Levitt, Norman, 621
Lewis, Wyndham, 610
liberation, transgression as, 371–72, 376
liberationist party, 357
Libeskind, Daniel, 32
Lichtenberg, Georg Christoph, 56
Lifton, Robert Jay, 406
Limet, Yun Sun, 537
linearity, 630
linguistic communication, model of, 35–36, 37
linguistic communities, 84, 548
linguistic interpretation, 200
linguisticity, 28, 36, 239
linguistic meaning, 80–81, 83–85, 161, 162
linguistic predicament, 596–97
linguistics, 25, 333; cultural, 127; fundamental principles, 149–57; language alone, 384
linguistic system, 127–28, 203, 384–85; discourse conflated with, 131–32; as negative, 128–29, 142n11. *See also* signification
linguistic turn, 28, 34, 123–25, 176–77, 202, 241
literal level of work, 644–47
literary autonomy, 413–14, 418
literary biography, 41

literary conventions, 73–74, 80, 83–85, 98
literary criticism: academicized, 60–61; critical conflicts, 655–60; emotional response, 66–67; literary scholarship distinguished from, 656–58; original contributions to knowledge, 656–57, 659; post-postcolonial, 308–10. *See also* literary theory; postcolonialism; Theory; theory
literary description, levels of, 644–47
literary history, 41–42, 48–49, 102; French, 319–22
literary imagination, 422–23
*Literary Into Cultural Studies* (Easthope), 361, 362
*Literary Knowledge* (Livingston), 623
literary meaning, 80–81, 83–85
literary scholarship, 656–58; globalizing studies, 297–98, 309; as study of history of civilization, 42–43; three main branches of, 41–42
literary sensibility, 509, 513, 587, 618–19
*Literary Theories: A Reader and Guide* (Wolfreys), 27
literary theory, 27, 442; confusion in, 147, 168–71; elements of a third conception of, 80–91; historical context, 35–37, 95–97, 101–2, 104–5; reading for the ethical, 87–90; text, author, reader triad, 81, 83–85; three phases of, 93–95, 103; tripartite system of classification, 81–83; truth in literature, 85–87. *See also* great dichotomy; literary criticism; Theory
*Literary Theory: An Introduction* (Eagleton), 79, 344–45
*Literary Theory: A Practical Introduction* (Ryan), 5
*Literary Theory at Work* (Tallack), 33
*Literary Theory* (Chadwyck-Healey), 35
literature: as arbitrary construct, 294; attack on concept of, 639–41; defense of concept of, 641–43; fiction identified with, 639–41; humanly interesting content, 639, 643, 646–47; lack of focus on, 2, 5–6, 8, 10, 16n16, 21, 50; as language, 123; mimetic aspect, 200, 234–35, 639, 643, 645–46, 650; reality, reference to, 49, 58–59; as repository of human values, 588; saying and showing, 648–49; as socially constructed,

363–64; specificity of, 361–64; study of, 9, 41; as term, 670, 682n4; theme and subject, 647–48; as writing, 318–19. *See also* literary criticism; literary theory; Theory; theory

*Literature Against Itself* (Graff), 234

literature departments, 236

*littérateur*, 334–35

Livingston, Paisley, 588, 623

localization, 388–89, 392, 500

local knowledges, 526, 575; postcolonial defense of, 578–79

locution, 196. *See also* speech act

Lodge, David, 236

logic, 322, 323, 643

logical positivism, 103, 157, 218, 221, 546

logocentric model, 202

Lorenz, Konrad, 627

Lovejoy, A. O., 43, 47

Lyotard, Jean François, 144n20, 288

Macaulay, Thomas Babbington, 306–7

McCabe, Colin, 30

McClintock, Ann, 300

McGowan, John, 470

MacIntyre, Alasdair, 517–18

MacKillop, Ian, 620n14

MacKinnon, Catharine, 436–37

McKinson, Cary, 676–77

*Madwoman in the Attic, The: The Woman Writer and the Nineteenth-Century Literary Imagination* (Gilbert and Gubar), 444

Maggiori, Robert, 537

Mailloux, Stephen, 194

male writers, as misogynist, 412–13

*Mansfield Park* (Austen), 304, 452, 483–89, 490n4

Marcus, Leah, 615

Marcus, Steven, 76

Marcuse, Herbert, 503

marginality, 403–4, 500, 579, 580

"Marginal Notes on the Prose of the Poet Pasternak" (Jakobson), 673

Margolies, David, 459

Marius, Richard, 614

Marks, Elaine, 9, 398

marks (written text), 202–3, 205; intentionality and, 158–62; iterability of, 165–66

*Marriage of Heaven and Hell, The* (Blake), 209

Martin, Biddy, 420

Marvell, Andrew, 414

Marx, Karl, 36, 38, 226, 383, 464–65, 600

Marxist criticism, 7, 22, 31–32, 43, 464–65; competition with Theory, 260–61; Foucauldians and, 238–39; Habermas's view, 222–24; limitations of, 227; normative theories, 82; objectivity, view of, 551–52; presentism and, 288; as relativist, 240; scientism of, 238; subjective/objective distinction, 468–69; values, view of, 57–58

mass culture, 600–601

Masson, Jeffrey Mousaieff, 436

masturbation, 433, 434, 435–37

materiality, 383

mathematics, 500

Matthews, Brander, 354

May 1968 student uprisings, 226, 228

meaning: as active, 138; authorial intention and, 163–65; Background of, 149–50; context of, 45–46, 82–83, 133; conventional, 158–59; deconstructionist view of, 114–15, 142n8, 165–70; deferral of, 29–30, 100, 108n23, 132–33, 204, 211n12; fiction and, 637; form and, 234–35; indeterminacy of, 124, 147, 173, 192, 206, 622; indirect, 196–97; indirect speech acts, 155, 156; intentionality and, 83–84, 158–59, 163–68, 593; ironical, 155, 156; linguistic, 80–81, 83–85, 161–62; literary, 80–81, 83–84; metaphorical, 155, 156; natural, 194, 198n11; production of, 55–56, 145n21; sentence meaning, 83–84, 154–57, 160, 167–68; speaker meaning, 154–57, 160, 167–68, 170; of text, 52, 59, 147; verbal, 194

"Meaning of July Fourth for the Negro, The" (Douglass), 504–5

*Meaning of Meaning, The* (Ogden and Richards), 182–83

mechanics, 74–76, 442

*Mediterranean, The* (Braudel), 220

Megill, Alan, 215, 235–36, 243

Mehlman, Jeffrey, 276

memory, cultural, 608

Menand, Louis, 559

mention-use distinction, 153

*Men Writing the Feminine* (ed. Morgan), 415, 416–17

Merquior, J. G., 215–16

*Metahistory* (White), 102, 675

metaphor, 538, 595, 623

metaphorical meaning, 155, 156

metaphysical picaresque, 241

metaphysics: of cultural studies, 374–75; Derrida and, 204–5, 211n15, 244; of presence, 44, 595

meteorite example, 553–54

method, 513, 547, 593

Meyer, Michael, 671

Meyer, Susan, 302

Michaels, Walter Benn, 84, 147, 158–65

Mill, John Stuart, 230–31n3

millennium, 618

Miller, J. Hillis, 125, 258; canny and uncanny critics concept, 205, 207–8; on deconstruction, 55, 207–8, 260; on de Man, 272, 273–74; interpretation, view of, 199–201, 205–10

Miller, Seumas, 22–23, 78, 91

Millett, Kate, 7

Milovanovic, Dragan, 137–38, 142n12

mimesis, 200, 234–35, 639, 643, 645–46, 650

mind-independent reality, 566

minimalist approach, 491

"Minute on Indian Education" (Macaulay), 306–7

"Minute on *Jane Eyre*" (Spivak), 307–8

mirror stage, 134

misapprehension, 255

misdescription, 254–55

*mise en abyme*, 207, 208, 210, 268n28

*Misérables, Les* (Hugo), 321, 323

misinterpretation, 46, 49, 156, 206

Mitterand, François, 543

"Modern Fiction" (Woolf), 636

modernism, 72, 74, 289–90, 602, 609, 636; New Criticism and, 62–63

modernity, 363, 576, 607; repudiation of, 243–45. *See also* Renaissance

Modern Language Association of America (MLA), 11, 18n31, 260, 420, 421, 614–15; *PMLA*, 342, 346, 420

*Modern Literary Theory* (ed. Rice and Waugh), 9, 17n24

Moi, Toril, 464–65

*Moll Flanders* (Defoe), 644

Montagu, Mary Wortley, 412, 413

Moon, Michael, 429, 438–39

*Moonstone, The* (Collins), 304

Moore, Arthur K., 236

moral agent, 88–91

morals/morality, 118, 510, 594, 597; academic moralism, 441–48

*Morphology of the Folktale* (Propp), 30

Morrison, Toni, 445

Morton, Donald, 426, 459, 469

Morton, Michael, 624

mountain example, 566–67

Moussa, Helene, 563

*Mr. Sammler's Planet* (Bellow), 90–91

Mueller-Vollmer, Kurt, 193, 195, 197–98n7

Mulhern, Francis, 617

multiculturalism, 37, 402, 409, 559–60

Murdoch, Iris, 596

Myers, D. G., 10, 316

mystification, 255

myths, 129–30, 244

Nagel, Thomas, 526, 567

naïve objectivism, 626–28

naïve realism, 177

Namier, Lewis, 218

Nanda, Meera, 500–501, 525, 526

Nandy, Ashis, 576, 578, 579, 581

Napoleon example, 182–83

narrative, 100, 623, 628–29; equated with fiction, 630–31; postcolonial literary studies and, 298–99

narrativity, 628–29

narratology, 50

National Association of Scholars (NAS), 24–25

National Endowment for the Humanities (NEH), 669

nationalism, 49, 539. *See also* Hindu rightwing leaders

*Nationalist Thought and the Colonial World: A Derivative Discourse?* (Chatterjee), 576

natural meaning, 194, 198n11

*Natural Supernaturalism* (Abrams), 199, 689

necessary complicity, 295

Neely, Carol, 262
negative culpability, theory of, 468
Nelkin, Dorothy, 572
neoconservative critics, 515
neologisms, 24, 49, 215. *See also* worlding
neo-Platonism, 622
neopragmatism, 622–24
nerd identity, 390
Network, 150–51, 163, 166–68
New Criticism, 16–17n16, 22, 36, 38, 123, 325;
    Barthes, view of, 326–27; close readings,
    61–63, 67, 100, 234–35; emphasis on po-
    etry, 637; formalist view of, 164; methods,
    513; modernism and, 62–63; origins of,
    344; political agenda attributed to,
    458–59
New Historicism, 31, 38, 96–97, 217, 254; col-
    lage technique, 293–94; feminist theory
    and, 261–62; presentism and, 293–95
*New Historicism, The: A Reader* (Veeser), 294
new Left, 401–2. *See also* left intellectuals
Newton, Isaac, 343, 540
*New York Review of Books*, 66
Nietzsche, Friedrich, 43, 201, 243; Derrida on,
    75–76; *Nachlass*, 168–70; past, view of,
    287–88; radical aestheticism of, 243–44;
    *The Will to Power*, 201
Nietzschean stance, 238–39
nihilism, 43, 49, 124, 186
*Nineteen Eighty-Four* (Orwell), 56, 602
1960s movements, 226, 228, 425–26, 442
*No Man's Land: The Place of the Woman
    Writer in the Twentieth-Century* (Gilbert
    and Gubar), 444
nonmodern intellectuals. *See* Hindu right-
    wing leaders
non-person, 179
Noon, William T., 677
normative theories, 81, 82, 103
Norris, Christopher, 273
*Norton Anthology of Literature by Women,
    The: The Tradition in English* (Gilbert
    and Gubar), 444
*Norton Anthology of Theory and Criticism*
    (*NATC*), 2, 3–4, 6, 8–9
*Notebooks* (James), 430–31
Nottingham University Theory Group, 33
*nouveau roman*, 331, 429

novel, 290; fiction *vs.*, 636–37; historical con-
    text, 484–85; imperialism and, 482–83. *See
    also Jane Eyre*
*Novel Gazing: Queer Readings in Fiction* (ed.
    Sedgwick), 431–32
Novy, Marianne, 467
Nussbaum, Martha, 12, 355
Nuttall, A.D., 235, 253, 260, 264

object, 176–77; of theory, 80, 87
objectivism, 263–64; anti-objectivist argu-
    ments, 508–9; naive, 626–28
objectivity, 47; aesthetics and, 516; cultural
    studies view of, 365–66; dismissal of,
    99–101, 250–54, 548; identity politics
    and, 404, 510–11, 516; ideology critique
    and, 508–11, 516; Marxist view, 551–52;
    science studies and, 550–51; skeptical
    view of, 508–9; social constructionist
    view of, 342–43. *See also* disinterest-
    edness
O'Connor, Erin, 217
"Ode on a Distant Prospect of Eton College"
    (Gray), 647
Oedipus complex, 134
"Of the Standard of Taste" (Hulme), 592
Ogden, C. K., 182–83
Ohmann, Richard, 342
Old Leftists, 34
Olsen, Stein Haugom, 255, 259–60, 264, 588,
    663–64
*Omphalos* reasoning, 415–16, 417
*On the Aesthetic Education of Man* (Schiller),
    517
ontology, 169, 170; of works of art, 654–55
*Ontology of Art, An* (Currie), 654–55
opaque criticism, 235
operative intention, 194
oppositional stance, 451–52, 458, 485, 614;
    anachronistic readings, 462–64; context
    of silence and, 470–71
oppressed, alliance of, 578
oppression, 31, 47, 466–67; culture and,
    371–72, 376
oral communication, 126
Orgel, Stephen, 346
*Origin of Geometry* (Husserl), 337
origin of language, versions of, 187–88

Orwell, George, 4, 16n10, 56, 327, 491, 511, 602, 603

Osborn, Bob, 678

Other, 31, 37, 124; of language, 181, 188; as moral agent, 91; Victorian novel as, 307

other-directed personality, 406–7

oversimplification, 254–55

Panofsky, Erwin, 606

panoptic gaze, 31

paradox, 487–88

paranoia, 433

Park, Clara Claiborne, 315–16

*parole*, 29, 131, 146n24. *See also* speech act

particularity, 372–73, 392, 393

Passes-for Fallacy, 558

past, 287; burden of, 49; control of, 602–3; dismissal of, 216–17, 608–9

Patai, Daphne, 16n10

*pathos*, 671

patriarchy, 467

Patterson, Annabel, 256–57

Paulson, Ronald, 519

Pavel, Thomas, 249, 250, 258–59

Pechter, Edward, 97, 107n14

pedagogy, 61, 390–91

Peirce, Charles Sanders, 101, 108n28, 152, 351, 559–61

people of color, 409

perception, 177

performance, 389

periods, 289, 607

perlocutionary effects/intents, 196

Perloff, Marjorie, 281, 589

Perry, Ralph Barton, 109

Perseus image, 605–6

personal as political, 404–5, 443

perspectivists, 510

philosophical aesthetic, 653–55

philosophical analysis, 665

*Philosophical Investigations* (Wittgenstein), 593

*Philosophische Diskurs der Moderne, Der* (Habermas), 243

philosophy, 594; American, 441; of language, 124, 171, 173; literary component of, 391–92; of representation, 177; of science, 101–2, 568. *See also* linguistic turn

*Philosophy and Literature*, 354–56, 358

*Philosophy of Right* (Hegel), 44

Philp, Mark, 220

phonemes, 29

Piaget, Jean, 627, 633

"Piano" (Lawrence), 68, 70

Picard, Raymond, 320, 325, 326

Pickering, Andrew, 565

Plato, 571, 672, 675, 680

pleasure, 680–81

Pleistocene era, 626

pluralism, 199–200, 263–65, 408; of Theory, 33–34

Poe, Edgar Allan, 324

poetics, 41, 83, 658; as study of literature, 670–72

*Poetics* (Aristotle), 631, 674–75, 681

poetry, 36, 49, 589, 596, 637; as cultural production, 674–76; as one of the arts, 672–73; as truth/knowledge, 672

polarization of discourse, 261–65, 348; as misleading, 509–10; in Shakespeare criticism, 265–66

polemical techniques, 259–60, 269–70n52, 305, 346–47

political correctness, 400, 515

political criticism, 10; as ineffectual, 12, 17n25, 18n31, 425

political philosophy, 390

*Political Shakespeare* (Sinfield and Dollimore), 465

political sphere, 482–84

political system, as evil, 466–67, 471

*Political Unconscious, The* (Jameson), 599

politics, 4–5, 8, 258–59, 308–9, 519; attributed to New Criticism, 458–59; cultural studies and, 365, 366, 374–75, 378n24; deconstruction and, 116–17, 119–20; ethics and, 58, 88; feminist, 261–65; feminist criticism as, 416–17; objectivity and, 550–51; outside agitator trope, 460; personal as political, 404–5, 443; in Shakespeare criticism, 256–57; social constructionism and, 344–45; Theory and, 8, 10, 93–94, 451–53; Theory as institution and, 116–17. *See also* identity politics

"Politics and the English Language" (Orwell), 4, 511

Pollak, Ellen, 412–13, 414

Pope, Alexander, 398, 412–13, 591

Popper, Karl, 546, 625

positivism, 582; as form of rationalism, 251–52; opposition to, 222–24; rejection of, 250–51

post-, as term, 609–10

postcolonialism, 31, 217, 289, 291–93, 526; allegories in, 308; alliance of the oppressed, 578; defense of local knowledges, 578–79; as epistemological project, 577–78; generalization in, 303–4; on *Jane Eyre*, 300–306, 592; as project, 305, 577; right-wing alignment with, 579–83; role of facts, 300–301; science studies, 578–83. *See also* colonialism

postmodernism: as epistemic break, 608–11; liberation from Theory, 613–14; as movement, 608; presentism and, 289–90; professionalization and, 387–88; reading, 282–83; vocabulary of, 12

"Postmodernism, or the Cultural Logic of Late Capitalism" (Jameson), 599–600

postness, 216–17, 289, 297

post-Orientalist historiography, 576–77

post-postcolonial literary criticism, 308–10

post-Saussureanism, 123, 127, 135, 139, 142n12; absence of self and, 134–38; absence of speaker and, 131–33; referent and, 136–37

poststructuralism, 127, 190, 228; Anglophone, 238; authority *vs.* rationality, 639–40; dualisms and, 622, 632–33; emphasis on mechanics, 74–75; jargon, 22, 76, 236; *Kulturkritik* and, 243–45; Marxist opposition to, 57–58; modernism as basis for, 289–90; negative effect on criticism, 22; nihilism of, 4–5; political context, 344–45; radical politics and, 464–65; representatives of, 335; as term, 53; theorhhea and, 240–43. *See also* deconstruction; Derrida, Jacques; Foucault, Michel; post-Saussureanism; pragmatism; Theory

"Poverty of Theory, The" (Thompson), 598

power, 31, 317, 328, 498–99, 603; cultural studies and, 366, 378–79n37; deconstructionist view, 54–55; knowledge as, 404; Theory as, 385–86; truth and, 499–500, 623

practical criticism, 36, 41, 60–62, 654–55, 671; communal basis of, 64; development of, 65–66; emotion and, 69–70; emphasis on mechanics, 74–75. *See also* Barthes, Roland

*Practical Criticism* (Richards), 22, 65, 67–71

*Practising Theory and Reading Literature: An Introduction* (Selden), 33–34

pragmatism, 22, 33, 34, 53, 55–56, 179, 559; neopragmatism, 622–24

Prague Linguistic Circle, 49, 50, 94

Prakash, Gyan, 576–77, 580

Preis, Ann-Belinda S., 500

presence, 44, 132, 134; metaphysics of, 44, 595; transcendental signified and, 143–44n15

present, control of, 602–3

presenticentric predicament, 47

presentism, 216–17, 287–97; denial of historical agency, 295–96; New Historicism and, 293–95; rejection of historicism, 287–88; rejection of progressive ideas, 288–89

*Present Philosophical Tendencies* (Perry), 109

primary texts, 290–91

principles, 118

*Principles of Criticism* (Richards), 42

privileging, 228

"Problem of Belief, The" (Isenberg), 637

proclamation, rhetoric of, 607, 609

producer/consumer relationship, 242

professional habits, 315, 316, 452

professionalization, 386–87, 393; interpretive frameworks and, 477–78, 482; postmodernism and, 387–88

pronouns, personal, 179–80

proof, 531, 534

*Prophets of Extremity* (Megill), 243

proposition, 196

Propp, Vladimir, 30

protocols, 67–68

Proust, Marcel, 91, 596, 597, 680–81

*Province of Literary History, The* (Greenlaw), 42

provincialism, 577–78

pseudo-inquiry, 560–61

psychoanalysis, 222n20, 226–27, 233n23, 261, 418; Habermas's view, 223–24; incoherence of, 356

publication criterion, 350–52, 560

*Publication of the Modern Language Association* (*PMLA*), 262–63, 342, 346, 420
publications, academic, 482
public intellectuals, 477
public sphere, 64
public style, 64
puns, 44
Putnam, Hilary, 231n8

quantity of criticism, 60–61
quantum theory, 549–50
quarks, 565
*Quarterly Review*, 65
"Queer Performativity: Henry James's *The Art of the Novel*" (Sedgwick), 389
queer theory, 31, 384, 389, 398, 424–25; anal strategy, 431–32; body and, 425–29, 438; focus on James, 431–32, 439–40; politics, 425–27
Quine, W. V. O., 441
quotation marks, use of, 558

*Rabelais and His World* (Bakhtin), 31
race, 302, 401, 408–9
race-gender-class theorists, 31–32, 39, 397; authorial intention and, 97–99; evaluation and, 102–4; ignorance of historical context, 95–97, 101–2, 105; reader-response criticism and, 100–101; rejection of objectivity, 99–100, 101
radical skeptical epistemology, 509, 621–22
Rajan, B., 615
rarity, 336–37
rational inquiry, 555; consistency, 529, 530; disembedded from world, 532–33; legitimacy of, 528–29; opposition to by left intellectuals, 528–36; proof and, 531, 534. *See also* rationality; science
rationality, 263–64, 525, 528; Nietzsche's stance, 243–44; positivism as form of, 251–52; subaltern, 580–81; undermining of, 639–40. *See also* rational inquiry
Rawls, John, 118, 219, 220
reader: ability to interpret, 200; emotionality, 38–39; production of meaning, 55–56
reader-response criticism, 26, 45–46, 81–82, 100–101, 147, 657

reading, 8, 22, 32; academically trained ways of, 478–79, 482; anachronistic, 462–64, 466; close, 61–63, 67, 100, 234–35; contrapuntal (Said), 488; for evil, 486–89; instrumental, 588; interpretive frameworks and, 481, 486–89; postmodernist, 282–83; students and, 423, 680; text, author, reader triad, 81, 83–85
Readings, Bill, 381
realism, 295–96, 503–4; basic goal of, 289–90; deconstruction of, 72–74
reality: language, relationship with, 4, 10, 17n25, 43, 124, 177, 191–92, 234; mind-independent, 566; organized by linguistic systems, 640–41; representation of, 85–86; social construction of, 365, 369–70, 640, 643
Rebatet, Lucien, 278–79
reconfigurability, 383–84
"Recovery of Open-Mindedness and the Revival of the Literary Imagination, The" (Alter), 422
*Redrawing the Boundaries* (MLA), 614–15
reductionism, 455, 509–10
referent, 54, 124, 176–77; analysis of language, 180–81; original misconception of notion of, 182–83; post-Saussurean theorists and, 136–37; semiological hypothesis, 177–78
referential function of language, 176–80
Regan, Tom, 346
regionalism, American, 502
relativism, 221, 223, 545–48; appeal of to academics, 551–52; apriorism, 250; cultural, 94, 95; epistemic, 242, 538; fallacy of, 548; framework, 623; Marxism as, 240; as tribalism, 558–59; truth and, 557–58
relativity, theory of, 549–50
*Religieuse, La* (Diderot), 398, 415, 417
religion, dismissal of, 291–92
*Religion Within the Limits of Reason Alone* (Kant), 112–13
Renaissance, 295–96, 466–67, 605–7, 614; as epistemic break, 608–9; as movement, 607
Renascences, 606–7
representation, 85–86, 493, 495; genre and, 86–87; object of, 176–77
repression, 224, 226

resistance: cultural studies as, 368–69; Foucault's view, 404–5; to theoreticism, 223–24; to Theory, 104; Theory as, 8–10, 12, 34–35, 296, 451

*Responses: On Paul de Man's Wartime Journalism* (ed. Hamacher, Hertz, and Keenan), 271, 278

responsibility, 114–15, 254

*Re-Thinking Theory: A Critique of Contemporary Literary Theory and an Alternative Account* (Freadman and Miller), 22–23, 78, 91

*Return of Grand Theory in the Human Sciences* (ed. Skinner), 215, 218–21

reviewing, 65–67

revisionism, 37–39

revolutionary academic, 454–57

*Rezeptionsaesthetik*, 45–46

rhetoric, 45, 102, 508, 671; of the End, 258–59; of proclamation, 607, 609

rhetorical techniques, 279–81

Rice, Philip, 9, 17n24

Richards, I. A., 22, 39, 42, 65, 67–71, 94, 182–83

Richelieu, Cardinal, 319–20

Ricks, Christopher, 6, 21, 112, 118

Ricoeur, Paul, 192

Riesman, David, 406

Right position, 599

*Rise and Fall of the Man of Letters, The* (Gross), 70

Robbe-Grillet, Alain, 429–30, 605

Robbins, Bruce, 501

Roberts, Jeanne Addison, 467

romantic aesthetics, 362, 374

romantic authors, 596

Romantic period, reviewing in, 65–67

Rooney, Ellen, 377n15

Rorty, Richard, 144n20, 238–39, 510, 566–67, 623; cynicism of, 490–91; linguistic turn concept, 123, 202; pragmatism of, 34, 559; science wars, view of, 571–72; on shift to cultural studies, 420–21

Ross, Andrew, 501, 541

Rousseau, Jean-Jacques, 499, 595

routinization, 336, 513

Routledge & Kegan Paul catalogue, 613

Rubin, Gayle, 429, 432–33

Runciman, W. G., 253, 254–55

Ruse, Michael, 628, 629

Rushdie, Salman, 292, 497–98, 506n22

Russell, Bertrand, 534, 539

Russian Formalists, 31, 36, 38, 123, 673; structural analysis and, 49, 53; systematic approach, 94, 100

Ryan, Kiernan, 459, 463, 466

Ryan, Michael, 5

Ryle, Gilbert, 492

Said, Edward, 53, 293, 298, 304, 305, 310n6; on Foucault, 248; interpretive frameworks and, 477, 478, 479; on novel, 299, 482–83; on professionalization, 477, 482; questions Theory, 11, 116–17, 251, 258, 265; reading of *Mansfield Park*, 452, 483–89, 489–90n3, 490n4; on social issues, 478, 479; *Works: Orientalism*, 577; *The World, the Text, and the Critic*, 266–67. *See also Culture and Imperialism*

*Saint Foucault: Towards a Gay Hagiography* (Halperin), 427, 429

Salam, Abdus, 501

*Sarrasine* (Balzac), 71–74

Sarraute, Nathalie, 429

Sartre, Jean-Paul, 220, 226, 239, 316; model of, 332, 333, 335

*Satanic Verses, The* (Rushdie), 497–98, 506n22

*sati*, 575

Saussure, Ferdinand de, 30, 95, 123, 141, 203, 384; *Cours de linguistique générale*, 28–29, 36, 43, 178–79; fundamental doctrines, 128–29; system-based analysis of language, 127–28

*savant*, 334–36

Sayers, Dorothy, 559

Schelling, Friedrich, 115–16

Scherzo Publishers, 334–35

Schleiermacher, Friedrich, 195

Scholes, Robert, 52–54, 56–58, 234

schools of theory, 94, 95

Schwartz, Stephen Adam, 317

science, 100, 348; attacks on, 525–26; critique of, 9, 17n24; cultural authority of, 571–73; cultural studies criticism of, 366–67; cutting edge of knowledge, 548–49; effect on academe, 218–19; E-knowledge example,

science (*continued*)
530, 531, 535; empiricism of, 222; feminism and, 577–78; institutions of, 556–57; intuition and, 549–50; literature compared with, 616–17; nonwhite practitioners, 534–35; philosophy of, 101–2; postcolonial view of, 577–78; progress in, 554–56; quantum theory, 549–50; as social construct, 547–48; Sokal's spoof, 32–33; state systems and, 529, 532; universalism and, 500–501; X example, 529–32. *See also* rational inquiry

science education, 366–67

science studies, 348, 525, 527n1, 541, 569; postcolonial, 578–83

scientificism, 25–26, 243

scientific method, 222, 231n8, 546, 548

scientists, leftist, 550–51

Scott, Joan, 273

Scruton, Roger, 667n18

Searle, John, 124, 345, 595, 646

*Second Sex, The* (Beauvoir), 564

Sedgwick, Eve Kosofsky, 309, 342, 389, 398, 426, 427; Foucault's influence on, 429–30; influence of, 434, 438; on James, 431–32; misunderstanding of information, 432–33, 436–37; on Shakespeare, 434–35; on Tomkins, 437–38

Selden, Raman, 33–34, 34

self: absence of, 134–38; end of, 597; as product of language, 130, 134–38; symbolic, 134. *See also* identity; subject

self-awareness, 126

self-consciousness, 47, 74, 127, 236

self-interest, 374–75, 516–17

self-other dichotomy, 631–32

self-presence, 165–66

self-reference, 64, 137–38

self-reflection, 223, 633

Semantic Definition of Literature, 637

semantics, 153–54

semiological hypothesis, 177–78, 183–84, 188

semiology, French school of, 178–80

semiotics, 28–29

sense, 591

*Sense and Sensibility* (Austen), 436

sentence meaning, 83–84, 154–58, 160, 167–68

sentence/utterance distinction, 152–53, 168, 198

separatism, 401–4

*Seven Types of Ambiguity* (Empson), 596

sexuality, 427–28; identity politics and, 384, 401; masturbation, 433, 434, 435–37

sexualization, 424–25

Seznec, Jean, 606

Shaftesbury, Earl of, 517–18

Shakespeare, William: historicist view of, 96–97; imagination of, 519; nonpolitical readings of, 465–68; sonnets, 434–35; *Works: Antony and Cleopatra*, 464; *Coriolanus*, 462, 468, 469; *Hamlet*, 256–57, 461, 467; *Henry V*, 463; *Julius Caesar*, 642, 649; *King Lear*, 463, 464; *Macbeth*, 463; *A Midsummer Night's Dream*, 256; *Othello*, 255–56, 269n47, 461, 462, 468; *The Taming of the Shrew*, 463–64; *The Tempest*, 265–66, 270n55, 293; *Titus Andronicus*, 464; *Troilus and Cressida*, 463; *As You like It*, 461

*Shakespeare and the Popular Voice* (Patterson), 256–57

Shakespeare criticism, 254, 459; feminism and, 261, 262–63, 265; interpretation, 255–57; oppositional stance, 451–52, 459–69, 467; polarization in, 265–66; political agenda in, 256–57; silence and, 460–62, 467

*Shakespeare Our Contemporary* (Kott), 47

*Shame and Its Sisters: A Silvan Tomkins Reader* (ed. Sedgwick), 437–38

Sharpe, Jenny, 303

Shattuck, Roger, 241

Shelley, Percy Bysshe, 595

Showalter, Elaine, 6, 16n16

Sicherman, Carol, 462, 464, 469

Sidney, Philip, 323, 671

Siegel, Carol, 416–17

Siegel, Lee, 398

sign, 30, 203–4; arbitrariness of, 127–28, 141, 367, 384–85; classic theory of, 211n12; cloakroom system model, 184–89; misconception about, 183–84; semiological hypothesis, 177–78, 183–84, 188. *See also* symbols

significances, 194

signification, 8, 28–30; difference and, 203–4; trace and, 205–6. *See also* linguistic system

signified, 29, 30, 128–29, 131; transcendental, 143–44n15, 186, 204, 367

signifier, 29, 30, 54, 128–29, 131; floating, 367; free play of, 143n15, 147, 203–5, 204–5, 211n14, 663; sliding, 37

silence, 402, 431; context of, 470–71; oppositional stance and, 451–52; as supportive of dominant ideology, 460–62, 464, 466–69

Sinfield, Alan, 458, 459, 463, 465–66, 468

Sircello, Guy, 93, 106n4

skepticism, 54, 55, 99, 235, 250, 382–83, 456

Skinner, Quentin, 215, 218–21, 222, 230

slavery, 504–5; in *Mansfield Park*, 483–87

sliding signifier, 37

Sloterdijk, Peter, 490

*Small Boy and Others, A* (Moon), 438–40

Smith, Barbara Herrnstein, 512

Snow, C. P., 218, 221, 616

social anthropology, 254–55

social construction, 562–63; of belief, 563–64, 567–71; cultural authority of science, 571–73; of reality, 365, 369–70, 640, 643; of things, 564–67; of truth, 623–24

social constructionism, 316, 341–42, 526; benefits to right-wing Hindus, 579–83; criticism of, 345–46; discovery/justification, 343–44, 346; as dogmatic, 342, 346–48; genetic fallacy and, 343, 344, 346; institutional nature of, 341–42, 349–53; origins, focus on, 344–45; strong constructivism, 621, 624, 630–31; weak constructivism, 621

*Social Construction of What?, The* (Hacking), 563

"Social Construction of Women Refugees, The" (Moussa), 563

social issues, 31; interpretive frameworks and, 478–79, 489

Socialist Realism, 37, 38

social realism, 38

social sciences, 218, 242, 531

social standing, early literary criticism and, 66–67

*Social Text*, 32–33, 501, 537, 541, 542

sociobiology, 625

sociology of knowledge, 569

*Soir, Le*, 271

Sokal, Alan D., 32–33, 501, 525–26, 537, 541–44, 548, 550–51

Sontag, Susan, 328, 329, 429

Sophocles, 612

Souljah, Sister, 409

sources, 62–63

*Sovereignty of Good, The* (Murdoch), 596

speaker, 195, 196; absence of, 131–33; deixis of, 132, 136, 137–38, 142n11; other *vs.*, 414

speaker meaning, 154–57, 160, 167–68, 170

speech act, 85; Background of, 149–50; conflated with system of signification, 131–33; consciousness and, 129, 130; context of, 140–41; dissolution of subject, 130–38; indeterminacy of, 167–70; indirect, 155, 156; sentence meaning *vs.* speaker meaning, 154–57, 160, 167–68, 170

speech-act, 124–25, 196–97

spider's web metaphor, 206–7, 208–9

Spiller, Robert, 102

Spitzer, Leo, 100–101

Spivak, Gayatri Chakravorty, 143n15, 217, 298–306, 307–8, 498, 592; on epistemic violence, 575–76

Sprinker, Michael, 472

Stalinism, 598

Standard Model, 565

standpoint epistemology, 397, 578

Stanford University, 669

star map example, 605–6

star system, 21, 315, 317, 381–82, 385–87, 393

state, 602–3

status quo: anachronistic readings, 462–64, 466; silence as support of, 468; supported by silence, 460–62, 464. *See also* dominant ideology

Steiner, George, 126, 682

Stephen, Leslie, 624–25

Stich, Stephen, 559

Stoic philosophers, 428

Stolnitz, Jerome, 516

Storey, Robert, 631, 632

stories, invented, 641. *See also* fiction

strategic essentialism, 580–81

Streuver, Nancy S., 671

Strickland, Geoffrey, 50
strong constructivism, 621, 624, 630–31
structural anthropology, 30, 332
structuralism, 30, 36, 38, 53, 100, 127, 191, 621; analysis of myths, 129–30; canny and uncanny critics, 205, 207–8; Czech, 49, 50, 94; dualisms in, 632; introduction into America, 27, 225; representatives of, 335; science, view of, 251–52
*Structuralism and Semiotics* (Hawkes), 29
*Structuralism or Criticism?* (Strickland), 50
structuralist poetics, 50, 83
*Structure of Scientific Revolutions, The* (Kuhn), 101–2, 108n28, 204–25
*Structures élémentaires de la parenté, Les* (Lévi-Strauss), 251
student guides, 27, 33, 34
students, 9; critical skills needed, 9–13, 17n25; dedicated to literature, 611–12; effects of Theory on, 42, 679; female, 447; identity politics and, 403; literary imagination and, 422–23; *Norton Anthology of Theory and Criticism* and, 3–4; reading and, 423, 680; teacher relationships with, 390–91
Sturrock, Jonathan, 27
style, 64, 511–12
subalternity, definitions, 580
subject, 8, 28, 397, 647–48; dissolution of, 131–38; emancipation of, 79–80; thick notion of, 81. *See also* identity; self
subjectivity, 99; as linguistic act, 134–38; thick description and, 495–96
subject level, 649–50
subject matter, 675–77
sublime, 512–13, 514, 519
subliterature, 48, 110
surely, use of as term, 346
Swift, Jonathan, 44, 436
symbol, as fusion of image and idea, 596
symbolic capital, 669
symbolic credit, 336
symbolic domination, 335–36
symbolic self, 134
symbolism, triangle diagram, 182–83
symbols, 124, 182–83. *See also* sign
symmetry principles, 569
symptomatics, 194, 198nn. 11, 12, 252
synchronic point of view, 185

synecdochal reasoning, 305–6
syntax, 157; compositionality, 153–54; as relative to intentionality, 163; as relative to language, 161, 175n18; unrelated to physics, 157, 163

Taine, Hippolyte, 49
Tallack, Douglas, 33
Tallis, Raymond, 123
Taylor, Charles, 371, 497–98
Taylor, Mark, 308–9
teaching, 419–21; distance from student, 390–91
"Teaching Literature, Changing Cultures" (Martin), 420
*techne*, 672
teleological theories, 82
tenure system, 454, 613, 659; meetings, 349–50; publication criterion, 350–52, 560
text, 8, 22, 32, 43; authority of, 45; boundaries of, 98; history as, 238; illocutionary intentions and, 160–61; interpretation as source of, 164–65; literature as, 123, 588; as material entity, 383; meaning and, 52, 55, 59, 80, 83, 147; New Criticism focus on, 61–63; as opportunity for self-display, 76; as secondary to work, 642; as self-deconstructive artifact, 207; sociohistorical context, 89–90; as undecidable, 46, 53–55, 129, 142n8; written, 126, 205–6
text, author, reader triad, 81, 83–85
"Textual Feminism" (Furman), 423
textualism, 594
textuality, 36; as game, 29–30, 31
*Textual Power* (Scholes), 52, 53
thematic level of work, 646–47, 650
theme, 647–48
theoreticism, 221–23, 225, 250; resistance to, 223–24
*theoros*, 26
theorrhea, 236, 240–43
Theory: anthologies, 2–4; antitheoretical reaction, 388–89; as approach, 5; apriorism, 215, 221; Bad Theory, 23, 92, 104; as belief system, 15n6, 23, 109–10; claims to truth, 9–10, 34; critical challenges to, 1–2, 12, 111–12; critical examination by students, 11–13; critique of science, 9, 17n24; culture

of, 104–6; cycles of, 100–101; destroyed from within, 22, 42, 50–51; deterioration of, 94–98, 103; domestication of, 34; excluded approaches/authors, 3, 34; generalizations, 658; as idea, 5; as imperialist, 235–36, 259–60; incoherence of, 5, 7, 21, 93, 95, 97, 103; as ineffectual, 296–97, 402–3, 451–52, 470, 481, 497–98; as institution, 110–11, 115–16, 385–86; as intellectual colonizer, 22, 28; as intolerant, 8, 34, 99, 215, 216, 442–43; jargon, 22, 64–65, 76, 92, 105, 236; as label, 26–28; lack of focus on literature, 2, 5–6, 8, 16n16, 21; liberation from, 613–14; limitations of, 92–93; Marxism, competition with, 260–61; modes of, 93, 104; as opportunistic, 33–34, 98, 348; as origin of star system, 382; origins, 7–8, 21; penetration of other disciplines, 8, 11, 21–23, 27–28, 32, 95, 235–38, 317; pluralism of, 33–34; political agenda, 8, 10, 93–94, 451–53; as practice, 386; professionalization of, 315–17; rejection of progressive ideas, 288–89; as resistance, 8–10, 12, 34–35, 104, 296, 451; schools of, 94, 95; scientificism of, 25–26; skepticism of, 382–83; specializations and subfields, 8, 27; as systematic, 384; terminology, 7, 12–13, 22, 24–25, 389, 498; universality of, 33; university linked to outside world, 382–83; zones of, 35–36. *See also* critics of Theory; literary criticism; literary theory; theory; thought-systems

theory: as approach, 1; definitions of, 104; development stages, 94–95; generic, 81; insubstantiated, 221–22; local considerations, 110–11; meanings of term, 3, 5, 16n13, 23; object of, 80; as practice, 8; principles required, 545; usefulness of, 110–11. *See also* Theory

*Theory of Literature* (Wellek and Warren), 22, 50, 62, 94, 97

*Theory of Morals, A* (Rawls), 118

*Theory of the Avant-Garde* (Bürger), 679

thesis, 648

*Thick and Thin* (Walzer), 491

thick description, 452, 491–94; aestheticism of, 493, 495–96

*Thief's Journal* (Genet), 44

"Thinking Sex" (Rubin), 429, 432

third person, 179

Third World theorists, 303, 397

Thompson, Ann, 261

Thompson, E. P., 248, 260, 369, 535–36, 598

Thomson, Virgil, 248

thought, three spheres of, 244

thought-systems, 247–48, 257; verification and, 251–54

"Three Women's Texts and a Critique of Imperialism" (Spivak), 298–99, 300–306, 592

*Times Literary Supplement* (London), 25

Timpanaro, Sebastiano, 254, 270n52

Todorov, Tzvetan, 22, 177–78, 215, 239–40; defense of humanism, 641–42

"To His Coy Mistress" (Marvell), 414

tokens, 157, 161; intentionality of, 167–68; type *vs.*, 152, 153

Tolstoy, Leo, 646

Tomkins, Silvan, 309, 437–38

total intellectuals, 332

totalitarianism, 57, 602, 623

totalities, 623

trace, 203–4, 205–6

traditional societies, 363

"Traffic in Women, The" (Ruben), 432–33

*Trahison des clercs, La* (Benda), 619

transcendental appearance, 188

transcendental idealism, 565–66

transcendental signified, 143–44n15, 186, 204, 367

"Transgressing the Boundaries: Toward a Transformative Hermeneutics of Quantum Gravity" (Sokal), 32–33, 541

transgression, 241, 427

transparency, 235, 511–12

transvestism, literary, 416–17

Traub, Valerie, 467

tribalism, 558–59

Trilling, Lionel, 442, 610, 670

tripartite system of classification, 81–83

Trollope, Anthony, 86

true impression, 91

truth, 23, 99, 452, 490; as construct, 345; as contextual, 502–3; correspondence theory of, 623–24; of fiction, 636–37; interpretation and, 592–93; knowledge, relationship to, 552–53; in literature, 85–87; as nonex-

truth (*continued*)
istent, 526; Passes-for Fallacy, 558; post-colonial view of, 578; power and, 499–500, 623; as relative, 557–58; as socially constructed, 623–24. *See also* verification

*Truth, Fiction, and Literature: A Philosophical Perspective* (Lamarque and Olsen), 639

*Truth and Method* (Gadamer), 45, 220

Tulane University, 386–87

Turner, John, 463

Turner, Mark, 633–34

"Two Cultures, The: The Significance of C. P. Snow" (Leavis), 616–17

"Two Cultures and the Scientific Revolution, The" (Snow), 218, 616

Tyler, Patrick, 460

types, 152, 153, 158, 161, 168

Tyson, Lois, 9–10, 17–18n25

UbuWeb, 678

*Ulysses* (Joyce), 675–77

uncanny critics, 205, 207–8

uncertainty, intolerance of, 553

unconscious, structured like language, 30, 127

universalism, 111, 375; in art and criticism, 503–4; flight from, 497–98, 500–502; Marxist criticism of, 57–58; scientific, 500–501

university courses, 24–26, 34

*University in Ruins, The* (Reading), 381

University of Chicago meeting, 2, 12, 687

university presses, 350, 352

use-mention distinction, 153, 174n7

utterance/sentence distinction, 152–53, 168, 196

vagueness, 147–49, 166–67

*Validity in Interpretation* (Hirsch), 194

values, 54, 102–3, 362, 643, 653; facts as, 88, 363–66; Marxist view of, 57–58; of signified, 128–29

Vedic science, 581–82

Veeser, Aram, 294

Vendler, Helen, 322, 326

verbal densities, 324–25

verbal icon, 36, 46

*Verbal Icon, The* (Wimsatt and Beardsley), 413–15

verbal meaning, 194

verbal texts, 205

verification, 222, 231n8, 251–54, 295

Vickers, Brian, 15n6, 216

Vico, 47

Victorian novel, 36, 217; as instance of imperialism, 298–300; as Other, 307; postcolonial approach to, 307. *See also Jane Eyre; Mansfield Park*

Victorientalism, 217, 305

*Village in the Vaucluse* (Wylie), 322

Vincent, John, 431

voice, 370–71

Voltaire, 323

*Vulgarization of Art, The: The Victorians and Aesthetic Democracy* (Dowling), 517–18

Wagner, Richard, 244

Walker, Alice, 462, 468

Wallen, Jeffrey, 452

Walzel, Oskar, 94

Walzer, Michael, 491

*War and Peace* (Tolstoy), 646

Warhol, Andy, 599

Warminski, Andrzej, 281, 282–83

Warner, Michael, 426–27, 433, 438

Warren, Austin, 22, 50, 62, 94, 97

Warren, Robert Penn, 325

Wasserman, Earl, 443

Watkins, William J., 504

Waugh, Patricia, 9, 17n24

weak constructivism, 621

Weber, Max, 336, 337, 339

Weber, Samuel, 282

Weisbuch, Robert, 668, 677

Wellek, René, 22, 50, 62, 94, 97

well-wrought urn, 36, 46

*Well-Wrought Urn, The* (Brooks), 62

*Western Canon, The* (Bloom), 421, 512–13, 518

Western Culture, traditional historians of, 199–200

"What Ails Feminist Criticism?" (Gubar), 445

*What's Happened to the Humanities* (ed. Kernan), 611

*What Was Literature?* (Fiedler), 48

White, Hayden, 102, 675
Whitehead, Alfred North, 503–4
white studies, 389–90
Whitman, Walt, 323, 433
"Who Killed Feminist Criticism?" (Gubar), 445
Widdowson, Peter, 458, 467
Wiener, Jon, 272
Wilde, Oscar, 44
Williams, Bernard, 567
Williams, Raymond, 31, 38, 369, 371, 491
Wilson, E. O., 626
Wilson, George, 159
Wimsatt, William K., 97–98, 100, 398, 411, 442, 591. See also "Intentional Fallacy, The;" Verbal Icon, The
Wings of the Dove (James), 431
Wittgenstein, Ludwig, 123, 593, 600–601; Zettel, 593, 600–601, 673
Wolfreys, Julian, 27, 34
Wollheim, Richard, 663, 666n4

Wood, James, 16n16
Woolf, Virginia, 289–90, 616, 636
Woolgar, Steve, 565
Wordsworth, William, 597, 601; "Lines Composed A Few Miles above Tintern Abbey," 644–45, 646; The Excursion, 66–67; "A Slumber Did My Spirit Seal," 158
working-class culture, 535
works, 588, 641. See also fiction; text
worlding, 298, 301, 302, 305–6, 577
writing: literature as, 318–19; as prior to speech, 138, 173, 202–3, 595
written text, 126, 205–6
Wylie, Lawrence, 322, 326

X example (science), 529–32

Zambaco, Demetrius, 436–37
Zangwill, Nick, 667n18
Zavarzadeh, Mas'ud, 469
zeitgeist, 96–97